PSYCHOLOGY

 MIDWIFERY

PSYCHOLOGY

FOURTH EDITION

CAMILLE B. WORTMAN
State University of New York at Stony Brook

ELIZABETH F. LOFTUS
University of Washington

MARY E. MARSHALL

INTERNATIONAL EDITION

McGRAW-HILL, INC.
*New York   St. Louis   San Francisco   Auckland   Bogotá
Caracas   Lisbon   London   Madrid   Mexico   Milan   Montreal   New Delhi   Paris   San Juan   Singapore
Sydney   Tokyo   Toronto*

PSYCHOLOGY

1 2 3 4 5 6 7 8 9 0 DOW DOW 9 0 9 8 7 6 5 4 3 2 1

ISBN 0-07-071918-7

This book was set in Palatino by Black Dot, Inc.
The editors were Christopher Rogers, Roberta B. Meyer, and
Elaine Rosenberg; the designer was Edward A. Butler;
the production supervisor was Kathryn Porzio.
The photo editor was Elyse Rieder.
R. R. Donnelley & Sons Company was printer and binder.

Credits for photographs, figures and tables appear on page C-1.
Original chapter opening art work was done by
Edward A. Butler.

Library of Congress Cataloging-in-Publication Data

Wortman, Camille B.
    Psychology / Camille Wortman, Elizabeth Loftus, Mary
Marshall. —4th ed.
      p.   cm.
    Includes bibliographical references and indexes.
    ISBN 0-07-071918-7
    1. Psychology.   I. Loftus, Elizabeth F., (date).
II. Marshall, Mary E.   III. Title.
BF121.W67   1992
150—dc20   91-37999

ABOUT THE AUTHORS

Camille B. Wortman is professor of psychology and Director of the Social/Health Psychology Training Program at the State University of New York at Stony Brook. A social psychologist, her major research interests include reactions to undesirable events, causal attribution, and reactions to stress and victimization. Wortman graduated summa cum laude from Duke University in 1969 and received her Ph.D. from Duke in 1972. She was a member of the psychology faculty at Northwestern for seven years. The introductory psychology course that she taught there was so successful that a lottery for enrollment had to be instituted because of student demand. In recognition of her excellence in undergraduate teaching, she won the Distinguished Teaching Award at Northwestern University. She then transferred to the University of Michigan where she taught and conducted research until 1989. Wortman has published numerous articles in every major journal in her field. She has also contributed chapters to a large number of edited books including *Advances in Social Psychology, New Directions in Attribution Research,* and the *Advances in Environmental Psychology* series. In recognition of her research, Wortman received the American Psychological Association's Distinguished Scientific Award for an Early Career Contribution to Psychology.

Elizabeth F. Loftus is professor of psychology at the University of Washington, Seattle. A specialist in learning and memory, she has been nationally recognized for her research on eyewitness testimony. Her first book on the subject, *Eyewitness Testimony,* was published by Harvard University Press in 1979 and won an APA National Media Award, Distinguished Contribution, in 1980. Another book, *Eyewitness Testimony: Psychological Perspectives,* which she co-edited, was published in 1984. *Memory* appeared in 1980; *Essence of Statistics* and *Mind at Play,* both co-authored,

appeared in 1981 and 1983, respectively. Loftus's latest book, co-authored with Katherine Ketham, is *Witness for the Defense: the Accused, the Eyewitness, and the Expert Who Puts Memory on Trial* (St. Martin's Press, 1991). Loftus received her B.A. with highest honors in mathematics and psychology from UCLA in 1966, and an M.A. (1967) and Ph.D. (1970) in psychology from Stanford University. In 1982 she received an honorary doctor of science degree from Miami University of Ohio. Loftus was a Fellow at the Center for Advanced Study in the Behavioral Sciences, Stanford, 1978–79. She has published numerous articles, and travels extensively to present papers at college and university colloquia and to the legal profession. She has twice been the APA nominee for the NSF Waterman Award for outstanding contributions to science. Loftus has served as president of the Western Psychological Association (1984). She is also past president of the Psychology and Law Division and the Division of Experimental Psychology of the American Psychological Association. Loftus is on the board of directors of the APS and serves on the governing board of the Psychonomics Society. In 1990 she received an honorary doctorate from Leiden University, the Netherlands. In 1991 she was elected an Honorary Fellow (conferring lifetime membership) of the British Psychological Society.

Mary E. Marshall, until she became a psychology writer in 1979, was manager of special projects at the college department of Random House. During her ten years in college publishing, she supervised the development of introductory texts such as *Psychology Today, Abnormal Psychology* (2nd and 3rd eds.), and *Understanding Psychology* (2nd ed.). Marshall is a graduate with distinction of Connecticut College, Phi Beta Kappa and magna cum laude.

CONTENTS

Now in its fourth edition, *Psychology* has come to be regarded as the book with a conscience. Rather than just offering facts and theories to help students pass their exams, we've also given them tools to use in their lives—tools for helping them gain insight into their own behavior and their relationships with others. *Psychology* will help students understand and think critically about human behavior long after this course has ended.

UNDERSTANDING HUMAN BEHAVIOR

We frequently encourage students to draw from course material to gain insight into both their own lives and the world around them. For example, a student may be surprised when he agrees to do something that he does not really want to do, or even that he believes is morally wrong. By understanding the pressures of conformity, which are described in Chapter 18, the student can gain insight into what leads to this behavior and how it can be avoided. A young woman may be terrified that her boyfriend is going to leave her, and may wonder whether her fear is realistic or groundless. By learning how her current orientation toward relationships may be influenced by events that happened earlier—parental death or divorce, for example—she can gain perspective on her current feelings. Finally, students may wonder how to make sense of things they read in the newspaper—for example, a description of a brutal incident of discrimination (such as the police beating a man in Los Angeles) or a gang rape of a woman by students at a nearby college. By learning about the complex

causes of human behavior, they will gain insight into such events.

FOSTERING CRITICAL THINKING

Perhaps the most important part of teaching students to think critically about what they read and experience is encouraging them to ask questions about how "facts" are obtained. In this way, we hope to promote a healthy skepticism toward ideas derived from inadequate research methods. Such skepticism is invaluable in today's society, where people are exposed to a barrage of popular "psychologizing"—everything from tests in the Sunday supplement to evaluate one's marriage to the numerous "self-improvement" books that line the bookstore shelves. We have tried to provide students with the critical skills needed to question the validity of popularized psychology. Students will forget particular facts and the details of specific studies, but we hope that these critical thinking skills will remain with them.

In short, we encourage students not to take their own behavior, the behavior of others, or what they read at face value. We teach them not to accept simple answers to complex questions. We teach them to weigh opposing arguments and reach their own conclusions about what they observe and read. Critical thinking skills are also fostered in several of the special features described below.

FEATURES OF THIS TEXT

Since the first edition, a number of special features have distinguished this book from others and have been responsible for its success. These include (1) an integration of theory and research with applications, and a strict departure from the idea that an introductory psychology book has to resort to gimmicks; (2) a focus, throughout the book, on the process of scientific inquiry—that is, how psychologists develop testable hypotheses, how they gather and interpret data, and how they arrive at conclusions; (3) a comparison of empirical data with common-sense ideas; and (4) In Depth discussions of important issues.

INTEGRATING THEORY, RESEARCH, AND APPLICATIONS: THE BOOK WITHOUT GIMMICKS

Some texts have a strong research orientation, with little apparent concern for readability or student interest. Others are research-oriented in some parts and are interspersed with separate sections on applications and other high-interest topics. Many authors have filled their texts with an array of "special features"—newspaper clippings, boxed inserts of various kinds, even stories and vignettes. Indeed, many current books seem to be based on the assumption that the only way to make scientific content palatable to students is to offer them a panoply of gimmicks and titillating topics. We still believe that psychology can be exciting and engaging without resorting to gimmicks or sacrificing scientific integrity.

As in previous editions, our aim is to integrate conceptually sophisticated theories and research with applications and topics of current concern to students. We feel that separate boxes, vignettes, and other added-on features have several serious drawbacks. They disrupt the flow and coherence of a chapter, often making it hard for readers to grasp how topics interrelate. In addition, such added-on extras are based on the false assumption that students need a breather from their toils as they wearily plod through scientific material. For those who disagree, we offer an alternative view: By fully interweaving theories and research with applications, *all* of introductory psychology can be made fascinating and meaningful to students.

Increasingly, researchers in different areas are finding that concepts presented in one subfield are relevant to concepts in another. We continue to tie these interrelated concepts together to enrich students' overall understanding of psychology. For instance, the concepts of limited human capacity for processing information and of schemas are introduced in Chapter 4, which deals with sensation and perception. In Chapter 6, we discuss the role of schemas in learning. In Chapter 7 we pick up the thread again when discussing the limitations of human memory. The ideas appear again in Chapter 8, where we examine how people go about solving problems and making decisions. In Chapter 9 we see how cognitive development is affected by limited short-term memory storage space. Still later, in Chapter 18 on social psychology, we relate the very same ideas to social cognition, especially to how people employ schemas in forming impressions of others. In this way we hope that students will perceive some of the important consistencies in how we humans think and act.

FOCUS ON THE PROCESS OF SCIENTIFIC INQUIRY

In the fourth edition we continue to make every effort to emphasize the *process* of scientific inquiry. Repeatedly we focus on how psychologists develop testable hypotheses, how they gather and interpret data, and how they arrive at conclusions. We try to show how early studies form the foundation for later research, which in turn often refines our understanding by ruling out alternative explanations. Chapter 2 describes the research process: how psychologists define research objectives, select a method of inquiry, gather and interpret their data, rule out alternative explanations, and deal with the theoretical dilemmas that research sometimes poses. We then carry these themes throughout the book by repeatedly encouraging students to evaluate the theories and research we present.

COMPARING EMPIRICAL DATA WITH COMMON SENSE IDEAS

Another technique we use to develop critical thinking is to contrast "common sense" myths about psychology with conclusions based on empirical data. One of the frustrating things about teaching introductory psychology is discovering the large number of students who believe that psychology is nothing more than "common sense." We try to show that while empirical data sometimes support our common-sense notions, they often do not. For instance, common sense leads us to believe that the more motivated people are, the better they will perform on a task. Drawing from theoretical and empirical work, we demonstrate in Chapter 1 how simplistic this assumption is.

Similarly, common sense tells us that we remember events exactly as they happen. In Chapters 2, 5 and 7, we counter this popular misconception. We present information on memory distortions—especially the fascinating cases of children's court testimony to show that our memories can be distorted by questions, suggestions, and our own moods. By highlighting such discrepancies between common sense and empirical findings, we hope to emphasize that people cannot trust their intuitions when it comes to human behavior. A careful evaluation of available evidence is always essential.

IN DEPTH SECTIONS

Perhaps the most important way that we try to encourage critical thinking skills is in the section of each chapter labeled "In Depth." Most psychology texts give a very even, almost homogeneous, coverage of all of the main concepts in psychology. We felt that there would be enormous advantages in providing a closer look at how psychologists have approached a given problem, exposing students to the process of psychological inquiry. All In Depth features have several key qualities. Each one explores a topic that is interesting to students and that flows directly into the narrative. They are not boxed or set apart.

In Depths give shape to the process of psychological inquiry. Each one discusses a problem and reviews the initial studies designed to address it. Then we discuss how later scientists challenged the earlier findings and sometimes came up with alternative hypotheses. We describe additional research that builds on and often challenges the conclusions of the early studies. Finally, we discuss current thinking regarding the problem in question, summarizing what is known and widely accepted, and what is still being debated. We also discuss studies currently in progress that are designed to further clarify the subject.

Finally, just as we do throughout the text, the In Depths challenge students to think about implications. For example, society continues to be upset about TV violence, especially on shows for children. Does viewing violence on TV have anything to do with apparent increases in crime or changes in the crimes that are occurring? In the In Depth on the effects of TV violence (Chapter 2), students will find both answers and additional questions about this important area of research. Are people influenced by things that they are not even aware of? In Chapter 4, an In Depth introduces students to the nature of unconscious processes. Whether subliminal stimuli cause people to do things they wouldn't otherwise do is an important question that is thoroughly explored. Recent research conclusions in this area support the idea that people are influenced by stimuli that they are not even aware were presented. However, there is virtually no evidence that stimuli below the level of awareness make people do complicated things such as buy items they would not otherwise buy or do things they would not otherwise do.

The In Depth in Chapter 7 takes students into the laboratory and into the courtroom. We explore the research and controversy over the malleability of memory and discuss the implications for the justice system. In the In Depth in Chapter 13, we discuss the Type A behavior pattern. There is considerable evidence that Type A behavior is bad for your health. But does this mean that if people become less competitive, the health risk will disappear? The In Depth appearing in Chapter 19 presents evidence suggesting that pornography can increase men's sexual aggression toward women. Should pornography therefore be banned? In Chapter 11 the In Depth explores the problem of obesity. We review the theoretical and empirical work of Schachter, Nisbett, Rodin, Herman and Polivy, and others, with particular attention to how these investigators have built on one another's work. Throughout the discussion, the reader is led to see that the problem of significant, permanent weight loss is a complex one to which there are no simple answers.

WHAT'S NEW IN THIS EDITION?

The fourth edition of *Psychology* is a major revision. About three-quarters of the chapters have been heavily revised as we've strived to be contemporary and comprehensive. We have made a special effort to include "cutting edge" research that is changing firmly entrenched notions in our field—including research on neurophysiology, judgment and decision making, intelligence, social cognition, and health psychology. Below are some examples of changes that reflect new findings and important areas of research:

- Chapter 2   How reliable is children's testimony? Clarke-Stewart's "Chester the Molester" study introduces students to the research process. This fascinating study has very important "real world" implications.
- Chapter 3   New material on cognitive neuroscience; updated In Depth on left–right hemispheres of the brain.
- Chapter 6   A revised classical conditioning section brings us up to date on the way behaviorists view this process. Numerous changes throughout clarify important concepts. New material links learning to Richard Thompson's research cited in Chapter 3.
- Chapter 7   Includes new research on short-term memory and working memory. In an updated In Depth, Elizabeth Loftus discusses reactions to her research on eyewitness testimony. Implications for the judicial system are stressed.
- Chapters 9 and 10   In the two development chapters, we've expanded coverage of adulthood, updated research on gender similarities and differences, and discussed genetics and personality.
- Chapter 13   Randy Larsen provided important information on new developments in personality psychology, including work on the behavior genetic approach to understanding personality. We've included fascinating new research on twins with similar personalities and new work by Nancy Cantor and her associates on the life tasks that people face. The concepts behind her theories are described in a study of making new friends in college.
- Chapter 15   This new chapter, Health, Stress and Coping, includes the following topics: Can stress make you sick? How can negative thinking affect your life? What does the latest research show on

the best ways to deal with addiction to alcohol or cigarettes? A section on AIDS discusses current research designed to ameliorate the pain of those suffering from this disease.
- Chapter 16   It includes a discussion of twin and adoption studies. We evaluate the evidence that genetics may be an important cause of particular psychological disorders, including schizophrenia and generalized anxiety disorder.
- Chapters 18 and 19   Under the advice of John Bargh, important changes were made in the social psychology chapters, incorporating more "cutting edge" work on social cognition.

IN DEPTHS

About one-third of our In Depth features are new; the rest have been updated. The new additions are:
- Memory Enhancement and Hypnosis (Chapter 5)
- Do Cognitive Differences Develop between the Sexes? (Chapter 9)
- What Is So Deadly about "Type A" Personality? (Chapter 13)
- The Psychological Consequences of Abortion? (Chapter 15)
- Treating Suicidal People (Chapter 17)
- Pornography: What Is Its Relationship to Rape? (Chapter 19)

ACKNOWLEDGMENTS

Thanks to Chris Rogers and to Suzanne Thibodeau for their creative problem solving which kept this project moving along, and to Rochelle Diogenes, who helped to shape our revision plan. Special thanks are due to our editor, Roberta Meyer, whose contribution to the book was simply enormous. In terms of development of ideas and themes for the book, her contributions were equally as important as ours. We also want to thank Elaine Rosenberg, our editing supervisor, for her outstanding work. Our photo editor, Elyse Rieder, and our designer, Ed Butler, have created a bold new look for the fourth edition of our book.

We must also express our thanks for the many useful comments and suggestions provided by the following reviewers: Clark E. Alexander, Arapahoe Community College; Raymond R. Baird, The University of Texas, San Antonio; John Bargh, New York University; Jonathan Baron, University of Pennsylvania; Jay Belsky, Pennsylvania State University; Donald D. Chezik, Marshall University; Francis A. Colletti, Jr., United States Military Academy; Lynn A. Durel, University of Miami, Coral Gables; Leslie E. Fisher, Cleveland State University; Russell G. Geen, University of Missouri; Mary Alice Gordon, Southern Methodist University; Robert L. Gossette, Hofstra University; Gary W. Heiman, State University of New York, Buffalo; Joseph Hughey, University of Missouri, Kansas City; Walter L. Isaac, East Tennessee State University; Ken Kallio, State University of New York, Genesee; Keith R. Kluender, University of Wisconsin, Madison; Lois Layne, Western Kentucky University; Marc A. Lindberg, Marshall University; Steven Mewaldt, Marshall University; Douglas G. Mook, University of Virginia; Leslie C. Morey, Vanderbilt University; David I. Mostofsky, Boston University; Lawrence A. Pervin, Princeton; E. Jerry Phares, Kansas State University; John B. Pittenger, University of Arkansas, Little Rock; Craig A. Smith, Vanderbilt University; Diedrick Snoek, Smith College; Lisa A. Spielman, New York University; John Vitkus, Barnard College; Jennifer Vookles, New York University; Lori Van Wallendael, University of North Carolina, Charlotte; Paul J. Watson, University of Tennessee, Chattanooga; Heidi A. Wayment; David H. Westendorf, University of Arkansas, Fayetteville; Macon L. Williams, Illinois State University; Jeremy M. Wolfe, Massachusetts Institute of Technology; Dianna S. Woodruff-Pak, Temple University; and, James L. Zacks, Michigan State University.

Finally, we give special thanks to Randy Larsen, University of Michigan, for his help on Chapters 11, 12, and 13; Stephen Klein, Mississippi State University, for his expert advice on Chapter 6; and Shelley E. Taylor, University of California, Los Angeles, for her expertise in health psychology in Chapter 15.

Camille B. Wortman

Elizabeth F. Loftus

PSYCHOLOGY

CHAPTER 1

THE DIMENSIONS OF PSYCHOLOGY

When you hear the word *psychology*, what comes to mind? A laboratory where scientists run rats through mazes, trying to understand what influences learning and performance? Or do you picture a therapist listening to someone's problems, analyzing dreams, or providing guidance on how to raise children? Although these are common preconceptions about psychology, they provide only a limited view of what the field and this book are all about. But each one touches on an important aspect of the subject you are about to explore. The first emphasizes that psychology is a *science*, a set of procedures for systematically observing facts and organizing them into generalizations about why things occur as they do. The second stresses that psychology is *a means of promoting human welfare*, a body of information that can be applied to help solve a variety of human problems. We begin this chapter by examining these two aspects of **psychology**, which can be defined as the study of behavior and mental processes.

ASPECTS OF PSYCHOLOGY

PSYCHOLOGY IS A SCIENCE

Psychology may not seem as much of a science to you as biology or chemistry does. Psychologists, after all, often study things that cannot be put into test tubes or looked at under microscopes. A psychologist might want to know why identical twins can develop quite different personalities; why women in general seem to be more emotionally expressive than men; why people sometimes persist in behaviors that threaten their health or undermine their happiness; and why we are occasionally so attracted to another person that we say we are in love. Are such questions really appropriate for a scientist to study?

The answer is that a science is defined not by *what* it studies, but by *how* it studies it. Psychologists, like other scientists, adopt a special approach to obtaining and organizing knowledge. They use systematic methods to gather data about the things that interest them, methods you will read about in Chapter 2. Once these data have been collected, they carefully analyze the data and interpret the meaning of their findings as objectively as they can. Along with conducting research, they develop general principles or theories about why things happen as they do. A **theory** is an attempt to fit all the known, relevant facts into a logical explanation. Once formulated, a theory can serve as a framework for collecting more data. "If this theory is true," psychologists reason, "people should respond in the following way in this set of circumstances." Psychologists then gather more evidence to verify these predictions. As new facts emerge, they often modify their theories to make them more accurate or more comprehensive. In this way scientific knowledge grows.

Of course, applying scientific methods to psychological questions is often more challenging than this brief description implies. Psychologists cannot dismantle human beings to learn what makes them tick. Studying the how and why of human behavior often takes ingenuity. Later in this chapter and throughout the rest of this book we shall look at how psychologists have skillfully designed studies to answer some of the many questions we all have about human behavior.

SCIENCE VERSUS COMMON SENSE

There are certainly ways of "knowing" things other than through science. People often rely for their knowledge on tradition and "common sense." Aren't these other sources of information just as reliable as science? The answer is "no," they generally are not, because the knowledge derived from these other sources has never been put to systematic test. Instead, it is simply accepted because it *seems* logical and right. Scientific knowledge, in contrast, has always been tested systematically. Such systematic testing is the hallmark of science.

How often does scientific knowledge disprove what "common sense" tells us? More often than one might think, psychologists have found. Suppose you are an arithmetic teacher who notices that some students do poorly because they give up trying as soon as a problem seems hard. How can you help these children? Common sense might suggest that you assign them many easy problems to build their confidence. Then later, when they encounter harder problems, they should be so sure of eventually succeeding that they will tend to persist until they do.

Psychologist Carol Dweck (1975) decided to test this common-sense approach against another approach suggested by her scientific research. In some of her earlier studies she had found that children whose performance deteriorates after failure usually explain their failure in terms of things they cannot change, such as innate lack of ability (Dweck and Reppucci, 1973). Such children feel helpless in prob-

lem-solving situations. They believe that there is no reason to keep on trying, since nothing they do will make a difference. Dweck suspected that if these children were taught to attribute failure to something they *could* change (such as insufficient effort), they might persist longer at problems and experience more success.

To evaluate the effectiveness of this alternative approach against the common-sense one, Dweck chose twelve children who were known to give up in the face of failure. She divided the children into two groups and gave each group twenty-five days of special training with math problems. The first group was presented only with easy problems and so experienced nothing but success. The second group was given a mixture of easy and difficult problems. Whenever these students began to give up, they were encouraged to believe they were simply not trying hard enough. At the end of the training period, both groups were tested on new arithmetic problems. Contrary to the common-sense idea that many successes should build confidence and lead to greater persistence, the "success only" children continued to quit when they once again experienced failure. In contrast, the children who had been taught to attribute failure to insufficient effort persisted longer at the problems and performed much better than they had before.

Dweck's study is just one of many that shows how scientific findings about human behavior often contradict common-sense notions (Brown, 1984). To take another example, consider the common-sense idea that if people under hypnosis remember details about the past that they did not recall before, then hypnosis must be an effective memory aid. This conclusion seems so logical, you are probably sure it is right, but psychologists have found that it isn't. Scientific tests reveal that the memories of hypnotized people are often less accurate than those of people who are not hypnotized. Hypnotized people may report many new recollections that they did not report before, but sometimes they have just manufactured those recollections because they *seem* appropriate. Of course, hypnotized people may also retrieve correct information that they could not recall when not hypnotized. But most of this memory improvement can be explained by factors that have nothing to do with hypnosis per se. You will find out what these factors are when you read about hypnosis in Chapter 5 of this book. The point for now is that scientific

Psychologists have disproved many commonsense beliefs. For example, people who might otherwise give up on a difficult task are more likely to persist and succeed, not when they are given easier tasks to build their confidence, but when they are persuaded to try harder.

findings about hypnosis or any other aspect of behavior sometimes contradict our common-sense views.

Another common-sense idea contradicted by scientific findings is the assumption that, to eliminate discriminatory behavior toward ethnic minorities, we must first eliminate prejudiced attitudes toward them. The overwhelming majority of people accept this common-sense view, yet psychologists have challenged it (Vaughan, 1977). In one experiment conducted many years ago, psychologist Richard LaPiere (1934) traveled around the United States with a Chinese couple, expecting to be denied service at hotels and restaurants because of the anti-Oriental attitudes prevalent at the time. But this was not what happened. "In something like ten thousand miles of motor travel," LaPiere wrote, "twice across the United States, up and down the Pacific Coast, we met definite rejection just once from those asked to serve us" (LaPiere, 1934, p. 233). LaPiere followed up his travels by writing a letter to each of the 251 establishments he and his Chinese friends had visited, asking whether they would provide food or lodging to Orientals. Of the 128 that responded, more than 90 percent answered with a flat "no," showing that their attitudes were very prejudiced. Apparently, people do not always act in accordance with their attitudes, as common sense would have us believe. In Chapter 18 we shall explore the conditions under which

inconsistency between attitudes and behavior is most likely to occur.

That psychology sometimes contradicts intuitive judgments about human behavior is an important theme of this book. As you read this text and learn more about psychology, you may be surprised to learn just how many of the "facts" about human nature that you accept as valid fail to hold up under scientific scrutiny.

THE ONGOING NATURE OF SCIENCE

In exploring how psychologists sometimes challenge common-sense notions, we have described just a few examples of the imaginative detective work that researchers do. But note that few scientific questions are ever fully and unequivocally answered. Like any science, psychology is an ongoing field of study. The findings of different investigators inevitably lead to new problems, new directions, new possibilities. This is what makes psychology so exciting: There is always more to learn.

An excellent example of the ongoing nature of psychological investigations is research on how a person's way of attributing causes can affect his or her performance. Remember Dweck's research on how children who attribute failure to their own lack of ability tend to give up trying as soon as tasks become difficult. You can think of Dweck's experiment as one of the *initial studies* on this important topic. Because Dweck's findings seemed so interesting and important, other psychologists quickly responded to them with their own ideas about the subject.

In general, the responses of other psychologists to a colleague's work take several forms. Some *criticize* how the initial studies were conducted. They might, for example, find flaws in the design of the research, such as how participants were selected and assigned to groups. Or they might question whether behavior observed in the laboratory is really representative of how people act in the "real" world. Others offer *alternative interpretations* of the initial findings. For instance, a psychologist analyzing Dweck's results might suggest that the students who learned to persist longer at difficult tasks could have been influenced more by the pattern of rewards they experienced than they were by the fact that they were taught to attribute failure to lack of effort. In Chapter 6 you will discover that when people receive a reward only occasionally, the behavior for which they are being rewarded tends to become strong and persistent. Since Dweck's students who underwent "attribution retraining" were rewarded with success only some of the time, perhaps this is what caused them to acquire greater perseverance.

To find out which of two alternative interpretations has greater validity, psychologists would have to conduct *further research.* This would entail studies designed to compare one explanation with another, just as Dweck's initial study compared her attributional theory with one based on common sense. Often this becomes a spiraling process, with the results of each new study giving rise to additional insights, which in turn spawn more research, and so the process continues. Dweck's research, for instance, helped ignite an explosion of studies on the topic of causal attributions. We will discuss some of this research in several later chapters. The important point to remember here is that all of it emerged because scientists never accept any initial set of findings as the ultimate truth. They always seek additional data, search for additional insights, and try out different perspectives from which to view a topic.

This theme of science as a dynamic, ongoing process will be found throughout this book, but especially in the sections of later chapters that are labeled "In Depth." In these sections we will take a close look at particularly intriguing research questions, the ways investigators have tackled them, the discoveries they have made, and how other psychologists have reacted to the findings. To make this ongoing scientific process easier to follow, we have divided each in-depth section into three subsections: "The Initial Studies," which explains how research on the topic began; "Criticisms, Alternatives, and Further Research," which describes reactions to the initial studies on the part of other psychologists; and "Patterns and Conclusions," which helps you to see where scientific knowledge on the topic now stands. These subsections stress how one idea leads to another and how scientists gradually build on research that has gone before. Only in this relatively slow, incremental fashion does scientific knowledge expand.

PSYCHOLOGY IS A MEANS OF PROMOTING HUMAN WELFARE

The two main professional organizations for American psychologists are the American Psychological Association (APA) and the American Psychological Society (APS). The aims of both are to advance the basic science of psychology and to promote the use of research findings to benefit society. The wide variety of interests that members of these organizations have is reflected in Figure 1.1.

The deliberate use of research findings to solve practical problems or improve the quality of life is generally called **applied science. Basic science,** in contrast, aims at understanding a subject without regard to whether that understanding will have immediate practical effects. Probing the brain to discover which particular areas are involved in remembering information is an example of basic research. In contrast, researchers who use their knowledge of the brain's mechanisms of memory to help alleviate memory impairments are engaged in applied science. At times, of course, basic and applied research cannot be distinguished so neatly. Psychologists sometimes discover a new "basic" fact when they are working on an "applied" problem, and vice versa.

Some people have trouble seeing the potential benefits of basic research. They are quick to label many such studies frivolous, a criticism that is usually groundless. Why does the public so readily jump to this conclusion? One reason is a lack of understanding about how science progresses. What may seem at first a trivial finding can turn out to provide a small

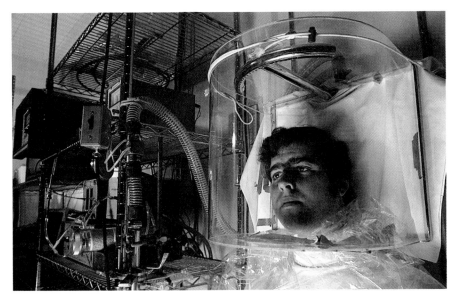

Basic research can be useful across scientific disciplines. What physiologists learn about the breathing rate of a person at rest can aid psychologists studying the effects of emotional arousal.

but vital clue in a larger and more important puzzle. The progress of science, as we have said, is often slow and incremental. But without the many small contributions accumulated over years of basic research, great breakthroughs in applied science—the first human heart transplant, the first landing of people on the moon—would never have been possible.

Another reason why many people underestimate the practical value of basic research is that the full implications of a particular study are seldom spelled out for them. Suppose you heard that the government was funding a study on hearing problems in pigs. Would you think this research was a silly waste of the taxpayers' money? A number of years ago, when such research was described in the press, many Americans thought just that. But this was because they were not informed of the potential implications. That study of pigs has helped researchers develop a way to diagnose hearing problems in human infants early enough so that they can be corrected (Walgren, 1982).

One difficulty in judging the value of basic research is that it is often hard to see where a certain line of research might lead. For instance, many years ago the work of B. F. Skinner (1904–1990), who eventually became one of the most influential twentieth-century psychologists, was attacked as frivolous. Skinner was interested in the effects of rewards and punishments on learning. To explore this topic he conducted a great many studies on "lower" animals,

such as rats and pigeons. A pigeon, for example, might be rewarded with a bit of grain whenever it pecked at a key, or a rat might be rewarded with a pellet of food whenever it pressed a bar. Seemingly simple studies like these enabled Skinner to develop the theory of learning for which he ultimately became famous. Yet his first book, *The Behavior of Organisms* (1938), sold a mere eighty copies in its first four years in print. Much of the resistance to Skinner's early work was due to the belief that his findings had limited application. How likely is it, critics asked, that an organism as complex as a human being would respond to rewards and punishments in the same predictable way that a rat or a pigeon does?

Applied research in the past several decades has challenged Skinner's early critics. People seem to be every bit as susceptible to rewards and punishments as lower animals are. Consider the work of Nathan Azrin, who was a graduate student under Skinner. He has divided his very productive career between basic research on learning and applied research on how rewards and punishments can be used to solve human problems. Azrin began his applied work by designing procedures to teach severely retarded people to feed and dress themselves, to use the toilet, and to stop such negative behaviors as bed-wetting and sprawling on the floor. These training programs proved so successful that Azrin soon expanded his efforts to common problems among normal children

and adults. He has developed widely accepted therapies for problems as diverse as stuttering, nail biting,
alcoholism, and marital conflict. We will say more
about such practical applications of learning theory in
Chapters 6 and 17.

The APA is extensively involved in informing
lawmakers and the public about the value of psychological research to many aspects of human welfare.
Every year, the APA's Public Affairs Office generates
thousands of news stories about developments in
psychology that could have implications for improving the quality of human life. In addition, the APA's
Public Interest Directorate focuses on major social
issues to which psychological knowledge can be
productively applied, issues such as the plight of the
homeless and the treatment of people with AIDS. Its
programs and activities encourage further research
on these issues, public awareness of the many problems they entail, and government funding to help
find solutions.

Besides doing research, both basic and applied,
psychologists are involved in promoting human welfare in more direct ways too. They work as counselors
and clinicians in many settings: schools, hospitals,
businesses, community health centers, and private
practices. Many students who take psychology courses do so because they are attracted to careers that
involve helping other people. We will discuss several
such careers later in this chapter.

PSYCHOLOGY'S PAST AND PRESENT

Few things can be fully understood without some
sense of where they came from and how they have
evolved. This is true of psychology. In the following
sections we shall explore the ideas of some of the
people who helped to build psychology into what it is
today. We begin with a look at the major figures who
created this new field of study in the nineteenth
century. They were responsible for first establishing
psychology as a separate discipline and a science.
One of these was a professor at the University of
Leipzig in Germany. His name was Wilhelm Wundt.

A NEW DISCIPLINE EMERGES

Wilhelm Wundt (1832–1920) was dissatisfied with
the armchair introspection of philosophers who stud-

The German
physiologist Wilhelm
Wundt (1832–1920)
taught the first course
in scientific
psychology in 1862 at
the University of
Heidelberg, and set up
the first experimental
psychology laboratory
at Leipzig in 1879.

ied the mind (Blumenthal, 1985). He felt that mental
processes could be investigated with objective techniques similar to those that scientists in other fields
used. So he set out to create a "new domain of
science," the science of psychology (Wundt, 1904). At
the University of Leipzig, where he taught for many
years, Wundt officially established the first psychology laboratory in the fall of 1879. This laboratory was
greatly expanded in the decades that followed. By
1897 it had been moved to a new building constructed just for the purpose of doing psychological research (Hothersall, 1984).

Wundt and his students conducted studies on a
broad range of topics, including sensation and perception, attention, emotions, word associations, and
reaction times to various stimuli. They strove to be
systematic and precise in taking measurements by
using a variety of laboratory instruments in their
research. These methods set them apart from most
earlier scholars, who had studied the human mind
simply through introspection. Because of his insis-
tence on rigorous scientific methods, Wundt is aptly
known as the father of modern psychology.

Wundt's ideas influenced a whole generation of
psychologists. Many of his students went on to be
prominent researchers in their own right, establishing
laboratories and departments of psychology across
Europe and the United States. One of these students
was Edward Tichener (1867–1927), who started a
psychology laboratory at Cornell University. Tichener believed that the job of psychologists was to
analyze human consciousness in terms of its
component parts, much as chemists analyze matter in

terms of its component molecules and atoms. The principal components of consciousness, Tichener argued, were fundamental sensations and feelings, which ultimately combine to form the structure of the mind. Because of his emphasis on how mental structure is built up from parts, Tichener's perspective came to be known as **structuralism.**

Just two years before Tichener began working at Cornell, an American psychologist at Harvard published what was to become one of the most influential books in all of psychology. That book was William James's *Principles of Psychology* (1890), a text that taught a whole generation of future psychologists (Hothersall, 1984). Taking twelve years to write and running to nearly 1,400 pages, it is filled with provocative insights about such topics as human habits, emotions, and consciousness.

James (1842–1910) had little patience with the structuralist belief that our mental states can be broken down into smaller components. To him this was an obscure idea at odds with his own observations. James maintained that consciousness was not "chopped up in bits," but rather was a continuous whole that flowed like a stream. Influenced by Charles Darwin's theory of biological evolution, James believed that the human mind was constantly evolving as it adapted to new information from the environment. As such, the human mind serves the vital function of mediating between the environment and a person's needs.

Other American psychologists at the time, including some students of James, likewise began to focus on how the mind adapts to environmental information and so helps people survive. This view came to be known as **functionalism,** because its adherents stressed the functions that our mental processes serve. They also emphasized the dynamic operations of the mind, in contrast to the structuralists, who focused on the mind's more static components. Structuralists and functionalists were soon debating the proper subject matter for their new and growing discipline. These debates, however, were not enduring. With the turn of the twentieth century, other psychological perspectives began emerging, perspectives that would eventually overshadow structuralism and functionalism. Still, debates among the proponents of these two early schools of thought helped set the stage for a discipline filled with controversies and differing viewpoints.

THE DEVELOPMENT OF CONTEMPORARY PERSPECTIVES: PSYCHOLOGY IN THE TWENTIETH CENTURY

Five perspectives have come to dominate psychology in the twentieth century. One is the neurobiological perspective, which explains thoughts, feelings, and behaviors in terms of the workings of the brain and nervous system. Another is the behaviorist perspective, which looks for explanations in the environmental stimuli that shape and control a person's actions. A third contemporary viewpoint is the psychoanalytic perspective. Its explanations for behavior lie in powerful unconscious wishes and conflicts. In contrast, the humanistic perspective explains what people do in terms of their motivation for self-fulfillment and the obstacles that sometimes thwart it. Finally, the cognitive perspective explains behavior by looking at a person's particular ways of reasoning and thinking.

Although these five perspectives are all very different, they are not necessarily opposed to one another. It is more productive to think of them as simply viewing behavior from different angles. Consider three people viewing a sunset. The first, an artist, considers how the various colors work together to produce a beautiful scene. The second, a meteorologist, considers how the earth's atmosphere affects the rays of light and so creates what we see. The third, a physicist, considers the light waves themselves and how the energy in them travels millions of miles. Notice how all three of these analyses, while very different, make valuable contributions to understanding the whole. The same is true when psychologists view behavior from different perspectives. Each may arrive at a different explanation, but all may have some validity. Thus, it is best to think of the five perspectives in modern psychology as complementing one another. Each contributes valuable pieces to the puzzle of why people think and act as they do. With this in mind, let us look at what these perspectives entail and how they developed.

THE BEHAVIORIST PERSPECTIVE

The **behaviorist perspective** arose in the early twentieth century, led by the brilliant but brash young scholar John B. Watson (1878–1958). It was partly a reaction against the functionalist preoccupa-

John B. Watson (1878–1958) formulated the goals of behaviorism in 1913, proposing that its methods of study be modeled on those of the natural sciences.

tion with studying consciousness. Consciousness, the behaviorists argued, was not a proper topic for scientific inquiry, for it is too hard to measure objectively. Thus, if psychology was to be a science, it must stop trying to study what goes on in people's heads. Instead, it must be limited to the study of observable behavior.

This narrower definition of psychology led the early behaviorists into a new kind of research. They began to investigate how environmental stimuli can cause an animal to learn particular responses. Watson and his associates were strongly influenced by the pioneering work of the great Russian physiologist Ivan Pavlov (1849–1936). In a now-famous experiment, Pavlov rang a bell a few seconds before giving a dog some meat, a stimulus to which the dog responded by salivating profusely. After repeating this procedure many times, Pavlov found that the dog salivated upon hearing the bell alone, even if no food was given. The bell, in short, now had the power to trigger a certain behavior (salivation), because the dog had learned an association between the bell and food.

Watson took the extreme position that *all* behavior represents learned responses to particular stimuli. He rejected the notion of innate differences in ability or temperament. He believed that, by controlling environmental stimuli, he could shape a person's character in any way he wished. "Give me a dozen healthy infants," Watson boasted, ". . . and my own specified world to bring them up in, and I'll guarantee to take any one at random and train him to become any type of specialist I might select—doctor, lawyer, artist, merchant-chief, and yes, even beggar-man and thief, regardless of his talents, penchants, tendencies, abilities, vocations, and race of his ancestors" (Watson, 1924, p. 82). Fortunately for the babies, Watson never got the chance to do this experiment.

Other American psychologists were also influential in developing behaviorist thought. One was Edward L. Thorndike (1874–1949), who conducted a series of studies with cats. Each cat was placed in a box from which it could escape if it pulled or pushed the right mechanism (a string or lever, for example) attached to the box's inside. Although the cat's first successful responses were largely a matter or chance, it gradually learned to perform the desired action as soon as it was placed in the box. This research emphasized the importance of rewards to learning, because the cat received a tasty bit of food when it found its way out. Thorndike argued that if an animal comes to associate a particular response with a reward, that response will strengthen and increase in frequency. Conversely, if an animal comes to associate a particular response with punishment, that response will weaken and decrease in frequency.

Behaviorist B. F. Skinner, like both Watson and Thorndike before him, spent a good part of his career studying learning among animals. But Skinner went far beyond his predecessors in arguing that behaviorism's insights can and should be applied to human society as a whole. His widely read novel *Walden Two* (1948) portrays a behaviorist utopia: a small community in which people are trained from birth to be productive and satisfied citizens. For example, through the application of rewards and punishments, children in Walden Two are taught to shun excessive materialism and the destruction of the environment. Skinner believed that this type of society is essential to the survival of the human species in light of the seemingly insurmountable environmental and social problems that confront us today. To those who are disturbed by this degree of control over people's lives, Skinner replied that we are already heavily controlled by others, but are often unaware of it. In his utopia, control is open and aboveboard, planned by parents, teachers, and others for the good of all.

Skinner's brand of behaviorism is called "radical" not because of his social philosophy, but because of his ideas about the role the mind plays in determining people's behavior. To Skinner, the concept of mind was totally unnecessary to explain why someone acts in a certain way. All that is needed is a knowledge of the rewards and punishments that are affecting the person's behavior. For instance, if you know that a man who has served time in prison is no longer committing crimes, you do not need to know his inner thoughts and feeling in order to explain his actions. It does not matter that he deeply regrets injuring others in the past. In fact, mentioning this subjective feeling tends to divert our attention from the true cause of the man's behavior: the fact that his crimes resulted in a punishing consequence.

Radical behaviorism has been widely criticized in recent years. The critics charge that we cannot ignore people's thoughts and feelings if we are to understand their actions. What goes on within people's minds while learning and responding is extremely important to understanding their behavior, these psychologists say. Consider two men who have gone to prison for the same number of years. When they are released, one resumes criminal activity while the other one does not. Why is there this difference if both men have experienced the same punishment? According to psychologist Albert Bandura and others with similar views, it depends on how each man *interprets* his personal experiences. Suppose the first man sees prison as just a temporary setback. He believes that he will not have to serve time again because he has learned from other prison inmates how to avoid police. The second man, in contrast, dreads another prison term; he is convinced that those who break the law will ultimately be caught. These two men, in short, have very different mental outlooks that help explain why they behave so differently. This focus on how individual beliefs and expectations mediate the impact that rewards and punishments have is a contemporary slant to the behaviorist perspective that you will see again in later chapters.

THE PSYCHOANALYTIC PERSPECTIVE

No discussion of modern psychology would be complete without mention of the **psychoanalytic perspective** developed by Sigmund Freud. Freud (1856–1939) was a physician in Vienna, Austria, who specialized in disorders of the nervous system. He observed that some of his patients had nothing physically wrong with them, even though they had symptoms of physical illness (headaches, exhaustion, insomnia, and so forth). He suspected that mental conflicts lay behind these symptoms—conflicts that had been pushed out of normal awareness and into a

Sigmund Freud (1856–1939), one of the major figures of the twentieth century, developed the theory of psychoanalysis and its techniques for the treatment of psychological disorders, which he believed were caused by unconscious conflicts.

part of the mind Freud called the **unconscious.** Freud was impressed with the results that another Viennese doctor, Josef Breuer, had obtained in his treatment of a woman suffering from psychosomatic paralysis. Breuer found that if he hypnotized the woman, she was able to discuss the psychological roots of her disorder quite freely, and after such discussion her condition tended to improve. Freud became convinced that if unconscious conflicts could be brought into a patient's awareness, they would lose their power to control that person's life.

One of Freud's challenges was how to uncover unconscious conflicts. Although he started by using hypnosis, he became dissatisfied with it because often it did not reach deeply enough into a person's buried memories. Eventually he developed a method called **free association,** in which the patient was asked to lie comfortably on a couch and say whatever came to mind, no matter how irrelevant or foolish it sounded. The patient's apparently random talk, Freud believed, would eventually contain themes related to unconscious conflicts. Freud also encouraged patients to talk about their dreams, because he believed that dreams are full of symbolic hints as to what is bothering the dreamer. With these verbal clues, Freud helped his patients interpret and understand their symptoms. He called his approach to treatment **psychoanalysis.**

Freud gradually developed an elaborate theory of personality based on his observations. For instance, he found that when a patient's unconscious was probed for critical events that had initiated psychological problems, the most significant memories were usually those of some forbidden sexual impulse during childhood. Freud took this as evidence that human beings, like other animals, are driven by powerful biological urges, especially sexual ones. In humans, however, such urges often conflict with society's moral standards, so people must learn to restrict and inhibit them. A major part of this learning, according to Freud, takes place during childhood, when the rules of society are first imposed. Thus, in Freud's view, psychological problems arise when early conflicts between society's demands and innate sexual urges are never satisfactorily resolved. In the Victorian age in which Freud wrote, his stress on childhood sexuality was often seen as shocking, and today many criticize Freudian theory for being hard to verify scientifically. Nevertheless, Freud made lasting contributions by calling attention to the frequent importance of early life events and to the existence of unconscious motives in people.

Even while Freud was still alive, some of his followers began to work their own ideas into psychoanalytic theory. In general, subsequent psychoanalytic thinkers have placed less emphasis on innate biological urges as the basic human motivators and more on the thinking, planning, rational side of the human psyche. They have also focused more on how interactions with others and society as a whole shape who we become; and they tend to see personality development as extending beyond childhood, into adolescence and even adulthood. For example, Erik Erikson, a contemporary psychoanalyst, has proposed a theory of personality in which people face a series of challenges from infancy to old age, each challenge arising from new demands that society makes as people mature. How someone meets these challenges shapes the kind of person that individual becomes. You will read more about Erikson's views in Chapters 10 and 13 of this book.

THE HUMANISTIC PERSPECTIVE

The behaviorist and psychoanalytic perspectives flourished in the early part of this century, but by mid-century reactions against them began to set in. One was strong opposition to their deterministic outlooks. By deterministic we mean that both behaviorist and psychoanalytic theory assume that people's thoughts and actions are often shaped by forces beyond their control. To behaviorists these determin-

ing forces are environmental stimuli, especially rewards and punishments; to psychoanalysts the uncontrollable forces are unconscious drives and conflicts. Psychologists who adopt a **humanistic perspective** reject the idea that people are not masters of their own destinies. According to them, we are free to reach our fullest potential, to become whatever we are capable of being. The humanists, in fact, see a striving for **self-actualization** (for becoming all we can be) as the pinnacle of human motivation. This highest of all our motivations is stressed in the writings of Abraham Maslow (1908–1970), a noted personality theorist who took a humanistic view.

Of course, environmental situations and the actions of other people can sometimes thwart a person's efforts toward self-actualization. Psychotherapists with a humanistic perspective believe this is a major cause of psychological problems. When people are prevented from achieving self-fulfillment, when they are forced into being something other than their "true" selves, they feel anxious and unhappy, manipulated rather than free. One widely influential psychotherapist with a humanistic view was Carl Rogers (1902–1987). He believed that people can be helped to find self-actualization when a therapist treats them with empathy and understanding, giving them emotional and psychological support regarding anything they want to be or do. Like others who take a humanistic perspective, Rogers stressed the positive side of human nature. He argued that when people are genuinely free, they are automatically constructive in their actions and seek to build caring relationships with others. This view is very different from traditional Freudian theory, in which instinctual urges often propel people toward selfish, sometimes aggressive acts. You will read more about both Rogers and Maslow in Chapter 13 of this book.

Although the views of humanistic psychologists have been criticized as vague and unscientific, they have nevertheless had a strong impact on modern-day thinking. The stress on fulfilling individual potential, establishing close relationships with others, and fashioning lives that are meaningful strikes a responsive chord in contemporary society, where huge bureaucracies and anonymous urban living seem to threaten our fundamental humanness. Not surprisingly, the last few decades have seen a proliferation of group therapies aimed at helping people to grow psychologically and experience more joy in their lives.

The work of humanistic psychologists has led to the various group therapies so widespread today. Whether labeled "New Age," "human potential" or "personal growth," all these approaches are intended to help group members feel happier with themselves and more comfortable with other people.

THE COGNITIVE PERSPECTIVE

We have already mentioned the modern trend among psychologists who study learning to consider how people interpret the events and stimuli around them, fashioning their actions according to their individual understandings. Such understandings, thoughts, expectations, and perceptions are known as **cognitions,** a term that refers to all mental processes. Contemporary psychologists who take a **cognitive perspective** study a wide range of cognitive topics, including learning, memory, concept formation, problem solving, decision making, and language.

The cognitive movement in America began to take hold in the 1950s, but even before then some psychologists had turned their attention to mental processes. One was an Englishman, Sir Frederic Bartlett. In studying human memory he came to the conclusion that we do not just duplicate in memory precisely what we see and hear (Bartlett, 1932). Instead, our minds actively interpret our experiences on the basis of what we know and believe. It is these interpretations, or **schemas** as Bartlett called them, that we store in memory. Once formed, our schemas constantly guide our subsequent thoughts and actions.

Many cognitive psychologists have incorporated the concept of schemas into their views of how the human mind works. For instance, Jean Piaget (1896–1980), a Swiss psychologist, proposed that schemas undergo fundamental change from infancy to adolescence. According to Piaget, a baby does not interpret objects the same way that adults do. In the mind of a very young infant, an object actually ceases to exist when it is out of the child's view. Only with experience do babies come to realize that objects have permanence. Thus, in Piaget's theory, experience plays a crucial role in the development of increasingly mature schemas (Piaget, 1952, 1954).

Many other concepts, besides schemas, have helped to form the cognitive viewpoint. One is the idea of **mental strategies** first proposed by Jerome Bruner and his colleagues in an influential book called *The Study of Thinking* (1956). Bruner suggested that people use mental strategies when trying to identify the defining features of an unfamiliar concept. They essentially test out various hypotheses until they zero in on the correct response. In a similar vein, psychologist George Miller proposed that *plans* are enormously important in guiding people's actions. Plans, in Miller's view, allow us to initiate behaviors that will close the gap between our current state and a goal we want to reach (Miller et al., 1960).

Researchers in fields other than psychology have also had an impact on the development of the cognitive perspective. For instance, communications engineers helped provide cognitive psychology with a useful analogy between the human mind and an **information-processing system.** According to this analogy, the mind takes in information, processes it in various ways, and produces outputs in the form of ideas, words, and behaviors. The information-processing analogy encouraged computer scientists to try to program computers to simulate human thought. Two pioneers in this effort were Alan Newell and Herbert Simon. They developed a program called the General Problem Solver which attempted to mimic the way human beings reason their way to solutions (Newell and Simon, 1972). Although the General Problem Solver turned out to have some major limitations as a model of human thought, it nevertheless helped to make the study of mental processes scientifically acceptable. Today, a great many psychologists take a cognitive perspective and are engaged in researching cognitive topics. You will read about their theories and findings in almost every chapter of this book.

THE NEUROBIOLOGICAL PERSPECTIVE

Psychologists have long acknowledged that the brain must ultimately control all of human thought, feeling, and behavior. This idea gave rise to the **neurobiological perspective,** *neuro* meaning having to do with the nervous system, of which the brain is the central part. During the 1930s and 1940s, however, interest in neurobiology waned. The behaviorists, who dominated American psychology at that time, felt that our understanding of neurobiology was so sketchy that we should postpone theorizing about the brain's role in learning and other important psychological processes. This attitude persisted until about 1950, when advances in technology started to make possible new, more effective methods of studying the brain.

One group of researchers at Berkeley—David Krech, Edward Bennett, and Mark Rosenzweig—helped to launch the modern exploration of brain chemistry. They believed that the various chemicals released in the brain played major roles in controlling human thought, feelings, and behavior. Identifying these chemicals and determining each one's effects in specific parts of the brain became a major preoccupation among neurobiological researchers. This preoccupation continues today as we discover more and more about the complexities of the brain's chemical systems. For instance, brain chemicals are strongly

implicated in some serious psychological disorders, such as major depression and schizophrenia. We will say more about the chemistry of the brain in a number of later chapters.

Another major interest of psychologists with a neurobiological perspective is mapping the brain to find out which areas are involved in controlling specific kinds of behaviors. One technique is to stimulate different cells in the brain of an experimental animal and observe how the animal responds. Depending on which cells are stimulated, the animal might cower in fear, fly into a rage, begin eating voraciously, or react in any number of other ways. Neurobiological researchers also record the spontaneous activities of brain cells while an animal is performing some task. For example, using this method, psychologist Richard Thompson and his colleagues are well on the way to identifying the specific cells involved in simple kinds of learning. Such findings make the neurobiological perspective a very exciting part of modern psychology.

APPLYING DIFFERENT PERSPECTIVES: AN ECLECTIC APPROACH

The five perspectives in modern psychology all add to our understanding of why human beings behave as they do. Thus, for any given question about human behavior, psychologists with different perspectives have different things to say. Each tackles the issue from another angle, contributing different insights. You can see this more clearly by considering a specific kind of human behavior to which all five of these perspectives can be applied. Why, for example, do people sometimes explode in acts of extreme violence toward others? Why in the spring of 1989 did a band of teenage boys go on a rampage of violence in New York's Central Park? When the rampage was over they had beaten several men unconscious and so brutally raped and beaten a woman jogger that she nearly bled to death. That same year the small town of Stockton, California, had its own encounter with extreme violence. A man with an automatic weapon walked into an elementary school yard and fired randomly at the children and teachers. Many were wounded and some were killed. This incident is reminiscent of another that occurred in Texas some years earlier. Charles Whitman, a student at the University of Texas, armed himself with an arsenal of weapons—three rifles, a sawed-off shotgun, two pis-

Modern psychology's different perspectives can each contribute insights into shocking incidents like the sniper shooting of several children in a Stockton, California, schoolyard in 1989. They can also provide ways of helping survivors and eyewitnesses cope with the trauma.

tols, a Bowie knife, five gallons of gasoline—and climbed to the top of a twenty-seven-story tower. From there he proceeded to fire at people below, killing thirteen and injuring thirty-two. The night before, he had shot his mother and stabbed his wife to death. A note left behind explained that he wanted to spare his wife the embarrassment that his actions would surely cause her.

What could explain this bizarre behavior from someone who was an honor student, a dormitory counselor, and an Eagle Scout? Psychologists with different perspectives would search for different kinds of answers. Those with a neurobiological perspective would look for answers in Charles Whitman's brain. Might he have a tumor or some serious neurochemical imbalance? Not surprisingly, an autopsy revealed a walnut-sized tumor in a part of Whitman's brain involved in emotion and aggression.

This tumor probably predisposed him to some form of extreme violence.

But was the tumor the whole cause of Whitman's tragic actions? Some psychologists would say not. Even before the brain tumor developed, Whitman had displayed unusual aggression. He was court martialed from the Marine Corps for excessive fighting. He physically abused his wife. Once he threw a fellow college student out of a classroom when the other student sat in Whitman's chair. Why did Whitman show these earlier aggressive tendencies?

Psychologists with a behaviorist perspective would look for rewards that might have encouraged unusual aggression. Did Whitman gain social approval for being "tough"? Did he gain a sense of superiority by dominating others? If so, his aggression was being encouraged by these positive consequences.

Psychologists who take a cognitive perspective would offer further insights. Many would look to the schemas of aggressive behavior that Whitman had acquired. As a child, he had often seen his father beating his mother and siblings. Perhaps these experiences had fashioned in his mind an image of men as "strong" and "aggressive," which he then used as a model for his own behavior.

Psychologists with a psychoanalytic perspective would adopt still a different outlook. Some might concentrate on the fact that Whitman hated his father, whom he described as "brutal, domineering, and extremely demanding." When Whitman's parents separated, he moved his mother to Texas, where she took an apartment near him. Subsequently, his father had spent over $1,000 a month in telephone calls to Whitman, begging him to get the mother to return. In this complicated web of stormy relationships, we can see the outline of what Freud called the Oedipus conflict. This is a situation in which a little boy loves his mother and wants to surpass his father as an object of the mother's affections. But he also fears that the father will be jealous and punish him for these desires. Perhaps this childhood conflict lingered unresolved in Whitman, influencing his emotions and behavior as an adult.

Finally, psychologists with a humanistic perspective would focus on how Whitman's progress toward self-actualization and fulfillment had been blocked. If his efforts to achieve what he wanted in life had continually been thwarted, if others were constantly devaluing him and limiting his future choices, he

Do violent movies like the 1990 hit *GoodFellas* make angry, frustrated people more likely to behave violently? Psychologists consider such questions as part of their effort to explain human behavior.

might respond with frustration and resentment that built to dangerous levels, periodically triggering acts of violent aggression.

Don't be dismayed by the fact that psychology offers so many different explanations for acts of unusual violence. Such differing viewpoints often complement each other, together providing a far richer understanding of human behavior than any one view could alone. In this book we take an *eclectic approach* to understanding behavior—that is, we draw insights from all five of these perspectives and more.

THE THREE GOALS OF MODERN PSYCHOLOGY

So far we have focused mainly on psychologists' ideas about *why* people behave in the ways they do. But offering explanations for behavior is just one of the goals of psychology. Psychologists also seek to describe and predict how people behave. Let us look more closely at these three goals and how they relate to one another.

DESCRIPTION

Understanding human behavior must begin with careful *descriptions* of how people think, feel, and act in specific situations. To begin understanding the violence of a Charles Whitman, for example, we must know in detail what he did that was violent, when

these acts of violence were triggered, and how Whitman himself viewed them.

Psychologists collect this descriptive data as objectively as they can. Ideally, they try to observe the behavior of interest first-hand, recording it precisely in written notes or on tapes or videocassettes. Of course, in most incidents of sudden, explosive violence, no curious psychologists are there to watch and record what happens. But researchers can carefully reconstruct such incidents through the testimonies of participants and eyewitnesses. We will say more about the techniques used to gather descriptive data in Chapter 2, on research methods.

EXPLANATION

Describing human behavior is not enough, however. We also want to know *why* it happens—that is, we want to *explain* it. We have already talked about the different explanations that psychologists with different perspectives might offer. This is a critically important part of psychologists' work. Without insights into why people think and act as they do, psychologists would have purely descriptive information and no meaningful understanding of it.

But theories, in themselves, are not enough either. We need evidence to support or disconfirm them; otherwise we would not be engaged in science. Psychologists conduct studies for this express purpose. For instance, researchers have conducted studies to test the theory that people who are frustrated and angry are more apt to lash out with violence if they are exposed to some aggressive cue, such as a gun or a violent movie. Such studies tend to support the idea that aggressive cues *can* sometimes encourage violence under the right emotional circumstances (Berkowitz and Geen, 1966; Berkowitz and LePage, 1976). We will return to the evidence supporting this and other theories of violence in Chapter 19 of this book.

PREDICTION

A study designed to test a theory usually involves making a prediction that people will behave in a certain way in a certain set of circumstances. If the prediction is upheld, the theory is supported; if it is not, it is unsupported. Thus, the ability to make *predictions*—to say in advance how someone is likely to act—lies at the heart of doing certain kinds of psychological research.

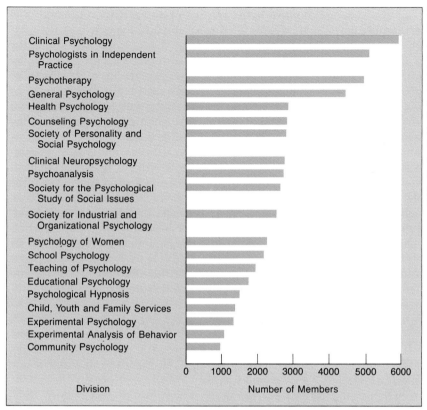

FIGURE 1.1 Membership in the twenty largest divisions of the American Psychological Association's forty-four divisions in 1990. Note that members may belong to more than one division. In the American Psychological Society, the subfields with the largest number of members are: general and historical (16.5 percent); experimental and perceptual (16 percent); clinical, community, counseling, and health (12.5 percent); and social and personality (13 percent).

When psychologists have a broad understanding of a particular behavior, they can make *many* accurate predictions about it. For instance, psychologists with a broad understanding of human violence should be able to predict with a fair degree of accuracy who is most likely to be involved in such behavior (their age, sex, social class, personal histories, and so forth), what immediate circumstances tend to trigger it, and what if any factors can restrain it. Of course, no such predictions prove accurate 100 percent of the time. Human behavior is highly complex, and unanticipated factors can always influence it. But if psychologists cannot predict a behavior at least some of the time, they are not very far along in understanding it.

CONTEMPORARY FIELDS OF SPECIALIZATION

Psychology is usually a single department in colleges and universities, yet psychologists are far from uniform in their professional interests. Psychology is made up of many highly specialized subfields, each

with not only its own subject matter, but also its own theories and sometimes even its own research methods (see Figure 1.1). In the following pages we will acquaint you with some of the major subfields in psychology today, as well as the kinds of research being done in them.

EXPERIMENTAL PSYCHOLOGY

Where would you put something if you wanted to be sure you could find it again when needed? Would you try putting it in some very unusual place, assuming that such an odd location could never be forgotten? This memory aid seems logical enough. How well does it work? Psychologists have found that the answer is not very well at all. One experiment showed that people have a harder time recalling unusual places where things have been put (an airline ticket put in a shoe, a set of car keys put in a light fixture) than they do recalling more logical "safe-keeping" places (Winograd and Soloway, 1986). In Chapter 7 you will read about many other experiments that have been conducted on human memory. This is just one of a large number of topics that **experimental psychologists** explore.

The term *experimental psychology* is a bit of a misnomer. It implies that this subfield is the only one in psychology that relies on experimentation as a data-gathering method. This is definitely *not* the case. Researchers in many other areas of psychology also conduct experiments. So, to define experimental psychology we must look as much to its subject matter as to its methods. Experimental psychologists study one of several "basic" processes—"basic" both in the sense that they are shared by a variety of animal species and in the sense that they are often involved in other aspects of behavior. These basic processes include sensation, perception, learning, memory, problem solving, communication, emotion, and motivation. Experimental psychologists often do their research in a laboratory, and frequently they use animals other than humans as their experimental subjects.

NEUROPSYCHOLOGY

Like experimental psychologists, **neuropsychologists** also study basic processes, but they focus on a certain aspect of them. They study how basic processes are controlled by the nervous system, of which the brain is the central part. For instance, if asked to explain why memory sometimes declines in old age, a neuropsychologist would probe the brain for signs of a breakdown in the network of nerve cells thought to be involved in remembering. Or if asked what causes a person to persistently overeat, a neuropsychologist would suspect a malfunction in the brain's mechanisms for regulating hunger. Like experimental psychologists, too, neuropsychologists often use other animal species as subjects.

In recent years neuropsychologists have made great strides in understanding the neurological basis of many behaviors. Today modern technology allows them actually to look inside a human brain at work. For example, researchers have used PET scans to study activity in the brains of hyperactive adults. Hyperactive people have both difficulty remaining still (they seem to be in constant motion) and difficulty focusing their attention for very long. The researchers found that adults with a history of hyperactivity, who also had hyperactive children, had markedly reduced activity in areas of the brain that control body movement and attention (Zametkin et al., 1990). Of course, lifelong hyperactives with hyperactive children may be a subgroup of all the people who suffer this disorder, a subgroup for whom the disorder is largely genetic in origin. But the insights from this study may still provide clues for treating hyperactivity. You will be learning about many other exciting new findings in neuropsychology throughout the rest of this book.

Experimental psychologists and neuropsychologists are often affiliated with colleges and universities, for centers of higher education can provide the facilities needed for their research. Many others, however, work in business or government. Pharmaceutical companies, for instance, hire neuropsychologists to assess the effects of new drugs. As scientists learn more about how the brain works, **psychopharmacology** (the study of the link between drugs and behavior) has become a rapidly growing field.

PERSONALITY PSYCHOLOGY

If given a choice between a date who was rather unattractive physically but friendly and sensitive and a date who was very attractive physically but moody and self-centered, whom would you choose? Psychologists have found that your answer depends greatly on your personality—that is, your relatively stable style of thinking, acting, and responding emotionally. In one study, male college students were assessed for a personality trait called self-monitoring, a measure of how concerned a person is about the image he or she conveys (Snyder et al., 1985). High self-monitors are very conscious of what others think of them, so they watch their own behavior closely to make sure it meets with others' approval. Low self-monitors, in contrast, do not know or do not care much about others' opinions of them. Their behavior is generally based on their *own* beliefs and feelings. The researchers found that when high and low self-monitors were given the choice described above, the great majority of "highs" selected the attractive partner, while the great majority of "lows" selected the personable one. Apparently, a need to project a favorable image to other people steers high self-monitors toward relationships with those who "look good."

This study is just one example of the kinds of issues that **personality psychologists** explore. Personality psychology is concerned with describing and

Personality psychologists explore the reasons for differences in people's behavior. Why, for example, are some people naturally more comfortable than others in the same situation?

explaining individual differences in behavior. To what extent is one person more self-monitoring than another, more manipulative, more outgoing, more obedient to authority? How can we account for differences in personality? Is there something "inside" that makes us think, feel, and act in certain ways? Do we largely inherit personality traits? Or do "outside" factors—our personal histories, our culture, the times in which we live, the pressures of the immediate situation—shape the ways we respond? How, in other words, does personality develop? And can personality change over time? These are the central questions that personality psychologists ask. We will investigate them in detail in Chapters 10 and 13.

SOCIAL PSYCHOLOGY

Suppose you were in a crowded store and a man collapsed before you, clutching his chest and gasping for breath. Would you try to help him? What would you think of people who just stood by and watched, as often happens in such situations? Are these people heartless and uncaring? If not, why do they stand idly by? In a classic series of studies, psychologists John Darley and Bibb Latané tried to answer these questions by staging bogus emergencies and observing bystanders' reactions (Darley and Latané, 1968; La-

tané and Darley, 1968). In one experiment, people heard someone in the next room crash to the floor and moan in pain (actually a tape-recorded performance); in another, someone was heard having a violent seizure (also simulated); in a third, the experimenter pretended to be severely shocked by electrical equipment. Latané and Darley found that willingness to help was *not* related to individual personality traits, such as sensitivity to others. Instead, a bystander's reaction was shaped largely by the social situation. A person was far more apt to offer help when witnessing an emergency alone than when seeing it in a group. We will suggest some reasons for this difference in Chapter 19.

If you are thinking that this powerful influence of other people must be unique to emergencies, you are wrong. **Social psychologists** have shown repeatedly that our behavior is not just the result of our personalities and predispositions. Environmental factors, especially the presence of others, greatly affect what we think, say, and do. This finding sheds light on many incidents that would otherwise be hard to explain. How could a company of American soldiers have massacred nearly 500 civilians, most of them women and children, in the Vietnamese village of My Lai? Social psychologist Stanley Milgram (1963) has demonstrated the incredible extent to which average people will inflict severe pain on their fellow humans

Developmental psychologists study the differences in human behavior at various stages of life. For instance, young children are afraid of people in costumes, even Santa Claus, while infants generally couldn't care less.

if an authority figure tells them to do so. How can groups of intelligent, well-informed adults make decisions so terrible, so poorly thought out, that any casual observer can point out their flaws? Social psychologist Irving Janis (1972) believes the answer sometimes lies in "groupthink," the enormous pressure for unanimity that arises in closely knit groups, to the point where group members can no longer appraise things realistically. In Chapters 18 and 19 we will explore these and many other examples of how our perceptions, motivations, beliefs, and behaviors are influenced by situational factors, especially by the actions of other people. This is the unique and fascinating perspective of social psychology.

Where do social psychologists work? Like experimental psychologists, they work largely in two types of settings: colleges and universities; and business, government, and nonprofit agencies.

DEVELOPMENTAL PSYCHOLOGY

Suppose you show a three-year-old a red toy car behind a green filter so that the car appears black. You remove the car from behind the filter and hand it to the child so that he or she can see the car's true color. Then you place the car back behind the filter and ask the child: "What color is that car? Is it red or black?" The child quickly answers "black." So you rephrase the question: "What color is it *really and truly?* Is it *really* black or *really* red?" Again the child answers "black." If you asked this same question of a seven-year-old, he or she would say "red." Unlike a three-year-old, a seven-year-old does not have trouble distinguishing appearance from reality on such simple tasks. Yet even seven-year-olds do not yet think about appearance–reality distinctions in the same way adults do. Children this age have difficulty talking about appearance and reality in abstract terms. It is not until they are about age twelve that they acquire a relatively sophisticated grasp of these two concepts (Flavell, 1986).

Developmental psychologists try to describe and explain the systematic changes that occur in people throughout the life cycle. How ways of thinking and reasoning change as people grow older is just one of many topics developmental psychologists study. In fact, most fields of psychology—from sensation and perception to learning and memory, thinking and problem solving, emotion and motivation, personality and social interaction—can be studied from this perspective. Do newborn infants perceive the world differently than adults do, and if so in what ways? Why will a four-year-old tell you that a lump of clay grows "bigger" as it is rolled into a snake, whereas an eight-year-old can easily see that the amount of clay stays the same? What about intellectual skills in adulthood? Do they decline in old age as many people assume? Answers to these and many other questions about developmental changes are explored in Chapters 9 and 10. These chapters also explore another issue of interest to developmental psychologists: how can we explain the individual differences that develop in people? As you will learn, the answers lie in a complex interplay of genes and environment.

Developmental psychologists work in a variety of settings, including colleges and universities, health-care settings, or business, government, and nonprofit agencies. In addition to doing academic research, developmental psychologists may be involved in evaluating children who are not developing normally and advising parents on how these children can be helped.

INDUSTRIAL AND ORGANIZATIONAL PSYCHOLOGY

Have you ever heard of "sick building syndrome"? This is a set of symptoms people sometimes experience when they work in offices suspected of having air pollution. The symptoms include irritated eyes, nose, throat, or skin, frequent headaches, and mental fatigue. But are these symptoms always caused by poor indoor air? Probably not. When researchers recently studied over 3,000 workers in eighteen office buildings, none of which had a history of indoor air pollution, they discovered that many of the workers still experienced sick building syndrome (Hedge et al., 1990). And the ones most likely to complain of it were women who spent a great deal of time at computer monitors, felt stressed at work, and were dissatisfied with their jobs. Apparently, to make people feel healthier in the workplace, we must pay attention not only to the quality of their physical surroundings, but also to the psychological effects of the work they do.

The question of how work can be made more satisfying and more productive is just one of the issues of interest to **industrial and organizational psychologists.** These psychologists are concerned with all aspects of behavior that relate to the workplace. Some, like the researchers just mentioned, try to identify the causes of problems that result in lowered morale and motivation among workers. Others design programs to alleviate such problems, such as introducing changes that help make work less repetitive and boring. Still others create employee training programs, administer counseling, and set up systems for evaluating job performance. Many industrial and organizational psychologists work in the subfield of **personnel psychology,** which is concerned with screening, hiring, assigning, and promoting workers. Two-thirds of those in industrial or organizational psychology work in private business, government, and nonprofit agencies.

A major issue confronting industrial and organizational psychologists in the 1990s is finding ways to help working women deal with the stress of handling their dual responsibilities at home and in the office. Women make up a sizable and growing part of the American workforce, and many today are in demanding managerial and professional jobs. Yet most working women still perform the lion's share of child-care and housekeeping duties at home, and they usually have the primary responsibility for seeing that all these tasks get done. This is true even in families where the woman earns as much as her husband (Biernat and Wortman, in press). How women workers can be helped to cope with this reality of modern-day life is a critically important question that industrial and organizational psychologists can help to answer.

EDUCATIONAL AND SCHOOL PSYCHOLOGY

If you were a teacher who wanted to increase student participation in class discussions, how would you go about it? Would it even occur to you that where students sit might influence how much they speak? This possibility *has* occurred to **educational psychologists,** who specialize in analyzing and improving formal education. In one study, researchers observed children in each of six elementary school classrooms as the teacher led a brainstorming discussion about an upcoming writing assignment (Lambert et al., 1985). In some of the classrooms the desks were arranged in traditional rows; in others the desks were in small clusters; and in others the children sat in a circle. Participation in the discussion varied directly with the openness of the seating arrangement: children in rows participated least, children in clusters more, and children in circles most of all. This study suggests that how we structure a classroom physically can substantially affect the process of education.

Educational psychologists are concerned with *all* aspects of the learning process. What factors, they ask, generally affect performance in the classroom? How important is motivation? IQ? Personality? The use of rewards and punishments? The size of the class? The expectations of the teacher? The ways in which students and teacher interact? Educational psychologists are also involved in evaluating student performance by designing and administering tests of various kinds.

To educational psychologists, the setting and seating arrangement of a class are subjects of interest as influences on learning.

Educational psychologists do not work only in colleges, universities, and school systems. Some have careers in health-care settings, where they are often concerned with planning and supervising special education—classes for learning-disabled children, for example. Of those who work in private industry, government, and nonprofit agencies, many are engaged in developing tests or in planning, setting up, and evaluating training programs.

In contrast to educational psychologists, who seek to learn about learning, **school psychologists** focus on applying psychological knowledge. Almost two-thirds of the school psychologists in this country work in elementary and secondary schools. They may be involved in training teachers in how to deal with difficult students, in counseling such students and their parents, in administering standardized tests and interpreting the results, and in assessing students with learning difficulties.

CLINICAL AND COUNSELING PSYCHOLOGY

Clinical psychologists are practitioners in the subfield of psychology that deals with the diagnosis and treatment of psychological disorders, many of which are far more severe than the normal problems we all experience from time to time. Clinical psychologists also investigate the causes of these disorders, for theories about causes are the foundation for developing treatments. As in every other area of psychology, there are many ideas about causes. Some believe that psychological disorders arise from a person's unresolved conflicts and unconscious motives. Others maintain that some of these problems are merely learned responses that can be unlearned with training. Still others contend that there are biological bases to certain psychological disorders, especially the most serious ones. As you will discover in Chapter 17, these different views have yielded a variety of different treatments for problems as diverse as phobias, depression, paranoia, and drug dependence.

Not surprisingly, close to three-quarters of all clinical psychologists are employed in hospitals, clinics, and private practice. There they often work closely with two other specialists in the mental health field: the psychiatrist and the psychoanalyst. Unlike clinical psychologists, who have earned a Ph.D. and have completed specialized training in diagnosis and psychotherapy, **psychiatrists** first earn an M.D. and complete a medical internship, as other physicians do. Then, during a three-year residency program in psychiatry, nearly always in a hospital, they receive specific training in the treatment of psychological disorders. As physicians, psychiatrists can prescribe drugs and use other medical procedures that clinical psychologists cannot. Some psychiatrists go on to become **psychoanalysts,** practitioners of the form of therapy originally developed by Freud. To become a psychoanalyst, psychiatrists must study psychoanalytic theory extensively, undergo psychoanalysis themselves, and analyze clients under the supervision of an experienced analyst. Psychoanalytic institutes that provide such training are located in several major cities.

Whereas clinical psychologists and psychiatrists generally treat people with serious psychological disorders, **counseling psychologists** usually help those with milder problems of social and emotional adjustment. Some counseling psychologists specialize in particular areas, such as marriage and family life. They may also help normally adjusted people with such tasks as setting vocational goals. About half of all counseling psychologists work in health-care settings or in private practice.

HEALTH PSYCHOLOGY

Is your personality hazardous to your health? It may be if you are a cynical, hostile type of person. In a recent study, forty-five married couples were given a test to measure their cynical hostility (that is, their general suspiciousness that others are antagonistic toward them and therefore deserve to be treated with anger, resentment, and contempt). The couples were then presented with a hypothetical situation in which a school district was about to lay off staff (Smith et al., 1991). Each husband and wife was given a different list of people who should *not* be laid off, and they were asked to defend their own list to their partner using arguments the researchers supplied. Some of the subjects were also given a financial incentive to "win." Significantly, men who scored high in hostility, especially those with a financial incentive, had much higher increases in blood pressure during the experiment than other men did. This is one more piece of evidence suggesting that cynically hostile people are prone to elevated cardiac responses that may raise their risk of heart disease.

Health psychologists study these kinds of relationships. They believe that the mind plays a role in many physical disorders, from ulcers and heart disease to the common cold and cancer. In fact, some health psychologists suspect that psychological factors may be involved in the onset and progress of *all* diseases.

Health psychologists are making many important contributions to modern health care and disease prevention. They are identifying psychological factors related to disease (such as hostility, stress, and depression). They are devising ways to test people for these factors, and thus for their possible susceptibility to illness. They are also trying to understand how a psychological factor such as hostility or stress can have harmful physical effects. At the same time, they are searching for the psychological and social reasons why people sometimes behave in ways that can harm their health, such as smoking, overeating, ignoring early symptoms, and neglecting medical treatment once an illness has been diagnosed. They are also helping to identify psychological strategies for coping with serious illness, for psychological responses have an impact on recovery.

Like clinical and counseling psychologists, many health psychologists work in health-care settings. But many, too, are affiliated with colleges and universities, where they conduct research.

EMERGING FIELDS OF SPECIALIZATION

In addition to the subfields we have just described, a number of new specialty areas in psychology are growing in importance. One of these is **artificial intelligence (AI),** the science of programming computers to perform tasks that would ordinarily require human cognitive capabilities. One of the goals of AI researchers is to develop models of complex mental processes such as solving problems, making decisions, recognizing visual patterns, understanding language, and even having creative insights (see Boden, 1981; Winston and Rendergast, 1984). They reason that if we can construct computer models that duplicate aspects of these cognitive activities, we will have a better understanding of how humans perceive and think. Other AI researchers have a more applied orientation. They are using artificial intelligence to help solve practical problems. There are now AI programs that help doctors diagnose illness and geologists search for oil, to mention just a few applications (Waldrop, 1984). We will say more about artificial intelligence research in Chapters 4 and 8.

Another growing field of specialization is **environmental psychology.** Inspired by the concern for environmental quality that developed in the 1960s and early 1970s, environmental psychology focuses

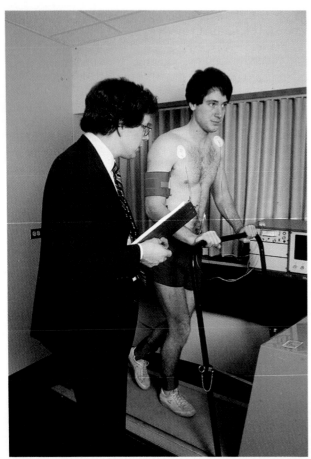

Health psychologists study the relationship between psychological factors, especially stress, and physical condition as measured by devices like this treadmill test, which assesses the cardiovascular system's response to exertion.

information with professionals in other fields. The subject matter of environmental psychology is of interest not just to psychologists but to sociologists, engineers, urban planners, physicians, and architects as well. In addition, research in environmental psychology reflects a growing concern among psychologists about the application of their findings to the world outside the laboratory.

This outward look has spawned a new subfield: **peace psychology,** or the study of how war, especially nuclear war, can be avoided. Researchers in this field focus on a wide variety of topics, including the personalities of world leaders, perception and misconception in international conflict, how different styles of political decision making affect the escalation of international crises, and negotiation and bargaining among political officials. It is hoped that sound, scientific information about such critical topics can help public policy makers manage future international crises better.

Other researchers interested in war and peace are focusing attention on the psychological effects of living with the threat of nuclear destruction. They are trying to determine why fear of nuclear war does not motivate more people to become involved in working toward world peace. How, they ask, can we transform people's fears and anxieties into effective political action? Here, as elsewhere, the special perspectives and skills of psychologists are being brought to bear on an issue of great importance to human welfare, one that may even involve the very survival of our species.

PSYCHOLOGY'S VALUE TO YOU

Psychology is a very popular vocation in the United States. The American Psychological Association, to which most psychologists belong, had approximately 60,000 members in 1990. The number of people entering this field is growing rapidly. Of the 30,000 doctoral degrees in science and engineering awarded annually in this country, about 3,000 (or 10 percent) are in psychology. In addition, each year roughly 8,000 students earn master's degrees in psychology (Strickland, 1987). Apparently, a fascination with human behavior draws a great many people to psychology as a career.

Even if you do not go on to earn a graduate degree in psychology, taking psychology courses can

on the relationships between people and their physical and social surroundings. Environmental psychologists ask questions such as: Does high population density in urban areas increase stress and contribute to crime? Are high-rise apartment buildings as suitable for people to live in as smaller-scale housing? Does exposure to noise from airplanes harm people who live near major airports? Are certain kinds of noises more stressful than others and why?

These questions reflect two trends emerging in psychology as a whole but especially evident in environmental psychology. One is the tendency for psychologists to broaden their focus and to share

greatly help you in your future work. If you major in psychology you might find a job in some directly related field, such as working in a rehabilitation program, a correctional institution, or a community mental health center. Other careers have indirect ties to a knowledge of psychology. A person who gets a job in advertising, for instance, will probably find courses in social psychology, human motivation, and human learning invaluable. Similarly, a person who enters the field of personnel management will make much use of information on personality, individual differences, and testing. Psychological knowledge also has important applications in such careers as teaching, social work, nursing, business, engineering, and law.

And the value of psychology to a college student is not just vocational. Even if you take no psychology courses beyond this one, you will still learn much about yourself and others from this broad introduction to psychological findings and principles. How can I improve my memory? My study habits? How can I get someone I know to stop smoking? When people pressure me to do something I would rather not do, why do I sometimes go along? Whenever I babysit for my infant nephew, he cries continually unless I hold him. What can I do to change his behavior? I get so tense when I sit down to take a test that my mind goes completely blank. Is there a way I can get over this? A variety of answers to these and many other questions of great personal interest are contained in this book.

Finally, the study of psychology has the important benefit of giving you a perspective for evaluating new psychological findings reported in newspapers and popular books, and on TV. Consider, for example, a startling news story that was widely publicized a number of years ago. A team of medical researchers in England found that chronic marijuana use was associated with cerebral atrophy, a wasting away of the brain (Campbell et al., 1971). This conclusion was based on brain X rays of ten habitual marijuana users compared with brain X rays of nonusers of the same age. On the surface, this evidence may seem very convincing. But consider some questions that a critical psychologist might ask. What evidence is there that the cerebral atrophy did not occur *before* the marijuana use? If there is good evidence to rule out this possibility, could the brain damage be due to some other cause? As it turned out, the conclusion of this study was suspect. Of the ten marijuana users

How accurate is eyewitness testimony? What prejudices are certain jurors likely to have? Do rape victims always appear distraught? Being sophisticated in psychology can be immensely helpful to lawyers in the courtroom. (Here, Glenn Close portrays an attorney in a scene from *The Jagged Edge.*)

with wasted brain tissue, all had also used the hallucinogen LSD, some more than twenty times; eight had used amphetamines, another powerful drug; and several had frequently taken sedatives, barbiturates, heroin, or morphine. In addition, one young man had a medical history of convulsive seizures, and four had suffered substantial head injuries in the past (Kolodny, 1974). Thus, there was very good reason to believe that the cerebral atrophy revealed by the brain X rays might have been caused by some factor other than marijuana.

This example nicely illustrates the perspective of the scientist. A good scientist is an incurable doubter. He or she is always asking: What is the evidence, and how reliable is it? Was this study designed and carried out carefully enough? Were all other possible influences controlled before conclusions were drawn? Are alternative interpretations possible, and if so, what additional information is needed to rule them out? Exposure to the methods of psychology will help you develop this questioning, critical approach yourself. By the end of this course, you should share with the psychologist a healthy skepticism of the sweeping generalizations and psychological cure-alls you read and hear about so often. This newly acquired outlook, and the critical thinking skills it encourages, should make you a more sophisticated interpreter of all information that can affect your life.

SUMMARY

1. **Psychology,** the study of behavior and mental processes, is first of all a science. It is a set of procedures for systematically observing facts about behavior and organizing them into testable generalizations about why people think, feel, and act as they do. The three major goals of the science of psychology are to *describe* behavior and mental processes, to try to *explain* them, and to *predict* their characteristics in specific circumstances.

2. Psychology is also a means of promoting human welfare, a body of information that can be applied to help solve a variety of human problems. Research that is purposely directed toward this goal is called **applied science.** In contrast, research that is conducted purely to add to our store of knowledge is called **basic science.**

3. Wilhelm Wundt is generally considered the founder of modern psychology. In the late nineteenth century he established the first laboratory for the express purpose of investigating human mental processes. Wundt and his students conducted studies on a broad range of topics. Their efforts to use precise and systematic methods of measurement launched psychology as a science.

4. Five perspectives have come to dominate psychology in the twentieth century. Rather than seeing these as opposing viewpoints, it is better to view them as complementary. Each can provide valuable insights, and together they enrich our understanding.

5. One important approach in modern psychology is the **behaviorist perspective,** which first arose in the early twentieth century. The early behaviorists insisted that psychology focus only on data that can be objectively observed and measured. The pioneering work of Ivan Pavlov, John Watson, E. L. Thorndike, and B. F. Skinner established the behaviorists' enduring interest in how learned associations give rise to specific responses. In the United States, the study of how rewards and punishments control behavior became the hallmark of behaviorism.

6. Sigmund Freud emphasized the role of **unconscious** drives and feelings, often stemming from unresolved childhood conflicts, to explain the psychological problems that adults sometimes experience. He felt that unconscious conflicts can be deprived of their power to dominate a person's life if they are brought into awareness through a process called **psychoanalysis.** While few psychologists wholly accept Freud's

ideas today, his influence on twentieth-century thought has been enormous. The modern **psychoanalytic perspective** in psychology still shows the influence of Freud's views.

7. Psychologists with a **humanistic perspective** have reacted against the deterministic views of both behaviorism and Freudian psychology. They maintain that people are free to become whatever they are capable of being. Humanists have developed forms of psychotherapy that stress the human potential for **self-actualization** and fulfillment.

8. A modern trend among psychologists who study learning is to consider how people interpret the events and stimuli around them, fashioning their actions according to their individual understandings. Such understandings, thoughts, expectations, and perceptions are known as **cognitions.** Psychologists who take a **cognitive perspective** study a wide range of topics, including learning, memory, concept formation, problem solving, decision making, and language.

9. Psychologists who take a **neurobiological perspective** stress that all human thought, feeling, and action is ultimately controlled by the nervous system, of which the brain is the central part. Many researchers with this perspective try to map the different areas of the brain involved in controlling specific kinds of behaviors. Others seek to understand the workings of the brain's complex chemical systems.

10. Contemporary psychology has researchers working in many specialized subfields. **Experimental psychologists** rely largely on laboratory experiments to investigate basic behavioral processes, such as sensation, perception, memory, and learning. **Neuropsychologists** also study basic processes, but they focus on how those processes are controlled by the brain and other parts of the nervous system. **Personality psychologists** measure and explain individual differences in behavior, **developmental psychologists** explore changes in thought and behavior throughout the life cycle, and **social psychologists** look at the influence of social situations on human thought and actions. **Educational** and **school psychologists** are concerned with the processes of formal education, while **industrial and organizational psychologists** focus on the relationship between people and their work. **Clinical psychologists** specialize in the diagnosis and treatment of mental and emotional disorders, while

health psychologists focus on psychological factors involved in physical illness and recovery from it. In addition to these established subfields, new ones are emerging, including **artificial intelligence (AI), environmental psychology,** and **peace psychology.**

11. While psychology is very useful in many careers you might pursue, it also has practical value as a perspective on human behavior. It can help you answer many questions you have asked about yourself and others. At the same time, it can help you be more perceptive in evaluating psychological information you read and hear about.

SUGGESTED READINGS

American Psychological Association. (1986). *Careers in psychology.* Washington, DC: American Psychological Association. A useful booklet describing current career opportunities in various subfields of psychology. A copy can be obtained by writing to the American Psychological Association, 1200 Seventeenth St. NW, Washington, DC 20036.

Graduate study in psychology and associated fields, 1990. (1990). Describes requirements for admissions and degrees, tuition, and financial aid at over 600 departments of psychology. Includes extensive lists of specialties and types of degrees offered. Washington, DC: American Psychological Association.

Hothersall, D. (1984). *History of psychology.* New York: Random House. An interesting presentation of psychology's past that allows the reader to see the field as a whole and to better understand recent trends.

Rubinstein, J., and Slife, B. D. (1982). *Taking sides: Views on controversial psychological issues* (2nd ed.). Guilford, CT: Dushkin. This book contains both sides of many controversial issues in psychology, including the effects of TV violence on aggression, the nature of hypnosis, and psychosurgery.

Woods, Paul J. (Ed.), with Wilkinson, Charles S. (1987). *Is psychology the major for you? Planning for your undergraduate years.* Offers guidance in deciding whether to major in psychology. Describes careers available to psychologists and offers advice on finding a job. Washington, DC: American Psychological Association.

CHAPTER 2

THE METHODS OF PSYCHOLOGY

Everyone asks questions about human behavior. Why did I do so poorly on my biology exam even though I *knew* the material? Why do smokers disregard warnings that cigarettes are hazardous to their health? Why do some people need at least eight hours of sleep nightly, while others do fine with six or fewer? Why do I sometimes go along with other people's opinions even though I really disagree? Psychologists ask the same kinds of questions about human behavior, but the difference between psychologists and other people lies in how they seek the answers.

Consider how psychologist Alison Clarke-Stewart and her colleagues tried to answer a question that thousands of other Americans have asked in recent years: how accurate is the testimony of young children who are being interrogated about alleged incidents of child abuse? The researchers were struck by cases in which children's testimonies of abuse were later proved false. For instance, in 1985 a two-year-old boy in Berkeley, California, was questioned extensively by social workers, doctors, and police about what looked like a burn on his knee, which his mother could not explain. Based on the boy's testimony, authorities tentatively concluded that he had been abused, and they placed him in a foster home. Only later did an astute nurse point out that the so-called burn was really a bacterial infection. This incident is not an isolated one. In a sizable number of such cases the reports of young children have not been accurate. What could account for these misleading testimonies? Why do children sometimes fail to tell the truth about things that are so important to themselves and their families?

Clarke-Stewart and her colleagues proposed an interesting answer. Perhaps, they reasoned, these youngsters are being placed in situations that they do not fully understand and so they look to cues from their interrogators to interpret what has happened to them. The Berkeley boy, for example, had no idea where the wound on his knee came from, but since authority figures were suggesting that a member of his family might have caused it, his two-year-old mind decided that this in fact must be what happened. This is precisely the kind of **hypothesis**—a tentative statement about how or why something happens—that any observer might propose. But unlike an ordinary observer, Clarke-Stewart and her colleagues did not stop there. As research psychologists, they went on to conduct a study to test their proposed explanation (Clarke-Stewart et al., 1989).

The researchers staged an incident involving a janitor named Chester, whom they jokingly referred to among themselves as Chester the Molester. Chester came into a playroom where a five- or six-year-old child was alone and proceeded to dust and empty the waste basket. Then he turned his attention to the toys, which included a doll of the same sex as the child. For half the children studied, Chester cleaned the doll's face with water, checked under its clothes for more dirt, straightened its arms and legs, and bit off a loose thread. He talked strictly about cleaning and straightening up the toy: "This doll is dirty. I'd better clean it. I'd better see if it's dirty here, too. . . ." And so forth. For the rest of the children studied, Chester performed the same behaviors, but his words were very different: "Oh goodie," he exclaimed. "Here's a doll. I like to play with dolls. I like to spray them in the face with water. I like to look under their clothes. I like to bite them and twist their arms and legs."

About an hour after Chester left, his "boss" arrived and questioned the child about what Chester had done. For some of the children the questions were worded in a relatively neutral way ("What did Chester do? Did he spray water on the doll? Did he look under its clothes? Why did he do that?"). For others the questions were accusatory of Chester ("I don't believe he was just cleaning these toys. He was playing with them, right? You don't need to protect Chester. Chester wasn't really cleaning the toys, was he?"). For still others the questions suggested that Chester had done what a good cleaner *should* do ("Chester was probably just cleaning the doll. This doll needed to be cleaned. Did you see how dirty it was? Maybe he pretended to play with the doll, but he was really cleaning it. You shouldn't say he did something wrong unless you are sure. He wasn't really playing, was he?"). The researchers were interested in comparing the answers given by children interrogated *in*consistently with what they had seen (they saw Chester playing and the adult interpreted his actions as cleaning, or they saw Chester cleaning and the adult accused him of playing). Would these children stick to the truth, or would they be swayed by the adult's interpretation?

The results showed that young children will usually go along with an authority figure's view, even though that view does not match their own initial understanding of what happened. In this case, about a third of the youngsters exposed to inconsistent leading questions went along with the adult com-

pletely, and another quarter compromised by saying that Chester had both cleaned *and* played. Moreover, when a second adult conducted another interrogation, also filled with incorrect leading questions, only one child managed to hold out and maintain that Chester had *not* been doing what the interviewer suggested. In contrast, children interrogated with neutrally worded questions were almost always able to describe Chester's actions and motives correctly.

This study, of course, did not prove that all instances of incorrect testimony by children are the result of an interrogator's leading questions. But Clarke-Stewart and her colleagues *had* collected concrete evidence that inaccurate testimony can sometimes arise in this way. Systematically gathering concrete evidence is what separates the scientist from the average observer. Scientists are not content with mere speculation; they demand hard data on which to base their conclusions. In the following sections we will describe many of the procedures that psychologists use to collect and analyze such data.

Knowing something about these procedures is of great value. Psychologists have much to say about important issues, from child care to education to mental health, race relations, and sex roles. The more you know about the methods they use to reach their conclusions, the better able you will be to understand and evaluate what they say. A grasp of scientific methods, in short, is essential to acquiring the critical thinking ability we discussed in Chapter 1.

But perhaps you feel that scientific methods are too dry and complicated to be interesting. Many introductory psychology students draw this hasty conclusion, only to find out later how mistaken they were. Psychological research has all the fascination of solving a complex mystery. Like detective work, it begins with puzzling questions, proceeds to tentative conclusions, and involves imaginative suppositions, logical reasoning, and carefully conducted tests. The eventual findings, moreover, are always worth the effort, because they shed light on a subject of great intrinsic interest: you.

GATHERING DATA

Imagine that you are a psychologist interested in determining people's attitudes toward smoking. You want to find out what percentage of smokers intend to go on smoking indefinitely, what percentage hope to

Based on an inadequate sample of early election returns, the *Chicago Daily Tribune* ran a banner headline proclaiming Republican candidate Thomas E. Dewey the winner of the 1948 presidential campaign. The next morning, more complete returns revealed that Harry Truman, the Democratic candidate, was the actual winner. Truman is shown here triumphantly displaying the premature headline.

quit someday, what percentage hope to quit in the near future, and what percentage are trying to quit right now. How would you go about doing your research? Most likely you would conduct a survey; that is, you would ask a number of smokers about their attitudes and plans regarding smoking. Now suppose your interest shifts to the question of which method of quitting smoking is more effective: cutting down slowly or stopping "cold turkey." Would a survey be adequate to answer this question? Probably not, because you are no longer dealing with people's opinions and intentions. This example shows that the research method a psychologist uses to gather data depends in part on the nature of the question being asked. Each method is better suited to some kinds of questions than to others. You will see this clearly as you read about the major data-gathering techniques. First, however, let us consider a task common to most psychological studies: selecting a sample.

SAMPLING

The saying, "You don't have to eat the whole ox to know that the meat is tough," could have been coined by a psychologist doing scientific research. Few questions about human behavior permit researchers to study every single member of the population they want to generalize about. The number of people who would have to be considered is usually far too large. Fortunately, researchers have an alternative. They can select a segment of a population and draw their conclusions on the basis of this **sample.** In a sense, they sample parts of the ox to determine its overall toughness.

The size of a sample is extremely important for many of the topics psychologists study. For instance, a poll intended to reflect the opinions of all the Democrats in the United States could not sample only five people, for such a small sample would be likely to be biased. Just by chance, for example, one of these people might have highly atypical views—views shared by only a tiny minority of Democrats. In a sample of only five, however, this person's opinions would represent 20 percent of the total. The larger the sample, the greater is the likelihood that such atypical views or behaviors will be "lost in the crowd." By the same token, a large sample helps to ensure that the views of sizable and important minorities are not inadvertently left out.

Another requirement of a good sample is that the members be chosen randomly. A **random sample** is one in which everyone in the total population has an equal chance of being included. Suppose you want to draw a random sample of the student body at your school. You could get the names of all currently enrolled students, write those names on cards, put the cards in a large bowl, and draw out 20 percent. As long as the total student population is sufficiently large and the cards are shuffled adequately, this technique will probably produce a sample that mirrors the whole student body in many ways. For instance, if 60 percent of all students support lengthening midsemester recess, roughly 60 percent of your sample probably will too.

But sometimes a psychologist 'wants to make certain that a sample includes members of specific subgroups. To understand why, consider again our example of sampling Democrats in the United States. It is widely known that the views of southern Democrats frequently differ from those of their northern counterparts; so a good sample of all Democrats would probably have to include appropriate numbers from each regional subgroup. The goal here is to deliberately assemble a **representative sample,** that is, one in which important subgroups are represented according to their incidence in the population as a whole. Public opinion pollsters routinely construct their samples in this way. They include certain proportions of each sex, each ethnic and age group, each geographic region, each income level, and so forth, so that the resulting sample accurately reflects all people in the nation.

Failure to construct a truly representative sample was the cause of a now-classic polling error. In the 1930s, political surveying was dominated by the *Literary Digest,* a magazine that had correctly forecast the results of every U.S. Presidential election since 1916. The *Digest* conducted its surveys by sending out millions of requests for candidate preferences to people whose names appeared in telephone directories and automobile registration records. George Gallup, a young man from Iowa who had developed his own sampling techniques, realized the flaw in the *Digest's* approach. In the early part of this century, people who had cars and telephones were much wealthier than most and so were not representative of all voters. The test of Gallup's view came in 1936, when the *Digest* predicted that Republican Alf Landon would beat Democratic incumbent Franklin D. Roosevelt. Although Gallup thought that Landon would do well among affluent voters, he believed that much of the rest of the nation (suffering from the Great Depression) would opt for the more liberal

Roosevelt. Gallup's prediction was ridiculed right up to the eve of the election, but the next morning Roosevelt had won by a landslide (Reeves, 1983). Gallup went on to build his techniques of polling into a widely respected research organization.

Notice that large size alone does not make a sample representative. The *Digest's* sample was huge by today's polling standards, yet it failed to tap the views of the population as a whole. To reinforce what makes a sample representative, consider another example. In 1987 researcher Shere Hite published a book about women's views on love and their intimate relationships based on an extensive survey that she had conducted. Hite reported that the overwhelming majority of American women were frustrated and disillusioned with men. For instance, 95 percent of her sample felt harassed by the men in their lives. Many said that their men were condescending and judgmental toward them, prone to inappropriate teasing, insults, and other acts of hostility. Also, 77 percent complained that their men didn't listen to them, and 87 percent found their deepest emotional relationship existed not with a man, but with another woman.

Hite obtained her data by distributing 100,000 questionnaires to clubs and organizations across the country that had women members or clients. These included church groups, voting and political organizations, women's rights groups, counseling centers, senior citizens' homes, and many others. Of the original 100,000 questionnaires, 4.5 percent were filled out and returned, giving Hite a sample of 4,500. Hite felt that this was a large enough number to provide representative information. After all, the statistical breakdown of respondents by race, income, place of residence, marital status, labor-force participation, and political affiliation quite closely mirrored that of the female population as a whole. Shouldn't this make the sample adequately representative?

Can you think of any reason to question the representativeness of Hite's sample? If you can, you are like some psychologists who have criticized her work. These critics charge that women who join organizations do not represent the full spectrum of the female population. Moreover, the 4.5 percent who took the time to answer Hite's lengthy questionnaire were probably more apt to be unhappy with their intimate relations, more likely to have dissatisfactions to express. And, in fact, other national surveys using random samples have not found such widespread discontent with intimate relationships as Hite found (e.g., Peplau and Gordon, 1985). Figure 2.1A describes some other research procedures based on unrepresentative samples. Can you detect the flaw in each one?

Although psychologists recognize the advantages of drawing generalizations on the basis of truly representative samples, those who conduct laboratory research are seldom able to meet this sampling ideal. An example will illustrate why. Suppose you are a social psychologist interested in why people sometimes seek human companionship, yet at other times prefer to be alone. To investigate this question, you design an experiment placing people in various conditions you suspect might promote affiliation. But what are your chances of persuading hundreds of people from every part of the country and from all age brackets, ethnic groups, income levels, and so forth to come to your laboratory and participate in your research? The chances are slim. Although such a procedure would increase the representativeness of your sample, you will probably have to settle for a more homogeneous group.

Like many researchers, you might use students from the university where you teach, often those taking introductory psychology. In fact, in over 80 percent of the human studies published in some of the leading psychology journals, college students serve as subjects (Korn and Bram, 1988; Sears, 1986). The data gathered in such studies have provided much valuable information about how people think and act and why they behave as they do. But some psychologists point out that college populations may not really mirror the human population as a whole. Researchers must therefore be cautious in using findings based on samples of students to generalize about the behavior of all people everywhere.

RESEARCH METHODS

Psychological research is intended to accomplish one or more of three basic goals: to *describe* behavior, to *explain* behavior, and to *predict* the circumstances in which a certain behavior might occur again. Each of the various data-gathering methods we are about to describe is more useful for achieving some of these aims than others. Observation in a natural setting, for example, allows researchers to describe behavior and to generate possible explanations, but it is not well suited to testing hypotheses about why certain responses occur. Surveys also allow researchers to describe behavior, including people's attitudes and

1. A senator is interested in whether his constituents favor the death penalty. His staff reports that letters about the death penalty have been received from 458 constituents and that 398 favor it.

2. A cookie manufacturing company wants to know what percentage of Dallas residents make cookies from scratch. A sample of 1,000 residential addresses is chosen and interviewers call these households during regular working hours on weekdays.

3. A newspaper is interested in finding out what proportion of drivers in the city wear seat belts. Some reporters go to a Ford Motor Company plant and record the number of employees who fasten their seat belts when they leave work.

FIGURE 2.1A Three sampling procedures. Can you spot the flaws in these examples? The answers can be found in Figure 2.1B on the next page.

feelings, but surveys also have major limitations for determining causes. An experiment, in contrast, allows explanations to be tested under highly controlled conditions and so helps to pinpoint causes, but it may not reveal the complexities of behavior as it occurs outside the researcher's lab. Different research methods, then, often complement one another, and together they enrich our understanding of human behavior.

But using a specific research method is not really a researcher's first step. The process of exploring human behavior begins with much more casual observations, coming up with hunches, and wondering how to find out more (Jones, 1985). Many initial ideas must then be discarded as too unlikely, too unwieldy, or too difficult to pursue. Only after this early period of speculation does research become systematic and directed toward specific goals. But don't discount the importance of this earliest stage in scientific work. It is from imaginative initial speculations that some of the best research studies have been born.

THE EXPERIMENT

The **experiment** is a research method designed to answer questions about cause and effect. Its main advantage over other data-gathering methods is that it permits the researcher to control conditions and so rule out—to as large an extent as possible—all

WHAT'S WRONG:

1. People who write to their representatives in Congress tend to have strong opinions. The opinions of this group are often systematically different from those of the population as a whole.

2. This sampling technique tends to exclude working people, whose responses may be very different from those given by people at home on weekdays. Thus the sample is not representative.

3. People who work for an auto company are probably not representative of all people on an issue having to do with cars. They may, for example, be more safety conscious than the average driver.

FIGURE 2.1B

influences on subjects' behavior *except* the factors being examined. This advantage motivated Clarke-Stewart and her colleagues to choose an experiment in order to test their hypothesis as to why young children sometimes give incorrect testimony about things they have witnessed. These researchers created the factor they wanted to assess (leading questions during an interrogation) while excluding other factors that could also influence what children report. In this way, they gathered evidence about causes. But experiments have one potentially important disadvantage. Eliminating all extraneous influences can sometimes create such an unnatural situation that you wonder if the results are applicable to behavior in the real world.

The basic procedures of an experiment are best explained with an example. Consider the social-psychological question we raised earlier: under what conditions are people more likely to want to be with others rather than alone? Of the many experiments on this topic, we will focus on a classic one performed over thirty years ago by Stanley Schachter (1959). Schachter was one of the first psychologists to suggest that the desire to affiliate does not depend simply on individual personality traits. Affiliation, he proposed, also depends on the situations in which people find themselves, and among the situations most conducive to affiliation are those that arouse fear. This was Schachter's hypothesis.

Schachter's first step in testing his hypothesis was to design an experiment in which subjects would experience fear. The method he chose was devious

but highly effective. He arranged for a number of students who had volunteered to participate in an experiment to be met at the laboratory door by a white-coated man who identified himself as Dr. Gregor Zilstein from the medical school's Department of Neurology and Psychiatry. Surrounded by an impressive array of electrical equipment, the doctor told the students that they were part of a very important study on the physiological effects of electric shock. Each of them would undergo a series of shocks while pulse rate, blood pressure, and other physical reactions were recorded. The shocks, the doctor warned in an ominous tone, would be extremely painful, because only intense shock could provide the information required. But, he added with a tight smile, the shocks would cause no permanent tissue damage.

The students who encountered this diabolical doctor composed what is called the **experimental group.** An experimental group consists of those subjects who experience the experimental condition—in this case, exposure to a fear-arousing situation. Most experiments also use a **control group** to provide a source of comparison. Control subjects experience all the conditions the experimental subjects do except the key factor the psychologist is evaluating. Thus, in Schachter's experiment, the control subjects were also greeted at the door by a white-coated doctor who told them that they were about to participate in an experiment on the effects of electric shock. But this time, instead of grimly warning that the shocks would be extremely painful, the doctor said in a kindly manner that they would produce only a mild, not unpleasant, tingling sensation.

Note that subjects were placed in either the experimental or the control group completely at random. This is a way of compensating for the fact that experimenters cannot possibly control for everything about their subjects. In this study, for instance, some people may have been naturally more outgoing than others, more eager to affiliate when given a chance. Schachter could not erase such tendencies in his subjects by the stroke of some magic experimental wand. But he could try to make sure that all the extroverts (the outgoing people) did not end up in one group while all the introverts (the shy people) ended up in the other. The ideal would be to place a similar number of extroverts and introverts in each of the two groups. In this way, any biases they might impose on the study would balance out. This is where random assignment of subjects comes in. When a sample is sufficiently large, random assignment tends to produce a good shuffling, so to speak, not only with regard to introversion and extroversion but also with regard to other factors that might otherwise bias the experiment's results. Consequently, any observed differences in the behavior of the two groups are not likely to have been caused by inherent differences in the people who form those groups.

After Schachter had created appropriate experimental and control groups, one last step remained. He had to give his subjects the opportunity to affiliate with others in order to observe the effects, if any, of fear. So, after describing the upcoming experiment, Dr. Zilstein announced that everyone would have to wait ten minutes while the experimental equipment was prepared. Each subject was given the choice of waiting alone in a private room or waiting with other subjects. These choices provided the experimental data. Once the subjects had expressed their preferences, the experiment ended and no shocks were ever given.

The results of Schachter's pioneering study are shown in Figure 2.2. They suggest that the tendency to affiliate does indeed increase in fear-arousing situations. Students subjected to the experimental condition (where the doctor's words were ominous and his smile sadistic) were much more likely to want to wait with others than were subjects who experienced the control condition (where the doctor's words were reassuring and his manner kindly). Thus, Schachter's hypothesis that fear can promote affiliation was supported by his data.

Let us summarize how Schachter's procedures met the requirements of an experiment. An experiment is a controlled method of exploring the relationship between factors capable of change, called **variables.** The factor that the experimenter deliberately manipulates is called the **independent variable.** In Schachter's study the independent variable was the degree to which the doctor's words and manner were fear-inducing. The **dependent variable,** which nearly always involves some form of behavior, is what is expected to change when the independent variable is manipulated, provided the experimenter's hypothesis is right. Changes in the dependent variable, in other words, *depend* on changes in the independent one. In Schachter's experiment the dependent variable was the choice that subjects made between waiting alone or waiting with others.

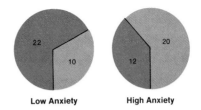

Low Anxiety   High Anxiety

● Subjects who chose to be alone or did not care
● Subjects who chose to affiliate

FIGURE 2.2 Results of Schachter's experiment. Using an experimental group and a control group, he tested the effects of anxiety aroused by fear on people's need to affiliate.

It will help you identify these two key variables in any experiment if you phrase the researcher's hypothesis as an "if/then" statement. For Schachter's experiment the if/then statement would be: "If a person is exposed to a fear-arousing situation, *then* the desire to affiliate with other people should increase above normal levels." The factor that follows the word *if* is the independent variable; the factor that follows the word *then* is the dependent variable. An if/then statement stresses that a cause-and-effect relationship occurs in one direction only. Change in the independent variable causes change in the dependent variable, but not vice versa. Because an experiment provides a means of establishing causality, it is the data-gathering method of choice for many psychologists.

But note that Schachter's experimental findings barely scratch the surface in asking important questions about the motivation to affiliate. Does fear *always* produce a desire to be with other people, or only under certain circumstances? And exactly why, in Schachter's study, did fear have this effect? Did Schachter's fearful subjects want to be distracted? Did they want to express their anxious feelings to a sympathetic ear? Or were they looking for a chance to compare their own emotions with those of others in the same predicament? What about other factors that encourage affiliation? Which are the most important ones, why do they have this effect, and how powerful are they compared with fear? In order to get a full understanding of affiliation, we would need additional research to answer these and similar questions. Thus, a comprehensive understanding of any complex human behavior can be gained only from a

Does lack of parental discipline cause young people to join gangs and possibly engage in delinquent behavior? This is the kind of question that does not lend itself to investigation through a true experiment. It would be unethical for researchers to encourage parents to be either harsh or lax in disciplining their children in order to study whether delinquency resulted. Such questions about cause and effect must be studied through quasi-experiments or correlational research.

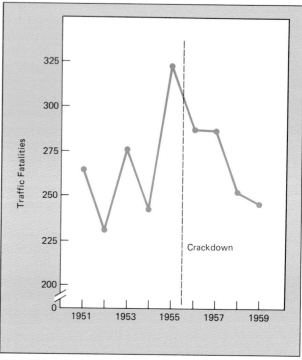

FIGURE 2.3 A time-series experimental evaluation. When the number of traffic deaths in Connecticut peaked at 324 in 1955, state officials instituted a crackdown on speeding. The dramatic drop in fatalities between 1955 and 1956 does not indicate, however, that the crackdown caused the decline. Decreases in accidents had been registered in 1952 and 1954, without the crackdown, and a decline could have been expected in 1956 following the unusually high fatality rate in 1955. But the continued decline in deaths from 1955 to 1959 may indicate that the prolonged crackdown had a genuine effect. *(After Campbell and Ross, 1968.)*

large number of studies that build and expand on one another.

QUASI-EXPERIMENTAL DESIGNS

Sometimes, however, psychologists cannot study a cause-and-effect question by means of a true experiment. Certain variables, for one reason or another, cannot be experimentally manipulated. For example, a psychologist interested in how effectively the death penalty deters murder would be unable to arrange a true experiment. Death penalties are imposed and lifted through changes in public attitudes, not through experimental whim. Other factors are, for ethical reasons, not open to manipulation. For instance, a psychologist might suspect that overly harsh or overly lax parental discipline leads to juvenile delinquency, but he or she could certainly not encourage these potentially harmful parenting practices in order to find out.

How can researchers investigate questions about cause and effect that do not lend themselves to experimental manipulations? One way is to wait for "experimental" and "control" groups to form naturally—that is, in real life. This approach creates a research design that approximates an experiment. But because the investigators have far less control over variables than they do in true experiments, and because they cannot assign subjects randomly to conditions, such studies are called **quasi-experiments** (*quasi* means "resembling but not identical to").

There are several types of quasi-experimental designs (Campbell and Stanley, 1966). In the **time-series** design, a researcher repeatedly observes or measures the dependent variable both before and after the independent variable changes. This design was used to evaluate the effectiveness of a prolonged crackdown on speeding in Connecticut after a record number of traffic deaths occurred in 1955. Figure 2.3 shows that the highway fatality rate did indeed drop in 1956 and continued to fall over the next three years. But in order to label the speeding crackdown a success, we would have to be certain that this decline was larger than what might have happened by chance alone. Because the 1955 fatality rate was so unusually high, it is likely that traffic deaths would have dropped somewhat anyway, even without a crackdown on speeding. Using statistical procedures to take this fact into account, researchers concluded that the observed decline *was* significantly greater than any decline likely to have occurred just by chance. This finding suggests that the crackdown was effective (Campbell, 1978).

Problems arise from making inferences about causes on the basis of quasi-experiments, however. This is because a quasi-experiment does not provide the powers of control that a true experiment does. Think about the Connecticut traffic-fatality study. Perhaps some other change occurred at the time of the crackdown on speeding that could also have affected the number of deaths on the highway. For instance, maybe car makers introduced new safety features, such as seat belts, padded dashboards, or more shatter-resistant windshields. If so, then highway fatalities could have dropped for reasons that had nothing to do with the crackdown on speeding. In contrast to a true experiment, a quasi-experiment does not allow researchers to eliminate such additional factors. All they can do is try to take these additional factors into account when drawing their conclusions. Needless to say, this task is difficult. Something important may easily be overlooked. This is why quasi-experiments are not as reliable for drawing causal inferences as true experiments are.

CORRELATIONAL RESEARCH

Another approach that can be helpful when a true experiment is not feasible is **correlational research.** Suppose an investigator wants to determine the extent to which two variables—parental discipline and juvenile delinquency—are related. The investigator might randomly select a large number of children and interview their parents to determine the severity of discipline in the home. The researcher might ask such questions as "How often do you spank your child?" and "What would you do if your child told a lie?" On the basis of each parent's

Research on correlations makes it possible to assert that it is more likely—though not inevitable—that people with higher IQs will get better grades.

responses, he or she could then be assigned a severity-of-discipline score. The children's behavior could next be assessed, perhaps with the help of school or court records, to see which ones had committed delinquent acts, and how frequently. Finally, the researcher could calculate a numerical value called a **correlation coefficient,** which would indicate the strength and direction of the relationship between discipline and delinquency.

We will return to correlation coefficients later in this chapter. For now we simply want to point out that the results of correlational studies vary. Sometimes the relationship between two variables is close and positive: a high rank on one is usually accompanied by a high rank on the other. There is a strong **positive correlation,** for example, between intelligence as measured by IQ tests and academic performance. People who score high on IQ tests tend to get high grades. Other times, the relationship between two variables is close but negative: a high rank on one is usually accompanied by a low rank on the other. There is a strong **negative correlation,** for example, between musical ability and tone deafness (inability to distinguish the pitch of musical notes). The more difficulty a person has perceiving pitch, the less likely he or she is to be able to play a musical instrument well. In still other instances, little or no relationship, positive or negative, exists between two variables. There is no relationship, for example, between eye color and academic success, or between hair color and tone deafness.

Correlations allow psychologists to make predictions about behavior. If you know that a woman has a high IQ, you can predict that she is likely to get good grades. If you know that a man is tone deaf, you can predict that he is not likely to play a piece of music you would care to hear. Note that in either case your prediction, although probable, could prove to be wrong, for very few relationships are perfectly correlated.

But though a correlational study can show that two variables are related, it cannot establish that one factor *causes* the other. A third factor, related to each of the other two, may also be involved. Consider a study of motorcycle accidents that the U.S. Army once conducted. It attempted to correlate the number of accidents a person had with such variables as income and age. The best predictor of whether a person had been involved in a motorcycle accident turned out to be the number of tattoos that person had! Obviously, tattoos do not cause motorcycle accidents, nor does being in a motorcycle accident prompt a person to get tattooed. Instead, some third factor, perhaps a desire for personal display, probably caused both tattooing and dangerous motorcycle driving.

Assessing whether causality exists between two correlated factors is seldom this easy, however. Often two factors that logically *might* be causally connected turn out not to be. This is where the need for experiments comes in. Only through experiments, or very well constructed quasi-experimental designs, can researchers demonstrate cause-and-effect relationships.

THE SURVEY

In all correlational studies, the initial data about the variables being considered must be collected by some means. Frequently this means is a survey. A **survey** is an attempt to estimate the opinions, characteristics, or behaviors of a particular population by investigating a representative sample. Researchers conducting a survey gather the data of interest to them through interviews, questionnaires, or sometimes public records. Interviews have the advantage of letting the researchers see or speak with their subjects and of allowing them to modify their questions when clarification is needed. Questionnaires, on the other hand, take less time to administer and so are

particularly useful when information is being gathered from a large number of people.

Although survey data may be used to look for correlations between factors, they may also have importance in their own right. Probably the most famous survey in this century is the one that resulted in the Kinsey reports, published in 1948 and 1953. Alfred Kinsey and his staff interviewed more than 10,000 men and women about their sexual behavior and attitudes—a radical thing to do at the time. Kinsey found, among other things, that sexual behaviors often considered abnormal in the 1940s (such as masturbation, homosexual activity, and oral-genital sex) were much more common than most people supposed. Methods similar to Kinsey's are still being used today to study sexual behavior, attitudes, and knowledge (Reinisch and Beasley, 1990).

Many factors contribute to a survey's validity. One is the wording of the questions. Leading questions can completely bias the results. Even very subtle changes in wording can alter a person's responses. Elizabeth Loftus (1975) found that people who were asked "Do you get headaches frequently and if so how often?" reported an average of 2.2 headaches a week, whereas people asked "Do you get headaches occasionally and if so how often?" reported a weekly average of 0.7 headaches. Even when a question is worded neutrally—for example, "Do you get headaches?"—people can still give misinformation. Some invariably answer "yes," just to be agreeable. Others seem to have a built-in tendency to say "no." If a survey contains questions that reflect on ability or character, people frequently present themselves in a more favorable light than is warranted (Cannell and Kahn, 1968; Myers and Ridl, 1979). Similarly, if a survey covers a touchy area, such as race relations, people are likely to claim that they believe what they think they *ought* to believe.

The characteristics of the person doing the questioning can also make a difference. In one study conducted in the late 1960s, a period of racial conflict, black residents of Detroit were asked if they felt they could trust most whites. When the interviewer was white, 35 percent of respondents answered "yes" to this question, whereas only 7 percent said "yes" when the interviewer was black (Moore, 1979).

Psychologists conducting surveys try to anticipate and prevent such inadvertent biases. When they suspect that some characteristic of an interviewer (race, for example) might encourage "polite" lying, this should be taken into account in pairing interviewers and respondents. Alternatively, a mail-in questionnaire could be used. Steps can also be taken to counteract potential problems with the wording of survey questions. A researcher can include several differently worded questions on the same topic and see how consistent a person's answers are. This kind of careful construction of a survey greatly increases the likelihood that the findings will accurately reflect what people really think and do.

NATURALISTIC OBSERVATION

As careful as researchers may be in gathering data through surveys or by means of experiments, sometimes the very act of filling out a questionnaire or being in a laboratory changes the way a person is inclined to feel or behave. Imagine investigating the effects of alcohol on social aggressiveness by means of an experiment. Even if you tried to design a laboratory to look just like a bar, as at least one researcher and his colleagues have done (Collins and Marlatt, 1981; Marlatt and Nathan, 1978), could you completely rule out the possibility that subjects were controlling their behavior because they knew they were being watched? Probably not. The only way around this problem would be to do your observing in a natural setting where the drinkers did not know they were being studied. The cardinal rule of such **naturalistic observation** is that the investigator stay out of the way.

Many questions lend themselves to naturalistic observation. An organizational psychologist might use this method to study leadership roles in small corporations. A developmental psychologist might use it to study the way four-year-olds interact in a preschool classroom. Such observation is sometimes done through a one-way window so that the presence of the psychologist cannot interfere with routine behavior. Alternatively, psychologists sometimes use **participant observation,** in which they join an existing group to record thoughts and feelings accessible only to group members. In one such study, three social psychologists joined a secretive group that predicted a great flood would end the world at a certain time on a certain day (Festinger et al., 1956). When the fateful moment came and went, the psychologists observed how disconfirmation of the

The one-way window is a great aid to naturalistic observation. The subjects see only a mirror, while the researcher can observe them through the glass. Unaware of the researcher's presence, the subjects behave more naturally.

prophecy influenced the group's behavior. Instead of disbanding, as one might expect, group members became more public. In an attempt to attract new followers, they announced that their belief had saved the world.

In observational research it is crucial to record data in ways that avoid subjective interpretations. How do we know, for example, that members of the doomsday group became less secretive after disconfirmation of their prophecy? We know because the researchers kept careful records of what they saw and heard. Such records help other researchers to detect biases in the initial investigators' views. In the case of the doomsday group study, moreover, three researchers were involved, so they could compare observations among themselves to make sure they were in agreement. When the independent observations of several observers do, in fact, agree, we have added reason to believe that their viewpoints are right.

Although naturalistic observation is extremely valuable for investigating many types of questions, it also has limitations. The main problem is that a researcher cannot control the situation and so cannot test cause-and-effect hypotheses. If the psychologists in our hypothetical barroom study observe that customers get rowdier as they drink more, is it necessarily the alcohol that is inducing their behavior? What if, as the evening wears on, the bar becomes packed with people? Perhaps increased aggressiveness is due less to the amount of alcohol consumed than to the extent of crowding. The degree to which a particular factor is causally related to another can be inferred only through an experiment or a very well constructed quasi-experimental design.

THE CASE STUDY

Most of the data-gathering methods we have discussed so far involve collecting information from a representative sample of people ideally chosen at random from a much larger population. But some things of interest to psychologists occur too rarely to be studied in this way. Consider the psychological disorder commonly called multiple personality, in which one person has two or more distinct personalities, at least one of which is typically unaware of the thoughts and actions of the others. Because relatively few cases of multiple personality have ever been reported, psychologists cannot study it by means of, say, correlational research. Instead, they must rely on intensive investigation of those people known to have the disorder. Such in-depth analysis of a single individual is called a **case study.** In this instance, a case study would involve probing the past of the disturbed person to discover any unusual factors that might have contributed to the condition.

In other instances, psychologists conducting a case study may know the unusual factors that pertain to a particular person but not the exact effects that those factors have on behavior. The factors may simply occur far too rarely. Case studies of children who have been raised in near-total isolation from other human beings are one example. One such child was Genie, a girl who from the age of one to the age of thirteen had been imprisoned alone in a small room in her parents' house (Curtiss, 1977; Pines,

1981). During the day she was harnessed in a sitting position, and at night she was often bound in a cagelike crib. Her psychotic father beat her whenever she made noise, and he forbade her mother ever to talk to the child. When authorities finally discovered Genie, she was a frail, pitiful creature who was unable to stand erect or speak. Through much subsequent training, she gradually acquired some language, but even after years of effort she still had not mastered many of the rules of grammar. Does Genie's slow and difficult progress provide evidence that language must be learned during a critical period early in life? Psychologists are not yet certain, but the case study of Genie has given them some important clues.

Case studies, then, not only provide a wealth of descriptive information about a particular phenomenon, they may also suggest important principles underlying it. In the hands of a brilliant psychologist, the case-study method can be a powerful tool indeed. Sigmund Freud's theory of personality, described in Chapter 13, was based on case studies of the patients who came to him for treatment. Similarly, Jean Piaget's theory of intellectual development in childhood, described in Chapter 9, began with intensive observation of his own three children as they were growing up. Insightful as they may be, however, case studies can never *prove* that suspected principles of behavior actually operate. Still, subsequent researchers can learn much by attempting to corroborate the patterns of behavior observed in case-study investigations.

MEASUREMENT TECHNIQUES

In discussing the data-gathering methods psychologists use, we have not had a chance to say much about how they measure the factors they study. Yet careful measurement is just as important to the success of an investigation as the careful choice of a research method or the careful selection of a sample. If variables cannot be measured accurately, we can never really be certain about what a study shows. Psychologists use two major criteria, validity and reliability, to determine the adequacy of their measurement devices.

VALIDITY AND RELIABILITY

A measurement device is **valid** if it does in fact measure what it is intended to measure. If you tried to

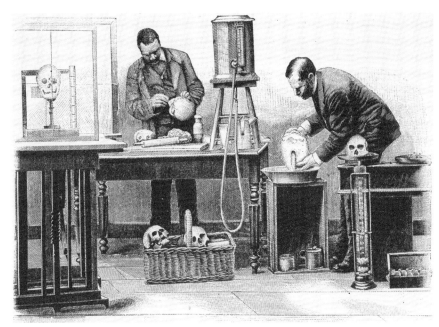

For many years, scientists believed that skull size was an indicator of intelligence. However, although scientists could reliably measure skull size, size is not a valid measure of intelligence.

gauge intelligence by measuring the shape of a person's head, you would be using an invalid yardstick because head shape has virtually nothing to do with IQ. Of course, it is not always this easy to tell if a measurement tool is invalid. Sometimes a yardstick that seems valid at first turns out not to be so when it is considered more closely. Asking questions about the validity of measurement devices is therefore an important part of critically assessing psychological research.

Just as measurement tools must be valid, they must also be **reliable;** that is, they must yield reasonably *consistent* results. This means that the results must not fluctuate widely from one measurement session to another. Measuring the shape of a person's head is certainly a reliable yardstick. If you performed such a measurement ten times in a row, you would get almost identical results. Yet this reliable yardstick is still invalid as a means of assessing intelligence. This example shows that reliability and validity need not go together. That a certain measurement tool yields the same scores at different times does not necessarily mean that it is measuring what it purports to measure. We will say more about reliability and validity in Chapter 14, which discusses psychological testing and assessment. For now, just keep in mind that whenever a psychological study is conducted, the

reliability and validity of its measurement tools must be taken into account.

THREE APPROACHES TO MEASUREMENT

Psychologists use a wide variety of measurement devices. Often they custom design a measurement technique to suit the particular needs of their research. Many of these techniques, however, can be grouped into three major types: self-reports, behavioral measures, and physiological assessments.

When **self-reports** are used as a measurement device, people are asked how they think, feel, or are inclined to act in a given situation, and their responses are recorded and tallied. Self-reports, of course, form the basis of all surveys, and they figure prominently in many other types of research. In Stanley Schachter's classic study of affiliation, for example, both the assessment of how fear-inducing the experimental condition was (the sadistic Dr. Zilstein and his painful electric shocks) and the assessment of whether subjects wished to wait by themselves or with others were gathered through self-reports.

But however useful self-reports may be in many kinds of studies, they do have limitations. If you were interested in measuring social aggression in a barroom, for example, it is unlikely that you would set

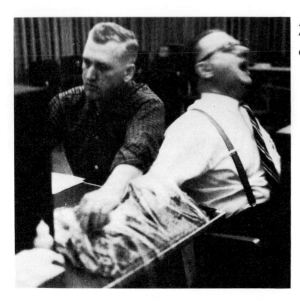

A subject in Milgram's experiment on obedience forces a "victim's" hand onto a plate that the subject believed would deliver a painful electric shock.

about the task by questioning all the patrons about their aggressive feelings. To do so would almost certainly influence the very phenomenon you were trying to measure, since many drinkers would become annoyed at your inquisitiveness. A more reliable approach would be to use what psychologists call **behavioral measures**—that is, objective, quantifiable assessments of how people actually behave. In this case, you might try unobtrusively to count the number of verbal or physical acts of aggression that occurred in the bar during a given period of time. Such unobtrusive behavioral measures are also useful when it is suspected that people might distort their answers in order to present themselves in a more favorable light. Thus, if you wanted to know how much beer the students at a fraternity party consumed, counting the empty bottles would probably be a more accurate approach than asking the drinkers outright (Webb et al., 1966).

Often the tendency to misreport what we have done or are likely to do is not at all conscious. We may honestly think that we would act one way, only to behave quite differently when a real-life test arises. This was demonstrated in an alarming study of obedience to authority conducted by Stanley Milgram (1963). Subjects were ordered to deliver increasingly painful electric shocks to a supposed fellow subject as part of a bogus learning experiment. Milgram used a behavioral measure in his study—the extent to which people continued to increase the voltage when they were told to do so. He found that a surprisingly large

percentage of subjects delivered the maximum voltage (despite the victim's convincing screams of protest) simply because a stern experimenter told them that they must. Before conducting this experiment, Milgram asked people he knew how they thought *they* would react if they were a subject in it. Most said that neither they nor anyone else would administer painful shocks to another person. In short, his friends and colleagues were totally wrong in predicting how people would behave. This important study and the controversy it has created are discussed more fully in Chapter 19. The point here is that, without behavioral measures, psychologists would have little idea how strong certain tendencies are in human beings.

But though behavioral measures often have advantages over self-reports, they have some limitations of their own. For one thing, they are not appropriate for studying certain topics, such as dreams and fantasies (too mental) or people's sexual practices (usually considered too private to be observed). In addition, behavioral measures are often more troublesome to collect than subjective ratings, questionnaires, and other kinds of self-reports. These potential drawbacks will usually be weighed in a researcher's choice of measurement techniques.

Physiological assessments are a third kind of approach to measurement, and they too have pros and cons. Their great value lies in providing objective data on things that are difficult to measure in other ways. Consider the problem of determining when subjects in studies on sleeping are actually asleep.

You certainly cannot rely on self-reports in this instance. Nor can you trust to simple observations of behavior, such as the fact that the subject's eyes are closed. Fortunately, a device called an electroencephalograph can provide a physiological measure. By reading the brain's electrical activity from outside the skull and tracing it on rolling graph paper, the electroencephalograph allows researchers to tell whether someone is asleep and if so which of several stages of sleep that person is in.

Similarly, psychologists who want to know what parts of the brain are involved in learning, memory, reasoning, speaking, and other mental activities certainly cannot solicit self-reports. People have no idea how their brains accomplish all the things that they do. A modern-day solution is to eavesdrop on activities within the brain by using physiological assessments. One technique is to implant tiny electrodes into the brains of experimental animals and record the electrical activities of small groups of cells, or even single cells. Psychologist Richard Thompson and his colleagues have used this technique to map the brain circuits involved in learning simple responses, such as blinking upon hearing a sound which signals that a puff of air is about to strike the eye (Thompson, 1988). Thompson has verified these maps of brain circuits using behavioral measures. By making small cuts in the brain tissues that physiological measures show are involved in this kind of learning, he has directly observed the resulting learning deficits in experimental animals.

This use of more than one approach to measurement is advantageous because it helps to guard against misinterpretations of data. In fact, contemporary psychologists may simultaneously use all three of the measurement approaches we have described. Consider the measurement of depression (John et al., 1988). Psychologists can solicit self-reports (asking patients what they are thinking and feeling); they can observe certain kinds of behavior (general activity level, appetite, sleep patterns, and so forth); and they can monitor activity in the brain, looking for patterns associated with depression. Each type of measurement helps to compensate for any limitations in the others.

ASSESSING DEVELOPMENT OVER TIME

One special measurement problem that psychologists face is assessing how and why people change over time. Imagine that you are trying to find out whether children with parents who are warm and affectionate tend to grow up to be caring, empathetic adults. You might randomly select a group of adults, assess each person's degree of empathy and caring, and then try to discover, by reconstructing their pasts, how warm and affectionate their parents were toward them. But this approach would probably require you to rely on people's memories to a large extent, and memories of events that happened years ago are notoriously unreliable. A more accurate way to answer the same question would be to conduct a **longitudinal study,** one in which the same group of people is examined over a number of years. Thus, you might select a group of children, assess how their parents treat them, and then assess the empathy and caring they display when they become adults. Researchers who have conducted such studies have made an unexpected finding. Simply having parents who are warm and affectionate does *not* by itself mean that the child will become a caring and empathetic adult. Apparently, parents must also set firm limits on their children's behavior and encourage self-sacrifice in them in order for the children to grow up showing sensitivity and concern toward others.

Longitudinal studies are time consuming, however. An alternative approach that psychologists sometimes take is to study a population cross-sectionally by age. In a **cross-sectional study,** the population is divided into subgroups on the basis of certain criteria (in this case, age), the subgroups are randomly sampled, and the members of each sample are then surveyed, tested, or observed. If you were conducting a cross-sectional study of intelligence by age, for instance, you might administer an IQ test to people of various ages—some ten years old, some fifteen, some twenty, and so forth—and then draw conclusions about intelligence at different stages of the life cycle on the basis of the results. Such studies usually show that the high point of intellectual development is somewhere around age thirty, after which intelligence consistently declines.

There is a serious problem with cross-sectional studies of intellectual development, however. The older people sampled have had very different educations and life experiences from the younger ones. This age-related difference in intellectual stimulation can easily influence the test results. And in fact, longitudinal studies of intelligence over the life span have shown this factor to be highly significant. When psychologists examine the *same* people at different points in their lives, they generally find that some measures of intellectual performance either increase or stay the same until the age of fifty or sixty (Baltes et al., 1977). Thus, longitudinal studies have in some instances produced findings that are more valid than those obtained when a population is studied cross-sectionally by age.

This does not mean that the longitudinal approach is always better, however. Both longitudinal and cross-sectional studies have certain advantages and limitations that make each more or less useful in answering particular types of questions. A combination of the two methods is probably ideal. Cross-sectional research is less expensive, the data can be gathered in a much shorter time, and a larger number of subjects can usually be studied. When cross-sectional studies are used for preliminary investigations, they can often provide important directions for later, more extensive longitudinal research. You will meet the complementary use of these two approaches again in Chapters 9 and 10 on human development.

Questions about the negative effects of televised violence on children have concerned adults since the 1950s. Studies by psychologists have uncovered many parts of the puzzle, but no single research method can reveal the complete picture.

IN DEPTH

Exploring the Effects of TV Violence

Other kinds of research methods can likewise be used in a complementary way. Often, however, there is no "best" approach to a research problem. Several methods must be used together to provide the fullest insights into how, when, and why a certain behavior occurs. You can see the value of using many research methods by looking at how psychologists have studied the impact of television violence on children.

THE INITIAL STUDIES

American TV programs have always contained a great deal of violence. People have wondered if this daily exposure to fistfights, shootings, car crashes, bombings, and other violent acts might not be detrimental to viewers. Of particular concern has been the effect of TV violence on children, especially very young, impressionable children. Some early laboratory research seemed to justify this concern. In one classic study (described in Chapter 19), nursery school children who watched an adult assault an inflated plastic doll quickly acquired a whole set of violent behaviors: later, when they had been mildly frustrated, the children used the same behaviors on the same doll (Bandura et al., 1961).

Might not children learn other violent behaviors from watching the battles of their TV heroes? In addition, could watching TV violence have a disinhibitory effect? Might it loosen normal social inhibitions, causing viewers to strike out at others over minor provocations? At the same time, could TV violence inure children to the effects of actual violence? Could it encourage them to think that the victims of real aggression are injured far less than they actually are (Linz et al., 1989)? One way to find out if exposure to TV violence has any of these negative effects is to conduct an experiment in which TV violence is the independent variable and subsequent aggression in young viewers is the dependent one.

In one early experiment (Liebert and Baron, 1972), elementary school children were shown one of two video clips. The first, shown to experimental subjects, was an excerpt from the TV program "The Untouchables," a series about government agents fighting organized crime during the 1930s. This clip had a chase scene, two fistfights, two shootings, and a knifing. The second clip, shown to control subjects, was an excerpt from a series of athletic events (running, jumping, and so forth) that were fast-paced but nonviolent. After the videos, each subject was shown a gray metal box with wires leading through the wall. On the box were two buttons: a red one marked "hurt," and a green one marked "help." The subject was told that in the next room another child was playing a game that required a handle to be turned. (The wires presumably connected that handle to the gray box.) Either the subject could help the other child by pushing the green "help" button and making the handle easier to turn, or the subject could hurt the other child by pushing the red "hurt" button and making the handle too hot to touch. Subjects who had just seen the violent TV program were more likely than the control group to press the red button. And later, when placed in a free-play situation, these same children were also more likely to act aggressively, especially the youngest boys. The researchers' hypothesis that TV violence can prompt aggression seemed to have been supported. Other psychologists who have conducted similar laboratory experiments have usually drawn the same conclusion, especially when the children involved are already prone to aggression and especially when they are exposed to violent cues, such as a "hurt" button (Andison, 1977; Josephson, 1987).

CRITICISMS, ALTERNATIVES, AND FURTHER RESEARCH

But many psychologists have wondered if it is valid to generalize from these laboratory findings to behavior in the real world. After all, watching a brief TV excerpt picked especially for its violence is not necessarily the same as watching an entire TV program. Whole programs often contain pro-social messages (helping people in trouble, seeing that justice is done) along with displays of violence. Furthermore, in real life people are rarely given a specific invitation to injure someone else, as when offered a "hurt" button to push. Such situations may be so contrived that subjects respond in unusual ways. Then, too, laboratory studies often artificially eliminate the normal social context of watching TV. In the real world, children often watch TV with family or friends, not in isolation. The influence of these other people could easily alter reactions to violence. Such misgivings about generalizing from laboratory findings are part of a methodological issue called **ecological validity.** Ecological validity refers to the concern that conditions in a laboratory experiment may not always mirror those in real-life settings.

To address the issue of ecological validity, psychologists have designed experiments conducted in natural settings, called **field experiments.** For in-

stance, Ross Parke and his colleagues conducted three field experiments in institutions for juvenile delinquents (Parke et al., 1977). Groups of boys living in different cottages saw different kinds of films, usually a different film each night for an entire week. For some groups, the films contained a great deal of physical violence; for others, the films contained little violence. The boys' behavior was carefully observed at three stages: before the experiment, during the week the films were shown, and during a follow-up period. In all three studies, exposure to violent movies was followed by increased aggression.

But the problem is that not all field experiments have produced the same results. While some have offered evidence that TV violence increases aggression, others have found no such link. Some psychologists believe this is reason to doubt that exposure to TV violence has predictable effects on behavior in real life (Freedman, 1984). Others, however, argue against this view. They point out that experiments in natural settings are usually quasi-experiments. (The Parke study, for example, was a quasi-experiment because the subjects were not randomly assigned to groups, as is required in a true experiment; rather, the groups were preexisting ones.) Quasi-experiments do not offer the power of control that laboratory studies do. In natural settings it is hard to be sure that all factors are being held constant *except* the independent variable. Inadvertently, some of these other factors could be having an effect, leading to different results in different studies.

Many psychologists go on to argue that we cannot ignore these additional factors that may be enhancing or diminishing the effects of viewing television violence. What is needed, they say, are theories that consider how various factors interact to promote or inhibit aggression. Some researchers have tried to identify the most important of these factors by means of correlational research. The strategy was to study large groups of people and find out what experiences and characteristics the most aggressive ones have in common.

In one such study, researchers collected data on hundreds of children and their parents at several times during a three-year period (Huesman and Eron, 1983). Consistent with most earlier correlational studies, they found a small but positive relationship between extensive viewing of television violence and a higher-than-average level of

Although it has not been proved that watching televised violence causes aggressive behavior, there is evidence that many children identify with violent television characters and believe that what they see on TV reflects reality.

aggression. They also found aggression to be related to a number of other factors, including low popularity among peers, low achievement in school, strong identification with TV characters, and a belief that behaviors seen on TV reflect real life.

As you know, cause-and-effect relations cannot be identified strictly from correlational data. But researchers can speculate on how all these variables fit together. Leonard Eron (1982) suggests the following circular pattern: Aggressive children may be unpopular because they bully and injure other children. As a result, peers reject them, and the aggressive youngsters spend more time alone watching television, including many violent programs that mirror their own personal styles. This heavy diet of televised violence tends to reinforce their aggressive responses, particularly if they lack the intellectual skills needed to grasp that most television solutions to problems are unrealistic. When they then try out the aggressive solutions of their TV heroes in their own lives, they become even more alienated from peers and are driven to more television viewing. A vicious circle thereby perpetuates itself. This, of course, is only conjecture. Experimental studies would be needed to test for the existence of this complex circle of events. At the same time, there are undoubtedly other factors that also enter into the equation. For instance, researchers have found that parents' use of physical punishment tends to

be related to higher-than-average aggression in their children (Singer and Benton, 1989). Ironically, then, parents who spank their children to deter them from behaving in the violent ways they see on television are probably helping to instill the belief that physical aggression is a "solution" to problems.

PATTERNS AND CONCLUSIONS

Psychologists have been studying the impact of TV violence for over thirty years. Why has it been so hard to determine if and how exposure to televised violence increases viewer aggression in real-life situations? One reason is that each research method available to psychologists has certain limitations, which means that no one kind of study can provide the full answer. Another reason is that the causes of human aggression are far from simple. Case studies of people who are abnormally aggressive show that their lives are filled with learning experiences that could promote a tendency toward extreme aggression. Watching a great deal of televised violence is only one of those experiences, and it never operates in a vacuum. Always there are interacting factors that encourage and discourage aggressive responses. This is what makes psychological research so challenging. A variety of methods must be used to fully understand most complex human behaviors (Greewald et al., 1991).

ANALYZING DATA

So far we have focused primarily on how psychologists gather their data. But inevitably we have also touched on the closely related topic of data analysis. Survey responses, test scores, or observed behaviors in people cannot "speak for themselves." Researchers must summarize them in some way to make clear what they mean or suggest (Kimble, 1989). Usually this involves some form of **statistics**—mathematical methods for analyzing data and presenting them in summary form. There are two main kinds of statistics: descriptive and inferential. A student of psychology should have some knowledge of each.

DESCRIPTIVE STATISTICS

Looking at research data in its initial, unorganized state can be a bewildering experience for a person with an untrained eye. But by using various procedures for presenting quantitative information, psychologists can summarize even vast amounts of data in forms that are brief, meaningful, and easy to grasp. These procedures are collectively called **descriptive statistics.** In this section we will show how descriptive statistics enable researchers to accomplish two important goals: specifying at a glance how scores in a sample are distributed, and conveying in a shorthand manner how closely two factors are related.

DESCRIBING DISTRIBUTIONS OF SCORES

Suppose a group of psychologists wants to find out if participating in a support group for cancer patients can help women with breast cancer survive. So they locate nearly a hundred such women willing to take part in their study and randomly assign them to experimental and control groups. All receive the standard medical treatment for breast cancer, but the experimental subjects are also organized into support groups. These groups meet once a week for an hour and a half, during which time the women have a chance to form close friendships, share their feelings about having cancer, and discuss with one another and their group leader how best to cope with the disease. During the ten years following the start of the study, the researchers periodically assess how each of their subjects is faring. They find that some die in the first few weeks of the study; others survive for a number of months; and still others live for years. The survival periods of those in the experimental group vary between 1 month and 120 months, and so are said to have a **range** of 119 months (120 − 1 = 119). The survival periods of those in the control group vary between 4 months and 83 months, and so have a range of 79 months (83 − 4 = 79). Calculating these two different ranges is the first step in meaningfully organizing the data.

Measures of Central Tendency   The next step is to choose some method of calculating the central tendencies of the two distributions. A **central tendency** is the most characteristic score in a distribution. One measure of central tendency is the **mean,** or arithmetic average. To find the mean, you add all the scores in a sample and divide by the total number of scores. The mean survival time in our study of breast cancer patients is 36 months for the women who participated in a support group and 18 months for the controls.

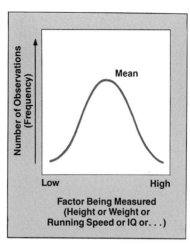

FIGURE 2.4   A normal curve. The "bell" shape of an ideal normal distribution of frequencies. The highest point of the curve represents the mean.

These mean scores are not just hypothetical. Psychologists recently conducted a study just like the one we described and got just these results (Spiegel et al., 1989). The findings suggest that participating in a support group does indeed help women with breast cancer live longer than they otherwise would.

The mean is just one measure of central tendency. Two others are the median and the mode. The **median** is the score that falls in the exact middle of a distribution of numbers arranged from highest to lowest. For example, for the numbers 74, 74, 68, 57, and 50, which represent the ages of five women in our study of support groups and cancer survival, the median age is 68. The **mode** is the score most frequently obtained in a distribution, in this case 74. The mean in this example is 64.6. The mean, median, and mode are often different, as they are here, but not always. For some distributions these three measures of central tendency are equal.

One example of a distribution in which the mean, median, and mode are equal is plotted as a graph in Figure 2.4. This bell-shaped curve is called a **normal curve,** and the distribution in this case is called a **normal distribution.** Normal curves are most nearly approximated when a very large number of randomly selected subjects are measured regarding some trait for which individuals vary from a maximum to a minimum, with smooth gradations in between. If, for instance, you were to administer an IQ test to a random sample of 100,000 Americans and you plotted the frequency of each score obtained, you would probably get a curve much like the one in Figure 2.4. A large proportion of scores would fall close to the mean, a much smaller proportion would

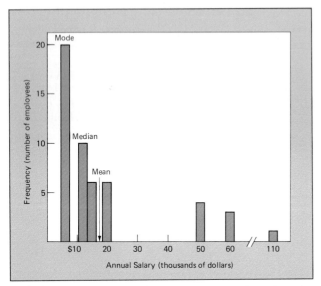

FIGURE 2.5 The distribution of incomes in an imaginary company. The mean, median, and mode are not identical in this distribution. Frequency distributions of this and many other kinds are commonly used in psychology.

be a moderate distance away from it, and only a very small percentage would be extremely far from the average. Note, however, that just by looking at a curve and observing that it has a roughly bell shape, you cannot tell for sure whether it is a normal curve. Normal curves are formed only by a very specific distribution of scores. In psychological research few sets of scores have this exact distribution.

Those distributions that are not normal are *skewed*. In such cases the mean, median, and mode are not equal. How, then, does a psychologist decide which measure of central tendency to use? The answer depends in part on exactly how the scores are distributed.

Suppose someone told you that the mean income at a certain company was $19,000 a year. What would this suggest to you? Look at Figure 2.5, the salary distribution for a hypothetical firm employing fifty people. The president of the company earns $110,000 a year; he pays three executives $60,000 and four executives $50,000 each; six supervisors earn $20,000 each and six salespeople earn $15,000 each; the remaining thirty manual and clerical workers all earn $12,000 or less, and most of them earn only $6,500.

The mean of all fifty salaries is $19,000, but this is not really a fair representation of the actual distribution of incomes. It seems too high. In this case, a better measure of central tendency would be the median, the salary level at which the number of people who earn more than this amount and the number who earn less are the same. This level is $12,000. Because the mode, or most frequent salary, is only $6,500, it is as misleading an indicator of the overall distribution as the mean.

Why would anyone go to the trouble of calculating a measure of central tendency? The reason is to organize a mass of numerical data into a form that can show findings simply. It is much easier, for example, to tell someone that the median salary earned at a particular company is $12,000 than it is to say, "One person earns $110,000, three people earn $60,000, four people earn $50,000," and so on. Central tendencies, then, like other statistical tools, provide a kind of quantitative shorthand. They also enable us to easily compare the distributions of variables in two or more groups.

Measures of Variability But a measure of central tendency does not tell the whole story. To describe a distribution of numbers more fully, we also need information about the **dispersion,** or degree of scatter among the individual numbers. Are scores clustered closely together or are they widely spread out? To understand why this question is important, imagine that you learn you have a serious illness with a median life expectancy of only eight months after the initial symptoms arise. Would you assume that you will *necessarily* die before the year is out? Probably not, for the median tells you only the middle score in a distribution. You would certainly ask your doctor about the dispersion of life expectancies among people with your condition. Do some live less than eight months and others more? And among any longer-lived patients, what percentage go on for years?

Biologist Stephen Jay Gould found himself asking just these questions after surgery for a rare form of cancer. Because of his training in statistics, he knew that an eight-month median rate of survival was not necessarily a death sentence, and, in fact, he has survived (Gould, 1985). Of critical importance in assessing his chances was the extent to which survival among different patients *varied* from the median or other measure of central tendency. The statistical

TABLE 2.1 Calculating the Standard Deviation

Step 1: Calculate how much each score deviates from the mean: Group A (mean: 78)				
Value	52	65	78	95	100
Deviation from mean	−26	−13	0	+17	+ 22

Step 2: To equate the positive and negative deviations, square each deviation:				
Deviation	−26	−13	0	+17	+22
Deviation squared	676	169	0	289	484

Step 3: Find the mean of the squared deviations:

$$\frac{676 + 169 + 0 + 289 + 484}{5} = 323.6$$

Step 4: To convert the squared figures back into the same units as the original values, find the square root of the mean deviations. This is the standard deviation.

$$\sqrt{323.6} = 18$$

Now calculate the standard deviation for group B.

techniques for expressing this information are called **measures of variability.**

The range, mentioned earlier, is one measure of variability. But it can be deceptive. A single extreme score can dramatically affect a range. For example, suppose high profits at our hypothetical company allowed the president to take a raise of $20,000 a year. The range would leap from $103,500 ($110,000 − $6,500) to $123,500 ($130,000 − $6,500), even though the amount of variation among the remaining forty-nine salaries remained exactly the same. Clearly it would be helpful to have a more sensitive measure of variability—one that would take into account all the scores in a given set of data.

The **standard deviation** is such a measure of variability. It indicates the average extent to which all the scores in a particular set vary from the mean. The more dispersed scores are, the higher is the standard deviation; the less dispersed, the lower is the standard deviation. Which of the following sets of scores would you guess has a larger standard deviation?

Group A: 52 65 78 95 100 (mean = 78)
Group B: 85 89 91 97 98 (mean = 92)

If you guessed group A, you are right. Its standard deviation is 18, while that of group B is 5. Table 2.1 explains the steps involved in calculating the

standard deviation. The important point to remember is that the standard deviation tells you immediately whether a set of scores varies widely from the mean or is clustered closely around it. The greater the standard deviation, the wider is the variation.

CORRELATION COEFFICIENTS

Earlier in this chapter, when we discussed correlational research, we said that psychologists assess the strength of a correlation (the degree of relatedness between two variables) by calculating a correlation coefficient. Now we are ready to describe this statistical tool in more detail. A correlation coefficient is a number ranging from −1, which indicates a perfect negative correlation, through 0, which indicates no correlation, to +1, which indicates a perfect positive correlation. Thus, the closer a correlation coefficient is to +1 or −1, the stronger the relationship—positive or negative—between the two variables.

It is important to remember that a correlation coefficient of, say, −.65 is just as strong as a correlation coefficient of +.65. The strength of a correlation is determined not by the sign of its coefficient (+ or −) but by the absolute value of the coefficient. To test your understanding of this potentially confusing point, suppose that researchers at a certain university find that grade-point average and number of traffic violations have a correlation of −.42, while grade-point average and running speed have a correlation of +.26. Which relationship is stronger? In this fictitious example, a stronger correlation exists between traffic violations and grade-point average than between running ability and grade-point average, because 42 is larger than 26. Note that the minus sign in front of .42 has nothing to do with the strength of the relationship being measured. It simply indicates that the relationship is negative: as traffic violations *increase*, grade-point average *declines*, and vice versa.

To summarize, correlational studies are a way of discovering the extent to which two variables are related, and the correlation coefficient is a quantitative means of expressing this relationship. At one extreme, a correlation coefficient of 0 indicates that there is no relationship between the variables in question: they vary independently of one another. At the other extreme, a correlation coefficient of −1 or +1 indicates that a perfect relationship exists: if you know the quantitative change in one variable, you can state the accompanying change in the other precisely. Most of the relationships that psychologists study fall somewhere between these extremes.

INFERENTIAL STATISTICS

Descriptive statistics enable researchers to convey the highlights of their findings with only a few words and figures. They can reduce a mass of numerical data to a form that is more manageable and easier to understand. But often the investigators' task is not over when they have finished "describing" their data. Many times the goal of research is to explore hypotheses, and for this purpose psychologists must turn to **inferential statistics.**

Inferential statistics provide ground rules or conventions for determining what conclusions can legitimately be drawn from data. Remember that psychological researchers begin with a hypothesis—a conjecture about behavior that they want to test. They then collect quantifiable data (scores, ratings, behavioral measures, and so on) about the way people in a sample actually behave under specific conditions. Next they summarize their data by means of descriptive statistics, like those discussed in the preceding section. Finally, they make use of inferential statistics to infer (draw a reasonable conclusion about) whether the data support their hypothesis. Were the results

due primarily to chance, or was there indeed a significant pattern or relationship? To see how they answer this question, we must enter the world of odds and probability.

PROBABILITY

Probability is a complex area of mathematics that is frequently misunderstood. Our intuitions about "what the odds are" are not always correct. Assume, for example, that you have been tossing a coin and it has landed heads up ten times in a row. You are about to toss the coin again. What do you predict will happen? If you say that tails will turn up, you are committing a common error known as the "gambler's fallacy." The odds of getting heads on any given toss of an unbiased coin are always 50–50, no matter how many times heads has already appeared.

Suppose we know the odds of getting a single head is 50–50, or 1 chance out of 2. What are our chances of getting several heads in a row? We can figure this out by multiplying the probability of getting one event (heads one time) by the probability of getting each subsequent one. The probability of getting two heads in a row, therefore, is $1/2 \times 1/2$, or $1/4$. For four heads in a row, the odds would be $1/16$ (that is, $1/2 \times 1/2 \times 1/2 \times 1/2$). The probability that a coin will come up heads ten times in a row is $1/2$ raised to the tenth power, which is $1/1,024$. That is, the odds against this event occurring by chance with a fair coin are 1,024 to 1, which is why you might begin to suspect in such a case that the coin is biased. What you are doing when you form this suspicion is making a judgment about the meaning of an event (ten heads in a row) based on the odds of its occurring purely by chance. Because the likelihood of this being a chance occurrence is so slim, you might favor some alternative explanation. This is exactly the kind of logic that psychologists use when they use inferential statistics to judge the significance of their data.

STATISTICAL SIGNIFICANCE

The crux of the problem psychologists face is that the influence of chance can never be eliminated. Whenever a researcher conducts an experiment, there will invariably be some difference, based strictly on chance, between the performance of one group and the performance of another. If you gave a hearing test to 100 people with brown hair, and the same test to 100 blonds, you might find that the blonds, on

Gamblers rely more on luck than on statistics, but psychologists seek to separate causes from chances, to identify the conditions that cause something to happen again and again.

average, can hear slightly better. Hearing, however, has nothing to do with hair color, so you can assume that in this case the difference was caused entirely by chance. This means that if you ran the same test again with a different group of people, you would be just as likely to get the opposite results. But how do you assess the influence of chance on a relationship that is far more plausible? What you need is a statistical test to help decide when a given difference in performance is reliable—that is, when we can expect it to occur again and again under the same circumstances. Such a test is called a measure of **statistical significance.**

An example will help clarify the importance of being able to calculate statistical significance. Suppose an experimental group of rats has been given an injection of caffeine, the stimulant in coffee. On average, these rats learn to run a maze in thirty trials. A control group of animals is injected with a **placebo** (a substance that has no physiological effect) to ensure that the two groups will not perform differently merely because one has received an injection and the other has not. The control group learns to run the same maze in an average of thirty-eight trials. Is the difference between thirty and thirty-eight trials large enough to warrant concluding that the caffeine increased the speed with which the experimental animals learned the maze? Or, alternatively, might these results have occurred merely by chance?

Psychologists and other scientists have adopted an arbitrary convention for making such decisions. By various methods they calculate the probability that the outcome of the study could have occurred by chance alone. If this probability is quite low, say .05 (5 times out of 100), they then have good reason to reject the "chance" explanation and to conclude instead that the independent variable under study caused the results. In this instance, the researchers would report that the data had attained the .05 level of statistical significance. Some investigators choose more stringent levels, say .01 (1 time out of 100). In each case, however, the investigator computes the probability that the results occurred solely by chance. Only if that probability is low does the researcher assert that the results support the hypothesis.

META-ANALYSIS

So far we have been talking about statistical analysis of data obtained in single studies. As you know, however, science is a cumulative process, with new studies building on those conducted before. With so many psychologists doing research today, there are often a great many studies done on any given topic, and those studies do not always yield the same results. Consider the issue of the short-term effects of school desegregation (discussed in Wachter, 1988). Does creating a better racial balance in American schools raise the achievement test scores of black students? One hundred and fifty-seven known studies have been conducted on this topic, but of these only nineteen have had reasonably well controlled designs (Wortman and Bryant, 1985). Nineteen would not be too large a number to cope with if most of these studies had findings that were fairly similar. The problem is that they do not. About a third show small negative effects of school desegregation on blacks' achievement test scores. The rest show positive effects, mostly small ones, but some of moderate size. What are we to make of these varied findings? Does desegregation boost black achievement test scores? And if it does, is the effect small or moderate?

One tool for helping to answer these questions is called a **meta-analysis.** Meta-analysis is a method of synthesizing the results of different studies by using a set of statistical procedures to compute, select, and combine data (Hedges and Olkin, 1985; Rosenthal, 1984; Wolf, 1986). In the case of the school desegregation issue, the National Institute of Education

One of the most intriguing—and frustrating—hazards of psychological research is the self-fulfilling prophecy. Teachers who were told that some randomly selected children were late bloomers treated those students differently from the others; by the end of the school year, that group of children did indeed do better on IQ tests.

asked six different researchers to review a meta-analyses using the nineteen studies mentioned. Each reviewer generally agreed with the results of the meta-analysis: although the results of the separate studies varied substantially, desegregation had a positive effect on the test scores of black children equal to almost two months educational gain in one year (Wortman and Bryant, 1985).

Meta-analyses must be conducted carefully, of course. Researchers cannot just take all the studies in existence, compute a statistical average in outcome, and assume that they have drawn a worthwhile conclusion. Studies must first be screened for weaknesses in their methods, and those found to have serious flaws must be eliminated. In the case of the desegregation issue, 138 of the initial 157 studies were discarded for this reason. If this important step had not been taken, far too much weight would have been given to methodologically questionable research, thus calling into question the meta-analysis too (Wortman, in press).

But even a carefully conducted meta-analysis is not necessarily the last word on an issue. We still need to analyze the individual studies for clues as to why their results varied. What are the differences in the studies' designs that could account for the differences in their findings? Answers to this question may point the way to additional research that could be conducted to help clarify the issue.

SOME PITFALLS IN PSYCHOLOGICAL RESEARCH

Good research is difficult in any scientific field. It requires a broad knowledge of available tools for collecting and analyzing data, as well as careful attention to details when performing these tasks. At the same time, good research demands creativity in asking the initial questions and in putting together an effective research strategy. It also calls for an awareness of the various pitfalls inherent in doing scientific research. We will look at four of these pitfalls in the following sections.

THE SELF-FULFILLING PROPHECY

The term **self-fulfilling prophecy** refers to the fact that people often find what they *expect* to find. More than that, they may even unwittingly *create* what they are seeking. Applied to psychological research, the self-fulfilling prophecy means that investigators may inadvertently make their own hypotheses "come true" (or at least appear true). If, for example, a researcher conducting an interview smiles faintly when a subject's response corroborates the theory under investigation, this inadvertent act can easily affect the subject's answers to subsequent questions.

If this seems hard to believe, consider the following experiment.

Robert Rosenthal (1966) told a group of elementary school teachers that certain pupils had obtained high scores on some special tests and therefore were sure to show unusual intellectual development later in the school year. Actually, these potential "late bloomers" were no different from other pupils who had not been so labeled. But a few months later the teachers rated the late bloomers as more interested, more curious, and happier than other students. And when all the children were given IQ tests at the end of the year, many of those who had been labeled late bloomers, especially the first and second graders, showed a significantly greater gain in IQ than did their classmates. In this study it was the teachers, not the experimenter, who fulfilled the prophecy of academic success through their differential treatment of the supposed late bloomers. But an experimenter, even one who is fully aware that self-fulfilling prophecies occur, can also sometimes unintentionally create the expected results.

To avoid self-fulfilling prophecies, a researcher might employ the **double-blind technique,** in which neither the experimenter nor the subjects know who is in the experimental group and who is in the control group. (This procedure differs from the **single-blind technique,** in which the experimenter knows who is in which group but the subjects do not.) In a double-blind experiment to test the effects of a tranquilizing drug, for example, the experimental group would be given the tranquilizer, whereas the control group would receive a placebo, perhaps in the form of a sugar pill. Only some outside party, such as the pharmacist who supplied the pills, would know which group received which kind of pill, and the outsider would not give that information to the experimenter until after the effects of drug and placebo on the two groups had been recorded. In other types of studies, similar techniques can be used. Psychologists looking for a possible positive correlation between IQ and psychological adjustment, for example, would assess psychological adjustment first, without knowing the subjects' IQ scores. In this way they could avoid seeing better adjustment in high-IQ subjects than was actually present.

DEMAND CHARACTERISTICS

Even if a researcher uses the double-blind technique, there is still a possibility that subjects will invalidate

research findings by trying to behave like "good" subjects. Most people who volunteer for an experiment want to do well at the experimental task, so they search for clues as to what the experiment is about. The clues they uncover have been called **demand characteristics,** because subjects feel that these clues *demand* a certain kind of response (presumed "correct") on their part (Orne, 1962). An example illustrates the distorting effects that demand characteristics can have.

Suppose you have volunteered for a psychological experiment. At the laboratory, the researcher tells you that the study involves memory of fast-moving events. She shows you a series of slides depicting successive stages in an automobile accident and then asks you twenty questions about them. One of the questions is "Did another car pass the red Datsun while it was stopped at the stop sign?" This question puzzles you. The sign you remember seeing at the corner was a yield sign, not a stop sign. You conclude that the experimenter must be trying to trick you. But why? Later you believe you detect the experimenter's intentions. She shows you several pairs of very similar slides and asks which of each pair you saw previously. One pair shows the Datsun stopped at an intersection with either a stop sign or a yield sign at the corner. "Aha!" you say to yourself. "She expects me to choose the stop sign because that's what she mentioned in her question. Well, perhaps I should. After all, I'd hate to ruin her experiment." If you select the stop sign knowing full well that it is the wrong sign, you have succumbed to demand characteristics. In doing so, you have made it more difficult for the researcher to interpret the results correctly.

How can researchers counteract demand characteristics? One approach is to question subjects carefully after an experiment to see if demand characteristics influenced them. At the end of an experiment on memory similar to the one just described, Loftus and her colleagues (1978) revealed their true purpose. They told subjects that they were trying to determine the effects of false information on eyewitness testimony by showing slides of an automobile accident and later asking questions about them. One of those questions, the researchers confessed, may have contained false information about the traffic sign located at the intersection. Would the subjects now please indicate which sign they *really* remembered seeing? In this way, Loftus and her colleagues were able to get some idea of the extent to which demand characteristics had influenced their results. The conclusion they drew at the end of this procedure? Demand characteristics had affected subjects' responses hardly at all.

There are problems with this end-of-experiment questioning, however. Sometimes even the most careful and sensitive questioning may not reveal the real reasons behind a person's behavior. Subjects may be unwilling to admit to reasons that place them in an unflattering light, or they may be only vaguely aware of the complex motivations that prompted a particular response.

There are several ways of minimizing the problem of demand characteristics. One is to try to conceal the true purpose of the experiment through deception. In the study by Stanley Milgram (1963) described earlier, subjects were led to believe that the experiment concerned the effect of punishment on learning. The real question, of course, was whether subjects would obey an authority figure even if doing so meant delivering painful electric shocks to another person. (We will discuss the ethics of using deception in psychological research at the end of this chapter.) Another way to reduce the effects of demand characteristics is to automate an experiment as much as possible in order to avoid personal sympathy or hostility toward the experimenter. For example, a researcher might avoid face-to-face contact with subjects by using tape-recorded instructions and anonymous responses. A third approach is to increase the use of unobtrusive measures. If subjects are not aware that a particular behavior is being recorded, they are unlikely to distort it in an effort to please the experimenter.

THE HAWTHORNE EFFECT

More than fifty years ago, researchers at the Hawthorne plant of the Western Electric Company had a mystery on their hands. They were trying to determine the effects of various environmental conditions on the output of workers, but the results they were getting did not seem to make sense. In one set of studies, they varied the amount of lighting that people were given to work by. As the brightness of the lighting increased, worker productivity did too, but so did the output of workers in a control group whose lighting stayed constant. Later the researchers tried decreasing the lighting. Again productivity rose, as did that of the control subjects. It wasn't until the lighting for the experimental subjects had become so

dim that it was almost nonexistent that productivity finally began to fall! The researchers wondered what was going on. Why did these people keep working more effectively despite the unfavorable environment, or, in the case of control subjects, despite no change at all? The mystery deepened as other experiments varying other working conditions yielded similar findings. Productivity kept rising almost no matter what the researchers did.

The investigators concluded that there is something about just being a subject in a study that alters a person's behavior. This phenomenon came to be called the **Hawthorne effect.** But what exactly is the "something" that causes the Hawthorne effect? Is it the novelty of the situation in which people are placed? The extra attention they receive? Or perhaps simply the awareness that someone is watching them? After all the years that have gone by since the Hawthorne studies, psychologists still are not sure about the answers to these questions (Adair, 1984).

What they do know is that the subjective meaning people give to being in a study can easily affect their behavior. For instance, if participating in a study makes you feel special, even slightly superior, you may try extra hard to perform better than average. Conversely, if you resent having to take part in an experiment, your behavior may be careless, even deliberately hostile. Psychologists who conduct research on humans must constantly remind themselves that a subject may have feelings, thoughts, and motivations that the researchers are not aware of. Since these subjective factors can color a study's results, it helps to question people thoroughly after an experiment to find out why *they* believe they acted as they did.

DRAWING PREMATURE CONCLUSIONS

During their training, psychologists are taught to anticipate and overcome the kinds of methodological problems we have been describing. Nevertheless, errors and oversights still occur. This is why it is essential to avoid drawing firm conclusions on the basis of a single study, or even several studies. Yet the temptation to do so is often powerful, as the following example illustrates.

In the early 1970s, two pediatricians, Marshall Klaus and John Kennell, tested an intriguing hypothesis. They questioned the wisdom of the standard hospital procedures that followed the birth of a baby. The new mother was given just a glimpse of her child

Workers at Western Electric's plant in Hawthorne, Illinois, outside Chicago, were the subjects of pioneering research on productivity in the 1920s. The mysterious phenomenon known as the Hawthorne effect was identified in these studies. For reasons that are still not clear, mere participation in a study will affect subjects' behavior.

before the infant was whisked away to be medically examined and cared for. Klaus and Kennell were aware that in some animal species contact during the period immediately after birth is often critical for the development of a normal mother–infant bond. For instance, if a ewe is separated from her lamb immediately after giving birth, she will often reject the lamb several hours later, even though she would have nurtured it earlier (Collias, 1956). Klaus and Kennell believed that if such a sensitive period occurs in humans, existing hospital procedures were less than ideal for mother–infant bonding.

To test their hypothesis, Klaus and Kennell created experimental and control groups. The control group consisted of fourteen mothers and their firstborn infants. These mothers were briefly shown their babies right after delivery, and during the next three days they were given their infants every four hours for routine feeding. In contrast, the fourteen mothers in the experimental group were allowed a private hour with their babies right after delivery and were given an extra five hours each day to interact with them. Klaus and Kennell found that, a month after giving birth, mothers in the experimental group on average were more attentive toward their infants in a routine medical exam, more inclined to look at and fondle them, and more reluctant to leave them with babysitters than were control mothers (Klaus et al., 1972). Even when the children were a year old, the experi-

mental-group mothers seemed more concerned and attentive in certain situations than did the control mothers (Kennell et al., 1974).

These findings made nationwide headlines. The two pediatricians went on to write a popular book in which they claimed that optimal child development depended on bonding in the first hours after birth (Klaus and Kennell, 1976). Concerned parents pressured the medical establishment to change hospital procedures. By the late 1970s it had become standard practice for parents to be given time alone with their newborns so that proper bonding could occur.

It was not long, however, before other researchers began to point out serious problems in Klaus and Kennell's study. For one thing, doctors and nurses might have biased the results by inadvertently giving the experimental women more encouragement as new mothers. And what about the size of the samples —fourteen women and infants in each group? With samples this small it is certainly possible for differences to exist just by chance alone. The experimental mothers might have been more attentive because of preexisting personality traits, or because their infants' temperaments just happened to elicit such responses. Questions of this kind prompted several psychologists to try to replicate Klaus and Kennell's findings.

Replication is an essential part of scientific research. Other investigators reconstruct the basic features of the original study and see if their results are similar. In the case of early mother–infant bonding, other researchers' results did not always match those of Klaus and Kennell. Sometimes there were no significant differences between experimental and control groups. Other times a few differences appeared, but not always the same ones that Klaus and Kennell had found. These patterns led to the suspicion that any differences were due simply to chance. Certainly the combined evidence showed that the universal importance of early mother–infant contact claimed by its proponents was far from an established fact (Lamb and Hwang, 1982).

The history of research into early mother–infant bonding underscores the importance of avoiding premature conclusions. Even when the results of a new study sound convincing, psychologists must be careful to place these findings in proper perspective. Additional investigations, using adequate-sized samples, are essential to verify the initial results (Rosnow and Rosenthal, 1989). And even if a given study is replicated successfully, many questions remain. Are there particular circumstances under which the ex-

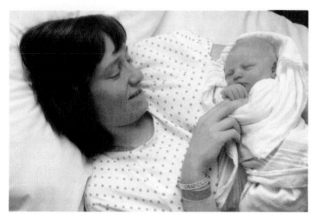

Attempts to replicate studies about the importance of early mother–infant bonding raised many questions about the original research. Replication is essential for confirming initial findings and for generating additional questions that will ultimately lead to fuller understanding of human behavior.

perimental outcomes are more likely? Are there other ways in which the current findings might be interpreted? Such constant questioning is fundamental to scientific work.

THE ETHICS OF RESEARCH IN PSYCHOLOGY

Several times in this chapter we have said that, for ethical reasons, certain research could not be done. For example, we said that psychologists could not encourage a group of parents to severely discipline their children from birth to adolescence in order to assess the relationship between harsh child rearing and delinquency. Such an experiment could cause irreparable harm. So could a true experiment investigating the effects of smoking on human health. Those assigned to the experimental group and required to smoke a certain number of cigarettes daily would be asked to do something that could lead to a fatal illness. But the propriety of many other psychological studies is not so clear-cut. Consider these two examples.

Suppose you volunteer for an experiment that allegedly is about the effects of hypnosis on creative problem solving. After being hypnotized and then brought out of your trance, you and two other subjects are asked to write a story about a picture. The other two begin to laugh and talk, but you can't hear

what they're saying. You grow increasingly sure they are making fun of you. If you find out later that you had been given the posthypnotic suggestion that you would be partially deaf, would you feel unfairly manipulated? Would the researcher's true goal of investigating the effects of partial deafness on paranoia justify the distress you experienced? Now suppose that you are riding a New York City subway, and the passenger beside you collapses at your feet, blood trickling from his mouth. You become extremely upset but don't know what to do. If you later learn that the victim was a confederate in an experiment designed to investigate bystander apathy, would you feel that this deception was justified?

These are actual experiments that psychologists have conducted (Piliavin and Piliavin, 1972; Zimbardo et al., 1981). As you can see, it is hard to say whether the deceptions were justified or not. Psychologists have an obligation to find answers to important questions, such as the causes of paranoia or the reasons for bystander apathy. But they also have an obligation to protect the dignity and welfare of the people who participate in their research. These two obligations can sometimes conflict. When they do, how can a researcher decide whether or not to proceed with a particular study?

The American Psychological Association (APA) has helped to answer this question by issuing ethical guidelines for studies involving human subjects (APA, 1990). These guidelines require that researchers avoid all procedures that would in any way cause lasting harm to people. "Harm" includes psychological as well as physical injury. Subjects should not leave an experiment feeling degraded or mistreated. If they do, their rights have been violated. Whenever the possibility of physical or mental discomfort exists, the researcher should inform subjects of this fact and secure their consent beforehand (see Figure 2.6). If it becomes essential to deceive subjects, the researcher must later explain why this deception was needed. A subject's participation must always be voluntary. And if a subject decides to withdraw from a study for any reason, that decision must be respected. Finally, subjects have a right to privacy. The researcher should not reveal subjects' identities unless the subjects themselves authorize such disclosure.

The American Psychological Association is not the only organization concerned about the ethics of psychological research. The federal government too requires that all research sponsored by U.S. government grants be reviewed for ethical standards by a

FIGURE 2.6   **This letter was given to all subjects in an experiment performed by a psychologist in an American university.**

INFORMED CONSENT

The present study consists of several stages. The first stage of the study merely consists of having you complete a few brief questionnaires. The rest of the study consists of several short stages in which you watch a series of slides and respond to them while we monitor your physiological responses, such as heart rate and skin conductance.

In order to record your physiological responses we will need to place sensors on you in several locations.

First, we will place small sensors on your cheek and forehead: two right above your right eyebrow and two on your right cheek. Next we will tape sensors to the first and third fingers of your non-dominant hand, and then a clip will be placed on the thumb of that same hand. All of the sensors are merely attached to the surface of your skin, and the procedures are quite simple and painless.

You will then watch several series of slides, some of which may depict scenes which some people find emotional. These slides will be pictures you might see in such magazines as Time or Life. You may also be given instructions while you watch the slides. After viewing some of the slides, we will ask you to respond to some questions about the slides.

All of the data you provide will be kept strictly confidential. Your data will be identified by a random number, and this number will in no way be associated with your name.

You may decline to participate in the described study now, or at any time during the study, without penalty, and we will immediately discard any data collected from you.

I have read and understood the above, and I hereby freely consent to participate in Study # 88-66.

_____
Signature

---

panel of qualified people. Some government research agencies have also developed procedures for dealing with suspected ethical misconduct in studies that they fund (Miers, 1985). In addition, most universities require that all research on human subjects conducted at their facilities receive the approval of their own ethics review board.

Public and private institutions also impose strict standards for the treatment of animal subjects. Nevertheless, the issue of animal rights has become increasingly heated in recent years. Critics charge that experimental animals are being subjected to unnecessary suffering, either for findings of little or no practical value or for results that could have been obtained in some other way. The most radical of the animal-rights activists want to ban experimentation on animals from all branches of science (Holden, 1988) while developing alternate ways of testing.

Psychologists and other scientists strongly disagree with these radical critics. While readily acknowl- edging their ethical responsibility to treat experimental animals humanely, they feel that today, due to modern regulations, abuse of research animals is very rare (Koshland, 1989). Animal studies, moreover, continue to be vital to the advancement of knowledge, the scientific community argues. They have given us crucial insights into such highly important topics as ways of recovering from nerve damage, the link between stress and disease, the effects of noise on hearing loss, new methods for reducing pain, drugs for combating mental illness, and new treatments for brain disorders (Miller, 1985b). They will undoubtedly play a major role in finding cures for cancer, AIDS, and other diseases that still plague society. Furthermore, animal research benefits animals as well as people. Vaccines for deadly diseases in dogs, cats, sheep, cattle, and many other species have been developed using animal experimentation. In most cases, findings obtained from animal research cannot be obtained in any other way. They are essential parts of many socially important scientific programs (Kaplan, 1988). This is not to say that animal research should be given a completely free rein. The benefits to be gained from such studies should always be carefully weighed against the methods used.

Whether a particular researcher is adequately meeting ethical standards is not always easy to decide (Sieber and Stanley, 1988). Consider, for instance, another example of research on human beings. Suppose psychologists studying the transmission of AIDS discovers some people who carry the AIDS virus and routinely have unprotected sex with partners who do not know about the carrier's medical condition. Should the researchers try to contact the partners and advise them of the risks they face? In doing so, they would be violating the subjects' right to privacy. But is there a point at which this right is overshadowed by the obligation to protect other people from harm?

What if, by informing the partners, the researchers make it more likely that other carriers of AIDS in the future will simply lie about engaging in irresponsible sex? Has disclosure of these cases then done more harm than good? Difficult questions such as these are still being hotly debated (Melton and Gray, 1988).

But even though some unresolved ethical issues remain, psychologists, as a whole, seem to be doing quite well maintaining ethical standards in contemporary research. During the five years between 1983 and 1987, for example, no complaints about the care and treatment of animals in psychological research and only three complaints about psychological research involving human subjects were filed with the ethics committee of the American Psychological Association (APA Ethics Committee, 1988). Perhaps ethical review boards at universities and other institutions have successfully screened out ethically questionable research projects.

SUMMARY

1. Psychologists usually investigate a **sample,** or selected segment of the population relevant to the issue they want to explore. In a **random sample,** every member of the population has an equal chance of being included. In a **representative sample,** subgroups with distinct characteristics are included according to their proportions in the total population.

2. The **experiment** is a method that allows researchers to infer causes because it holds constant (to as large an extent as possible) all influences on subjects' behavior except those being explored. Experimenters work with two groups of subjects: the **experimental group,** which experiences the experimental condition; and the **control group,** which does not. All experimenters set out to test a **hypothesis,** a tentative statement about how or why something happens. To do so they examine the relationship between **variables,** or factors that can change. The variable that the experimenter deliberately manipulates is called the **independent variable.** The one that is expected to change when the independent variable changes is called the **dependent variable.**

3. Sometimes psychologists use **quasi-experiments** to try to infer causal relationships. These take advantage of "experimental" and "control" groups that have

formed naturally in real life. But because the investigators have little or no control over variables and cannot assign subjects randomly to conditions, quasi-experiments are not as reliable as true experiments for inferring cause and effect.

4. **Correlational research** allows psychologists to determine the extent to which two variables are related to each other. A **positive correlation** means that a high incidence of one variable tends to be accompanied by a high incidence of the other, while a **negative correlation** means that a high incidence of one variable tends to be accompanied by a low incidence of the other. Both the direction and the strength of a correlation are indicated as a numerical value called the **correlation coefficient.**

5. One way to collect data for a correlational study is by means of a **survey**—an attempt to estimate the opinions, characteristics, or behaviors of a population by asking questions of a usually large representative sample. In contrast, a **case study** is a research method in which one individual is explored in depth.

6. In order to record behavior as it occurs in real life, psychologists use **naturalistic observation,** that is, observation in a setting where the subjects are naturally found. In **participant observation,** the research-

ers actually join the group to be studied in order to record thoughts and feelings accessible only to group members.

7. Psychologists use a variety of tools for measuring psychological factors. Such tools include **self-reports, behavioral measures,** and **physiological assessments.** These tools must be both **valid** (they must measure what they are intended to measure) and **reliable** (they must consistently yield similar results).

8. To study how behavior changes over time, researchers may use either a **longitudinal study,** in which the same group of people is examined at intervals over a period of years, or a **cross-sectional study,** in which people of different ages are assessed simultaneously. The longitudinal approach is more reliable, but it is very time consuming.

9. To interpret the data they collect, psychologists use **statistics**—mathematical methods for assessing and presenting data in summary form. **Descriptive statistics** enable researchers to present their findings in a concise manner. One goal is to convey how scores in a sample are distributed. This may involve calculating measures of **central tendency,** such as the **mean** (arithmetic average), **median** (middle score), and **mode** (most frequent score). It may also involve calculating **measures of variability,** such as the **range** (the distance between the highest and lowest scores) and the **standard deviation** (a measure of the average extent to which all scores in a set vary from the mean).

10. **Inferential statistics** enable researchers to judge whether their data support their hypothesis, or whether the results could have occurred by chance. They use measures of **probability** to answer this question. Only when results have **statistical significance** is the explanation of chance rejected.

11. **Meta-analysis** is a method of synthesizing the results of different studies on the same topic by using a set of statistical procedures to compute, select, and combine data. Meta-analyses must be conducted very carefully. Studies with serious methodological flaws must not be included in order to avoid giving undue weight to questionable findings.

12. Among the possible pitfalls in conducting psychological research is the **self-fulfilling prophecy,** or tendency for researchers' expectations to influence their results. One way to avoid self-fulfilling prophecies is to use the **double-blind technique,** in which neither the researcher nor the subjects know who has been assigned to the experimental or the control conditions. (In the **single-blind technique,** the experimenter knows who is in which group, but the subjects do not.) Two other pitfalls in psychological research occur when subjects succumb to **demand characteristics** (clues about the responses they think the researcher wants them to make) or to the **Hawthorne effect** (in which subjects behave in unusual ways simply because they are part of a scientific study). Finally, there is the pitfall of drawing premature conclusions on the basis of a single study. Research findings must be **replicated** many times in order for psychologists to accept them as generally valid.

13. Psychologists are expected to meet strict ethical standards in conducting their research. Various organizations provide guidelines for the ethical treatment of human as well as animal subjects.

SUGGESTED READINGS

Dooley, D. (1990). *Social research methods.* Englewood Cliffs, NJ: Prentice-Hall. Detailed coverage of a broad range of research designs, plus a chapter on library use and research report style.

Fernald, L. D. (1983). *The Hans legacy: A story of science.* Hillsdale, NJ: Erlbaum. Research methods in psychology presented through lively examples, including Freud's classic study of Little Hans, a boy who was abnormally fearful of horses.

Rowntree, D. (1982). *Statistics without tears.* New York: Scribner's. An introduction to the main concepts of statistics, explained through words and diagrams rather than through formulas and equations.

Rubinstein, J., and Slife, B. D. (1990). *Taking sides: Clashing views on controversial psychological issues* (6th ed.). Guilford, CT: Dushkin Publishing Group. As the subtitle states, this book explores opposing sides on controversial issues in psychology, including the use of deception in research and experimentation on animals.

Shaughnessy, J. J., and Zechmeister, E. B. (1990). *Research methods in psychology.* New York: McGraw-Hill. A general introduction to social science research, covering many different research methods.

CHAPTER 3

THE BIOLOGICAL FOUNDATIONS OF BEHAVIOR

Imagine yourself hiking through a forest. A steady drizzle has set in and you are looking for somewhere to take shelter until the rain stops. Around the next bend you come to a small clearing with a dilapidated cabin that appears to be deserted. Cautiously, you push the door open and step inside. To your left you hear a faint rustling noise. Your leg and arm muscles freeze as you turn toward the sound, looking and listening intently. Suddenly, a snake slithers out across your path. Startled, you jump back; your heart is pounding, you feel yourself tensed to run. But the snake, seemingly oblivious to your presence, slithers out the door.

These responses seem so simple, so automatic, you never stop to think of the biological events that make them possible. Yet inside your body millions of cells are reacting to make you move, see, hear, and feel emotions such as fear. For example, in a fraction of a second, nerve cells leading from your eyes pass electrical and chemical signals along circuits in your brain. These signals allow you to analyze the light waves that reflect off your surroundings as identifiable objects with specific shapes, colors, and movements. At the same time, an area at the base of your brain sends messages rapidly upward, arousing your higher brain centers and helping you to focus on the possible danger you face. And simultaneously, another region in your lower brain triggers physiological reactions throughout the rest of your body. These include not just the pounding heart and other changes you are aware of, but also a flood of hormones from glands you may not even know you have. Such responses interact with further signals racing through your brain, signals that give rise to the feeling of fear springing up inside you. Before you know it, your body is pulsing with energy, ready to flee or defend itself if need be.

The biological changes that give rise to sights and sounds, to movements and motivations, to memories and emotions, are the subject of this chapter. Here we discuss some basic features of the body's two communication networks: the nervous system, of which the brain is a part; and the endocrine system, with its hormone-secreting glands. Together these two closely interconnected systems regulate all of human behavior. Exactly how they do so is a story that extends into many subsequent chapters. In this chapter we simply provide the foundations needed to begin understanding yourself as a biological organism.

THE BODY'S CONTROL SYSTEMS

THE NERVOUS SYSTEM

With its billions of interconnected cells that radiate throughout the body, the human nervous system is one of the most complex creations in the living world. You could never consciously control such a vast and intricate network. Hundreds of billions of tiny atoms and molecules have to be shuttled back and forth across cell membranes at a split second's notice. Cells have to be kept constantly busy churning out all the chemicals needed to carry out the nervous system's work. These chemicals have to be delivered to precisely the right locations and used at just the right moments, in just the right amounts. Error, indecision, or napping on the job could have disastrous results. With such precise and ceaseless demands on the human nervous system, it is reassuring that it operates so automatically, without our conscious awareness, let alone our conscious control. Yet we *can* consciously use the brain, a central part of the nervous system, to explore this remarkable network and understand its complex workings.

The cells of the human nervous system are highly specialized. **Receptor cells,** embedded in the sense organs, are specialized to receive various types of stimulation from the environment. During each waking second, receptor cells in your eyes, ears, skin, and other parts of your body receive about 100 million signals, which are then transmitted to your brain. **Effector cells,** in contrast, are embedded in muscles and glands, and are specialized to contract the muscles and to stimulate the glands to secrete hormones. To perform even a relatively simple behavior, such as swinging a tennis racket, your brain must issue millions of commands via effector cells.

Neurons, or nerve cells, are specialized to conduct signals from one part of the body to another. They connect receptor cells to effector cells, directing and coordinating their activities. Neurons, in short, are the fundamental building blocks of the nervous system. Even the smallest action, such as blinking your eyes, involves many thousands of neurons working together. There are literally billions of neurons in the human body, about 100 billion in the brain alone. The tissues we call **nerves,** which run throughout the body, are actually the long, fibrous parts of many neurons bundled together.

Surrounding neurons are cells called **glia,** which are usually smaller than neurons but about ten times more numerous. *Glia* means "glue," and this word describes one of the functions that glial cells serve: they hold neurons in place. In addition, glial cells carry nutrients to neurons, remove their waste products, help repair damaged neurons in the peripheral nervous system, provide a barrier that protects neurons from certain harmful substances that can get into the blood, and play a role in the propagation of nerve impulses. They may even be involved in assembling and disassembling neural circuits (Hatton, 1985).

Glial cells, then, are very important in enabling neurons to carry out their work, but neurons themselves play the major role in creating our perceptions, thoughts, feelings, and behaviors. That is why we focus on neurons in this chapter. But before describing the structure and workings of neurons in some detail, let us step back and take a look at the nervous system as a whole.

DIVISIONS OF THE NERVOUS SYSTEM

The brain and spinal cord, which lie within the bony casings of the skull and spinal column, together form the **central nervous system (CNS),** so called because it provides the ultimate control over all human behavior. Branching out from the central nervous system and leading to all parts of the body is the **peripheral nervous system.** (See Figure 3.1.) Some neurons of the peripheral nervous system convey signals from sensory receptor cells to the spinal cord and brain. These neurons form **afferent pathways** (pathways leading *toward* the central nervous system). Other peripheral nervous system neurons transmit messages from the brain and spinal cord to effector cells in muscles and glands. These neurons form **efferent pathways** (those leading *away from* the central nervous system).

Efferent pathways, in turn, have two divisions: the somatic and the autonomic. The **somatic nervous system** consists of nerve fibers running to skeletal muscles—that is, the muscles that move the bones. These fibers control actions that are under voluntary control. When you raise an arm or wriggle a toe, you are using nerves in the somatic division. The **autonomic nervous system,** in contrast, controls the muscles of internal organs (blood vessels, heart, intestines) and the glands. Autonomic activity is

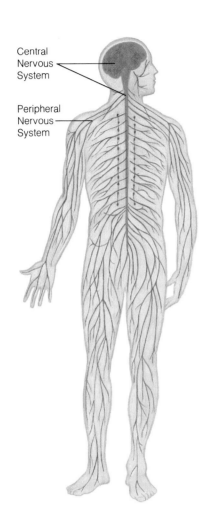

Central Nervous System

Peripheral Nervous System

FIGURE 3.1 **The central nervous system (CNS) and the peripheral nervous system (PNS) in the human body. Both of these systems are made up of billions of nerve cells, or neurons, each capable of transmitting a train of chemical-electrical signals. They work together through synapses that conduct in only one direction. In the CNS, these neurons and their synapses form an immensely complex network that organizes, stores, and redirects vast quantities of information. In the PNS, neurons in every pathway transmit information either from receptors (such as the sense organs) toward the CNS or away from the CNS to effectors (in the muscles, for example). There is a close match between information going to the CNS and information coming from it. Every muscle, for example, not only receives directions from the CNS to contract, but also sends back information about its present state of contraction or relaxation.**

nerves by both of these divisions. In general, these two divisions can be viewed as having broadly opposite effects. The **sympathetic nervous system** is usually involved in mobilizing the body's resources. In an emergency or a stressful situation, such as meeting a snake in a deserted cabin, it responds by increasing blood sugar, raising heart rate and blood pressure, and inhibiting digestion. The **parasympathetic nervous system,** in contrast, dominates under conditions of relaxation and tends to conserve the body's energy. After you eat a large meal, for example, your parasympathetic system works to aid digestion, at the same time decreasing heart rate and blood flow to the skeletal muscles. The actions of the sympathetic and parasympathetic divisions, of course, do not always divide as neatly as this. Many behaviors require a combination of sympathetic and parasympathetic activity.

THE STRUCTURE OF NEURONS

Neurons can be categorized according to the structures between which they conduct their signals. As Figure 3.3 shows, **sensory neurons** carry information from the sense organs to the brain and spinal cord, while **motor neurons** carry signals from the brain and spinal cord to the muscles and glands. **Interneurons** connect neurons to other neurons and integrate the activities of the sensory and motor neurons. It is the relationships among interneurons

usually considered involuntary, because it occurs more or less automatically. Most people do not consciously control the contractions of their stomach, for instance, or the beating of their heart. Apparently, however, people can learn to influence such "involuntary" responses when appropriate feedback is available. This procedure, called biofeedback, is discussed in Chapter 15.

The autonomic nervous system has two divisions of its own: the sympathetic and the parasympathetic. (See Figure 3.2.) With few exceptions, any given internal muscle or gland in the body is supplied with

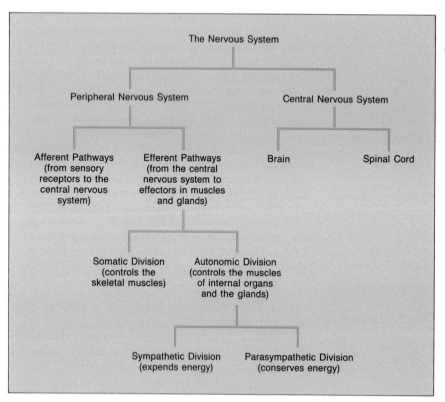

FIGURE 3.2   The relationships among the parts of the nervous system.

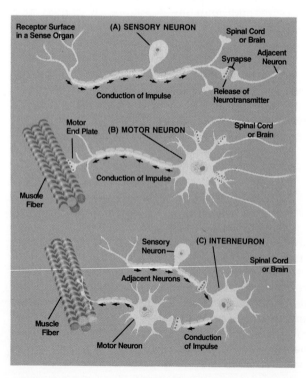

FIGURE 3.3   The three types of neurons. (A) A sensory neuron. (B) A motor neuron. The motor end plate releases a neurotransmitter that can change the electrical state of the muscle to which it is connected. (C) An interneuron. The interneurons, working through their synapses, either inhibit or excite the motor neurons that supply opposing muscles. For example, when the interneuron receives information from a sensory neuron, it sends inhibitory impulses to the connecting motor neuron, which then inhibits the extensor muscle, and the arm withdraws from a painful stimulus. (*Adapted from Williams and Warwick, 1975.*)

that somehow become translated into thoughts, feelings, perceptions, and memories. In humans, interneurons are much more numerous than sensory and motor neurons. It has been estimated that for every motor neuron there are more than 4,000 interneurons.

Neurons vary greatly in size and shape, depending on their location in the nervous system. Despite this diversity, however, most neurons have three major parts: the cell body, the dendrites, and the

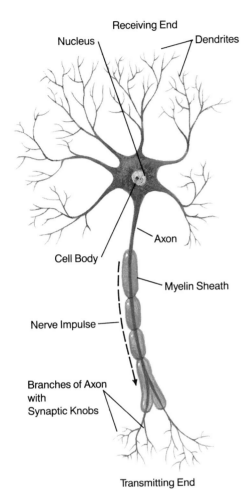

Receiving End

Nucleus

Dendrites

Axon

Cell Body

Myelin Sheath

Nerve Impulse

Branches of Axon
with
Synaptic Knobs

Transmitting End

FIGURE 3.4 A typical neuron. Most neurons have a single axon with branches called collaterals. A neuron may have many dendrites, each with its own branches. Most dendrites have short projections called dendrite spines on which they receive terminals from the axons of other neurons.

axon. (See Figure 3.4.) The **cell body** is the life-support center of the cell and provides the energy for all the cell's activities. The **dendrites** and the **axon** are two types of fibers that branch out from the cell body and are involved in communications. The numerous and relatively short dendrites can be thought of as the neuron's "antennae." They have specialized areas for receiving messages transmitted by other neurons. (Some cell bodies and axons have such specialized receiving areas as well.) The relatively long axon, in

A photomicrograph (microscopic photograph) of two human neurons with their axons and dendrites. (*Dan McCoy/Rainbow.*)

contrast, can be thought of as the cell's "outgoing message line." It carries neural signals down its length to affect the muscle fibers, glandular cells, or other neurons with which its outer end connects.

HOW NEURONS FORM CIRCUITS

The simplest set of connections between neurons is the **reflex arc,** which links a sensory input to a motor response. Reflex arcs are located throughout the nervous system, but those within the spinal cord, with no direct relay to the brain, have been the most extensively studied.

One well-known spinal reflex arc is the knee jerk, which is elicited by a tap on the tendon below the kneecap. It involves only two kinds of neurons: sensory neurons, which convey to the spinal cord information about stimulation of the tendon; and motor neurons, which stimulate the muscle groups in the thigh to contract, causing a kick. This two-neuron

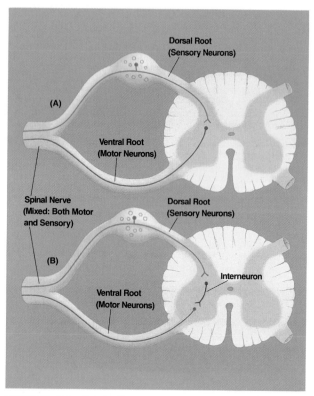

Dorsal Root
(Sensory Neurons)

(A)

Ventral Root
(Motor Neurons)

Spinal Nerve
(Mixed: Both Motor
and Sensory)

Dorsal Root
(Sensory Neurons)

(B)

Interneuron

Ventral Root
(Motor Neurons)

FIGURE 3.5   **(A) A diagram of a two-neuron reflex arc, such as the one present in the knee-jerk reflex. This is the simplest form of reflex arc. (B) A diagram of a three-neuron reflex arc, the pain reflex, which causes a quick withdrawal from the painful stimulus. This type of reflex arc involves one set each of motor and sensory neurons (as in the two-neuron reflex arc), but an interneuron is also present in the gray matter of the spinal cord. (*Gardner, 1975.*)**

reflex arc is illustrated in Figure 3.5A. Most reflexes, however, are more complicated than the two-neuron knee jerk. Figure 3.5B shows a pain withdrawal reflex arc, which involves three kinds of neurons. The additional neurons in such chains are interneurons, which connect sensory and motor neurons. These interneurons make possible more complex responses. For example, when you pull back a foot after stepping on a thorn, the interneurons pass information to your other leg, prompting your body weight to shift automatically.

Although spinal reflexes can occur without control by the brain, the brain still plays a role. The stimulation that triggers a withdrawal reflex, for instance, must travel to the brain in order to be

experienced as pain. This trip takes time, so the subjective feeling of pain often occurs after the reflex has begun. You probably can recall touching a very hot object, withdrawing your hand, and only then feeling the burn. The neurons that travel the length of the spinal cord and lead to and from the brain also permit some voluntary control over reflexes. You can demonstrate this by having someone tap the tendon below your kneecap to elicit the knee-jerk reflex. Then have the person tap in the same place while you concentrate on preventing the response. The pathways that link the brain to the spinal cord should enable you to hold your leg steady.

You can better understand the roles of these neural pathways by considering what happens to a paraplegic—a person whose spinal cord has been severed and hence cut off from its link to the brain. Paraplegics have no sensation in the lower part of their bodies, and they cannot move their legs voluntarily. Since the nerves in the spinal cord (like the neurons in the brain) cannot regenerate, this condition is permanent. Reflexes controlled by the spinal cord still operate, however, so a paraplegic continues to show the knee-jerk response when a leg is tapped. But unlike people with an intact spinal cord, paraplegics are not able consciously to prevent the knee jerk; nor can they feel the leg kick. They will not even know that their leg has moved unless they are watching it.

Reflex arcs, as we have said, are the simplest kinds of neural circuits. Far more complex ones also exist in the human nervous system. In fact, most of the things you do involve activation of more than one neural circuit, and the more complex the task is, the more numerous and elaborate these circuits are. When you consider all the nervous system's many circuits, the picture becomes staggeringly complex. There are probably a quadrillion connections between neurons in the human body—that is, a *million billion* (Rosenzweig and Leiman, 1989). Sometimes a single neuron has tens of thousands of connections to neighboring cells (Baskin, 1985). This incredibly complex circuitry, far too intricate to map in detail, underlies our impressive abilities to learn and remember, reason and solve problems, communicate with language, and perceive the world.

HOW NEURONS COMMUNICATE

How do the cells that make up neural circuits relay messages to each other? Scientists have known for many years that neural signals are partly electrical in nature, but the details of those signals remained a mystery until we developed the technology to measure responses in a single nerve cell. These measurements revealed that neural impulses are conducted by means of an electrical *and* chemical process. We will examine the electrical part of the process first, before turning to the brain's chemical messengers.

In discussing how electrical impulses are generated in the brain, we will look at a case in which the impulse travels from a neuron's dendrites to its cell body and down the length of its axon to connections with other cells. This is a very common pathway in the nervous system, which is why we focus on it. But bear in mind that it is not the only route that a nerve impulse can take. Sometimes an impulse flows from neuron to neuron via the dendrites alone. Other times it bypasses the dendrites completely and travels from the axon of one neuron to the cell body or axon of another. This is all part of the enormous complexity we mentioned earlier. When it comes to forming connections within a human brain, there are very few simple rules that apply universally. With that in mind, let us now explore how a nerve impulse is born.

Generating a Nerve Impulse The fluids in the body contain electrically charged particles called **ions.** Especially important to a neuron's electrical activity are organic ions (An^-) and chloride ions (Cl^-), both negatively charged, and potassium ions (K^+) and sodium ions (Na^+), both positively charged. The outer membrane of a neuron selectively regulates the passage of these ions into and out of the cell. The An^- ions, because of their large size, are trapped inside the neuron, while the smaller Cl^-, K^+, and Na^+ ions can pass through the membrane. The membrane, however, is not equally permeable to all of these other ions. When the membrane is in its resting state (that is, when it is not being stimulated), K^+ ions move much more freely outward than the Na^+ ions move inward. As a result, the cell membrane becomes **polarized:** negatively charged on its inside surface relative to its outside surface. This electrical imbalance across the cell membrane is known as the **resting potential.**

The resting potential is not permanent, however. Consider what happens when a certain threshold level of excitatory stimulation reaches the axon of a neuron. (By "threshold level" we mean a level of stimulation great enough to produce an effect.) The axon's membrane at the point of stimulation suddenly becomes completely permeable to sodium. Sodium channels, which were previously closed, now spring open, and sodium ions rush inside, pulled by the negative charge on the inner surface of the cell membrane (remember that opposite charges attract each other). For an instant, then, the inside of the membrane becomes positively charged relative to the outside. This abrupt reversal in electrical charge across the cell membrane is called the **action potential.** The action potential travels down the axon as sodium channels consecutively open along the axon's length. This process is somewhat similar to a spark traveling down a fuse. But the axon, unlike the fuse, very quickly restores itself, and so is able to conduct a burst of many action potentials—up to 1,000 per second.

The speeds at which action potentials travel down axons range from about 1 to 120 meters per second—that is, from about 2 to 270 miles per hour. The exact speed depends on the properties of the axons. One important property is the presence of a **myelin sheath,** a fatty whitish substance made up of certain glial cells which wrap around the axon. (Myelinated axons form the white matter of the nervous system; nonmyelinated axons, dendrites, and cell bodies form the gray matter.) Between each glial cell in a myelin sheath is a gap, called a **node of Ranvier.** These nodes enable an action potential to "leap" along an axon from gap to gap, thereby moving faster.

Not surprisingly, extensive damage to myelin sheaths severely hinders the workings of the nervous system. The disease called multiple sclerosis, for example, is caused by progressive destruction of myelin in the spinal cord and brain. The myelin is replaced by a hard, intermeshing plaque, and the axons that lie within it can no longer conduct nerve impulses. The result is progressive loss of muscle control.

We have described how a nerve impulse travels down an axon, but where does the stimulation come from that triggers this action potential? The answer lies in the dendrites of the neuron, the fibrous projections that receive messages from other neurons. The membranes of dendrites also have a resting potential, similar to that of axons, and they too undergo changes in electrical charge when stimulated. But there is a major difference in the electrical reactions of the two kinds of fibers. Axons produce action potentials in response to a particular threshold level of excitatory stimulation. When that level is reached, the axon

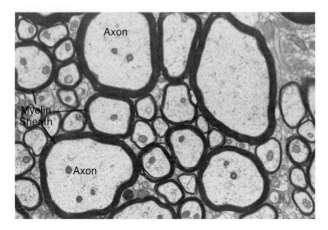

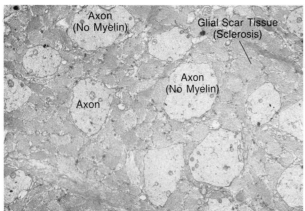

These photomicrographs show normal spinal axons (*top*) and axons damaged by multiple sclerosis (*bottom*). The thin myelin sheath around each axon has been destroyed, and sclerotic scar tissue has developed among axons.

fires. The amount of stimulation *above* the threshold is not important. The axon fires in exactly the same way as long as the threshold level is reached. This is referred to as the **all-or-none response.** Dendrites, in contrast, do not respond in an all-or-none fashion. When a dendrite is stimulated, the electrical charge across its membrane changes *in proportion* to the amount of stimulation. These relative changes in electrical potential are called **graded potentials.**

Graded potentials enable a neuron to "add" and "subtract" the amount of stimulation being received at different points on its dendrites or at the same point close together in time. Suppose a dendrite is stimulated at two nearby locations. If both stimuli are excitatory (causing **depolarization,** or a *decrease* in the electrical imbalance associated with the resting state), then the overall graded potential will be the *sum* of the electrical changes produced by the two. If, in contrast, one stimulus is inhibitory (causing **hyperpolarization,** or an *increase* in the electrical imbalance associated with the resting state) while the other is excitatory, then the graded potential will reflect the *difference* between the two. Only when graded potentials reach the axon's threshold level of excitatory stimulation will an action potential be triggered.

Transmitting Signals between Neurons We have said that when action potentials reach the end of an axon, they stimulate the muscle fibers, glandular cells, or other neurons with which that axon connects. But how can this stimulation occur, given that every axon is separated from adjacent cells by tiny gaps called **synaptic clefts?** (The area surrounding a synaptic cleft, including the tip of the axon on one side and the receiving cell's membrane on the other, is called a **synapse.**) The answer depends on the size of the synaptic cleft involved. Sometimes these gaps are so small that the electrical current in the axon can flow right across it to the cell on the other side. When synaptic clefts are wider, however, as they are in most cases, this method of communication is not possible. How, then, do most neurons send messages to other cells?

The answer lies in chemical substances known as **neurotransmitters,** which are stored at the terminals, or endings, of axons. When action potentials reach an axon terminal, they stimulate the release of these neurotransmitters, which diffuse across the synaptic cleft and activate receptor sites on the adjacent cell. Figure 3.6 illustrates this process in a simplified way. Although the diagram shows two synaptic connections, a typical neuron has between 1,000 and 10,000 synaptic connections on its surface (Stevens, 1979). The receptor sites on a "receiving" neuron are activated because the molecular structure of the incoming neurotransmitter fits them, much as a key fits a lock. Different neurotransmitters have different molecular structures, so those that activate certain receptors do not activate others.

Scientists have isolated more than sixty neurotransmitters, and undoubtedly many more are still to be discovered. Some experts think there may be several hundred (Snyder, 1984). Why are there so many chemical transmitters? No one knows for sure. At this point, researchers are concerned primarily

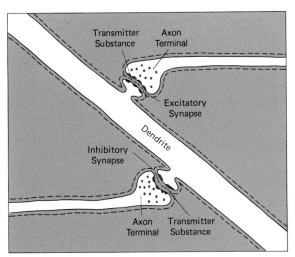

FIGURE 3.6 Two axon terminals forming synapses with one of the dendrites of another neuron.

Many animal species' natural toxins work on the neurotransmitters of their prey. The black widow spider's venom causes a flood of acetylcholine, producing muscle contraction, paralysis, and death.

with identifying these substances, mapping their receptor sites, and discovering the behavioral processes in which they are involved.

One of the best understood of the neurotransmitters is **acetylcholine,** or **ACh** for short. It is found in various parts of the peripheral nervous system, in the spinal cord, and in specific regions of the brain. In the peripheral nervous system it activates receptor sites embedded in muscles and glands. For instance, ACh operates at the synapses between motor neurons and skeletal muscles, where it has an excitatory effect. Thus, it is instrumental in making the body move. ACh is also a major neurotransmitter in the parasympathetic nervous system, where its effects are inhibitory: it slows down the actions of certain internal organs. In the brain, ACh is involved in a number of processes, including arousal, attention, learning and memory, and motivated behaviors, such as aggression and sexuality. In general, ACh's activities in the brain help an organism focus attention and muster appropriate responses (Panksepp, 1986).

Knowledge of the roles that neurotransmitters play at various receptor sites has provided important insights into how certain drugs work. For instance, curare, the poison that South American Indians use on their arrows, occupies the neuromuscular receptors that ACh molecules normally activate and so prevents ACh from functioning. The result is temporary paralysis, or sometimes death if the muscles that control breathing are affected. The lethal poison

botulin, which develops in improperly preserved food, also causes paralysis through its effects on ACh synapses, but these effects are quite different from those of curare. Botulin appears to block the release of ACh from axon terminals. Interestingly, the venom of the black widow spider has the opposite effect: it causes a flood of ACh into neuromuscular synapses. The result is violent and uncontrollable muscle contraction. Many psychoactive drugs also affect the activities of neurotransmitters. For example, amphetamines, which are stimulant drugs, increase the actions of a group of transmitters that include dopamine and norepinephrine, both of which are associated with arousal and motor activity.

Abnormalities in the activities of neurotransmitters have been implicated in many serious disorders. As you will see in Chapter 16, low levels of the neurotransmitter serotonin seem to be related to depression, while irregularities in the dopamine system seem to be involved in at least some of the symptoms of schizophrenia. In fact, the drugs called phenothiazines, which are widely used to treat schizophrenia, are believed to inhibit the action of dopamine receptors in certain parts of the brain. In other brain regions, degeneration of dopamine-releasing neurons is related to the muscular rigidity and uncontrollable tremors of Parkinson's disease (Kety, 1979). Deficiencies of another neurotransmitter, called GABA for short, have been found in the brains of people afflicted with Huntington's chorea, a neurological condition marked by total mental deterioration beginning in middle age (Iversen, 1979). And Alzheimer's disease, a degenerative brain disorder that leads to severe memory loss among other cognitive symptoms, has been linked in part to deficits of acetylcholine in areas of the brain critical to memory. Neurons that normally release acetylcholine to these brain regions undergo massive degeneration in severe Alzheimer's cases (Whitehouse et al., 1982). Such insights may provide important clues to possible treatments for these and other disabling disorders. We will be discussing some of the latest such treatments at the end of this chapter.

Our understanding of the nervous system was enhanced greatly by the discovery of a whole class of brain chemicals: the **neuropeptides.** Many of these chemicals were first identified as hormones elsewhere in the body, serving a variety of functions unrelated to nerve cell communication. Among the most fascinating of the neuropeptides are the **endogenous opioids.** These chemicals, which occur naturally within the central nervous system (the term *endogenous* means "originating from within"), have molecular structures that are very similar to those of morphine and other opium-based narcotics. In fact, opiates bind to the same receptor sites to which the endogenous opioids bind. This is what gives opiates their painkilling effects (Snyder, 1980). Apparently, the endogenous opioids serve as our bodies' natural pain fighters, among several other important functions. When exposed to painful stimuli, such as electrical shocks, we produce increased amounts of them (Bolles and Fanselow, 1982).

There is evidence that certain pain-relieving substances and procedures (placebos and acupuncture, for example) may work by triggering release of these chemicals in the nervous system (Watkins and Mayer, 1982). It has also been speculated that the pain caused by running may stimulate the flow of endogenous opioids and thereby produce the feeling of euphoria commonly called the "runner's high" (Carr et al., 1981; Colt et al., 1981). Interestingly, levels of endogenous opioids increase during pregnancy and peak right before and during labor, thus probably helping to ease the pain of giving birth. After delivery, however, these opiatelike chemicals diminish sharply, which may be a factor in the postpartum depression that some women experience (Hopson, 1988).

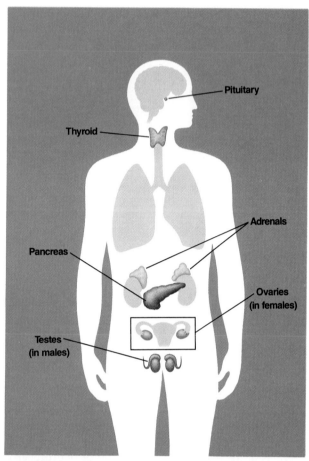

FIGURE 3.7   The major endocrine glands. The pituitary, the thyroid, the adrenals, and the gonads (ovaries or testes) produce hormones crucial to both body functions and behaviors.

The more scientists learn about the workings of neurotransmitters, the more incredibly intricate the human nervous system seems. This complexity is apparent even at the level of a single synapse. For instance, we now know that most axons release more than one neurotransmitter. While some of these chemicals affect nearby neurons directly, others affect them indirectly by modifying the activities of different neurotransmitters (Chan-Palay and Palay, 1984). Self-regulatory processes also occur at synapses. A neuron transmitting one message may change its activities depending on the feedback it receives from neighboring cells (Baskin, 1985). Similarly, receptors may become more or less sensitive to stimulation with decreased or increased use (Hokfelt et al., 1984).

As we look beyond the synapse to interconnections among many neurons, we see even greater complexity. Each neurotransmitter system is widely dispersed in the brain, not confined to a single small region. This means that in most areas of the brain, many neurotransmitters are at work. Not surprisingly, more than one neurotransmitter is involved in virtually everything we do, from feeling joy on a warm spring morning to studying for a final exam. The same neurotransmitter can also have very different effects depending on which circuit in the nervous system it is affecting. Acetylcholine, for example, is excitatory when it contacts receptor cells on the skeletal muscles, but inhibitory when it contacts receptors on the heart and the intestines. Thus, it helps to think of the nervous system as an incredibly intricate computer in which different circuits of neurons are involved in different functions. We will say more about these complex neural circuits in later sections of this chapter and in other parts of this book.

THE ENDOCRINE SYSTEM

The complex network of billions of cells that form the nervous system enables the human body to respond to a vast range of situations. The speed with which it does so is impressive. Because a nerve impulse can travel through the body in a mere hundredth of a second, we can pull back a hand from a hot stove almost instantaneously. For situations in which the body responds more slowly, such as sexual arousal and physical growth, the endocrine system provides an effective means of internal communication.

The **endocrine system** is a chemical communications network: Its messengers are chemical substances called **hormones,** which are produced by the **endocrine glands** and secreted into the bloodstream. (See Figure 3.7.) Although these hormones circulate throughout the body, each acts only at specific **target organs.**

Probably the most influential endocrine gland in the body is the **pituitary,** a structure only about half an inch in diameter, which lies at the base of the brain just below a region called the hypothalamus. Despite its small size, the pituitary controls a wide range of body functions via its many hormones. Particularly

important is **growth hormone,** which plays a key role in physical development. Dwarfism results from a severe deficit of growth hormone during childhood. If an excess of growth hormone is produced at an early age, a person will become a giant. Some pituitary giants have grown to heights of nearly 9 feet (Crapo, 1985). The pituitary is often called the "master gland," because some of its hormones regulate the output of other endocrine glands. One of these affects the thyroid gland; another affects the cortex of the adrenal glands; and two affect the output of the sex glands, or gonads.

The **thyroid gland** is located in the neck, on either side of the windpipe and esophagus (the tube that carries food to the stomach). Under the influence of the thyroid-stimulating hormone that the pituitary secretes, the thyroid produces several hormones of its own. One of these hormones is **thyroxin,** which plays an important role in regulating the body's metabolism. Too much thyroxin speeds up metabolism and leads to a condition called hyperthyroidism. The victim suffers from weight loss, an elevated body temperature, profuse sweating, intense thirst, accelerated heart rate, general excitability, and often difficulty in sleeping. The opposite disorder—too little thyroxin, or hypothyroidism—slows metabolism and creates a range of related symptoms including obesity, a slowed heartbeat, lowered body temperature, reduced sweating, physical lethargy, and lack of mental alertness. Hypothyroidism can have devastating effects on infants. If untreated in newborns, it leads to a condition called cretinism, characterized by severely retarded mental and physical development.

The **adrenals** are a pair of glands that lie just above the kidneys. Each adrenal actually consists of two glands, an inner region called the medulla and an outer region called the cortex. The adrenal medulla produces **epinephrine** and **norepinephrine,** the same two chemicals that in the nervous system act as neurotransmitters. In their roles as hormones, these chemicals are also called **adrenalin** and **noradrenalin.** Both are involved in the body's reaction to stress. Suppose you are severely frightened or subjected to intense pain. The outpouring of epinephrine from your adrenal medulla increases your heartbeat and blood pressure, releases more sugar into your bloodstream, accelerates your rate of breathing, and increases the flow of blood to your skeletal muscles. (Norepinephrine has very similar effects.) These

Growth hormone, which is secreted by the pituitary gland, produces a wide variation in human body size. John Hollinder is 7 feet, 5 inches tall; Patty Malone is 3 feet, 2 inches.

changes help prepare you to deal with the threat you face. You may have noticed that these responses closely parallel those produced by activation of the sympathetic nervous system. When the body's resources must be mobilized in emergencies, the activities of the nervous system and the endocrine system greatly overlap. We will return to the hormones of the adrenal medulla in Chapter 15, which deals with stress and coping.

The other portion of the adrenal glands, the adrenal cortex, is probably the most diversified hormone factory in the body. It produces at least fifty hormonelike chemicals, and perhaps many others that scientists have not yet identified. Some of these chemicals help regulate the supply of sugar in the blood; others help regulate the relative concentrations of minerals and water in the body; still others act as sex hormones, chiefly male hormones, called **androgens.** Overproduction of adrenal androgens in women can promote the growth of facial and chest hair, a deepening of the voice, and the development of muscular arms and legs.

Another set of endocrine organs are the sex glands, or **gonads,** the testes in males and the ovaries in females. These glands secrete hormones very similar in structure and function to the sex hormones the adrenal cortex produces, although in much larger amounts. They are particularly involved in sexual development and reproduction.

For clarity, we have described the endocrine system separately from the nervous system, but in fact, these systems are constantly interacting. You can see this in how the menstrual cycle is regulated (Marx, 1988). A region of the brain called the hypothalamus is itself a source of hormones, one of which affects the output of two hormones from the pituitary, which in turn influence secretions from the ovaries. Ovarian hormones, for their part, affect the output of the initial hormone from the hypothalamus, and so a complex feedback loop exists. There are similar feedback loops regulating other endocrine glands. Thus, the body's two communication networks—the nervous and endocrine systems—are intimately interconnected, with the brain having the ultimate task of coordination. The brain, in short, is the body's master control center. We will spend the rest of this chapter discussing it.

THE BRAIN

Dr. P was an accomplished musician and a greatly respected teacher whose family and friends were baffled by the bizarre things he started to do. When walking down the street, for example, he would stop and affectionately pat fire hydrants on the head, as if they were small children. He even spoke to the carved knobs on wooden furniture and then seemed perplexed when the knobs did not reply. Once, when he was looking for his hat and spied his wife's head, he reached out and tried to put it on! It seemed he had mistaken this round, hair-topped object for his favorite felt fedora. And yet, if you met Dr. P you would find him a charming person, cultured and erudite. The neurologist who examined him was sure, upon first meeting, that there couldn't be anything seriously wrong with this man—that is, until he asked Dr. P to put a shoe back on. Dr. P seemed dumbfounded. "Is *that* my shoe?" he asked, pointing to his foot. Apparently, it was impossible for him to identify objects visually. The best he could do was to guess at an object's identity based on key features he spotted (Sacks, 1985).

The cause of this strange affliction lay in Dr. P's brain, that complex mass of billions of cells, composed mostly of water and a host of chemicals. When fully grown, the human brain weighs less than 3 pounds, yet it is responsible for all the phenomena that psychologists seek to explain. Our perceptions and thoughts, our plans and actions, our feelings and dreams—all are produced by activities in the central nervous system, of which the brain is the main component. In Dr. P's case, extensive damage occurred to parts of the brain responsible for taking pieces of visual data and putting them together into the perception of meaningful wholes. This tells us something fascinating about how the brain works. The brain is, to some extent, compartmentalized, with particular regions taking part in specific functions. Thus, injury to a certain area of the brain can disrupt one aspect of visual perception while leaving other aspects of it intact. That such specific syndromes can result from damage to particular brain regions indicates that certain functions are *localized* in the brain (Coltheart, 1989). You will see this localization of function again and again as our discussion of the brain unfolds.

PROBING THE BRAIN'S DEVELOPMENT

A good place to begin our exploration of the brain is with its development. How has the brain evolved over millions of years into the complex structure it is today? And how is a brain built from the seemingly scanty materials contained in a single fertilized egg cell? We will offer some answers to these questions before moving on to a detailed look at the adult human brain.

EVOLUTION OF BRAIN STRUCTURES

The human brain is very similar to the brains of other mammals, and remarkably similar to the brains of other primates (the apes and monkeys, our closest living relatives in the animal kingdom). This fact reminds us that the brain, like any other biological organ, has been shaped by millions of years of evolution, during which its structures and functions have responded to selective pressures from the environment. Those features that have helped animals to survive and reproduce in their particular habitats have tended to be retained from one generation to the next. Thus, although humans and other species have gone their own separate evolutionary ways, we still have many basic brain features in common, features that have proven generally advantageous to survival. These shared features allow us to draw inferences about the human brain by studying the brains of other animals. As we will see later in this chapter, many exciting and useful discoveries about brain function have come from such animal studies.

But while there are many similarities in the nervous systems of different species, there are also differences. These physical differences are assumed to underlie differences in abilities and behaviors. For instance, researchers have recently found that one part of the human brain is much thicker on the left side than it is on the right. Since the ability to use language tends to be localized on the brain's left side, this physical difference has been linked to human language skills. Does the same thicker region on the left side of the brain occur in other primates—for example, in chimpanzees? We don't yet know the answer to this question. But if this thicker brain region is indeed related to language, we would expect it to have certain unique properties in humans, whose use of language far surpasses that of other species. This is not to say that humans are the only animals with **lateralized brain structures** (structures that appear on one side of the brain but not on the other). Such asymmetries exist in many other species, includ-

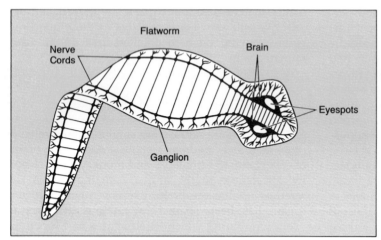

FIGURE 3.8 An invertebrate nervous system. In the flatworm, a nerve cord runs down each side of its body, with ganglia at various points. Enlarged ganglia at the front form a primitive brain. (*Adapted from Wessells, 1988.*)

ing both mammals and birds. We will return to the topic of lateralized brain structures toward the end of this chapter.

When we study the biological differences among species, a major distinction is made between animals with backbones, the **vertebrates,** and those without backbones, the **invertebrates.** Both vertebrates and invertebrates possess neurons as the basic building blocks of their nervous systems, but in these two categories of species the organization of neurons can differ substantially. The jellyfish, for example, which is a very simple invertebrate, has its neurons connected into a nerve net. When one neuron is stimulated, it affects the entire net, causing the body to contract. In contrast, flatworms, which are slightly more advanced invertebrates, show signs of both this primitive nerve net and a new structure: the **nerve cord.** (See Figure 3.8.) A nerve cord is a tubular bundle of nerve cells that runs the length of the body, one on each side. At various points along these cords are aggregates of neurons, or **ganglia,** which serve as processing centers for information gathered in that particular region. Enlarged ganglia at the front end play a role in coordinating the various other ganglia. Here we can see the early forerunner of the vertebrate brain.

Vertebrae, the bony segments that form a spinal column, protect the cells of the nervous system. The evolution of vertebrae made possible the emergence of extensive networks of neurons and, eventually, the brain. The basic structure of the vertebrate brain

shows the effects of growing out of what is essentially a tube. Over the millenia, this tube has been overlaid with successive new structures—structures that have proved to be advantageous in an ever-changing environment.

A popular, if oversimplified, way of thinking about vertebrate brain evolution is to imagine that a new layer of structures emerged at each of three critical junctures in the evolutionary history of animals. This could help explain the human brain's three major regions: the **hindbrain,** the **midbrain,** and the **forebrain.** Structures in the hindbrain and midbrain, which form the lower parts of the brain's central core, supposedly reflect our reptilian heritage and are said to permit only reflexive actions. Structures that grew up around this primitive region, including parts of the emerging forebrain, presumably constitute our inheritance from the earliest mammals. These areas are said to be concerned with emotions and basic motivations, such as hunger, sexuality, and aggression. Forebrain structures that surround these regions, and which blossom out in humans to occupy much of the skull, supposedly constitute our inheritance from more recent mammals. The fullest flowering of this latest brain development is the cerebral cortex, assumed to provide the basis for rational thought. (See Figure 3.9.) This three-part model of brain evolution is popular partly because it reinforces the satisfying notion that humans possess the greatest amount of "higher" brain structures—those concerned with reasoning and logic. Studying the brains of other

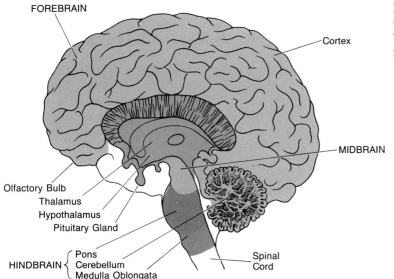

FOREBRAIN

Cortex

MIDBRAIN

Olfactory Bulb
Thalamus
Hypothalamus
Pituitary Gland

Pons
HINDBRAIN Cerebellum
Medulla Oblongata

Spinal
Cord

FIGURE 3.9 **The human brain showing the hindbrain, midbrain, and forebrain. The cerebral cortex is the site of thinking, memory, and language.** (*Adapted from Wessells, 1988.*)

animals allows us to evaluate such theories of brain evolution, with their far-reaching implications for understanding human nature.

HOW DO BRAINS GROW?

More than *100 billion* nerve cells are generated in the nine months before a baby is born, which means an average of over a quarter of a million every single minute! These cells migrate to the appropriate brain regions, where they send out axons and dendrites, which manage to make the right connections with thousands of other nerve cells. How is the formation of this incredibly complex network possible? How do the cells "know" in which directions to travel, where to extend their various fibers, and when they have made the proper synapses? Essentially, the answer is that developing neurons come equipped with the ability to search out, "read," and use various signposts and roadways that mark the routes they are to take. Let us take a closer look at one part of this intricate process: sending out axons and dendrites.

When an axon or dendrite grows out from an immature nerve cell, the way is led by a clublike extension called a **growth cone.** Many hairlike filaments extend from the leading tip of the growth cone. These filaments serve as advance scouts, so to speak, searching the environment and picking out the route

for the axon or dendrite to follow. When growth cones first start to invade a region of tissue, their filaments may crawl along preformed channels and bridges provided by glia and other non-neuronal cells (Kuwada, 1986; Silver and Rutishauser, 1984). But later, when a complex network of axons and dendrites has developed, other mechanisms are needed in order for a cell to find its way through the dense jungle of fibers. One of these other mechanisms seems to involve chemical markers on nerve cells. As the filaments of a growth cone probe the environment, they encounter axons of other neurons to which they have a special chemical attraction. The filaments adhere strongly to the surface of these "labeled" axons, pulling the leading tip of their growth cone along behind them. Over time, the attraction of filaments to specific axons changes, allowing the filaments to find their way through different stages of their journey (Goodman and Bastiani, 1984). Meanwhile, certain chemicals released from target cells (those cells toward which the filaments are ultimately extending) may lure the growing axons and dendrites like magnets, guiding them toward their final destinations (Dodd and Jessell, 1988).

So far you may have gotten the impression that axons and dendrites grow out from neurons, make connections with other nerve cells, and the wiring of

The brain grows extremely rapidly during gestation. At the tenth week of pregnancy, this fetus's brain is already clearly identifiable.

the brain is complete. The story, however, is far more complex. The various synapses that neurons form are often open to change, as cells respond to environmental stimulation and compete with one another for positioning (Rodgers, 1986). In fact, the immature nervous system produces many more neurons and synapses than it ultimately needs, and then, with further development, the excess is eliminated. Perhaps as many as 50 percent of the neurons originally created die during early development, and the same percentage of synapses may also atrophy (Kolb, 1989). It is as if a sculptor takes a lump of clay much larger than he actually needs and pares away until the desired shape emerges. Apparently, this process is one of fine-tuning. It adjusts the size of a particular group of neurons, and the interconnections among them, to the size and nature of the tasks those cells must perform. Having an overabundance of neurons to start with is a way of making sure that the developing nervous system will be able to cope with many different possible demands. At the same time, eliminating many neurons and synapses provides an important chance to get rid of any cells and connections that have found their way to the wrong places (Cowan et al., 1984).

This ability of the developing nervous system to modify itself in response to changing conditions has been studied many times in the laboratory. For instance, when one of a baby rat's nostrils is blocked for a period of weeks, the part of the brain that receives smell sensations from that side of the nose undergoes measurable atrophy as cells there die in unusually large numbers (Meisami, 1978). The developing brain seems to follow the rule: "use it or lose it." If a certain region of the brain is not actively employed, neurons there will be eliminated to a commensurate degree.

By the same token, when parts of a developing brain are used extensively, they tend to undergo greater than normal growth. By this we do not mean that a great many new neurons are added to these regions, for in mammals the creation of new neurons is quite limited after birth. Existing neurons can readily grow larger, however, and they can form additional connections with neighboring cells. Apparently, both these important changes occur in areas of the brain that undergo a great deal of stimulation (Greenough, 1986).

This was shown in a classic study of baby rats from the same litter who were raised in two very different environments (Rosenzweig et al., 1972). One was an enriched environment consisting of wheels, ladders, slides, and a variety of other toys that the rats could explore. The toys were changed often to ensure a steady stream of new learning experiences. The remaining rats were placed in an impoverished environment that consisted of an empty cage located in an isolated room. After nearly three months, the brains of the young rats were compared. The differences were dramatic. The outermost layer of the forebrain in the enriched-environment rats was significantly thicker and heavier. This was due to an increase in three factors: the size of neurons, the number of supporting glial cells, and the density of blood vessels. Subsequent research has shown that rats raised in an enriched environment also have a greater number of dendrite spines on many neurons, dendrite spines being the structures where other neurons form synapses (Diamond, 1984). Thus, early stimulation can promote the formation of richer connections between nerve cells, thereby enhancing how well those cells function as a unit. This process, by implication, occurs not just in rats, but in other animal species too, including humans.

Note again the advantage of this **plasticity,** the ability of the brain to modify itself in response to new conditions. Because early brain circuits are often open to change, they are able to adapt to the diverse circumstances that an animal might face. Plasticity, in short, helps to fine-tune neural connections in line with environmental experiences. Although some forms of neurological plasticity are lost with maturation, others continue to exist throughout life. The very fact that we can learn new information until the day we die shows that our brains must be perpetually able to form new synapses, or at least to enhance the strength and efficiency of existing ones (Edelman, 1987; Reeke and Edelman, 1988). In Chapter 7 we will say more about the changes in the brain associated with learning and memory.

METHODS OF BRAIN RESEARCH

How have scientists managed to learn what they know about the brain? Over the years they have developed a variety of increasingly sophisticated research methods. Let us look first at the oldest method of mapping the brain—clinical studies of people with localized brain damage.

CLINICAL OBSERVATIONS

Nineteenth-century doctors noticed that damage to certain brain areas typically caused very specific disorders—blindness, deafness, paralysis of a certain body part, speech difficulties, and so forth—depending on the brain region involved. The theories of brain organization developed from these early findings helped to guide later research on brain–behavior relationships. More recent clinical observations continue to bring us insights about the workings of the brain. Sometimes pieces of information that one would think the brain would process through exactly the same pathways turn out to be processed through significantly different routes. For example, people with extensive damage to certain areas at the back of the brain often cannot identify pictures of familiar faces, even the faces of their own relatives. Yet the same people can identify pictures of animals or objects with virtually no hesitation or error (Geschwind, 1979). Equally surprising is the person with damage to the left side of the brain who has completely lost the ability to read words but retains the ability to read numbers. Such a person might be able to interpret the symbols MIX as meaning 1,009 in Roman numerals, yet not be able to see them as an English word (Gardner, 1975). Such unexpected clinical findings remind us that the logic of the brain's

organization need not conform to the logic of the minds that analyze it (Shallice, 1988).

BRAIN STIMULATION AND LESIONS

Because neural activity is electrochemical, it can be induced by tiny amounts of electrical or chemical stimulation applied to nerve tissue. Scientists have taken advantage of this fact in their efforts to explore the brain. When chemicals are used, the investigator implants an extremely slender tube for transferring liquid into an animal's brain so that the tip touches the area to be stimulated. Then a tiny amount of a chemical is delivered through the tube. When electrical stimulation is used, weak electrical currents are delivered through electrodes implanted in the brain regions under investigation. Both these techniques have yielded a wealth of information.

Another technique for mapping connections between the brain and behavior involves making brain lesions in laboratory animals. A **lesion** is produced by surgical destruction or removal of a small amount of brain tissue. After the surgery, the researchers carefully assess deficits in the animal's behavior. The results of brain stimulation procedures and brain lesion techniques are closely related. In general, if electrical stimulation of a certain area *increases* a certain behavior, lesions in that same area will *decrease* the behavior. Conversely, if stimulation tends to block a behavior when it is normally appropriate, lesions may cause the behavior to occur more vigorously.

RECORDING ELECTRICAL ACTIVITY

You may already know that scientists can trace the electrical signals of a human brain by taking an electroencephalogram, or EEG. In a typical EEG procedure, electrodes are attached to various areas of the scalp, and the voltage emitted by the brain beneath causes a pen to record its patterns on rolling graph paper. A standard EEG, as you will learn later in this book, is useful in many types of psychological investigation. It has serious limitations, however, for a researcher who wants to determine how a particular stimulus—such as a flash of light or a mild shock to the fingers—affects electrical activity in the brain. The problem is that the brain emits a mass of electrical signals. How is the researcher to distinguish

This is the standard setup for an electroencephalogram, a device for recording the brain's electrical signals.

the specific electrical response evoked by the stimulus being tested? One solution is quite simple. Researchers present the stimulus many times and use a computer to average out the responses recorded from the brain. Over a large number of trials, electrical activity unrelated to the stimulus will be sometimes negative and sometimes positive, and so will average to zero. What emerges, then, is the pattern of electrical activity that the stimulus has *caused*.

This technique has helped scientists to chart many reactions in the brain. When the notes of the musical scale are played to a person, for example, electrical activity arises in a rather orderly fashion in a major hearing center of the brain. Low notes produce potentials at one end of this region, high notes at the other end, and middle notes in between (Woolsey, 1961). Similar kinds of orderly arrangements have been found for other sensory areas.

But the brain does more than just register sensory stimuli from the outside world. In the process of analyzing and understanding information, the brain routinely emits distinctive patterns of electrical activity. For instance, if you were listening to a repetitive series of sounds and they suddenly and unpredictably stopped, your brain would register its surprise by emitting a large, positive electrical voltage beginning three-tenths of a second after the sounds ceased. Similarly, if you read a sentence that ended with a word that did not fit the context, your brain would reveal its effort to make sense out of nonsense with a negative voltage beginning four-tenths of a second after you encountered the troublesome word. Researchers are now discovering that a wide variety of other mental processes are accompanied by their own characteristic patterns of electrical activity (Renault et al., 1982; Ritter et al., 1982).

It is not difficult to imagine the important diagnostic tools that such patterns could provide. Scientists working in this area have developed tests to help spot learning disabilities, the early stages of senility, alcoholism, and various mental disorders, including schizophrenia and depression (Shucard et al., 1984). This they do by mapping abnormalities in the brain's electrical activities. Different brain disorders apparently have their own distinctive electrical patterns, which differ measurably from the patterns produced by normal, healthy people. Taking a reading of a patient's brain activities can therefore help confirm a diagnosis based on behavioral symptoms. Some day such readings may identify people who are merely *susceptible* to a certain disorder by finding characteristic "markers" in the electrical signals their brains emit (John et al., 1988).

The electrical recording techniques we have discussed so far involve placing electrodes on the surface of the scalp to monitor the brain's activities. Consequently, the data obtained come from the electrical signals of many different neurons. But modern technology has also made it possible to record the electrical response of a *single* neuron, which at its widest has a diameter of only about one-thousandth of an inch. Such recording is done with the use of a microelectrode that is placed into or very close to an individual nerve cell in the brain of an experimental animal.

The single-neuron recording technique has provided important insights into the functional organization of the brain. For example, single-neuron

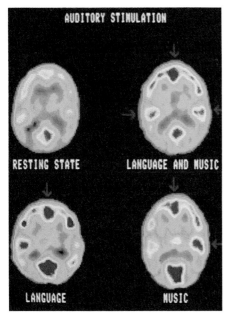

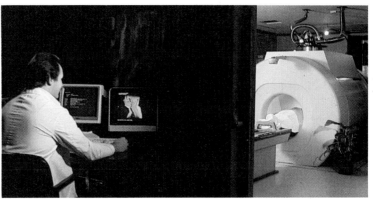

Two new techniques for recording brain activity by illuminating active parts of the brain: positron emission tomography (PET) scan (*left*) uses radioactive injections; magnetic resonance imaging (MRI) (*right*) uses nuclear scanning techniques. In the PET scan shown, the dark red parts of the brain are most active. (*Dan McCoy/Rainbow; Peter Menzel.*)

recordings from a visual region of a monkey's brain have provided fascinating insights into how these animals perceive faces (Perrett et al., 1987). Some of the cells in this region respond very strongly to faces (both human and monkey), but not to other complex objects, even ones that resemble faces, such as an alarm clock. These face-responsive cells can be further classified depending on the perspective of the head that they prefer (front, back, left profile, right profile, head raised, head lowered). Some even have a preference for a *particular* face, as if they are involved in the process of identifying faces. We will say more about this high degree of selectivity in the responses of certain neurons when we talk about sensation and perception in Chapter 4.

Some scientists are now using the data obtained from single-neuron recordings to develop computer models of how neurons work together (Sejnowski et al., 1988). Computers, of course, cannot yet mimic the way in which a brain simultaneously performs many different functions, each involving thousands of interconnected cells. They can, however, model some limited aspects of how a brain works, such as how cells of the visual system detect and compute distance, or how cells of the auditory system detect and compute the location of a sound. Such models can be used to make predictions about how a brain will respond to particular kinds of stimulation. By comparing these predictions to experimental results, new hypotheses can be developed to help guide future research.

CHEMICAL LABELING TECHNIQUES

The ability to label neural pathways with "traceable" chemicals has opened up whole new lines of brain research. For instance, researchers can inject experimental animals with radioactive forms of amino acids that are building blocks of a neurotransmitter, or they can directly inject a neurotransmitter that has been given fluorescent properties. The labeled chemical is then selectively taken up by the axons that normally use it. Later, when thin sections of brain tissue are placed on radiation-sensitive film or viewed under a fluorescent microscope, the researchers obtain a picture of how the various cells using that chemical interconnect. As a result of such techniques, we now know a great deal about the distribution within the brain of many neurotransmitters.

In addition to mapping the pathways of neurotransmitters, chemical labeling techniques are also used to map the patterns of brain activity that accompany various types of behavior. (See the photograph above.) One such method takes advantage of the fact

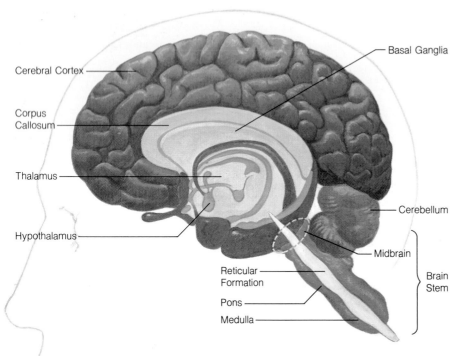

Cerebral Cortex

Corpus Callosum

Thalamus

Hypothalamus

Reticular Formation

Pons

Medulla

Basal Ganglia

Cerebellum

Midbrain

Brain Stem

FIGURE 3.10 This illustration shows the right hemisphere of the brain as it would appear if the head were sliced exactly in half from front to back. The structures illustrated are the first to receive incoming information, and they regulate the most fundamental processes of the body. The reticular formation, which controls the most general responses of the brain to sensory input, is located in the area that connects the brain to the spinal cord and to the rest of the nervous system. The thalamus is centrally located, and the hypothalamus controls the pituitary gland, which controls the activity of the other endocrine glands.

that the more a particular brain cell participates in controlling a thought or action, the more sugar it absorbs from the bloodstream, because sugar is the brain cell's fuel. Under normal circumstances, of course, absorbed sugar is broken down almost as soon as it is taken up, in order to release energy. But researchers have found that if they inject into the blood a radioactive substance very similar chemically to sugar, it will be taken up by neurons just as regular sugar is, but it will not be "burned" away. Instead, this radioactive substance will temporarily accumulate in the brain cells. Most important, the amount absorbed by different brain cells while an animal is performing some experimental task provides a measurable record of the extent to which those cells are involved in controlling that behavior. Thus, a researcher might flash a light previously paired with a mild electrical shock and then observe which parts of an animal's brain are activated in the response to this learned association. The latest technology, called a **PET scan** (PET stands for positron emission tomography), allows researchers to trace the path of the radioactive substance from outside the skull (Montgomery, 1989).

Another revolutionary procedure for examining neural activity is the **CAT scan** (CAT stands for computerized transaxial tomography). A rapidly rotating X-ray beam takes pictures of the brain from hundreds of different angles. These pictures are then processed by computer to yield a three-dimensional, cross-sectional image. The CAT scan is especially useful in medical diagnosis. Within half an hour, a neurologist can examine a brain for tumors, lesions, atrophy, or abnormal enlargements, without the need for exploratory surgery (Kolb and Whishaw, 1990). The CAT scan does have some disadvantages, however. It uses X rays, which are potentially hazardous, and it reveals only the relative density of brain tissue. Another new diagnostic technique, called magnetic resonance imaging, or **MRI**, overcomes these problems. MRI makes use of magnetic fields, which are not known to be harmful, and it can provide data about the chemical contents and environments of cells. This method can be used to detect cancer, diagnose strokes, examine blood vessels, and evaluate the effects of drugs, as well as to provide information about brain–behavior relationships (Andreasen, 1988: Edelson, 1983).

MAJOR REGIONS OF THE HUMAN BRAIN

Through these research methods we have learned a great deal about the workings of the human brain, including its complex organization and the roles its various parts play. To lead you though the labyrinth of the human brain, we will organize our discussion around two major regions: the central core and the cerebral hemispheres.

THE CENTRAL CORE

The **central core** of the human brain is sometimes called the "old brain," because in appearance and function it is similar to the brains of more primitive animals. In fact, the central core varies little among vertebrates. It includes structures that together carry out the functions most basic to survival, such as sleeping and waking, breathing, and feeding. The structures that make up the central core are shown in Figure 3.10. They include the hindbrain (consisting of the medulla, the reticular formation, the pons, and the cerebellum), the midbrain, and the thalamus and hypothalamus.

The Hindbrain If you follow the spinal cord up the neck and into the base of the skull, you will come to an area that swells out slightly. This is the **medulla,** the first structure of the **hindbrain.** The medulla plays an important role in many autonomic activities, such as circulation and breathing, and it is also involved in chewing, salivation, and facial movements. Above and extending forward from the medulla is the **pons** (meaning "bridge"), which connects the two halves of the cerebellum lying above it. The pons transmits to the cerebellum information about body movements that it receives from higher brain centers and from the spinal cord. The pons also seems to be involved in circuits that control sleep, which you will read more about in Chapter 5.

Running up the stem of the hindbrain, through the medulla, pons, and midbrain, and into the thalamus, are clusters of neurons and nerve fibers collectively called the **reticular formation.** The reticular formation seems to function as a sentry, arousing the forebrain when information related to survival must be processed and permitting periods of sustained attention. The reticular formation also appears to help screen out extraneous sensory input, especially during sleep. Severe damage to the reticular forma-

The cerebellum helps us maintain our sense of balance.

tion can cause a person to lapse into a permanent coma. You will encounter the reticular formation again when we talk about optimum levels of arousal in Chapter 12, on motivation.

Another major area of the hindbrain is the **cerebellum.** This name, which means "little brain," derives from the fact that the cerebellum is divided into two hemispheres and so looks like a miniature version of the forebrain. Different parts of the cerebellum have different connections to the higher brain and spinal cord, and they serve different functions. One area is involved in maintaining a sense of balance and equilibrium. Another is involved in coordinating muscular movements, ensuring that they are smooth and efficient. Thus, damage to the cerebellum can cause *ataxia*, a condition characterized by uncoordinated movement, lack of balance, and severe tremors. A person who has ataxia lacks the control needed for even simple reaching movements, and so may accidentally hit a friend in the stomach while reaching out to shake hands. Still another part of the cerebellum is involved in the learning and remembering of simple motor tasks (Thompson, 1983). We will say more about this in Chapter 7, when we discuss the physiological basis of memory.

The Midbrain   Above the hindbrain is a small structure known as the **midbrain.** All information passing back and forth between the forebrain and the spinal cord goes through the midbrain. The midbrain contains important centers for regulating body movements in response to visual and auditory stimulation. For example, your startle reflex in response to a sudden, loud noise is controlled by an area of the midbrain. The sizes of the visual and auditory areas of the midbrain vary depending on how important those centers are to survival. Birds that sight, track, and capture prey in flight, for instance, have very prominent and bulging visual midbrain regions. In contrast, bats, which use sound rather than sight to locate their prey, have small visual midbrain centers but very prominent auditory ones.

The Thalamus and Hypothalamus   Above the midbrain and deeply embedded in the central mass of the cerebral hemispheres are the thalamus and hypothalamus. The **thalamus** consists of many quite separate clusters of neurons called nuclei, each of which relays information to and from specific parts of the nervous system. For example, in Chapter 4 you will read about nuclei in the thalamus that relay information from sensory receptors in the peripheral nervous system to specific parts of the forebrain. One of these is concerned with the relay of visual information, a second with the relay of auditory information, and a third with the relay of information about touch, pressure, temperature, and pain. Don't take the term *relay* to mean that these thalamic nuclei are nothing more than passive waystations. The neurons of the thalamus actively process information as they pass it along. The thalamus, then, exerts its own influence on data as it shuttles it from one part of the nervous system to another.

The **hypothalamus** is a small structure (about as big as the tip of your index finger) located just below the thalamus. It too consists of various nuclei, each with different functions. Some of these nuclei are involved in very basic behaviors, such as eating, drinking, sexual activity, fear, and aggression. For example, stimulation of the lateral (side) area of the hypothalamus causes an animal to eat voraciously, even if it has just consumed a meal, while stimulation of the ventromedial (lower middle) area of the hypothalmus prompts an animal to stop eating, even if it is starving. These hypothalmic nuclei, it seems, are involved in an animal's ability to recognize when it is

hungry and full. We will say much more about them when we take up the topic of eating in Chapter 12.

Other nuclei in the hypothalmus are involved in regulating the body's internal environment. For instance, a part of the hypothalmus controls the body's internal temperature, and hypothalamic regions coordinate the activities of the autonomic nervous system. As we said earlier, the hypothalamus also regulates the activities of the pituitary gland, the hormones of which influence secretions from other glands throughout the body. Thus, despite its small size—only 0.3 percent of the brain's total weight—the hypothalamus is a vitally important brain region.

THE CEREBRAL HEMISPHERES, OR FOREBRAIN

The **cerebral hemispheres** are the two large structures that lie above the brain's central core, one on the left side, the other on the right. The cerebral hemispheres, also known as the **forebrain,** are the most recent development in the brain's long evolutionary history. These prominent structures are involved in the processes of learning, memory, language, and reasoning. We will be discussing two parts of the cerebral hemispheres: the limbic system and the cortex.

The Limbic System   Directly above the central core is the **limbic system,** so named because it forms the innermost border of the cerebral hemispheres (*limbic* means "bordering"). The limbic system contains some half-dozen interrelated structures, shown in Figure 3.11. These structures form a loop around the top of the central core and are closely connected with the hypothalamus and the inner surface of the cortex. Because the forward-most limbic structures— the olfactory bulbs—are intimately involved in the sense of smell, researchers once speculated that the other limbic regions probably evolved to process smell-related data too. As it turns out, this early hypothesis has proved incorrect. Although we do not yet fully understand all the roles the limbic system plays, each of its structures appears to serve different functions, often quite unrelated to the sense of smell. You will see this as we review some of what is known about three limbic regions: the hippocampus, the amygdala, and the septal area.

In humans, extensive damage to the **hippocampus** is linked to severe problems forming new memo-

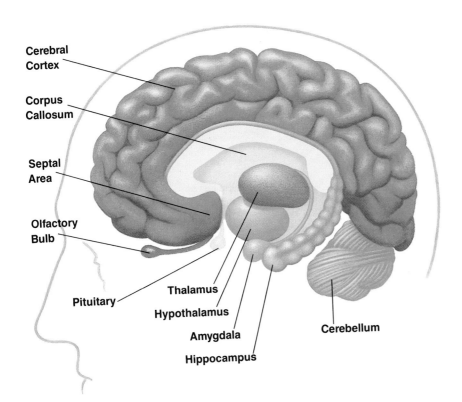

Cerebral Cortex

Corpus Callosum

Septal Area

Olfactory Bulb

Pituitary

Thalamus

Hypothalamus

Amygdala

Hippocampus

Cerebellum

FIGURE 3.11 The human limbic system. Structures within this system play a significant role in a variety of emotional behaviors. Damage to various regions of the limbic system may cause wild animals to become tame, or tame animals to become vicious. Other limbic or hypothalamic lesions may radically alter sexual and feeding behavior. The olfactory bulb (responsible for the sense of smell) is closely associated with other limbic structures, suggesting the importance of this sense to several functions of the limbic system.

ries. People who suffer such damage on both sides of the brain are often unable to consciously retain new information (Mishkin and Appenzeller, 1987). They cannot remember what they were doing or who they were with just moments after turning their attention to a new activity. They cannot find their way to a new location (one they never visited before their brain damage) even though they have been taken there over and over again. Not surprisingly, malfunction of the hippocampus seems to be involved in Alzheimer's disease, the symptoms of which include extensive memory impairment. We will say much more about the role of the hippocampus in learning and memory in Chapter 6. For now you should bear in mind that this important limbic structure probably serves some other functions as well. For instance, the hippocampus appears to be involved in the organization of movement and in spatial organization (Kolb and Whishaw, 1990). Thus, the hippocampus, like the other major brain regions we have talked about so far, seems to have multiple roles.

Like the hippocampus, the **amygdala** also seems to be involved in learning and memory (Zola-Morgan et al., 1982). The amygdala appears to be especially

important regarding memories with emotional components (Thompson, 1985, 1986). Not only may it play a role in linking feelings with other experiences, it may also strengthen perceptions that have emotional associations, making them more memorable (Mishkin and Appenzeller, 1987). In addition, scientists have long known that the amygdala is deeply involved in certain forms of emotional expression. For instance, lesions in parts of the amygdala of a lynx, a cat so wild it must be handled with nets, make the animal docile and tame (Kluver and Bucy, 1939). Similarly, stimulation of areas of the amygdala can prompt an animal to act fearful and try to flee (Goddard, 1964). We will return to the amygdala in Chapter 11, where we examine the brain's role in emotion.

The **septal area,** a third region of the limbic system, may also be involved in emotions, but in different ways than the amygdala is. In 1954 James Olds and Peter Milner accidentally discovered that rats will quickly learn to press a lever in order to receive mild electrical stimulation to parts of the septal area. The pleasure that this stimulation produces is apparently intense. A hungry rat hurrying to

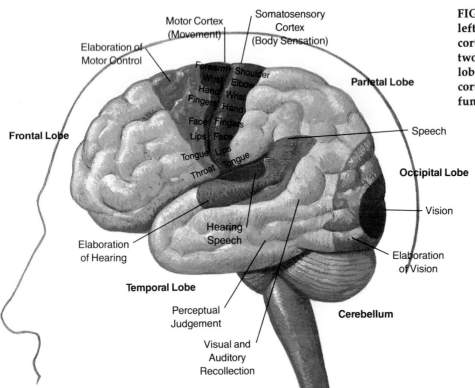

Motor Cortex
(Movement)

Somatosensory
Cortex
(Body Sensation)

Elaboration of
Motor Control

Parietal Lobe

Forearm Shoulder
Wrist   Elbow
Hand   Wrist
Fingers Hand
Face Fingers
Lips Face
Tongue Lips
Throat Tongue

Frontal Lobe

Speech

Occipital Lobe

Vision

Hearing
Speech

Elaboration
of Hearing

Elaboration
of Vision

Temporal Lobe

Cerebellum

Perceptual
Judgement

Visual and
Auditory
Recollection

FIGURE 3.12   A view of the left hemisphere of the cerebral cortex. The diagram shows the two major fissures, the four lobes, and several other cortical areas and their functions.

the feeding tray will stop in its tracks to receive it, and will remain there as long as the stimulation continues, even when food is only inches away. When allowed to stimulate their own septal areas by pressing a bar that connects the current, rats have been known to press frenetically, thousands of times an hour. What could the nature of such intense pleasure be? Humans who have undergone similar septal area stimulation (usually during treatment of some neurological disorder) report that they experience a rush of extremely good feelings, feelings that some have compared with the buildup to an orgasm. Exactly how stimulation of these septal regions is related to such behaviors as feeding and mating, also influenced by the limbic system, is still largely unknown. Bear in mind, too, that the septal area is not the only area of the brain where stimulation is pleasurable and rewarding. The brain, apparently, has dozens of these locations (Wise and Rompre, 1989). We will say more about the pleasure centers of the brain when we talk about the effects of certain drugs in Chapter 5.

The Cortex   The outermost area of the cerebral hemispheres is a thin layer of gray matter called the

cortex (the term means "bark" or "outer covering"). The cortex is the most recent evolutionary development of the nervous system. It is only about a twelfth of an inch (2 millimeters) thick, but it has so many convolutions that it contains more than 9 billion neurons. If the human cortex were flattened out, its area would be about 2.5 square feet.

The external surface of the cortex has several landmarks. The most prominent are the two deep fissures that subdivide each hemisphere into its principal areas, or lobes. As Figure 3.12 shows, a **central fissure** separates each frontal lobe from the parietal lobe that lies behind it, while a **lateral fissure** marks the top boundary of each temporal lobe. Dividing lines between the two occipital lobes and their neighboring lobes are much less clear, but researchers still consider these distinct regions. What functions do the cortical areas of these various lobes play?

The cortex of the **frontal lobe** next to the central fissure is concerned primarily with regulating voluntary movements and so is called the **motor cortex.** Figure 3.13A, which maps the motor cortex, shows that the amount of cortex concerned with movement

FIGURE 3.13 (A) The areas of the motor cortex and (B) the somatosensory cortex that control specific body parts. Areas of the body capable of the most complex and precise movements are linked to the largest quantities of space in the motor cortex. For example, the eyelid and eyeball (capable of many precise movements) have a larger area than the face. Large areas of the somatosensory cortex receive impulses from the more sensitive body parts (such as the fingers and the lips). Although for simplicity's sake these drawings make it appear as if each part of the body is represented only once in the motor and somatosensory cortices, in fact each body part has multiple representations. (*Penfield and Rasmussen, 1950.*)

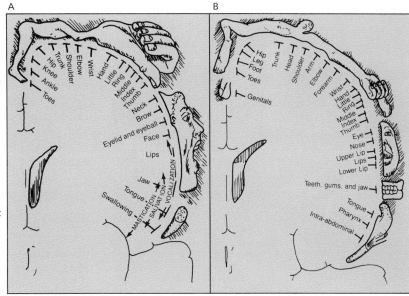

in a particular body part depends not on the size of that part, but rather on its degree of motor control. The fingers, for example, which can make very precise movements, have much larger representation in the motor cortex than does the trunk of the body. Also note that the motor cortex of the *right* hemisphere controls movement on the *left* side of the body, whereas the motor cortex of the *left* hemisphere controls movement on the body's *right* side. This is called **contralateral control** and is a basic principle of brain organization.

Brain anatomists once believed that the prefrontal areas of the frontal lobe cortex (the areas at the very front of the brain) are the site of our intellectual abilities. Most modern researchers reject this notion, however, for some people perform just as well on standard intelligence tests after massive amounts of prefrontal tissue have been removed. The cognitive deficits resulting from damage to the prefrontal areas, it now appears, include the abilities to order stimuli, sort out information, analyze steps leading to solutions, and maintain attention in the face of distraction, not so much the kinds of specific mental skills typically measured by IQ tests (Struss and Benson, 1984). Interestingly, because of its special role in handling serial information (information about how things follow one another in time), the prefrontal cortex may help us to differentiate the present from the future and to anticipate events. It is probably also the storehouse for serial-action plans—that is, plans

for the steps involved in upcoming thoughts and behaviors (Ingvar, 1985).

Behind the frontal lobes, on the opposite side of the central fissures, lie the **parietal lobes.** The parietal lobes contain the **somatosensory cortex,** the primary receiving area for the skin senses (touch, pressure, heat, pain) and for the sense of body position. Like the motor cortex, the somatosensory cortex shows contralateral control: this region in the *right* hemisphere is linked to sensations in the *left* side of the body, while this region in the *left* hemisphere is linked to sensations in the body's *right* side. Also like the motor cortex, the somatosensory cortex is *not* laid out according to the size of a body part. Instead, it is a particular part's sensitivity to stimulation that determines the amount of cortical tissue devoted to it. The lips, for instance, which are small but extremely sensitive to touch, have a relatively large representation in the somatosensory cortex, as shown in Figure 3.13B.

The somatosensory cortex lies at the most forward part of the parietal lobes, right next to the central fissure. The parietal lobe cortex more toward the back of the brain is involved in a different function. That function is to integrate visual, auditory, and somatosensory information received and passed on by other areas of the cortex (Kolb and Whishaw, 1990). Thus, a person with damage to the back of the parietal lobes (called *posterior* parietal lobe damage) is still able to see, hear, and feel sensations

Touch and the other skin senses are controlled by the somatosensory cortex of the brain's parietal lobes.

on the skin. But that person may have great difficulty integrating these different sources of sensory data into a single perception of an object or event. For instance, suppose such a person is given a pencil to feel with the fingers but is prevented from seeing it. The person is then asked to select the object held in the hand from an array of different objects presented visually. Whereas this task is very easy for people with normal brains, it can be very hard, even impossible, for a person with posterior parietal lobe damage.

The same integrative function performed by areas of the posterior parietal lobe cortex extends into posterior regions of the temporal lobe cortex as well. Figure 3.13 shows that the **temporal lobes** lie below the parietal lobes, more or less beneath the ears on either side of the head. In addition to housing regions that integrate sensory information and help people attend to distinctive features of it, the temporal cortex also has areas where auditory signals are first received and processed by the brain. You will read about this

auditory cortex when we discuss the sense of hearing in Chapter 4.

The last of the brain's lobes, called the **occipital lobes,** lie at the very back of each cerebral hemisphere. A major role of the occipital lobe cortex is to conduct the initial stages in analyzing visual information. In humans, injury to these portions of the cortex can produce blind spots in the visual field. Chapter 4 will say much more about the visual areas of the brain, including visual areas in the temporal lobe cortex.

THE BRAIN'S ROLE IN COMPLEX BEHAVIORS

Exploring the various structures of the brain to discover their different functions is the primary interest of neuroanatomists and neurophysiologists. *Neuropsychologists,* in contrast, look at the brain from a different angle. They want to understand the brain's role in complex behaviors, such as perception, learning, memory, language, and emotion. For this they must determine how various brain structures are part of broader neural circuits that govern thought and action. In this section we introduce the general perspective of the modern neuropsychologist. Then, in later chapters, we explore in detail how the brain controls some of the most interesting and complex human behaviors.

LOCALIZATION AND INTEGRATION

Many years ago neuropsychologist Karl Lashley attempted to locate specific areas of the cortex that were responsible for the learning and remembering of particular behaviors. In one set of studies, he trained rats to run mazes after making lesions in their cerebral cortices. The locations of the lesions overlapped considerably, so no area of the cortex was left unexplored. Lashley found that no lesion completely obliterated the rats' ability to learn a maze, although each of the lesions interfered with learning to some extent. He found in addition that the degree to which learning was impaired by a lesion was related directly to the lesion's size: the larger the lesion, the greater the learning deficit. This was particularly true with regard to learning more complex mazes. Based on these findings, Lashley concluded that learning a specific task did not appear to be localized in any particular area of the cortex. Instead, the entire cortex seemed to be involved in any given instance of learning and remembering (Lashley, 1929).

Today we know that Lashley's conclusion was essentially incorrect. Specific areas of the brain *are* involved in specific behaviors. **Localization of function** is a basic principle of brain organization. Why, then, couldn't Lashley locate the key structures involved in learning and memory? One reason was that he confined his search to the cerebral cortex. As you know, subcortical regions, particularly parts of the limbic system, seem to play critical roles in learning and memory. At the same time, Lashley downplayed the extent to which localization of function *and* integration of activities work together. Functions in the brain *are* localized to a large degree, but localized areas never operate in isolation. Localized regions are integrated into larger neural systems that provide the ultimate control over complex behaviors. Thus, learning a maze that leads to a goal box involves the simultaneous processing of *many* different kinds of information: sights, odors, tactile sensations, associations between behaviors and their consequences, basic drives such as hunger and curiosity, and emotions related to eventually obtaining the food reward. All these different parts of the maze-learning task involve different combinations of brain regions. This is why it was impossible for Lashley to pinpoint *the* learning and memory center in the brain. Single regions with this broad a function do not exist in the brain. Instead, the brain operates by integrating the activities of many different regions, each with functions more limited in scope (Squire, 1986; Thompson, 1986).

For example, lift up the page you are now reading and explore its shape and texture with your hand. Nerve signals travel from receptor cells in your fingers to your spinal cord or brainstem, and then via a nucleus in your thalamus to the so-called primary region of your somatosensory cortex. Here vertically connected neurons form narrow columns that run from the surface of the cortex to its base. These columns act as miniprocessing units, firing in response to the location and quality of each sensation you experience. More specifically, each column responds to a certain type of stimulation (light touch, for example) on a certain small part of the body (the tip of the thumb, for instance). Nerve signals from all the many columns that are activated when you touch the page are then passed on to secondary and tertiary parts of the parietal lobe cortex, where the various tactile qualities are assessed and given meaning, combined into a unified perception, and linked to auditory and visual sensations. Note that this proc-

essing follows a hierarchical route: each step in the sequence involves increasingly complex analysis of the sensory data. The overall process is one of localization *and* integration. The various local units, or modules as they are often called (the cortical columns, the different somatosensory regions), are performing specialized tasks, but their activities are ultimately integrated into a larger information-processing system (Churchland and Sejnowski, 1988).

IN DEPTH

Studying the Two Sides of the Brain

Another place where the themes of localization and integration can be seen very clearly is in studying the two sides of the brain. Remember that the two cerebral hemispheres are not completely symmetrical. Each side of the brain has some specialized functions that the other side lacks. How researchers came to discover these **lateralized functions,** as they are called, and how they came to understand how the two sides of the brain work together, is a fascinating story that we will describe in depth.

One of the first indications that the two hemispheres might serve somewhat different functions came in the early 1860s, when the French physician Paul Broca found that a specific area of the left frontal lobe was involved in the ability to speak. Broca's view was based on numerous autopsies of patients who had suffered speech defects after damage to the left frontal lobe. Broca was struck by the fact that damage to the right frontal lobe in precisely the same location had no effect on language ability. Soon additional evidence that the left hemisphere is the brain's language center began to pile up. For instance, the German neurologist Carl Wernicke discovered that when a portion of the left temporal lobe is damaged, speech is also impaired. But whereas damage to Broca's area tends to result in speech that is labored and fragmented (much like a slow, cryptic telegram), damage to Wernicke's area tends to result in speech that is still very fluent but oddly devoid of meaning (Geschwind, 1979). Such early findings quickly led to the generalization that the left side of the brain houses most of our higher intellectual functions (such as speaking and writing), while the right side is essentially a mute relay station, shuttling information back and forth between the left side of the body and the thinking left hemisphere. The right hemisphere, in short,

FIGURE 3.14 Experimental apparatus for testing split-brain patients. When a picture of an object is shown on a screen in one-half of the visual field, this information is transmitted exclusively to the opposite hemisphere. In split-brain patients, the hemispheres are disconnected, therefore their independent functions can be studied. If a picture of a spoon is presented in the *right* half of the visual field (transmitted to the left hemisphere), and a patient is asked to name the object she sees, she answers "a spoon." If the same picture is shown in the *left* half of the visual field (transmitted to the right hemisphere), she cannot name the object, because speech mechanisms are found in the left hemisphere. Although the right hemisphere cannot name the object, it "knows" what the object is and is able to instruct the left hand to select the spoon, as shown here. (*Springer and Deutsch, 1989.*)

was viewed as little more than an automaton. We humans were considered to be "half-brained" creatures (Levy, 1985).

This view predominated well into the twentieth century. Granted, there were some who tried to defend the disparaged right hemisphere, arguing that it too seemed to have some specialized functions. For instance, one extensive study of more than 200 brain-damaged patients found that those with injury to the right hemisphere tended to have trouble filling in missing parts to a pattern, assembling various kinds of puzzles, and manipulating geometric shapes (Weisenberg and McBride, 1935). Other research showed that right-hemisphere damage was sometimes linked to distortions in depth and distance perception and the ability to orient oneself in space. But these discoveries were slow in coming and did not do much to raise the general image of the right hemisphere. The right brain's functions were still widely considered nonintellectual ones.

Then, quite unexpectedly, a dramatic set of studies sharply changed psychologists' view of the two sides of the brain. These studies arose as a by-product of a new surgical treatment for severe epilepsy. The treatment involved cutting the large cable of nerve cells, called the **corpus callosum,** that connects the two cerebral hemispheres. With the hemispheres separated, the random neural firing that causes epileptic convulsions is confined to the side of the brain where it begins, thus greatly reducing the severity of a seizure. But the person is left with two cerebral hemispheres that can no longer communicate directly with each other. Psychologists saw in these so-called split-brain patients an extraordinary opportunity to conduct some important research on the specialized abilities of the two sides of the brain.

THE INITIAL STUDIES

One of the pioneers in research on split-brain patients was neuroscientist Roger Sperry, who has since won a Nobel prize for his work in this field. When Sperry and his colleagues tested their first split-brain subjects, the results were startling. Imagine yourself in their laboratory observing a middle-aged woman sitting at a table with a screen in front of her, her eyes fixed on a dot at the screen's center. (See Figure 3.14). A projector behind the screen flashes a picture for a fraction of a second to the left or the right visual field. Since the left visual field sends messages to the right side of the brain, while the right visual field sends messages to the brain's left side, this procedure is a way of ensuring that visual images are projected to one cerebral hemisphere only. Suppose that a picture of a spoon is flashed to the right visual field. The experimenter asks the woman what she saw, and she quickly answers "a spoon." So far, there is nothing unusual about the woman's responses. But now consider what happens when a picture of a spoon is flashed to her left visual field. The woman reports seeing nothing! Is her right hemisphere unable to perceive a visual image? No, this cannot be the case. When asked to use her left hand (controlled by her right hemisphere) to identify the object from among a group of things hidden behind a screen, the hand unhesitantly selects the spoon. What can explain these seemingly contradictory responses?

The explanation requires an understanding of the tasks for which the two cerebral hemispheres are specialized. When the spoon was flashed to the right visual field, its image was sent to the brain's left hemisphere. Since the left hemisphere is proficient at speech, the woman could identify the object verbally. However, when the same picture was flashed to the right hemisphere, which is *not* adept at language, the woman could not *say* what she saw. So the left hemisphere spoke up to fill the silence, reporting quite correctly that *it* had seen nothing. The right hemisphere, of course, had recognized the spoon and needed only a chance to show its knowledge in some nonverbal way.

Studying split-brain subjects allowed researchers to establish in greater detail those tasks at which the right and left hemispheres excel. Of particular interest were the capabilities of the right hemisphere, for so long considered the lesser of the two sides of the brain. Investigators discovered that the right hemisphere's abilities were more impressive than had previously been believed. This was strikingly demonstrated in a film that Roger Sperry and his colleague Michael Gazzaniga made of a split-brain patient in their laboratory (described in Springer and Deutsch, 1989). The subject, W.J., is given a set of four blocks, each of which has two

FIGURE 3.15 Researchers Roger Sperry and Michael Gazzaniga gave a split-brain patient a set of four blocks with differently colored and patterned surfaces and asked him to arrange the blocks to match patterns on cards. The patient could accomplish the task easily with his left hand, but not with his right—an indication of the right hemisphere's superior spatial ability. (*After Springer and Deutsch, 1989.*)

white surfaces, two red surfaces, and two surfaces divided diagonally into red and white halves. He is to use the blocks to duplicate a series of simple geometric patterns, like the ones in Figure 3.15. Starting with his left hand (controlled by the right hemisphere), W.J. moves along confidently, duplicating the patterns with little effort. Then he is asked to switch to his right hand (controlled by the left hemisphere). His performance plummets. The right hand moves slowly and hesitantly, making many mistakes. At one point the left hand reaches toward the blocks, apparently to help the awkward right hand out. The experimenter moves the left hand back down to W.J.'s lap, and the right hand continues along in its sadly inept way.

This and many other experiments with split-brain patients have led researchers to believe it is wrong to think of the right hemisphere as always cognitively inferior to the left (Sperry, 1982). It is more accurate to say that each has some specialized abilities at which it excels. For the left hemisphere these skills include the perception of words, letters, and speech-related sounds, and the performance of

TABLE 3.1   Principles of Cerebral Asymmetry*

Function	Left Hemisphere	Right Hemisphere
Visual system	Letters, words	Complex geometric patterns Faces
Auditory system	Language-related sounds	Nonlanguage environmental sounds Music
Somatosensory system	?	Tactual recognition of complex patterns Braille
Movement	Complex voluntary movement	?
Memory	Verbal memory	Visual memory
Language	Speech Reading Writing Arithmetic	
Spatial processes		Geometry Sense of direction Mental rotation of shapes

*Summary of data on cerebral lateralization. Functions of the respective hemispheres
that are predominantly mediated by one hemisphere in right-handed people.
Source: Kolb and Whishaw, 1990.

mathematical calculations. For the right hemisphere
they include the perception of complex geometric
patterns, human faces, and nonlinguistic sounds, as
well as the senses of direction and location in
space. Table 3.1 summarizes these and other functions believed to be the specialties of one or the
other hemisphere.

CRITICISMS, ALTERNATIVES, AND FURTHER RESEARCH

This conclusion raised some fascinating questions
about the workings of a normal brain, one in which
the corpus callosum is intact and functioning. Does
the right side of a normal brain perform largely
visual-spatial tasks, like putting together a geometric pattern or finding one's way in a new neighborhood? What about the left hemisphere in a normal
brain? Is it responsible largely for verbal tasks, such
as reading, writing, and speaking? Is it the side of
the brain we primarily rely on to solve an arithmetic problem or to engage in analytical reasoning?
The only way to answer such questions is to explore the actual workings of a normal human brain
while it is in the process of doing different kinds of
tasks. Researchers quickly put their imaginations to
work devising ways that such explorations could be
carried out.

One technique involves mapping the blood
flow in a person's brain, for blood carries the raw
materials that neurons need to carry out their work.
Some researchers have found that blood flow to the
left hemisphere is indeed greater than blood flow to
the right when a person is engaged in a verbal task.
Conversely, when a person is engaged in a visual
perception task (such as trying to identify pictures
that are drawn with very few lines), blood flow to
the right hemisphere is greater than to the left (Gur
and Reivich, 1980; Risberg et al., 1975). Such
findings suggest that the two sides of the brain are
unequally involved in some behaviors.

Other psychologists believe that additional evidence comes from the study of lateral eye movements. These are the small side-to-side glances that
the eyes often make, such as glancing upward and
to the left or right when answering a question.
Some researchers speculate that the direction of
these eye movements is a measure of activity in the
opposite side of the brain. Thus, a glance to the left
is said to indicate activation of the right hemisphere, while a glance to the right is said to show
activation of the left hemisphere. A number of studies in which people answer questions while their
lateral eye movements are recorded have indeed
found that questions requiring verbal or mathemati-

Research findings about the dominance of the left and right brain hemispheres in different areas have created a popular debate about hemisphere superiority that is largely pointless. After all, there seems little reason to try to decide whether artistic ability is "better" than mathematical aptitude.

cal analysis tend to elicit rightward glances, while those involving visual-spatial skills tend to elicit eye movements to the left (e.g., Galin and Ornstein, 1974). This pattern, however, is far from totally consistent, and we do not yet even know if lateral eye movements are a valid measure of cerebral hemisphere activity (Beaumont et al., 1984). Nevertheless, the possibilities are intriguing.

PATTERNS AND CONCLUSIONS

What can we conclude from all this data about the two sides of the brain? Some psychologists have proposed very speculative theories. For instance, psychologist Robert Ornstein has argued that coexisting in each of us may be two distinct minds: the left logical and analytical, the right intuitive and artistic (Ornstein, 1977). The impression that the mind is unitary, Ornstein says, may simply be an illusion produced by constant and instantaneous communication between the hemispheres. Others have wondered if there might not be "right-brained" and "left-brained" people, individuals who tend to depend on one side of the brain more than the other. One art teacher has written a best-selling book which purports to tell students how to suppress the analytical left hemisphere when drawing and "turn on" the more artistic right hemisphere instead (Edwards, 1979). There are now even workshops for corporate executives which claim to teach how to tap the underused potential of the supposedly creative right side of the brain (McKean, 1985).

Most psychologists are dismayed by such popularized programs. They see them as stemming from misinterpretations of scientific data—efforts to use research findings in ways that are unwarranted. Some who work in this field have tried to set the record straight (e.g., Levy, 1985). First, they stress that although the two hemispheres do have some different specialized functions, the idea that each has its own general style of thinking is still only speculation. This hypothesis is far from proven by the available scientific facts. Second, popular writers tend to greatly exaggerate left brain/right brain differences. Human beings seem to vary significantly in the extent to which their brain functions are lateralized (Hellige et al., 1988). In some people such lateralization is not great at all. And even in those with marked asymmetry between the two cerebral hemispheres, this asymmetry is not *the* major principle of brain organization. As far as the control of different behaviors is concerned, the particular site within the brain is just as important as, if not more important than, the side involved (Kolb and Whishaw, 1990). Thus, although the left frontal lobe contains Broca's area while the right frontal lobe does not, the two frontal lobes have far more in common, functionally speaking, than either does with any of the other regions of its own hemisphere.

Finally, it is important to realize that the various sides and regions of the brain *always* cooperate with one another. No one part ever carries out its work alone. Although opposite sides of the brain and specific areas within each side are more prominently involved in some tasks than in others, human thought and behavior are made possible by activation of many quite widely distributed brain regions (Kinsbourne, 1982; Springer and Deutsch, 1989). This is clearly revealed in studies of blood flow within the brain. They consistently show the involvement of *both* hemispheres in any activity a person may do (Lassen et al., 1978; Posner et al., 1988). Thus, when someone is reading or speaking, behaviors often labeled left-hemisphere activities, blood-flow studies show that the right hemisphere is intimately involved as well. And it is not just that the left brain is feeding the right brain information as the left performs the task alone. In some cases, input from the right brain is essential for optimal performance of the left, and vice versa (Gazzaniga, 1989). The brain, in short, requires integration of activities in order to perform its multifaceted functions.

TREATING BRAIN DISORDERS

He had been a successful writer for more than 40 years, celebrated for his ability to remember the details of a complex story virtually without using notes. But . . . at age 68, he began to experience difficulty in finding the right words to express himself, and he frequently appeared to lose the thread of his thoughts. Within months, he couldn't remember his schedule for the day. In a few years, he couldn't even remember if he had just eaten. (Fischman, 1984, p. 27)

This man was diagnosed as having Alzheimer's disease, a degenerative brain disorder in which memory and other cognitive functions steadily deteriorate, until eventually, performing even the simplest task is impossible. Alzheimer's disease, which is most common among the elderly, is just one of the neurological problems we have touched on in this chapter. Others include Parkinson's disease, multiple sclerosis, Huntington's chorea, severely damaging strokes, and extensive lesions due to neurosurgery. What hope does modern neuroscience hold for people who suffer such disorders? Research is helping to develop three different kinds of treatment: drug therapies, tissue implants, and therapies that involve relearning.

DRUG TREATMENTS

A major breakthrough in the treatment of Parkinson's disease emerged from the finding that this disorder is linked to a deficiency of the neurotransmitter dopamine. Parkinson's, as we noted earlier, is characterized by severe muscular rigidity, uncontrollable tremors and other involuntary movements, as well as by difficulty walking and maintaining a normal posture. We now know that people with Parkinson's disease have massive degeneration in an area of the midbrain called the substantia nigra. Cell bodies located in the substantia nigra normally send dopamine-releasing axons into a group of forebrain nuclei (the basal ganglia) which are involved in movement. In Parkinson's patients, 80 to 90 percent of these axons no longer function. You might think that Parkinson's could be treated simply with doses of dopamine, but this approach does not work. Dopamine molecules are too large to cross the membrane barrier that separates brain tissue from the bloodstream. So instead, doctors give Parkinson's patients large doses of L-DOPA, a critical building block of dopamine. L-DOPA *can* diffuse from the blood into the brain, and has had good results in reducing symptoms of the disorder. But L-DOPA is not a cure for Parkinson's. It cannot halt the slow and steady progress of the disorder, and it can have negative side effects, so doses must be monitored closely. Over years the body may also become unresponsive to L-DOPA. For these reasons, researchers are currently testing other drug treatments for Parkinson's disease (McDonald, 1988).

In dealing with more complex brain disorders, the problems with drug treatments become multiplied. For instance, it was once thought that administering the substance choline to people with Alzheimer's disease would help to overcome their memory losses. This is because choline is a building block of acetylcholine, a neurotransmitter found to be deficient in Alzheimer's patients. But choline therapy for Alzheimer's has proved disappointing (Bylinsky, 1986). Why this failure when L-DOPA has worked so well for Parkinson's disease? One reason is our still limited knowledge about the precise chemicals needed to increase or decrease the supplies of many neurotransmitters in the brain. Another reason is that acetylcholine deficits, it now appears, are just one part of a complex problem in Alzheimer's disease. For example, Alzheimer's is also characterized by **senile plaques,** insoluble clumps consisting of a certain brain protein surrounded by degenerating axon terminals and glial cells. Some researchers think that abnormal accumulation of this protein may come first, followed by plaque formation, cell death, and loss of acetylcholine. Alternatively, cell degeneration may precede accumulation of the protein and perhaps be its major cause (Marx, 1989). Until scientists know more about how Alzheimer's develops, they will not know what kind of drug treatment will be most effective.

But despite such obstacles, drug research remains a very active area in the fight against brain disorders. For instance, scientists are now exploring the potential use of a body chemical called nerve growth factor (NGF) to treat Alzheimer's disease. NGF seems to support the functioning of neurons that normally degenerate in this disorder (Phelps et al., in press). Researchers must be cautious with NGF, however, for it may inadvertently trigger more build-up of the protein involved in the formation of senile plaques (Marx, 1989). It remains to be seen how many people may ultimately be helped by this line of research.

TISSUE IMPLANTS

An equally active area of research is tissue implants—taking nervous system tissue from a donor source and grafting it into the brain of someone with a brain disorder (Fine, 1986). Some grafts seem able to serve as bridges for axons to grow across. In one study, for instance, researchers cut fibers that normally supply a rat's upper hippocampus with acetylcholine (Kromer et al., 1981). They then transplanted a piece of hippocampus from the brain of a rat embryo into the gap made by the cut. Nerve fibers grew through the graft and into the hippocampus. Apparently, the embryonic tissue enabled the damaged neurons to undergo new growth, something that mature neurons of the central nervous system cannot normally do.

Brain grafts may not only be able to serve as bridges for existing axons to grow through, they may also be able to serve as sources of completely new and functional cells. This possibility made headlines several years ago when a team of Mexican neurosurgeons announced that they had successfully implanted dopamine-producing cells (taken from adrenal gland tissue) into the brains of patients in advanced stages of Parkinson's disease (Madrazo et al., 1987). Videotapes showed amazing before-and-after pictures. Patients who had been so impaired they could not talk, walk, or even hold a glass of water were seen a few weeks after their operations walking, talking, eating unassisted, even mowing their lawns and playing soccer (McDonald, 1988).

The excitement that a cure for Parkinson's had been found was short-lived, however. When other doctors tried the same procedure on their own severe Parkinson's patients, the results were often disappointing. Only some of the patients were significantly helped by the procedure, and never to the extent that their impairments were eliminated completely. It now appears that the transplanted adrenal gland tissue does not really supply the basal ganglia with dopamine after all. Instead, something in those transplanted cells seems to be capable of sometimes promoting limited recovery of the damaged neurons in the substantia nigra (McDonald, 1988). Researchers are now trying to modify their transplant procedures in order to get a new source of dopamine into the critical brain region of Parkinson's patients.

THERAPIES THAT INVOLVE RELEARNING

Other researchers are trying treatment methods that do not involve manipulating damaged brain circuits. Instead, these therapies involve attempts to use intact pathways in the brain to compensate for those that have been injured or destroyed. In one study, for example, researchers attempted to teach memory-impaired patients how to perform simple tasks on a computer (Glisky et al., 1986). Many repetitions of the training were needed before the patients were able to perform the tasks without error. The most severely impaired of the group were unable to remember the training sessions in which they

learned the procedures. Nevertheless, they gradually mastered the correct series of responses. How could they do this if they could not recall ever having worked at a computer before?

One possibility is that they mastered the procedures *not* by means of their damaged pathways for conscious learning and remembering. Rather, mastery may have taken place by means of brain circuits that operate more or less automatically, without much conscious awareness. In Chapter 7 we will say more about these brain circuits and the kinds of procedural information that is normally processed through them. The point for now is that brain damage may sometimes be overcome by relearning skills through the use of *un*injured parts of the brain. People who manage to make unexpected recovery from severe traumas to the brain are probably doing so through this kind of learned "rerouting" of information.

SUMMARY

1. The human nervous system, an intricate communication network that radiates throughout the body, consists of billions of interconnected, highly specialized cells. The most fundamental of these cells are **neurons,** which control and coordinate all of human behavior. Most of the body's neurons are found in the **central nervous system (CNS),** which consists of the brain and spinal cord. Branching out from the central nervous system to all parts of the body is the **peripheral nervous system.** Its two divisions, the **somatic nervous system** and the **autonomic nervous system,** are related to control of the skeletal muscles and the internal organs, respectively. The autonomic system can be further subdivided into the **sympathetic** and **parasympathetic nervous systems.** The first is involved in mobilizing the body's resources, while the second is involved in conserving them.

2. Most neurons have three structural components: the **cell body,** which contains the cell's life-support systems; the relatively short **dendrites,** along which impulses travel to the cell body; and a long **axon,** along which impulses travel away from the cell to muscle fibers, glandular cells, or other neurons. The simplest set of neural connections is a **reflex arc,** in which a sensory input is linked to a motor response via the spinal cord.

3. Nerve impulses are transmitted by means of an electrochemical process. The electrical part of this process involves a sudden change in the relative electrical charge across a neuron's membrane. In the resting state, the inside of the membrane is negatively charged relative to the outside. Then, when the cell is stimulated to a threshold level, this condition is abruptly reversed, giving rise to an **action potential,** which rapidly travels the length of the axon.

4. Every axon is physically separated from adjacent cells by a gap called a **synapse.** When an action potential reaches the end of an axon, a chemical called a **neurotransmitter** is released from the axon terminal and diffuses across the synapse to activate receptor sites on adjacent cells. Depending on the chemistry of the neurotransmitter and the nature of the receptor sites, the message conveyed may be excitatory or inhibitory. Scientists are compiling an ever-growing list of neurotransmitters, each of which acts in complex ways in different parts of the nervous system.

5. The body's second communications network, which closely interacts with the nervous system, is the **endocrine system.** Its messengers are chemicals called **hormones,** which circulate in the bloodstream and have their effects on specific **target organs.** The endocrine system affects physical growth, metabolism, re-

productive functioning, and other physiological processes.

6. The brain is the body's master control center because it ultimately regulates all behavior. It consists of three overlapping regions, the **hindbrain,** the **midbrain,** and the **forebrain,** each representing a consecutive stage in the brain's evolution. The process by which a brain grows, neuron by neuron and synapse by synapse, has been studied extensively. Axons and dendrites seem to find their ways to the correct locations by reading chemical markers on other cells. The initial synapses that form are not necessarily permanent. Instead, they are often open to change as cells respond to environmental stimulation and compete with one another for positioning. Such **plasticity** allows an animal's neural connections to be fine-tuned in early stages of development.

7. Researchers have developed a variety of techniques to study the relationships between the brain and behavior. Some have observed brain-damaged people in order to link injury in a certain brain region to a particular behavioral deficit. Electrical or chemical stimulation has also helped to clarify the role of certain brain areas in specific feelings and actions. So has the technique of making brain lesions in experimental animals by surgically destroying a small area of brain tissue. Scientists employ sophisticated electronic equipment to monitor the brain's electrical activity. They are also using various labeling techniques to map the brain's numerous pathways.

8. The **central core** of the adult human brain is concerned with functions basic to survival, such as sleeping, waking, respiration, and feeding. Its major areas include the **hindbrain** (consisting of the **medulla,** the **pons,** the **reticular formation,** and the **cerebellum**), the **midbrain,** and the **thalamus** and **hypothalamus.** Above the central core lies the **forebrain** or **cerebral hemispheres,** the innermost borders of which are marked by the **limbic system.** The limbic system is involved in the regulation of behaviors that satisfy basic emotional and motivational needs, such as fighting, fleeing, and mating. Among its highly interrelated structures are the **hippocampus,** the **amygdala,** and the **septal area.** The outmost layer of tissue covering the cerebral hemispheres is called the **cortex.** It is intimately involved in the processes of learning, speech, reasoning, and memory.

9. **Localization of function** is a basic principle of brain organization, but the activities of localized regions are always integrated into larger neural networks. One area where the themes of localization and integration can be seen quite clearly is in the study of the two sides of the brain. Each cerebral hemisphere has some specialized functions, which means that for certain tasks one hemisphere may tend to be more active than the other. However, in any human behavior both hemispheres are always involved.

10. Researchers are trying to apply their knowledge of the brain to treat brain disorders. Areas currently under investigation include drug treatments, tissue transplants, and therapies that involve relearning information using uninjured neural pathways. Many of these treatments are still experimental, but there is reason for optimism concerning our ability to help brain-damaged people.

SUGGESTED READINGS

Bishop, J. E., and Waldholz, M. (1990). *Genome: The story of the most astonishing scientific adventure of our time—the attempt to map all genes in the human body.* New York: Touchstone/Simon & Schuster. This book highlights current research on genetic defects that cause such illnessess as Huntington's disease and muscular dystrophy. The authors focus on advances made in this area and examine ethical issues as well.

Klawans, H. L. (1990). *Newton's madness: Further tales of clinical neurology.* New York: Harper & Row. This collection of case studies of patients with neurological disorders is fascinating and informative. It offers personal accounts of twenty-two individuals with detailed descriptions of diagnosis and treatment.

Kolb, B., and Whishaw, I.Q. (1990). *Fundamentals of human neuropsychology* (3rd ed.). New York: Freeman, 1990. An excellent, and up-to-date account of research on the human brain, including much information on brain disorders.

Sacks, O. (1985). *The man who mistook his wife for a hat.* New York: Summit. A bestselling book that gives case studies of some fascinating brain disorders. The author is a practicing neurologist and a master storyteller.

Springer, S. P., and Deutsch, G. (1989). *Left brain, right brain* (3rd ed.). San Francisco: Freeman. A very interesting discussion of 100 years of research into the hemispheric differences in humans and other animals. The authors present findings on asymmetries in brain-damaged, split-brain, and normal subjects, and explore the implications for human behavior.

CHAPTER 4

SENSATION AND PERCEPTION

Imagine yourself walking to class on a bright autumn morning. As you hurry along, light waves from the sun reflect off objects and bombard your eyes. Pulses of air molecules, set in motion when anything moves or vibrates, constantly impinge upon your ears. Vaporized molecules from many different substances drift through the air around you, assailing the sensitive membranes of your nose. With so many sensations reaching you at once, why aren't you overwhelmed by them? The answer is that your brain interprets the sensations you receive, imposing order and meaning on them. As a result, you do not see a kaleidoscope of shapes and colors, but rather the trees, buildings, roads, and people that make up your college campus. You do not hear a cacophony of noises, but rather the hum of cars, the chatter of voices, and the rustle of fallen leaves. In short, you perceive a structured world.

Sensation and perception are so important because they are the starting points for all your other psychological processes. They supply the data you use for learning and remembering, for thinking and problem solving, for communicating with others, for experiencing emotions, and for being aware of yourself. Without access to the environment through sensation and perception, you would be like a person in a coma, devoid of any thoughts or feelings.

Psychologists have traditionally differentiated between sensation and perception. **Sensation** is the process whereby stimulation of receptor cells (in the eyes, ears, nose, mouth, and surface of the skin) sends nerve impulses to the brain, where they register as a touch, a sound, a taste, a splash of color, and so forth. **Perception,** in contrast, is the process whereby the brain interprets sensations, giving them order and meaning. Thus, hearing sounds and seeing colors may be largely sensory processes, but following a melody and detecting depth in a two-dimensional picture are largely perceptual ones. We say *largely* because in everyday life it is almost impossible to separate sensation from perception. As soon as the brain receives sensations, it automatically interprets or perceives them, and without sensations of some kind, perception could not occur. This is why some contemporary psychologists think that the distinction between sensation and perception is not as useful as it was once considered. Both processes, they argue, are part of a single information-processing system.

One fact that has emerged from the study of sensation and perception is that animal species differ in their views of the world. Consider sound detection

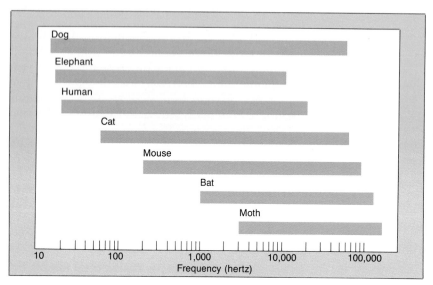

FIGURE 4.1 **A comparison of the range of sound frequencies audible to various species.** (*Hefner and Hefner, 1983.*)

(Figure 4.1). Many animals can hear sounds that are too high pitched or low pitched for humans to detect. A dog's range of hearing is substantially greater than ours, which is why it can hear a very-high-pitched whistle that many people cannot hear at all. Bats are true virtuosos at high-pitched sound detection. A bat sends out a shrill stream of ultrasonic cries, listens for the echoes bouncing off surrounding objects, and so navigates as it flies. But even though a flying bat is constantly emitting powerful noises, it seems soundless to us because the human ear is tuned too low to detect most of its cries. Interestingly, from a bat's perspective we humans also appear mute, for the sounds we normally make are just below the pitch level that stimulates a bat's hearing.

Sensory and perceptual capabilities also vary among members of the same species. Here is an example in taste detection. We all know that some people like their coffee black, while others add a great deal of cream and sugar. Although a number of factors may contribute to these different taste preferences, most people who use lots of cream and sugar find the taste of black coffee very bitter. How, they wonder, could anyone drink such bitter-tasting stuff? One answer is that the black-coffee drinkers do not perceive coffee as being particularly bitter. This may be due to inherited differences in their taste receptors, which make them less sensitive to coffee's bitter flavor (Bartoshuk, 1974). One important cause of sensory-perceptual differences, then, is variation in how sensory-perceptual systems are structured.

Another cause of differences in sensory-perceptual experiences is that each person brings to the task of "reading" the world a somewhat different set of knowledge, beliefs, and expectations. These higher-order processes can work downward to shape how we perceive, attend to, and interpret incoming sensations. Consider, for instance, the fact that postsurgery patients are much more likely to request painkilling drugs than are soldiers who are severely wounded in battle (Beecher, 1959; Fordyce, 1988). Apparently, the postsurgery patients, lying in their comfortable hospital beds, actually suffer *more* from their pain than men whose bodies have been torn apart by bullets, grenades, and mortars. Why? Part of the answer is a difference in mental outlook. To postsurgery patients, severe pain is an upsetting by-product of the cures they are undergoing; it has no positive meaning at all. To wounded soldiers, in contrast, severe pain is a ticket to evacuation, where they will be safe from enemy fire. For soldiers, in other words, pain means relief from combat, which helps explain why it causes them less distress than it would in other circumstances.

Later in this chapter we will discuss more examples of how higher cognitive processes work downward to influence perception. The main point to remember for now is that processing information about the world is not just a one-way street. In addition to information flowing upward from your sense organs to your brain (called **"bottom-up"** or **data-driven processing**), knowledge stored in your

Cultural background can have a powerful effect on our sensory perceptions. Most Americans would enjoy a taste of these "sausages"—but would be revolted when told that they're actually grubs (insect larvae considered delicacies in other parts of the world, including Australia, as here).

brain exerts a force downward, causing you to perceive things partly according to what you believe and expect (called **"top-down"** or **conceptually driven processing**). Your perceptions, in short, are the product of the particular sensory systems you possess, coupled with your beliefs and expectations about the world. As a way of stressing this important point, we begin this chapter by considering *psychophysics*, the study of the relationship between physical stimuli and the subjective experiences these stimuli create (Luce and Krumhansl, 1988).

STIMULI, SENSATIONS, AND PERCEPTIONS

If a tree falls in a forest where no one is there to hear, does it nevertheless make a sound? This question is perplexing at first because it clouds the distinction between a physical stimulus (sound waves produced by a falling tree) and a subjective sensation (hearing a crash). The two, of course, are not synonymous. A **stimulus** (pl., **stimuli**) is any form of energy (sound waves, light waves, heat, pressure) to which an organism is capable of responding. A sensation is a response to that energy by a sensory system. Stimuli and sensations, then, have a cause-and-effect relationship.

Most sensory systems respond to differences in both the quality and the quantity of stimuli. The *quality* of a stimulus refers to the kind of sensation it produces. Color is a quality related to visual stimulation; musical pitch is a quality related to auditory stimulation. *Quantity*, in contrast, refers to the amount of stimulation present. Thus, brightness represents the perceived quantity of light and loudness the perceived quantity of sound.

Remember, though, that such characteristics as color, brightness, pitch, and loudness are ways in which a person *experiences* a stimulus. They are not necessarily completely accurate reflections of the physical properties of a stimulus. That is why psychologists have extensively studied the relationship between stimuli and sensations. In doing so, they have examined several important processes. Among them are stimulus detection (the point at which we perceive very faint stimuli) and stimulus discrimination (the ability to differentiate between two similar stimuli).

STIMULUS DETECTION

How much light must be present before a person sees it? How much pressure must be applied to the skin before a person feels it? The answers to such questions involve the concept of **sensory threshold,** the minimum stimulus needed for a person to detect it.

You might think that for every stimulus there is some absolute level of intensity above which a person will *always* detect that stimulus and below which he or she will *never* detect it. This, however, is not the case. Suppose you sit in a dark room and watch for light beams of different intensities to be projected onto a wall. There will indeed be extremely dim lights that you will never report seeing, and other, brighter lights that you will always be able to see. But between these two categories will be a range of intensities for which the likelihood of seeing the light gradually changes from low to high. How, then, should we define your threshold for light? The decision must be an arbitrary one. Many researchers simply take the midpoint and define the threshold as the lowest intensity of light that you can see 50 percent of the time.

The ability to hear another person's voice above the background noise of a party depends on a number of factors, including motivation—the degree of desire to hear what the other person is saying.

But why is there a range of intensities (for light or any other stimulus) that sometimes you detect and sometimes you do not? The answer is that detecting a stimulus is not just a matter of how sensitive your sensory systems are. A number of other factors can substantially restrict or enhance the ability to perceive something.

One of these factors is the existence of competing stimuli, often referred to as background **noise** (Cohn and Lasley, 1986). You can probably think of many occasions when auditory noise impaired your ability to detect a particular sound—perhaps when you tried to hear what someone was saying at a very loud party. But "noise" can affect other senses as well. For example, an inexperienced person viewing a radar screen usually has great difficulty distinguishing the blips made by an airplane from those made by stormy weather, a form of visual noise. In much the same way, you would be hard-pressed to smell the fragrance of a delicate flower in a smoke-filled room. And noise need not always arise from external sources. Some of the cells in our sensory systems produce a form of noise due to their own spontaneous activities (Hudspeth, 1985). You can prove this to yourself by standing in a totally lightless room (a windowless basement or closet works well). Surprisingly, you do not see just blackness. Instead, you see a kind of gray mist, broken at times by what look like tiny, pinpoint

flashes of light. These sensations are caused by random activity of cells in your visual system. When such internal noise competes with the processing of very faint external stimuli, it is often hard to tell whether the external stimuli are really there or not.

Motivation can also affect detection of a stimulus. Sometimes people have reason to set very strict criteria for saying that they perceive something. (A *criterion* is simply the basis on which a person decides to say "yes," a faint stimulus is present, or "no," it is not.) Consider a man who has called the police about a prowler several nights in a row, with each report turning out to be a false alarm. The man will be very cautious in deciding that he hears a prowler again. He will, in short, set a strict criterion for detecting suspicious sounds in the night, because the embarrassment of another error would be very great. Conversely, there are times when people are motivated to set a very liberal criterion for stimulus detection. A radiologist, for instance, may see a tiny tumor on the X ray of a person who later turns out to be tumor-free. Here the radiologist is strongly motivated to perceive even the faintest possible signs of cancer because the patient's survival is at stake.

Expectations, too, affect a person's criteria for reporting a faint or ambiguous stimulus. If you often hear your car make a slight rattling noise, you are apt to say quite readily that you hear the noise again. If, on the other hand, you do not expect your car to make unusual noises, your criterion for saying that you hear one is likely to be much stricter.

Many factors, then, affect the ability to detect a stimulus. Psychologists have tried to take these various factors into account with **signal detection theory.** According to signal detection theory, some of these influences have to do with the stimulus itself (How intense is it? How muffled by background noise?), while others have to do with the person's sensory system (Is the system sensitive, or is it somehow impaired?). Equally important are factors that affect the criterion the person uses in deciding whether to ignore faint or ambiguous stimuli. (Does the person *expect* the stimulus to occur? Are rewards or punishments affecting the motivation to detect things?) Signal detection theory stresses that the detection of any stimulus varies with these factors. That is why two people with the same physical sensitivity may nevertheless perform quite differently on a stimulus detection task.

You will need three quarters, two envelopes, and your shoes. Take one quarter and put it in an envelope and put the remaining two quarters in the other. If you now gently lift each envelope and put it down (use the same hand), it is quite easy to distinguish the heavier envelope. Now insert one envelope into one of your shoes and the other envelope into your second shoe, and lift them one at a time. The weight difference should be almost imperceptible.

FIGURE 4.2 Weber's law. A demonstration for the perception of heaviness. Note that changes in an intense stimulus must be large before they can be noticed, while small changes in a weaker stimulus are easily distinguished. (*From Coren, Porac, and Ward, 1979, p. 2.*)

After a few minutes of exposure to the strong odors of a cheese shop, the aromas become much less noticeable as a result of sensory adaptation.

STIMULUS DISCRIMINATION

In addition to their interest in stimulus detection, psychologists are also interested in people's ability to notice a difference or change in stimulation—that is, to discriminate among stimuli. Research in this area began in the mid-nineteenth century, when Ernst Weber discovered that although people can perceive small changes in weak stimuli, they notice only large changes in strong stimuli. You can demonstrate this to yourself by following the instructions in Figure 4.2. After further study, Weber's brother-in-law, Gustav Fechner, specified the nature of this relationship more precisely (Fechner, 1860). Fechner noted that the amount by which a stimulus must be increased to produce a **just noticeable difference** tends to be a constant proportion of the initial stimulus intensity. In honor of his brother-in-law, Fechner called this **Weber's law.**

The proportional increase in an initial stimulus that is needed to create a just noticeable difference varies with the kind of stimulus. For weight, the proportion is 2 percent. This means that the average person will just notice a difference when a single pound is added to a backpack initially weighing 50 pounds (50 × 0.02 = 1); but 2 pounds must be added to a backpack weighing 100 pounds (100 × 0.02 = 2) in order for a difference to be detected. (In both cases the *proportional* increase remains constant.) The proportions for some other sensations are 7.9 percent for brightness, 4.8 percent for loudness, and 1.3 percent

for electric shock (Teghtsoonian, 1971). Although Weber's law does not hold true for very weak or very strong stimuli, it is quite accurate for stimulus intensities in a broad middle range. This makes it a useful way of summarizing our general ability to discriminate among stimuli.

SENSORY ADAPTATION

All sensory systems display **sensory adaptation**— reduced ability to provide information after prolonged, constant stimulation. When you enter a room with a distinctive odor, the smell is very noticeable at first, but soon it seems to fade. This decline in sensory sensitivity is due to adaptation. Some senses, such as smell and touch, adapt quite quickly; others, such as pain, adapt very slowly. All, however, do adapt.

Sensory adaptation occurs because the sense receptors in your body are designed to be maximally sensitive to *changes* in stimulation. This makes sense. You do not need to be constantly reminded, for example, that your shoes are securely on your feet. Thus, when you stimulate the touch receptors in your skin by putting on a shoe, and that pressure is held constant, the rate at which nerve impulses are generated steadily declines. Such adaptation also occurs in the visual receptors of your eyes. In fact, if you were truly able to stare at something, it would gradually disappear! Fortunately, you cannot lock your gaze onto a single point. Whenever you try to do so, your eyes involuntarily move very tiny amounts at a rapid rate, thus shifting the incoming light waves to different visual receptor cells. These involuntary movements prevent any single group of cells from adapting so much to an unchanging stimulus that vision fades away.

Because sensory adaptation affects sensitivity to stimuli, it can change the sensation produced by any given amount of stimulation. You can experience this effect with a simple procedure. Place one hand in ice-cold water and the other in bearably hot water. After your hands have adapted to these two temperatures, plunge them into a bucket of warm water. What temperature does this water feel? Oddly, it feels both hot (to the hand that was in cold water) and cold (to the hand that was in hot water), even though you know it is neither.

This example reinforces an important point raised at the beginning of this chapter: the way we view the world is not always an accurate reflection of the physical stimuli that exist there. Note, however, that distortions in perception are not necessarily caused by abnormal sensory systems, as many people assume. They are frequently caused by using normal sensory systems in unusual situations. As such, they provide important clues to the ways the senses normally work. We will say more about this later when we explore visual illusions.

THE HUMAN SENSES

Your eyes, ears, nose, tongue, and skin are the organs that link you to the outside world via the familiar senses of vision, hearing, smell, taste, and touch. But you possess considerably more senses than just these basic five. Your skin alone contains receptors for at least five sensations, and an organ in your inner ear gives you a sense of balance and equilibrium. In addition, sensory systems related to muscles and joints make you aware of your body position and movements, and many other internal receptors supply your brain with vital information about body temperature and blood chemistry. Although the following discussion is largely restricted to the classic five senses, those omitted are no less important to normal human functioning.

VISION

Vision is the richest of the human senses. Your eyes receive light from surrounding objects and translate it into nerve impulses that travel to your brain. When they reach their destination, you experience the vast array of shapes, colors, textures, and movements that make up your visual world. To understand how this remarkable system works, you must first know something about the basic stimulus for vision—light.

THE NATURE OF LIGHT

Light is a form of electromagnetic energy. Several hundred years ago, Sir Isaac Newton (1642–1727) proposed that light behaves as if it were a stream of tiny particles. Modern physicists call these subatomic particles of light radiation **photons.** An important characteristic of light is that it travels in wavelike patterns rather than in straight lines. Different streams of light have somewhat different **wavelengths**—that is, different distances between the crest of one wave and the crest of the next, as illustrated in Figure 4.3. These varying wavelengths of light (usually measured in billionths of a meter, or nanometers) largely determine the colors we see. The brightness of any color is determined mainly by the **intensity** of light—that is, by how densely the photons in the light wave are packed.

Figure 4.3 shows that the light energy to which our eyes are sensitive is just one small part of the total electromagnetic spectrum. This spectrum also includes longer wavelengths, such as radio waves and infrared waves, as well as shorter wavelengths, such as ultraviolet rays, X rays, and gamma rays. If our eyes were structured a little differently, we might see some parts of the electromagnetic spectrum that are now invisible to us. For instance, people who have had the lenses in their eyes removed because they have become clouded by cataracts see slightly more ultraviolet light than other people do, because the eyes' lenses absorb a great deal of ultraviolet radiation.

THE STRUCTURE OF THE EYE

Your visual system begins with your eyes, through which light enters. The structure of the human eye is shown in Figure 4.4. Light passes first

FIGURE 4.3   The spectrum of electromagnetic energy. Electromagnetic energy comes to us in varying wavelengths. Each step on the scale (*top*) corresponds to a tenfold increase in the wavelength of the electromagnetic radiation. The very short wavelengths at the *left* of the scale and the very long ones at the *right* are not visible as light. The visible spectrum—the small region to which the human eye is sensitive—is shown on an expanded scale with the wavelengths measured in nanometers (one-billionth of a meter).

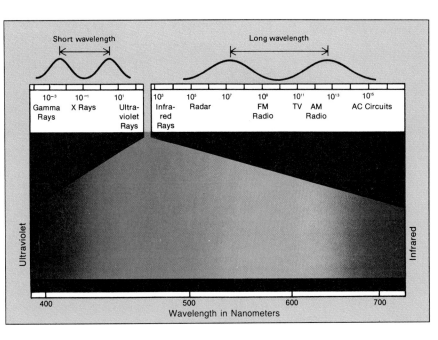

through a tough, transparent "window," called the **cornea,** which covers the front of the eyeball. Because the cornea is deeply curved, it bends the rays of incoming light and helps to focus them. Behind the cornea is a pouch of liquid that helps maintain the cornea's rounded shape. To its rear lies the **iris,** a ring of pigmented tissue that gives the eye its color. Contraction and relaxation of muscle fibers in the iris close and open the **pupil,** the opening in the center of the eye, which appears black. In this way the amount of light entering the eye is regulated. You can observe the action of your own iris by turning on a bright bulb in a dimly lit room and watching your pupil in a mirror. It will rapidly contract to a very small hole, thus reducing the amount of light that can pass through the pupil to the lens behind it. The **lens** is a transparent, elastic structure that allows the eye to adjust its focus in accordance with an object's distance. This adjustment is accomplished by **ciliary muscles,** which change the shape of the lens, flattening it to focus on more distant objects and allowing it to become more spherical to focus on near objects. The incoming light is then projected through the liquid that fills the center of the eyeball and onto the **retina,** the eye's light-sensitive inner surface.

You can easily see the close relationship between the eye's structure and function by considering the causes of near-sightedness and far-sightedness. In younger people these vision defects are typically due to a gradual misshaping of the eyeball. With far-sightedness the eyeball becomes shorter from pupil to retina, causing light waves to strike the retina before they completely converge and focus. With near-sightedness the opposite happens: The eyeball becomes elongated, causing light waves to converge and focus before reaching the retina. This means that by the time light finally strikes the retina, it is out of focus again.

HOW LIGHT BECOMES SIGHT

After light strikes the retina, how is it transformed into visual experiences? The answer lies in a network of millions of nerve cells. The outermost layer of each retina contains two types of receptors, the **rods** and the **cones,** so named because of their characteristic shapes. Rods are long, thin cells, while cones are more bulbous, tapering nearly to a point at one end. Rods and cones absorb light energy, and when they do they generate small electrical signals.

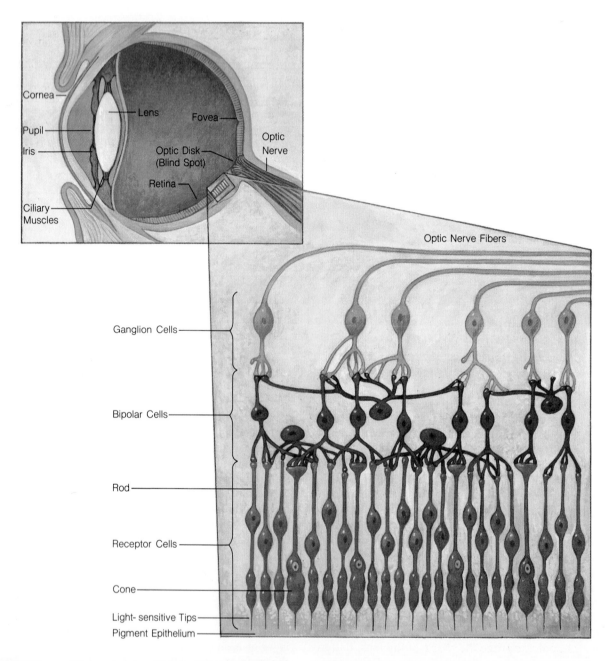

FIGURE 4.4   The structure of the human eye and the retina. Incoming light passes through the cornea, pupil, and lens, and hits the retina. As the *inset* shows, light filters through several layers of retinal cells before hitting the receptor cells (rods and cones), located at the back of the eyeball and pointed away from the incoming light. The rods and cones register the presence of light and pass an electrical impulse back to the adjacent bipolar cells. They relay the impulse to the ganglion cells. The axons of the ganglion cells form the fibers of the optic nerve, which transmits the impulses received to the brain.

The strength of these signals is determined by the amount of light absorbed. As Figure 4.4 shows, the receptor cells then stimulate the neighboring **bipolar cells,** which in turn stimulate the neighboring **ganglion cells.** The ganglion cells form the fibers of the **optic nerve,** which carries visual information from the eye to the brain.

The Role of Receptor Cells   As the starting point in this nerve network leading to the brain, the receptors in the retina—the rods and the cones—play a vital role. So let us examine them in some detail before turning to the vision-related areas of the brain. Rods and cones each serve a different visual function. Rods are involved in nighttime or dim-light vision, while cones are involved in daytime or bright-light vision. Cones are also the primary mechanism for color vision. Thus, you see little color by moonlight because there is not enough light to stimulate your cones; but you can see shades of light and dark because moonlight *is* adequate to stimulate your rods. A rod, in fact, is capable of responding to just a single photon of light (O'Brien, 1982).

Cones are far less numerous than rods are (there are about 5 million cones in each human retina, compared with about 120 million rods). But the cones are highly concentrated in and near the center of the retina, an area known as the **fovea.** In Latin the word *fovea* means "small pit," and this is exactly how the fovea of your eye appears—a pitlike depression about 1.5 millimeters in diameter. Many thousands of cones are packed into the fovea. In fact, this area contains no rods at all. When you want to inspect something closely, you look at it with your foveal cones, because they provide your sharpest, most detailed vision. Not only are the cones very dense there, they are also heavily exposed to light, since the blood vessels and nerve cells that cover all rods and cones form only a thin layer over the fovea. In addition, many cones in the fovea are connected to their own bipolar cells, which in turn are connected to their own ganglion cells. This gives many foveal cones their own private "lines" to the brain.

In contrast to the sharp and detailed images produced when cones are stimulated, images produced by the stimulation of rods are much fuzzier. The reason has to do with how rods connect to the next layers of cells in the visual system. Many rods may be linked to a single bipolar cell, which in turn

Carlsbad Caverns owes much of its mysterious appeal to the human eye's process of adaptation from light to dark and back again.

may be one of many such cells connected to a single ganglion cell. As a result, the signals from rods are usually blended, giving rise to indistinct lines and contours. This is why objects at night appear coarse and ill defined: you are seeing them mainly with your rods. The sharp drop in visual acuity that occurs at night is one cause of automobile accidents. Many people overestimate their nighttime ability to see obstacles on the road ahead. As a result, they drive too fast to stop in time when something blocks their way (Liebowitz and Owens, 1986).

Regardless of the differences in the images they produce, both rods and cones convert light into neural signals by means of chemical reactions. These reactions involve light-sensitive pigments. The pigment contained in the rods is called **rhodopsin,** or "visual red," because of its deep red color. When light strikes a rod, it changes the chemical structure of rhodopsin by bleaching it (Wald, 1968). This bleaching, in turn, generates neural activity, which, after some transformations, travels to the brain. Similar processes take place in the cones, although different pigments are involved.

Because light breaks it down, rhodopsin must be continually regenerated if the rods are to continue working. In very bright light, the speed of rhodopsin production cannot keep pace with the speed of its breakdown, and the pigment becomes depleted. Rhodopsin will replenish itself in the dark, but this process takes time. In humans, full recovery of the rods' rhodopsin supply can take up to half an hour, depending on the intensity and duration of the light to which the eyes were previously exposed. This is why you have difficulty seeing when you first enter a dark room from bright sunlight: your supply of rhodopsin has not yet had a chance to replenish.

Although most people's rods gradually become quite sensitive to dim light, some people have persistent difficulty adapting to dark. This condition, known as night blindness, can be caused by several factors, but perhaps the most common is an inability to use or store vitamin A, which is needed for rhodopsin production. For this reason an increase in vitamin A is often prescribed for night blindness.

The Role of Brain Regions Beyond the rods, cones, and other cells of the retina, fibers of the optic nerve form several pathways through the brain. The most important is the one that leads first to an area of the thalamus that serves as a relay station. From there the nerve network radiates out and travels to the primary visual cortex, located at the very back of the brain. It is here that the nerve impulses initiated when light hits the retina begin to give rise to the visual sensations we call sight. But analysis of visual information is not completed here. That information is passed along to other areas of the cortex, where it is further analyzed as to color, form, orientation, depth, and movement, and integrated into a coherent, meaningful whole. How this complex process actually takes place is still not fully understood, but scientists have discovered many important pieces of the puzzle.

In 1981 psychologists David Hubel and Torsten Wiesel at Harvard University won a Nobel prize for their work in this fascinating area (Hubel and Wiesel, 1959, 1979). Hubel and Wiesel found that each neuron in a higher mammal's primary visual cortex is activated by a very specific stimulus. For instance, one neuron might fire in response to a thick vertical line in the center of the visual field, while another might fire in response to a thin line oriented on the diagonal and moving from left to right. Apparently, each neuron in the primary visual cortex is specially adapted to detect certain visual features.

More recent research has provided additional information about the responses of neurons in the visual system and how they may be linked to one another. For example, beyond the primary visual cortex, nerve impulses seem to be fed into at least three separate processing systems: one for analyzing shapes; one for analyzing colors; and one for analyzing movement, location, and depth (Livingstone, 1988; Livingstone and Hubel, 1987). This three-part arrangement can be seen very clearly in the secondary visual cortex, which lies right next to the primary visual cortex. When tissue from the secondary visual cortex is stained, you can see that its cells are organized into three alternating columns: a thick one, a thin one, and one that is paler in color. Cells in the thick column seem to be concerned with processing depth, cells in the thin column with processing color, and cells in the pale column with processing shape. These cells, in turn, send signals to the tertiary visual cortex, where further analysis takes place. The thick columns, for instance, send projections into a part of the temporal lobe that is concerned with movement and depth perception, while the thin columns send projections into another cortical region concerned with the perception of color (Zeki, 1980).

The fact that different systems in the brain are involved in different aspects of visual perception can account for some interesting effects in art. For instance, when you look at a pointillist painting from a certain distance, you can see that it is composed of a great many dabs of paint, but the colors of those dabs blend together. Apparently, your neural system for analyzing shapes has keener ability to distinguish among stimuli than does your neural system for analyzing colors. In order for you to see both the shape of the dabs *and* their individual colors, you must stand much closer to the painting (Livingstone, 1988).

It may seem odd to you that different aspects of visual perception are handled by different systems in the brain. After all, when you look at a pointillist painting, you do not get a sense that your perception of color is separate from your perception of shape, both of which are separate from your perception of location, movement, and depth. Instead, you get an image that is a well-integrated whole. This shows how smoothly your brain integrates related perceptions. How such remarkable integration occurs with so little cognitive effort is one of the fascinating questions that remains about the workings of our sensory systems.

Le Cirque by the nineteenth-century French artist Georges Seurat, who devised the pointillist technique. He "built" each painting by applying tiny dots of pure color. From a normal viewing distance, the eye blends the individual dots into subtle shadings.

UNDERSTANDING HOW WE SEE COLORS

As surprising as it may seem, the colors you see are not inherent in objects. An apple, for instance, is not really red, a leaf is not really green, and the sea is not really blue. Instead, the colors you see are essentially the products of how your visual system interprets the different wavelengths of light that reflect off objects and strike your eyes. When those wavelengths measure 670 nanometers, you see a vivid red; when they measure 530 nanometers, you see a rich green; when they measure 470 nanometers, you see a clear blue. In short, color is created by the workings of your visual system. If you close your eyes and cease to look at the objects around you, they no longer have any colors (only the potential for producing them).

Theories of Color Vision But how does your visual system translate different wavelengths of light into the perception of colors? This brings us to various theories of color vision that psychologists have proposed. One is the **trichromatic** (or three-color) **theory,** first proposed by the Englishman Thomas Young at the turn of the nineteenth century and reformulated some fifty years later by the German physiologist Hermann von Helmholtz. Proponents of the trichromatic theory reasoned that color vision is not likely to arise from separate receptors for each of the hundreds of colors that humans are able to see. If so many different receptors were involved, relatively few would be activated for each shade we detect, and our color vision would be much weaker than it is. But if there are not hundreds of different kinds of color receptors, how can we possibly see this many shades? The trichromatic theory's answer is that we do so by ''mixing'' colors. In fact, by mixing just three colors of light (blue, green, and red) it is possible to make *every* color on the visible spectrum. This means that the eye

FIGURE 4.5   The phenomenon of afterimages can be demonstrated with this reverse American flag. Rest your eyes for a few minutes and then stare intently at the lower right-hand star in the flag for forty-five seconds. Now look at a white surface, such as a blank sheet of paper. You should see an American flag in its correct colors—blue instead of yellow, red instead of green, and white instead of black. Similarly, people usually report seeing yellow shortly after a brief flash of an intense blue light, and green after a brief flash of red light.

needs only three kinds of cones—one kind that is sensitive to short-wave light (the blue band), another that is sensitive to medium-wave light (the green band), and a third that is sensitive to long-wave light (the red band).

But other scientists were not satisfied with the trichromatic theory. One of the things they wanted to explain was the phenomenon of color afterimages. An **afterimage** is a visual impression that persists after removal of the stimulus that caused it. An example is given in Figure 4.5. Follow the instructions in the caption. Why does your visual system produce these sensations?

The **opponent-process theory** of color vision provides one answer. First proposed by the German physiologist Ewald Hering in the latter half of the nineteenth century, it has subsequently been revised and updated (Hurvich and Jameson, 1957; Jameson and Hurvich, 1989). Basically, the opponent-process theory argues that there are four primary colors, not three, as the trichromatic theory claims. These primary colors are red, green, blue, and yellow. Red-green and blue-yellow are called *complementary*, because when light waves of these color pairs are mixed together we see a colorless gray or white. (In fact, as Figure 4.6 shows, the true complementary color for green is a purplish red and for yellow it is a purplish blue, but for convenience we refer to the pairs as red-green and blue-yellow.) These color pairs, ac-

cording to the opponent-process theory, are linked in the brain to form "opponent systems." One opponent system contains cells that are excited by red and inhibited by green. This system also contains cells that are excited by green and inhibited by red. A second opponent system responds in the same manner to blue and yellow: some of its cells are excited by blue and inhibited by yellow, while others are excited by yellow and inhibited by blue. (A third opponent system, responding essentially to light and dark, is thought to enable the perception of brightness.)

Here is how the opponent-process theory explains color afterimages. When you look at the green stripes in Figure 4.5, you are stimulating the green response in your red-green opponent color system. Soon, however, this response adapts and becomes less vigorous. You then shift your gaze to a white surface. Normally you see this surface as white because the light reflected from it stimulates your red and green responses equally, giving rise to a colorless sensation. But because your green response in a striped pattern has been depressed through adaptation, your red response dominates and you see a set of red stripes.

The trichromatic theory and the opponent-process theory were originally proposed as competing explanations of how we see colors. Recent evidence suggests, however, that both have validity; they just operate at different levels of the visual system (Boyn-

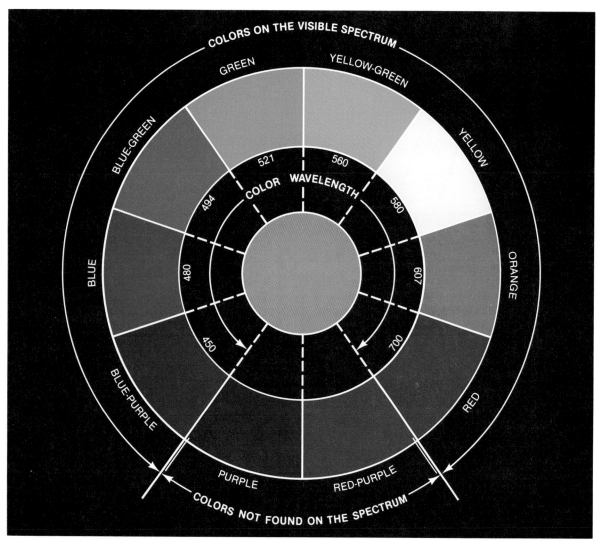

FIGURE 4.6 The color wheel. Any two colors that are opposite to each other are complementary; this means that combining them produces gray or white. Thus, when red is mixed with its opposite (really a blue-green, not a pure green), we see a grayish-white color. The numbers on the spokes of the wheel are wavelengths measured in nanometers. Spectral colors are shown in their natural order, but not at uniform intervals by wavelengths because of space limitations. The nonspectral reds and purples are also shown.

ton, 1988). At the level of the receptor cells the trichromatic theory applies. Researchers have identified three types of cones, each containing a slightly different form of a light-sensitive pigment called **iodopsin.** (This pigment should not be confused with rhodopsin, found in the rods.) Each form of iodopsin responds most strongly to a different band of light waves: a short-wave band (the purple-to-green range, centering on blue), a medium-wave band (the blue-to-yellow range, centering on green), and a long-wave band (the green-to-red range, centering on a yellowish red) (MacNichol, 1964; Mollon, 1982). These three overlapping response ranges are shown in Figure 4.7.

Beyond the cones and their trichromatic pigments, an opponent-process system comes into play.

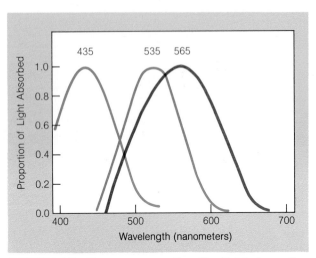

FIGURE 4.7   Curves representing the light-absorption sensitivity of the three types of cones. One group of cones is maximally sensitive to short wavelengths (around 435 nanometers), another to medium wavelengths (535 nanometers), and a third to long wavelengths (565 nanometers). The thrichromatic theory explains that the perceived color of a light depends on the *relative* intensity of activity caused by the light's absorption in the three types of cones.

Investigators have found ganglion cells, cells in the thalamus, and cells in the visual cortex that respond as expected by the opponent-process theory (Daw, 1968; De Valois and De Valois, 1975). For instance, when some of these cells are stimulated by diffuse green light, they increase their rate of firing; for other cells, the same green light causes a decrease in firing. If the researcher then switches to a complementary red light, the cells that were previously excited by green now become inhibited, while those that were previously inhibited by green now become excited. With a light that contains both green *and* red, the opposing reactions cancel each other out and these cells show little response. The same patterns can be found in cells that react to blue and yellow. When blue light is excitatory, yellow is inhibitory, and vice versa.

Figure 4.8 shows how chemical responses in the *three* types of cones may become converted into neural responses involving *four* complementary colors (Sekuler and Blake, 1990). The blue-yellow op-

ponent-process pathway (or *channel*, as it is often called) weighs the difference between signals from the short-wave (blue) cones, on the one hand, and signals from the medium-wave (green) cones *plus* the long-wave (red) cones, on the other hand. (When adding colors of light, pure green plus pure red produces yellow.) Similarly, the red-green opponent-process channel weighs the difference between signals from the medium-wave (green) cones, on the one hand, and signals from the short-wave (blue) cones plus the long-wave (red) cones, on the other. (Remember from Figure 4.6 that the complement of a pure green is a red mixed with some blue, or a purplish red.) Of course, scientists are still debating many of the details of this complex process. Future research will undoubtedly shed more light on how responses in the cones interact with those of neurons higher up in the visual system.

Color Blindness   There are several kinds of color blindness, each caused by a different defect in the visual system. About 8 percent of Caucasian males and 0.5 percent of Caucasian females have some type of color blindness. For Asians, blacks, and native Americans, the percentages are lower, reflecting their different gene pools (Sekuler and Blake, 1990). The accompanying photographs show how the world looks to people with three of these color-vision defects.

Usually color blindness is caused by abnormalities in the composition of iodopsin, the visual pigment in the cones. A person with normal color vision has three forms of iodopsin, each sensitive to a different range of wavelengths. Such a person is called a normal **trichromat.** A small minority of people, in contrast, are totally color blind. They see the world in shades of gray, like the pictures on a black-and-white TV. Most of these people are **monochromats;** they have only one kind of iodopsin, which is insufficient to differentiate wavelengths of light.

More common is partial color blindness caused by a lack of just one of the three kinds of iodopsin (Mollon, 1982). Such a person is called a **dichromat.** Most dichromats lack either the middle-wave (green) visual pigment or the long-wave (red) one. In either case, they tend to confuse the colors along the middle- to long-wave end of the spectrum (from

FIGURE 4.8 How chemical responses involving three types of cones may be converted into neural responses involving four complementary colors. The blue-yellow opponent-process channel is shown with striped arrows; the red-green opponent-process channel is shown with black arrows. (*After Sekuler and Blake, 1990.*)

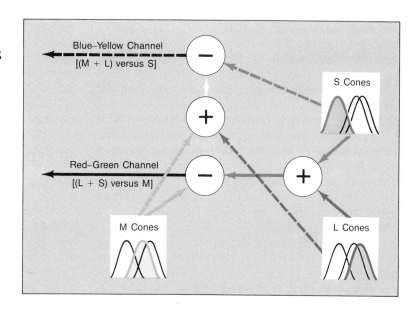

A

B

C

D

The same scene as perceived by a person with normal vision (A), and by people with three kinds of color blindness. (B) A person who is red-green blind sees everything in shades of blue and yellow. (C) Someone who is blue-yellow blind sees the world in shades of red and green. (D) Someone who is totally color blind sees in black, white, and shades of gray. (*Boulton-Wilson/Jeroboam.*)

green to red), because they have only one pigment absorbing light in that range. John Dalton, an English scientist who lived in the late eighteenth and early nineteenth centuries, had this condition and wrote about it. Rather than seeing four basic colors on the right-hand side of the visible spectrum (green, yellow, orange, and red), Dalton saw only one, which he called yellow. We assume that Dalton lacked the long-wave (red) visual pigment, because he saw even pure crimson as a dark, neutral tone. A Quaker who was supposed to shun bright colors, Dalton was dismayed and embarrassed to learn that the academic robes he sometimes wore were not black, but a vibrant red.

Much rarer than dichromats like Dalton are dichromats who lack the short-wave (blue) cone pigment. These people are usually blind to bluish purples, and they confuse shades in the blue-to-bluish-green range. The condition is rare because the gene for the short-wave pigment is not carried on the X (female) chromosome, as middle- and long-wave pigment genes are, but rather on another chromosome. Consequently, regardless of sex, a person always inherits *two* short-wave pigment genes, one from the mother and one from the father. Since it is very unlikely that both these genes will be totally defective, complete lack of the short-wave pigment is very uncommon. In contrast, color blindness in the red-green range is much more frequent, at least among males. Males have only one X chromosome (inherited from their mothers), so they also have only one each of the genes for the middle-wave and the long-wave pigments. If either gene is defective, they have no second gene as a "backup" (Nathans, 1989).

A milder form of color blindness occurs among people who have three cone pigments, just as they should, but one of those pigments—typically the middle-wave (green) or the long-wave (red) one—is abnormally structured. In vision tests, these people require unusually large amounts of the affected color to produce a mixed hue. Psychologists often refer to such people as "color weak."

Recent research suggests that the range of defects in color-vision pigments may be even more diverse than those we have described. Apparently, some people formerly considered red-green dichromats can nevertheless perceive red under the right conditions (Boynton, 1988). These people may not completely lack a third visual pigment, as was originally believed. Instead, their third pigment may be highly defective, and functioning only under certain circumstances. This finding suggests that a range of defects in iodopsin can occur, from ones that make the pigment malfunction somewhat (color weakness), to others that make it malfunction most of the time, to still others that make it virtually nonexistent and produce true monochromats and dichromats.

HEARING

WAVES OF SOUND

Sit back, close your eyes, and simply listen for a minute. Even in a room that you thought was quiet, you can still hear many sounds. These sounds arise when changes in the pressure of the atmosphere cause air molecules to vibrate. When you turn on a radio, for example, the amplifier makes the speaker vibrate. The vibrating speaker alternately pushes against the surrounding air, compressing it, and pulls away from the air, allowing it to become less dense, or rarefied. When these waves of compressed and rarefied air molecules strike your eardrum, they push and pull it in the same pattern as the vibrating speaker, although with much less intensity. This is the first step in producing a sound. Other sound-producing stimuli—a rustling piece of paper, a honking horn, a vibrating set of vocal cords—create sound waves in the same way.

The number of compression–rarefaction cycles per sound determines a sound wave's **frequency.** (One cycle per second equals 1 hertz, abbreviated Hz.) Frequency, in turn, largely determines the pitch we perceive: the higher the frequency, the higher the pitch. The human ear is capable of hearing frequencies from about 20 Hz to 20,000 Hz. Since human voices range from 100 Hz to 3,500 Hz, we can easily hear them. In fact, our ears are most sensitive to sounds in the frequency range of human speech. This is a good example of how an important human ability—communication through language—has been facilitated by the coevolution of our mechanisms for speech and hearing.

The intensity of a sound wave, the amount of pressure it exerts, corresponds to its **amplitude**—that is, to the distance of its peaks and valleys from a baseline of zero. The greater the amplitude of a wave, the louder it sounds to a listener. Amplitude is expressed in units of measurement called decibels. Conversation usually takes place at about 50 to 60

During more than twenty-five years of playing highly amplified rock music, Pete Townshend (*foreground*) of The Who has estimated he lost about half of his hearing.

decibels, but humans can also hear sounds of much lower amplitude. It has been calculated that a person can actually hear the sound of one air molecule striking the eardrum! This feat can be accomplished only under ideally quiet conditions, however. Normally, background noise makes such acute hearing impossible. At the other extreme, sounds above 120 decibels are likely to be painful to the human ear, and people who are frequently exposed to such sounds can suffer permanent hearing loss through damage to delicate portions of the inner ear. Rock musicians, for example, sometimes become partially deaf, as do workers who are constantly exposed to the roar of heavy machinery. Even exposure to moderately loud noises can cause a temporary upward shift in a person's auditory threshold. This is why your hearing may seem less acute right after you leave a loud concert or a noisy party (Miller, 1978).

BASIC WORKINGS OF THE AUDITORY SYSTEM

The human ear is a masterpiece of engineering. Into a space of about 1 cubic inch are packed all the amplifying mechanisms needed to make audible the buzz of a tiny mosquito or the splash of a single drop of water. To understand how the ear works, you must understand the structure and function of its three interrelated parts: the outer, the middle, and the inner ear (see Figure 4.9).

Sound is funneled into the outer ear through the **pinna,** the skin-covered cartilage visible on the outside of the head. From the pinna, sound travels down the **auditory canal,** a passageway about an inch long that is sealed off at its inner end by a thin membrane called the **eardrum.** Because of its long, narrow shape, the auditory canal resonates as sound passes through it, and so the sound is amplified. It has been calculated that for frequencies between 2,000 and 5,500 Hz, the pressure exerted at the eardrum is about twice that exerted at the entrance to the auditory canal.

The eardrum responds to changes in air pressure by moving in and out. Its movement, however, is extremely slight. When you listen to a normal speaking voice, your eardrum vibrates only about 100 millionths of a centimeter. Nevertheless, this is enough to set into motion three tiny, interconnected bones on the inner side of the eardrum in the area known as the middle ear. These bones, called the **hammer,** the **anvil,** and the **stirrup** because of their distinctive shapes, are positioned and linked in such a way that movement of the eardrum moves the hammer, which in turn moves the anvil, which in turn moves the stirrup, which ultimately presses against the **oval window,** a membrane stretching across an

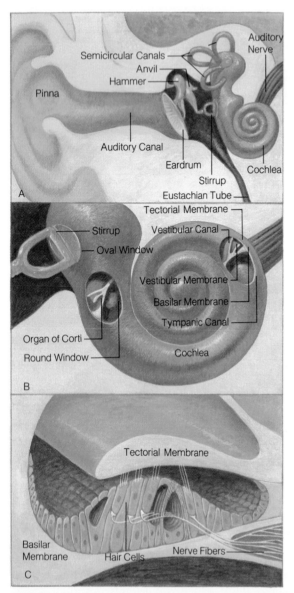

FIGURE 4.9 Structure of the ear. (A) A cross section showing the outer, middle, and inner ear. Sound waves pass through the auditory canal and are transformed into mechanical vibration by the eardrum. The three small bones—the hammer, anvil, and stirrup—amplify this motion and transmit it to (B) the oval window of the cochlea. The motion of the oval window sends pressure waves through the fluid in the cochlea. (C) Closeup cross section of the Organ of the Corti, within the cochlea. Waves in the cochlear fluid cause the basilar membrane to vibrate, which in turn disturbs the hair cells, the receptors of auditory, or hearing, information.

opening to the inner ear. The hammer, the anvil, and the stirrup are the smallest bones in the human body, no bigger than the letters on this page.

But why are these bones needed? Why isn't the ear constructed so that sound energy passes directly from the eardrum to the inner ear? The answer lies in the fact that the inner ear is filled with liquid, and liquid is much more difficult to compress than air. Consequently, the pressure that sound waves typically exert on the eardrum must be substantially amplified if the liquid in the inner ear is to be set in motion. This amplification is accomplished in two ways. First, the bones of the middle ear act as a series of levers, each one increasing the pressure on the next. Second, the fact that the oval window is up to thirty times smaller than the eardrum means that the pressure per square millimeter it receives is likewise increased. The end result is that the pressure exerted by the stirrup on the oval window can be up to ninety times greater than the pressure that the original sound wave exerted on the eardrum.

The importance of this amplification can be seen in people who suffer from various forms of **conduction deafness.** Conduction deafness involves malfunctions of the outer or the middle ear that impair the ear's ability to amplify sound waves. These malfunctions include excessive accumulation of wax in the auditory canal, fluid buildup in the middle ear that may rupture the eardrum, or bone disease that decreases the effectiveness with which the stirrup presses on the oval window. Depending on the particular problem, conduction hearing loss may be treated by thoroughly cleansing the ear (in the case of wax buildup), by antibiotics (if infection is involved), by microsurgery (if the eardrum or bones of the middle ear need replacement), or in chronic cases by means of a hearing aid that amplifies sound electronically.

When amplified pressure reaches the oval window, it is transmitted to the fluid in the spiral-shaped part of the inner ear called the **cochlea.** The cochlea is divided into several canals separated by membranes. Within the central canal is a string of many thousands of receptors, called **hair cells** because of their many hairlike projections. The hair cells are positioned between two membranes, one of which, the **basilar membrane,** is quite elastic, and the other of which, the **tectorial membrane,** is relatively rigid. Movement of the fluid in the inner ear pushes the basilar membrane, which in turn pushes the hair cells against the tectorial membrane, bending and rubbing them in the process. This movement of the hair cells triggers neural impulses. The impulses travel via the adjacent **auditory nerve** to the brainstem, and from there ascend through the thalamus to the auditory cortex, where the perception of sound and its patterns begins.

Because the basilar membrane and hair cells initiate nerve impulses in the auditory system, damage to them can produce what is called **neural deafness.** A new technology designed to help people who suffer severe neural deafness is called a **cochlear implant.** In the most sophisticated cochlear implant developed to date, twenty-two microelectrodes connected by a cable are surgically positioned at various points along the cochlea. The cable is then run to a tiny plug implanted in the skull above the ear. The person wears a small receiver, which picks up sounds and sends them first to a pocket-sized processor for analysis. The processor next relays the signals to the microelectrodes, which in turn transmit electrical impulses to fibers of the auditory nerve (Schmeck, 1984). Although cochlear implants can give some totally deaf people the ability to hear, that ability is nowhere near as rich as normal human hearing (Loeb, 1985). People with even the most sophisticated of these devices have trouble deciphering speech, and a complex mixture of sounds (as occurs when listening to an orchestra, for instance) is totally confusing to them. Thus the new technology of cochlear implants, as impressive as it may be, serves to demonstrate what a truly remarkable organ the human ear is.

THEORIES OF PITCH

How the brain distinguishes tones of different pitches is not yet fully understood. Just as with color vision, there are two classic theories, both dating back to the nineteenth century. One was first proposed by Hermann von Helmholtz, the physiologist who helped formulate the trichromatic theory. He and others argued that each pitch we hear depends on the area of the basilar membrane that a given sound wave vibrates the most. This view is aptly called the **place theory** of pitch.

In 1961, Georg von Bekesy won a Nobel prize for his research in support of the place theory. Bekesy (1959) found that sound waves of different frequencies do indeed vibrate places on the basilar mem-

brane in a nonuniform manner. High-frequency waves have their maximum effect on the region near the oval window, while mid-frequency waves have their maximum effect near the cochlea's inner lip. Moreover, when small groups of neurons leading from different parts of the basilar membrane are electrically stimulated, people hear sounds of different pitches (Simmons et al., 1965). This finding led directly to the development of the cochlear implant, in which each microelectrode positioned along the cochlea creates the perception of a different pitch when it is stimulated. As you would expect, damage to selected portions of the basilar membrane tends to affect only certain tones. With age, for instance, many people gradually lose their sensitivity to high-frequency tones, so that by the age of seventy quite a few people cannot hear frequencies greater than 6,000 Hz. This high-tone hearing loss is caused by deterioration of receptor cells close to the oval window.

But vibration of the basilar membrane does not occur in such a completely tidy fashion as the place theory predicts. Particularly troublesome is the fact that low-frequency sound waves tend to vibrate the membrane fairly uniformly across its surface. The second major theory of pitch detection overcomes this problem by focusing not on the location of the basilar membrane's vibration, but on its frequency. According to this **frequency theory,** the basilar membrane vibrates in exactly the same frequency pattern (the same number of cycles per second) as the original sound wave, thus causing neural impulses to fire in that pattern too. These different patterns of neural firing determine the pitches we hear.

The frequency theory has problems of its own, however. Remember from Chapter 3 that each time a nerve impulse travels down an axon, the cell must have a brief time to restore its firing potential before another impulse can be triggered. This fact imposes a limit on the number of nerve impulses that a single cell can transmit in any given period. A thousand impulses per second is probably the maximum. How, then, can the rate of firing of the auditory nerves mimic the frequencies of many of the sound waves we can hear? The human auditory system is capable of detecting frequencies of up to 20,000 Hz. No single nerve cell could possibly fire this fast.

Although this problem at first seemed perplexing, Ernest Wever and Charles Bray (1937) ultimately proposed an answer, which they called the **volley principle.** It is based on the assumption that the

To the sensible runner, the sensation of warmth produced by exertion is a valuable indicator of when the body has had enough.

frequency of neural firing that the brain detects is determined not by the rate of firing of single neurons, but rather by *groups* of neurons. Think of the auditory nerve as consisting of squads of rifle-firing soldiers (related groups of neurons). Each soldier must take time to reload after firing, and so can fire only a small number of shots in any given period. But if the squad of soldiers fires in a volley pattern, so that some are always firing while others are reloading, the group as a whole can substantially increase the total number of shots per time unit. The neurons of the auditory system, Wever and Bray argued, operate in a similar way. This is why they can follow sound frequencies above 1,000 Hz—up to about 4,000 Hz.

Thus both the place theory and the frequency theory help explain how we perceive pitch. Many psychologists believe that the two probably operate together to give us our powers of pitch discrimination. For sounds of intermediate and high frequencies, the place theory seems to apply. The location of maximum vibration on the basilar membrane does indeed change with changes in sound frequencies within this range. In fact, for higher frequencies there seems to be a one-to-one correspondence between the area of the basilar membrane being affected and the area of the auditory cortex being activated. At lower frequencies, however, vibration of the basilar membrane seems to be too diffuse to support the place theory. In this

range, the frequency theory provides a better explanation of pitch perception. But note that there is a lower-intermediate frequency range in which *both* mechanisms may operate. This may help explain why our pitch perception is so acute for sounds within this range—a range that corresponds to the frequency levels of normal human speech.

THE SKIN SENSES

We tend to think of vision and hearing as our primary senses, the ones that provide the most vital information about the world. And yet we have senses from receptors in our skin that are also crucial to us (Loomis and Lederman, 1986). These include our senses of touch, pressure, warmth, cold, and pain. Just think how hard it is to walk when your foot has gone to sleep. There is nothing wrong with the muscles that move the affected limb or the bones that support your weight. But because your foot's senses of touch and pressure have been lost, you find that even a step or two is clumsy and unsteady. Clearly, your skin senses are extremely important to performing even the simplest tasks.

Figure 4.10 shows that within and below the skin lies a forest of sensory receptors, some 17,000 just in the smooth and hairless parts of a hand (Johansson and Vallbo, 1983). These receptors are structured in many different ways and lie at different depths in the body tissue. All connect with neurons that transmit information to the central nervous system, usually first to the spinal cord and then through the thalamus to the somatosensory area of the cortex.

How are the various receptors embedded in our tissues related to the different skin sensations that we feel? Stimulation of receptors around the roots of hair cells seems to produce the sensation of touch on the skin's surface, as does stimulation of the Meissner's corpuscles, which are abundant in hairless areas, such as the fingertips, palms, and lips. What you feel when you stroke your hand across a page of this book probably involves stimulation of both these kinds of receptors. Lying below these two receptors are the Merkel disks and the Ruffini endings, both of which seem to be involved in the sensation of steady pressure on the skin, as when you press the end of a pencil against the palm of your hand. Even deeper beneath the skin's surface are the Pacinian corpuscles. They are extremely sensitive to touch and very light pressure. When you blow gently on a finger and feel the air, you are likely activating some of your Pacinian corpuscles.

Researchers once believed that free nerve endings embedded in our tissues (in contrast to encapsulated nerve endings) are associated exclusively with the sensation of pain. But the cornea of the eye, which contains almost nothing but free nerve endings, is responsive to pressure and temperature as well as to pain (Geldard, 1972). Thus, to understand pain, as to understand any other sensation, we must look beyond the various neural receptors.

An explanation of pain must be able to account for all of this sensation's unusual characteristics. One such charactertistic is the fact that people sometimes continue to experience pain after its original cause has disappeared. For instance, sufferers of neuralgia (an infection of the peripheral nervous system) may complain of persistent pain even after the infection has cleared up (Barlow and Mollon, 1982). Another striking feature of pain is that psychological factors can greatly alter the experience of it. In one study, for example, people with backaches who were subtly encouraged to think that their pain would subside in a limited amount of time tended to suffer less from their conditions than did those with equally severe back problems who lacked clear ideas about how long their suffering would last (Fordyce, 1988). How can such phenomena be explained?

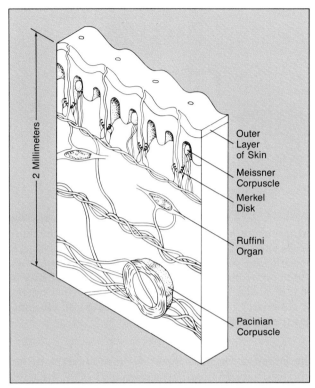

FIGURE 4.10 A cross section through the skin of a fingerpad showing the location of various receptor cells. (*After Sekuler and Blake, 1990.*)

One model that has tried to account for all pain's features is the **gate-control theory** (Melzack and Wall, 1965). Gate-control theory argues that the neurons that carry messages of pain up the spinal cord to the brain receive input from several different types of peripheral nerve fibers. Some (called C fibers) are small in diameter and relatively slow in conducting, while others (called A fibers) are large in diameter and relatively fast in conducting. Within a region of the spinal cord are certain interneurons that serve as "gate cells." These cells are inhibited by activation of the C fibers and excited by activation of the A fibers. When the interneurons are excited, they block the transmission of pain messages up the spinal cord. Thus high activation of the A fibers relative to the C fibers can actually close the pain "gate," causing the brain to sense little or no pain.

This theory can explain some of pain's unusual features. For instance, persistent pain after a wound or infection has healed may be caused by damage to

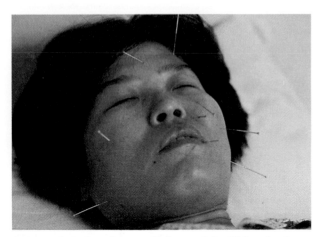

Acupuncture has been widely used in China for hundreds of years and is becoming more popular in Western societies for pain relief and anesthesia. No one knows exactly how the technique works, but one possibility is that it causes *A* fibers in the peripheral nervous system to stimulate "gate cells" in the spinal cord into blocking the transmission of pain messages.

the A fibers. Because the A fibers involved can no longer stimulate the interneurons and close the pain gate, the person feels chronic pain. Similarly, psychological and emotional factors from higher brain centers are assumed to send messages downward through the spinal cord to affect the activities of the interneurons, thus accentuating or reducing pain sensations.

The physiological details of gate-control theory have been criticized (Kelly, 1981). Some researchers have found that the peripheral nerve fibers and spinal cord neurons do not operate in precisely the ways that gate-control theory predicts (Whitehorn and Burgess, 1973). Yet therapeutic treatments based on gate-control theory have often been quite successful. For example, electrical stimulation of A fibers has been found to relieve pain in chronic pain sufferers for up to thirty minutes (Wall and Sweet, 1967). It has even been suggested that gate-control theory may explain how acupuncture works. With acupuncture, pain is alleviated when small needles are inserted into various points on the body and twirled or electrically stimulated. Perhaps this activates the A fibers and closes the pain gate.

Much more research needs to be done before the mysteries of pain are solved. Even if gate-control theory is eventually replaced by other physiological models, it nevertheless has served an important

purpose in emphasizing that pain does not just involve sensory signals traveling up the spinal cord to the brain. Instead, pain is also a psychological process in which the brain works downward on incoming sensations, determining which will be given attention and which will be ignored, which will be considered distressing and which bearable (Rachlin, 1985).

SMELL AND TASTE

SMELL

The sense of smell, or **olfaction,** can be a real source of pleasure, as anyone knows who has ever enjoyed the sensual fragrance of a rose or savored the aroma of a favorite food. Although many animals are more sensitive to odors than human beings are, the human sense of smell is still quite keen. For instance, a person can detect the musky odor of mercaptan, the scent that makes skunks so unpopular, at concentrations as low as 1 part mercaptan to 50 trillion parts of air (Gelard, 1972).

Smell requires that vaporized molecules of a substance enter the nasal passages and contact the **olfactory membranes** that line the roofs of these cavities. Within the olfactory membranes are some 10 million receptor cells, each with hairlike projections reaching out into the circulating air. When molecules of certain airborne substances contact these receptors, nerve impulses are generated (Lancet, 1984). These impulses travel directly to the **olfactory bulbs** at the forward base of the cerebral hemispheres. From there, nerve signals are relayed to various other parts of the brain, where the odor is consciously perceived and analyzed (Cain, 1988).

Psychologists are not sure why people can smell some substances and not others, nor why certain groups of odors smell alike. One theory is that the quality of an odor is related to the size and shape of the molecules that produce it (Amoore et al., 1964). Molecules of various sizes and shapes might fit into different receptor cell slots, much as keys fit into locks. The different receptor cells could then stimulate different nerve fibers leading to the brain (Mair et al., 1982). Whether the process really works in this way, however, is still speculative.

TASTE

Most people can discriminate among hundreds of odors, yet they appear to sense only four basic

A professional smeller—called a "nose"—has a highly developed ability to detect very small amounts of the many different substances that may be blended to produce a perfume.

categories of taste: sweet, sour, salty, and bitter. Other tastes are generally regarded as mixtures of these four or as some combination of taste and smell (Bartoshuk, 1988). Interestingly, the sensation of bitter, which can be so unpleasant, is probably crucial to our survival. Most poisonous substances in plants are extremely bitter tasting, which serves as a warning to us not to eat them (Akabas et al., 1988).

Our organs of taste are the **taste buds,** some 10,000 of which cover the upper surface of the tongue. Most taste buds are embedded in hill-like projections called **papillae.** It is the papillae that make the top of your tongue appear bumpy. Each taste bud, in turn, contains receptor cells that are quite sensitive. A salty or sweet solution applied to the tongue for only a tenth of a second is enough to generate responses in appropriate receptors and trigger an identifiable taste sensation (Kelling and Halpern, 1983). Figure 4.11 shows that different areas of the tongue are especially sensitive to one or more of the four basic categories of taste. The front of the tongue is particularly sensitive to sweet and salty, the sides to sour, and the back to bitter.

Taste sensations are transmitted from the tongue to the brain via nerve fibers that connect to the receptor cells in the taste buds. In some animal species, the individual nerve fibers respond to more than one kind of taste stimulus. This suggests that the neural code for different tastes may be based on different patterns of activity in the thousands of nerve fibers leading from the tongue (Erickson, 1984). Alternatively, each nerve fiber could carry a message regarding only one of the basic taste sensations. As yet, however, there is little evidence that nerve fibers leading from the tongue respond this selectively.

INTEGRATION OF THE SENSES

Smell and taste are closely interrelated. When describing how food "tastes," we usually include its odor, which circulates from the back of the mouth up into the nasal cavity. The intimate connection between taste and smell is most noticeable when the sense of smell is temporarily blocked. Try biting into an apple and then a raw potato while holding your nose. You will probably have difficulty distinguishing between the two tastes. For the same reason, food has a flat, uninteresting flavor when you have a bad head cold.

Although taste and smell are more interconnected than most of our other senses, none of our sensory systems operate in isolation. Information gained from one tends to "inform" the others about what sensations to expect and how to interpret them (Acredolo and Hake, 1982). For example, when you feel an object in your pocket and identify it by touch, this

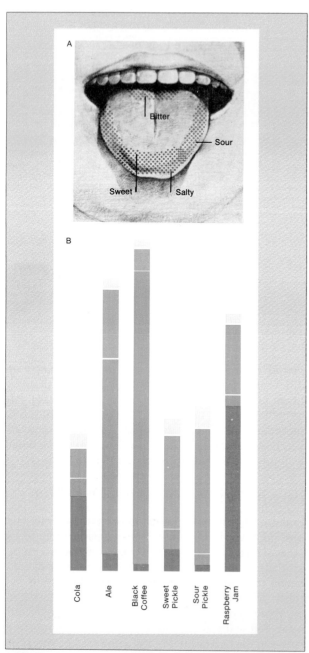

FIGURE 4.11   A map of the human tongue (A) shows the areas of maximum sensitivity to the four fundamental kinds of taste sensation. (B) The tastes of six foods analyzed into the four components of taste shown in part A. The length of the colored bars indicates the amount of each component judged to be present in the taste of the food by subjects in a psychological experiment. (*Data from Beebe-Center, 1949.*)

information gives you clues as to what the object will look like. Similarly, when you see a food that looks very unappetizing, you develop expectations about how it will taste. These expectations may be so powerful that the food will actually taste bad, even though, if you ate it blindfolded, you might find it perfectly all right.

Thus it seems that people strive to "match" information from their various senses, to make the different pieces of data coordinate with each other. You do this every time you go to a movie theater and hear the voices coming from the speakers rather than from the people you see on the screen. There may be a moment at first when you are aware of this disparity, but it doesn't last long. Soon you have coordinated sights and sounds into an integrated whole.

PERCEIVING A COMPLEX WORLD

Earlier we defined perception as the process whereby the brain interprets the sensations it receives, giving them order and meaning. We also pointed out that it is hard to separate sensation from perception because the first so quickly and effortlessly leads to the second. Certain ambiguous stimuli, however, can help us distinguish between them. Look, for example, at Figure 4.12. From a sensory perspective this picture amounts to just a series of black patches on a white background. But if you look long enough at the right-hand side, the form of a Dalmatian dog will probably emerge. This form is a perception, an organization of sensory data as a result of how your brain processes that information.

But how did your brain come up with the perception of a Dalmation? In answer to such questions, psychologists have proposed two different perspectives. The **direct perspective** emphasizes the contribution of the sensory data presented to your eyes (Gibson, 1950, 1966, 1979). According to this view, all the information you need to see the right-hand patches as a unified object is right there in the drawing. When this visual information is passed from the retina, along the optic nerve, and on up into higher and higher regions of the brain, it is automatically structured into the perception of a meaningful whole. The direct perspective is closely related to what we earlier called "bottom-up" or data-driven processing.

FIGURE 4.12 When you first look at this drawing, your visual system will probably register a set of black patches, but after a longer look you will probably see the form of a Dalmatian dog. This perception is encouraged because the text tells you what to look for and because you already know what a Dalmatian looks like.

In contrast to the direct view is the so-called **indirect perspective** or **constructivist view** (Gregory, 1970; Rock, 1984). It holds that all we process directly are sensory cues about the environment. In order to make sense of these cues we must supplement them with additional information stored in memory. Thus we take our knowledge about dogs (how they look and act) and use that as a hypothesis for organizing the patches in Figure 4.12 into a recognizable picture. This hypothesis works downward from higher brain centers, guiding our exploration of the drawing and offering a possible solution. In this way we actively construct our final perception. The indirect perspective or constructivist view stresses what psychologists call **schemas**—mental representations of objects and events against which incoming data can be compared and interpreted. Schemas, in short, direct our search for meaning in the world. You will encounter the concept of schemas in many chapters of this book, including those on learning, memory, thinking, and social psychology.

The direct and indirect perspectives on perception are not mutually exclusive. Although in some cases one may seem to apply better than the other, it is best to think of these as complementary viewpoints, both of which add to our understanding of how we perceive.

SOME BASIC PERCEPTUAL PROCESSES

Over the years psychologists have studied many basic perceptual processes. Some have been interested in what is called **form perception,** the ability to detect unified patterns instead of a hodge-podge of sensory data. Others have investigated **perceptual constancy,** the tendency to see objects as having stable properties even though the visual information we receive about them is constantly changing. Still others have been intrigued by **depth perception,** the ability to see the visual world in three dimensions even though the images that strike our retinas are in two dimensions only. In the following sections we will explore all three of these aspects of perception.

FORM PERCEPTION

One group of researchers interested in form perception were known as **gestalt psychologists.** The gestalt movement began in Germany in the early twentieth century. Its proponents, such as Max Wertheimer, Kurt Koffka, and Wolfgang Kohler, believed that it is impossible to understand form perception simply by analyzing each of the many sensations registered in the brain when we see, hear, smell, taste, or touch something. Often, they argued, our percep-

According to the indirect perspective or constructivist view of perception, we use our schemas about what a human being should look like to organize this Cubist painting—Picasso's *Seated Woman*—into a recognizable figure.

FIGURE 4.13   This drawing shows only three unrelated circles with a wedge missing from each and three unrelated 45° angles. What we perceive, however, is a white triangle overlaying three complete circles and another triangle.

tions are *more* than the sensations that give rise to them. That "more" is a meaningful pattern or whole, which in German is called a *Gestalt*. Thus gestalt psychology got its name.

The Dalmatian seen in Figure 4.12 is an example of a gestalt. Another example appear in Figure 4.13. You do not see this drawing as simply three unrelated circles with a wedge missing from each one, plus three unrelated 45° angles. Instead, you see a white triangle projecting forward at the center of the drawing, as if it is partially covering another triangle and three complete circles. All the pieces seem to be integrated into a single pattern, a unified gestalt. So "real" looking is the white triangle tying the other pieces together that it even seems to have distinct contours or edges. These perceptions are called **subjective contours**—lines or shapes that appear to be present but are not physically there (Kanizsa, 1976).

The early gestalt psychologists were interested in determining the "rules" the brain uses to order sensory information into wholes. So in their research they typically presented people with various stimuli —often dots or musical tones—and asked them to describe what they saw or heard. From their data they developed principles related to the perception of gestalts. These researchers had much in common with those who take a direct perspective on perception (McBurney and Collings, 1984). The gestalt psychologists believed that the brain automatically gives form to sensory data on the basis of the perceptual rules by which it operates.

Some of these rules are referred to as principles of **perceptual grouping** and are illustrated in Figure 4.14. In drawing A, dots of equal size are evenly spaced across a field, and we perceive no stable distinguishing pattern. In drawing B, the spacing between the dots has been changed so that we see them as forming four parallel lines. This effect demonstrates the principle of **proximity:** stimuli that are close together tend to be seen as a group. In drawing C, the dots in part B have been slightly rearranged so that we now perceive two curved lines. In this case

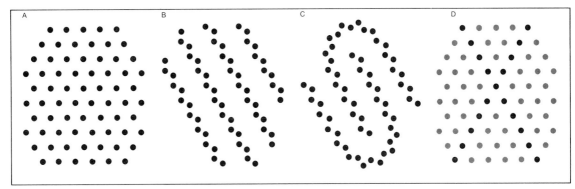

FIGURE 4.14 A demonstration of some of the gestalt principles of grouping. The pattern of equally spaced identical dots in (A) is not easily organized. It is seen either as an undifferentiated field or as a set of unstable overlapping patterns. In (B) a stable perception of parallel lines emerges because of the *proximity* of some dots to others. When some of these lines are made *continuous* with one another in (C), dots that are physically quite distant from one another are seen as belonging to a single curved line. In (D) a stable organization suddenly emerges because some of the dots have been made *similar* to one another and different from the rest.

the principle of **continuity** overrules the influence of proximity: dots that form a single, continuous grouping are seen as a gestalt. Another organizing principle, illustrated in drawing D, is **similarity.** Here we perceive an X in the same pattern of dots as in part A because the dots that form the X are a similar color.

Although contemporary psychologists acknowledge the importance of gestalt principles of perception, many feel that the early gestalt psychologists underestimated the extent to which prior knowledge works downward to shape how we organize sensory data. For instance, it may surprise you to learn that your perception of the gestalt in Figure 4.13 is influenced by your prior knowledge of and experience with triangles. If the subjective figure in the middle were instead some unusual shape, your brain would have much more trouble creating a whole from the disparate parts (Wallace and Slaughter, 1988). Try it with the drawings in Figure 4.15.

Another example of how bottom-up and top-down processing combine to give us form perception can be seen in our division of stimuli into **figure and ground.** When we look at most scenes we automatically separate regions that represent objects, or *figure,* from regions that represent spaces between objects, or *ground.* This ability to distinguish objects from space does not depend entirely on past experience. When people who have been blind from birth are given sight through surgery, they are very quickly

FIGURE 4.15A This figure is constructed very similarly to Figure 4.13, but here you probably do not see clear subjective contours. The reason is that the form in the middle (see Figure 4.15B) is an unusual shape, one you are not as accustomed to seeing as a triangle. Consequently, your brain has trouble creating a whole from the various parts. (*After Wallace and Slaughter, 1988.*)

able to separate figure from ground (Senden, 1960). But when stimuli are ambiguous, experience helps in this process. For instance, your knowledge of what a vase and a human profile look like is enormously helpful in perceiving the two images in Figure 4.16.

PERCEPTUAL CONSTANCY

When the sun sets and casts a rosy light on the world, you do not see trees and grass as suddenly

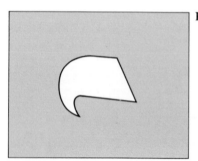

FIGURE 4.15B

FIGURE 4.16 Is this a white vase against a black background or two black facing profiles against a white background? Depending on your perspective, it may be either, and most people can easily switch from one perception to the other. Interestingly, if you were to draw a small line anywhere on the white portion of this figure, the clarity of that line would vary greatly as you reversed figure and ground (it would be distinct on figure and much fainter on ground) (Wong and Weisstein, 1982). Experiment and see. This effect occurs because your brain always emphasizes figure at the expense of ground.

turning reddish; and when you walk out of the sunshine into the shadow of a building, your skin does not suddenly look gray. Instead, you tend to ignore such temporary changes in color in favor of a view of the world that is constant and predictable. Similarly, although the image of a departing car rapidly becomes smaller, you do not perceive the car as shrinking; nor, when it turns a corner and you see it from the side instead of from the rear, do you think that it has changed shape. How does your brain maintain such perceptual constancies in a world of ever-changing stimuli?

Let us consider size constancy as an example. An object's distance and the size of the image it projects on the retina are inversely related: the greater the distance, the smaller is the image. This relationship has a ratio of 1 to 1. When an object's distance from the eye is doubled, for instance, its projected size is halved; when distance is tripled, size is cut to a third. The brain takes these facts into account when judging true size. Thus, if a tree 200 feet away looks half the size of one that is 100 feet away, a person will automatically perceive them as being equal in height.

But this perceptual analysis of size can operate effectively only if distance cues are clear. If they are not, a person can easily be fooled about size. The reverse, of course, is also true: if an object is not the size you expect it to be, you can easily misjudge its distance. The Allies took advantage of this fact during their invasion of Normandy in World War II. In the early-morning twilight they dropped 2-foot-tall dummies of paratroopers onto fields away from the planned landing site on the coast. When the dummies hit the ground, the impact set off a series of small explosions, simulating rifle fire. In the poor light and general confusion, the Germans thought the dummies were real paratroopers attacking from a substantial distance. Only when they moved close enough to

see the dummies did they realize that size had misled them about distance. In the meantime, the Allies had gained extra time for their landing.

DEPTH PERCEPTION

What the Allies actually did with their 2-foot dummies was to exploit the influence of relative size on depth perception, the ability to tell how far away an object is. Because the images cast on the retina are in two dimensions, not three, depth perception cannot be explained by the eye's structure. Instead, depth perception, like perceptual constancy, must be an outcome of the way the brain organizes and gives meaning to sensory information. Let us examine some of the ways this process works.

First, depth perception is partly the result of the fact that the brain receives visual input from two eyes rather than one. Since the eyes are set apart from each other, each views the world from a slightly different angle, giving the two retinas slightly different images. This difference in retinal images is called **binocular disparity.** You can demonstrate binocular disparity to

FIGURE 4.17   The positioning of light and shadow are important clues to depth. The spheres in the left, right, and middle columns look like bulges, while those in the other two columns look like hollows. Now try turning the book upside down. The former bulges now become recessed and the former hollows now protrude. These striking changes in depth perception are caused by a shift in shading from the bottom to the top of a sphere, and vice versa. (*After Sekuler and Blake, 1990.*)

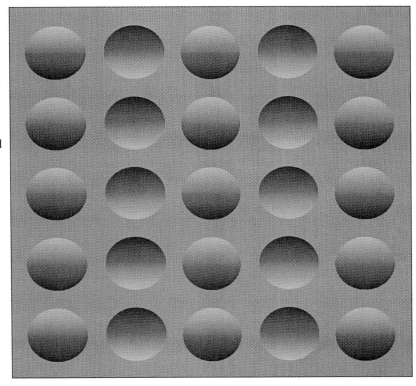

yourself by holding a finger in front of you and looking at it with one eye at a time. The image registered by the right eye will be slightly left of center, while that registered by the left eye will be slightly right of center. Now line up your finger with some other object that is farther away, and look at both your finger and that object with one eye at a time. As you switch from eye to eye, your finger will seem to jump back and forth in relation to the more distant object because the binocular disparity of objects farther away is less than that of nearer ones. The brain uses such binocular disparity cues to help judge distance and to give a sense of depth.

It is not necessary to have two eyes to perceive depth, however. Several monocular cues—that is, cues potentially available to one eye only—augment depth perception. One of these cues is **motion parallax,** the differences in the relative movements of retinal images that occur when we change position. An easy way to demonstrate motion parallax is to look toward two objects, one very near you, the other some distance away, and move your head back and forth. The near object will seem to move more than

the far one. This difference explains a perception you have as you look out the side window of a car as it moves along a highway. Nearby trees seem to zip by, while distant mountains appear hardly to move at all. We use such differences in apparent movement between near and far objects to help perceive depth.

Other monocular depth cues do not depend on movement. One, mentioned earlier, is **relative size.** When you think that two objects are the same size, you perceive the one casting the smaller retinal image to be farther away. **Relative closeness to the horizon** is also a monocular depth cue: objects that are closer to the horizon are generally seen as more distant. Another monocular cue is **linear perspective,** produced by the apparent convergence of parallel lines as they recede into the distance. **Texture gradient** also influences depth perception. In a highly textured scene, near objects appear coarser and more distant ones finer. Then, too, we judge distance by the **partial overlap** of objects. When one object appears to cover another, we perceive the object that is covered as farther away. **Light and shadow** give us a sense of depth as well. In Figure 4.17, the spheres in

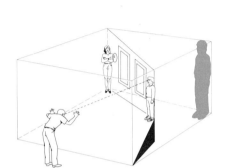

FIGURE 4.18   The Ames room. The illusion is produced by trapezoidal windows that run parallel to the sloping floor, making the room look rectangular (*right*). In (*left*), the actual construction of the room is compared with the way the room is perceived. The brain infers that both people standing against the back wall are at the same distance from the eye and interprets the difference between the size of their images as a real difference in size.

the left, right, and middle columns seem to bulge out, while those in the other two columns appear sunken. These different perceptions of depth are caused by differences in how the shadows are drawn. Your brain assumes that lighting comes from above, as does light from the sun (Ramachandran, 1988). So when the bottom of something is in shadow, you see it as projecting forward; and when, conversely, the top is in shadow, you see it as recessed.

EXPLAINING ILLUSIONS

Usually the perceptual processes we have been discussing serve us quite well. But when these processes are applied in unusual circumstances, they can sometimes give rise to **perceptual illusions**—that is, perceptions that differ from the true characteristics of objects. In these cases our perceptual processes are being fooled.

Illusions of this sort provide important insights into how our perceptual processes normally operate. At first this statement may seem a contradiction. How can illusions shed light on normal perceptual func-

tioning? To help answer this question, examine the room shown in Figure 4.18, known as the Ames room after its inventor, Adelbert Ames. Using one eye only, viewers peer into the room through a small hole in the front wall, thus eliminating the depth cues normally provided by binocular disparity. Since the viewers cannot move their position, depth cues from motion parallax are also eliminated. What observers see is astonishing: a dwarf seems to be standing side by side with a giant. Logically, most people know that this is an illusion. But what gives rise to it?

The answer is that, lacking the depth cues of binocular disparity and motion parallax, observers must rely mainly on linear perspective to judge the shape and depth of the room. However, linear perspective is distorted by, among other things, the way the "windows" are painted on the rear wall. These windows are really trapezoids (taller on the left side than on the right), but they appear to be rectangular because they parallel an angled rear wall and a downward-sloping floor. So viewers get the impression of a normal rectangular room in which each of the two people stands at an equal distance from the

FIGURE 4.19 Two famous illusions. The vertical lines of the figures in the Muller-Lyer illusion part A are identical in length, but they do not appear to be. An explanation for this illusion, suggested in (B), is that the arrow marking on the lines in part A causes you to perceive them as three-dimensional objects that have corners. The corners seem to induce a size constancy effect: the vertical line that appears to be distant is perceived as larger. The horizontal lines in the Ponzo illusion (C) are also identical in length. As the photograph in (D) suggests, this figure, too, could easily be perceived as three-dimensional, and again size constancy would cause the apparently more distant "object" to be scaled up in an apparent size relative to the "nearer object." (*After Gregory, 1970.*)

peephole. Note that this illusion does not involve a breakdown of normal powers of perception. Instead, viewers are applying the perceptual processes that serve them well in everyday life to a stimulus that has been purposely designed to produce perceptual error. To understand this important point more fully, study Figure 4.19, which demonstrates two other vivid illusions apparently caused by a misapplication of normal perceptual processes.

Illusions like these are of more than just theoretical interest. They can be purposefully applied in practical situations to create a desired effect. For example, a motorist driving at a constant speed over evenly spaced horizontal lines will become accustomed to the constant amount of time it takes to drive from one line to the next. If the lines are then spaced progressively closer together, the motorist will experience the illusion of increased speed even though the car has not accelerated (Denton, 1971). This trick has been used to encourage drivers to slow down as they leave high-speed roads or approach toll booths.

HOW DO PERCEPTUAL PROCESSES DEVELOP?

How did you come to perceive the world as you do? What factors led you to organize your perceptual environment according to the principles we have described? Historically, there have been two schools of thought on this issue. The first, called the **empiricist view,** holds that perceptual processes are largely a matter of learning. Babies, it claims, enter the world with little or no ability to see form, depth, perceptual constancies, and so forth. To them the world is "one great blooming, buzzing confusion," as psychologist William James (1890) once put it. Only gradually do infants learn adultlike perceptions on the basis of cues the environment provides. In sharp contrast is the **nativist view** of perceptual development. It holds that not all perceptual processes can be accounted for by learning. These processes also arise from the way our sensory systems work. Note how these two views are closely related to the two general perspectives on

FIGURE 4.20　Perceptual set. Most people see this well-known reversible figure as a rabbit. When they shift their attention to the left side of the figure, the image changes into a bird.

FIGURE 4.21　The stimulus above the handwriting can be interpreted as either 15 or IS, depending on its context.

perception we talked about earlier. The empiricist view is linked to the indirect or constructivist perspective, which says that knowledge must be imposed on sensory data in order to organize it. The nativist view, in contrast, is tied to the direct perspective, with its stress on how sensory information is automatically structured.

Most contemporary psychologists believe that neither the empiricist nor the nativist viewpoint is adequate in itself. They say that only through the interaction of inherited biological factors *and* experience do our perceptual processes unfold. Thus, what we see, hear, feel, and so forth is partly the result of how our sensory systems are programmed and partly the result of what we are exposed to.

This modern **interactionist view** of perceptual development is vividly illustrated by research into depth perception and the brain. To understand this research you must first know more about how cells in the visual cortex operate. In a newborn kitten or monkey (two animals that have been studied extensively), most visual cortex neurons receive input from *both* eyes (Singer, 1986). These so-called **binocular neurons** play a vital role in perceiving depth. Researchers have wondered if early life experiences can alter how binocular neurons function. To find out, Blake and Hirsch (1975) denied newborn kittens the simultaneous use of both eyes. On one day they

covered the left eye with an opaque contact lens; on the next they covered the right eye, continuing in this manner over a period of several months. When the kittens were finally given a chance to use both their eyes together, they had trouble perceiving depth. What had happened to them? The answer lay in the visual cortex. The experimental treatment had prompted the development of two distinct sets of cells: one set activated by the left eye, the other by the right. The normal pattern of neurons connected to *both* of the kittens' eyes had to a large extent disappeared. Thus two-eyed visual experience early in life seems to be essential to maintaining binocular neurons and normal depth perception.

This is an excellent example of the brain's plasticity, its ability to change in response to environmental conditions. This example also clearly shows that perceptual abilities are not just a product of biology *or* experience. Only through the interaction of both do perceptual processes develop (Wall, 1988).

EXPECTATIONS AND PERCEPTION

Although learning and experience are only part of the explanation of why we perceive things as we do, psychologists have studied these factors extensively. In this section, therefore, we take a closer look at some of the ways in which learning and experience mold our expectations, which in turn shape our perceptions. Two important concepts involved in this process are perceptual set and schema.

PERCEPTUAL SET

Suppose you are told that Figure 4.20 is a drawing of a rabbit. Is that what it looks like to you? Most people answer "yes" without hesitation, but now look again at the picture. This time you are viewing a

FIGURE 4.22 Perception and familiarity. These scrambled and unscrambled scenes illustrate how our familiarity with the normal relations among objects speeds up perception. (From Biederman et al., 1973.)

drawing of a bird. Does your perception of the image suddenly change? Do ears now become a beak? This example illustrates the concept of **perceptual set,** a frame of mind that "sets" a person to perceive things in a certain way. Perceptual sets establish expectations that guide our perceptions. We perceive what we think we *should* perceive.

A perceptual set can arise from what other people tell us, or it can stem from our own experiences or desires. Context is one factor that can lead us to perceive things in a particular manner. Look, for instance, at the two lines in Figure 4.21. Did you notice that the "IS" in the top line is the same as the "15" below it? Probably not, because the contexts were guiding your perceptions, causing you first to see a series of letters, then a string of numbers.

EXPECTATIONS BASED ON SCHEMAS

General knowledge of the world in the form of schemas also shapes our expectations, and hence what we perceive. This has been shown clearly in the work of Irving Biederman. Biederman and his colleagues have been intrigued by how quickly people process the information in photos of real-world scenes, such as a city street, a kitchen, or the top of someone's desk (Biederman et al., 1973; Biederman et al., 1974). When people view such scenes for only a tenth of a second, they can remember almost half the objects that the scenes contain. How is this rapid visual processing accomplished? Is perception really *that* automatic and instantaneous? Apparently not if people don't have help from their knowledge of the world, for when pictures are cut into six equal pieces and randomly rearranged, observers are much slower at processing what they see. They have trouble both identifying the objects in the pictures and remembering them when the pictures are removed. Figure 4.22 gives examples of photos that Biederman has used in his studies. When people process the one on the left, they seem to do so with the aid of a "city street" schema that partially tells them what to expect. With the photo on the right, this schema is no longer useful and perception becomes much harder.

Biederman has also discovered that schemas and the expectations they trigger can prompt people to overlook things that don't "belong" in a scene (Biederman et al., 1981; Biederman et al., 1982). To test this process, take a very quick look at Figure 4.23 and see if you spot anything odd about it. With only a quick glance, people are not very good at perceiving the sofa in the upper right-hand corner. Here again expectations are affecting what we see.

KNOWLEDGE AND EXPECTATIONS IN COMPUTER MODELS

Knowledge-based, expectation-guided models of perception are now being incorporated into computer vision systems (Gevarter, 1985). Researchers in this

FIGURE 4.23 In this drawing, the presence of the floating sofa is inconsistent with the natural relations among the rest of the objects. (*From Biederman et al., 1982.*)

area are motivated by two goals. One is to develop computer systems that can recognize specific patterns, such as addresses on envelopes or defects in machine parts. The other goal is to develop models that can help us understand how human perception works. There is widespread agreement that a general-purpose visual system, like the one humans possess, must have access to a great deal of knowledge in order to operate. But exactly how does this knowledge enter into visual processing?

One idea used in computer programs is that of different levels of analysis (Treisman, 1986). At lower levels, a major task is to distinguish the various features that make up a visual stimulus (lines, angles, edges, and so forth). In living organisms this task is partly performed by the feature-detecting cells in the visual cortex. Some researchers think that the process probably occurs in two steps: the first involves an instantaneous picking out of the most conspicuous features, and the second involves an attentive scanning of the stimulus to extract additional details (Julesz, 1984). Beyond the feature-detection level, higher-order processes comes into play. Here the task is to use symbolic representations of things we know to identify and interpret incoming visual data. A simple example is using a symbolic representation of what a dog looks like to correctly identify various four-footed creatures as dogs. This is the level at which schemas and prior knowledge have such important roles.

In the human brain these knowledge-based interpretive functions seem to be carried out in regions separate from those that perform feature detection. This is suggested from studies of people who suffer from **agnosias,** various kinds of inabilities to recognize objects. For instance, some people have trouble identifying everyday objects such as a watch or a telephone, even though they can clearly see the object's component parts. (Remember the man who mistook his wife for a hat, discussed in Chapter 3.) Here is how one such person responded when asked to identify a picture of a pair of eyeglasses: "There is a circle . . . and another circle . . . a cross bar . . . why it must be a bicycle?" (Luria, 1973). A woman with the same problem could not visually identify her own car in a parking lot. Rather than finding the car by appearance, she had to laboriously read each and every license plate (Damasio et al., 1982). Visual agnosias are related to damage in specific parts of the brain—especially forward portions of the occipital lobes and various parts of the temporal lobes.

Computer researchers have not even come close to duplicating the marvelous efficiency of human vision. In a normal human brain, knowledge is effortlessly brought to bear on incoming sensory data, giving it structure and meaning. What we know and remember help us make sense of what we see and hear. But at the same time, what we see and hear becomes an essential building block for acquiring more knowledge of the world. Thus, perception and other higher cognitive processes, such as learning and memory, *mutually* influence each other. None of these processes is ever completely isolated from the others.

IN DEPTH

Can We Perceive without Awareness?

So far we have assumed that all perceptions are conscious ones, that people are aware of the things they are perceiving and of how they interpret them. But is this the only kind of perception humans are capable of? Is it possible that we might be able to detect very fleeting or faint stimuli at some subconscious level? This brings us to the topic of **subliminal perception,** the brain's ability to register a stimulus presented so briefly or weakly that it cannot be consciously perceived. Subliminal perception is very controversial, as you will discover when you read about it in depth.

Some computer programs are approaching the sophistication of human vision. Programs that can project 3D images are useful in aerospace research.

THE INITIAL STUDIES

In the summer of 1957 a marketing executive named James Vicary conducted a six-week study that was soon to ignite an explosion of interest in subliminal perception. The site of the study was an unimposing movie theater in Fort Lee, New Jersey, just across the Hudson River from New York City. What Vicary did was very simple, and some might even think ludicrous. He superimposed on the regular film some verbal messages that appeared so briefly they could not be consciously detected. One message told the unsuspecting moviegoers "Eat popcorn," while another instructed them "Drink Coke." According to Vicary, popcorn sales surged upward by an impressive 58 percent, and Coke sales rose by a very respectable 18 percent (Morse and Stoller, 1982).

Vicary's study made national headlines. Many people were outraged at such underhanded practices. But others couldn't resist trying out their own subliminal messages (Moore, 1982). One radio station in Seattle launched a subliminal campaign against its archrival, television, by broadcasting such subaudible slurs as "TV's a bore." A few department stores in Toronto even played subliminal antishoplifting messages over their public address systems. As shoppers browsed through kitchenware and tried on shoes, a subaudible voice repeatedly warned them, "If you steal, you'll get caught." Many psychologists were fascinated. Some were eager to find out if subliminal perception was even possible, let alone whether such perceptions could actually influence behavior. Conducting controlled experiments was the best way to answer these intriguing questions.

One of the earliest such experiments was conducted by William Bevan (1964). He gave people mild electric shocks to the wrist and asked them to judge the severity of each one. When brief subliminal shocks were administered before a test shock, the subjects tended to describe the test shock as significantly stronger. It was as if their brains were subconsciously adding up the subliminal shocks *plus* the consciously perceived one and reporting the total sensation. In the early 1960s other psychologists also gathered data suggesting that subliminal perception may be possible in certain situations. For instance, when signal detection researchers asked subjects to express their degree of confidence that a very weak stimulus was or was not presented, they found that a person's confidence was related directly to the intensity of the stimulus—*even* for a stimulus that the person reported *not* detecting (Green and Swets, 1966; Swets, 1961). On some level, therefore, the subject must have registered "undetected" stimuli.

In spite of strong evidence that subliminal elements do not make advertisements more effective, some observers still insist that these hidden messages are widely used. Ice cubes shown in liquor and soft-drink ads are popular focuses for such claims. Some people perceive a skull in this ice cube, an image intended to make the viewer want to drink to forget the fear of death.

Still more support for subliminal perception came from work by Robert Zajonc and his colleagues. In one study they took advantage of the fact that repeated exposure to a stimulus often breeds a liking for it, an effect we will talk about further in Chapter 17. They presented people with polygons of various shapes, each for only a thousandth of a second. Later they showed the subjects the same polygons plus new ones, giving them as long as they needed to rate how much they liked each one and whether they recognized it. Significantly, most subjects tended to like the previously seen polygons better than the ones they had never seen, even though they could not consciously distinguish between the "old" and the "new" (Kunst-Wilson and Zajonc, 1980). Once again, it appeared that at some level people do process subliminal information.

The most recent evidence that subliminal perception is sometimes possible comes from studies based on the "priming" effect. Suppose you are shown the word *doctor* preceded by another word, known as the prime. When the prime is related to *doctor* (for example, *nurse*), you can determine that *doctor* is a meaningful word more quickly than when the prime is *un*related to it. Subliminal-perception researchers have taken advantage of this fact by prime masking—that is, interrupting a brief presentation of the prime with randomly arranged letters so that people cannot reliably say what the prime is (Cheesman and Merikle, 1985; Marcel, 1983). Yet even when the prime is masked and people say they cannot read it, they still process a second word more quickly when the prime is related to it. It appears that they are able to perceive the prime on a subliminal level.

But it is one thing to say that subliminal perception is sometimes possible and quite another to assert that such perceptions can actually change behavior. What evidence is there that subliminal messages can prompt people to do things they otherwise would not? One of the few early studies appearing to support this view was conducted by Marvin Zuckerman (1960). He displayed a series of thirty pictures about which subjects were to write descriptive stories. For the first ten pictures, experimental and control subjects were treated exactly alike. The pictures were presented individually, and the subjects wrote a story after viewing each one. This procedure established a baseline level of writing for each group. Then, for the experimental subjects (but not for the controls), Zuckerman accompanied the next ten pictures with the subliminal message, "Write more." Finally, the experimental subjects received the subliminal instruction, "Don't write," with the last ten pictures they saw. Zuckerman found that the experimental subjects *did* write more than the baseline level during the subliminal "Write more" message, and they decreased their level of writing slightly when the "Don't write" message was given. He interpreted this to mean that the experimental subjects had indeed followed his subliminal directives.

CRITICISMS, ALTERNATIVES, AND FURTHER RESEARCH

But other psychologists were not so ready to concede support for the power of subliminal messages. They pointed out that other interpretations of Zuckerman's results were possible (Moore, 1982). It seems that even from the beginning, Zuckerman's experimental subjects were more enthusiastic writers than his control subjects were. During the baseline condition, they spontaneously wrote much more about each picture than those in the control group did. Later, when the subliminal "Write more" was presented to them, they *did* increase their levels of output, as a subliminal-perception interpretation would predict; but so did control subjects who received no such message. The fact that the experimental subjects increased their writing more than the control subjects did may simply have been due to their natural enthusiasm for writing. Finally, the small drop in writing output that the experimental subjects showed when the subliminal "Don't write" message was given to them may have been nothing more than a "wearing out" effect. If you had written twenty stories as diligently as you could, it wouldn't be surprising if you wrote a little less in the next ten. In short, Zuckerman's findings by no means strongly support the ability of subliminal instructions to direct behavior. This may help explain why no other researchers appear to have replicated Zuckerman's results.

But what about the Vicary study mentioned earlier? Didn't it provide some convincing evidence that people sometimes follow what subliminal messages tell them? The answer here is "no, not really." When you look carefully at the study's design, you will find that it has serious flaws. Vicary's research is an example of a quasi-experiment. As we pointed out in Chapter 2, a quasi-experiment does not provide the powers of control that a true experiment does. Perhaps other factors were systematically influencing Coke and popcorn sales after Vicary introduced his subliminal messages. Maybe the weather grew hotter and people were thirstier. Or perhaps some lengthy movies were shown during the six-week period, so that people simply got hungrier as they were watching the shows. If so, purchases of Coke and popcorn might have risen for reasons that had nothing to do with Vicary's subliminal ads. Since Vicary apparently made no effort to take such additional influences into account, we cannot conclude that subliminal advertising caused his reported effects.

PATTERNS AND CONCLUSIONS

From all the studies conducted to date, what can we conclude about the effectiveness of subliminal messages? First, it seems that under certain carefully controlled laboratory conditions, people may sometimes perceive things without conscious awareness (Kihlstrom, 1987). In natural settings, however, it is not easy to meet the conditions needed for subliminal perception. For one thing, individuals have quite variable sensory thresholds, so it is hard to find a single stimulus intensity that will be below threshold for an entire group of people, yet not so far below that it has no effect whatsoever on the brain. In addition, it is hard to display subliminal stimuli in a barrage of consciously perceived ones. On a motion picture screen, for instance, the ongoing movie will almost inevitably overpower any fleeting subliminal ad (Dixon, 1971). The same seems to be true of subliminal messages on audio cassettes that claim to help instill desirable behaviors (such as assertiveness, self-control over drug use, improved reading skills, and heightened sexual responses). These messages are embedded in consciously heard sounds, including music and the sound of waves breaking on a shore. When researchers tested to see if people could subconsciously perceive these messages, they found no evidence that they could (Merikle, 1988). (Even analysis by electronic equipment could not detect them.) Thus, when subliminal perception is possible, it is only under conditions when people can maximally focus their attention on the faint or fleeting stimulus.

At the same time, there is virtually no evidence that subliminal messages can get people to do things they would not ordinarily do (Moore, 1988). Human beings, after all, are not robots. Even if they do detect a subliminal message, there is no reason to think that many of them will automatically follow its directives. People are not that easy to sway with overt appeals to change their behavior. Why would they be so much more susceptible to weak and fleeting ones? There are many compelling reasons, then, why most psychologists agree that subliminal perception is not an effective method of persuasion.

SUMMARY

1. **Sensation** is the process whereby stimulation of receptor cells in various parts of the body sends nerve impulses to the brain, where they register as a touch, a sound, a taste, a splash of color, and so forth. **Perception** is the process whereby the brain interprets the sensations it receives, giving them order and meaning.

2. Sensations and perceptions are not exact representations of what is "out there" in the environment. Instead, they are products of our particular sensory systems coupled with the beliefs and expectations we hold. Because of this, psychologists have spent a great deal of time studying the relationship between **stimuli** and sensations.

3. The sensation of sight begins when light waves pass through the eye's **cornea, iris, pupil,** and **lens** and strike the light-sensitive surface called the **retina** at the back of the eyeball. Here receptor cells convert light energy into nerve impulses, which travel via the **optic nerve** to the brain, where they give rise to the perceptions of shape, color, depth, texture, movement, and so forth.

4. The receptors in the eyes are of two kinds, rods and cones. Both convert light into electrical signals by means of chemical reactions involving light-sensitive pigments. **Rods** mediate low-light-intensity vision, while cones mediate high-light-intensity sight. **Cones** are also involved in the perception of color. Part of the explanation of color vision lies in the fact that our cones contain three different forms of pigment, each maximally sensitive to light of different wavelengths. According to the **trichromatic theory** of color vision, the many colors we see are caused by different relative activations of these three types of cones. This explanation alone, however, has proved to be incomplete. Investigators have also found that nerve cells in the visual system respond in an opponent on–off fashion to complementary color pairs. These cells provide support for what is called the **opponent-process theory.**

5. Sound waves travel down the **auditory canal** to the **eardrum,** which responds to changes in air pressure by moving in and out. Its movements set in motion three tiny bones, called the **hammer, anvil,** and **stirrup,** which amplify the pressure eventually exerted on the **oval window** leading to the inner ear. Within

the inner ear's spiral-shaped **cochlea** are thousands of receptors called **hair cells,** which trigger nerve impulses when they are bent and rubbed by movement of the **basilar membrane.** These impulses then travel via the **auditory nerve** to the brain, where the perception of sound occurs.

6. There is still debate over how sound waves of different frequencies are translated into the perception of different pitches. According to the **place theory,** each pitch depends on which part of the basilar membrane a given sound wave vibrates the most. According to the **frequency theory,** pitch depends on the patterns with which auditory nerve cells fire, these patterns presumably matching the frequencies of the original sound waves. Both these theories seem to have merit.

7. The skin senses include touch, pressure, warmth, cold, and pain. From receptors lying at different depths in the body tissue, these sensations are transmitted to the brain. Understanding how pain occurs is particularly difficult, both because it can sometimes arise with no physiological cause, and because thoughts and emotions can greatly affect the perception of it. The **gate-control theory** of pain holds that gate cells in the spinal cord serve to block or release the transmission of pain messages to the brain.

8. The senses of smell and taste are closely linked. Smell, or **olfaction,** occurs when vaporized molecules of a substance enter the nasal passages and contact receptor cells in the **olfactory membranes,** which in turn send neural messages to the brain. Different areas of the tongue are especially sensitive to one or more of the four basic taste categories we perceive: sweet, sour, salty, and bitter. **Taste buds,** grouped on the upper surface of the tongue in hill-like projections called **papillae,** contain receptor cells connected to nerve fibers that carry taste information to the brain. Although our other senses are not as closely interconnected as smell and taste, we nevertheless are constantly integrating information from them.

9. Psychologists have studied many aspects of perception. The **gestalt psychologists** have been among those interested in **form perception.** They have looked at how the brain unifies sensory data into meaningful wholes, called **gestalts.** Two major ways it does this is through **perceptual grouping** and through division of stimuli into **figure** (objects) **and**

ground (spaces between objects). Another way that we routinely impose order on sensory information is through **perceptual constancy,** the tendency to see objects as having stable properties even though the visual information we receive about them is constantly changing. A third important perceptual process is **depth perception,** the brain's tendency to see the world in three dimensions even though the images that strike our retinas have only two dimensions. Depth is perceived partly as a result of **binocular disparity.** Monocular depth cues include **motion parallax, relative size, relative closeness to the horizon, linear perspective, texture gradient,** the **partial overlap** of objects, and **light and shadow.**

10. When perceptual processes are applied in unusual circumstances, they can sometimes give rise to **perceptual illusions.** Such illusions provide important insights into the way our perceptual processes normally work.

11. Perception involves not just **"bottom-up"** or **data-driven processing,** but **"top-down"** or **conceptually driven processing** as well. Those who stress these aspects of perception are said to take an **indirect perspective** or **constructivist view** (as opposed to a **direct perspective**). They emphasize such concepts as **perceptual set** (a frame of mind that "sets" people to perceive things in certain ways) and **schemas** (mental representations of objects and events against which incoming data are compared and interpreted). Knowledge-based, schema-guided models of perception are now being incorporated into computer vision systems.

12. People have long been fascinated by **subliminal perception**—the apparent ability of the brain to register a stimulus presented so briefly or weakly that it cannot be consciously perceived. There is evidence that, in carefully created laboratory situations, subliminal perception may in fact occur. But the ability of such perceptions to influence behavior is very much in doubt.

SUGGESTED READINGS

Coren, S., and Ward, L. M. (1989). *Sensation and perception* (3rd ed.). New York: Academic Press. A useful textbook that covers modern research on sensation and perception.

Hubel, D. H. (1988). *Eye, brain, and vision.* San Francisco: Freeman. David Hubel, a Nobel prize winner, writes about his intriguing experiments probing the complex processes of vision. He pays special attention to color vision, face recognition, and development of the visual system, including the effects of early visual experiences.

Rock, I. (Ed.). (1990). *The perceptual world: Readings from Scientific American.* San Francisco: Freeman. This collection of articles highlights important research developments in visual perception, from discoveries of specific brain mechanisms to the nature of illusions and computer simulation of vision.

Sacks, O. (1989). *Seeing voices: A journey into the world of the deaf.* New York: Harper Perennial. An intimate portrait of the experiences of the deaf, this book will challenge hearing readers' misperceptions and help them gain a new understanding and appreciation of what the deaf encounter.

Sekuler, R., and Blake, R. (1990). *Perception* (2nd ed.). New York: McGraw-Hill. A very readable text that stresses vision and hearing, but covers smell and taste as well.

CHAPTER 5

THE NATURE OF CONSCIOUSNESS

Doctors have little trouble telling when someone is deeply unconscious. The person is totally unresponsive to the surrounding world. A prick of the finger causes no pain; a loud noise causes no startle reaction. At the same time, the cerebral cortex shows virtually no electrical activity, no indication that the person has any thoughts or feelings at all (Kihlstrom, 1984). A conscious person, in sharp contrast, actively processes a rich array of mental information. In fact, **consciousness** is often defined as an active awareness of all the many thoughts, images, perceptions, and emotions that occupy the mind at any given time (Natsoulas, 1983). Psychologist William James (1842–1910) likened consciousness to a stream that perpetually flows. Stop reading for a moment, and try to make your mind an absolute void. Even if you close your eyes, you will find it impossible to do so, for sensations, thoughts, feelings, and fantasies keep intruding into your consciousness. You hear, you feel, you analyze, you let your mind wander. Your mental stream, in other words, keeps flowing on.

Because consciousness is such a subjective experience, early behaviorists thought that it had no place in psychology. If we cannot objectively see into consciousness to measure and analyze its components, they argued, then consciousness is not a proper subject for scientific study. But most contemporary psychologists disagree with this view. In fact, there are even some renowned experimental psychologists who think that psychology should be redefined as the study of consciousness. This is because consciousness is so central to human functioning. Consciousness is what allows us to monitor ourselves and our environments as we make our way in the world. It is what enables us to exert some control over what we do and experience, to choose among alternative ways of thinking, feeling, and acting (Kihlstrom, 1984; Mandler, 1984). It is also what gives us a sense of continuity, a way of linking experiences into a past, a present, and a future. Without consciousness, in other words, we would have no sense of being, no sense of self (Rychlak, 1986).

How is consciousness related to brain activity? The answer is still unclear. We know that the reticular formation, a part of the hindbrain, plays a key role in maintaining consciousness. Stimulation of the reticular formation causes hyperalertness, whereas injury to it produces coma. Because the human brain has the most highly developed cerebral cortex in the animal kingdom, and because humans also seem to have the most highly developed sense of consciousness, many

"Jet lag" is a minor hazard of travel across time zones, temporarily disrupting daily rhythms of sleep and waking.

researchers assume that the cortex must also be involved in our conscious awareness. But the nature of this involvement is not yet understood. Some neuroscientists suspect that consciousness may simply be the sum total of all brain activity going on at any given moment. Others, however, are not so certain. For instance, Nobel laureate Roger Sperry (1976) points out that consciousness seems to have a role in *guiding* brain activity. If consciousness and brain activity are one and the same, does consciousness then guide itself? Such questions compound the mysteries of human consciousness. To Sperry the basis of consciousness remains one of the greatest unknowns in all of science.

But even though psychologists still have much to learn about the physiological basis of consciousness, they have extensively explored the subjective experience of it. In doing so, they universally agree that consciousness has many modes (Wallace and Fisher, 1987). Think of some of the cyclical changes in consciousness that occur during a typical day, the kinds of changes that can come and go naturally at periodic intervals, with no deliberate effort to create them. Sleep is an obvious example of a cyclical change in consciousness, and daydreaming is another. We will be exploring both in this chapter. In addition, we will look at changes in consciousness that people deliberately induce, either in themselves

or in others. These include drug-induced states of consciousness, meditative states, and hypnotic trances. Though it may seem that this is a broad range of topics for a single chapter, keep in mind the thread that ties them all together: in each of these states, a person's awareness of perceptions, thoughts, and feelings has distinctive qualities. Each, in short, is a different state of consciousness.

CYCLICAL STATES OF CONSCIOUSNESS

Many biological factors change predictably according to daily cycles called **circadian rhythms.** (The term *circadian* comes from the Latin *circa*, meaning "about," and *dies*, meaning "day.") For example, blood pressure, body temperature, and various chemicals in the bloodstream all rise and fall in circadian rhythms. Consciousness too changes according to a daily pattern called the *sleep–wake cycle*. When unaffected by external influences, especially day and night, this cycle spans a total of about twenty-*five* hours (not the twenty-four hours it takes the earth to rotate on its axis). Thus, when people are placed in windowless rooms with no indications of sunrise and sunset, they tend to go to bed about an hour later each day. Under normal conditions, however, we automatically reset our biological sleep clock to the twenty-four-hour light–dark cycle. This relatively minor adjustment is easy. Larger adjustments can be harder. That is why, when you travel by airplane across several time zones, it may take awhile for your sleep patterns to accommodate. It is also the reason why workers placed on rapidly rotating shifts (midnight to 8 A.M. one week, 4 P.M. to midnight the next week, 8 A.M. to 4 P.M. the following week) often complain of health problems, sleep disorders, and lower productivity (Czeisler et al., 1982).

The portion of the sleep–wake cycle that most interests us in this chapter is the time we spend asleep. This is because every other chapter of this book is devoted to the waking state of consciousness. When we talk about perception, learning, memory, emotion, motivation, and all the other psychological processes covered in this text, we are talking about thoughts, feelings, and behaviors that occur when people are awake. This is the only place we talk about the state of consciousness that occupies our *non-waking* lives. What have researchers learned about this sleeping state, in which we spend about a third of each day?

SLEEP

Considering how much time people spend asleep, we know relatively little about why we enter into this state of consciousness. For years scientists have searched for chemicals in the brain that build up and cause sleep to occur. They have found that increased amounts of certain neurotransmitters (serotonin, for example) can sometimes promote sleep, as can another chemical extracted from the blood of sleeping animals (Schneider-Helmert, 1985). But it is not clear that these chemicals are what normally cause sleep. In one study, for example, newborn Siamese twins who shared the same blood supply tended to fall asleep at different times, even though they also shared many of the same biochemicals (Lenard and Schulte, 1972).

More agreement exists about the neural circuits that control the sleep–wake cycle. The brain's wake center seems to be located in an area of the reticular formation. When that area is lesioned, an animal lapses into a permanent coma; when that area is stimulated, a sleeping animal wakes up. The brain also contains sleep circuits that extend from the lower hindbrain to the thalamus and the cortex. The activation of these circuits seems to inhibit the wake center

in the reticular formation, which causes sleep to take over.

BRAIN ACTIVITY FROM WAKEFULNESS TO DEEP SLEEP

The most revealing data concerning sleep as a distinct state of consciousness come from the use of the electroencephalograph, a device for recording the brain's electrical activity. The chart of brain-wave tracings that an electroencephalograph produces is called an **electroencephalogram (EEG).** In a typical laboratory study of sleep, a volunteer is hooked up to an electroencephalograph by means of electrodes attached to the scalp and the face. The volunteer then settles down in bed to sleep away the night. As the hours pass, an electronic pen records the person's brain waves on rolling graph paper. By morning, the chart is more than 1,000 feet long (Hauri, 1982).

As Figure 5.1 shows, the pattern of brain waves changes distinctively when a person drops from wakefulness into light sleep and then into deep sleep. Notice the reductions that occur in the speed of the brain waves. These reductions are known as changes in *frequency* and are measured in cycles per second. (Refer to Figure 5.1 as we describe what these changes in frequency entail.)

The EEGs of people who are fully awake and alert with eyes open usually show a predominance of **beta waves**—rapid or high-frequency brain waves, measuring 14 or more cycles per second. When people close their eyes and relax, their brain-wave patterns begin to change. Now somewhat slower **alpha waves** start to appear in the record. These alpha waves measure from 8 to 12 cycles per second. When people begin to fall asleep (stage 1 in Figure 5.1), even slower **theta waves** (3 to 7 cycles per second) become mixed in with the alphas, and every now and again a burst of betas is seen. As sleep becomes progressively deeper, the alpha pattern disappears (stage 2 in Figure 5.1). Then gradually, very slow **delta waves** $\frac{1}{2}$ to 2 cycles per second) begin to dominate the record. In the deepest stage of sleep (labeled **delta sleep** in the figure), delta waves occupy more than 50 percent of the EEG. This very deep sleep is accompanied by marked relaxation of muscles, slow and regular breathing, and significant drops in body temperature and pulse rate.

The production of delta waves is related to the amount of time a person has previously stayed awake.

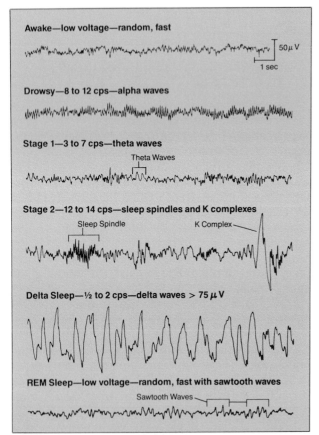

Awake—low voltage—random, fast

50 μ V

1 sec

Drowsy—8 to 12 cps—alpha waves

Stage 1—3 to 7 cps—theta waves

Theta Waves

Stage 2—12 to 14 cps—sleep spindles and K complexes

Sleep Spindle   K Complex

Delta Sleep—½ to 2 cps—delta waves > 75 μ V

REM Sleep—low voltage—random, fast with sawtooth waves

Sawtooth Waves

FIGURE 5.1   These EEG patterns show the electrical activity of the human brain in the various stages of sleep. Note that as sleep becomes deeper, the high-frequency, small-amplitude (small-sized) waves give way to lower-frequency, large-amplitude waves that are also more rhythmic, or synchronized. This change is thought to reflect the fact that the neurons in the brain are all firing at about the same level and in about the same pattern. Note also that the EEG pattern in REM sleep is very similar to the awake pattern. (*Hauri, 1982.*)

The longer the last period of wakefulness, the greater the number of delta waves emitted and the greater their amplitude or strength. This finding has led some researchers to suspect that delta waves may be associated with physiological changes or stresses that take place during waking consciousness (Feinberg and Fein, 1982). In one study, for example, delta sleep increased dramatically for two nights after long-distance runners had completed a 92-kilometer foot-

race (Shapiro et al., 1981). We also know that people deprived specifically of delta sleep sometimes report physical discomfort, such as tenderness in the muscles and joints and greater sensitivity to pain (Moldofsky et al., 1975; Moldofsky and Scarisbrick, 1976). So perhaps delta sleep is somehow related to restoring the ability of skeletal muscles to do their work efficiently (Hauri, 1982).

The nature of consciousness during delta sleep is also something of a puzzle. It is hard to awaken people from this deepest stage of sleep. They almost seem to be in a coma. So by the time the sleeper wakes up and is asked if any thoughts were just occupying consciousness, we cannot be sure if the thoughts reported happened during the delta sleep or during the waking-up period. It seems certain, however, that the brain must actively process both internal and external stimuli during delta sleep, because most episodes of sleepwalking, sleeptalking, and intense nightmares occur during this stage.

REM SLEEP

The nature of sleep is even more complex than our discussion so far implies. You do not merely fall into progressively deeper sleep and then gradually awaken. Instead, the cyclical state of sleep itself has a cycle that recurs about every ninety minutes (see Figure 5.2). First, you fall into deeper and deeper sleep, then gradually return to what superficially resembles a stage 1 or waking pattern; but you do not actually wake up. You remain sound asleep, although your eyes move rapidly back and forth under your closed eyelids. This stage, called rapid eye movement or **REM sleep,** recurs on average four or five times a night. Together, these episodes consume about one and a half to two hours, which is roughly 25 percent of total sleep time (see Figure 5.3). Since the discovery of REM sleep many years ago, psychologists have realized that the sharpest and most important distinction between the various stages of sleep is that between REM sleep and all the other stages, collectively called **non-REM sleep.**

REM Sleep and Dreaming   When researchers first observed REM sleep, they suspected that it was linked to dreaming. To explore this possibility, they woke subjects during the various stages of sleep and asked them to report any mental thoughts or images they

FIGURE 5.2 A typical night's sleep, showing the stages mentioned in the text. A new cycle of stages begins about every 90 to 110 minutes. Note that cycles early in the night are shorter and have more of the deepest stages of sleep (characterized by slow delta waves). Sleep becomes shallower as the night progresses and REM periods become longer.

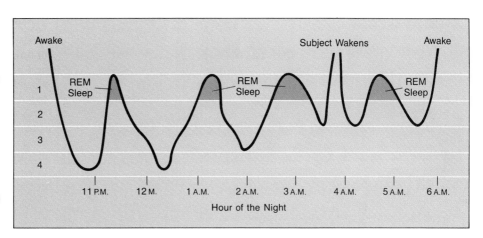

had been experiencing. The results were dramatic. During REM periods, dreams with vivid visual imagery, in which the dreamers felt that they were actively participating, were reported about 80 percent of the time. During non-REM periods, reports of storylike episodes occurred far less frequently. The exact percentages reported depended on how *dream* was defined, because much non-REM mental activity seems more like drifting, unstructured thinking than what we typically call a dream (Hauri, 1982).

With the discovery that rapid eye movements and dreams often go together, it was natural to speculate that sleepers' eyes move as they "watch" activity unfolding in their dreams. This theory, called the **scanning hypothesis,** was first proposed by sleep researcher William Dement (1976) on the basis of data collected in his laboratory. For example, when Dement awakened one subject who showed only horizontal eye movements during a particular REM period, the person reported that he had been dreaming about a Ping-Pong match. The problem with the scanning hypothesis, however, is that the relationship between rapid eye movements and dream content is rarely this clear-cut. A complicated mixture of eye movements, with few distinct patterns, occurs during most dreams.

Most researchers therefore suspect that dreaming is not the cause of rapid eye movements, as the scanning hypothesis suggests. Instead, rapid eye movements and dreaming may be two parallel outcomes of the brain's unusually high state of activation during REM sleep (Chase and Morales, 1983). According to one theory, this high state of activation is

triggered when a part of the pons (a region of the hindbrain) periodically "turns on" during sleep. When it does, it both produces rapid eye movements and bombards higher brain regions, especially the visual and motor systems, with random stimulation. The cortex then tries to make sense of these random neural signals by interpreting them as meaningful sights, sounds, and actions and weaving them together into a dream (Hobson, 1988; Hobson and McCarley, 1977).

The Paradoxes of REM Sleep One curious fact about REM sleep is that in some respects it seems similar to the waking state. The rapid, irregular brain waves that dominate the EEG record during REM periods look very much like those that occur when a person is wide awake. Other physiological signs during REM sleep also resemble those of a wide-awake person. Heartbeat, breathing, and blood pressure are irregular and varied, and there is evidence of sexual arousal. Usually, these patterns would be observed in a person who is not only awake but also excited. It is therefore not surprising that heart attacks, acute ulcer pains, and attacks of emphysema seem to occur more often during REM periods of sleep than in other sleep stages (Armstrong, 1965; Trask and Cree, 1962).

Paradoxically, however, the REM sleeper is *soundly* asleep, not just dozing lightly. He or she often sleeps on through the sound of a voice or the touch of a hand on the shoulder. Moreover, although many signs of arousal are present, the major muscles of the

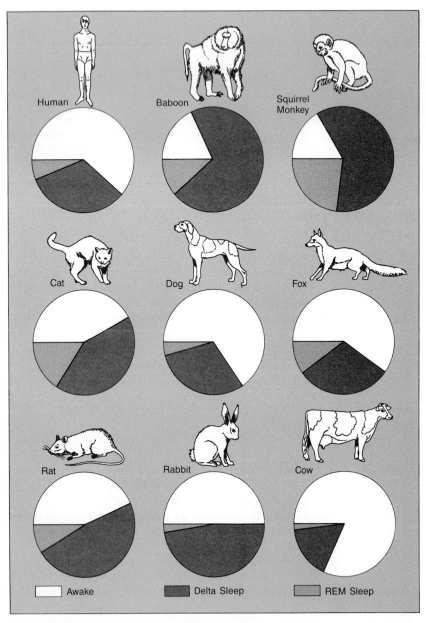

FIGURE 5.3 A comparison of the sleep–wake cycle in different kinds of animals. Although both humans and baboons are primates, and so are related in the animal kingdom, baboons spend much less time awake than we do. The shortest sleeper shown here is the cow, with about half the total sleep time daily of a human. Scientists do not yet know why animals differ so much in their daily amounts of delta sleep, REM sleep, and wakefulness. (*After Rosenzweig and Leiman, 1989.*)

body lose their tone and become limp, to the point where the person is literally unable to move. It is again an area of the pons that seems responsible for this condition. When that area was destroyed in the brain of a cat, REM sleep still occurred, but the animal no longer lay still. Instead, it jumped up and moved about, even though it was still asleep (Jouvet, 1967).

This study suggests an odd possibility: if our muscles were not paralyzed during REM sleep, our bodies might act out our dreams.

Do We Need REM Sleep? Suspecting that REM sleep might somehow be essential to psychological well-being, Dement (1960) deprived people of it for several consecutive nights. Whenever he saw the beginning of a REM period, he awakened the sleeper. With each successive REM episode, Dement found that it became harder and harder to arouse many of his subjects. A few eventually had to be hoisted onto their feet before they finally opened their eyes. And the longer Dement denied REM sleep, the more often his subjects entered REM periods. Whereas people normally have only four or five REM episodes nightly, Dement's subjects had to be awakened an average of ten or twelve times, even on the first night of REM-sleep deprivation. By the third night, Dement was running in and out of the subjects' rooms so fast that he could hardly keep up the pace. Finally, on the fifth night, he let the sleepers go into REM sleep without interruptions. The result was a **REM rebound:** the subjects spent about double the normal time in REM sleep.

Judging from the fact that our bodies automatically compensate for the loss of REM sleep, we can assume that people need it, but we do not know why. People sometimes become tired or irritable as a result of REM deprivation, but they do not display marked impairment during their waking hours. At most, they are slightly more prone than normal to unconventional thoughts and behavior (Dement, 1960; Kales et al., 1964; Sampson, 1965). Still, REM sleep may serve some special function that relatively short-term experiments do not reveal.

One suggestion is that the brain adapts to unusual life experiences during REM periods. In one study, for example, people wore goggles with distorting lenses for several days, and at night their sleep patterns were monitored. While becoming accustomed to the weird lenses, they showed a greater than usual amount of REM sleep. Once they had adapted, however, their REM time dropped back to normal (Luce, 1971). Learning unusual information, such as sentences containing incorrect words, also seems to be facilitated by REM sleep. So perhaps REM sleep helps consolidate into long-term memory information or experiences that require a good deal of effort to absorb (Pearlman, 1982). This theory could help explain why the amount of time spent in REM sleep steadily declines as a person grows older. (Newborns spend about half their sleep time in REM sleep; infants under two years, 30 to 40 percent; adolescents and young adults, about 20 to 25 percent; and elderly people, less than 5 percent.) In general, more infor-

mation and experiences are novel to an infant or a child than they are to an older adult; therefore we see more REM sleep in the young.

Other researchers speculate that REM sleep may provide a way of reducing some of the energy built up when our biological needs go unsatisfied. Support for this idea comes from observations of laboratory animals deprived of REM sleep for long periods, far longer than those normally inflicted on human subjects. The animals tended to show increased appetites for both food and sex. Laboratory cats, for example, after long-term REM-sleep deprivation often attempt to copulate with any available partner, even one that normally is not sexually arousing (Dement, 1969). In short, prolonged loss of REM sleep seems to intensify basic drives. This suggests that ordinarily REM sleep may serve as a kind of physiological release valve.

Researchers do not yet know if REM sleep serves this function in humans as well as other species. Some clues, however, come from studies of people who naturally sleep unusually long or unusually short periods (nine or more hours each night versus six or fewer hours). People who sleep for short periods, on average, experience only half the REM time nightly that long sleepers do. Significantly, these people also tend to have higher energy levels and greater aggressive drive than do people who sleep for long periods (Hartman et al., 1975; Webb and Agnew, 1970). In view of this finding, some clinical researchers have tried prolonged REM-sleep deprivation as a treatment for the severely depressed, who are chronically tired and apathetic. In one study, half the severely depressed patients who were deprived of REM sleep and received no other treatment recovered enough to leave the hospital after about seven weeks (Vogel, 1975; Vogel et al., 1975). Future research may provide many more clues to the possible functions of REM sleep.

THE DREAMS OF SLEEP

By age seventy, the average person will have had about 150,000 dreams (Snyder, 1970). Does this mean 150,000 fascinating adventures? No, not at all. When people are awakened randomly during REM sleep and asked what they have just been dreaming, the reports are often ordinary, even dull (Hall and Van de Castle, 1966). Usually these uneventful dreams are quickly forgotten, probably because they are never consolidated into long-term memory (Kihl-strom, 1984). The dreams that people store long enough to recall when they awaken tend to be emotion-laden, bizarre, or sexy, the kind of dreams that typically occur toward the end of a night's sleep (Hauri, 1982; Webb, 1975). Some psychologists, especially psychoanalysts, find great symbolic meaning in such dreams. Are they right that these dreams have deeper significance, and if so, what determines their content?

What Determines Dream Content? A papyrus in the British Museum dating from the tenth century B.C. instructed the ancients in interpreting their dreams. Today, more than 3,000 years later, people still wonder about the hidden meaning of dreams. Sigmund Freud believed that dreams reflect the repressed needs and desires of the unconscious, needs and desires that often arise from unresolved psychosexual conflicts of childhood. In *The Interpretation of Dreams* (1900), Freud distinguished between the manifest content and the latent content of a dream. The **manifest content** is the readily perceived plot or story line, including the actors, the setting, and the events that take place. The **latent content** is the deeper meaning of the dream, the underlying, largely unconscious wishes it expresses. For instance, one new mother who found herself up at all hours tending to her newborn baby reported to her analyst a dream in which she gave birth to identical twin boys, one of whom then died. According to the analyst, the latent content of the dream was an unconscious wish to be rid of the infant who had destroyed a formerly peaceful, well-ordered way of life. Such a resentful, "unmotherly" wish is particularly hard to admit to, however. To avoid confronting it directly, the woman's mind fashioned a more benign manifest dream plot (*two* babies, only one of whom dies) (Foulkes, 1985). This veiling of the dreamer's unconscious wishes in more acceptable symbolic images is what Freud called "dream work."

But not all psychoanalysts have accepted Freud's views on dreams. Alfred Adler (1870–1937), a close early colleague of Freud, rejected many aspects of Freudian doctrine, including the meaning of dreams. Adler (1936) argued that dreams do not embody unconscious wishes, as Freud believed. Instead, he saw dreams as a continuation (cloaked in visual metaphors) of whatever thoughts and feelings were dominating a person's consciousness during waking

hours. Many contemporary therapists share this perspective (Foulkes, 1964; Gelman, 1989; Ullman, 1962). To them, the student who dreams that he goes to take an exam, opens the door to the classroom, and finds the room dark and deserted is not trying to fulfill some unconscious sexual desire, as a strict Freudian might say, but instead is simply worried about failing an upcoming final.

Implicit in this view is the idea that during nighttime hours we continue to try to cope with our current concerns and problems. Psychologist Rosalind Cartwright (1979) has studied this process in the laboratory. In one experiment, she had people identify a personality trait they disliked in themselves. Then, as they were falling asleep, they repeated a wish to change that trait. Over and over, they said to themselves, "I wish I were not so sarcastic," "I wish I were not so timid," or whatever. Thus, the subjects created a conflict in themselves: they acknowledged having a characteristic that they would rather not possess. Would dreams help them resolve this conflict? For some of the subjects, the answer seemed to be "yes." They dreamed about the worrisome trait more than would be expected by chance. And when they did, they tended to fashion scenes in which the negative trait was entirely justified!

Can We Control Our Dreams?

It was late Sunday night, and Jill Day was having a nightmare. She had watched a violent movie about a serial murderer and, recognizing that her dreams were often affected by such stories, she knew as she fell asleep that she had probably not seen the last of the killer. Perhaps because of that awareness, when the movie psychopath appeared in her dream and threatened to kill her, Day suddenly recognized that he was not real. "I know this is a dream," she yelled at the man. "Now go away and get out of here!" The image of the man dissolved, as did all other images, and she slowly drifted into the obscurity of dreamless sleep (Gackenbach and Bosveld, 1989, p. 27).

People often assume that emotionally negative dreams, which frighten, anger, or disturb us, simply cannot be avoided. Such dreams seem to come when they want to, like uninvited guests, and they stay until we finally awaken to discover that they are not real. But researchers are showing that these common as-

Psychologists disagree about the significance of the content of dreams and about whether and to what extent people can control what they dream about.

sumptions are not entirely right. People *can,* to some extent, control their dream lives, as Jill Day did.

A dream in which the sleeper becomes fully aware that he or she is only dreaming (and yet the dream continues) is called a **lucid dream,** because the person perceives the true situation clearly. Lucid dreams have proven to be excellent opportunities for people to take charge of their dream lives. Psychologist Stephen La Berge (1981) developed a technique for cultivating lucid dreaming for this purpose. The technique involves telling yourself after you awaken from a dream: "The next time I'm dreaming, I want to remember I'm dreaming." At the same time, you repeatedly picture yourself dreaming and then realizing, while still asleep, that you are only dreaming. When La Berge used this method himself, he averaged more than twenty lucid dreams a month, sometimes as many as four a night. More important, these lucid dreams allowed him to resolve many of his nighttime conflicts in emotionally satisfying ways.

With the recognition that people can potentially control dream content, some psychologists have tried to develop dream-management techniques as a form of psychotherapy (Begley, 1989). The theory is that, if

people can incorporate constructive conclusions into dreams related to their current life problems (divorce, loss of a job, failure at school, and so forth), their self-image and outlook may improve significantly. But not all psychologists feel that *control* of dream content is the best form of dream therapy. Some contend that we should use lucid dreams not just to give our nighttime fantasies pleasant endings but also to explore what they mean.

One way to do this is to actively engage dream characters in conversation. German psychologist Paul Tholey, who has studied lucid dreaming for many years, tells of how his father used to appear in his dreams as a hostile, threatening figure, full of criticisms and insults (Gackenbach and Bosveld, 1989). If Tholey turned lucid during one of these dreams, he would sometimes beat his father, transforming him into a primitive creature and making him go away. Tholey felt triumphant on these occasions, but in subsequent dreams the father would reappear. Then one night when Tholey dreamed that he was running from a tiger, he became lucid and asked the tiger who he was. The tiger turned into his father, who began criticizing again. But this time, instead of banishing the dream father, Tholey began talking to him, saying that he hated his threatening manner, although some of the criticisms were justified. The two eventually grew friendly, shook hands, and became one. Tholey was never again troubled by the memory of his father, and he also overcame the problems he had always had dealing with authority figures in his life.

We do not yet know to what extent such dream manipulation can influence other kinds of troubling feelings and behaviors. Nor do we know how many people are capable of taking charge of their dreams in this way. The possibilities are intriguing, however. Apparently, people may have more capacity to deliberately shape their nighttime fantasies than was ever imagined.

EXPLORING SLEEP DISORDERS

The most common sleep disorder is **insomnia,** difficulty in falling asleep or in staying asleep all night. About 20 percent of all people have insomnia at some time in their lives (Schneider and Tarshis, 1986). Brief episodes of insomnia are usually caused by transient worries and stress, but the insomnia is often worsened by the way in which the sufferer deals with it (Hauri, 1982). Many people become upset after several nights of poor sleep, to the point that getting into bed increases their state of arousal. The increased arousal makes sleep all the less likely, further increasing the distress and arousal, so that a vicious circle sets in. Such insomnia is often treated with a combination of relaxation training, sleep medications, and stimulus-control therapy, in which the person avoids staying in bed when he or she is not really sleepy (Hauri, 1982).

When insomnia fails to respond to this kind of treatment and continues unabated over a long period of time, some biological factor may be involved as well. One biological condition that can contribute to insomnia is **sleep apnea.** People with severe sleep apnea literally stop breathing shortly after falling asleep and then quickly wake up, gasping for air. They then drift back to sleep again, and the cycle is repeated—in extreme cases, every minute or almost 500 times a night (Schneider and Tarshis, 1986). By morning they feel exhausted, as if they had not slept at all. Sleep apnea is often caused by an overrelaxation of the muscles in the throat as the person falls asleep, which causes the air passage to be cut off.

Another cause is a central nervous system disorder in which the diaphragm, the muscle that controls the lungs, stops working during sleep (Kolb and Whishaw, 1990). Treatment depends partly on the source of the problem.

People who have relatively mild cases of sleep apnea are sometimes only partially awakened by the repeated shortages of oxygen during the night. Consequently, these people are usually unaware of their condition. Rather than complaining of insomnia, they tend to complain of excessive sleepiness during the day (Kelly, 1981). A more extreme cause of excessive daytime sleepiness is the condition called **narcolepsy,** in which a wide-awake person suddenly loses muscle control and quickly collapses into sleep. Narcoleptics often enter a REM period *immediately* upon falling asleep, as if the REM circuit in the brain suddenly and unpredictably turns on and overrides waking consciousness. The disorder is often treated with drugs that both enhance wakefulness and inhibit REM sleep (Hauri, 1982).

DAYDREAMING

Walter Mitty dutifully drives his wife to the shop where she is to have her hair done. "Remember to buy those overshoes," she orders, "and put on your gloves!" Mitty nods in resignation and slowly drives away. As he passes the hospital on his way to find parking, his thoughts take a flight of fancy. He is a world-renowned surgeon, held in awe by the hospital staff. As a wealthy banker lies near death on the operating table, a vital piece of high-tech equipment suddenly breaks down. The other doctors panic, but Mitty steps forward to save the day. Ingeniously, he repairs the machine using a fountain pen for a spare part. But the repair will last only ten minutes. Who could possibly perform the operation in such a short amount of time? The specialists called in from New York and London turn pale with apprehension. "Would you take over, Mitty?" they ask. "If you wish," he confidently replies. Just then a loud voice interrupts the reverie. "Wrong lane, Mac," shouts the parking lot attendant, and Mitty sheepishly backs out of the exit.

This memorable character in James Thurber's story "The Secret Life of Walter Mitty" clearly enters a different state of consciousness when he begins to daydream. A **daydream** is a train of thought that departs from a person's immediate situation and whatever tasks are at hand. For a few moments the daydreamer loses "touch" with the outside world and focuses attention instead on some internal drama (Klinger, 1987). Often these dramas contain elements that do not usually occur in the daydreamer's real life. In daydreams the timid can become assertive, the dull brilliant, the inept competent, the poor wealthy, the house-bound world travelers.

You may think that daydreams occur randomly throughout our waking hours, summoned to our minds whenever we feel like letting our imaginations roam. The occurrence of daydreams, however, is more regular than this. In fact, most people enter this state of consciousness at regular intervals during the day, intervals that are roughly 90 to 100 minutes apart (Lavie and Kripke, 1981). This is true of people in their everyday settings, as well as in specially created environments that lack cues about the time of day. Notice that the 90- to 100-minute daydreaming cycle is very similar in length to the cycle of nighttime dreaming that occurs during REM periods (see Figure 5.1). Some psychologists think that this similarity is not coincidental. Perhaps, they say, the human brain has a fundamental rest–activity cycle that underlies both REM-sleep dreaming and the kind of daytime fantasizing that occupies our minds when current tasks do not demand our full attention (Kleitman, 1969).

Although we do not yet know what prompts a person to drift into a daydream, we do know that when a daydream is occurring it activates some of the same brain regions involved when a person actually perceives and acts in the real world. For instance, self-generated visual imagery, such as occurs during a daydream, activates regions of the occipital and temporal lobes of the cortex, where visual signals from the outside world are also processed. In this case, however, the outside world is tuned out and an inner world unfolds. Interestingly, too, in most people, the brain's right hemisphere becomes more active during daydreams with visual imagery, the right hemisphere being the side of the brain that tends to specialize, among other things, in the perception of complex scenes (Goldstein, 1984).

Some researchers have studied the content of daydreams, hoping to find insights into their functions. Freud believed that daydreams, like the dreams of sleep, are fulfillments of our ambitions and erotic

Daydreams, like nighttime dreams, may help people come up with solutions to problems.

wishes. If sometimes they do not seem wish-fulfilling to us, it is because the wishes that are involved are cloaked in symbols. Most contemporary researchers, however, disagree with Freud's view. Daydreams, they argue, are not *all* wish-fulfilling, just as all nighttime dreams are not (Erdelyi, 1985). In fact, most daydreams, they say, simply focus on a current concern that is important to the person. Often these current concerns pose some special challenge, or require some decision or action soon (Klinger, 1987). College students, for instance, often daydream about their relationships with other people (lovers, friends, family members), their studies and schoolwork, and their future careers (Gold and Gold, 1982). Daydreams, then, may be one way of helping to cope with the problems of everyday life.

INDUCED STATES OF CONSCIOUSNESS

A man with a blood alcohol level of 0.25 percent becomes confused when driving his car at night. The reflectors marking the lanes look to him like lights on a runway. Convinced that he has somehow driven onto an airfield, he swerves to turn the car around and crashes into a fence.

On a bitterly cold night high up in the Himalayas, a Tibetan yogi sits outdoors, deep in meditation. Although he is clad only in a thin cotton robe, he is able to keep his body temperature high enough to melt surrounding ice.

A woman who has witnessed a brutal murder says that she remembers virtually nothing about the killer's face. But later, when hypnotized, she "relives" the trauma and sees the face in perfect detail.

Although these incidents seem very dissimilar, they have a common thread: each involves a change in consciousness that has somehow been *induced*. By "induced," we mean that the change did not naturally arise as a result of the brain's normal cyclical activities. Instead, some deliberately sought-out influence —taking a psychoactive drug, engaging in meditation, undergoing hypnosis—has caused the new state to occur. In the rest of this chapter we will explore the three induced states of consciousness introduced above: drug-induced states, meditative states, and hypnotic trances.

DRUG-INDUCED STATES

If a **drug** is any substance that can alter the functioning of a biological system, hardly a person alive is not a drug user. Many substances fall within this broad definition of a drug, from aspirin and antibiotics to vitamin C. The drugs of special interest in studying consciousness, however, are those that interact with the central nervous system to alter a person's mood, perception, mode of thinking, or behavior. These are called **psychoactive drugs.**

Although all psychoactive drugs alter consciousness, different ones affect it in different ways. Some, like alcohol, are depressants: they slow down the activities of the central nervous system. Others, such as cocaine, are stimulants: they arouse the central nervous system while also driving up heart rate, blood pressure, and muscle tension. Still others, such as LSD, are hallucinogens: they prompt the brain to produce hallucinations. In the following sections we will examine in more detail the effects of each of these three classes of drugs.

CONSCIOUSNESS AND DEPRESSANTS

A **depressant** is a drug that acts on the central nervous system to reduce pain and anxiety, to relax and disinhibit, and to slow down intellectual and motor responses. The major depressants are alcohol, sedatives, and tranquilizers, such as Librium and Valium, which we will discuss in Chapter 17. Because alcohol is the most widely used depressant in this country (in fact, the most widely used of *any* mind-altering drug), we will explore it as our central example of the effects that depressants have on consciousness.

When administered slowly and in small doses, alcohol is often regarded as a social wonder drug. It seems to relax inhibitions and often makes people more gregarious. Under the influence of a moderate amount of alcohol, a collection of ill-at-ease strangers can be transformed into a group of laughing, boisterous friends. But remember that alcohol is a depressant, a drug that *inhibits* nerve impulses. How, then, can it have these seemingly stimulating effects?

One reason alcohol appears to stimulate is that, among other things, it slows down the ability to think critically and to be cautious. As a result, people with as little as 0.05 percent alcohol in their bloodstreams may say and do things they would never ordinarily do. (See Figure 5.4 for the way alcohol influences the ability to drive safely.) As a person consumes more alcohol, a steady deterioration of all body functions results. Perception becomes distorted, speech begins to slur, and the drinker has trouble controlling simple movements. How soon these symptoms arise depends on how rapidly alcohol enters the bloodstream, on how much alcohol is consumed relative to body weight, and on individual differences in reactions to the drug (Wilson and Plomin, 1986). For everyone, however, serious impairments eventually set in.

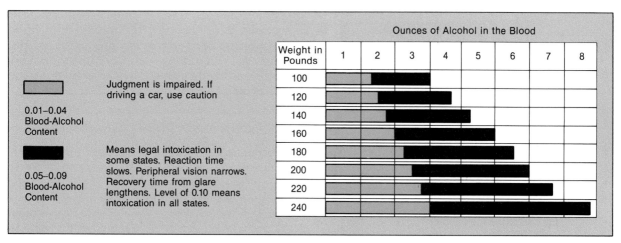

FIGURE 5.4   How alcohol affects driving a car. (*After* **U.S. News & World Report.** *1983. April 4:74. Reprinted by permission.*)

When blood alcohol reaches a level of 0.3 to 0.4 percent, it severely disrupts activity in the brain's reticular formation, which maintains consciousness, so the person lapses into a coma. At a blood-alcohol level of about 0.5 percent, heartbeat and breathing stop, and death occurs (Combs et al., 1980; Dusek and Girdano, 1987).

Traditionally, people assumed that all the behavioral changes associated with alcohol were caused entirely by the drug. But research has shown that people's *expectations* about the effects of alcohol can also influence their behavior. In one study, men were given either vodka and tonic or plain tonic to drink. (It is hard to taste any difference between the two.) Half of the vodka-and-tonic drinkers were correctly told that they were drinking an alcoholic beverage; the other vodka-and-tonic drinkers were incorrectly told that they were consuming a nonalcoholic drink. The same procedure was followed with the plain tonic drinkers: half were told truthfully that their drinks were nonalcoholic; the others were told untruthfully that they were drinking alcohol. At the end of the drinking session, all the men were placed in a situation that might elicit aggressive behavior. The results were surprising. Those who *believed* they had consumed alcohol, whether or not they actually had, were significantly more aggressive on average than those who believed they had simply been sipping tonic (Critchlow, 1986; Marlatt and Rohsenow, 1981). Other studies have produced similar results. In one, increased sexual arousal following alcohol consump-

tion was found to be due more to expectations than to chemical effects (Hull and Bond, 1986). Such findings demand that we rethink our assumptions about why social inhibitions weaken when people drink. Expectations that alcohol will weaken our social restraints are often partly responsible for this widely observed effect.

Beyond its effects on social inhibitions, alcohol also affects many *non*social behaviors (Hull and Bond, 1986). Take memory, for instance. Heavy drinking can cause new information to evaporate from memory as soon as attention shifts. This is because alcohol can impair the long-term storage of information (Parker et al., 1976). Heavy drinkers may therefore have great trouble remembering the names of people they meet while under alcohol's influence. They may even experience an **alcoholic blackout,** fragmentary or even total memory loss of events that occur while drinking.

In view of alcohol's adverse effects on memory, people sometimes wonder if alcohol can permanently affect the brain. For alcoholics, such dangers are very real. About 10 percent of those who seek help for alcoholism are discovered to have brain damage (NIAAA, 1982). Sometimes this damage produces irreversible memory impairment. In severe cases, the person can remember almost nothing about events that occurred since the disorder set in. This acute condition is called **Korsakoff's syndrome.**

In addition, chronic alcoholics may show a number of other symptoms related to the brain damage

With a powerful stimulant like cocaine, it is easy to move rapidly from occasional "recreational" use to dependency.

their prolonged and heavy drinking has produced (Oscar-Berman and Ellis, 1987). For instance, they may have trouble selectively attending to new information, or maintaining attention long enough to process that information fully. As a result, they may comprehend things slowly and often at only a superficial level. They may also show a flattening of their emotional responses. In situations that would normally be very emotionally arousing, they may show little or no emotion at all. At the same time, they may tend to repeat previous actions in a rote, mechanical manner. When trying to solve a puzzle, for example, they may keep repeating the same response over and over again, even though it clearly does not work. Oddly enough, they may even be able to tell you that they should try a different approach and yet be unable to make themselves do so. It is as if their ability to execute new responses has been impaired. Which of these and other symptoms arise in chronic alcoholics, and how marked those symptoms are, depends on the location and severity of the brain damage incurred.

What about those people who are merely social drinkers? Need they worry about long-term effects of alcohol on the brain? Probably not. Research shows that many gallons of alcohol consumed over a lifetime have little, if any, effect on cognitive abilities as long as a person does not regularly indulge in bouts of heavy drinking. Social drinkers who run the greatest risk are those who may go for days without drinking but then consume large quantities in a single session (Parker and Noble, 1977).

CONSCIOUSNESS AND STIMULANTS

Stimulants are drugs that produce physiological and mental arousal. Specifically, they can decrease fatigue, increase talkativeness and physical activity, enhance endurance, diminish appetite, produce a state of alertness, and for a time elevate mood, often to the point of euphoria. Stimulants vary widely in their potency. Some, such as the caffeine in coffee and colas and the nicotine in tobacco, are relatively mild. Others are extremely powerful. Here we focus on two of the powerful stimulants, cocaine and amphetamines.

The effects of cocaine and amphetamines seem to result from activation of the reticular formation and regions of the forebrain, including certain pleasure centers that lie close to the septal area (Jones-Witters and Witters, 1983). Stimulation of these pleasure centers probably accounts for the euphoria, or greatly elevated mood, that cocaine and amphetamine users often experience. Such euphoria may be one basis for the psychological dependency these drugs can cause (remember from Chapter 3 how experimental rats allowed to stimulate their own septal-area pleasure centers abandoned all other activities in order to turn on the electrical current). Research also indicates that cocaine and amphetamines enhance the activities of two neurotransmitters: norepinephrine and dopamine. As you learned in Chapter 3, increases in norepinephrine tend to elevate attention and sensory responses, while increases in dopamine tend to raise motivational excitement and produce an eagerness to act (Panksepp, 1986). Cocaine and amphetamines, however, do have somewhat different effects on consciousness (Palfai and Jankiewicz, 1991).

Cocaine   Cocaine is a substance obtained from the leaves of certain coca plants native to South America. Years ago it was one of the ingredients in Coca-Cola, originally sold as an invigorating tonic. (The leaf material, with the cocaine extracted, is still used as a flavoring in Coca-Cola.) Although cocaine is illegal, addictive, and dangerous, it is quite widely used. About 22 million Americans report having used cocaine at some time during their lives, and about 5 million currently use it (Higgins, 1989). Until fairly recently, cocaine was expensive, so its regular users tended to be mostly middle- and upper-class white-collar workers and executives. But now this pattern has changed. Cocaine use has spread to many segments of the population, including the working class and the young (White, 1988).

Prepared in the form of a fine white powder, cocaine is usually inhaled or snorted into the nostrils and absorbed into the bloodstream through the mucous membranes. It can also be ingested orally, absorbed through the lungs by smoking, or injected into the body with a hypodermic needle. A more elaborate procedure is "freebasing," in which the powder is heated with ether—a process that frees its base, its most powerful component—and is then smoked.

The euphoria cocaine produces can last from forty-five minutes to two hours, depending on the size of the dose and its potency (Dusek and Girdano, 1987). Users not only experience an elevated mood, they also have an inflated sense of their own abilities and accomplishments. Under the drug's influence, people become convinced that they are thinking more clearly and performing much better than they ever have before. Often, however, they overestimate their own capacities and the quality of their work. In addition to this effect on conscious awareness, cocaine, like other stimulants, also provides a short-term boost in energy. But because it does not replenish energy stores, users pay the price in physical exhaustion after the drug wears off and the body comes down or crashes. Post-high depression and fatigue can be extreme when large doses of the drug are taken (VanDyke and Byck, 1982).

Chronically heavy use of cocaine has more disturbing effects. It can cause a general mental deterioration, persistent agitation, and feelings of paranoia. Cocaine taken frequently in large doses can also produce hallucinations, one of the most horrifying of which is the sensation of bugs crawling beneath the skin. This hallucination may be caused by drug-induced hyperactivity of the nerve cells embedded in the skin. In excessive doses, especially by injection, cocaine can produce headache, nausea, hyperventilation, convulsions, coma, and sometimes even instant

death. A tolerance develops with regular use of cocaine, meaning that more of the drug must be taken to produce the same effects as before. Chronic heavy users experience severe withdrawal symptoms that may begin only half an hour after a dose is taken (Palfai and Jankiewicz, 1991).

During the 1980s, cocaine began appearing on the streets in the form of crack. Crack is sold in small chunks or rocks, which are smoked in a pipe. Like freebase, it is exceptionally powerful, producing in seconds an intense rush that then quickly wears off. Because crack is relatively inexpensive, its advent has placed cocaine within the reach of most American adolescents. Today, its use has reached epidemic proportions in large cities, and it has spread rapidly into suburban and even rural areas of the country.

Amphetamines The amphetamines—commonly called speed, uppers, or bennies—are a group of synthetic drugs. Before all the risks of amphetamines were known, they were sold by prescription under various trade names, such as Dexedrine and Benzedrine. Many people—truckers on long hauls, students studying for exams—used them to help stay awake. Others, particularly women, used them to suppress appetite and help burn off fat.

Amphetamines produce a boost in energy, arousal, and alertness, as well as confidence. Users get the feeling that they can take on the world, solve any problem, achieve any goal. Are people really more capable under the influence of amphetamines? No, they are not. Studies show that amphetamines improve neither problem-solving ability nor performance on any other complex cognitive task (Tinklenberg, 1971).

As long as they are taken irregularly and in low doses, amphetamines do not appear to cause any measurable harm. But the problem is that people develop a tolerance for them and must take larger and larger doses to achieve the same high. If intake of the drug becomes chronic and excessive, users begin to develop ungrounded suspicions. They may imagine that people are staring at them in a peculiar way or talking behind their backs. They may also imagine objects on their skin or get caught up in meaningless, repetitive behaviors and meandering trains of thought. The symptoms of extreme amphetamine use are often strikingly similar to the symptoms found in certain kinds of schizophrenia, a psychological disorder also believed to be related to overactivity of dopamine pathways in the brain (Jones-Witters and Witters, 1983). As a heavy dose of amphetamines begins to wear off, the chronic user typically sinks into a depression that may last for days and may sometimes be severe enough to prompt attempted suicide. Amphetamine abuse can also cause serious brain damage (Palfai and Jankiewicz, 1991).

CONSCIOUSNESS AND HALLUCINOGENS

Hallucinogens, or drugs that are capable of producing hallucinations, are derived from plants as well as being produced synthetically. Among the most common hallucinogenic plants are marijuana, henbane, mandrake, jimson weed, peyote cactus, some varieties of morning glory, and many kinds of mushrooms. Of these, the best known in this country is probably marijuana. Marijuana and hashish come from the same marijuana plant. The two drugs are often referred to as minor hallucinogens because their effects are considerably milder than those of the major hallucinogens, which include mescaline and the synthetic drugs LSD and PCP. Examining the effects of LSD, PCP, and marijuana will give you a good idea of the range of effects on consciousness that hallucinogens can have.

LSD   Lysergic acid diethylamide (LSD) is the most extensively studied of the hallucinogens and also the most potent. It is 100 times stronger than the psilocybin in hallucinogenic mushrooms, and 4,000 times stronger than mescaline, which comes from the peyote cactus. A dose of between 100 and 200 millionths of a gram (just a small speck) alters consciousness in thirty to sixty minutes, producing a "trip" that lasts from ten to twelve hours (Combs et al., 1980).

We do not yet know how LSD produces its powerful effects. We do know that it influences the activity of serotonin, a neurotransmitter that plays a role in promoting sleep and generally inhibiting emotional responses (Panksepp, 1986; Thompson, 1985). But the exact nature of this influence is not completely clear. It is probably not just a simple reduction in serotonin that LSD promotes, for other drugs that inhibit serotonin do not induce the hallucinations that LSD does (White and Appel, 1982).

Thus, we have much more to learn about the special ways that LSD affects the brain.

The hallucinations that LSD produces are often dramatic. Visual hallucinations can progress from simple geometric forms to complex images and then to dreamlike scenes (Siegel, 1977). The user may encounter perceptual distortions so extreme that familiar objects become almost unrecognizable. A wall, for example, may seem to pulsate and breathe. The senses may also seem to intermingle. Sounds may be seen and sights heard. A person may experience a mental dissociation into one self who observes and another who feels. Distortions of time are common, too. Events may seem to race by at a dizzying pace or crawl along in slow motion. A single stimulus may become the focus of attention for hours, perceived as ever changing or newly beautiful and fascinating.

Thinking, as measured by the ability to perform simple tasks, is also impaired by LSD, even though users may feel they are thinking with incredible logic and depth. Lifelong problems may suddenly seem resolved, or the need to resolve them unnecessary. The person often experiences the great-truth phenomenon, a sense that ultimate truths have suddenly been revealed. When the trip is over, however, the magnitude of the discoveries shrinks, and the solutions reached often turn out to be untenable (Jones-Witters and Witters, 1983).

During an LSD trip a person can experience any number of emotions, often quite intense and rapidly changing. The person's mental set—his or her pre-drug mood, expectations, and beliefs—and the circumstances under which the drug is taken can greatly affect the experience, making it euphoric or terrifying. Panic reactions are the most common of LSD's unpleasant side effects. They usually occur when a person tries to change or get rid of the drug's effects, only to find it impossible. Medical attention is sometimes needed for intense panic reactions.

PCP   Powerful hallucinations can also be induced by another synthetic drug sold on the illegal market—phencyclidine (PCP), often called angel dust, among many other street names. In small doses, PCP tends to produce depersonalization, a feeling of being cut off from one's normal self. Larger doses cause more dramatic changes in consciousness. Heavy users experience insomnia, agitation, mental confusion, delusions and hallucinations, and the urge to behave violently. These negative effects often last for days.

Studies of PCP in laboratory rats suggest that molecules of the drug bind to specific receptor sites in the brain, especially in parts of the limbic system, which are involved in motivation and emotion (Zukin and Zukin, 1979). Scientists have not yet identified a naturally occurring neurotransmitter that normally binds to these same sites, but undoubtedly one will eventually be found. One clue to the function the sites may serve comes from the fact that PCP was first used by medical researchers as a powerful painkiller, only to be outlawed later when the disturbing side effects of higher doses were discovered. Thus, PCP may act on some pain-reducing or pleasure system in the brain. Significantly, laboratory monkeys administer PCP to themselves repeatedly, even when they must forgo food to do so.

Marijuana Marijuana, a minor hallucinogen, has been used in Eastern cultures for centuries. Before the early 1960s, marijuana use in the United States was common only among members of certain subcultures, such as jazz musicians and artists living in big cities. In the 1960s, however, college students discovered marijuana, and with that discovery its rate of use greatly increased. Today more than 50 million Americans, perhaps many more, have tried marijuana; and some 10 to 15 million, most under age twenty-five, consider themselves regular users (Dusek and Girdano, 1987; Palfai and Jankiewicz, 1991).

The active ingredient in marijuana is a complex molecule called tetrahydrocannabinol (THC), which occurs naturally in the marijuana plant, a common weed with the Latin name *Cannabis sativa*. Marijuana is made by drying the flowers and the leaves of the plant. Hashish, a gummy powder made from the resin (cannabin) exuded by the plant's flower tops, is five to ten times stronger than marijuana, because the resin contains much more THC than do the flowers and leaves. Both marijuana and hashish are usually smoked, but they can also be eaten in food.

Although the effects of marijuana vary somewhat from person to person and depend partly on the setting in which the drug is taken, regular users agree about marijuana's effects on consciousness (Tart, 1970). For one thing, most sensory experiences are greatly augmented. Music sounds fuller, colors are brighter, smells are richer, foods taste better, and sexual sensations are more intense. The sense of time may also be greatly distorted. A short sequence of events may seem to last for hours. A musical phrase of a few seconds' duration may seem so prolonged as to be isolated from the rest of the composition, and the listener perceives it as never before.

Elevations in mood are common, too, under the influence of marijuana. The world seems more meaningful, and even the most ordinary events may take on a kind of extraordinary profundity. Users may become so entranced with a common everyday object that they sit and stare at it for many minutes, marveling at its newly discovered qualities. Marijuana may also heighten negative moods, however. If a person is frightened or depressed to begin with, the drug can intensify those feelings. In some cases marijuana appears to have helped bring on psychological disorders in people who were already unstable.

Marijuana also tends to decrease a person's ability to direct thoughts at will. Ideas and perceptions extraneous to the person's current focus keep intruding into consciousness. As a result, users often have trouble sustaining goal-directed behavior because they cannot keep their minds on the task at hand (Melges et al., 1970, 1971). Their speech also shows that attention frequently wanders, causing a train of thought to be lost (Weil and Zinberg, 1969).

Researchers have studied the effects of marijuana on memory as well. Like alcohol, marijuana impairs the transfer of new information to long-term storage (Darley et al., 1973; Miller et al., 1977, 1978; Wetzel et al., 1982). It seems to reduce the release of the neurotransmitter acetylcholine (ACh) in various pathways in the brain's limbic system (Miller and Branconnier, 1983). One structure within the limbic system, the hippocampus, seems particularly involved in consolidating new information into long-term storage. Marijuana may affect memory by temporarily impairing some of the activities that the hippocampus carries out.

Little sound information exists on the long-term effects of marijuana. Some studies of American teenagers suggest that those who use marijuana regularly do more poorly in school than nonusers do, are more apathetic, have less motivation, and show lower self-esteem (Glantz, 1984). But these characteristics

  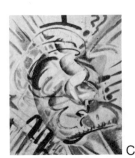  

A   B   C   D   E

FIGURE 5.5 Drawings done by a man under the influence of LSD. (A) Twenty minutes after the first dose, the drug had not yet taken effect. (B) Twenty-five minutes after the second dose was administered, the subject experienced the first alterations in perception. He saw the model correctly but could not control the sweeping movements of his hand. (C) Two hours and forty-five minutes after the first dose, the subject experienced the most intense effects of the drug. (D) After five hours and forty-five minutes, the effects of the drug began to wear off. (E) After eight hours, the effects were almost gone. (Triangle, The Sandoz Journal of Medical Science, *1955, 2, 119–123.*)

often *precede* the marijuana habit, so it is hard to say just what the long-term effects of the drug are (Maugh, 1982; National Academy of Sciences, 1982b).

One problem with understanding the effects of marijuana from earlier research is that the potency of the 1990s' varieties is much greater than the potency of the 1970s. In 1970 the typical marijuana cigarette might have 10 to 15 mg of THC. Today it may have 150 mg. The effects of such high-potency varieties have not yet been thoroughly studied (Palfai and Jankiewicz, 1991).

DRUGS AND CREATIVITY

Some writers and artists have attributed creative outputs to the use of drugs. Writer Ken Kesey, for instance, used peyote and LSD while writing parts of the novel *One Flew over the Cuckoo's Nest*. It is also suspected that Robert Louis Stevenson was under the influence of cocaine when he wrote the classic story *Dr. Jekyll and Mr. Hyde* in a mere six days (Jones-Witters and Witters, 1983). Can drugs really enhance creativity, as these examples suggest? Or is the effect, at best, limited?

One study of college students who took LSD in a laboratory on three separate occasions found that enhanced creativity was more illusion than fact (McGlothin et al., 1967). The students were no more imaginative, insightful, or clever at performing a variety of tasks after the LSD experience than they had been before it. Yet many of them *felt* that they were more creative as a result of the drug. How can this paradox be explained?

The answer lies partly in the fact that drugs like LSD have two kinds of effects. On the one hand, they induce general changes in consciousness that can easily make people think they have enhanced creative capacities. Users may feel more relaxed and open, with heightened sensory awareness and a better ability to fantasize freely. But the problem is that these traits are accompanied by other changes that can hinder creative output (see Figure 5.5). Users often experience a diminished capacity for logical thinking, a reduced ability to concentrate or to control things they imagine, and a tendency to become absorbed in the drug-induced state of consciousness itself. The capacity for self-criticism is frequently blunted, too, a fact that can be seen in a story about psychologist William James. James had several mystical revelations during experiments with nitrous oxide (laughing gas), but he was never able to record them before blacking out from the drug. One night, though, he managed to write down his monumental thoughts before losing consciousness. Upon returning to his normal state, James rushed to find out what he had written. It was:

> Hogamous, higamous,
> Man is polygamous.
> Higamous, hogamous,
> Woman monogamous.

Thus, although drugs may sometimes open new

To meditate, it is necessary to empty the mind to distracting thoughts by focusing on a simple pattern or idea. In some forms of meditation, the individual concentrates on a visual pattern such as the mandala shown here, which continually returns the gaze to its center.

perspectives and foster new ideas, it is often hard to translate what is experienced during a drug-induced state into a valuable creative product (Leavitt, 1974).

MEDITATIVE STATES

A yogi sits in a laboratory in India with legs crossed and eyes closed, deep in meditation. From his head a forest of electrodes leads to equipment for producing an electroencephalogram (EEG). A team of psychologists watch intently as the yogi's brain waves are traced on paper. When the EEG shows that his brain is emitting a steady flow of slow, rhythmic alpha waves, the testing session begins. A psychologist strikes a tuning fork and holds it next to the yogi's ear. The alpha waves stream on, unbroken—a sign that the yogi is not aware of the sound. The test is repeated with a hand clap and a hot test tube applied to the yogi's arm—all with the same result: his brain, deep in meditation, registers no reaction to the stimuli. The yogi is in *samadhi*, a state in which his awareness appears to be separated from his senses through intense concentration on a single thought or object (Anand et al., 1961).

This investigation of a yogi's brain waves during **meditation** was one of the first scientific attempts to study how people can deliberately induce a special state of consciousness in themselves without using drugs. In one form or another, meditation has been incorporated into every major religion, including Judaism and Christianity. Vast differences exist among the many kinds of meditation practiced in the world today, but most share a common element: the meditator focuses attention on a single stimulus, which greatly restricts sensory input and ultimately produces a change in consciousness (Goleman, 1977). For example, in the form of meditation called *zazen*, which is practiced by a sect of Japanese Zen Buddhists, the meditators concentrate on the normal flow of their breathing, without trying to control it in any way. Other common stimuli on which people focus to enter a meditative state are short prayers, a sacred picture, a candle flame, or a spot on the lower abdomen.

What physiological changes occur during meditation? One is a slowing of metabolism marked by a drop in oxygen consumption, a decreased rate of heartbeat and breathing, a decline in blood pressure,

Buddhist monks have long known that it is possible to induce an altered state of consciousness simply through meditation, without the use of drugs or any other substance.

This device induces an increase in slow theta waves—a high-tech, Western approach to the Eastern tradition of meditation.

and a rise in the skin's resistance to conducting electricity (Wallace and Benson, 1972). But these changes can also occur in people who are merely resting. What is it about meditation that makes it a unique state of consciousness? To find out, we must turn to the study of brain waves. Whereas the relaxed person shows only modest changes in brain-wave patterns compared with those seen during normal waking consciousness, the meditator's brain waves change markedly. The specific type of brain-wave activity during meditation depends to a large extent on the kind of meditation being practiced. For instance, one study found that the EEGs of Buddhist monks who practiced *zazen* registered alpha waves as soon as the monks started meditating, even though their eyes were wide open (Kasamatsu and Hirai, 1966). Alpha waves are normally abundant only in people whose eyes are closed. As the meditation session progressed, the monks' alpha waves changed

gradually to slower theta waves—very unusual in people with their eyes open.

How could a person with open eyes display theta brain-wave patterns? Although the answer is still far from complete, studies on the effects of restricted awareness provide some insight. Remember from Chapter 4 that whenever you try to fix your gaze on a single point, your eyes move involuntarily. This movement prevents your photoreceptor cells from adapting to constant stimulation and subsequently ceasing to respond. Researchers have demonstrated the startling effect on visual perception that a truly steady gaze would have. One ingenious technique uses a tiny projector attached to a contact lens. As the subject's eye moves, the contact lens moves with it, and so does the miniprojector. The result is that the projector steadily casts its image on one part of the retina. People who volunteered to wear this strange device reported that the picture they saw gradually disappeared. And when it did, the person's visual cortex suddenly emitted the preponderance of alpha waves generally found only when the eyes are closed (Lehmann et al., 1967). Meditation may involve a similar loss of awareness of the outside world, precipitated by a restricted focus on an unchanging stimulus (Ornstein, 1977).

Supporters of meditation claim that it has psychological benefits. They say that it neutralizes stresses, enriches life experiences, and enhances overall contentment (Bloomfield and Kory, 1976). Psychologists have therefore used meditation in the treatment of anxiety, mild hypertension, insomnia, alcoholism, drug abuse, stuttering, and other stress-related problems. Although few psychologists dispute that people can benefit from such programs, some contend that resting produces equivalent results (Holmes, 1984). Thus, a quiet time in an easy chair may reduce stress just as well as entering a meditative state of consciousness does.

THE HYPNOTIC STATE

The scene is a college classroom. Thirty students who have scored high in susceptibility to hypnosis are sitting in straight-back chairs. A hypnotist is speaking to them in a soft, monotonous tone: "I want you to relax your body and become comfortable. Just relax and let yourself go limp. You will find yourself becoming warm, at ease. Now you are becoming drowsy and sleepy, drowsy and sleepy. . . ." One by one, the students close their eyes and lower their heads. When everyone is still, the hypnotist tells them: "Now clasp your hands together tightly, as though they were locked together by a steel band. Try as you might, you can't get them apart. Try to separate them. You can't." The students strain to pry apart their hands, but their fingers remain interlocked. Finally, the hypnotist breaks the tension: "Stop trying, and relax. Your hands are no longer locked together." The straining stops, and everyone's hands easily separate. The entire class relaxes, awaiting the hypnotist's next instruction.

Such demonstrations of hypnosis create the popular impression that a hypnotized person is in a special kind of trance, cut off from normal waking awareness and self-control. Does this impression agree with what scientific studies of hypnosis show? The answer is not clear-cut. Although some psychologists believe that hypnosis is indeed a special state of consciousness, others are not so certain. The skeptics point out that even after years of investigation, we still have trouble defining hypnosis except by simply describing how hypnotized people act. This has led some to doubt whether hypnosis is a unique state of consciousness after all. We will return to the debate over the "reality" of hypnosis at the end of this chapter and let you decide for yourself. But first, let us take a look at susceptibility to hypnosis, as well as at the uses to which hypnosis has been put.

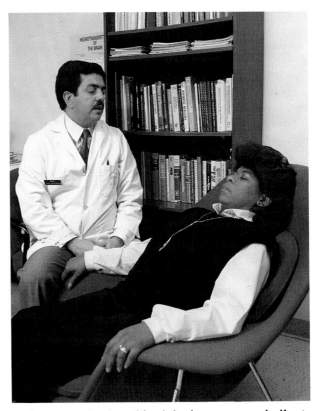

Under hypnosis, the subject's brain waves are similar to those of a person who is awake. This lack of an objective difference in consciousness is one reason that the hypnotic state is so difficult to describe except by referring to the behavior of a hypnotized subject.

HYPNOTIC SUSCEPTIBILITY

According to one estimate, about nineteen out of twenty people can be hypnotized to some degree *if* they want to be and *if* they trust the hypnotist. But some people are much more easily and deeply hypnotized than others. Psychologists measure the trait of **hypnotic susceptibility** by means of various standardized tests. Using the Stanford Hypnotic Susceptibility Scale, for example, the hypnotist first attempts to bring the subject under hypnosis and then makes a series of suggestions, such as "Your left arm will become rigid" and "You will be unable to say your name when asked." If the subject is unable to bend the arm more than 2 inches in ten seconds or is unable to say the name within ten seconds, he or she receives a positive rating. If ratings are positive on the rest of a dozen suggestions, the person is classified as *highly susceptible* to hypnosis. In one study of more than 500 college students, about 10 percent were so classified (E. Hilgard, 1965).

What are the characteristics of people who score high in hypnotic susceptibility? Many often become so absorbed in activities such as reading a novel, listening to music, or appreciating the beauty of nature that they lose track of time (Crawford, 1985). In general, these people have a greater than average ability to focus on a task, ignore extraneous perceptions, and become deeply involved in imagination. Many occasionally enter trancelike states in which they feel somehow separated from things as they usually experience them (K. Bowers, 1983). Hypnotic susceptibility may develop early in life. People who are highly susceptible to hypnosis are likely to have had a history of daydreaming and imaginary companions as children (J. Hilgard, 1970, 1974). As adults, they often have a marked facility for switching from reality to fantasy, from analytical thinking to free-flowing modes of thought (Crawford, 1985). These patterns are not universal, of course. Not all people who fantasize a lot are highly hypnotizable, and some people who can be deeply hypnotized have poor imaginative abilities (Lynn and Rhue, 1988). In general, however, fantasy, imagination, and susceptibility to hypnosis tend to go together.

THE USES OF HYPNOSIS

In the past several decades, hypnosis has been put to a growing number of uses. Some doctors find it a drug-free way to help relieve pain. In fact, on the battlefields of World War II, hypnosis was sometimes used to treat the wounded when painkillers were not available. Today, pregnant women with a history of painful childbirths sometimes seek out hypnosis to aid in labor and delivery. Psychologically caused migraine headaches have also yielded to hypnosis (Harding, 1967). Even the intractable pain of terminal cancer has sometimes been alleviated by it (J. Hilgard, 1974). Thus, there is no doubt that hypnosis is an effective pain reliever (Kihlstrom, 1985). But how it works remains a puzzle. Some think that the answer may lie in the deep relaxation associated with hypnosis, for anxiety can greatly intensify pain (see Chapter 4).

In addition to its role in alleviating pain, hypnosis is also used in treating certain behavioral problems. A longtime smoker, for instance, may seek the help of a hypnotist to break the cigarette habit. Under hypnosis, the person is usually told that cigarette smoking will no longer be enjoyable, and then he or she is instructed to forget that this idea came from the hypnotist. For some people in some circumstances, this approach has worked (Johnston and Donoghue, 1971; Spiegel, 1970). Hypnotic suggestions have also been used with some success for other problems, including psychosomatic allergies, insomnia, and compulsive overeating.

The most controversial use of hypnosis is as a tool for probing human memory. Under hypnosis, people often recall events so clearly and fully that they seem to be tapping into memories that are not available to normal consciousness. We say *seem* to be tapping, because the evidence regarding memory retrieval and hypnosis is ambiguous. While some argue that hypnosis is an excellent memory enhancer, other contend just as adamantly that it is not. Psychologists, of course, are deeply involved in this debate. Because the issue of memory enhancement has such important implications for our law enforcement and judicial systems, we have decided to examine it in depth.

IN DEPTH

Memory Enhancement and Hypnosis

By the late 1980s, over a dozen state supreme courts had barred or restricted testimony obtained from hypnotized witnesses (Grisham, 1987). Why are courts so concerned about hypnosis as a method of obtaining evidence? Why have supreme court justices taken the time to investigate this issue and pass judgments on it?

The reason is that hypnosis may pose certain risks. For one thing, it may make people more susceptible to leading questions, especially people who are easily hypnotized. When under hypnosis, these people may run a significantly greater than normal chance of incorporating the interviewer's suggestions into their own recollections (Laurence and Perry, 1983; Bothwell, 1989). In addition, people who are easily hypnotized may suffer an inflated confidence in the accuracy of the memories they retrieve under hypnosis. Compared with *un*hypnotized people who are also very susceptible to hypnosis, they may be more apt to say they are *certain* that what they remember is right (Orne et al., 1984; Bothwell, 1989). This is unfortunate, because jurors tend to be swayed by witnesses who maintain that they are sure of their testimonies, whether or not those testimonies contain errors. Finally, deeply hypnotized people may be unusually prone to "creating" recollections. In one study, for instance, hypnotized subjects recalled more details regarding a pickpocketing incident they had witnessed, but they also distorted more details than nonhypnotized subjects did (Sheehan and Tilden, 1984). Apparently, they were more inclined to fabricate memories when genuine ones were not available for recall. It is not yet clear how widespread these potential problems with hypnosis are (Spanos et al., 1989). Until additional research has been conducted, however, many state courts have been cautious in allowing testimony obtained under hypnosis.

But isn't the information gathered through hypnosis often worth the risks? Hypnosis, after all, has a reputation for being able to help witnesses retrieve deeply buried memories. Why should law enforcement agents give up a tool for extracting information that is as valuable as this? To understand why, let us take a look at two views of the issue: that of law enforcement agents and that of research psychologists who study hypnosis.

THE INITIAL STUDIES

Police records are filled with cases which seem to testify that hypnosis is an effective means of improving the memories of eyewitnesses. One of the most widely publicized such cases occurred in 1976 when a busload of twenty-six children and their driver were kidnapped at gunpoint. The captives were taken in vans to an abandoned stone quarry, where they were sealed inside an underground pit. Eventually, the driver and two of the older boys escaped, led police to the deserted quarry, and the remaining children were rescued. The kidnappers, however, were still at large, and there were few leads to their identities. The busdriver had tried to memorize the license plate numbers of two of the vans, but now he couldn't recall them. So police called in a hypnotist. Under hypnosis, the driver saw the events of the crime unfolding, as if he were watching a movie. Suddenly he saw the license plate numbers and called them out. One was correct except for a single digit, and the kidnappers

were apprehended. They are now in prison serving life sentences (Kroger and Douce, 1979).

In many similarly dramatic cases, hypnotized eyewitnesses have sometimes recalled details of a crime that have greatly helped police. Under hypnosis, distinctive markings on a getaway car have been remembered, or some unusual piece of clothing that the suspect was wearing. Surely such cases of enhanced recall are strong evidence that hypnosis is very effective in refreshing people's memories.

Unfortunately, psychologists see a major flaw in this logic: the absence of a control group. How do we know it was the hypnosis per se that aided memory in these cases? Might not some other aspect of the interrogation process, that just happens to occur simultaneously with hypnosis, be responsible for whatever recall improvement occurred? We have no way of ruling out this possibility unless we conduct a true experiment. Here a control group of subjects would experience all the conditions the experimental subjects do, *except* being hypnotized. By comparing the memory performance of the two groups, we can then tell if hypnosis aids recall.

Early studies of this kind provided no clear-cut evidence that hypnosis per se is a memory enhancer. In one such study, hypnotized people who were highly susceptible to hypnosis showed a modest gain in memory performance when they were encouraged to try their hardest and remember everything they could about material they had learned before. But a very similar gain in memory performance was also recorded for subjects low in susceptibility to hypnosis who were simply asked to "make a real effort" and were *not* hypnotized. In fact, even control subjects who were exposed to no special conditions, just given another recall test, showed at least some improvement in memory compared with a previous recall effort (Dhanens and Lundy, 1975). Findings like these do not do much to convince us that hypnosis is some kind of magical key for unlocking memories. And yet many law enforcement officers still believe that it is. "Whatever its nature or however it works," one FBI agent has contended, "it *does* work with many people" (Ault, 1980, cited in Smith, 1983). How can we explain these conflicting perspectives? Why have laboratory studies like the one just described consistently failed to show that hypnosis has the memory-enhancing effects that law enforcement officers think it does? To answer this question we need further research.

CRITICISMS, ALTERNATIVES, AND FURTHER RESEARCH

One possibility is that significant differences exist between the kinds of memory retrieval studied in the laboratory and the kinds that eyewitnesses attempt during criminal investigations (Smith, 1983). For instance, early laboratory studies investigating the effects of hypnosis on memory looked at recall of verbal material (lists of words or nonsense syllables, brief prose passages), *not* recall of episodes that happen in real life. Moreover, the verbal material studied was unemotional in content, *not* the emotionally arousing, often stressful situations surrounding a serious crime. Could it be that hypnosis is effective only in improving recall of the kinds of information that eyewitnesses to crimes encounter?

This possibility has been explored in a number of studies. In one of them, researchers showed to people who scored high in susceptibility to hypnosis a very realistic ninety-second film of a bank robbery (McEwan and Yuille, 1982). A week later, they asked the subjects questions about the incident, aimed at getting eyewitness descriptions of the two armed men involved. Half the subjects were hypnotized during questioning, the others were not. The researchers found no difference between the hypnotized and nonhypnotized groups in the amount of correct information recalled. Other studies, using similar procedures, confirm this result (e.g., Buckhout et al., 1982; Putnam, 1979). Apparently, it is not the use of verbal material that prevents hypnosis from enhancing recall. In controlled experiments, hypnotized people do no better at recalling real-life events than do nonhypnotized ones.

The same is true when the real-life events that have been witnessed promote a great deal of stress. In one study, for instance, subjects who scored high in susceptibility to hypnosis saw a film showing serious workshop accidents, such as one in which a man's finger was suddenly cut off and another in which a sharp piece of wood, thrown from a circular saw, killed a man by impaling him (Zelig and Beidleman, 1981). The subjects were then asked questions about what they saw, half of them under hypnosis. Hypnosis did not improve recall, even though the episodes witnessed were very traumatic and stressful, as are many of those associated with serious crimes.

Of course, the researchers in this study tested subjects' recall ability soon after they viewed the film. Perhaps hypnosis refreshes memories of trau-matic events only when those memories have had more time to fade. A recent meta-analysis explored this possibility. It found that hypnosis *does* seem to improve memory retrieval when the recall test is delayed for at least a day (Bothwell, 1989). This improvement is small, however. The average is only a 5 percent increase in accuracy over attempts at recalling in a normal waking state.

PATTERNS AND CONCLUSIONS

So we are still left with the question of why many law enforcement agents remain convinced that hypnosis is an excellent memory aid. Laboratory research provides little evidence that hypnosis is a good memory enhancer, and yet police are often eager to use it with witnesses who are having trouble recalling evidence. Surely if hypnosis had only a very small effect on memory performance, police detectives would have long ago abandoned it. What explains their steadfast belief in the powers of hypnosis? Why do they see more improvements in recall among hypnotized people than psychologists in the laboratory do?

The answer probably is that the memory enhancement observed when hypnosis is used in police investigations is due largely to factors other than hypnosis, factors that just happen to be linked with the use of hypnosis for this purpose (Smith, 1983). For example, it could be that when people are hypnotized and asked to recall the details of a crime, the hypnotist routinely encourages them to imagine themselves back at the scene. Studies show that such reconstruction of the context in which something was originally learned can indeed improve recall of it, even when a person is *not* hypnotized. In one study (Malpass and Devine, 1981), college students witnessed a very convincing (but actually staged) act of vandalism. Five months later, they were asked to pick out the culprit from a set of photographs. The researchers helped half the subjects to reconstruct the context in which they encountered the vandal by encouraging them to recall the room, their thoughts and feelings on that evening, their reactions to what they witnessed, and so forth. Those who were given this guided memory tour accurately identified the culprit 60 percent of the time, compared with only 40 percent among those who simply looked at the photos.

Another possibility is that witnesses in police investigations remember more under hypnosis partly because they are being given another attempt at recalling. This phenomenon of improved recall on second and third trials is called *hypermnesia* and has been demonstrated in the laboratory (e.g., Erdelyi and Kleinbard, 1978). Perhaps with repeated recall trials people have had a chance to organize information in ways that aid retrieval (Roediger and Payne, 1982). In any case, since hypnosis in police investigations is almost always used *after* other recall efforts have failed, it could easily be that whatever improvements in memory occur under hypnosis are due more to hypermnesia than to the powers of hypnosis itself.

HYPNOSIS AND CONSCIOUSNESS: TWO VIEWS

In a laboratory at Stanford University in California, a hypnotized subject plunges his forearm into a tank of circulating ice water and holds it there for sixty seconds. The young man has been given the hypnotic suggestion that his arm will remain numb, as if made of rubber, so he will feel no pain. Every five seconds he is asked to say how much pain, if any, he is experiencing, using a rating scale from 0 to 10 (Hilgard et al., 1975). The numbers the young man calls out are very low, indicating that he perceives the severe cold as relatively painless. At the same time, however, his free hand tells a different story. Covered by a box and out of sight, the free hand presses a key to indicate that the experience is *very* painful, just what you would normally expect a person to say. Why this difference between the subject's verbal ratings and what he expresses by pressing the key? The answer lies in the fact that the young man has been told that his free hand is controlled by a part of his awareness that is cut off or "hidden" from his hypnotized self. This hidden self is said to have access to thoughts and feelings that the hypnotized self does not. Thus, while the hypnotized self feels no pain, the hidden self does, so the two report different pain sensations.

What accounts for this special kind of hypnotic pain reduction called the **hidden observer** phenomenon? One explanation, supported by Ernest Hilgard and others, is called the *dissociation view*. It holds that, under hypnosis, people often experience a mental **dissociation,** a split in consciousness that causes certain thoughts, feelings, and behaviors to operate independently from others (Hilgard, 1973, 1975). You

may have at some time experienced a dissociation yourself. For instance, in everyday life people often respond correctly to a message they thought they didn't hear. Their conscious awareness apparently did not process what was said, but another part of them did. Similarly, people with severe phobias often insist that they have no idea what caused their irrational fears, yet their emotional reaction to the feared object is that of a person who remembers a traumatic incident all too well.

Dissociations, according to Hilgard and other psychologists who favor this theory, occur routinely under hypnosis. Consider posthypnotic amnesia, for instance. A hypnotist can instruct a subject to forget all that happened during hypnosis until a cue to remember is given. The subject, upon coming out of the hypnotic trance, adamantly maintains that he or she remembers nothing, as if the memories were somehow split from normal conscious awareness. On cue, however, the person remembers everything, as if the split in consciousness were suddenly bridged. Similarly, a person who insists that an arm in icy water is not painful, but then presses a key that indicates *great* pain is felt, could be experiencing a dissociation between two parts of conscious awareness, each with different pain sensitivities.

But other psychologists doubt that we need to appeal to dissociations in order to explain what goes on during hypnosis. They contend that hypnosis is not a special state of consciousness at all, but rather just a special case of role-playing. According to this *cognitive role-enactment view*, the hypnotized person, like a good actor immersed in a part, is deeply involved in acting as if he or she is hypnotized. The hypnotist prepares the subject to play the role of a hypnotized person by establishing expectations. The subject is given specific instructions about what is to happen, and the hypnotist reinforces those expectations by playing the role of competent hypnotist. The transition to the role of hypnotized person is complete when the subject continues to meet the hypnotist's role demands as they change. Thus, the experiences that subjects report are determined by what they believe is appropriate and proper in the situation (Sarbin and Coe, 1972).

Now let us return to the young man in the hidden-observer study and consider his behavior from this second perspective. He verbally reported that he felt no pain but pressed a key indicating that he did. According to the cognitive role-enactment view, he did this because he was trying hard to act like a good hypnotic subject. Note that the young man was not faking or deliberately lying to the researcher. He was just deeply engrossed in the role he was playing (Spanos and Hewitt, 1980). As such, he used certain cognitive strategies to bring about the desired effects. When the hypnotized self was asked to talk, he shifted attention away from the arm in the icy water, to the point where the discomfort was much less. Then, when the hidden self had a chance to express its feelings, he focused intently on the pain sensations, thereby intensifying them. In this way, he seemed to possess both pain-resistant and pain-sensing parts of consciousness.

To gather evidence in support of this perspective, researchers have conducted studies in which people are either hypnotized and told that they will feel no pain or not hypnotized and just encouraged to try their hardest to reduce pain in any way they can. In all these studies, the reductions in reported pain have been the same regardless of the method used to achieve them (Spanos, 1986). It is significant, too, that when people in these studies were later asked how they managed to reduce pain, hypnotic and nonhypnotic subjects reported using much the same attention-shifting strategies. How could this be, the researchers ask, if hypnosis is supposedly a special state of consciousness that involves genuine dissociations in awareness?

But proponents of the dissociation view are not persuaded by these critics. They say that the typical hidden-observer study may not be the best test for comparing the experiences of a truly hypnotized person and a nonhypnotized one who is simply trying hard to comply with the hypnotist's requests. When we study people who are *deeply* hypnotized, dissociation theorists argue, they can sometimes do things that are hard to explain by the cognitive strategies available to us in normal waking life. Consider, for instance, the case of a boy with severe burns on one leg (Graham, 1986). He screamed and writhed in agony whenever the doctor cleaned and redressed his wounds. Then the doctor tried hypnosis. After just a few sessions with a hypnotist, the child literally smiled and laughed while the burns were being handled. Was he simply shifting his attention away from the intense pain? And if so, why can't everyone who suffers acute pain eliminate it in this way?

The debate over the nature of hypnosis may be in need of a compromise (Kihlstrom, 1984, 1986; Laurence and Perry, 1983). Ultimately, a full understanding of hypnosis will probably require a combination of both the dissociation perspective and the cognitive role-enactment one. From the first we learn that the human mind is capable of sometimes dividing its awareness of perceptions, thoughts, and feelings. Such mental dissociations may help to explain how people behave under hypnosis. Interestingly, some recent studies suggest that during hypnosis the brain's right hemisphere becomes more active in relation to the left, perhaps because the left side is somehow inhibited (Crawford, 1985). Proponents of the dissociation perspective hope that such findings may someday lead to physiological evidence supporting a split in consciousness. At the same time, however, we cannot ignore the fact that hypnotic induction is filled with cues about how a hypnotized person is *expected* to act. When people are trying their best to be good hypnotic subjects, they may use a variety of cognitive tactics to conform to these expectations. Researchers who study hypnosis must repeatedly try to assess the extent to which such demand characteristics are influencing their results.

SUMMARY

1. **Consciousness** is our awareness of the many thoughts, images, sensations, and emotions that occupy the mind at any given time. This awareness varies significantly depending on the situation. People experience cyclical changes in consciousness every day (sleeping and daydreaming, for instance). They also induce distinctive states of consciousness in themselves (by taking psychoactive drugs, practicing meditation, or undergoing hypnosis, for example).

2. Psychologists have distinguished several stages of sleep by monitoring people's brain waves. After a person has been in the deepest stage of sleep for a while (known as **delta sleep**), he or she seems to return to a waking brain-wave pattern. Yet the person remains sound asleep, with eyes moving rapidly back and forth beneath closed eyelids. This stage is known as rapid eye movement or **REM sleep** and is closely associated with dreaming.

3. People compensate for lost REM sleep on one night by entering the REM state more often during their next night's sleep (**REM rebound**). This finding has led to theories that REM sleep serves some special physiological function. One possibility is that REM sleep helps the brain adapt to disturbing or unusual life experiences. Another possibility is that REM sleep helps release pent-up energy associated with unsatisfied physiological needs.

4. People have debated the meaning of dreams for centuries. Although Freud believed that dreams embody people's unconscious wishes, disguised in symbolic form, many contemporary therapists believe that dreams are usually direct attempts to deal with the concerns and problems that dominate waking consciousness. There is also evidence that people can occasionally control the content of their dreams, making the outcomes more emotionally satisfying.

5. A **daydream** is a train of thought that departs from a person's immediate situation and whatever tasks are at hand. For a few moments the daydreamer loses "touch" with the outside world and focuses attention instead on some internal drama. Interestingly, most people daydream at regular intervals during the day, intervals that are roughly 90 to 100 minutes apart. Daydreams tend to focus on current concerns that pose some special challenge and so may be a way of helping to cope with the problems of everyday life.

6. Distinctive states of consciousness involving changes in mood and thought can be induced by various **psychoactive drugs,** including the **depressant** alcohol, the **stimulants** cocaine and amphetamines, and the **hallucinogens** LSD, PCP, and marijuana. Each has distinctive effects on human functioning, and each is suspected of working by altering the normal operation of neurotransmitters in the brain. Certain drug-induced states of consciousness may seem, on the surface, to be conducive to creativity. But psychoactive drugs can actually hinder creativity by diminishing the capacity for well-ordered thought.

7. An ancient technique for inducing a special state of consciousness without the use of drugs is **meditation.** Although there are many varieties of meditation, most involve focusing attention on a single stimulus until sensory input from the outside world is greatly restricted. During meditation, a person's metabolism may undergo a measurable slowing, and brain-wave patterns may also slow. Exactly how these changes occur is still being explored.

8. Many law enforcement agents strongly believe that hypnosis can enhance the memories of people who have witnessed serious crimes. But research psychologists can find no evidence that hypnosis is, in fact, a very good memory enhancer. Probably the memory improvement observed when hypnosis is used in police investigations is due largely to factors other than hypnosis, factors that just happen to be linked with the use of hypnosis for this purpose.

9. The precise nature of the state of awareness called hypnosis is uncertain, despite its medical and therapeutic uses. Some researchers propose that when a person is hypnotized, a **dissociation** or split in consciousness occurs. But others contend that hypnotized people are merely trying hard to follow the hypnotist's directives by using a variety of cognitive strategies available to them in the normal waking state.

SUGGESTED READINGS

Bowers, K. S. (1983). *Hypnosis for the seriously curious.* New York: Norton. A good introduction to the phenomenon of hypnosis and its many applications.

Empson, J. (1990). Sleep and dreaming. Winchester, MA: Faber & Faber. The author presents new research on sleep and dreaming for the general reader. Explains what scientists have learned about the experience of sleep and dreaming and the various types of sleep disorders.

Hobson, J. A. (1989). *Sleep.* San Francisco: Freeman. Describes the nature of sleep in nontechnical language. Includes recent research on sleep and its functions from an interdisciplinary perspective.

Julien, R. M. (1988). *A primer of drug action* (5th ed.). San Francisco: Freeman. Up-to-date information on the actions and side effects of drugs that affect the central nervous system. Covers a wide variety of drugs, including alcohol, opiates, and psychedelics.

Wallace, B., and Fisher, L. E. (1987). *Consciousness and behavior* (2nd ed.). Boston: Allyn & Bacon. Provides a brief history of the study of consciousness as well as information about the physiology of consciousness. The authors speculate about the future of the psychology of consciousness.

LEARNING

Albert Einstein didn't begin to speak until he was three. His mastery of speech was so slow that his family feared he would never learn to talk (Jakobson, 1982). Thomas Edison had trouble mastering grammar and spelling. Even in his late teens, his writing skills were terrible (Thompson, 1971). Agatha Christie, the world-renowned mystery writer, couldn't master spelling either. She once dropped the word *Caribbean* from the title of one of her books because she was tired of struggling to spell it correctly. As a child, Christie also struggled to learn the alphabet. Her old copybooks are full of shaky B's and R's, which she seemed to have had great trouble distinguishing (Siegel, 1988).

Psychologists have devoted a great deal of time to studying the various difficulties in learning that people may experience and trying to understand their causes. The reason for this attention to learning problems is that learning is so crucial to our lives. Through learning we not only acquire academic skills, such as reading and writing, we also acquire the knowledge we need to function in everyday life. When you master the techniques of driving a car, cooking a meal, or doing your laundry, you are engaged in forms of learning. Learning, in fact, has an impact on almost everything you do. In this chapter we explore the important subject of learning and psychologists' perspectives on it.

THE NATURE OF LEARNING

How do we know when learning has occurred? Often we cannot just ask people if they have learned, because sometimes people are not sure if they have or not, and sometimes they tend to gloss the truth. We may also wish to study learning in infants or animals, who are not able to say what they know. The way around these problems, proposed by the early behaviorists, is to infer learning by observing changes in *performance*. Thus, a psychologist can create a controlled situation that is conducive to learning and then objectively measure performance at different times. If performance changes, we may be able to say that the change indicates learning. Of course, the experimental situations must always be carefully controlled, because factors other than learning (emotion, motivation, maturation, fatigue, health, and so forth) can also influence performance. Only when such other influences can be legitimately ruled out may researchers infer that a change in performance is most likely due to learning.

FIGURE 6.1 The apparatus used in early studies of classical conditioning. Saliva dropping from a tube inserted into the dog's cheek strikes a lightly balanced mechanical arm. The resulting motion is transmitted hydraulically to a pen that traces a record on graph paper attached to a revolving drum. Pavlov's discovery of conditioned salivation was an accidental by-product of his research into the activity of the digestive system.

But though performance is useful for measuring learning, someone who has learned need not always show it through a change in performance. Sometimes we learn but do not have an opportunity to demonstrate that learning. Or sometimes we simply are not motivated to show what we have learned. Nevertheless, learning always gives us the *potential* for a change in performance. This potential should be mentioned in any definition of learning. A definition of learning should also differentiate between learning and all the other factors that can influence performance. To distinguish learning from factors that temporarily affect performance (such as emotion or fatigue), learning can be called a *relatively permanent* change in performance potential. And to distinguish learning from physical factors, such as maturation or illness, learning can be called a change in performance potential that results from *experience*. Putting all these elements together gives us the following definition: **learning** is a relatively permanent change in performance potential that arises from experience (Gordon, 1989).

Throughout this chapter we will look at some of the different kinds of learning in which humans and many other animals engage. One is learning to associate one event with another, called **associative learning.** Suppose your car develops a strange sputtering sound. A few seconds later the engine stalls, and you respond by feeling annoyed. If after a while you feel

annoyed as soon as you hear the sputter (even *before* the engine stalls), psychologists would say that you have acquired a **classically conditioned response.** You have learned an association between the sputter and the stall and now respond to the sputter almost as if it were the stall. **Classical conditioning** is a very basic kind of learning in which a previously neutral stimulus (in this case a sputtering sound) comes to elicit an involuntary action or feeling (such as annoyance) because it signals the onset of another stimulus (a stalled engine) that naturally elicits the same response.

Another kind of associative learning is called **operant conditioning.** It involves learning to change your voluntary actions because of the consequences they bring. Suppose you find that if you press your car's accelerator sharply every time your engine sputters, you can avoid the frustration of stalling in the middle of the road. Psychologists would say that the lurching style of driving you are sure to develop is a **conditioned operant response.** It results from a learned association between a particular action (quick pressure on the gas pedal) and a desirable consequence (an engine that does not stall).

Some psychologists have argued that virtually all learning can be explained by classical and operant conditioning. But others contend that, while these two forms of learning are important, much of human learning does not fall neatly into either category.

FIGURE 6.2 (A) Acquisition of a conditioned response (CR). On early test trials, with the tone alone, there is little salivation. Later in the series, the tone alone (CS) elicits considerable salivation and a CR has been acquired. (B) Extinction of a CR. When the tone-food pairings are eliminated, the amount of salivation (CR) to the tone alone (CS) drops steadily until the relationship between CS and CR no longer exists.

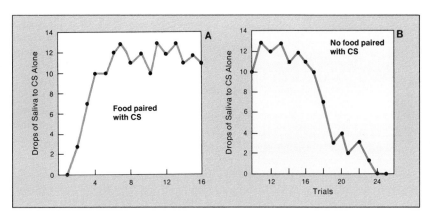

Cognitive learning, they say, is also crucial. Cognitive learning involves the formation of concepts, schemas, theories, and other mental abstractions. For instance, when your car develops its sputter, you acquire a mental expectation that this sputter will be followed by a stall. At the same time, you acquire a general rule for circumventing the problem (quickly stepping on the gas). Behaviorists maintain that cognitions like these are too vague and subjective for scientific study. To cognitive psychologists, however, people's thought processes are just as important as their overt behaviors. We will conclude this chapter by looking at learning from the cognitive psychologists' perspective. But first we turn to classical and operant conditioning.

CLASSICAL CONDITIONING

Ivan Pavlov, a Nobel-prize-winning Russian physiologist, discovered classical conditioning in the early twentieth century. Like many great discoveries, this one was largely accidental. Pavlov was studying how the mouth prepares itself for food by secreting saliva. In a series of experiments with dogs (1927), he found that the mouth also secretes saliva when food is merely seen or smelled. He called this salivation a "psychic secretion" because it is caused by psychological processes, not by food actually being placed in the mouth. Pavlov also found that when a dog first sees an unfamiliar food, it does not salivate. Only when it has learned the particular sights, odors, or other stimuli associated with a desirable food do

psychic secretions occur. These discoveries provided the foundation for Pavlov's subsequent investigations into classical (sometimes called Pavlovian) conditioning.

ACQUIRING A CLASSICALLY CONDITIONED RESPONSE

BASIC PROCEDURES

Figure 6.1 shows one of Pavlov's dogs in an experimental apparatus. The dog has a tube inserted in its cheek so that saliva flows from the salivary gland into a container. The mechanical device at the far left monitors the amount of saliva secreted. Pavlov began by presenting the dog with a neutral stimulus, such as a tone. (The tone was "neutral" with regard to salivation: it neither evoked nor inhibited the salivation response.) Several seconds after the tone, Pavlov dropped food into the dog's feeding tray. When the dog put the food in its mouth, it salivated. As the pairing of the tone and the food continued, the tone began to elicit salivation by itself, even when no food was given. The outcome of this conditioning process is illustrated in Figure 6.2.

In Pavlov's terms, the food in the mouth is the **unconditioned stimulus (UCS),** which elicits the **unconditioned response (UCR)** of salivation. The word *unconditioned* indicates that the connection between this particular stimulus and response does not have to be learned. The new stimulus that comes to elicit salivation is called the **conditioned stimulus (CS),** and the animal's salivation in response to it is called the **conditioned response (CR).** The word

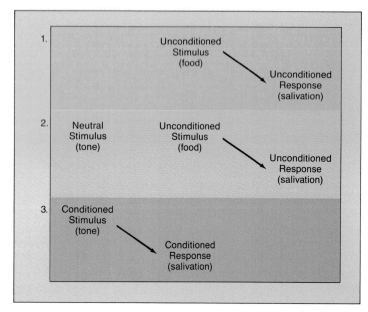

FIGURE 6.3   Elements of the classical conditioning situation used in Pavlov's experiments. (1) An unconditioned stimulus (food in the mouth) elicits an unconditioned response (salivation). (2) A neutral stimulus (such as a tone) is then repeatedly presented right before the dog is given food and salivates. (3) The tone soon becomes a conditioned stimulus that elicits a conditioned salivation response. (*After Gordon, 1989.*)

conditioned indicates that this new response is learned through an association of events (in this case an association between the tone and the arrival of food). This process is shown in Figure 6.3. Pavlov found that a large number of auditory, visual, or tactile sensations—including the ticking of a metronome, the flash of a light, or a brush on the skin—can serve as conditioned stimuli for salivation. He also found that, using procedures similar to those just described, he could condition involuntary responses other than salivation.

THE IMPORTANCE OF PERCEIVING RELATIONSHIPS

In the past, classical conditioning was characterized as a very mechanical process in which control over some involuntary reaction is passed from a stimulus that naturally elicits it (the UCS) to another that normally does not (the CS) as a result of a pairing of the two stimuli. But many modern behaviorists see classical conditioning as being more complex than this (Rescorla, 1988). They stress the information that one stimulus gives about another and the fact that the responding organism perceives a relationship between the two. According to this view, Pavlov's dogs perceived a connection between the tone and the food such that the tone seemed to signal that food was about to arrive. It is usually easiest to establish this

perceived relationship when the conditioned stimulus is presented a little before the unconditioned one, a procedure called **forward conditioning.** Pavlov, for example, usually presented the tone (the CS) five seconds before the food (the UCS) and in some cases continued the tone until the food was given. In contrast, **backward conditioning** (presenting the CS *after* the UCS) is generally less effective in creating a classically conditioned response (Hrudova et al., 1987).

When there is *no* consistent relationship between an unconditioned stimulus and some neutral stimulus, classical conditioning is apt to be weak or does not occur at all. Robert Rescorla (1968) demonstrated this by repeatedly sounding a tone for a period of time, during which experimental animals received one or more brief electric shocks. The animals in each of two groups received the same number of shocks while the tone was sounding. But those in one of the groups also received shocks alone, when the tone *was not* turned on. Rescorla found that the animals in this group developed a much weaker classically conditioned fear of the tone. Apparently, because they had also experienced shocks without the tone, it was harder for them to learn to perceive the tone as a signal that a shock was about to come. Such studies suggest that classical conditioning involves more than just mechanically "stamping in" an association between two stimuli paired with one another in time.

Instead, it seems to depend on whether the organism learns to use the CS to predict the arrival of the UCS (Mackintosh, 1983; Rescorla, 1988; Staddon and Ettinger, 1989).

EXTINCTION OF A CLASSICALLY CONDITIONED RESPONSE

How long do classically conditioned responses last? Did Pavlov's dogs forever salivate at the sound of bells and tones? The answer depends on whether the CS and UCS continue to be paired, at least occasionally. If occasional pairing does not occur, the conditioned responses will gradually disappear. For example, if a dog has been trained to salivate in response to a tone paired with food, and then the tone is repeatedly presented *without* the food following, the number of drops of saliva secreted will gradually decline toward zero, as shown in part B of Figure 6.2. This slow weakening and eventual disappearance of a conditioned response is called **extinction.**

Sometimes when a conditioned response seems to be totally extinguished, it reappears in the original learning situation. Suppose we sound a tone over and over in the presence of a dog trained to salivate at this sound, but we no longer deliver any food. Eventually, the dog will stop salivating when it hears the tone. The next day we bring the dog back into the lab and sound the tone again. The dog is apt to salivate yet another time, although not as strongly as before. This process, called **spontaneous recovery,** probably occurs because old perceptions of relationships die hard. In the past the tone was often a signal that food was about to arrive. Perhaps it will be again. Of course, if still no food follows the tone, extinction will reoccur rapidly.

STIMULUS GENERALIZATION AND DISCRIMINATION

Suppose you have classically conditioned a dog to salivate at the sound of a dinner bell. Can you expect the dog also to salivate if it hears a set of chimes, a ringing telephone, or high-pitched notes on a piano? Conversely, can you train the dog to salivate only when it hears a *particular* bell and to ignore all other bells? The first process is called **stimulus generalization**—performing a learned response in the presence of similar stimuli. The second is called **stimulus discrimination**—learning to make a particular response only to a particular stimulus.

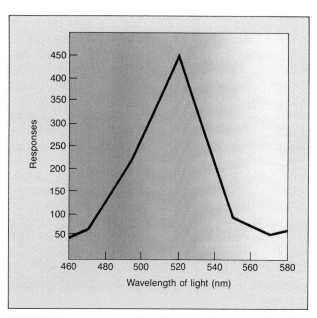

FIGURE 6.4   An example of a stimulus generalization gradient showing the pecking responses of a pigeon to keys of different colors. The bird has been trained to peck at a green key in order to receive a food reward. The more dissimilar another color is to the green used in training, the less the bird pecks. (*After Gordon, 1989.*)

Generalization of a classically conditioned stimulus happens frequently. In a famous experiment that many now criticize as unethical, John B. Watson and his student Rosalie Rayner showed just how readily generalization occurs (Watson and Rayner, 1920). They classically conditioned an eleven-month-old boy named Albert to fear a harmless laboratory rat by repeatedly pairing presentation of the rat with a sudden loud noise. Soon little Albert began to show fear at the sight of the rat alone, without the noise following. And his fear appeared to generalize to other furry objects—a rabbit, a dog, a sealskin coat, even a bearded Santa Claus mask.

The more similar a subsequent stimulus is to the one that prevailed during learning, the more likely it is that generalization will occur. Conversely, the more a new stimulus *differs* from the original conditioned stimulus, the less likely it is to elicit a conditioned response. Little Albert, for instance, showed fear at the sight of a live furry rabbit, but he would probably have shown much less fear if presented with a picture of one. This decreasing tendency to display a conditioned response as the resemblance between a new stimulus and a conditioned one becomes weaker is called a **generalization gradient** (see Figure 6.4).

People display generalization gradients because they can discriminate: they can perceive the dissimilarities between two stimuli and so respond to them differently. Animals can also do this, but in animal research a procedure called **discrimination training** is often used to enhance stimulus discrimination. Discrimination training makes critical use of extinction. Consider again the dog that has been conditioned to salivate at the sound of a dinner bell. It will probably also salivate when it hears a set of chimes, although not as much as in response to the bell. To reduce the response to the chimes still further, a researcher could ring the dinner bell alternately with the chimes, but present food only after the bell. Soon the dog's salivation in response to the chimes will extinguish. It has now learned to discriminate sharply between the two stimuli.

Generalization and discrimination often work together to help us respond in appropriate ways. For example, if you have been stung by bees and develop a conditioned fear of them, it is advantageous to generalize that wariness to wasps and hornets too. At the same time, it is helpful to discriminate between stinging and nonstinging insects, or else you will waste a great deal of time avoiding things that are harmless.

APPLYING CLASSICAL CONDITIONING PRINCIPLES

Pavlov's experiments in classical conditioning had an enormous influence on American psychology. John B. Watson was so impressed by Pavlov's work that he based most of his analysis of behavior on it. All learning, he argued, can be explained within the framework of classical conditioning. Today few psychologists, even behaviorists, take this extreme a view. Still, most believe that classical conditioning is an important form of learning. Emotional responses are particularly susceptible to it. Suppose that in several consecutive arithmetic lessons a child is asked a question and does not know the answer. He feels anxious each time, and soon the very mention of arithmetic causes him anxiety. This response may be difficult to extinguish, for the fact that the child is upset may cause him to perform poorly, thus maintaining the association.

Watson and his colleagues were among the first psychologists to study how classically conditioned

fears might be reduced or eliminated (Jones, 1974). Mary Cover Jones (1924), a graduate student of Watson's, pioneered the most successful approach. She began with a two-year-old boy named Peter, who had learned to fear furry animals and objects, especially rabbits. Jones put a caged rabbit in the same room in which Peter was eating, and gradually moved the cage closer and closer to him, always while Peter was enjoying food. In this procedure, a form of **counterconditioning,** the conditioned stimulus (a rabbit) was repeatedly paired with another stimulus (food) that elicited a response (pleasure) very different from the conditioned response (fear). Eventually, the rabbit came to be associated with food and the pleasure that food produced. As a result, Peter lost his fear of rabbits.

A similar technique, called **systematic desensitization,** is used to treat people with strong, persistent, debilitating fears known as phobias. This technique involves teaching a person (in graduated steps) to relax totally in the presence of the fear-arousing stimulus, thus introducing a response that is incompatible with fear. For example, a woman with an elevator phobia would be trained to relax her muscles while imagining a series of increasingly fear-arousing situations connected with elevators. Once she mastered this task, she would then attempt to remain relaxed during successive stages of an actual ride in an elevator. We will look more closely at systematic desensitization as a form of behavior therapy in Chapter 17.

Classical conditioning principles can be used not only to extinguish undesired behaviors but also to *instill* desired ones. One example is a treatment for children who wet their beds (Mower and Mower, 1930). This treatment uses a bed pad that causes a bell to ring the moment it is moistened with urine. The bell serves as the unconditioned stimulus, which elicits the unconditioned response of waking up. The physical sensation of a full bladder becomes the conditioned stimulus that repeatedly precedes the sound of the bell. In time the child should awaken at the bladder cue alone, as if in anticipation of the bell ringing. Research has shown that this can be an effective way to stop bed-wetting (Ross, 1981; Wilson, 1982).

Classical conditioning has applications beyond behavior therapy. For instance, medical researchers have classically conditioned a reduction in blood pressure among rats with hypertension by repeatedly pairing a distinctive odor with the injection of a blood-pressure-reducing drug (Spencer et al., 1988). After many such pairings, the distinctive odor alone comes to elicit the same effects as the drug. Such findings could eventually lead to new nondrug treatments for hypertension and high blood pressure.

OPERANT CONDITIONING

Even before Pavlov's experiments in classical conditioning, the innovative and highly influential American psychologist Edward L. Thorndike was investigating another form of associative learning. In one classic experiment, he placed a hungry cat in a "puzzle box" (1898, 1932). If the cat made a certain combination of moves, the door to the box would fly open, allowing the animal to escape and eat a piece of fish.

Thorndike found that initially the cat's behavior in the box was erratic. It would scramble about and make the desired response only accidentally. But in repeated trials the animal gradually became more proficient at escaping, until eventually it could oper the door almost immediately. Thorndike concluded that the cat had learned to escape because the escape responses were associated with a desirable consequence: food. Previously, he had summarized this relationship in the **law of effect** (1911), which states that responses that lead to satisfying consequences will be strengthened and are likely to be repeated, whereas responses that lead to unsatisfying consequences will be weakened and are unlikely to occur again. The law of effect provided the foundation for later studies concerning the effects of rewards and punishments on learning.

THE CENTRAL ROLE OF REWARDS AND PUNISHMENTS

B. F. Skinner, the leading behaviorist in modern psychology, became interested in some of the same problems that had interested Thorndike. Our environment, Skinner argued, is filled with positive and negative consequences that mold our behavior as surely as the piece of fish molded the behavior of Thorndike's cat. Our friends and families control us with their approval or disapproval. Our jobs control us by offering or withholding money. Our schools control us by passing or failing us, thus affecting our access to jobs. Positive or negative consequences

A parent's pride, as well as the trophy, provides reinforcement for this athlete's achievement.

shape our actions in all areas of life. To Skinner, in fact, the distinctive patterns of behavior that each person has are merely the product of all the many consequences that person has experienced (Skinner, 1985).

Learning to make or to withhold a particular response because of its consequences has come to be called **operant conditioning.** An important difference between operant and classical conditioning is that classical conditioning usually involves reflexive or involuntary responses, whereas operant conditioning usually involves voluntary ones. **Operant behaviors,** in other words, are actions that organisms emit of their own accord. For instance, no particular stimulus is needed to induce a rat to sniff and move about its cage. Such behavior is as natural to a rat as flying is to a bird or swinging through trees is to a monkey. Psychologists say that the rat is voluntarily "operating" on its environment, not responding involuntarily to a particular stimulus.

But though operant behaviors are voluntary, they can still be influenced by external factors—in particular, by their own consequences. These consequences can either increase or decrease the frequency of an operant response. A consequence that causes a behavior to be repeated (to increase in frequency) is called **reinforcement** or reward. A consequence that suppresses a behavior (decreases its frequency) is called **punishment.** Of course, what is considered rewarding or punishing can vary from person to person. For example, a child who hits a playmate and makes him cry may be spurred on to increase this form of bullying, but another child who experiences the same consequences may feel sorry and thereafter refrain from hitting others. For the first child the consequence (the crying) serves as reinforcement; for the second it serves as punishment. This example emphasizes why behaviorists avoid defining reinforcement and punishment as "good" versus "bad" consequences. *Good* and *bad* are subjective terms, which depend on an individual's viewpoint. It is much more objective, behaviorists argue, to define reinforcement and punishment in terms of their effects on subsequent behavior—that is, whether they increase or decrease the frequency of the response.

Occasionally, though, subjective definitions are helpful, even though strict behaviorists avoid them. This is true in distinguishing between positive and negative reinforcement, both of which *increase* the frequency of a response. In **positive reinforcement,** the frequency of a response increases because that response causes the *arrival* of a subjectively satisfying stimulus. When a hungry rat presses a lever and receives a pellet of food, lever pressing is being positively reinforced and is likely to occur again. In **negative reinforcement,** the frequency of a response increases because that response causes the *removal* of some subjectively unpleasant stimulus. When a rat presses a lever that turns off an electric shock, lever pressing is being negatively reinforced. Here the rat is engaging in **escape learning:** pressing the lever allows it to escape from the shock. Alternatively, pressing the lever might enable the rat to stop the shock from being turned on and so avoid it. This is called **avoidance learning.** Both escape and avoidance responses can be established through negative reinforcement.

Negative reinforcement and punishment both involve aversive stimuli (such as electric shock), so it is easy to confuse them. The trick to keeping the distinction straight is to focus on whether the aversive stimulus is being added to or removed from the environment and how the individual's behavior consequently changes. When a behavior is followed by the *arrival* of an unpleasant stimulus, punishment occurs. Punishment tends to *decrease* the frequency of the response that precedes it. The organism tries to prevent the unpleasant stimulus from occurring another time by *not* performing the behavior again. In contrast, when a behavior is followed by the *removal* of an unpleasant stimulus, negative reinforcement occurs. Negative reinforcement tends to *increase* the frequency of the response that precedes it. The organism tries to escape from or avoid the unpleasant stimulus by performing the behavior that enabled it to do so before. An example will further help to distinguish these two concepts. When a boy's sister hits him for grabbing her favorite toy, his action is being punished and he is less likely to grab the toy again. In contrast, if the boy gets his sister to *stop* hitting him by temporarily taking away her toy, his behavior is being negatively reinforced and he is likely to do the same thing again in similar circumstances.

In these examples, a cause-and-effect relationship exists between a particular behavior (taking a toy) and the outcome that follows it (being hit or getting relief from being hit). Sometimes, however, a behavior does not actually produce a consequence but is just accidentally linked with it. In such cases, people may still act as if the behavior caused the outcome. Behavior that increases or decreases as a result of such a chance relationship is called **superstitious behavior.** We can see this kind of behavior in a gambler who blows on the dice before every roll, or a football coach who wears his "lucky" hat to every game. Probably, at some time in the past these behaviors were accidentally linked with a winning streak and so were reinforced. Now they persist even though they never really caused the winning streak to occur.

ACQUIRING A CONDITIONED OPERANT RESPONSE

The general procedure for establishing a conditioned operant response is to control the consequences of behavior by manipulating rewards and punishments. One requirement is that the behavior and its consequences must be close enough together in time so that the individual perceives a cause-and-effect relationship between them. The occurrence of the consequence must seem to *depend* on the performance of the behavior. When a substantial time gap intervenes between the response and the consequence, the relationship may become clouded, and learning is more difficult. B. F. Skinner (1983) felt that a clouded relationship between war and its consequences is the reason why we humans go to war so readily. Too much time intervenes between the actions that lead to armed conflict and the punishing consequences such conflict brings (the massive death and destruction).

To condition operant behaviors in animals, psychologists have created many devices. One of the best known is the **Skinner box,** or operant chamber, developed by B. F. Skinner (1938). It is a small compartment in which a reward is automatically delivered right after an animal performs some target behavior, such as pressing a lever or pushing a button. Skinner created this invention one day when using another piece of operant conditioning equipment in which a rat must run down an alley to reach a food reward. He grew tired of always having to pick up the rat and return it to the starting point, so he designed a chamber in which a press of a lever sent a pellet of food tumbling into a feeding tray. The Skinner box has been an aid to researchers because it allows easy measurement of the rate and consistency of an animal's responses.

One potential problem in establishing a conditioned operant response is to get the subject to perform the target behavior the first time, before it knows that this behavior will be rewarded. Researchers usually make the task easier by selecting a behavior that comes naturally to the subject. For instance, pigeons need no special inducement to peck: they peck at virtually everything. So, when establishing a conditioned operant response in a pigeon, psychologists usually select some form of pecking as the target behavior (pecking at a special button, for example). Before long the bird accidentally hits upon the object the researcher wants it to peck. When the food reward is delivered, the pigeon begins to learn the association between this particular behavior and the rewarding consequence.

But suppose an animal is slow to perform the desired behavior. Physically forcing the response would probably make the animal too frightened to learn. Must the researcher simply wait for a lucky accident? A much quicker solution is to use a proce-

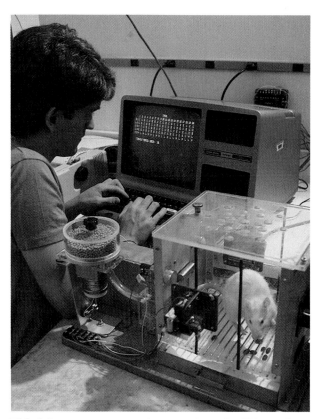

This laboratory rat occupies a version of a Skinner box, which automatically dispenses food pellets as rewards whenever the rat emits the desired behavior.

dure called **shaping.** With shaping, the researcher systematically reinforces each closer and closer approximation of the desired response. To understand how shaping works, imagine that you are trying to get a reluctant rat to press a bar. You begin by reinforcing the first response that shows the rat is on the right track—in this case, approaching the bar. After a few reinforcements, the rat will interrupt its other activities to walk toward the bar. Now you withhold reinforcement until the rat not only approaches the bar but also raises its front paws off the floor. Finally, you make the reward contingent on actually pressing the bar. When the animal learns this contingency, the desired behavior has been shaped. But note that each successive approximation of the target response must be only a small step beyond what the subject was previously doing; otherwise, the procedure will fail.

Shaping has been used to train animals to perform complicated tricks. Chickens, for example, have

Workers who are paid after completing a certain number of units each day or each week are on a fixed-ratio schedule of reinforcement.

been taught to play a simple Mozart piece on the piano. Shaping is used to modify human behavior too. Consider how parents often teach preschoolers to write their names. At first they praise mere scribbles on the paper, but gradually only more accurately shaped letters are rewarded, until eventually the child writes the name legibly. Campaign speeches are another example of shaping. Voters' responses to a candidate's speeches (cheers and applause versus stony silence) prompt the candidate to repeat well-received viewpoints and eliminate poorly received ones. Gradually, the speeches come to mirror what people want to hear. Shaping is also important in modern behavior therapy (Wilson, 1982). For instance, severely retarded children have been taught to dress and feed themselves by being systematically rewarded for closer and closer attempts at tying their shoes, using a fork, and so on.

MAINTAINING A CONDITIONED OPERANT RESPONSE

Once an operant response has been established, how can we make sure it will last? The key to maintaining operant behavior is keeping up the reinforcement, but the schedule of reinforcement also makes a difference. By altering the contingency on which reinforcement is delivered, an experimenter can change both the frequency and persistence of virtually any conditioned operant response.

SCHEDULES OF REINFORCEMENT

Consider a woman who is paid by the piece to assemble computer chips. This method of payment

represents a **schedule of reinforcement,** one that encourages very rapid work. The faster the woman can complete the chips, the more she will be paid. People in other situations are similarly affected by the schedules on which they receive rewards. At school, on the job, and in the laboratory, the prevailing schedule of reinforcement considerably affects behavior.

A **continuous reinforcement schedule**—providing a reward each time the desired behavior occurs—works best for establishing a conditioned operant response. For example, researchers might give a rat a pellet of food every time it presses a bar in order to firmly establish the bar-pressing response. Once a response has been established, however, often the best way to maintain it is to use a **partial reinforcement schedule** and withhold the reward some of the time. In this case, the rat receives food for only *some* of its bar-presses. Skinner discovered the power of partial reinforcement quite by accident. One weekend he ran low on food pellets and so tried rewarding his trained rats intermittently, for every second or third lever-press. Instead of diminishing their conditioned response, the rats responded more vigorously than before (Staddon and Ettinger, 1989).

But on what basis should you deliver the reward on a partial reinforcement schedule? Should you give food to a rat, say, every ten bar-presses? Or would it be more effective to wait, say, every two minutes? The first approach (a reward every ten bar-presses) is an example of a **fixed-ratio schedule.** Here the behavior is rewarded after it occurs a specific number of times. The rat experiencing a fixed-ratio schedule tends to press the bar at a more rapid rate than it would if it were rewarded continuously, for the faster the rat performs the *un*rewarded responses, the sooner it will finally get a piece of food. In the same way, our computer chip assembler who is paid for each ten chips she completes will work as quickly as she can.

The second approach—a reward once every two minutes—is an example of a **fixed-interval schedule,** delivering a reward the first time the behavior occurs after a certain interval of time has elapsed. A rat reinforced on a fixed-interval schedule will learn not to bother pressing the bar until the time of the next available reward approaches. In the same way, we learn not to bother checking a mailbox until near the regular time of delivery. A fixed-interval schedule tends to yield a relatively low frequency of response, because extra effort does not pay off with additional rewards.

While fixed-ratio and fixed-interval schedules deliver rewards regularly and predictably, other partial reinforcement schedules are irregular and unpredictable. For instance, a reward might be given after a variable number of responses: sometimes after ten responses, sometimes after seven, still other times after fifteen or twenty, and so on. This is called a **variable-ratio schedule.** Alternatively, a reward may be given after a variable time interval has elapsed: half a minute before the first reward, two minutes before the second, one minute before the third, and so forth. This is called a **variable-interval schedule.**

How do you think such reinforcement patterns affect the frequency of behavior? Because variable-ratio and variable-interval schedules are unpredictable, they encourage constant "testing" for the reward, and so tend to produce very high rates of response. They also produce responses that are very persistent. Consider a slot machine. Because the amount and schedule of its rewards are so varied, a slot machine has a compelling effect on behavior. Players continue to harbor the hope that the next pull of the handle will bring the big jackpot. So they keep on playing coin after coin.

Because irregular schedules of reinforcement are so powerful, they can easily maintain behaviors unintentionally. Consider a two-year-old who flatly refuses to go to bed. When his parents insist, he throws a tantrum. Usually the parents continue with bedtime preparations, but sometimes one parent can stand the roar no longer and the boy is allowed to stay up and play "just this once." The parents do not understand why, at age three, he is still having tantrums. What is going on in this situation? Unwittingly, these parents have been rewarding the boy's tantrums on a very effective variable-ratio schedule. To halt his bedtime rebellion, behaviorists would recommend that the parents resist even occasionally letting the boy stay up and play when he has a tantrum (Travris, 1982). At the same time, the parents should reward cooperative bedtime behavior with praise and attention, or perhaps the privilege of engaging in some special activity.

STIMULUS CONTROL

Besides controlling the strength and frequency of operant responses, reinforcement has another important effect. It relates a particular behavior to stimuli associated with the learning situation. Suppose that a rat has been conditioned to press a bar for a reward whenever a bulb in a Skinner box lights up. The Skinner box and the lighted bulb have become associated with reinforcement and the behavior of bar pressing. Whenever these stimuli are present, the rat is likely to press the bar again. This is called **stimulus control,** because the stimuli prevailing at the time of reinforcement have come to control the organism's response.

People also experience stimulus control. In fact, anyone who lives in a university dorm with low water pressure has benefited from this kind of learning. Flushing the toilet sharply reduces the amount of cold water being fed to the shower. So if you hear the toilet flush while you are in the shower, you learn to step back to avoid being sprayed by scalding water. What, psychologically, has happened here? First, you have acquired an operantly conditioned response: stepping back from the shower spray. Second, this behavior is under the control of a specific stimulus: the sound of the toilet flushing. You move back when you hear this cue.

Note that when you distinguish the flush from other sounds, you are engaging in stimulus discrimination. The flush has become a **discriminative stimulus** controlling your behavior. Helping establish discriminative stimuli is an important part of some behavior therapies. People who are overweight, for instance, often associate eating with all kinds of stimuli, such as watching television, reading a book, going to a movie, or sitting on a beach. One way to get them to decrease their eating is to ask them to confine it to the dining table. This location then becomes a discriminative stimulus, and other stimuli

Enjoying a home-cooked meal is the primary reinforcer of a chain of operant behaviors that includes buying and preparing the ingredients.

that used to be associated with eating gradually lose their power of control through lack of reinforcement.

Of course, just as people discriminate among stimuli that can control their behavior, so they also generalize about them. For instance, someone who has once slipped on an icy stairway learns to take great care on icy roads and sidewalks too. Without the ability to generalize in this fashion, people would profit little from their experiences.

SECONDARY OR CONDITIONED REINFORCERS

Typically, in operant conditioning experiments, the reward that establishes and maintains the conditioned response is a **primary reinforcer,** such as food or water—something that satisfies a basic biological need. The effects of a primary reinforcer can generalize, however, to a **secondary (or conditioned) reinforcer,** a stimulus which signals that a primary rein-

forcer is on its way. Suppose a chimpanzee is given a plastic token shortly before it receives a piece of fruit. After a while, the chimp will come to view the token as a signal that a primary reinforcer, food, will soon arrive. If a token consistently precedes the arrival of food, it may itself acquire the power to reinforce a learned response. The chimp, in short, will perform new behaviors in order to receive tokens.

Secondary reinforcers are extremely important in the world outside the laboratory, where it is rare for a learned behavior to be followed immediately by a primary reward. Behaviorists argue that secondary reinforcers are the reason people perform many of the activities they do. By rewarding each of a series of related responses with a secondary reinforcer, it is possible to maintain long sequences of behavior. For instance, although people derive many kinds of satisfaction from their jobs, the behavior of working is maintained in part by the secondary reinforcer of a paycheck. The behavior of going to the bank and cashing that paycheck is maintained by the secondary reinforcer of obtaining paper money. The behavior of spending that money in the supermarket is maintained by the secondary reinforcer of taking home a bagful of food. And finally, the behavior of cooking and serving a meal is maintained by the primary reinforcer of eating. Learning such a sequence of operant behaviors that eventually ends in a primary reward is called **chaining.** Each link in the chain is presumably maintained by its own secondary reinforcer.

EXTINCTION OF A CONDITIONED OPERANT RESPONSE

A conditioned operant response that is no longer reinforced gradually decreases in frequency and eventually disappears. This extinction process is illustrated in Figure 6.5. For the rat in a Skinner box, bar pressing diminishes after food pellets are no longer given. For the rebellious two-year-old, tantrums eventually decline after the parents stop giving in to them. During the early stages of extinction, however, the response tends to be even more forceful than before. For example, if you stop giving a pigeon food for pecking at a light, the bird typically becomes agitated and exaggerates the formerly rewarded behavior. Similarly, the child whose defiant screams stop paying off in rewards will probably scream even louder for a while.

FIGURE 6.5 Extinction of an operantly conditioned response. Initially, the animal's responding is reinforced. After twelve and a half minutes, reinforcement is withheld, and responding steadily declines. After forty minutes, the animal is removed from the chamber. When it is returned, its response begins again at nearly the original rate, even though there is *no* reinforcement. This spontaneous recovery may result from an association between the chamber and being rewarded.

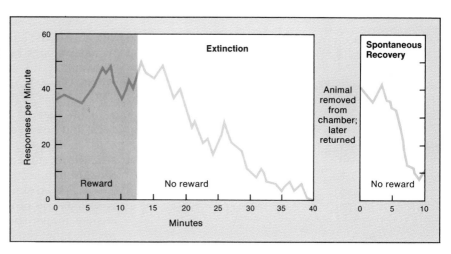

You can probably think of instances of this reaction in your own experience. Suppose your front door lock, which usually works well, does not open one day. In the language of operant conditioning, the previously reinforced response of inserting the key and turning it is no longer rewarded by entry into the house. Before you give up, however, your efforts to unlock the door will probably become more forceful. You may jiggle the key, rattle the doorknob, or give the door a kick before looking for another way into the house.

Now suppose you have been away from home for several days. When you return, are you likely to try the front door again? Most people would. In the same way, if an animal is removed from an experimental chamber for a while after a response has been extinguished and then is put back in, the response will usually reappear to some extent (Figure 6.5). This is the phenomenon of spontaneous recovery we discussed in the section on classical conditioning. The individual is responding once again to old controlling stimuli. In the past, a certain behavior was reinforced in this particular situation. Why not another time? Of course, without reinforcement, a spontaneously recovered behavior will diminish over time until it is again extinguished.

APPLYING OPERANT CONDITIONING PRINCIPLES

In the last twenty years, operant conditioning has gradually found its way out of the laboratory, with its experimental rats and pigeons, and into many areas of human life. Operant learning principles have been applied in schools, hospitals, prisons, drug rehabilitation centers, offices, factories, even homes. Two of the most important outcomes of this trend have been the educational method called programmed instruction and the therapeutic approach called behavior modification.

PROGRAMMED INSTRUCTION

However it is presented, whether by means of specially written textbooks or brightly colored graphics on a computer screen, **programmed instruction** emphasizes reinforcement in a learning situation. Every response the student makes elicits immediate feedback. The program presents information sequentially in small segments, and the learner goes on to a new unit only after demonstrating comprehension of the present one. Furthermore, instead of always moving through the same progression of steps, the program can branch off into supplementary lessons. For instance, students who are having trouble can be directed to remedial work in the area that is causing them problems, while those who are learning easily can be offered more advanced instruction (Hill, 1985).

There are several methods for presenting programmed instruction. One is the programmed textbook; another is the teaching machine, which B. F. Skinner helped develop in the 1950s; and a third, the most sophisticated, is **computer-assisted instruc-**

Computer-assisted instruction (CAI) can enable children to master educational material at their own pace, and designing their own programs can motivate children to become more creative problem solvers.

tion. One advantage of computer-assisted instruction is that it greatly increases the possibilities for branching off into supplementary lessons. A computer can also maintain a record of each student's progress and use this information to structure subsequent work. In addition, many teaching programs are fun for children. They use synthesized speech, sound effects, and color graphics as arresting as anything in a video game (Loftus and Loftus, 1983).

Besides improving specific skills, computers can also enhance children's ability to think. For instance, mathematician Seymour Papert (1980) has devised a computer language called LOGO, which enables children to do their own programming. The experience of teaching a computer how to "think," Papert argues, encourages children to explore how they themselves think. At the same time, learning to program gives students a chance to be creative in their work with computers, which can help to motivate the more imaginative child.

BEHAVIOR MODIFICATION

The scene is a classroom. A boy of eight takes out a large watch, places it in front of him, and selects a set of addition problems from a nearby table. He works on the problems quietly and steadily. When he has finished, he notes the time and calls the teacher. She corrects his work, smiles, and says, "Very good.

You get ten tokens for this." The boy takes his tokens and crosses the hall to another room, where he trades them for a large candy bar. Smiling, he returns to his classroom in this institution for emotionally troubled youth. When he came to the institution this boy's behavior was highly disruptive. He refused to stay seated, screamed at his teachers, pushed other children, and knocked things off shelves. Now he can sit still for relatively long periods and concentrate on schoolwork to an extent that many people once thought him incapable of.

This is an example of **behavior modification,** the conscious use of operant conditioning principles to change human behavior. The concept of behavior modification comes from B. F. Skinner's stress on behavior as the proper focus of psychological study. As early as the 1950s, Skinner argued that we must stop thinking of the behavioral aspects of psychological disorders as mere "symptoms" of some deeper, underlying cause (Skinner, 1953). Instead, we must address the problem behaviors in their own right, for if we eliminate these, we effectively eliminate the problem. Soon some of Skinner's students, armed with operant conditioning techniques, set out to apply this perspective outside the laboratory (Wilson, 1982). Today the deliberate use of rewards and punishments to change human behavior is also known as **contingency management** (Masters et al., 1987). This term derives from the fact that the psychologists involved are managing the contingencies (or relationships) between behaviors and their consequences.

Using Rewards to Change Behavior Some of the earliest behavior modification programs were established in mental hospitals and other institutions for people with severe behavior problems. In all of these early programs, **token economies** played a key role. The boy described above was participating in a token economy. As operant conditioning principles prescribe, he was immediately reinforced for performing a relatively complex task—sitting still long enough to solve some arithmetic problems. His reward was a handful of tokens (secondary reinforcers) that could be exchanged at any time for primary reinforcers, such as candy bars.

Behavior therapists deliberately manipulate rewards to try to cure many other problems, from smoking, overeating, truancy, stuttering, and shyness, to poor study habits, volatile tempers, and lack

"Time out," in the form of brief separation from the rest of the class, has proven effective in modifying a child's undesirable behavior.

of self-assertion. Employers have used this approach to raise worker productivity and government officials to deter littering in public parks. In all cases the procedure is much the same: eliminate inadvertent rewards for the problem behavior, while systematically reinforcing a more desirable alternative response. Thus, a teacher trying to engage a shy boy in group activities would avoid giving him attention when he withdraws from the class, but encourage and praise him when he interacts with others.

The Use of Punishment Although many parents and teachers turn first to punishment as a way of changing a child's behavior, its usefulness as a method of behavior modification is limited (Axelrod and Apsche, 1983; Klein, 1991; Martin and Pear, 1983). Inhibition of the problem behavior is apt to be only temporary unless the punishment is immediate, consistently given, and severe. Severe punishment, however, may have "backfire" effects, such as anger and aggression, and it can also prompt such strong anxiety that the original problem worsens. Punishment can also cause the situation related to it to become an "aversive stimulus," to be escaped from or avoided. For instance, a child punished at school for misbehav-

ing may come to dislike school even more. Finally, punishment signals only what should *not* be done. It does not establish a positive response to replace the undesirable one. Consequently, one undesirable behavior may simply replace another. This is why punishment is most effective when used in conjunction with positive forms of behavior modification. Punishment can temporarily prevent some very negative behavior, such as excessive physical aggression, so that a more acceptable response can then be rewarded and strengthened.

Proponents of behavior modification consider it to be one of the most important innovations ever made in the treatment of psychological problems (Hill, 1985). But critics charge that it often brings only temporary solutions that last no longer than the rewards that maintain them. Some people are also uncomfortable with controlling human behavior in such a deliberate way. Behavior therapists answer that they have often been able to maintain reinforcement over long periods of time, and they see no problem in controlling behavior if it benefits the people involved. We will say more about behavior modification in Chapter 17, where we discuss the treatment of psychological disorders.

Pigs are physically equipped for jumping (though not very high), so training them to jump through a hoop is relatively easy because it is based on such prepared learning.

BIOLOGICAL CONSTRAINTS ON ASSOCIATIVE LEARNING

THE CONCEPT OF PREPARED LEARNING

So far you may have gotten the impression that classical and operant conditioning can be applied in unlimited ways. If so, this impression is mistaken. Both these forms of associative learning are subject to important biological constraints. Why is it so easy to teach a dog to "shake hands" but very hard to teach a cat the same trick? Why do you feel nauseated when you smell a food that once made you sick, but not when you see the table where you ate it? Why do researchers routinely teach rats to run mazes but usually do not present a pigeon with this task? The answers lie in what is called **prepared learning**— learning that a particular kind of animal is biological-ly prepared to do. When an organism is *not* biological-ly prepared to learn a certain task, learning is slow and often fraught with problems.

Keller and Marion Breland, two former students of Skinner's, learned this lesson many years ago. The Brelands organized a show in which animals per-formed unusual tricks taught to them through shap-ing (Breland and Breland, 1961). For instance, they trained a pig to deposit wooden "nickels" in a large piggy bank, and a chicken to eject a capsule from its cage after pulling a cord that made the capsule roll down a chute. All went well until, suddenly, the performers started misbehaving. The pig began push-ing the nickels around with its snout, as if it was rooting in the dirt; and the chicken became so caught up in pecking at the capsule that it failed to do the very thing that would earn it a food reward. The Brelands concluded that the animals were reverting to instinctive feeding and foraging responses that com-peted with the behaviors they had been taught. Perhaps these instinctive responses were elicited by the food rewards the animals expected to get (Timber-lake and Lucas, 1984). In any case, the Brelands called this process of natural reversion **instinctive drift.**

Instinctive drift explains why, even with rewards, it can be hard to maintain operantly conditioned responses that oppose an organism's "built-in" ten-dencies (Gould, 1986; Lefrancois, 1982). Moreover, when a particular response is very uncharacteristic of an animal's behavior (pigeons exploring mazes, cats shaking one paw), it can be difficult to instill that response in the first place, despite careful shaping. In the same way, it is hard to establish a classically conditioned association between two stimuli that an animal is not biologically prepared to connect. On the other hand, organisms readily acquire conditioned responses and associations that they are prepared to learn. Studies of learned taste aversions demonstrate this clearly.

IN DEPTH

Studying Learned Taste Aversions

The time is the mid-1950s. Just a decade earlier, physicists working to develop an atomic bomb had succeeded in tapping the secrets of nuclear fission. But how serious were the hazards of nuclear wastes and fallout? Many concerned scientists were anx-ious to find out. Among them was a psychologist named John Garcia.

In the course of his investigation into the effects of radiation, Garcia made a puzzling discovery (Garcia et al., 1956). Rats placed in a radiation chamber for eight hours weekly, and exposed to moderate levels of radiation, progressively lowered their intake of water, as though they were learning *not* to drink. Yet when the rats were returned to their home cages, they drank as usual. It was only the water in the radiation chamber that they refused to touch. In fact, while in the chamber they avoided water even when no radiation was given. What could explain this strange behavior? Garcia suspected that it must reflect some kind of associative learning. But what specific stimuli were involved?

Later Garcia believed that he had deduced the answer. This behavior, he proposed, was a case of classical conditioning. The water bottles in the radiation chamber were made of plastic, while those in the home cages were made of glass. Apparently, the plastic bottles gave a peculiar taste to the water. It was this taste that served as the conditioned stimulus. The unconditioned stimulus was stomach upset caused by exposure to radiation; it elicited the unconditioned response of nausea. After being repeatedly paired with stomach upset, the plastic-tasting water came to evoke nausea on its own, so the rats avoided it. Thus, Garcia hypothesized that animals can acquire classically conditioned taste aversions when a distinctive flavor is repeatedly paired with stomach upset. His next step was to design a set of controlled experiments to test this interesting possibility.

THE INITIAL STUDIES

Garcia's first experiments involved spiking water with various novel flavors and administering illness-inducing agents to laboratory rats. As predicted, the rats seemed to acquire a classically conditioned taste aversion to any new flavor that had been paired with severe stomach upset. Furthermore, this learning occurred with remarkable speed and was extremely persistent. In one of Garcia's studies, a single pairing of salty water with illness was enough to cause the rats to shun salty water when they encountered it again more than a month later (Garcia et al., 1974).

But why, Garcia wondered, had the rats developed an aversion specifically to the water? Why hadn't they also developed an aversion to the sight of the experimental chamber? After all, it too had been associated with illness. Yet his studies showed that it was very hard to get a rat to avoid the *place* where it had become sick (Garcia et al., 1961). Was there something special about certain kinds of relationships that made them easier or more difficult to learn? If so, this contradicted one of the basic assumptions about classical conditioning prevalent at the time—the assumption, dating back to Pavlov, that virtually any formerly neutral stimulus could serve as a conditioned stimulus to elicit virtually any involuntary response. Garcia's work suggested that this long-held belief might be wrong. The nervous system of an organism might be structured in such a way as to facilitate the learning of certain relationships and hinder the learning of others.

CRITICISMS, ALTERNATIVES, AND FURTHER RESEARCH

To investigate this theory, Garcia and his colleague Robert Koelling designed a clever experiment in which various kinds of stimuli were paired with various aversive outcomes (Garcia and Koelling, 1966). One group of rats was presented with saccharin-flavored water, and as soon as they drank it they either received a paw shock or were induced to become ill. Another group of rats was presented with water that, when sipped through a drinking tube, set off an impressive display of flashing lights and loud noises. Drinking this "bright, noisy water" was again followed by either a paw shock or illness. The results of this experiment are shown in Table 6.1. Whether a rat subsequently avoided the water to which it had been exposed depended on the water's characteristics and what happened after the animal drank it. An aversion developed when saccharin-flavored water was paired with illness and when bright, noisy water was paired with shock. But no aversion resulted when these stimuli were paired in the opposite way—that is, saccharin water with shock, and bright, noisy water with illness. Garcia concluded that the ease with which an animal learns a given association seems to depend on some intrinsic relationship between the cue (the CS) and its perceived consequence (the UCS).

Why should this be the case? Garcia believes that to answer this question we must analyze the problem from an evolutionary perspective. Natural selection, he argues, has favored a nervous system that allows rapid learning of relationships common

TABLE 6.1   Results of the Bright, Noisy Water Experiment

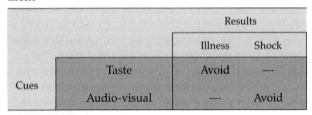

Cues		Results	
		Illness	Shock
	Taste	Avoid	—
	Audio-visual	—	Avoid

From Relation of cue to consequence in avoidance learning. J. Garcia and R. A. Koelling (1966), *Psychonomic Science, 4*, 123–124.

in a species' environment and crucial to its survival. Consider the dietary habits of rats. These animals eat virtually anything they can find. While this practice expands their food supply, it also increases a rat's risk of eating something poisonous. Thus, a rat whose nervous system is "programmed" to remember foods that make it ill will clearly have a better chance of surviving and reproducing. In this way, a built-in facility for learning to avoid dangerous foods may have evolved. From an evolutionary viewpoint, it makes sense that taste, but not noise or flashing lights, would be an effective conditioned stimulus for eliciting nausea.

An evolutionary perspective also helps explain why learned taste aversions violate another traditional rule of classical conditioning—that the UCS must follow the CS within a matter of seconds if learning is to occur. In his earliest experiments, Garcia noticed that a learned taste aversion develops even when a fairly long delay occurs between the taste of a new flavor and the onset of illness. Other studies have shown that the lapse between the CS and the UCS can be anywhere from three to twelve hours, depending on the circumstances (Andrews and Braveman, 1975; Kalat and Rozin, 1971). Furthermore, in many cases tastes intervening between the CS and the UCS do not prevent a strong aversion to the CS from forming, provided that the flavor of the CS is novel and salient enough (Revusky and Bedarf, 1967). Such findings are understandable if you assume that organisms have biological predispositions to learn adaptive behaviors. In nature, substantial time gaps often occur between ingestion of a toxic substance and the subsequent feeling of illness. Any organism capable of learning despite such gaps would clearly have a survival advantage.

Ilene Bernstein has extended Garcia's path-breaking research to the study of human beings. After all, most of us know at least one person who loathes the very sight of a certain food that was once associated with a severely upset stomach. Does this mean that humans, too, have a built-in facility for learning aversions to tastes associated with illness? To find out, Bernstein has studied cancer patients, suspecting that the loss of appetite that they often suffer may involve classically conditioned taste aversions. Bernstein has found that cancer patients do indeed acquire learned taste aversions due in part to a pairing of food with the stomach upset caused by chemotherapy (Bernstein, 1978; Bernstein et al., 1982). In addition, the toxins and hormones that tumors produce may also act as unconditioned stimuli in acquiring taste aversions (Bernstein, 1986). In either case, learned taste aversions exacerbate the patients' problems by encouraging them to undereat and further jeopardize their health.

PATTERNS AND CONCLUSIONS

Garcia and Bernstein's work shows that many animal species, including human beings, rapidly learn aversions to tastes associated with illness. This rapid learning results from how the nervous system is programmed. Evolution has endowed us with the ability to learn very quickly those associations that could be important to our survival. Unfortunately, such learning occurs even when the food in question is just *coincidentally* associated with illness, when it is not actually the *cause* of getting sick, as in the case of food paired with illness-inducing chemotherapy. Can anything be done to "short-circuit" learning in these cases? Luckily, it can. For instance, Bernstein and her colleagues found that when a novel food (such as an unusual-flavored ice cream) is given to cancer patients right before chemotherapy, a learned aversion tends to develop to that novel taste, not to the foods that the patients usually eat (Bernstein, 1985). The novel food, in other words, serves as a kind of scapegoat, allowing the patients to continue eating their normal diets. Bernstein has also found that patients who eat little or nothing before chemotherapy are less likely than others to develop food aversions. This suggests that pretherapy fasting for cancer patients may be another useful approach. Findings like these are an excellent example of how scientific research often leads to ideas for overcoming human problems.

LEARNING AND COGNITION

Most early behaviorists explained associative learning in a very mechanistic way. They argued that when an organism makes a response to a certain stimulus, and that response is reinforced, a stimulus–response (S–R) connection forms in the brain. Subsequent reinforcement of the same response strengthens this neural connection, until eventually the behavior will almost always occur in the presence of the controlling stimulus. Thus, the pigeon that pecks at a button as soon as it lights up, the dog that sits by the table when dinner is to be served, and the person who answers the telephone whenever it rings are simply exhibiting automatic stimulus–response patterns that in the past have been rewarded.

ASSOCIATIVE LEARNING: THE COGNITIVE VIEW

But many contemporary psychologists reject the traditional behaviorist perspective because it completely ignores an organism's perceptions and thoughts. In almost any learned association, they argue, mental processes intervene between the stimulus and the response. One of the earliest proponents of this **cognitive view** of associative learning was Edward Tolman, an American psychologist who worked at a time when strict behaviorists dominated psychology in this country. Tolman argued in favor of the then unorthodox idea that many animals are capable of thinking about the consequences of their behavior and selecting the most rewarding course of action in a purposive way. While he was alive, Tolman's ideas were overshadowed by the behaviorist perspective, but today the cognitive view that he helped start is very influential in all areas of learning.

Central to the cognitive view of associative learning is a concern for the *expectations* that an organism develops—that is, for its mental representations of how things in the environment typically respond or are related to one another. For example, a dog being classically conditioned develops the expectation that a previously neutral stimulus—say, a flashing light—will be followed by food or some other unconditioned stimulus. It is that expectation which brings about the conditioned response (Edelman, 1987). This cognitive view seems to be supported by an anecdote about one of Pavlov's dogs that had been conditioned to respond to the ticking of a metronome. When the metronome was turned off, the dog planted himself

Illness caused by eating one bad oyster is enough to establish a strong taste aversion, making us think twice about eating any kind of shellfish.

in front of it and proceeded to whine and beg. If this story is true, more seems to be going on here mentally than the development of a mechanistic stimulus–response association.

A strong motivation to learn exists when our current expectations are violated in some way. In this situation we are anxious to find out what new contingencies apply. Conversely, when our current expectations are serving us quite well, we often disregard new associations; we tend *not* to learn them. The same is true of other animal species. For instance, suppose you have conditioned a rat to expect a shock after it hears a tone. If you then flash a light when you sound the tone, will the rat learn to view the light as a signal for shock as well? Probably not, because the light provides no additional information about the delivery of shock. The tone continues to signal shock, just as it always has done, so there is no need to learn another association. When prior conditioning to one stimulus prevents conditioning to another, **blocking** is said to have occurred. Blocking suggests that many animals are intelligent, adaptive learners. Instead of acquiring *all* associations in a mindless way, they seem to mentally "screen" them and focus mainly on those that are useful to learn.

LEARNING WITHOUT REINFORCEMENT

Evidence that learning can occur without reinforcement also bolsters the cognitive view. Recall that in

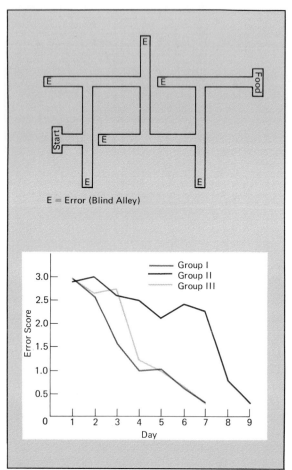

E = Error (Blind Alley)

FIGURE 6.6   Latent learning. Tolman and his colleagues argued that learning is a result of cognition—a thinking process that involves more than just the association of stimulus and responses through reinforcement. Support for this idea came from a series of experiments like the one shown (Blodgett, 1929). Rats in group I were put in the maze once a day for nine consecutive days; they always found food at the maze's end. Group II rats were also put in the maze, but not rewarded until the seventh day. Group III found rewards on day 3. At first, the rats in groups II and III made many errors in getting through the maze, but the errors dropped abruptly on the day *after* the reward was first introduced. Thus, during the *nonrewarded* trials, the rats had learned more than they exhibited; the reward improved their performance in the maze, but did not determine their learning to get through it.

the strict S–R model, an association will be formed only if it is reinforced. Yet cognitive psychologists maintain that much of human learning occurs without the meting out of overt rewards or punishments. Two types of learning that fall into this category are latent learning and learning through observation.

LATENT LEARNING

When an organism learns a new behavior but does not demonstrate this knowledge until an incentive to do so arises, the learning is called **latent learning.** In an early demonstration of latent learning, Tolman and Honzik (1930) permitted some rats to explore a maze in the absence of any reward. Meanwhile, they presented other rats with food whenever they reached the goal box. As expected, the rewarded rats soon learned to run the maze quickly and without error. The unrewarded rats, in contrast, seemed to wander aimlessly. However, when the previously unrewarded rats were also given food for reaching the goal box, they abruptly performed just as well as the first group (see Figure 6.6). Apparently, they had learned from their earlier explorations, but this learning remained latent (not visible) until a reward for reaching the goal box was introduced (Dickinson, 1989). Humans similarly learn many things without specific rewards, even though they may not immediately demonstrate what they know. For example, you can learn the way to an unfamiliar part of town if someone simply tells you how to get there. You store the route in memory as a kind of cognitive map and use it when the need arises. Reinforcement and repeated practice are not necessary for such learning to occur.

OBSERVATIONAL LEARNING

The research on latent learning suggests that animals acquire a great deal of knowledge largely through observation—looking, listening, touching, and so forth—in the course of normal activities. When it comes to human learning, a large proportion of these observations are of other people. What do we acquire from observing what other people say and do? According to **social learning theory** (also known as social cognitive theory), we acquire a wide variety of strategies, outlooks, and rules about behavior that we imitate, avoid, or modify to our advantage. Once again, we need no particular reinforcement to accumulate this information. We do so naturally in the course of cognitively processing what those around us do. This fashioning of our own behavior by observing the behavior of others is called **observational learning.**

How Rewards and Punishments Relate to Observational Learning Social learning theorists do not say that rewards and punishments are unimportant to human behavior. Their point is that reinforcement is not essential for learning to occur. According to Albert Bandura (1977a), one of the leading proponents of this view, reinforcement is much more important in getting people to perform a learned behavior than it is in teaching that behavior in the first place. For example, a little girl who observes her older brother clearing his dishes from the dinner table adds these actions to her knowledge of possible behaviors even without reinforcement. But if she observes that her brother is warmly praised for his helpfulness— that is, if she sees him rewarded—she will be more inclined to copy him and clear her own dishes too. Reinforcement, then, mainly affects the likelihood of performance. The acquisition of new ideas and strategies through observation does not require rewards.

Bandura also conceptualizes rewards and punishments more broadly than strict behaviorists do (Bandura, 1986). We are influenced, he says, not only by the consequences of our own behavior (the behaviorists' view) but also by the consequences we see other people experiencing, as in the case of the girl who saw her brother praised for clearing away his dishes. Bandura calls such "second-hand" consequences **vicarious reinforcement and punishment,** and he correctly points out that they can have important effects on our behavior. In addition, Bandura stresses the importance of **intrinsic reinforcement and punishment.** By this he means that our actions are regulated not just by the environmental consequences we observe but by our own reactions as well. We measure our own performance against our internalized standards of behavior. If we exceed our own standards, we feel self-esteem, a powerful form of reinforcement; if we fall short, we feel self-reproach, a potent form of punishment.

But remember that, to Bandura, none of these various forms of reward and punishment is essential for learning to occur. For him, learning is a change in acquired information (and hence in performance potential) that can occur just by virtue of being an observer in the world. As you will see in later chapters, Bandura and others have conducted experiments showing that such observational learning can take place without reinforcement. In a typical study, groups of children observe a model who responds to a situation in some unusual way. Then the experimenter puts the children in a similar situation and notes the number of imitative responses they make. Such studies suggest that children may learn and imitate a new behavior with no external inducement at all. Where external inducements are often most important is in *maintaining* a new behavior, especially over the long run (Deguchi et al., 1988).

What Do We Acquire through Observational Learning? According to social learning theorists, we do not take cameralike snapshots of other people's behavior when we observe them. There are simply too many details to take in, too many things that are not really relevant to our interests and objectives. Instead, we form abstract representations that capture the essence of what other people do. Another word for these abstract representations is *schema*, a term we introduced in Chapter 4. The schemas we form from watching and listening to others can then be used to guide our own thoughts, feelings, and actions (Bandura, 1986).

Everyday experience is full of examples of how people form schemas through observation. Consider what some people learn from watching television. Surveys have shown that adults who are heavy TV watchers (over four hours a day) often form very stereotyped schemas of life in our society—ones that match the networks' portrayal of what Americans are like (Gerbner and Gross, 1976). These viewers tend to believe, for example, that the elderly are a very small segment of our population; that a large percentage of people are professionals, such as doctors and lawyers; and that the chances of being the victim of violent crime are exceedingly high. Outside the world of television, not one of these statements is true. But schemas formed by repeated observation of TV programs seem to help make them appear true to many people.

Social-learning theorists point out that once such distorted schemas are formed, they tend to persist unless contrary observations disconfirm them. And because people often see what they *expect* to see, this disconfirmation process may never occur. The woman who fears she will be the victim of violent crime, for example, may look for signs of bad intentions in all the strangers who approach her. As a result, she tends to see strangers as far more threatening than they actually are. One way to help free this person of her distorted perspective might be through a program of observational learning. Such a program would repeatedly demonstrate to her that walking on the streets seldom results in assault or robbery, and that most strangers are not dangerous, but quite law-abiding.

Psychologists have in fact developed forms of psychotherapy based on observational learning. Their treatment of phobias, for instance, rests on the belief that if phobic people can observe someone else performing the activity that they so greatly dread, they are likely to develop confidence that they, too, can perform it safely (Bandura, 1977b). The most effective of these therapies appear to be those in which people are gradually encouraged to perform the feared activity themselves after first watching others do so. Apparently, disconfirmation of a false belief is more powerful when we actually demonstrate it to ourselves.

Observational learning is clearly very widespread, as are other forms of cognitive learning (Flaherty, 1985). Cognition is an almost constant part of human experience, and learning theories that do not consider the role of mental activity and knowledge seem to ignore a crucial facet of human life. Cognitive theories of learning contribute to many areas of psychology, including personality and social development, psychological disorders, and psychotherapy. They provide the foundation for our next chapter, on human memory.

SUMMARY

1. **Learning** is a relatively permanent change in performance potential that arises from experience. **Associative learning** involves learning how various events are related to each other. One kind of associative learning is **classical conditioning,** in which a previously neutral stimulus comes to elicit an involuntary action or feeling because it signals the onset of another stimulus which naturally elicits that response. Another kind of associative learning is **operant conditioning,** in which we learn to perform or withhold a voluntary behavior because of its consequences. Some psychologists emphasize **cognitive learning,** which entails forming expectations and mental schemas of objects and events.

2. Pavlov discovered classical conditioning while studying the physiology of digestion. He found that the **unconditioned stimulus (UCS)** of food in a dog's mouth elicited the **unconditioned response (UCR)** of salivation. When a neutral stimulus—the sound of a bell, for example—repeatedly preceded the UCS (the food), the dog eventually salivated in response to the bell alone. The bell had therefore become a **conditioned stimulus (CS),** and the learned reaction to it was a **conditioned response (CR).** To maintain a **classically conditioned response,** the conditioned and unconditioned stimuli must continue to be paired at least occasionally; otherwise the conditioned response will weaken and eventually undergo **extinction.**

3. Once a classically conditioned response has been established, the individual may begin responding to stimuli similar to the CS, as if they were the CS itself. This process is called **stimulus generalization.** The more similar a stimulus is to the CS that prevailed during learning, the more likely it is for generalization to occur. Organisms also engage in **stimulus discrimination**—learning to make a particular response only to a particular stimulus.

4. Some psychologists have applied classical conditioning principles to the treatment of certain psychological disorders. For instance, the technique of **systematic desensitization,** developed from procedures for extinguishing classically conditioned responses, has been used to treat phobias.

5. According to Thorndike's **law of effect,** responses that result in satisfying consequences tend to be repeated, while those that lead to unsatisfying consequences tend not to be. A consequence that increases the frequency of a behavior is called **reinforcement** or reward. A consequence that decreases the frequency of a behavior is called **punishment.** In **positive reinforcement,** the frequency of a response increases because that response causes the *arrival* of a subjectively satisfying stimulus. In **negative reinforcement,** the frequency of a response increases because that response causes the *removal* of some subjectively unpleasant stimulus. **Superstitious behavior** can occur when a response is strengthened or weakened because it happens by chance to precede reinforcement or punishment.

6. Researchers have studied operant conditioning by manipulating rewards and punishments in such devices as the **Skinner box. Shaping**—a technique in which a subject is reinforced for displaying closer and closer approximations of a desired response—has

been used to establish new behaviors in both humans and other animals.

7. The **schedule of reinforcement** greatly affects a conditioned operant response. A **continuous reinforcement schedule**—reinforcement each time the response occurs—is very effective for establishing a new behavior. A **partial reinforcement schedule**—withholding the reward some of the time—is very effective for maintaining a behavior. Schedules of partial reinforcement include a **fixed-ratio schedule,** in which a reward is given for a fixed number of responses, and a **fixed-interval schedule,** in which a reward is given for the first response after a fixed time interval has elapsed. Two schedules that result in high rates of response that are quite resistant to extinction are the **variable-ratio schedule** and the **variable-interval schedule,** both of which derive their power from their unpredictability.

8. Besides controlling the strength and frequency of an operant response, reinforcement also brings behavior under the control of stimuli prevailing at the time of reinforcement. The individual tends to make the conditioned response when these particular stimuli are present. This is called **stimulus control.**

9. The effects of **primary reinforcers** (those satisfying biological needs) can generalize to **secondary (or conditioned) reinforcers** (those signaling that primary reinforcement is on its way). Learning a sequence of operant behaviors, each one maintained by its own secondary reinforcer and eventually leading to a primary reward, is called **chaining.**

10. A **conditioned operant response** gradually disappears when it is no longer reinforced. But sometimes a response (whether operantly or classically conditioned) will reappear after it seems to have been extinguished, a phenomenon called **spontaneous recovery.** The organism seems to be retesting old relationships.

11. Operant conditioning principles have been applied in both **programmed instruction** and **behavior modification.** In the behavior-modification approach called the **token economy,** tokens earned can be exchanged for more basic reinforcers, such as a desirable food or a special privilege. Today, such deliberate use of rewards or punishments to change human behavior is often called **contingency management.**

12. When a conditioned response is in conflict with an animal's genetically based tendencies, it may tend to weaken despite reinforcement. This process, called **instinctive drift,** shows that biological constraints influence learning. A good example of biological constraints can be seen in the study of learned taste aversions. Apparently, natural selection has favored a nervous system that allows easy learning of relationships between unusual tastes and subsequent illness, but not between unusual sights or sounds and illness.

13. Psychologists who support the **cognitive view** of associative learning believe that important thought processes intervene between the stimulus and the response in most instances of associative learning. In particular, both humans and other animals tend to develop expectations that one event will be followed by another. Cognitive psychologists also maintain that much human learning does not depend on the meting out of overt rewards or punishments. Two examples of learning without reinforcement are **latent learning** (learning that occurs but is not demonstrated until there is an incentive) and **observational learning** (learning that results simply from observation of other people's behavior).

SUGGESTED READINGS

Gordon, W. C. (1989). *Learning and memory.* Pacific Grove, CA: Brooks/Cole. A solid, readable text that covers the field of learning and ties it to memory.

Hill, W. F. (1985). *Learning: A survey of psychological interpretations* (4th ed.). New York: Harper & Row. A paperback text that discusses the work of many leading learning theorists.

Klein, S. (1991). *Learning: Principles and Applications* (2nd ed.). New York: McGraw-Hill. A clear, up-to-date discussion of basic learning and memory processes. Plentiful examples relate the material to students' experiences.

Skinner, B. F. (1971). *Beyond freedom and dignity.* New York: Knopf. A highly readable account of Skinner's work and beliefs.

Staddon, J. E. R., and Ettinger, R. H. (1989). *Learning: An introduction to the principles of adaptive behavior.* San Diego: Harcourt Brace Jovanovich. A basic text that concentrates on the study of learning in animals. It describes a variety of basic learning phenomena along with their theoretical underpinnings.

CHAPTER 7

MEMORY AND FORGETTING

When psychologist Peter Polson first spotted waiter John Conrad in a Boulder, Colorado, restaurant, he was understandably impressed. Conrad had the uncanny ability to remember elaborate dinner orders without writing anything down. He once served a table of nineteen people without making a single mistake. Not only were all the meats, the vegetables, the salads, and the dressings just as each customer had ordered, but Conrad remembered without hesitation precisely who had ordered what. And this feat of gastronomic recall did not even begin to tap the limits of Conrad's memory capability. He maintained that he could remember orders for up to thirty dinners at a time before his powers of recall began to break down (Singular, 1982).

For those of us who have trouble remembering where we left the car keys, John Conrad's feats of memory seem awesome indeed. It may therefore surprise you to learn that his impressive accomplishments are well within the bounds of ordinary human memory. Even though we seldom devote the energy to memorization that John Conrad has done, we are all endowed with a substantial capacity for remembering information. Who were your closest friends in high school? When was the American Revolution? In which state is Chicago? What is the melody of "The Star-Spangled Banner"? How does a Christmas tree smell? You immediately know the answers to these and hundreds of thousands of other questions. In its breadth and flexibility, the capacity of human memory far exceeds that of the most advanced computer.

Memory is very closely related to learning. Whereas learning is the process of acquiring new information or skills, memory is the retention of what you have learned as well as its retrieval for future reference or use (Squire, 1987). Learning and memory, therefore, work together. You cannot really learn if you are unable to remember, and unless you acquire new data (that is, learn it), you have nothing for memory to store.

Psychologists usually divide memory into three types: sensory, short-term, and long-term. **Sensory memory** is the momentary lingering of sensory information after a stimulus has been removed. If you touch the palm of your hand with the point of a pencil, for example, you continue to feel the sensation for several seconds after the point is withdrawn. That momentary storage of tactile information is just one example of sensory memory. Actually, we seem to have separate sensory storage systems for each of our different senses. We can store a great deal of information in these sensory registers, but only for an instant or so.

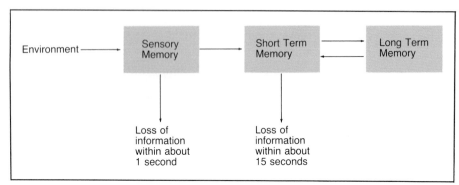

FIGURE 7.1   A diagram of the human memory system, showing the relative durability of information from the environment in sensory memory, short-term memory, and long-term memory.

Short-term memory is far more durable than sensory memory is. **Short-term memory** contains the contents of your conscious awareness: what you are actively thinking about at any particular time. If you are trying to retain a phone number you have just looked up, if a tune keeps playing itself in your mind, if you recall the image of someone you know, you are processing this information through short-term memory. Short-term memory, moreover, is not just a passive storehouse of data, as older conceptions of it sometimes implied. Rather, it is a dynamic arena for processing information—for thinking, reasoning, and solving problems (Waldrop, 1987). That is why today many cognitive psychologists prefer to call it **active memory** or **working memory**. As we will discuss later, this short-term, working memory system holds only a limited amount of information at any one time, and its contents fade in about twenty seconds if they are not actively renewed.

Long-term memory, in contrast, can store things indefinitely without active effort. It can be thought of as a library of information, and its capacity is believed to be limitless. Figure 7.1 shows how many psychologists view the relationships among sensory, short-term, and long-term memory.

In this chapter we will answer many questions about these three memory systems. Why is it usually so difficult to remember a long string of numbers but so easy to remember a sentence with the same number of words? Why do some people seem to have remarkable powers of recall while others appear to be constantly forgetting? If you are often dissatisfied with your own memory performance, how can you improve it? In this chapter we will also explore the biological side of memory. How do the neurons of the brain store information? Findings in this area are

providing an exciting new dimension to our understanding of how memory works. Finally, we will examine one of the frustrating experiences of daily life, the experience of forgetting. How much do we really forget over a lifetime? Is it possible that everything we have ever learned is still stored somewhere in memory and that we simply lack the right keys with which to retrieve it? These are some of the many issues we will raise in this chapter. We begin with the entry of new information into memory via sensory storage.

SENSORY MEMORY

Glance for just an instant at the pattern of letters and numbers in Figure 7.2. Then close your eyes and try to list out loud as many as you can. You will probably find that your powers of recall are rather disappointing. In fact, the results of many carefully controlled experiments show that most people can remember only about four or five out of twelve unrelated items that are flashed to them very briefly. Yet such findings seem to contradict much of everyday experience. When we glance quickly at something and then look away, we are usually left with the impression of a complete and accurate image, however fleeting that image may be. If visual sensory memory is indeed as rich as everyday experience suggests, why does it seem so poor in laboratory tests?

This puzzle intrigued a young psychology graduate student named George Sperling. Perhaps, Sperling reasoned, previous researchers had been testing visual sensory memory in the wrong way. So he set about to devise a new test (Sperling, 1960). He flashed a twelve-item pattern like the one in Figure

7.2, but he did not ask people to specify *all* the letters and numbers they had seen. Instead, upon removing the pattern, he immediately sounded a high, medium, or low tone to indicate which line the subjects should report. Under these conditions, people could often report correctly all of the four items in *any* of the three rows. Sperling's research demonstrated that the ability to process information through the senses is indeed better than verbal reports suggest. The instant after we scan a multi-item pattern, we usually retain a fairly complete image of it. This visual memory is fleeting, however; it lasts for only about a second. So during the time it takes to report four or five items, the remaining images fade from visual sensory storage.

Why do we need these sensory storage bins if the memories they hold are so fleeting? Apparently, our sensory registers enable us to start the process of identifying stimuli, of giving meaning to them (Ellis and Hunt, 1989). Imagine trying to understand a sentence that someone is saying without auditory sensory storage. While you were placing the first few words in working memory and retrieving their meaning from long-term storage, you would have no way of temporarily "holding" the other words that followed. Auditory sensory memory gives you this ability, just as visual sensory memory gives you the ability to read smoothly and quickly. While you are recalling the meaning of the first words in this sentence, the next words are being scanned and entered into your visual sensory storage until you can process them further.

Some psychologists think that people who have great difficulty reading (despite normal intelligence) may be suffering from a deficit in the ability to retain or use information held in visual sensory storage. In one test of this theory, sixth graders were briefly shown circles made up of eight figures, some of which were letters, others shapes (Morrison et al., 1977). When each circle of figures disappeared from the screen, it was replaced by a marker at the point where one of the figures had previously been. The children were then given a card of figures and asked to pick out the one that had been where the marker now was. As long as the marker appeared one- or two-tenths of a second after the figures had vanished, poor readers performed just as well at this task as good readers did. But with longer time intervals, the poor readers suffered. It was as if they had lost the information that had been in visual sensory storage more quickly.

FIGURE 7.2 A typical test for visual sensory memory. When exposed to this array of unrelated items for a brief period, people typically recall no more than four or five of them. But if subjects are signaled immediately after the exposure to recall just one of the lines, they can almost always remember all four items correctly. This evidence suggests that people "read" the information from some sort of complete sensory image of the stimulus, which fades in the time it takes to say the names of a few of the letters and numbers in the image.

Just as some children can have deficits in their visual sensory storage system, other children can have a system that is remarkably good. A few even have the ability to retain vivid visual images of complex objects for up to several minutes after those objects have been removed (Haber, 1969, 1979). These youngsters do not have the sense that these so-called **eidetic images** are just imagined in their minds. Instead, the images seem to linger before their eyes, almost as if the objects that produced them were still there. An eidetic image is usually so clear that the child can "read" detailed information off it. Interestingly, the ability to form eidetic images usually disappears by adolescence, for reasons psychologists do not yet understand. To test your own capacity for eidetic imagery, hold any highly detailed picture against a neutral-colored surface and look at it for half a minute; then take the picture away. Do you still see it? Probably not. Adults with the ability to form eidetic images are extremely rare.

Hold this photograph or any other detailed picture against a neutral background and examine it for thirty seconds, then look away. If you can still see the picture, you're one of the few adults who has the capacity to form eidetic images.

SHORT-TERM OR WORKING MEMORY

Of course, not all the information that enters sensory storage is worth giving our active attention to. In other words, it is not worth placing in short-term or working memory. If we tried to attend to all the many sights, sounds, odors, tastes, and tactile sensations that bombard us from all sides, we would surely be overwhelmed. Some kind of selectivity is essential. One process that is crucial to getting the more interesting and important information placed in short-term memory is called selective attention.

PLACING INFORMATION IN SHORT-TERM MEMORY

SELECTIVE ATTENTION

When you are having a conversation at a crowded party, your ears receive a great deal of extraneous information. You hear not only the person you are speaking with, but also the din of other voices, the clink of glasses, and perhaps the sound of music too. Yet despite this potentially confusing mix of sounds, you manage to follow your companion's conversation. You do this by screening out some of the information entering a particular sensory channel (in this case your ears) and focusing on only a portion of it. This process of restricting your focus is called **selective attention.**

When attending selectively to someone's voice, however, you do not completely ignore all the other sounds around you. Instead, you give peripheral sounds an elementary form of attention. For example, at a crowded party you may suddenly hear your name mentioned in one of the conversations you thought you were ignoring. Clearly, you must have been processing that conversation to some extent.

Psychologists have studied this "cocktail party phenomenon" extensively. Cherry (1953) used a **dichotic listening** technique in which people wearing earphones simultaneously heard one message played into the left ear and a different message played into the right ear. Cherry asked his subjects to "shadow" one of the messages—that is, to repeat it aloud as they heard it. (The subject's voice, like a shadow, trails along immediately behind the recorded message.) Later he tested to see if the subjects could recognize or recall material from the unshadowed message, the one that had entered the other ear. In general, the meaning of the unshadowed message eluded the subjects, except for an occasional word that had special significance for them (a familiar name, for instance). But the subjects *could* detect the physical characteristics of the unshadowed message, such as its pitch or volume. The same results have occurred in many subsequent studies. They suggest that when different stimuli enter the same sensory channel, we discriminate among them more on the basis of their physical characteristics than their meanings (Broadbent, 1958). Thus, it is mainly differences in the physical characteristics of voices—their pitch,

Whenever there's a lot of going on, we must pay selective attention if we want to remember one out of the many stimuli that are bombarding us.

volume, rhythm, and so forth—that allow us to attend to a single speaker at a crowded party.

This is not to say that meaning plays no part in selective attention. Of course it does. When people are instructed to follow only what is played into one of their two ears, they often involuntarily begin listening with the *other* ear if the words that continue the message's meaning start entering on that side (Treisman, 1960). Selective attention, then, is probably based on both physical traits *and* meaning. At first we may attend to the physical characteristics of a message (where it comes from, what the voice qualities are), but we may then switch our attention to the message's content when we have gathered enough information to make sense of what is being said (Treisman, 1964).

ENCODING

Look back at Figure 6.1 in Chapter 6 and try to remember it. As you do, note the thoughts going through your mind. If you are like most people, you do not simply try to take a mental snapshot of this drawing. You also retrieve from long-term memory the words you associate with what you see—dog,

harness, food, tubes, perhaps even Pavlov and classical conditioning. These verbal associations are part of what you store as you attempt to memorize the drawing. Now try another memory task. Read and place into memory the following list of words: *tree, flower, squirrel, staircase, house*. You may find that in addition to saying the words to yourself, you also try to picture them based on visual memories you have stored. Notice, in both cases, that when you place information into memory, you often elaborate or transform it in some way. This elaboration process is part of what is called encoding. More specifically, **encoding** is the act of converting sensory stimuli into a form that can be placed into memory, often using old information to analyze or manipulate the data. The methods you use to carry out this process, such as naming objects or mentally picturing words, are called **encoding strategies**.

The instances of encoding we have just discussed are examples of effortful encoding. **Effortful encoding** involves a deliberate attempt to put something into memory. You deliberately *tried* to encode the details of Pavlov's experimental equipment shown in Figure 6.1; you actively *worked* to place into short-term memory the list of five nouns. When most

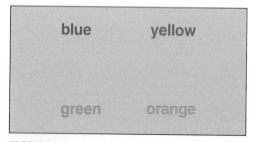

FIGURE 7.3   Look at the words in the figure and then, from memory, try to name the colors used to print the words.

people think of putting information into memory, this is the kind of encoding that often comes to mind. But there is a second kind of encoding that is also very common, a kind that seems to happen with no deliberate effort and so is called **automatic encoding.**

To demonstrate how much you acquire through automatic encoding, answer the following questions:

1. What route did you take to get to school when you were in the sixth grade?
2. Where did you sit the last time you were in a large lecture hall?
3. What time of day was it when you last stopped by your college book store?
4. How many movies have you seen in the last three months (not including those on TV)?
5. Are there more words in the English language ending with *e* or more words ending with *p*?
6. Which is a more common last name in this country: Williams or Skahill?

You probably had no trouble answering any of these questions, although you don't remember ever deliberately trying to retain the information. It is as if your memory just soaks up this kind of data with no conscious effort. Researchers have found that information about your location in time and space (questions 1–3) and how often you experience different kinds of stimuli (questions 4–6) are among the things you typically encode automatically (Hasher and Zacks, 1984).

Why did our brains evolve the capacity to encode certain things automatically? Probably because the ability to learn certain things very swiftly helped our early ancestors to survive. For instance, if you had to laboriously keep track of where you are in space, finding your way in a new setting would be very difficult. The fact that your brain automatically en-

codes how an environment is laid out is enormously helpful in allowing you to get around in the world. Automatic encoding of your location in time has equally clear-cut value. But why we automatically encode information about the frequency with which things happen is not so obvious. One possibility is that frequency information allows us to estimate the likelihood that a particular thing will happen (Hasher and Zacks, 1984). This, in turn, enables us to categorize harmful things as either rare (and therefore of little concern) or common (and therefore to be watched for and avoided).

Through practice you can learn to encode other kinds of data automatically. For example, when you were a child, you had to work hard to encode written words into short-term storage, but now, as an adult with many years of practice at reading, this task is effortless. Psychologists have demonstrated just how effortless it is by presenting adults with color names written in inks inconsistent with those colors (Stroop, 1935). The word *red*, for instance, might be written in blue, the word *orange* might be written in green. The subjects are asked to identify the ink colors. Significantly, responding takes longer than when subjects are given simple squares of color to name. It seems that they automatically encode the written words too, in addition to the visual colors, so that they hesitate a moment as their minds register the visual/verbal inconsistency. Try this experiment yourself by naming the colors used to print the words in Figure 7.3. You will find it is almost impossible to ignore what the words say. You have developed this automatic processing of written language over many years of practice. (Ellis and Hunt, 1989).

SHORT-TERM, ACTIVE STORAGE

Once information has been attended to and encoded, it must be kept active in short-term memory in order to be retained. After looking up a telephone number, for example, you probably repeat it several times, either aloud or mentally, while reaching for the phone. Then you dial quickly, knowing that you will not remember the number for long if you stop saying it. If you get distracted for a few seconds and interrupt this repetition, you will probably have to look up the number again. This example illustrates a basic fact about short-term memory: information entering it is lost rather quickly unless it is renewed through **rehearsal.**

Rehearsal usually involves some kind of speech —either overt, as when you repeat a telephone number aloud, or implicit, as when you repeat a number mentally. Rehearsal seems to maintain information in short-term memory this way: a person says the information aloud or silently, hears what is being said, and then re-stores it. Rehearsal, in other words, often maintains things *phonetically:* it is the *sounds of the words* that are repeated and stored (Baddeley, 1982).

Exactly how long can new information stay in short-term memory without rehearsal? Studies suggest no more than half a minute. For example, when people are briefly shown a short series of consonants —say, *CPQ*—and then asked to count backward by threes from, say, 270 (267, 264, 261 . . .), they are very likely to forget the letters within about twenty seconds (Brown, 1958; Peterson and Peterson, 1959). The backward counting is an interfering task, a device psychologists use to prevent rehearsal. If the interfering task is ineffective and subjects manage to rehearse *CPQ* secretly while appearing to take a deep breath between counts, their memory of the letters will probably last longer. The exact duration depends on the amount of rehearsal they are able to squeeze in.

Other factors also affect the duration of short-term memory. For one thing, its duration depends on the degree to which new material happens to be associated with information held in *long*-term storage. Thus, if *CPQ* happens to be a person's initials, that person is likely to recall them no matter how distracting an interfering task may be. In addition, the duration of short-term memory is affected by whether or not a person is motivated to remember. If someone who has viewed three consonants is then distracted by a backward-counting task when not expecting ever to have to recall the letters again, those letters fade from short-term storage with astonishing speed —often within a mere two seconds (Muter, 1980). This finding suggests that the ability to retain new information in short-term memory depends on how a person processes it in the first place. Information deemed insignificant is likely to disappear quickly, whereas information you want to remember has a better chance of being recalled despite a few seconds of distraction.

Just as important as short-term memory's duration is its capacity. How much information does short-term memory hold? In 1956 George Miller published a paper titled "The Magical Number

To retain anything in short-term memory, we must rehearse it verbally so that our brain can "hear" the words.

Seven, Plus or Minus Two." In it he summarized the results of many experiments, all of which indicated that the majority of people can hold only between five and nine items in short-term memory at any one time. Most psychologists agree that the capacity of short-term memory is very near this range.

At first researchers were puzzled by the human ability to process large amounts of information despite the limited capacity of short-term memory. How, they wondered, can we read and comprehend even a very brief sentence if we are unable to handle more than seven letters at once? George Miller again provided an answer: we expand our limited capacity by **chunking** information. We see groups of letters as words (small chunks), groups of words as phrases (larger chunks), and series of phrases as sentences (even larger chunks). Short-term memory can hold only about seven chunks, but each chunk may contain a great deal of information. In this way, we greatly increase the amount we can process at any one time.

The process of chunking uses material already stored in long-term memory to categorize new information entering short-term storage. The number 1492 is easier to recall than the number 2769, for example, if you think of 1492 as the year that Columbus sailed to America. Here you are using your knowledge of history to reduce your memory load to a single date instead of four separate digits. Conceivably, you could hold in short-term memory a string of twenty-eight numbers if they could be chunked into seven familiar dates.

Researchers have shown that almost anyone can become a short-term memory whiz by means of appropriate chunking (Waldrop, 1987). In one study (Ericsson et al., 1980), psychologists worked with a college student named Steve Faloon, average in both intelligence and short-term memory capacity (he could remember a string of approximately seven random digits). After twenty months of practice recalling random digits, Faloon could remember a staggering eighty digits presented at the rate of one every second! The key to his phenomenal improvement lay in a clever chunking technique he devised. Faloon was an accomplished long-distance runner, and he hit upon the scheme of categorizing digits whenever possible according to running times. Thus he would encode into short-term memory the sequence 3492 as "3 minutes, 49.2 seconds, near the world record mile time." Faloon would then take clusters of three or four digits encoded by running times and think of them as one larger chunk containing several related pieces of information. Several other strategies supplemented this one to give him his impressive recall ability. But note that Faloon's short-term memory *capacity* never really increased. When the researchers suddenly switched from presenting random digits to presenting random letters, his memory span plummeted from eighty back to seven. What Faloon had improved was his skill at using his limited short-term memory capacity through learned techniques of chunking.

Chunks need not be verbal. The following task requires visual chunking. First study the chessboard in Figure 7.4A for five seconds, then turn the page and see how many of the pieces you can draw correctly on the empty board (Figure 7.4B). If you are unfamiliar with the game of chess, your limit will probably be close to the magical number seven. In fact, you may recall far fewer than seven pieces, because storing each one requires several bits of information: what the piece looks like, its row, and its

American tourists who learned a foreign language many years before are often surprised at how much of it they remember when they travel abroad.

column. Yet master chess players can reproduce the entire arrangement after just a five-second look. Does this mean that chess masters have exceptional memories? Research suggests that they do not (De Groot, 1965; Simon and Gilmartin, 1973). When pieces are arranged on a chessboard in a random pattern, the chess master's memory is no better than anyone else's. But when pieces are arranged in a pattern that might possibly occur in a game between good players, the master can easily encode the pattern as a number of large chunks, making the entire arrangement fit well within the capacity of ordinary short-term memory. How many such visual chunks can chess masters identify? Somewhere between 25,000 and 100,000. Although this seems amazing, it is not so remarkable when you consider that an educated speaker of English has a vocabulary of about the same size.

Mathematical equations are among the rule-based kinds of information that we store as semantic memories.

FIGURE 7.4A Visual chunking. Study this arrangement of chess pieces for five seconds. Then turn to the empty chessboard on the next page and try to reproduce the arrangement. The amount you are able to recall correctly represents approximately seven of the chunks you have developed for processing information about chess games.

LONG-TERM MEMORY

A few pages back we discussed the process of looking up a phone number and holding it in short-term memory. The number remains available only as long as you repeat it. If you are distracted for even a few seconds, it is likely to evaporate. Obviously there is more to memory than this short-term "holding pattern," or else you would have to spend your days continually repeating your own name just to remember who you are!

Learning and intelligence are made possible through what is called long-term memory. Because of long-term memory, your experiences are not lost the moment you cease to think about them. Instead, you can retain the past and use your memories of it in the present. As the repository of all your accumulated knowledge, long-term memory must contain an extraordinary amount of information, some of which you are hardly aware of until you have reason to recall it. For instance, people who learned Spanish in school, especially those who studied it for a number of semesters, retain large portions of this information even after fifty years, during which time they rarely use the language (Bahrick, 1984). And this is an example of only one small part of the contents of long-term memory. If you consider the many thousands of other facts, ideas, and perceptions you store away over a lifetime, the capacity of long-term memory seems almost beyond comprehension.

Long-term memory contains several different kinds of information. Some of what you retain in long-term storage are learned associations between stimuli and responses. You hear the phone ring and immediately reach to pick up the receiver; you see a stop sign and quickly put your foot on the brake. These learned associations are called **procedural memories.** They allow you to respond to things around you in adaptive ways. In addition, you have a wealth of **semantic memories**—mental representations of objects, states, and qualities in your world, as well as ideas about how these things are related to each other (Chang, 1986). When you retrieve conceptual knowledge, such as a rule of English grammar or a chemical formula, you are drawing on your broad semantic knowledge. Finally, you possess a great number of **episodic memories.** These are recollections of personal experiences, dating back to early childhood. We seem to be able to "replay" them, somewhat like clips from a movie: going on a grade school trip, spending a day with a special friend, first setting foot inside a college classroom.

FIGURE 7.4B   Turn to Figure 7.4A, on the preceding page, if you have not already looked at it, and study it for five seconds. Then try to produce the arrangment shown there on this empty chessboard. See the text for an explanation of the results.

Some psychologists argue that the brain stores these different kinds of memories—procedural, semantic, and episodic—in three separate long-term memory systems (Tulving, 1985). But others think that there is not enough evidence to draw this conclusion, especially to propose separate systems for semantic and episodic memories (McKoon et al., 1986). We will return to the question of different kinds of memory systems when we explore the physiology of learning and remembering. But first we turn to the general processes of long-term storage and retrieval.

LONG-TERM STORAGE

The way information enters long-term memory is not completely understood. The process depends partly on the amount of time we rehearse things: the longer the rehearsal, the more likely is long-term storage. But even more important is the *type* of rehearsal. If we simply repeat something to ourselves without giving it thought (as when we rehearse a telephone number), that information seldom becomes part of our long-term knowledge. In contrast, if we take a new piece of information and mentally do something with it—form an image of it, apply it to a problem, relate it to other things—it is more likely to be deposited in long-term storage.

These different approaches can be described as **shallow processing** or mere **maintenance rehearsal** versus **deep processing** or **elaborative rehearsal** (Craik and Lockhart, 1972). Emphasizing the mean-

ing of a stimulus is especially conducive to deep processing. In one study, people were presented with words and asked questions about them (Parkin, 1984). Sometimes the question had to do with the word's meaning (Is it a synonym for *large*? Is it a type of vehicle?). At other times, the question concerned the word's appearance (How many vowels does it have? Is it printed in all capital letters?). Afterward the subjects were unexpectedly asked to remember as many of the words as they could. Words that had been processed for meaning were recalled significantly more often.

The value of stressing meaning when trying to store something in memory is clear in the case of Steve Faloon, the random-digit recall wizard. After an hour-long practice session, Faloon could recall over 80 percent of all the number sequences he had seen that day. He could even recognize many of the sequences he had seen a week earlier (Ericsson et al., 1980). Clearly, the way in which he chunked the digits and related them to meaningful things facilitated their transfer from short-term to long-term storage. The opposite kind of processing—processing that is shallow, inattentive, and concerned only with superficial features—is undoubtedly the cause of many common memory lapses. Why, for instance, do you sometimes forget a person's name just minutes after you have been introduced? Probably because you are so concerned about making appropriate small talk that you fail to think actively about the name you have just heard (Baddeley, 1990).

But though shallow processing is less effective in getting information into long-term storage, you should not conclude that what we process in this way is always completely forgotten. In one study, for instance, subjects were asked to remember various four-digit numbers while repeating "distractor" words out loud (Glenberg et al., 1977). They did not anticipate ever having to remember these distractor words again, so they repeated them in an almost mindless, rote fashion. But later, at the end of the experiment, they were asked to identify the distractors. When this surprise memory test consisted of simply naming as many of the words as they could, the subjects performed poorly, just as you would expect. However, when given a long list of words that included the distractors, they were reasonably successful at picking out the distractors. This result suggests that what we process shallowly is not always lost completely. But we may need special help to

Both kinds of retrieval from long-term memory—recognition of people and objects, and recall of particular things and events—are required of courtroom witnesses.

retrieve it, probably because we seldom bother to link it to other things in long-term storage, a process that creates valuable retrieval cues. In the following section we will discuss more fully just how important such retrieval cues are.

RETRIEVAL FROM LONG-TERM MEMORY

Most people can read at a steady rate of 300 to 600 words per minute, or five to ten words per second. This skill requires an amazingly efficient system for retrieving the meanings of words. But because we are so accustomed to our remarkable powers of information retrieval, we seldom stop to think how truly impressive they are.

Psychologists have studied two basic kinds of retrieval from long-term storage: recognition and recall (Brown, 1976). **Recognition** involves deciding whether you have ever encountered a particular stimulus before. Identifying a suspect in a police line-up is an example of recognition. **Recall,** in contrast, entails retrieving specific pieces of information, usually guided by retrieval cues. To ask a witness to a robbery "What did the thief look like? Do you remember what he was wearing?" is to demand that the person recall. The witness must search through memory and come up with a description.

Recognition, unlike recall, is little more than a matching process. When asked if we recognize something, we consider its features and decide if they match those of a stimulus that is already stored in memory. In doing so, we tend to evaluate not the object as a whole, but rather its various parts (Adams, 1980). If all the parts match, the object is quickly recognized. If, however, some of the parts match while others do not, we are left with a feeling of only vague familiarity. Such partial matches can easily occur when we meet a person again after many years. Some of the old acquaintance's features immediately match our memory (the eyes and smile, for example), but others do not (body weight some fifteen pounds heavier and hair decidedly thinner). The result is the uncomfortable feeling, "Do I know you?" This process of partial recognition may also account for the phenomenon called *déjà vu*, the sense that something is familiar even though you have never encountered it before. In this case you may be partially matching a novel experience with a similar but unidentifiable past event.

Recall involves more mental operations than recognition does. When we try to recall something, we must first search through long-term memory to find the appropriate information. Then we must determine, as in recognition, whether the information we come up with matches the correct response. If we think it does, we give the answer; if we think it does not, we search again.

Retrieval cues are especially important to the success of the search component of recall. In one experiment (Tulving and Pearlstone, 1966), subjects read lists of words that included both category names (animals, fruits, furniture, for example) and the name of one or more members of each category (dog, plum, chair). The subjects were asked to remember only the names of specific items, not the categories. When the time came to recall the words, half the subjects were given the category names as retrieval cues. These subjects remembered about 50 percent more words than those who were not given the categories to help them recall. Without adequate retrieval cues, then, things that are stored in memory may be difficult to find.

The importance of retrieval cues to successful recall should come as no surprise. We have all had the frustrating experience of being unable to recall something that we know is stored in memory. Sometimes this experience produces what is called the **tip-of-the-tongue phenomenon.** We feel that an answer is poised to emerge, but somehow we just cannot get it out. How do we pry these uncooperative facts loose from memory? Usually we use a variety of retrieval cues based on bits of information about the target word that we are able to recall. Suppose you were asked to remember the word for "a small Chinese boat propelled by a single oar over the stern and with the deck usually covered by a roof." You might grope your way through a string of similar-sounding words —"Cheyenne . . . Siam . . . Saipan"—until you eventually arrived at the correct response, "sampan" (Brown and McNeill, 1966). Similarly, when shown a picture of Dustin Hoffman and asked to remember his name, you might first recall his profession and the name of one of his films: "Movie actor . . . starred in *Rainman* . . . Dustin Hoffman." When we store information in long-term memory, we also seem to create a number of retrieval pathways to it. These pathways typically involve both sounds (particularly the first letter of a word) and associated facts and meanings (Reason and Mycielska, 1982). Try to recall the names of the people shown in the photographs below and see what retrieval pathways you use.

Of course, retrieval pathways based on the sound of a word can be a mixed blessing. Sometimes we become so fixated on a word that sounds like the one we want to recall that retrieval of the real word is blocked (Jones, 1988). You may have had this experience when trying to remember someone's name. If a name that is very close in sound enters your head, you find you have trouble discarding it. The similar-sounding name keeps popping into mind and thwarts your efforts to find the right name. The best solution in this case is to stop the search for a while, until your brain

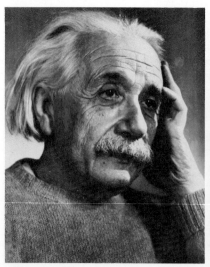

(A)

(B)

(C)

Do you know who these famous people are? As you try to recall their names, see whether you can follow the retrieval pathways that you use.

(A) Albert Einstein, (B) Leo Tolstoy, (C) Marie Curie.

1. **Shopping lists.**

2. **First-letter memory aids.** The first letters of "Richard of York gave battle in vain," for example, give the first letters of the colors of the rainbow.

3. **Diary.**

4. **Rhymes.** "In fourteen hundred ninety-two Columbus sailed the ocean blue," for example, helps you to remember the date 1492.

5. **The place method.** Items to be remembered are imagined in a series of familiar places. When recall is required, one "looks" at the familiar places.

6. **Writing on your hand** (or any other part of your anatomy or clothing).

7. **The story method.** Making up a story that connects items to be remembered in the correct order.

8. **Mentally retracing a sequence of events or actions** in order to jog your memory; useful for remembering where you lost or left something, or at what stage something significant happened.

9. **Alarm clock** (or other alarm device) for waking up only.

10. **Kitchen timer with alarm** for cooking only.

11. **Alarm clock** (or other alarm devices such as watches, radios, timers, telephones, calculators) used for purposes other than waking up or cooking.

12. **The keyword method.** "One is a bun, two is a shoe, three is a tree," etc., as a method of remembering lists of items in correct order (Figure 6.7).

13. **Turning numbers into letters.** For remembering telephone numbers, for example.

14. **Memos.** Writing notes and "To do" lists for yourself, for example.

15. **Face-name associations.** Changing people's names into something meaningful and matching them with something unusual about their faces. Red-bearded Mr. Hiles, for example, might be imagined with hills growing out of his beard.

16. **Alphabetical searching.** Going through the alphabet letter by letter to find the initial letter of a name. For example, does a particular person's name begin with A...B...?Ah, yes, C! C for Clark.

17. **Calendars, wall charts, year planners, display boards, etc.**

18. **Asking other people to remember things for you.**

19. **Leaving objects in special or unusual places** so that they act as reminders.

FIGURE 7.5 How many of these memory aids do you use, and how frequently do you use them? Researcher John Harris (1980) distributed a questionnaire among university students and found that the devices used most frequently by that group were items 3, 8, and 13. (*After Baddeley, 1982.*)

stops activating the stumbling block (Reason and Lucas, 1984).

Since recall always involves a search through memory to find the correct response, is recall necessarily more difficult than recognition? Frequently it is. As a student you have probably noticed this yourself. Most students find that multiple-choice questions (recognition tests) are substantially easier than fill-in-the-blanks (recall tests). The reason is that in multiple-choice tests the answer is right there before you. All you have to do is match it with information learned previously. So as long as you are familiar with the correct answer, and the possibilities offered are not confusingly similar, you will probably make the right choice.

FACTORS AFFECTING LONG-TERM MEMORY PERFORMANCE

Most of us complain about our memories. We are annoyed when others' powers of recall seem much better than our own. What accounts for differences in long-term memory performance? Can anything be done to improve your own ability to remember?

USE OF MNEMONIC DEVICES

Some simple techniques, like those in Figure 7.5, can greatly improve almost anyone's powers of recall (Cook, 1989; Higbee, 1988). These include external aids (such as written lists of reminders) as well as

One is a bun.	Six is sticks.
Two is a shoe.	Seven is heaven.
Three is a tree.	Eight is a gate.
Four is a door.	Nine is a line.
Five is a hive.	Ten is a hen.

FIGURE 7.6 A mnemonic aid. These are *key words* commonly used as learning aids in learning a series of items in order. Say that you want to remember to buy eggs, milk, candy, flowers, and a newspaper, in that order. First learn the rhyming key words that correspond to the numbers; then visually associate each shopping item with the appropriate key word. Thus you might imagine an egg on a bun, drinking from a shoe, pieces of candy hanging from a tree, flowers growing up a door, and a newspaper jammed into a hive.

internal aids (such as name–face associations). Internal aids are also called **mnemonic devices,** from the Greek word *mneme,* which means "memory."

Many mnemonic devices involve clever ways of organizing material when it is stored in long-term memory. The **method of loci,** for example, involves associating items to be remembered with a series of places, or loci, that are already firmly fixed in memory. Suppose you had to learn, in chronological order, the names of all the Presidents of the United States in the twentieth century. You would simply visualize a familiar place—say, your home—and imagine each President in a particular location. Teddy Roosevelt, carrying a big stick, might greet you at the front door. Stout William Howard Taft might be found talking to a thin, bespectacled Woodrow Wilson in the entrance hall. On you would go, through the living room, up the stairs, until you finally came to the attic window, through which you would spot a smiling George Bush sunning himself on the roof.

One of the most famous memory whizzes of all time—a Russian newspaper reporter named Shereshevskii, who was studied for many years by psychologist Aleksandr Luria—often used this system to remember long lists of unrelated words. When each word was presented to him, he would form a concrete image of it and place the image along Gorky Street in Moscow. Then, to recall the list, he took an imaginary walk down Gorky Street, meeting each of his visual images along the way. Luria (1968) claimed that with

this system Shereshevskii could conjure up a string of fifty words presented to him only once—even after an interval of fifteen years! A somewhat similar mnemonic device is called the **peg word system,** by which you associate items to be learned with appropriate key words that are easily visualized (see Figure 7.6).

USE OF VISUAL IMAGERY

Although the method of loci and the peg word system are based primarily on organization, they also rely on imagery. Research shows that people can remember verbal material better if they relate the words to be learned to visual images of some kind (Paivio, 1971). For example, you would probably have an easier time remembering that the French word *escargot* means "snail" if you pictured a snail carrying a cargo of *S*'s on its back. This strategy would leave you with the paired images "*S*-cargo" and "snail." The waiter John Conrad we mentioned earlier used imagery extensively to perform his feats of recall (Singular, 1982). For one thing, he always tried to make visual associations between customers' faces and the entrées they ordered. Thus, a woman who ordered chicken might be remembered for her thin, birdlike nose, while a man who ordered a sirloin steak might be recalled for his beefy jowls.

Think back to the imagery we suggested using to store the meaning of *escargot* and notice that the snail and the "*S*-cargo" are not simply side by side. Instead, the two images are interacting; the snail is *carrying* the *S*-cargo. This kind of interactive imagery has been found to be especially effective for remembering pairs or clusters of words (Bower, 1972). You do not need to make your interactive images bizarre and dramatic in order to have them work as mnemonic devices. The interactive quality matters more than how unusual the imagery is (Kroll et al., 1986).

We are not sure why imagery is such a powerful memory tool. One possibility is that by encoding information in two different ways—verbally and visually—we are twice as likely to remember it (Paivio, 1971). However, even people who have been totally blind since birth show above-average recall of words that normally produce strong visual images (Jonides et al., 1975). This suggests that more may be involved in the encoding of these words than just the processing of a set of speech sounds accompanied by a mental picture.

RECONSTRUCTING CONTEXT AND MOOD

Another powerful memory aid is reconstructing the context in which information was learned. Suppose you were asked to recall the names of your high school classmates. You would probably reconstruct various scenes from your high school days and then try to name all of the classmates you picture there. This approach often enables people to remember the names of a large number of classmates even after many years (Williams, 1976).

Even information that seems impossible to retrieve may suddenly emerge through reconstruction. Suppose you were asked to recall what you were doing at 1:30 in the afternoon on April 27 two years ago. Your initial response to this question might be "Ridiculous!" But try breaking the problem down into smaller subproblems. What day of the week was it? Were you in school at the time? What courses were you taking? At what hour did each class meet? In this way, you could probably reconstruct the broad outline of that particular afternoon. Retrieval, then, becomes a problem-solving task in which the right answer comes from asking the right questions (Lindsay and Norman, 1977).

Psychologists have wondered if reconstructing a particular emotion might likewise serve as a memory aid. If a person is experiencing a strong emotion when certain facts are learned, might not reliving that emotion cue retrieval of the information? This is what apparently happened to Sirhan Sirhan, the man who assassinated Senator Robert Kennedy, brother of President John F. Kennedy. Sirhan was in a highly agitated state when he shot the senator in a crowd of campaign aides and reporters. Afterward he denied committing the crime. Yet when, under hypnosis, he was placed back into the agitated state in which he had pulled the trigger, the events of the moment came flooding back in vivid detail (Bower, 1981; Diamond, 1969; Kaiser, 1970). Sirhan's was an extreme case of **mood-dependent memory,** that is, a memory that is easier to retrieve when in the emotional state in which it was originally stored.

Less extreme examples of mood-dependent memory have been seen in the laboratory. In one study, subjects learned one list of words when happy and another list when sad (these two emotions were induced through hypnosis). When they were later given recall tests, the subjects remembered each list better if they were reexperiencing the mood in which

A high school reunion is the classic "trip down memory lane," in which the participants recall long-forgotten information by reconstructing the original context.

that list was learned (Bower et al., 1978). This effect is not widespread, however, and sometimes it is hard to replicate (Bower and Mayer, 1985; Wetzler, 1985). Apparently, only under special circumstances does good retrieval *depend* on being in the same emotional state as you were when you first learned something (Blaney, 1986).

But this does not mean that emotions do not often serve as effective memory cues. Quite frequently, people tend to remember information that matches their current mood (Blaney, 1986). If they are depressed, for example, they tend to dwell on negative thoughts and situations, screening out more positive memories; if they are happy, they tend to do the opposite (Gilligan and Bower, 1984; Teasdale and Fogarty, 1979). This retrieval bias is called **mood-congruent recall.**

One explanation of mood-congruent recall is based on a **network model** of memory (Bower, 1981). There are many network models of memory, but most stress that the ideas and concepts stored in memory are linked to one another by means of their various relationships (Chang, 1986). Thus, our memory storehouse resembles a complex network of pathways leading from each piece of information to numerous related pieces. Suppose that you are elated over getting an *A* on an exam. As this happy situation is stored in long-term memory, it becomes linked to other pieces of information that you also associate with happiness. In the process, some of these other memories are reactivated, and they pop into mind one after the other. Soon you are engaging in a chain of effortless mood-congruent recall.

Network models of memory fit within what is called the **connectionist framework** for viewing cognitive processes (McClelland, 1988). By emphasizing the connections between stimuli and responses, between the cognitive system's inputs and outputs, this framework helps us to understand how retrieval cues work. When a cue is activated, it in turn activates other data units to which it is linked, especially those where the links involved are strong. So if you strongly associate a certain high school classmate with the play in which he had the lead, chances are that remembering that play will trigger automatic recall of the person.

LONG-TERM MEMORY DISTORTIONS

Although there is much we can do to improve our powers of long-term recall, human memory is far from completely reliable. People commonly confuse what happened one time with what happened another. When memories are vague, people fill in the gaps with what they *believe* to be true. In short, the process of piecing together the past is often prone to distortion. This tendency to distort is one of the most fascinating aspects of the way humans remember.

SCHEMAS, EXPECTATIONS, AND INFERENCES

An Indian legend tells of two young men who go down to the river to hunt, whereupon the weather becomes foggy and calm. Out of the fog appears a war party of five men in a canoe. The five urge the two to accompany them to a battle. One of the young Indians refuses; the other accepts. During the fighting he is wounded, but he feels no pain. It is then that he realizes that the war party is made up of ghosts. He returns home and tells his people what has happened to him. The next day at sunrise he falls over dead. Psychologist Frederic C. Bartlett (1932) used this Indian legend to study how information becomes

distorted in the process of remembering it. After reading the legend, Bartlett's first subject was instructed to tell the story to another subject, who in turn told it to a third subject, and so on down the line, much as children play the game of telephone. As in that game, the story changed substantially after being retold by many people, but Bartlett noticed that the changes were not haphazard. Several patterns emerged.

First, subjects tended to "flatten" details that did not fit within their existing viewpoints. For example, by the time the tale was told by the tenth subject, all references to ghosts had been dropped. Bartlett argued that this was because mystical references are not easily assimilated into the average Westerner's concepts of life, warfare, and death. For a similar reason, other details tended to be sharpened. In the original story, for instance, the second Indian declined to join the war party because his relatives would not know where he had gone. The tenth subject said that the Indian refused because his elderly mother was dependent on him—an expansion of the story that fits Western concepts of a son's responsibilities. Finally, many subjects added a moral to the story, because this kind of ending is typical of the folktales we are used to.

Bartlett was one of the first psychologists to propose that such distortions reflect how human memory works. He argued that people unconsciously process new information through mental structures built up from the knowledge and beliefs they already have about the world. We talked about such mental structures in Chapters 4 and 6 when we discussed how prior knowledge and expectations affect perception and learning. These mental structures, or schemas, filter new experiences and give meaning to them.

Contemporary psychologists believe that schemas influence memory in a number of ways (Alba and Hasher, 1983; Brewer and Nakamura, 1984). First, we tend to select what is relevant or important on the basis of our schemas. For instance, if you were encouraged to read the description of a house from the perspective of planning a robbery, you would likely remember the exact location of the burglar alarm, but not the color of the tile on the bathroom walls. Your burglary schema would direct your attention to certain pieces of information and cause you to gloss over others (Anderson and Pichert, 1978). Second, schemas help you interpret the meaning of new information. For example, try reading the following passage:

> The procedure is actually quite simple. First you arrange things into different groups. Of course, one pile may be sufficient depending on how much there is to do. If you have to go somewhere else due to lack of facilities, that is the next step; otherwise you are pretty well set. It is important not to overdo things. That is, it is better to do too few things at once than too many. In the short run this may not seem important, but complications can easily arise. A mistake can be expensive as well. At first the whole procedure will seem complicated. Soon, however, it will become just another facet of life. It is difficult to foresee any end to the necessity for this task in the immediate future, but then one never can tell. After the procedure is completed, one arranges the materials into different groups again. Then they can be put into their appropriate places. Eventually they will be used once more, and the whole cycle will then have to be repeated. However, that is part of life. (Bransford and Johnson, 1973, p. 400)

It will probably be hard to make much sense out of this description until you are given the hint to use a clothes-washing schema. Now the meaning is clear, because the schema gives you a framework with which to understand and encode the material.

Schemas also allow you to elaborate on what you learn, fleshing out the details according to your expectations. For example, if you hear that John arrived at an exam at 9 A.M. and left an hour later, your exam schema allows you to infer that he also sat at a desk, was given a test, and tried to answer the questions. This inference process can be very helpful, because it enables you to "know" more than you are actually told. But the problem is that people's inferences are sometimes incorrect. This was illustrated in a classic set of studies using the picture in Figure 7.7 (Allport and Postman, 1947). Among other things, it shows a black man in a subway car apparently talking to a white man who is carrying a razor. The researchers asked one person to look at this picture and

FIGURE 7.7 A test of how stereotypes can influence visual memory. This is the original drawing used in Allport and Postman's experiment (1947).

describe it to a second person who could not see it first-hand. The second person then retold the description from memory to a third person, who retold it to a fourth, and so on until the description had passed through six or seven people. Significantly, in over half the experiments, the razor migrated from the white hand to the black hand at some point in the retelling process. It seems that the then-common schema of blacks as more violent than whites influenced what subjects recalled. Allport and Postman conducted relatively few of these experiments, so we must be cautious in drawing far-reaching conclusions from them (Treadway and McCloskey, 1989). Nevertheless, these studies suggest that human memory does not function like a video camera, accurately recording every image and sound. Instead, memory is a process of active construction in which old knowledge, beliefs, and expectations are constantly shaping what we store and retrieve.

The tendency of people to make inferences on the basis of expectations can be illustrated in many ways. For instance, look very briefly at the top drawing in Figure 7.8A. Then turn away and try to reproduce from memory this sketch of a pair of eyeglasses. If you are like most people, your drawing will look very similar to the one at the top of the left-hand

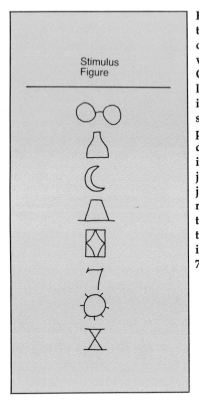

Stimulus
Figure

FIGURE 7.8A   A test of how preconceptions influence visual memory. In Carmichael and colleagues' (1932) experiment, subjects were shown these line patterns, which were described as drawings of various objects. When the subjects were asked to reproduce the patterns they had seen, they made the drawings shown in Figure 7.8B.

column in Figure 7.8B. Although the original sketch consisted of two circles joined together by a short, straight stick, people who are told that this is a representation of eyeglasses tend to connect two circles with a slightly curved and elevated line—much as we think eyeglasses should look. In contrast, people who are told that the same initial sketch is a picture of a dumbbell tend to reproduce the drawing as shown in the right-hand column of Figure 7.11B. Memory for visual material, in other words, is easily distorted by what we are *told* we see (Carmichael et al., 1932).

These findings have serious implications for our legal system. Witnesses to accidents or crimes are almost always questioned before a trial takes place. Could something said during these interrogations alter the witness's later recollections? If so, when are such alterations most likely to occur? Research on the accuracy of eyewitness testimony provides some interesting answers.

Studying Eyewitness Testimony—
How Accurate Is It?

Much of the work in the area of eyewitness testimony has been conducted by Elizabeth Loftus, one of the authors of this book. Loftus has been intrigued by cases in which the memories of eyewitnesses have later proved to be grossly incorrect. In one such case, a Roman Catholic priest stood trial for a series of armed robberies in the Wilmington, Delaware, area (Loftus and Ketcham, 1991). Someone notified police that Father Bernard Pagano looked remarkably like a sketch of the robber being circulated in the local media. Accusing a priest of the crimes made some sense when you realize that this particular robber was dubbed the "gentlemen bandit" because of his impeccable grooming and politeness. *Seven* eyewitnesses identified Father Pagano as the thief. At his trial the prosecution's case seemed airtight. But then, in a turn of events that could have come from a TV melodrama, the trial was abruptly halted when another man confessed to the crimes. He knew details about them that only the true gentleman bandit could have known.

How could this case of widespread mistaken identity have happened? The two men are not lookalikes, as their photos clearly show. Apparently, before presenting pictures of suspects to witnesses, the police let it be known that the robber might be a priest. Since Father Pagano was the only suspect wearing a clerical collar, the witnesses could have been strongly primed to identify him. Loftus has wondered if such expectations acquired after witnessing an event can alter a person's recollection of what actually happened. To find out, she designed a series of experiments.

THE INITIAL STUDIES

In one experiment, Loftus and her colleagues showed subjects thirty color slides of successive stages in an automobile accident involving a red Datsun (Loftus et al., 1978). The critical slide was of the Datsun stopped at an intersection before it eventually turned right and hit a pedestrian. Half the subjects were shown a slide with a stop sign at the corner; half were shown a slide with a yield

FIGURE 7.8B Giving specific names to the patterns shown in Figure 7-8A (see the word lists) influenced the subjects perceptions of the objects, as shown in the drawings they reproduced. (*After Carmichael et al., 1932.*)

Reproduced Figure	Word List	Word List	Reproduced Figure
	Eyeglasses	Dumbbell	
	Bottle	Stirrup	
	Crescent Moon	Letter "C"	
	Beehive	Hat	
	Curtains in a Window	Diamond in a Rectangle	
	Seven	Four	
	Ship's Wheel	Sun	
	Hourglass	Table	

sign. After viewing all the slides, subjects answered questions about them. The critical question mentioned either a stop sign or a yield sign. For half the subjects the sign that was mentioned was the same as the one they had seen; for half it was different (a yield sign when they had seen a stop sign, or a stop sign when they had seen a yield sign). Next the subjects performed a distracting task, and finally took a recognition test. The researchers showed them fifteen pairs of slides and asked them to choose the one slide out of each pair that they had seen before. How do you think the subjects re-

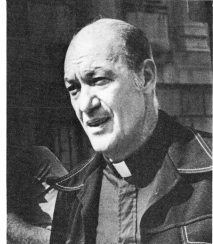

Father Bernard Pagano (right) was almost convicted of armed robbery when seven eyewitnesses mistook him for Ronald Clauser (left), the real culprit.

sponded when they were shown two views of the intersection, one with a stop sign and one with a yield sign?

When the critical question had mentioned a traffic sign *consistent* with what the subjects had seen, they chose the correct slide 75 percent of the time. In contrast, when the critical question mentioned a traffic sign *in*consistent with what they had seen, they made the correct choice only 41 percent of the time. Loftus concluded that misinformation introduced after an eyewitness observation seems to be capable of altering the witness's memory. If the witness initially thought he or she saw a stop sign, the subsequent mention of a yield sign might change that recollection. The likelihood of such mistakes can be substantially increased, moreover, by a change in the timing of the misinformation. If subjects are exposed to inaccurate information a week after they witness an accident, when the true details are more difficult to retrieve, they are susceptible to the misinformation 80 percent of the time (Loftus et al., 1978).

Within a few years Loftus had collected substantial evidence that when people witness an important event, such as a crime or accident, their memory of the various objects involved can be distorted by subsequent misinformation. Loftus wondered if the same thing is true about memory for faces. After all, legal evidence often involves eyewitnesses' accounts of whom they saw at the scene of a crime. Could these witnesses easily be led astray by prejudicial information, as apparently happened in the Father Pagano case?

To find out, Loftus and Greene (1980) presented subjects with a three-minute film that showed a man parking his car on the street, entering a grocery store, buying a few things, and then returning to his car, where he found a young man who appeared to be breaking into it. The two argued for a few seconds and then the young man ran off. After seeing the film, the subjects performed an unrelated task for twenty minutes. Then they were given a one-page description of the incident supposedly written by a professor who had also seen the film. Control subjects received a completely accurate description, while experimental subjects received a description that was wrong in only one small detail (it said that the suspected thief had wavy hair when in fact he had straight hair, that he had a thin moustache when actually

he was clean-shaven, or that he had crooked teeth when actually his teeth were straight). Next all the subjects performed an unrelated task for forty-five minutes, after which they were asked to write their own description of the incident and suspect. They were instructed to write down *only* what they had seen themselves, *not* things they had picked up from the professor's account. Yet despite this explicit instruction, 34 percent of those who had encountered an incorrect detail in the professor's account included that same detail in their own descriptions. What they had learned from the professor's account seemed to have blended with their own recollections, leaving them unable to distinguish one from the other. Control subjects, in contrast, hardly ever included one of the three inaccurate details in their descriptions.

In a second study, Loftus and Greene found that subjects also *misidentify* suspects on the basis of subsequent misinformation. After viewing a man in the midst of other people and later being told that he had a moustache (when actually he did not), the subjects picked out a face with a moustache 69 percent of the time when given a number of mugshots from which to identify the "culprit." In contrast, control subjects, who had received no misinformation, selected a mugshot with a moustache only 13 percent of the time. It was as if the misinformed subjects had unconsciously added to their memories a detail they had not actually seen, but had only heard about later. Such findings make Father Pagano's case seem not so surprising after all.

CRITICISMS, ALTERNATIVES, AND FURTHER RESEARCH

Loftus's research has led to much concern about the accuracy of eyewitness testimony. But some psychologists argue that we should not make premature judgments about the fallibility of human memory. They interpret Loftus's findings in ways that make memory seem less open to distortion. Consider, for example, Loftus's stop sign/yield sign study, this time from a different perspective.

Remember that in this study some subjects were shown a stop sign at the corner where an accident later took place. In subsequent questioning, it was suggested to half of these subjects that the sign had actually said "Yield." Loftus contended that, for many of the misled subjects, memory of

Spectators cannot possibly observe and remember every detail about a major sporting event. They often incorporate information acquired later, from media reports, into their own accounts of what they saw.

the original stop sign was transformed. But Michael McCloskey and Maria Zaragoza (1985) have proposed an alternative. Perhaps, they say, many of the misled subjects never encoded the stop sign into memory in the first place. If so, they were forced to guess when later asked to decide whether it was a stop sign or a yield sign that they had seen. At this point, they may have remembered that a yield sign was mentioned during questioning and so opted for that choice as the most likely one. Notice that in this case no memory distortion occurs. The subjects merely guess about what they previously saw on the basis of later information. McCloskey and Zaragoza have gone on to conduct experiments which suggest that this alternative explanation may be appropriate in some cases.

PATTERNS AND CONCLUSIONS

But though this explanation may account for some of the instances in which people misidentify things they had seen previously, it cannot account for all the findings that have emerged from Loftus's research. Consider one of the studies by Loftus and Greene that we mentioned earlier. In it, people's memory of faces became distorted even though they were explicitly asked *not* to include in their descriptions any facts learned merely through another witness's account (the unidentified professor's). The subjects were told that if they could not recall anything about a certain feature of the suspect, they were not required to write about that feature. And yet a third of the subjects who had been exposed to an incorrect detail in the professor's account chose to include that detail in what

they themselves wrote. It was as if they could not distinguish these later-learned facts from their own initial perceptions. Such memory distortion may not necessarily involve a *transformation* of originally encoded information, but, at the very least, it entails a supplementation of original memory. Furthermore, people who make such additions to their memories may not even know they have done so.

Robert Belli (1989) calls this unconscious adoption of later-learned, incorrect facts **misinformation acceptance.** It occurs when people, for whatever reason, fail to record into memory certain details about an event they have seen. Then later, when they hear or read someone else's eyewitness account, they take facts from that other person's description and incorporate them into their own recollections. Belli has conducted research which shows that misinformation acceptance plays a major role in studies like those that Loftus has done. In addition, Belli's findings suggest that misinformation may also interfere with originally encoded memory in some cases. By "interfere with," he means that the misinformation either weakens or distorts original memory, or it causes confusion about the sources of the various facts that have been learned. Such memory interference, however, seems to play a lesser role in explaining the results of a typical eyewitness testimony study.

After reviewing Belli's studies and other similar ones (e.g., Tversky and Tuchin, 1989), Loftus agrees that misinformation acceptance probably made a major contribution to her own research findings (Loftus and Hoffman, 1989). But the fact that this process does not involve a *distortion* of original memories does not make it unimportant, Loftus contends. If people can unconsiously add facts to their recollections, sometimes to the point where they become convinced that they witnessed those facts first-hand, we are dealing with a process of great importance both to our system of justice and to our understanding of how human memory works. One focus of future research will be to assess the extent to which this process actually affects the details of an eyewitness's report.

THE PHYSIOLOGY OF MEMORY

Some of the most compelling questions about memory concern its physiology: how are information and experiences recorded, stored, and recalled? The answers lie in the billions of neurons that form the human brain. In recent decades scientists have made dramatic progress toward understanding what happens inside the brain when a memory is formed (Matthies, 1989). Some think that we are now in the critical "breakthrough" stage, during which more and more vital pieces to the puzzle are emerging (Thompson, 1988).

EXPLAINING THE BASIS OF SHORT-TERM MEMORY

Some of the earliest clues to the biological basis of memory came from clinical findings. For instance, in 1933 doctors recorded the case of a twenty-two-year-old man who was accidentally thrown from his motorcycle and received a severe blow to the head. When he regained consciousness, he insisted that the year was 1922 and that he was only eleven. Gradually over the next ten weeks he recalled the past decade, beginning with the most distant years and working up to the recent ones. But no matter how hard he tried, he could never remember the minutes just before the accident (Baddeley, 1982). Such a condition, called **retrograde amnesia,** involves memory loss for a segment of the past only, *not* for new events. Retrograde amnesia is fairly common among people who receive severe blows to the head. This implies that information stored in short-term memory at the time the head injury occurs is held far more fragilely than information stored in long-term memory.

Many researchers believe that short-term memory involves a temporary circulation of electrical impulses around complex loops of interconnected neurons (Goddard, 1980; Hebb, 1949, 1972). This theory is supported both directly and indirectly. Some indirect evidence comes from the fact that any event that either suppresses neural activity (such as a blow to the head, carbon monoxide poisoning, or heavy anesthesia) or causes neurons to fire incoherently (such as electroconvulsive shock) can erase information held in short-term storage. More direct evidence comes from studies in which researchers have probed the brains of experimental animals with electrodes and found that different circulating patterns of electrical activity are associated with attention to different stimuli (Vereano et al., 1970). How such activity relates to short-term memory, however, is not yet fully known.

EXPLAINING THE BASIS OF LONG-TERM MEMORY

Over forty years ago, an experiment with laboratory rats gave some important insights into the physiology of long-term memory. In his now classic experiment, Duncan (1949) trained rats to run from a darkened compartment when a light flashed in order to avoid electrical shock to their feet. After each training session, the rats were given electroconvulsive shock (ECS) administered through their ears. (Electroconvulsive shock involves the passage of enough electrical current through the brain to induce unconsciousness.) The timing of the ECS varied. Some rats were given it only twenty seconds after training, others after intervals of as long as fourteen hours. As you might expect, the rats that received the ECS shortly after training showed almost no recollection of what they had previously experienced about darkness and flashing lights. Significantly, however, the rats that had received ECS up to an hour after training *also* showed memory deficits. Thus, it seems to take at least an hour for an experience to become firmly fixed in long-term storage, and in some cases even longer (Squire, 1986). Apparently, a series of solidifying events occurs when a long-term memory trace is formed. If ECS is given *after* this so-called **consolidation** is complete, then little or no memory loss occurs.

Because most long-term memories are so resistant to ECS, head blows, and other factors that temporarily disrupt neural activity, they must reflect relatively permanent alterations in the ways that neurons communicate with each other. Remember from Chapter 3 that electrochemical messages are transmitted from neuron to neuron across tiny junction gaps called synapses. Long-term memory traces probably involve some sort of change at synapses. Such change could be either structural or chemical, or both. Structural change means a change in the cell membranes, axon terminals, or receptor sites that surround the synapses. Chemical change means a change in the amount or composition of the transmitter substances that carry neural messages across the synapses.

The neural activity associated with short-term memory probably initiates the physical changes that create long-term memory traces, or at least the first step in those changes (Squire, 1987). Evidence for this link comes from the fact that high-frequency stimulation of a neuron can produce long-lasting change in that neuron's communications across synapses. This change is reflected in persistently higher levels of response in neurons that receive signals from the stimulated neuron, as if the circuits involved are somehow enhanced. Such a change is just what we would expect to find when a long-term memory trace is formed.

Scientists are exploring possible causes of this effect. Gary Lynch, for example, has discovered that high-frequency firing of certain neurons in the forebrains of mammals causes channels for calcium ions to open on the target side of synapses. He hypothesizes that a sudden inflow of calcium in turn causes an enzyme in the membranes of the target cells to briefly become active. This enzyme, called calpain, "chews up" a meshwork of proteins that normally maintains the cells' shape, so the cells can undergo structural changes that make them more sensitive to neurotransmitters. As a result, the neural circuits work more readily than they did before (Lynch, 1984; Lynch and Baudry, 1984). This theory of how memory traces are formed has not been confirmed, however (Johnson, 1987). Other scientists have other ideas about the physiological basis of long-term memory (e.g., Alkon, 1984; Kandel, 1979, 1984). This continues to be a very active area of research.

In addition to exploring the physiology of long-term memory traces, neuroscientists also want to know which particular areas of the brain are involved in learning and remembering. One area of interest is the hippocampus, a part of the limbic system that lies beneath the cortex on both sides of the brain. H.M., whom we introduced in Chapter 6, had surgical damage to the hippocampus, as well as to some neighboring brain regions. As you may recall, H.M. had severe trouble remembering anything new. He could hold information in short-term memory as long as he paid attention to it, but as soon as he was distracted, the information vanished. If you were to talk with H.M. for half an hour, leave the room, and return just a few minutes later, he would not remember you. Yet H.M. can readily recall things that he learned *before* his operation. H.M.'s condition is called **anterograde amnesia,** a loss of memory for *new* events and information, not for things stored in the past.

What exactly has happened to people with anterograde amnesia? What neurological mechanisms have they lost? Psychologists once assumed that most had lost the ability to consolidate new memories into long-term storage. This assumption is now questioned, however. It may be the ability to consciously retrieve new data that H.M. and others like him have lost (Ellis and Hunt, 1989). Evidence for this comes from studies in which people with anterograde amnesia are given pairs of unrelated words and asked to create sentences using them (Graf and Schacter, 1985). Next, they are given a long list of word stems, each consisting of the first three letters of a word. They are asked to complete each word stem to make a whole word. The researchers do not mention that some of the stems are the starts of words in the previously seen pairs. They simply ask the subjects to think up a word that begins with each of the three letters shown. Surprisingly, the amnesia patients complete many of the stems using the words they have just seen, far more than they would complete that way by chance. Yet if asked to intentionally recall those words, they cannot remember a single one! It is as if their brains have stored the words but cannot consciously retrieve them.

Damage to the hippocampus also seems to affect the ability to consciously retrieve new procedural memories. In one study, for example, H.M. was presented with a puzzle called the Tower of Hanoi, consisting of three pegs and five blocks of different sizes, stacked in a pyramid on the central peg (Cohen and Corkin, 1981). To solve the puzzle, the blocks must be moved one at a time to the various pegs, until finally all are pyramid-stacked on the peg at the right. In the process, no block can ever be placed on top of a

William Shakespeare's Hamlet is one of the longest roles in the English language. To master this difficult part, Mel Gibson and all the other actors who have played it over the years undoubtedly had to mobilize many different areas of the brain.

smaller one. Over several days H.M.'s performance steadily improved, just as it does in normal people, and in time he solved the puzzle in the minimum number of moves. Yet each time he worked on it, he insisted he had never seen it before and that he had no idea how to solve it. In short, he seemed to have stored in memory a set of automatic procedures leading to the solution without any conscious memory of what those procedures were.

The hippocampus is not the only part of the brain that participates in memory processes. Other areas include the amygdala (another limbic system structure), which may be involved in memory storage, and a cluster of neurons in the thalamus (a part of the brain's central core), which may play a role in the initial encoding of information (Kolb and Whishaw, 1990; Squire, 1986; Winocur, 1984). We say that these areas *participate* in memory processes, but they are probably not the sites where memories are actually held. Many long-term memory traces are probably stored in the cerebral cortex, and for any complex piece of information there is probably more than one trace in more than one location (Woody, 1986). These multiple storage sites are apt to be the same areas of the brain (sensory, perceptual, analytical, and so forth) involved in originally learning the data (Squire, 1986; Thompson, 1986).

This seems to be the case regarding the storage of simple classically conditioned responses (such as

blinking an eye at the sound of a tone previously paired with a puff of air). Learning such responses involves the cerebellum, a structure of the hindbrain, and this is where the memory traces of them are stored, at least in certain lower species (Thompson, 1988; Thompson et al., 1983). This finding supports the general idea that the brain carries out different kinds of memory storage using different neural systems.

Scientists still have much more to learn about the biological bases of memory. Even after the mechanisms of short-term and long-term storage are better understood, many other mysteries will remain. One is memory retrieval. The average adult can quickly recall any one of many thousands of facts and experiences stored in the brain. How is such remarkably efficient retrieval accomplished? Scientists do not yet have the answer, but research in the frontier areas of neuropsychology continues to probe for explanations.

FORGETTING

How many times have you forgotten the name of a person you know you have met? How many times have you searched for your keys or struggled to remember doing something you are reasonably sure you did? Psychologist Marigold Linton (1978), frustrated by the unreliability of her own memory, set out in the early 1970s to investigate how readily people forget their personal experiences. Following the lead of the nineteenth-century memory researcher Hermann Ebbinghaus (1885), Linton used herself as the subject of her study. For six years she recorded on file cards two or more things that happened to her each day. The entries varied from the ordinary (eating dinner at a Chinese restaurant) to the unusual (interviewing for an important job). Every month she tested her recall of the dates of about 150 events selected at random from the card file, as well as some other information related to those incidents. The results were not encouraging. By the end of 1978, Linton had slowly but steadily forgotten almost one-third of the events she had considered memorable enough to record six years earlier.

THEORIES OF FORGETTING

Psychologists have suggested three major causes of persistent forgetting: decay of memory traces, interference from similar information, and the motivation to forget.

DECAY OF MEMORY TRACES

Perhaps the oldest theory of forgetting is that memories simply fade away or **decay** as time passes if they are not renewed through periodic use. The memory of a movie seen last year is usually weaker and less detailed than the memory of a movie seen last week.

Important questions have been raised about decay theory, however. One is why some long-term memories *do not* seem to fade over time. Motor skills, for instance, are particularly resistant to decay. An adult who has not ridden a bicycle for twenty years usually has no trouble demonstrating this skill to a child. Another question concerns the physical basis of memory decay. If long-term memories do, in fact, fade over the years, then the chemical or structural changes in the brain that originally stored those memories must also decay in some way. Why would this process regularly occur? No one yet knows.

INTERFERENCE

Another proposed cause of forgetting is **interference:** the confusion of one memory with another, similar one. Marigold Linton was surprised at how much of her forgetting was due to this kind of confusion. As a string of similar events in her life became longer (the sixth time she ate at a certain restaurant or the twelfth time she attended a certain professional meeting), she found it increasingly difficult to distinguish one episode from another. The details of the separate episodes blended together, until none could be recalled clearly (Linton, 1982).

Psychologist Willem Wagenaar (1988), who like Linton has studied his own memory for personal experiences extensively, believes that interference often works by making old retrieval cues no longer specific enough. For instance, the retrieval cue, "dinner with Bill at Firehouse Pizza," is fine for recalling an event that has happened only once in your life. But if you have eaten with Bill at this restaurant six or seven times, your formerly effective cue becomes too general to pinpoint a particular incident.

Just as interference can hinder recall of personal experiences, it can also hinder recall of verbal information. You may have encountered this form of interference when studying for exams. If you memorize the names of various bones of the body for a test on human anatomy, reading about the related muscles may cause you to confuse the two sets of facts. When information learned later interferes with information learned earlier, psychologists say that **retroactive interference** has occurred. Conversely, when material learned earlier interferes with the recall of material learned later, **proactive interference** has taken place.

Sleep seems to be a good temporary safeguard against interference. Research has shown that people forget substantially less if they sleep for several hours after learning (Benson and Feinberg, 1977; Schoen and Badia, 1984). In one classic experiment, people who stayed awake for eight hours after learning new information recalled only about 10 percent of it, whereas people who slept for eight hours remembered about 60 percent of the same material (Jenkins and Dallenbach, 1924). Presumably those who went to sleep were not subject to interference. These findings can be applied to your own study habits. Getting a good night's sleep after studying for an exam will probably increase your powers of recall in the morning.

MOTIVATED FORGETTING

Sometimes, it seems, we forget because we *want* to. Such **motivated forgetting** is, in fact, the foundation of Freud's psychoanalytic theory. According to Freud, people often push unacceptable, anxiety-provoking thoughts and impulses into their unconscious so as to avoid confronting them directly. This psychological defense mechanism is called **repression.** Repression seems to be quite common among people known to have committed violent crimes of great passion; it occurs in an estimated one out of every three such cases (Bower, 1981).

A landmark case that went to trial in 1990 suggests that witnesses of violent crimes may also experience motivated forgetting. The defendant, George Franklin, Sr., 51 years old, stood trial for a murder that occurred over 20 years ago. The victim, 8-year-old Susan Kay Nason, was murdered on September 22, 1969. Franklin's daughter Eileen, only 8 years old herself at the time of the murder, provided the major evidence against her father. What was unusual about the case is that Eileen's memory of witnessing the murder had been repressed for over 20 years.

Eileen's memory did not come back all at once. Her first flashback came one afternoon in January 1989 when she was playing with her 2-year-old son, Aaron, and her 5-year-old daughter, Jessica. At one particular moment, Jessica looked up and asked her mommy a question like, "Isn't that right, Mommy?" A memory of Susan Nason suddenly came back. Eileen recalled that look of betrayal in the eyes of Susie just before the murder. Later, more fragments would return, until Eileen had a rich and detailed memory. She remembered her father sexually assaulting Susie in the back of the VW van. She remembered that Susie was struggling as she said, "No, don't," and "Stop." She remembered her father saying "Now Susie" and mimicked his actual intonation (preliminary hearing testimony, 1990). Next, her memory took the three of them outside the van, where she now saw her father with his hands raised above his head with a rock in them. She remembered screaming. She remembered walking back to where Susie lay, covered with blood, the silver ring on her finger smashed. Interestingly, media reports from 20 years before (December 1969 when the body was found) were filled with some of these same details—skull fractured on the right side, crushed silver Indian ring found on the body.

Eileen's memory report was believed not only by her therapist, by several members of her family, and by the San Mateo Country District Attorney's office which chose to prosecute her father, it also was believed by the jury, which convicted George Franklin, Sr., of murder in December 1990.

Eileen's memory experience of repression followed by reported recovery raises a number of interesting psychological questions. How does the mind "know" to repress memories that are painful? Why do the memories return? When they do return, are they accurate reflections of the past? This extreme form of "motivated forgetting" needs much more research for these issues to be fully understood.

Not all motivated forgetting is a defense mechanism against severe anxiety, however. People generally forget unpleasant experiences more readily than pleasant ones, even when the unpleasant experiences are not overwhelmingly threatening. When Willem Wagenaar (1986) explored his own ability to remember personal experiences over a period of six years, he was surprised at how much more he forgot about negative events than about positive ones. When asked questions about very unpleasant past experiences he could answer correctly only 34 percent of the time. In contrast, he could answer correctly questions about very pleasant past experiences 53 percent of the time. Negative memories, it appears, are banished more readily than positive ones.

Not only do we selectively remember the better things about our past, we also unconsciously skew our recollections to cast ourselves in a more favorable light (Myers and Ridl, 1979). For example, people often remember themselves as having held more responsible, better-paying jobs than they actually did. They also recall donating more to charity, voting more frequently, and raising more intelligent children than objective records show (Cannell and Kahn, 1968). These often unintentional distortions probably reflect a desire to maintain our self-esteem. Since most of us try to maintain a generally positive self-image, we automatically edit our personal memories to make ourselves more like we *want* to be (Barclay cited in Rubin, 1985).

HOW MUCH DO WE REALLY FORGET?

The theories of interference and motivated forgetting suggest an interesting possibility. Perhaps many of the things we fail to remember are not completely lost. Perhaps they lie somewhere in the recesses of the brain, awaiting the right retrieval cues to find them. Is there any evidence supporting this view that informa-

Many psychologists now believe that nothing is ever truly forgotten. An older person's long-buried memories can suddenly return to awareness when triggered by some stimulus, such as a young person's questions or a look at an old photograph.

tion lingers on in memory long after we think it has been forgotten?

Brain surgeon Wilder Penfield thought he had collected such data. While electrically stimulating the brains of patients in preparation for neurosurgery, Penfield found that the patients sometimes reported what seemed to be vivid memories of long-forgotten events (Penfield, 1969). For example, when a mild electrical current was passed through a region of one patient's cortex, he claimed to hear an old tune being played. Another patient "relived" the birth of her child, while a third "revisited" the midway of a traveling circus. In these and other instances, Penfield reported, it was as if a former stream of consciousness was made to flow again with all the clarity of the original experience.

Other evidence also suggests that long-term memories may be indelible even if they are hard to retrieve. For instance, you have probably had the experience of suddenly remembering an event from the distant past. You might be walking by the building where you attended grade school and unexpectedly remember something that happened in the playground when you were very young. This memory had been buried somewhere in your brain for many, many years. Similarly, some psychologists have been impressed with the apparent ability of people under hypnosis to give detailed reports of events from long

ago. The hypnotist may ask a man to describe his sixth birthday, and the man complies with a detailed account of a children's party. People undergoing psychoanalysis also seem to dredge up deeply repressed events from the past which they thought they had long forgotten. Surely these are strong indications that virtually all our experiences stay permanently locked away in memory. All we need are the proper keys to retrieve them.

As compelling as these findings may seem, however, all of them can be explained in other ways. Of the small percentage of Penfield's patients who actually experienced lifelike memories from brain stimulation, some reported events as though they were observing them from the sidelines, much as we often do when dreaming. Others recalled being in places where in all probability they had never been. It is likely, then, that many of Penfield's cases of memory "retrieval" did not involve accurate retrieval at all. Instead of reliving the past, these people may simply have been reconstructing it. Similarly, although hypnotized people are usually convinced that what they report is true, objective evidence often contradicts them, as we discussed in Chapter 5. It can frequently be shown that they have committed an error called **confabulation.** When unable to retrieve a certain fact from memory, they manufacture something else that seems appropriate. Thus, the man who is asked to remember his sixth birthday may combine his recollections of several children's parties and invent the missing details. The same may be true of many people who appear to recover memories through psychoanalysis (Rosenfeld, 1988).

The existing evidence for memory permanence, then, is not as strong as it appears at first glance. But this fact alone does not necessarily mean that some memories are irrevocably lost. Even if we fail to retrieve a certain memory, that does not prove the memory trace no longer exists. Still, if we can show that rigorous efforts to recall the information are unsuccessful, we at least have an indication that complete memory loss *may* occur.

Loftus performed such rigorous tests in variations of the eyewitness testimony studies discussed earlier. First she subtly suggested to people that they had seen a traffic sign other than the one they had actually seen. Most subjects later reported that they had seen the suggested sign rather than the real one. But was the correct information stored in memory somewhere? Loftus tried to find out. She provided powerful incentives for correct responses—up to $25 in cash—and still most people clung to the misinformation. She offered them a second chance to give the correct response (out of three possible choices), but their performance on the second try was no better than sheer guesswork (Loftus, 1979). Of course, it is not clear if this was really a case of forgetting, or simply a case in which most of the subjects failed to instate the correct information into long-term storage in the first place. It would be better to test for recall of *known* information days, months, or even years after storage of that data had been clearly shown. It would also be revealing to vary the retrieval cues used in such studies in order to see if some are more effective than others.

At this point, psychologists cannot say how many memories are permanent. More research is required before any firm conclusions can be drawn. But even if a great many of them do last for a lifetime, there is no doubt that we also sometimes forget, perhaps thankfully so. Imagine what life would be like if we *never* forgot. The remarkable Russian newspaper reporter studied by Aleksandr Luria had a so-called "perfect" memory (Luria, 1968). This man remembered everything in astonishing detail. Images of each experience haunted him for hours. Whatever he had seen, done, read, or heard—pleasant or unpleasant, trivial or important, from his earliest childhood to his old age—stayed in his memory, shifting, combining, piling up. He was left with a junk heap of impressions. Often he got confused and frustrated. The mere thought of such complete and total recall is probably enough to make most of us content to have an ordinary memory—one that lets us remember most of what we want or need to recall while the rest is allowed to slip quietly away.

SUMMARY

1. **Sensory memory** is the momentary lingering of sensory information after a stimulus has been removed. A person can store a great deal of information in sensory memory, but its duration is very brief—only a second or so.

2. **Short-term memory** is often called **active memory** or **working memory.** Whatever you are actively thinking about or working on at a given moment is held in this memory system. Information taken into short-term memory must be limited, otherwise we would be overwhelmed by sensory stimuli. One process that is crucial to preventing short-term memory overload is **selective attention,** a screening out of some of the information entering a given sensory channel while attention is directed to other information entering that channel.

3. When you attend selectively to a piece of information, often using old information to analyze or manipulate the data, and then place the results into memory, you are engaging in the process of **encoding. Effortful encoding** occurs when you use deliberate **encoding strategies** (verbal labeling, mental picturing, and so forth) to put something into short-term memory. In contrast, **automatic encoding** takes place with no intentional effort. Information you encode automatically includes your location in time and space and how often you experience various stimuli.

4. Once information is placed in short-term memory, it will fade in less than half a minute if it is not renewed by **rehearsal.** Rehearsal usually involves a verbal process, either overt (saying the information aloud) or implicit (repeating it mentally).

5. Short-term memory is limited in capacity: it seems to hold only between five and nine items. Through **chunking** (perceiving related items as a larger unit or cluster), however, we can greatly increase the amount

of information we process in short-term memory at any one time.

6. Unlike short-term memory, **long-term memory** stores information indefinitely, and its capacity is essentially limitless. Successful transfer of information from short-term to long-term storage depends on both the amount and the type of rehearsal. **Deep processing** or **elaborative rehearsal** is generally more effective than **shallow processing** or **maintenance rehearsal.**

7. Retrieval from long-term memory is measured in two basic ways: **recognition** and **recall.** Recognition seems to involve a kind of matching process. We consider a given stimulus and decide whether it matches something already stored in memory. Recall appears to be more complex. It demands that we first search through memory and locate appropriate information before we test for a match. This search is largely directed by retrieval cues. When retrieval cues are weak, we may have difficulty recalling. Sometimes such difficulty gives rise to the **tip-of-the-tongue phenomenon.**

8. Several factors can affect performance on long-term memory tasks. One is the use of **mnemonic devices.** Most are clever ways of organizing information when it is stored in memory; many make effective use of imagery. Recalling a context or mood that is linked to material we wish to remember is another memory aid. The success of this technique provides support for **network models** of memory.

9. One fascinating aspect of long-term memory is the extent to which it appears to involve a process of active construction. New information is assimilated within the framework of existing knowledge and beliefs, so that we tend to recast or dismiss facts that do not fit our expectations. At the same time, information acquired after an event has taken place can affect our memory of that experience. This process is especially important to the accuracy of eyewitness testimony.

10. Scientists have learned a great deal about how the brain manages to store information. The current thinking is that short-term memory somehow involves a temporary circulation of electrical impulses around complex loops of neurons. Long-term memory, in contrast, is thought to involve some kind of permanent change—either structural or chemical, or both—in the way that neurons interconnect. We are also learning more about the various brain structures involved in different kinds of learning and remembering. Most likely, there are multiple storage sites for any complex piece of information, and these sites are very apt to be the same areas of the brain that participated during the original learning of the data.

11. In addition to studying memory, psychologists have also investigated the process of forgetting. Three major causes of forgetting have been proposed. The theory of **decay** suggests that memories simply fade away with the passage of time if they are not renewed through periodic use. The concept of **interference** holds that forgetting is basically due to the confusion that results when we encounter very similar stimuli. Finally, forgetting may also be **motivated;** we may forget because we want to forget. A complete account of forgetting should probably include all three of these explanations.

12. Psychologists are not yet certain how much of what we learn over a lifetime is retained and how much is forgotten. Some have argued that we permanently retain almost everything we learn, but we often lack the retrieval cues needed to bring these memories to the surface. Others believe that at least a portion of the information we acquire is permanently altered or lost.

SUGGESTED READINGS

Ashcraft, M. H. (1989). *Human memory and cognition.* Glenview, IL: Scott, Foresman. A readable text on a variety of cognitive topics, such as language and decision making, but with an emphasis on human memory.

Baddeley, A. (1990). *Human memory.* Boston: Allyn & Bacon. A very up-to-date text containing all the latest research and information on human memory.

Gruneberg, M. M., Morris, P. E., and Sykes, R. N. (1988). *Practical aspects of memory: Current research and issues: Volume 1, Memory in everyday life; Volume 2, Clinical and educational implications.* New York: Wiley. This two-volume series describes current research and issues pertaining to many practical aspects of memory, such as recognizing faces, learning course material, and generally improving memory performance.

Rosenfield, I. (1988). *The invention of memory.* New York: Basic Books. A fresh look at memory which proposes that the brain is not the passive repository of recollections, but rather the active constructor of them.

CHAPTER 8

COGNITION AND LANGUAGE

Two men play five games of checkers. There are no ties, yet each man wins the same number of games. How could this happen? If at first this situation sounds impossible, don't give up. Reread the first two sentences carefully. If each man won the same number of games out of five and there were no ties, the two men could not have been playing one another. They must have been playing *different* people.

The fact that you can solve such a problem shows that there is more to human cognitive capabilities than learning and memory alone. Although you held in memory all the separate facts needed to find the answer, you had to combine these facts in a certain way to reach the correct response. This process of organizing information in your mind to accomplish some desired end is the essence of what we call thought. In our ability to engage in complex thinking —to ponder, to reason logically, to have sudden bursts of creative insight—we humans are unsurpassed in the animal kingdom.

Discovering *how* people think is a difficult task, however. Even if we take great pains to ensure that people describe their thoughts as carefully as they can, those descriptions may not be accurate. One reason is that we do not always have access to some of our cognitions, as a classic study by Norman Maier showed.

From the ceiling of his laboratory, Maier (1931) hung two long strings far enough apart so that a person could not hold the end of one and reach the other. Subjects were asked to figure out how the two strings could be tied together with the help of objects found in the lab, such as pliers, clamps, extension cords, ringstands, and poles. Every time a subject came up with a solution, such as tying an extension cord to one string and pulling it toward the other, Maier would say, "Now do it another way." One solution was particularly elusive. This was the pendulum technique. When a pair of pliers or some other heavy object was tied to the end of one string, that string could be set swinging and grasped as it approached the other string. Although few people thought of this solution on their own, most were susceptible to a hint. When Maier saw that someone was stumped for another approach, he would walk by one of the strings and casually set it in motion. Within less than a minute the subject was busy constructing a pendulum. Clearly, the sight of a swinging string had caused the person to think of this solution. Yet when they were asked what had triggered the pendulum idea, very few subjects mentioned this factor. Most gave vague answers, such as "It just dawned on me" or "It was the only thing left." Apparently, they were unaware of their own thought processes.

Subsequent research has shown that this is not an isolated case. In a lengthy series of studies, Nisbett and Wilson (1977) found that people can easily make mistakes in assessing the impact that something has on their behavior, especially when that impact differs from what they would normally expect. Under these circumstances, people often maintain that a truly influential factor had no effect on them, or they insist that a noninfluential one was indeed important. Nisbett and Wilson argue that people tend to assess a factor as influential if logic suggests that it *should* be influential. In short, our estimates of the causes of our own behavior may be little more than plausibility judgments. We are, of course, aware of the content of our thoughts at any given moment, but we apparently have very limited access to the processes involved in creating those thoughts. As a result, many psychologists avoid using introspection as a way of exploring cognitive processes. Instead, they focus on mental activities with results that can be observed and measured.

In this chapter we will examine four such mental activities: thinking in terms of concepts, solving problems, making decisions, and using language. These may seem to be diverse mental activities, but they all have something in common. They all depend on knowledge derived from perception, learning, and memory. Consequently, you will encounter in this chapter many concepts that were introduced in Chapters 4, 6, and 7.

CONCEPTS

If you were asked what you see in front of you at this moment, you would probably answer with a series of one- or two-word labels: a page, a book, a coffee mug, a lamp, a desk, a wall. These answers reveal an important fact about human cognition. Although the world consists of a multitude of objects and events, each in many ways unique, we tend to simplify and order our surroundings by classifying together those things that have features in common. The mental constructions involved in making such classifications are called **concepts.**

It is difficult to overstate the importance of concepts to cognitive processing. Concepts are truly the building blocks of thought. They allow us to impose structure and predictability on a world that would otherwise be a welter of unrelated stimuli. They do this partly by organizing information into manageable units. With concepts, we take things that are similar to each other, but not exactly the same, and treat them as though they were equivalent (Neisser, 1987; Wattenmaker et al., 1986). Thus, one lamp is not really identical to another, but we think of them as members of the same concept and so treat them similarly (we plug them in and turn them on). With concepts, we can also formulate rules about how things are related. Consider the concepts *flame* and *heat.* We have an implicit rule that the first causes the second, so whenever we see a flame, we do not touch it. With concepts, then, we form general rules that can be applied to particular situations. Such generalizations make complex thought possible.

HIERARCHIES OF CONCEPTS

A moment's thought will reveal that your world is very neatly structured into hierarchies of concepts. The object you are sitting on may be an instance of the concept *desk chair,* or *kitchen chair,* or *lawn chair,* which in turn is an example of the more general concept *chair,* which in turn is an instance of the even broader concept *furniture.* Similarly, we classify and subclassify a great variety of other objects, qualities, and behaviors that have shared characteristics.

Concepts at the intermediate or basic level in our hierarchies are the ones we use most often in everyday speech (Rosch et al., 1976). For example, you seldom tell someone to pass the Bic fine-tipped felt marker or to give you the writing instrument. You say instead: "Hand me the pen." Using the lower (subordinate) or the higher (superordinate) level of classification seems artifical to us. The first is too specific; the second is too vague. The basic level, in contrast, seems just right. It gives ample information without unnecessary details.

THE STRUCTURE OF CONCEPTS

Whenever you ask yourself, "What is that?," you are searching for a concept or set of concepts in which to place an unfamiliar stimulus. What does this search entail? Apparently, when you encounter something new, you compare it with your knowledge of concepts already stored in memory. If you find a "match," at least along key dimensions, you label the stimulus an instance of that concept. The caption to the accompanying photograph gives one example of this process.

But how is knowledge of a concept structured in your mind? How is it stored in your memory? Researchers once believed that it is stored as a set of fairly unambiguous defining features. *Bachelor*, for instance, would be stored in memory as an "adult," "male," who is "currently unmarried." These three features together define the concept. Anyone who possesses them is automatically a bachelor, and any bachelor must, by definition, have all three. But do most concepts that are used every day have defining features that are this clear-cut? Psychologist Eleanor Rosch (1978), among others, argues that they do not. Granted, some concepts, such as *bachelor*, do have a set of clearly defined features that all instances of the concept share. But try to list the defining features of a concept like *furniture, candy,* or *fruit.* You will probably find this difficult. Although it is possible after careful thought to define these and other so-called **natural concepts,** you are not accustomed to thinking about them in this way.

Rosch has proposed that we do not encode most natural concepts into memory in terms of a list of defining features. Instead, we encode them in terms of a **prototype**—that is, an example that best illustrates the concept—plus an implicit understanding of the degree to which stimuli can vary from the prototype and still be regarded as instances of the concept. This theory can explain why some things are considered better instances of a natural concept than other things are, even though, technically speaking, they all have the same "defining" features. For example, you would probably agree that a robin or a sparrow is a better instance of the concept *bird* than a pelican or an ostrich. In fact, if you were asked for an example of the concept *bird*, you would probably name a robin or a sparrow (Mervis et al., 1976). For Rosch, this is because robins and sparrows are very close to our prototypical birds, whereas pelicans and ostriches are not. If a natural concept is learned only in terms of a list of defining features that all instances of that concept possess, Rosch asks, why isn't one example as good as another?

Rosch and others have gone on to perform many experiments designed to show that the prototype model of concepts is closer than the **feature-based model** to the way we actually categorize things in everyday life. Figure 8.1 is drawn from one such study. You should be able to respond to part A faster than to part B. Why? Rosch argues that it is because

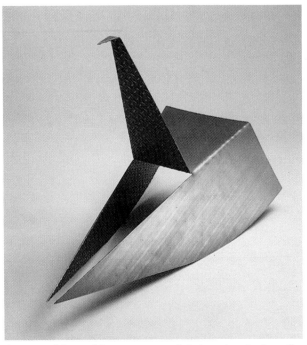

Concept hierarchies are essential for structuring the world and communicating about it. This object, for instance, fits into the general concept *chair*; specifically, it's a diamond-plated steel rocking chair designed by artist Gail Fredell.

the examples in part A are much closer to our prototypes of the concepts *bird, fruit,* and so forth, than are the examples in part B. We process the information in part A faster because we do not have to stop and think: How close is that to my prototype image of an X?

Although the prototype model was originally proposed as a criticism of the feature-based model, the two may not be incompatible. One way to partly reconcile them is to think of many of the features in a feature-based model as merely "characteristic" traits, not essential ones (Smith and Medin, 1981). The ability to fly, for example, is a characteristic trait of birds, even though not *all* birds can fly. Thus, part of what we encode into memory when we learn a new concept may be a set of characteristic features that the "best" example (the prototype) of that concept has.

Another way to reconcile feature-based and prototype models is to think of some concepts as having a feature-based "core," which is used to distinguish one concept from another (Medin and Smith, 1984). The concept *boy*, for example, has the feature-based

PART A

1. A sparrow is a bird.
2. An orange is a fruit.
3. A dog is a fish.
4. A hammer is a tool.
5. A bean is a vegetable.
6. A chair is an example of furniture.
7. A shirt is an example of clothing.

PART B

1. An ostrich is a bird.
2. A tomato is a fruit.
3. A whale is a fish.
4. A crane is a tool.
5. Rice is a vegetable.
6. A telephone is an example of furniture.
7. A bat is a bird.

FIGURE 8.1   Here are two sets of statements involving prototypes. Indicate whether each statement is true or false, and determine whether you take longer to respond to part A or to part B. As the text explains, your response time will probably be shorter for part A. (*From Matlin, 1983*.)

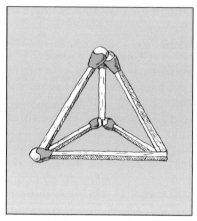

FIGURE 8.2   The match problem is solved by building a three-dimensional pyramid; most people assume that the matches must lie flat, as they were first perceived.

core: "human, juvenile, male." You might consider this core if asked to describe the difference between a *boy* and a *man* or a *boy* and a *girl*. When it comes to identifying a particular person as an instance of a *boy*, however, you are more apt to use a prototype procedure. You recall your mental image of a "typical" boy and then determine if the person before you is reasonably similar (small in size, with relatively short hair, dressed in boys' clothes, and so forth).

There is evidence that people do indeed use a prototype procedure when identifying instances of a concept that has a feature-based core (Armstrong et al., 1983). In one study, researchers presented people with concepts that are clearly defined by specific features, such as the concept *even number* (defined by the feature "evenly divisible by 2"). Most people thought that 4 was a much better example of an even number than, say, 34 or 106. The reason may be that 4 is closer to the prototype that is generally used to identify a number as even. The most important point

about this study is its implication that at times prototype and feature-based models of concepts may coexist in our minds.

PROBLEM SOLVING

A knowledge of concepts and relationships among them makes problem solving possible. To understand why, observe the role that concepts play in solving this puzzle: Take six matches of the same size and assemble them so that they form four equilateral triangles with every side equal to the length of one match. Most people find this task difficult. If you see the solution, it is undoubtedly because of your knowledge of the concepts *triangle* and *pyramid* and the way they relate to each other. Only by building a three-dimensional structure, as shown in Figure 8.2, can you perform the task. The solutions to other problems also call on some of the many concepts you have stored in memory.

STAGES IN SOLVING PROBLEMS

Psychologists sometimes divide problem solving into three stages: initially representing the problem, devising strategies for reaching a solution, and deciding when a satisfactory answer has been found (Posner, 1973). These three stages are a useful way to organize our discussion.

INITIALLY REPRESENTING THE PROBLEM

No single aspect of problem solving has a greater impact on the speed and likelihood of finding a good solution than the way in which the problem is represented. "Represented" means how the problem solver thinks about and interprets the task. Consider Figure 8.3. It shows a circle with a radius of 5 inches. In it is drawn a right-angled triangle, *xdl*. What is the length of side *1*, that is, of the triangle's hypotenuse? If you are trying to remember the formula for calculating the length of a hypotenuse, you are representing this problem in a more difficult way than you need to. Instead of viewing figure *xdl* as a triangle, try viewing it instead as half of a rectangle. Now the solution may be obvious. Line *1* is one diagonal of a rectangle, the other diagonal extending from the center of the circle to the point where *x* and *d* meet—that is, the circle's radius. Since you know that the radius is 5 inches, *1* too must be 5 inches. Thus, what at first appeared to be a difficult problem suddenly becomes much easier when represented in a different way.

Paradoxically, then, when you interpret a problem quickly and decisively, you may sometimes be hindering your ability to solve it. Once you have committed yourself to representing a problem in a certain way, you automatically structure available information accordingly, and your chances of seeing better alternatives are reduced. This is why psychologists often suggest that people avoid settling on a specific representation as soon as they encounter a seemingly difficult problem. Instead, they should view the question from various angles, searching for different ways to perceive it. With that in mind, try to solve the following problem: A dog has a 6-foot chain fastened around his neck and his water bowl is 10 feet away. How can he reach the bowl? The solution appears in Figure 8.4.

Changing your perspective on a problem is not always easy. Many things can steer you toward an unproductive point of view. One is the fact that the critical aspects of a problem may sometimes be embedded in irrelevant information. Consider, for instance, this problem: "If you have black socks and brown socks in your drawer, mixed in the ratio of 4 to 5, how many socks will you have to take out to make sure of having a pair the same color?" (Sternberg and Davidson, 1982). If you didn't know immediately that

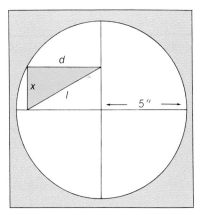

FIGURE 8.3   Problem illustrating the importance of the initial representation.

the answer is three, it was probably because the 4:5 ratio misdirected your attention. The ratio of black socks to brown socks is irrelevant information. If you have only *two* colors of socks in the drawer and the first two socks you take out do not match, the third sock *must* match one of the others. Thus, when irrelevant information (like the color ratio) dominates your thinking, flexible representation of a problem is harder.

Much the same thing can happen when you become locked into perspectives you have always held in the past. For example, people often perceive objects as having only their customary functions, a tendency called **functional fixedness.** Functional fixedness may help explain why people faced with Maier's problem of tying together two widely spaced strings seldom think of the pendulum solution. A pair of pliers or some other object likely to be found in a laboratory is not ordinarily used as a pendulum weight. Consequently, this alternative function is not apt to occur to people. Another problem whose solution may be hindered by functional fixedness is illustrated in the photograph of candles, matches, thumb tacks, and string on page 224 (Duncker, 1945). How would you use the materials shown to mount a single lighted candle on a vertical wooden wall? Because the boxes in this picture are serving the function of containers, you may fix on this function for them and ignore other possible ones. But a box can also serve as a platform on which to mount a candle, as shown in the photograph on page 226. If you were flexible in your representation of this problem, you probably arrived at this solution.

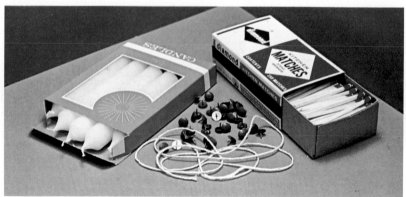

A problem used by Duncker (1945) to demonstrate functional fixedness: He gave subjects the materials shown and asked them to mount a candle on a wall so that it could be used to give light. Try to solve the problem yourself. (The use of the term "functional fixedness" gives you a clue to the solution of the problem that Duncker's subjects did not have.) The solution is shown on page 226.

Not all people are equally skilled at representing problems. Experts, for example, are often better than novices at effectively assessing problems in their particular field. What gives experts this cognitive advantage? Part of the answer lies in the schemas they possess. Remember that a schema is a mental representation of objects and events through which we filter incoming information and give meaning to it. Doctors, for instance, possess an intricate schema of how the body can break down, and this schema gives them a framework for interpreting patients' symptoms. That is why a doctor is far better at diagnosing illness than the average person is.

Research confirms the role of schemas in giving the expert a problem-solving edge. In one study, experts in physics categorized problems from a physics textbook differently than college students did (Chi et al., 1982). While the students grouped problems by similarity in appearance ("These two both deal with blocks on an inclined plane"), the experts grouped problems by similarity in underlying principles ("These two can both be solved by Newton's second law"). Thus, the experts' complex schemas about the laws of physics led to problem representations more likely to bring about solutions.

People can learn to represent problems in more effective manners, even though they are not experts. For instance, psychologist A. B. Lewis (in press) has taught people who have trouble solving arithmetic word problems how to represent such problems more clearly using simple diagrams. Those who take Lewis's two-hour training program are significantly better at grasping the requirements of word problems than are those who merely practice solving word problems on their own. Apparently, effective representation of these problems is a skill that can be learned.

DEVISING SOLUTION STRATEGIES

Most problems cannot be solved instantaneously even when they are represented in an effective way. Often the problem solver must go on to manipulate the data in some fashion before the final answer emerges. But the human ability to manipulate data is unavoidably constrained by the limited capacity of short-term memory. Remember from Chapter 7 that short-term memory can hold only about seven pieces of information at any one time. Consequently, we must often use problem-solving strategies that reduce

FIGURE 8.4   The dog can simply walk to his bowl if the chain is not attached to anything but his own neck. (*Adapted from Solso, 1988, p. 424.*)

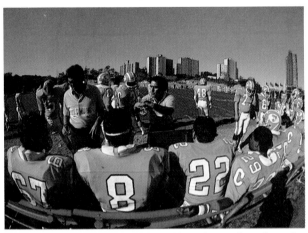

Like most other games, football involves subgoal analysis. The coach continually analyzes the possibilities and chooses the play that is most appropriate at a given point, aiming at the ultimate goal of winning the game.

the demands placed on it. In the following sections we examine some of these strategies.

Algorithms and Heuristics Some problems can best be solved by a strategy called an **algorithm:** a precisely stated set of rules for solving problems of a particular kind. The formula πr^2, for example, is an algorithm for finding the area of a circle given its radius, whether that radius is measured in millimeters or miles. The major advantage of an algorithm is that it guarantees success if it is applied in the right circumstances and followed correctly.

But the use of algorithms is not always practical. Consider the task of rearranging the letters *bnirg* to form an English word. An algorithmic solution would be to arrange the letters systematically in all possible ways until a meaningful combination appeared. Obviously, this procedure could be enormously time-consuming, for five letters can be combined in 120 different ways. Most people, therefore, would follow a short-cut strategy. They would focus on letter combinations that are likely to appear in the English language, such as *br* at the beginning of a word or *ing* at the end. Using this approach, they would probably discover the word *bring* quite quickly. A rule-of-thumb problem-solving strategy like this one is called a **heuristic** (from a Greek word meaning "to discover"). Although heuristics do not guarantee success, they frequently pay off with speedy solutions. This is why we use them so often. In "The Adventure of the Dancing Men," Sherlock Holmes, an expert in deduc-

FIGURE 8.5A Match your skill against that consummate expert in deductive problem solving, Sherlock Holmes. The case of Hilton and Elsie Cubitt began when client Hilton handed Sherlock the first hieroglyphic fragment. Several days later Sherlock received three more samples; shortly afterward the last example came. Sherlock then rushed into action after seeing the last fragments, realizing that they were addressed to Elsie. Why? What message did these last figures contain? How would you solve this puzzle of the "dancing men"? What heuristics, or rules of thumb, might be helpful? Check your solution with the one that is explained in Figure 8.5B.

tive problem solving, used a heuristic strategy to decode the puzzling set of hieroglyphics shown in Figure 8.5A. Knowing that each man represents a letter, what heuristics would you use to decipher this cryptic five-part message? (See page 226.)

The heuristics used for solving anagrams (scrambled word problems) or coded messages are very specific to these particular tasks. But there are also some very general heuristics that people commonly use in solving problems of all kinds (Newell and Simon, 1972). One is **subgoal analysis.** Consider a

"Having recognized . . . that the symbols stood for letters, and having applied the rules which guide us in all forms of writing, the solution was easy enough. The first message was so short that it was impossible to do more than say that the symbol $\mathcal{X}$ stood for E. As you are aware, E is the most common letter in the English alphabet . . . [so] it was reasonable to set this down as E . . . in some cases, [this] figure was bearing a flag, but it was probable, from the way in which [they were] distributed, that they were used to break the sentence up into words. I accepted this as a hypothesis . . . I waited for fresh material . . . [In message 4] I got the two E's coming second and fourth in a word of five letters. It might be 'sever' or 'level' or 'never' . . . The latter as a reply to an appeal is far the most probable. . . . Accepting it as correct, we are now able to say that the symbols $\mathcal{X} \dashv \mathcal{X}$ stand respectively for N, V and R." And so on. The last fragment was a threat of murder against Mrs. Cubitt: "ELSIE PREPARE TO MEET THY GOD." (A. Conan Doyle, "The Adventure of the Dancing Men," in *The Return of Sherlock Holmes* [New York: Ballantine Books. © 1975.])

FIGURE 8.5B   The heuristics that Holmes used to solve the "dancing men" puzzle involve certain facts about how words and sentences are constructed in English. These are facts you normally don't think about. For example, there must be some signal to indicate the separation of words in a sentence (in writing, that signal is a black space; in the hieroglyphic, it was a "figure bearing a flag").

A close analysis of the parts of the match box shows it can function as a candle platform. Seeing this new use for the box breaks "functional fixedness" and leads to the solution for Duncker's problem.

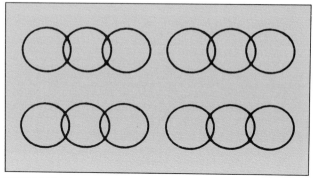

FIGURE 8.6A   Means–end analysis of a problem. A man has four chains, each three links long. He wanted to join the four chains to form a single closed chain. Having a link opened cost 2 cents, and having a link closed cost 3 cents. The man had the chains joined into a closed chain for 15 cents. Without spending too much time, can you figure out how he did this? Check your solution with the one given in Figure 8.6B.

chess player. A person beginning a game of chess could never consider all of the 10^{120} play sequences that are theoretically possible. Even if the person could evaluate one play every billionth of a second, it would still take billions upon billions of centuries to consider all the alternatives. Clearly, chess players must have some way of limiting their focus. Their strategy is to break down the problem of winning the game into a series of smaller problems, or subgoals, each of which is of manageable scope. For example, a player may first determine if the king is in danger of attack and, if so, concentrate on moves that protect the king. If the king is safe, the player may proceed to the next most important subgoal: ensuring that all other major pieces are safe. If the other pieces are not in danger, the player may then work through a series of offensive subgoals. In this way the demands on the player's limited information-processing capabilities are substantially reduced, even though there is no guarantee that the player will spot the best move.

Subgoal analysis is not the only general heuristic that people use. Another is **means–end analysis.** This strategy involves comparing your current position with a desired end point and then trying to find a means of closing the gap between the two. To take a very simple example, if you have to get to work on a morning when your car has broken down, means–end analysis would tell you that you have a distance of, say, 5 miles between you and your destination. You might cover this distance on foot, by bicycle, or by bus. Note, however, that means–end analysis has

FIGURE 8.7   The backward-search strategy. In this problem, the water lilies double in area every twenty-four hours. At the beginning of the summer, there is one water lily on the lake. It takes sixty days for the lake to become covered with water lilies. On what day is the lake *half* covered? (*After Sternberg and Davidson, 1982.*)

a built-in bias: it encourages you to focus on reducing the *existing* distance between where you are and where you want to be. If, alternatively, a problem can best be solved by first *increasing* the gap between your current state and your desired goal, means–end analysis may actually divert you from the best solution. Keep this bias of means–end analysis in mind as you try to solve the three-chain problem in Figure 8.6A.

A third general heuristic is the **backward search,** in which a person begins at the end point of a problem and then works backward. Consider the problem in Figure 8.7. If you try to work forward toward the answer, beginning with one water lily and doubling the area every twenty-four hours, you will remain hopelessly stumped. But if you begin on the sixtieth day and work backward, the solution is simple. If the lake is completely covered on the sixtieth day, it must be *half* covered on the fifty-ninth. The backward search is most helpful in circumstances like these, where the end point in a problem is very clear-cut (a lake totally covered with water lilies) while the starting point is surrounded by many options or questions (How big is a water lily? How big is the lake?). For this reason, you might also try a backward search when solving a maze puzzle, in which many paths leads away from the starting point but only one path leads to the goal (Matlin, 1989).

The Need to Remain Flexible   Algorithms and heuristics are useful tools when they are used correctly. But if you chose one that is inappropriate to a certain problem, you may end up with a poor solution or no solution at all. That is why you should always try to remain open to alternative solution strategies, just as you should always try to remain open to other ways of representing problems.

The danger of being closed-minded when using a solution strategy was demonstrated in a classic experiment by Abraham Luchins (1946). If you were a subject in one of his experiments, you were given six problems to solve, like those in Figure 8.8. Each requires that you imagine three jars, labeled A, B, and C, with the capacities listed from left to right in the columns of the table. You are to use these jars to measure out the amount of water shown at the far right, under the heading "Obtain." In problem 1, for example, you are to use jars with capacities of 21, 127, and 3 quarts to measure out 100 quarts. A moment's thought will probably give you the solution. You fill jar B (127 quarts), pour off enough to fill jar A (21 quarts), and then pour off enough to fill jar C (3 quarts) twice. You will be left with 100 quarts of water in jar B [127 quarts − 21 quarts − (2 × 3 quarts) = 100 quarts]. Now solve the remaining five problems.

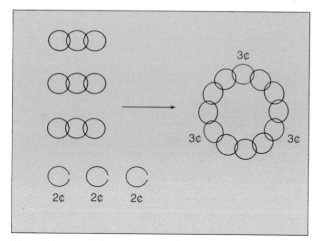

FIGURE 8.6B The answer to the four-chain problem in Figure 8.6A. Take one chain completely apart, for 6 cents, and use its links to join the remaining three chains for 9 cents. Most people find it extremely difficult to solve the chain link problem, perhaps because they rapidly employ a means–end analysis, but are unaware of its bias toward decreasing the *apparent* gap between the means and the goal. If the problem is to join four chains into a single circular chain, taking apart one of the chains completely seems to be working in the wrong direction because it appears to increase the gap between the means and the end. Yet opening and closing only three links is the way to produce the desired result.

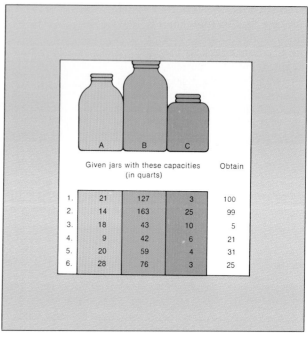

	Given jars with these capacities (in quarts)			Obtain
	A	B	C	
1.	21	127	3	100
2.	14	163	25	99
3.	18	43	10	5
4.	9	42	6	21
5.	20	59	4	31
6.	28	76	3	25

FIGURE 8.8 Luchins's (1946) classic demonstration of mental set in problem solving. For each of the problems in this series, you must work out how you could measure out the quantities of liquid indicated on the *right* by using jars with the capacities shown on the *left*. Try the series yourself before reading on. After solving the first five problems, nearly two-thirds of Luchins's subjects were unable to solve the sixth. The sixth problem actually requires a simpler strategy than the first five, and it could be solved easily if the mental set established in solving the five prior problems had not interfered with normal mental flexibility.

If you breezed through problems 2 through 5 but were stumped by problem 6, you probably encountered the same obstacle that two-thirds of Luchins's subjects did. You became so accustomed to using "jar B minus jar A minus twice jar C" that you failed to explore other possibilities. Actually, the solution to problem 6 is very easy. You simply fill jar A and subtract jar C. Luchins found that almost anyone could solve this problem if he or she had not already learned the steps for solving the other five problems. But a person who had acquired the B − A − 2C rule was very likely either to give up on problem 6 or to insist staunchly that the previously successful formula still worked—that 76 − 28 − 2(3) did in fact equal 25!

This inclination to use an old perspective in new situations is called a **mental set**. Mental sets, when inappropriate, cause stalemates in solving problems. The person treats the situation in an unthinking fashion, governed by strategies that have worked in the past but are not effective now. Such rigid adherence to a mental set has been called "mindlessness"

(Langer, 1989). Psychologist Ellen Langer gives a tragic, real-life example of it. On a snowy evening in 1985, a plane leaving Washington, D.C., en route to Florida crashed into the Potomac River shortly after take-off because its wings had become covered with ice. The pilot and copilot had gone through their preflight checklist, but when they came to the anti-icer control they left it turned off. Apparently, they were accustomed to flying in warm climates, so the "off" response was habitual. But now the mindless repetition of an old solution caused a disaster.

One way to break free of habitual mental sets is to get away from the problem for a while—that is, to provide a period of incubation. Psychologist Jeanette Silveira (1971) found that when people worked steadily on the three-chain problem (Figure 8.6A) but could not see the answer, a temporary break greatly increased their chances of later success. One reason might be that the period of incubation helped them discard inappropriate mental sets. In addition, they may have continued searching for the solution on an unconscious level while engaged in other activities. The extent to which such unconscious processes actually contribute to solving a problem is not yet known, but the possibility is intriguing. We will say more about unconscious processes later in this chapter, when we look at how very creative people sometimes come up with solutions.

DECIDING WHEN A SOLUTION IS SATISFACTORY

For some problems, deciding when a solution is satisfactory is no trouble at all. If you solved the matchstick-pyramid problem, or the water lilies one, you were absolutely sure that you were right when you perceived the answer. Unfortunately, the "right" answer is not always so clear-cut. How, for example, would you determine if you have chosen the "best" topic for a term paper? Or if you have made the "best" move in a game of chess? It is not easy to say.

In fact, when people grapple with problems like these, they often settle for a less-than-ideal solution if finding a better one overly stresses their cognitive capacities (Posner, 1973). This concession makes sense. To function effectively, a person must avoid cognitive overload, and one way to do so is to accept a solution that may not be perfect but is good enough. This is why you sometimes return to a previously rejected solution after devoting a great deal of time to a problem. Searching for a better solution no longer seems worth the effort. We will say more about the effects of cognitive limitations later in this chapter.

PROBLEM SOLVING BY COMPUTER

Much of the recent research on problem solving has been done in the field of **artificial intelligence (AI)**, the science of getting computers to perform tasks that would ordinarily require human cognitive capabilities. Sometimes AI researchers deliberately try to make computers mimic the human mind. Both humans and computers, after all, are information-processing systems. They take in information, manipulate it in various ways, store things to be remembered, and retrieve them again when needed. Can computers be made to perform these functions much like humans

The computer uses "expert systems" to solve problems, imitating—and sometimes surpassing—the human brain's ability to identify and evaluate a wide variety of possible solutions.

do? Some researchers think that they can. It is their efforts to simulate human thought in a computer, particularly human problem solving, that are of interest to us here.

An early problem-solving program, called the General Problem Solver (GPS), was developed by Allen Newell and Herbert Simon in the early 1960s (Newell and Simon, 1964). The General Problem Solver was based on information gathered by having people think aloud as they solved different kinds of problems. The major heuristics that they used were incorporated into the program. Chief among these were subgoal and means–end analyses.

The General Problem Solver was successful at solving a variety of problems, but it did have limitations (Waldrop, 1988a). For one thing, it was, as its name suggests, an incurable generalist. It worked by applying the same general strategies to problems of

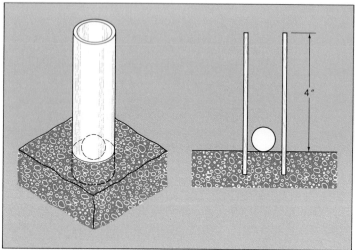

FIGURE 8.9   Assume that a steel pipe is imbedded in the concrete floor of a bare room as shown in the drawing. The inside diameter is 0.6 inch larger than the diameter of a Ping-Pong ball (1.50 inches) that is resting gently at the bottom of the pipe. You are one of a group of six people in the room, along with the following objects: 100 feet of clothesline, a carpenter's hammer, a chisel, a box of Wheaties, a file, a wire coat hanger, a monkey wrench, and a light bulb. How can you get the ball out of the pipe without damaging the ball, the pipe, or the floor? (*After Adams, 1976.*)

many different kinds. As such, it was very plodding, faithfully following prescribed heuristics even when they led down blind alleys. It was not capable of the rapid insights that an expert in a certain problem area might have. Psychologists began to wonder if problem-solving programs would be "smarter" if they focused instead on specific areas of knowledge and were modeled after the ways in which experts in those areas think. Experts, it seems, have information about the particular actions needed in any one of many situations that might arise in their fields of expertise (Langley et al., 1987). These situations are "indexed" in long-term memory according to their various features, and the features, in turn, serve as cues to trigger appropriate problem-solving actions. It is estimated that an expert in a particular field may have learned over 50,000 of these cue–action pairs (Chase and Simon, 1973).

These insights led to the development of "expert systems" for computers, which sometimes outperform even the human experts they mimic. Expert systems are built around a great many interrelated rules in the form of "if/then" statements. If condition X prevails, the computer might be told, then do A—provided that Y does not exist, in which case do B. Using such rules, computer programs have been created for diagnosing illnesses, interpreting medical tests, and even helping geologists decide where to drill for oil (Waldrop, 1985).

But an expert system, too, has limitations (Waldrop, 1988a). When confronted with conditions that are not included in its program, a strictly expert system grinds to a halt. It has not been instructed how to go back to basics and reason as a generalist would. One way around this problem is to develop a computer program that can perform both as an expert (when it has sufficient knowledge) *and* as a generalist does. Newell and his colleagues John Laird and Paul Rosenbloom have developed one such program, which they call SOAR. SOAR has many impressive capabilities (Waldrop, 1988b). For one thing, it is resourceful in novel situations. When it encounters a situation to which none of its many "if/then" rules applies, it returns to basic principles and tries to reason away the impasse. It is also able to learn from its experiences. Every time it overcomes an impasse, it remembers how it did it, so if similar conditions arise again, it immediately knows the solution. In short, SOAR is capable of expanding its own expertise.

Despite SOAR's impressive capabilities, however, it is still not a human brain. Far from it. In a human brain, many different circuits, each composed of millions of neurons, act upon information simultaneously. In SOAR, too, different "if/then" rules can all fire together, but this parallel processing is not nearly as extensive as it is in humans. SOAR also has very limited perceptual capabilities, and it completely lacks the human capacities of emotion, motivation, and self-awareness. Finally, when it comes to creativity and sudden bursts of unusual insight, no computer program has yet matched the human mind at its best. In the next section we will look at just what it is that highly creative problem solvers possess.

HIGHLY CREATIVE PROBLEM SOLVERS

The ancient Greek scientist Archimedes (287?–212 B.C.) was a highly creative problem solver. When King Hiero suspected that his new crown was not made of pure gold as ordered, but instead was a blend of gold and silver, he asked Archimedes to determine the truth. Archimedes knew how to calculate what an object of a particular volume would weigh if it was made of either gold or silver, but he had no idea how to measure the crown's volume without first melting it down. Then one day, while sitting in his bathtub and seeing the water rise, the solution leapt to mind. He could determine the volume of the crown by immersing it in water and measuring the amount of water it displaced!

We call Archimedes' solution *creative* because it had several traits. First, it was novel. No one had ever thought of measuring volume in this way before. In fact, Archimedes had to break free of previous approaches to measurement that might otherwise have impeded his thinking. In addition to being novel, Archimedes' solution was also practical. It was easy to measure volume by the method he devised. This is another hallmark of creative thinking. The idea must not only be unusual, it must be workable (Murray, 1959; Stein, 1956). See if you can arrive at a solution with both these traits for the problem illustrated in Figure 8.9.

What factors facilitate creative thinking? One is often the effective use of analogies (Bransford and Stein, 1984). Consider how the German chemist Friedrich Kekulé (1829–1896) discovered the molecular structure of benzene, a highly volatile and flammable liquid. Chemists had not yet figured out why benzene has the chemical properties it does. The answer had to lie in the way its six atoms of carbon and six atoms of hydrogen were connected, but no one had been able to determine the structure. Then one evening when Kekulé was dozing in front of his fire, he envisioned sets of benzene atoms linked together like a snake. Suddenly the snake grabbed

hold of its tail and whirled around. Kekulé awoke with a start. The snake analogy had given him the answer. The carbon atoms of benzene must form a closed ring, with a hydrogen atom attached to each carbon.

Another aspect of Kekulé's creative insight is the suddenness and unpredictability with which it occurred. This is characteristic of many creative ideas, as you saw in the case of Archimedes. The solution suddenly comes to mind when the person is not deliberately trying to produce it. Some psychologists suggest that in such cases the creative idea may be the result of unconscious thought (Ghiselin, 1952).

But unconscious thought must also have a base of information on which to work. Creative ideas seldom just pop into the minds of people who have no background in the problem area (Wood, 1983). Creative solutions are far more likely to occur with a broad knowledge base on which to build. "The apple that fell on Newton's head and inspired him to develop a general theory of gravity struck an object filled with information" (Solso, 1988, p. 444).

Equally important is strong motivation and persistence, a willingness to work exceptionally hard (Gruber, 1981). When psychologist Anne Roe (1946, 1953) studied very creative scientists and artists, she found that hard work was the one element they all had in common. This finding is supported by what we know about some of history's greatest musicians, painters, and writers. Beethoven, for example, found composing music torturous. He would agonizingly write, discard, and rewrite over and over again. Similarly, Thomas Mann, the Nobel-prize-winning author, struggled to turn out just three pages a day (Gardner, 1982). For these and many other creative geniuses, great works have been partly the products of great perseverance.

Are highly creative people more intelligent than others? Perhaps. Studies show that creative problem solving and intelligence do tend to go together (Guilford, 1967; Sternberg and Davidson, 1982). But intelligence is not enough to guarantee creative insights. While people who score high in creativity also tend to score high in intelligence, many intelligent people are not very creative (Roe, 1946, 1953).

Whether people can be trained to be more creative is uncertain. A number of creativity training courses have attempted to teach people how to

Leonardo da Vinci (1452–1519) is perhaps best remembered today as an artist (*Mona Lisa, The Last Supper*), but he was also a scientist, architect, mathematician, and engineer. His notebooks and drawings express his genius as a problem solver. As Cesare Borgia's military engineer, he designed this device, in which men work at a treadmill to charge a giant crossbow.

generate new ideas (Dormen and Edidin, 1989). While various claims are made for the value of these courses, it appears that they typically improve performance only on the kinds of tasks used during training. The skills that are learned do not often generalize to other situations (Mayer, 1983). There is also a question as to whether some of the skills taught in these courses are crucial to genuine creativity. For instance, some courses teach what is called **divergent thinking,** the ability to generate many different answers to a question (How many uses can you think of for a brick? List all the consequences of humans suddenly growing an extra finger on each hand.) Although divergent thinking may *seem* the same as creativity, this is not necessarily the case. When researchers gave tests of divergent thinking to groups of scientists, the most creative scientists were not the ones who scored the highest on the tests, and the highest scorers were not the most creative in their work (Weisberg, 1986). Apparently, there is more to scientific creativity than simply being able to generate a large number of ideas.

Psychologist Dean Simonton (1988, 1989), who has extensively studied scientists who make "break-through" contributions to their fields, believes that these people are distinguished most by an unusual willingness to take risks. The creative greats of science bet on long shots. They are willing to adopt a theory or line of research that everyone else thinks is far-fetched. Interestingly, their nonconforming ideas prove wrong about as often as they prove right. But the mistakes are usually forgotten quickly, while the successes are viewed as brilliant.

DECISION MAKING

Although creativity is a great asset in many areas, it does not help people make sound judgments in the hundreds of decisions they make every day. Some of these decisions have far-reaching consequences. Deciding whether to get married, to have children, to go to graduate school, or to change careers can greatly alter a person's life. And political decisions made by voters and government officials can affect a nation, the world, even the course of history. What do psychologists have to tell us about decision making?

Composer Aaron Copland, like other creative people, combined knowledge, intelligence, motivation, and hard work.

RATIONAL MODELS OF DECISION MAKING

Suppose you are faced with the following decision. Your friends are planning a weekend ski trip, but you have an exam scheduled for Monday morning. Although you have already studied, you are not certain how difficult the exam will be. And because it is early in the ski season, conditions on the slopes may be only fair. Should you go with your friends or not?

According to psychologists, two sets of variables will probably influence your decision. One is the value you place on possible outcomes—often called their **utility.** How much pleasure will you derive from a weekend of fun and relaxation? How much satisfaction from doing well on your exam? How unhappy will you be if you miss this ski weekend? How distressed if you do poorly on the test? But estimates of utility, although important, are not really enough. In addition, you must also estimate the **probability** that a possible outcome will actually happen. What are the chances that insufficient snow will ruin the skiing? What are the odds that this particular instructor will give a difficult exam? Your decision, then, involves a combined evaluation of both utility and probability. This is true of many decisions you make.

If you were a completely rational creature, you might tackle this problem as a mathematician would. You would start by assigning a utility value to each potential outcome of forgoing additional studying and spending the weekend skiing. You might use a scale of, say, -10 to $+10$, negative numbers being assigned to unpleasant outcomes and positive numbers to pleasant ones. You would then multiply these figures by your estimated probability that each outcome will occur. Tallying up these figures would give you a plus or minus number—minus telling you to stay at home, plus telling you to go skiing.

How closely does this rational approach match the way that people actually make such decisions? Sometimes we may intuitively approximate this strategy, although we seldom make our calculations in a formal, mathematical way. Lee Beach and his colleagues, for instance, asked married couples who were contemplating having a child to assign relative utilities to a number of possible outcomes associated with parenthood. The couples then estimated the probability that each outcome would actually happen if they decided to have a child. From these figures the researchers calculated an overall score that could be used to predict whether a particular couple would have a child in the next two years. This score proved

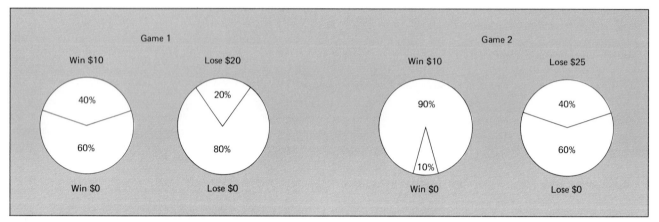

FIGURE 8.10   Which of these games should you play? If you made a quick choice based on the 90 percent probability of winning in game 2, then narrowing your cognitive focus made the choice a poor one. A consideration of the probabilities of winning and losing, together with the respective amounts of money at risk, should lead you to prefer game 1. In game 1, the odds are that you will break even: in ten tries, for example, you will probably win $40 and lose $40 (40% × 10 tries × $10 = 20% × 10 tries × $20). In game 2, you are likely to lose money: in ten tries, probability says that you may win $90 (90% × 10 tries × $10 = $90) but lose $100 (40% × 10 tries × $25 = $100). (*See also Slovic et al., 1977.*)

reasonably accurate: it predicted the decision correctly more than 70 percent of the time (Beach et al., 1979).

Not all decisions conform to a rational model, however. Studies show that people often ignore information that is important to a good decision. For example, grocery shoppers who want to buy the most economical products may still choose relatively expensive items despite the fact that unit prices are posted on the shelves (Russo et al., 1975). Why do people act this way? Why do they sometimes fail to consider all the pertinent facts when making choices?

Much of the answer lies in the limited capacity of working memory, which places a ceiling on the amount of information we can process at any one time. So when a decision is fairly complex, we tend to simplify our choices by concentrating on a few of the relevant facts and largely ignoring others. Often this approach serves us quite well: it pays off with speedy decisions that turn out to be good. Other times, however, this tactic leads to choices that are not ideal. Figure 8.10 allows you to demonstrate this. It offers you a choice between two games. In game 1, you have a 40 percent chance of winning $10 but also a 20 percent chance of losing $20. In game 2, you have a 90 percent chance of winning $10 but also a 40 percent chance of losing $25. Decide in the next thirty seconds which game you prefer to play, say, ten times in a row.

If you are like most people, you failed to multiply the probability of winning or losing by the amounts to be won or lost. Instead, you made a rough estimate of which game looked most favorable. Perhaps you reasoned that game 2's 90 percent chance of winning looked very good indeed. This game did involve a somewhat higher chance of losing, and the amount at risk was also slightly higher. But over all, 90 percent odds in your favor were too good to pass up. If game 2 was your choice, you did not make a good decision, as the caption to Figure 8.10 explains. In this case, narrowing your cognitive focus mainly to the probability of winning led to a decision that made little sense from a strictly logical point of view. In terms of your limited time, attention, and short-term memory, however, the strategy you used was understandable.

Many people are disturbed by this tendency to limit cognitive focus. After all, we like to think of ourselves as rational decision makers who carefully assess all the facts before making informed choices. Is it possible that people's sense of themselves as competent decision makers is, in many cases, an illusion? This question has generated heated controversy. On the one hand are those who emphasize the skill that people often show in making daily choices. On the other hand are those who stress the errors that our rule-of-thumb decision-making strategies sometimes bring. Much of the research related to this controversy deals with the topic of how people make decisions that involve estimating odds. This is the topic we turn to next.

HOW GOOD ARE WE AT JUDGING ODDS?

In June 1979, NASA informed the public that its 79-ton *Skylab* satellite would fall out of orbit within a matter of weeks. But there was no great cause for worry, the space agency hastened to add. The odds were 151 to 1 *against* the plummeting *Skylab* causing harm to human beings. And the chance that the spacecraft would injure any given person was 600 billion to 1. Such odds are astronomical, most people reasoned; the chance is almost nonexistent that it will ever fall on me.

A desire to know the odds is common in everyday life. Should I have my car serviced or wait another month? What are the chances that something will go wrong if I neglect it? Should I study this evening or go to a movie? What are the chances that my instructor is planning a surprise quiz for tomorrow? Should I get married or stay single? What are the chances that either choice will affect my career? In such matters the odds are uncertain. We must try to estimate them for ourselves. Most of us, however, are not statisticians. How do we approach the task?

Psychologists have found that people do not usually take the approach of a statistician when making such probability judgments. Instead they rely on heuristics, or rule-of-thumb strategies, to simplify the problem. Two very common heuristics are representativeness and availability. When people overlook the limitations of these heuristics, errors in judgment can occur.

WHEN HEURISTICS LEAD US ASTRAY

The Representativeness Heuristic   Read the following description of Jack, who was picked at random from a sample consisting of thirty engineers and seventy lawyers (Tversky and Kahneman, 1973).

> Jack is a forty-five-year-old man. He is married and has four children. He is generally

We like to calculate the odds of success for many of our activities, but accurate assessments are more crucial in some activities than in others.

> conservative, careful, and ambitious. He shows no interest in political or social issues and spends most of his free time on his many hobbies, which include home carpentry, sailing, and mathematical puzzles.

Given this brief personality profile, what would you estimate the chances to be that Jack is a lawyer? That he is an engineer? Write your answers, in percentages, on a sheet of paper before reading further.

How did you arrive at your probability estimates of Jack's line of work? If you are like most people, you relied on what is called the **representativeness heuristic.** You compared what you knew about Jack's personality with your ideas about what an "average"

The scoring system used in a game of squash shouldn't affect either player's chances of winning, right? Wrong! To find out why the representativeness heuristic is misleading in this instance, read the accompanying text.

or "representative" lawyer or engineer is like. The extent to which Jack matched each of these stereotypes determined your estimate of the probability that he was employed in that occupation. The job to which you gave the highest odds was undoubtedly engineer. Lawyer, you thought, was probably much less likely.

The representativeness heuristic is a useful device as long as it does not blind you to other relevant information. The problem is that it sometimes does. What other factors, besides similarity to occupational stereotypes, might enter into your estimates of what Jack does for a living? A moment's thought may tell you that the relative proportion of lawyers and engineers in the sample should also influence your judgment. Because their are over twice as many lawyers as engineers, a person drawn at random from this sample is more likely to be a lawyer. Did you consider this factor before? Probably not. When asked a question of this type, most people employ the representativeness heuristic and completely ignore what statisticians call prior probabilities. As a result, their judgments can sometimes be misguided.

Another error that reliance on representativeness can create is illustrated in the following problem:

A game of squash can be played to either 9 or to 15 points. If A is a better player than B, which scoring system will give A a better chance of winning? (Kahneman and Tversky, 1982).

When they are asked this question, most people maintain that the scoring system should not matter. Did you think this too? If so, you'll be surprised to learn that your answer is wrong. By assuming that each type of game would be equally representative of the two players' skills, you overlooked an important fact discussed in Chapter 2. The smaller the size of a sample, the greater the likelihood that, just by chance, people's behavior will not conform to expectations. Thus, the shorter game offers player B a better chance of winning, despite his lesser skill. It is the longer game that benefits player A.

The Availability Heuristic Suppose you travel about 10,000 miles a year by car and are a driver of average skill. How would you estimate the odds that you will someday be involved in a car accident? In order to make such a judgment, you would probably try to determine the frequency of automobile accidents from past experience. Have you or anyone you know ever been involved in one? Have you ever witnessed a collision? How often do you hear about traffic accidents in the news? What you are doing here

DENTAL ANESTHESIA KILLED KID: CORONER

5 FAMILY MEMBERS DIE IN NEWARK FIRE

BOY, 10, NABBED IN CENTRAL PARK MUG ATTEMPT

25 DEAD IN COLORADO JET CRASH

Media publicity can distort our use of the availability heuristic, because it makes negative events—crimes, fatal accidents, and the like—seem more common and therefore more probable than they really are.

is assessing the probability of an event according to the ease with which instances come to mind. Events that are easy to remember are perceived as more frequent and therefore more probable than events that are difficult to recall. This approach is called the **availability heuristic,** and it makes a good deal of sense. In general, the present probability of an event is related directly to its frequency in the past, and the more often an event has been experienced previously, the easier it is to remember. But note the qualification "in general." Like any rule-of-thumb device, the availability heuristic has limitations that people sometimes ignore.

The basic problem is that some things come more readily to mind than others, for reasons that have nothing to do with the frequency of past instances. A person who has just seen a highway accident is far more likely to remember it than a person who saw one ten years ago, for recency affects availability. The vividness of an event affects availability as well. This is why you are more likely to remember a five-car collision you saw than one you merely read about. Things are also more readily remembered when they are related to strong emotions. Are you convinced that you always pick the "slow" line at the store whenever you are in a hurry? If so, it is probably

because these delays are associated with great annoyance and therefore come quickly to mind (Dawes, 1988). Familiarity, too, can make it easier to recall things. For instance, when people are shown a list composed of an equal number of famous women and not-so-famous men, they later tend to describe it as consisting primarily of women (Tversky and Kahneman, 1973). The fame of the women apparently makes them easier to remember and so distorts perceptions concerning their relative frequency.

The availability heuristic is often used in estimating risks. In one study, people were asked to estimate the likelihood of dying from different possible causes (Slovic et al., 1976, 1980). They greatly overestimated the risks from things that were both highly publicized and very dramatic—tornadoes, nuclear accidents, and homicides, for example. At the same time, they greatly underestimated the risks from diseases such as diabetes, tuberculosis, and asthma, which are only rarely reported as causes of death in the news. Apparently, recollection of death from various causes is affected by media coverage, and because media coverage is unrelated to mortality rates, reliance on the availability heuristic can cause misperceptions.

Psychologists who study such misperceptions do not say that heuristics are useless (Sherman and

Corty, 1984). They acknowledge that these intuitive strategies can save us cognitive effort and often produce quite accurate judgments. But when heuristics blind us to other relevant information, we become prone to systematic mistakes. Even experienced research psychologists, trained extensively in statistics, often make the very same errors when estimating odds (Tversky and Kahneman, 1971, 1981). According to one view, then, humans are generally earnest but rather error-prone judgers of odds. They are not always able to recognize the limitations of their own heuristics.

A MORE POSITIVE PERSPECTIVE

The problem with this view is that it contradicts the way we tend to see ourselves. Most of us do not have the sense that we muddle through uncertainly, repeatedly miscalculating our chances, seldom learning from our mistakes. Could we really be so consistently poor at judging probabilities and yet be totally oblivious to our own incompetence? A number of researchers strongly suspect not.

Then what are we to make of the decision-making errors demonstrated in the laboratory? Certainly the evidence documenting them is too extensive to be ignored. Some psychologists urge caution before drawing conclusions, however. For one thing, the findings are not completely consistent (Evans, 1982). For example, it is not *always* true that the vividness of what we witness distorts our later recall of how frequently events occurred. Apparently, whether or not we do so depends on the situation (Taylor and Thompson, 1981). The same is true of our reliance on other probability-judging heuristics. The reason that people misuse these heuristics so often in laboratory studies may be that the deck there has been stacked against them. Consider the study that asked subjects to estimate the probability that a certain personality profile belonged to a lawyer or an engineer. Did you really think that the profile of Jack was drawn at random from a real-life sample? Jack seemed so stereotypical of an engineer that it is hard to believe the experimenters did not create him on purpose (which, of course, they did). In this respect, they were encouraging the subjects to base their judgments on representativeness (Lopes, 1989). Significantly, when a personality profile is drawn from a sample of *real* lawyers and engineers, people are much more inclined to consider prior probabilities as they should (Gigerenzer et al., 1988).

The deck is also stacked against subjects in the typical odds-judging study in that they do not have a chance to acquire feedback about their mistakes and modify their answers accordingly (Hogarth, 1981). In real life, for instance, skilled squash players are likely to deduce after a period of time that a longer game gives them an added advantage over less skilled players. Humans, after all, are usually very good learners. Studies show that we can easily learn to reason about everyday events using statistical concepts like sample size and prior probabilities (Nisbett et al., 1987). Even brief feedback regarding these concepts can enhance our ability to judge odds.

Finally, the use of heuristics is not guaranteed to misguide us, as some experiments seem to imply (Lopes, 1989). In real life, heuristics do not always lead to wrong answers. Sometimes they are both quick *and* accurate ways to judge odds, just as they are often valuable short-cuts to solving different kinds of problems. Depending on the circumstances, then, we can be both intuitively perceptive and intuitively naive. This is what makes our decision making so fascinating to study.

LANGUAGE

Another fascinating cognitive process is the use of language. Human language is an incredibly rich communication system. There is virtually nothing you might want to express that you cannot say with words. What makes language so remarkably flexible and efficient?

One reason is that language is *symbolic*; it involves the use of sounds to symbolize or represent objects, events, and ideas. As a result, language is tied to neither the concrete nor to the present. You can talk about things removed in time and space as well as things immediately before you. When you say the sounds that make up the word *book,* for example, you are symbolically referring to the collection of bound, printed pages in front of you, or to any other book ever produced. Your use of these sounds to represent this object is completely arbitrary. A German conveys the same meaning with the word *Buch,* an Italian with the word *libro.* Language is simply a set of conventions that speakers agree to share.

FIGURE 8.11 Practice reading these sentences until you can read them smoothly. Then read them to a friend. Ask your friend to report which word in each sentence was mispronounced and to identify which sound in the word was incorrect (Matlin, 1989).

1. In all the gunfusion, the mystery man escaped from the mansion.
2. When I was working pizily in the library, the fire alarm rang out.
3. The messenger ran up to the professor and handed her a proclamation.
4. It has been zuggested that students be required to preregister.
5. The president reacted vavorably to all of the committee's suggestions.

Another reason why language is so versatile is that linguistic rules allow words to be combined in an enormous variety of ways. As a result, what we can say with language is virtually unlimited. It has been estimated that it would take 10,000 billion years, nearly 2,000 times the estimated age of the earth, merely to say all the possible twenty-word sentences in English.

UNDERSTANDING AND PRODUCING LANGUAGE

Humans use and understand language with extraordinary facility. When we speak, our thoughts seem to be converted into words with little or no effort. It is only occasionally that we struggle to express our ideas. Similarly, when we listen to someone else talk, we process roughly 200 syllables every minute, quickly combining the stream of sounds into words and phrases, and retrieving the meaning of what we hear. These tasks seem so easy to us, and yet they are far from simple. Very complex mental processes underlie them both. Let us begin by exploring what is involved in understanding speech.

FROM SPEECH SOUNDS TO WORDS

Humans can produce a great number of vocal sounds, and each language uses a few of these sounds as its fundamental building blocks. Linguists divide the sounds of a particular language into categories called **phonemes.** A phoneme is a class of slightly varying sounds that speakers of a language perceive as being linguistically similar. In English, the sound of the *k* in *kite* is a phoneme, the same phoneme that is also represented by the *c* in *carrot* and the *ch* in *character. Kite* has two other phonemes, the sound of the long *i* and the sound of the *t.* These sounds are

combined to form a **morpheme,** a meaningful unit of speech that cannot be subdivided without losing its meaningfulness. Most English morphemes are words that can stand alone (*kite, play, stop,* for instance), but some are prefixes and suffixes that must be combined with free-standing morphemes in order to convey meaning (play*er, non*stop).

We say the phonemes in words so quickly that they tend to run together, with the sound of one still being heard as the sound of the next one begins. This means that each phoneme is modified by the sounds of its neighbors, making the job of perceiving phonemes quite difficult. And yet we do not feel that we struggle to identify phonemes. In fact, we feel that we hear them with great clarity. How do we manage to perceive the sounds of everyday speech so readily?

One answer is that the human brain has circuitry specialized for perceiving phonemes (Liberman and Mattingly, 1989). This circuitry is said to be separate from that which we use to identify nonspeech noises. Evolution has adapted it to recover distinct phonemes from the blur of sounds we hear in everyday speech. It does this quickly, almost instantaneously, without the need for higher-level cognitive processing.

Not all psychologists agree with this view, however. Some suspect that we hear phonemes as clearly as we do because the brain anticipates the speech sounds we are apt to encounter based on the meaning of the speaker's message. In fact, most people do not even notice when a phoneme is completely omitted from one of the words in a sentence (Warren, 1970). Their brains simply fill in the missing phoneme, giving them the illusion that they have heard it (Warren, 1984). Figure 8.11 allows you to demonstrate this process using sentences in which incorrect phonemes appear. The chances are that the people to whom you read these sentences will hear the right phonemes instead. In much the same way, this theory

The apparently simple act of reading calls into play our entire repertoire of cognitive skills.

goes, our brains are constantly "shaping" the phonemes we hear, using cues drawn from the context in which those phonemes are embedded (Cole and Jakimik, 1980). This makes phonemes seem to be pronounced more correctly and distinctly than they actually are.

Of course, if we lack knowledge about the context of words being spoken, we may misperceive speech sounds. Think of the mistakes that young children often make when they learn to sing adult songs they don't understand. Psychologist Margaret Matlin (1989) tells of one student who remembered singing a Christmas carol in which shepherds "washed their socks by night" (instead of "watched their flocks"). Another student as a child had sung this rendition of "O Come, All Ye Faithful": "O come, all ye hateful: Joy, Phil, and their trumpet." Clearly, even if we have neurological structures specialized for perceiving phonemes, understanding the context is another important factor in helping us to hear speech sounds correctly.

PROCESSING WRITTEN WORDS: READING

A different challenge is involved when we process written language (Bower and Morrow, 1990). Here we are not presented directly with phonemes, but rather with strings of letters that represent the sounds of words. How do we manage to identify what these strings of letters mean?

One theory is that the mind leaps directly from the sight of a word to retrieving that word's meaning. There is, in other words, a direct link between the visual stimulus (a particular set of letters) and what that stimulus symbolizes (a certain object, action, or idea). Another theory is that readers first translate written words into mental representations of how they sound before retrieving their meaning. The sound of a word, in short, is an intermediary step needed to gain access to semantic memory.

There is evidence supporting both of these theories. For instance, when people are asked to read out loud word pairs such as *mown–down* and *horse–worse*, they read the second word more slowly than the first because the different pronunciations create a minor stumbling block. But when people read the same words silently, this stumbling block disappears. It seems that during silent reading it is not essential to encode words by their sounds (Bradshaw and Nettleton, 1974). And yet there are studies which suggest that sound *is* involved in extracting the meaning of writing. In one such study, people were given a category name ("four-footed animal," for instance) and then shown a word and asked to say if it was an example of the category (Van Orden et al., 1989). Subjects often answered "yes" to words that merely

FIGURE 8.12 A tree diagram— so-called because it represents an upside-down tree—of the constituents of the sample sentence in the text.

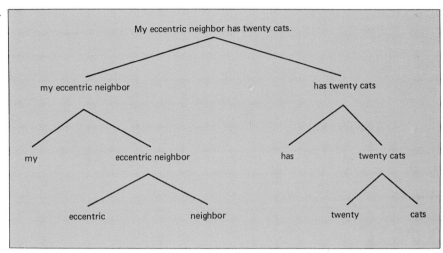

sounded the same as a genuine correct answer (saying that "dear" is indeed an animal). And they made the same error even when the word presented was not a real word (saying that "sute" is an article of clothing). In these cases, sound must be playing a role in word identification. But exactly what that role is, and how often it is important, are topics still being debated.

FROM WORDS TO PROPOSITIONS

Of course, much more is involved in understanding written or spoken language than retrieving the meanings of separate words. We must also extract the overall message that the writer or speaker intends. How do we do this? Most researchers believe that when people read a sentence, they automatically dissect it into phrases and subphrases called constituents. A **constituent** is a group of words that make sense together. Thus the sentence "My eccentric neighbor has twenty cats" divides naturally into two major constituents: the noun phrase "my eccentric neighbor" and the verb phrase "has twenty cats." These phrases in turn further divide into smaller constituents, as Figure 8.12 shows. It is from such constituents that people extract the underlying **propositions,** or units of meaning, that a sentence contains. And it is the gist of these propositions, not the sentence verbatim, that people represent in long-term memory (Kintsch and Glass, 1974; Ratcliff and Mc-Koon, 1978).

Psychologists are not yet certain how people identify constituents, or how they build propositions

from them. One line of reasoning, the so-called **syntactic approach,** holds that listeners rely heavily on clues related to **syntax**—that is, to the way in which words and their prefixes and suffixes are combined. Consider the opening lines of Lewis Carroll's poem "Jabberwocky":

'Twas brillig, and the slithy toves
    Did gyre and gimble in the wabe:
All mimsy were the borogoves,
    And the mome raths outgrabe.

The words are nonsensical, yet somehow we feel they convey meaning. Why? We are probably using function words (articles, conjunctions, prepositions, and the like) plus prefixes and suffixes and an occasional English verb to divide this string of words into constituents and to identify the role that each constituent plays in the sentence. From here it is presumably a short step to extracting the meaning of a sentence when the content words are ones we know.

One problem with the syntactic approach, however, is that the function words, prefixes, and suffixes on which we are said to rely when dividing a sentence into its constituents are the very words that are most likely to be spoken quickly and enunciated poorly (Pollack and Pickett, 1964). Out of context, in fact, these words are often unintelligible. How, then, can they provide the only clues to the constituents of a sentence? The answer is that they cannot. Consider the sentence, "The vase that the maid that the agency hired dropped broke on the floor" (Stolz, 1967). If we use a purely syntactic approach, this sentence is very

Assertion Commercial	Implication Commercial	Test Sentence
Aren't you tired of the sniffles and runny noses all winter? Tired of always feeling less than your best? Taking Eradicold Pills as directed will get you through a whole winter without colds.	Aren't you tired of sniffles and runny noses all winter? Tired of always feeling less than your best? Get through a whole winter without colds. Take Eradicold Pills as directed.	If you take Eradicold pills as directed, you will not have any colds this winter.

FIGURE 8.13   **A sample of advertising excerpts and a paired sentence presented to college students by Harris (1977). Those students who heard the implied version in the second column were almost as likely as those who heard the explicit version in the first column to say that the advertisement had made the claim as represented by the test sentence.**

hard to interpret, for one relative clause ("that the agency hired") is confusingly embedded within another ("that the maid dropped"). Yet you can probably guess the meaning of this sentence just by hearing the major content words alone: *vase, maid, agency, hired, dropped, broke, floor.* According to the **semantic approach** to sentence interpretation, key content words spoken in a given context allow us to form plausible hypotheses about the underlying propositions that someone is trying to convey. In actual conversations, of course, we undoubtedly use both syntactic and semantic clues to make sense of other people's speech.

THE IMPORTANCE OF LINGUISTIC INFERENCES

But our ability to understand language can still not be fully explained by our grasp of the rules of syntax combined with our knowledge of the meaning of words. If these were the only tools we had for deciphering language, much of what we hear each day would be incomprehensible. To understand why, consider the following sentence: "The policeman held up his hand and stopped the car" (Schank and Abelson, 1977). This statement seems simple enough, but think about it some more. Did you consider the possibility that the policeman, in superhuman fash-

ion, literally stopped the car with an upraised hand? Probably not. This is because part of our skill at understanding language comes from our ability to make inferences about what we hear.

Artificial intelligence researcher Roger Schank (1983) was one of the first to call attention to this important process. He and his colleagues tried to program a computer to understand English by giving it a dictionary, a set of semantic rules, and the rules of English syntax. They found that the machine was a hopeless failure at interpreting many sentences that people understand easily. The reason was that the computer knew nothing about the world to which language refers. We humans, in contrast, have a large base of knowledge that we readily use to draw inferences. When presented with our sentence about the policeman, for example, we automatically make inferences on the basis of what we know about a police officer's work and how automobiles are driven. We infer that the policeman is directing traffic, that he holds up his hand as a signal to stop, and that the oncoming motorist applies the brakes that actually stop the car. If we did not make all these inferences, we would miss the sentence's intended meaning. Schank and his colleagues are now supplying their language-processing computers with a broad base of knowledge. Part of this knowledge is in the form of **scripts,** the sequences of actions that can be expected in particular situations. A "directing traffic" script, for instance, is enormously helpful in getting a computer to interpret the sentence above correctly.

But it is not just a general knowledge of objects and events that enables us to make linguistic inferences. To see why, consider this bit of conversation:

A: I've got a headache. Do you have any aspirin?
B: There's a store around the corner.

What knowledge do you need to figure out the meaning of B's reply? To a great extent you need an understanding of the implicit rules of English conversation. You need, for instance, an expectation that speaker B is trying to be cooperative—that he or she is not changing the subject by suddenly mentioning a store. You also need an expectation that B's response is relevant—that the store being referred to is in fact one where aspirin is sold. Users of language are constantly making inferences on the basis of these and other implicit rules of conversation (Howard, 1983; Miller, 1981; Tracy, 1984).

Our readiness to make inferences about language is often very helpful, for it spares us the need to communicate *everything* through explicit speech. But the tendency to make inferences also poses risks. If people want to mislead us, they can often do so simply by using sentences that encourage incorrect inferences. This was clearly demonstrated in a study in which subjects were presented with a series of commercials (Harris, 1977). Some of the subjects heard a version of each commercial that made a very explicit statement about what the product could do, while others heard a version that merely implied the same benefit. (Figure 8.13 gives an example of the two versions for a fictitious cold remedy.) When asked immediately afterward about the content of the commercial, the "implied version" subjects were almost as likely as the "explicit version" ones to say that the advertised claim had been made *explicitly*. They seemed to believe that their own inferences were actually part of what they had heard. To test your own susceptibility to this effect, try interpreting the advertised claims in Figure 8.14.

SPEECH IN SOCIAL CONTEXT

Linguistic inferences are part of the complex process of comprehending speech. But the process of producing speech is equally complex. Not only must

Consider the following advertisers' claims:

Scientific studies show that our brand (brand A) is unsurpassed by any other brand on the market.

Dogs prefer our brand of food by a ratio of two to one.

Write down your interpretations of these claims before you read the caption.

FIGURE 8.14 Did you assume that brand A is better than all other brands? If so, your inferences misled you. The word *unsurpassed* simply means that no other brand is better than A. In actual fact, all available brands could be absolutely equal. How about the claim for the brand of dog food? Did you think that dogs prefer it to some competing brand? If so, you again made an unwarranted inference, for the ad never says what other food (or even that food itself) was used as a basis of comparison. (*From Bransford and Stein, 1984, pp. 75–76.*)

we transform the propositions we want to express into grammatically correct sentences, we must also construct those sentences in ways that are appropriate to the social situation. The goal of speaking, after all, is to influence other people, to make them understand our ideas and intentions, and to get them to respond to us in favorable ways (Clark, 1985). To do so, we must follow certain socially accepted conventions about how people talk to one another. The study of how we do this is part of a growing field called pragmatics. **Pragmatics** explores the many social rules we use in structuring language (Miller and Glucksberg, 1988).

One example can be seen in how speakers of English phrase requests. Although it would often be easier to give a direct order ("Dust the living room"), social rules encourage more polite, indirect forms ("Don't you think the dust is getting pretty thick here?" or "Isn't it your turn to dust?"). People do not answer such questions with a simple "yes" or "no." Instead, they interpret them as a request to perform some behavior (Labov and Fanshel, 1977).

To add even more complexity to the social rules governing speech, these rules tend to vary with the

The social context is a powerful influence on the production of speech. For example, we would address Derek Bok, the former president of Harvard University, differently at this garden party than at a formal meeting, and we would speak to him differently as students than as educators.

particular social context. For instance, a woman would probably phrase a request to mow the lawn differently to her husband than she would to her teenage son. In the first situation the social equality between the two speakers demands a more indirect phrasing ("Were you planning to mow the lawn today?"). In the second situation the power differential allows a blunter approach ("Get that lawn cut before you go off with your friends"). Even between the same two speakers, styles of speech vary depending on the topic. Two doctors discussing a diagnosis use much more formal language than the same two people discussing yesterday's tennis match. All these and many other social conventions are part of our implicit knowledge of how sentences should be formed (Levinson, 1983).

LANGUAGE AND THOUGHT

Psychologists have long wondered about the relationship between language and thought. Some speculate that language determines *how* people think, as well as what they are able to think *about.* "The limits of my language," wrote philosopher Ludwig Wittgenstein, "mean the limits of my world" (1963). Yet the relationship between language and thought cannot be strictly one-sided. If language is able to influence thought, thought must also be able to influence language. At the very least, human cognitive capabilities must impose some limit on how language can be structured and used. And since language is a means of communication, a way of conveying information about objects and events, it seems likely that language will be influenced by what people experience and learn.

HOW LANGUAGE INFLUENCES THOUGHT

One of the strongest proponents of the idea that language shapes thought was the linguist Benjamin Lee Whorf. Whorf (1956) argued that the way people perceive the world is determined largely by the unique vocabulary and structural rules of their native language. English, for example, has a single word *snow*, while Eskimo has more than twenty terms for various types of snow—fluffy, drifting, packed, and so forth. This difference has important implications, according to Whorf. He argued that when Eskimos gaze out across a winter landscape, their language forces them to perceive certain qualities of snow that the typical speaker of English is apt to ignore. This tendency is called **forced observation.** Whorf believed that the grammatical rules of a language affect thought in a similar way. Consider one of the differences he noted between English grammar and the grammar of the Hopi Indian language. Whorf called

Hopi a "timeless" language because it does not force a speaker to distinguish between the present, past, and future. English, in contrast, always does so. English speakers must either inflect their verbs to show tense ("He talks," "He talked") or otherwise designate timing through their choice of words ("Tomorrow I talk"). Whorf reasoned that this grammatical convention forces English speakers to keep careful track of time, and no one can deny that people in our society are indeed very time conscious. The idea that language influences thought in such ways is called the **linguistic relativity hypothesis.**

Does language actually influence thought to the extent Whorf believed? Research suggests that his claims were too sweeping. Consider the perception of color. Although people tend to think of their own way of naming colors as the natural way, other languages have different systems. In fact, the number of basic color terms in a language (those terms that consist of one word and are not subsumed under another color) varies from two to eleven. Do people whose language has only a few basic color terms perceive the same distinctions in color as people whose language has many more such terms? According to Whorf they should not. Yet studies show that they do (Berlin and Kay, 1969). Languages, then, may categorize stimuli in different ways, but people still perceive their physical surroundings in much the same manner. This suggests that Whorf overestimated the control that language exerts over thought.

HOW THOUGHT INFLUENCES LANGUAGE

What about the influence of thought on language? Are there basic ways of looking at and thinking about the world that structure the languages we create? The well-known linguist Noam Chomsky (1972) believes that there are. He maintains that different languages have much in common structurally, and that these similarities reflect the workings of the human mind.

Chomsky's view has led to a search for **linguistic universals:** features found in *all* languages as a result of shared characteristics of thought. Color terms again provide a good example. Because of the structure of the human visual system, most people see the color spectrum in much the same way. This leads to great regularity among cultures in the selection of basic color terms (Berlin and Kay, 1969). Regardless of the number of such terms used, those

terms always have their focal points in the colors that speakers of English call black, white, red, yellow, green, blue, brown, purple, pink, orange, and gray. Furthermore, color terms are generally incorporated into a language in a set order. If a language has only two such terms, they are always the colors black and white (often more appropriately translated *dark* and *light*.) If a language has a third color term, that term will invariably be red. If a fourth color term exists, the choice is usually made from among the colors yellow, green, and blue. Thus there is a universal pattern to the ways in which languages select their basic color terms, a pattern that is due to perceptual processes that all humans tend to share. In much the same way, other universal human cognitive processes seem to generate other linguistic universals.

IN DEPTH

Can Other Animals Learn Language?

In a primate research center a chimpanzee helps his trainer carry a tray of objects over to an electronic keyboard. The chimp touches one of the objects—a small piece of string—and then turns to the keyboard where he presses a symbol that his trainer has designated as the "word" for string. Next the chimp hands the piece of string to the trainer, chattering away excitedly as if anticipating a reward. The trainer responds by praising the chimp and giving him a piece of candy (based on Savage-Rumbaugh et al., 1983).

Since our discussion so far has stressed the complexity of human language, it may surprise you that this chimpanzee seems to be "speaking" to his trainer. Is the chimp really able to use language in a rudimentary way, or is this just an illusion created by careful operant conditioning? Doesn't language demand some special, uniquely human form of intelligence? Or is it something that other higher animals can learn to use as well? These questions have generated several efforts to teach language to other intelligent mammals, especially chimpanzees. So fascinating are the results of these efforts that we will explore them in depth.

THE INITIAL STUDIES

As far back as the 1940s, psychologists realized that chimpanzees would never be able to learn spoken

Come

More

Clean

Toothbrush

Clothes

Go

FIGURE 8.15   Hand signs used by the Gardners' chimpanzee Washoe within twenty-two months of the beginning of training. The signs are presented in order of their becoming part of her repertoire. After learning eight to ten signs, Washoe began to combine them spontaneously to form statements similar to those children make when they are learning spoken language. The most common combinations involved signals the Gardners called *emphasizers* (signals for "please," "come-gimme," "hurry," and "more"), with one other signal. Washoe also used sequences of more than two signs involving names or pronouns, such as "You go gimme," "Roger you tickle," or "Please Roger come."

language (Hayes and Hayes, 1951). Chimps lack the specially adapted tongue, lips, teeth, facial muscles, and palate that allow humans to produce such a wide variety of speech sounds. So researchers have instead tried to teach chimps some visual form of language. For example, Beatrice and Allen Gardner (1969, 1972) experimented with American Sign Language (or ASL), the language used by many deaf people in North America. ASL is based on a

system of gestures, each corresponding to a word. Since chimpanzees are extremely nimble-fingered and use gestures spontaneously, they seemed ideally suited to learn ASL.

The Gardners began their research with a one-year-old chimp named Washoe, whom they raised almost as though she were a child. The Gardners and their associates signed to Washoe and to one another just as deaf parents might. Whenever Washoe signed correctly, she was rewarded. Because Washoe was raised among her caretakers, she had rich opportunities to learn signs in the course of daily interactions. After four years of training, Washoe had acquired about 160 signs. A few of them are shown in Figure 8.15.

The Gardners saw many parallels between Washoe's progress and that of a young child learning spoken language. Once she had learned a particular sign, Washoe appropriately generalized its use to other activities or objects. For instance, after learning the sign *more* to request more tickling, she used the same gesture to request more swinging and more food. Many of her mistakes seemed to resemble those children commonly make, as when she overgeneralized the sign for flower to refer to all kinds of smells. Furthermore, as soon as she had learned her first eight or ten signs, Washoe began to use some of them spontaneously in combinations, forming such statements as "More sweet" and "Roger come." Later she combined three or more signs: "Hurry gimme toothbrush" and "You me go there in." The Gardners felt that by the age of five Washoe's command of language resembled that of a three-year-old child.

Washoe's accomplishments were not unique. In another research project, psychologist David Premack (1971a, 1971b) taught a chimpanzee named Sarah a language based on small plastic symbols of varying colors and shapes, each of which stood for a word. Sarah learned to construct simple sentences by arranging the symbols on a magnetized board. Premack's system is easier for the chimp than ASL is. Since the symbols were right in front of her, Sarah could use them as cues to recall the associated meanings. A major drawback, however, was that Sarah became mute when she did not have her symbols.

In yet another approach, Duane Rumbaugh and colleagues (1963) taught a chimp named Lana to operate a special typewriter linked to a comput-

A young researcher signs with Nim Chimpsky, whose name is a pun on that of Noam Chomsky, a noted linguist who revolutionized the study of language with his theory of generative grammar.

er. The machine had fifty keys, each displaying a geometric configuration that represented a word. When Lana typed a configuration, it appeared on a screen in front of her. She learned to correct herself by checking the sequence of configurations as they appeared. Not only did Lana respond to humans who conversed with her via her computer, she also initiated conversations. And when confronted with an object for which she had not been taught a word, Lana sometimes created one. For example, when shown a ring for the first time, Lana identified it, using words she already knew, as a "finger bracelet."

Can chimpanzees be said to use language as humans do? Some researchers, such as the Gardners, believe the answer is "yes." They argue that Washoe and other language-trained chimps use symbols meaningfully and accurately. Like humans, they are able to refer to things removed in time and space (such as an apple they saw a while ago but that is now in the refrigerator). There is also some evidence that chimps can create novel and appropriate word combinations based on simple grammatical rules. (Lana's "finger bracelet," for instance, combines a noun and a modifier correctly.) Such word combinations suggest that chimps have at least some capacity for understanding elementary syntax.

CRITICISMS, ALTERNATIVES, AND FURTHER RESEARCH

Not all researchers agree with this view, however. David Premack (1976) has wondered if the linguistic creativity of chimpanzees may not be limited to word substitutions in restricted sentence structures —"Mary eat apple," for example, transformed to "Mary wash apple." Psychologist Herbert Terrace, who spent nearly four years teaching sign language to a young male chimp named Nim Chimpsky, has expressed similar reservations (Terrace, 1979). While working with Nim, Terrace became convinced that his chimp was indeed combining words into grammatical units comparable to a child's first sentences. But upon analyzing the data he had collected, Terrace began to doubt that Nim's achievements were really as sophisticated as a child's. For one thing, a child's sentences quickly grow in both length and complexity, as more and more rules of

Dolphins are among the most intelligent of all animals, but their ability to master the complexity and versatility of language does not equal that of the average human child.

syntax are mastered. Nim did not progress in this way. Although he sometimes produced fairly lengthy sequences, his grasp of syntax did not expand. Furthermore, analysis of videotapes showing conversations with Nim revealed that many of his utterances were partial imitations of things a teacher had just said. This finding led Terrace to believe that subtle prompting by human trainers, coupled with the delivery of rewards, may play a primary role in a chimp's use of language. Chimps, Terrace argued, may have the *potential* to create grammatical sentences, but no one has yet proven that they do.

Another issue is whether or not chimps truly understand that words are symbols for something else. Perhaps their signs are merely operant behaviors used to gain some desired object or action (Savage-Rumbaugh et al., 1983a). Just as a rat learns to press a lever to release a pellet of food, so a chimp may learn to form the sign for apple to get an apple as a reward. No one would try to argue that the rat thinks a press of the lever is a symbol

for the concept "food." Perhaps the chimp, too, perceives the hand gesture not as a symbol but merely as a behavior that leads to a desired end. In short, perhaps the chimp has no awareness that the gesture is a "name" for something. If so, then chimps would be using words in a very different way than children do. Children quickly discover the principle of naming, which is why toddlers are constantly asking "What that?" (Locke, 1980). Chimpanzees, in contrast, seldom ask the names of new objects or actions. And they rarely use words to call others' attention to things they are doing or seeing. Is this because they do not think of words as linguistic labels? Answering this question is critical to assessing just how close to a child's use of language a chimpanzee's use of language is.

Savage-Rumbaugh and her colleagues (1983a) tried to teach the principle of "naming" to two chimpanzees, Sherman and Austin. The chimps were taught to use symbols on an electronic keyboard to represent words for objects, qualities, and actions. In one procedure, the researchers placed five to seven different kinds of foods on a table out of sight of the chimpanzees' keyboard. Each chimp was then allowed to go to the table, look over the foods, decide which one he wanted to eat, and return to the keyboard to "state" his choice. One of the researchers next gave the chimp permission to retrieve the desired food. If the animal came back with the right item, he was allowed to eat it. If not, the researcher expressed dismay and pointed to the symbol the chimp had used. Both Sherman and Austin learned to perform this and similar "naming" tasks with very few errors. Their trainers concluded that the animals indeed understood that the keyboard symbols "stood for" particular things.

PATTERNS AND CONCLUSIONS

But some researchers are not convinced that Sherman's and Austin's behaviors prove they have a true grasp of words as symbols. We still cannot conclude that apes who "talk" are using the same cognitive processes as humans do, these critics argue (Sugarman, 1983). Savage-Rumbaugh and her colleagues (1983b) answer that they never intended to draw such a conclusion. We should not expect chimpanzees and children to be cognitive equals, they say. These are two different species, one with much greater intellectual ability than the other. Children also have a built-in predisposition to mas-

ter language that chimpanzees lack, which is why children pick up language with no apparent effort, whereas chimps acquire it only with long and arduous training. Thus, the reason for trying to teach language to chimpanzees at all is to learn more about both the similarities *and* the differences between our species and theirs.

Other psychologists have likewise acknowledged the differences between apes and humans when it comes to learning language. For instance, one of the most impressive language-trained apes so far is a female gorilla named Koko, who after eight years acquired nearly 400 ASL signs. Yet this achievement is tiny compared with that of a well-educated human, whose speaking vocabulary often encompasses tens of thousands of words. There are also definite limits to the kinds of things that apes can use language to communicate *about*. In discussing animal intelligence, Bertrand Russell once commented: "No matter how eloquent a dog is, he cannot tell me that his father was poor but honest" (quoted in Hunt, 1982). Other animals, in short, are not capable of conveying the rich and complex thoughts that humans take for granted (Premack, 1983). All these important differences point to one conclusion: although other animals may have some capacity to learn the basic features of language, the flexible, virtually unlimited use of language remains the domain of humans.

SUMMARY

1. **Concepts**—the mental constructions involved in classifying together those things that have features in common—enable us to make generalizations and thus to engage in complex thought. The **prototype** model offers a good description of how we mentally structure the **natural concepts** we use every day. According to this model, we acquire a mental image of a "best example" or prototype, plus an implicit sense of how far a stimulus can vary from this prototype and still be an instance of the concept.

2. A knowledge of concepts and relationships among them makes problem solving possible. A critical step in solving a problem successfully is the initial representation, that is, the way we first view the problem's

components. Viewing a problem from different angles can help produce more effective representations. Such flexibility can also break **functional fixedness,** the tendency to see objects as having only their customary uses.

3. After representing a problem, we must often manipulate data to reach a final solution. One approach to this task is called an **algorithm,** a precisely stated set of rules that works for solving all problems of a particular kind. An alternative approach is to use a **heuristic,** or rule-of-thumb strategy. One general heuristic is **subgoal analysis,** by which a person breaks down a large problem into smaller problems of more manageable size. Another general heuristic is

means–end analysis, by which a person tries to narrow the gap between a current position and a desired goal. A third general heuristic is the **backward search,** by which the problem solver starts at the end point and works backward to discover how to get there. Just as flexibility is important when initially representing a problem, so it is also important when selecting a problem-solving strategy. Unfortunately, there is a common tendency to stick with approaches that have worked in the past. Such **mental sets** can hinder problem solving.

4. It is not always easy to determine when you have found the best solution to a problem. Experimenting with different solutions is often necessary before making a final choice. People are frequently willing to settle for a less-than-perfect solution if a continued search for the ideal one places too great a demand on cognitive capacity.

5. Much recent research on problem solving is being done in the field of **artificial intelligence (AI),** the science of getting computers to perform tasks that we usually think of as requiring human cognitive abilities. Although computer models have enriched our understanding of human problem solving, they are still far from being able to match all the capacities of a human brain.

6. Creative solutions to problems may come suddenly and unpredictably, often when the person is not actively working on the task. This has led some researchers to suspect that many creative inspirations are partly the products of unconscious thought. Other factors, such as knowledge, strong motivation and persistence, and a willingness to take risks, also contribute to creativity.

7. According to rational models of decision making, we systematically consider two basic factors in making choices: the **utility** or value of each potential outcome and the **probability** or likelihood that those outcomes will occur. We are not always rational decision makers, however. When a decision is fairly complex and requires that we process substantial amounts of information, we tend to reduce our choices to simpler ones by concentrating on a few of the relevant factors and largely ignoring others. In short, we make many choices by using heuristics.

8. The use of heuristics can be seen in decisions that involve estimating odds. Sometimes we assess odds by judging how representative a given stimulus is to a larger class of stimuli. This is called the **representativeness heuristic.** Other times we estimate odds by the ease with which instances of something come to mind. This is called the **availability heuristic.** When either heuristic causes us to ignore pertinent information, our resulting decisions may be poor.

9. Another important cognitive process is the use of language, a highly rich and flexible means of communication. The processes of producing and comprehending language are very complex. Language production involves transforming units of meaning, called **propositions,** into a spoken or written sentence. In order for that sentence to be understood properly, it must be correct both grammatically and in terms of the social rules that govern language (an area of study called **pragmatics**). Comprehending language is essentially the reverse process. We transform a sentence into its underlying propositions. In doing so we seem to rely on both syntactic cues and the meaning of key content words. We are also constantly making inferences about other people's speech based on our general knowledge of the world and our expectations about conversations.

10. Psychologists are also interested in the relationship between language and thought. Linguist Benjamin Lee Whorf argued that the vocabulary and syntax of a language strongly affect how people perceive the world, a view called the **linguistic relativity hypothesis.** But Whorf has been challenged by evidence that all humans tend to perceive their surroundings in similar ways, regardless of differences in their languages. There is more support for the idea that thought influences language. Researchers have found that broadly shared patterns of human cognition seem to give rise to **linguistic universals** (features common to all languages).

11. Efforts to teach language to other primates have shown that apes may be capable of learning a communication system with some of the basic features of human language. But even the smartest ape's aptitude for language is very limited compared with that of a normal human.

SUGGESTED READINGS

Dawes, R. M. (1988). *Rational choice in an uncertain world.* New York: Harcourt Brace Jovanovich. Compares principles of rationality with actual behavior in making decisions. Charming anecdotes are used liberally as a teaching device.

Evans, J. S. (1989). *Bias in human reasoning: Causes and consequences.* Hillsdale, NJ: Erlbaum. Presents laboratory data on biases that occur in human reasoning and considers the practical implications for decision making in the real world.

Honeck, R. P., Case, T. J. S., and Firment, M. J. (eds.) (1991). *Introductory readings for cognitive psychology.* Guilford, Conn.: Dushkin Publishing Group. A collection of readings in the area of cognitive psychology that conveys the excitement and in-depth analysis of ongoing research in the area.

Levine, M. (1988). *Effective problem-solving.* Englewood Cliffs, NJ: Prentice-Hall. Excellent "how to" book that gives advice on solving problems more effectively, including interpersonal problems.

Matlin, M. W. (1989). *Cognition* (2nd ed.). New York: Holt, Rinehart & Winston. Solso, R. L. (1988). *Cognitive psychology* (2nd ed.). Boston: Allyn & Bacon. Two excellent texts in cognitive psychology, both of which cover a broad range of topics.

Taylor, I. (1990). *Psycholinguistics: Learning and using language.* Englewood Cliffs, NJ: Prentice-Hall. An excellent basic text on the psychology of language.

COGNITIVE DEVELOPMENT

Adult: What makes clouds move?
Child: When we move along they move along too.
Adult: Can you make them move?
Child: Yes.
Adult: When I walk and you are still, do they move?
Child: Yes.
Adult: And at night, when everyone is asleep, do they
       move?
Child: Yes.
Adult: But you tell me that they move when somebody
       walks.
Child: They always move. The cats, when they walk, and
       then the dogs, they make the clouds move.

(Piaget, 1930/1969, p. 62)

Clearly, this preschooler's understanding of the world is not the same as yours and mine. Young children think and reason differently than adults do. They have different ideas about how things work and why they are the way they are. The cognitive differences that exist in people at different stages of the life cycle are part of what developmental psychologists study. **Developmental psychology** seeks to describe and explain *all* the patterns of growth and change that occur in people from conception to old age.

In this chapter we introduce some general developmental principles and then turn our attention to cognitive development—that is, to changes in how people think, reason, remember, use language, and carry out a variety of other mental tasks. In Chapter 10 we examine social and personality development, the ways in which people's interactions with others and their habitual ways of behaving are formed over time. You will find that cognitive and social development are intimately interconnected, with each influencing the other in ways that may surprise you.

THE PROCESS OF DEVELOPMENT

DEVELOPMENTAL SEQUENCES

A fundamental principle of human development is that change occurs in broadly predictable patterns, or developmental sequences. Nowhere are these sequences more apparent than in physical growth and maturation (see Figure 9.1). At birth a human infant is, physically speaking, far from just a miniature adult. Aside from the newborn's relative weakness and lack of muscular coordination, a baby's body is proportioned very differently than an adult's. A baby's head is huge compared with the torso, and the

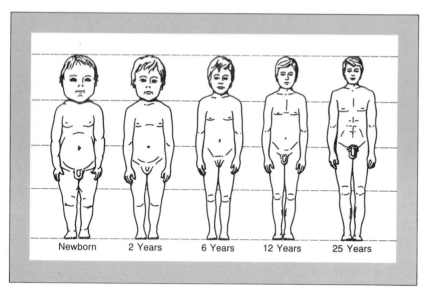

FIGURE 9.1   Human development follows predictable patterns. This drawing shows the development of the human male from infancy to young adulthood. Note the changes in the proportion of the head and limbs in relation to the size of the body. (*Adapted from Robbins et al., 1986.*)

Newborn   2 Years   6 Years   12 Years   25 Years

legs are bent and stubby. But all this changes dramatically over the next several years. By the time children enter school, their bodies have taken on more mature proportions, in addition to increasing in strength, coordination, and height. Then, at puberty, further physical changes occur, usually quite rapidly. A boy's shoulders broaden; a girl's breasts and pelvis enlarge. Less sudden but equally predictable are the physical changes that occur through adulthood. With middle age the body generally thickens and the muscles begin to lose their tone. By old age, changes in the skeleton often cause the body to shorten, and posture may become slightly stooped.

Although the sequences associated with physical development are probably the most apparent, they are not the only ones. Similar developmental sequences occur in other areas, from perceptual abilities to intellectual skills to styles of social interaction. Of course, all people develop differently in many respects. Some, for instance, reach puberty much sooner than others. Some age quite quickly, while others age very gradually. All, however, eventually undergo much the same developmental changes. Most of the research we will be discussing focuses on these broadly shared sequences of change.

HEREDITY AND ENVIRONMENT

In addition to describing *how* people change as they grow older, developmental psychologists also want to know *why* these developmental sequences occur and why some people differ developmentally from others. The answers lie in two interacting factors: heredity and environment. **Heredity** refers to the inherited set of developmental instructions that help to make us who we are, which are transmitted to us by the **genes** we are born with. **Environment** refers to all the nongenetic influences that we encounter, influences that can vary with gender, social class, ethnic background, historical era, and so forth. Many environmental factors arise outside our bodies. Examples are our physical surroundings (such as our houses, schools, and offices, our tools, books, toys, and other objects) and the people with whom we interact (people with their own individual values, beliefs, and behaviors). Together such factors create our external environment. Each of us also has an internal environment, made up of nongenetic factors within our bodies. Examples are the nutrients we eat and the toxins, bacteria, and viruses to which we are exposed. Some researchers try to determine the relative contributions of environmental and hereditary factors to differences in human thought and behavior. This area of study is known as **behavioral genetics,** a term that is something of a misnomer because the field assesses the contributions of environment as much as those of genes (Bouchard et al., 1990; Plomin, 1987, 1989, 1990).

We have said that heredity and environment are *interacting* influences. What exactly do we mean by this? Perhaps the best way to answer is to start at the moment of conception, when a sperm penetrates an egg cell. Both sperm and egg contain twenty-three **chromosomes,** structures within the cell nucleus that carry the organism's genes. All other cells in the human body contain twenty-three *pairs* of chromosomes, or forty-six in all. The sperm and egg are different because toward the end of their development they undergo a form of cell division called **meiosis.** During meiosis, the twenty-three chromosome pairs are split, rearranged, and distributed to two "daughter" cells, each of which receives twenty-three single chromosomes. The need for such a process is easy to understand. At the time of fertilization, the twenty-three chromosomes in the father's sperm combine with the twenty-three in the mother's egg to yield forty-six, the number needed to carry a complete set of genetic instructions for a new human being. And because meiosis involves a shuffling of genes and chromosomes (a different combination of them gets distributed to each daughter cell), it also guarantees variety in future generations.

It is only within the last several decades that scientists have begun to understand exactly how chromosomes and the genes they carry influence development. Chromosomes are essentially long, spiral-shaped molecules of a complex substance called deoxyribonucleic acid, or **DNA.** A gene is a small portion of a DNA molecule that contains the code for producing one of the many proteins from which the body is built. Genes, in other words, are the chemical "blueprints" for building and maintaining a living organism.

That organism is also shaped by the internal environment in which the blueprints are "read." The instructions in particular genes may or may not be followed, or they may be modified, depending on biochemical changes within the body (Plomin, 1987). This can be seen in the development of the male reproductive organs. All genetically male embryos contain within their cells a so-called Y chromosome, which differentiates them from females. About six weeks after conception, some change in the embryo's internal environment activates the genes on a small portion of the Y chromosome, which begin promoting the production of certain proteins. Some of these proteins cause a part of the primitive reproductive structures (until then identical in genetic males and females) to grow into male sex glands, or testes. Soon thereafter the cells in the testes start to produce the

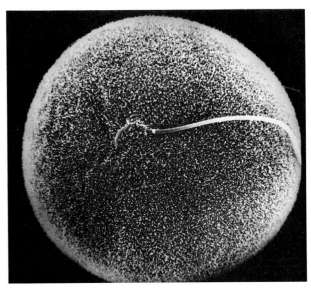

Fertilization, the union of sperm and egg (shown here magnified thousands of times), combines the father's and mother's chromosomes. At this moment the baby's biological inheritance is determined.

male sex hormone testosterone, which further changes the embryo's internal environment. It is this testosterone that stimulates embryonic tissue to form the remainder of the male genital organs. If something goes awry and *no* testosterone is secreted, a genetic male will be born who looks like a female. Conversely, if genetically female embryos are exposed to high levels of testosterone during a critical time in their development, they will turn out to have malelike external genitals. Thus, development is guided not by genes alone, but by a complex interplay of genes *and* environment.

Since environment is so critical to development, it is not surprising that the substances a woman ingests during pregnancy can seriously affect her baby. For example, if a woman abuses alcohol during pregnancy, her baby may be born with *fetal alcohol syndrome.* Such children are mentally retarded and have distinctive physical abnormalities including widely spaced eyes, a flattened nose, and curvature of the spine. Even just one or two drinks daily during the first few months of pregnancy can slow a child's reaction times and create attention problems throughout childhood (Streissguth et al., 1984).

Many other substances are now known or suspected to be **teratogens**—things that when intro-

Heredity and environment interact to make us the individuals we are. A child whose genetic inheritance is normal but whose mother drinks to excess during pregnancy (providing a toxic environment) may be born with fetal alcohol syndrome, a combination of physical defects and mental retardation.

duced into the prenatal environment raise the risk of developmental abnormalities. Teratogens usually do the most harm when introduced early in pregnancy, the time when the basic structures of the body are being formed. One of the most tragic examples occurred during the early 1960s, when doctors in some countries were prescribing a drug called thalidomide for "morning sickness." Women who took thalidomide four weeks after conception, when the embryo's limbs were "budding," gave birth to children without arms or legs. Women who took the drug after the eighth week of pregnancy generally had normal babies, for by then the basic body parts had all been properly formed. Other teratogens, however, can affect development at later stages. For example, substances that disrupt brain cell growth are most devastating during the final stages of pregnancy, because of the accelerated brain development.

Genes and environment continue interacting long after birth. People affect their internal environments through the food they eat, the water they drink, even the air they breathe. In addition, information is constantly being stored in memory, a process that affects the physiology of the brain. And the things that people encounter can provoke a wide range of emotions, which are often associated with intense responses in various nerves and glands. All these factors can and do affect the ways in which genes are expressed. Consider the impact of emotional deprivation on physical growth. When a baby is raised by indifferent care givers, the child may be sickly, stunted in size, and slow to mature. It is thought that the emotional barrenness is linked to reduced secretions from the pituitary gland, including its growth hormone (Gardner, 1972). Lack of physical contact (touching, cuddling, caressing) may have something to do with this effect. In one study, baby rats that were physically handled every day experienced changes in the brain that reduced secretions of stress-related hormones (Meaney et al., 1988). Perhaps human infants who *lack* physical contact with others experience the reverse effect: changes in their hormones that adversely influence their development.

Because environments so vitally affect how genes are expressed, scientists often try to change environments to reduce the impact of defective genes. A good example concerns children with Down's syndrome, a condition caused by inheriting three (instead of two) of the chromosomes called number 21. Children with Down's syndrome are usually retarded and lack normal physical coordination. In the past, they were often considered hopeless cases. But recent studies show that if Down's syndrome children are given intensive training in physical and cognitive tasks, especially during infancy, their performance improves substantially (Cicchetti and Sroufe, 1978). Thus, a change in the learning environment can make an enormous difference in the way this genetic abnormality is expressed. Genetic makeup, in other words, should never be viewed in isolation. All human traits are influenced by both genes *and* environment. For complex behavioral traits the influence of environment is enormous. Almost no such trait has more than half its variability explained entirely by genetic differences among people (Plomin, 1987).

Newborn babies can see well enough to detect and imitate changes in an adult's facial expression. These are frames from videotape recordings of two- to three-week-old infants reproducing an experimenter's expressions.

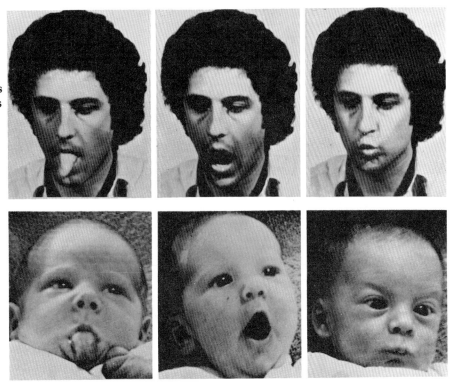

THE COMPETENCY OF THE HUMAN INFANT

People used to think that human newborns were largely oblivious to the world. Some parents even wondered if their newborn babies could see or hear at all. In the last several decades, however, research on the newborn has expanded greatly, and a very different view has emerged. We now know that humans are born with sensory systems that are impressively able. They process information and learn about their surroundings from the very moment of birth.

PERCEPTUAL CAPABILITIES

Findings regarding the newborn's visual capabilities have done much to foster this view. Although babies at birth have only about 20/300 vision (they can see the amount of detail in an object 20 feet away that an adult with perfect vision can see at 300 feet), they can nevertheless see fairly clearly when things are held close enough (Banks and Salapatek, 1983). Their vision is sharpest at a distance of about 7 to 8 inches,

which is about the distance at which adults hold infants when feeding them. From the very beginning, then, babies gather information about their caregivers' faces. Newborns' ability to fixate on objects and to track slowly moving stimuli with their eyes helps them to inspect this important part of their world visually.

Newborns even seem to be able to detect changes in facial expressions. In one study, babies on average only thirty-six hours old were able to discriminate among happy, sad, and surprised expressions that an adult displayed (Field et al., 1982). The researchers could tell this by the fact that the babies tended to look less and less at an expression that was presented repeatedly, as if they were growing bored with that particular face. (This boredom stems from **habituation,** a simple form of learning in which the response to a given stimulus grows weaker and weaker the more that stimulus is presented.) Yet the babies showed renewed interest as soon as an old expression was replaced by a new one. Apparently, they could tell that the new expression was different,

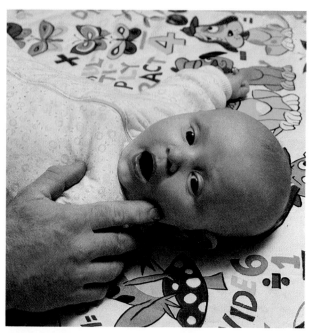

Exhibiting the rooting reflex, this baby instinctively turns its head toward any object that touches its cheek.

and because it was different they found it more interesting.

These same babies also showed a tendency that had been seen before in newborns: imitation of an adult's facial expression (Meltzoff and Moore, 1977). They often spread their lips and crinkled their eyes when they looked at a happy face, furrowed their brows and pouted when they saw a sad expression, and opened their mouths and widened their eyes when they saw a look of surprise. In a follow-up study, newborns who were less than three days old (some as young as seven hours) were able to imitate an adult who opened his mouth and stuck out his tongue (Meltzoff and Moore, 1983). This is not to say that babies this young deliberately mimic others. As yet they have no sense of "self" and "other," no knowledge of the similarities between their own expressions and someone else's. Their behavior in this case is akin to a reflex—an unpremeditated "matching" of their own facial movements with those of another person (Kaye and Marcus, 1978). Yet the newborn's ability to attend so carefully to human faces is undoubtedly an important foundation for future social and emotional development.

And even in this very early behavior, we see individual differences which will help to shape the infant's development. Babies who are, perhaps by innate temperament, very responsive to their parents or other adults tend to get more responses *from* them. In turn, these responses encourage the infants to continue being responsive and sociable (Heimann, 1989).

Adding to this foundation is the newborn's impressive ability to differentiate sounds (Aslin et al., 1983). Newborns can even distinguish the sound of their mother's voice from that of a female stranger; in one study, babies even preferred hearing stories that their mothers had read aloud while pregnant (De Casper and Fifer, 1980; De Casper and Spence, 1986). At an early age, babies can also distinguish between speech sounds, even ones as similar as the consonants *b* and *p* (Brody et al., 1984; Eimas et al., 1971). No wonder infants only two weeks old often respond differently to the sound of their own name (Pines, 1982).

Newborns can differentiate odors as well. In one study, two-day-old babies showed changes in activity, heart rate, and breathing whenever they were first presented with a new odor, suggesting that they perceived it as new (Engen et al., 1963). Infants only five or six days old can even distinguish the scent of their mother from that of another woman (Macfarlane, 1977). This keen sense of smell may help young babies "navigate" in their environment—locating their mother's nipple, for example.

Another capacity that infants are born with is the ability to coordinate certain kinds of sensory responses. If supported properly, newborns will turn their entire head in the direction of a sound (Muir and Field, 1979). Such innate coordination between seeing and hearing is very important, for it increases the speed with which young babies learn associations between sights and sounds. Furthermore, information gained by one sense can be transferred to and used by another (Walker-Andrews and Gibson, 1987). For example, babies who are given objects they can touch but not see will recognize them in pictures (Rose et al., 1981a, 1981b).

The perceptual capabilities of a newborn, then, are quite mature and well integrated. With these perceptual systems a baby can interact with people and objects from the very first moments after birth. Such early interactions have a profound effect on both cognitive and social development.

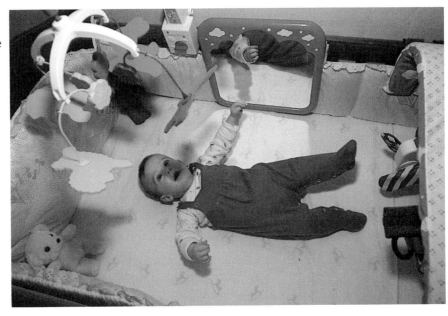

Exposure to a variety of stimulating objects can aid in the development of a baby's cognitive and motor skills.

REFLEXES AND MOTOR SKILLS

Infants also come into the world with a number of reflexes—that is, involuntary responses to specific stimuli. One is the **rooting reflex,** a baby's tendency to turn the head toward any object that gently touches a cheek. This reflex helps the child locate a nipple for feeding. Newborns also have a strong **grasping reflex.** If you place them on their backs and put a finger on one of their hands, they usually grasp the finger firmly. Sometimes grasping newborns can even be lifted up by one of their arms! This reflex may be a vestige from our evolutionary past. If our early ancestors carried their young on their backs or undersides, as many apes and monkeys do, the ability to cling tightly to the mother would have great survival value (Prechtl, 1982). These and other newborn reflexes usually disappear between three and four months of age.

Developmental psychologists have long been interested in the appearance and disappearance of newborn reflexes. One reason is that these reflexes are considered a measure of how well the central nervous system is functioning. Weak or absent reflexes may mean that something has gone wrong with neural development. The later disappearance of newborn reflexes is thought to be a sign that more

advanced motor and cognitive abilities are emerging as the cerebral cortex matures (Smolak, 1986). Behaviors that were at first controlled automatically by lower brain regions are now coming under voluntary control by the cortex.

What are the changes in the cortex that allow this important development? One is the growth of dendrites, the parts of neurons that receive incoming messages. A second is the formation of many new synapses, or connections between neurons. And a third is the formation of myelin sheaths, the fatty casings that surround certain neural fibers, helping them to conduct their signals more efficiently. As a result of these three processes, plus an increase in the volume of nerve cell bodies and a proliferation of glial cells, the thickness of the human cortex more than triples between birth and about four years of age (Rabinowicz, 1986).

As soon as a baby's nervous system becomes mature enough, and muscles and bones are sufficiently strong, the child is intrinsically motivated to try to master new motor skills. Early motor skills such as rolling over, picking up a toy, sitting alone, crawling, walking, and so forth emerge in a fairly predictable order at much the same ages in most children. Table 9.1 lists the ages at which 25, 50, and 90 percent of infants reach some of the major milestones in motor development.

TABLE 9.1   Milestones of Motor Development

Skill	25 Percent	50 Percent	90 Percent
Rolling over	2 months	3 months	5 months
Grasping rattle	2½ months	3½ months	4½ months
Sitting without support	5 months	5½ months	8 months
Standing while holding on	5 months	6 months	10 months
Grasping with thumb and finger	7½ months	8½ months	10½ months
Standing alone well	10 months	11½ months	14 months
Walking well	11 months	12 months	14½ months
Building tower of two cubes	12 months	14 months	20 months
Walking up steps	14 months	17 months	22 months
Jumping in place	20½ months	22 months	36 months
Copying circle	26 months	33 months	39 months

Note: Table shows approximate ages when 25 percent, 50 percent, and 90 percent of children can perform each skill.
Source: Adapted from Frankenburg, 1978.

LEARNING AND MEMORY IN YOUNG INFANTS

As soon as they are born, babies are capable of learning how their own actions are related to other events in the world (Kolata, 1984). For instance, babies only a few days old have been taught to turn their heads upon hearing a tone when a sip of sugary water awaits them as a reward (Werner and Siqueland, 1978). They will even learn when the "reward" for doing so is nothing more than a flash of light (Papousek, 1969). Apparently, learning such relationships is rewarding in itself. Older babies show great pleasure when they learn a relationship between one of their own behaviors and something that happens around them. Suppose that a nine-month-old has learned to kick her left leg vigorously in order to move a mobile which is attached to that leg by a string. The researcher then changes the relationship so that the *right* leg moves the toy. The baby will again search for the solution and coo vigorously when she finds it (Monnier et al., 1976). It is as if solving the problem is a source of intellectual pleasure for her, as it is for older children and adults (Watson, 1972).

Exactly how long does a baby's memory for such new relationships last? Do infants forget things as soon as they are distracted, much as adults forget an unfamiliar number as soon as they close the phone book? Many people assume that babies' memories *are*

this fleeting, particularly given how little we remember about our own infancies. Yet recent research shows that babies' memory capabilities are much better than we think (Rovee-Collier, 1990). Two-month-olds, for instance, can remember the relationship between kicking a certain leg and making a mobile move for at least a few days after learning it, and eight-month-olds can recall this relationship even a week later (Greco et al., 1986). Apparently, very young infants can often remember for fairly long periods. This ability helps them greatly in other aspects of their cognitive development.

But if babies' long-term memories are relatively good, why do adults have such trouble recalling events from their own first few years? Why can't we remember sitting in a highchair, drinking from a bottle, or taking our first few tottering steps? Psychologists do not yet know the reasons for this blackout of episodic memories from infancy, a phenomenon called **infantile amnesia** (Kail, 1990). One theory is that we have trouble *retrieving* these early experiences. The memories are there, stored away in our brains, but we lack the keys to unlock them. This was essentially Freud's explanation for infantile amnesia. He believed that because of the sexual nature of many early life experiences, the whole period is repressed and unavailable for recall. Some contemporary researchers likewise focus on retrieval problems, but from a different angle. They suggest that we lack the visual retrieval cues needed to recall experiences from infancy because the world now looks so different to us than it did then. (Remember that people may be twenty times or more larger by weight than they were as newborns.) Another theory holds that infantile amnesia arises because babies do not process information deeply enough. In particular, they do not process it using language (they do not *label* what they see and hear), and this may be essential for memories to persist. Finally, there are those who contend that early life experiences are probably stored just as well as later ones, but early memories are disrupted and lost due to changes in the brain. This disruption may be related to the development of the cerebral cortex, with its rapid growth of dendrites and new synapses during infancy.

All these theories of infantile amnesia are certainly plausible, and researchers have found evidence in support of many of them. At the same time, however, there is also counterevidence that makes none of these explanations unquestionably right. For this reason psychologists continue investigating the puzzle of why we remember so little from our earliest years.

COGNITIVE DEVELOPMENT IN INFANCY AND CHILDHOOD

Cognitively speaking, tremendous development occurs during the first dozen years of life. By the time children enter school, they have mastered the intricacies of language. They can count, recite the alphabet, narrate the plots of their favorite stories, and explain the rules of many games. They can also operate mechanical equipment such as TV sets, telephones, and video game machines. Upon leaving elementary school six years later, they can read, write, do arithmetic, and tell you much about history, science, geography, and more. How does human intellect develop from the basic abilities present at birth to the impressive skills exhibited in middle childhood?

CHANGES IN THINKING AND REASONING

Swiss psychologist Jean Piaget (1896–1980) was one of the first researchers to provide answers to this question. Piaget was a gifted observer of children's behavior. He looked beyond the superficial things that youngsters do and say to probe the underlying nature of how they view the world. The quotation from a child explaining what makes clouds move,

which appeared at the start of this chapter, is taken from Piaget's research. The theory of cognitive development that Piaget proposed on the basis of his findings has tremendous breadth, covering from the very first days after birth through adolescence. This has helped to make it of enduring importance. In recent decades, however, many of Piaget's ideas have been criticized, especially by those who take an information-processing view. It will help you to understand the nature of these criticisms if you know more about these two perspectives on cognitive development.

TWO PERSPECTIVES

Piaget's Theory Piaget saw cognitive development as a series of *qualitatively different* stages. At each new stage children construct a more mature view of reality, which in turn changes how they think about the world and assimilate new information. In Piaget's view there are four major stages of intellectual growth: the **sensorimotor period,** which encompasses the first two years of life; the **preoperational period,** which occurs during the preschool years; the **concrete-operational period,** which occupies the elementary school years; and the **formal-operational period,** which begins around adolescence and continues throughout adulthood (Piaget and Inhelder, 1969). In each, cognitively speaking, the individual is a fundamentally different person.

How do we advance from one cognitive stage to another? To Piaget the answer lay in three interrelated processes: assimilation, accommodation, and equilibration. **Assimilation** involves incorporating new information into old ways of thinking or behaving. Suppose a five-year-old girl thinks that "living things" refers only to animals such as dogs, cats, rabbits, birds, and people (Siegler, 1991). She then takes her first trip to the zoo and sees an elephant. Although her notion of the size of living things has to be modified, she is able to assimilate this new example into her existing understanding. This is not true when the child is later told that a tree is a living thing too. The girl must now **accommodate;** she must fundamentally alter her old way of thinking to adapt to new information. Thus, her concept of living things becomes more abstract as she focuses on such qualities as the abilities to grow and reproduce. Note how this change in thinking restores the child to a state of equilibrium in which the various pieces of her knowledge all fit together. Piaget called this process **equili-**

This infant of about six months has not yet developed the concept of object permanence. She looks intently at a toy elephant that is in front of her, but when the toy is blocked from her view, she gives no indication that she understands that the toy is still present.

This older infant realizes that the disappearance of an object does not necessarily mean that it is no longer present. When a towel shields the object from his view, he crawls under the towel to search for it.

bration. Through accommodation and equilibration this child will advance from Piaget's preoperational period (in which she focuses mainly on the external appearance of things) to the period of concrete operations (in which she can think more abstractly).

Information-Processing Theory Not all psychologists agree with Piaget's stage approach, however. Some believe that many of the contrasts in cognitive ability between younger and older children can be explained not by qualitative differences in how they view reality, but rather by *quantitative differences* in how they process information. By "process information" we mean how children mentally represent what they see and hear, how they operate on that information, and how their memories impose limits on the data they can handle (Siegler, 1986). From this perspective, a ten-year-old's ability to understand concepts that elude a five-year-old is not due to fundamental differences in how the two construct reality. Rather, it is due to the older child's more advanced capacity for processing information, a capacity that emerges gradually, not in an abrupt "giant-step" way.

Both the qualitative and quantitative approaches to cognitive development have some validity. We will consider evidence for each as we explore children's thinking from infancy through the elementary school years.

COMPARING PERSPECTIVES DURING THE EARLY YEARS

Infancy Piaget argued that the central cognitive task of infancy is constructing a view of the world that incorporates a basic understanding of objects and of cause-and-effect relationships. This the child does by exercising what Piaget called sensorimotor intelligence. The term **sensorimotor intelligence** implies that babies do not think abstractly, as older children do. They do not analyze problems, plan out strategies, and wonder what the consequences will be. Instead, babies come to know the world strictly by perceiving and acting in it. Their understanding is derived solely from what they sense and do.

Piaget proposed that an understanding of objects during infancy develops in a series of substages. At first a baby has no awareness that objects have a permanent existence. When a child can no longer perceive something with the senses, it ceases to exist for him or her. Piaget drew this conclusion after observing infants' reactions when an object "disappears." Suppose a toy that has captured a baby's attention is partially hidden from sight by a piece of paper, as shown in the accompanying photo. Piaget noticed that babies up to the age of about four months do not search for the missing toy either with their eyes or with their hands. They act as if it has vanished completely. Piaget interpreted this behavior to mean that babies this young lack any notion of the toy as an enduring entity. By the age of four to eight months, in contrast, infants *do* recognize and reach for partially covered objects. They also look downward to find an object they have dropped, implying that they expect it still to be there. By eight to twelve months infants also search for *totally* covered objects (see photos on page 262).

In some ways, however, babies eight to twelve months old still have an immature concept of objects. Consider what would happen if during the "curtain" game the hourglass were suddenly hidden behind a second towel, still in the child's full view. Babies this age would continue to look for the object behind the *first* towel. They would simply repeat the action that had produced the toy earlier, rather than look for it where it was last seen. It is only by the age of twelve to eighteen months that infants can deal with such displacements. And it is not until the age of eighteen to twenty-four months that children can deal with displacements they have not actually seen (as when a toy hidden in one hand is surreptitiously passed to the other hand). This milestone marks the final stage in acquiring the object concept.

Piaget's descriptions of infants' behavior toward objects have proved to be quite reliable. Babies all over the world have been found to pass through these developmental sequences, searching for hidden objects in predictable ways at different ages. But some researchers have questioned Piaget's conclusions about what these patterns mean. They wonder to what extent it is the child's construction of reality that is shaping his or her behaviors—whether failure to look for a hidden toy necessarily means that the baby sees objects as impermanent things that come and go at random.

One alternative explanation is that infants' behavior in these situations may reflect their memory limitations (Kagan et al., 1978). Imagine a three-month-old shown a toy, which is then hidden by a paper. To find the toy, the baby must hold in mind an image of this briefly viewed object after the paper covers it. Then the child must coordinate that memory with a visual and manual search. This may be beyond the cognitive capabilities of someone so young.

If memory limitations are indeed the major stumbling block in Piaget's object concept studies, how well do babies really grasp the fact that hidden objects do not simply vanish? Some researchers have tried to answer this question with studies that avoid making

When what Piaget called representational thought develops at about two or three years of age, the child becomes able to pretend that one object is another.

young infants conduct a search for a hidden thing. Instead, they show babies possible and impossible events involving objects and record their reactions. In one such study (Baillargeon et al., 1985), five-and-a-half-month-old babies were shown an object that appeared to move through the space occupied by another object that was temporarily hidden from sight. If the infants thought that the temporarily hidden object no longer existed, they should not show surprise when the second object passed through its space. Instead, however, this odd event grabbed the babies' attention, suggesting that they have a sense of objects as solid, permanent things. Follow-up studies have shown that four-and-a-half-month-old infants, and even many babies only three and a half months old, look significantly longer at this impossible event than at one that does not defy the laws of solid objects (Baillargeon, 1987).

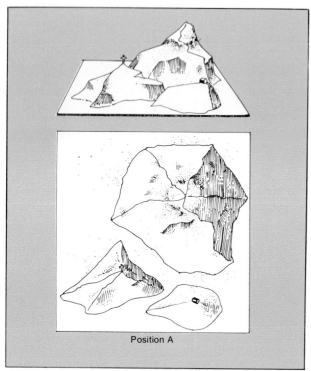

Position A

FIGURE 9.2   A model used to demonstrate egocentrism.
Piaget and Inhelder first had children walk all around
the model and look at it from all sides. Then they seated
children of various ages at position A and asked them
how the scene would appear to observers at other positions. Preoperational children regularly indicated that
the scene would appear as it did from position A, no
matter where the observer was located. Their thinking
did not allow them to reconstruct the scene mentally
from a point of view other than their own. (*After Piaget
and Inhelder, 1956.*)

Such discoveries of previously unsuspected cognitive abilities in infants have emerged in many other
recent experiments. They imply that Piaget's conclusions about cognitive development were not completely right. At the very least, children may possess
the early precursors of certain cognitive abilities at a
younger age than Piaget thought.

The Preschool Period   Between the ages of two
and three, children leave the cognitive world of
infancy far behind. One of the key intellectual accomplishments is **representational thought,** the ability to
represent things mentally when those things are not
present physically. Children can now imagine, and by

doing so, they expand their world far beyond the
limits of their immediate perceptions. One sign that
preschoolers can think representationally is their
ability to imitate someone else's actions long after
they have seen them. Another is their ability to play
"make-believe," pretending, for example, that they
are astronauts and that a large cardboard box is a
spaceship. But the most important indication of representational thought is the ability to use language, an
intellectual accomplishment that greatly expands the
child's powers of reasoning and communication. We
will say much more about the development of language later in this chapter.

As impressive as preschoolers' cognitive advances are, however, they still have cognitive limitations.
One is the fact that their thought is often **egocentric.**
This means that preschoolers do not always understand that different people have different perspectives
and that their own view is merely one among many.
In one demonstration of egocentrism, Piaget and his
colleague showed preschool children a large model
composed of three mountains in a triangular arrangement (see Figure 9.2). After a child had walked
around the model and become familiar with it, he or
she sat in a chair facing one of the mountains. The
experimenter sat in a chair facing another mountain
and asked the child which of several pictures showed
what the *experimenter* saw. Children this age repeatedly chose the picture depicting their own perspective
(Piaget and Inhelder, 1969).

While there is little doubt that preschool youngsters do show egocentrism, psychologists have debated its cause. Piaget believed it is due to a subjectively
structured view of the world. When asked to describe
another person's perspective, Piaget argued, children
this age cannot help but describe their own. But other
psychologists answer that the cause of egocentrism
may lie more in the preschooler's still limited information-processing capabilities. In one study, for instance, preschoolers were asked to hide a Snoopy doll
behind a screen so that an experimenter could not see
it from where she sat (Flavell et al., 1978). Even
two-and-a-half-year-olds were able to do this, suggesting that in certain situations they *can* adopt
another person's perspective. And sometimes they do
so quite cunningly. When no one is watching, a
three-year-old will hide his one-year-old brother's
favorite blanket and then watch as the frustrated baby
searches in vain to find it. Such behavior shows a
sophisticated understanding of the point of view of
others (Dunn, 1988).

Perhaps, then, failure on the mountain-range problem has more to do with the complexity of this particular task. The child, after all, must encode the entire landscape into memory, recall the experimenter's viewpoint, and retain this mental image while considering the various pictures (Huttenlocher and Presson, 1979). Faced with such difficult requirements, most preschoolers may simply fall back on a simple rule: Choose the picture that matches what *I* see.

Middle Childhood Around the time children enter school, they begin to think more logically than younger children do. Piaget felt that the major intellectual accomplishment of middle childhood is the ability to perform what he called **concrete operations.** This term refers to a variety of mental transformations (all of which can be reversed) that the child can carry out on concrete or tangible objects. The ability to perform concrete operations develops between the ages of about six and twelve. An excellent example can be seen in the emergence of what are called **concepts of conservation:** the recognition that certain features of things remain the same (are conserved) despite changes in other features.

Suppose you show a four-year-old two identical short, wide beakers of water and ask the child to say whether beaker 1 or beaker 2 contains more. The child will probably answer correctly that the two beakers contain equal amounts. Now suppose you pour the water from beaker 1 into a third beaker, which is tall and thin. If you now ask the child which beaker contains more water, beaker 1 or beaker 3, the child is very apt to say that beaker 3 has more. The youngster seems to fixate on the height of the water, concluding that the taller one has "more." On the basis of such experiments, Piaget and others have argued that preschoolers lack the concept of conservation of liquid quantity. Children of this age fail to understand that the amount of liquid does not change simply because it is poured into a container of a different shape.

Nor have children this young grasped other concepts of conservation. For instance, if you show a preschooler two parallel rows of six identical-sized marbles, with the marbles in each row touching one another, the child will say correctly that both rows contain an equal number. But if you then spread out the marbles in one row, as shown in Figure 9.3, the child will say that the lengthened row has more, even though the number of marbles remains the same. Psychologists say that the child does not yet under-

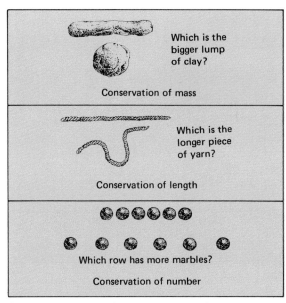

FIGURE 9.3 Conservation problems. Before they reach the stage of concrete operations, children cannot imagine the changes that occur in each of these problems. For example, preoperational children will answer that there are more marbles in the bottom row than in the top one. By age eight, they understand that the lengths and quantities are the same in each case.

stand conservation of number. He or she believes that number can vary with an irrelevant change in appearance, such as an increase in spacing. Parents sometimes take advantage of this error in reasoning. They may spread out a pile of candies, for example, so that preschoolers think they are getting more. Figure 9.3 shows two other conservation problems, conservation of mass and conservation of length, which are also beyond the grasp of children this young.

Older children gradually come to understand concepts of conservation. A girl of eight, for example, will probably be able to coordinate her thoughts about a change in the height of a quantity of water with her thoughts about the width of each container, concluding that thinner compensates for taller. She will also be able to picture the reverse operation mentally: pouring the water back into the original beaker so that its surface is again even with that of the water in the other beaker of the same shape. As a result, she will answer correctly that the amount of water in the two containers remains the same.

Do their differences in performance on conservation tasks mean that preschoolers and older children

After about the age of seven, most children understand that when identical amounts of fluid are poured into two different-sized containers, the amount does not change —"taller" is not necessarily "more." In Piaget's terms, this ability demonstrates the concept of conservation.

have qualitatively different views of reality, different logical structures they apply to the world? Piaget thought so, but other psychologists are not so sure. One piece of evidence against Piaget's conclusion is the existence of inconsistencies in the tasks children can perform. For instance, many youngsters can perform Piaget's conservation-of-number task at age six, yet they cannot perform his conservation-of-mass problem until age eight, nor his test for conservation of weight until age ten (Elkind, 1961; Katz and Beilin, 1976; Miller, 1976). If the ability to understand conservation of number reflects the development of a new, more advanced logical structure, why can't children immediately apply that new understanding to *all* conservation problems? This question has encouraged psychologists to search for additional factors underlying cognitive constraints and change.

Some researchers have wondered if preschoolers may fail traditional conservation tests for reasons that are unrelated to an understanding of conservation. Consider the standard conservation-of-number task. Might some preschoolers say that there are more marbles in the longer row simply because they as-

sume that *more* is a synonym for *longer?* Or might their attention be misdirected when they are instructed to watch as the experimenter spreads out the marbles in one of the rows? So later, when asked again, "Which row has more?," the children may conclude that this is a question about length. Both these explanations are certainly possible. Is either of them right?

Psychologist Rochel Gelman (1972) designed an experiment to test whether preschoolers were in fact deceived by the language or conduct of typical conservation tests. She presented children ages three to six and a half with two plates. On one plate was a row of three toy mice fastened to a strip of Velcro. On the other plate was a row of two toy mice fastened similarly. The children were told that they were about to play a game in which they had to identify the "winning" plate. Gelman pointed to the plate with three mice and said that it would always be the winner. But she never described the plate in any way. The children had to decide for themselves which attributes—the number of mice, the length of the row, the spacing between the mice—made that plate the winner. This was Gelman's way to avoid using the words *more* and *less,* which might have meanings slightly different for preschoolers than for older children.

Now Gelman began her experiment. She covered each plate with a large lid and shuffled them. The child was then asked to pick the lid under which the "winning" plate lay. Whenever the child picked the three-mouse plate, he or she was given a prize. After several rounds of shuffling and picking, Gelman made the critical transformation. She surreptitiously changed the three-mouse display, either by moving the mice closer together or farther apart or by removing one mouse entirely. The fact that these transformations were made covertly was Gelman's way of making sure that she did not call attention to the change and so bias the child's thinking.

Gelman's findings showed that most of the children, even the youngest ones, considered number the relevant attribute differentiating the two plates. Almost no child claimed that a change in the length of the three-mouse row disqualified it as a "winner." Many children, in fact, failed even to notice such a change. In contrast, almost all subjects noticed removal of a mouse from the previously "winning" plate. Many showed great surprise that one of the mice was missing, exclaiming, "Where is it?" "Where'd it go?" "Where'd ya put the threes?" Oth-

According to Case's theory of cognitive development, an infant's capacity for short-term memory is limited. With practice, the baby learns to "chunk," or combine, the steps needed to research for and grasp an object. This frees storage space for other mental tasks, even though total memory capacity has not increased.

ers searched for the vanished toy—under the lids, beneath the table, all around the room. Even more important, the overwhelming majority of children doubted whether a three-mouse plate with one of its mice missing could still be considered a "winner." Over two-thirds said emphatically that the plate had now become a "loser." The only way to fix things, they said, would be to add another mouse. Clearly these children understood that number can be changed only by addition or subtraction—the essence of the conservation concept.

Why did Gelman's youngest subjects perform well on this game but would probably fail if given Piaget's conservation-of-number test? Perhaps the traditional conservation-of-number test is confusing to them for reasons that have nothing to do with a grasp of conservation. If this is the case, the intellectual differences between younger and older children may not be so qualitative as some psychologists believe. At the very least, the beginnings of an understanding of conservation may emerge at an earlier age than Piaget proposed.

CASE'S INTEGRATIVE THEORY

Despite the differences between Piaget's perspective and the information-processing view, these two are not mutually exclusive. In fact, in recent years some psychologists have tried to combine the best of both perspectives into a single integrated theory of cognitive development. One of these psychologists is Robbie Case (1985).

Case believes that children progress through a series of developmental stages. Each of his proposed stages is characterized by the most advanced kind of mental operations that the youngster is able to carry out: sensorimotor operations in infancy, representational operations in the preschool years, and logical operations during middle childhood. In this regard, Case's theory is very similar to Piaget's.

But Case draws heavily on information-processing theory for his ideas about constraints on development, as well as for his explanations of how children progress within and between developmental stages. Here he stresses both limitations and changes in short-term memory capacity. Case argues that, as children mature, the size of their **short-term storage space** increases. By short-term storage space he means the memory capacity available actively to think about problems and work out solutions. Case maintains that the total physical capacity of short-term memory is under fairly strict biological control and does not change much over the years. How, then, does the size of short-term storage space grow? Case's

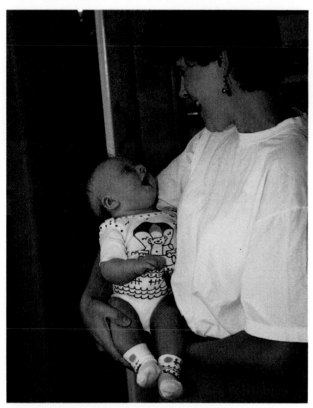

An infant's cooing and babbling are not speech, but they unmistakably represent communication.

mental tasks, allowing the baby to coordinate reaching and grasping with other behaviors. In this way the child makes more storage space available, even though the total capacity of short-term memory is no bigger than before.

The availability of short-term storage space in a given domain (such as reaching and grasping or counting and using numbers) sets limits on a child's ability to construct what Case calls new **executive control structures.** Executive control structures are the child's current ways of representing the world coupled with the child's current strategies for dealing with specific kinds of problems. As youngsters move from one major stage of development to another, they acquire new executive control structures that are fundamentally more advanced than before.

According to Case, a more advanced executive control structure may appear in one domain before another depending on two things: (1) how efficiently short-term storage space is used in each domain, and (2) how complex each new control structure is. This aspect of Case's theory explains seeming inconsistencies in some of the tasks children can do. Even when two tasks involve the same logical insights, they may still differ in the type of executive controls needed to perform them. For instance, a problem in conservation of number has much in common logically with one about conservation of liquid volume. But solving the first merely entails accurate counting (how many marbles are in each row?), whereas solving the second requires consideration of two different dimensions at the same time (how does the decreased width of this water compensate for its increased height?). Thus, a six-year-old who has become efficient at counting has probably freed up enough short-term storage space to acquire the relatively simple executive controls needed to perform conservation-of-number tasks. The same child, however, may not yet be very efficient at dealing with quantities of liquid. As a result, the control structures that conservation-of-liquid-volume tasks require remain beyond the child's current capabilities.

Because it can account for inconsistencies in children's performance, Case's theory has better explanatory power than Piaget's does. This is an example of how science progresses. First, Piaget and his followers put forth an explanation of cognitive development. Next, a group of critics demonstrated problems with that explanation. And finally, Case responded to those critics by modifying Piaget's

answer is that we gradually make more efficient use of the total capacity we have.

Consider an infant who has just learned to reach for and grasp objects. The process of mentally coordinating this series of actions consumes all of the child's short-term storage space. Thus, if you place an object in front of another one that the baby wants to hold, the child is apt to become frustrated. He or she does not have enough working memory available to come up with the solution of first removing the second object before securing the desired one. Gradually, however, the behaviors of reaching and grasping become more efficient, and the child performs them not as a series of separate steps (extend arm, touch object, uncurl fingers, grasp firmly), but rather as a single smooth action. This is a form of *chunking*, which we talked about in Chapter 7, processing smaller pieces of information as a larger single unit. Chunking frees up short-term storage space for other

TABLE 9.2   Milestones in Language Development

Milestone	Approximate Age
Cooing	2 to 3 months
Babbling	By 5 months
First words	10 to 14 months
Ten words in usable vocabulary; comprehends about fifty	12 months
Two-word sentences	21 to 24 months
Two hundred words in vocabulary	24 months

Source: Steinberg and Belsky, 1990.

original explanation. Although Case's theory may not withstand the critical assessment of those who disagree with Piaget's approach in *any* form, it is still important in its effort to combine the best of the Piagetian and the information-processing views.

DEVELOPMENT OF LANGUAGE SKILLS

Thinking and reasoning in increasingly sophisticated ways is far from the only cognitive accomplishment of infancy and childhood. Another is the mastery of spoken language. Listen to these two four-year-olds as they struggle to express themselves:

Girl: [on toy telephone] David!
Boy: [not picking up second phone] I'm not home.
Girl: When you'll be back?
Boy: I'm not here already.
Girl: But *when you'll be back?*
Boy: Don't you know if I'm gone already, I went *before* so I can't talk to you?

(Miller, 1981)

Besides grappling with the idea of past, present, and future, these two children are still learning to phrase questions. Soon they will learn that in an English question the auxiliary verb goes before the subject, and "When you'll be back?" will become "When will you be back?" Another rule of language will be mastered.

Although the human capacity for language begins to develop soon after birth, infants come into the world totally speechless. In fact, the word *infant* comes from the Latin word *infans,* which means "without speech." Yet in a few years all children of normal intelligence are highly skilled speakers and listeners. How does a child progress in so short a period from the newborn's sounds to the mastery of words and sentences?

MILESTONES IN LANGUAGE ACQUISITION

Although children grow up in different cultures, they seem to go through a similar sequence in learning to speak their native language (Bloom, 1970; Brown, 1973). One child may reach a particular stage before another does, but all children learn language in a similar way. (See Table 9.2.)

Prespeech Communication From the earliest weeks of life, the sounds that babies make attract the attention of others and communicate with them. Newborns communicate mainly with their cries, which vary in tone and rhythm depending on what the baby is feeling (hunger, pain, anger, and so forth). Most parents quickly learn to distinguish among these cries, and so they are better able to respond appropriately to the baby's needs (Wolf, 1969).

As infants grow older, they begin to produce more varied sounds. By three months they can coo, which they do both alone and in "conversations" with adults. A mother says something to her baby, who answers with cooing noises and then pauses as if waiting for the mother to reply. By age four months this turn-taking has the structure of a real conversation, with each speaker allowing the other to pause for roughly the same amount of time (Beebe et al., 1988). Interestingly, young babies who experience this turn-taking pattern in verbal exchanges with adults tend to sound different than other babies their age do. More of their vocalizations sound like genuine syllables rather than just coos and gurgles (Bloom, 1988; Bloom et al., 1987). People often remark: "That baby is really *talking!*"

By six or seven months of age infants can babble —that is, chant various syllabic sounds in a rhythmic fashion. Infants' early babbling, a type of play and experimentation, is not limited to the sounds used in their parents' speech. Sometimes they also make sounds that are part of other languages. (The baby of English-speaking parents, for instance, may utter a rolled *r* or a guttural German *ch*.) For the first six months deaf babies babble like children who can hear, a further indication that these early vocalizations are spontaneous and relatively independent of what the child hears. It is only later that children develop the capacity to imitate the sounds that others make.

Although older prespeech babies communicate many things through actions and gestures, they also express themselves through intonation. In one study, the patterns of pitch in the sounds babies made to convey frustration, satisfaction, a question, or a command corresponded closely to the typical adult patterns (Tonkova-Yampol'skaya, 1973). For example, babies seven to ten months old expressed commands with the same sharply rising and falling pitch that adults use: "Stop that!" Some months later, the children began to use the intonation that signifies a question, distinguished by a sharp rise in pitch at the end: "Are you going?" Such intonations are important in helping to convey meaning throughout a person's life.

First Words   By the end of the first year, children know the names of a few people and objects, and they begin to produce their first words. To reach this stage they must understand that sound can be used to express meaning. Simply pronouncing an English word in an appropriate context is not enough. For instance, some prespeech babies, following prompting by adults, say *bye-bye* while waving at someone. But because they do not yet grasp the rather abstract meaning that this string of sounds conveys, it cannot be considered a genuine word. Children's true first words usually refer to the immediately tangible and visible (Nelson, 1973, 1981; Schwartz and Leonard, 1984). They label people, objects, and everyday actions (*dada, car, sit*) and issue simple commands (*down!*). What these words have in common is a focus on the here and now.

This is the stage when children tend to over- and underextend the meanings of words (Clark, 1983; Kuczaj, 1982). A girl who has learned the word *dog* for the family pet may apply it at first to any animal she sees. This is a case of overextension. Conversely, another child may use the word *dog* correctly to label the neighbor's retriever but fail to apply it appropri-

ately when she first encounters a chihuahua. This is a case of underextension. Through over- and underextension and feedback about mistakes, a child gradually develops essentially the same mental representation of *dog* that other speakers of the language possess.

First Sentences   Once children have acquired a basic vocabulary, they are ready for the momentous step of combining words into sentences. But just as the first step on their own feet must await a certain level of motor control, so the emergence of sentences must await a certain level of neurological maturation. This maturation partly involves a rapid increase in the number of synapses that occur in the cerebral cortex around the age of one and a half to two (Milner, 1976).

Children's first sentences are very simple. They are short, usually two words long, and limited largely to concrete nouns and action verbs. Nonessential words, such as articles and conjunctions, are omitted, as are prefixes and suffixes (Brown et al., 1968). The child's talk sounds rather like the terse wording used in telegrams, which is why it is sometimes called **telegraphic speech.** But despite this terseness, people who know the child usually understand what is being said, and they often respond by expanding the child's sentences into well-formed adult ones. Here are examples of a toddler's sentences and his mother's interpretations of them (Brown and Bellugi, 1964):

Child	Mother
Baby highchair	Baby is in the highchair.
Eve lunch	Eve is having lunch.
Throw Daddy	Throw it to Daddy.
Pick glove	Pick up the glove.

Even at this early stage, speech is quite structured. Often toddlers combine words in an order that follows adult syntax. While gobbling a cookie, for instance, a toddler may say, "Eat cookie," correctly putting *cookie* after *eat* (Maratsas, 1983). This tells the listener that the cookie is the object being eaten rather than the actor doing the eating. Not all toddler's sentences are simply reduced versions of adult sentences, however. The sentence "All-gone sticky" (after washing hands) is just one example of the kind of utterances unique to young children. But even though such sentences are not predictable from adult rules, they are predictable from the child's rules.

One way a researcher can know for sure how a young child is interpreting adult sentences is to have the child act the sentences out. This boy has been handed two dolls and a washcloth and asked by an experimenter to "Show me 'The boy is washed by the girl.' " The boy treats this sentence as though it were "The boy washes the girl." The grammatical rules that he has acquired so far are inadequate to process correctly a sentence in the passive voice.

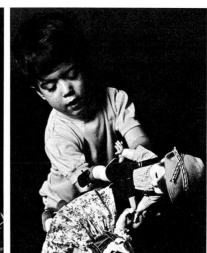

The range of meanings children express with two-word sentences is impressive, from identification ("That Daddy") to location ("Doggy here"), recurrence ("Tickle again"), possession ("My ca"), negation ("No touch"), nonexistence ("All-gone bubble"), agent–action or agent–object ("Mommy throw"/ "Throw ball"), attribution ("Baby little"), and question ("Where kitty?") (Brown, 1973). It seems that sometime prior to their second birthday, children around the world start to put two words together to express the same concepts. These concepts form the core of all human language. Indeed, a large part of later language development is simply a matter of elaborating and refining basic ideas that are already present at this early stage.

Acquiring Complex Rules Two-word sentences are usually difficult to interpret out of context. "Baby chair," for example, could mean "This is the baby's chair," or "The baby is in the chair," or "Put the baby in the chair," or even "This is a little chair." Someone has to be there when the sentence is spoken to know what the child means. The grammatical information contained in adult sentences reduces this dependence on context. The sentence "The baby is in the chair" is unambiguous because of the addition of the verb *is* and the locational preposition *in*. Thus, mastering complex grammatical rules enables the child to communicate beyond the immediate situation.

This stage in the acquisition of language occurs largely between the ages of two and five. By the time they enter school, most children have a good grasp of

the grammar of their native language. This is not to say that children memorize a set of textbook rules. They do not. Even many adults have trouble stating grammatical rules, although they are able to apply them correctly. What children acquire during this period is an implicit sense of how to organize words into increasingly complex sentences. At the same time, their vocabularies grow rapidly. As one expert put it, "Their minds are like little vacuum pumps designed by nature to suck up words" (Miller, 1981, p. 119). A larger vocabulary further facilitates the ability to communicate clearly with language.

Children learn grammatical rules in a fairly predictable order, with little variation from child to child. Certain rules are acquired in gradual steps. A good example is the use of the negative (Bellugi, 1964). Two-year-olds have a very simple rule for forming negative sentences. They simply add *no* at the beginning (or occasionally the end) of a positive statement: "No get dirty." As children grow older, however, this simple rule is often insufficient to express what they wish to say. So they acquire more elaborate rules of negation, rules that build toward the appropriate ones for their native language. In English, a child's next step is to learn to place *no* or *not* just before the verb: "I not get it dirty." The last step is to add the required auxiliary verb: "I won't get it dirty."

As they learn the rules of their language, preschoolers often commit errors of **overregularization:** they overextend a grammatical rule to instances where it does not apply (Bellugi, 1970; Slobin, 1972).

By about age four, children understand the need to adjust their speech to fit the social context. They will speak differently to a younger child than to an adult.

Psychologists are interested in overregularizations because they show that children have noticed general rules of grammar and are trying to apply them. For this reason, overregularizations can be thought of as "smart" mistakes. These smart mistakes are committed by children around the world (Howard, 1983).

Overregularization is the way children learn forms of the past tense in English. At first they use certain irregular past-tense verbs, such as *fell* and *came*, correctly. Each word probably enters their vocabularies as a separate item. But then they learn the rule for forming the regular past tense by adding a *d* or *t* sound to the end of the base, as in *hugged* and *walked*. Once they have acquired this rule, they try to apply it to the irregular verbs as well, and such sentences as "He goed to the store" and "I falled down" begin to appear in their conversations. It may take a year or even longer before these exceptions are finally mastered (Ervin, 1964).

Speech in Social Context: Pragmatics We have concentrated on how children acquire grammar because this is such an important part of early language development. Yet speaking a language involves more than just knowing proper word order and verb tense. People must also use language appropriately within a given social context. Studying how children acquire this ability is part of the field called **pragmatics.**

Researchers have found that children start to shape their use of language to suit the social context at quite an early age. In one study, four-year-olds showed marked differences in the way they went about describing a new toy to a two-year-old and to an adult (Shatz and Gelman, 1973). Figure 9.4 shows the descriptions that one child gave. When addressing the two-year-old, this child used many attention-getting words: "Look," "Watch," "Perry" (the younger child's name). Such attention-getters were not deemed necessary when the child was addressing the adult. The sentences directed to the two-year-old were also shorter and simpler, assuming much less competence. Clearly, this four-year-old knew that different listeners demand different kinds of speech. Although the child's ability to tailor speech to fit the situation will become more skilled in the years ahead, this important principle of language use is established in the preschool years.

EXPLAINING LANGUAGE ACQUISITION

Nativist Theories Why do children acquire language as readily as they do? **Nativist theories** propose that language acquisition is controlled by the genetically programmed development of certain neural circuits in the brain. According to Noam Chomsky (1979), the most influential proponent of the nativist view, the brain has a structure called the language acquisition device (LAD), which automatically analyzes the components of the speech a child hears. This structure is present in all normal humans, but not in other species.

Nativists point to several lines of evidence to support their view. One is the fact that children acquire very different native languages in much the same way (Slobin, 1982). Remember our discussion of the earliest rule that children use to form negative sentences: they simply add "no" at the beginning of a positive statement. In every language studied so far, two-year-olds have been found to use this same rule of negation, even though it is never part of the adult grammar they hear (Slobin, 1973). This suggests that humans are born with innate tendencies to structure language in particular ways. Nativists also point to the fact that different children receive different levels of encouragement for acquiring language. Some parents speak to their babies often, while others do so much less. Some parents regularly expand on what a toddler says, while others provide fewer such learning experiences. Yet despite these different language-learning environments, all children end up acquiring about the same linguistic knowledge at much the same age. Finally, nativists point to the speed with which language is mastered. Between the ages of two and five, children acquire a vocabulary of about 10,000 words. This rapid rate of language acquisition would seem unlikely without some innate propensity to master speech.

Learning Theories But even if humans have a built-in facility for acquiring language, learning mechanisms must also come into play. No child has ever mastered language without regular exposure to speech. This exposure provides vital information that guides language development. Exactly what, however, is involved in the learning process?

Parents often believe that they help their children master language by praising them for correct speech and expressing disapproval of mistakes. In other words, they think they use reinforcement to shape language development. There is some evidence that reinforcement does encourage language learning, but not to the extent that many people assume. When one team of researchers studied tapes of actual parent–child conversations, they found that adults greatly overestimate the roles of praise and criticism in children's acquisition of language (Brown et al., 1968). Parents corrected gross mistakes in a young child's grammar, and they occasionally corrected errors in pronunciation. But in most cases it was the truthfulness of a remark, not the accuracy of the grammar, that elicited approval or rejection. For instance, when one child produced the grammatically perfect sentence, "There's the animal in the farmhouse," the mother corrected her because the building was, in fact, a lighthouse. Most parents pay relatively little attention to grammar as long as they can understand what the child is trying to say and as long as the child's statements conform to reality. Reinforcement, then, cannot be the only mechanism of language learning.

> **Four-year-old to two-year-old:** ...Watch, Perry. Watch this. He's backing in here. Now he drives up. Look, Perry. Look here, Perry. Those are marbles, Perry. Put the men in here. Now I'll do it.
>
> **Four-year-old to adult:** You're supposed to put one of these persons in, see? Then one goes with the other little girl. And then the little boy. He's the little boy and he drives. And then they back up. And then the little girl has marbles....[Questions from adult and responses from child] And then the little girl falls out and then it goes backwards.

FIGURE 9.4   **Speech in social context in a four-year-old.** (*Schatz and Gelman, 1973.*)

Simple imitation cannot be the only mechanism either. All children produce sentences they have never heard before. Children who say "All-gone sticky" or "I seed two mouses" are not mimicking adults. Adults do not speak this way. Even when asked to reproduce exactly what an adult says, a child may make mistakes. Consider this conversation between a little girl and her mother:

Child: Nobody don't like me.
Mother: No, say "Nobody likes me."
Child: Nobody don't like me.
            (*Eight repetitions of this dialogue.*)
Mother: No, now listen carefully; say "*Nobody likes me.*"
Child: Oh! Nobody don't *likes* me.

(McNeill, 1966)

Clearly, this little girl is not imitating her mother directly. She is filtering what she hears through her own linguistic rules.

This is not to say that reinforcement and imitation have no role in language development. Certainly they do. When children learn to say something that other people understand, this experience in itself is reinforcing, because it enables the child to communicate thoughts, needs, and desires. Grammatically correct constructions tend to be repeated not because they are praised by adults, but because they get results.

Similarly, although children do not imitate what adults say exactly, adult modeling does influence the development of grammar. One researcher was able to accelerate two-year-olds' acquisition of certain grammatical forms by providing repeated examples of them (Nelson, 1977). For instance, when a child asked, "Where it go?" the researcher modeled the future tense in responding to the question: "It will go there" and "We will find it." Soon the children began using the new forms in their own speech. Notice how the psychologist in this study was attentive to the children's statements, building on them to get her own points across. Research shows that this style of talking to young children (using what the child says to help model more complex grammar) can significantly facilitate language learning (Rice, 1989). Such learning, of course, is not mechanical. Language learning is part of a creative process in which children come to grasp the rules of speech by screening what others say through their own current levels of understanding.

MEMORY DEVELOPMENT

If you have ever asked a five-year-old to help remember a grocery list, you know how limited a preschooler's memory can be. The child may remember a few things that are especially appealing (cookies and ice cream, for instance), but the rest of the list will probably be forgotten. Yet six or seven years later the same child may be quite adept at memorization. Psychologists wonder what accounts for this marked improvement in memory. Is a preschooler's brain not as able as an older child's? Or does the explanation lie in the different ways younger and older children process information?

CHANGES IN INFORMATION-PROCESSING STRATEGIES

Recent research suggests that information-processing factors may be extremely important. For one thing, younger children use far fewer deliberate strategies for storing and retrieving information than do older children (Flavell and Wellman, 1977). In one study, six-, eight-, and eleven-year-olds viewed pictures of three related objects along with a card that could serve as a memory cue (Kobasigawa, 1974). For example, one group of pictures showed a bear, a monkey, and a camel, while the cue card showed a zoo with three empty cages. The experimenter explicitly related the card to the pictures by pointing out that the zoo is the place where these animals live. Later, some of the children were given the stack of cue cards and asked to recall the three pictures associated with each one. They were told that they could look at

the cards if that would help them remember. Significantly, most of the six-year-olds virtually ignored the cards. They seemed not to grasp the relationship between these cues and the ability to retrieve information. The eleven-year-olds, in contrast, used the cues quite effectively, often recalling all three items associated with a card before moving on to the next one. The eight-year-olds were somewhere in between. They sometimes used the cue cards, but their strategy was more haphazard than that of the older children. It is interesting that when all the children were *required* to use the cue cards, age differences in recall disappeared. Thus, some of the improvements in memory we find as children grow older probably have to do with learning effective storage and retrieval strategies. This is not to say that very young children use no cognitive strategies at all in trying to remember things. Even preschoolers sometimes spontaneously employ deliberate tactics to aid in memory storage and retrieval (DeLoache and Todd, 1988; Wellman, 1987). But these early tactics tend to be quite unsophisticated and therefore have limited effectiveness.

Another information-processing factor that contributes to improved performance is greater familiarity with the items to be recalled. In general, the more familiar material is, the easier it is to remember, and the older children get, the more knowledge and experience they acquire (Chi and Ceci, 1986). This link between familiarity and good memory is related in part to effective storage and retrieval strategies, especially to categorization (organizing things to be remembered into groups, which can then be stored and recalled as chunks). The more a child knows about a particular topic, the easier it is to categorize new information in this fashion, thus reducing the demands placed on memory.

CHANGES IN METACOGNITION

If you asked preschoolers to study a set of pictures until they were sure they could remember each and every one, you would probably find that they greatly overestimated their ability to remember the drawings. A quick look through the stack and a preschooler may announce, "I'm ready," only to make a dismal showing on the subsequent recall test. An older child, in contrast, is much more apt to *know* when he or she has fully memorized a list. This ability to monitor one's own thoughts—whether on a memory test, a problem-solving task, or some other cognitive activity—is called **metacognition.** It is another important intellectual capacity that emerges in middle childhood. Of course, even young children have *some* understanding of their own memory powers. For instance, four-year-olds realize that adults can recall more information than they can, and they also realize that it is easier to remember a short list of items than a long list (Wellman et al., 1981). But older children have much more accurate and realistic understanding of their memories than younger children do (e.g., Yussen and Berman, 1981).

Studies have shown how dramatic these age-related metacognitive differences can be. In one of them, first, second, and third graders were asked to evaluate a set of oral instructions about how to play a card game (Markman, 1977). The instructions were lacking a vital piece of information, so no one could possibly understand them. Yet most of the first graders assured the researcher that the instructions were perfectly clear. Only when they tried to play the game did they realize the problem. Most of the third graders, in contrast, spotted the blatant gap in the instructions far sooner.

Perhaps the younger children failed to process the instructions deeply enough—by trying to imagine them being carried out, for example. There is evidence suggesting that this is the case. In one study, researchers asked children where a good place would be to leave a note reminding themselves to visit a friend on the way to school (Fabricius and Wellman, 1983). It was not until fifth grade that youngsters consistently realized that leaving the note in their desk at school was not a good idea if the visit was to be made *before* school. Apparently, the youngest children were either unwilling or unable to imagine themselves enacting the visit.

What explains these age-related differences in the monitoring of thought processes? One answer may be younger children's limited exposure to metacognitive techniques such as self-testing or enacting an event in their minds. When researchers encourage young children to use metacognitive processes, they perform better on certain cognitive tasks (Brown and Kane, 1988). It is unlikely that differences in experience alone provide a full explanation. Very young children who are taught metacognitive strategies often quickly forget them or fail to use them in subsequent situations. Thus, there are probably age-related constraints on the development of metacognition.

Young children are likely to overestimate their ability to remember—insisting, for example, that they can recall an entire set of pictures after glancing at them once.

COGNITIVE DEVELOPMENT IN ADOLESCENCE AND ADULTHOOD

THE COGNITIVE SKILLS OF ADOLESCENTS

Around the beginning of adolescence a new set of cognitive capabilities starts emerging. For the first time children can carry out systematic tests to solve problems. They also become able to think hypothetically and in abstract terms. These cognitive changes, which Piaget called **formal operations,** herald the onset of adultlike thinking.

Piaget created many tests to measure formal operations. One involves four beakers of colorless, odorless liquids labeled 1, 2, 3, and 4, plus a smaller bottle, labeled *g*, also containing a colorless, odorless liquid (Piaget and Inhelder, 1969). The subjects are given some empty glasses and asked to find the liquid or combination of liquids that will turn yellow when a few drops from bottle *g* are added. The combination that produces the yellow color is 1 plus 3 plus *g*. The liquid in beaker 2 is plain water and has no effect on the reaction, and the liquid in beaker 4 prevents the yellow from appearing. To make these discoveries

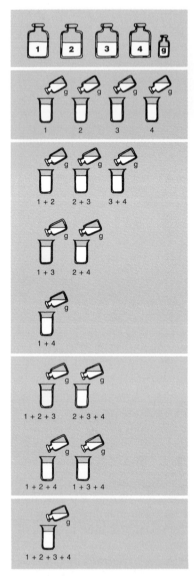

FIGURE 9.5 A problem that requires the systematic examination of hypotheses for its resolution. The chemicals selected by Piaget and Inhelder for this problem have unexpected interactions. It is virtually impossible to determine how the color yellow is produced without trying every possible combination of the liquids, as shown here, and keeping track of the results. Not until children reach the formal-operational period can they conceive of such a procedure. (*After Piaget and Inhelder, 1969.*)

Premise 1:	If Rupert is a dog, then Rupert walks on four legs.
Premise 2:	Rupert is not a dog.
Conclusion:	Rupert does not walk on four legs.

FIGURE 9.6 When adults are asked to judge whether the reasoning displayed in arguments such as this one is correct, over 75 percent answer that it is. In fact, the conclusion is incorrect. One cannot say from the information given in the premises whether Rupert walks on four legs or not. Rupert may be a cat or a human, so the conclusion given here does not necessarily follow from the premises. (*Brainerd, 1978.*)

and to be certain of them, the subjects must try all the possible combinations shown in Figure 9.5.

When presented with this task, elementary school children often begin by systematically trying out all the single possibilities. They may test 1 plus *g*, then 2 plus *g*, then 3 plus *g*, then 4 plus *g*. When none of these produces yellow, they are likely to say, "I tried them all and none of them works." With a little prompting from the experimenter, they may realize that more than one liquid can be combined with *g*. But they then mix the liquids haphazardly and often become confused. Most adolescents, in contrast, can

consider all possible combinations systematically. They may need a paper and pencil to keep track of those they have tried, but they nevertheless understand how to generate the full set.

Although Piaget's conclusions about the emergence of formal operations seem reasonable enough, not all researchers have been able to verify them. Consider the problem in Figure 9.6. It is a task in logical reasoning that, according to Piaget, many adolescents should be able to solve. Yet research shows that only between 5 and 25 percent of adolescents, college students, and college-educated adults manage to give the right answer (Brainerd, 1978). Large proportions of teenagers and adults also fail on other formal operations (Donaldson, 1984; Gardner, 1985; Wason and Johnson-Laird, 1972). Piaget was aware that such failures occur, but he offered an explanation for them. He argued that just because a person has reached the stage of formal operations, it does not necessarily mean that he or she will always reason logically. A person may misunderstand the demands of a particular problem or find its solution too difficult. Many adults, in fact, may be capable of using formal thinking only in their own areas of expertise (Ault, 1983).

Piaget believed that the stage of formal operations was a fundamentally new way of understanding the world. According to him, teenagers are, mentally speaking, very different beings than elementary school children. Teenagers, in Piaget's view, have overcome the cognitive limitations of middle childhood and are now free to think and reason in more advanced ways. Not all psychologists agree with this perspective, however (Keating, 1980, 1988). Some feel that the changes we observe in adolescents' performance on formal-operational tasks may be due simply to having gradually acquired better information-processing skills. These skills include the regular use of memory storage and retrieval tactics, as well as a tendency to consistently monitor one's own ideas and thoughts. How much of teenagers' cognitive performance is accounted for by such factors is still open to debate. Certainly, information-processing skills *do* improve during adolescence, a fact that undoubtedly affects what teenagers can do.

IN DEPTH

Do Cognitive Differences Develop between the Sexes?

Brian scored a 770 on the math SAT this year. Any high school senior would be delighted with this accomplishment, but Brian's achievement is particularly impressive because he is only thirteen years old. He has just finished the seventh grade and is now attending a summer camp for mathematically gifted youth. If you eavesdropped on him and his friends in the dining hall one evening, you would hear a peculiar mix of talk about skateboards and Nintendo combined with debate over how best to approach the most difficult calculus problems in tonight's homework assignment. You would also notice that these gifted youngsters are predominantly male. In fact, the male-to-female ratio is 13 to 1.

Brian's case conforms to our stereotyped notions about gender differences in cognitive skills. Most people think of males as being more "mathematical" than females, while they think of females as being more "verbal" than males. Is there any truth to these stereotyped assumptions about the sexes? This question is so intriguing to many people that we will explore it in depth.

THE INITIAL STUDIES

In 1974 researchers Eleanor Maccoby and Carol Jacklin published an influential book on the psychology of sex differences. After reviewing many studies, they concluded that cognitive differences between the sexes exist in three areas: verbal abilities, mathematical abilities, and spatial abilities (tasks such as mentally rotating a figure or creating a map fall into this last category). In keeping with traditional ideas about the sexes, Maccoby and

Research has shown that, contrary to widespread popular opinion, boys are not somehow innately "better" at mathematics than girls.

Jacklin found that females have an edge in certain verbal abilities, while males have an advantage in certain mathematical and spatial skills. Interestingly, too, many of these cognitive differences did not emerge reliably until early adolescence.

Maccoby and Jacklin's conclusions were widely publicized. Most often, they were reported in summary fashion, just as they are here, without any discussion of the extensive data that Maccoby and Jacklin analyzed. When presented in this manner, it appears that cognitive differences between the sexes are both consistent and very significant. A high school guidance counselor who read such a summary might easily conclude that boys are indeed well suited for careers in math and engineering, while girls are better at jobs that entail working with words. But are these assumptions valid? To what extent do actual research findings support such gender stereotypes?

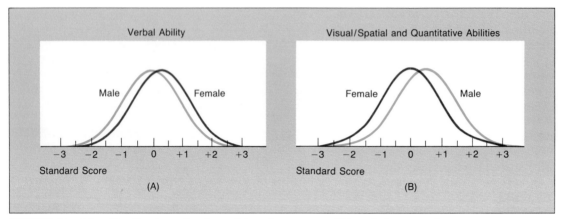

FIGURE 9.7   The distribution of male and female scores on (A) verbal tests and (B) tests of visual–spatial and quantitative skills. On both kinds of tests the differences are very small. (*After Frankel, 1988.*)

CRITICISMS, ALTERNATIVES, AND FURTHER RESEARCH

A look at the studies that Maccoby and Jacklin reviewed show that cognitive differences between the sexes are really quite variable. Consider the differences regarding performance on tasks that require a person to visualize spatial relationships. Of the thirty such studies that Maccoby and Jacklin analyzed, nine had differences favoring males, two had differences favoring females, and nineteen reported *no* significant gender differences (Frankel, 1988). Thus, when sexual differences appeared, they were indeed more likely to show that males perform somewhat better on such tasks, but by far the most common outcome in these studies was a lack of any differences at all. A male advantage was, in short, far from universal.

It is also the case that any differences we find in the cognitive skills of the two sexes are small in absolute terms. Figure 9.7 shows the distributions of male and female scores on verbal tests and on visual-spatial and quantitative ones. Notice how much the curves overlap and how close together the means (the peaks of the curves) are. Such differences are much too slight to allow us to predict the cognitive performance of any given person based on that person's sex alone. In fact, the sex of a person accounts for less than 5 percent of the overall variability in performance on tests of visual-spatial abilities, and only a scant 1 percent of the variability on verbal tests (Hyde, 1981; Hyde and

Linn, 1986). Some researchers feel that differences of this size are too small to be very meaningful (Caplan et al., 1985).

Moreover, male–female gaps in cognitive abilities have been closing in recent years. Some researchers now report *no* gender differences in scores on tests of verbal abilities, and gender differences in quantitative skills are becoming much, much smaller (Feingold, 1988; Hyde and Linn, 1988). This suggests that at least some of the former gender differences in cognitive performance were caused by differences in what males and females were traditionally encouraged to learn. Inherited differences between males and females simply do not change this fast. As two researchers have put it, the former gender gaps in cognitive abilities are now closing faster than the gene can travel (Rosenthal and Ruben, 1982).

One big exception to the general rule of disappearing cognitive differences between the sexes is the gender gap that remains at the highest levels of performance on tests of high school math. When mathematically gifted youngsters like Brian are given the math SAT (the Scholastic Aptitude Test, normally used as a college entrance exam), *thirteen* times more boys than girls score 700 or higher by the age of thirteen (Holden, 1987). But such ratios are to be expected when we look at extremes in performance. In Figure 9.7B, the male distribution extends slightly farther to the right, meaning that there is a certain *extremely* high level of performance reached exclusively by a small number of boys. This is not to say that some girls do not score very high as well. Of course they do. But if we consider only those youngsters who score beyond some rare extreme, the resulting sample is bound to be made up mostly of males. The danger here is when people try to make generalizations about the whole population based on what we find at the extremes. At the vast majority of levels on tests of mathematics, male–female performances are very much the same, which is why the two curves overlap so much.

PATTERNS AND CONCLUSIONS

A fascination with male–female differences is widespread in our society, perhaps the world over (Jacklin, 1989; Doyle and Paludi, 1991). People love to talk about the ways the sexes differ, including any differences in their cognitive abilities. This fascination can cause us to give more importance to gender differences than they really merit. Male–female differences in cognitive performance are by no means great. A few, however, are fairly reliable, which is why psychologists continue to study them and try to understand their causes.

One theory of why males have a small advantage in spatial abilities and higher mathematics has to do with differences in male and female hormones at puberty. This is the time when boys undergo a surge of male sex hormones, which could affect their developing brains so as to facilitate certain skills. Remember that the male edge in spatial abilities and higher mathematics doesn't really come into its own until adolescence. This fact could be explained if differences in hormones were at least partly responsible for the gender gap. In keeping with this theory, one longitudinal study found that the more masculinized adolescents become physically (due to the presence of male hormones), the better their spatial abilities (Petersen, 1976). On the other hand, it could simply be that the more masculine looking a teenager is, the more people think that he or she *ought* to be good at tasks traditionally considered the province of males, and so they encourage these skills (Eccles et al., 1983). Hopefully, future research will help to sort out such alternative explanations of the gender differences that still exist in cognitive abilities.

COGNITIVE CHANGE DURING ADULTHOOD

As most people know, cognitive development does not end at adolescence. Most people proceed through broadly similar sequences of intellectual change from early to middle to later adulthood.

Early adulthood (from age twenty to roughly age forty) is a time of peak intellectual performance. On any kind of learning or memory task, young adults usually do better than they ever have before. And if success at a task depends on how fast it is done, they probably do a little better than they ever will again. Early adulthood also tends to be the time when people are most intellectually flexible. They can usually accept new ideas quite easily, and they can readily shift their strategies for solving problems.

Provided a person remains healthy, verbal skills and reasoning ability are likely to get even better during middle adulthood—roughly the years between ages forty and sixty. Long-term studies of intellectual performance find that IQ generally increases into middle age (Eichorn et al., 1981; Kangas and Bradway, 1971). And since middle-aged adults continue to learn and store new information, they are often more knowledgeable than they were in their younger years (Schaie, 1984). In addition, the ability to think flexibly, to shift one's mental set to solve a problem, is likely to be as good as it was in early adulthood. When declines in flexible problem solving occur, they do so very gradually, achieving no practical importance until the sixth decade of life or later (Schaie, 1984). Only when people are asked to do tasks involving hand–eye coordination do they tend to perform less well than they used to. This is because motor skills often decline in middle age (Baltes and Schaie, 1974). In all other ways, however, adults in their middle years remain in their intellectual prime.

What about cognitive skills after the age of sixty? Do they decline in late adulthood, as many people assume? Most recent findings on this topic are quite encouraging. For one thing, the average age at which measurable declines in cognitive abilities occur is much greater than most people think. In some studies such declines have not been detected until the mid-seventies (Schaie, 1989). Nor does the detection of some cognitive declines with advancing years mean that *all* of a person's cognitive abilities are becoming poorer. For most elderly people, at least some of their cognitive skills remain as good as ever. Consider short-term memory, for example. The capacity of

A decline in cognitive ability does not necessarily accompany aging. Deficits that do occur in elderly people are often the result of environmental factors such as isolation and depression.

short-term memory—the amount of information it can hold—remains virtually the same as people grow older (Craik and Byrd, 1982). When short-term memory decrements are found among the elderly, they are usually extremely slight.

A somewhat different picture emerges, however, when we consider long-term memory, for many elderly people do experience some decline in this area of performance. In one study, for example, researchers tested the memories of nearly 2,000 people for a tense, fast-paced film clip from the movie Z (Loftus et al., 1991). This study took place in a science museum in San Francisco. Visitors viewed the film clip on a large screen near the museum entrance. Then later, when they had made their way to the memory exhibit, they were asked ten questions about what they had seen. The researchers found that people over age sixty-five answered fewer questions about the clip correctly than did subjects in any other age group. The average score for all the other age groups was 74 percent right, whereas the average score for the elderly was only 56 percent.

But such age-related declines in long-term memory performance can be compensated for. For instance, when elderly people are given extra time to learn and recall information, they perform much better than they do under pressure (Canestrari, 1963;

Eidorfer et al., 1963; Monge and Hultsch, 1971). And when people are specifically advised to use mnemonic strategies, the elderly sometimes profit more than the young do, again narrowing the gap between them (Craik and Simon, 1980; Erber et al., 1980; Perlmutter and Mitchell, 1982). Such findings have led some researchers to suggest that any long-term memory advantage of young over old has more to do with younger people's quicker response times, greater knowledge of test-taking tactics, and so forth than it does with physiologically based differences in long-term memory per se (Datan et al., 1987; Reese and Rodeheaver, 1985).

This is not to say that there are no physiologically based differences in memory performance between young and old. When people receive extensive practice in remembering lists using the method of loci (a mnemonic technique discussed in Chapter 7), elderly subjects usually reach the limits of improvement sooner than college students do, which probably has something to do with the physiological limits of the aging brain (Kliegl et al., 1989). Most elderly people, however, are perfectly capable of becoming virtual experts in long-term memory storage and retrieval. Thus, in everyday life any limits to their abilities at the upper reaches of memory performance would not have any practical significance.

Memory abilities among the elderly, then, are nowhere near as poor as many people believe. Although the elderly themselves will usually tell you that their memories are not what they used to be, this assessment is often due more to negative assumptions about aging than it is to genuine memory declines (Hultsch et al., 1987; Tavris, 1987). In fact, some elderly people suffer no measurable decline in cognitive functioning whatsoever (Schaie, 1984; 1990). If there is one indisputable fact about aging, it is that its effects are widely varied. Psychologists are eager to learn why.

Biology is one factor underlying intellectual performance in later adult life. Identical twins are more alike in their cognitive functioning some forty or more years after finishing school than are unrelated individuals or even fraternal twins (Jarvik, 1975). Of course, these similarities do not necessarily mean that people have a genetically programmed timetable for aging (Fries and Crapo, 1981). It may be that what identical twins share is a predisposition toward, or resistance to, certain degenerative diseases, which in turn affect cognitive functioning. But whatever the link, biology appears to account for at least some of the wide variation in cognitive decline among the elderly.

Equally important, however, are environmental factors. Conditions that promote loneliness and de-pression can contribute to cognitive deficits (Miller, 1975). So can mere expectations of intellectual decline with aging, for there is some evidence that actual performance often mirrors people's expectations (Perlmutter, 1983). The amount of stimulation in a person's environment also appears to be critical (Dutta et al., 1986; Gribbin et al., 1980). If older people keep active and involved in interesting and challenging activities—if, in short, they continue to *use* their minds—their intellectual powers will very likely not be blunted at all.

An interesting, challenging environment even seems able to reverse cognitive declines that have already occurred. In one study, researchers selected over a hundred people ages sixty-four to ninety-five, all of whom had shown a decline in cognitive performance over the previous fourteen years (Schaie and Willis, 1986). These elderly subjects were then given five one-hour training sessions on either inductive reasoning or spatial problem solving. In a substantial number of cases, the training totally erased cognitive declines that had previously occurred in those areas. Such findings encourage a critical look at cognitive deficits in the aged. Although these deficits may seem to be caused by physical deterioration, in fact the cause may often be disuse. If so, relatively simple intervention programs may be able to eliminate the problem.

SUMMARY

1. The branch of psychology that seeks to describe and explain the regular patterns of growth and change that occur during the life cycle is called **developmental psychology.** Answers to the "why" of human development are generally sought in two interacting factors: **heredity** and **environment.** Efforts to determine the relative contributions of heredity and environment to human differences in thought and behavior belong to a field called **behavioral genetics.**

2. Human infants are born with impressive perceptual, motor, and learning capabilities. They process information and interact with their surroundings from the very first moments after birth. These early interactions in turn help to shape the child's cognitive, social, and emotional development.

3. Two major views of cognitive development have been proposed. One, which is closely associated with Jean Piaget, sees cognitive development as a series of qualitatively different stages. In each stage the child's construction of reality becomes more mature. The second view, which stems from the information-processing perspective, argues that quantitative differences in children's cognitive skills and knowledge account for the changes we see.

4. Piaget believed that infants exercise **sensorimotor intelligence.** They come to know the world strictly by perceiving and acting in it, not through any abstract kind of thinking. Then, in the preschool years, youngsters become capable of **representational thought,** the ability to represent things mentally when those things are not physically present. Intellect is still limited in some respects, however. For instance, in many cases preschoolers are quite **egocentric;** they fail to take into account the perspectives of

others. Piaget felt that the major intellectual accomplishment of middle childhood was the ability to perform **concrete operations,** a variety of reversible mental transformations carried out on tangible objects. One example involves **concepts of conservation,** the recognition that some characteristics of objects remain the same (are conserved) despite changes in other features.

5. Some psychologists have questioned Piaget's account of how thinking and reasoning develop. One reason is the existence of inconsistencies in the kinds of tasks children can perform. For instance, if six-year-olds can perform conservation-of-number tasks, why can't they solve conservation-of-mass or -weight problems until they are two to four years older? One answer is that changes in children's thinking and reasoning have as much to do with quantitative advances in such factors as short-term memory as they do with qualitative advances in how youngsters structure reality. Robbie Case is one psychologist who has recently tried to integrate this information-processing viewpoint with the stage approach of Piaget.

6. Besides making impressive advances in thinking and reasoning, young children also master spoken language. Children of all cultures appear to go through similar sequences in acquiring language. By the age of one, most produce their first words, often over- or underextending the meaning until the underlying concept is grasped correctly. Around age two, children begin to use what is known as **telegraphic speech**—short sentences made up of nouns and action verbs. The ability to organize words into increasingly complex sentences develops most prominently between the ages of two and five. Children seem to acquire an implicit knowledge of grammatical rules in a fairly stable order. By the end of the preschool years they also display some understanding of how speech should be modified to suit different social contexts.

7. Children acquire language as readily as they do because of a number of interrelated factors. Some of these are processes of learning, such as learning through reinforcement and observational learning. It is doubtful, however, that these learning processes alone can account for the rapid pace and highly predictable order seen in language development. Most likely the human brain has specialized regions that automatically analyze the components of speech a child hears, thus greatly facilitating language learning.

8. During childhood, people also become increasingly adultlike in their memory capabilities. This is partly because they learn to use more effective encoding and retrieval strategies, and partly because they are more familiar with the information to be recalled. Over the years youngsters also develop an increasingly sophisticated capacity for **metacognition,** the ability to monitor their own thoughts.

9. Around the beginning of adolescence, people start to be able to carry out systematic tests and to think hypothetically and abstractly. Piaget called this the ability to understand **formal operations.** In various tests of formal operations, however, teenagers and adults often fail to perform well. This suggests that even when people are capable of logical reasoning, they may not apply it in all situations.

10. Although people often think of males and females as having different cognitive abilities, in fact such gender differences are really very small. Males have a slight edge in certain spatial skills and in higher mathematics, while females have a slight advantage on certain verbal tasks. In recent years these gender gaps have been narrowing, however.

11. Cognitive development continues throughout adulthood, as knowledge and experience expand. Intellectual abilities do not usually decline sharply in old age, as many people fear. In fact, cognitive decline with aging is by no means inevitable. There is wide variation among individuals due to both biology and environment. Providing a more stimulating and challenging environment even seems to reverse many cognitive declines.

SUGGESTED READINGS

Bjorklund, D. F. (1989). *Children's thinking: Developmental function and individual differences.* Pacific Grove, CA: Brooks/Cole. This book provides a good grounding in the basics of cognitive development by clearly describing theories and research regarding how children think. Research findings are also applied to the tasks of raising and educating children.

Bower, T. G. R. (1989). *The rational infant: Learning in infancy.* San Francisco: Freeman. A well-known developmental psychologist demonstrates that infants are far more rational in their exploration of the world than is often assumed. This book describes both classic studies and contemporary findings, including those of the author.

Doyle, J. A., and Palud, M. A. (1991). *Sex and gender* (2nd ed.). New York: William C. Brown. A current research-based view of sex and gender. Includes a discussion of how social institutions play a central role in thinking about gender.

Kail, R. (1990). *The development of memory in children.* San Francisco: Freeman. A general text on memory development that covers both classic studies and important contemporary research. Memory is treated as a process that is basic to all cognitive and social activities.

Stern, D. (1990). *Diary of a baby.* New York: Harper Collins. Stern's style of describing events in an infant's life from both the observer's and the child's perspectives is an intriguing approach which makes his book informative yet personal. The chapters detail events such as eating and interacting with others while integrating scientific research into an easy-to-read text.

CHAPTER 10

SOCIAL AND PERSONALITY DEVELOPMENT

My mother had a good deal of trouble with me but I think she enjoyed it. She had none at all with my brother Henry, who was two years younger than I, and I think that the unbroken monotony of his goodness and truthfulness and obedience would have been a burden to her but for the relief and variety which I furnished in the other direction.

MARK TWAIN, *Autobiography*

People everywhere are fascinated by personality differences. Even children in the same family, such as Mark Twain and his brother, can be so startlingly different that we wonder how such differences could arise. Some of the reasons psychologists give are explored in this chapter, which deals with both social and personality development. By **social development** we mean how a person's interactions and relationships with others change as that person grows older. By **personality development** we mean the emergence of distinctive styles of thought, feeling, and behavior which make each human being a unique individual. Personality and social development are closely interconnected. How you interact with others can affect who you become (that is, your distinctive styles of behavior), and your distinctive styles of behavior can, in turn, affect the nature of your social relationships.

We will say more about the origins of personality in Chapter 13, which is devoted entirely to personality theories and research. In this chapter we lay some groundwork by looking at social and personality development during the various stage of life, from infancy to old age. First, however, we give a broad overview of the major perspectives in this area of psychology.

PERSPECTIVES ON SOCIAL AND PERSONALITY DEVELOPMENT

One of the earliest perspectives on social and personality development was the psychoanalytic theory of Sigmund Freud. Freud believed that the first five years of life significantly shape later development. For Freud the key factor was how a person deals with various sexual and aggressive urges during childhood. You will learn much more about Freud's theory in Chapter 13. In this chapter we will discuss only selected aspects of his views.

Erik Erikson, a contemporary psychoanalyst, rejected Freud's belief that the resolution of sexual and

TABLE 10.1   Erikson's Eight Stages of Psychosocial Development

Developmental Challenge	Possible Outcomes
Birth to one year: Basic trust versus mistrust	Babies learn to trust others to satisfy their basic needs. Those who receive neglectful or inconsistent care grow to mistrust people.
One to three years: Autonomy versus shame and doubt	Children start to be independent by mastering simple tasks. Those who fail to develop this autonomy doubt themselves and feel shame.
Three to six years: Initiative versus guilt	Children take intiative in trying out new activities. When this initiative brings them into conflict with others, guilt may arise. Too much guilt can inhibit initiative, so children must learn to balance initiative against others' desires and needs.
Six years to puberty: Industry versus inferiority	Children must learn the skills of their culture. Those whose industry enables them to do so develop a sense of mastery and self-assurance. Those who fail at this task feel inferior.
Adolescence: Identity versus role confusion	Adolescents must develop a personal identity, an integrated sense of who they are as distinct from other people. Those who fail to do so feel confused about their future roles.
Early adulthood: Intimacy versus isolation	Young adults strive to form intimate friendships and fall in love with another person. Those who fail feel lonely and isolated.
Middle adulthood: Generativity versus stagnation	Middle-aged adults achieve generativity if they develop a sense of responsibility to guide the next generation and be meaningfully productive in their work. Those who do not become bored, self-indulgent, and stagnant.
Old age: Self-integrity versus despair	Older people achieve a sense of self-integrity if they can look back on their lives and see them as productive and satisfying. If instead they view their lives as wasted, they feel despair.

Adapted from Sroufe and Cooper, 1988, p. 33.

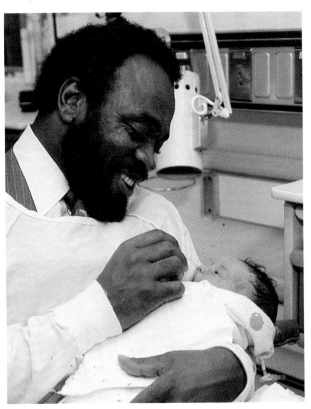

Thousands of unwanted babies were born in Romania during the harsh rule of dictator Nicolae Ceausescu, who prohibited abortion and all forms of birth control in order to increase his country's population. Abandoned in orphanages (*left*), these children may never develop the basic trust in other people that Erikson considered crucial to healthy development. Babies whose needs are consistently and lovingly met (*right*) have a much more secure foundation.

aggressive urges during childhood form the roots of personality. Instead, he proposed a set of nonsexual challenges that people face at each of eight stages from infancy to old age. The family and other social settings are the arenas in which these challenges unfold. Each challenge has an outcome, either favorable or unfavorable, which affects a person's social and personality development. A favorable outcome results in positive outlooks and feelings, which in turn make it easier to cope with subsequent challenges. An unfavorable outcome, in contrast, leaves a person troubled and at a disadvantage in future developmental stages. Table 10.1 summarizes Erikson's eight challenges and the two possible outcomes for each one.

Looking more closely at one of these challenges and how it might be resolved will help you to understand Erikson's theory better. Consider the first of Erikson's eight stages. In the first year of life,

children are totally dependent on others to take care of them, so the major issue they face is whether their needs will be met adequately. Many infants' needs *are* met promptly, consistently, and with affection. According to Erikson, such babies learn to trust other people, to see them as reliable and loving. As a result, they have a foundation of confidence when they begin to seek autonomy in their second and third years of life (Erikson's next stage). In contrast, babies who are neglected, or whose needs are met inconsistently, will come to *mistrust* others. Erikson believed that they will be insecure in their subsequent strivings toward independence, and perhaps also in their dealings with others at later points in development.

Another view of social and personality development is the social learning perspective. Unlike Erikson and Freud, with their focus on people's inner challenges and conflicts, social learning theorists look to the external environment for factors that shape behavior. According to them, social and personality development results from the same processes of learning we discussed in Chapter 6. One such process is observational learning. Social learning theorists say we are constantly observing how other people act, and sometimes we imitate the behaviors we see, especially when the people observed are ones we love and admire. Thus, a little boy may learn to be sympathetic toward an injured playmate by imitating how his parents act toward *him* when *he* is hurt. At the same time, the parents may praise such acts of kindness (a form of reward) and rebuke uncaring behavior (a form of punishment). To social learning theorists, then, personality and social behavior are largely the products of what people learn from their interactions with others.

A fourth view of social and personality development is the cognitive developmental perspective. It argues that a child's understanding of the world changes with age, and that the understanding which exists at any given stage in development significantly affects behavior. For instance, children are not born with the understanding that they are boys or girls. Understanding this aspect of their world does not begin until about the age of two. According to the cognitive developmental perspective, as this new understanding emerges it has important effects on how children act. Boys begin to act more "boyishly" than they did before, while girls begin to act more "girlishly." In the cognitive developmental view this is because new knowledge of what is "right" for boys and girls is influencing the children's behavior.

Finally, social and personality development can be viewed from a biological perspective—that is, as partly the product of inherited biological tendencies. Some of these tendencies are shared by all human beings as a result of their common evolutionary history. One example is the young infant's tendency to smile at human faces. Babies around the world develop this behavior at approximately the same age, suggesting that it is not something parents *teach* their infants to do. Psychologists with a biological perspective search for ways that innate behaviors like this one help people adapt to their environments and flourish in them. At the same time, biologically oriented researchers try to assess the extent to which individual differences in personality and social behavior can be attributed to genetic differences.

In the following sections you will read about all of the various perspectives we have outlined here.

Rather than trying to decide which of them is right, think of them as complementary viewpoints. Each adds valuable ideas about how human social and personality development unfolds.

SOCIAL AND PERSONALITY DEVELOPMENT IN INFANCY

THE BEGINNINGS OF SOCIAL RELATIONSHIPS

Robert was a well-muscled, well proportioned baby who was active right after delivery. . . . Everyone in the delivery room was struck with how competent and controlled this alert little boy was just moments after birth. His father leaned over, talking to him in one ear. Immediately, Robert seemed to grow still, turning his head to the sound of the voice, his eyes scanning for its source. When he found his father's face, he brightened as if in recognition. His father said, "Oh, what a great, big handsome boy!" He picked Robert up to handle him. As he was cuddled, Robert turned his body into his father's chest and seemed to lock his legs around one side of his father. Robert reached up to grasp and hold onto his father's gown, looking up into his face. By this time, his father was about to burst with pride and delight. When he put Robert up on his shoulder, the brand-new, still-slippery baby nestled against his father, his legs still seeming to hold on, his hands and arms up on his father's shoulder, his head cocked and nestling into the crook of his father's neck. His beaming father pulled him even closer to contain and cuddle him. (Brazelton and Cramer, 1990, pp. 76–77)

A major task of infancy is to acquire social competence—that is, to learn to engage in the reciprocal give-and-take of social relationships. This task seems enormous when you consider that at birth a child does not even know that other people exist. Fortunately, however, babies have an inherent tendency to respond to the faces and voices of others in ways that induce not only social interaction, but nurturance and protection too (Bowlby, 1969). What is it about a baby's appearance and behavior that helps to set these important processes in motion?

The social smile is an infant's irresistible invitation to interaction with the parent.

Adults respond lovingly to infants partly because of their inherent "cuteness." This cuteness is a product of the baby's round face, chubby cheeks, and large, wide-open eyes. Robert was an especially cute infant, particularly for a newborn. Undoubtedly, his big searching eyes and soft, babyish features were part of what made his father want to cuddle him. In addition, just by looking at the sight and sound of his father, Robert increased his chances for social interaction. This is because adults are prone to talk to and smile at an infant who reinforces their attention by looking back. In a few more weeks, Robert will start to stimulate social exchanges when he produces his first **social smile,** a heart-warming grin triggered by just the sight of a human face. The social smile is believed to strengthen the bond between infant and parents. In fact, Charles Darwin, the founder of evolutionary theory, argued that the social smile helps the infant survive by instilling feelings of joy in adults and so encouraging care giving.

Why is it so important for babies to encourage others to nurture and protect them? The answer is that human infants enter the world at a stage when they are incapable of "doing" for themselves—even more incapable than the young of many other species. This is because they must be born when the large human head is still able to fit through the mother's birth canal. If birth were delayed until the baby's brain development was more advanced, the head would be so large that both mother and child would be at risk. Being born so early, however, means that the child's parents must provide a great deal of care. Thus, inherent cuteness and the social smile set the stage for the loving attention that will help the child survive.

But early parent–child interaction is not rigidly programmed to unfold in a particular way. The nature of this interaction is also influenced by the characteristics of the people involved and their current situations. The parents, for one thing, have their own emotional styles, products of their inherited tendencies, their developmental histories, and many factors in their present lives. At the same time, the baby has his or her own **temperament,** or behavioral predispositions. Aspects of temperament that vary in infants include activity level, "soothability," "talkativeness," attention span, fearfulness in new situations, display of positive emotions (frequency of smiles and laughter), and display of negative emotions (frequency of crying, irritability, and distress) (Bates, 1987; Rothbart, 1986). Interestingly, the frequencies of positive and negative emotions are not always inversely related. Although some infants who smile and laugh often are seldom irritable, and vice versa, there are also babies who show positive and negative moods with equal frequency, and others who remain for the most part emotionally neutral (Belsky et al., 1991; Goldsmith and Campos, 1991).

What causes these individual differences in infant temperament is still being debated, but many psychologists think they are substantially influenced by heredity (Campos et al., 1983; Smolak, 1986). They reason that temperament differences appear too soon after birth to be significantly shaped by different external environments. They also point to recent research findings that personality differences among adults have relatively strong genetic components (Bouchard and McGue, 1990). We will discuss the biological basis of adult personality differences in Chapter 13. For now, bear in mind that the behavioral differences of newborn babies are partly the result of biological factors.

The temperament that a baby brings to parent–child interactions has an impact on the personalities of the mother and father, who are also being influenced by their current situations and the level of contentment in their lives. Consider a baby with a tendency to be irritable and fussy. If the parents are generally confident and easy-going, and if they are not currently experiencing significant stress, they will probably respond calmly to the baby's fussiness, searching for clues as to what the child wants and learning to be more soothing in their care giving. If, on the other hand, the parents are emotionally immature and are having financial or marital troubles, they could easily "turn off" to their fussy infant and grow impatient with the child. In both cases, the parents' own traits and situations affect how they respond to the baby's temperament, and their responses, in turn, then affect the child's behavior. If the parents become more soothing, the baby is likely to fuss less, and if the parents become annoyed and impatient, the baby is apt to be even more difficult. Here we see a **bi-directional influence** between parent and child. Both are continually affecting one another as their relationship grows.

The development of early social relationships is an excellent example of how heredity and environment interact. A child may be born with certain tendencies that are largely genetic in origin, but these tendencies can be modified and channeled by the baby's experiences. One way of describing this important process is with the concept of reaction range. **Reaction range** refers to the range within which

inherited tendencies can vary by virtue of environmental influences. Genes, in other words, do not rigidly determine a person's characteristics. Instead, what we inherit at birth is a set of developmental *possibilities,* any of which can be encouraged or thwarted by the things that happen to us (Scarr, 1984a). Thus, a baby with a strongly outgoing disposition (smiles early and vigorously at other people) may end up reserved, even withdrawn, if adults ignore his social overtures (Kagan, 1984). Likewise, a very active baby can be encouraged to overactivity or helped to be more relaxed depending on the experiences that other people provide. Infant temperament, in other words, is not fixed and immutable. It is a set of behavioral tendencies that is open to change through environmental influences (Belsky et al., 1991).

THE FORMATION OF ATTACHMENTS

During the second half-year of life babies show signs of having developed enduring emotional bonds or **attachments** to their principal care givers, including mother, father, day-care provider, and even older siblings (Lamb, 1986). Attachment can be seen in the joyous greetings the baby gives the care giver. For instance, a seven-month-old will smile, gurgle, and coo with delight when mother or father comes to get her in the morning, and she would probably cry loudly if the parent suddenly turned and left the room. When babies are old enough to crawl, they often try to follow a care giver wherever the person goes (Maccoby and Martin, 1983). They want to maintain at least visual contact with the attachment figure, as if the person is an important source of security for them.

EXPLAINING ATTACHMENT FORMATION

Researchers have wondered what attributes of the care giver tend to encourage the baby's attachment. Is it the fact that the care giver provides food and other necessities, as Freud proposed, or is it more the emotional comfort that a care giver offers? Thirty-some years ago, psychologist Harry Harlow and his colleagues set out to answer these questions. They separated newborn monkeys from their natural mothers and provided them instead with various kinds of "surrogate mothers." In one study, for instance, Harlow raised each baby monkey in a cage that contained two surrogate mothers, one made of stiff, bare wire and the other covered with soft terrycloth (Harlow, 1958; Harlow and Harlow, 1966, 1969). Even when the wire mother was equipped with a milk dispenser, the babies still preferred the terrycloth mother. They spent a great deal of time clinging to its soft body, just as baby monkeys cling to their real mothers. And it was always the terrycloth mother to which the infant monkeys ran when alarmed. Thus, the tactile sensations a mother provides seem to have something to do with attachment formation in monkeys.

In human infants the formation of attachment is undoubtedly more complex. The baby's emotional bond to the care giver seems to grow not simply from the tactile experience of being held and cuddled, but from many, many hours of social interaction as well. Since in most families such repeated interactions occur with fathers as well as with mothers, infants typically become attached to *both* their parents at approximately the same age (Lamb, 1981).

VARIATIONS IN THE QUALITY OF ATTACHMENTS

Although virtually all children form attachments of some kind during infancy, the quality of those attachments can vary greatly depending on the sensitivity of the care giving received. This has been demonstrated in extensive research by Mary Ainsworth and her colleagues (1978, 1989). They have found that when the care giver responds to the baby's needs promptly, appropriately, and consistently, the child tends to develop a **secure attachment**. The infant seems to acquire the expectation that the care giver will be available and responsive—that he or she will quickly and effectively remedy any distress the child may experience. In contrast, a baby who develops an **anxious attachment** typically has a care giver who cannot be counted on for comfort when it is needed. Some of these care givers are emotionally indifferent or even rejecting toward the baby, often showing these feelings in an intrusive, overcontrolling style of care that totally ignores the infant's needs. Others try to be responsive to the baby some of the time, but at other times they fail to do so and only add to the child's distress—in short, they are inconsistent.

Subsequent research has shown that the security of an infant's attachment can have important implica-

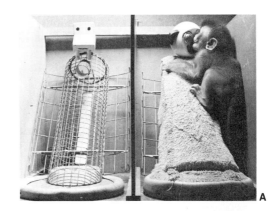

(A) One of Harlow's monkeys clings to its terrycloth surrogate mother. (B) A monkey stays in contact with the terrycloth mother even as it nurses from the wire mother. (C) Typical posture of a monkey raised in isolation.

tions for future development. Children who were securely attached as infants are generally less dependent and more socially competent as preschoolers than their anxiously attached peers (Plunkett et al., 1988; Sroufe et al., 1983; Waters et al., 1979). As preschoolers they also tend to have fewer behavior problems, especially excessive aggression and noncompliance with adults. It is children who were *insecurely* attached as infants who are more apt to have these behavior problems, and when they do the problems often persist into later childhood (Renken et al., 1989). Such findings are consistent with Erik Erikson's theory that development of basic trust through early parent–child relationships is the single most important emotional task a person accomplishes during the first year of life. Apparently, a secure attachment is an emotional foundation that makes a child better able to cope with the new demands and challenges that come as he or she grows older (Sroufe, 1988).

Why are some parents less able to foster secure attachments in their children? The answer seems to lie in a number of interacting factors, including the personalities of the parents, the levels of stress and social support in their lives, and the temperament of their infant (or at least their *perceptions* of the baby's temperament). Consider the results of one study which followed first-time parents and their babies from the mother's last few months of pregnancy until the baby was one year old (Belsky and Isabella, 1988). The researchers found that babies who were insecurely attached at twelve months tended to have mothers who scored low on two key personality traits: emotional stability/maturity and empathy toward others. The insecurely attached infants also tended to have mothers who had experienced the greatest decline in marital satisfaction since the baby was born, who perceived the baby as becoming more difficult with age, and who viewed their social environment as relatively unfriendly and unsupportive. These factors contributed to insecurity of attachment in an additive way. Women who experienced all of them almost always raised an insecurely attached baby, whereas women who experienced none of them almost always raised a child who was securely attached.

Of course, this single study only begins to tap the many factors that can increase a child's risk of becoming insecurely attached. In addition to the stresses of a difficult baby to care for, marital dissatisfaction, and lack of psychological support, parents can also expe-

rience many other kinds of stresses in their lives that affect their children. These include work-related stresses (fatigue from long working hours, concerns about job performance, unhappiness with one's job), strained relationships with family members other than one's spouse (parents and in-laws, for example), and the stress of financial worries and hardships. All these factors can affect the quality of parenting and hence the risk of raising an insecurely attached child.

What about the amount of time that mothers spend with their infants? If a secure attachment is the product of the trust that comes from many hours of responsive care, wouldn't babies who are often separated from the mother be more at risk of feeling insecure in their relationship with her? This is precisely the question millions of Americans are now asking because of our widespread use of day care for the children of working mothers. The issue, in fact, has become so important that it deserves an in-depth look.

IN DEPTH

Studying the Effects of Infant Day Care on Emotional Development

Dianne C. began looking for day care for her first child three months before the baby was born. Six months later, with her maternity leave from work about to end and still no day-care arrangements made, she was growing desperate. "I would go to visit some of the places that had openings," Dianne explained, "but I just couldn't imagine leaving my little girl there. Some were chaotic. Toddlers fighting over toys, screaming 'Mine!' at each other, and babies crying in the background. But even worse were the places where the kids weren't making any noise at all. Sometimes they'd have a bunch of older babies just bouncing up and down in those jumper things. It was awful! And even when I did eventually find a good place, it wasn't easy leaving Katie there. That first morning after I handed her over, I could hardly make myself drive away. But there was no question that I had to work. I had to pay the bills."

As women have become more career-oriented, as the cost of living has spiraled, and as divorce has become more common, a growing number of women with young children now work outside the home. Today, 50 percent of all the babies in the United States have a working mother, twice the percentage as in 1970 (Clark-Stewart, 1989). These mothers must secure some form of day care and be away from their children for substantial amounts of time. What effects are these substitute care arrangements having on emotional development? Are they hindering the formation of a secure attachment between mother and child? In recent years psychologists have been conducting studies designed to help answer these questions.

THE INITIAL STUDIES

In one of the first studies to examine the relationship between early day care and emotional development, Mary Blehar compared twenty two- and three-year-olds enrolled in full-time day care with twenty youngsters the same age cared for by their mothers at home. Blehar (1974) found that the day-care children, as a group, seemed less securely attached to their mothers. In a laboratory situation in which each mother repeatedly left her child alone with a stranger, the day-care children became more upset. They cried more, engaged in more oral behavior (thumb sucking, for instance), avoided the stranger more, and were inclined to ignore or resist the mother each time she returned. Early day care, in short, seemed to be related to less emotional resiliency in children.

CRITICISMS, ALTERNATIVES, AND FURTHER RESEARCH

But many psychologists stressed the need for caution in interpreting Blehar's results. Some pointed out that the observers who scored the children's behaviors often knew beforehand which group the youngsters belonged to, the day-care group or the home-reared one. This knowledge could have biased their perceptions, inclining them to see what they *expected* to see. In fact, when one group of researchers repeated Blehar's study with scorers who were unaware of the experiment's purpose and each youngster's child-care background, they could not replicate her findings (Moskowitz et al., 1977). Instead, they found that children who had experienced day care were no different emotionally from those who had not.

Other psychologists argued that Blehar may have been observing only a short-term reaction to day care. Her day-care subjects had been enrolled in group care for only four and a half months. Perhaps they were still adjusting emotionally to this new experience. If so, any insecurity they showed would not be comparable to the long-term insecurity of children whose parents are emotionally rejecting or inconsistent in the responsiveness of their care. In support of this hypothesis, one team of researchers found that the longer children had been in day care, the fewer negative reactions they showed (Blanchard and Main, 1979). In another study, children who had been in day care an average of nine and a half months seemed no different emotionally from similar-aged children raised at home by their mothers (Portnoy and Simons, 1978). Thus, although children might go through a period of stressful adaptation to day care, regular care outside the home may not by itself result in any long-term emotional harm.

But some psychologists were not satisfied with the data that had been gathered so far. They argued that much of the research on day-care children had focused on those attending high-quality, university-affiliated centers with excellent staffs and programs. How comparable, they asked, are these centers to ones that most American preschoolers with working mothers attend? In addition, much of the research to date had focused on children who entered day care at a relatively late age, when attachment to the mother was already firmly established. What about babies who are placed in day care before they are one year old, when the attachment process is still going on or has not even yet begun? Do these infants stand a higher-than-average chance of developing an insecure attachment, with all the risks for future development which that insecurity entails?

Brian Vaughn and his colleagues were among the first to try to answer these questions (Vaughn et al., 1980). They chose for study 100 economically disadvantaged mothers and their infants. These mothers could not afford top-quality day care. They had to make do with whatever child-care arrangements were within their budgets—often a neighborhood woman willing to babysit in her home for a modest fee. Vaughn and his colleagues assessed the quality of the children's attachment to the mother at ages twelve and eighteen months. They found a higher proportion of secure attachments among those children who had been raised exclu-

The ratio of children to caregivers is one of the most significant factors in evaluating the quality of day care. Researchers have recommended that each adult be responsible for no more than three infants or six preschoolers.

sively at home. Children placed in day care before the age of one were especially likely to avoid the mother in stressful situations, a pattern that Ainsworth says arises when a mother is emotionally inaccessible to her baby. This pattern has been linked to serious social and emotional maladjustments later in childhood (Sroufe, 1979, 1983). Thus, poor-quality day care begun at a very early age seems to be particularly harmful to children's development.

Other studies have drawn similar conclusions. For instance, Sandra Scarr and her colleagues conducted a six-year study of day care on the island of Bermuda, where 90 percent of children are tended by someone other than their mothers by the time they are two years old (McCartney et al., 1982;

Scarr, 1984a, 1984b). The Scarr team carefully evaluated the quality of ten day-care centers and the progress of children who had attended them for six months or longer. They found that entry into day care before the age of one, coupled with a low level of verbal interaction between child and care givers, was generally associated with emotional maladjustment. Children who experienced this combination of early separation from the mother and relatively poor-quality care were more likely than other preschoolers to be anxious, hostile, and hyperactive. In another more recent study, Carollee Howes (1990) assessed a large group of children from the time they were babies until they entered kindergarten. She found that preschoolers who had experienced poor-quality day care beginning in infancy were less compliant and less able to exert self-control, more hostile and less considerate of others, more distractible and less able to focus on a task, and had more problems with their peers.

Studies such as these suggest that the quality of day care is extremely important, especially when a child is placed in day care very early in life. Researchers are therefore trying to specify exactly what comprises good- or poor-quality day care. The study by Sandra Scarr and her colleagues and the one by Carollee Howes suggest that a critical factor is care-giver involvement with the children. Day care in which adults frequently talk to the youngsters, share discoveries with them, and show affection and concern are most conducive to favorable emotional development. These characteristics are usually found in settings with a low child-to-care-giver ratio and, generally, a small number of children overall (Howes and Rubenstein, 1981). Many child-care specialists recommend no more than three infants or six toddlers to each care giver (Kagan et al., 1978; Clarke-Stewart, 1982).

Another significant factor contributing to quality day care is continuity in care. In the study by Brian Vaughn and his colleagues, 80 percent of the children from low-income homes experienced at least one change in day-care provider during their first eighteen months of life (Vaughn et al., 1980). As a group, these children were especially likely to suffer insecure attachment to the mother. This finding is echoed in another study in which children were observed as they were dropped off at day care each morning (Cummings, 1980). Those who were left with an unfamiliar care giver were much more

When a two-year-old says, "I'll do it," her drive for independence often outstrips her know-how.

distressed than those left with a familiar one. Note that having more than one care giver, in and of itself, does not seem to be detrimental to young children. Preschoolers cared for by several different adults can be expected to thrive as long as those adults provide stable relationships (Clarke-Stewart and Fein, 1983).

PATTERNS AND CONCLUSIONS

What can we conclude about the effects of early day care on children's emotional development? Apparently, it is not *where* children are raised that makes a difference, but rather *how* they are cared for (Belsky, 1988; Scarr et al., 1989). If our society can offer high-quality day care to the children of working parents—day care that meets the children's needs for interaction, affection, and enduring relationships with adults—there is every reason to expect no adverse effects. Setting high minimum standards for day care has therefore become a top priority among many developmental psychologists. Unfortunately, high standards for day care is not always a top priority among state legislators. In some states, the law allows each day-care worker to care for up to seven babies or twenty preschoolers at once! Most states also lack high standards for the training of day-care workers. Twenty-six have no preemployment educational requirements for them,

and nine do not even require that inexperienced people receive at least some child-care instruction after they begin providing day care (Vandell and Corasaniti, 1990).

We must be careful not to assume that the link between early, poor-quality day care and developmental problems in children necessarily means that the poor-quality day care is causing all the trouble. Day-care quality and family characteristics tend to be related (Howes, 1990). Parents who are more stressed, with more problems in their lives, tend to choose lower-quality day care (perhaps in part because they lack the time and energy to evaluate day-care options more thoroughly). This makes it hard to pick apart the various influences leading to the behavior problems that we see. Nevertheless, improving the quality of day care can only be beneficial. When day-care providers create a stable base of affection and involvement in young children's lives, they can help to compensate for any sources of stress in the youngsters' home environments.

SOCIAL AND PERSONALITY DEVELOPMENT IN CHILDHOOD

In the course of interacting with the world around them, especially with other people, babies begin to develop a sense of self (Mahler et al., 1975). By "sense of self'' we mean an awareness of being a separate person, distinct from and independent of others. How do psychologists know that a sense of self is emerging? One way has been to dab a bit of rouge on a baby's nose and watch how the child responds to his or her image in a mirror. An eight-month-old might show interest and reach out to touch the nose's mirror image, but she won't touch her *real* nose to see if there is anything on it. It is as if she does not yet fully grasp that she is the baby in the mirror. By eighteen months, however, this same child *will* touch her nose to find out what the red mark is. She now seems to have a schema of what her face *should* look like, a schema that is part of her growing sense of self (Bertenthal and Fischer, 1978).

At least by the end of the second year, then, and probably earlier, most children have developed a concept of self. With this awareness that their own thoughts and actions are distinct from those of others, two-year-olds begin to strive for greater autonomy. This can be seen in their persistent efforts to master simple tasks without the assistance of adults. (Children this age are constantly telling their parents "No! *Me* do it!") Erik Erikson saw such striving for autonomy as the overriding challenge of the second and third years of life. This stage of budding independence helps mark the baby's entry into the social world of childhood.

EXPLAINING INDIVIDUAL DIFFERENCES

We opened this chapter by quoting Mark Twain's description of the differences between himself and his younger brother Henry. Mark Twain was the mischief maker, always getting into trouble, while Henry was the model of all that is good and honest. Such marked differences between brothers or sisters are not at all uncommon. Consider the differences between the noted nineteenth-century psychologist William James and his brother Henry James, the famous novelist. Even as a child William was very active and energetic, with a buoyant, gregarious, effervescent style. Henry, in contrast, was much quieter and shyer, much more of a social loner. What causes such marked differences in personality to develop? How can two children turn out to be so different from one another? The answer, as you know, lies in a complex interplay of genes and environment.

In this section we will explore some of the genetic and environmental factors that influence per-

sonality development during childhood. Because psychologists often study these factors apart from one another, we too will first look at environmental and genetic forces separately. But then we will turn our attention to gene–environment interaction, which ultimately gives rise to the distinct personalities we see in people.

ENVIRONMENTAL INFLUENCES

Parenting Styles Psychologists have long suspected that parents may have a major impact on the personalities their children develop. Consequently, they have spent a great deal of time exploring which aspects of parents' behavior influence children the most. One researcher who has studied this topic extensively is Diana Baumrind (1967, 1984). She began by identifying three basic personality profiles in nursery school children on the basis of fourteen weeks of observation. Children in group 1 (the mature group) were energetic, emotionally positive toward peers, and high in curiosity, self-reliance, and self-control. Children in group 2 (the disaffiliated group) were moody, apprehensive, easily upset, passively hostile, and either negative in their relations with peers or socially withdrawn. Children in group 3 (the immature group) were impulsive, undercontrolled, and low in self-reliance, but more cheerful and resilient than those in group 2.

Baumrind then assessed the parents of these children through personal interviews, home observations, and laboratory studies. She found three distinctive styles of parenting. Parents of the mature children were nurturant and responsive, but firm in setting limits. They were also flexible in their thinking and encouraged their children toward independence. Baumrind called this **authoritative** parenting. In contrast, parents of the disaffiliated youngsters were unresponsive to their children's wishes, inflexible in their thinking, and harsh in controlling behavior— what Baumrind calls an **authoritarian** style. Parents of the immature youngsters were somewhat nurturant, but they failed to set firm limits or to require age-appropriate behavior, thus hindering the development of self-control in their children. Baumrind labeled them **permissive** parents. Five years later, Baumrind still found the children of the authoritative parents to be the most mature. Apparently, a parenting style characterized by warmth and nurturance, the encouragement of independence, but the setting

Sexual abuse by a parent or other relative is probably the most devastating betrayal of a child's trust.

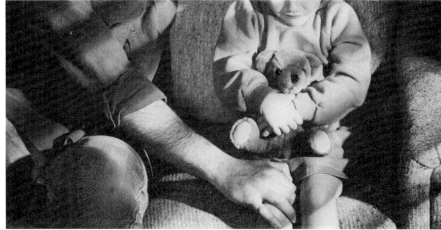

"Made available as a public service by the Sunny von Bulow National Victim Advocacy Center"

MOST PEOPLE IGNORE VIOLENT CRIME. UNTIL IT TOUCHES SOMEONE THEY LOVE.

Some 125,000 cases of child sexual abuse were reported in 1984. Battered child reports climbed 200% over a five year period. Over 28,000 youngsters were listed as missing in 1985. When it comes to violent crime, innocence is no defense.

Support victims' rights in our community.

of firm rules when needed is associated with very positive outcomes in children.

Unfortunately, we cannot say with certainty exactly what this association means. As you know from Chapter 2, a correlation between two factors (such as a certain style of parenting and certain traits in children) does not necessarily prove that one *caused* the other. Perhaps some third factor, such as the genes parents and children share, is contributing to the observed behaviors of both the parents and the children. In order to rule out genetic influences, researchers would have to repeat Baumrind's study using adopted children as subjects, since they are genetically *un*related to their adoptive parents. In the meantime, though, it seems reasonable to suggest that environmental influences were probably at work as well. That is to say, the parents' behaviors (not just their genes) were probably helping to shape the behavior of their children. And the environmental influences were probably bi-directional. Adults with an authoritative style of parenting probably tend to raise children who are happy, self-reliant, and self-controlled. These positive traits, in turn, probably promote in authoritative parents more favorable perceptions of their children than authoritarian or per-

missive parents have (Greenberger, 1989). Such positive perceptions would foster continued warmth and nurturance and an expectation of mature behavior from the children. In this way, barring unusual stresses in the family, the cycle would perpetuate itself.

An overly restricting style of parenting would also tend to be self-perpetuating. Parents who control their children in a harsh, severe manner would tend to raise youngsters who are moody, negative, passively hostile, and easily upset. These traits could encourage the parents to believe that their children are in need of even stricter discipline and so they become still harsher toward them. Repeated negative exchanges between parents and children would also create more stress in the home, which could cause the parents to lose their patience and react in more volatile ways. When this happens, a harsh parenting style is in danger of escalating into child abuse.

Child Abuse

What I remember most about my mother was that she was always beating me. She'd beat me with her high-heeled shoes, with my father's belt, with a potato masher. When I was eight, she black-and-blued my legs so badly I told her I'd go tell the police. She said, "Go, they'll just put you into the darkest prison." (*Time*, September 5, 1983, p. 20)

Tragically, child abuse is far from rare in our society. About 2 million cases are reported every year, and undoubtedly a great many more go unreported (Children's Defense Fund, 1987). The most visible form of child abuse is physical maltreatment—that is, the use of corporal punishment beyond the limits considered acceptable in our society (Daro, 1988). Physical abuse includes beatings and other acts of physical aggression that cause cuts, bruises, burns, internal injuries, or broken bones. Children can also be abused sexually, forced or persuaded to submit to the sexual advances of an adult. A third form of child abuse involves neglect, failure to adequately clean, feed, clothe, or give medical care to a child. Such physical neglect is often accompanied by emotional neglect, failure to meet the child's basic need for affection. Emotional maltreatment can also take the form of extreme verbal aggression. Parents who constantly berate their children and repeatedly ridicule their efforts are being emotionally abusive toward them (Garbarino and Garbarino, 1986).

Abuse can have devastating effects on children. Apathy, blunted emotions, insecure attachment to the parent, low self-esteem, and increased risks of depression, suicide, and drug addiction are just some of the effects seen (Garbarino et al., 1986; Schneider-Rosen and Cicchetti, 1984; Widom, 1991; Youngblade and Belsky, 1989). Other effects are heightened aggressiveness, distractibility, and noncompliance, less caring and helping toward others, and a tendency to respond to other people's distress with anger, hostility, and even physical attack (Egeland, 1991; Howes and Eldredge, 1985; Main and George, 1985). The scars of abuse can also be very enduring. Because abused children are victimized by the very people they look to for care and affection, they often feel abandoned, betrayed, and distrustful of others, even into adulthood (Aber and Allen, 1987; McCrae and Costa, 1988). Very often, too, when they try to explain why the abuse happened, they are unable to do so. This inexplicability can make them view the world in general as an unpredictable place that defies understanding (Silver et al., 1983). Abused children who seem to be at the greatest long-term risk include those for whom the entire atmosphere in the family is chaotic, unsupportive, or violent, and who suffer multiple episodes of mistreatment, which may not be acknowledged until much later in life (Figley, 1989; Mowbray, 1988).

You may think that parents who abuse their children must be by nature hostile and violent, perhaps even mentally disturbed, but this is seldom true (Brunnquell et al., 1981). Most child abusers are simply people who are ambivalent about being parents, who lack knowledge about young children and how to manage them, and who are currently experiencing high levels of stress in their lives, often brought on by economic troubles (Sedlack, 1989). Many, too, have a history of being abused themselves as children; essentially, they are re-creating in the next generation the family roles they grew up with. Child abusers also tend to be socially isolated. They lack supportive other adults who can help them deal with the day-to-day tasks of child rearing (Crockenberg, 1986). Providing parents who are experiencing stress with a network of other people who can give them emotional support may be one of the best ways to help prevent child abuse.

The Impact of Divorce   Divorce is another environmental factor that can shape how a child thinks, feels, and acts. Every year, over a million American children experience the divorce of their parents (Wegman, 1986). Estimates are that roughly half of all the babies born in the United States today will spend at least some of their young lives in a one-parent home (Newberger et al., 1986). Many more will witness repeated conflict between their parents that does not end in divorce. Exactly how do these negative experiences in the family affect children?

During the period immediately following the breakup of their parents' marriage, most children feel some anger and resentment, anxiety, depression, and perhaps even guilt. But then, following the initial crisis, reactions tend to vary (Hetherington, 1989). Some children are very resilient and bounce back remarkably well, while others suffer sustained problems, including increased aggression, noncompliance with parents, and general acting out, coupled with declines in academic achievement and the quality of peer relationships. There are also children who seem to be adjusting for a time, only to suffer delayed reactions, especially in adolescence. Why these individual differences in children's responses to divorce? The answers seem to lie in both biology and environment.

Most of the environmental factors contributing to differences in reactions to divorce are related to the amount of stress the child experiences. For instance, continued conflict between the divorced parents is associated with behavior problems and poor adjustment in their children (Camara and Resnick, 1988; Forehand et al., 1988). So is a negative change in the custodial parent's style of parenting. When a custodial parent becomes more erratic, inconsistent, punitive, or permissive due to the stress of divorce, children may respond badly (Hetherington et al., 1989). Children who do best tend to have some stable sources of love, psychological support, and guidance in their lives. Parents (both custodial and noncustodial), grandparents, and teachers can all serve this role, as can siblings and close friends to a lesser extent (Furstenberg, 1988; Hetherington, 1988; Wallerstein et al., 1988; Zill, 1988).

At the same time, a child's temperament also affects reactions to divorce. Temperamentally difficult children tend to be more vulnerable, both because parents under stress tend to criticize them more often and because they are less able to cope with adversity (Hetherington, 1988). Other traits in children that are associated with poor adjustment to divorce are low self-esteem, overdependence, and a tendency to blame themselves (Masten, 1986; Nolen-Hoeksema et al., 1989; Rutter, 1987; Werner, 1987). We are not yet certain why these detrimental traits develop. It may be that inherited tendencies help to make some children less resilient to stress, including the stress of divorce. Thus, resilient and nonresilient children may be filtering similar experiences through different, partly genetic inclinations and predispositions. In the next section we will examine the entent to which personality differences in people are in fact genetic in origin.

GENETIC INFLUENCES

The idea that genes significantly influence human behavior has been gaining new acceptance in recent years. The reason is a growing body of evidence from studies of twins and adopted children, both of which allow scientists to estimate the relative contributions of heredity and environment to human differences. Consider the logic of twin studies, for instance, particularly twins who were separated at birth and raised apart from each other. Some are fraternal twins, who have, on average, only about half their genes in common; while others are identical twins, who developed from the same fertilized egg and so have *all* the same genes. If pairs of fraternal twins raised apart are no more dissimilar regarding a certain trait than pairs of identical twins raised apart, genetic differences among the fraternals cannot be making a contribution to their individual variability on this trait. If, on the other hand, pairs of fraternal twins raised apart are very dissimilar to each other, while pairs of identical twins raised apart are not dissimilar at all, heredity must be virtually the entire cause of the fraternal twins' individual variability. More commonly, of course, identical twins will be dissimilar to each other, but not as dissimilar as fraternal twins are. This means that both genes and environment are contributing to the variability we see. In this case, behavioral geneticists can estimate the percentage contribution that heredity is making to the siblings' differences by subtracting the variability among the pairs of identicals twins from the variability among the pairs of fraternals.

The estimates they are currently making say that heredity exerts a sizable influence on personality differences. For instance, in one intensive study of over seventy sets of twins raised apart, the contribution of heredity to most of the personality traits the researchers measured was about 50 percent (Bouchard and McGue, 1990). Personality differences among people in sociability, emotionalism, and general activity level seem to have especially strong contributions from genes (Plomin, 1989). Individual differences in other personality traits have smaller genetic contributions, but almost none have no genetic contributions at all.

THE INTERPLAY OF GENES AND ENVIRONMENT

These findings showing a sizable contribution of genes to human differences in behavior could cause some people to jump to the wrong conclusion. They might think that genes virtually determine why one person acts a certain way, while a second person acts another. This, however, is not the case. The same findings that show a strong contribution from genes to human differences show an equally strong contribution from environment. Even if the contribution of heredity to personality differences averages 50 percent, the remaining 50 percent not accounted for by genes must be accounted for by environment (Dunn and Plomin, 1990).

Even when parents try to treat their children the same, some differences are almost inevitable. The birth of a sibling, with its extra demands on parents' time and attention, is bound to affect the older child's responses.

But there is a surprise in the most recent findings concerning environmental influences. The environmental influences that people share by virtue of being raised together do not seem to have much of an impact on personality at all! Twins who are raised together are about equally alike in terms of most psychological dimensions as twins who are raised apart (Tellegen et al., 1988). Similarly, biologically *unrelated* children who are adopted into the same home do not usually develop many personality resemblances, even though they seem to have many environmental influences in common (Loehlin et al., 1981; Scarr et al., 1981). When you compare their results on personality tests, the correlation coefficient turns out to be only about .05, a *very* weak relationship (Plomin, 1989).

Does this mean that previous researchers have been wrong in stressing parenting styles and other home environment influences to explain the personality differences that children develop? No; it just means that we may have to reconceptualize how such influences are exerted. Having the same parents apparently does not mean that children in the same family will experience the same parenting influences. Instead, environmental influences in the family are *specific* to each child, not general for all of the siblings. This means that in some cases parents treat their children differently, perhaps by virtue of the differences among them, such as differences in sex, temperament, health, physical appearance, and so forth. Parents may not be aware that they do this; they may try hard to treat all of their children alike. But despite good intentions, differences in treatment can easily arise. For example, a shy, quiet boy in generally poor health could easily elicit more permissiveness from a parent than a boisterous, active brother who constantly seems to be "getting into trouble." In two recent studies the majority of mothers admitted to treating their children differently in terms of affection, attention, and amount and type of discipline (Dunn and Stocker, 1989; Stocker et al., 1989). These differences do not usually go unnoticed by the children. In another study in which older children were asked about their family experiences, nearly half reported that their parents treated them and their siblings differently (Daniels et al., 1985). Table 10.2 lists the questions used in this study.

And even if some parents *do* treat their children alike most of the time, each child could still respond to that treatment differently, by virtue of their different temperaments and different personal experiences in the world. An inherently sensitive child who has experienced difficulty making friends might feel deep rejection when a parent or teacher reprimands him.

TABLE 10.2   How Similar Are Siblings' Experiences?
Parental Interactions with You and Your Sibling

This questionnaire is designed to ask how similarly your mother and father treated you and your sibling. Compare yourself to your sibling (or one of your siblings) when you were growing up and living at home. Answer first for your mother and then for your father. Scoring instructions and comparison scores appear below.

1 = much more this way toward my sibling than me
2 = a bit more this way toward my sibling than me
3 = the same toward my sibling and me
4 = a bit more this way toward me than my sibling
5 = much more this way toward me than my sibling

	Toward Sibling Much More		Same		Toward Me Much More
1. Has been strict with us	1	2	3	4	5
2. Has been proud of the things we have done	1	2	3	4	5
3. Has enjoyed doing things with us	1	2	3	4	5
4. Has been sensitive to what we think and feel	1	2	3	4	5
5. Has punished us for our misbehavior	1	2	3	4	5
6. Has shown interest in the things we like to do	1	2	3	4	5
7. Has blamed us for what another family member did	1	2	3	4	5
8. Has tended to favor one of us	1	2	3	4	5
9. Has disciplined us	1	2	3	4	5

Scoring: Separately for the mother and father items, add your answers for items 2, 3, 4, 6, and 8 and divide by 5 to create an affection score. A control score is obtained by adding 1, 5, 7, and 9 and dividing by 4. For both scales for mothers and fathers, young adult siblings yield an average score of 3.0. The extent to which your affection and control scores are below or above 3.0 indicates how differentially you view your parents' treatment of you and your sibling.
Source: Adapted from Dunn and Plomin, 1990, p. 65, Table 4.1.

In contrast, a confident child who is well-liked by peers would probably be less affected by occasional scoldings from adults. Thus, even environmental factors that seem the same may be *experienced* differently by dissimilar people (Bouchard and McGue, 1990.) This suggests that the factors contributing to personality differences are far more complex than we previously assumed.

EXPLAINING GROUP DIFFERENCES: THE CASE OF GENDER ROLES

> In a thickly carpeted room same-sex trios of four-year-olds are left alone to play with a small trampoline, a beach ball, and a large inflated Bobo doll. Trios of girls spend most of their time jumping on the trampoline. Their play is active but seldom rough-and-tumble. Almost never does one girl throw herself on top of another, and end up laughing and wrestling with the first. Trios of boys, in contrast, routinely interact this way. They push and pounce, wrestle and roll, giggling and squealing in high spirits. When records of the children's behavior are compared at the end of the study, boys have engaged in over six times more rough-and-tumble play than girls. (Maccoby, 1988)

At a very early age most children begin to acquire the behavior patterns associated with their sex. One-year-old boys, for example, tend to play more vigorously than girls the same age do (Maccoby and Jacklin, 1974), and by the age of about one-and-a-half, boys start to prefer cars and trucks as playthings, whereas girls prefer soft, cuddly toys (Smith and Daglish, 1977). During the preschool years, children also start to gravitate toward members of their own sex as playmates, a tendency that is quite pronounced by the early elementary school years (Luria and Herzog, 1985; Maccoby and Jacklin, 1987; Thorne, 1986). These same-sex groups often show significant differences in behavior, as in the study described above. In addition to boys' greater amount of rough-and-tumble play, boys also tend to be more aggressive in asserting their desires than girls are, and they try more to dominate each other, often with physical force. Girls, in contrast, are usually less impulsive than boys are, more compliant, and more sensitive to their playmates' views and feelings (Charlesworth and Dzur, 1987; Maccoby, 1988; Maltz and Borker,

1983). Such differences are signs that children are adopting **gender roles,** patterns of behavior characteristic of the members of their own sex.

Gender roles are different from individual differences in personality. While members of the same sex often vary greatly in their personality traits, girls *in general* display certain patterns of behavior different from those that boys *in general* display. Why do these group differences in behavior develop? Again, the answer must lie in an interplay of heredity and environment. However, the relative contributions of heredity and environment to group differences in personality are not necessarily the same as those associated with individual differences. Nor can we use the same research methods (twin studies, adoption studies) to investigate the causes of group personality differences. Instead, we must turn to different kinds of studies, each suggested by a different type of theory as to why gender roles develop. We begin by looking at what psychologists with a biological perspective have to say.

THE IMPACT OF BIOLOGY

It is difficult to assess the impact of biology on masculine and feminine behavior, for biological tendencies begin to interact with experiences almost immediately after birth. There are, however, some behavioral differences between the sexes that appear before the social environment has had much of a chance to exert an influence. Newborn boys are generally more active than newborn girls, and they also tend to cry more and sleep less than girls do (Moss, 1967; Phillips et al., 1978). What this means in terms of future personality and social development is hard to say. Perhaps these initial differences cause male and female babies to experience different kinds of care giving and different patterns of social interaction. A very active, squirming infant, for instance, may be played with more energetically, but hugged and cuddled less. Similarly, a high level of activity could prompt a baby to explore the physical environment more extensively, and this, in turn, could encourage certain patterns of personality development. In short, innate differences between boys and girls in activity level alone could interact with environmental factors to gradually produce a variety of behavioral differences.

But some psychologists now believe that biology may play an even greater role in male–female behavioral differences. For instance, males who are born

Boys are certainly capable of the gentle, nurturing behavior traditionally expected of girls. Developmental psychologists seek to explain how rigid gender roles arise and why they persist. According to social learning theorists, children learn "appropriate" behavior for boys and for girls by observing and imitating their parents and other adults.

with female-looking genitals and therefore are raised as girls sometimes begin to behave more masculinely upon reaching puberty, when male hormones start to surge (Imperato-McGinley et al., 1979). Aggressive tendencies may be especially influenced by biological factors, perhaps even by hormones present in males before birth.

But though biological factors may produce some gender-related differences in behavior, it is extremely doubtful that biology alone is responsible for all the behavioral differences between the sexes. If such differences were primarily genetic in origin, then males and females everywhere would exhibit the same gender-role patterns. This, however, is not the case. Anthropologists have observed marked differences among the world's cultures in the behaviors and personality traits ascribed to men and women (e.g., Mead, 1935). In the next sections we will look at the major environmental theories of gender differences. As we do, keep in mind that these theories are not

mutually exclusive. Each may contribute a piece to the puzzle and together enrich our understanding.

THE FREUDIAN PERSPECTIVE

According to Freud, gender-role learning results from the **Oedipus conflict,** which presumably occurs between the ages of three and six. This is the time when most children discover the genital differences between the sexes, and this discovery, according to Freudian theory, prompts children to see themselves as rivals of the same-sex parent for the affection of the parent of the opposite sex. Eventually, however, the child comes to realize that this longing for the opposite-sex parent is not likely to be fulfilled. So the child compromises. Instead of trying to possess the opposite-sex parent, he or she tries to be like, or identify with, the parent of the same sex, adopting that parent's values, attitudes, gender role, and so forth. This process of **identification,** according to Freud, is crucial to normal development, including the acquisition of appropriate sex-typed behaviors.

THE SOCIAL LEARNING PERSPECTIVE

Unlike Freudians, social learning theorists believe that the acquisition of sex-typed behavior is not initiated by a single event in a child's life, but rather is a gradual process of learning that begins even in infancy. Parents and other adults, social learning theorists argue, shape the child's behavior to conform to established gender roles by reinforcing "appropriate" responses and discouraging "inappropriate" ones. In addition, adults, as well as older brothers and sisters, provide numerous gender-role models for the child to imitate. As a result, the behavior expected of a boy or a girl has begun to emerge as early as the age of one-and-a-half to two.

Studies reveal that fathers especially encourage traditional sex roles in their children by treating sons and daughters differently (Siegal, 1987). For instance, fathers typically regard their baby sons as stronger and hardier than their baby daughters, whom they are inclined to regard as more fragile and more in need of protection. In keeping with these perceptions, fathers encourage more physical play in their infant and toddler boys, as well as more independence and exploration. Similar patterns of influence continue as children grow older. In general, fathers are more physical in their interactions with sons, and they are also stricter and firmer in disciplining them. Toward daughters, in contrast, they are usually gentler and more affectionate.

This gender-role channeling is not necessarily conscious and deliberate. Ironically, even parents who set out to treat their sons and daughters similarly may still end up responding in sex-typed ways. This was suggested in a study in which young adults were asked to evaluate a baby's emotional responses to four stimuli—a teddy bear, a jack-in-the-box, a doll, and a loud buzzer (Condry and Condry, 1976). Half the subjects were told they were watching a boy, while half were told they were watching a girl. In reality, they were all watching the same nine-month-old child, who had previously been filmed on videotape. When the baby cried after being presented with the jack-in-the-box several times, the subjects who believed they were observing a boy attributed the reaction to anger, whereas those who believed they were observing a girl attributed the response to fear.

In an ambiguous situation, the common stereotype that females are more fearful than males tended to influence the subjects' thinking. It is easy to imagine that as parents these same people might respond in very different ways to a crying son and a crying daughter—not because they think boys and girls merit different treatment, but because they perceive each child to be expressing a different emotion.

Once a child becomes old enough to play cooperatively with peers, gender-role lessons may intensify. Children, especially boys, are often staunch defenders of gender roles. By the age of five or six, most boys have firm ideas about sex-appropriate dress and behavior, and they expect ostracism for deviating from the norm (Damon, 1977). These expectations are warranted. Observation of school-age children has shown that a boy who tries to enter a girls' game on the playground (jump rope, for instance) will be both shunned by the girls and ridiculed by other boys (Thorne, 1986). Thus, peer pressure seems to play an important part in gender-role learning.

THE COGNITIVE DEVELOPMENTAL VIEW

Researchers interested in the cognitive aspects of early childhood development have contributed yet another perspective on how gender roles are acquired. They argue that it may not matter whether other people encourage children to act in sex-appropriate ways. In their view, children have a built-in motivation to imitate the behaviors that society expects of their sex. Children, they say, strive to be competent at all things—including the actions and attitudes associated with being a boy or a girl. Thus, once youngsters have the cognitive ability to understand the concepts of male and female and to recognize that one of these concepts applies to them, they will automatically want to adopt behaviors considered right for this newly discovered status (Kohlberg, 1969).

Cognitive psychologists go on to argue that sex-typed behaviors should become more pronounced as a child's understanding of gender matures. And, in fact, this is what happens. In one study, for instance, researchers showed children ages four to nine three sets of unfamiliar objects and told them that one was for boys, another for girls, and another for boys *and* girls. In reality, the objects (a burgler alarm, a hole puncher, a phone index, and so forth) are *not* normally sex-typed. The older children ex-

According to social learning theorists, this child will avoid repeating his assault on his little sister if he knows he'll be scolded for doing so.

plored the objects said to be appropriate for their own sex more than they explored those called appropriate for both sexes, which in turn they explored more than those said to be for members of the opposite sex (Bradbard et al., 1986). The age at which this pattern emerged coincided closely with the age at which most youngsters have developed a good understanding of gender constancy—that is, an understanding that gender cannot be changed simply by changing hairstyle or clothing. This suggests that a relatively mature grasp of gender is often needed for children to show a consistent preference for "sex-appropriate" objects and behaviors.

Can we change children's notions of "sex-appropriate" things simply by showing them examples of people acting in *non*-sex-typed ways? Not easily, cognitive psychologists say. Once traditional stereotypes of "boy things" and "girl things" are firmly established in a child's mind, they tend to color and even distort what the child perceives and remembers. For instance, if you showed a child some pictures of boys playing with dolls and girls playing with trucks, several days later the youngster would probably report that the toys and genders had been reversed: that the pictures showed the *girls* playing with the dolls and the *boys* playing with the trucks (Martin and Halverson, 1981). Apparently, people often perceive and remember what their stereotypes tell them is

"right," a point we raised in Chapter 7. This makes it hard to change gender stereotypes just by exposing children to a small number of *non*-stereotypical experiences.

SOCIALIZATION AND MORAL DEVELOPMENT

An important developmental task of childhood is **socialization,** learning the expectations and values of one's society. The basic goal of socialization is **internalization**—incorporating society's values into the self to such an extent that violation of these standards produces a sense of guilt. In this section we will discuss an area of child development in which socialization plays a key role: the development of moral thought and behavior. By this we mean the development of children's thinking and actions concerning what is right and wrong. Infants enter the world totally amoral, bent on nothing more than the satisfaction of their own immediate desires. How is this totally self-centered baby transformed over the years into a person who is sensitive to the needs and rights of others? Three of the perspectives we explored regarding gender-role acquisition—the Freudian, the social learning, and the cognitive developmental—also provide answers to this question.

THE FREUDIAN PERSPECTIVE

According to Freud, a child internalizes the moral code of the same-sex parent during resolution of the Oedipus conflict. This process results in a dramatic change in the child's moral orientation. A strong sense of right and wrong emerges where previously there was none. The child, in other words, quite rapidly develops a conscience, which in Freudian theory is called a **superego.**

Research has not provided a great deal of support for Freud's view of moral development. Children do not seem to acquire a conscience as the result of a single developmental crisis, as he suggests. Moral development appears to be a gradual process that begins during the preschool years and continues into adulthood (Hoffman, 1976; Kohlberg, 1969).

THE SOCIAL LEARNING PERSPECTIVE

Unlike the Freudian view, the social learning perspective can accommodate the gradualness of moral development. Social learning theorists say that children act morally because over the years they are reinforced for "good" behavior and punished for "bad" behavior, and because they also have moral models to imitate. Research has provided some support for these contentions. For example, studies show that children often behave generously after observing an unselfish adult (Bryan, 1975), and they frequently behave aggressively after watching an aggressive model (Bandura et al., 1961). Also in keeping with the social learning perspective, the degree to which a child is inclined to imitate such actions often depends on whether the model's behavior is observed to be rewarded or punished.

Research has also shown that how parents socialize their children can affect the extent to which the children internalize moral rules and principles. Excessive use of power-assertive techniques of punishment (spankings, withdrawal of privileges, physical coercion, and threats of force) tends to be associated with low levels of moral development (Hoffman, 1976). In contrast, reasoning with children about their behavior—explaining why a certain act is right or wrong, pointing out how the behavior affects others—appears to be associated with high levels of moral development, including consideration for others, capacity for moral reasoning, and feelings of guilt over wrongdoing (Aronfreed, 1969; Hoffman, 1976; Hoffman and Saltzstein, 1967). Such lessons in moral reasoning, moreover, must be heartfelt to be effective. The adult must convey kindness and caring with intense feelings about the issues involved (Radke-Yarrow and Zahn-Waxler, 1984).

THE COGNITIVE DEVELOPMENTAL PERSPECTIVE

The social learning view of moral development implicitly assumes that acquiring a conscience depends more on the amount and type of training that a child receives than it does on the child's age and level of maturation. The cognitive developmental view reverses the importance of these two sets of factors. It argues that a child progresses through distinct stages of moral reasoning, and that these stages reflect changes in the child's cognitive capabilities, which are broadly related to age.

The psychologist most closely associated with the cognitive developmental view of moral learning is Lawrence Kohlberg (1963, 1969). Kohlberg maintained that the stages of moral reasoning occur in an invariable sequence, each developing out of its predecessor and each cognitively more complex than the one before. He assessed a person's current level of moral thinking by presenting a series of moral dilemmas and asking how each should be resolved and why. Here is one example:

> In Europe a woman was near death from cancer. One drug might save her, a form of radium that a druggist in the same town had recently discovered. The druggist was charging $2,000, ten times what the drug cost him to make. The sick woman's husband, Heinz, went to everyone he knew to borrow the money, but he could only get together about half of what it cost. He told the druggist that his wife was dying and asked him to sell it cheaper or let him pay later. But the druggist said, "No." The husband got desperate and broke into the man's store to steal the drug for his wife. Should the husband have done that? Why? (Kohlberg, 1969, p. 379)

What mattered to Kohlberg was not the particular decision a person makes (whether Heinz's behavior was right or wrong), but the explanation for that decision. Table 10.3 presents typical explanations given at three major developmental levels, each of which has two stages. At the **preconventional** level, a child adheres to the rules of society in large part out of fear of the consequences of breaking them. The

TABLE 10.3 Motives for Stealing or Not Stealing the Drug at Various Levels of Moral Development

	For Stealing Drug	Against Stealing Drug
Preconventional Level		
Stage 1: obedience, or reward, orientation		
Action motivated by avoidance of punishment, and "conscience" is irrational fear of punishment.	If you let your wife die, you will get in trouble. You'll be blamed for not spending the money to save her and there'll be an investigation of you and the druggist for your wife's death.	You shouldn't steal the drug because you'll be caught and sent to jail if you do. If you do get away, your conscience would bother you thinking how the police would catch up with you at any minute.
Stage 2: instrumental exchange, or marketplace, orientation		
Action motivated by desire for reward or benefit. Possible guilt reactions are ignored and punishment is viewed in a pragmatic manner.	If you do happen to get caught, you could give the drug back and you wouldn't get much of a sentence. It wouldn't bother you much to serve a little jail term, if you have your wife when you get out.	He may not get much of a jail term if he steals the drug, but his wife will probably die before he gets out so it won't do him much good. If his wife dies, he shouldn't blame himself, it wasn't his fault she had cancer.
Conventional Level		
Stage 3: conformist, or "good boy, good girl," orientation		
Action motivated by anticipation of disapproval of others, actual or imagined.	No one will think you're bad if you steal the drug, but your family will think you're an inhuman husband if you don't. If you let your wife die, you'll never be able to look anybody in the face again.	It isn't just the druggist who will think you're a criminal; everyone else will too. After you steal it, you'll feel bad thinking how you've brought dishonor on your family and yourself; you won't be able to face anyone again.
Stage 4: "law-and-order" orientation		
Action motivated by anticipation of dishonor—that is, institutionalized blame for failure of duty—and by guilt over concrete harm done to others.	If you have any sense of honor, you won't let your wife die because you're afraid to do the only thing that will save her. You'll always feel guilty that you caused her death if you don't do your duty to her.	You're desperate and you may not know you're doing wrong when you steal the drug. But you'll know you did wrong after you're sent to jail. You'll always feel guilty for your dishonesty and lawbreaking.

(continued on page 308)

child, in other words, acts "good" to avoid punishment. The overwhelming majority of seven-year-olds are still at the preconventional level. At the second major level, the **conventional,** a child is concerned about winning the approval of others and meeting their standards and expectations. He or she is often inclined to follow the dictates of established authority. About half of all ten-year-olds have advanced to the conventional level. The final level of moral reasoning, the **postconventional,** is not reached during childhood. In fact, it is attained by only a small percentage of adults (Shaver and Strong, 1976). A

TABLE 10.3 Motives for Stealing or Not Stealing the Drug at Various Levels of Moral Development (continued)

	For Stealing Drug	Against Stealing Drug
Postconventional Level		
State 5: social-contract, legalistic orientation		
Concern about maintaining respect of equals and of the community (assuming their respect is based on reason rather than emotions). Concern about own self-respect—that is, about avoiding judging self as irrational, inconsistent, nonpurposive.	You'd lose other people's respect, not gain it, if you don't steal. If you let your wife die, it would be out of fear, not out of reasoning it out. So you'd just lose self-respect and probably the respect of others too.	You would lose your standing and respect in the community and violate the law. You'd lose respect for yourself if you're carried away by emotion and forget the long-range point of view.
Stage 6: universal ethical principle orientation		
Concern about self-condemnation for violating one's own principles.	If you don't steal the drug and let your wife die, you'd always condemn yourself for it afterward. You wouldn't be blamed and you would have lived up to the outside rule of the law but you wouldn't have lived up to your own standards of conscience.	If you stole the drug, you wouldn't be blamed by other people but you'd condemn yourself because you wouldn't have lived up to your own conscience and standards of honesty.

Adapted from Kohlberg, 1969.

person at this level recognizes that universal ethical principles can transcend the laws of society. Failure to adhere to these principles brings self-condemnation.

The fact that a person's level of moral thinking is age-related suggests that it is also related to level of cognitive development. Research supports this conclusion. In general, the more complex the intellectual tasks a youngster can perform, the higher the stage of moral reasoning that child tends to exhibit (Kuhn et al., 1977; Selman, 1976). One demonstration of the link between moral and cognitive development is seen in the research of Robert Selman (Selman, 1980; Selman and Byrne, 1974). Selman presented children of varying ages with stories that involved dilemmas. For example:

Holly is an 8-year-old girl who likes to climb trees. She is the best tree climber in the neighborhood. One day while climbing down from a tall tree she falls off the bottom branch but does not hurt herself. Her father sees her fall. He is upset and asks her to promise not to climb trees again. Holly promises. . . . Later

that day, Holly meets Sean. Sean's kitten is caught up in a tree and cannot get down. Something has to be done right away or the kitten may fall. Holly is the only one who climbs trees well enough to reach the kitten and get it down, but she remembers her promise to her father. (Selman and Byrne, 1974, p. 805)

Selman then asked the children a series of questions designed to assess their ability to take various perspectives: Holly's, her father's, and that of "most people." He found a clear developmental trend in the children's responses. The youngest ones could think only in terms of their own perspective. They either failed to realize that their own perspective was not shared by others, or they were unable to gauge others' points of view. Older children, in contrast, understood that the viewpoints of others could differ from their own, and they were able to imagine what those other viewpoints might be. At the same time, they were able to look at the views of several people through the eyes of a third party. This ability to take the perspectives of others is an important cognitive achievement. In Piaget's theory of cognitive development it is one of the accomplishments that distinguish older children from preschoolers. As children mature, they are increasingly able to transcend egocentrism and see things from a broader point of view. The ability to take broader and broader perspectives is also the essence of Kohlberg's stages of moral thinking. Thus, cognitive development and moral development often go hand in hand.

Kohlberg's cognitive theory of moral development has been criticized, however. Some have pointed out that a person's stage of moral reasoning does not always closely match his or her actual behavior (Kurtines and Greif, 1974). Someone may talk about ethical principles yet fail to adhere to them when faced with a moral dilemma (Gibbs and Schnell, 1985). Someone could even cheat and steal and still be capable of abstractly reasoning at Kohlberg's most advanced level (Santrock and Bartlett, 1986). If this is so, it is appropriate to ask how significant Kohlberg's stages really are.

Critics have also charged that Kohlberg's stages are biased because they fail to consider the values that people are taught to emphasize (Gilligan, 1977; Harkness, 1980; Hogan, 1975; Holstein, 1976; Sampson, 1978; Simpson, 1974). It may not be fair, for instance, to apply these stages to people of other cultures—cultures that value social consequences more highly than abstract principles or stress obligations to family above all else. Similarly, Kohlberg's stages may be biased against women. According to psychologist Carol Gilligan (1982, 1989), Kohlberg's theory ignores the fact that males are socialized into a different hierarchy of values than females, values that foster different forms of moral reasoning in adulthood. Specifically, men are prone to detachment from others; their self-worth stems from a sense of autonomy. This inclines them to reason morally in terms of abstract concepts, such as equity and justice (Kohlberg's postconventional level). Women, in contrast, are prone to attachment; their sense of self is linked to interconnectedness with family and friends. As a result, they are inclined to think about moral dilemmas in terms of personal relationships and social obligations (Kohlberg's conventional level). Such criticisms have helped to introduce well-deserved caution when assessing what a person's style of moral reasoning suggests about that person's level of cognitive development. Nevertheless, many psychologists believe that Kohlberg's theory offers a useful way to

think about changes in moral reasoning from early childhood to adulthood (Hoffman, 1977).

SOCIAL AND PERSONALITY DEVELOPMENT IN ADOLESCENCE

The word *adolescence* comes from the Latin word *adolescere*, meaning "to grow into maturity." And so the beginning of adolescence is marked by the onset of **puberty,** the period of sexual maturation. Puberty is triggered by changes in the body's hormones, especially an increased output of pituitary gland hormones that stimulate physical growth and the production of hormones from the sex glands. In boys puberty begins around the age of twelve and in girls around the age of ten or eleven.

One of the most obvious indications that puberty is underway is a sudden spurt in height. Boys grow about 5 inches in a single year and girls about 4 inches. **Primary sexual characteristics** also emerge, meaning that the sex organs develop. The testes, scrotum, and penis mature in boys, and the ovaries, vagina, and uterus in girls. The development of the uterus is accompanied by **menarche,** the start of the menstrual cycle. In industrialized nations, the age of first menstruation has declined over the last few generations. In mid-nineteenth-century America a girl typically began to menstruate at age sixteen; today the average age is twelve-and-a-half (Hamburg and Takanishi, 1989). This decline is thought to be due to the better nutrition that most girls in modern societies get (Tanner, 1982). Sexual maturation, of course, is accompanied by other physical changes. A boy's voice lowers, his shoulders widen and get more muscular, and he grows hair on his face, chest, underarms, and pubic region. A girl also grows pubic and underarm hair, and her breasts develop while her hips enlarge. These physical changes are called **secondary sexual characteristics.**

The timing of puberty can have important consequences. Boys who mature early are physically stronger than late-maturing boys, and so they tend to excel at sports. This can give them more poise and self-confidence, and make them more desirable in the eyes of both peers and adults (Conger, 1977). For girls the consequences of early maturation can be more negative. Dramatic changes in height and body shape may lead to temporary problems of social adjustment, particularly if these changes are sexually attractive to boys. Early maturation in a girl that occurs simultane-

A difference in height that would be insignificant among adults may cause a young adolescent girl to feel gawky and self-conscious.

ously with graduation to a higher-level school can be particularly stressful and give rise to feelings of depression (Petersen, 1989). Parents can help their early-maturing daughters avoid these negative outcomes by teaching them effective strategies for coping with changes.

The changes of puberty bring with them a new sense of self. Adolescents, with their emerging adult bodies, can no longer view themselves as children. They have now become teenagers, young people on the brink of early adulthood. Their improved cognitive abilities, which we talked about in Chapter 9, enable them to see the self in more psychological terms (Damon, 1983; Sprinthall and Collins, 1984). When asked for self-descriptions they tell you not just their physical traits, but also their feelings, beliefs, values, and characteristic ways of behaving. Adolescents can be very introspective. They search for a deeper, underlying core to the self, a core that explains and integrates their surface characteristics.

Adolescents also develop a need to establish an independent identity, especially to distinguish themselves as separate from their parents. This striving to gain a sense of themselves as separate, autonomous people becomes a major preoccupation. In fact, Erik Erikson labeled the search for a secure, well-integrated personal identity *the* overriding challenge of adolescence.

According to Erikson (1950), who introduced the concepts of **identity** and **identity crisis** to psychology, the physical, sexual, and social demands on adolescents foster in them a need to clarify who they are as individuals, and how they relate to society and the adult world they are soon to enter. Part of doing this is to try out different adult roles. Thus, one teenager may try her hand at acting, become more avant-garde in her style of dress, and get involved in political causes. By experimenting with a variety of possible choices, adolescents acquire some idea of the life-styles associated with different roles, without committing themselves irrevocably to any one. Of course, trying out different adult identities is much more possible in some societies than others. While an American teenager has a prolonged period of adolescence during which to experiment and many alternatives to choose from, young people in nonindustrialized societies are often forced soon after puberty into the adult roles that tradition dictates.

Another aspect of adolescent social development is relationships with peers. In keeping with their new capacity for self-understanding, teenagers also develop a more mature capacity for understanding others. As a result, their friendships take on a new degree of intimacy. Girls, especially, spend hours in self-disclosure and sharing of confidences (Sprinthall and Collins, 1984). This new intimacy extends first to peers of the adolescent's own sex and then to opposite-sex partners.

Adolescence is also the time when psychological intimacy may expand to include sexual intimacy as well. In one nationwide survey of American teenagers, 61 percent of the boys and 53 percent of the girls had experienced sexual intercourse by the age of seventeen (Louis Harris and Associates, 1986). The age of sexual initiation varies, however, with gender (most boys experience intercourse earlier than girls), race (blacks tend to be initiated earlier than whites), and the norms that prevail in a teenager's particular peer group (Brooks-Gunn and Furstenberg, 1989). When asked why most teenagers do not postpone sexual activity until they are adults, adolescents give a variety of reasons. In the nationwide survey just mentioned, boys and girls often listed curiosity as a motive, and boys cited sexual drives too. Some (roughly 10 percent) said that they had had sex because they were in love. The most frequently mentioned reason, however, was peer pressure. Half the boys and nearly three-quarters of the girls gave this explanation, with a quarter of both sexes reporting that they themselves had succumbed to pressure to do more sexually than they really wished to do.

Does this mean that adolescents are *over*influenced by peers, as many parents argue? There is little doubt that adolescence is a time when peers do become increasingly influential. If parents attempt to separate their teenage children from their friends, they usually meet with strong resistance (Steinberg, 1991). Young people probably oppose such parental interference partly because of a fear of being ridiculed by their peers. But the tendency of adolescents to oppose their parents and side with peers instead is often greatly overstated. Strong peer influence among teenagers does not entirely remove parental influence. Parental influence tends to remain fairly high, especially concerning the basic values the young person holds (Chassin and Sherman, 1985).

SOCIAL AND PERSONALITY DEVELOPMENT IN ADULTHOOD

Many people assume that personality development slows and eventually ceases once a person reaches adulthood. In fact, Freud argued that basic personality traits are essentially fixed in childhood and that adult identity is established around the end of adolescence. Some contemporary psychologists have found that, usually, adult personality traits are indeed quite stable, at least the most basic ones (Costa and McCrae, 1980; McCrae and Costa, 1984). But others who have a broader conception of what personality entails argue that our habitual ways of thinking and acting continue to change during adulthood (Levinson, 1986). At the very least, people face different challenges, have different concerns, and find different sources of satisfaction at various points in their adult lives. These differences in life experiences can make the attitudes and outlook of a person who is twenty-five significantly different from those of the same person twenty or forty years later. What are some of the changes in outlook that Americans can

Some adolescents use exaggerated styles of dress as a way of establishing their identities, fitting in with their peers—and, perhaps, annoying their parents.

expect as they move through the adult years? Researchers who view adult development as occurring in a series of stages have offered some answers to this question.

THE STAGE PERSPECTIVE

EARLY ADULTHOOD

If adolescence is a time of searching inward for personal identity, early adulthood is a time of looking outward to the tasks of launching a career, a marriage, and perhaps a family. In one study of the feelings, concerns, and activities of more than 500 men and women, those between the ages of twenty-two and twenty-eight were found to be busy making commitments, taking on responsibilities, and focusing their energies on the attainment of goals (Gould, 1972, 1978). Thus, rather than being a period of deep introspection, the early and mid-twenties are usually a period of action.

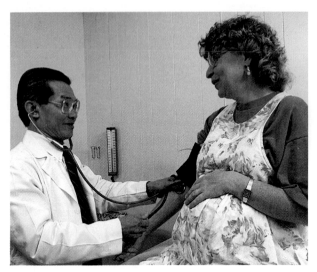

More women are choosing to postpone having children until they are in their thirties or forties. In 1987 (the most recent year for which statistics are available), 1 million women aged thirty and over had babies, compared to 660,000 in 1970.

The decade from age twenty to age thirty poses a special challenge to women. A young woman today is faced with a much wider range of choices than was her grandmother or probably even her mother. Like generations of women before them, many women in their twenties today still see marriage and motherhood as major life goals (Roberts and Newton, 1987). But a growing number are postponing childbearing in favor of first establishing a career. This means that many women are starting families at a significantly older age (Shreve, 1982). Most mothers today also continue to hold jobs outside the home even when their children are young. For these women, the balance between family and career is often adjusted several times during early and middle adulthood (Roberts and Newton, 1987; Sheehy, 1976).

The attitudes and concerns of adults gradually start to change in their early thirties. Many of those between the ages of twenty-eight and thirty-four begin to question the commitments they have made in the past decade, the values they have chosen, and the goals they have worked so hard to achieve. In short, this is a time of life when many people stop and ask themselves: "What is life all about now that I have done what I am supposed to do?" (Gould, 1972, 1978). Such misgivings, of course, can often lead to difficult and very painful reversals. Marriages may end, careers may be abandoned, and entire life-styles

may be changed. People in their early thirties sometimes feel that any unsatisfactory aspect of their lives must be rectified immediately, because soon it will be too late. This period of life has been called the age-thirty crisis (Levinson et al., 1978).

As the questioning and changes that accompany the age-thirty crisis subside, a person enters a new period of adulthood. For working men and women, the years between thirty-five and forty can be especially productive ones. In one study of both professional and working-class men, this was a time of "making it"—of establishing oneself in the world and of actively carving out a niche (Levinson et al., 1978). Usually this meant moving up the ladder of prestige and achievement in the person's chosen career.

MID-LIFE AND BEYOND

At about the age of forty the period of early adulthood comes to an end and a mid-life transition begins. For women who have devoted their adult lives to the roles of wife and mother, a crisis may occur when the children begin to leave home. To adjust to these changes, these family-oriented women may now search for satisfying work outside the home, returning to an interrupted career or perhaps starting a new one. Interestingly, middle-aged women who during their twenties and thirties already had involvements outside the home are not so affected when their children eventually leave the family nest (Roberts and Newton, 1987).

For men the mid-life transition usually centers around questions about both personal life and career. Like women at this stage, they may wonder: "What have I done with my life? What have I accomplished? What do I still wish to do?" In the study of men conducted by Daniel Levinson and his colleagues (1978), which revealed the stages shown in Figure 10.1, fully 80 percent of the sample experienced the mid-life transition as a moderate to severe crisis, characterized by a questioning of virtually every aspect of their lives.

This widespread questioning at mid-life is consistent with the seventh stage in Erik Erikson's theory of social and personality development. The challenge now, according to Erikson, is to learn how to reach out beyond one's own immediate welfare, to become concerned with the well-being of future generations and the impact that one's own efforts will have on them. Erikson calls this goal *generativity*. The person who fails to achieve generativity experiences stagnation, an embittered preoccupation with the self. In a thirty-year study of ninety-five men, beginning with their graduation from college, George Vaillant (1977) found that middle-aged people who excelled were indeed meeting Erikson's goal of generativity. In contrast, those who fared poorly were characterized by a bored self-indulgence, just like Erikson's concept of stagnation.

After the critical mid-life transition, the middle adult years are for many people a period of greater stability than they have ever known. Income is typically higher than at any time in the past. People usually have confidence in the skills they possess, and their productivity is often at its peak. But with middle age comes a new sense of time. People are increasingly aware that life is finite. They are constantly reminded of their own advancing years. When parents and friends die, when their own children have children, when they gradually become one of the oldest people at work, and when their bodies no longer perform as they once did, people are faced with the reality of growing old (Karp, 1988). "Within the last five years," one man in his fifties put it, "both my parents died. I became the oldest in my family. I'm the patriarch of the family now. Maybe that's when old age [begins]" (Karp, 1988, p. 731).

And so people start to think more in terms of priorities, in terms of focusing their remaining time on the things that really matter to them. This is a stage when personal relationships often become more important. Many people report greater satisfaction with their marriage, warmer ties with their children, and an increased value placed on friends. For many, these values and outlooks continue into the late adult years (Gould, 1972, 1978).

INDIVIDUAL DIFFERENCES

The stage perspective on social and personality development in adulthood stresses the events and transitions that many people have in common at specific ages. There are, however, differences in people's life stories that make each individual develop in some ways uniquely. For instance, not everyone experiences major milestones in life at the same time. Especially in the last several decades, our society has become more tolerant of those who proceed through life "off schedule" so to speak (Neugarten and Neugarten, 1987). Thus, the man or woman who is still unmarried at age thirty-five, the couple that decides to have

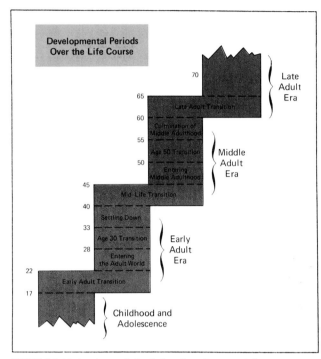

FIGURE 10.1 **A model of the developmental sequence of a man's life developed by Daniel Levinson. The major life eras are childhood and adolescence, early adulthood, middle adulthood, and later adulthood: within each era there are distinctive stages, and between eras a major transition occurs. This model emphasizes that development is a continuing process that requires continual adjustment. (*After Levinson, 1978.*)**

children after they are in their forties, and the career-minded people who continue to work into their seventies and eighties are no longer viewed with quite the surprise they used to be. For these people life follows a different pattern from the mainstream one.

Research underlines the importance of individual differences in adult development. In one study, for instance, the stages women experienced were found to be much less related to their ages than to the timing of events in their own particular lives (Reinke et al., 1985). Nor did all the women studied experience the same set of transitions and stages. It all depended on each woman's particular life history. Such studies remind us that human lives are not programmed to unfold in a uniform fashion. Each of us is in some ways a unique individual, subject to our own personal experiences, needs, and rhythms.

In Erikson's view, ideally, old age should bring a sense of satisfaction with the kind of life one has led.

COPING AND SATISFACTION IN ADULTHOOD

In Erik Erikson's theory, the final stage of life should result in a sense of wholeness, a recognition of purposes accomplished and a life meaningfully lived. Those who do not achieve this sense of fulfillment experience regret over wasted opportunities and poor choices. They long for another chance and so despair about death in ways that those who have found fulfillment may not.

What factors are associated with a sense of satisfaction in a person's later years? In one study of men and women that extended over much of their lives, people who were content at age seventy were the same ones who had reported positive feelings about their health, work, and marriages forty years earlier (Mussen et al., 1982). We can assume that people with no chronic diseases or physical handicaps would probably be content with their health. But what characteristics are related to satisfaction with a marriage and a job? Other studies have provided clues. For instance, people who are very happily married tend to describe their marital relationship as having certain traits. Most important is the emotional security that the relationship brings, followed by the partners' mutual respect, their ability to communicate well, the help and enjoyment they give one another, their sexual intimacy, and their loyalty (Reedy et al., 1981). In the area of job satisfaction, other traits tend to emerge. People who are content with their occupations often derive satisfaction from the independence and self-reliance that those occupations bring (Sears, 1977).

Involvement in meaningful activities may also be a factor in promoting satisfaction with life, not just during a person's working years, but into old age as well. In one study, for instance, researchers arranged weekly visits between nursing home patients and a college student in which the two shared personal experiences (Langer et al., 1979). At the end of each visit, the student asked the elderly patient to think about a specific topic to be discussed the following week. This mental activity appeared to make a large difference, both in the elderly patients' memory ability and their emotional well-being, as measured by nurses' ratings of their awareness, alertness, sociability, activity, and health. Patients who were not involved in these weekly student visits did not fare as well. Apparently, elderly people who continue to be mentally active are able to cope more successfully with old age and to live more meaningful lives than those who become inactive.

SUMMARY

1. Babies appear to be biologically "programmed" to interact with other humans, responding especially to their voices and faces. An infant's **social smile,** triggered by the sight of a human face, has survival value because it strengthens the bond with the care giver. Each baby is also born with his or her own **tempera-ment,** or behavioral disposition. But biology alone does not determine how we develop. Rather, what we inherit at birth is a range of developmental possibilities, a **reaction range,** which can be fulfilled or thwarted depending on experiences.

2. The formation of emotional bonds with care givers,

known as **attachment,** is a central factor in development during infancy. Depending on how responsive the care giver is, a baby may form a **secure attachment** or an **anxious attachment.** The kind of attachment, in turn, can affect later social and personality development. People have wondered if a secure attachment to the mother is jeopardized if a baby is placed in day care while the mother works. Research suggests that the answer is "no," as long as the mother continues to be responsive to her baby and the day care is good.

3. Parenting styles can be classified as **permissive** (lacking rules for appropriate behavior), **authoritarian** (harsh, inflexible, and unresponsive to the child's wishes), and **authoritative** (warm, responsive, and flexible, but setting firm limits when needed). Children with permissive parents tend to be impulsive and lacking in self-reliance; those with authoritarian parents tend to be moody and have problems with peers; and those with authoritative parents tend to be friendly, independent, and in control of themselves.

4. Various forms of child abuse can have devastating effects on children. Apathy, blunted emotions, and low self-esteem are just some of the reactions seen in the victims of abuse by parents. Parents can also negatively affect their children by marital conflict and divorce. But a strong, caring relationship with at least one of the parents can do much to overcome any adverse reactions.

5. **Gender roles** are the patterns of behavior that males and females in general tend to have in common, despite their individual differences in personality. Although biology may contribute to the behavioral differences between the sexes, learning also plays an important part.

6. **Socialization** is the process of instilling society's values into children. The basic goal of socialization is **internalization**—incorporating social values to such an extent that their violation produces guilt. Socialization plays a key role in the development of moral thought and behavior. According to Freud, a child internalizes the moral code of the same-sex parent during resolution of the **Oedipus conflict.** Social learning theorists claim that children acquire morality gradually by observing good behavior in others, being rewarded for their own good deeds, and experiencing punishment when they are bad. The cognitive developmental view holds that children progress through stages of moral reasoning, each of which reflects their current cognitive level.

7. Adolescence, the transition from childhood to adulthood, involves important physical, psychological, and social changes. Adolescence is marked by the onset of **puberty,** the period of sexual maturation. The mature sex organs that develop are called **primary sexual characteristics,** while the other physical traits of a man or a woman are called **secondary sexual characteristics.** With their more advanced cognitive capabilities, adolescents are able to analyze the self more abstractly than they did as children, often raising probing questions about who they are. Erik Erikson labeled this search for a personal **identity** *the* overriding challenge of adolescence.

8. Social and personality development continues throughout adulthood in the sense that people continue to face new challenges and new roles. Although people often experience similar feelings and outlooks at the same points in their adult lives, individual differences in adult development are important too. The final years of life can be ones of pleasure and fulfillment, especially for people who have found satisfaction in their marriage, family, and work and who continue to be mentally active.

SUGGESTED READINGS

Belsky, J. K. (1990). *The psychology of aging.* Pacific Grove, CA: Brooks/Cole. A noted researcher explores classic and contemporary topics in the psychology of aging.

Kotre, J., and Hall, E. (1990). *Seasons of life: Our dramatic journey from birth to death.* Boston: Little. The authors argue that human development revolves around three time clocks: the biological, the social, and the psychological. They provide rich examples of how people pass through each of these stages across the life span.

Llewelyn, S., and Osborne, K. (1990). *Women's lives.* New York: Routledge, Chapman, & Hall. This book details the unique challenges that women experience throughout life, ranging from the teen years to adult sexuality issues.

Miller, P. H. (1989). *Theories of developmental psychology* (2nd ed.). San Francisco: Freeman. Concise introduction to various theories of developmental psychology, including those of Piaget, Freud, and Erikson.

Steinberg, L. (1991). *Adolescence* (2nd ed.). New York: McGraw-Hill. A multidisciplinary survey of theories and research on adolescent development, including a look at the effects of the different contexts in which adolescents grow.

CHAPTER 11

PERSPECTIVES ON EMOTION

He could not help but observe in his mother's actions a concealed nervousness, an irresolution as if under the strain of waiting. Unlike the fluent, methodical way in which she habitually moved about the kitchen, her manner now was disjointed, uncertain. In the midst of doing something or saying something, she would suddenly utter a curious, suppressed exclamation like a groan of dismay, or lift her hand in an obscure and hopeless gesture, or open her eyes as though staring perplexedly and brush back her hair. Everything she did seemed insecure and unfinished. She went from the sink to the window and left the water running and then remembering it with an odd overhastiness, turned, missed the handkerchief she was pegging to the clothesline and let it fall into the yard.

HENRY ROTH, *Call It Sleep*

[A young musician recalls]
All of a sudden nothing seemed to matter except the music. . . . The things I practiced seemed to just come out. I never thought about which fingering I would use or when I would breathe. It just came out naturally. All I thought about was expressing myself in the way that I thought the piece should sound. I never noticed there was an audience after the first eight bars of music. . . . Even now I don't remember their applause but only my feeling of satisfaction in playing the piece the way I actually felt it should be played. (Privette and Landsman, 1983, pp. 195–196)

Emotions are so much a part of our daily existence that it is difficult to imagine life without them. Try to picture yourself standing in a two-hour line without annoyance, winning a $100,000 lottery without elation, learning of a loved one's death without grief. Such lack of emotions is almost inconceivable. Emotions set the tone of our experiences and give life its vitality. Without the ability to feel rage, grief, joy, and love, we would hardly recognize ourselves as human.

Yet as familiar as emotions are to us, it is not easy to frame a general definition of the term. Consider the passages at the beginning of this chapter. They clearly describe anxiety and satisfaction. But what do these two states have in common? What attributes do all emotions share?

Reviewing the literature on emotions, Paul and Anne Kleinginna (1981) found many different defini-

Intensely absorbed in their music, performers can lose touch with everything else around them.

mon. Thus, **emotions** may be defined as patterns of reactions that include physiological and bodily changes, expressive and/or goal-oriented behavior, and subjective experiences.

Many older theories depicted emotions as disorganized and maladaptive (e.g., Angier, 1927). According to this view, emotions are primitive, physiological responses that interfere with logical, rational action. People become emotional when they are unable to cope with a situation, and their emotions make them even more confused, further undermining their ability to cope. The idea that emotions are disruptive is part of our popular culture. Often we dismiss someone by saying, "Don't mind her, she's just being emotional."

Most modern theories, in contrast, emphasize the *functional* aspects of emotions (Smith, 1989; Smith and Ellsworth, 1985; Tomkins, 1980). To be sure, emotions may be disruptive. In the first passage above, the mother's nervous anxiety interferes with her ability to carry out ordinary, everyday activities. But emotions can also be adaptive, as in the second passage, where the young musician's joy may have enhanced his performance.

According to the modern view, one function of emotions is to prepare and motivate us to deal with challenges in our environment. Anger, for example, prepares and motivates us to get rid of an obstacle or an irritant; fear prepares and motivates us to avoid or escape danger. Emotions operate somewhat like instincts in lower animals: they prompt us to adjust to a change in the environment. But emotions are more flexible than instincts, allowing us to fine-tune our responses. When a wolf is threatened, it attacks; when a rabbit is threatened, it runs. These instinctive responses are part of their species' biological programs. Emotions alert us to conditions that require adjustment, but give us many more options. When threatened and afraid, we may choose to flee or stand our ground, to fight or attempt to negotiate.

Emotions are also a signal to others. They reveal how we are feeling and, thus, how we are likely to behave. The boy in the first passage knew without being told that his mother was upset; the audience senses the musician's joy. Other animals are able to communicate their "feelings" and "intentions": When a strange wolf invades another wolf's territory, the home wolf snarls, letting the intruder know that it had better clear out or prepare to fight. But the wolf's bared fangs are a biological reflex, like a sneeze.

tions, but general consensus on three points. First, emotions involve physiological changes. Although these bodily manifestations are not described specifically in these passages, we can imagine the mother's racing heart, tight throat, and shaky hands; the energy flowing through the musician's fingers, and the deep sense of muscle relaxation he experiences after his performance. Second, emotions often, but not always, lead to expressive and/or goal-directed behavior. The mother's actions—her odd, uncoordinated movements, exclamations, and facial expressions—all stem from her emotional state. Musicians often look "carried away"—that is, they are so concentrated on the music, they seem unaware of anything else around them. Third, and perhaps most obviously, emotions are subjective experiences or internal states, often brought on by external circumstances. Human emotions run the gamut from sorrow and despair, through envy and hate, to joy and ecstasy. But all have these three dimensions in com-

Again, emotions are more flexible. We can act *as if* we are burning with anger or consumed by grief when in fact we feel totally indifferent. And we can play it cool when inside we are seething with rage or shaking in fear. So rather than viewing emotions as disruptive, psychologists today see emotions in a more positive light, as adaptive and functional.

We begin this chapter by analyzing the three basic dimensions of emotion—physiological changes, expressive behavior, and internal states. Then we take an in-depth look at one emotion, happiness. What makes people happy? Why are some of us happier than others? Can people learn to be happy? Next we consider the long-standing theoretical debate over where emotions come from. Are emotions "gut reactions," or are emotions largely "in our head"? (The answers may surprise you.) Finally, we look at emotional reactions to crises and the process of recovery.

THE PHYSIOLOGY OF EMOTION

When we are feeling frustrated or anxious we say, "My nerves are on edge." When we are overjoyed we say, "I'm flying." These are not mere figures of speech. Rather we are expressing what psychologists have demonstrated time and again in the laboratory: strong emotions are associated with physiological arousal, or more specifically, with changes in the peripheral nervous system.

EMOTION AND THE PERIPHERAL NERVOUS SYSTEM

As we discussed in Chapter 3, the peripheral nervous system is comprised of two main parts, the somatic (or voluntary) nervous system and the autonomic (or involuntary) nervous system. The somatic nervous system innervates our smooth muscles (including facial muscles), making it possible for us to interact with our physical and social environment. To understand how important the somatic nervous system is, imagine being without it. Would you have emotions without the somatic nervous system? Perhaps, but you would not be able to express these emotions or to act on them. At very least, emotions would lose their purpose.

The innervation of facial muscles is of particular interest to emotion researchers. Most of our smooth

The movie *Mr. and Mrs. Bridge,* **based on Evan Hunter's novels and starring Joanne Woodward and Paul Newman, portrays a couple whose marriage is damaged by the husband's inability to express—or even acknowledge—his emotions and by his insensitivity to his wife's feelings.**

muscles are attached to the skeleton; they enable us to move around. The facial muscles are attached to skin and connective tissue, not bone. Their sole function is to move skin on the face, producing changes in facial expressions. As you will learn in later sections of this chapter, the face has a fascinating relation to the experience of emotion. The autonomic nervous system regulates the body's internal environment and usually functions without conscious control. It is composed of two subdivisions, the sympathetic and the parasympathetic, both of which connect to almost every muscle of the internal organs and also to every gland. The two divisions have broadly opposite effects. In general, the sympathetic division dominates during emergencies or stress and promotes energy expenditure. It encourages the increased blood sugar, heart rate, and blood pressure needed for sustained

Tennis player Andres Gomez gives a clear demonstration of the link between strong emotion and physiological arousal.

physical activity, and at the same time it inhibits digestion. The parasympathetic division, in contrast, dominates during relaxation and promotes energy conservation. It works to decrease heart rate and blood flow to the skeletal muscles, while also promoting digestion. Not surprisingly, most of the physiological changes associated with strong emotion, such as intense anger and fear, are caused by activation of the sympathetic division.

What exactly happens when the sympathetic nervous system is activated? Suppose it is 2:00 A.M. and you are walking to your car, which is parked on a deserted city street. Suddenly a man emerges from a dark alley. What physiological changes would occur in this fear-arousing situation?

1. *Vascular changes:* The blood vessels leading to your stomach and intestines would constrict, and digestion would virtually stop. At the same time, the vessels leading to your larger skeletal muscles would expand, diverting the oxygen and nutrients carried in your blood to where they might be needed for fight or flight.

2. *Hormonal changes:* Your pancreas would secrete the hormone glucagon, which would stimulate your liver to release stored sugar into the bloodstream. The sugar would supply extra energy to your skeletal muscles should they need it. In addition, your adrenal glands would secrete the hormone epinephrine, which would help sustain many of the other physiological changes brought about by activation of the sympathetic nervous system.

3. *Respiratory changes:* Your breathing would become deeper and more rapid, and your bronchioles (the small air passages leading to your lungs) would expand. These changes would increase the supply of oxygen to your blood—oxygen needed to burn the sugar being sent to your skeletal muscles.

4. *Circulatory changes:* Your heartbeat rate would increase, perhaps more than doubling, thus speeding the circulation of blood and hastening the delivery of oxygen and nutrients to your skeletal muscles.

5. *Visual changes:* The pupils of your eyes would dilate, thereby taking in more light.

6. *Sweat gland changes:* The activity of your sweat glands would increase. The sweat glands on the palms of your hands, in particular, would secrete moisture.

7. *Muscular changes:* The muscles just beneath the surface of your skin would contract, causing hairs to stand on end. For our furry ancestors the erection of body hair may have been part of a threat display, but we relatively hairless humans simply break out in "goose bumps" (Lang et al., 1972). The muscles of your neck and shoulders would quickly tense, orienting your eyes and face toward the source of threat. And the muscles over your eyebrows would contract, pulling your brows together and pushing them out, partially covering your eyes. This is part of the fear expression, and may help to protect your eyes should a fight ensue.

Activation of the sympathetic and somatic nervous systems has sometimes made possible feats of great strength and endurance. Cases have been reported in which a woman managed to lift a car to free her child trapped beneath the wheel, or a man somehow swam against a powerful current to reach safety. This is not to say that arousal suddenly endows a person with superhuman powers. Rather, physiological arousal enables us to use our muscles more effectively and for longer periods of time than we ordinarily could.

Once a threatening situation is over, diverse physiological changes again take place. Suppose that your would-be attacker turned out to be a police officer on patrol. Almost immediately the opposing effects of the parasympathetic nervous system would begin to reassert themselves. Your heart rate, respiration, glandular secretions, blood flow, and muscular tension would all return to normal, and the bodily sensations associated with fear would subside. This general cycle of physiological arousal—caused by assertion of the sympathetic nervous system over muscles and glands, followed by reassertion of the parasympathetic division—is the cycle associated with most strong emotions.

MEASURING THE PHYSIOLOGY OF EMOTION

In extreme cases (such as the encounter with a stranger in dark alley), we feel as if our senses are turned up full blast; an observer can easily perceive what we are feeling. More often, however, the physiological changes associated with emotion are so slight that others do not notice. How can psychologists monitor and record such subtle activities in the peripheral nervous system?

The emotion researcher's primary tool is a machine called a **polygraph,** which literally means "many pens." In a sense, a polygraph works like a radio communication system. A radio detects small electrical impulses in the air (radio waves), amplifies these electrical signals, and transduces or converts them into energy to drive a speaker, producing sound. Similarly, the polygraph detects small changes in the subject's nervous system, transduces these changes into electrical signals, and uses them to drive pens on a moving roll of paper, producing a strip chart. (See Figure 11.1.) Modern polygraphs also send the electrical signals into a computer, which converts them to numbers for statistical analysis.

A polygraph can be used to take a number of different physiological measurements simultaneously. One of the most widely used in emotion research is *electrodermal activity* or EDA (formerly called *galvanic skin response,* or GSR) (Fowles et al., 1981). When the autonomic nervous system is aroused, sweat glands concentrated in the palm of the hand quickly fill up with water (the "sweaty palm syndrome," a frequent cause of embarrassment on first dates and job interviews). Water conducts electricity. The more aroused the autonomic nervous system, the more water in the glands, the more electricity the skin

conducts. Researchers can pass a tiny current (too weak to be felt) across the subject's palm and detect the slightest change in conductance, thereby measuring autonomic nervous system activity.

Cardiovascular measures are also popular among emotion researchers (Cacioppo and Tassinary, 1990). The most common is the *electrocardiogram* or EKG, which uses electrodes attached to the subject's chest to measure changes in heart rate. (The "K" in EKG comes from the original German spelling.) Another sensor attached to the thumb may be used to measure the time it takes the contraction pulse to travel from the heart to the thumb, and thus how constricted or relaxed the subject's arteries are. A rubber tube (called a *pneumograph*) around the subject's chest assesses changes in the rate and depth of breathing. Blood pressure is measured with the standard inflatable cuff, routinely used in physical examinations.

Emotion researchers have become increasingly interested in the muscles that produce facial expressions (Dimberg, 1990). As noted earlier, the somatic nervous system controls the facial muscles. When these muscles contract, they give off small electrical potentials, on the order of a few microvolts (or millionths of a volt). The *electromyogram* (EMG) can pick up, and the polygraph amplify, changes in facial muscle actions that are so small and fleeting they do not produce any visible movement—that is, any visible change in facial expression (Cacioppo et al., 1986). Finally, researchers who are interested in the brain's role in emotion (discussed below) use an *electroencephalogram* (EEG) to record brain activity.

Psychologists use the polygraph to investigate a wide range of questions. For example, polygraphs have been used to measure changes in fear reactions among phobic persons undergoing treatment. Polygraphs are also widely used in biofeedback research, where, for example, subjects might be taught to control their heart rate or brain waves by receiving feedback from the polygraph. (See Chapter 15 for further discussion of biofeedback.)

To many people, however, the polygraph is associated with lie detector tests. The use of polygraphs in this context is both widespread and widely misunderstood. A million or more lie detector tests are given in the United States each year (Ekman, 1985). Until recently, the majority of these tests were given by private employers—ranging from banks to fast-food outlets such as McDonald's—to prescreen employees and to control internal crime. Federal law now prohibits the use of polygraphs for preemployment

The polygraph, set up as shown here, is used to record the subtle changes in the peripheral nervous system that signal the degree of emotional arousal being experienced by the subject.

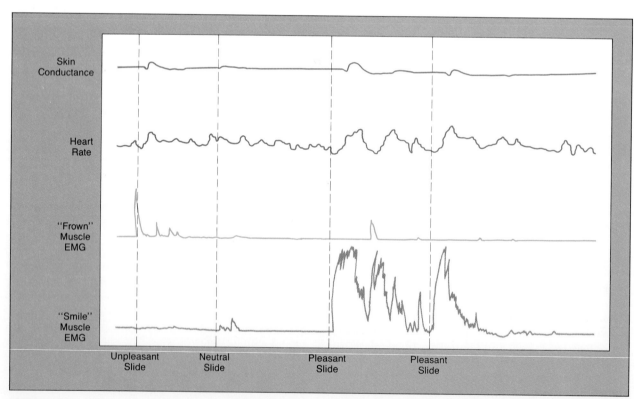

FIGURE 11.1   Polygraph output from an experiment on emotion. The subject was asked to look at several photographic slides. The unpleasant slide was of a terrorist bombing. The pleasant slides were of children playing and a clown. The neutral scene was of a parking lot. The output shows changes in several physiological systems in response to the emotional content of the slides. *(Courtesy of Randy J. Larsen.)*

screening in the private sector, but not for examining employees suspected of theft or other crimes. A second common use of the polygraph as a lie detector is in criminal investigations—not only to assess the guilt or innocence of criminal suspects, but also to test the credibility of witnesses and victims. Although many states do not permit the results of a polygraph to be reported in a trial, some do, if the defendant agrees. Another large user of lie detector tests is the federal government, which reserves the right to pre-screen job applicants who would have access to classified material. The government also uses polygraphs to examine employees suspected of crimes (including espionage) or of "leaking" sensitive information to the press. Periodic random screening of current government employees who have security clearance—the "dragnet" approach—is highly controversial. At present, government agencies cannot require an employee to submit to a polygraph unless there is evidence that the person might have violated a rule or law. But laws and regulations in this area are constantly changing.

In a typical lie detector test, the subject is first asked a series of neutral, control questions to establish a baseline: "Is your name John Doe?" "Do you live on Elm Street?" "Did you eat eggs for breakfast?" These are followed by questions that would indicate "guilty knowledge," facts known only by the criminal. How accurate is this procedure? First, polygraphs *do not* detect lying. Rather, as described above, they measure changes in a person's nervous system activity. Only if we assume that lying produces such changes can we infer that a polygraph catches lies. But many other, extraneous factors can cause physiological arousal (including surprise, pain, anxiety, joy, and novelty). Moreover, individuals vary widely in their physiological responses. Just as some people can lie with "a straight face," others can lie with cool palms and a steady heartbeat.

Second, most people think of accuracy only in terms of detecting guilt. The other side of accuracy is often overlooked—namely, how good are polygraphs at detecting *innocence?* Polygraph operators can make two types of mistakes: believing a lie and disbelieving the truth. Actually, polygraphs are fairly accurate in detecting guilt, but have a poorer record in detecting innocence. In other words, they tend to err in convicting the innocent. Unfortunately, a truly innocent person is likely to volunteer for a polygraph (whether in a criminal investigation or employment

setting) in the mistaken belief that he or she has nothing to lose and everything to gain.

Despite these weaknesses, polygraphs are still widely used. If you look in the yellow pages of the phone book under "Lie Detection," you will find that most cities have at least one and often several companies providing these services.

EMOTION AND THE BRAIN

Although the peripheral nervous system most clearly exhibits the physiological changes associated with emotion, this system is coordinated by the brain. The hypothalamus and certain areas of the limbic system, in particular, are involved in a number of emotional reactions, including anger, aggression, and fear (Pribram, 1981). This has been demonstrated by research on experimental animals in which different parts of these brain regions were mildly stimulated or surgically removed. Research with cats, for example, has shown that stimulation of particular areas of the hypothalamus can induce intense activation of the sympathetic nervous system and an emotional display that can be interpreted only as feline rage. The cat's pupils dilate; the fur on its back stands erect; the animal flattens its ears, arches its back, unsheathes its claws, and hisses and snarls intensely (Flynn et al., 1970). In contrast, surgical lesions in areas of the amygdala produce extremely docile behavior.

In humans, exaggerated emotional behavior may accompany damage to certain areas of the limbic system. Such damage can take place before, during, or after birth, and it can arise from a variety of causes, including diseases that affect the brain, drug abuse, and trauma due to auto accidents, athletic injuries, or gunshot wounds. You may recall from Chapter 1 the example of Charles Whitman, who shot and killed thirty-eight people. An autopsy revealed a malignant tumor on his amygdala (Sweet et al., 1969).

Documentation of other cases in which damage to the limbic system has been associated with uncontrollable violence has led some researchers to suggest that many extremely volatile people may be suffering from brain disease or injury of some sort (Mark and Ervin, 1970). This possibility generated renewed interest in psychosurgery—the removal or destruction of parts of the brain—as a form of treatment (see Chapter 17). Although such a procedure may control violent behavior, it can also alter an individual's personality in very adverse ways. For this reason it is

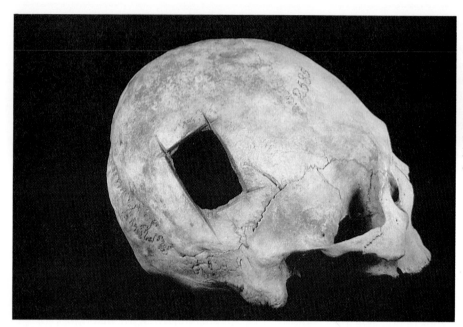

Psychosurgery, in which parts of the brain are removed or destroyed to treat certain forms of mental illness, is rare but hardly new. Archeologists have unearthed a number of skulls like this one, which show that brain surgery was practiced thousands of years ago by the Inca and other ancient civilizations.

highly controversial and relatively rare (see Valenstein, 1986).

For a long time psychologists believed that the brain's control over emotion was exerted largely through such "primitive" structures as the hypothalamus and the amygdala. More recently, however, it has become clear that the cerebral cortex is intimately involved in emotion as well. Evidence is accumulating that the cortex's role in emotion is asymmetrical: the left frontal cortex is associated with positive feelings, and the right frontal cortex with negative feelings (Heller, 1990). Laboratory experiments have shown that when pleasant emotions are induced in subjects, the left hemisphere shows greater activation; whereas when unpleasant emotions are induced, the right hemisphere shows greater activation (Davidson et al., 1990). Other research has shown that individual differences in resting hemisphere activity predict readiness or predisposition to respond to events with positive or negative emotions. In one study (Davidson and Fox, 1989), ten-month-old infants who showed relatively greater right-hemisphere activation during a quiet, baseline period (a negative predisposition) were more likely to cry when later separated from their mothers. Conversely, infants who showed greater left-hemisphere activation during the baseline period (a positive predisposition) were less likely to cry.

In a similar study of adults (Tomarken et al., 1990), the researchers used an electroencephalogram (EEG) to measure hemispheric asymmetry under quiet, neutral conditions. They found no relationship between greater right- or left-hemisphere activity and self-reported mood ratings under these conditions. Then they showed the subjects film clips designed to invoke pleasant emotions (a puppy playing with flowers and monkeys cavorting in a zoo) or negative emotions (a nurse training film showing a leg amputation and third-degree burns). Subjects whose EEGs suggested a right-hemisphere predominance described more intense feelings of fear while watching the nurse training film than did subjects whose EEGs suggested a left-hemisphere predominance. Other studies have shown that depressed patients have a much higher level of activation in the front portion of the right hemisphere than do people who are not depressed (Davidson, 1984).

The growing field of *psychoneuroimmunology* has found significant links among emotions, the brain, and the immune system. (See Chapter 15.) In one study (Stone et al., 1987), dental students were asked to record their daily mood and provide a saliva sample three times a week, for a period of two months. Antibodies in the saliva were analyzed to measure the subjects' immune system functioning.

The researchers found that the subjects' antibodies were low on days when their mood was negative and high on days when their mood was positive. In Chapter 15 we discuss in more depth how emotionally stressful events, such as the death of a spouse, can affect the immune system.

Another growing field of research concerning emotions and physiological changes focuses on brain chemistry. Depression, for instance, is now known to be associated with reduced levels of the neurotransmitter norepinephrine. (See Chapter 3.) Drugs that deplete norepinephrine produce depression, while antidepressant drugs usually stimulate norepinephrine secretion or prevent its reuptake, thus allowing more to remain active in the synapse for the transmission of nerve impulses (Beckham and Leber, 1985). (Also see Chapter 17.) Moreover, anger, which is often provoked therapeutically to counteract depression, is also related to increased secretions of norepinephrine (Dienstbier, 1978). Granted, just a few such patterns have so far been discovered. But keep in mind that only very recently have advances in technology allowed scientists to trace neurotransmitters with any precision. Many suspect that in the future the relationship between brain chemicals and emotions will become clearer.

What can we conclude about the relative contributions of the brain and peripheral nervous systems to emotions? Some years ago the psychologist George W. Hohmann (1966), himself a paraplegic, interviewed twenty-five Army veterans who had severed spinal cords. He found that the nature and intensity of certain emotions, especially anger and fear, were significantly different from normal emotional reactions. In general, the higher the lesion on the spinal cord, the more extensive the disruption of sympathetic arousal and the greater the change in emotional experience. The veterans still perceived the significance of emotion-arousing situations, and even displayed much of the behavior associated with strong emotion, but the *quality* of their emotional experience was often altered. Something was missing. As one man explained, "Sometimes I get angry when I see some injustice. I yell and cuss and raise hell, because if you don't do it sometimes I've learned people will take advantage of you. But it just doesn't have the heat it used to. It's a mental kind of anger." This research was often cited as evidence that autonomic arousal and feedback are an essential part of emotional experience.

In a recent study (Chwalisz et al., 1988), researchers compared university students with spinal-cord injuries, students with other problems that confined them to a wheelchair (such as a broken leg), and nonhandicapped students. They found that students with spinal-cord injuries experienced the full range of emotions: joy, love, sentimentality, anger, sadness, and fear. All reported emotional highs and lows. But, in general, the intensity of their emotional experiences was somewhat lower than that of other subjects. The researchers concluded that feedback from the autonomic nervous system may amplify emotional experience, but it is not essential. In their view the essential organs of emotion are the brain and the face. "The excitation of particular brain pathways and accompanying facial expressions may be sufficient for emotional experience" (Chwalisz et al., 1988, p. 821).

THE BEHAVIORAL EXPRESSION OF EMOTION

Consider the photograph on page 326 of a couple in their kitchen. They are saying nothing, but communicating plenty. The man's folded arms, the tilt of his head, his averted eyes—all suggest a stubborn form of anger. The woman, in contrast, conveys resignation and despair by her bowed head, stooped shoulders, and the way she has buried her face in her hand. We would be incredulous if someone tried to tell us that this domestic scene involved a casual conversation about a neighbor's new car. Powerful emotions are obviously being expressed here. Psychologists have wondered why people show their emotions in such recognizable patterns. Are these patterns purely the product of socialization, or do they form a part of our genetic heritage?

THE BIOLOGICAL BASIS OF EMOTIONAL EXPRESSION

In his book *The Expression of the Emotions in Man and Animals* (1896), Charles Darwin argued that many of our patterns of **nonverbal communication** are inherited—that they evolved because they had survival value. Darwin approached the topic of emotions from a functional perspective. "Why do emotional expressions exist?" he asked. His answer was that the primary function of emotional expression is to broadcast information about our internal state. By telling others how we feel, we also tell them how we are

People can often express their emotions perfectly clearly without saying a single word.

likely to behave. When we are enraged, for example, we commonly grimace and bare our teeth. Other animals also bare their teeth to alert others that they are prepared to fight. In most cases a threat is sufficient. Advance warning enables others to take action to avoid violence (backing off, signaling deference or friendly intentions, etc.). For social animals who live in groups, such as humans, this rapid communication of internal states is highly adaptive. Much actual fighting is avoided. The human grimace may be left over from a time in our evolutionary past when we fought with our teeth—a weak form of preparatory action that had *previously* been adaptive. Although human aggression today seldom involves biting, the grimace still communicates that we are angry and might become aggressive in other ways. Our snarl is part of our species's biological equipment and a product of evolution.

By showing how the expression of emotions is adaptive, Darwin extended his theory of evolution. The laws of natural selection apply not only to physical, biological characteristics, but also to behavior patterns. At the same time Darwin advanced our understanding of emotional expression by providing a functional perspective.

If emotional expressions are a product of evolution, Darwin held, they should be universal: people from remote places, who do not understand one another's *spoken* language, nevertheless should have no trouble understanding each other's *expressive* language. Darwin was able to document some degree of cross-cultural similarity; later researchers have found extensive evidence for the universality of certain emotional expressions. In one study, people from different countries were asked to identify the emotions expressed in a series of photographs of faces, some of which are shown in Figure 11.2. Anger, fear, disgust, surprise, sadness, and happiness were consistently recognizable, regardless of the culture from which a person came. Even members of New Guinea tribes, who had had little previous contact with Westerners and their characteristic patterns of expression, had little trouble labeling these basic emotions (Ekman and Friesen, 1974). Other research has found that the facial expressions of interest, shame, and contempt are virtually the same across cultures (Ekman and Friesen, 1986; Izard, 1971). Such findings support Darwin's view that certain characteristic patterns of emotional expression are, at least in part, genetically transmitted (Izard, 1984).

Additional evidence for the biological underpinnings of emotional expression comes from the study of a ten-year-old girl who had been deaf and blind from birth (Goodenough, 1932). Because the little girl could not have learned appropriate emotional expression by observing the people around her, her behavior was presumed to reflect primarily her innate tendencies. When the girl displayed pleasure on finding a doll hidden in her clothing, she "threw herself back in her chair. . . . Her laughter was clear

Photograph Judged						
Judgment	Happiness	Disgust	Surprise	Sadness	Anger	Fear
Culture			Percent Who Agreed with Judgment			
99 Americans	97	92	95	84	67	85
40 Brazilians	95	97	87	59	90	67
119 Chileans	95	92	93	88	94	68
168 Argentinians	98	92	95	78	90	54
29 Japanese	100	90	100	62	90	66

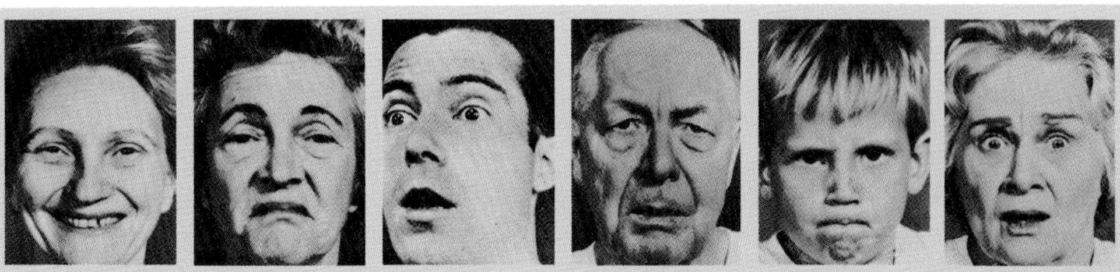

FIGURE 11.2 **The meaning of facial expressions. As this chart indicates, there is general agreement among the members of different cultures about the meaning of facial expressions. This suggests that we are biologically programmed to recognize and produce the emotions conveyed by certain facial expressions.** (*After Ekman et al., 1972.*)

and musical, in no way distinguishable from that of a normal child." The girl also showed anger in very characteristic ways. "Mild forms of resentment are shown by turning away her head, pouting the lips, or frowning. . . . More intense forms are shown by throwing back the head and shaking it from side to side, during which the lips are retracted, exposing the teeth which are sometimes clenched." Thus, the way this child expressed common emotions was remarkably similar to the patterns of emotional expression in most normal ten-year-olds. Other studies of disabled children have produced similar findings (Eibl-Eibesfeldt, 1970). So have studies of infants who seem too young to have acquired their emotional expressions through learning. Naive observers (who were not informed of the situation) could easily recognize the facial expression of pain in two-month-old babies who were receiving injections (Izard et al., 1983) and the facial expression of anger in four-month-old babies who were frustrated because their bottle, pacifier, or toy had been taken away (Stenberg and Campos, 1990). In short, the evidence suggests that

patterns of basic emotional expression are innate and present from a very early age.

EMOTION AND ACTION TENDENCIES

Emotions predispose us to behave in specific ways. Happiness, for example, leads us to relax and recuperate after attaining some goal; sadness, to appeal for support from others; fear, to withdraw or flee; anger, to threaten or attack; disgust, to get rid of some noxious object; and so on. Emotions tend to exert some control over action, and thus serve as the *motivational* link between experience and behavior (Frijda, 1986; Frijda et al., 1989). Emotions can create a state of readiness or *un*readiness to interact with the environment—as when a person "freezes with fear."

Felt **action tendencies** or "motivational urges" are what distinguish emotions from mere feelings of pleasantness or unpleasantness. They also *differentiate* between different emotional experiences. Consider fear and anger. Both emotions are associated with high levels of unpleasantness. Both are accompanied by similar patterns of physiological arousal (a racing heart, sweaty palms, and so on). But they are linked with quite different action tendencies: fear is associated with the action tendency to withdraw, and anger with the action tendency to attack. Physiological arousal prepares the body to effectively carry out this urge.

THE ROLE OF LEARNING IN EMOTIONAL EXPRESSION

To say that certain expressions of emotion are prewired, and that emotions prepare us to act in a specific way (fight or flight), does not rule out learning. Culture dictates when it is appropriate to express or suppress an action tendency. In Japan people are expected to smile and be polite, even when seething with rage; a woman of the Kiowa Indian tribe is supposed to scream and tear her face when her brother dies, whether she liked him or not (Tavris, 1982). People of different cultures also vary in their use of certain nonverbal cues to express emotion. In Chinese literature, the expression "He scratched his ears and his cheeks" is supposed to let the reader know that the person is happy (Otto Klineberg, 1988). In Western culture, this description might be interpreted as indicating that the person is anxious, even distraught. The Profile of Nonverbal Sensitivity (PONS) measures an individual's ability to decode nonverbal messages. After administering it to more than 2,000 subjects from twenty nations, one group of researchers found that people from cultures similar to that of the United States (where the test was developed) performed best. Although all subjects did better on the test than would occur by chance, the differences obtained strongly suggest that some aspects of nonverbal expression are culturally learned (Hall et al., 1978).

Additional evidence for the role of learning in nonverbal expression is provided by the fact that men and women differ in their nonverbal display of emotion. When Ross Buck (1976) showed the same series of emotion-arousing pictures to a group of men and women, observers could guess the content of the pictures much more easily from the faces of the women than from those of the men. Even though the men often reacted with increased heart rate and sweating palms, they kept their faces "masked." Significantly, according to Buck, this sex-based difference in emotional expressiveness is not found in preschool children. Although young children vary in their responses to emotion-arousing pictures, their varied reactions are a function of personality, not of gender. In the process of growing up, boys apparently learn to control certain aspects of emotional expression.

Ekman and his associates (Ekman et al., 1983; Levenson et al., 1990) have taken the study of facial expression a step further. They contend that facial muscle movement is closely tied to the autonomic nervous system, which controls heart rate, breathing, and other essential involuntary functions. Thus, if one adopts the facial expression characteristic of a certain emotion, this may trigger the related physiological changes. In a typical experiment, Ekman and his colleagues asked subjects to combine the following actions: raise the eyebrows, pull the eyebrows together, raise the upper eyelids, tighten the lower lids, drop the jaw, and stretch the lower lip wide. Simultaneously, the volunteers' brain waves, heart rate, breathing rate, and skin temperature were monitored. Although the subjects were not told that they were mimicking an expression of anger, they showed the physiological effects associated with anger. Similar findings apply to such emotions as disgust, fear, sadness and, possibly, surprise and contempt (Rensberger, 1985). Ekman conjectures that the contraction or relaxation of certain facial muscles triggers a specific response in the nervous system which in turn produces hormones capable of changing our mood (McDonald, 1985). The work of other researchers is buttressing Ekman's notion that there are unique brain pathways controlling each major emotion (Davidson, 1984).

INTERPRETING EMOTIONAL EXPRESSIONS

Our ability to interpret behavioral expressions of emotion is, like the unspoken communication itself, partly biological and partly learned. We appear to be "preattuned" to pick up the meaning of certain faces and gestures (Dimberg, 1990; Dimberg and Ohman, 1983). Presented with a novel situation or a new toy, infants check their mother's facial expression before deciding how to act (Lamb and Campos, 1982). If she looks happy or relaxed, the infant generally will approach; if she looks frightened, the infant will try to avoid the new situation or even flee.

In the course of socialization we learn which expressive behaviors to notice and which to ignore.

Women are generally better at detecting emotional undercurrents than men are, perhaps because girls are socialized to be more sensitive to the feelings of others (Ekman, 1982; Rosenthal et al., 1974).

Whatever their skill at interpreting emotional expressions, people tend to trust these nonverbal messages (Ekman, 1985; Ekman and Friesen, 1969; Mehrabian, 1972). When verbal and nonverbal information is contradictory—if, for example, a person denies that she is angry while repeatedly clenching and unclenching her fist—an observer generally concludes that the nonverbal message is the true one. This is because most people believe that body language is relatively difficult to control. Psychologists have shown that there may be some truth to this common assumption. Body movement *is* particularly difficult to disguise—more so than facial expressions. In one experiment designed to test people's control over nonverbal cues (Ekman and Friesen, 1969, 1974), subjects watched a gory film showing amputations and burn victims. They were then asked to conceal the true nature of the film in describing it to others. When observers could see only a speaker's head and face, they could not distinguish the subjects, who were lying, from the members of a control group, who were truthfully describing a pleasant film. But when given the opportunity to view the rest of the speaker's body, many of the observers could perceive deception. Apparently the liars managed to mask their feelings with a pleasant smile, but their anxiety showed in the movements of their bodies. Of course, whether the people we are trying to deceive do indeed notice such "leaks" through our nonverbal channels depends on a number of factors, including the strength of the emotions we are trying to conceal and how well our observers know us (Miller and Burgoon, 1982). Trained observers can usually (but not always) distinguish between a felt and a false smile.

EMOTIONS AS SUBJECTIVE STATES

Emotions are subjective or internal states, what we commonly call "moods" and "feelings." Often we have difficulty translating these feelings into words. If we ourselves have difficulty describing our feelings, how can psychologists develop models and measures of subjective states? How do they know what emotions people are feeling in a given situation?

This woman's smile looks real enough, but most people would rely on her exuberant gesture to conclude that she is genuinely happy.

Most contemporary emotion researchers view emotions in terms of opposing or bipolar states, such as relaxed versus anxious, elated versus bored. Further, most agree that the two most important dimensions of emotion are pleasant-to-unpleasant and high-to-low activation (Larsen and Diener, in press). These two dimensions are the basis of the **circle of emotions**, first popularized by James Russell (Russell, 1980; Russell et al., 1989) and shown in Figure 11.3. (In the scientific literature, this model is known as the *circumplex model of emotion*.) In principle, all emotions can be located on this circle. Some are characterized by high or low degrees of activation; some by high or low degrees of pleasure; and others by various combinations of the two. Thus excitement is a pleasant state of activation; nervousness is an unpleasant state of activation; relaxation is a pleasant state of low activation; and so on. Empirical studies show that most of us conceive of emotions in terms of these two basic

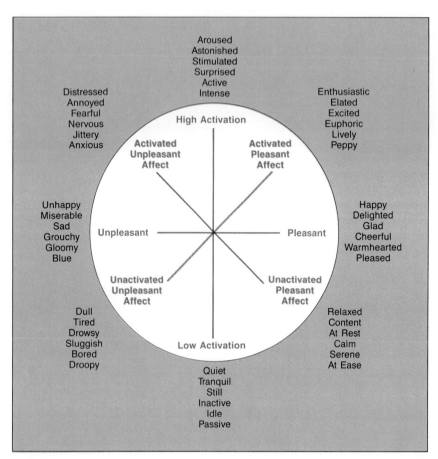

Aroused
Astonished
Stimulated
Surprised
Active
Intense

Distressed
Annoyed
Fearful
Nervous
Jittery
Anxious

High Activation

Activated
Unpleasant
Affect

Activated
Pleasant
Affect

Enthusiastic
Elated
Excited
Euphoric
Lively
Peppy

Unhappy
Miserable
Sad
Grouchy
Gloomy
Blue

Unpleasant

Pleasant

Happy
Delighted
Glad
Cheerful
Warmhearted
Pleased

Unactivated
Unpleasant
Affect

Unactivated
Pleasant
Affect

Dull
Tired
Drowsy
Sluggish
Bored
Droopy

Low Activation

Relaxed
Content
At Rest
Calm
Serene
At Ease

Quiet
Tranquil
Still
Inactive
Idle
Passive

FIGURE 11.3 The circumplex model of emotions, showing typical adjectives that define the dimensions of emotional experience. (*From Larsen and Diener, 1992./© 1992 by Sage Publications. Reprinted by permission.*)

dimensions (Watson and Tellegren, 1985; Watson et al., 1988).

Not all emotion researchers agree with this approach, however. Some feel that a two-dimensional model glosses over important distinctions between emotions. For example, fear and anger are both characterized by highly activated unpleasant feelings, but they *feel* quite different to the person experiencing them. (They also lead to different action tendencies, as noted earlier.) For this reason some researchers prefer models that identify specific emotional categories, such as anxiety, hostility, and depression (e.g., Zuckerman and Lubin, 1985).

STUDYING THE SUBJECTIVE EXPERIENCE OF EMOTION

Researchers in this area face two main challenges: how to create or induce moods in subjects, and how

to measure subjective feelings. The most widely used tool for inducing emotions in the laboratory is the *Velten Mood Induction Procedure* (Velten, 1968; see Larsen and Sinnett, in press, for a review). Subjects are given a list of sixty statements designed to evoke either elated, depressed, or neutral feelings (see Figure 11.4). They are asked to read each statement aloud and think about it for about fifteen seconds. Presumably the act of concentrating on the statements induces the subjective feelings. Another technique for producing moods is *false feedback.* Subjects are given a fake test of intelligence or some other ability. Subjects are then told that they scored in the top or bottom 25 percent of the group (Larsen and Ketelaar, 1989). In reality, the tests are never scored and the feedback is entirely false; the point is to induce positive or negative feelings in the subjects. In a variation, subjects are given a bogus test called the Indiana Digit Identification Orientation Test (or the

Sample statements:

Depressed

I have too many bad things in my life. I feel unhappy, things seem pointless and gloomy. I'm fed up with it all. I feel so tired and gloomy I would rather just sit than do anything.

Elated

This is great, I really do feel good, I am elated about things. I feel alert, happy, full of energy. Life is so full of interesting things it is great to be alive. Right now I feel like smiling.

Neutral

Utah is the beehive state. This book or any part thereof may not be reproduced in any form.

FIGURE 11.4   Can reading about an emotion make it happen? The Velten Mood Induction Procedure was designed to find out. (*Velten, 1968./© 1968, Pergamon Press. Reprinted with permission.*)

Putting the customer in a relaxed, confident mood increases the chances of making a sale.

IDIOT) (Notarius et al., 1982). Their task is to cross out either all of the letters or all of the digits in a booklet, an extremely tedious job that takes about twenty minutes. The experimenter leaves the room, returning when the time is up to examine the booklet. "Idiot," the experimenter exclaims. "You were supposed to cross out the letters, not the numbers." The experimenter then rips up the booklet and storms out of the room. One can imagine the feelings of anger and/or humiliation this exercise creates. Other techniques for inducing moods in the laboratory include: asking subjects to recall or imagine very pleasant or unpleasant events; exposing subjects to pleasant or unpleasant slides and films (as in the facial-expression experiments described above); and asking subjects to imitate facial expressions or postures associated with different emotions (Riskind, 1984).

Manipulating moods is surprisingly easy, as Alice Isen's experiments in natural settings demonstrate. In one (Isen and Levin, 1972), she asked subjects to make a call from a public phone booth and arranged for some of them to find a dime in the coin-return slot. These subjects were more likely to spontaneously help a confederate who dropped a stack of papers than were subjects who had not found a dime. Apparently, even a very small amount of money puts people in a temporary good mood, and being in a good mood promotes helpfulness. Another of Isen's experiments (Isen et al., 1978) was conducted in a shopping mall. To induce good moods, a

confederate posing as a sales representative offered subjects a free gift (a note pad or nail file, worth only 29 cents), explaining that this was part of a promotional campaign. Shortly thereafter another confederate asked the subject to participate in a "consumer opinion survey." If they agreed, subjects were asked to rate the performance and service records of their television set or automobile. Isen found that subjects who had received a gift, and presumably were in a good mood, gave higher ratings than did subjects who had not received free gifts. The practical implications of these experiments are clear. If you need help (say, to borrow notes from a classmate), you will have better luck if you start by putting the target of your request in a good mood ("Gee, that's a great looking sweater"). By the same token, if a salesperson or an advertiser puts you in a good mood, you will be much more susceptible to the pitch. No wonder advertisers use babies and puppies to promote everything from detergents to tires!

An intense positive emotion is exhilarating while it lasts, but is hard to sustain and not closely related to a person's overall level of happiness.

In many cases, researchers need to measure their subjects' moods for use as an independent or dependent variable. The most direct way to determine what emotions people are feeling is simply to ask, to solicit self-reports. For example, subjects might be shown a list of mood adjectives and asked to rate how much of each emotion they are feeling, on a scale from 0 (not at all) to 7 (very, very much). Because self-reports are not always honest or accurate, researchers also have developed indirect measures of emotion (Mayer and Bremer, 1985). Subjects may be asked to estimate the probability of various good and bad events occurring in their lives (for example, "What is the probability that you will win some lottery?" and "What is the probability that you will develop cancer?"). The better the subject's mood, the more likely he or she is to be optimistic (and vice versa). Subjects may be presented with a series of emotion-laden words and asked to free-associate: the more words they produce, the more likely they are to be feeling that emotion. Or subjects may be asked to perform a monotonous task: the faster they work, the more likely they are to be in a positive mood. In general, indirect measures are better at assessing the pleasant-to-unpleasant dimension of emotion than the active-to-inactive dimension (Larsen and Diener, in press).

Is manipulating subjects' moods in the laboratory ethical? In general, the effects of these procedures are slight and brief (usually lasting less than ten minutes). Nevertheless, researchers take strict precautions. Subjects are not "tricked" into participating in an experiment. Researchers always obtain informed consent, using a form such as the one that appears in Chapter 2. After the procedure, they are "debriefed." If they have looked at unpleasant slides, for example, researchers tell them that it is *normal* to feel bad. The experimenters may also show them a series of pleasant slides or give subjects a small gift (a pen or candy) to counteract unpleasant feelings.

EMOTIONAL TRAITS

So far we have been talking about emotional states. States are transient and temporary; they come and go. Many people become anxious when called upon to make a public speech, for example. But when the speech is over and they hear applause, they relax. Emotions can also be thought of as traits—as relatively stable and consistent ways that people differ from one another (see Chapter 13). Some people are anxious most of the time, worry about little things, and seem unable to enjoy success or to relax. When the speech is over, they continue to fret. ("Are they applauding just to be polite? Will they ask me to speak again?") Anxiety is more than an occasional experience for such people; it is part of their enduring

FIGURE 11.5 Daily mood data of two subjects. Over the three months of observation, subject 21 showed relatively stable moods, whereas subject 23 showed much more intense and variable moods. Subjects were experiencing similar events in their lives during the course of this study. (*From Larsen and Diener, 1992./© 1992 Sage Publications. Reprinted by permission.*)

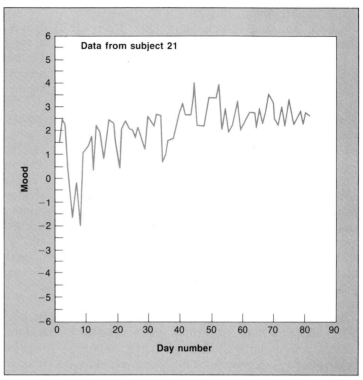

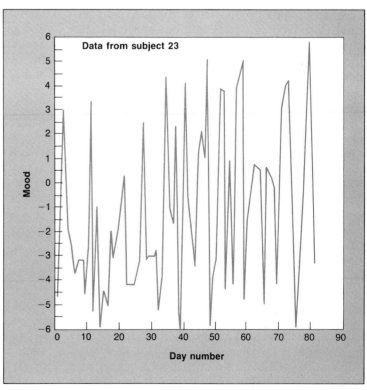

psychological makeup. The distinction between emotional states and traits is an important one. Everyone has experienced the *state* of anxiety, but not everyone has the *trait* of being anxious.

Some of the most interesting insights into emotional traits grew out of the (scientific) pursuit of happiness. What distinguishes people who are generally enthusiastic and cheerful from those who are chronically worried and blue? One answer is the *frequency* of positive as opposed to negative emotions. Everyone experiences emotional ups and downs. People who describe themselves, and are described by others, as happy report more pleasant than unpleasant emotions. In most studies, a majority of people put themselves in the happy category. For example, when asked to estimate the percent of time that they feel happy, unhappy, or neutral (so that the percentages add up to 100), college students typically report that they are happy about 70 percent of the time (Larsen et al., 1985).

When one looks at the *intensity* of happy emotions, however, a different picture emerges. Reports of extreme emotional highs—jubilance, rapture, bliss, euphoria—are relatively rare. Moreover, individuals who report great emotional peaks are not necessarily happy people. To the contrary, they also report deep emotional valleys. Upon reflection, this surprising finding makes sense. Suppose you are going to a college football game. You want to have a good time, you get yourself "psyched up," you cheer a lot, and you get very engaged in the game. If your team wins, you will be much happier than someone who remained emotionally indifferent to the game. If your team loses, however, you will be much *un*happier than someone who remains indifferent. Over the long run, then, happiness seems to depend on being able to sustain pleasant feelings (even at a low level, as in calm contentment), not on intense moments of bliss (Diener et al., 1989).

Studies of happiness led researchers to the discovery of an another emotional trait, *affect (or emotional) intensity* (Larsen and Diener, 1987). People who are high in this trait tend to experience their emotions quite strongly. They react quite strongly to both the good and bad events in their lives, even to things that other people might consider trivial, such as losing a pen or receiving a compliment. Their emotional lives are also highly variable, with many mood swings. People who are low in this trait tend to experience their emotions quite mildly. They take everyday

successes and frustrations in stride. Their emotional lives tend to be quite stable, with only minor fluctuations. Evidence for these two patterns of emotional life come from records of subjects' daily moods reported over a period of eighty-four days. (See Figure 11.5.)

What is interesting about this trait is that it applies to *both* positive and negative emotions. On Randy Larsen's Affect Intensity Measure (AIM), subjects are asked to rate their emotional reactions on a scale of 1 (for never) to 6 (for always). Some sample items are: "Seeing a picture of some violent car accident in a newspaper makes me feel sick to my stomach"; "When things are good I feel 'on top of the world'"; "When I'm nervous I get shaky all over"; and "When someone compliments me, I get so happy I could burst." It turns out that people who endorse the negative items also endorse the positive items. In other words, when good things happen to people who are high in affect intensity, they feel happier than people who are low in affect intensity; and when bad things happen, they feel worse. As the old adage suggests, the higher you climb, the harder you fall (emotionally speaking) (Larsen, 1987).

Individuals who are high and low in affect intensity also experience emotions differently (Larsen and Diener, 1987). The former experience happiness as exuberance and are typically zestful and enthusiastic; the latter experience happiness as contentment and serenity and are typically calm and easygoing. Apparently, there are different styles of happiness.

Many questions still remain. What makes people happy? Why do some people experience more positive than negative emotions over their lifetimes? Can people learn to be happy? We will explore these questions in depth.

IN DEPTH

What Makes People Happy?

Psychologist Michael Fordyce reports, "When I ask people, 'What's the most important thing in life?' about half of them immediately say, 'Happiness'" (in Swanbrow, 1989). Each person has his or her personal definition of happiness. But most would agree that **happiness** is an enduring, positive emotional state that includes satisfaction with one's life and self as well as active pleasures and accomplish-

Social comparison studies indicate that happiness is relative. Seattle has been rated one of the most livable cities in the United States, with its recreational opportunities, low crime rate, and other attractions.

ments (Warr, 1978). The real question is how one achieves this state.

Aristotle answered, "by living the virtuous life." The French philosopher Jean-Jacques Rousseau held that the critical ingredients were "a good bank account, a good cook, and a good digestion." Probing deeper, the founder of American psychology, William James, offered a formula. Happiness, according to James, was the ratio of one's accomplishments to one's aspirations:

$$\text{Happiness} = \frac{\text{accomplishments}}{\text{aspirations}}$$

The closer individuals come to achieving their goals, the happier they will be. By implication, there are two routes to happiness: working harder to achieve success, or limiting how much one tries to accomplish, that is, "lowering one's sights."

In the years since James declared happiness a subject worthy of scientific study, psychologists have come closer to understanding what makes people happy.

THE INITIAL STUDIES

Suppose a researcher asked you, "How happy or satisfied are you with your life?" *Social comparison theory*—one of the earliest and most enduring the-
ories of happiness—holds that you would answer by looking at the people around you and comparing your life to theirs. If you judged that you were doing better than most, you would probably say that you were happy. If you judged that you were not doing as well as others, you would probably say you were unhappy. Simply put, happiness equals "keeping up with the Joneses," or more accurately, one step ahead of the Joneses.

Empirical research has often supported the social comparison theory of happiness. One of the first pieces of evidence in its favor came from a survey of soldiers during the 1940s (Merton and Kitt, 1950). The survey revealed a number of puzzling paradoxes. For example, soldiers who lacked a high school diploma were much less likely to be promoted than were soldiers with a high school education or better. Yet the men with *less* education were generally *more* satisfied with the army's promotion policies than were their better-educated counterparts. The reason apparently had to do with each group's sources of comparison. Compared with similarly educated men in the civilian world, the more educated soldiers were doing quite poorly, but the less educated soldiers were doing quite well. As a result, the former were very dissatisfied while the latter were reasonably content.

Such findings suggest that if we could only change the sources of comparison people use to gauge their degree of fortune, we might be able to change their self-perceived happiness. Advertisers, in fact, regularly try to do this. By bombarding us with pictures of people whose possessions are far more elegant than our own, they try to induce us to compare ourselves with these more fortunate others and so to feel discontented (Brickman, 1978). The reverse, of course, is also possible. If unfavorable sources of comparison are eliminated, people may be more satisfied with their lives. It has been argued that Cuban president Fidel Castro may have raised the satisfaction of his people considerably just by eliminating the rich American tourists who used to flock to Cuba each year (Brickman and Campbell, 1971). This ability to change people's perceived happiness simply by changing the sources of social comparison available to them has been demonstrated experimentally. In one study, for instance, Milwaukee residents who read vivid descriptions of how terrible life in their city was at the turn of the century reported more satisfaction with their current circumstances than did residents who read a glowing description of Milwaukee's earlier years (Dermer et al., 1978).

Outside the laboratory, however, the sources of comparison available to us are seldom so tightly controlled. As a result, people have a choice about which group of others they will compare themselves with. And research suggests that, when given such a choice, people are often strongly motivated to enhance their feelings of well-being by comparing themselves with *less* fortunate others (Wills, 1981). This has been clearly demonstrated in interviews with cancer patients who had every reason to think of themselves as worse off than almost everyone else. Remarkably, however, even these victims found ways to think of themselves as relatively lucky (Taylor et al., 1983). Women who had had a malignant tumor removed from one of their breasts compared themselves with less fortunate women who had undergone mastectomies (removal of the entire breast). The mastectomy patients, in turn, focused on others still worse off than themselves— perhaps those whose cancer was spreading despite the operation, or those whose surgical amputations were more disfiguring (loss of an arm or leg, for instance).

Thus people not only make upward social comparisons (what we usually mean by "keeping up with the Joneses"), but also downward social comparisons. When we are feeling low, we often buck ourselves up by thinking of people who are *less* fortunate (for example, the starving people in Africa) and tell ourselves, "Gee, I don't have it so bad after all."

Social comparison (upward or downward) is only one of the measures we use to evaluate our lives. We also use our own past as a standard (Smith et al., 1989). In addition to asking ourselves, "Am I better off than most people I know?," we ask, "Am I better off today than I was last year?" For example, the poet T. S. Eliot suffered through a long and miserable first marriage (Ackroyd, 1984). When he married for a second time in the last decade of his life, he felt rejuvenated. Comparing his current to his past marital life, he considered himself an extraordinarily happy man. Furthermore, people may apply different standards to different areas of their life. Eliot was more successful than most other poets of his generation, in terms of both recognition and income (social comparison). He admitted to being happy about his "fame and fortune," even during his wretchedly unhappy first marriage. Thus Eliot used social comparison in judging his *professional* life, but past-self comparisons in judging his *marital* life. The key point is that the degree of satisfaction people experience may be due, not so much to the absolute value of their current affairs, but to how their situation compares to those of their friends and peers, and to how their present compares to their past.

CRITICISMS, ALTERNATIVES, AND FURTHER RESEARCH

Most contemporary researchers still consider social comparison an important element of happiness (e.g., Emmons and Diener, 1985; Schwarz and Strack, 1990). But it is only one element, not the complete story. A major flaw in social comparison theory is its failure to explain why a person who is extremely fortunate in relation to others can still be unhappy. One study has shown, for instance, that winners of a million-dollar state lottery report no more satisfaction with life than less financially fortunate people (Brickman et al., 1978). How could this be if happiness depends on social comparison alone? Clearly, some other psychological factors must be involved as well.

Adaptation theory provides one such set of factors (Brickman and Campbell, 1971; Helson, 1964).

Social comparison theory is flawed because it does not explain why lottery winners are no happier than other people. Adaptation theory suggests that as the new millionaires adjust to their wealth, it becomes "old hat" to them—the thrill is soon gone.

It argues that when something highly positive happens, we quickly adapt to our new level of fortune —that is, we accept it as an integral part of our lives. As a result, several things tend to happen. First, in the short run, simple things that once gave us pleasure tend to lose some of their appeal because they seem so much less exciting than our recent windfall. This is called the "contrast effect." Second, in the longer run, the pleasure derived from the windfall itself tends to erode. What once seemed a thrilling stroke of fortune gradually loses its luster and becomes the status quo. This is called the "habituation effect." In short, pleasure depends on change.

Unpleasant emotions, in contrast, endure so long as the conditions producing them continue. While we adapt quickly to comfort, we never get used to continuing humiliation or harassment. Hope fades, but fear can go on forever. Nico Frijda (1988) offers an evolutionary explanation for this negative balance. The function of emotions is to alert us to conditions that require action. The emotions are part of our evolutionary equipment for survival. When alertness and action are no longer required, when we experience satisfaction, the emotions "switch off." But this does not mean that we are doomed to chronic unhappiness. In Frijda's

words, "Enduring happiness seems possible, [but] it does not come naturally, by itself. It takes effort" (p. 354).

To test adaptation theory, Philip Brickman and Dan Coates (1978) interviewed twenty-two big winners in the Illinois state lottery and twenty-two other people with similar backgrounds who had never experienced such a financial windfall. Brickman and Coates found that, as predicted, the lottery winners described themselves as no more happy than the nonwinners did, and they also tended to derive less satisfaction from such simple pleasures as watching television and eating a good breakfast. Apparently, winning a lottery is not nearly so rich a source of happiness as we might expect. Although winners may initially compare themselves with others and think how lucky they are, the contrast and habituation effects may eventually lessen the overall pleasure they experience.

Some people might interpret these findings in an optimistic light: great wealth, fame and power, all the fabulous things we will probably never acquire, would not make us very happy anyway! But a pessimistic interpretation is also possible. These same findings can be used to argue that the pursuit of happiness is a kind of pleasure-seeking treadmill, whereby today's great joys tend to overshadow simpler pleasures and may eventually seem lackluster themselves. According to this perspective, great happiness can never be permanent unless our circumstances are *constantly* improving—something that is very unlikely.

Many psychologists take issue with this pessimistic outlook, however. They point out that in surveys a sizable number of people report being "very happy," and that those who are tend to stay that way over long periods of time (Andrews and Withey, 1976; Gurin et al., 1960; Palmore and Kivett, 1977). What could account for these chronically happy people if we assume that relatively few of them can have constantly improving life circumstances?

One possibility is that certain personality traits (or combinations of traits) foster happiness. This is what psychologists Paul Costa and Robert McCrae (1980, 1986) argue. In a correlational study of personality traits and subjective well-being, they found that extroverted traits (sociability, warmth, involvement with other people) are strongly associated with positive emotions, while neurotic traits (a tendency to worry, be irritable and anxious) are strongly associated with negative emotions. Moreover, a follow-up study found that these personality traits predicted levels of happiness and unhappiness ten years later. Thus a person's overall potential for happiness may be thought of as the sum of these two personality dimensions. A person who is high in extroversion and low in neuroticism has the greatest potential for happiness, while a person who is high in neuroticism and low in extroversion has the greatest potential for unhappiness.

The weakness of the Costa and McCrae personality theory of happiness is that it is based on *correlational* studies, and therefore does not tell us about the direction of cause and effect. Perhaps extroverts and neurotics create or choose different life-styles, and these different life-styles—not personality traits per se—are responsible for their general happiness or unhappiness. In other words, are extroverts predisposed to enjoy life, or are they happy because they lead active social lives, and sociability promotes good moods? Are neurotics predisposed to unpleasant emotions, or are they unhappy because their emotional instability fosters difficult life situations, and these situations make them unhappy?

To answer these questions, Randy Larsen and Timothy Ketelaar (1989, in press) conducted a series of laboratory experiments with college students. On the basis of standard personality tests, the students were identified as extroverted or introverted, neurotic or stable. All were exposed to mood-induction procedures (either false feedback or imagery) and then asked to fill out mood self-reports. The researchers found that extroverts responded strongly to positive mood induction (such as imagining they had won a $50,000 lottery) and about average to negative mood induction. Neurotics responded strongly to negative mood inductions (imagining being expelled from college under embarrassing circumstances) and about average to positive mood induction. Because all the subjects were in the same situations, the results support a personality theory of happiness. Extroverts appear to be *predisposed* to experience high levels of pleasant emotions, while neurotics appear to be *predisposed* to experience high levels of unpleasant emotions. This conclusion is supported by a recent study by William Pavot and his colleagues (Pavot et al., 1990), which found that extroverts are happier than introverts even when they are not in social situations.

Research on personality and happiness also exposed a common misunderstanding. Common sense suggests that the more happiness you experience, the less unhappiness you will suffer. Happiness and unhappiness are seen as opposite sides of the same emotional coin. What could be more logical? In this case, logic is wrong. Happiness and unhappiness appear to be distinct feelings, which rise and fall independently (Swanbrow, 1989). The extroverts in Larsen and Ketelaar's study had strong positive emotions, but average (not low) negative emotions. Likewise, the neurotics had strong negative emotions, but average (not low) positive reactions. Thus extroverted traits contribute to enjoyment and satisfaction, but do not inoculate a person against unpleasant experiences. Neurotic traits contribute to anxiety and distress, but do not diminish the capacity to enjoy pleasant experiences. By implication, personality traits do not dictate whether a person will be happy or unhappy; other factors come into play.

Another set of factors we have not yet mentioned are specific life circumstances. Intuitively,

Wealth doesn't guarantee happiness, but it does provide opportunities—for leisure activities, better education, and better health care, among other advantages—that can contribute to happiness.

most of us believe that such life circumstances as wealth, youth, and prestige contribute greatly to happiness. The relationship between income or wealth and happiness is particularly intriguing to most Americans. Many of us pay lip service to the idea that "you can't buy happiness," but secretly believe that you can. After all, the rich don't have to worry about how they will pay next month's bills. They can go skiing or sailing, to the opera or the Superbowl, and engage in other pleasurable activities more often than people of average or low income. When misfortune strikes, they have greater resources for coping (they can afford the best medical care, legal advice, and so on). Moreover, the rich enjoy more power and respect than the average person. As the saying goes, "Money talks." The rich have fewer worries than the rest of us.

Does money lead to happiness? What are the facts? We mentioned Brickman and Coates's study of big lottery winners earlier; they found that the euphoria of "striking it rich" wore off quickly. To test this and similar findings, Ed Diener and his colleagues (Diener et al., 1985) studied the very wealthy. Subjects were selected from *Forbes* magazine's 1983 list of the 400 wealthiest Americans. The average net worth of subjects in this sample was $125 million or more and most had incomes of over $10 million per year. Rich subjects were matched to control subjects from the same geographic location (whose average net worth was $120,000 and mean family income, $36,000). Both groups were asked to fill out questionnaires designed to measure life satisfaction. Diener found that the super-rich tended to be slightly happier than the nonwealthy control subjects. But the differences between them were small: the rich said they were happy 77 percent of the time; the controls, 62 percent of the time. Moreover, 37 percent of the wealthy subjects reported being less happy that the average nonwealthy control, and 47 percent of the nonwealthy controls reported being much happier than the average multimillionaire. In short, great wealth may contribute to happiness, but it is certainly not a guarantee.

In a review of the literature, Diener (1984) found that other life circumstances, including age, gender, education, religion, and health, have surprisingly little relationship to subjective well-being. The single most important life circumstance predicting great happiness is a satisfying marriage and family life (Campbell et al., 1976; Glenn and Weaver, 1981).

A satisfying family life has been found to be the single best predictor of an individual's happiness.

PATTERNS AND CONCLUSIONS

Can psychologists generalize about what makes people happy? Can they recommend ways for people to bring more happiness into their lives? Happiness researcher Michael Fordyce (1988; see Swanbrow, 1989) has translated empirical and theoretical studies into a practical program. Happiness is within reach, but it requires work. Fordyce outlines eight steps to happiness:

1. *Spend time with your loved ones.* Of all the characteristics and circumstances that happy people share, loving relationships stand out. All too often people take their family and close friends for granted, knowing they will always be there. Instead, make time with loved ones a priority.
2. *Seek challenging, meaningful work.* If love is the first priority, work is the second. Happy people work hard and enjoy what they do. If your current job (or college major) is not rewarding, consider switching to one that is. People need to feel that they are using their abilities to accomplish something they consider worthwhile.
3. *Be helpful to others.* There are two "selfish" reasons for being altruistic. First, doing good makes you feel good about yourself. It enhances self-esteem. Second, helping a friend solve a problem, being kind to a stranger, or devoting time to a worthy cause may relieve stress.

It takes your mind off your own troubles and leaves you refreshed.
4. *Make time for activities you enjoy.* Most people know what makes them happy, but waste a lot of their free time doing things that leave them feeling empty or bored. (Watching TV is a prime example.) Think about what makes you happy—whether it is organizing a party, going to a museum, or fixing the kitchen sink—and make the time to do it.
5. *Keep fit.* It does not matter what you do—run, bike, swim, play a sport, dance—so long as you keep in shape. No one knows exactly why aerobic exercise increases subjective well-being, but there is abundant evidence that it does.
6. *Be organized, but flexible.* Planning ahead is important (especially if you include plans for fun). But you should not be so tightly scheduled that you cannot take advantage of an unplanned opportunity to try something different. People who seek new experiences —go places they have never been, play games they have never played, do things on the spur of the moment—are happier than people who stick to the "tried and true."
7. *Think positively.* Trite as this sounds, your general attitude makes a difference. If you expect good things to happen, you generally get what you are looking for (and vice versa).

8. *Keep things in perspective.* Everybody has emotional highs and lows, but try to stay on an even keel. If you let your hopes soar too high, you are likely to crash; if you let little things get you down, you may have trouble pulling yourself back up. Emotional extremes exact a cost.

Fordyce advises that wishing for happiness won't make it happen, but planning can. The key is getting your priorities straight.

THEORIES OF EMOTION

So far in this chapter we have concentrated on the experience and consequences of emotion. Here we want to focus on the question: What *causes* emotion? A number of theories have been proposed. These theories can be divided into two broad categories: those that emphasize physiological arousal, and those that emphasize cognitive activity.

THE IMPORTANCE OF PHYSIOLOGICAL AROUSAL

Many early psychologists considered emotions too varied, too vague, too private and personal for scientific consideration. William James (1890) disagreed. For James, the key to understanding emotions was physiological arousal.

THE JAMES-LANGE THEORY

Common sense holds that emotions cause physiological arousal and behavior. When we see a mysterious figure in a dark alley, we feel frightened, and this emotion (fear) causes our heart to pound, and we run. In other words, events in the environment trigger a psychological state—an emotion—which in turn gives rise to physiological responses. James turned this common-sense notion upside down.

> My theory, on the contrary, is that *the bodily changes follow directly the perception of the exciting fact, and that our feeling of the same changes as they occur IS the emotion . . .* we feel sorry *because* we cry, angry *because* we strike, afraid *because* we tremble. . . . (James, 1890).

According to James, then, we do not act because we feel; rather, we feel because we act. Our perception of certain stimuli (what James called "exciting facts") triggers changes in the body. These changes cause sensory messages to be sent to the brain and produce the actual experience of emotion. James held that each emotional state is signaled by a unique physiological pattern. In his original formulation he proposed that feelings might arise from changes in the viscera (or abdominal organs), respiration, circulation, the skin, the muscles, and even posture. Danish psychologist Carl Lange proposed a similar theory at about the same time. Where James depicted emotion as a whole-body experience, Lange located emotions in the autonomic nervous system and the viscera. In his later writings James embraced Lange's position (Izard, 1990a). The idea that emotions arise from perception of bodily changes became known as the **James-Lange theory** (Lange and James, 1922).

THE CANNON-BARD THEORY

The James-Lange theory stimulated a great deal of research on emotions, much of it designed to disprove that theory's claims. In 1927 Walter Cannon, a pioneer in the study of the autonomic nervous system, published a powerful critique. Cannon's main argument was that the physiological changes are *uniform* across different emotional states. Both fear and rage, for example, are associated with a pounding heart, sweaty palms, tremors, and so on. If the James-Lange theory were correct, if we feel emotions by interpreting our bodily sensations, then each emotion must be characterized by a somewhat different set of physiological changes. But this is not the case, at least according to the research techniques available at the time. Note that Cannon did not deny that physiological arousal plays a role in emotion; rather, he argued that bodily changes are too generalized and diffuse to permit discrimination among different emotions (Blascovich, 1990).

Cannon also cited evidence that physiological arousal alone is not sufficient to induce emotion. In one study, Gregorio Maranon (1924) produced physiological arousal artificially, by injecting several hundred subjects with the hormone epinephrine (adrenalin) and asked them to report the effects. About 71 percent said that they experienced only physical symptoms—rapid heartbeats, tightness in the throat —with no emotional overtones at all. The remainder reported emotional responses of some kind, but most described what Maranon called "as if" emotions. These subjects said, "I feel *as if* I were afraid" or "I feel *as if* I were happy." Their feelings, then, were similar to emotions but clearly not identical to them.

Furthermore, emotional responses are often quite rapid: we feel the car skidding out of control and experience immediate panic; we spot an old friend and feel instantaneous joy. Yet the viscera are relatively insensitive organs, with few nerve endings, and slow to change. How, Cannon asked, can the viscera be regarded as the source of sudden emotion?

In addition to pointing out the shortcomings of James's theory of emotions, Cannon (1927) and his associate L. L. Bard proposed a theory of their own. According to the **Cannon-Bard theory,** the part of the brain called the thalamus plays a key role in emotions. In an emotion-arousing situation stimuli from the senses are passed to the thalamus, which acts as a relay station. The thalamus simultaneously transmits the information to two parts of the body: upward to the cerebral cortex (resulting in the subjective experience of emotion) and downward, by way of the autonomic nervous system, to the body's internal organs (resulting in physiological responses). Thus, bodily reactions occur along with feelings of emotion; they do not produce emotions, as James believed.

Later researchers have refined the basic ideas in the Cannon-Bard theory. For instance, anatomist James Papez (1937) pointed out the critical roles of the hypothalamus and parts of the limbic system. The hypothalamus, Papez argued, is ultimately the brain region that triggers physiological arousal, while the limbic system is intimately involved in the subjective experience of emotions. This basic view is supported by many studies and is widely accepted today, along with the idea of the cortex's involvement that Cannon and Bard first proposed (Buck, 1985; Panksepp, 1982).

Cannon (1929) also added a motivation function to emotion: the function of emotion is to prepare the body to deal with "emergency" situations, as in the urge toward "fight or flight."

THE FACIAL FEEDBACK HYPOTHESIS, A MODERN JAMESIAN PERSPECTIVE

For many years the case against the James-Lange theory appeared to be closed. Then, in the 1960s and

1970s, when researchers began to test Darwin's theory of the universality of facial expressions of emotion, they came upon some ideas that previously had been overlooked. "The free expression by outward signs of an emotion intensifies it," Darwin wrote. "On the other hand, the repression, as far as this is possible, of all outward signs softens our emotions" (1872, p. 365). Eighteen years later, James had made a similar observation: "Refuse to express a passion and it dies . . ." (1890, p. 463). Both believed that sensory feedback from the face could stimulate or inhibit emotion. Was it possible that James had had the right idea, but looked for evidence in the wrong place (the viscera instead of the face)?

As often happens in science, rereading old sources led to new insights (Adelmann, and Zajonc, 1989; Izard, 1990a). The **facial feedback** hypothesis holds that facial expressions play a key role in initiating or at least modulating the experience of emotion. According to this view, facial expressions are not merely the outward expression of emotion: they contribute to the feeling itself.

To test this hypothesis, researchers had to devise ways to have subjects simulate emotional expressions without knowing why. In one experiment (Strack et al., 1988), subjects were told they were participating in a study of people's ability to use parts of their body to perform unusual tasks, as they might have to do if they were injured or handicapped. Some of the subjects were asked to hold a pen in their teeth. This can only be done by pulling the lips back, as we do when we smile. Other subjects were asked to hold a pen with their lips, which relaxes the cheek muscles and prevents smiling. While holding the pen in their mouth, they were asked to rate cartoons on a scale from 0 (not at all funny) to 9 (very funny). As the facial feedback hypothesis predicts, subjects who held the pen in their teeth (the simulated smile) rated the cartoons as funnier than those who held the pen in their lips (the inhibited smile). Other studies (reviewed in Adelmann and Zajonc, 1989; Izard, 1990b) have led to the same conclusion: the simple act of smiling or frowning can alter subjective emotional feelings.

The question of how facial feedback works has not been resolved, however. Some psychologists have proposed that sensory feedback from the skin and facial muscles has a direct impact on the brain centers responsible for the experience of emotion (Izard, 1971; Tomkins, 1962). Others have proposed that facial feedback is a matter of self-perception: when we feel ourselves clenching our teeth, we infer "I must be angry" (Buck, 1985; Laird, 1974, 1984). Still others see facial feedback as the result of classical conditioning, where specific facial expressions have been repeatedly paired with specific emotions (Cacioppo et al., 1986). A new proposal holds that when certain facial muscles are tightened or relaxed, they raise or lower the temperature of the blood flowing to the brain. This, in turn, influences the activity of the brain centers that regulate emotion. Smiles cool the blood, causing pleasant feelings, while frowns heat the blood, causing unpleasant feelings (Zajonc et al., 1989). Only future research will tell which, if any, of these explanations is correct.

Most contemporary psychologists accept the view that physiological arousal and facial expressions are an integral part of emotion (a weak version of the James-Lange theory and facial feedback hypothesis). But many do not accept the idea that physiological arousal and/or facial expression play a causal role in emotion (a strong version of James-Lange and facial feedback). According to these critics, neo-Jamesians have greatly improved our *description* of emotional experience, but they have not *explained* where emotions come from. A racing heart may be an essential part of the experience of fear. But why does a person feel afraid in the first place?

THE ROLE OF COGNITION

When people are asked to describe their emotions, they typically begin with a descriptive term—excited, angry, frightened, peaceful—and then immediately launch into an explanation. "I just got a job in summer stock theater" (excited). "They broke into my car—again" (angry). "My mother has to have an operation" (frightened). And so on. Cognitive theories of emotion hold that understanding how people interpret events is one key to understanding emotion.

SCHACHTER AND SINGER'S THEORY OF COGNITIVE AROUSAL

Stanley Schachter and Jerome Singer (1962) were pioneers in the study of emotion and cognition. In a sense they provided a bridge from earlier physiological theories of emotion to contemporary cognitive theories. Schachter and Singer accepted James's view that physiological arousal plays a primary role in emotion. They also accepted Cannon's view that arousal is general and diffuse. How, then, do we

know what we are feeling? Schachter and Singer hypothesized that in order to explain our feelings to ourselves, we search our surroundings for a reasonable cause. Depending on the environmental cues available, we might decide that the same state of arousal is joy, love, jealousy, or even hate. This **cognitive arousal** interpretation enables people to label a *general* state of physiological arousal as a *specific* emotion (Schachter, 1964).

To test this hypothesis, Schachter and Singer gave subjects injections of adrenaline, under the pretext that they wanted to test the effects of "vitamins" on vision. Some of the subjects were correctly informed about side effects (heart palpitations, hand tremors, etc.). Some were deliberately misinformed (told the shot might cause itching or headaches). Others were told the shot had no side effects (the ignorant condition). As a control, still others were given saline injections, which have no side effects. Schachter and Singer predicted that both misinformed and ignorant subjects, lacking an adequate explanation for their aroused state, would search the environment for information to explain how they felt.

After the injection, each subject was asked to fill out a questionnaire while he or she waited for the "vision test" in a room with another person. The other person was actually a confederate in the experiment. In some cases the accomplice acted very happy and frivolous, throwing paper airplanes, laughing, and playing with a hula hoop. In other cases the accomplice grew increasingly sullen and irritable, complained about the questionnaire, and finally tore it up and stormed out of the room. Meanwhile the researchers watched through a one-way mirror.

The results of this experiment gave some support to Schachter and Singer's theory. The misinformed and ignorant subjects, who had no logical explanation for their aroused state, did tend to adopt the mood of the accomplice in the waiting room. Many of those with the euphoric accomplice also reported that they felt "good or happy." The informed and control subjects were less likely to behave as the confederate did.

Critics were quick to point out flaws in both the experiment and in Schachter and Singer's conclusions (Kemper, 1978; Plutchik and Ax, 1967; Zimbardo et al., 1974). One common criticism is that Schachter and Singer seemed to be saying that a single, undifferentiated state of arousal leads to the entire array of emotions. This seems implausible at best. In fact, researchers have begun to identify

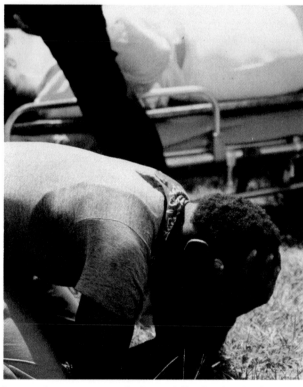

Cognitive theories of emotion maintain that the individual's interpretation of events plays a casual role in his or her emotional response. Thus, in normal people receiving good news causes elation, while the death of a loved one is perceived as a tragedy.

emotion-specific patterns of autonomic nervous system activity (e.g., Levenson et al., 1990). (James may have been right after all!) A second criticism is that Schachter and Singer assumed that their subjects' behavior and self-reported mood were based solely on the cues provided by the exuberant or irritable confederate. By implication, cognitive interpretation of arousal is based on rapid and uncritical assimilation of information in the immediate environment. But the subjects' responses might have reflected something that had happened earlier that day; previous experiences with injections or tests; memories touched off by the experimenter who gave the shot, by the confederate, or even by the room; or by a general predisposition to enjoy or feel nervous in new situations.

To be fair, Schachter and Singer never intended this one experiment to become the sole basis for a theory of emotion. Nevertheless, the notion of cogni-tive arousal filled a void. The idea that emotions are "nothing more" than feelings (implied in the James-Lange theory) struck many psychologists as false. Despite criticism, the theory of cognitive arousal dominated emotion research for almost two decades. Then, in the 1980s, researchers began to look more closely at the role of cognition in emotions.

EMOTION AND COGNITIVE APPRAISAL

For Schachter, Singer, and their followers, cognition provided the missing link between physiological arousal and emotion. For many contemporary psychologists, cognition plays a central, *causal* role in emotion.

Richard Lazarus (1990) is a leading proponent of **cognitive appraisal** theory. "Emotions," writes Lazarus, "are organized psychophysiological reactions to good news and bad news about ongoing relationships with the environment" (pp. 13–14). People continually search the environment for meaning. We want to know not only how to act, but also how to feel (Smith and Ellsworth, 1985). Emotions arise when we judge that a situation or encounter has personal meaning, that it might be helpful or harmful to our current well-being and our long-term goals. Appraisal is more than information gathering; it involves judgment of what that information *means*. The information that someone has threatened or insulted us, by itself, does not cause emotion. If the threat comes from a child playing with make-believe guns, we do not feel fear; if the insult comes from a friend with whom we have a long-standing joking relationship, we are unlikely to feel anger. But if the offense is committed by someone we appraise as extremely powerful and capable of causing us future harm, our response will likely be fear.

Our emotions are the result, not of the objective situation in which we find ourselves, but of our *appraisal* of that situation, relative to our needs, wants, and resources. Lazarus distinguishes two levels of cognitive appraisal. In *primary appraisal* we assess whether what is happening is relevant to our personal well-being, or how the event might affect us; in *secondary appraisal* we evaluate our options and resources, or how we might handle the problem.

Cognitive theorists hold that people appraise events and situations in terms of a limited number of specific dimensions (Smith and Ellsworth, 1985), including:

Attention: Does this require my full attention, or can I safely ignore or avoid it?

Novelty: Does this meet or violate my expectations? Should I examine it closely or walk away?

Certainty: Do I know what will happen, or is the outcome unpredictable?

Control: Can I cope with this situation myself? or is it controlled by others or by forces beyond anyone's control (as in an earthquake)?

Pleasantness: Is this agreeable and satisfying? Will it help me to achieve my positive goals (and avoid negative ones)?

Perceived obstacle: Is someone or something standing in my way?

Responsibility and legitimacy: Who set this chain of events in motion? Is the outcome deserved or undeserved?

Anticipated effort: Does this require action, or can I relax or withdraw?

Analyzing emotions in terms of these dimensions helps psychologists to understand not only the nature of distinct emotions, but also the relationships among emotions. The appraisal that someone else is causing an unpleasant situation leads to anger; the appraisal that one has only oneself to blame for an unpleasant situation, to guilt; the appraisal that an unpleasant situation was nobody's fault and no one can change it, to sadness.

In an investigation of this model, Craig Smith and Phoebe Ellsworth (1985) found that students associated anger with receiving an unfair grade, having personal property stolen, and in one case, having wine poured over one's head in a restaurant. They felt guilt about stealing, lying, spreading gossip about a friend, and failing to meet an obligation. Several linked sadness to the death of a loved one; one mentioned being sad when she learned that her parents were getting divorced, "because I didn't want it, I knew it had to be, and yet I didn't want it" (Smith and Ellsworth, 1985, p. 834).

Cognitive appraisal theorists see emotions as functional (see Figure 11.6). Specific appraisals lead to specific emotions, and these in turn motivate us to take appropriate action. Thus anger motivates us to remove an irritant or obstacle; guilt, to adhere more closely to our personal standards and societal norms; sadness, to seek comfort. In addition, each emotion is accompanied by a distinct pattern of physiological arousal, which presumably prepares us to cope with the problem, and by an identifiable facial expression, which communicates our intentions to others (Smith, 1989).

ARE COGNITIONS ESSENTIAL TO EMOTION?

Cognitive appraisal theory has attracted considerable attention, but it is not universally accepted. In particular, the question "Are cognitions essential to emotion?" has generated much debate.

Lazarus (1990), as one might expect, argues that they are. In his view, emotion and cognition are inseparable. Unless a person is cognizant of what is happening, emotion would be mere activation, without purpose or direction. People do not experience fear in the abstract; they are afraid *of* someone or something. They do not simple flee, they flee *from* the source of danger. Indeed, the dissociation of information and meaning (or emotion) is a primary symptom or neurological or psychological disorder.

FIGURE 11.6 Theories of emotion. This flow chart compares the sequence of events outlined in the James-Lange, Schachter-Singer, and cognitive appraisal theories. (*Courtesy of Randy J. Larsen.*)

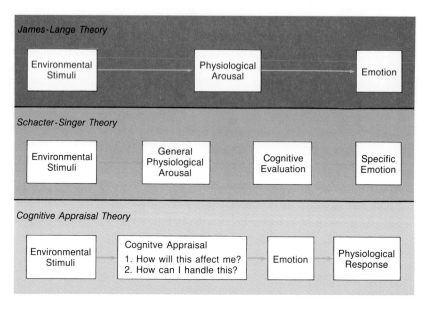

R. B. Zajonc (1980, 1984) disagrees. To help us understand why, he invites us to consider some of the emotions we experience in everyday life (Zajonc, 1980). When we meet a stranger, for example, we sometimes feel that we like or dislike the person instantly—long before we have a chance to evaluate the person's characteristics. How, Zajonc asks, could a cognitive appraisal be meaningfully involved in such a quick response?

Zajonc has gone on to compile empirical evidence in support of his belief that emotion and cognition are two separate psychological processes, so that a person may experience emotion *without* cognitive appraisal. In one experiment (Zajonc, 1980), he used a tachistoscope to present subjects with nonsense syllables (KAQ, LOZ, and the like). The syllables were presented so quickly that subjects did not know they had seen them and could not identify them in a list of three-letter syllables. Nevertheless they later said they liked the syllables they had "seen" (subliminally) more than others. Thus they had an emotional response (liking) in the absence of cognitive activity (conscious recognition). Zajonc concludes that feelings do not require thinking. Lazarus counters that subliminal perception represents low-level cognition.

In the end, the debate hinges on how one defines cognition (Buck, 1990). Most psychologists would agree that such basic emotions as preference or liking may occur very quickly, with little or no cognitive effort. But more complicated human emotions, such as jealousy or indignation, probably require a certain amount of high-level cognition.

EMOTIONAL REACTIONS TO CRISIS

Most of us encounter tragedy at some point in our lives. We or someone we love may be the victim of a violent crime, a disabling accident, or a life-threatening illness. How do people respond emotionally to such experiences? Do they progress through discrete stages in attempting to cope with misfortune? Do they eventually recover, or at least learn to live with their adversity? These are very important questions that psychologists have recently begun to answer.

VARIABILITY IN RESPONSES TO CRISIS

One thing that has become increasingly clear is that popular expectations about the way people will react to adversity—expectations often shared by those in the medical and other helping professions—are often incorrect (Silver and Wortman, 1980; Wortman and Silver, 1989). Imagine a young woman who has just been raped. She arrives at the police station to fill out a report. How does she feel at the time? Filled with anger and hatred toward her assailant? Enraged enough to want him harshly punished? Such reactions sound appropriate to most people. It may therefore surprise you to learn that relatively few women feel anger immediately after being raped—in one study as few as 20 percent (McCombie, 1975).

And it is not just that we often misjudge how people will react to any given crisis. The very assumption that there is some "typical" response is itself a misconception. People respond with much variability to tragedy (Wortman and Silver, 1989). In one survey of women who had recently lost their husbands, the initial emotional reaction to the husband's death ranged from intense shock and numbness to anxiety, depression, and anger (Parkes, 1972). There is even variation in whether or not *any* emotion is expressed. In a series of interviews with rape victims a few hours after their assaults, half the women showed intense emotions (crying, sobbing, severe tension, and restlessness), while the other half appeared outwardly quite controlled (Burgess and Holmstrom, 1974). Unfortunately, a rape victim who appears controlled immediately after her attack is often judged more negatively—even viewed as less credible—than is a more outwardly emotional victim (Calhoun et al., 1985).

The idea that emotional response to crisis follows a predictable sequence of stages is also widespread, but it, too, is probably unwarranted. One of the best-known proponents of a stage model of coping is Elisabeth Kübler-Ross (1969). She has proposed that the terminally ill pass through five discrete stages: denial, anger, bargaining (for example, promising to become a better person if given more time), depression, and, finally, peaceful acceptance of their fate. Most of the evidence for this view comes from anecdotal accounts and researchers' subjective impressions. The few pertinent empirical studies do not seem to support a stage model. In a study of permanent paralysis from spinal-cord injury, for instance, N. C. Lawson (1976) attempted to determine whether victims experienced a stage of depression. Multiple measures of depression were taken five times a week

over an average of twenty-four weeks. Surprisingly, not a single patient was consistently depressed for even as short a period as one week. Such findings raise considerable doubt as to whether a stage model of response to crisis is valid.

Yet despite the scarcity of evidence in support of the stage model, most people continue to believe in it, even those in the medical and helping professions. As a result, people who experience life crises are often told by well-meaning professionals how they *should* react. Worse still, when a person does not conform to these expectations, the helpers may lose patience. One researcher has reported that because of wide acceptance of Kübler-Ross's stage theory of dying, terminally ill patients "who did not follow these stages were labeled 'deviant,' 'neurotic,' or 'pathological' diers. Clinical personnel became angry at patients who did not move from one stage to the next" (Pattison, 1977, p. 304). And if patients' emotional reactions are dismissed as "just a stage," legitimate complaints may be ignored. When one hospitalized cancer patient complained because she had been given the wrong tests, a nurse was overheard telling a coworker: "Don't worry about Mrs. A; she's just going through the anger stage" (Dunkel-Schetter and Wortman, 1982). Such responses from others may only compound the dying patient's problems.

ARE LIFE CRISES ALWAYS OVERCOME?

What about the prognosis for successfully overcoming a life crisis? Does "time heal all wounds," as many people believe? This common assumption, too, may not hold true for many people. There is considerable evidence that those who manage to recover from trauma do so less quickly and less completely than they or others expect. A large minority of people continue to be extremely upset long after their tragedy has occurred. One study found that fully 44 percent of widows and widowers continued to experience moderate to severe anxiety two to four years after their loss (Parkes, 1975). The sudden death of a loved one appears to produce the most severe and long-lasting distress (Parkes and Weiss, 1983). Even four to seven years after the loss of a spouse or child in an auto accident, for example, survivors have been found to exhibit depression and other psychiatric difficulties and to have problems functioning socially

Our culture accepts expressions of grief immediately after someone dies, but surviving spouses and close family members find that they are expected to recover quickly from their loss—even though they are actually likely to continue to feel depressed and anxious for months or years.

(Lehman et al., 1987). Similar slow recovery from adversity has been observed in many victims of rape. One survey found that 26 percent of rape victims still felt that they had not completely recovered four to six years after the assault (Burgess and Holmstrom, 1978).

Reviewing the literature, Wortman and Silver (1989, in press) identified four distinct styles of coping with irrevocable loss (the death of a spouse or loss of an infant due to sudden infant death syndrome). About half of the survivors accepted their loss: although saddened, they did not experience intense anxiety, depression, or grief. Approximately 30 percent reported extreme distress and depression immediately after the trauma, but gradually, after varying amounts of time, recovered. Another 18 percent were classified as "chronic grievers": they continued to report distress and depression for months, even years, after the trauma. Two percent were "delayed grievers": they seemed well adjusted immediately following their loss, but were deeply distressed a year later.

The recent research on emotional reactions to crisis reminds us that our intuitions about human behavior are not always correct. We tend to empha-

size the remarkable adaptability of people faced with adversity—their impressive ability to cope with the trauma and to recover emotionally. Although this highly resilient image may fit some victims of trage-dy, it tends to divert attention from the many who experience distress much longer than is commonly expected. Outsiders should be sensitive to the fact that for many people a life crisis is never put entirely behind them. The emotional scar is carried with them for the rest of their lives (Silver and Wortman, 1980; Wortman and Silver, 1989).

Despite such findings, health-care professionals, as well as friends and relatives, often expect quite rapid emotional recovery from adversity. They urge the victims to "get back on their feet," to go on with their lives as soon as possible. Bereaved widows report that remarriage is often tactfully mentioned within a few days or weeks of the husband's death, especially when the widow is young (Glick et al., 1974; Maddison and Walker, 1967). Similarly, par-ents who have lost a newborn baby are often immedi-ately encouraged to "put the death behind them" and have another child (Helmrath and Steinitz, 1978). So strong is the expectation that victims of misfortune should bounce back rapidly that those who fail to do so may be viewed in a negative light. Researchers have found that women who are still highly dis-tressed six months after being raped are often viewed by others as maladjusted and generally less likable than more resilient rape victims (Coates et al., 1979).

From the victim's or bereaved person's perspec-tive, such attitudes are often upsetting. Widows often resent the early hints that they should date and remarry (Glick et al., 1974). In addition, by encourag-ing the widow or victim to "get back on her feet," other people may subtly convey the message that her feelings and behaviors are inappropriate or even indicative of a psychological disorder. Ironically, vic-tims who have such feelings may be reluctant to seek professional help. In one study, a third of the young women who had undergone a hysterectomy one year earlier were still extremely upset, yet they "were hesitant to seek medical or psychological help be-cause they thought that they should be able to cope with this normal crisis" (Kaltreider et al., 1979, p. 1503).

Can the process of coping with trauma be accel-erated? James Pennebaker and his colleagues have

College freshmen move into their dormitory, beginning a phase of life that is likely to provide the most intense enjoyment—and anxiety—they will ever experience. Some researchers suggest that if the homesickness and other stresses of starting college are not acknowledged and dealt with, health problems may result.

gathered evidence that it can (Pennebaker et al., 1987, 1990). Numerous studies have shown that people who try to cope with stressful events by controlling, repressing, or denying their emotions experience more health problems than do people who talk about their trauma. Traumatic events are, by their very nature, difficult to understand and accept; talking promotes insight and recovery. But many people are reluctant to confess or confide in others—both because reliving an unpleasant experience is painful and because they fear embarrassment, disapproval, or punishment. This is a case where short-term pain results in long-term gain. In one study Pennebaker's team focused on a common but often unacknowledged problem: homesickness and anxiety upon entering college (Pennebaker et al., 1990). They divided freshman volunteers into two groups. The experimental group was asked to write down their thoughts and feelings about entering college for twenty minutes a day for three consecutive days. The control group wrote about emotionally neutral topics. The researchers found that the freshmen who wrote about their feelings had better health (measured in terms of fewer physician visits) than the control group throughout the year. Although they reported more homesickness and anxiety two to three months after the writing assignment, they were equal or superior to control subjects in positive moods and grade-point average by the end of the year.

Much more needs to be learned about emotional reactions to crisis. The more information researchers obtain, the better able we will be to help people cope with tragedy. Of course, it is also important to examine the physical responses that often accompany the emotional responses to adversity. As you will see in the following chapter, highly stressful life events can have a marked effect on physical well-being, sometimes contributing to the onset of serious illness.

SUMMARY

1. **Emotions** are largely involuntary responses involving visceral changes, visible expressive changes, and subjective feeling changes. Many older theories viewed emotions as primitive and disruptive, but most modern theories consider emotions functional and adaptive.

2. One of the defining features of emotion is physiological arousal. Numerous studies have shown that strong emotions are associated with activation of the peripheral nervous system; such changes can be measured with the **polygraph.**

3. The brain coordinates the activities of the peripheral nervous system. Psychologists used to believe that emotional responses were centered in the "primitive" regions of the brain, especially the hypothalamus and the limbic system. New research shows that the cerebral cortex is also involved in emotional experience.

4. Behavioral expression is also an integral part of emotion: often our face and posture say more about what we are feeling than the words we use. Darwin believed that many patterns of **nonverbal communication** are the product of evolution and served the adaptive function of alerting others to our state of mind and how we are likely to act (or **action tendencies**). Recent studies show that many facial expressions are the same across cultures and are universally recognized. But which emotions we express freely or attempt to conceal, and how well we read emotional expressions, are largely the result of cultural learning.

5. Emotions are also subjective states, what we call "moods" and "feelings." The **circle of emotions** model holds that emotions vary along two primary dimensions: pleasant-to-unpleasant and high-to-low activation. Numerous techniques have been developed to induce emotions in the laboratory. Many contemporary researchers are interested not only in emotional states, but also in emotional traits. Individuals differ from each other in the frequency and the intensity of their emotions.

6. Theories of emotions can be divided into two broad groups. The first emphasize physiological arousal. At the turn of the century, William James and Carl Lange proposed that our perception of bodily changes is itself the emotion, and that each emotional state is signaled by a unique physiological pattern. This view was challenged by Walter Cannon and L. L. Bard, who held that physiological arousal is too vague, diffuse, and slow to cause emotions. But new research on **facial feedback** suggests that physiological changes in the face may initiate, or at least modulate, the experience of emotion.

7. The second group of theories emphasize the role of cognition in emotion. Schachter and Singer's theory of **cognitive arousal,** which held that we interpret physiological arousal by reading cues in our environment, attracted both support and criticism. A more contemporary view, **cognitive appraisal,** holds that emotions arise from how we appraise events in our environment in relation to our short- and long-term goals and our abilities and resources for coping. The question of whether cognitions are essential to emotions has not been resolved, however.

8. Ideas about how people cope with crisis are clouded by stereotypes. Contemporary research suggests that people respond to extreme pain and irrevocable loss in a variety of ways; that time does not necessarily heal all wounds; and that encouraging people to talk about traumas, rather than urging them to "pull themselves together," may speed the process of recovery.

SUGGESTED READINGS

Buck, R. (1988). *Human motivation and emotion.* New York: Wiley. A text designed for use in an undergraduate class on emotion. A good review of scientific studies on emotion. Good discussion of research on how people send and receive emotional signals.

Cacioppo, J. T., and Tassinary, L. (1990). *Principles of psychophysiology: Physical, social, and inferential elements.* Cambridge, England: Cambridge University Press. An edited volume with chapters that focus on the different response systems (e.g., electrodermal, cardiovascular, the brain) and how physiological data may be used in psychological research. The chapters have been written by experts in the various techniques. This will be the standard handbook for psychophysiological methods for years to come.

Csikszentmihalyi, M. (1990). *Flow: The psychology of optimal experience.* New York: HarperCollins. The author presents his ideas and research on the topic of "flow" in a lively and engaging manner. Flow is a pleasant state of absorption in what one is doing. There is an excellent chapter on happiness, as well as suggestions for working toward happiness.

Ekman, P. (1985). *Telling lies: Clues to deceit in the marketplace, politics, and marriage.* New York: Norton. The author summarizes his many years of research on facial expressions in this book written for the popular audience. Through many examples and illustrations, the author instructs the reader in how to recognize felt from false emotions through facial expressions. There is also an excellent chapter on lie detection through polygraph techniques.

Ortony, A., Clore, G. L., and Collins, A. (1988). *The cognitive structure of emotions.* Cambridge, England: Cambridge University Press. As the title implies, this book details the authors' theory about the cognitive causes of different emotions. This book provides one of the most detailed accounts of how different appraisals of events gives rise to different emotional responses.

Stein, N. L., Leventhal, B., and Trabasso, T. (1990). *Psychological and biological approaches to emotion.* Hillsdale, NJ: Erlbaum. An edited collection of chapters by experts representing an effort to present current perspectives on both cognitive and biological approaches to emotion. This book also has a section on emotional development, covering research on emotions in infants and young children.

CHAPTER 12

THE DYNAMICS OF MOTIVATION

Why, in the early 1950s, did two men endure weeks of bitter wind and cold, scarcity of oxygen, and treacherous icy terrain in order to be the first people to set foot on the top of Mount Everest? Why do you sometimes do things that seem to be against your best interest, such as drinking too much at a party on the night before a big exam, or compulsively overeating when you know you should lose weight? Why do some students leave most of their reading for the week before finals, while others keep up throughout the semester? The answers to all such questions are bound up in the complex web of human motivation.

By **motivation,** psychologists mean that which gives impetus to behavior by arousing, sustaining, and directing it toward the attainment of goals (Madsen, 1959). Because motivational factors are so diverse, this chapter necessarily covers a variety of topics, ranging from biological forces that propel us to satisfy physiological needs, to motives we seem to acquire purely through learning. We begin with a look at the development of motivational concepts in order to give you an overview of psychologists' perspectives on this subject. We then turn to two motivations with strong biological components: the urge to eat and the urge to obtain sexual gratification. In the process of exploring eating, we also examine weight control, a persistent problem for many Americans today. Next, we turn to the idea that organisms strive to maintain an optimum level of arousal. As you will see, findings in this area help explain why your performance often drops when you are over- or understimulated. We then take up the related topic of high-arousal activities, such as hang gliding and parachuting. What motivates people to risk their lives in these dangerous sports? Finally, we investigate a learned motivation that is important to success in life, the motivation to achieve and excel.

THE DEVELOPMENT OF MOTIVATIONAL CONCEPTS

Like psychologists in other fields, those interested in motivation have developed a number of concepts that help guide their research. One of the earliest was the concept of instincts, innate motivations inherited through genes.

INSTINCTS AND GENETIC INFLUENCES

An **instinct** is an innate force, found in all the members of a species, which directs behavior in

Much animal behavior is instinctive. The male bower bird, for example, has an innate drive to build an elaborate bower of grass and twigs, which he decorates with feathers and other found objects, in order to attract a mate.

predictable ways when the right eliciting stimulus is present (Weiner, 1972, 1980). An example of an instinct is the "imprinting" of baby geese to their mother—following her as soon as they are able to walk. Ethologist Konrad Lorenz discovered that the stimulus eliciting this instinctive behavior is the first moving object that the newly hatched goslings see, which in nature is invariably the mother. By separating newborn goslings from the mother and showing them other moving things, Lorenz got them to faithfully follow a variety of "peculiar" objects, such as a wooden box on wheels, and even himself.

At the turn of the century, with the growing popularity of Darwin's theory of evolution, people began to wonder if they, too, had instincts. If the behavior of lower animals is largely instinctual, scientists reasoned, and if we humans are in fact related to other living things, perhaps some of our behaviors are also motivated by instincts. Such speculation launched a widespread effort to identify human instincts.

One of the most influential of the instinct theorists was William McDougall (1871–1938), who in 1908 proposed a list of human instincts that included curiosity, pugnacity, self-abasement, flight, repulsion, self-assertion, reproduction, gregariousness, acquisition, and parental care. Other investigators proposed different lists, and the number of instincts grew

as researchers tried to account for more and more human behaviors. A survey in the 1920s found that more than 2,500 human instincts had so far been proposed (Bernard, 1924). One researcher facetiously suggested that humans must also have an instinct to believe in instincts (Ayres, 1921)!

With the popularity of behaviorism in the mid-twentieth century, and its stress on *learned* responses, interest in instincts waned. In recent years, however, there has been a resurgence of interest in them and their role in human motivation. One example of a modern instinct theory is John Bowlby's view that babies have a built-in tendency to become attached to the adults who care for them (Bowlby, 1982). This tendency probably evolved because it served the important function of encouraging infants to stay close to their parents, thus affording them protection. Human instincts, of course, are less rigid and automatic than those of many other species, more open to variations due to different learning experiences (Eibl-Eibesfeldt, 1975). For instance, unlike the imprinting of baby geese, which occurs quickly, cannot be changed once established, and is identical for every member of the species, the attachment of human babies to their parents is the product of a great many hours of interaction, leaves room for attachment to other care givers, and can vary greatly in quality due to learning.

Freud believed that the sublimation of sexual urges was the unconscious motivation for such sensual works of art as Titian's *Bacchanal*.

The renewed interest in inborn behavioral tendencies has spawned a field called **evolutionary psychology** (Buss, in press). Researchers in this field focus on the genetic bases of a wide range of animal and human social behaviors, including aggression, cooperation, competition, sex roles, and altruism, especially altuism toward those who share one's own genes. Evolutionary psychologists argue that organisms are inherently motivated to pass their genes on to future generations and to ensure that the ''carriers'' of their genes survive, even if they themselves do not. Thus, a mother may sacrifice her own life to save her child, for the child will carry her genes into the next generation.

Some psychologists have criticized evolutionary psychology, arguing that human behavior is far too flexible to be controlled to a great extent by genes (Cantor, in press). These critics also feel that a focus on genetic factors downplays the influence of nongenetic ones. Still, few deny that genes play some role in human motivation. Most accept the idea that human behavior is the product of genes interacting with environment.

FREUD AND UNCONSCIOUS MOTIVATION

Like many other turn-of-the-century psychologists, Sigmund Freud looked to instincts as a way of explaining human behavior. But Freud's list of instincts included just two basic ones. The first was the urge toward life, procreation, and self-preservation, which included the drives for food, water, warmth, and, above all, sex. The second was the urge toward death and self-destruction, a return to the inanimate matter of which all living things are composed. Freud speculated that we often resolve the conflict between these two basic instincts by turning our self-destructive energies outward, against others—hence, the human tendencies to compete, to conquer, and to kill.

Freud believed that the dual urges of sex and aggression, if unsatisfied, create tension in people, and the desire to reduce this tension motivates behavior. But people cannot always reduce the tension directly by engaging in sex and aggression whenever they please. Doing so is often forbidden by the norms and laws of society. So people learn to push forbidden urges deep into the unconscious, a process called **repression.** A repressed urge still has power, however. It demands an outlet of some kind. Often, it encourages **sublimation,** or unconsciously finding some substitute behavior that is more socially acceptable. For example, Freud proposed that many of the beautiful nudes that Renaissance artists created on canvas and in marble were the products of sublimated sexual impulses. Similarly, we may unconsciously express anger toward our parents by losing or accidentally breaking one of their cherished possessions or by showing up late for a special holiday dinner. The possibility that our behavior is controlled by unconscious motives—motives that arise from deeply repressed urges—is one of Freud's most important contributions. We will discuss Freudian theory further in Chapters 13 and 16.

DRIVE-REDUCTION THEORY

At the same time that Freud's ideas were attracting interest in Europe, American behaviorists were arguing for an approach to motivation that emphasized observable influences in the environment, not innate or unconscious factors that are difficult or impossible to measure. A person behaves aggressively, they said, not because of an aggressive instinct, but because he or she has learned to do so by being rewarded for such behavior in the past.

Soon, however, problems became apparent for those who tried to argue that goal-directed behavior could be explained entirely by learning. For instance, researchers found it hard to condition a dog that had just been fed. Should we conclude that feeding produces some kind of learning deficit? Not likely. It makes more sense to say that learning is often encouraged when an animal is motivated by biological need. This led many psychologists interested in motivation to begin focusing on the role of physiological drives.

Behaviorist Clark Hull (1884–1952), widely considered the most influential psychologist of the 1930s and 1940s, argued that **drive** was the outcome of an animal's state of biological need. As a result of drive,

an animal becomes more active, thus increasing the likelihood that it will perform a drive-reducing response (Hull, 1943). A hungry rat, for instance, becomes agitated, begins to roam about its cage, and soon hits the bar that delivers a pellet of food. When the rat eats, its drive state declines, and reinforcement occurs. This increases the likelihood that the same actions will be repeated when a similar drive is aroused. According to Hull, then, drive (a motivator of performance) and reinforcement (a key to learning) work together to help an animal acquire adaptive responses.

But does the concept of drive, as Hull defined it, really provide a comprehensive theory of human motivation? This **drive-reduction theory** certainly helps explain why we eat, sleep, avoid pain, engage in sex, and so on. But how can it explain the large number of behaviors that seem to be unrelated to biological needs? Why, for example, do people seek out contact with other humans? Not because of any known biological need. What, then, motivates their behavior? To answer such questions, Hullian theorists proposed a distinction between primary and secondary drives. **Primary drives** are the most fundamental—the ones that arise from needs built into our physiological systems. **Secondary drives,** in contrast, were said to be learned through association with primary drives and their reduction. Thus, when a child's contact with adults is repeatedly paired with the reduction of hunger or pain, that contact itself soon becomes a secondary reinforcer, and the urge to obtain it becomes a secondary drive. By appealing to the concept of secondary drives (a form of what are often called **learned motives**), drive-reduction theorists believed they could explain the impetus for a wide range of behaviors.

BEYOND DRIVES AND DRIVE REDUCTION

For many years drive-reduction theory was extremely popular. The concept of drive was something that researchers could study in the laboratory. They could deprive experimental animals of food and other biological necessities for specified lengths of time and then measure the behavioral outcomes, all in controlled environments. Many hundreds of such studies were performed by Hull and other researchers, and the information gathered helped to refine their theories. Gradually, however, it became apparent that the

Young monkeys become engrossed in a problem-solving situation.

drive-reduction model had serious limitations. It simply could not account for certain facts that psychologists were uncovering.

For one thing, researchers were finding that animals of all kinds are strongly motivated to explore their environments and manipulate objects, even though no physiological needs are being served (Berlyne, 1950; Harlow, 1953). Rats, for instance, will endure electric shock in order to explore unfamiliar settings, and monkeys will become totally engrossed in solving puzzles, such as opening the clasp that fastens a door. These behaviors, moreover, occur despite never having been paired with food or other primary reinforcers, so secondary drives cannot explain them. What, then, is the motivation?

In a provocative paper, psychologist Robert White (1959) suggested that humans and other animals have a basic need to deal effectively with their environment and to master new challenges. We saw evidence of this in Chapter 9, where we described the reaction of human infants who figured out how to make a mobile move (Monnier et al., 1976). When the babies finally found the solution, they smiled and cooed vigorously, in apparent delight. White and others have argued that the reward in performing such behaviors lies in the intrinsic satisfaction of acting competently. This kind of **intrinsic motivation,** many now believe, explains much of human behavior (Deci and Ryan, 1980; Dwek and Leggett, 1988). It is probably the reason why one person

spends an entire Sunday morning doing a difficult crossword puzzle, while another meticulously tends a garden and then gives away all the vegetables. Whenever people perform actions in the absense of extrinsic payoffs, we might wonder if they are being intrinsically rewarded just by the pleasure of doing something well.

Another reason why people may perform actions in the absense of extrinsic payoffs is that they are motivated to maintain an optimum level of arousal (Hebb, 1955). Thus, a bored animal confined to a cage may be motivated to raise its level of arousal by exploring unfamiliar things. Later in this chapter we will examine some of the findings in support of this theory, as well as the implications of those findings.

But the tendency to explore unfamiliar things is not the only behavior that drive-reduction theorists had trouble accounting for. Researchers were also finding that animals sometimes refuse to satisfy a biological need even though the means to do so are readily available. For instance, you may remember a time when you felt extremely hungry and yet refused to eat when presented with unappetizing food. Hull's original model had no way to explain such behavior. Nor could it explain why you devour a delicious dessert at the end of a large meal, even though your need for food has already been fully met. Contemporary psychologists say that in such cases the rewards and punishments offered you are acting as **incentives** and motivating your behavior.

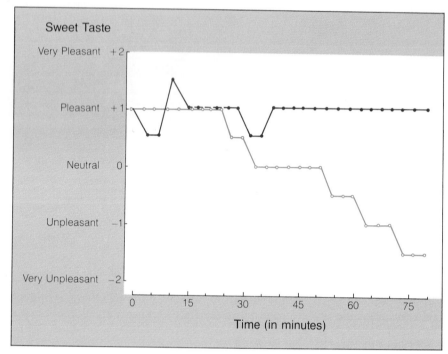

FIGURE 12.1 Graph of Cabanac's (1971) findings in his experiment on changes in the palatability of a sweet solution. The closed circles represent the response of a subject who sampled the solution without swallowing it. The open circles represent the response of a subject who swallowed the solution. Such changes in taste occur when hunger is appeased and may be a factor regulating food intake. (© 1971 by the AAAS. Used by permission of the AAAS and Professor M. Cabanac.)

Incentives are a product of experience—of coming to learn which stimuli in the environment are pleasant or unpleasant. You devour an ice cream sundae, even though you have just eaten, because you have learned in the past how good an ice cream sundae tastes. Incentives differ from primary drives, which are not dependent on experience. No learning is needed to feel hunger pangs, for instance. They arise automatically from changes within the body. Thus, an animal's total motivation can be seen as resulting from two different forces: the external pull of incentives on the one hand and the internal push of primary drives on the other.

Although Hull eventually acknowledged a role for incentives in later versions of his theory, many psychologists felt that he had not gone far enough. Cognitive psychologists argued that his view of incentives was too mechanistic. Animals, they said, especially humans, are intelligent creatures. They are not simply drawn to rewards in a mindless, unthinking fashion. Instead, they develop expectations about what their behaviors will lead to, and they attach subjective values to receiving or avoiding certain consequences. Out of these ideas emerged **expectan-**

cy-value models of motivation (Lewin, 1951; Tolman, 1959). They explained motivation by taking into account both the expectancy of achieving a particular goal and the value placed on it. One of the topics to which expectancy-value theory has been applied is achievement motivation—the urge to succeed and excel (Atkinson, 1964). Achievement motivation is discussed at the end of this chapter, after we have explored the motivations involved in eating, sexual behavior, and seeking stimulation.

EATING AND WEIGHT CONTROL

A remarkable aspect of the motivations that underlie eating is their ability to balance energy intake (food consumed) against energy expenditure (calories burned away). For most adults, weight does not fluctuate very widely. It stays much the same year after year. This stability in body weight is all the more impressive when you consider that an excess food intake of only 100 calories a day—about the number in a handful of peanuts—can theoretically add a hundred pounds to body weight in just ten years. For

Taste cues are one of the ways in which we control the amount we eat. A hungry person is likely to find a sweet-tasting food very pleasurable at first, but less so as his or her stomach becomes full.

most of us, fortunately, this does not happen. To understand why, we must look first at the physiological factors that regulate hunger.

PHYSIOLOGICAL FACTORS REGULATING HUNGER

What makes us feel hungry, and how do we decide when we have had enough to eat? Early researchers suspected that the answers lay in the stomach contractions we call hunger pangs and in the feeling of a full stomach. To investigate the role of hunger pangs, physiologist Walter B. Cannon (1871–1945) persuaded his assistant to swallow a specially designed balloon, which he then inflated and used to measure stomach contractions. As expected, the contractions were highly correlated with subjective feelings of hunger (Cannon and Washburn, 1912). Later findings suggested that distention or stretching of the stomach likewise plays a role in the cessation of eating. When one team of researchers loaded a large bulk of nonnutritive material directly into a dog's stomach (via a surgical incision), the animal ate less than normally or not at all (Janowitz and Grossman, 1949, 1951). For a time, then, stomach cues seemed adequate to explain why we start and stop eating.

But then it dawned on researchers that the stomach contractions Cannon had measured might not have been hunger pangs after all. Instead, they might have been the result of the stomach trying to digest the balloon that was inside it. This, in fact, turned out to be the case. When the electrical activity of contracting stomach muscles was measured from the surface of the body, the contractions were *least* strong and *least* frequent when the stomach was empty (Davis et al., 1959). Later evidence confirmed that cues from the stomach are of only secondary importance in regulating hunger and eating. Rats whose stomachs have been removed still learn mazes to obtain food, so apparently they can still feel hungry, and humans who have had their stomachs removed because of ulcers or other diseases continue to report hunger pangs (Janowitz, 1967; Penick et al., 1963).

Other investigators have suggested that eating may be partly regulated by changes in the sensation of taste. As Figure 12.1 shows, the hungrier a person is, the more likely he or she is to judge a sweet-tasting food as pleasant. Once full, the person rates the same food as unpleasant (Cabanac, 1971). Thus, the first bite of a food may taste better than the last, regulating intake accordingly. But taste cues, like cues from the stomach, must be of only secondary importance in

After destruction of the ventromedial area of the hypothalamus, this rat has overeaten to such as extent that it weighs 1,080 grams. (The dial has gone beyond the 1,000-gram capacity of the scale and registers an additional 80 grams.) A normal rat would weigh about 320 grams.

controlling eating (Woody et al., 1981). When humans and other animals must press a lever to receive an injection of liquid food delivered through a tube directly into the stomach, they are able to control their body weight quite well despite the fact that they never taste what they are fed (Epstein and Teitelbaum, 1962; Jordan, 1969). An animal fed this way can maintain a stable weight even when the experimenter varies the amount of food delivered with each bar-press. Clearly, some control system other than taste is at work.

The messages in this other system seem to be carried in the blood (Whalen and Simon, 1984). When the blood from a rat that has recently eaten is transferred to a food-deprived rat, the latter no longer appears hungry. It nibbles indifferently at food it would otherwise devour (Davis et al., 1969). This finding suggests that something in the blood of the recently fed rat signals satiation. But what, exactly, is the signal or signals involved?

One is probably the amount of a hormone called cholecystokinin (CCK), which is released during digestion. CCK suppresses eating under certain conditions, and so is probably a satiation signal that works in conjunction with other still-to-be-identified chemicals (Muurahainen et al., 1985). Another signal involved in regulating eating is the amount of sugar in the blood (Mayer, 1952). Blood sugar, however, is probably more important in *initiating* eating than in stopping it (Logue, 1991). When the blood sugar available to the body is low, people tend to feel hungry and seek out food.

But signals like blood sugar and CCK are short-term regulators of eating. Their levels rise after a meal (signaling satiation) and fall five or six hours later (signaling hunger again). If these were the only kinds of signals we had, our bodies would never be able to correct for times when we ate more than we needed and stored the excess calories as fat. And yet, as we have said, most animals maintain remarkably stable weights over many years. How is this long-term weight regulation achieved?

The answer seems to lie in signals derived from the total amount of fat in the body. Each of the 30 billion or so fat cells in a normal human is a warehouse for storing liquefied fat, microscopic droplets that look much like the fat in a jar of cooking oil. As more fat accumulates, the fat cells swell, sometimes more than doubling in size. At the same time, every fat cell is continually spilling into the bloodstream a substance known as glycerol (within the cell, glycerol is attached to the fat molecules). Thus, the more fat molecules are crammed into a fat cell, the more glycerol is discharged into the blood. This glycerol, some researchers suspect, serves as an eating signal. According to their theory, when glycerol reaches the cells of the brain, it provides information about the size of the body's surplus energy stores. Depleted stores encourage additional eating, while overabundant stores curb the appetite. This theory is supported by the finding that rats injected with extra glycerol virtually stop eating (Bennett and Gurin, 1982). Another theory of long-term weight regulation focuses on the amounts of free fatty acids in the blood, fatty acids being another component of fat molecules. When the body is breaking down stored fat, free fatty acids are released, which seems to serve as a signal to eat more. Conversely, when the body is storing fat, the amount of free fatty acids in the blood gets depleted, which apparently serves as a signal to eat less.

But how does the brain "read" the various signals involved in regulating eating? Much of the answer is found in a part of the brain called the

Bulimia—bouts of gorging, often followed by purging—most often occurs among young, white, middle-class women.

hypothalamus. Electrical or chemical stimulation of the lateral (side) region of the hypothalamus causes a previously satiated rat to eat voraciously (Anand and Brobeck, 1951). This suggests that the lateral hypothalamus helps to process information in the blood about the need to initiate eating. Not surprisingly, when the lateral hypothalamus is destroyed, a rat refuses to eat. Another area of the hypothalamus, the ventromedial (middle front) region, has opposite effects. Stimulation of it turns off hunger, while destruction of it usually causes an animal to gorge (Hetherington and Ranson, 1940; Hoebel and Teitelbaum, 1962). Thus, the ventromedial hypothalamus helps to process information that signals satiation.

Bear in mind that these two regions of the hypothalamus do not act as isolated control centers. The lateral and ventromedial hypothalamus are important parts of much larger neural networks that radiate through many areas of the brain (Grossman, 1975; Schwartz, 1984). In addition, other neural pathways related to other motivations cross the hypothalamus. This is why an animal with a lesioned hypothalamus typically shows a mixture of symptoms. For instance, lesions in the ventromedial hypothalamus produce not only a voracious appetite but also a short temper and general irritability (Schachter, 1971a). Apparently, an intact ventromedial hypothal-

amus plays a role in restraining emotions as well hunger.

EATING DISORDERS: ANOREXIA AND BULIMIA

Some people become so obsessed with the subject of weight control that they literally starve themselves to death in an attempt to shed pounds. This condition is known as **anorexia nervosa,** and it is far more prevalent in women than in men. About 95 percent of anorexics are females—most of them teenagers and young adults. These women have lost at least a quarter of their weight (some as much as two-thirds), and so look like walking skeletons. Yet, despite their emaciated appearance, their sense of body image is so distorted that they continue to insist they are too fat and must drastically restrict their diets (Bemis, 1978; Bruch, 1980).

About half of all anorexics suffer from an additional eating disorder called **bulimia,** which involves periodic gorging. On a typical binge of a few hours, the average bulimic consumes 4,800 calories, the equivalent of several days' worth of food. Often, bulimics eat everything available—a loaf of bread, a jar of peanut butter, a half-gallon of ice cream, a barrel of fried chicken, several bags of cookies, a quart of potato salad—before the compulsive eating stops. Afterward, most bulimics either fast to avoid weight gain, or purge their systems by vomiting or taking laxatives. Not surprisingly, bulimics have a love–hate relationship with food. They tend to be people who derive psychological comfort from eating and who use food as their major self-reward (Lehman and Rodin, 1989). But they also feel guilty and negative about themselves after eating many kinds of foods (Ruggiero et al., 1988).

Although bulimia is often found in anorexics, most bulimics are of average or even above-average weight. Virtually all, however, have strongly internalized the value our culture places on being thin. And most are very dissatisfied with their own weight; they think they are too heavy even if they are not (Ruderman and Grace, 1988; Williamson et al., 1988). This dissatisfaction with body image helps to explain why bulimia usually begins after a period of stringent dieting. Some authorities think that the hunger caused by dieting may exacerbate a tendency toward binge eating (Polivy and Herman, 1985; Smead, 1988). At the same time, social learning may also play a part in the onset of bulimia. College women living in large-group housing (where the eating patterns of many others can be observed) have a rate of bulimia more than twice as high as that of other college women (Drewnowski et al., 1988).

THE GENETICS OF WEIGHT CONTROL

Genes strongly influence individual differences in weight relative to height. Identical twins, who have all their genes in common, are more similar in fatness or thinness than are fraternal twins, who have on average only half their genes in common. This is true even when the identical twins are raised apart (Stunkard et al., 1990). Similarly, parents and their biological children are more alike in weight than are parents and children they have adopted (Foch and McLearn, 1980). Researchers have also found that they can breed animals with a propensity to fatness just by selectively mating the fattest ones in each generation (Bray and York, 1971).

But what weight-related factors are passed on through genes? One possibility is a certain metabolic rate—that is, a certain rate at which food energy is burned away. This possibility was strongly suggested in a study of male identical twins (Bouchard et al., 1990). Twelve pairs of identical twins were housed together in a closed-off section of a dormitory where their diets and exercise were carefully controlled. Each of the men received an extra 1,000 calories a day above the level he needed to maintain a stable weight. This overeating continued six days a week for a total of twelve weeks, and involved enough excess calories to produce 21 pounds of fat. But the different pairs of twins did not all gain 21 pounds each. Their weight gains ranged from 9 to 29 pounds, with each of the twins in any given pair both gaining very close to the same amount. It was as if each set of twins had inherited a tendency to burn calories at a certain rate given a situation of prolonged overeating.

Researchers have wondered what other inherited factors make a person naturally prone to gaining weight or staying slim. One idea has been that people might inherit different sensitivities to external cues regarding eating—that is, different susceptibilities to the sight, smell, and taste of good food. Psychologist Stanley Schachter proposed this interesting theory some twenty years ago. Other scientists' responses to it, and to one another's findings, have built our current understanding of the major causes of obesity. Since this is a subject of such enormous interest in our weight-conscious society, we will examine it in depth.

IN DEPTH

Studying the Causes of Obesity

THE INITIAL STUDIES

Schachter's ideas about eating and obesity grew from his theory of human emotion, which we discussed in Chapter 11. As you may recall, Schachter argued that an emotion has both a cognitive and a physiological component, both of which are needed for the emotion to be complete. Hunger, he reasoned, might also involve these two interacting factors. On the one hand are cognitions regarding external eating cues (Is it time for a meal? Does the food look tempting?). On the other hand are internal changes associated with hunger (stomach contractions and changes in blood chemistry, for example). Schachter proposed that people differ in their sensitivity to internal versus external factors. Some are more controlled by internal forces, while others are more controlled by external ones. This idea, in turn, led him to his theory of obesity: if people who are very sensitive to external eating cues live in an environment where such cues abound, they are apt to constantly overeat and become very fat (Schachter, 1971b).

To test his theory, Schachter designed a series of clever experiments. Most were aimed at showing that overweight people are indeed unusually sensitive to external eating cues and relatively insensitive to internal ones. In one study, obese and average-weight men were asked to skip a meal and come to the experiment hungry (Schachter et al., 1968). Upon arriving, half were fed roast beef sandwiches, while the others remained hungry. Each subject was then given five kinds of crackers and asked to rate the taste of each (salty, cheesy, garlicky, and so forth). He was told that he could eat as many crackers as he wanted to ensure the accuracy of his ratings. Actually, the experimenters didn't care about the ratings; they were interested only in the number of crackers each man ate. As expected, normal-weight subjects ate fewer crackers if they had been given a sandwich beforehand, but obese subjects did not. The amount they ate was unaffected by whether they had eaten a sandwich or not. Schachter concluded that this was because obese people are less sensitive to internal eating cues and more sensitive to external ones.

CRITICISMS, ALTERNATIVES, AND FURTHER RESEARCH

Schachter's theory of obesity attracted widespread interest, but it soon became apparent that there were a number of problems with it. For one thing, not all obese people were found to be highly sensitive to external eating cues, nor were all people *with* such sensitivity found to be overweight (Rodin, 1981). Thus, unusual sensitivity to external cues cannot be the only cause of obesity. Moreover, even among obese people who *are* highly sensitive to food cues, the nature of this link is not clear. Hypersensitivity to food cues could just as well be the *result* of obesity rather than its cause; or perhaps some third, unidentified factor causes both the other two.

Psychologist Richard Nisbett has focused on this second possibility (Nisbett, 1972). He has suggested that some obese people are actually starving themselves from their brains' perspective, which accounts for both their large appetites and their heightened responsiveness to food cues. Nisbett

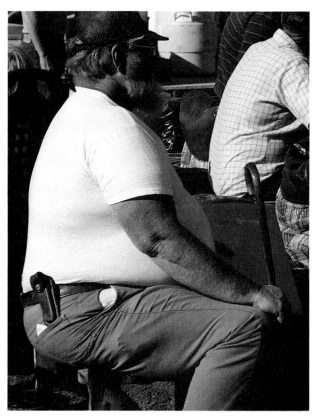

People may have a setpoint, a proportion of body fat that the brain is programmed to consider normal. Thus, even an obese person may be chronically hungry because he or she is eating less than the body needs to maintain its setpoint and meet its energy needs.

came to this surprising conclusion after reviewing information on the effects of prolonged hunger. He noticed some striking behavioral similarities between severely hungry people and many people who are obese. Both are highly sensitive to food cues; both tend to be easily frustrated and upset; and both generally lack energy and interest in sex. In addition, both have abnormally high levels of free fatty acids in their blood, a sign that body fat is being broken down to help meet energy needs. This led Nisbett to suspect that some obese people are in a state of chronic energy deficit, which gives rise to persistent hunger. Persistent hunger, in turn, causes both a tendency to overeat and a tendency toward overresponsiveness to food cues.

But how can an obese person be hungry when he or she eats more than enough to maintain a

TABLE 12.1   Eating Restraint Scale

1. How often are you dieting? Never; rarely; sometimes; often; always. (Scored 0–4)
2. What is the maximum amount of weight (in pounds) that you have ever lost within one month? 0–4; 5–9; 10–14; 15–19; 20 +. (Scored 0–4)
3. What is your maximum weight gain within a week? 0–1; 1.1–2; 2.1–3; 3.1–5; 5.1 +. (Scored 0–4)
4. In a typical week, how much does your weight fluctuate? 0–1; 1.1–2; 2.1–3; 3.1–5; 5.1 +. (Scored 0–4)
5. Would a weight fluctuation of 5 pounds affect the way you live your life? Not at all; slightly; moderately; very much. (Scored 0–3)
6. Do you eat sensibly in front of others and splurge alone? Never; rarely; often; always. (Scored 0–3)
7. Do you give too much time and thought to food? Never; rarely; often; always. (Scored 0–3)
8. Do you have feelings of guilt after overeating? Never; rarely; often; always. (Scored 0–3)
9. How conscious are you of what you are eating? Not at all; slightly; moderately; extremely. (Scored 0–3)
10. How many pounds over your desired weight were you at your maximum weight? 0–1; 1–5; 6–10; 11–20; 21 +. (Scored 0–4)

Source: Herman and Polivy, 1975. (© 1975 by the American Psychological Association. Reprinted by permission.)

normal weight? Nisbett believes that the answer lies in the concept of a **setpoint** for fat—that is, a level of fat which the brain is "set" to consider normal. This setpoint seems to vary from one person to the next. Some people, Nisbett argues, have a setpoint for fat that is far above average. As a result, their bodies are constantly telling them that they are hungry and in need of food. A high setpoint for fat may be partly caused by a large number of fat cells, which in turn can be caused by either genetics or overeating at some point in life (Bennett and Gurin, 1982; Knittle and Hirsch, 1968). Someone who has acquired a great many fat cells can never be rid of them. Even with extreme weight loss, fat cells do not disappear, they just shrink in size. Thus, a large number of fat cells all clamoring to be filled with fats could help produce the chronic state of hunger that Nisbett talks about.

Nisbett has gone on to argue that some people respond to this chronic hunger by letting their bodies have their way. These are the people who eat until they are satisfied and grow to gargantuan proportions. But many other naturally obese people do not want to be fat. Obesity is considered unattractive in our society, so the fat person is under great pressure to lose weight. These people, according to Nisbett, find themselves in perpetual conflict. Their bodies tell them that they are hungry and need to eat more, while society tells them that they are fat and need to lose weight. These are the people who end up undereating for their setpoints and so display the behavioral symptoms of chronic hunger.

Some intriguing evidence supports Nisbett's theory. For instance, the *grossly* obese usually do not display the behavioral symptoms of hunger. Presumably these people have given up any effort to remain slender and so eat as much as they want. It is people who are only moderately obese and who are constantly watching their weight who tend to display the emotionalism, lack of energy, and high responsiveness to food cues that are characteristic of severe hunger (Hibscher and Herman, 1977).

This finding raises an interesting possibility. Some people who are of normal weight, or even very slim, may be "starving" themselves from their bodies' viewpoint in order to achieve thinness. Psychologists Peter Herman and Janet Polivy (1975) have called such people **restrained eaters.** Whether they are currently fat, slender, or in between, restrained eaters would gain a great deal of weight if they "let themselves go" regarding eating. Herman and Polivy have developed the scale in Table 12.1 to measure eating restraint. You can use it to assess your own eating behavior. If you score high on this test—totaling 14 or more points—you are apt to be frequently dieting. And when your eating restraint is for some reason broken, you may not just eat, you may binge.

The effects of breaking eating restraint among normally restrained eaters has been demonstrated in experiments. In the first such study, subjects arrived at the laboratory shortly after lunch or dinner and were given either nothing to eat or one or two milkshakes as part of a bogus taste test (Herman and Mack, 1975). Each person was then left alone to taste and rate three flavors of ice cream. The subjects were told that after rating the flavors they could eat as much of the ice cream as they wished. Enough ice cream was provided so that someone could gorge without making an embarrassing dent. As expected, ice cream eating and milkshake drinking were related: For unrestrained eaters (those who described themselves as rarely giving a thought to dieting), the more they drank, the less they ate. Restrained eaters, as predicted, did the opposite. Those who drank *more* milkshakes also ate *more* ice cream, with those who had downed two milkshakes gobbling up substantial amounts! Why did overeating breed more overeating in normally restrained eaters? Apparently, after indulging in the milkshakes, the restrained eaters reasoned that all hope of dieting for that day was lost. The result was a collapse of their normal restraint and a sizable eating binge. Many subsequent studies have replicated this tendency of restrained eaters to overeat once they have been induced to go off their diets (Herman and Polivy, 1980). Some of the naturally occurring factors that can prompt restrained eaters to abandon their normal restraint are negative emotions, such as anxiety and depression, and the use of alcohol (Wardle and Beales, 1988).

The concepts of setpoint and restrained eating go beyond Schachter's concept of heightened sensitivity to food cues as a way of explaining why some people are chronically obese. The theories of Nisbett and Herman and Polivy, Schachter admits with good humor, are "really closer to the way God sees things. . . . They can incorporate far more data than any scheme I know of, including my own" (quoted in Bennett and Gurin, 1982, p. 44). This is not to say that some overweight people are not also very responsive to food cues. Many of them are. But heightened responsiveness to food cues may more often be a product of hunger than an innate tendency. High responsiveness to food cues, in any case, makes it hard not to overeat. People with this reaction experience a boost in insulin levels at the very sight of something good to eat. Insulin, in turn, accelerates the process by which sugar is removed from the blood (taken up by body cells and by the liver), which makes people feel even hungri-

er than before and increases the likelihood that they will eat (Rodin, 1979).

PATTERNS AND CONCLUSIONS

With all these physiological factors working against them, what chances do chronically obese people have of losing weight? Popular diets that slash calories may produce some weight loss, but many have serious drawbacks. A few, if used without medical supervision, can actually cause severe harm by eliminating essential nutrients. And even if fad diets cause no measurable harm, there is no evidence that they succeed in the long run. The biggest problem with such diets is recidivism: An estimated 95 percent of "successful" dieters regain their lost pounds (Adler and Gosnell, 1982).

The concept of a high setpoint for fat can help explain why. Once they have lost weight, people with a high setpoint for fat receive strong hunger signals from the brain. These signals continue until the person eats enough to reach setpoint again. In addition, physiological processes help ensure that setpoint will be reestablished. For instance, a dieter who has lost a great deal of weight has elevated levels of a certain body chemical (lipoprotein lipase) that promotes the storage of fat (Adler and Gosnell, 1982). As a result, any food the person eats in excess of energy needs is used to generate fat. And such a person can have remarkably *low* energy needs. The metabolism of a stringent dieter usually shifts downward in an apparent effort to use meager food supplies efficiently. The person is able to get along on fewer and fewer calories, until eventually anything more than the most Spartan of diets is enough to start putting on weight (Keesey and Powley, 1986).

Experts believe that the best approach to combating obesity is to combine a sensible diet with regular exercise, behavior therapy, and a long-term program of maintenance monitoring (Perri et al., 1988). A sensible diet limits calorie intake while providing essential nutrients. Regular exercise burns calories and may sometimes raise a person's metabolic rate for several hours following (Thompson et al., 1982). This means that even after the person *stops* exercising, more calories than normal are being burned away. Behavior therapy involves

In addition to a sensible eating plan and exercise, the group support and regular monitoring provided by organizations like Weight Watchers are helpful to people trying to lose excess weight.

restructuring a person's environment to reduce stimuli that trigger overeating, providing rewards for eating restraint and adherence to an exercise program, and carefully monitoring relevant information, such as calorie intake, time spent eating, and weight lost or gained. This last factor—monitoring—should be continued even after a desirable weight is reached. When people who are prone to overeating keep track of their eating behavior, they are more likely to exercise self-restraint (Polivy et al., 1986). It is also important that people who are trying to keep off weight have another person to consult with regarding the problems they encounter (Wadden et al., 1988). Such a person can help the formerly obese person to cope with the many eating temptations that can undermine self-restraint.

SEXUAL BEHAVIOR

Although external cues play an important role in the motivation to eat, they are even more important in

sexual motivation. Sexual stimuli of some kind (real or imagined) are essential for the process of sexual arousal to begin. Consider a male rat that has lived alone for several weeks. He walks about his cage sniffing and exploring, occasionally nibbling at food or taking a sip of water. There are no external or internal signs that the rat is in a state of deprivation. Then a female rat in heat is placed in the same cage. The male's behavior changes dramatically. He begins to court the female, seeking to mount her and copulate. Although the male's actions are strongly influenced by hormone changes within his body, those changes, in turn, are triggered by the sight and smell of the receptive female. In short, the animal's sexual behavior is under the influence of two interacting factors: the presence of sexual stimuli, which tend to elicit certain physiological changes; and the physiological changes, which help to heighten and sustain sexual activities (Bolles, 1975). In this section we will examine these interacting influences.

HORMONES AND SEXUAL RESPONSIVENESS

The role that hormones play in energizing sexual responses is still controversial. In lower animals hormones seem to be especially important. Female rats, for instance, are sexually responsive only when their ovaries secrete a high level of the female hormone estrogen, which, in turn, triggers the release of egg cells for possible fertilization. Not surprisingly, when the ovaries of a female rat are removed, she becomes totally unreceptive to males, unless she receives estrogen injections, which restore her normal sexual responsiveness.

In humans, in contrast, sex hormones may help promote sexual activity, but they certainly do not control it. Although some women report that sexual responsiveness seems to increase during the middle of the menstrual cycle, when estrogen levels peak, objective evidence shows that for most women no such increase in responsiveness occurs (Hoon et al., 1982). Nor do most women experience any cyclical decrease in the ability to become sexually aroused. The vast majority of women can become aroused *throughout* the normal rise and fall of estrogen levels (Adams et al., 1978). In fact, even complete removal of the ovaries tends to have only a negligible effect on a woman's sexual responsiveness. It appears that the sex hormones secreted by the adrenal glands may have a greater effect on female arousal than those secreted by the ovaries. When diseased adrenals are surgically removed, a woman's sexual urge often

Our expectations may be what gives perfumes their power as sexual attractants. Other animals are aroused by natural body odors but are indifferent to perfume.

drops appreciably. But even in the case of adrenal hormones, the effects are not clear-cut. Some women continue to be sexually responsive even after adrenal surgery. This finding suggests that, although some degree of hormonal influence over sexual receptivity may exist in women, that influence is far from all-powerful.

In the human male the influence of hormones on sexual responsiveness is also less than in other species. If the testes (which produce the male hormone testosterone) are surgically removed from an adult, a loss of sexual interest and responsiveness is not inevitable. Consider a study of over a hundred Scandinavian men whose testes were removed, either because of disease or as punishment for repeated sex crimes (Bremer, 1959). In a third of the men, sexual activity persisted for more than a year, and in some it continued for as long as ten years, even though they all eventually lost their ability to ejaculate during orgasm. Loss of the testes before adolescence, however, seems to have a more predictably negative effect. With some exceptions, most castrated boys who do not receive hormone therapy grow up to have little sexual interest or ability, nor do they develop secondary sex characteristics, such as facial hair and a deep-pitched voice (Money and Ehrhardt, 1972).

Hormones, of course, interact with the central nervous system. The hypothalamus, in particular, stimulates the anterior pituitary gland to release hormones, which, in turn, stimulate both the gonads (the ovaries and the testes) and the adrenal glands to secrete sex hormones. The sex hormones then travel in the bloodstream back to the hypothalamus, where they activate nerve networks involved in sexual arousal. One area of the hypothalamus that plays a key role in these nerve networks is the preoptic region (Giantonio et al., 1970). Electrical or chemical stimulation of the preoptic region greatly increases mating in both male and female rats (Fisher, 1956, 1967; Malsbury, 1971). Males so stimulated mount other males if females are not available, and they can ejaculate at a rate of once every 27 seconds—more than ten times faster than the normal rate.

THE ROLE OF AROUSING STIMULI

Hormones reaching the hypothalamus serve only to prime sexual responses. Sexual stimuli are also needed for full-fledged sexual arousal. In humans a wide variety of visual and tactile sensations are known to serve this purpose, from the sight of a nude body to the touch of someone's lips. But what about less obviously sexual stimuli, such as olfactory ones (those received by the sense of smell)? Are humans as sexually aroused by certain odors as other species are?

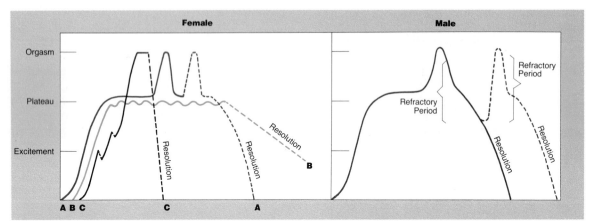

FIGURE 12.2 Masters and Johnson's description of coitus in the human female and male. The phases—excitement, plateau, orgasm, and resolution—are defined by physiological changes. In both sexes, excitement leads to a plateau phase that may be maintained for considerable periods without orgasm. The female may have one orgasm or several orgasms in succession (line A), not achieve orgasm at all and return relatively slowly to an unaroused state (line B), or, rarely, have a single prolonged orgasm followed by rapid resolution (line C). The male has only one pattern of response after the plateau phase: he ejaculates quickly in orgasm, and his arousal decreases rapidly. In the refractory period after ejaculation, he is incapable of another ejaculation. He may repeat the orgasmic phase several times before returning to an unaroused state.

In many species, including some mammals, odors are powerful sexual signals (Carr and Caul, 1962; Michael and Keverne, 1968). Male dogs and monkeys, for example, are especially attracted to the scent of the female's vaginal secretions (Beach and Merari, 1970; Michael et al., 1971). In rats, the sexual odors of nursing females play a major role in arousing males when a sexually receptive female is near (Fillion and Mass, 1986). Some researchers think that humans, too, emit sexually arousing odors, although we are seldom consciously aware of them (Wiener, 1966). It is believed that these scents may arise from the sweat glands and from secretions that accumulate in the genital regions (Comfort, 1971; Morris and Udry, 1978).

An intriguing question is why people develop sexual responsiveness to some stimuli but not to others. Do we *learn* to find certain sights, scents, and actions arousing, or are we born with these tendencies? As with most other sources of human behavior, the causes of sexula motivation are both varied and complex. Biological processes occurring before a child is even born may influence adult sexual behavior. But from birth on, social learning, family dynamics, and other life experiences will also play a role.

HUMAN SEXUAL RESPONSES

It is one thing to study the stimuli that people find sexually arousing and quite another to study sexual acts themselves. For many years, psychologists considered this subject far too private for scientific investigation. Then, in the late 1950s, William Masters and Virginia Johnson started a revolution in the study of human sexuality. They were the first to conduct extensive laboratory observations of what actually happens in the human body during sexual activity. Using cameras and other devices to record internal and external responses, Masters and Johnson studied nearly 700 male and female volunteers engaged in intercourse, masturbation, and other sexual behaviors. In all, the research team directly observed more than 10,000 sexual orgasms. A detailed summary of their findings was published in the book *Human Sexual Response* (1966).

THE SEXUAL RESPONSE CYCLE

Masters and Johnson found that men and women respond quite similarly during sex. Both experience the same four physiological stages, called the

sexual response cycle (see Figure 12.2). In the first stage, the **excitement phase,** breathing, heart rate, and muscular tension increase as arousal begins. Blood rushes into the genital organs, causing erection of the penis in a man and swelling of the clitoris in a woman. The lining of the vaginal walls becomes lubricated as drops of moisture, resembling perspiration, begin to form on it. The nipples of the woman—and sometimes of the man—typically become erect.

During the **plateau stage,** arousal heightens and brings a further increase in breathing, heart rate, and muscle tension. A man's penis achieves maximum erection, and the glans, or head, turns a purplish color. Drops of fluid, which can contain active sperm, are usually secreted from the opening of the penis. The testes increase in size and are pulled up tightly against the scrotum. In women, the vagina is further lubricated to facilitate insertion of the penis. The inner two-thirds of the vagina balloon up into a sac to receive semen, and the outer one-third decreases in diameter to put pressure on the penis. At the same time, a woman's clitoris retracts under its hood.

In the **orgasmic phase,** the muscles in the pelvic region and around the anus of both sexes undergo a series of contractions. In a woman the muscles of the vaginal walls and the uterus contract rhythmically, as do the muscles in and around the penis in a man. Contraction of the penile muscles leads to ejaculation, the expulsion of semen, a milky white fluid that contains sperm. Most of the ejaculate is expelled during the first few contractions, but the contractions typically continue for a few more seconds. The contractions of a woman may last longer, from ten to thirty seconds. Orgasm in a woman arises from penile stimulation of either the clitoris or the vaginal walls. Other muscles, particularly in the face and limbs, also contract involuntarily. In both sexes, blood pressure and heartbeat rise further, frequently reaching the level experienced by athletes at peak physical exertion. This state of extremely heightened arousal is accompanied by feelings of intense pleasure as muscle tension releases.

During the **resolution stage,** blood pressure, heart rate, and respiration gradually fall to normal. Men enter a refractory period, during which they are incapable of being stimulated to another orgasm for some time. Some women, in contrast, are capable of a series of multiple orgasms before passing into the resolution phase.

Although Masters and Johnson's model of the sexual response cycle is widely considered important, it has been criticized. Some complain that Masters and Johnson never fully described the methods they used to collect their data, so their studies cannot be replicated precisely. Others question the universality of Masters and Johnson's stages, arguing that they may not apply equally well to all people. More research needs to be done using standardized measurement techniques in order to resolve the issue of universality (Geer and Head, 1990).

SEXUAL DYSFUNCTIONS

Masters and Johnson's work was not only important basic research, it also had applied significance. It laid the foundation for understanding and treating sexual dysfunctions. A **sexual dysfunction** is any persistent or recurring problem that prevents a person from engaging in sexual relations or from reaching orgasm during sex.

There are several different kinds of sexual dysfunctions. In men, **erectile failure** is the inability to achieve or maintain an erection. In rare cases, the man has never been able to have an erection, a condition called **primary erectile failure.** More often, the man has problems maintaining an erection only in some situations, a condition called **secondary erectile failure.** For other sexually dysfunctional men, arousal is not the problem. They acquire an erection easily enough but ejaculate before they or their partners would like. This **premature ejaculation** is the most common sexual complaint among male college students (Werner, 1975). Still other men have the opposite sexual problem. They are *unable* to ejaculate during sex with a partner. This is called **inhibited ejaculation.**

One of the sexual dysfunctions of women is **vaginismus,** involuntary muscle spasms that cause the vagina to shut tightly so that penetration by a penis is extremely painful or even impossible. Other women engage in, and often enjoy, sexual intercourse but do not experience orgasm. The term **primary orgasmic dysfunction** refers to cases in which the woman has never experienced an orgasm through any means. The term **secondary orgasmic dysfunction** refers to cases in which the woman experiences orgasms sometimes (through masturbation, for exam-

The sexual themes of romance novels, though quite repetitious (as their covers indicate), appeal primarily to women, perhaps even increasing their motivation to have sex.

ple), but not with her primary sexual partner or not during sexual intercourse.

When sexual difficulties are chronic and very distressing, people may seek the help of a sex therapist. Masters and Johnson were pioneers in the development of sex therapy. In their approach (1970), the couple is treated as a unit by a pair of sex therapists, one male and one female. The focus is on the sexual relationship, on education, and on the reduction of sexual anxiety. Usually, to lessen the fear of failure, the couple is told not to engage in sexual intercourse for the time being. Instead, they are assigned "nondemanding" sensual exercises, such as massaging one another. Gradually, more sexual activities are introduced, and the couple is instructed in how to respond freely while giving each other pleasure.

A diagnosis of sexual dysfunction should not be made hastily. Many people experience the problems we have described at one time or another. Only when these problems are extremely persistent and upsetting should they be called dysfunctional. For instance, a woman's difficulty achieving orgasms would not automatically be labeled a dysfunction. In fact, research indicates that about a third of all women do not regularly have orgasms during intercourse. If these women enjoy sex and can reach orgasm through oral or manual manipulation, most sex therapists would consider them sexually normal (LoPiccolo and Stock, 1986).

THE MIND'S ROLE IN HUMAN SEXUALITY

The fact that the vast majority of sexual dysfunctions have no physiological basis, but instead are caused psychologically, attests to the powerful role of the mind in human sexuality. Similarly, the fact that people can become highly aroused just by sexual fantasies also attests to the mind's role in sexual behavior. In studies in which sexual arousal is measured while subjects merely think about erotic stimuli, researchers have found that the more explicit the erotic imagery, the more heightened the arousal (Dekker and Everaerd, 1989).

Studies also show that erotic imagery plays an important role in most people's daily sex lives. In a study of nearly a hundred men, a large majority reported imagining various sexual acts during both intercourse and masturbation, and they also fantasized sexual scenes at least once daily *outside* any kind of overt sexual activity (Crepault and Couture, 1980). Such mental images seem to heighten erotic arousal and increase the motivation to engage in sex. The same processes occur in women. The large majority of women fantasize sexually both during and outside the physical act of sex (Crepault et al., 1977; Hariton and Singer, 1974). Such erotic images are often used to enhance sexual responsiveness.

Because of the critical role of the mind in human sexuality, psychologists have proposed models of sexual arousal that emphasize cognitive processes. According to one of them, arousal begins when erotic cues trigger *expectations* of arousal (Barlow, 1986). If the person finds these expectations pleasant, he or she will focus more intently on the cues (noticing more details about them, for example). This serves to trigger physiological arousal, which helps to direct even more attention to the cues, which heightens the physiological arousal, and so on in a feedback loop. Ultimately, if the erotic cues are processed long enough and arousal rises to a sufficiently high level, the person will seek some overt form of sexual activity.

But what if erotic cues produce arousal and no willing partner is available? Might the sex drive eventually build to such a level that it encourages acts of sexual aggression such as rape? As logical as this reasoning may seem, scientific evidence does not tend to support it. (See Chapter 19, In-Depth essay.) Studies have shown that exposure to violent pornography does not make men any more prone to sexual arousal when they view depictions of rape (Ceniti and Malamuth, 1983). Thus, many psychologists now believe that rape and other acts of sexual violence are the product of deep-seated anger, not sexual motivation that has been heightened by pornographic cues (Gray, 1982). Such anger would continue to find expression in sex crimes even if pornography were banned. However, pornography, especially when it depicts masochism and violence, may perpetuate sexually callous attitudes toward women, even if it does not directly influence overt sexual aggression.

STIMULUS SEEKING AND AROUSAL

If you give a monkey a mechanical puzzle, such as a metal clasp used to fasten a door, it manipulates the object with great curiosity, searching diligently for the solution (Harlow et al., 1950). Humans have a similar penchant for puzzles of all kinds. What makes a person stay up all night to finish a mystery novel? Why do people spend hours playing video games? One answer lies in the theory that people have an optimum level of arousal that they try to maintain.

THE OPTIMUM-LEVEL-OF-AROUSAL CONCEPT

By the middle of this century, psychologists had collected a wealth of information related to motivation. Among their data was a fascinating set of findings concerning arousal and the brain. In particular, scientists had learned that, when sensory stimuli impinge on an organism, they activate not one but two pathways in the brain. First, there is a pathway that leads from receptor cells to the thalamus and then to appropriate sensory and other areas of the cortex. Second, there is a pathway traveling to the reticular formation (a part of the brainstem) and from there upward to produce diffuse arousal of the *entire* cortex.

Most important for an understanding of motivation, this cortex-wide arousal seems to be essential to perform a goal-directed response (Lindsley, 1951). When the diffuse cortical arousal induced by the reticular formation is slight, the chains of neurons associated with goal-directed behaviors may be unable to fire effectively. The result is lethargy and stupor. Conversely, when an excessive amount of diffuse cortical arousal is induced by the reticular formation, the neural circuits associated with goal-directed behavior may become blocked, causing a person to feel paralyzed. For instance, at the height of a fierce battle an estimated 75 to 85 percent of soldiers are so immobilized by fear and excessive sensory stimulation that they never fire their rifles (cited in Hebb, 1955).

Figure 12.3 shows the general relationship between diffuse cortical arousal and efficiency of performance. As you can see, the relationship is an inverted U: as arousal increases, performance first improves and then declines. These findings led psychologist Donald Hebb and others to suggest that organisms have an **optimum level of arousal,** a level at which their goal-directed behaviors are most effective (Duffy, 1957; Hebb, 1955). According to Hebb, people automatically tend to maintain their arousal within the optimum range. Others have argued that humans, with their high levels of self-awareness, often consciously and actively seek an optimum level of arousal (Berlyne, 1960).

Many researchers have tried to test the notion of an optimum level of arousal by inducing different levels of arousal using various means (stimulant drugs, mild electric shock, aversive noises, bogus threats, monetary incentives, and so forth). They then observe how a certain level of arousal is related to performance on some task. Although there has been substantial variation in the outcome of such studies, there is general support for the idea that a moderate level of arousal is associated with enhanced performance, while very high and very low arousal is

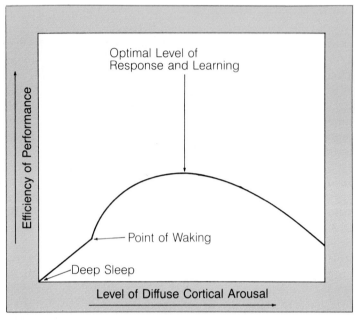

Optimal Level of
Response and Learning

Efficiency of Performance

Point of Waking

Deep Sleep

Level of Diffuse Cortical Arousal

FIGURE 12.3 **The relationship of efficiency to cortical arousal. As the level of cortical arousal increases, performance increases until it reaches an optimal level; then, it decreases. Higher animals may be attracted to risk taking and mild fear, or to problem solving and mild frustration, because these serve to increase arousal. (*After Hebb, 1955.*)**

associated with performance decrements (Anderson, 1990).

But a problem with these studies is that the independent variable (the factor being manipulated) is never "pure" arousal (Neiss, 1988, 1990). When researchers do something to arouse a person physiologically, they inevitably affect that person's emotions and thoughts as well. So how can we say that arousal alone is the cause of any changes in performance? Maybe one or more other factors are also playing a part. This could help explain why negative states of high arousal (fear or grief, for example) are more apt to cause performance decrements than are positive states of equally high arousal.

Some critics think it is now time to refine the concept of an optimum level of arousal as a way of explaining differences in performance. They argue that researchers should develop more complex models of why performance varies in different situations related to arousal. Using modern techniques to study cognition, emotion, and other physiological changes in the body, some psychologists will probably start to do just that.

EXPLAINING SENSORY DEPRIVATION AND SENSORY OVERLOAD

The concept of an optimum level of arousal captured great interest partly because it helped to explain the results of **sensory deprivation** studies. In sensory deprivation studies, a person's sensory input is drastically reduced for a prolonged period of time. Consider one such study conducted just a few years before Hebb published his theory that organisms tend to maintain an optimum level of arousal. Male college students were paid $20 a day to remain in an environment with very low levels of sensory stimulation (Bexton et al., 1954). Each subject lay on a bed in a small room, as illustrated in Figure 12.4. A hollowed pillow enveloped his ears, muffling the only sounds —the low, monotonous hums of an electric fan and an air conditioner. The subject's eyes were covered with translucent goggles that diffused light, so the few objects around him appeared blurred and indistinct. Because he wore only loose-fitting pajamas, he did not even feel the pressure of a belt or a shoe. Cardboard tubes encased his arms from elbow to fingertips, cutting off the sense of touch. On demand, he received food or water and was allowed to use the bathroom. Otherwise, he heard almost nothing, saw almost nothing, and felt almost nothing.

A drive-reduction theory of motivation would predict that a person should remain happily quiescent under such conditions. After all, his needs for food, water, relief from pain, and so forth were being admirably met. But this is not what happened. Many of the subjects quit the experiment after only a few days. Subsequent sensory deprivation studies have shown that about a third of all participants drop out before the end (Goldberger, 1982). Why this negative reaction?

Part of the explanation probably has to do with the stress of social isolation (Suedfeld, 1975), but a less than optimum level of sensory stimulation seems to play a role as well. Subjects in such experiments grow bored and apathetic. Their minds wander; they have trouble concentrating; and their brain waves sometimes show patterns more characteristic of sleep than alert wakefulness. At the same time, they seem to develop a strong desire for sensory stimulation of *some* kind (Bexton, 1953). This desire for stimulation is consistent with optimum-level-of-arousal theory, which predicts that very low levels of stimulation will prompt a quest for higher levels.

Also in keeping with optimum-level-of-arousal theory is the fact that performance on certain mental tasks often decreases with sensory deprivation (Goldberger, 1982; Suedfeld, 1975). In one study, subjects were given the task of thinking up as many uses as they could for common household objects. After thirty-six hours of sensory deprivation, their performance dropped markedly (Landon and Suedfeld, 1972).

If people tend to be impaired when arousal levels fall too low, it seems logical that the opposite extreme would also cause problems. That is, excessively high levels of arousal should likewise be detrimental to performance, making it harder for people to sustain goal-directed behavior. Researchers have investigated this subject in the laboratory by bombarding people with high-intensity sights and sounds for several hours. In a typical study, a person lies down in a specially designed room where sounds blare from all directions and the walls are ablaze with rapidly changing and vividly colored patterns. Most people find this kind of **sensory overload** even more aversive than sensory deprivation. They become aroused and disoriented with regard to time and space, perform poorly on many cognitive tasks, and after a while may sometimes even have hallucinations (Goldberger, 1982).

Similar reactions have been observed in real-life situations that involve sensory overload, especially those that also pose serious threats to life (Kaminoff and Proshansky, 1982). For instance, in one study of people's responses to such life-threatening disasters as fires and flash floods, at least 75 percent of the victims showed impairment in their ability to react rationally (Tyhurst, 1951). Many behaved in ways that

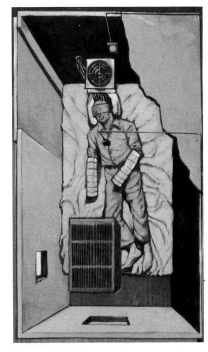

FIGURE 12.4 A sensory deprivation experiment. In a classic series of experiments in the 1950s, subjects were isolated in sound-resistant cubicles. A foam pillow and the continuous hum of the air conditioner and fan made input to the ears low and monotonous. Except for eating and using the bathroom, the subjects did nothing except lie on the bed. Few chose to remain longer than three days.

simply did not make sense, such as wandering aimlessly rather than seeking a viable escape route. A full 12 to 25 percent were hopelessly disoriented. They screamed and cried hysterically or remained frozen to one spot. Apparently their extremely high levels of arousal, caused by sensory overload and intense emotion, made them unable to act in goal-directed ways.

WHY PEOPLE TAKE RISKS

It was nearing noon that Sunday when a stiff, warm breeze suddenly materialized. Brent Hansen, a 29-year-old student . . . had been waiting for it most of the morning. Helmetless, he picked up the control bar of his multi-colored hang glider, fastened his harness, and ran 10 yards along the top of a 600-foot cliff. . . . But no sooner was he aloft than he

What makes some people willing to engage in such dangerous work as high-steel construction? The pay is good, but all the money in the world wouldn't be enough to get most of us out on one of these girders. An opponent process may be involved, in which the initial intense fear is countered by exhilaration.

got into serious trouble. Somehow he had become tangled in his harness. "I'm caught! I'm caught!" he screamed. But his friends below could only watch as he dove nose first into the ground at roughly 40 mph. After three days in the intensive-care unit . . . he recovered, only to hang glide again. (Greenberg, 1977, p. 17)

Although optimum-level-of-arousal theory can help explain the tendency to seek *some* degree of stimulation, it cannot explain why certain people risk their lives in high-arousal activities, such as hang gliding. What made Brent Hansen and many others like him return to a sport that nearly killed them? What is it that draws the race-car driver back to the track and the sky diver back to the sky?

THE OPPONENT-PROCESS MODEL

One model that provides a possible explanation was proposed by Richard Solomon and J. D. Corbit (1974). Beginning with the assumption that organisms seek to maintain a biological and psychological balance, Solomon and Corbit argued that, when a strong emotion disrupts that balance, an *opponent process* is activated. By **opponent process** they mean an opposite response. If the initial emotion is negative, the opponent process is positive and vice versa. Usually the opponent process reduces and eventually cancels out the original emotion, thus reestablishing an emotionally neutral state. If, however, the stimulus that caused the initial emotion is suddenly removed, the opponent reaction will temporarily be experienced by itself and can be overwhelming.

Applied to a high-arousal sport, such as sky diving, the opponent process model says that, on the sky diver's first leap from a plane, he or she is likely to feel a moment of utter terror. Almost immediately, however, an opponent process begins to counteract the intense fear, and soon the jumper, though still highly anxious, is no longer terrified. Once the diver lands safely, fear evaporates, and only the pure opposing emotion is left. The novice sky diver now feels relieved and happy.

This pleasurable sensation helps to coax the person back for another jump. According to Solomon and Corbit, each additional dive serves to *intensify* the positive experience because an opponent process is strengthened every time it is elicited. Consequently, if a sky diver continues to jump, the opponent process becomes more and more powerful until eventually a jump provokes only mild anxiety. Furthermore, upon landing, the diver is exhilarated, a feeling that can sometimes last for hours. It is this euphoria that presumably draws even the previously injured diver back jump after jump.

The opponent-process model has been used to account for a variety of experiences, some of which are otherwise hard to explain (Solomon, 1980, 1982). For instance, people generally find that running becomes less agonizing after a certain distance, as if an opponent process counteracts their physical pain. And experienced runners often report euphoria at the end of a run, suggesting that what they may be feeling is an intensified opponent process taking over when the stress of running ends. This postrun euphoria is said to be one reason why people get hooked on running. Using the same logic, some researchers suggest that the exhilaration students sometimes feel after taking a difficult exam may be an opponent process set in motion to counteract their test-taking anxiety (Craig and Siegel, 1979).

The opponent-process model has received support in studies not only of humans but of laboratory animals as well (Mineka et al., 1981). Yet the theory is not without critics. Some wonder if *every* emotion necessarily induces an equal and opposite response. The answer is probably not. In one study, researchers generated happiness or revulsion in people by repeatedly exposing them to positive or negative pictures (a picture of a smiling bandleader, for example, versus one of a man with a facial disease) (Sandvik et al., 1985). They found that emotional reactions did tend to weaken as people viewed the same pictures over and over again. This is in keeping with the idea that an emotion is automatically counteracted by an opposing one. Contrary to opponent-process theory, however, people who had become inured to negative pictures were no happier upon seeing positive ones than were people who had not become inured. The same was true of people inured to positive pictures who were suddenly shown negative ones. Their feelings of revulsion were no more intense than those of other subjects. It was as if there was no opponent process at work boosting their "reverse" emotion. Perhaps these findings mean that stronger initial emotions are needed to start an opponent process going. If so, psychologists must conduct more research to find out the limits of opponent-process theory.

INDIVIDUAL DIFFERENCES IN SENSATION SEEKING

The opponent-process model provides one rationale for the drawing power of dangerous sports, but it does not explain why some people are more attracted to risk than others. An answer proposed by psychologist Hans Eysenck (1967) is that people vary greatly in their need for stimulation as a result of differences in their brains. According to Eysenck, these brain differences explain the dissimilarities in behavior between introverts (people who are generally withdrawn) and extraverts (those who are generally sociable and lively). The reticular formation of an introvert, in Eysenck's view, is activated to a relatively high degree by sensory inputs. Consequently, the introvert has a naturally high level of cortical arousal. Such a person needs little external stimulation to achieve an optimum arousal level and so prefers

quiet, solitary activities. The extravert, in contrast, has a reticular formation that is activated to a relatively low degree by sensory inputs and so has a naturally low level of cortical arousal. As a result, the extravert requires a great deal of external stimulation to boost arousal to an optimum level, which explains the extravert's preference for noise, excitement, and companionship. High-sensation seekers may also be extraverts, people who need a great deal of external stimulation to attain an optimum level of arousal.

Psychologist Marvin Zuckerman has tried to assess the needs of high- and low-sensation seekers for other kinds of stimulation. He has developed a personality scale that includes items ranging from preferences for exotic vacations and spicy foods to the desire to try risky sports or hallucinogenic drugs. (A brief version is shown in Table 12.2.) More than 10,000 people have taken this test. The results show that the drive for excitement and diversity is seldom confined to one area of life, just as Eysenck's theory predicts. "The high-sensation seekers," Zuckerman wrote, "are likely to have not just one but a number of adventurous tastes, from an eagerness to try risky sports such as sky diving to a desire for variety in sexual partners" (Zuckerman, 1978, p. 40). Whether such adventurous tastes can be explained entirely by naturally low cortical arousal is still a matter of debate. Zuckerman later suspected that the activities of certain neurotransmitters in the brain also play a part (Carrol et al., 1982; Zuckerman, 1979). But regardless of cause, the fact remains that for certain people the quest for stimulation is virtually a way of life. Many high-sensation seekers do not even seem to care whether the stimulation they experience generates emotional highs or emotional lows (Kohn and Coulas, 1985; Larsen and Zarate, 1990). They seem interested only in being stimulated somehow— positively *or* negatively—in order to compensate for underarousal.

What are the implications of these findings for adjustment to life and to other people? Zuckerman suggested that high-sensation seekers react badly if they feel trapped in unstimulating situations. They often do poorly in academic settings that lack creative outlets. And when tied down to dull, routine kinds of work, they may, according to Zuckerman, turn to excessive use of alcohol or other drugs. Moreover, even when high-sensation seekers are able to select schools, jobs, and hobbies that meet their needs, they may still be misunderstood by low-sensation seekers, who consider some of their actions "reprehensible,

TABLE 12.2   Sensation–Seeking Scale

1. A. I would like a job that requires a lot of traveling.
   B. I would prefer a job in one location.
	9. A. I enter cold water gradually, giving myself time to get used to it.
	   B. I like to dive or jump right into the ocean or a cold pool.

2. A. I am invigorated by a brisk, cold day.
   B. I can't wait to get indoors on a cold day.
	10. A. When I go on vacation, I prefer the comfort of a good room and bed.
	    B. When I go on vacation, I prefer the change of camping out.

3. A. I get bored seeing the same old faces.
   B. I like the comfortable familiarity of everyday friends.
	11. A. I prefer people who are emotionally expressive even if they are a bit unstable.
	    B. I prefer people who are calm and even-tempered.

4. A. I would prefer living in an ideal society in which everyone is safe, secure, and happy.
   B. I would have preferred living in the unsettled days of our history.
	12. A. A good painting should shock or jolt the senses.
	    B. A good painting should give one a feeling of peace and security.

5. A. I sometimes like to do things that are a little frightening.
   B. A sensible person avoids activities that are dangerous.
	13. A. People who ride motorcycles must have some kind of unconscious need to hurt themselves.
	    B. I would like to drive or ride a motorcycle.

6. A. I would not like to be hypnotized. B. I would like to have the experience of being hypnotized.	**Scoring** Count one point for each of the following items that you have circled: 1A, 2A, 3A, 4B, 5A, 6B, 7A, 8A, 9B, 10B, 11A, 12A, 13B. Add up your total and compare it with the norms below.
7. A. The most important goal of life is to live it to the fullest and experience as much as possible. B. The most important goal of life is to find peace and happiness.	1–3 Very low on sensation–seeking 10–11 High 4–5 Low 12–13 Very high
8. A. I would like to try parachute-jumping. B. I would never want to try jumping out of a plane, with or without a parachute.	6–9 Average

Source: Zuckerman, 1978.

foolish, and even crazy. The 'highs,' for their part, consider the caution of the 'lows' prudish, stuffy, timid, or inhibited. High- and low-sensation seekers do not understand one another, and this can be an unfortunate state of affairs if they are a therapist and patient, or a husband and wife'' (Zuckerman, 1978, p. 99).

LEARNED MOTIVATION: THE CASE OF ACHIEVEMENT

Arousal of the cerebral cortex sheds much more light on some motivations than others. Why are you willing to go out of your way to do a favor for a friend? Why does a college student work weekends and abandon other interests to win acceptance to medical school? Why does a politician submit to a grueling campaign and spend a personal fortune trying to become President of the United States? For answers to these and similar questions, we must look to the motivations people learn in the course of growing up,

including the motives for achievement, power, social approval, and companionship. By concentrating on one of these learned motivations—achievement—we can explore the factors that underlie a learned motivation and the benefits that scientific knowledge of these factors brings.

INDIVIDUAL DIFFERENCES IN ACHIEVEMENT MOTIVATION

To measure individual differences in achievement motivation, researchers typically use pictures from the Thematic Apperception Test (TAT), discussed in Chapter 14 (Atkinson, 1958; McClelland et al., 1953, 1976). In the TAT, people are presented with ambiguous pictures (such as a man standing by a machine or a boy apparently daydreaming) and are asked to write a brief story about each one. These stories presumably express their own motivations. Stories that receive high scores for achievement motivation are those in which the major character performs at a high level or accomplishes something unique, is concerned

High achievement needs and expectation for success spur these Olympic hopefuls toward their goal.

with standards of excellence or the pursuit of a long-term goal, expresses pride in success or shame at failure, or displays other achievement-related feelings and behaviors.

People who test high and low in achievement motivation differ in several important ways. Those with a high **need for achievement** persist longer and show better performance on exams than do those with a low need for achievement (Atkinson and Raynor, 1974). This is especially true when an authority figure stresses the need for excellence (McClelland, 1985). People with a high need for achievement also tend to select occupations that require individual initiative, such as owning their own business. People with a low need for achievement, in contrast, tend to be attracted to such jobs as routine office work, which demand little individual initiative (McClelland, 1955). Those high in achievement motivation tend to set challenging but realistic goals. Their opposites set their sights far lower or unrealistically high, as if they were aiming more toward failure than success. In one study, for instance, researchers measured how far each subject chose to stand from the target when playing a ring-toss game. Those who scored high in achievement motivation stood at an intermediate distance, making the game challenging but not impossible. Those who scored low in achievement motivation usually stood either very close to the target or very far from it

(Atkinson and Litwin, 1960). Similarly, students with a high need for achievement tend to seek challenge in their majors and future careers but also tend to be realistic in these choices. Students with a low need for achievement, in contrast, tend to choose either very easy or extremely difficult majors (Isaacson, 1964).

Researchers have wondered what factors underlie achievement striving or its absence. They have found, for one thing, that people who avoid realistic challenges and fail to persist at difficult tasks tend to have a relatively high *fear of failure*. This fear helps explain the outcome of the ring-toss experiment and similar findings. Those who select very easy goals virtually assure their own success, and those who select very difficult goals provide a way of explaining failure that preserves their self-esteem ("No one could succeed at a task *this* hard!"). Anxiety about failure, then, is an important determinant of achievement behavior. People seek challenge and accomplishment only if their motive to achieve success is stronger than their motive to avoid failure (Atkinson, 1964).

Another factor that helps explain differences in achievement strivings is the *expectations* that people hold regarding their own potential for success or failure. If people expect to do well on a task, they are likely to devote more effort to it than they do if they anticipate failure. But why do some people have confidence that they will ultimately prevail, while

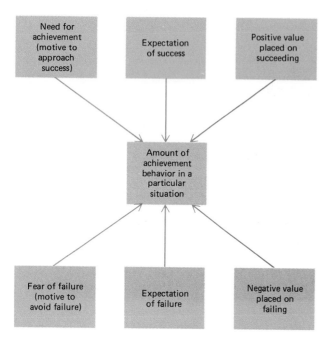

FIGURE 12.5 **Factors affecting achievement behavior.**

when people decide whether or not to strive for achievement. Figure 12.5 shows how incentives related to values fit into an overall model of achievement behavior.

Thus, a complex relationship exists among the values people assign to specific successes and failures, the causes they attribute to them, their emotional reactions to doing well or poorly, and their tendencies to seek or avoid challenge. People who attribute achievements to their own abilities often place high value on success. Their self-esteem is raised by their accomplishments, so they tend to seek out challenges. In contrast, people who attribute success to external causes and failure to themselves do not generally find accomplishment very rewarding, but they do find failure highly threatening. As a result, they tend to avoid challenges. And because they believe that inability causes their lack of success, they seldom persist when failure threatens. Ironically, then, they often give up in challenging situations, thereby ensuring the failure they so greatly dread (Heckhausen, 1977).

others are filled with doubts? One answer is that people differ in the ways they explain past performance (Dweck, 1975; Weiner, 1974; Weiner et al., 1972). When people attribute their successes to the enduring factor of ability, they are likely to develop high expectations that they will succeed again and again. The same is true of people who attribute their failures to controllable factors, such as amount of effort. When people who fail are convinced that their failure was caused by too little effort, they develop the expectation that more effort will bring success. Now consider some ways of explaining past performance that tend to breed *lack* of confidence. When people attribute failure to an enduring lack of ability, they have every reason to expect additional failures in the future. And when they attribute success to variable factors, such as luck or the ease of the task, they have little reason to be confident that more successes will come their way.

Yet a third factor that underlies achievement efforts is the positive or negative *value* that someone places on success or failure (Parsons et al., 1978; Spenner and Featherman, 1978; Tesser, 1985). Will doing well or poorly on a particular task affect the person's self-image or sense of self-worth? Will it facilitate or block the future fulfillment of important goals? Such questions are undoubtedly considered

ENCOURAGING ACHIEVEMENT BEHAVIOR

There is strong evidence that achievement behavior develops during childhood and is influenced, both positively and negatively, by a child's parents. One early study found that mothers of eight-to-ten-year-old boys who scored high in achievement motivation had long expected their children to be independent in various ways—getting themselves ready for bed, earning their own spending money, choosing their own clothes, and so forth (Winterbottom, 1958). In addition, these mothers controlled their children's behavior mainly through rewards, such as praise and affection, rather than through punishment. Parents of boys with low achievement motivation, in contrast, tended to relate to their children in either an aloof or a domineering way, and they tended to emphasize conformity traits, such as good manners and obedience. Subsequent studies have tended to confirm these general findings (Rosen and D'Andrade, 1959; Weiner, 1980).

Although we cannot really specify causes from such correlational data, it is easy to imagine how these childhood experiences might help to foster achievement behavior. When children are encouraged to be independent, to do things for themselves, they seem more apt to develop a sense of being the masters of their own fates. Being controlled through rewards rather than punishments would probably help to generate a similar sense of autonomy, a feeling that one's behavior is not coerced, but rather comes from within. These outlooks, in turn, could easily affect children's willingness to strive for goals —that is, their achievement motivation.

But if achievement strivings are strongly influenced by experiences in childhood, is it still possible to instill them when a person is an adult? Psychologist David McClelland and others believe that it is. In one study, for instance, McClelland and Winter (1969) encouraged and guided college students in the creation of success fantasies, and the students subsequently improved their academic performance. It is not entirely clear why this strategy worked. Perhaps just by making the rewards of success salient, fantasies encourage people to try harder. Or perhaps the act of mentally creating successes makes people see themselves as being in control.

In a more ambitious study, called the Kakinada project, the same researchers tried to increase the achievement strivings of all the businessmen in a village in India. The businessmen were encouraged to have high-achievement fantasies, to make plans that would help them realize their goals, and to communicate with one another about their goals and methods. McClelland does not know exactly why the program succeeded, whether one technique worked more than others or whether all contributed equally. But succeed it did. The businessmen became significantly more productive. They started several large industries, enlarged their existing businesses, and hired a total of 5,000 workers (McClelland and Winter, 1969). Moreover, unlike many other economic development projects, which succeed only in the short run, the Kakinada project appeared to have a continuing effect for more than a decade (McClelland, 1978). McClelland suspects that the success was due to the program's stress on achievement motivation, not just business knowledge. Apparently, by making people more aware of the possibilities of success and the methods of attaining it, it is possible to boost achievement strivings in many different kinds of situations.

ACHIEVEMENT BEHAVIOR AMONG WOMEN

In the many studies of achievement motivation researchers have found a peculiar but persistent pattern: a need for achievement did not predict the behavior of women as well as it predicted the behavior of men.

Women who scored high in the need for achievement did not always set themselves challenging goals, nor did they always persist in achievement-oriented tasks. In fact, the performance of some women actually declined in certain competitive situations. Psychologists wondered why.

EARLY RESEARCH ON WOMEN AND ACHIEVEMENT

One answer that generated a great deal of controversy was proposed by Matina Hunter (1965). To explain the differences in behavior between men and women with high achievement motivation, Horner (1965) argued that achievement-oriented women are propelled in opposite directions by two powerful forces. On the one hand, they are pushed toward achievement by their desire to obtain the psychological satisfaction associated with accomplishment. On the other hand, they have learned from childhood that success for a woman is unfeminine and socially disapproved, especially by men. Consequently, they are also motivated to avoid success.

Horner (1970) devised a way to measure the fear of success, as it came to be called. She gave male and female college students an opening sentence and then asked them to complete the story. For the ninety women in the study, the opening sentence was: "After first-term finals, Anne finds herself at the top of her medical school class." For the eighty-eight men in the study, the sentence was the same except that the name *John* was substituted for the name *Anne*. Horner reasoned that, if a subject was fearful of success, that fear should be reflected in the story he or she wrote about a highly successful medical student of the same sex. Specifically, if a story contained references to social rejection, anxiety, or negative self-image as a result of success; if it linked success to abandonment of a medical career; or if it denied that such success was possible, the story was said to include fear-of-success imagery.

The results of the study confirmed Horner's predictions. The women showed significantly more evidence of fear of success than did the men. But the most striking feature of Horner's results was the magnitude of the differences. More than 65 percent of the women wrote stories containing fear-of-success imagery, compared with fewer than 10 percent of the men.

Horner's research made headlines in the popular press, prompting many women to wonder if their slow climb in the business world was not due to deep-seated fear of success. The widespread interest helped to generate a wave of subsequent research. Later findings, however, did not always support Horner's original conclusions. In sixty-one studies in which subjects were asked to write stories in response to an achievement cue (such as Anne at the top of her medical school class), the percentage of women expressing fear of success ranged from 11 to 55 percent, and the percentage of men expressing such a fear ranged from 14 to 86 percent. Fear of success, in other words, was not always dramatically greater in women. In fact, in seventeen of thirty-six studies that included men, the men expressed *more* fear of success than did the women (Tresemer, 1974, 1977). If fear of success is a stable personality trait found primarily in women, how can those results be explained?

Important clues began to emerge when researchers looked for patterns in the circumstances surrounding fear-of-success imagery. Some psychologists extended Horner's experimental design by having men write about Anne's success and women write about John's. Under those circumstances, the men envisioned many negative outcomes related to achievement, whereas the women envisioned relatively few (Monahan et al., 1974). The findings indicated that men were less able to envision favorable implications of success for a woman than for a man, and women found it easier to imagine positive outcomes for a successful man than for a successful woman. In addition, the amount of negative or positive imagery a subject expressed could be increased or decreased by changing the achievement situation. Women, for example, wrote much less fear-of-success imagery about Anne when they were told that half of Anne's classmates were women (Katz, 1973) or that Anne was at the top of her *nursing* school class (Alper, 1974). Similarly, men wrote far more fear-of-success imagery when they discussed John's success in nursing school (Cherry and Deaux, 1975).

On the basis of such findings, many researchers have concluded that Horner's original experiment may not have been measuring a fear of success at all. Instead, she may have been measuring women's assessments of the social rejection likely to be caused by deviation from traditional sex roles (Frieze et al., 1979). And those assessments were probably warranted. In one study some men did, indeed, dislike being outdone by a girlfriend and so preferred to work alone, rather than with the girlfriend, on achievement tasks (Condry and Dyer, 1976). The message to the girlfriend was clear: "If you outperform me, I will be threatened and avoid you." Such social rejection may have been what women in Horner's study were fearing when they reacted ambivalently to Anne's success in a male-dominated field. Compounding that fear may have been the fact that many women at the time of Horner's study (about twenty years ago) were probably sex-role traditionalists. Research has shown that women who adhere to traditional sex-role values are more likely than other women to have lower career aspirations, to rate themselves as less intelligent, and to perform more poorly than otherwise when required to compete with a boyfriend (Peplau, 1976).

SEX DIFFERENCES IN INTERPRETING FAILURE

But some researchers now suspect that a fear of deviating from traditional sex roles and being rejected by men may be only part of the reason why some women who score high in the need for achievement fail to persist at achievement tasks or refrain from setting challenging goals for themselves. Another possible explanation has emerged from recent research by psychologist Carol Dweck, whose studies we mentioned in Chapter 1. Dweck has found that some people are inclined to attribute failure to lack of ability, rather than to a lack of effort, and, as a result, stop trying to succeed. As it turns out, the tendency seems to be more prevalent in girls than in boys. Whereas girls are more likely than boys to view their academic failures as signs of low ability, boys are more likely than girls to see such failures as due to simple lack of effort. That is the case regardless of the fact that during the early school years girls equal or surpass their male classmates in all areas of academic work (Dweck and Goetz, 1978; Dweck et al., 1980; Nichols, 1975). Certainly, if that negative way of interpreting failure came to undermine one's general sense of competence, it could easily prompt achievement-oriented women to behave in the puzzling ways they sometimes do.

Dweck wondered just what it is in a young girl's experience that encourages her to interpret failure in that negative fashion. One fact that she thinks may be important is the behavior of the average American teacher. Dweck and her colleagues (1978) found that, when most grade school teachers criticize their girl students, they focus almost exclusively on the child's intellectual inadequacies. ("You spelled that word wrong." "You forgot to carry the two.") Boys, of course, also receive that kind of negative feedback.

High school physics—where are the girls? As with mathematics, girls may opt out, if upper level science classes do not relate to their career goals.

But, in addition, boys are often criticized for *non*intellectual aspects of their work. ("You did this sloppily." "You weren't trying very hard.") As a result, Dweck argues, when girls experience failure, they are more apt than are boys to conclude that their poor performance is caused by lack of ability. To demonstrate the power of those patterns, Dweck conducted a study in which she reversed the kind of criticisms boys and girls typically get. As expected, when the children were later confronted with failure, it was the boys who tended to act defeated, whereas the girls persevered and mastered.

SEX DIFFERENCES IN TASK INCENTIVES

Psychologist Jacquelynne Eccles concedes that attributing failure to lack of ability may sometimes be a factor in undermining girls' achievement strivings. That undermining may be particularly true early in life, when a girl's self-perception of competence is still forming. But Eccles disagrees with Dweck's view that a perception of lack of ability is the primary reason why girls sometimes fail to persist at achievement tasks. Eccles (1983, 1987) pointed out that Dweck's theory focuses only on the expectations that people hold about their future chances for success or failure. Equally important, Eccles argued, are the incentive values of the tasks that people face. Some achievement tasks, according to Eccles, may simply not be worth the effort from the average girl's point of view.

One such task apparently is higher mathematics. Eccles and her colleagues studied junior and senior high school students' attitudes and expectations toward current and future math courses (Eccles et al., 1984). They found that the value placed on mathematics is the single most important factor underlying the common decision among young women to stop taking math courses once math requirements are met. That finding is in keeping with the frequent finding that by the age of thirteen or fourteen boys are more likely than girls to regard math as important to their career goals (Dornbusch, 1974; Fennema and Sherman, 1977, 1978; Wise et al., 1979). In a larger study that included younger children and parents, Eccles and her coworkers tried to identify some of the forces that promote sex-typed differences in values (Eccles, 1987). They found that parents often reinforce the sex-stereotyped perception that higher math is more useful for men than it is for women. As would be expected on the basis of Dweck's work, parents also make different attributions for sons' and daughters' successful math performance. They tend to attribute sons' success at math primarily to talent, while attributing daughters' success more to effort or hard work (Yee and Eccles, 1988). Eccles and her associates have also identified the supportiveness of the teacher as an important factor in how much students value math. Students showed a sharp decline in their valuing of mathematics when they moved from a more-supportive to a less-supportive teacher (Midgley et al., 1989). This was especially the case for low-achieving students.

Thus we see that a complex set of factors can influence achievement choices. Behavior in many achievement settings is probably the result of inner needs, fears, and motives, appraisals of consequences, self-concepts of ability and expectations for success, plus the incentive value of the task at hand, all interacting with one another. The approach of Eccles is an improvement over earlier theories that focus on only a few of the factors involved in this complex process (Deaux, 1985). But researchers still have a long way to go before the process is fully understood.

SUMMARY

1. **Motivation** is what gives impetus to our behavior by arousing, sustaining, and directing it toward the attainment of goals.

2. One motivational factor is an **instinct,** an innate force, found in all members of a species, which directs behavior in predictable ways when the right eliciting stimulus is present. Sigmund Freud proposed that people have two basic instincts—one, the urge toward life, procreation, and self-preservation, which includes the sexual drive; the other, the urge toward death and self-destruction, which is often turned outward as aggression against others. Because people's ways of satisfying these impulses may conflict with society's moral standards, the impulses are often **repressed** and **sublimated** into more acceptable forms of behavior.

3. In the 1930s and 1940s, behaviorist Clark Hull and others developed **drive-reduction theories** of motivation. They saw biological needs (for food, water, relief from pain, and so forth) as the basic motivators of action. These needs gave rise to **primary drives.** By adding the concept of **secondary drives** (drives learned through association with a primary drive and its reduction), drive-reduction theories could account for a large number of behaviors.

4. But drive-reduction theories had limitations. They could not explain certain behaviors that seemed to involve **intrinsic motivation.** Nor could they account for actions that seemed to be as much the product of **incentives** as of drives. Recognizing the need for a more cognitive approach to motivation, psychologists began to develop **expectancy-value models.**

5. Many researchers who study the motivations behind eating believe that humans regulate their food intake largely through chemical messengers carried in the blood. Blood sugar is an important short-term regulator, and substances released from fat cells are important long-term regulators.

6. Some people become so obsessed with being thin that they literally starve themselves to death, a condition called **anorexia nervosa.** Most anorexics are teenage girls. Some suffer from an additional eating disorder called **bulimia,** which involves periodic gorging.

7. Genes seem to strongly influence individual differences in weight relative to height. Chronically obese people may have a partly inherited high **setpoint** for fat tissue that their bodies try to defend. Thus, when an obese person tries to become thin by dieting, the body may react as if it were underfed, giving rise to a constant state of hunger.

8. Hormones secreted by the ovaries, testes, and adrenal glands help to initiate and sustain sexual activity. But sexually arousing stimuli are also needed to activate sexual responses. In humans the **sexual response cycle** is quite similar for men and for women and has been found to have four phases: **excitement, plateau, orgasm,** and **resolution.** The mind plays a crucial role in interpreting sexual signals and in directing sexual behavior toward appropriate goals.

9. Psychologist Donald Hebb, among others, has proposed that there is an **optimum level of arousal** for effective behavior, which organisms try to maintain. This theory can help explain why both **sensory deprivation** and **sensory overload** hinder performance on complex cognitive tasks.

10. One intriguing question in motivation research is why people take risks. According to the **opponent-**

process model, a strong emotion activates an opposite response. So when a high-risk activity is over and the anxiety associated with it ends, the person is left with the opponent feeling: pure exhilaration. It is this euphoria that draws the person back to the activity again and again. Of course, some people are more attracted to risks than others. One possible reason is that the brain of a person who enjoys taking risks and engaging in other very stimulating activities needs a great deal of external stimulation in order to attain an optimum level of arousal.

11. Many human motivations are learned, among them the urge to achieve. People who score high in **need for achievement** persist longer and do better on difficult tasks and tend to set realistic but challenging goals for themselves. Other factors that underlie achievement strivings include low fear of failure, strong confidence in one's own ability, high expectations of attaining success, and a high value placed on accomplishing the task at hand.

12. Achievement strivings seem to be influenced by experiences in childhood, especially encouragement toward independence by a child's parents. But achievement efforts can be fostered at any age and in all kinds of circumstances.

SUGGESTED READINGS

Brumberg, J. J. (1990). *Fasting girls: The history of anorexia nervosa.* New York: Plume/New American Library. A comprehensive and readable discussion of anorexia.

Logue, A. W. (1991). *The psychology of eating and drinking.* New York: Freeman. A highly readable account of scientific research on factors that influence eating, weight control, food preferences, and alcohol use.

Konner, M. (1990). *Why the reckless survive.* New York: Viking Penguin. In this thought-provoking collection of essays, the author attempts to explain why we, as a species, often unknowingly make dangerous choices in our lives.

Strelau, J., and Eysenck, H. J. (1987). *Personality dimensions and arousal.* New York: Plenum. A collection of chapters written by researchers working in the area of arousal and arousal regulation, including Marvin Zuckerman, who has studied high-sensation seekers.

Tavris, C., and Offir, C. E. (1984). *The longest war* (2nd ed.). New York: Harcourt Brace Jovanovich. A witty, highly readable exploration of social science findings about the battle of the sexes, including research on gender differences in achievement motivation.

CHAPTER 13

PERSONALITY THEORIES AND RESEARCH

Suppose you were asked to write a letter describing yourself to a total stranger. What would you say about yourself? How could you paint an accurate self-portrait in words? You might begin with a few simple facts (I am a man or woman; I am a student; I am a member of certain ethnic group). Then you would describe your personal traits—your ways of responding to various situations. Are you thick-skinned or sensitive? Outgoing or shy? Aggressive or timid? Emotional or restrained? Try to list at least five or six traits that you think describe you quite well. Now answer this question: Do you think these traits will still describe you in ten or twenty years? Most people answer with a qualified yes. Although they recognize that ways of thinking and acting can and do change, they think of themselves as having certain fundamental features that will endure across the years. These features together form one's personality. More formally defined, **personality** consists of all the relatively stable and distinctive styles of thought, behavior, and emotional response that characterize a person's adaptations to surrounding circumstances (Maddi, 1976; Mischel, 1976).

Psychologists who study personality ask two key questions. The first concerns the origins of differences among people. When several people encounter the same situation, why don't they all react alike? Why does one person confronted with a group of strangers find it easy to make conversation, while another feels uncomfortable and shy? Why does one student assigned a paper begin the research promptly, while another almost always puts it off until the last minute? Clearly, people have different personalities, but why do these differences develop? As you will see later in this chapter, psychologists have given a variety of answers. Some have stressed the influence of early life experiences and childhood conflicts, some have stressed the influence of people's biological makeup, while others have stressed the influence of learning. Many factors undoubtedly play a role in shaping the traits that people display.

The second major question that personality theorists ask concerns the power of people's individual differences. Do shyness, friendliness, punctuality, and other traits exert such a strong impact on behavior that they cause people to act with great predictability? Or are people often inclined to let the situation determine their response? For instance, might a student be scrupulously honest in handling a campus

What makes some people outgoing and friendly in almost all situations?

club's funds but be willing to cheat on exams if given the opportunity? Or would the student's honesty cause him or her to behave with integrity in both of these situations? Psychologists have come up with different answers to such questions.

As you will also discover in reading this chapter, theories of personality are highly varied. Some theorists have concentrated on specific traits, such as honesty and shyness, asking how each person's cluster of traits can best be measured and described. Others have stressed factors that integrate personality, such as the concept of the self. Still others have emphasized internal feelings (anxiety, conflict, self-fulfillment) that seem to be associated with various personality makeups. These diverse perspectives are what make the field of personality so challenging—and so frustrating. Just when you are convinced that one theory is correct, you may come upon another that seems equally persuasive. The best way to cope with this situation is to think of the theories you are about to encounter as complementary rather than competing. Each sheds valuable light on certain, but not all, aspects of the subject. Consequently, none is

completely adequate in and of itself. Together, however, they paint a rich portrait of why individuals behave as they do.

In this chapter we will be discussing five major perspectives in personality. The first is the **psychoanalytic approach,** which began with Sigmund Freud. This school of theories emphasizes childhood experiences as critically important in shaping adult personality. They also stress the role of the unconscious in motivating human actions. Rather than probing for hidden motives, **trait theories** hold that human personality can be described in terms of observable, measurable characteristics or traits (aggression, friendliness, emotional stability, and so on). Individual differences are the result of different combinations of traits in varying strengths. **Social cognitive approaches** are based on the principles of learning and information processing. These theories focus on the different ways in which individuals interpret events, and how these interpretations shape their styles of coping with the problems of everyday life. The **humanistic approach** emphasizes the human potential for growth, creativity, and spontaneity. Those who take this approach reject both the Freudian preoccupation with the irrational and sometimes destructive instincts and the social cognitive emphasis on rational calculation. **Biological approaches** focus on behavior patterns that may be a result of adaptive pressures that existed in our evolutionary past, the genes individuals inherit from their parents, and physiology. As you will see, despite their widely varying emphases, all of these perspectives offer valuable insights into the questions of why people behave as they do, and why individuals differ from one another.

PSYCHOANALYTIC THEORIES

Psychoanalytic theories of personality are rooted in the work of Sigmund Freud (see Chapter 1). Although his concepts have been expanded and modified, all psychoanalytic theories have two themes in common. First, they are concerned with powerful but largely unconscious motivations believed to exist in every human being. Second, most maintain that human personality is governed by conflict between opposing motives, anxiety over unacceptable motives, and defense mechanisms that develop to prevent anxiety from becoming too great.

In Freud's psychoanalytic theory, even such apparently random and trivial behavior as fiddling with a pencil or doodling can be an indication of unconscious impulses.

BASIC CONCEPTS OF FREUDIAN THEORY

Freud is generally considered the single most important theorist in the field of personality. His ideas have had a profound impact not only on psychology, but also on twentieth-century art, literature, and philosophy. Some of his concepts, such as "Freudian slips," or slips of the tongue, are known by people who never opened a psychology text. Because of his enormous influence, we will discuss Freud's theory in some detail.

THE UNCONSCIOUS

Freud's concept of the unconscious was a major contribution. Before Freud's time, psychologists were concerned only with people's conscious thoughts and feelings. Freud likened the mind to an enormous iceberg, of which consciousness is only the small exposed tip. The massive structure of the iceberg that lies beneath the surface is the vast region of the unconscious. To Freud the unconscious was both a reservoir of instinctual drives and a storehouse of all the thoughts and wishes we conceal from conscious awareness because they cause us psychological conflict. In fact, Freud maintained that the unconscious is *the* major motivating force behind human behavior. According to him, much of what we say and do is either an effort to find some socially acceptable way

of expressing unconscious impulses or an effort to keep those impulses from being expressed.

One provocative aspect of Freud's view is that even seemingly trivial words and actions often have deeper meanings. Accidents, forgetfulness, mislaying objects, the mispronunciation of a name, or an attempt at making a joke were to Freud all signs of unconscious drives, wishes, and conflicts. Even the most seemingly purposeless acts—doodling, twirling a button or lock of hair, humming a tune to oneself—had deeper significance to Freud. Each was believed to afford a glimpse into the subterranean world of the unconscious.

A number of experiments with subliminal stimulation demonstrate the unconscious at work (Geisler, 1986; Silverman, 1976, 1982). Undergraduates were asked to study a passage presented on a screen. Before the passage appeared, subjects were flashed a subliminal message, one too quick to register consciously. In some cases the message was designed to be reassuring (for example, "Mommy and I are one"); in other cases the message was upsetting ("I am losing Mommy"). A group of control subjects were shown an emotionally neutral message ("People are walking"). Subjects who were shown the reassuring message remembered considerably more of the passage, and subjects who were shown the upsetting message significantly less, than did the controls. Thus the emotionally charged messages influenced their

"ALL I WANT FROM THEM IS A SIMPLE MAJORITY OPINION ON THINGS."

behavior, even though they were not consciously aware of having received it. Hardaway (1990) reviewed fifty-six studies that used unconscious stimulation with the "Mommy and I are one" phrase. He found that the subliminal effect, though moderate, is very real. Studies in many different laboratories, using many different subject samples, have found that this phrase affects subjects' emotional state without their conscious awareness.

STRUCTURE OF THE HUMAN PSYCHE

Freud divided the human psyche into three separate but interacting elements: the *id*, the *ego*, and the *superego*. As you read about these elements in the discussion that follows, do not make the mistake of viewing them as three distinct entities, locked in perpetual combat. True, Freud himself often suggested this very image in order to dramatize his points. But he did not intend to be taken literally. The id, the ego, and the superego are *not* physical divisions of the brain. Instead, they are names given to strong psychological forces, the existence of which is inferred from the ways that people behave.

Freud described the **id** as a reservoir of psychic energy, the pool of biological drives that arise from

our needs for food, water, warmth, sexual gratification, avoidance of pain, and so forth. Freud believed that these drives power and direct all human behavior. The id is an unconscious force, with no link to objective reality. It seeks one thing only: the discharge of tension arising from biological drives. The id's exclusive devotion to gratification—without regard for logic or reason, reality or morality—is called the **pleasure principle.** The id is like a demanding, impulsive, selfish child. It seeks only its own pleasure, has no inhibitions, and cannot abide frustration or deprivation of any kind.

The id seeks satisfaction of bodily needs, but has no way of determining which means of doing so are safe and which are dangerous. This task falls to the ego. The **ego,** according to Freud, begins to develop soon after birth, but does not become apparent until the age of about six months. The ego's primary role is to serve as a mediator between the id and reality (Freud, 1920, 1932). Unlike the id, most of the ego is conscious. And whereas the id operates according to the pleasure principle, the ego operates according to the **reality principle:** taking into account past experiences, it seeks the best time to obtain the most pleasure with the least pain or damage to the self. The ego cannot banish the id entirely. Rather, like a patient parent, it seeks to restrain, divert, and protect the id.

As if the job of taming the irrational, insistent id were not enough, the ego must also contend with the superego. The **superego** is the component of personality that represents the ideals and moral standards of society as conveyed to the child by his or her parents. It is roughly equivalent to what we call "conscience." Like the id, the superego is oblivious to reality. It does not consider what is realistic or possible; nor does it distinguish between desires and actions. It constantly commands that sexual and aggressive urges be stifled, and pleasure be postponed, in the pursuit of lofty ideals of moral perfection. It backs these commands with rewards for "good" behavior (feelings of pride and self-esteem) and threats of severe punishment for even thinking about "bad" behavior (feelings of guilt and inferiority). The superego can be a harsh, punitive taskmaster that does not take either the individual's capabilities or the limitations of the situation into account, and is never quite satisfied.

The ego must perform a delicate balancing act. Somehow it must satisfy both the pleasure-seeking demands of the id and the equally powerful perfection-seeking commands of the superego. For exam-

Taking a course in white-water rafting safety is a realistic way of coping with one's fear of such an exciting but potentially dangerous activity. A person who used the defense mechanism of denial would repress all awareness of fearing the experience.

ple, a child spots her favorite candy bar in a store. The id shouts "I want it now! Take it!" The superego intones, "Thou shalt not steal." The ego must contend not only with these two opposing forces, but also with the constraints of reality. "I could ask Mommy to buy it for me, but she might say no."

ANXIETY AND DEFENSE MECHANISMS

Given the conflicting goals of the id and the superego, as well as the constant demands of reality, how does the ego ever manage to carry out its work? This important question brings us to a second part of Freud's theory, his ideas about anxiety and defense mechanisms.

According to Freud, the signal that the ego is losing its struggle to reconcile the divergent demands of the id, the superego, and reality comes in the form of **anxiety,** a state of psychic distress. Anxiety arises when the ego realizes that expression of an id impulse will lead to some kind of harm and/or that the superego is making an impossible demand. The resulting inner struggle is felt as anxiety. Anxiety, in turn, serves as an alarm signal that tells the ego something must be done to resolve the conflict. That something is usually a **defense mechanism,** a mental strategy the ego uses to block the harmful impulse while at the same time reducing anxiety.

The most basic defense mechanism is **repression:** pushing unacceptable id impulses back into the unconscious. In effect, the ego is saying, "What I don't know—or what I can't remember—can't hurt me." According to the psychoanalytic theory of repression, the content is in fact not forgotten but remains unconscious and active, and it can influence thoughts and behavior. Individuals who frequently use repression as a defense mechanism often report that they are not feeling anxious when physiological measures clearly indicate that they are (their hearts are pounding, their palms are sweating, and their muscles are tense). They are not lying about their subjective feelings; rather they have shut them out of consciousness.

In several recent studies (Davis, 1987; Davis and Schwartz, 1987; Hansen and Hansen, 1988), questionnaires were used to identify "repressors" (who rarely reported experiencing anxiety or other negative emotions) and "nonrepressors" (who experienced high or low levels of anxiety). The subjects were then asked to recall times in childhood when they felt angry, embarrassed, sad, or afraid. The repressors reported fewer negative emotional memories than the nonrepressors, implying that they had successfully banished many anxiety-provoking experiences from consciousness. From this study we do not know whether repressors actually experienced fewer negative *events* in their childhoods than did nonrepressors, or whether they had fewer *memories* of those events. Other research (e.g., Davis, 1987), however, shows that in learning new information about themselves, repressors remember fewer negatives than nonrepressors, suggesting that the difference lies in their memories of negative information about the self.

Pioneering studies on the nature of unconscious processes bearing on repression have been conducted by Howard Shevrin and his colleagues. Shevrin (1988, 1990) has attempted to study unconscious processing as it occurs by presenting emotionally charged words subliminally, and examining electrical activity of the brain in response to such words. In these studies, clients with a psychological disorder, usually a phobia, participate in a number of clinical interviews. Clinical judges select words from the interviews believed to reflect an unconscious conflict that the client is struggling with. For example, there was evidence in the interviews of one client to suggest that he had longstanding problems with aggressive sexual impulses directed at women. Words selected for this client included "beating up" and "screaming." Shevrin has found that when presented subliminally, or below conscious awareness, such words are recognized earlier by the brain than are control words with no special meaning. But when presented supraliminally—that is, above the threshold for consciousness awareness—the words are recognized later than control words. The results suggest that there is indeed a highly selective and inhibitory process screening out stimuli that arouse anxiety, as the psychodynamic theory of repression would predict.

Repression is both a defense mechanism in its own right and the aim of all other defense mechanisms. For no matter what one's specific strategy for coping with anxiety may be, the ultimate aim is to make sure that "forbidden" thoughts and feelings stay out of consciousness. Among the most important strategies are denial, regression, reaction formation, projection, displacement, and sublimation.

Denial is refusal to acknowledge a threat. For example, a student who is afraid that she might not be accepted into medical school might deny that she wants to become a physician and tell herself and others that the only reason she is taking the medical boards is to please her parents. By convincing herself that she does not care, she protects herself from fear of failure.

Regression occurs when a person made anxious by threatening thoughts and feelings behaves in ways characteristic of an earlier stage in life, before the present conflict began. A middle-aged man who is having difficulties with his wife, for example, may resort to taking long afternoon naps on weekends, just as he did as a small child.

Reaction formation is the replacement of an anxiety-producing impulse or feeling by its direct opposite. A person who is strongly attracted to pornography, for instance, may vehemently insist that all sexually explicit material is filthy and disgusting. Thus many of those who lead crusades against pornography—those who "protest too much"—may in reality be displaying a reaction formation.

Projection occurs when people unknowingly attribute their own objectionable impulses to others. A man who has had many extramarital affairs, for example, may begin to accuse his wife of being unfaithful, thereby transferring his own shortcomings to her. Similarly, people who constantly accuse the young of being sexually promiscuous may simply be projecting their own sexual urges onto others.

Displacement is the transfer of unacceptable feelings from their appropriate target to a much "safer" one. A familiar example is the man who is constantly belittled by his boss and so vents his anger on his secretary, a store clerk, his children, or anyone else unlikely to retaliate. Thus wife beating and child abuse may sometimes be forms of displaced aggression.

Sublimation is a kind of displacement in which forbidden impulses are redirected toward the pursuit of socially desirable goals. In *Civilization and Its Discontents* (1930), Freud argued that civilization itself came about through such a rechanneling of primitive drives. In *Leonardo Da Vinci: A Psychosexual Study of Infantile Reminiscence*, Freud suggested that da Vinci's urge to paint Madonnas was a sublimated expression of his longing for reunion with his mother, from whom he had been separated at an early age.

Defense mechanisms are useful ways of coping with the unpleasant experiences life sometimes throws our way. When we are in a situation that arouses anxiety, they prevent us from making the situation worse by worrying. Short-term use of denial or other defense mechanisms may be helpful in getting people through an initial crisis period, thus buying them time to formulate a more effective coping strategy (Hamburg and Adams, 1967). For example, one study found that victims of heart attacks who denied the severity of their condition were less depressed and anxious and resumed normal activities more rapidly than did those who were more "realistic" (Stern et al., 1976).

Defense mechanisms become harmful when carried to an extreme. Freud held that the hallmarks of psychological adjustment in adulthood are the ability to love and work, to be sociable and productive. Defense mechanisms are counterproductive when they become a person's main or only way of coping with problems, and hence interfere with these goals. For example, a person who constantly projects his or her weaknesses onto others may have difficulty keeping friends. A person who habitually defends against a fear of failure by practicing denial, and so lacks any ambition, may miss opportunities for more creative and rewarding work. Repressors, as discussed earlier, have an impoverished memory for negative events (Davis, 1987). As a result, they have a smaller repertoire of experiences to call upon when they find themselves in a difficult interpersonal situation. Repressors tend to avoid conflict of any kind, and so may find themselves shut off both from other people and from opportunities to learn how to relate to others effectively.

HOW PERSONALITY DEVELOPS

Freud developed an extensive theory about the shaping of adult personality by early life experiences. Freud argued that at each stage in a child's life, the drive for pleasure centers around a particular area of the body: first the mouth, then the anus, and finally the genitals. All these id urges he loosely labeled "sexual" to emphasize that the earlier strivings for sensual pleasure emanate from the same reservoir of psychic energy as does the striving for genital sex. Freud believed that adult personality is shaped by the way in which the conflicts between these early sexual urges and the requirements imposed by society (weaning, toilet training, prohibitions against masturbation, and so forth) are resolved. According to him, failure to resolve any of these conflicts can result in **fixation,** in which the person becomes "stuck" in that particular psychological battle, repeating the conflict in symbolic ways. To understand these ideas more fully, let us consider Freud's five stages of psychosexual development.

The Stages of Psychosexual Development Freud believed that during the first year of life—the **oral stage**—a child's sexual pleasure focuses on the mouth. Since sucking is the only way for a baby to obtain food, it is not surprising that this activity is an important aspect of the child's life. But Freud argued that to a baby the significance of sucking goes far beyond the basic satisfaction of hunger. Sucking, he maintained, is a source of intense pleasure in its own

Psychoanalytic theorists consider toilet training to be a developmental turning point because it usually represents the child's first encounter with society's rules regarding acceptable behavior.

right. According to Freud, this is why babies suck, lick, bite, and chew virtually anything they can get into the mouth. Fixation at the oral stage can occur for a variety of reasons. For example, when babies repeatedly experience anxiety over whether food will be given or withheld, they may come to learn that they are totally dependent on others. This lesson may lead to a passive, overly dependent, unenterprising adult.

The next stage of development in Freud's scheme is the **anal stage.** It occurs during the second year of life, when children begin to develop voluntary control over bowel movements. As a result, they come to derive great sensual pleasure from holding in and expelling feces. But no sooner are these pleasures established than the demands of toilet training are imposed. Toilet training, according to Freudians, is a crucial event because it is the first large-scale conflict between the child's id impulses and society's rules. If this conflict is not resolved satisfactorily, fixation may occur. Children who undergo strict, punitive toilet training, for example, may learn to repress completely the urge to defecate in a free and enjoyable manner. Repeated repression of this urge may result in personality traits that are very much the opposite of uninhibited defecation—such traits as fastidious orderliness and excessive neatness.

Freud's third stage of development, the **phallic stage,** spans the years from about three to five or six. During this time the child's erotic pleasure focuses on masturbation, that is, on self-manipulation of the genitals. The phallic stage is said to be particularly important to a person's psychological development because this is the period when the Oedipus conflict presumably occurs. As we discussed in Chapter 10, this conflict involves an intense desire to take the place of the same-sex parent in the affections of the parent of the opposite sex. Freud saw this desire as explicitly sexual. He argued that "when the little boy shows the most open sexual curiosity about his mother, wants to sleep with her at night, or even attempts physical acts of seduction, the erotic nature of his attachment to her is established without a doubt" (Freud, 1935, p. 342). But the child naturally fears that the jealous same-sex parent will seek retribution for these incestuous longings. The child is therefore plagued by conflict—drawn toward the parent of the opposite sex, but fearful of being punished. The healthiest resolution, according to Freud, is for the child to recognize that he or she can never physically possess the opposite-sex parent. So instead the child tries to become like the person who does enjoy this privilege, striving to adopt the attitudes, behaviors, and moral values of the *same*-sex parent. This identification with the same-sex parent is believed to be crucial to development of the child's conscience, or superego. At the same time, striving to be like the same-sex parent is also a form of defense. By becoming like the powerful person who poses a potential threat, the child feels less likely to be the victim of punishment.

After the phallic stage, children presumably move into the fourth stage of psychosexual development, a period of **latency.** From the age of five or six until puberty, sexual impulses appear to remain in the background while the child is busy learning a range of social and cognitive skills. Finally, during adolescence, sexual feelings reemerge and the **genital stage** begins. The focus in this last period is on the pleasures of sexual intercourse. Feelings of dependency and Oedipal strivings that were not resolved earlier may resurface during this time. In fact, Freud maintained that the turmoil of adolescence may be partly due to such conflicts. With their successful resolution, however, a person is capable of forming deep and mature love relationships and of assuming a place in the world as a fully independent adult.

Even mature adults do not live without conflict and anxiety. Life constantly provides challenges and threats to which we must adjust. Even if everything goes well during personality development, there is no guarantee of happiness in adulthood. In fact, Freud believed that sometimes the best hope for therapy is to turn a patient's misery into common, everyday unhappiness. The hallmark of adequate personality development is not necessarily happiness; rather it is the ability to form relationships and to be productive. As you will see in Chapter 16, when a person has consistent problems with relationships or trouble being productive, we would consider using the term *neurotic.* A person who is merely unhappy, however, is not considered to be the product of abnormal personality development.

Freud's theory of psycho*sexual* personality development shocked his Victorian contemporaries. How perverse, they charged, to attribute sexual thoughts and behavior to innocent little children. But they were missing the point. Freud was not attempting to uncover the "sins" of childhood, but rather to emphasize that all human beings are born with biological drives. Human sexuality does not suddenly emerge out of nowhere when a person reaches puberty, he reasoned. It is more logical to think that erotic impulses are present all along, but take different forms at different ages. More contemporary psychologists have also criticized Freud's emphasis on sexuality, but for different reasons, as we will see in the next section.

OTHER PSYCHOANALYTIC THEORISTS

In spite of—or perhaps because of—the controversy over his ideas, Freud attracted many followers. From all over Europe and the United States, young people flocked to Vienna to study with Freud. And so the psychoanalytic movement was born. Like Freud himself, some of these students were highly creative thinkers. Not surprisingly, they began to expand and modify Freud's original ideas.

Although it is difficult to summarize briefly all the different directions that later psychoanalytic thinking has taken, three trends in particular stand out. First, post-Freudian theorists have tended to give an increased importance to the ego and a decreased importance to the id. Freud viewed the ego as simply

Carl Jung proposed that, in addition to the individual unconscious, there is a collective unconscious, in which humanity's memories are stored and transmitted through the centuries and across cultures. The existence of the collective unconscious could explain why sun worship is found in cultures as widely separated in space and time as the Assyrians of western Asia (c. 1100–600 B.C.) (*left*) and the Incas of South America (c. A.D. 1200–1540) (*right*).

the id's dutiful servant, trying as best it can to satisfy id instincts without neglecting reality or causing the superego remorse. Most later psychoanalytic thinkers, in contrast, have abandoned the idea that id drives always take center stage. Instead, they have focused on the ego as an important force in its own right, capable of much creativity, rational planning, and the formation of satisfying goals. Second, later psychoanalytic theorists have emphasized the importance of social interaction in explaining how human personality develops. Instead of seeing a person's nature as solely the outcome of conflicts over id impulses, they have seen it as much more the product of a child's relationships with significant others in his or her life. Finally, later theorists have tended to extend the period of critical developmental stages. While Freud believed that psychosexual development runs from birth to puberty, he emphasizes the phallic stage, especially the Oedipus conflict. Some later psychodynamic theorists have placed greater emphasis on infancy, while others have argued that personality continues to develop throughout the life span.

Of all the deviations from orthodox Freudian theory that occurred during his lifetime, the ones that distressed Freud most were instigated by two of his closest colleagues, Carl Jung (1875–1961) and Alfred Adler (1870–1937). Jung disagreed with Freud on two important points. One was the nature of the unconscious. Jung held that the unconscious consists not only of the individual's repressed urges and desires (as Freud taught), but also contains the collective memories of the human race, inherited from our distant ancestors. This is why, Jung argued, the same symbols (or *archetypes*) recur in myths and fables from different cultures and times, in religion and art, and in dreams. Second, where Freud saw the adult's personality as reflecting unresolved conflicts left over from childhood, Jung saw personality development as a lifelong process of striving to reconcile opposing urges (for example, toward introversion and extraversion, "feminine" passivity and "masculine" assertiveness).

Alfred Adler's main disagreement with Freud concerned the primary source of psychic energy. Adler believed that the great motivation in human life is not the striving for satisfaction of sexual urges, but rather the striving upward toward "superiority" (Adler, 1930). By this he did not mean social distinction or prominence. He meant instead an inner quest for self-perfection. Adler proposed that all children are born with a deep sense of inferiority because of their small size, physical weakness, and lack of knowledge and power in the world of adults. In fact, it was Adler (1931) who coined the widely used term **inferiority complex.** He argued that the way parents interact with their children has a crucial effect on the children's ability to overcome feelings of inferiority and so to achieve competency later in life. Thus Adler saw

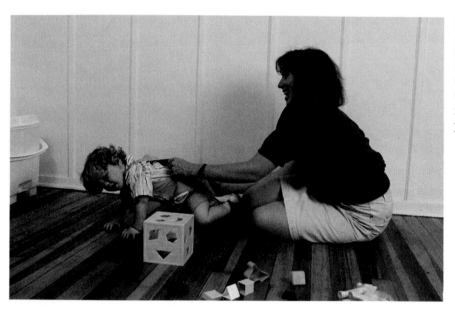

Erik Erikson believed that childhood conflicts are essentially social, not sexual. The young child begins to exert his or her will in conflicts with the parents, who represent society, over such issues as picking up toys after playtime.

personality as heavily influenced by the quality of early social relationships.

Other psychoanalytic thinkers have elaborated this view of the self as a product of social relationships. The writings of the psychoanalyst Karen Horney (1885–1952) provide a good example. Like Freud, Horney saw adult personality as largely shaped by childhood experiences. But unlike Freud, she focused on social relationships (especially with parents) rather than on the resolution of id-related conflicts (Horney, 1945). In particular, Horney argued that when parents' behavior toward a child is indifferent, disparaging, and erratic, the child feels helpless and insecure. Horney called this feeling **basic anxiety.** Accompanying basic anxiety, according to Horney, is a feeling of deep resentment toward the parents, or **basic hostility.** This hostility cannot be expressed directly, because the child needs and fears the parents and strongly wants their love. So the hostility is repressed, leading to increased feelings of unworthiness and anxiety. The conflict between basic anxiety and basic hostility leads the child, and later the neurotic adult, to adopt one of three modes of social interaction: moving *toward* others, moving *against* others, or moving *away* from others. Someone who moves toward others becomes compliant, always anxious to please in order to gain affection and approval. The person who moves against others is attempting to find security through domination. The

goal of the person who moves away from others is to find security by becoming aloof and withdrawn, never allowing close relationships. Clearly all of these self-protective strategies give rise to many interpersonal problems.

Erik H. Erikson is another student of Freud's who broke with the master (see Chapter 10). Erikson agrees with Freud that a person's basic personality orientation is established in early childhood. But he maintains that the conflicts of childhood are primarily social, not sexual, in origin. For example, the basic conflict in Freud's anal stage is not over the pleasure of holding in or letting go feces, but over cooperating with or distressing parents. For the first time the child is able to exercise will power. Depending on how this first battle of wills with parents is resolved, the child may develop a sense of autonomy or suffer feelings of shame and doubt. Erikson agrees with Freud's concept of "fixation"—that if a person does not adequately resolve a conflict at one stage, elements of that conflict may carry over into later stages of development. But whereas Freud held that personality is more or less determined by the conflicts of early childhood, Erikson holds that every stage in life presents the individual with new psychosocial challenges, up to and including old age. The challenge of adolescence is developing an identity (versus role confusion); of young adulthood, intimacy (versus isolation); of middle age, generativity (versus stagnation); and of old age, integrity (versus doubt). Thus Erikson offers a theory of adult development, something not found in the writings of Freud.

In addition to emphasizing social relationships and lifelong development, many post-Freudians have forged a new view of the ego. One **ego psychologist** was Heinz Hartmann (1939). He argued that the ego develops independently of the id and has its own autonomous functions. It does not just mediate conflicts between the id and the superego or the id and reality. Instead, the ego has its own "conflict-free" domain, including such cognitive processes as memory, perception, and learning. This view of the ego has brought the psychodynamic perspective closer to the mainstream of contemporary psychology, where cognitive processes are given a great deal of attention.

An important merging of this focus on the ego with an emphasis on social relationships can be seen in a modern approach called **object relations theory** (Klein, 1967; Kohut, 1971; Winnicott, 1965). The term *object* here refers to the people to whom an infant becomes attached, especially the child's mother. Object relations theory emphasizes the importance of these early attachments to the development of the child's ego, the child's feelings about the self, and later interpersonal relationships. Personality development is viewed in terms of the person's strivings to relate to other people in emotionally satisfying ways.

One influential object relations theorist was Margaret Mahler. Her major contribution was to chart the process by which infants psychologically separate themselves from their mothers, a process she called separation–individuation (Mahler, 1968; Mahler et al., 1975). Mahler felt that the success of this process determines the child's psychological future, for the features of the crucial relationship with the mother will be repeated in later intimate relations. Thus, if the mother hurries the separation process or tries to resist it, the child's personality development will probably be disturbed.

Like Mahler, Heinz Kohut, another object relations theorist, was interested mainly in the psychological consequences of early parent–child relations. Kohut proposed that the development of the self, or core of the personality, depends on the child's receiving two essential supports. One is confirmation of the child's sense of vigor and "greatness." The other is a sense of calmness and being in control, the feeling that everything will ultimately be all right (Kohut and Wolf, 1978). Parents encourage these two psychological outlooks through their daily behaviors. When they exclaim over the child's small successes or reassure the child when he or she is upset, they are building the foundations of a strong, self-confident ego in Kohut's view. Conversely, when parents fail to provide these supports, personality problems are apt to develop and the child may have very fragile self-esteem.

EVALUATING PSYCHOANALYTIC APPROACHES

Like all controversial ideas, psychoanalytic theories of personality face strong and persuasive criticisms. The first charge is that supporting data have not been collected and analyzed in rigorous scientific ways. Following Freud, most theorists in this school have relied exclusively on case studies, usually of individuals undergoing psychoanalysis. Psychoanalytic sessions are private, so there is no way of checking what was actually said. The analyst may influence what patients recall by showing more interest in some topics than others. In reporting on sessions, the analyst may selectively recall statements that confirmed his or her hypotheses and overlook others.

In addition, the sample on which psychoanalytic theories is based is small and atypical—namely, individuals undergoing psychoanalysis. Freud himself reported only twelve cases in detail, most of whom were upper-class, emotionally disturbed women. Indeed, he relied heavily on his own self-analysis. Contemporary theorists face the same problem. Individuals who seek psychoanalysis are usually young or middle-aged, white, above average in intelligence, and relatively well-to-do. A large proportion work in mental health fields. Does this select group justify a universal theory of personality?

A more serious charge is that many Freudian concepts are untestable—that is, they are defined in such a way that they can neither be proved nor disproved. For example, in precisely what behaviors must a little boy engage to be considered embroiled in an Oedipus conflict? Are signs of strong attachment to the mother enough? Or must the boy's words and actions have explicit sexual overtones? Furthermore, some of Freud's concepts are defined in ways that allow virtually *any* behavior to be used as evidence in their support. If a person acts in a blatantly sexual or aggressive manner, for instance, he or she can be said to be expressing an unbridled id instinct. But if the person acts in the *opposite* manner, he or she may also be said to be driven by the very same impulse, only this time the impulse is surfacing as a reaction formation. In fact, many different actions can be interpreted as forms of compromise between a particular id impulse and the demands of conscience and reality. This looseness of Freudian theory makes it particularly challenging to test. At present, a number of investigators are attempting to develop innovative ways to measure unconscious processes objectively and to study their effects on behavior using vigorous experimental methods (Balay and Shevrin, 1988).

Finally, Freud's writings showed a strong gender bias. According to Freud, when little girls notice that they lack a penis, they "feel themselves heavily handicapped . . . and envy the boy's possession of it" (1925, p. 327). And this, said Freud, is the beginning of a long slide into inferiority. Freud reasoned that because a girl lacks a large and visible external genital organ, she cannot experience as intense an Oedipus conflict as does a boy. A boy, Freud argued, often comes to fear that his father will punish his Oedipal longings by cutting off his penis. This terrible dread, called **castration anxiety,** is presumably so powerful that it propels the boy toward identification with the father and the development of a strong superego. Because a girl feels she has already been castrated, she has less motivation to identify with her mother and develop a strong superego. As a result, Freud argued, women feel less pressure to strive to achieve. They are also less likely to condemn themselves for violations of moral standards.

Psychoanalyst Karen Horney was the first to publicly oppose Freud's notion of penis envy. In 1926 she argued that Freud, lacking exposure to women in other societies and to women in his own society who had no serious psychological problems, was in a poor position to know what normal, healthy girls think as they are growing up. According to Horney (1967), it is not girls who see themselves as "castrated," but boys who perceive girls as deficient—in part to compensate for their envy of a female's capacity to give birth. The more general criticism of Freud's treatment of women is that he used males as the standard or prototype of all human personality development. As a consequence, he not only overlooked female experiences and perspectives, but also implied that females should strive to be like males.

Despite these strong criticisms of Freud, his influence on twentieth-century thought has been profound. Such Freudian concepts as anxiety, repression, and defense mechanism are used by psycholo-

gists and lay people alike. The fact that we often analyze an individual's personality in terms of early childhood experiences or worry about the way we toilet-train our children testifies to Freud's enduring impact. Psychoanalytic theories offer the most detailed and explicit theory of personality *development.* Most other theorists deal with adult personality only, with little effort to explain how a person came to be this way. Although Freud may not have been a rigorous scientist, he was a keen observer of human behavior. The enormous originality of his thinking, his perseverance in the face of severe criticism, the comprehensiveness of his theories, and even the controversies his work continues to inspire have earned him great distinction in the history of psychological thought.

TRAIT THEORIES

Psychoanalytic theories deal with *how* personality develops; trait theories are concerned with *what* personality is made of. What are the fundamental elements, the building blocks of personality? An analogy can be drawn between the structure of personality and that of color. The human eye can perceive an almost infinite array of colors. Yet every possible color, from chartreuse to vermillion, is simply a combination of the three primary colors (red, blue, and yellow). Likewise, human beings exhibit an almost unlimited variety of personalities. Yet perhaps each is simply a combination of a few primary personality traits. Discovering what these primary characteristics are is a major objective of trait theory.

A **trait** is defined as "any relatively enduring way in which one individual differs from another" (Guilford, 1959). This definition highlights three assumptions underlying trait theory. First, personality traits are relatively *stable over time.* Thus a person who is shy at parties at age twenty is likely still to be shy at parties five, ten, even twenty years later. There is a good deal of evidence to support this view (Block, 1971; Block and Block, 1979, 1980; Costa and Mc-Crae, 1986; Thomas et al., 1970). For instance, when James Conley (1985) compared the personality traits of several hundred adults at three different times in their lives, he discovered that extraversion, neuroticism, and impulse control hardly changed over a forty-five-year period.

The second assumption is that personality traits are *consistent over situations.* A person who is domi-

Trait theorists explore the stability, consistency, and combination of the characteristics that make up the individual personality. From child movie star to adult diplomat, Shirley Temple Black has consistently shown personality traits associated with sociability.

neering at work is likely to be domineering at home, at parties, in stores, and other settings. To be sure, certain situations call for behavior that is out of character: even the most sociable, talkative person will be quiet during a funeral service. Nevertheless, trait theories assume that, on average, people will act in the same way in many different situations. This view, too, has been supported by research (Epstein, 1983). For example, Nancy Cantor and her colleagues (1985) found that college freshmen used consistent strategies to pursue such varied goals as getting good grades and making friends. Some decided on a plan and followed through, working hard at their assignments and their social lives; others primed themselves by imagining worst-case scenarios, in class and at parties. But none used different strategies for different goals; their approach to the many challenges of the first year of college was consistent.

The third assumption is that *individual differences* are the result of differences in the strength, number, and combination of traits a person possesses. No two people are identical, but the differences among us are largely a matter of degree. For example, everyone can be classified as more or less sociable. Sociability is best seen as a continuum, with extreme extraversion at one end of the scale and extreme introversion at the other. Most people fall between these extremes.

These variations can be quantified, for example, by asking people to rate themselves on a scale of 1 to 10. Ideally, these ratings can then be used to predict behavior. People who rate themselves high in sociability probably would enjoy careers in sales; people who give themselves a low rating probably would not.

To some degree, all of us are trait theorists. When we learn that John's hobby is racing motorcycles, we assume that he seeks excitement in other areas and would not enjoy such sedentary pastimes as stamp collecting or needlepoint (consistency). We can imagine him racing around the playground on a tricycle as a child (stability). And we contrast him to our super-cautious friend Paul, who will not board a plane until he has checked the weather reports and purchased life insurance (individual differences). The trait theorists we will introduce have endeavored to translate this common-sense approach into a science of personality.

ALLPORT'S TRAIT APPROACH

Gordon Allport was a pioneer in trait psychology. He wrote the first textbook on personality, published in 1937, and continued to develop and refine his ideas for almost forty years (1961, 1966). Allport believed

In Gordon Allport's trait theory, certain "central traits" unify a person's behavior. General Colin Powell, the first black chairman of the Joint Chiefs of Staff, might be said to have central traits dealing with ambition, achievement, and service to country.

that the words people use to describe themselves and others provide a window to personality. One of his first steps was to comb an unabridged dictionary for words used to describe people (Allport and Odbert, 1936). He found almost 18,000. Even after he eliminated words used to evaluate a person's character (such as *worthy* and *insignificant*) or to describe a temporary state (for example, *joyous* or *flustered*), 4,000 to 5,000 terms remained. Allport found that when people are asked to characterize an individual, they tend to use the same or similar words, and these words fall into categories such as "honest," "gregarious," and "independent." He called these *central traits.*

Allport believed that traits unify and integrate a person's behavior by causing that person to approach different situations with similar goals or plans in mind. A person who is highly competitive, for instance, will view a variety of situations as opportunities to "beat" other people, to show that he or she is superior in strength, intelligence, or talent. Although acknowledging that situations do influence behavior, he maintained that the way a person interprets situations depends on his or her inner disposition. Thus a

person who is highly competitive would see a political discussion as an opportunity to "one-up" the other participants; a person who is highly cooperative will see the same discussion as an opportunity to share information and arrive at a consensus. "The same fire that melts the butter hardens the egg," wrote Allport, meaning that different people respond to the same situation in ways that reflect their individual traits.

Allport also believed that two people who possess the same trait often express that trait in different ways. For example, one ambitious person may strive to achieve in the business world; another becomes a social climber; another is a marathon runner. Allport saw each individual as having a unique personality profile, regardless of any general traits he or she shares with others. For this reason, he is sometimes referred to as an *idiographic* theorist: that is, his primary focus was on the unique, idiosyncratic cluster of traits that distinguishes each person from all others. He maintained that individuals can be only partially understood by administering standardized tests and comparing the results to group norms. In-depth case studies are necessary to do justice to the uniqueness of each human being. In contrast to the idiographic strategy is the *nomothetic* approach, which searches for general, all-encompassing laws of personality. One nomothetic theorist is Raymond Cattell.

CATTELL'S RESEARCH APPROACH

Raymond Cattell earned a bachelor's degree in chemistry before turning to psychology in his graduate studies. This background played an important role in his approach to the study of personality. Cattell firmly believed that psychology could become as exact and rigorous a science as chemistry, and that it should be possible to identify the basic elements of personality, classify them in a manner similar to the periodic table, and understand the general laws by which the elements combine. In six decades of research, he has never abandoned this conviction. "The clinician [or idiographic theorist]," Cattell wrote, "has his heart in the right place, but perhaps we might say that he remains a little fuzzy in the head" (1959, p. 45).

Like Allport, Cattell believed that the vocabulary people use to describe themselves and others provided essential clues to the structure of personality. The problem was how to identify the basic or primary traits underlying the huge array of descriptive adjectives. Cattell found a solution in factor analysis. **Factor analysis** is a mathematical technique for identifying underlying sources of consistency. Suppose, for example, that researchers find that people's scores on math tests are correlated with their grades in chemistry: people who score high on math tests usually (but not always) do well in chemistry, and vice versa. Math scores are less highly correlated with grades in history, and have little relationship with grades in English. But high grades in English are highly correlated with high grades in history. Analyzing these patterns, the researchers might conclude that two distinct underlying factors are at work: mathematical ability and verbal ability. This, in a nutshell, is how Cattell approached personality traits.

Cattell greatly expanded the data base for trait theory, in the belief that if there are basic elements of personality, we should be able to find them by many different measures. He applied factor analysis to subjective ratings of peers (how people describe one another) in order to identify underlying or source traits. He used this information to devise questionnaires which were administered to thousands of

TABLE 13.1 Cattell's Sixteen Personality Traits

1. Reserved	Outgoing
2. Less intelligent	More intelligent
3. Stable, ego strength	Emotionality/neuroticism
4. Humble	Assertive
5. Sober	Happy-go-lucky
6. Expedient	Conscientious
7. Shy	Venturesome
8. Tough-minded	Tender-minded
9. Trusting	Suspicious
10. Practical	Imaginative
11. Forthright	Shrewd
12. Placid	Apprehensive
13. Conservative	Experimenting
14. Group-dependent	Self-sufficient
15. Undisciplined	Controlled
16. Relaxed	Tense

Pervin, 1987, p. 306. (© 1987. Used by permission of John Wiley & Sons.)

people of different ages and backgrounds. He also used several hundred "objective tests" to explore how traits might be expressed. For example, is the tendency to be assertive associated with quick reflexes?

Cattell concluded that personality is composed of sixteen primary or source traits, which he described in terms of opposing tendencies (Table 13.1). Virtually all trait theorists credit Cattell with introducing and refining the quantitative approach to the study of personality. But many feel that his table of personality elements is too complex, that it includes too many "surface" (as opposed to underlying "source") traits. One of these is Hans Eysenck.

EYSENCK'S DIMENSIONS OF PERSONALITY

Like Cattell, Hans Eysenck relied heavily on standardized tests and statistical tools for assessing and comparing personalities. But Eysenck initially concluded that personality can be essentially reduced to major dimensions (1970). One dimension is neuroticism versus emotional stability, the degree to which people have control over their feelings. At one extreme is the highly neurotic person—anxious, moody, touchy, restless, quick to fly out of control. At the other extreme is the very emotionally stable person—calm, even-tempered, reliable, almost never falling to pieces. The second of Eysenck's major dimensions is extraversion versus introversion, the

	Yes	No
1. Do you usually take the initiative in making new friends?	____	____
2. Do ideas run through your head so that you cannot sleep?	____	____
3. Are you inclined to keep in the background on social occasions?	____	____
4. Are you inclined to be moody?	____	____
5. Do you very much like good food?	____	____
6. When you get annoyed do you need someone friendly to talk to about it?	____	____
7. Do you usually keep "yourself to yourself" except with very close friends?	____	____
8. Do you often make up your mind too late?	____	____

FIGURE 13.1 The Eysenck Personality Inventory. Questions 1, 3, 5, and 7 measure extraversion versus introversion. Questions 2, 4, 6, and 8 measure neuroticism versus emotional stability. Eysenck's third major personality dimension, psychoticism, is not represented here. With the results of all three dimensions, psychologists should be able to predict much about a person's behavior.

extent to which people are socially outgoing or socially withdrawn. On the one hand are those who are active, gregarious, impulsive, and excitement-oriented. On the other are those who are passive, quiet, cautious, and reserved. The third dimension is what Eysenck calls "psychoticism," or what American psychologists usually call "psychopathology": a lack of feeling for others, a tough manner of interacting with others, and a tendency to be different, to defy social conventions. Figure 13.1 lists some of the items from a questionnaire developed by Eysenck.

Having identified what he believed were the three basic dimensions of personality, Eysenck went on to explore individual differences. He concluded that differences in personality have a biological basis. Consider extraversion–introversion. As we saw in Chapter 12, Eysenck hypothesized that people who are extraverted have a naturally low level of arousal in the cortex of the brain. As a result, they seek high levels of external stimulation to raise cortical arousal to an optimum level. The introvert, in contrast, already has a naturally high level of cortical arousal and is easily overaroused by high external stimulation. So the introvert seeks out situations that minimize stimulation, thus preventing cortical arousal from becoming too great. To test these hypotheses, Eysenck and his colleagues turned to the experimental method. They found, for example, that introverts take longer to fall asleep and are more sensitive to pain than extraverts, suggesting that their brains are somehow more alert. And alcohol, which lowers cortical arousal, makes introverts more extraverted. Conversely, when extraverts take amphetamines, which increase cortical arousal, they become more introverted.

More recent experiments (discussed below) have confirmed and refined Eysenck's biological hypothesis. These studies show that introverts and extraverts differ not in their resting or baseline levels of arousal, but in their response to stimulation or arousability (Stelmack, 1990). Studies of identical twins add further evidence that Eysenck's speculations may be on the right track. Inherited biological factors *do* seem to make a major contribution to individual differences along the extraversion–introversion dimension of personality (Shields, 1976).

The extraversion–introversion dimension has been found to have interesting implications for college students. When trying to study, extraverts generally prefer more background noise and opportunities for socializing than introverts do. Extraverts are also inclined to take more study breaks than their introverted peers (Campbell and Hawley, 1982). These differences in study habits may be related to the fact that introverts usually do better in school than extraverts, particularly in higher-level subjects (Pervin, 1984). The introvert's preference for studying in quiet places with few interruptions may be more conducive to academic achievement. In addition, introverts have a tendency to be more thorough and careful than extraverts, which could also contribute to scholastic success (Wilson, 1978). Whatever the causes, extraverts are more likely to drop out of college for academic reasons than introverts are.

THE NEW CONSENSUS

For decades, trait theorists have debated whether personality is composed of a large number of traits (Cattell's sixteen to twenty-one) or a small number

Who goes to rock concerts? If Eysenck was right about differences in cortical arousal, introverts will be in short supply both in the crowd and on the stage.

(Eysenck's three). In recent years, however, a new consensus has emerged (Digman, 1990; McCrae, 1989). Both new research and reanalysis of older studies indicate that people of different ages, different walks of life, and even different cultures repeatedly and consistently refer to five major dimensions of personality (sometimes called the "Big Five"). These are:

Extraversion: socially active, assertive, outgoing, talkative, fun loving—the opposite of shy

Neuroticism: emotionally unstable, frequent negative emotions (anxiety, worry, fear, distress), poor emotional control, irritable, hypersensitive—the opposite of well adjusted

Agreeableness: helpful, cooperative, friendly, caring, nurturant—the opposite of hostile and self-centered

Conscientiousness: achievement-oriented, dependable, responsible, prudent, hardworking, self-controlled—the opposite of impulsive

Openness to experience: curious, imaginative, creative, original, intellectually adventuresome, flexible—the opposite of rigidity.

Many personality psychologists regard the development of the "Big Five" trait model as a major scientific breakthrough. This model provides psychologists with a framework for understanding and integrating the large body of research on personality traits and a set of broad dimensions to characterize the major ways that people differ from one another. Measures of these dimensions have proven both reliable and valid (Digman, 1990).

To return to the analogy we used at the beginning of this section: if three primary colors combine to produce the infinite range of visible hues, then five primary personality traits combine to produce the infinite range of human character. Or so many trait theorists believe.

EVALUATING TRAIT THEORIES

Like other approaches, trait theory has been vigorously criticized. In contrast to the psychoanalytic approach, the trait approach lacks a theory of development. Personality is seen as essentially static. Even if one accepts the "Big Five" model of personality, many questions remain. Where do traits come from? Why does an individual develop one set of traits instead of another? Can traits change? Trait theory is largely silent on these questions. Because it does not deal with the issues of development and growth, the trait approach is the only personality theory that does not include a strategy for personality change or therapy, such as psychoanalysis.

A second charge is that the trait approach relies too heavily on simple mathematical techniques to analyze massive amounts of data. Statistics create the impression of objectivity and scientific precision. In

contrast to psychoanalytic speculation, trait theory seems to offer "hard facts." But statistics do not speak for themselves; they have to be interpreted. And this opens the door to theoretical bias. Cattell did not discover sixteen traits, nor Eysenck three traits, under a microscope. Their different conclusions were based in part on what they expected to find, in part on the methods of analysis they chose.

Third, Walter Mischel (1968) and others have argued that trait theories greatly exaggerate the consistency of human behavior. Casual observation reveals that the most agreeable person may turn disagreeable on occasion. Someone who is assertive, even domineering, in the office may be shy and hesitant in social situations. A good deal of research supports the notion of human *in*consistency. For example, in a classic study of honesty (Hartshorne and May, 1928), children were exposed to a range of temptations. The researchers found little correlation in the way an individual child behaved in different situations. Thus a child who lied to save face in an interview might pass up an opportunity to steal money, while a child who cheated on a test might admit this misdeed later. Mischel and others have argued that we want to see

ourselves and others as consistent because this makes us feel we can predict what will happen in a given situation. Personality may not predict what a specific person will do in a specific situation, but rather predict average tendencies to behave in certain ways over many situations.

Perhaps the most serious criticism is that trait theories can lead to circular reasoning. Why does Jane go to so many parties? Because she is extraverted. How do we know she is extraverted? Because she goes to so many parties. Put another way, trait theories tend to confuse description with explanation. The label "extravert" may be an accurate description, but this by itself does not explain *why* Jane is the way she is.

In the final analysis, trait theories are better at describing than explaining personality. This is an important part of the study of personality, but it is only a part.

IN DEPTH

What Is So Deadly about Type A Personality?

In May 1983, psychologist Logan Wright was told that he would have to undergo coronary bypass surgery. Wright was shocked. In a decade of annual physicals, he had always had good blood-pressure readings and low cholesterol levels. He did not smoke. He was not overweight. And he led an active life, exercising regularly. "Why me?" Wright asked. As a psychologist, he had heard of the Type A personality, but he had never given the idea much thought. "Bypass surgery," he later wrote, "has a way of getting one's attention" (1988, p. 2). As a result of his own experience, Wright was drawn into research on the link between personality and health.

Coronary heart disease (CHD) is one of the deadliest diseases affecting Americans, accounting for over half of all mortalities in any given year. People with high blood pressure, high levels of serum cholesterol, and who smoke cigarettes are six times as likely as individuals who do not to develop CHD. Even so, these physiological risk factors account for only a small proportion (about 14 percent) of heart disease. Identifying other risk factors for CHD is a major goal for medical researchers (Dembroski and Costa, 1987).

THE INITIAL STUDIES

In the 1950s two cardiologists, Meyer Friedman and Ray Rosenman, noticed that many of their patients possessed similar personality traits: they were high-powered, ambitious, competitive "workaholics," who seemed unable to slow down and relax. Friedman and Rosenman defined the **Type A personality** as "an action-emotion complex that can be observed in any person who is aggressively involved in a chronic, incessant struggle to achieve more and more in less and less time, and if required to do so, against the opposing efforts of other things or other persons" (1974, p. 37). (**Type B personality** was defined as the absence of these traits.) Could Type A personality characteristics play a role in CHD?

Rosenman (1978) developed a Structured Interview to identify the Type A behavior pattern. Subjects are asked twenty-five questions about how they would respond to situations likely to provoke Type A behavior (such as waiting in a long line or working with a slow partner). The interviewer also attempts to elicit Type A behavior during the test (for example, by speaking slowly and hesitantly). Scores are based both on the content of the subjects' answers and on their behavior during the interview.

Using the Structured Interview, Friedman, Rosenman and their colleagues divided a group of 3,000 subjects into Type A and Type B groups and followed them over eight-and-a-half years (Rosenman et al., 1975). They found that Type A subjects were twice as likely to develop some form of CHD as were Type B subjects. The results of this impressive study attracted widespread attention in the medical community and the mass media. At a 1978 conference sponsored by the National Heart, Lung, and Blood Institute, a panel of scientists announced that the risks of Type A personality were *equal to or greater than* the risks of high blood pressure, cholesterol, or smoking.

CRITICISMS, ALTERNATIVES, AND FURTHER RESEARCH

No sooner had scientists embraced the link between Type A personality and CHD than contradictory evidence and criticisms began to appear. At least seven major studies (reviewed in Dembroski and MacDougall, 1985, and Matthews and Haynes, 1986) failed to find a significant link between the two. Attempts to create other measures of Type A

personality also failed. Some critics (O'Rourke et al., 1986; Shekelle et al., 1985) argued that Type A personality predicts risk for CHD only among white middle- and upper-class men, and does not apply to blacks or to blue-collar working men, who are already at high risk. Nor does it predict CHD among women (Eaker and Castelli, 1988). Others found that the Structured Interview overpredicts risk for CHD: 70 percent of adult males in a random sample, and 85–90 percent of top executives and senior military officers, tested positive for Type A personality—many more than will develop CHD (Dembroski and Costa, 1987).

Gradually a consensus began to build that the original concept of the Type A behavior pattern did not describe a single personality type, a unified syndrome, but rather a cluster of distinct traits (impatience, workaholism, striving to achieve, generalized hostility, and so on). But these characteristics do not necessarily appear together; for example, people who are highly involved in their jobs are not necessarily hostile. Moreover, some of these traits (such as achievement motivation and job involvement) are not linked to CHD. But the possibility remained that even one of these traits might predict risk for CHD.

PATTERNS AND CONCLUSIONS

In the mid- to late 1980s scientists began to zero in on the "toxic" element in Type A behavior. Reviewing both old and new studies to discover which measures had or had not predicted CHD, researchers found that one stood out: hostility (Booth-Kewley and Friedman, 1987; Dembroski and Williams, in press). In this context, *hostility* is defined as a tendency to become angry, irritable, and resentful in response to everyday frustrations, and/or a tendency to be antagonistic, rude, surly, critical, and uncooperative in everyday interactions (Dembroski and Costa, 1987).

Much current research indicates that hostility is a major factor in CHD, if not the only predictor (Dembroski and Williams, in press; Wright, 1988). Indeed, one reason Friedman and Rosenman found a strong correlation between Type A personality and CHD was that their Structured Interview focused on hostility, whereas other measures gave more weight to other traits, such as pressure to achieve and work involvement.

The Structured Interview includes three overlapping measures of hostility. One is the content of the subject's response. Subjects score high in hostility if they admit to becoming angry in a variety of goal-blocking situations, such as getting stuck behind a slow-moving automobile, a delay in being seated in a restaurant, waiting in line, and waiting for someone who is late. Logan Wright, whom we introduced at the beginning of this discussion and a self-confessed Type A, argues that time urgency is a major factor, because people who feel pressed for time become angry when others slow them down. In his view, time urgency is not a symptom of hostility, but a frequent cause.

The second measure is the intensity of the subject's response. Subjects who score high in hostility report not just that they feel irritated when they have to wait in line, but that they feel *infuriated!* Their interviews are filled with emotion-laden words (such as "hate"); profanity (calling a slow driver a "stupid sonofa_____"); and negative generalizations (for example, saying that coworkers are "all lazy"). They often shout or hiss their answers, rather than speaking in a normal tone of voice.

The third measure is the subject's style of interaction with the interviewer. Subjects who score high in hostility tend to be disagreeable and uncooperative. They may act arrogant ("What is that supposed to mean?"), bored ("Aren't we finished yet?"), argumentative ("How would you answer that?"), or condescending (calling a female interviewer "honey" or "toots"). The interview is tape-recorded, and all three measures are factored into the score.

Type A personality is related to two of the five major personality traits described earlier. The first is agreeableness—or rather its opposite, antagonism. People who score high in hostility are predisposed to be critical, callous, cynical, "cold-blooded," manipulative—in short, antagonistic. Hostility is also related to some aspects of neuroticism—to being chronically negative, temperamental, high-strung, or "hot-blooded."

Evidence that hostility is the lethal element of Type A personality is mounting. Nevertheless, many questions remain (Booth-Kewley and Friedman, 1987). The first is: Where does hostility come from? Like trait theorists in general, researchers who study hostility and CHD rarely consider the developmental origins of this trait. Wright (1988) found that many of his cardiac patients report a high need to achieve, early successes that caused them to strive harder, and frequent exposure to timed activities (such as sports or jobs where speed was rewarded). But this suggestion has not been followed with more detailed research.

A second question is: How does hostility affect the cardiovascular system? One hypothesis (Eliot and Buell, 1983) is that a Type A behavior pattern causes mechanical stress to the artery walls. When a person is angry, the arteries constrict and the heart pumps faster. When someone is chronically angry, this might cause small tears in the artery walls where particles lodge, eventually causing blockage. A second hypothesis is that the chemicals released under stress damage the artery walls. Stress mobilizes body chemistry for "fight-or-flight." When a person experiences stress occasionally, or works it off (for example, by jogging), these chemicals appear to be harmless or even beneficial. But when a person is continually mobilized and does not take physical action to dispel stress, the same chemicals may cause damage. But again, these hypotheses have yet to be proved.

A third question is: Is there any way to intervene in this process, to reduce hostility in Type A personalities and thus reduce the risk of CHD? Can people learn to reduce their hostility? Programs for "hostility management" (generally referred to as "stress management") usually begin by making people aware of their physiological responses (how they feel), behavioral responses (what they do), and cognitive responses (what they think and say) to frustration. Next they are taught to imagine and then practice relaxing under trying circumstances (such as the longest line in the supermarket). Several researchers have reported success with Type A counseling (Friedman et al., 1984; Gill et al., 1985). But as Wright (1988) points out, these therapies have a built-in liability: there is always a danger of throwing out the "baby" (ambition and drive) with the "bathwater" (hostility and risk of CHD). More research is needed on teaching people how to pace themselves—"that is, to run the race of life like a marathon and not a series of 100-yard dashes" (Wright, 1988, p. 13). (We will say more about health, stress, and stress management in Chapter 15.)

According to social cognitive theory, our behavior in various situations—such as being introduced to an attractive person—is determined by our interpretation of the situation, which in turn is influenced by our cognitions (beliefs and expectations).

SOCIAL COGNITIVE THEORIES

Whereas psychoanalytic and trait theories focus on the stable, underlying structure of personality, social cognitive theories emphasize the active, conscious dynamics of personality. For social cognitive theorists, the key to explaining our actions lies in our thoughts. Specifically, these theorists argue that how we think about ourselves and our experiences shapes our behavior. Consider how two different men behave at a party. Tom, who has never had much luck with the opposite sex, sees meeting an attractive woman as a threat to his self-esteem. As a result of his outlook, he is shy and awkward when they are introduced and she soon excuses herself, confirming his belief that he is not attractive to women. Larry, who believes he has a good deal of sex appeal, sees meeting an attractive woman as an opportunity. Because of this attitude, he is confident and friendly when they are introduced and she accepts his invitation to dinner the next night, confirming his belief that he does well with women. If she turns him down, he is likely to believe whatever reason she gives (rather than assuming that she is making a polite excuse); if she is more direct and says she is not interested in seeing him, he is likely to conclude that there is something wrong with her, not him.

The cognitive approach to personality is rooted in the work of Julian Rotter (1954) and George Kelly (1955). Individuals, they reasoned, may interpret the same event quite differently, as a result of their different memories, beliefs, and expectations. Their mental interpretation of the event affects the way they behave; the way they behave affects their experience of the event; and that experience shapes their expectations of future events—as in the examples of Tom and Larry.

OBSERVATIONAL LEARNING

One form of social cognitive theory stresses **observational learning.** As we discussed in Chapter 6, observational learning is the process of learning complex patterns of behavior by watching other people perform them. Through observational learning we acquire cognitive representations of behavior patterns we see, which may then serve as models for our own behavior. Social cognitive theorists argue that many of our habitual ways of responding in situations—our personality styles—have been influenced by observational learning.

Consider what is being learned in the following incident.

Children learn the behavior that adults expect from them by observing adults in social situations.

Jim, age five, found a dead rat, picked it up by the tail, and brought it over to Rita, also age five, waving it in front of her, and evidently hoping to frighten her. Rita showed interest in the rat and wanted to touch it, much to Jim's apparent disappointment. He then took the rat to Dorothy, age seven, who reacted with apparent disgust and fear and ran away from Jim toward Rita, screaming. When Jim pursued Dorothy, Rita also ran away from Jim and the rat and began to scream. Later, when Jim showed up with his rat, Rita ran and showed fear even though Dorothy was not around any more. (Corsini, 1977, pp. 422–423)

Rita has not only learned overt acts (running and screaming at the sight of a dead rat) through her observations, but a number of related cognitions as well. She might have learned that dead animals are dirty and disgusting. The fact that Dorothy ran to her and not a boy for support taught her that girls, in particular, fear dead animals, and further, that girls should stick together when boys do nasty things. At first she may have imitated Dorothy to win the older girl's approval. But then she incorporated fear of dead animals into her idea of how girls should behave, and acted accordingly on her own. In contrast, a boy might have anticipated ridicule from other boys if he

imitated Dorothy and therefore made every effort *not* to show fear.

In short, people do not respond to events in mechanical, unreflexive ways. Instead, they filter events through their own past experiences and develop expectations accordingly. Social cognitive theorists stress that our behavior is shaped not only by the objective event, but also by our *expectations* (including expectations of reward or ridicule). These expectations are not set (in the manner of a personality trait or a Freudian fixation), but are continually revised through observational learning.

According to Albert Bandura (1977a, 1982, 1986), one of the most important consequences of observational learning is an estimate of our own capabilities. In Bandura's terms, when people believe they are capable of dealing effectively with a situation, they possess a sense of **self-efficacy** about it. Self-efficacy is important to personality development because it greatly affects whether or not a person will even *try* to behave in a certain manner. If a little girl is convinced, for instance, that she cannot touch a dead rat, she is likely to avoid dead animals, and such squeamishness may become characteristic of her. Bandura points out that our degree of self-efficacy in any given situation depends both on our own past experiences and on the experiences of others that we observe. In Chapter 17 we will see how instilling a

TABLE 13.2   When Making Friends Is Hard: The Social Schemas and Self-Protective Strategies of Social Pessimists

Task Appraisal	Self-Appraisal	Actions	Other Directedness
Low social expectations Avoids thinking about possible good outcomes (social) Finds social tasks in general to be stressful	Sees discrepancy between actual and ideal social self-concepts Makes self-deprecating comments Feels others are more appealing than self Focuses attention on self after social failure	Obsesses/ruminates over multitude of potential actions/outcomes	Is comfortable with and wishes to have structure imposed by others Judges self according to others' (external) standards Seeks to make own tasks similar to others Thinks about having social support Uses perceived similarity of self to typical others in situations as a guide in decision making

Adapted from Langston and Cantor, 1989, p. 655. (© 1989 by the American Psychological Association. Used by permission.)

sense of self-efficacy may help people overcome a variety of maladaptive behaviors, from acute shyness to irrational fears.

OTHER SOCIAL COGNITIVE THEORIES

In recent years social cognitive theorists have turned to the question of how and why expectations (or more generally, personality styles) are maintained over time. Nancy Cantor (1990) identifies three basic elements of personality functioning that distinguish one individual from another: schemas, tasks, and strategies. **Schemas,** as we have noted before, are organized sets of knowledge about particular domains of life, including the self. Schemas function as a personalized cognitive filter, coloring the way we perceive events, what sorts of things we pay attention to and remember, and how we feel about ourselves and others. For example, an individual with a "shyness schema" will view the slightest misstep in a social situation as a disaster, quickly recall the many social blunders she has made in the past, and perceive other people as everything she is not—outgoing, charming, and totally at ease. Equally important, she will *not* process the information that no one else noticed that she pronounced a name incorrectly, that other people feel awkward and ill at ease too, that many times people have chosen to speak to her at a

party, or other positive social feedback. Her shyness schema filters out this information.

Tasks are the goals we set for ourselves, the ideals for which we strive. Everyone is faced with a wide array of culturally prescribed goals and biologically based demands. From these we choose a small selection that are personally important to us. In so doing we may overlook social realities in favor of dreams, and not consider "alternative possibilities for the self in the future" (Cantor, 1990, p. 737). For example, a college student may focus on the task of making friends to such an extent that he or she neglects alternative life tasks, such as getting good grades and maintaining family relationships.

Strategies are the specific techniques or procedures people use to work on their life tasks. Depending on the schemas they have developed, the tasks they have set, and the context, an individual might adopt a strategy of looking on the bright side, expecting the worst, acting helpless, taking risks, avoiding difficult situations, and many more. Strategies are a combination of thoughts, feelings, and actions; of anticipation, planning, effort, and self-monitoring.

The concept of strategies was examined in a study of making new friends in college (Langston and Cantor, 1989). Most of the students saw making friends as an important task, but only a minority

The college years can be a great opportunity for developing strategies for coping with life tasks. Few other settings offer such a variety of new people and situations that the individual must learn to deal with.

perceived this task as extremely difficult. These "social pessimists" were competent in other areas, but harbored extreme self-doubt about their social capabilities. Some elements of their negative social schemas appear in Table 13.2. Such students adopted a self-protective strategy in social situations, taking their cues from other people. For example, instead of seeking other people out, they waited for people to come to them. In getting-acquainted conversations they asked questions, but rarely volunteered information about themselves. When they did speak out, it was to endorse what other people were saying, not to express themselves. This other-directed stance may have helped these students avoid social anxiety, but at a high cost. Cantor suggests that the more they looked to others for social guidance, the more personally inadequate they felt. Always on the alert for rejection, they rarely enjoyed social encounters. Moreover, their self-protective strategy probably cost them friends: people who always "hold back" and "play it safe" are not much fun. In their junior year these students were much more likely than others to express the feeling that they were dissatisfied with their social lives.

Where Cantor stresses strategies, other social cognitive theorists emphasize **self-schemas:** an organized set of knowledge about the self that guides perception and interpretation of information in social situations. Like other schemas, the self-schema acts as a filter, letting in some information and blocking out other data. In a series of experiments on self-schemas, Hazel Markus (1977) had subjects rate themselves on an independent–dependent scale, then divided the group into Independents, Dependents, and Aschematics (who did not show clear tendencies one way or the other). She found that Independents were quicker than Dependents or Aschematics to recognize words that described independence (adventurous, self-confident, etc.), wrote more detailed descriptions of past actions that demonstrated independence, predicted that they would behave in a similar manner in future situations, and rejected information suggesting that the original test results were false.

More recently, Markus and others have been investigating the notion that each of us has not one but several self-schemas (Markus and Nurius, 1986). These **possible selves** include the type of person we think we might become, the type of person we would like to become, and the type of person we are afraid of becoming. Each of these schemas acts as a framework for interpreting information about the self. In interpreting past events and planning future actions we consider all these self-schemas, and strive toward our ideal self and away from our undesired self.

EVALUATING SOCIAL COGNITIVE THEORIES

Social cognitive theories have become increasingly popular and influential. Nevertheless, their usefulness as a comprehensive theory of personality is limited. For one thing, social cognitive theorists assume that the ways we think about ourselves (schemas) determine our actions. But it is just as plausible to assume the reverse, that behavior determines schemas. In other words, we form a self-image in the same way as we develop images of others: by observing what they do and inferring general characteristics from specific actions.

Second, social cognitive theories tend to neglect emotions. Human beings are portrayed almost as information-processing robots, calculating the best strategy to achieve a given task. Too little attention is paid to the passionate and spontaneous aspects of human behavior—to joy, love, hate, envy, anger, and sorrow.

Third, this approach tends to be quite narrow. Whereas the other theories we have described seek consistency over a variety of situations, social cognitive theories focus on responses to this or that specific situation. Why, for example, does John race motorcycles? A social cognitive theorist might answer, because he has developed an expectation that this sport will earn him status in the eyes of his friends, or that taking risks is part of his self-schema. But this does not provide a coherent picture of John as an overall person. Is this activity central to John's personality? Does he take risks in other situations? How do his behaviors in different settings relate to one another? Social cognitive theorists have not addressed these questions.

Despite these drawbacks, the social cognitive approach has added to the study of personality by focusing on life as it is lived, in ordinary, everyday settings. Cantor's work in particular emphasizes the problems and tasks of everyday life, how people develop strategies for attaining goals, and what outcomes are important to individuals.

HUMANISTIC THEORIES

The humanistic approach to personality is based on two main assumptions. The first is that because subjective experiences are in many ways unique, we can understand another's personality only by trying

Carl Rogers maintained that children may do things—such as participate in organized sports—to obtain their parents' approval as well as for their own enjoyment.

to see the world through that person's eyes. The second is that people are free to become what they want, to fulfill themselves, to carve out their own destinies and write their own histories. At the heart of the humanistic approach is a strong belief in self-determination and individual potential. This view contrasts sharply with certain earlier perspectives, especially psychoanalytic theory, which holds that our actions are molded largely by forces beyond our control. Two historically influential thinkers from this school are Carl Rogers and Abraham Maslow: a major new voice within the humanistic tradition is Don McAdams.

ROGERS'S THEORY OF THE SELF

Carl Rogers (1902–1987), a clinical psychologist, developed his theory of personality from observa-

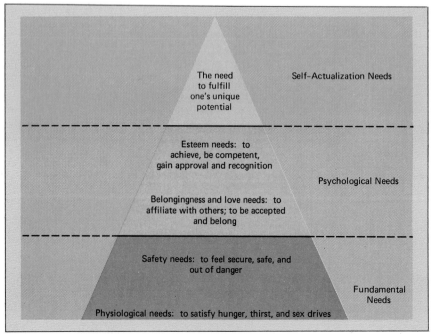

Physiological needs: to satisfy hunger, thirst, and sex drives

Safety needs: to feel secure, safe, and out of danger

Belongingness and love needs: to affiliate with others; to be accepted and belong

Esteem needs: to achieve, be competent, gain approval and recognition

The need to fulfill one's unique potential

Self-Actualization Needs

Psychological Needs

Fundamental Needs

FIGURE 13.2 Maslow's hierarchy of needs represented as a pyramid. According to Maslow, fundamental needs must be satisfied before a person is free to progress to psychological needs. These, in turn, must be satisfied before a person can turn to self-actualization. Maslow later added a need for transcendence—the experience of being able to see oneself in perspective—which is even a higher-level goal than the need for self-actualization. (*Eysenck 1970/Used by permission of Mathuen & Co.*)

tions he made while practicing psychotherapy. He noticed that his clients (a term he preferred to *patients* because it does not imply illness) repeatedly expressed an organized set of perceptions, feelings, and attitudes about themselves. They made such statements as "I haven't been acting like myself; it doesn't seem like me" and "I don't have any emotional responses to situations; I'm worried about myself." Such statements led Rogers to believe that the *self*—the body of perceptions we think of as "I" or "me"—is a vital part of human experience. Furthermore, he found that most people are constantly struggling to become their "real" selves. Rogers concluded that the overriding human motivation is a desire to become all that one truly is—to fulfill one's capabilities and to achieve one's total potential. This powerful, lifelong motive Rogers called a striving toward **self-actualization** (Rogers, 1970, 1971).

But Rogers also discovered from his clients that self-actualization is often thwarted by an existing self-concept that is narrow and restricting. His clients seemed to have learned during childhood that in order to obtain the regard of others, they had to feel and act in ways that distorted or submerged what they were really like. In short, they had to deny certain feelings and inclinations in order to be accepted by parents, relatives, or peers.

Rogers explained this denial or distortion of feelings by arguing that almost every child is the victim of **conditional positive regard.** By this he meant that love and praise are often withheld until the child conforms to parental or social standards. If a boy dislikes rough-and-tumble play, for instance, he may be admonished not to be a "sissy." Or if he enjoys long walks in the woods by himself, he may be cautioned that it is not good to be a "loner." Contact sports and group activities, though, may be rewarded with smiles and compliments. According to Rogers, children incorporate into the self these so-called **conditions of worth**—strong ideas about which thoughts and behaviors will bring positive regard and so are desirable and "good." At the same time, they suppress, distort, or deny those feelings and experiences that prevent positive regard, even though they are genuine and would be intrinsically satisfying.

Rogers saw two possible outcomes from these early life experiences. When the conditions of worth a person learns are few and reasonable, the self will usually be flexible enough to allow a wide range of feelings and behaviors. Rogers described such people as **fully functioning.** They are open, undefensive, realistic, creative, and self-determining, and have an underlying confidence in themselves. If, however, conditions of worth are severely restrictive, prohibiting many thoughts and actions in which the person would otherwise engage, self-actualization is blocked. The person is anxious, fearful, defensive, conforming, and unrealistic in self-demands. He or she feels manipulated rather than free.

Although Rogers counseled many people whose self-actualization had presumably been thwarted by unreasonable conditions of worth, his theory is nevertheless a very optimistic one. He maintained that humans always have the potential to break free from any beliefs and feelings that are hampering their personal growth. This optimistic view is in keeping with some research (Epstein, 1979). When college students were asked to describe the experience in their lives that had the most positive impact on their self-concept, many mentioned a situation in which they were at first evaluated *negatively* by others. Rogers would not have been the least surprised at this paradoxical finding. To him it would have suggested that people originally oppressed by unreasonable conditions of worth were managing to reassert their true selves and become more fully functioning. Thus a young woman whose career choice is greeted negatively by parents and friends may be forced to reconsider her goals and values, eventually strengthening her career commitment, and ending up with a greater sense of self-reliance and self-worth.

MASLOW'S SELF-ACTUALIZED PERSON

Like Carl Rogers, psychologist Abraham Maslow (1908–1970) began with the assumptions that people are free to shape their own lives and that their most important motivation is the desire to achieve self-actualization. A self-actualized person, as defined by Maslow, finds fulfillment in doing the best of which he or she is capable, not in competition with others, but in an effort to become "the best me I can be" (1971a, 1971b). Maslow criticized psychoanalysts for their pessimistic, negative, and limited conceptions of human beings. Where is the psychology, he asked, that takes account of gaiety, exuberance, love, and expressive art to the same extent that it deals with misery, conflict, shame, hostility, and habit (1966, 1968)? Accordingly, Maslow deliberately set out to create what he called a "third force" in psychology, one that would offer an appealing alternative to psychoanalysis and cognitive theories.

One of Maslow's key concepts is what he called **hierarchy of needs,** illustrated in Figure 13.2. Maslow believed that all humans face a series of needs in

In Abraham Maslow's view, the self-actualized person is the one who is able to fulfill his or her unique potential.

life, and that needs at more basic levels must be met before a person can go on to fulfill higher-level needs. At the bottom of Maslow's hierarchy are so-called **fundamental needs:** those associated with physical requirements, such as satisfying thirst and hunger, and those related to obtaining a safe and secure environment. Above these, Maslow identified a set of **psychological needs.** These include both the need to develop a sense of belonging and of being loved and the need to achieve competence, recognition, and high self-esteem. Finally, once all fundamental and psychological needs are met, a person can begin to fulfill the need for self-actualization, that is, the need to realize one's own unique potential. This includes not just excelling at one's lifework, but also devoting oneself to higher social goals, such as bringing about justice or stopping cruelty and exploitation. The self-actualized person, according to Maslow, does not seek fame and glory or the love and approval of everyone. Instead, he or she finds peace and content-

TABLE 13.3   Characteristics of Self-Actualized Persons

They are realistically oriented.	They identify with humankind.
They accept themselves, other people, and the natural world for what they are.	Their intimate relationships with a few specially loved people tend to be profound and deeply emotional rather than superficial.
They have a great deal of spontaneity.	Their values and attitudes are democratic.
They are problem-centered rather than self-centered.	They do not confuse means with ends.
They have an air of detachment and a need for privacy.	Their sense of humor is philosophical rather than hostile.
They are autonomous and independent.	They have a great fund of creativeness.
Their appreciation of people and things is fresh rather than stereotyped.	They resist conformity to the culture.
Most of them have had profound mystical or spiritual experiences, although not necessarily religious in character.	They transcend the environment rather than just cope with it.

Source: Maslow, 1954.

ment in the inner satisfaction that comes with being the best that one can be (Landsman, 1974; Maslow, 1971a).

Unlike Rogers, Maslow derived his theory of personality development largely from studies of healthy, creative, self-actualized people who made full use of their talents and capabilities. They included some historical figures—Abraham Lincoln, Henry David Thoreau, Ludwig van Beethoven, Eleanor Roosevelt, and Albert Einstein, for instance—as well as some of Maslow's own friends (Maslow, 1954). Their distinguishing personality traits are listed in Table 13.3. Maslow's critics point out that some self-actualized people do not seem to have scaled the hierarchy of needs in precisely the way Maslow predicted. Many writers and artists, for example, have created their masterpieces in spite of miserable childhoods, insecurity, social rejection, and poverty. To Maslow, however, these are the exceptions that prove just how strong the drive toward self-fulfillment is.

McADAMS'S THEORY OF PSYCHOBIOGRAPHY

Don McAdams's theory of psychobiography (1988) combines elements of humanistic theories with concepts adapted from Erikson's theory of psychosocial development. For McAdams, the key issue in the study of personality is identity. He argues that individuals construct their own identities through the stories they tell about themselves. "[T]he main thesis of my work," McAdams writes, "[is]: *Identity is a life story*—an internalized narrative integration of past, present, and anticipated future which provides lives

with a sense of unity and purpose" (1988b). In other words, individuals try to make sense of their lives by envisioning their life as a narrative with key scenes and a clear plot that leads toward an appropriate ending. Thus, in place of self-actualization, McAdams proposes what we might call a drive for self-coherence.

According to McAdams, the construction of a life story begins in adolescence when the young person asks: Who was I? Who am I now? Who will I become in the future? Adolescents answer these questions by selectively remembering (or even rewriting) scenes from the past that explain how they came to be a certain kind of person. But the adolescent's life story is often grandiose, a personal fable (Elkind, 1981) that depicts the teenager as totally unique. In young adulthood the life story becomes both more realistic and more complex. The young adult begins to realize that his or her story contains a number of distinct characters identified with the self, roughly equivalent to what Markus calls "possible selves." One of the tasks of young adulthood is to reconcile these differences and arrive at a more integrated image of the self. Another is to reconcile conflicting drives for love (intimacy, communion, cooperation, merger) and glory (power, mastery, control, and separation). In middle adulthood, individuals become aware of their mortality and realize that *the end* is nearer than they would like. This awareness calls up feelings of what Erikson called "generativity": a desire to leave a legacy to future generations, to invest in people, relationships, and work that will outlive the self. At each stage the life story is revised and rewritten to meet current needs. Ideally, the individual arrives at a life story that has no end.

McAdams argues that if identity is a life story, then identities (or personalities) can be analyzed in much the same way we analyze works of literature. The personality theorist's job, according to McAdams, is to collect autobiographies; to analyze these in terms of themes, settings, scenes, characters, and plot; to classify or catalog stories; and ultimately, to discover how one individual's life story is in some ways like all other stories, like some other stories, and like no other story (Kluckhohn and Murray, 1953).

EVALUATING THE HUMANISTIC APPROACH

The humanistic approach has attracted many followers—and many critics. One common complaint is that humanistic theories are oversimplified. Each of the theorists we have introduced here claims that all human behavior can be explained in terms of a single, overriding principle: self-actualization for Rogers, self-fulfillment for Maslow, and self-coherence (or identity) for McAdams. They do not attempt to explain where these drives come from; they simply assume that they exist. Nor do humanists deal with the possibility that individuals vary in their need for self-actualization, for example. The drive for self-fulfillment may explain some facets of personality and behavior, but surely it is not the full story.

A second criticism is that humanistic theories are unscientific. Maslow, for example, identified individuals he considered self-actualized, then searched for the characteristics they had in common. Had Maslow gone on to test whether the presence of these characteristics *predicted* whether an individual would become self-actualized, his conclusions might be considered scientifically valid. But he did not. Rogers was one of the first clinical psychologists to record therapeutic sessions and submit these records to quantitative analysis. But his explanations were difficult to prove or disprove, as he himself admitted (Rogers, 1985). For example, he never offered a clear definition of a fully functioning person; to the contrary, he maintained that behavior that constitutes progress and maturity for one person might indicate stagnation and immaturity for another. McAdams walks a fine line between scientific analysis and literary criticism.

Humanistic theories assign great importance to the possibility of change. Yet neither Rogers nor Maslow offered an explicit explanation of personality

The feeling of generativity that arises late in life reflects the desire to pass along one's wisdom and experience to the younger generation.

development. Are there predictable changes in the way people think, act, and feel over the course of development? Is there a pattern of change that can be charted and analyzed? Rogers and Maslow did not say. McAdams, however, has begun to correct this flaw, by adapting and refining concepts from Erikson's theory of psychosocial development.

Finally, the humanistic approach is widely criticized for being romantically naive. It is romantic in presenting an idealized picture of human nature, focusing on the positive, rational, and caring aspects of human nature and on the potential for growth, while ignoring the negative, irrational, and aggressive side of human nature and the potential for self-destruction. The humanistic approach is naive in its belief that one can apply scientific methods of inquiry to subjective experience with any certainty.

The primary appeal of the humanistic approach is its attention to human freedom and creativity, something that is conspicuously lacking in other theories (particularly the psychoanalytic approach, with its emphasis on the darker side of human nature). More specifically, both Rogers and Maslow questioned the Freudian notion that adaptation to the demands of society is necessary for healthy development. From their humanistic viewpoint, excessive adaptation produces conforming, unimaginative, inhibited, unfulfilled people. Although they recognized that some degree of accommodation is essential, they stressed the importance of transcending—of going beyond—social conventions. Likewise, McAdams questioned the mechanical aspects of the social cognitive approach, arguing that people's schemas are closer to literature and mythology than to computer programs. These are important additions to the study of personality.

BIOLOGICAL APPROACHES

In the second century A.D., the Roman physician Galen proposed that personality is determined by the amounts of certain fluids in the body. Galen held that there were four main bodily fluids or humors *(phlegm, black bile, blood,* and *yellow bile),* four main personality characteristics *(phlegmatic, melancholic, choleric,* and *sanguine),* and that these were directly related to one another. For example, an excess of phlegm was thought to produce a phlegmatic character (someone who is apathetic and lacks emotion). An excess of black bile was thought to produce a melancholic character (someone who is generally sad and anxious, and sees difficulties everywhere). Galen also thought that an individual's personality could be changed by correcting the imbalance of body fluids through bathing and diet. Although few people today believe the body fluid theory of personality, it is notable as one of the first truly biological theories of personality. Modern scientists have made significant progress in developing sophisticated theoretical models and precise research techniques for evaluating the relationship between biology and personality (Buss, 1990).

Biological views of personality can be divided into three basic categories: the evolutionary, behavioral genetic, and psychophysiological approaches.

THE EVOLUTIONARY APPROACH

At least since Freud, personality theorists have been concerned with defining human nature—with identifying the core human motives and basic psychologi-

cal mechanisms found in all (or most) members of our species (Buss, 1990). Thus Freud argued that human behavior is motivated by two basic instincts (sex and aggression); the human psyche is divided into three parts (the id, ego, and superego); and all human beings go through the same stages of psychosexual development (the oral, anal, phallic, latency, and genital phases). Maslow argued that human behavior is driven by the need to fill basic biological needs and achieve self-actualization. Contemporary trait theorists have identified five basic elements of personality.

From the evolutionary perspective, these attempts to pin down human nature are largely speculative. Psychologists who adopt the evolutionary perspective argue that to understand the human mind one must consider the adaptive problems human beings faced in our evolutionary past. In this view, human nature consists of the strategies that evolved among our ancestors to solve the twin problems of survival and reproduction.

In evolutionary theory, adaptation is measured in terms of "reproductive success." Individuals who possess traits that give them an advantage in acquiring resources, ensuring safety, and attracting mates produce more offspring than do individuals who do not possess these traits; their offspring inherit these traits and enjoy greater reproductive success in the next generation; and so the adaptive traits are passed to future generations. The laws of evolution apply not only to anatomy, but also to behavior (see Chapter 10). The evolutionary approach holds that just as our upright human posture and opposable thumbs are the product of evolution, so, too, are our styles of behavior the result of natural selection.

As an example of the evolutionary approach, consider Steven Gangestad and Jeffrey Simpson's analysis of patterns of female sociosexuality (1990). Gangestad and Simpson maintain that human females adopt one of two strategies in selecting mates. One is a *restricted strategy:* the female takes a relatively long time to select a mate, and requires strong attachment to, commitment from, and closeness with a potential partner before she enters into a sexual relationship. The second is an *unrestricted strategy:* the female takes a shorter time to select a mate, and requires less attachment, commitment, and closeness before engaging in sexual relations.

Gangestad and Simpson reason that both strategies are adaptive, but for different reasons. The

How much of an individual's personality is due to heredity? Several long-term studies of identical twins reared in different families have suggested that genes exert more influence on some personality traits than psychologists used to think. For example, as part of a long-term University of Minnesota study of more than 350 pairs of twins raised apart, these identical twins exhibited very similar personality traits for flexibility, self-control, and sociability. In fact, they both drive the same model blue Chevrolet, smoke the same brand of cigarettes, own dogs named Toy, and vacation at the same beach.

restricted female who requires commitment is likely to acquire a mate who will stay with her and help her to rear her offspring, thus enhancing their chances of survival. But she may not attract the fittest males, who have a wide choice of partners. The unrestricted female, who does not require a long courtship, is more likely to attract these males. But what she gains in fitness for her offspring (traits they inherit from the father), she loses in support and protection. Her offspring may have more reproductive success as adults, but they are somewhat less likely to survive to reproductive age.

Gangestad and Simpson hypothesized that the restrictive style will be most successful when females outnumber males, so that males have to compete for mates and females can afford to be "choosy." The unrestrictive style will be most adaptive when males outnumber females, so that females have to compete for mates. To test this hypothesis, they reviewed a number of population studies. Amazingly, they found that birth ratios conform to these predictions. In principle, the ratio of male to female offspring should be 50:50. But Gangestad and Simpson found that restricted females have slightly more female offspring, and unrestricted females slightly more male offspring. They do not speculate as to how this occurs or which comes first (the reproductive strategy or the imbalanced sex ratio). But biology and sociosexual style do appear to be synchronized.

THE BEHAVIORAL GENETIC APPROACH

While the evolutionary approach focuses on universal aspects of human behavior, the behavioral genetic approach seeks to explain individual variations. To answer the question, "Where does personality come from?," behavioral geneticists examine three sources: genetic contributions (traits or dispositions individuals inherit from their parents), shared environmental influences (parenting style, school training, neighborhood, and other environmental influences that siblings share), and idiosyncratic events (environmental influences that are unique to the individual, such as a childhood illness or friends).

We discussed research on genetic influences on personality in Chapter 10. To review: Comparative studies of identical twins reared together or apart, and of biological and adopted siblings, suggest that heredity plays an important role in personality development. For common personality traits (extraversion, emotional stability, and so on), about half the differences we observe among individuals are due to their genetic makeup. But idiosyncratic life events—the fact that parents treat siblings differently, and that siblings have different friends and teachers and different experiences—are equally important in shaping personality (Bouchard and McGue, 1990; Bouchard et al., 1990). Thus current behavioral genetic research suggests that personality is the result of the combination of, or interaction between, the traits individuals inherit from their parents and their unique life histories.

THE PSYCHOPHYSIOLOGICAL APPROACH

Psychophysiologists are interested in how inherited differences are translated from genes into personality and behavior. According to this view, differences in personality are due, at least in part, to differences in physiology, particularly in the nervous system. This approach posits *explanations* for why people behave differently, explanations that can be tested experimentally.

Research on the biological differences associated with introversion/extraversion is a classic example of this approach. Eysenck suspected that this dimension of personality had a biological basis and uncovered some evidence that he was correct. More recent research (reviewed in Stelmack, 1990) has pinpointed the difference. Introverts are more arousable, more reactive, to sensory stimulation than extraverts are. For example, introverts show a larger and faster startle response. But their nervous system is easily overwhelmed, so that they tend to avoid or shut out high levels of stimulation. This explains why they tend to seek out quiet environments and withdraw from crowds. Extraverts, in contrast, tend to seek stimulation to make up for their lower physiological reactivity. Put another way, extraverts are "stimulus hungry" (Gale, 1969) because their nervous system tends to dampen the effects of low or moderate sensory stimulation. So they tend to seek out noisy environments and the hustle and bustle of crowds. According to the psychophysiological perspective, extraverts are *not* extraverts because they have a psychological need to be around people, but because they crave the stimulation that lots of people provide. Likewise, introverts are not introverts because they dislike people, but because their nervous system cannot tolerate strong stimulation.

Future research may show that other traits, such as emotional stability versus instability or impulsive versus planful, are partly the result of physiological differences.

EVALUATING BIOLOGICAL APPROACHES

Many psychologists intuitively accept the possibility that personality differences have some biological basis. But many see flaws in both the theory and methods of current biological perspectives.

First, the evolutionary approach can (and often does) lead to circular reasoning. If a trait or characteristic is found in all or most people, it must be adaptive. How do we know it is adaptive? Because it is widespread. Much evolutionary theorizing simply fills in the gaps in this circle. The notion that the key to human nature lies in our species' evolutionary past means that the evidence for natural selection also lies in the very distant past. As a result, proving or disproving explanations of personality traits is all but impossible. Many of the behavior patterns evolutionary theorists have analyzed can just as easily be explained by other means. For example, different sociosexual strategies might be the result of social and cultural forces rather than natural selection. In a society where men are scarce, perhaps because many have been killed in hunting accidents or war, and a large number of women are competing for a small number of men, women might adopt the unrestricted strategy. In a society where women have few resources, because they are culturally prohibited from many types of work, they would be more likely to adopt a restricted strategy.

Second, the evolutionary and behavioral genetic approaches contain a built-in contradiction. According to the theory of evolution, natural selection leads to sameness. For example, all normal, healthy human beings are born with two legs, two arms, two eyes, two brain hemispheres. These characteristics must be adaptive because they show uniformity in the population. If a trait is adaptive, evolution tends to eliminate genetic variability. Yet in the case of personality we find, not genetic sameness, but genetic variability. How can this puzzle be explained?

On the surface, the psychophysiological perspective seems stronger. But here, too, critics point to a built-in flaw. The evidence that introverts are more arousable, and extraverts less so, does not necessarily tell us the direction of cause and effect. Psychophysiologists reason that high reactivity causes people to become introverts. But an equally plausible explanation is that introversion causes people to become highly arousable—that is, people who like quiet and solitude have less experience of high levels of sensory

One recurring theme in personality research is the importance of external influences on thought and behavior. Some psychologists believe that an individual's social environment and interactions with others have a strong effect on that person's self-concept.

stimulation than extraverts do, and so become more sensitive. Likewise, people who like noise and crowds become habituated to high levels of stimulation, and so need higher levels to become excited. Which comes first?

On the positive side, most psychologists welcome the "reunion" of biology and psychology. For decades personality and physiological psychologists have gone their separate ways, barely talking to one another. They pursued different questions, employed different research methods, and spoke different technological and conceptual languages. New efforts to bring the two together can only be seen as a step forward for psychology as a whole. Moreover, scientific examination of the biological bases of personality is a relatively new field, one almost certain to bear fruit in coming years.

INTEGRATING DIFFERENT APPROACHES TO PERSONALITY

Of all the theories of personality we have described, which one is right? In a sense, they all are. The human personality is extremely complex and can be viewed from different perspectives. Each of the theor-

ies covered in this chapter represents a unique perspective on human nature. Each also has its own strengths and weaknesses (as we have suggested in the evaluations sections following each theory). Most psychologists take an eclectic approach to personality, adapting the strong points of each theory, those points which seem most useful in helping them to understand, predict, and explain human behavior.

The overriding concerns of all personality theorists are: Why do people behave as they do? And why do individuals differ from one another? Because of their common interests, personality theorists of all persuasions tend to return to several common themes.

One such theme is *conflict*, first introduced to psychology by Sigmund Freud. According to Freud, conflict is inherent in the human psyche. The best we can hope for is an uneasy balance among competing forces. Although usually less pessimistic than Freud in their views on the inevitability and persistence of conflict, other psychoanalytic theorists also incorporated the conflict theme in their work. In addition, Carl Rogers introduced a conflict theme when he argued that clashes between a person's true inclinations and the values of others can cause denial and distortion of reality.

A second recurring theme in personality research is the importance of *external influences* on thought and behavior. You can see this theme in the work of psychoanalysts Alfred Adler and Karen Horney, who stressed that early social environments have a crucial impact on people's development. Carl Rogers also recognized the importance of social influences when he argued that a person's self-concept is partly shaped by the conditions of worth imposed by others.

Continuity and consistency are a third theme we find in personality theories. They were emphasized by Freud, who took the extreme view that personality is totally formed in the resolution of childhood conflicts and is thus very resistant to change in adulthood. The trait theorists also stress continuity and consistency—hence their efforts to identify and measure relatively enduring dispositions. Striving for consistency plays a key role in McAdams's theory of psychobiography.

Finally, we come to the theme of *self-fulfillment.* It can be seen in the writings of Adler, who viewed life as a kind of striving for self-perfection. But the fulfillment theme is most fully developed in the humanistic approaches both of Carl Rogers and Abraham Maslow. Here the striving to realize one's own potential becomes the overriding human motivation.

Although less optimistic than the humanists, Cantor sees the different ways people behave as strategies for dealing with the problems of everyday life and if not finding fulfillment, avoiding anxiety, at least temporarily.

In summary, then, personality theorists often differ sharply in their views, sometimes engaging in heated debates over seemingly irreconcilable ideas. Yet a broader look shows that all seem to be touching in different ways on many of the same themes. Do these themes together begin to provide a unified picture of human behavior? To some extent, they do. Contemporary psychologists see human personality as an immensely complex subject, influenced by a host of factors, yet still susceptible to scientific study (Mischel, 1981). We are at once shaped by past experiences and responsive to new conditions, yet at the same time we have an enormous impact on the people and events around us. Sometimes we find ourselves driven by motivations that seem to arise from unconscious needs and conflicts. But we are also quite capable of creatively resolving those conflicts and of using our impressive cognitive powers to set our own agendas and to seek our own fulfillment.

SUMMARY

1. **Personality** consists of all the relatively stable and distinctive styles of thought, behavior, and emotional responses that characterize a person's adaptations to surrounding circumstances.

2. The **psychoanalytic approach** to personality stresses the importance of childhood experience in shaping adult personality and focuses on the role of the unconscious in motivating human actions. Central to all psychoanalytic theories are the concepts of conflict between opposing motives, anxiety over unacceptable motives, and defense mechanisms to prevent anxiety from becoming too great.

3. Sigmund Freud was the founder of the psychoanalytic perspective. He originated the concept of the unconscious and considered it the motivating force behind all human behavior. Freud saw the human psyche as divided into three separate but interacting elements: the id, the ego, and the superego. The **id,** which is part of the unconscious, seeks only the satisfaction of bodily needs and is therefore said to operate on the **pleasure principle.** The **ego,** which serves as a mediator between the id and reality, is largely concerned with personal safety and thus is said to act according to the **reality principle.** The **superego,** which represents the moral standards of society, is equivalent to what we call "conscience."

4. When the demands of these three conflicting forces cannot be met, people experience **anxiety** and use **defense mechanisms** to try to reduce it. The most basic defense mechanism is **repression,** pushing unacceptable id impulses into the unconscious. Others are **denial, regression, reaction formation, projection, displacement,** and **sublimation.**

5. According to Freud, the child goes through five stages of psychosexual development—the **oral, anal, phallic, latency,** and **genital**—which are characterized by conflicts between the id and society. It is the resolution of these conflicts that presumably shapes adult personality. A person who fails to resolve any one of these conflicts may become **fixated,** or locked in a psychological battle that is expressed symbolically throughout life.

6. Post-Freudian psychoanalysts have tended to give decreased importance to the id and increased importance to the ego, which they see as capable of creativity, planning, and the formation of self-fulfilling goals. They have also come to see personality development as less the result of conflicts over id impulses than the product of a child's relationships with significant others. Among the important psychoanalytic theorists besides Freud have been Carl Jung, Alfred Adler, Karen Horney, Heinz Hartmann, Margaret Mahler, and Heinz Kohut.

7. Another approach to personality is called **trait theory.** A **trait** is any relatively enduring way in which one individual differs from another, and trait theorists focus on these various attributes to explain consistency in human behavior. One of the earliest trait theorists, Gordon Allport, adopted an idiographic approach, relying heavily on case studies. Raymond Cattell used sophisticated statistical analyses to identify sixteen source traits. Hans Eysenck believed that there were only three traits, and that these were rooted in biology and could be tested experimentally. In recent years trait theorists have arrived at a consensus on five major personality traits: extraversion/introversion, neuroticism/well adjusted, agreeableness/hostility, conscientiousness/impulsivity, and openness to experience/rigidity.

8. The announcement that a cluster of traits labeled **Type A personality** placed individuals at high risk for coronary heart disease (CHD) was premature. However, ongoing research (especially using the Structured Interview) found that one of these traits, hostility, does predict susceptibility to CHD. Important questions for future research are: What is the origin of this trait? And how does it damage the cardiovascular system?

9. **Social cognitive approaches** hold that differences among individuals are largely the result of differences in how people think about themselves and others.

Some theorists in this school emphasize **observational learning.** Others are concerned with how cognitive personality structures are maintained over time. Nancy Cantor identified three mechanisms: **schemas, tasks,** and **strategies.** Hazel Markus has investigated **self-schemas** and the concept of **possible selves.**

10. Another perspective on personality is offered by the **humanistic approach,** which stresses the individual's unique perception of the world and a belief in human potential. Psychologist Carl Rogers evolved a theory of the self according to which each person is engaged in a lifelong striving for **self-actualization.** Rogers found that many people are thwarted in this goal because, in order to receive approval from others, they have to deny their true selves and conform to those others' **conditions of worth.** Psychologist Abraham Maslow also saw self-actualization as an important human motive. But he proposed that one must fulfill a **hierarchy of needs** before reaching the goal of realizing one's own unique potential. Don McAdams holds that individuals actively construct their identity by "writing" a life story that explains how they got to be the kind of person they are and where they are headed, giving meaning to their experiences.

11. **Biological approaches** hold that common behavioral patterns might be the result of evolutionary forces, that personality traits might be to some degree genetically determined, and that some personality traits might be due to differences in physiological functioning.

12. While psychologists take many approaches to describing and explaining human personality, all have touched on at least some of the following four basic themes: conflict, external influences, continuity and consistency, and self-fulfillment. Most personality psychologists take an eclectic approach, incorporating what they consider the strongest points of various theories.

SUGGESTED READINGS

Buss, D., and Cantor, N. (1989). *Personality psychology: Recent trends and emerging directions.* New York: Springer-Verlag. A collection of chapters by active, contemporary personality psychologists who were asked to write their views of important and emerging issues in personality psychology.

Horney, K. (1973). *Feminine psychology.* Harold Kelman (Ed.). New York: Norton. A paperback edition of the classic discussion of the forces that influence the development and expression of personality in women.

Mischel, W. (1981). *Introduction to personality* (3rd ed.). New York: Holt, Rinehart & Winston. A survey of the research on a social learning approach to *aspects* of personality, such as frustration, aggression, and self-control.

Pervin, L. A. (1989). *Goal concepts in personality and social psychology.* Hillsdale, NJ: Erlbaum. Contains chapters on specific topics in personality (unconscious motivation, measurement of traits, and so on), written by researchers who have greatly contributed to our understanding.

CHAPTER 14

ASSESSMENT AND INDIVIDUAL DIFFERENCES

Is a man with an IQ of 80 who reads at the second-grade level capable of masterminding a complex financial fraud? The courts in England debated this question in the case of a man accused of fraud who scored this low on tests of intelligence and reading ability (Tunstall et al., 1982). Expert witnesses for the defense said it was impossible for such a person to play any significant part in planning or carrying out a complex financial operation. But prosecution experts argued that the test scores were deceptive because the defendant had dyslexia, a reading impairment caused by an abnormality in the brain. This condition, they said, made him appear less intellectually able on tests than he really was. In support of their view, they pointed out that the defendant had learned to speak four languages and regularly won large sums of money playing a complex card game called Kalookie. Could a man of truly low intelligence accomplish these things? What would you have decided if you had been on the jury that heard this case? Would you have had trouble making up your mind about what the test scores meant? If so, you are beginning to understand the controversy that surrounds the use of tests to assess people's abilities.

This controversy is important because in our society so much often hinges on the results of tests. Americans are among the most extensively tested people in the world (National Academy of Sciences, 1982). Tests are used in industry, hospitals and clinics, the military, and schools. Mental health professionals use them to diagnose psychological problems, help determine treatments, make evaluations for court cases, and assess disabilities (Piotrowski and Keller, 1989). In our public schools alone, more than 250 million standardized tests are given each year to measure academic abilities, perceptual and motor skills, emotional and social characteristics, and vocational interests and talent (Bersoff, 1980). You may take a dozen such tests yourself by the time you graduate from college. If you want to continue your education, more testing is needed. Medical schools require you to take the Medical College Admissions Test, law schools the Law School Aptitude Test, and graduate schools the Graduate Record Examinations. Graduates of professional schools must then take further tests to be certified to practice in their fields. Poor performance at any point in this extensive testing process can seriously jeopardize a career.

Psychologists stress both the virtues of testing and its inherent limitations. On the one hand, tests can tell whether someone has mastered a body of information. They can also help diagnose a less than obvious problem, such as identifying a child who is so far ahead of his class that he has lost interest in the curriculum and simply daydreams. On the other hand, tests must be used with caution. Many written tests place so much emphasis on language ability that it is hard for some people (such as dyslexics) to show what they really know. Tests may also overlook certain factors that are often important to success, such as creativity, motivation, and a willingness to cooperate with others.

At several points in this chapter we will look in more detail at the pros and cons of testing. But first we consider what is involved in constructing and evaluating a good test. What characteristics must a test have to be an accurate measurement device? We then turn to some of the specific types of tests that psychologists have developed, including intelligence tests, personality tests, tests to help people choose careers, and tests to screen job applicants. Finally, we discuss some of the ethical issues that surround testing.

CONSTRUCTING AND EVALUATING TESTS

An ad in the newspaper calls for a camp counselor to tutor emotionally disturbed children in math. You are a math major with a psychology minor, so this appears to be the perfect summer job for you. When you go to apply, you, along with the other applicants, are asked to take two tests. One assesses your knowledge of math, the other your emotional maturity. Does this seem like a good way to select counselors for the camp? Is this procedure fair to the applicants as well as in the best interests of the children who will be tutored? A great deal depends on how the tests were constructed and evaluated. A good test must be properly standardized and also both reliable and valid.

STANDARDIZATION

In the process of **standardization,** uniform procedures for giving and scoring a test are developed. Ideally, all people who take the test are subject to identical conditions—the same directions, the same materials, the same time limits, and so forth. If you were given only fifteen minutes to take each test for the tutoring job, while someone else had half an hour, the administration of the test would not be standardized. Without such standardized conditions it would be impossible to say that different scores are not just a reflection of different testing situations.

Standardization also involves establishing **norms,** or standards of performance for the test. This is done by administering the test to a large group of people representative of those for whom the test is intended and then determining the distribution of their scores. These norms tell us if subsequent scores are high, low, or in the middle range. It is essential that the group used to establish norms is representative of *all* those who will later be tested, otherwise subsequent scores may seem misleadingly high or low. For instance, if the test you take to determine your math ability was standardized on a group of junior high school students, your score would probably be deceptively high if you are a college sophomore. Similarly, the IQ of a child from a very poor family might be misleadingly low if the intelligence test given was normed on privileged, upper-middle-class youngsters. To avoid the problem of unrepresentative norms, many tests are developed with norms for people of different ages, ethnic backgrounds, and social classes.

RELIABILITY

A test is considered **reliable** if it consistently yields the same results. With an *un*reliable test, the same person may score very high on one occasion and very low on another, even though the two occasions are close together in time. These fluctuations tell us that such a test is tapping more than just the relatively stable traits it is designed to measure. Unwanted, variable influences are distorting the results.

Researchers have developed several procedures for measuring reliability. One is called **test–retest.** The same people take the test twice, and if their two scores are very similar, the test is considered reliable. One problem with test–retest is interpreting the meaning of the second score, for perhaps people are simply recalling the answers they gave before. To avoid this problem, the test can be given in two separate but equivalent forms, or the **split-halves** method can be used. With the split-halves method, the test items are randomly divided into two halves, and a person's scores on the two halves are correlated. If the test is reliable, the correlation coefficient should be about +.90, a very strong positive relationship. This measure of reliability is sometimes called

internal consistency. A test is internally consistent if a person responds much the same way to items that measure the same thing.

Of course, few tests are ever 100 percent reliable. People perform differently on different occasions for any number of reasons. A person may feel alert one day and drowsy another, ill one week and healthy the next. These unwanted sources of variation are hard to eliminate. A good test, however, is designed to make sure that nothing about the test itself—how it is given or how it is scored—contributes to individual inconsistencies in performance.

VALIDITY

Test reliability assures us that we have established reasonably consistent measures, ones that will not be distorted by variable influences within our power to control. An important aspect of test evaluation still remains, however. Are we sure our test is really measuring what we want it to measure? In other words, is it **valid?** In the case of the tests you take for the job of tutoring emotionally disturbed children, it is important to know if those who have previously been selected on the basis of these tests have done well in the job. Perhaps a math ability test identifies those who are skillful at math, but not those who can teach it the best. If so, that test is not valid for this particular use.

Validity can be assessed in several ways. One way considers **criterion validity.** Criterion validity is important for tests that are trying to identify people who have a specific trait or ability. The test validators determine the correlation between a person's score on the test and some other yardstick of the factor that the test presumably measures. For example, a psychologist might validate a paper-and-pencil test of depression by comparing the scores obtained on that test with the judgments of trained clinicians. Similarly, on-the-job performance might be used to validate the results of the tests for the math tutoring job. The measure against which the test scores are compared is called the criterion, hence the term *criterion validity.*

As the two examples given show, two kinds of criteria may be used to validate a test: a criterion immediately available and one measured in the future. If a test is validated by demonstrating a correlation with a criterion immediately available, it is said to have **concurrent validity.** A paper-and-pencil test of depression has concurrent validity if scores on it correlate highly with the professional opinions of clinical psychologists who simultaneously observe the patients. But if this other criterion is available, why develop the test? One reason is that a short paper-and-pencil test is convenient and economical to use. Second, once such a test has been validated, it can be given when alternative criteria are *not* available.

Sometimes an investigator is interested less in whether test scores correlate with other currently available criteria than in whether the scores are related to people's future performance. What types of students are likely to be successful in college? Which job applicants are likely to make an important contribution to the company? If test results can help answer such questions, the tests are said to have **predictive validity.** It takes many years of research to demonstrate predictive validity. The developers of the Scholastic Aptitude Test (SAT), for example, have invested a great deal of time and effort to establish that test's predictive validity regarding college grades.

The subject of test validity will come up again when we talk about public concerns over IQ testing. First, however, you need to know more about intelligence tests. We begin by exploring what intelligence is and how different psychologists have defined it. This is important because a researcher's definition of intelligence greatly affects how he or she tries to measure it.

MEASURING INTELLIGENCE

WHAT IS INTELLIGENCE?

We are all quick to size up people in terms of their intelligence. When you start a new class, for instance, you probably mentally categorize your classmates as smart, not so smart, and somewhere in between. But how, exactly, do you make these assessments? Why do you perceive one person to be intelligent and another not?

One group of researchers tried to answer this question by asking hundreds of people to list the behaviors they thought characterized intelligence (Sternberg et al., 1981). (If you were asked to do so, what behaviors would you list?) The researchers found much agreement between the answers of ordinary people like yourself and those of psychologists who specialize in studying intelligence. Many of the

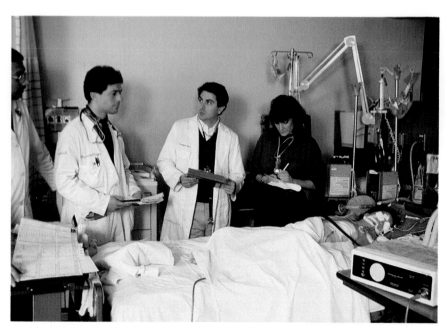

Will applicants who score high on medical school admissions tests make good doctors or good students? Testing alone can't identify the personal qualities that will affect the performance of even the highest scoring test-takers.

behaviors listed fell into two categories: *problem-solving abilities* ("sees all aspects of a problem," "poses problems in an optimal way," "gets to the heart of problems," "makes good decisions") and *verbal abilities* ("has a good vocabulary," "reads with high comprehension," "is verbally fluent," "converses easily," "is well read"). These researchers concluded that a definition of intelligence should encompass both these key categories. Consequently, we define **intelligence** as the capacities to acquire and retain knowledge and to understand concepts and relationships, capacities that an intelligent person uses effectively when solving problems and communicating.

But this definition still leaves unanswered some important questions about intelligence. One is how many basic cognitive abilities intelligence entails. More than just problem-solving and verbal abilities? And is there also a *general* intelligence factor that underlies *all* our cognitive skills? These questions are central to researchers who use a statistical technique called **factor analysis** to study intelligence.

THE FACTOR-ANALYSIS APPROACH

The factor-analysis approach is based on the assumption that intelligence has various components referred to as **factors**. Researchers try to identify these factors by giving people different kinds of mental

tests and calculating the correlations among the scores. Through factor analysis they then determine which groups of scores tend to cluster together—that is, they identify groups of tests on which people tend to perform similarly. Next, they make educated guesses as to what underlying factors explain the clusters. For instance, if strong positive correlations exist between scores on tests of vocabulary, sentence completion, and paragraph comprehension, researchers might hypothesize that all three reflect the underlying factor of verbal ability.

Different researchers have drawn different conclusions about the particular factors that are involved in intelligence. Some believe that a general intelligence factor exists, one that is measured by every item on an intelligence test. A leading proponent of this view was the British educational psychologist Charles Spearman (1927). His factor analyses suggested that scores on a wide variety of mental tests are to some extent related. That is, many people who score high on tests of verbal ability also do fairly well on tests of mathematical reasoning, spatial-perceptual skills, and so forth. Spearman concluded that a general intelligence factor, which he called the **g factor,** accounts for these positive correlations. Spearman's influence can be seen in contemporary IQ tests that yield a single score indicating *general* intelligence.

Older people tend to perform well on tests of crystallized intelligence, which represents what they have learned from experience over the years.

The idea of general intelligence was given a new twist by psychologist Raymond Cattell (1971). He wanted to explain why a person's IQ is influenced by both heredity and environment. Cattell proposed that there are two g factors, gf (for *fluid intelligence*) and gc (for *crystallized intelligence*). Fluid intelligence is the ability to reason abstractly, to make inferences from data, and to understand relationships. Analogy problems and problems in classification largely measure fluid intelligence. According to Cattell, fluid intelligence is strongly influenced by heredity. Crystallized intelligence, in contrast, is built up from what a person learns and retains from experience, and so is strongly influenced by environment. Tests of vocabulary size and general information largely measure crystallized intelligence. Since tasks on IQ tests demand the use of both fluid and crystallized intelligence, a person's IQ is affected by heredity as well as environment. Interestingly, performance on tests of fluid intelligence tends to decline in later adulthood, probably due to changes in the aging brain. But performance on tests of crystallized intelligence keeps on improving, at least until the age of sixty or so (Horn, 1982). This is not surprising when you consider that older adults continue to learn new information.

Not all researchers who have conducted factor analyses have agreed with the concept of a g factor.

One who took a different view was the American psychologist Louis Thurstone (1938). His factor analysis of scores from fifty-six different cognitive tests suggested that there are seven major intelligence factors, each relatively independent of the others. The seven factors and the kinds of tests used to measure them are shown in Table 14.1. Thurstone's influence can be seen in modern IQ tests that produce not one but several scores, each for a different mental ability. After a massive factor analysis, another researcher, J. P. Guilford (1982), proposed no fewer than 150 separate cognitive abilities.

Whose factor analysis provides the most accurate picture of human intelligence? Unfortunately, even after years of study, psychologists still cannot come to a consensus. The reason is that different mathematical techniques, each equally valid, can produce different results and lead to different conclusions (Gardner, 1983). Consequently, it is hard to decide whose ideas about the factors underlying intelligence are best.

THE INFORMATION-PROCESSING VIEW

For many years, factor analysis dominated research into human intelligence. But then, as the cognitive perspective gained ground in psychology, researchers began to look more closely at *how* people think and reason intelligently. They wanted to know

TABLE 14.1   Thurstone's Seven Primary Mental Abilities

Ability	Measure
Verbal comprehension	Test of vocabulary
Verbal fluency	Test that requires listing in a limited time as many words as possible that start with a given letter
Inductive reasoning	Tests of analogies and number series
Spatial visualization	Tests requiring mental rotation of pictures of objects
Number	Tests of computation and simple mathematical problem solving
Memory	Tests of pictures and word recall
Perceptual speed	Tests that require finding small differences in pictures

what goes on in a person's mind when solving a problem or performing some other cognitive task. This subject became the focus of researchers who took an **information-processing view** of intelligence.

Robert Sternberg (1984, 1985), a leader in this field, has tried to identify the mental operations involved in answering questions on intelligence tests. Chief among these are the operations involved in planning a strategy, monitoring its appropriateness, and evaluating the quality of the solution that is reached. Sternberg has found that a good test taker spends more time than a poor one in analyzing and understanding a problem before trying to solve it. This finding contradicts the common-sense assumption that someone who is good at taking tests works on problems quickly. Apparently, correct answers do not just leap into the minds of people who score high on intelligence tests. Instead, they do well by taking the time to analyze each question thoroughly.

Sternberg has suggested that psychologists try to develop intelligence tests which measure some of the mental operations that underlie "intelligent" thinking. Such tests would be quite different from the intelligence tests now in use, all of which are essentially based on the factor-analysis conception of intelligence. We will say more about new directions in intelligence testing later in this chapter. But before we do, we will take a look at the early history of intelligence testing and the major intelligence tests being used today.

THE EARLY HISTORY OF INTELLIGENCE TESTING

The idea for intelligence testing originated with an English scientist, Francis Galton (1822–1911). Galton, the youngest of seven children, was born into a distinguished family descended from the eminent physician and poet Erasmus Darwin (Fancher, 1985). Galton's precocious childhood led to high academic expectations that he never fulfilled to his satisfaction. Puzzled by his lack of distinction at boarding school and Cambridge, he concluded that he simply lacked the innate ability for intellectual brilliance. So he quit his academic career and became an African explorer and geographer. In the course of his travels, he made a study of ethnic diversity in psychological characteristics.

In 1859 Galton's half-cousin, Charles Darwin, published his theory of evolution in the book *On the Origin of Species*. Although Darwin wrote about the evolution of physical traits, Galton believed that psychological traits (such as intelligence and moral character) were genetically inherited too, and so capable of evolving. This idea led him to take up the cause of *eugenics*, the effort to improve the human species through selective breeding. Since Galton believed that superior ability could be passed from eminent parents to their children, he needed a way to identify young adults who were destined to become eminent. So he tried to devise a test to predict eminence in middle age. The high-scoring men and women could then be encouraged to marry one another and produce potentially eminent children.

Galton's test consisted of measures of reaction time, sensory acuity, physical energy, and head size, all of which he thought indicated differences in brain efficiency and thus in native intelligence. He set up a laboratory in a London museum where he tested thousands of people and kept records of the results. He hoped that the government would eventually provide a register (a "golden book of natural nobility") of all the highly intelligent and marriageable people in the country. But the predictive power of Galton's test was disappointing. High scores failed to correlate with more accepted indicators of intelligence or with actual accomplishments.

Though Galton's testing procedures were flawed and his theory questionable, he did establish the concept of the intelligence test, which subsequent researchers took further. Alfred Binet (1857–1911), a gifted and versatile French psychologist, was the first to develop a valid intelligence test. Binet's research on the measurement of children's intelligence, the work for which he is best known today, came at the end of a career that included degrees in both law and medicine and the writing of plays, psychological treatises, and books on hypnosis, zoology, and chess (Miller, 1962).

Binet's work departed markedly from prevailing methods of measuring intelligence. Like Galton, most psychologists at the time thought that people with high intelligence are likely to have keen motor and perceptual skills. After all, we come to learn everything we know by moving and perceiving in the world. So they set about testing such things as people's ability to estimate the passage of time, the efficiency of their hand–eye coordination, and their speed at finger tapping. Binet conducted these perceptual-motor tests on his two young daughters and found that when they paid close attention to the tasks they could duplicate the performance of adults. He concluded that these tests must not be good measures of adult intellectual abilities. Intelligence could be assessed only by examining the far more complex processes of memory, mental imagery, comprehension, and judgment (Kail and Pellegrino, 1985).

Binet and his assistants spent many hours administering various kinds of tests to a large number of schoolchildren. They found that cognitive tests did in fact work better than tests of motor skills in differentiating students who were successful in the classroom from those who were not. They also found that performance varied partly as a function of age. An average seven-year-old, for instance, would perform just the same as a slow learner considerably older, while a very bright seven-year-old would match the performance of an average older child. Binet reasoned that children whose performance surpassed that of others their age must be mentally older—more intelligent—than their peers.

By the early twentieth century the French educational system had taken a turn that would put Binet's research to use. The Minister of Public Instruction for the Paris schools wanted to develop a test that could differentiate between normally intelligent children and those who required special help. If educators had this information, he reasoned, all children could be educated according to their abilities and needs. Misdiagnosis of subnormal intelligence could also be better avoided, a goal that was very important to Binet. So in 1905, in collaboration with psychiatrist Theodore Simon, Binet introduced the world's first standardized intelligence test, consisting of thirty items arranged in order of increasing difficulty.

Binet originally defined as retarded any child whose score was two years or more below the average for all children of that age. One problem with that definition, however, was that children aged twelve who were two years behind their age group were considered just as retarded as children aged six who were two years behind their peers. Yet the six-year-olds would seem, intuitively, to be *more* retarded because the two-year disparity between them and their peers is a larger proportion of the children's total age. A German psychologist, William Stern (1914), suggested a solution: instead of using the absolute difference between mental age and chronological age, testers should use the *ratio* between the two ages. This idea resulted in the **intelligence quotient, or IQ.** It is computed by dividing a child's mental age (the average age of those who obtain that child's score) by the child's chronological age and then multiplying by 100 to eliminate the decimal point. If, for example, a child has a mental age of twelve and a chronological age of ten, his or her IQ is $12/10 \times 100$, or 120.

Binet did not regard a child's score on his test as a fixed measure of intelligence (Fancher, 1985; Kamin, 1974). For one thing, the construction of the test was subject to error. It was not a perfect measurement device. In addition, Binet believed that few people ever reach the upper limits of their intelligence, so improvement is always possible through education and experience. But this enlightened and cautious view has not always been shared by the educators who have used Binet's tests through the years.

One of those who considered IQ to be a fixed measure of innate intelligence was Lewis Terman, a professor at Stanford University (Baron, 1985). Terman is responsible for bringing Binet's test to America in a revised form known as the **Stanford-Binet** (Terman, 1916). Terman made the scoring of the test more exact and added some new items, but in other respects it closely resembled Binet's test. Terman's version (now in its fourth edition) is still widely used today.

An enthusiastic believer in eugenics, Terman regarded his test as particularly useful in diagnosing

Two tests of the Stanford-Binet Intelligence Scale being administered to a little boy. He would easily pass both tests unless he were severely retarded. In a performance test (*left*), the examiner has built a tower of four blocks and has told the child, "You make one like this." In a verbal ability test (*right*), the examiner shows the child a card with six small objects attached to it and says, "See all these things? Show me the dog," and so on.

borderline mental "defectives" so that they could be discouraged from having children and passing on their defective genes. He believed this would eliminate "an enormous amount of crime, pauperism, and industrial inefficiency" (quoted in Kamin, 1974, p. 392). Such views, shared by many other psychologists in the early part of this century, led a number of states to adopt sterilization laws in order to prevent the "feeble-minded" from reproducing.

During World War I the government called on psychologists to administer intelligence tests to almost 2 million army recruits. The tremendous amount of data obtained encouraged a great many studies. Perhaps the most controversial was conducted by Carl Brigham (1923), who focused on the IQs of immigrant draftees. Because he found that those born in Slavic and Latin countries performed much worse than those born in Scandinavian and English-speaking countries, he concluded that some ethnic groups were intellectually inferior to others. This assumption helped sway Congress to severely restrict immigration from southern and eastern Europe. Unfortunately, Brigham had not taken into account how long each group of immigrants had lived in America. Those recruits born in southern and eastern Europe were generally more recent arrivals than those born in northern Europe, a fact which would surely have affected their relative performances on an American

IQ test. Although Brigham retracted his conclusion in 1930, by then the new immigration act had been in force for six years (Kamin, 1974).

Thus the early years of intelligence testing were filled with incidents in which IQ scores were misinterpreted and misapplied. And six decades later we are still concerned about the potential abuses of IQ testing, a topic we will return to shortly. First, however, we will look at the tests themselves.

CONTEMPORARY INTELLIGENCE TESTS

INDIVIDUAL TESTS

Individual intelligence tests are given to only one person at a time. As a result, the test taker can answer oral questions and work on performance tasks (in which objects are manipulated) which would be hard to administer to a large number of people simultaneously. Two individual intelligence tests that are widely used today are the current version of the Stanford-Binet and the intelligence scales developed by David Wechsler.

The Stanford-Binet Test The fourth edition of the Stanford-Binet Intelligence Scale (Thorndike et al., 1985) is designed to assess the intelligence of children and adults who range in age from two to twenty-four. The Stanford-Binet contains a number of subtests, some of verbal ability and some of performance skills, that are grouped together by age level. The performance subtests include such activities as completing a drawing, reproducing a geometric pattern with colored blocks, and assembling an object.

Because the Stanford-Binet was originally designed for school-age children, the development of an adult version created a scoring problem. After early adolescence the pace of improvement on the test items slows, yet chronological age proceeds as always. Thus, if we applied the mental age divided by chronological age formula to adults, their IQs would inevitably decrease just because they were growing older. The solution to this problem was simple. Researchers assigned a score of 100 to the mean or average performance at any given age. Then they used standard deviation as a yardstick for measuring just how much better or worse than average a particular person did. Remember from Chapter 2 that the standard deviation indicates the average extent to which all scores in a given distribution vary from the mean. In the case of intelligence tests like the Stanford-Binet, the standard deviation is about 15. Consequently, a person who scores one standard deviation above the mean would receive an intelligence score of 115, someone who scores one standard deviation below the mean would receive an intelligence score of 85, and so on. Often, these scores are still called IQs, even though they are technically no longer quotients. But it is more accurate to think of them as standard-deviation-from-the-mean scores. Psychologists use the much shorter term *standard score.*

The Wechsler Scales The most frequently used individual intelligence tests are the **Wechsler scales.** They are also among the most reliable and valid tests used in clinical assessment (Parker et al., 1988). These tests include the Wechsler Adult Intelligence Scale (WAIS-R); the Wechsler Intelligence Scale for Children (WISC-R), used for ages six to sixteen; and the Wechsler Preschool and Primary Scale of Intelligence (WPPSI-R), used for ages four to six (Wechsler, 1949, 1955, 1967, 1974, 1981, 1989). Each of these tests has been revised and updated, hence the initial R in the names.

Like the Stanford-Binet, the Wechsler scales have verbal and performance parts, each with various subtests. Figure 14.1 lists some typical questions from

General Information
1. How many wings does a bird have?
2. How many nickels make a dime?
3. What is steam made of?
4. Who wrote "Paradise Lost"?
5. What is pepper?

General Comprehension
1. What should you do if you see someone forget his book when he leaves his seat in a restaurant?
2. What is the advantage of keeping money in a bank?
3. Why is copper often used in electrical wires?

Arithmetic
1. Sam had three pieces of candy and Joe gave him four more. How many pieces of candy did Sam have altogether?
2. Three men divided eighteen golf balls equally among themselves. How many golf balls did each man receive?
3. If two apples cost 15¢, what will be the cost of a dozen apples?

Similarities
1. In what way are a lion and a tiger alike?
2. In what way are a saw and a hammer alike?
3. In what way are an hour and a week alike?
4. In what way are a circle and a triangle alike?

Vocabulary
"What is a puzzle?"
"What does 'addition' mean?"

FIGURE 14.1   Tests similar to those in the various Wechsler intelligence scales. The questions are examples of five of the verbal subtests.

the verbal subtests. The performance subtests include picture arrangement (putting pictures in an order that tells a story), picture completion (identifying the missing part in a drawing), object assembly (constructing an object from various pieces, much like putting together a jigsaw puzzle), and coding (matching digits with the symbols they were previously paired with).

The Wechsler scales differ from the Stanford-Binet in several ways. For one thing, they include more performance tasks and so are less biased toward verbal skills. For another, the Stanford-Binet yields a single IQ score, whereas the Wechsler scales give separate scores for the various subtests, which are then combined into separate IQs for verbal and

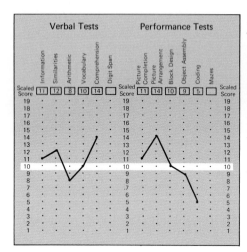

FIGURE 14.2   A simplified version of a WISC-R profile of a thirteen-year-old boy. (The digit span and mazes subscales—both optional—were not administered.) Scores on the subscales within the verbal and performance groupings are first converted into special scaled scores and plotted accordingly on the chart. Then individual subtest scores are added together, yielding a total verbal and a total performance score. Finally, the full-scale score is converted into the full-scale IQ score—in this case determining specific talents or deficits that might not have been apparent if only the overall IQ scores were reported. (*Adapted from WISC-R record form, © 1971, 1974, The Psychological Corporation.*)

	Scaled Score	IQ
Verbal Score	55	106
Performance Score	49	98
Full Scale Score	104	103

performance abilities. The scoring procedure for the WISC-R is summarized in Figure 14.2.

GROUP TESTS

Most group tests of intelligence are paper-and-pencil measures. There is no person-to-person interaction, as with individual tests, so the role of the test administrator is greatly simplified. The convenience and the economy of group tests have led to their use in schools, employment offices, and many other mass testing situations. One of the primary purposes of group tests is to classify large numbers of people. For example, the American military uses group tests to assess the general intelligence and special abilities of its recruits so they can be channeled into appropriate jobs.

Despite their economy, group tests have disadvantages. It is difficult to put the subjects at ease and to maintain their interest. The examiner is also unlikely to detect illness, fatigue, anxiety, or other variables that may hinder test performance. As a result, most experts suggest that, when important decisions about people are being made, scores on group tests be supplemented by individual testing or by information obtained from other sources (Anastasi, 1976; Baumaster, 1987).

College admissions officers generally heed this advice regarding the group test that many college-bound students takes: the **Scholastic Aptitude Test,** or **SAT.** Although the SAT is designed to measure aptitude for college, not a person's IQ, it measures some of the abilities often included on IQ tests. Studies show that college admissions staffs consider SAT scores as just one of several pieces of information, along with high school grades, letters of recommendation, and personal interviews. One survey found that only 2 percent of all colleges considered aptitude scores the most important factor in admissions choices (Hargadon, 1981). But this finding has not prevented critics from attacking the SAT. What is it about this test that some people find so objectionable?

Allan Nairn and his associates (1980), in cooperation with Ralph Nader's consumer advocacy group, launched one of the harshest attacks. Nairn argued that the SAT discriminates against minorities. Success on the test, he claimed, is more a product of an upper-middle-class background than a reflection of scholastic aptitude. Nairn also charged that the SAT is not a good predictor of success in college, a criticism that others have raised too. One recent study concluded that SAT scores add little or nothing over high school records as a basis for college admissions (Crouse and Trusheim, 1988).

But some knowledgeable statisticians have challenged these highly negative views (Kaplan, 1982; Linn, 1982). The correlation between SAT verbal and math scores and freshman grade-point average is in the range of +.40, far from insignificant. Moreover, there is little convincing evidence that the SAT is unfairly biased against minorities. The predictive validity of the test is quite consistent across income and ethnic groups (Linn, 1982). In fact, use of the SAT

Many people turn to study guides that promise to help them do better on group tests used to screen applicants to graduate and professional schools.

may actually *raise* the proportion of low-income students entering selective colleges, because it gives those who attend academically inferior high schools the chance to demonstrate superior aptitude in comparison with all college applicants (ETS, 1980; Kaplan, 1982).

There are two other reasons why use of the SAT may be fairer than its elimination. First, when high school grades and SAT scores are used *together* to predict performance in college, their combined power surpasses that of either yardstick alone (Kaplan, 1982; Linn, 1982). This makes sense. Two methods of measurement, neither of which is perfect, are bound to produce better judgments than one of them alone. Second, the SAT provides a way of demonstrating the scholastic potential of people who believe that their high school grades are misleadingly low. If the college entrance exams were abandoned, these applicants would lose an important second chance to prove themselves.

In recent years the development of private coaching services to raise SAT scores has further fueled the debate over these tests. Some people reason that, if coaching can improve results on the SAT, the test must be invalid, for it is supposed to measure innate abilities. This view reflects a total misunderstanding of what the SAT gauges. The SAT does not measure a fixed intellectual capacity, but rather skills in verbal

comprehension and mathematical reasoning that develop over many years of learning (Messick, 1980). These abilities *can* be improved by instruction. The instruction must be extensive, however. Short-term coaching is unlikely to make much of a difference. For instance, it has been estimated that boosting a person's SAT score by just thirty points (about three more correct answers) requires 45 hours of coaching for the math section and 260 hours of coaching for the verbal (Messick and Jungeblut, 1981). The average coaching service, therefore, is not apt to have much of an impact on SAT results (Kulik et al., 1984). Whatever small effects coaching does have are rarely enough to change the decisions of college admissions boards (Der Simonian and Laird, 1983).

Coaching will also have little impact on the *revised* SAT, scheduled to be put into use beginning in 1994. On the revised version, some of the math questions will no longer be multiple choice, which means that students can no longer be taught how to get some right answers simply by making educated guesses. The revised SAT will also have longer reading comprehension passages, with questions that focus more on overall context rather than on specific facts. In addition, students will be given more time per question, and for the first time they will be allowed to use calculators for the math section. The test developers are optimistic that the new SAT will be

Psychologists who study intelligence are beginning to realize that intelligence may include skills, such as the body abilities of dancers and athletes, that traditional IQ tests do not measure. (*Left*, Mikail Baryshnikov. *Right*, Allan Trammel)

as good or better than the old one at predicting success in college, but it will be many years before they are able to demonstrate this predictive validity (Moses, 1991).

NEW DIRECTIONS IN INTELLIGENCE TESTING

One of today's most prominent researchers in intelligence testing, Howard Gardner, argues that traditional IQ tests tell only part of the story. After observing the different ways that intelligence is defined in different cultures, Gardner has suggested that it has seven different components, most of which are not being gauged at all on traditional IQ tests (Gardner, 1986; Gardner and Hatch, 1989). These tests measure, at best, only three components: language ability, mathematical-logical reasoning, and spatial-perceptual skills. The other four components in Gardner's theory are musical ability (the ability to per-

ceive and create rhythmic patterns), bodily ability (the ability possessed by a prima ballerina or a skilled mime), intrapersonal ability (the ability to understand oneself), and interpersonal ability (the ability to understand others). To get a full picture of a person's cognitive capacities, Gardner says, we need to tap all these different skills that the brain controls.

Psychologist Robert Sternberg also believes that we must try to broaden what intelligence tests measure (Sternberg, 1984, 1988). Sternberg lists a number of capacities that are part of what we generally mean by intelligence but that are not included on standard IQ tests. One is the ability to adapt to novel or unexpected situations, such as quickly finding a way to an important appointment on a morning when your car breaks down (Sternberg and Gastel, 1989). Another is the capacity to have sudden insights when solving problems, such as suddenly seeing a link between the current problem and another you have solved before. A third is the ability to learn from

A Different Sort of I.Q. Test

Standard I.Q. tests measure, in the main, two varieties of intelligence—verbal and logical-mathematical. But according to critics like Robert Sternberg, a Yale psychologist, tests should measure other key elements of intelligence, such as insight. The first two questions on this quiz, which is taken from Dr. Sternberg's book "Intelligence Applied," are standard I.Q. questions that he says rely for their answers on specific skills a child learns in school. But the other questions, he says, measure the sort of intelligence not found on standard I.Q. tests and depend for answers on such mental skills as insight, thinking in novel ways and detecting fallacies. The answers appear below.

STANDARD I.Q. QUESTIONS:

1. *TENNIS is to RACQUET as BASEBALL is to:*
   a. Club
   b. Strike
   c. Bat
   d. Home run

2. *In the following series, what number comes next?* 3, 7, 12, 18 -
   a. 24
   b. 25
   c. 26
   d. 27

INSIGHT QUESTIONS

3. Aeronautical engineers have made it possible for a supersonic jet fighter to catch up with the bullets fired from its own guns with sufficient speed to shoot itself down. If a plane, flying at 1,000 miles an hour, fires a burst, the rounds leave the plane with an initial velocity of about 3,000 miles an hour. Why won't a plane that continues to fly straight ahead overtake and fly into its own bullets?

4. If you have black socks and brown socks in your drawer, mixed in a ratio of 4 to 5, how many socks will you have to take out to make sure of having a pair of the same color?

5. In the Thompson family, there are five brothers, and each brother has one sister. If you count Mrs. Thompson, how many females are there in the Thompson family?

NOVEL THINKING QUESTIONS

In solving the following analogies, assume that the statement given before the analogy is true, whether it actually is true or not, and use that assumption to solve the analogy.

6. *LAKES are dry.*
TRAIL is to HIKE as LAKE is to:
   a. Swim
   b. Dust
   c. Water
   d. Walk

7. *DEER attack tigers.*
LION is to COURAGEOUS as DEER is to:
   a. Timid
   b. Aggressive
   c. Cougar
   d. Elk

8. *DIAMONDS are fruits.*
PEARL is to OYSTER as DIAMOND is to:
   a. Mine
   b. Tree
   c. Ring
   d. Pie

INFERENCE QUESTIONS

The following problems require detecting the relationship between the first two items, and finding a parallel relationship between the second two. In answering, explain what those relationships are.

9. *VANILLA is to BEAN as TEA is to LEAF.*

10. *ATOM is to MOLECULE as CELL is to ORGANISM.*

11. *UNICORN is to SINGLE as DUET is to BICYCLE.*

12. *NOON is to EVE as 12.21 is to 10:01.*

ANSWERS

1. c
2. b
3. Gravity pulls the bullets down; thus unless a pilot consciously dives to run into the bullets, they will not hit the plane.
4. Three.
5. Two. The only females in the family are the mother and her daughter, who is the sister to each of her brothers.
6. d.
7. b.
8. b.
9. Vanilla comes from a bean, and tea from a leaf.
10. Atoms combine to form a molecule, cells combine to form an organism.
11. A unicorn and a single both refer to one of something, a duet and a bicycle both refer to two of something.
12. Each of the terms of the analogy is the same forward and backward.

FIGURE 14.3   These questions test abilities that are not measured by most IQ tests. (*After Goleman, *1986/© 1986 by the New York Times Company. Reprinted by permission.*)

context, not just from direct instruction (for example, figuring out the meaning of an unfamiliar word from the sentence in which it is used). And a fourth is the capacity to perform different tasks at once, as when someone carries on an intricate conversation while continuing to repair a broken toy (Hawkins et al., 1979; Lansman and Hunt, 1980). Examples of questions that tap some of these abilities are given in Figure 14.3. If these capacities are part of what we generally mean by intelligence, why not include them in IQ tests, Sternberg asks. He hopes that future tests of human intelligence will do just that.

EXTREMES OF HUMAN INTELLIGENCE

When large numbers of people take IQ tests, their scores form close to normal distributions. That is, when plotted on a line graph, they produce the characteristic bell-shaped curve we described in Chapter 2. Such a curve is shown in Figure 14.4. As

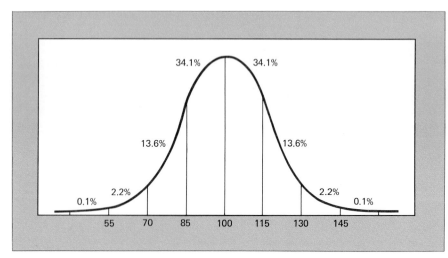

FIGURE 14.4 The normal distribution of IQ scores when large numbers of people are tested. The normal range of IQ scores is considered to be 85 to 115, with a mean score of 100. Over 95 percent of any large population tested will score between 70 and 130.

you can see, about 68 percent of all scores fall somewhere between the mean (100) and one standard deviation (15 points) to either side of it. That range of scores, 85 to 115, is generally considered the "normal" range. If we move one more standard deviation to either side of the mean, we encompass all the scores between 70 and 130. More than 95 percent of a large sample population falls within this range. Most of those who score between 70 and 85 are considered low normal, while most of those scoring between 115 and 130 are considered high normal. Beyond these scores are a small number of people of exceptionally low or exceptionally high intelligence. That tiny fraction of the population is the subject to which we turn next.

THE MENTALLY RETARDED

A person whose general intelligence has from childhood been significantly below average and who chronically has trouble functioning in everyday settings is usually classified as **mentally retarded** (Grossman, 1983). Different levels of retardation have traditionally been associated with certain ranges of scores on standardized IQ tests. Those who score between 70 and 50 on the Stanford-Binet have traditionally been classified as mildly retarded, those with scores between 49 and 35 as moderately retarded, those with scores between 34 and 20 as severely retarded, and those with scores below 20 as pro-

foundly retarded. You should not view these IQ ranges rigidly, however. A person's ability to function in everyday life is important to consider too. For instance, children whose test scores suggest moderate retardation, but who show some everyday skills (the abilities to communicate, interact socially, and feed, clean, and dress themselves), are more appropriately classified as mildly retarded. Table 14.2 lists the levels of everyday functioning associated with the different classifications of mental retardation.

The stigma of being labeled retarded has led educators to plead for greater care in evaluating children who appear to have below-normal intelligence. In the past, children from non-English-speaking families, emotionally disturbed children, and children with hearing and vision problems were sometimes mistakenly classified as retarded on the basis of a single intelligence test that was poorly chosen or administered. Federal law now prohibits school officials from assigning children to special classes for the mentally retarded on the basis of an IQ score alone. Children must be tested for normal hearing, vision, and health, and their linguistic and cultural backgrounds must be considered as well as their ability to function in everyday life. Children should be classified as retarded only if they exhibit *both* a low IQ and deficiencies in everyday skills, and only if these problems cannot be explained by linguistic or cultural barriers, physical handicaps, emotional disturbances, or ill health.

THE MENTALLY GIFTED

In our culture the genius is often expected to be a misfit, someone who has trouble coping in a world beyond test tubes and books, someone who is eccentric, socially awkward, physically frail, and prone to poor health. But in fact, this is a misleading stereotype, as studies since Lewis Terman's landmark research on the **mentally gifted** have shown.

In the early part of this century, Terman launched a study of 1,500 gifted children (Terman, 1916). His subjects, aged three to nineteen at the start of the study, all had IQs above 135. Over the years, as Terman continued to follow their development, his findings disproved most of the common myths about unusually intelligent children (Oden, 1968; Terman and Oden, 1947). Not only were gifted children generally superior to their peers in health, adjustment, and achievement, but their relative superiority continued as they moved through adulthood. They far exceeded persons with average IQs in educational attainment, occupational level, and income. In addition, their adult health and emotional adjustment were well above average. As a group, they suffered fewer divorces, fewer cases of alcoholism, less trouble with the law, and even fewer premature deaths than did people with lower IQs. Other studies have also indicated that gifted children typically are well adjusted, with fewer behavior problems than their less gifted peers (Horowitz and O'Brien, 1986).

Do these findings mean that high intelligence is a key to personal happiness and success? Not necessarily. Psychologists point out that most of Terman's subjects were originally nominated by their teachers for inclusion in the study. This selection process could easily have produced a bias in favor of bright children who were especially well adjusted, socially skilled, and motivated. We have no way of knowing whether the high-IQ children overlooked by their teachers turned out to be equally successful.

It is also possible that some other factors shared by Terman's high-IQ children could be responsible for the positive outcomes in their lives (McClellan, 1973). For instance, Terman's sample consisted heavily of middle- and upper-middle-class whites, a privileged group in our society. Perhaps his results show largely that the privileged have more opportunities than other people, and so do better in life. Interestingly, the 100 most successful men in Terman's sample

Intelligence test scores should not be the only measure of mental retardation. When the ability to function well in daily life is taken into account, many people with low IQ test scores are appropriately classified as mildly, not moderately, retarded.

(as measured by job status and income) were more likely to have had a professional father with a college education than were the 100 least successful men. In addition, the most successful tended to come from more intellectually stimulating home environments, where initiative and achievement were stressed. So maybe another critical factor in their success was early encouragement by parents.

Today's rapidly accelerated academic programs for gifted children do not seem to have any negative social or emotional effects (e.g., Fox and Washington, 1985; Stanley, 1983). This is not to say that some *very* gifted children (with IQs over 180) do not sometimes have problems of adjustment. But these problems often spring more from atypical social relations (with

TABLE 14.2   Characteristics of Mentally Retarded Children

Area of Functioning	Mild	Moderate	Severe and Profound
Self-help skills	Feeds and dresses self and cares for own toilet needs.	Has difficulties and requires training but can learn adequate self-help skills.	No skills to partial skills but some can care for personal needs on a limited basis.
Speech and communication	Receptive and expressive language is adequate. Understands communication.	Receptive and expressive language is adequate. Has speech problems.	Receptive language is limited to good. Expressive language is limited to poor.
Academics	Optimal learning environment, third to sixth grade.	Very few academic skills. First or second grade is maximal.	No academic skills.
Social skills	Has friends, can learn to adjust adequately.	Capable of making friends but has difficulties in many social situations.	Not capable of having real friends. No social interaction.
Vocational adjustment	Can hold a job. Competitive to semicompetitive. Primarily unskilled work.	Sheltered work environment. Usually needs constant supervision.	No employment for the most part. May be in an activity center. Usually needs constant care.
Adult living	Usually marries, has children. Needs help during stress.	Usually does not marry or have children. Dependent.	No marriage or children. Always dependent on others.

From Van Osdol and Shane, 1977, p. 68.

parents as well as peers) than they do from academic acceleration per se (Janos and Robinson, 1985).

A puzzle to those who study giftedness is why, in a time of greatly expanded educational and occupational opportunities, gifted women still achieve and earn less than gifted men. One answer is that many gifted women still adhere to traditional gender roles, which can lower their expectations of success in traditionally male careers and channel them into traditionally female occupations that do not use their talents fully (Eccles, 1985). If these influences are to be counteracted, parents, educators, and counselors must encourage gifted girls from an early age to broaden their horizons and consider all the career options open to them.

EXPLAINING VARIATIONS IN INTELLIGENCE

We all wonder why some people have IQs of 180, while others have intelligence in the broad "normal" range, and still others are mentally retarded. We wonder, in other words, about the causes of *individual differences* in intelligence. The answer lies in two sets of factors: hereditary and environmental. But what are the relative contributions of each to the individual differences we see? Behavioral geneticists try to answer this question by estimating IQ's *heritability factor* —that is, the proportion of the variation in intelligence that can be attributed to genetic differences in people.

It is important to understand at the outset what a heritability factor is and is not. A **heritability factor** is an estimate of genetic contributions to the individual differences in people who belong to the same population. Why did scores on the Stanford-Binet given to a group of middle-class first graders range from a low 80 to a high of 165? How much of the variation was due to genetic differences among the children and how much to environmental ones? A heritability factor helps to answer this kind of question.

But a heritability factor does *not* tell us about the relative contributions of genes and environment to any one person's development of some trait. How did Jane acquire an IQ of 140? Are her genes or her environment largely responsible? It is impossible to say. Any given person's development is always the product of *both* heredity and environment, interacting in complex ways that make it futile to try to disentan-

Well-planned academic programs challenge gifted children without putting excessive pressure on them.

gle them (Scarr and Carter-Salzman, 1982). For instance, if Jane inherits the genetic potential for high intelligence, she will probably be the kind of person who helps create for herself a stimulating environment (by asking many questions, avidly exploring new things, reading lots of books, and so forth). How could we possibly pry these interacting influences apart and assign numerical values to them?

To test your understanding of what heritability factors are, consider this fact: even if a certain heritability factor is 1.0, meaning that, in a certain population, *all* of the variation regarding that trait is due to heredity, any given person's development of the trait is still greatly influenced by environment and can always be changed by a relevant environmental change. Can you explain why this statement is true? If not, an example will help. The heritability factor for height among middle-class Americans is close to 1.0, or 100 percent. Does this high heritability factor mean that nutrition (an environmental influence) has almost nothing to do with how tall a middle-class American grows? No. The high heritability factor simply means that, given the similarity in diet among Americans of this social class, almost all the variation we see in their heights is due to differences in their genes. The height of any given person can still be affected by a change in diet, just as a person's IQ can always be affected by relevant environmental chang-

es. In fact, it is estimated that a person inherits the potential for an IQ that can vary by as much as 20 to 25 points depending on environmental influences (Cronbach, 1975; Scarr-Salapatek, 1971). Thus, even when a heritability factor is very high, the trait in question is *not* fixed and immutable. We will return to this important point a little later in this chapter. But first let us look at what heritability factors *do* tell us about IQ.

THE CAUSES OF INDIVIDUAL IQ DIFFERENCES

Over the years a huge amount of research has been devoted to determining heritability factors for individual differences in IQ. Many studies of twins, of adopted children, and of people with various degrees of blood relationships to one another have all been conducted to calculate this statistic. (See Chapter 10 for a discussion of twin studies, probably the most common method used.) Psychologists are now arriving at some consensus. Current estimates are that about 50 percent of the individual variability in IQ scores is due to genetic differences among people (Dunn and Plomin, 1990; Plomin, 1989).

This, of course, leaves an equally large influence from environment. If half the individual variability in IQ is due to genes, the remaining half (barring

Birth order may be a factor in IQ differences. First-born and only children tend to have higher IQs, possibly because of the extra time their parents can devote to guiding and encouraging them.

measurement error) *must* be due to environmental influences. The effect of the environment on intelligence often begins before birth. Ann Streissguth and her associates (1989) examined the relationship of prenatal alchohol exposure to the IQ of children at age four. They found that alcohol use during pregnancy was associated with a significant decrement in IQ, even after other factors, such as nutrition and birth weight, were considered. Also important are family experiences, such as different kinds of relationships between children and their parents. High achievers tend to have parents who provide encouragement, nurturance, and emotional support from an early age (Bloom, 1985). The family experiences that are important to intellectual achievement are not necessarily shared by all the siblings growing up in

the same home. Recent studies suggest that parents may treat each of their children quite differently, depending on each child's age, sex, temperament, talents, and number of siblings, a point we made in Chapter 10 (Dunn and Plomin, 1990). In fact, first-born children, who have a number of years "alone" with their parents, often have higher IQs than their later-born siblings (Albert, 1980; Zajonc, 1986). Of course, the family is not the only environmental factor influencing intellectual development. Each of us has different friends, different teachers, and different educational experiences. All these factors, and others, contribute to individual differences in IQ.

Today the nature–nurture issue regarding individual differences in intelligence is much less controversial than it once was. It is now quite widely accepted that genes and environment share a role in explaining individual variability in IQ (Snyderman and Rothman, 1987). More hotly debated are the reasons for certain *group* differences in IQ, especially those that exist between people of different races and ethnic backgrounds. For instance, black Americans as a group score an average of eleven to fifteen points lower on IQ tests than white Americans do. What explains this difference? The answers to this question are so important that we will explore them in depth.

IN DEPTH

The Causes of Racial IQ Differences

THE INITIAL STUDIES

In 1969 Arthur Jensen, an educational psychologist, was asked to write an article for the *Harvard Educational Review* on why compensatory education programs for minority groups had so far produced disappointing results. A number of years earlier Jensen had attended a lecture by an eminent English psychologist, Sir Cyril Burt, who specialized in studying the causes of variations in intelligence. Burt's data from 53 pairs of twins who had been raised apart suggested that, among the white population of England, individual differences in IQ were heavily influenced by heredity. His estimated heritability factors were consistently over .80. Jensen reasoned that, if variations in IQ *within* a white population were so heavily genetic in origin, perhaps the average IQ differences *between* whites and blacks were too. "It seems a not unreasonable hypothesis," Jensen wrote, "that genetic factors are strongly implicated in the average Negro–white intelligence difference" (Jensen, 1969, p. 82).

The ink was barely dry on Jensen's article before the news media began to report highly simplified and sometimes inaccurate versions of it. A piece in *Newsweek* (March 31, 1969), titled "Born Dumb?," summed up Jensen's theory as the belief that black intelligence is fixed at birth at a level far below that of whites, with the implication that no amount of compensatory schooling would ever make any difference. Jensen had actually never said this, but nearly every popular article on him drew that conclusion (Cronbach, 1975). The national political climate of the time helped fuel public outrage against him. The civil rights movement was in full swing, and just a year earlier, Martin Luther King, Jr., had been assassinated. Racial riots were erupting in cities across the country. Angry students who saw Jensen's theory as racist disrupted his speeches and classes. Jensen received so many threats of violence that the University of California, where he taught, had to hire bodyguards to protect him (Fancier, 1985).

Jensen's calmness in the midst of this storm of protest was beginning to win him respect when a related furor erupted in 1976. Investigators charged that some of the data on which Jensen's original conclusions had been based were at best questionable and possibly even fraudulent. An American psychologist, Leon Kamin (1974, 1976), and a reporter for the London *Sunday Times*, Oliver Gillie, carefully examined Sir Cyril Burt's published findings and discovered peculiarities in some of the figures. For one thing, identical correlations between twins' IQ scores (to three decimal places) kept showing up, regardless of how many new sets of twins were added to Burt's sample. The odds against this happening even once are many millions to one, but in Burt's research it happened twenty times (Gillie, 1977). In addition, it was impossible to locate two of Burt's alleged collaborators, who he said were responsible for collecting much of the raw data. Why, if these collaborators really existed, couldn't they be found?

People began to wonder if Burt had deliberately faked his findings. More evidence came in 1979 in a biography of Burt commissioned by his sister after his death. Searching through Burt's files, Les-

lie Hearnshaw, the biographer, could find no raw data whatsoever from studies of twins. He also discovered that during Burt's retirement, when he was supposedly testing many newly found pairs of twins raised apart, his detailed diaries made no mention of such testing. Equally indicting were the diary entries for the period immediately following a request by psychologist Christopher Jencks for Burt's raw data on the fifty-three pairs of raised-apart twins that he had presumably studied. Burt spent an entire week "calculating" the figures, which strongly suggests that he was fabricating them, not just making copies of his records. There was also no indication in Burt's private papers of contact with the two alleged collaborators whom Kamin and Gillie could not locate. These people were listed as the authors of two independent analyses corroborating Burt's conclusions. Apparently, Burt had written these analyses himself and gotten them published under fictitious names in a scholarly journal he controlled. Such fraud is probably the worst sin a scientist can commit, for it threatens to destroy the very foundations of science (Aronson, 1975, p. 115). If scientists cannot trust that each other's work is not deliberately falsified, they cannot build on each other's findings to accumulate and refine their knowledge.

CRITICISMS, ALTERNATIVES, AND FURTHER RESEARCH

Even before the Burt scandal, Jensen's critics had amassed powerful arguments against him. They correctly stressed that Jensen had made an unwarranted leap in logic when he suggested that heritability factors concerning variations *within* groups also provide clues as to the causes of variations *between* groups. In fact, the causes of differences *within* groups do not necessarily tell us anything at all about the causes of differences *between* groups. To understand why, consider a simple example. Suppose you had two groups of 100 seeds, group A and group B, the individual seeds in each group being equally diverse genetically. You plant group A seeds in fertile soil, with plenty of sunlight and water, and group B seeds in poor soil, giving them little light or moisture. Six months later you measure the heights of all the resulting plants. To what should you attribute any differences among them? Because all the plants within each group were exposed to exactly the same conditions, we can attribute any within-group differences almost entirely to

In the United States, many black children, native Americans, and members of other minority groups grow up in environments that can hinder development. Such deprivation tends to have negative effects on IQ scores—differences that are caused by environment, not heredity.

heredity. But what about the differences *between* the two groups? Should those differences also be attributed largely to heredity? Obviously not. Despite high heritability factors *within* each group, the differences *between* the groups were probably greatly influenced by the differences in their environments.

Jensen's critics point out that blacks and whites in this country likewise experience significant differences in their environments. At the most obvious level, a far higher proportion of blacks than whites live in poverty. As a result, they receive poorer prenatal care, poorer nutrition, inferior medical services, and greater exposure to certain pollutants and toxins, all of which can significantly hinder development. The higher risk of lead poisoning alone that poor black children face is an enormously important environmental difference between them and middle-class whites. In substandard

housing, young children can easily ingest lead-contaminated particles from old, peeling paint. The results can include significantly lowered IQ scores that persist into young adulthood (Needleman et al., 1990).

In answer to such criticisms Jensen has argued that, even when economic class is equated, blacks on average still score below whites on IQ tests. But in reasoning this way, his opponents contend, Jensen is greatly underestimating the range of environmental factors that can affect test performance. Simply matching people for income level across the races does *not* make the environments of whites and blacks comparable. Between American blacks and whites there are many cultural differences and differences in psychological environment that can affect the development of cognitive skills in complex ways (Block and Dworkin, 1976). Blacks are systematically exposed to levels of prejudice and discrimination that even the poorest whites never experience. Black children, in general, are also less exposed to the skills and knowledge required on a typical IQ test. When all these environmental differences between whites and blacks are considered, they provide a powerful alternative to Jensen's genetic explanation.

PATTERNS AND CONCLUSIONS

What can we conclude about the causes of racial differences in IQ scores? Even if we assume for the sake of argument that some of the average black–white difference is attributable to heredity, this conclusion in no way means that the IQ gap is somehow fixed and unchangeable. The development of any given person's intellectual abilities is always the product of heredity and environment together. This is true even if an observed *difference* in intelligence is 100 percent genetic in origin. Thus, changes in relevant aspects of the environment can always have significant effects on a person's IQ score.

This fact was clearly demonstrated in a study of black children adopted by white couples of higher-than-average socioeconomic status and above-average intelligence (Scarr and Weinberg, 1976). These black children had been born to biological parents of about average intelligence. Yet their IQ scores were, on average, six points above the mean and fifteen points above the average of other black children in that part of the country. Thus, a black child's range for potential intellectual development is at least as broad as and probably even broader than the current gap in IQ scores between blacks and whites.

Of course, environmental enrichment for a disadvantaged black child need not be as controversial as adoption into a white home. Many educational programs have raised the IQs of black children from low-income families who continue to live in their own communities. For example, Project Head Start, begun in the 1960s, was designed to stimulate learning in preschool children (both black and white) living in poverty. Sometimes teachers visited the children in their homes and engaged them in enjoyable learning activities, which the parents could later do too. Other times the children attended Head Start classes, where they received intellectual stimulation in groups. Most of the children in

The Head Start program was established in 1964 to help poor children prepare for elementary school. The value of such environmental interventions has been established, but they are available to fewer children as a result of government funding cuts.

these programs scored higher on standardized IQ tests when they entered kindergarten than did control children who did not experience Head Start. Other educational enrichment programs with the same goals as Head Start have also had success in boosting IQ scores. The increases are up to an average of fifteen points, the *entire* black–white IQ gap (McKey et al., 1985).

There has been debate over how enduring these increases in IQ are. Some children experience a gradual fading of IQ gains after they leave an enrichment program. But this may be due largely to a drop in the motivation that the program formerly gave them (Zigler and Seitz, 1982). If so, boosting academic motivation among disadvantaged blacks may be an important ingredient in permanently

The Dove Counterbalance Intelligence Test
by Adrian Dove

1. If they throw the dice and "7" is showing on the top, what is facing down?
   (a) "Seven"   (b) "Snake eyes"
   (c) "Boxcars"   (d) "Little Joes"
   (e) "Eleven"

2. Which word is most out of place here?
   (a) splib   (b) blood
   (c) gray   (d) spook
   (e) black

3. "Bird" or "yardbird" was the jacket jazz lovers from coast to coast hung on
   (a) Lester Young   (b) Peggy Lee
   (c) Benny Goodman   (d) Charlie Parker
   (e) Birdman of Alcatraz

4. Cheap "chitlings" (not the kind you purchase at the frozen-food counter) will taste rubbery unless they are cooked long enough. How soon can you quit cooking them to eat and enjoy them?
   (a) 15 minutes   (b) 2 hours
   (c) 24 hours
   (d) 1 week (on a low flame)
   (e) 1 hour

5. A "Handkerchief Head" is
   (a) A cool cat   (b) A porter
   (c) An "Uncle Tom"   (d) A hoddi
   (e) A "preacher"

FIGURE 14.5 The Dove Counterbalance Intelligence Test was devised by Adrian Dove to be culturally biased against whites—an extreme example of how an intelligence test may depend on knowledge specific to one culture. A population of urban blacks would probably score high on this test, and a population of suburban whites would probably score low. Even when a test's items do not show this kind of obvious culture loading, a test may have validity problems. For example, many subcultures within Western society place great emphasis on competence in test taking. In a subculture where such emphasis is lacking, the validity of almost any test is likely to suffer. (*Answers: 1.a, 2.c, 3.d, 4.c, 5.c*)

closing the average black–white difference in IQ. This was suggested in a study in which inner-city black children and middle-class white ones took the same IQ test (Johnson et al., 1984). Half the chil-

dren in each group were offered tokens for right answers, tokens which could later be traded for toys. While the offer of tokens had no significant effect on the performance of white children, it did on that of blacks. The black children who received tokens scored an average of thirteen IQ points higher than those who did not. This is enough of an increase to virtually eliminate average racial differences in IQ.

In summary, then, a person's IQ score can almost always be increased through the right environmental interventions. This is because almost no one is already performing at the peak of his or her genetic potential. So regardless of what the causes of the current racial gap in IQ are, that gap can be reduced significantly by making the educational environments of blacks and whites more similar.

PUBLIC CONCERNS ABOUT INTELLIGENCE TESTING

The controversy sparked by Jensen's hypothesis about racial IQ differences in turn sparked heated debate over the fairness of IQ tests. Blacks, Hispanics, and native Americans, as well as economically disadvantaged whites, were being *over*represented in special classes for the mentally retarded and *under*represented in programs for the intellectually gifted (Linn, 1986). Some blamed the IQ tests often used to track students, arguing that these tests assessed the knowledge and skills of the white middle class. Vocabulary items from IQ tests provide a good example. Someone who has never heard such words as *sonata* and *ingenuous* will perform poorly, but isn't that as much a reflection of the person's cultural background as of his or her intelligence? What if the test included words from the black culture, such as *chitlings* or *yardbird*? Would the average middle-class white get them right? (See Figure 14.5.)

Solving this problem by developing a culture-free test has not been easy. One approach has been to continue using a standard IQ test but to build into the scoring process adjustments for minority-group children. The best-known such effort is the **System of Multicultural Pluralistic Assessment (SOMPA)** (Mercer, 1979). Besides providing a culturally adjusted IQ score, the SOMPA also assesses a child's nonacademic performance and physical health. But some psychologists oppose the SOMPA's reliance, even in part, on a standard IQ test. They want to develop an assessment system in which the test items themselves are less culturally biased.

One intelligence test that attempts to reduce cultural bias is the **Kaufman Assessment Battery for Children (K-ABC).** It tries to minimize the effects of language skills on performance, so that what is assessed is closer to pure problem-solving ability. It also tries to separate pure problem-solving ability from performance based on the amount of knowledge that a child has acquired. The K-ABC has been reasonably successful in these efforts. The gap between the mean scores for black and white children is less than half that associated with traditional IQ tests (Klanderman et al., 1985).

But some psychologists wonder if the need to create culture-free IQ tests has not been exaggerated. They say that scores on standard IQ tests have just as much predictive validity regardless of whether the test taker comes from a minority group or the white majority (Schmidt and Hunter, 1981). Those who do poorly on these tests are said to lack skills which, like it or not, are important in our society.

Are the skills that IQ tests measure really important to success in life? Studies suggest that they are not the whole story. For instance, although IQ scores are good predictors of grades in school, they are not that good at predicting *exceptional* achievement in a person's career. Among Lewis Terman's 1,500 high-IQ subjects, there were no Nobel Prize winners, nor were there many millionaires (Goleman, 1980). Even more modest career achievements are not always related to IQ. In one study of professional racehorse handicappers (people who estimate the odds of each horse winning a certain race given the competition), IQ was found to have no correlation with handicapping skills (Ceci and Liker, 1986). Thus, IQ apparently misses some factors that are important to success. These probably include a person's interest level, motivation, creativity, and persistence.

And yet IQ tests continue to be used to screen people for certain jobs, even though the duties of those jobs have no apparent connection with the skills the tests measure. Here is one example:

> . . . suppose you are a ghetto resident in the Roxbury section of Boston. To qualify for being a policeman, you have to take a three-hour-long general intelligence test in which you must know the meaning of words like "quell," "pyromaniac," and "lexicon." If you do not know enough of these words or cannot play analogy games with them, you do not qualify and must be satisfied with some such job as being a janitor for which an "intelligence" test is not required by the Massachusetts Civil Service Commission. You, not unreasonably, feel angry, upset, and unsuccessful. Because you do not know those words, you are considered to have low intelligence, and since you consequently have to take a low status job and are unhappy, you contribute to the celebrated correlations of low intelligence with low occupational status and poor adjustment. Psychologists should be ashamed of themselves for promoting a view of general intelligence that has encouraged such a testing program, particularly when there is no solid evidence that significantly relates performance on this type of intelligence test with performance as a policeman. (McClelland, 1973, p. 4)

As a result of this kind of criticism, intelligence tests have come under something of a cloud. Some school systems have abandoned them entirely, and others no longer use them to track students into accelerated, average, and slow classes. Industry's reliance on intelligence tests to select among job applicants has also been decreasing, a fact that many applaud. But others caution that to throw such tests out completely may do more harm than good. Alternative means of assessment, such as personal interviews for job placement and teachers' judgments about assignment to classes, are even more likely to be biased and inaccurate than a good standardized test (Reschly, 1981; Tenopyr, 1981). So perhaps we should continue to use standardized IQ tests but try to improve how we select and administer them. Another suggestion is to supplement current IQ tests with tests of thinking and problem-solving skills in everyday, real-life situations (Frederiksen, 1986).

ASSESSING PERSONALITY

Psychological testing began with the goal of measuring human intelligence, but soon psychologists began to develop personality tests as well. These tests have found a number of uses. Clinicians and social workers use them to gain insight into people's social and emotional problems, thereby aiding in diagnosis and

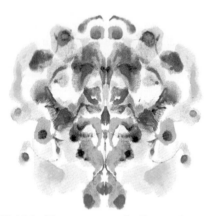
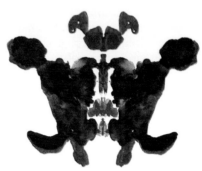

FIGURE 14.6 Two patterns similar to those on the Rorschach Inkblot Test, which is used for clinical psychiatric diagnosis. Three criteria are common to all methods of scoring the test: responses to *location* of the blots or details in them; responses to *determinants*, or qualities of the blots that are reflected in responses; and descriptions of *content* or what the subject "sees" in the blots. Many clinicians believe that certain types and patterns of responses on the test indicate various normal and abnormal personality traits.

treatment. School psychologists, industrial psychologists, and vocational counselors use them to help people select careers that suit their dispositions. And researchers interested in personality also use them to investigate some of the concepts and theories in their field.

The particular method psychologists choose to assess personality often depends on their theoretical approach. Those who see personality as a set of fairly stable characteristics select personality tests developed to measure such traits. Behaviorists, in contrast, regard personality as much more variable, more influenced by the immediate situation. As a result, they search for stimuli in the environment that either reinforce particular responses or set the stage for them. Their main assessment tools are direct observations of behavior and carefully compiled self-reports, in which people record instances of a problem behavior and the situations in which it occurs. Not surprisingly, psychologists with a psychoanalytic perspective use a different tactic. Because they believe that personality is shaped by unconscious conflicts, they favor techniques that allow a person's underlying motives and feelings to surface. One example of this kind of assessment method is a projective test (Elias, 1989).

PROJECTIVE TESTS

Projective tests assess the way people respond to and interpret ambiguous stimuli, such as inkblots and pictures in which the motives and feelings of the characters are not clear. The test takers describe what they see in these materials. Presumably, in doing so, they project their own unconscious feelings and conflicts. Thus, someone who repeatedly sees peering eyes and threatening figures in abstract blots of ink is projecting onto the inkblots the fears and suspicions typical of paranoia.

THE RORSCHACH INKBLOT TEST

Perhaps the best-known projective test for clinical diagnosis is the one developed in 1921 by Hermann Rorschach (1884–1922), a Swiss psychiatrist. In the **Rorschach Inkblot Test,** people look at ten inkblots (such as those shown in Figure 14.6) and report what they see in each one. The examiner notes not only what a person says, but also how the person says it—quickly or cautiously, with what kind of emotion, and so forth. After all ten cards have been presented, the examiner shows them a second time and asks the person why he or she gave the previous answer. If in one blot the subject saw two elephant heads, for instance, the examiner would ask what about that blot suggested this particular image.

The Rorschach is scored by considering what part or parts of the inkblot a person focused on, whether the shape, color, or some other aspect of it was significant, what kind of objects or activities the person saw, and how common or uncommon the person's responses were. Traditionally, certain answers on the Rorschach are assumed to indicate certain personality traits. For instance, if a person often focuses on the *entire* inkblot (not just a part of it), that person is assumed to be good at abstract, conceptual thought. Many responses to the *shape* of an inkblot supposedly suggests dispassionate thinking, while many responses to *color* suggests strong emotion and impulsiveness (McAdams, 1990). A skilled Rorschach examiner also interprets the overall pattern of answers a person gives to get a general picture of what that person is like. Consider a man who saw in one inkblot two headless people with arms touching, who might be women with bad figures; in another, some women trying to lift weights; and in a third, Count Dracula ready to suck blood and strangle a woman. This overall pattern of responses suggested to the examiner a man who was in conflict over his sexual orientation. While he seemed to want contact with a nurturing mother figure, he also seemed very angry and hostile toward women (Pervin, 1989).

The value of the Rorschach as a personality test depends on a person's perspective. Some say that people's answers are too easily influenced by transitory thoughts and feelings, and that the scoring procedures for the test are not standardized enough. Others say that the Rorschach is not a very good diagnoser of specific psychiatric disorders, that it simply helps clinicians identify general themes involved in people's psychological problems (Feshbach and Weiner, 1982; Korchin and Schuldberg, 1981). But those who use the Rorschach downplay these criticisms. They believe that projective tests like the Rorschach allow insights into people's minds that other types of personality tests do not. This helps explain why the Rorschach remains one of the top ten tests used today in outpatient mental health facilities (Piotrowski and Keller, in press).

THE THEMATIC APPERCEPTION TEST

The **Thematic Apperception Test (TAT),** developed by Henry Murray in 1935, is another

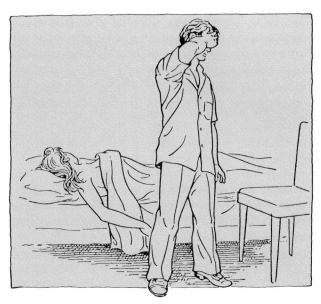

FIGURE 14.7   The TAT card shown here was interpreted as follows by a male college student, who seems to be distressed by sexual conflict: this is a young boy who's never had any experience with girls, to any extent. For some reason he finds himself with a woman, a few years older than he is, who expects that he's gonna go to bed with her. He wants very much to prove to himself that he's a man . . . but still, he's afraid. He doesn't know what to do. His fear . . . turns into disgust, when he thinks of himself being unable to act like a boy his age he believes is supposed to act. . . . He'll probably run out of the room, and block off his mind, to sex and to women, for a long time. . . . He may never be able to develop normally . . . because of things that have happened to him in the past and are manifesting themselves in his immaturity and self-hate. (*From Lamberth and Rappaport, 1978.*)

projective test that is widely used in both clinical work and studies of motivations (Piotrowski and Keller, in press). The TAT consists of a series of pictures of ambiguous scenes involving people. Usually, the person being tested is shown twenty or fewer of the pictures, chosen for their appropriateness to his or her age and sex. The person tells a story about each picture, including what led up to the scene, what the characters are thinking and feeling, and how the situation ends. Figure 14.7 shows one picture from the TAT and a college student's story about it.

In analyzing a subject's TAT stories, the examiner first determines the character on whom the subject has apparently projected aspects of him- or herself.

This is usually the story's central character. Other characters are thought to be given traits of people important in the subject's life. Murray originally suggested that TAT responses be analyzed for two things: the psychological needs of the subject (including the needs for achievement, affiliation, nurturance, aggression, dependency, power, and sex) and environmental factors in the subject's life that are helping or hindering need fulfillment. For instance, if the central character in several of a person's stories is striving hard for success but is constantly being thwarted by lack of social connections, a need for achievement and a concern over obstacles related to social status are presumed to be important in that person's life.

Like the Rorschach, the TAT has been subjected to criticisms that scoring is too open-ended and places too much reliance on the skill of the examiner. Nonetheless, the test continues to be used in a variety of clinical and research contexts to assess underlying motivations that may be difficult for respondents to express directly. In one study, for example, TAT stories were used to study respondents' feelings of ambivalence toward their same-sex siblings (Bedford, 1989). In another investigation, the test was used to study attitudes toward death among the offspring of Holocaust survivors (Schneider, 1988). The TAT test is also used in research to test aspects of psychodynamic theory—for example, to examine whether individuals with certain personality disorders show disordered orientations toward interpersonal relationships, such as a conception of others as malevolent or an incapacity to invest in relationships with others (Weston et al., 1990).

SELF-REPORT TESTS

Projective tests of personality may seem rather indirect ways of discovering what people are like. Couldn't we just ask people what they feel and how they usually act? Do you feel awkward in most social situations? Do you often say things you immediately regret? Do you think that most people can be trusted? Psychologists who favor a trait approach to personality have developed this type of **self-report test.** They believe that people's answers to such questions do indeed yield valid psychological profiles of them.

TEST CONSTRUCTION

But how do psychologists come up with the items to include on self-report tests? There are several different approaches and no consensus as to which is best. Usually, however, the test developers begin with a thorough and clear definition of the trait they want to measure, including all the elements they think compose it (McAdams, 1990). Suppose we want to develop a test of conscientiousness, one of the "Big Five" personality traits discussed in Chapter 13. There we defined conscientiousness as involving an achievement orientation, dependability, carefulness, hard work, perseverance, self-control, and a sense of responsibility. We could write test items that tapped all the various aspects of conscientiousness included in our definition. For instance: "I always make sure I finish the projects I start." "If someone gives me a job to do, I feel an obligation to do it well." "I am very careful and meticulous in most of the things I do." To identify people who tend to answer "yes" to everything they are asked, we would also include some "reverse" items, such as "I see nothing wrong with cutting a few corners to get a job done" or "When I lose interest in a task, I just put it aside and do something else." We should also include some items concerning aspects of a person that are closely related to those in our definition of conscientiousness (degree of honesty and unselfishness, for instance). This would allow us to establish the boundaries of what conscientiousness entails. In addition, we might throw in a few items that do not ask directly about a person's traits, but that may turn out to be good indicators of them nonetheless. "I would enjoy a career as a scientist" is one possibility. We are not directly asking people about their conscientiousness, but people who are *not* conscientious might not be very interested in the exacting work that scientists do.

To decide which items we should keep in our final version of the test, first we would administer the test to a large number of people. Then we would analyze answers to each of our items to see how they generally relate to a person's overall score. Those items that we found made only a negligible contribution to the total score could be eliminated. Finally, we would have to validate our test by making sure that it was in fact measuring what people generally consider to be conscientiousness. We could do this by seeing how closely scores on our test correlated with conscientiousness ratings made by people who knew the test takers well. Or we might conduct a laboratory experiment in which we gave the test takers a chance to behave in a conscientious or an unconscientious way. If we found that those who scored high on the test behaved the most conscientiously in our study,

FIGURE 14.8 (A) Sample MMPI items. (B) MMPI profiles for abusive and nonabusive fathers. The letters along the bottom of the graph correspond to the scales described in Table 14.3. Note that the two groups showed different profiles: fathers who abused their children scored much higher than nonabusive fathers on the depression (D), psychopathic deviate (Pd), and mania (Ma) scales. Although it appears that the MMPI can differentiate between abusive and nonabusive parents, further study would be necessary before a more conclusive profile of an abusive parent could be drawn. [*Minnesota Multiphasic Personality Inventory (MMPI™) Copyright © The University of Minnesota, 1943, renewed 1970. Profile form 1948, 1976, 1982.*]

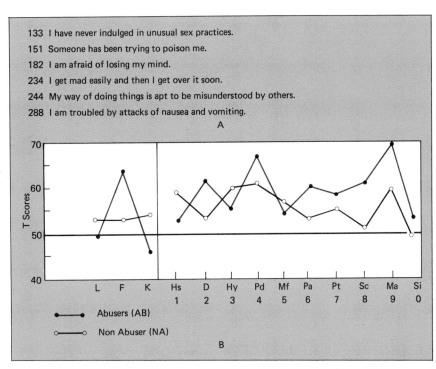

133 I have never indulged in unusual sex practices.
151 Someone has been trying to poison me.
182 I am afraid of losing my mind.
234 I get mad easily and then I get over it soon.
244 My way of doing things is apt to be misunderstood by others.
288 I am troubled by attacks of nausea and vomiting.

A

Abusers (AB)
Non Abuser (NA)

B

we would have some evidence that our test was indeed valid.

THE MINNESOTA MULTIPHASIC PERSONALITY INVENTORY

The **Minnesota Multiphasic Personality Inventory (MMPI)** is a widely used self-report test—in fact, it is the most widely used assessment test of any kind in outpatient mental health facilities (Piotrowski and Keller, in press). The MMPI was originally developed to aid in the diagnosis of psychiatric patients. The test developers tried out a variety of possible test items on groups of patients suffering from different psychological disorders: schizophrenia, depression, paranoia, hypochondria, and so forth. The same items were also given to a group of psychologically healthy people. Items that discriminated among the groups were incorporated into the test. For instance, of the original pool of test items, fifty-three were found to discriminate sharply between depressed and healthy people. Later, a few more items were added to sharpen the discrimination between people who are severely depressed and those with other psychiatric conditions (Winters et al., 1984). The result is the D, or depression, scale of

the MMPI. It is a highly sensitive indicator not only of major depression, but also of less severe downswings in mood.

The entire MMPI contains 550 test items, all of which can be answered *true* or *false*. (Sample items are given in Figure 14.8A.) A person's answers to the test items yield scores on each of the ten clinical scales listed in Table 14.3. When scores are presented graphically, it is easy to compare the personality profile of one person or group with that of another. Figure 14.8B compares the profiles of a group of fathers who abuse their children with a group of fathers who do not. As you can see, they differ substantially on many of the scales.

The original MMPI did have some problems, however. First, the group used to define a normal or average profile was not a representative sample of the general population. All of the individuals used to develop norms were white residents of Minnesota, and most were semi-skilled workers or farmers with an eighth-grade education. Second, many of the original items on the test were outdated (for example, "Horses that don't pull should be beaten or kicked") or were offensive to some respondents because they referred to content that was objectionable (for example, sexist items, items having to do with bowel and

TABLE 14.3 Scales of the MMPI

Clinical Scales	
1. Hypochondriasis (Hs)	Items selected to discriminate people who persist in worrying about their bodily functions despite strong evidence that they have no physical illness.
2. Depression (D)	Items selected to discriminate people who are pessimistic about the future, feel hopeless or worthless, are slow in thought and action, and think a lot about death and suicide.
3. Hysteria (H)	Items selected to discriminate people who use physical symptoms to solve difficult problems or avoid mature responsibilities, particularly under severe psychological stress.
4. Psychopathic deviate (Pd)	Items selected to discriminate people who show a pronounced disregard for social customs and mores, an inability to profit from punishing experiences, and emotional shallowness with others, particularly in sex and love.
5. Masculinity-femininity (Mf)	Items selected to discriminate men who prefer homosexual relations to heterosexual ones, either overtly or covertly because of inhibitions or conflicts. Women tend to score low on the scale, but the scale cannot be interpreted as simply upside down for women.
6. Paranoia (Pa)	Items selected to discriminate people who have delusions about how influential and how victimized they are or how much attention is paid them by other people.
7. Psychasthenia (Pt)	Items selected to discriminate people with obsessive thoughts, compulsive actions, extreme fear or guilt feelings, insecurity, and high anxiety.
8. Schizophrenia (Sc)	Items selected to discriminate people who are constrained, cold, aloof, apathetic, and inaccessible to others and who may have delusions or hallucinations.
9. Mania (Ma)	Items selected to discriminate people who are physically overactive and emotionally excited and have rapid flights of disconnected, fragmentary ideas; the activities may lead to accomplishment but more frequently are inefficient and unproductive.
10. Social introversion (Si)	Items selected to discriminate people who are withdrawn from social contacts and responsibilities and display little real interest in people.

Based on Dahlstrom, Welsh, and Dahlstrom, 1972.

bladder functions, and items focusing on religious beliefs).

In 1989, after several years of work, a revised and updated form of the MMPI was published—MMPI-2 (Butcher et al, 1989). The MMPI-2 contains 567 items. Original items with sexist wording or objectionable or outmoded content were modified or dropped. In order to make research on the original MMPI applicable to the MMPI-2, the scientists working on the revision left the ten original clinical scales as unchanged as possible (see Table 14.3). Three validity scales, designed to determine whether the test taker is

responding honestly to the test, also have been retained. One such scale is the Lie scale, which is designed to identify people who are faking their responses in order to appear better than they actually are. For example, a person who answers "yes" to statements such as, "I always tell the truth," would score high on such a scale, since most people tell a lie occasionally. A second validity scale, the F scale, is designed to identify people who are deliberately trying to portray themselves as more disturbed than they really are. Such people typically mark "true" to statements that seem to indicate pathology (for example, "I see

Behavioral assessment is a form of personality testing that involves observing problem behaviors to see how they cause distress in the person and how they might be changed. With young children, this approach may include observing behavior with toys and other props.

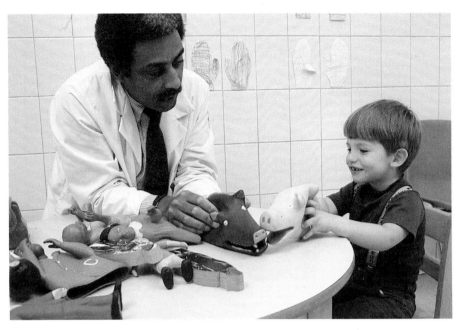

things, animals, or people around me that most people do not see") but that, in fact, are not endorsed by respondents who are truly disturbed. The K scale is similar to the Lie scale, but the items are more subtle (for example, "At times I feel like swearing"). Many false responses to such statements suggest that the respondent is being less than frank and is trying to conceal his or her distress.

In addition, several new scales have been developed for the MMPI-2, including a Post-Traumatic Stress Disorder scale, a Gender Role scale, a Shyness scale, and scales designed to measure a number of new content areas including Anger, Cynicism, Type A Behavior Pattern, Health Concerns, and Family Problems. Although research is continuing on the MMPI-2, it appears to be regarded by many clinicians as improved substantially over the MMPI. Thus far, the test has been widely adopted and has generated considerable enthusiam among clinicians.

BEHAVIORAL ASSESSMENT

Behavioral assessment of people is associated with the behaviorist and social learning perspectives in psychology. Behavioral assessment differs in important ways from self-report tests of personality or projective tests. In behavioral assessment the focus is on observable behavior. The assessors are not searching for hidden motives or mental-emotional traits presumed to make people act in certain ways. They are interested in behavior for its own sake, because some aspect of it is causing distress, *not* because they see behavior as an indicator of some underlying predisposition.

Because behaviorists believe that people are strongly influenced by outside stimuli, they look to situational factors for the causes and cures of problem behaviors. Generally, they have three goals: identifying specific situations that tend to trigger problem behaviors; describing the problem behaviors in detail, to know exactly what they entail and how severe they are; and identifying environmental consequences that might be reinforcing an undesirable response, consequences that could be changed to help alleviate the problem. This approach has been called the ABC assessment because it looks at *a*ntecedent conditions, at the nature of the problem *b*ehavior, and at *c*onsequences that may be maintaining the unwanted response (Pervin, 1989).

Most behavioral assessment occurs in the context of a behavioral therapy program. Suppose that a mother visits a behavioral therapist to learn how to stop her son's temper tantrums. Before advising anything, the therapist needs to learn about the tantrums—how often they occur, what tends to

Vocational interest tests can help the subject discover and analyze various abilities as they relate to the requirements of different occupations.

trigger them, and the consequences they produce. The therapist could ask the mother to write down what happens before, during, and after a tantrum. Or the therapist could make her own first-hand observations either in the child's home or in a clinical setting. Let us say that in this case the therapist discovers that the little boy screams, kicks, hits, and bites when he is denied something he wants. She also finds that the mother periodically tries to soothe the child by giving him a cookie or a piece of candy, behaviors that could inadvertently be reinforcing the tantrums. The therapist recommends that the mother put the boy in a "time-out" room whenever a tantrum begins and require him to stay there without toys, attention, or other rewards until he has calmed down. The mother is also asked to reward desirable behavior—for instance, praising her son whenever he is denied something he wants and *does not* have a tantrum. Behavioral assessment continues during this relearning process to keep track of the changes that occur.

Many behavior therapists today are broadening their approach to assessment. Some are starting to probe a client's thoughts and feelings, much as cognitive therapists do. For instance, a man who has persistent conflict with his coworkers would still be asked to keep a careful record of the situations and behaviors involved in the problem. But in addition, he might also be asked about his mental reactions: "What thoughts go through your mind when your boss criticizes your work?" "What do you think to yourself when someone else lands a big contract?" This information could give important insights into *why* certain situations trigger certain responses. Collecting it is a step toward using more diversified tools of behavioral assessment (Korchin and Schuldberg, 1981).

TESTS FOR CHOOSING CAREERS AND SCREENING EMPLOYEES

A number of tests have been developed to help people select appropriate careers and to help companies choose the best applicants for a job.

INTEREST TESTS: CHOOSING CAREERS

Identifying your interests can help you to find a career in which you are likely to succeed and find personal satisfaction. But why do you need a formal test to identify your interests? Aren't you aware of your interests already? Not necessarily. Many people never deliberately analyze their interests, and if they do, they may not know how those interests relate to the requirements of various jobs. A young woman who is very interested in science, for example, may think that she wants to be a doctor. But if she has no interest in dealing with other people's problems, she is overlooking an important part of a physician's work. Interest tests can help avoid such oversights by matching the full range of a person's interests with the demands of different types of jobs.

The **Strong-Campbell Interest Inventory (SCII),** originally developed in the 1920s by E. K. Strong, Jr., consists of 325 items, most of which list particular occupations, school subjects, activities (repairing a clock, giving a speech, raising money for charity), amusements, and people with whom someone might associate (old people, people who like to live dangerously, and so forth). The test taker marks each item *like, indifferent,* or *dislike.* Other items on the Strong-Campbell include pairs of activities to choose between ("Would you prefer to deal with things or to deal with people?") and simple self-descriptions that the person marks *yes* or *no* ("I make friends easily"; "I am always on time with my work").

All the subject's answers are then computer-analyzed in terms of three major scales. One is the Occupational Scale, which tells how similar a person's answers are to those of successful people in specific occupations (psychologist, architect, advertising executive, musician, army officer, and so on). A woman may find, for instance, that her answers on the test are very similar to those given by a group of engineers but very dissimilar to those given by a group of social workers. Dissimilar answers are believed to be more revealing than similar ones, and they can be used to eliminate career options (social worker in this case). The Strong-Campbell also has a Basic Interest Scale, which contains twenty-three vocational areas, such as agriculture, military, science, art, sales, writing, and teaching. In each area, the test taker receives a score showing his or her degree of interest in working in that field. Finally, the test has a General Occupational Themes Scale. It consists of six adjectives (realistic, conventional, enterprising, social, artistic, and investigative) describing general styles of thinking and acting. The test taker is rated as being high, medium, or low in each of these different styles. Occupations are also classified according to these six adjectives, so the test taker gains insight into which occupations seem to match his or her own personal style.

SCREENING TESTS: CHOOSING EMPLOYEES

As intelligence tests have become increasingly controversial as a method of assessing job applicants, employers are turning to other kinds of screening tests. Some administer aptitude tests designed to measure a person's potential to perform a specific task. For example, factories seeking workers to assemble tiny electronic components often give applicants a manual dexterity test. Aptitude tests can also help identify potential talent for working with computers and other types of machines. Job applicants may also be given current performance tests to demonstrate how well they currently do at tasks like typing or proofreading. Finally, some corporations use personality tests to match candidates to jobs. To enter an executive training program, for example, a person may have to rank exceptionally high in assertiveness and tolerance for stress and moderately high in conformity.

Of course, companies also assess job applicants through interviews, a screening method that many employers prefer because they say it allows them to get to know an applicant personally. When evaluated scientifically, however, interviewing does not fare well. Most studies have found choices made on the basis of interviews alone to be at best random and at worst unfairly biased (Tenopyr, 1981).

THE ETHICS OF TESTING

Because Americans use standardized tests so extensively, psychologists, government officials, and the general public are concerned about the ethical standards for testing. The American Psychological Association has issued several documents on the subject, legislators have already enacted laws, and some corporations have voluntarily tightened their policies regarding employee screening exams. *Standards,* a volume compiled by a Joint Committee on Testing Standards (AERA, APA, NCME, 1985), gives guidelines for a wide range of testing activities, from developing tests to interpreting them (Jones and

Applebaum, 1989). What are some of the issues regarding the ethics of testing that people are most concerned about?

One is the concern that people who use tests choose, administer, and evaluate them properly (London and Bray, 1980). Tests must be used only for appropriate purposes—that is, purposes for which the tests have been empirically demonstrated to be valid. Tests must also be fair to members of all the social groups that take them. No test that discriminates unfairly should ever be used. In addition, those who use tests must be aware of their limitations. Test scores never supply absolutely certain information. At best they provide only a good estimate of what they are designed to measure. That is why important decisions about a person should never be made on the basis of a test score alone. In addition, someone who does poorly on a test should at least be given the chance to retake it.

Another ethical issue in testing is the disclosure of test results. Who should have access to people's test scores? Only the test takers themselves unless they agree otherwise? In general, most ethics commit-tees stress the test takers' right to confidentiality. They say that test scores should not be released to outside parties without subjects' prior knowledge and often their express consent (London and Bray, 1980). Whether test takers also have a right to see exactly how a test was scored is a related ethical question that has been very controversial. Developers of tests often argue that, if both questions and answers are disclosed to people who have taken a test, new test items must constantly be generated to avoid possible cheating by others. Eventually, they reason, after many, many questions have been used, the new test items may gradually become inferior to the old. But though this may be true, public opinion has generally sided with test takers' right to know *why* they did well or poorly. In 1980, for example, New York State passed a law requiring that questions and answers on college entrance exams be made available to those who have taken these tests. This legislation has been part of a growing belief that tests in our society be administered for the benefit of *all* concerned—those who take the tests as well as those who give them.

SUMMARY

1. **Standardization** involves developing uniform procedures for giving and scoring a test, as well as establishing **norms,** or standards of performance, against which people's scores on the test can be evaluated. A good test must be both **reliable** and **valid,** meaning that it must consistently yield the same results and measure what it is intended to measure.

2. **Intelligence** involves the capacities to acquire and retain knowledge and to understand concepts and relationships, capacities that an intelligent person uses effectively when solving problems and communicating. One approach to studying intelligence is **factor analysis,** in which researchers try to identify different components of intelligence by seeing which scores on mental tests tend to cluster together. Psychologists who have conducted factor analyses disagree on how many such components exist and on whether there is also a general intelligence factor that underlies all a person's various intellectual abilities. Another approach to studying intelligence is the **information-processing view,** which looks closely at *how* people think and reason intelligently.

3. The first valid test of intelligence was developed by Alfred Binet, a French psychologist, in collaboration with psychiatrist Theodore Simon. This test measured **intelligence quotient** or **IQ,** a child's mental age divided by his or her chronological age. Lewis Terman, a professor at Stanford University, brought Binet's test to America in a revised version called the **Stanford-Binet.** Another set of widely used tests are the **Wechsler scales,** developed by David Wechsler. In addition to these individual tests of intelligence (those given to only one person at a time), there are also group tests, paper-and-pencil measures that many people can take at once. One group test that measures some of the abilities often assessed by IQ tests is the **Scholastic Aptitude Test (SAT).** Although it is often criticized, scores on it are reasonably good predictors of grades in college.

4. At one extreme of human intelligence are the **mentally retarded,** those whose IQs are significantly below average and who have trouble functioning in everyday life. In evaluating mental retardation today, educators are careful to take into account factors such

as vision and hearing, language skills, and cultural background, which can sometimes deceptively lower a person's IQ. At the other extreme of human intelligence are the **mentally gifted,** who, contrary to popular stereotypes, are not awkward, eccentric, and frail. But it is not clear that the success and good adjustment of high-IQ people should be attributed solely to their cognitive abilities. Other factors, particularly family background and motivation, also contribute to the tendency to excel.

5. A **heritability factor** is an estimate of the contribution heredity makes to the individual differences we observe in some trait such as intelligence. Current estimates are that about 50 percent of the individual variability in IQ scores is due to genetic differences among people. This leaves an equally large influence from environment, including such factors as different family experiences, different friends and teachers, different interests and hobbies, and different levels of encouragement to excel.

6. More hotly debated than the causes of individual differences in IQ scores are the causes of group differences between people of different races. Arthur Jensen proposed that heredity may be strongly implicated in these racial differences, but others have argued persuasively in favor of environmental explanations.

7. IQ tests have often been criticized as assessing mainly the knowledge and skills of the white middle class. Attempts have been made to create culturally unbiased intelligence tests, such as the **System of Multicultural Pluralistic Assessment (SOMPA)** and the **Kaufman Assessment Battery for Children (K-ABC).**

8. Psychologists have developed a number of tests to assess personality. **Projective tests,** such as the **Rorschach Inkblot Test** and the **Thematic Apperception Test (TAT),** are related to the psychoanalytic perspective because they assume that people project unconscious conflicts and needs into their interpretations of ambiguous test material. In contrast, **self-report tests,** such as the **Minnesota Multiphasic Personality Inventory (MMPI),** are associated with the trait approach to personality. These tests assume that valid personality profiles can be obtained by asking people straightforward questions about themselves. Finally, **behavioral assessment** is associated with those who take a behaviorist or social learning perspective. Their goal is to assess observable problem behaviors and the situational factors that trigger and reinforce them.

9. A number of tests have been developed to help people select appropriate careers for themselves and to help companies choose the best applicants for a job. An example of the first kind of test is the **Strong-Campbell Interest Inventory (SCII),** which measures people's interests and relates them to various occupations.

10. People have become increasingly concerned about the ethical standards that apply to testing. Among the issues raised are the uses to which tests are put and the people to whom test results are disclosed. Several organizations are attempting to set guidelines in these and other areas.

SUGGESTED READINGS

Anastasi, A. (1986). *Psychological testing* (5th ed.). New York: Macmillan. A survey of intelligence and personality tests, with useful discussions of test reliability and validity.

Fancher, R. E. (1985). *The intelligence men: Makers of the IQ controversy.* New York: Norton. Provides an excellent overview of the controversy surrounding Jensen, Burt, and Kamin in their attempts to understand whether there are, in fact, racial differences in IQ.

Gould, S. J. (1981). *The mismeasure of man.* New York: Norton. The history of misguided attempts to measure intelligence, written by a gifted science writer.

Kleinmuntz, B. (1982). *Personality and psychological assessment.* New York: St. Martin's Press. Ability and aptitude testing and measurements of attitudes and values are addressed from a systematic and objective point of view.

Lanyon, R. I., and Goldstein, L. D. (1982). *Personality assessment* (2nd ed.). New York: Wiley. Describes the usefulness of assessment methods in a variety of settings.

Shekerjian, D. (1990). *Uncommon genius: How great ideas are born.* New York: Viking. An insightful discussion of the conditions under which people can maximize their creative powers and develop important ideas.

CHAPTER 15

HEALTH, STRESS, AND COPING

It's exam week, and Sam is in the infirmary with the flu. For the past few weeks he has been studying around the clock; he has barely slept and often forgot to eat. When he was exposed to the flu virus, his run-down body succumbed.

Sara is in the hospital, recovering from injuries in a car accident. Normally she is a careful driver, but on the day of the accident her boyfriend of two years told her that he just wasn't ready for commitment and admitted that he was seeing someone else. Angry and hurt, she didn't see the stop sign.

In these explanations of Sam and Sara's problems, we see the new, biopsychosocial approach to health and health care.

Traditionally, our society has viewed illness and injury as strictly medical problems. According to the **biomedical model,** sickness is the result of a biological malfunction, and can be explained and treated without reference to the victim's psychological state or social situation. The mind and body are thought to be two separate entities; illness is a "technical" matter, best treated by trained medical practitioners. If a person is sick, he or she requires medical attention; if not, he or she is presumed to be healthy. The **biopsychosocial model,** in contrast, holds that social, psychological, and biological factors interact to affect our health. The biopsychosocial model views the mind and body as working together. Health and illness are seen as a continuum, rather than an either/or condition. And good health is viewed as an active achievement that people accomplish through their habits and life-style. Whereas the biomedical approach focuses on containing illness, the biopsychosocial approach seeks to promote health.

Traditionally, when treating a man in his forties who has suffered a heart attack, physicians emphasized continuing drug treatment, along with frequent monitoring of the condition. Today, however, many doctors, influenced by the biopsychosocial approach, would also emphasize the patient's life-style. Does he smoke? Drink? Eat properly? Exercise? A stop-smoking program, nutritional counseling, and a controlled exercise program might be recommended. The biopsychosocial practitioner would also be concerned about the man's personal life. A high-powered executive who works fourteen-hour days, six days a week, might be urged to re-order his priorities so that he spends more time with his family and at relaxing hobbies.

The biopsychosocial model is at the heart of the growing field of **health psychology:** the subfield of

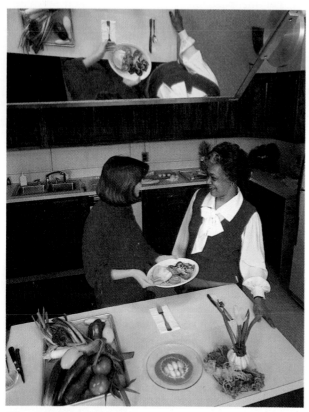

The trend toward health promotion increases people's sense of control over their physical well-being. At Duke University's Fitness Center, clients are taught the principles of healthy nutrition.

psychology dedicated to promoting good health and health care. One of its aims is to investigate the psychological and social factors that influence the prevention and treatment of illness, such as habits, stress, and personality traits. A second aim is to inform people about risky behavior and develop programs to help them lead healthier lives. Finally, health psychologists try to understand and improve the health-care system itself.

LIFE-STYLE AND HEALTH

Before the twentieth century, the major causes of death in the United States were acute infectious diseases such as influenza, tuberculosis, and pneumonia. Thanks to innovations in public health (im-proved sanitation, purified water, pasteurized milk) and medical technology (vaccinations and antibiotics), these diseases are far less common and less deadly than they once were. Instead, the major causes of disability and death today are such chronic, often incurable disorders as cardiovascular disease, cancer, diabetes, strokes, and automobile accidents. These health problems have been called diseases or disorders of *life-style* because they often can be traced to patterns of behavior, including smoking, overeating, alcohol consumption, or failure to use safety devices (such as seatbelts and motorcycle helmets). Tobacco consumption is a prime example of a life-style problem. Smoking accounts for approximately 125,000 deaths from cancer, and another 170,000 deaths from cardiovascular disease, in the United States each year (American Cancer Society, 1989). Smoking is also linked to chronic bronchitis, emphysema, deaths and injuries in fires, and pregnancy problems (Centers for Disease Control, 1989). AIDS and drug abuse also fall into this category. Disorders such as cardiovascular disease, cancer, and strokes also have a major impact on life-style: although some can be controlled, most cannot be cured, and their victims often live with them for many years.

As the role of life-style factors has gained recognition, more and more attention is being paid to health promotion, the process of enabling people to increase control over their health and improve it. Eating a balanced diet, cutting down on cholesterol and fat, exercising regularly, developing good preventive health behaviors (such as regular medical checkups)—and avoiding behaviors that compromise health (such as smoking, taking drugs, and drinking excessively)—are practices associated with the promotion of health.

BELIEFS, ATTITUDES, AND HEALTH

Walk into any grocery store and you will see dozens of products labeled "low salt," "no cholesterol," and "only 300 calories." Health clubs and exercise gear (especially athletic shoes) are big business. Almost every public facility has no-smoking areas. On the surface, Americans appear to be extremely health-conscious. But appearances can be deceiving.

Consider breast cancer. One in every eleven American women will develop breast cancer at some point in her lifetime. Yet little more than a third of women practice breast self-examination, and many of these do not use the right method (American Cancer

Alison Gertz never used intravenous drugs and never had a
blood transfusion, but contracted
AIDS after having sex one night
with a man whom she later
learned was bisexual. She is
using her own experience to
spread the message that no one is
immune to this deadly disease.

Society, 1989). Why don't more women take this simple step to safeguard their health? In general, research shows that four beliefs influence preventive health behaviors: (1) How severe do we perceive the threat to be? (2) How vulnerable to the health threat do we feel? (3) Do we feel that we can act to reduce the threat (self-efficacy)? (4) Do we believe that our response will overcome the threat (response efficacy)? (Bandura, 1986; Janz and Becker, 1984; Rogers, 1984). Most women know that breast cancer is serious, though they may not know how common it is. Young women see breast cancer as a disease that afflicts older women, and so postpone preventive measures. Older women may practice self-examination once or twice, but conclude they can't detect changes anyway. Finally, women may worry about what will happen if they *do* find a lump. Many would prefer not knowing to facing a possibly incurable problem (Gallup Organization, 1979). In the abstract at least, some women may feel they would "rather die" than have a breast removed.

One of the jobs of health psychologists is to disseminate accurate information. For instance, younger women should know that while breast cancer strikes more often after age forty-five, the age of onset is decreasing and more and more young women are affected. Statistics on successful treatment need to be publicized: when breast cancer is detected early, a woman has an 85 to 90 percent chance of being cured (American Cancer Society, 1989). Furthermore, in many cases a mastectomy (removal of the entire breast plus adjacent muscle tissue) is not necessary; cure rates with lumpectomies (removing only the cancerous lump and some surrounding tissue) are just as high. Finally, health practitioners should give women explicit instruction and practice in self-examination, and send monthly reminders (like those dentists mail regularly).

No disease needs more public attention than acquired immune deficiency syndrome (AIDS). AIDS is an incurable, fatal disease caused by the human immunodeficiency virus (HIV). The virus may produce no symptoms for as long as eight or nine years. Eventually, however, it attacks the immune system, leaving the victim vulnerable to a specific type of pneumonia or to a type of cancer known as Kaposi's sarcoma. These symptoms and the presence of other indicators in the blood lead to a diagnosis of AIDS.

Until a cure or a preventive vaccine is found, prevention is our only protection. Yet in spite of all that is known and all that has been written about the way AIDS is spread, fantasies, myths, and just plain ignorance abound. And even those who know how to protect themselves and others may not always do so. Again, knowledge does not necessarily translate into healthy behavior. Teenagers and young adults are the

"We're Most satisfied."

For that extra measure of satisfaction, choose not to smoke.

You don't have to smoke to be satisfied. In fact, if you don't smoke you're probably happier and healthier than someone who does. Take care of yourself. Don't smoke.

♥ American Heart Association

Teenagers: Smoking causes bad breath and yellow teeth.

Talk About AIDS

How About Dinner, A Movie, And A Talk About AIDS?

Marie: That's not exactly my idea of a great date.

Why?

Marie: Because it's kind of depressing.

When you think about AIDS and being single, what's the first thing that comes to mind?

Marie: Be careful!

AIDS scares you?

Marie: Sure. But, it's something I have to think about.

When you say you think about it, what do you mean?

Marie: I ask myself questions I never thought about before.

Do you ask guys?

Marie: I'm starting to.

How is that working out?

Marie: Actually, not so bad.

AMERICA RESPONDS TO AIDS
1-800-342-AIDS

Public-service announcements help to spread information about the risks of smoking, AIDS, drug abuse, and other health hazards. Health psychologists are working on effective ways of getting people to move from being aware of the dangers to changing their behavior.

IF YOU'RE INTO DOPE, YOU MIGHT AS WELL SMOKE THIS.

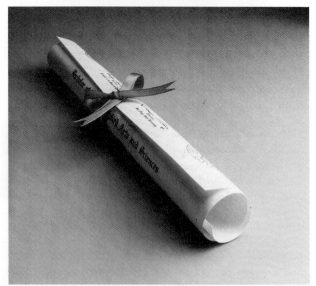

There's one sure way to see your future go up in smoke. Do drugs. Last year alone, America's businesses lost more than $60 billion to drugs. So this year, most of the Fortune 500 will be administering drug tests. If you fail the test, you're out of a job. The message is simple. Doing drugs could blow your whole education.

WE'RE PUTTING DRUGS OUT OF BUSINESS.

Partnership for a Drug-Free America

most sexually active age group in our population, and therefore highly vulnerable to AIDS (and other sexually transmitted diseases). But they are also the least likely to protect themselves. A survey of 1,000 adolescents found a good deal of confusion about who gets AIDS, how it is spread, and how to avoid infection (DeClemente et al., 1986). Even those who know how to protect themselves may not do so, for several reasons. First, many young people believe that AIDS is something that happens to "them" [homosexuals and intravenous (IV) drug users], not to "us" (drug-free heterosexuals). In fact, AIDS is spread through contact with the blood or semen of an infected person, typically via a blood transfusion, by sharing a needle (in IV drug use), or by having sexual contact— whether heterosexual or homosexual—without a condom. The receiving partner may be more at risk than the inserting partner. Second, using condoms is often considered "uncool," especially among adolescents (Collins and Aspinwall, 1989). And using condoms requires planning—someone has to buy them and have them. But teenage sex is often unplanned and secretive, and many teens are embarrassed to seem prepared. Third, young people often believe that they can tell from a person's appearance whether he or she is carrying the AIDS virus. Many assume that AIDS carriers are slovenly vagrants and that clean-cut, attractive, affluent people are not risky sexual partners. In fact, the reverse may be true. People who are attractive are somewhat more likely to have been sexually active and therefore may be more at risk for AIDS (Cochran and Mays, in press). Finally, young people usually do not talk about the intimate details of their past with a prospective partner until after they have become involved (i.e., had intercourse). This is particularly true for people who have been promiscuous or bisexual. In a survey of college students, a large proportion of men and an only slightly smaller proportion of women said that they would lie about their sexual history to a new partner (Cochran and Mays, in press). Thus the information that a partner is at risk usually comes too late.

To date, very few cases of AIDS have been reported in adolescents and college-age adults (reinforcing the belief among young people that it can't happen to them). But because the HIV virus may lie dormant for many years, those exposed to it in adolescence might not show symptoms until they reach their mid- to late twenties. The tragedy is that such early deaths might have been prevented through the use of condoms, which can be purchased inexpensively in a drug store by a person of any age and either sex.

The AIDS example illustrates that appeals through the mass media can help to alert the public to the need for a change in health behavior. Almost every day one reads about debates over mandatory AIDS testing. But media campaigns seem to be more successful in increasing public fear (sometimes irrationally) than in actually changing behavior (Lau et al., 1980). The challenge for health psychologists is how to translate concern into healthy behavior.

CHANGING HEALTH HABITS: THE COGNITIVE-BEHAVIORAL APPROACH

A person's behavior is the result of both external events, such as rewards, praise, and other reinforcements, and internal events, including how we *think* about our actions. The cognitive-behavioral approach to changing health habits is based on the observation that modifying behavior without modifying the atti-

tudes and beliefs people hold about their behavior is rarely successful. For example, most smokers want to quit. But self-doubt interferes with their motivation. They tell themselves, "I'll never be able to give up smoking" or "I've tried before and failed," and so they postpone active efforts to quit. In cognitive-behavioral therapy, both the unhealthy habit and the beliefs that accompany it are targets for change. Initially, cognitive-behavioral change may come from a therapist, a physician, or a formal group program (such as Smokenders). But ultimately it is the client who must carry out the behavior change on his or her own.

The most successful programs for health-habit change use a broad spectrum of learning techniques, or what is sometimes called the *multimodal* approach. A typical program might begin with *self-observation* and *self-monitoring*, in which the client keeps a detailed record of the target behavior. An obese client who needs to lose weight, for example, would keep a diary of when she ate, what she ate, and what else was happening at the time, including how she felt. This record helps the therapist and client identify the thoughts, feelings, or circumstances that elicit the unwanted behavior, as well as the dimensions of the problem. (Often people do not realize how often or how much they eat or smoke.)

The second step might be to remove the stimuli that trigger the undesirable behavior. A smoker would be advised to remove all ashtrays from his office and apartment; an obese client, to clear the refrigerator and cupboards of unhealthy, high-fat food. The goal of *stimulus control* is to eliminate unthinking, reflexive behavior and make it more difficult to indulge in the unhealthy behavior.

Next the therapist would help the client to change patterns of *self-reinforcement* that maintain the unhealthy habit. Drawing on the principles of operant conditioning, the smoker might set up a schedule of rewards for each day without cigarettes: a movie for day one, a new CD for day two, dinner with a friend for day three, and so on. Some people find that they cannot change their behavior all at once, or go "cold turkey." In these cases, the therapist would use the principles of *shaping*, with a schedule of rewards for cutting back from twenty to fifteen, ten, five, and finally no cigarettes. The goal of self-reinforcement is to change the consequences of behavior, so that not smoking (or snacking or drinking) is associated with rewards rather than experienced as punishment.

Another behavioral technique for changing health habits is **contingency contracting.** A person makes a contract with another individual detailing the rewards or punishments contingent on succeeding or failing to make a behavior change. For example, in one actual case a black woman attempting to control her use of amphetamines made a contingency contract with her therapist authorizing payment of $50 to the Ku Klux Klan each time she abused the drug. The contract was extremely successful (Thoresen and Mahoney, 1974).

The therapist would also help the client to correct self-defeating patterns of thought, through *cognitive restructuring.* People who are giving up old habits often feel as if they are losing a close friend. The therapist helps the client to reverse this cognitive pattern, by focusing on gains rather than losses. Thus the smoker might be taught to remind himself, "When I don't smoke, food tastes better, I can run without getting winded, my children are proud of me." Clients may believe, deep down, that they cannot change. Thus the dieter who sneaks one candy bar in the afternoon may say to herself, "I'm a hopeless case," and pick up a gallon of ice cream and an apple pie on the way home. The therapist would teach her to tell herself, instead, "I've been doing great; I can run extra laps tomorrow at the gym; think what my old friends will say when I've lost ten pounds."

Finally, the therapist may use *skills training* to help the client deal more adaptively with the situations that evoked the unwanted behavior in the first place. A client may have begun drinking to excess because he or she felt anxious in social situations, was under a great deal of stress at work, or was alone and lonely much of the time. Depending on the client, the therapist might work on developing social skills, finding healthier ways to relax after work (such as exercise or a hobby), or getting out (joining clubs, taking a class, and the like). The great advantage of the multimodal approach is that it allows the therapist to tailor a program to fit the needs and problems of each client. Let us look at some actual examples.

A PROGRAM TO CONTROL DRINKING

During the Persian Gulf crisis, American soldiers were stationed in Saudi Arabia, an Islamic country with a strict ban on alcohol (Shenon, 1991). The result was a "natural experiment" in alcohol with-

drawal. Most of the soldiers in the Gulf were young men in their late teens and early twenties, and many had been drinkers before they left for the Gulf. Stranded for months in the desert in a highly stressful situation, one might have expected them to rebel, set up home-made stills, and demand at least beer. With a very few exceptions, they did not. Many in fact reported being changed by the experience.

> Back in Germany, a lot of people get off work and go drink, and on weekends they go crazy. Alcohol can change your personality real quick, and there were a lot of fights in the barracks. You don't see that here.
>
> People are learning to deal with their problems here, and a lot of soldiers are seeing the best part of themselves.

Army officials agreed. The rate of disciplinary problems in Saudi Arabia was less than a third of that for troops stationed anywhere else in the world. Note though, that we have only a *correlation* here. It is not valid to conclude that no alcohol caused high morale and good discipline. After all, unlike soldiers in Germany or elsewhere, these soldiers were awaiting or experiencing combat in a war that was strongly supported at home. Other conditions, completely unrelated to drinking, could account for the lack of disciplinary problems.

Back in the states, drinking often begins in high school (or earlier). In national surveys, half of high school seniors say they drink every week, and more than a third say they got drunk (had five or more drinks on one occasion) during the past two weeks (Johnston et al., 1986). Between 70 and 95 percent of college students drink, and 15 to 25 percent describe themselves as heavy drinkers (Kivilan et al., 1989). Alcohol consumption generally peaks between ages eighteen and twenty-five (Dupont, 1988). Nevertheless, between 10 and 15 million adult Americans are either alcoholics or problem drinkers, and most began drinking in their youth.

Excessive drinking is not only a health risk in itself, it is also implicated in other health problems. Drinking and driving is a leading cause of death as a result of motor vehicle crashes. There is evidence that losing a spouse or child in such a crash causes intense grief, anguish, and problems in fuctioning that last for many years (Lehman et al., 1987). Many people are unaware of the length of time alcohol remains in the bloodstream, thus hampering performance. Al-

Alcohol is a popular "social lubricant" on college campuses, just as it is in other areas of society. But excessive drinking poses special risks to college-age young people who are particularly sensitive to peer pressure.

though there is variation from one person to another, the National Institute on Alcohol Abuse and Alcoholism estimates that if a person ingests three drinks in a half-hour period, it takes about six hours for that alcohol to leave the body (Ray, 1991). Although there are no hard statistics, many experts believe that drinking often plays a role in risky, unprotected sex (and, by extension, sexually transmitted diseases and unwanted pregnancies). Many college deans link alcohol to problems ranging from rowdiness and vandalism to racial confrontations and rape. Attempts to ban alcohol on campuses have generally failed to control the problem: parties simply move off campus. College-sponsored alcohol abuse programs attract only a few participants. A major reason is that most students do not regard drinking as a problem (Baer et al., 1989).

One eight-week training program focuses on helping students to *control* drinking rather than to eliminate it altogether (Baer et al., 1989; Land and Marlatt, 1983). This program draws on many of the techniques we have just described. Students are taught to monitor their drinking and identify the circumstances under which they are most likely to drink excessively (often at parties). Then they are taught a technique for controlling alcohol consumption, called **placebo drinking.** At parties, the student either consumes only nonalcoholic beverages that

look like alcoholic drinks, or alternates between alcoholic and nonalcoholic beverages.

Drinking among college students often is associated with peer pressure (a boy's friends dare him to drink a pint of scotch in an hour, or a girl's friends accuse her of being a wet blanket if she doesn't drink) and with social anxiety (feeling nervous at parties and other gatherings). The program includes training in facts about alcohol. Students are told, for example, that ingesting a large quantity of alcohol in a limited time period can result in death from acute alcohol poisoning. The program also emphasizes social skills: learning to recognize that other people feel shy, too; role-playing conversation starters and face-saving ways to handle rejection; and the like. For students who are more solitary drinkers, the program also includes stress management and relaxation techniques (discussed later in this chapter).

Equally important to the program is *life-style rebalancing* (Marlatt and George, 1988). Students are encouraged to take aerobics, eat better, stop smoking, and change their health habits in other ways. The theory is that students who become health-oriented will view excessive drinking as incompatible with their new life-style.

Initial evaluations indicate that this program has been fairly successful. Participants reported significant reductions in drinking compared to a control group that received only educational materials about the ill effects of drinking. Moreover, these gains persisted over a year-long follow-up period (Baer et al., 1989).

PREVENTING RELAPSE

After people break an unhealthy habit, we want to keep them from relapsing once the program ends. In fact, the rate of relapse runs from 50 to 90 percent for addictive disorders such as alcoholism, smoking, drug abuse, and overeating (Brownell et al., 1986). People may relapse because their bodies never fully adjust to abstinence, when they are under stress, when they are suddenly exposed to stimuli that evoke old associations (such as meeting an old "drinking buddy"), or simply because over time their motivation fades and their vigilance wears down.

Anyone who has tried to give up smoking knows how easy it is to slip back into the habit. A review of studies of people who tried to quit smoking on their own found that it often is a cyclical process (Cohen et al., 1989). In other words, over the course of a lifetime many smokers move from periods of smoking to abstinence to smoking again, and so on. The researchers found a median relapse rate of 24 percent among smokers who succeeded in quitting for six months, with heavy smokers having higher relapse rates than light smokers. In general, stop-smoking programs seem to be less successful than quitting on one's own: most studies find relapse rates of about 70 percent (Glasgow and Lichtenstein, 1987; Schwartz, 1987). But one reason for these results may be that these studies do not take into account the cyclical pattern of quitting; another, that hard-core smokers are the most likely to seek professional help.

To date, no one has found a solution to the relapse problem. Neither "booster sessions" (periodic check-up meetings with the therapist or group), contingency management (requiring substantial deposits that are forfeited if the person relapses), nor lifelong treatment have shown high rates of success. The problem with these strategies may be that they imply the individual cannot control the behavior him- or herself. The most promising technique to date seems to be building relapse protection into the initial program. Clients are encouraged to anticipate situations that might encourage them to relapse (such as romantic problems, job stress, or returning to a favorite bar or another environment where one practiced unhealthy behavior) and to work out strategies for coping (such as placebo drinking) in advance. Clients are also taught to think of single transgressions ("bumming" one cigarette, "pigging out" at a celebration) as missteps rather than signs that they lack willpower. As we pointed out earlier, self-efficacy (feeling that we can do something) and response efficacy (feeling that we know how to deal with this problem) are important factors in healthy behavior.

So far we have been talking about behavior patterns that are more or less voluntary. To be sure, there is evidence that obesity, alcoholism, drug abuse, and even smoking are partly hereditary. This does not mean that some people are "predestined" to lead unhealthy lives, but that they are genetically more vulnerable than other people are and more likely to become addicted. Even so, such behaviors as drinking, smoking, overeating, or taking drugs are typically a matter of choice. One thing that none of us choose, but all of us experience, is stress. In the sections that follow we will look at what causes stress, how it affects our health, and how we can cope with it.

STRESS

You have to catch a train and you can't find your keys. Your car won't start. It's Friday, your first exam is Monday, and you haven't begun writing a forty-page term paper due the same day. You were turned down for a student loan and don't know whether you will be able to earn enough over the summer for next semester's tuition, much less how you will pay this month's phone bill. You suspect that you (or your girlfriend) might be pregnant. You pick up the campus newspaper and discover that your best friend was murdered in a robbery attempt.

Everyone experiences stress, ranging from minor irritations to major traumas. Intuitively we recognize that stress has both physiological and psychological components. When we are under stress our palms sweat, our heart races, our neck and shoulder muscles tense, our head aches, and our stomach churns (physiological components of stress). We also have difficulty concentrating, get angry about little things, and tend to experience unpleasant thoughts, however much we try to push them out of our minds (psychological components).

The earliest models of stress focused on physiological reactions. One held that when an organism

Stress is a part of everyday life, but people differ greatly in their reactions to minor irritations, such as the daily commute, and to major life events, such as divorce.

perceives a threat, the sympathetic nervous system and endocrine system are aroused to enable the organism to attack the invader or to flee. This is called the **fight-or-flight response** (Cannon, 1932). Later, Hans Selye (1956) proposed a somewhat different model. He described a **general adaptation syndrome** with three phases. In the *alarm* stage, the organism becomes mobilized to meet a threat. This mobilization is directed by the adrenal glands, which promote sympathetic nervous system activity (breathing rate increases, heart rate and blood pressure increase, blood is directed to the muscles, digestion slows down, and so on; see Chapter 3). In the second stage, *resistance*, the organism tries to come to terms with the threat—for example, through confrontation. The third stage, *exhaustion*, occurs if the organism depletes its physiological resources in the process of trying to overcome a threat. This is why repeated or prolonged exposure to stress causes wear and tear on the body. According to Selye, the response to a stressful event is nonspecific. That is, regardless of the cause of stress, the individual will respond with the same physiological pattern of reactions.

Selye's work was important because it offered a general theory of reactions to a wide variety of stressful events over time, and provided a way of thinking about the interplay of physiological and environmental factors. The major criticism of Selye is that he virtually ignored psychological factors: all people do not respond to potentially threatening events in the same way.

The psychological view defines **stress** as that which we appraise as harmful, threatening, or challenging (Lazarus and Folkman, 1984; Lazarus and Launier, 1978). In contrast to Selye's model, this definition takes into account wide variations in the experience of stress. Clearly, some events (loss of a loved one, prolonged unemployment) are more stressful than others (losing a sweater, waiting in a long line). Moreover, individuals differ in the way they respond to similar events. Some people panic at the very thought of a deadline; others do their best when they are working under pressure. Some people thrive on parties: they love the crowd, the noise, and the excitement of meeting new people. Others find walking into a room full of strangers and striking up conversations excruciating. Some people are terrified of heights; others are passionate about mountain climbing. Some people recover fairly rapidly from divorce, and feel they are stronger and happier as a result; others remain hurt, angry, and socially and emotionally disoriented for years after (Wallerstein and Blakeslee, 1989). In short, what some people find stressful others find benign and even beneficial or

Psychologists and other health-care professionals are becoming more aware of the burden of stress imposed on those who must care for loved ones afflicted by chronic, degenerative illnesses. This man, walking with his wife and son, was a brilliant engineer; he now has Alzheimer's disease and needs constant supervision.

exciting. One determinant of whether or not we feel stress depends on how we evaluate or *appraise* a situation.

A classic study illustrated the importance of appraisal in the experience of stress (Speisman et al., 1964). College students viewed a graphic film depicting tribal initiation rites, including genital surgery. Before seeing the film, the students were assigned to one of four experimental conditions. One group heard a dry anthropological description of the rites. The second group listened to a lecture that emphasized the excitement of the initiates, rather than the pain they experienced. A third group was given a detailed description of the pain and trauma the initiates underwent. The fourth group received no preparation. Both measures of autonomic arousal (heart rate and skin conductance) and self-reports suggested that the first two groups, who were prepared to see the rites as a meaningful, even religious experience for participants, experienced far less stress than the second two groups, who focused on the pain.

In real life situations, appraisal involves two steps (Lazarus, 1990): whether we judge the event or situation as a threat to our well-being (primary appraisal), and whether we believe we have the resources to cope with the threat (secondary appraisal). The level of stress we experience depends on the balance between the two. When we perceive the threat as mild and our ability to cope as high, stress will be minimal. But when we perceive the threat as severe and our ability to cope as weak, stress will be substantial.

Much has been written in the popular press about the negative effects of stress on health. What are the facts? Psychologists have approached this issue from different angles. Some have investigated the impact of stress on the body. Others have focused on major life events, and the question of what kinds of events are most likely to compromise health. Still others are concerned with individual differences in the experience of stress.

STRESS AND THE IMMUNE SYSTEM

The 27-year-old army captain who commanded the ceremonial troops at the funeral of President Kennedy . . . died 10 days later.

A 39-year-old pair of twins who had been inseparable died within weeks of each other; no cause of death was mentioned.

A 64-year-old woman who was said never to have recovered from the death of her son in an auto accident 14 years earlier died 4 days after her husband was murdered in a holdup. (Adapted from Engel, 1971, p. 774)

For psychologists, cases of *sudden death syndrome* provide dramatic proof that stress can be dangerous to your health. But what exactly is the relationship between stress and illness? *How* does stress affect the body? Research has begun to establish a connection between stress and the immune system. Indeed, a new field—**psychoneuroimmunology**—has developed to examine how psychological factors alter the immune system and ultimately increase the risk of immune system–related diseases, such as AIDS, cancer, arthritis, infections, and allergies.

The **immune system** is the body's surveillance system: it guards the body against foreign invaders (called *antigens*). The primary tasks of the immune system are, first, to detect and identify antigens, and second, to neutralize them and remove them from the body. The cells which handle these tasks are produced in the lymph organs and bone marrow, and are known collectively as *lymphocytes*. When bacteria invade the body, *B-lymphocytes* coat them or neutralize their toxin. This activity attracts *macrophages* ("big eater cells"), which ingest and destroy them. When viruses, cancer cells, fungi, or parasites appear in the body, other cells spring into action. *T-lymphocytes* attack these invaders directly, breaking down their cell membranes. *Natural killer* (NK) cells attack cells already infected by a virus and secrete interferon, which inhibits viral reproduction in uninfected cells. (T-lymphocytes and NK cells are also responsible for the body's rejection of organ and tissue transplants.)

The term **immunocompetence** refers to how well the immune system is operating. Researchers assess immunocompetence by measuring the levels of lymphocytes and antibodies present in a person's blood or saliva and testing whether they are active by exposing them to natural and artificial "enemies" in the laboratory.

A growing body of research suggests that even commonplace stressors can suppress the immune system. Academic stress is a prime example. In a study of forty second-year medical students, researchers tested immune functioning six weeks before finals and again during final exams. The levels of lymphocytes, how active and responsive they were, and even the amount of interferon secreted by NK cells were all significantly lower during exams (Glaser et al., 1985, 1986). The implication was clear: academic stress compromises immunity, making students more vulnerable to illness.

Immunosuppression has been linked to a wide range of stressful conditions, including problems in interpersonal relationships. Researchers have found lowered immunity and higher rates of illness in women who have recently lost a spouse (Irwin et al., 1987), couples who have recently separated or divorced (Kiecolt-Glaser et al., 1987), and unhappily married couples (Levinson and Gottman, 1985). This is not to say that everyone whose marriage is disrupted suffers increased vulnerability and poor health. Men who initiated the divorce show better immune functioning than those who had divorce thrust upon them (Kiecolt-Glaser et al., 1988).

One of the most difficult interpersonal roles appears to be caring for a family member or friend who is suffering from a long-term illness, such as AIDS or Alzheimer's disease (Kiecolt-Glaser et al., 1987). The chronic stress of being a care giver results in significantly lower immunocompetence, as compared to people of the same age and general health status (including nutrition, caffeine consumption, alcohol use, and amount of sleep).

Acute and long-term stress can both lower resistance. For example, the *Apollo* astronauts experienced sharp declines in immune functioning following splashdown (Fischer et al., 1972). And people who lived near the Three Mile Island nuclear power plant after the accident there showed lower resistance as well (McKinnon et al., 1989). Daily hassles and even anticipated stress can affect the immune system (Kemeny et al., 1989; Moss et al., 1989).

In short, there is strong evidence of a connection between stress and lowered immune system function. A question for ongoing research is whether stress affects the immune system directly, by causing wear and tear on the system, or indirectly, as a result of depression, negative moods, poorer health habits, and other side effects of stress.

While the research we have been describing deals with the consequences of stress, other studies have looked at the origins of stress. What events or types of events are most likely to lead to stress?

STRESS AND LIFE EVENTS

Although the most negative events in our lives— death of a loved one, divorce, getting fired—cause the most stress, even happy events, such as getting married, having a baby, being promoted at work, or going on vacation, may cause stress as well. Two early stress researchers, Thomas Holmes and Richard Rahe (1967), found that *any life change*—whether positive or negative—is stressful. The reason is that changes

Adapting to a major life event, good or bad, always causes stress, but a stressful event isn't necessarily a threat to health. Some people dread their retirement as a kind of living death; for others, it's a chance to try new experiences and get more enjoyment out of life.

in the external circumstances of our lives force us to adapt; old habits must be given up and new patterns established. To assess the impact of life changes, Holmes and Rahe developed the **Social Readjustment Rating Scale (SRRS).** The scale lists forty-three items that were determined through extensive testing to be events that, on average, require people to make the most changes in their lives. Each item is given a point value that reflects the amount of adaptation required. Death of a spouse, for example, disrupts virtually every aspect of one's life, so it is given the highest number of points (100). Retirement demands fewer adjustments, and so is given a lower rating (45 points). A minor violation of the law is irritating but does not force a person to alter his or her life-style in major ways, and so is given the lowest rating (11 points). A researcher using this scale asks individuals to check off every event that has occurred in a given time period (usually the preceding year) and then totals up the points. According to Holmes and Rahe, people with scores of 300 or more are at high risk for illness and injury. For example, in a study of college football players, they found that 50 percent of those identified as high risk were injured that season, compared to 25 percent of those at medium risk and 9 percent of those considered at low risk (Holmes and Gregersen, 1974).

Other researchers, however, have found that this approach to assessing life stress is only moderately successful in predicting subsequent mental or physical health. One problem is that some of the items on the scale are ambiguous. For example, "personal illness" could mean anything from a cold to a heart attack. Second, people can experience the same events quite differently. One person may experience retirement as liberating, while another finds it disheartening. Third, the scale does not consider the context of life events. Surely, losing a job will be more stressful for someone who has just bought a new house and taken out a large mortgage than for someone with modest expenses and substantial savings. Another problem is that the scale is retrospective and does not attempt to assess the person's current state. A person who is under considerable stress at the time he or she fills out the questionnaire might recall an earlier illness as being more severe than it actually was, for example.

Because of such problems, many stress researchers have abandoned the use of simple rating scales like the SRRS. Instead, most try to obtain information about the context in which the event occurred, as well as information about how a given individual reacts to the event in question. Life events researchers are also increasingly interested in identifying the features of particular life events that make them more stress-enhancing, such as how predictable or controllable they are (Wortman et al., in press).

While some researchers who are interested in the impact of life events continue to study large samples of people who have experienced a variety of different events, others believe that we will learn more by focusing in detail on particular life events, such as bereavement, job loss, divorce, etc. (Wortman et al., in press). In such studies, the emphasis is typically on understanding the short- and long-term psychological consequences of the event, although some investigators have examined the impact of such events on subsequent physical health. As we noted in Chapter 11, one of the most fascinating aspects of studying life events is that reactions to any given event are usually extremely variable, with some people experiencing far more distress than others. As Gordon (1991) has written about the range of responses to abortion, "after having an abortion, some women get dressed and go to Burger King and some want to die."

To illustrate the issues that are faced in examining the impact of a particular life event, we will look at one potentially stressful event—abortion—in depth.

IN DEPTH

The Psychological Consequences of Abortion

Research on the psychological impact of abortion on women has been almost as controversial as abortion itself. Few areas of study have been as strongly influenced by personal convictions, political agendas, and theoretical assumptions. Nancy Adler (1991; Adler et al., 1990) has reviewed the history of abortion research and analyzed current findings. We will draw extensively on her work here.

THE INITIAL STUDIES

Studies conducted in the 1950s and 1960s were almost unanimous in asserting that abortion was a psychologically devastating experience for women, one from which few recovered completely (e.g., Simon and Senturia, 1966). Almost all of the early studies were based on individual case studies of women who sought psychotherapy following an abortion—by definition, a self-selected sample of women who were troubled by the experience. Abortions were still illegal in the United States, so studying a representative sample was virtually impossible. Nevertheless, the authors of these case studies often assumed that their patient's distress was typical of all women, and the studies often were cited as applying to women in general. The view that abortion was traumatic was seldom questioned.

One reason for widespread, uncritical acceptance of this view was that it fit prevailing notions of female psychology (Deutsch, 1945). According to psychoanalytic theory, abortion was a violation of the powerful "maternal instinct." (By implication, women who were not severely stressed by abortion were missing something.) One interesting study (Fingerer, 1973) found that psychoanalytic postdoctoral students predicted that women going to a clinic for an abortion would have far more negative responses than the women actually experienced, either before or after the procedure. The author concluded that "the psychological aftereffects of abortion seem to reside in psychoanalytic theory and societal myths." At the time, this was a minority view. Even today antiabortion groups often claim that abortion endangers a woman's psychological health. Some even hold that women experience a "post-abortion trauma syndrome" similar to the "post-traumatic stress syndrome" identified in veterans of the Vietnam war (Speckhard, 1987).

CRITICISMS, ALTERNATIVES, AND FURTHER RESEARCH

In 1988, President Ronald Reagan asked Surgeon General C. Everett Koop to review the literature and issue a report on the medical and physical dangers of abortion. By this time abortion on demand had been legal for fifteen years, and there were over 200 papers on the topic. Koop wrote a report, but did not release it to the public on the grounds that the results were inconclusive. Koop testified before Congress that although the psychological effects of abortion can be overwhelming for a given individual, this was rare—in his words, "minuscule from a public health perspective" (Committee on Government Operations, 1989, p. 14).

In 1989 the American Psychological Association (APA) assembled a panel of experts, including Adler, to review the literature on the psychological impact of abortion. Adler's analysis of the existing research (1991) identified three common methodological flaws.

First, many studies did not consider the circumstances under which the abortion took place. In particular, they did not differentiate between women who had undergone legal and illegal abortions. Illegal abortions typically were performed in clandestine, unsanitary settings, with no painkillers or other medications. Women who had illegal abortions risked life-threatening infections, not to mention legal reprisals. These circumstances—not the procedure itself—might have caused considerable stress. Second, many studies did not consider individual characteristics—such as the subject's age, her marital status, and whether she had children, much less how she felt about becoming pregnant. Third, many did not take into account the timing of the abortion or the type of procedure used. One study that did include these factors found that the later in pregnancy an abortion is performed, the more difficult it is, emotionally and psychologically (Kaltreider et al., 1979). The underlying assumption in most studies was that the termination of a pregnancy, no matter what the circumstances, was a stressful experience.

In order to draw valid conclusions about the psychological impact of abortion, the panel of experts focused their attention solely on those studies deemed to be methodologically sound. This panel established three minimal criteria for including a study in its review. First, the sample had to be limited to women in the United States (to rule out the effects of different cultural attitudes toward abortion). Second, the sample had to be limited to women who had legal abortions, with no institutional barriers (such as approval by a panel of physicians). Third, the study had to use standard data-collection procedures that allowed for statistical analysis. Only 20 of the 200 plus papers published on the effects of abortion met these minimal criteria.

The panel found that "the weight of the evidence from scientific studies indicates that legal abortion of an unwanted pregnancy in the first trimester does not pose a psychological hazard for most women" (Adler et al., 1990, p. 42). In fact, most studies found that stress is higher *before* an abortion than afterward. In other words, abortion seems to reduce the stress of an unwanted pregnancy (Cohen and Roth, 1984; Major et al., 1985). In one study (Lazarus, 1985), the most common emotion after abortion was relief, reported by 76 percent of the women. The most common negative emotion, guilt, was reported by only 17 percent.

Only two U.S. studies have compared women who had an abortion to women who gave birth. The first (Athanasiou et al., 1973) looked at three groups of women: those who had early abortions, late abortions, or term births. Subjects were matched for age, marital status, previous births, ethnicity, and socioeconomic status. A year to a year-and-a-half after the abortion or birth, the women were asked to complete the Minnesota Multiphasic Personality Inventory (MMPI). The researchers found no evidence of psychological disturbance in any of the three groups, and few differences in other characteristics. They concluded that the women were "startlingly similar."

In another study (Zabin et al., 1989), researchers interviewed 360 adolescent girls just after they had gone to a clinic for a pregnancy test, and again two years later. All of the girls showed high levels of anxiety in the first interview. (Apparently, none of them wanted to be pregnant.) In the second interview, girls who had chosen abortion showed a more positive psychological profile than those who had become mothers. Specifically, they were lower in anxiety, higher in self-esteem, and had a greater sense of internal control than the child-bearing group. Interestingly, these adolescents seemed to be better off than girls who turned out *not* to be pregnant after the first interview. One might speculate that the decision to have an abortion helped these girls to feel that they could take responsibility for their lives. (It is important to remember the age of these subjects, and the probability that the results are compounded by the difficulties of being an unmarried teenage mother.)

This is not to say that abortion has no negative consequences. The more difficulty a woman has making the decision to have an abortion, the more likely she is to experience negative emotions (such as regret, sadness, and guilt) (Adler, 1975). This is particularly true when the pregnancy was *wanted* (Major et al., 1985). For example, when a woman has an abortion because diagnostic genetic testing has found a major defect in the fetus, both she and her partner may be at risk for depression. Their marriage may also suffer (Blumberg et al., 1975). A study in Denmark (David et al., 1981) found that women who were separated, divorced, or widowed experienced more psychological problems following an abortion (as measured by admission to psychiatric hospitals) than did single or married women—

presumably because the termination of the pregnancy compounded their feelings of loss. Women who reported that they were pressured or even coerced into having an abortion, or that their partner or parents (in the case of adolescents) did not agree with the decision, are at higher risk than women who made the decision freely (Adler, 1975; Osofsky and Osofsky, 1972; Shusterman, 1979). So are women who blame themselves for an unwanted pregnancy, rather than blaming their partner, the situation, or chance (Major et al., 1985).

The APA panel concluded that while the effects of abortion generally appear to be mild, this is not always the case. "Women who are terminating pregnancies that are wanted and personally meaningful; who lack support from their partner or parents for the abortion; or who have more conflicting feelings or are less sure of their decision beforehand may be at relatively higher risk for negative consequences" (Adler et al., 1990, p. 43). But the impact of abortion seems more similar to other "normal life stressors" than to severe traumatic experiences.

PATTERNS AND CONCLUSIONS

The APA panel's review helped to "clear the air," but at the same time pointed out many blind spots in our knowledge of the impact of abortion.

Most studies have focused on the time just before and after abortion. To determine the full impact, a researcher ideally would begin with baseline measures of the women's psychological state and overall adjustment prior to becoming pregnant, and follow them through the discovery of pregnancy, the decision to have or not have a baby, and the aftermath. While such a prospective study would be an expensive, long-term undertaking, it is not impossible.

Most studies have treated abortion as a single event, rather than as part of a chain of events, beginning with the discovery of pregnancy. The impact of pregnancy on the woman's life (changes in her relationship with her partner and parents, friends' reactions, rescheduling of life plans, reevaluations of the self) may be greater than the impact of abortion itself.

Surely pregnancy means different things to different women. For some women, pregnancy might represent hope of saving a dying relationship or, alternatively, an obstacle to escaping from an unsatisfactory relationship. For a teenager, pregnancy might represent hopes for being recognized as an adult and becoming independent from her parents or, the ultimate dreaded event, even "punishment" for becoming sexually active. A woman who had tried for years to become pregnant, and failed, might see pregnancy as a "miracle"; a woman who used contraception erratically or not at all might see pregnancy as one more situation in which she had failed (Adler, in press). Existing studies show that for most women pregnancy is the crisis, and abortion is the solution. But this may be an oversimplification. Learning how a woman's appraisal of pregnancy affects her experience of abortion is an important area for new research.

We know very little about the long-term effects of abortion. (The longest follow-up in the studies the APA panel reviewed was only two years.) Perhaps some women who have an abortion regret the decision and become pregnant again and have a baby soon after. Abortion also may have delayed or "sleeper effects." Suppose, for example, that a woman has an abortion in her youth and then later, when she is older and married, has difficulty conceiving a child or complications with a wanted pregnancy. Do these later experiences lead to a reappraisal of the abortion, and perhaps guilt, feelings of remorse, and depression? We don't know.

In fact, we know very little about the impact of the social and political climate on women considering abortion. If anything, abortion has become more controversial and opinions more polarized in recent years. Depending on where she lives, who her friends are, and perhaps her religious affiliation, a woman may be under considerable pressure to have or not have an abortion. She also may be bombarded with propaganda, both pro and con. What effect do these politicized cross-currents have on a woman's personal experience of abortion?

In assessing the impact of abortion it is important to select an appropriate control group for comparison. An obvious choice would be women who carry a pregnancy to term, then give the baby up for adoption. In both cases the pregnancy is unwanted (at least in the sense that the mother feels she cannot take responsibility for a child). One reason such a study has not been undertaken is that the number of women putting babies up for adoption has declined more or less steadily (in part because of the legalization of abortion and in part

Abortion remains a controversial, emotionally charged issue. For most women who have had an abortion, however, the experience has not been permanently damaging.

because of greater cultural acceptance of single parenthood). More restrictive abortion laws might change this picture, however. Is completing an unwanted pregnancy more or less stressful than abortion?

In considering this question, it is equally important to investigate the effects of unwanted births, not only on women, but also on *children*. When a single teenager has a child, she is committing herself to a life path of limited educational and occupational opportunities, as well as to family responsibilities that will continue for years. Few teenagers are prepared for the demands of an infant and the limitations that motherhood places on their social lives. Stress on the mother may translate into stress on the child.

As a result of recent United States Supreme Court rulings, abortions may become less available to low-income mothers. Therefore there has been renewed interest in the consequences of denying abortions. A recent review of research in this area, conducted mostly in other countries, found that women who are denied abortions and subsequently keep their babies may have difficulties with parenting (Angier, 1991; Dagg, 1991). In one study, 34

34 percent of such mothers indicated that they felt angry and rejecting toward their unwanted child. They described the child as a burden they frequently resented, and they were less likely to breastfeed or cuddle their babies than most mothers.

Not surprisingly, studies focusing on the fates of the unwanted children born to these mothers suggests that they indeed suffer adverse consequences. In several studies conducted in Eastern Europe and Scandanavia, children who were born because an abortion was denied had more difficulties making friends at school, were more likely to drop out of school, were likely to have drug and alcohol problems, and had difficulties establishing good interpersonal relationships (David et al., 1988). In a similar study conducted in Sweden, 18 percent of the unwanted children were reported to welfare boards for delinquency compared with 8 percent of the wanted youngsters. The unwanted children were twice as likely to have sought psychiatric help and more than three times more likely to have committed crimes (Dagg, 1991). Taken together, the evidence suggests that denying abortions appears to have far-reaching personal and societal consequences.

CHRONIC STRESS AND DAILY HASSLES

Increasingly, researchers are looking at the impact of chronic stress on mental and physical health. Is continuing, unremitting strain, with no end in sight, more stressful than a single episode of acute strain? Chronic stress might affect people both directly, exhausting their resources for coping, and indirectly, making it more difficult to cope with other major life events or even with daily hassles.

Consider the wives of American soldiers who fought in the Persian Gulf war. Most were separated from their husbands for months even before the fighting began, and letters were few and far between.

> He reminded me before he left that for the 20 years of our marriage I knew that this could happen and that we had all trained for this. The difference now is that he is in harm's way and I don't know when he will be coming home. (Smothers, 1991)

Many had to adjust to the role of single parent (and reduced income), as well as the possibility that their husbands might be killed in combat. The hardest part was not knowing what might happen when. Wives often described themselves as "news junkies":

> I watch ABC while I tape CBS, then MacNeil/Lehrer. . . . I get The Christian Science Monitor and the World Monitor. Also the Louisville Courier-Journal and USA Today. And I watch CNN. (*Newsweek*, November 19, 1990, p. 33)

Many wives and mothers actually felt relieved when the war finally began.

> The anxiety of just waiting is so stressful so when the air war started that was the beginning of the end. This [the opening of the ground war] is now the middle of the end. They'll be home soon. (Smothers, 1991)

According to these wives, then, waiting and wondering (chronic stress) were worse than knowing their husbands were in combat (acute stress).

Some research supports this view (Brown and Harris, 1978; Eckenrode, 1984; Pearlin and Schooler, 1978; see also House, 1987). But in most cases it is difficult to separate the effects of acute from chronic

Saying goodbye was just the beginning of the chronic stress that military families experienced during the Persian Gulf war. For many, waiting for the ground war to begin was harder to bear than knowing their loved ones were in combat.

stress (Kessler et al., 1985). For example, loss of a job (a single event) has multiple, often long-lasting repercussions (struggling to pay bills, looking for a new job, finding ways to fill time, dependency on a spouse, and so on). Moreover, it is difficult to determine from subjective self-reports whether a person is under constant or intermittent stress (a mixture of good days and bad days). If a person were tested on a "bad day," he or she might report more anguish and strain than if tested on a "good day." Work is underway to develop better measures of chronic stress (such as inventories of a "typical week").

Other researchers have focused on the impact on health of daily hassles—such as getting stuck in traffic jams, waiting in line, and being behind in household chores. All of us experience such minor frustrations. Is it possible that these irritants can pile up to the point where our health suffers as a result? Using scales to measure the severity of daily hassles, several studies have tied the presence of these stresses directly to declines in physical health (Delongis et al., 1982; Holahan et al., 1984). Indeed, some psychologists hold that daily hassles may be more stressful and more harmful to our health than major misfortunes (Fleming et al., 1987). Others, however, wonder if subjects' reports of constant annoyances reflect an already existing state of psychological distress (Dohrenwend et al., 1984; Monroe, 1983). In other words, feeling "hassled" might be the symptom, not the cause, of mental and perhaps physical health problems.

CONTROLLABLE VERSUS UNCONTROLLABLE STRESS

The wives of the soldiers in the Persian Gulf were faced not only with chronic stress, but also uncontrollable stress. They had no say in whether the allied troops would engage Iraqi forces, when the war would begin, or how it would be conducted. Many studies suggest that uncontrollable situations are more stressful than controllable ones. For example, one team of researchers (Suls and Mullens, 1981) asked people to list which life events on the Holmes and Rahe scale they considered controllable. They found that the rate of illness was significantly higher among people who had experienced uncontrollable life events (such as death, injury, or mandatory retirement) than among those who had experienced controllable changes (such as divorce, moving, or changing to a different line of work). Another study (Baum and Valins, 1977) compared college students randomly assigned to small suites and short corridors to those assigned to live in rooms on long, crowded corridors, where, by necessity, they were constantly bumping into people—in the halls, on the stairs, in the bathrooms. The study found that the latter were less well adapted on a variety of measures. Apparently, the "crowded" students felt that they had no control over their interactions with others.

People who must live in institutions—prisons, mental hospitals, military barracks, nursing homes—often feel stripped of control. Studies of elderly residents of nursing homes illustrate how small amounts of control can improve health. In one (Langer and Rodin, 1976), residents were divided into two groups who were roughly equal in health status and socioeconomic background. In a meeting with the nursing home administrator, the first group was reminded of the many options available to them and that it was up to them to decide how to arrange their rooms, spend their time, and use the home's facilities. If they wanted to make changes, they should speak to the staff, who would be happy to oblige. "[I]t's your life and you can make of it whatever you want," the administrator concluded. Each patient was then given a potted plant and told it is "yours to keep and take care of as you'd like" (pp. 193–194).

The second group also met with the home administrator, but the tone of the meeting was subtly different. The residents were told that they were "permitted" to use all of the home's facilities, that the staff had tried to "make your rooms nice for you," and that if they had any complaints or suggestions, "Let us know how best we can help you." The administrator emphasized, "We feel that it's *our responsibility* to make this a home you can be proud of and happy in . . ." (p. 194, emphasis added). These residents were also given plants, but told "the nurses will water them and care for them for you." Thus, where the first group was encouraged to take control of their lives, the second group was encouraged to depend on the nurses.

The results of these simple interventions were dramatic. In the first three weeks after the meeting, both nurses and residents themselves reported that members of the first group were significantly happier, more active, and more assertive than those in the second group. In a follow-up study eighteen months later (Rodin and Langer, 1977), the researchers found that members of the first group had made significant health improvements in comparison to the second group. Moreover, the death rates in the two groups were different: seven of the forty-seven residents in the first group had died (15 percent), compared to thirteen of forty-four members of the second group (30 percent) and an overall death rate of 25 percent for the nursing home as a whole. These statistics

Elderly people in nursing homes do better when they are surrounded by their own possessions and have some control over their daily activities.

should be treated with caution: all of the subjects were elderly, and all had serious enough health problems to be institutionalized, so it is impossible to say how many would have died with or without this simple intervention. But at least one other study found similar improvements when elderly patients were given more control over their lives (Schulz, 1976). As a result of these studies, attitudes toward and treatment of nursing home residents have changed significantly (Hall, 1984).

POST-TRAUMATIC STRESS SYNDROME

Other researchers have concentrated on delayed reactions to stress, especially **post-traumatic stress disorder (PTSD).** This syndrome was first identified among combat veterans, as "battle fatigue" or "shell shock." PTSD may also occur in victims of rape, kidnapping (including hostages), natural disasters, and confinement to concentration camps. People who have been exposed to these traumatic experiences sometimes suffer psychological side effects and poor health for months or even years afterward. Symptoms include hyperalertness, sleep disturbances, guilt for having survived when others have not, memory loss,

and emotional distance (difficulty establishing and maintaining close relationships) (Frye and Stockton, 1982). Some psychologists estimate that as many as 50 percent of combat veterans suffer from PTSD, and the proportion may have been higher among Vietnam veterans. We discuss this disorder more fully in Chapter 16.

In summary, there is evidence that both major traumas and minor irritations can affect health. But the relationship between stress and illness is small (Kessler et al., 1985). The simple fact is that most people do not become ill after experiencing stress. And this fact has encouraged health psychologists to investigate the possibility that some of us are more vulnerable to stress than others.

INDIVIDUAL DIFFERENCES AND STRESS

Why do some people experience more stress and stress-related illness than others? Why do individuals react to the same events in different ways? Why do some appear to be frazzled or "charged up" most of the time, while others remain cool and collected under the most adverse circumstances? Why do some recover quickly from loss, disappointment, and even illness and injuries, while others suffer for months and even years? To answer these questions, researchers have looked for the personality traits that might make a person more or less vulnerable to stress.

TYPE A PERSONALITY, REVIEWED

We discussed Type A personality, and its association with coronary heart disease (CHD), in depth in Chapter 13. To review: Type A personality was originally defined as a behavioral and emotional style characterized by a constant struggle to achieve more and more in less and less time, often in opposition to others. Further research identified the "lethal" element in Type A personality (the one associated with risk for CHD) as hostility—especially a combination of cynicism, suspicion, resentment, antagonism, and frequent outbursts of anger. Individuals who are high in hostility are predisposed to appraise events and actions of others as threatening, and to see their only option for coping as striking out (fight, not flight or compromise). While this style might be adaptive in competitive situations (for example, business or sports), it is maladaptive over the long run, increasing stress and the risk of CHD.

OPTIMISM VERSUS PESSIMISM

Another personality dimension that has been linked to the experience of stress and the likelihood of illness is optimism versus pessimism. In one study (Scheier and Carver, 1985), students were asked at the beginning of the semester to fill out a questionnaire designed to measure their orientation toward optimism or pessimism. Subjects were told to answer "true" or "false" in response to each item, including the following:

1. In uncertain times, I usually expect the best.
2. If something can go wrong for me, it will.
3. I always look on the bright side of things.
4. I'm always optimistic about my future.
5. I hardly ever expect things to go my way.
6. Things never work out the way I want them to.
7. I'm a believer in the idea that "every cloud has a silver lining."
8. I rarely count on good things happening to me. (cited in Taylor, 1991, p. 240)

At the end of the semester, students who had scored high in optimism were less likely to report being bothered by physical symptoms (headaches, upset stomachs, and the like) than were students who had scored lower on the scale. Another study of college students found that pessimists had almost twice as many infectious diseases, and visited a physician twice as often, as optimists did (Peterson and Seligman, 1987).

The difference between pessimists and optimists is largely a matter of attribution. Pessimists tend to blame themselves for bad events and to see negative events as stable and global ("It's my fault," "It will never end," "This ruins everything"). Even a minor setback causes them to doubt their ability to cope. Optimists, in contrast, tend to attribute negative events to external circumstances and to assume that they are temporary and limited ("It wasn't my fault," "It won't happen again," "It's not the end of the world"). They are confident that good things will happen and that they will be able to manage whatever problems life throws their way.

Evidence that pessimism increases stress and vulnerability to illness is accumulating. In a longitudinal study (Peterson et al., 1988), researchers analyzed interviews that had been conducted with Harvard graduates of the classes of 1939–1944 when they were twenty-five years old. The researchers were particularly interested in the subjects' interpretations of negative events in their lives. For instance, they were asked about their experiences in World War II: what combat was like, how they got along with superiors, and whether they felt that they had dealt successfully with difficulties. The researchers coded each response as reflecting an optimistic or pessimistic style. A typical optimistic response was "My career in the Army has been checkered, but on the whole, characteristic of the Army." This man took the ups and downs of his military career in stride. A typical pessimistic response was "I cannot seem to decide firmly on a career. . . . This may be my unwillingness to face reality." This man dwelled on the negative and blamed himself. The subjects of this study are now in their late sixties, and have had physical check-ups every five years. Beginning at about age forty-five, those who had been pessimists at age twenty-five began to show significantly poorer health than those rated as optimists, a pattern that has continued as they enter old age. (Indeed, the pessimist quoted above died before age fifty-five.) By implication, pessimism can have lifelong negative effects.

Under stress, we may begin to eat "on the run"—quickly and haphazardly. For many people, this kind of behavior increases the risk of physical illness.

Other studies have focused on the effects of optimism versus pessimism on recovery from illness. One followed thirty-four women who had had a recurrence of breast cancer for five years (Levy et al., 1989). The pessimists died sooner than the optimists, regardless of the severity of the disease. Another study followed patients who had had coronary artery bypass surgery (Scheier et al., 1989). The researchers found that optimists recovered more quickly than pessimists did, left the hospital earlier, returned to normal activities sooner, and reported a higher quality of life six months later. By implication, optimism is good medicine.

Not all health psychologists are convinced of "the power of positive thinking," however. Some point out that while a little optimism can be healthy, too much can be maladaptive (Baumeister and Scher, 1988; Perloff, 1987; Weinstein, 1980, 1982). These psychologists argue that unrealistic optimism can lead people to deny problems until it is too late to cope (including physical illnesses that require early treatment), and to assume they have control in uncontrollable situations, such as gambling casinos or abusing addictive drugs. Other psychologists (e.g., Scheier et al., 1986) argue that the opposite is true. In their view, pessimists are more likely to engage in maladaptive behavior (denying stressful events and dwelling on their negative emotions rather than dealing with a problem), whereas optimists are more likely to use successful coping strategies (focusing on the positive aspects of a stressful situation, seeking social support, and attacking the problem directly). This issue remains controversial.

Another problem with viewing optimism as protection against stress and illness is that it can lead to "blaming the victim." For example, a woman who suffers a recurrence of breast cancer may blame herself (and be blamed by others) for worrying about her illness and not having a more positive, "I can lick this" attitude. The idea that individuals can ward off or conquer serious illness through sheer willpower is based on a misreading of the scientific literature (or reading too many popular sources that misrepresent the facts). No health psychologist would argue that optimism can "prevent" or "cure" cancer or any other illness. Rather, some health psychologists believe that there is evidence that, *all other things being equal,* optimists may be *less likely* to develop cancer and *more likely* to recover from or live for a longer time with the disease than are pessimists. In life, "all other things" (including genetic vulnerability, exposure to environmental toxins, life-style, and the many other factors associated with cancer) are rarely equal. Scientists attempt to reduce the influence of "other things" on research findings by comparing people with similar backgrounds, life-styles, and types of disease, but they can never eliminate them entirely. This is why results are reported in terms of *probabilities*, not cause and effect. But this important distinction is often lost when scientific findings are reported in popular media and passed on through word of mouth.

STRESS AND ILLNESS: A MODEL

What, finally, can we conclude about the connection between stress and illness? A review of the evidence suggests that there is a relationship, but it is not a simple one. Rather, stress affects health in a variety of ways. The first is the *direct route:* stress may produce physiological and psychological changes that contribute to the development of illness. For example, stress can lower immunity, making a person more vulnerable to colds, the flu, and other diseases. But not everyone who is under stress gets sick, suggesting that preexisting and/or intervening variables come into play. One preexisting variable is *personality.* People who rate high on hostility or pessimism, for example, may be more vulnerable to stress and thus more prone to illness and injury. A third possibility is that stress increases vulnerability to illness by *altering health behaviors.* For example, under the stress of exam week, students are more likely to sleep less, smoke more, eat poorly, and engage in other behaviors that can compromise their health. Fourth, stress may promote "illness behavior." That is, people who are under stress are more likely to treat fatigue, insomnia, anxiety, and depression as symptoms of illness and seek medical care (Gortmaker et al., 1982). Playing the sick role (staying home in bed) also allows a person to avoid a stressful situation and elicits concern and sympathy from others. Finally, these different factors may *interact.* The experience of stress, psychological vulnerability, or poor health behaviors alone might not be enough to cause illness, but a combination of these factors might.

COPING WITH STRESS

The federal Centers for Disease Control report that fewer than 30 percent of adults with AIDS live more than three years after the disease is diagnosed. Victims of AIDS are constantly reminded of the odds against them. They watch their friends die, and they live not knowing which infection will attack their weakened immune system next (Navarro, 1991). It is difficult to imagine a more stressful situation. Listen to how some AIDS patients cope:

> In the beginning, AIDS made me feel like a poisoned dart, like I was a diseased person and I had no self-esteem and no self-confidence. That's what I have been really working on, is to get the self-confidence and self-esteem back. (Reed, 1989)

> Even if something happens next week, if I'm diagnosed with a lymphoma, it's better for me to live my life as if I'm going to live another 20 years. (Navarro, 1991)

> I made a list of all the other diseases I would rather not have than AIDS. Lou Gehrig's disease, being in a wheelchair; rheumatoid arthritis, when you are in knots and in terrible pain. So I said, you've got to get some perspective on this, and where you are on the Great Nasty Disease List. (Reed, 1989)

Faced with an apparently hopeless situation—in effect, a death sentence—some AIDS patients undoubtedly give up. But many others strive to lead normal and productive lives and to live as long, and as well, as they can. In other words, they cope. "I don't know anybody who survives this by accident," said one AIDS patient. "You have to make a conscious decision" (Navarro, 1991).

Coping is the process of managing the internal and external demands that one appraises as taxing or overwhelming (Lazarus and Folkman, in press). Coping takes two main forms: *problem-directed coping*, or attempts to do something constructive about the stressful situation, and *emotion-focused coping*, or efforts to regulate the emotional consequences of a stressful situation (Lazarus and Folkman, 1984; Pearlin and Schooler, 1978). Often the two work together. For example, a couple who are having marital difficulties might see a marriage counselor to help sort out their differences and develop better ways of communicating with one another (problem solving), and at the same time strive to set aside feelings of anger and hurt and think about the good times they have had together (emotion-focused coping).

STRATEGIES OF COPING

Researchers who study different strategies for dealing with stressful situations often use the Ways of Coping Questionnaire. Subjects are first asked to list important events or experiences in their lives and rate them on a scale from 1 for "extremely stressful" to 5 for "not stressful." Then they are asked to indicate the thoughts and actions they have used to deal with these stressful events.

In one study (Folkman et al., 1986), married couples were interviewed once a week for a period of six months. After indicating their most stressful experiences, they completed the Ways of Coping Questionnaire. The study suggested that the specific coping methods used could be grouped into eight distinct strategies. Consider how you might use these to manage the stress of being fired from a job. One strategy is *confrontational coping*, or standing your ground and fighting for what you want. Thus you might demand to know why you were fired, and try to convince your boss to change his or her mind. A second strategy is to seek *social support*, turning to others for comfort and advice on how to handle the situation. A third strategy is *planful problem solving*, or devising a plan of action to solve the situation. Thus, you might read the want ads, visit an employment agency, and send your résumé to several prospective employers. All of these strategies are examples of problem-directed coping. At the same time, you would attempt to deal with your feelings about being fired. One emotion-focused strategy is *self-control*: "keeping your chin up" and not letting your feelings show. Another is *distancing*, or telling yourself, "I'm not going to let this get to me." You might try to immerse yourself in other activities to take your mind off the problem. A third emotion-focused strategy is *positive reappraisal*, or "looking for the silver lining." For example, you might reappraise getting fired as being the push you needed to look for a more interesting and rewarding job. Alternatively, you might *accept responsibility*, acknowledge that you brought this on yourself ("I was late all the time, I didn't try as hard as I could have, I antagonized the boss"), and try to learn from the experience. Finally, you might choose *escape/avoidance*—engaging in wishful think-

ing ("Maybe my boss will change her mind") or escaping through drugs, drinking, or overeating.

Which coping strategies are most effective for dealing with stress, and which are least effective?

AVOIDANCE VERSUS CONFRONTATION

A number of researchers have compared people who cope with stress by minimizing or avoiding it to those who use more confrontational or vigilant strategies, such as gathering information and taking action to change the situation (Holahan and Moos, 1987). In general, research shows that confrontation is more successful than avoidance. Individuals who deal with a problem directly are not only more likely to solve the problem but are also better prepared (emotionally and otherwise) to handle future stress. Indeed, some research suggests that chronic use of avoidance places people at risk for added stress and perhaps related health problems (Felton et al., 1984; Quinn et al., 1987). But avoidance as a coping strategy is not always bad. When people are faced with a minor, short-term threat, or with a stressful situation that they cannot control, avoidance may be more adaptive. For example, you might go to your physician with what you think is a minor complaint, but she is concerned and wants you to take a series of tests. You should take the tests, but at this stage, focusing on the risks, reading everything you can about your symptoms, and demanding that your physician tell you "the worst-case scenario" (a confrontational strategy) will only add to your stress. If, however, the tests reveal that you do have a serious health problem—say, diabetes—avoidance becomes dangerous. In this case, vigilance (taking insulin shots, following the prescribed diet, learning as much as you can about your disease, and so on) is far more adaptive.

The same principles apply to situations that are not health-threatening. For example, in a romantic relationship, vigilance may translate into unwarranted jealousy (confronting your girlfriend when you see her having lunch or merely talking with another man, constantly demanding to know where she was and with whom) that can undermine the relationship. However, if your girlfriend seems cool and distant much of the time, and constantly makes excuses for not being able to see you, avoidance (pretending nothing has changed) becomes maladaptive. She may have a problem that she is embarrassed to discuss

Some people may need the help of a support group to learn how to confront a stressful situation, but this direct approach to a problem is likely to pay off in reduced stress and fewer health problems. At meetings of Alcoholics Anonymous, for example, members try to confront and conquer their addiction to alcohol.

with you, or you may have done something to offend her, or she may be losing interest. In any of these cases, you are better off knowing and taking action (whether that means changing your behavior or facing the fact that the relationship is over). In short, vigilance and avoidance both have their uses, but too much or too little of either can be maladaptive.

In many cases, a combination of coping strategies is most successful (Collins et al., 1990). If your dog disappears, for example, you might cope best by minimizing the stress (telling yourself he is just lost, somebody probably took him in, and you'll get him back) and confronting the problem (calling the ASPCA lost and found, putting up posters in pet shops, etc.).

VENTING EMOTIONS

Another line of research has explored the value of venting emotions, or **catharsis** (from the Greek, "to cleanse"). We described a series of experiments in Chapter 11, in which some college students were asked to write about stressful events (including their feelings about college) and others were asked to write about trivial subjects (Pennebaker et al., 1987, 1990). The researchers found that venting emotions increases stress in the short term but produces long-term benefits, including fewer visits to the health center.

Another related study adds a qualification, however. The researchers assigned the same task to a group of sixty undergraduates (Greenberg and Stone, 1990), but this time the students were divided into three groups: those who had previously disclosed the traumatic events, those who were disclosing these events for the first time, and those who wrote about trivial topics. These researchers found that those who had previously disclosed the traumatic events exhibited far greater stress and more negative moods than members of either of the other groups. (And they found no differences in health, measured in health center visits and self-reports.) The researchers hypothesized that confiding in others about stressful events may intensify rather than reduce the negative emotions associated with the experience.

Reliving a painful experience over and over may delay the process of recovery. But most researchers have found that venting emotions has clear benefits. Talking with others can provide us with useful information about how to cope; it can also reassure us that we are not alone, that others have faced the same problems and feelings (Lazarus, 1966; Wortman and Dunkel-Schetter, 1979). Talking with others can help us to organize our thoughts and perhaps find meaning in the experience (Meichenbaum, 1977; Silver and Wortman, 1980). In the next section we will look more closely at the support others can provide in times of stress.

SOCIAL SUPPORT AND STRESS

How we manage stress depends not only on our internal resources but also on external resources—our social support system. *Social support* is the information we obtain from others that we are loved, cared for, valued, and included in a network of mutual concern (Cobb, 1976). This kind of information can help mute the effects of stress and reduce the risk of illness. The sense of support we get is more important than whom we get it from: sources of support can include friends, spouses, lovers, children, church members, club members, or even a devoted pet.

The various forms of social support fall into three categories: tangible assistance, information, and emotional support (House, 1981; Schaefer et al., 1981). *Tangible assistance* can take the form of a gift of money to tide a person over some bad times or even something so small as meals provided during a time of bereavement. *Information* from the support system may give a person ideas on specific actions to take to overcome a stressful situation. Perhaps most valuable of all is the *emotional support* given by family and friends, reassuring the individual experiencing stress that others care for him or her.

Research has shown that social support can effectively reduce distress at times of stress (Cohen and Wills, 1985). Social support can also lower the likelihood of illness, speed recovery from illness, and reduce the risk of death from serious disease (House et al., 1988; Kulik and Mahler, 1989). In one classic study, researchers asked 7,000 adults living in California about their social and community ties and then tracked their mortality rate over a nine-year period (Berkman and Syme, 1979). Those people who reported few social and community ties were more likely to die during this period than were people who claimed many ties. Women who had access to a social support system lived an average of 2.8 years longer and men an average of 2.3 years longer than those with few social contacts. Support from others also appears to lead to better health habits. People with high levels of social support are more likely to follow medication recommendations and to use health services (Umberson, 1987).

Still, we do not need great numbers in our social support system to feel its benefits. The most important aspect of support is having at least one confidante to whom one can turn. In fact, in some cases having too many people provide advice or support may actually increase stress. In addition, sometimes people trying to be helpful may provide the wrong kind of social support. Imagine, for example, that you are trying to decide which graduate school to attend. In an effort to help, relatives may offer facts and opinions about the schools. But their information may be conflicting, making the decision process more confusing and stressful for you. You might do better just to accept emotional support from them, reassuring you that you will make the right decision (Dakof and Taylor, 1990).

Sometimes emotional support can go awry. This situation often arises when friends try to comfort those who are bereaved. One study found that 60 percent of those coping with the loss of a spouse or a child reported that others had said or done something that was unhelpful (Wortman and Lehman, 1985). The four support tactics that were most commonly identified as unhelpful were giving advice ("You can always have another child"), encouraging recovery ("A trip would do you a world of good"), minimizing the loss or forcing cheerfulness ("It's a good thing you have other children"), and identifying with the feelings of the bereaved ("I know just how you feel"). Some tactics that were judged helpful were "just being there," providing an opportunity to discuss feelings, and expressing concern.

Another study has examined what kinds of support help or hinder a person's attempts to quit smoking (Cohen and Lichtenstein, 1989). More than 200 subjects who wanted to quit smoking were surveyed after their quit dates to determine the frequency of both positive and negative support behaviors they received from a partner or someone close to them. Among the positive behaviors listed in the questionnaire were "compliment you on not smoking," "tell you to stick with it," "express confidence in your ability to quit." Negative behaviors included "comment that the house smells of smoke," "refuse to let you smoke in the house," "talk you out of smoking a cigarette." The researchers found that success in quitting was not associated with the frequency of these behaviors but with the ratio of positive to negative behaviors. In every follow-up (one month, three months, six months, and twelve months), it was found that the greater the proportion of positive to negative behaviors the subjects reported receiving, the greater the rate of abstinence from smoking.

TRAINING IN STRESS MANAGEMENT

People who cannot reduce stress through either their own efforts or with the support of others may benefit from learning the techniques of *stress management.* Workshops in stress management are increasingly common in the workplace, where stress-related disorders are estimated to account for as much as $17 billion a year in lost productivity (Adams, 1978). Stress-management programs are also directed at people who suffer from or are at risk for stress-related illnesses or disorders, such as headaches, alcohol abuse, obesity, cardiovascular disease, and hypertension. Increasing numbers of college administrators also have made stress-management programs available to their students. Some of these programs make use of the cognitive-behavioral approach we introduced earlier in this chapter.

COGNITIVE-BEHAVIORAL TECHNIQUES

Many students find the first semester of college very stressful. Suddenly they find themselves in a noisy dormitory, full of strangers. Making friends, getting used to communal bathrooms and kitchens, and adapting to a roommate's habits can be difficult. Often, college courses are far more demanding than the classes they took in high school: a former A student may see her first C or even D. Furthermore, college students are given fewer daily or weekly homework assignments, and no one is checking to see that they are keeping up. In most colleges, students receive reading lists and due dates for papers and exams, and then are allowed to "sink or swim." Many begin to feel overwhelmed.

Stress-management programs for college students are given many different names, but the basic goal is to help students learn to cope with their new and stressful situations before they drop out or flunk out. Most such programs include three stages. The first is *education.* The counselor begins by assuring students that many young people find college stressful (they are not alone). He explains what stress is, emphasizing that stress depends more on how people appraise situations and their ability to cope than on the situations themselves. He talks about how stress can affect psychological and physical health, as well as academic performance and social behavior. He trains students to recognize the symptoms of stress in themselves (overeating, sleep problems, palpitations), and to keep a record of the situations that cause them stress and how they try to cope. He also trains students to listen to their interior monologue, and to recognize (and record) negative self-talk ("I always get tongue-tied when the professor calls on me" or "I'll never be able to write a forty-page term paper").

The next stage is *training.* This might include instruction in time management (establishing priorities, setting specific times for work and play, breaking large assignments down into small steps, and taking periodic breaks to stretch and relax), social skills (such as assertiveness, or confronting people who are causing one stress), good health habits (regular meals and exercise), and relaxation techniques (described below). Students are helped to establish realistic goals, use positive self-talk, and reward themselves for reaching their goals. The high school science whiz who was devastated by a C on her first chemistry quiz might aim for a C+ on the next quiz and a B− on her midterm. Whenever she began to feel discouraged, she would remind herself that the reason she got into the difficult pre-med program was that she showed potential in high school. A student who is terrified about being called on in a particular class might observe students who seem comfortable in class the first week, write down questions he would like to ask and rehearse them in private during the second week, then ask three questions the third week, rewarding himself with a movie when he succeeded. In addition to these "homework" assignments, students might role-play with one another. For example, a student whose roommate borrowed things without asking might practice asking him to stop with another student who tries to make the confrontation as difficult as possible.

The third stage is *practice*. Now students apply the skills they have been rehearsing in real-life situations, and report back to the group on their experiences. Ideally, this three-stage program enables students to "inoculate" themselves against stress (Meichenbaum and Deffenbacher, 1988).

BIOFEEDBACK

In the 1970s, a new technology for managing stress took the health professions and popular press by storm. **Biofeedback** is a specialized procedure for monitoring and controlling the physiological aspects of stress (and pain). The individual is given feedback on a body function that is normally outside conscious awareness and trained to recognize and control it. For example, a patient might be connected to a machine that translates heart rate into a tone, so that it is possible to hear how fast or slowly one's heart is beating. Through trial and error the patient gradually learns to control what was previously an automatic response. For example, a patient might find that shutting out all sound and concentrating on breathing slowly helps to reduce his or her heart rate.

At one time, biofeedback was recommended for the treatment of hypertension, chronic pain, muscle-contraction headaches, and migraines, as well as general stress. But this initial flurry of enthusiasm faded when careful research found mixed success. Biofeedback may help some people overcome some problems (especially in combination with other types of therapy). But others techniques that are much less costly and easier to implement are just as effective (Turk et al., 1979). One of the simplest and most successful is relaxation training.

RELAXATION TECHNIQUES

Relaxation is the counterpoint to stress. When we are relaxed, our body is in a state of low arousal, which means we are less susceptible to reacting to stress. Relaxation techniques help a person learn to shift the body into this pleasant state of low arousal and to reduce states of abnormal tension associated with stress. Relaxation techniques are considered effective for treating insomnia, hypertension, tension headaches, anxiety disorders, and general autonomic arousal.

One technique focuses on progressive relaxation of different muscle groups in the body (Everly, 1989). The idea is that since stress and anxiety are related to muscle tension (the contraction of muscle fibers), reducing the muscle tension can also lessen feelings of stress and anxiety. Progressive relaxation requires the subject systematically to tense and relax selected muscles, usually starting in the lower body and progressing up to the facial muscles, until the whole body is relaxed. Continual practice allows the subject to become accustomed to feelings of repose and to develop a less stressful attitude.

Another relaxation technique is controlled breathing. Because states of relaxation are associated with deep, long breaths, we can induce relaxation by intentionally trying to create this breathing pattern. First, one takes a long cleansing breath in which air in the lungs is blown out through the mouth. Deep breaths lasting as long as ten seconds then replace short, shallow breaths. This technique seems to have some effect in controlling the kinds of pains that are stress-related, such as headache or facial pain (Turk et al., 1979; Weisenberg, 1977).

Relaxation techniques that are practiced regularly appear to improve the functioning of the immune system. In one study, first-year medical students were assigned to either a relaxation group or a comparison group (Kiecolt-Glaser et al., 1984). Those in the experimental condition attended five to ten relaxation sessions that took place in the month before exams. At the time of the exams, both groups showed signs of decreased immune system functioning (fewer percentages of T-cells and lower killer cell activity), but the relaxation group reported feeling less anxiety and those members of the relaxation group who had more frequent practice had higher T-cell percentages than did those who had fewer sessions. Another study assigned forty-five elderly residents of an independent-living facility to one of three groups: those receiving relaxation training; those receiving social contact; and a control group (Kiecolt-Glaser et al., 1985). The members of the first two groups were seen

Regular aerobic exercise has numerous health benefits, including an increased tolerance of stress.

three times a week for one month. At the end of the month, the relaxation group showed significant increases in killer cell activity, as well as other signs of improved functioning of the immune system, and significant decreases in self-rated distress. A follow-up one month after the relaxation practice ended revealed that these effects were no longer significant, which suggests the importance of regular, long-term practice of relaxation.

EXERCISE

Stress prepares the body for "fight or flight" (increasing the blood supply to the heart, tensing the muscles, and so on). Stifling the physical expression of this response—getting "revved up" but not releasing this tension—may increase the risk of stress-related disorders. Exercise is a healthful way to use the body's preparation for action. Indeed, exercise has been called "nature's own prescription" for managing stress.

The best kind of exercise, in terms of physical fitness, is *aerobic*—swimming, walking, running, ski-ing, cycling, dancing, jumping rope—any activity that demands increased oxygen intake and thus gives the cardiovascular system a workout. The exercise should consist of coordinated rhythmic movements, performed for their own sake—not to "win" or prove a point. To be effective, aerobic exercise must be consistent. Healthy adults should exercise briskly and continuously at least three times a week for at least fifteen minutes at a time. Each session should consist of warm-up, exercise, and cool-down periods.

Numerous studies have found that regular exercise improves cardiovascular fitness, endurance, muscle tone and strength, flexibility, and optimal weight; can help to control hypertension (high blood pressure) and cholesterol levels; and increases tolerance of stress. For example, in one study that followed young people through adolescence, the researchers found that adolescents who exercised regularly experienced less stress in the face of negative life events and fewer illnesses than those who did not (Brown and Siegel, 1988).

Exercise can also improve moods and general sense of well-being, and help to reduce anxiety, depression, and tension—though perhaps not as much as popular articles imply. People who are committed to a regular exercise program tend to have a more positive self-image, greater self-esteem, and a higher sense of self-efficacy than those who exercise sporadically or not at all (Rodin and Plante, 1989). What researchers do not know is whether exercise affects psychological well-being directly (through some biochemical process as yet unidentified) or indirectly—because people often exercise with friends and enjoy the sociability, because they feel they are accomplishing something, or simply because they believe that exercise will improve their mood (Hughes, 1984; Hughes et al., 1986).

Physical fitness has almost reached the level of a fad in our culture, but long-term commitment to exercise is less widespread. It seems to depend on whether or not people see themselves as athletic or as the type of person who exercises (Kendzierski, 1990), the convenience of exercise facilities (Dishman, 1982), and habit (Valois et al., 1988). The first three to six months appear to be critical. People who exercise continually for three to six months are more likely to continue to do so, but before six months, even regular exercisers may drop off and become nonexercisers.

While more and more adults plunged into exercise routines in the 1980s, their children became less active, fatter, weaker, and slower. A ten-year study of more than 12,000 boys and girls in grades 1 to 12 found that in 1990 only 32 percent could satisfactorily complete physical fitness tests of strength, flexibility, and muscular and cardiovascular endurance, compared to 43 percent a decade earlier (*The New York Times*, May 24, 1990, p. B14). It appears that TV and cutbacks in physical education programs are taking their toll on the health and fitness of American youth.

The importance of exercise in promoting good health brings us back to the point that health is an *active* achievement. Protection from illness and injury is not a matter of "luck of the draw" or a question of "medical potluck." As this chapter has emphasized, people can play an active role in establishing healthy habits and learning to cope with stressful conditions: we can eat regular and nourishing meals, not smoke, not drink to excess, not abuse drugs, develop positive (yet realistic) attitudes, exercise routinely, and, occasionally, just slow down and relax.

SUMMARY

1. The idea that social, psychological, and biological factors can interact to affect our health is known as the **biopsychosocial model.** This model departs from the traditional view of illness as a purely biological malfunction—the **biomedical model.** The biopsychosocial model focuses on how the mind and body influence each other and how we can actively achieve health by developing healthy habits and life-styles.

2. The field of **health psychology** refers to the contributions that psychology can make to maintaining health, preventing illness, and improving health care and policy. Health psychologists are active in health promotion, enabling people to increase control over their health and improve it.

3. One way of promoting health is to publicize accurate information to correct people's misperceptions and to acquaint them with health facts about their life-styles. But knowing that behavior is risky does not necessarily cause people to change. For this reason health psychologists are also involved in designing programs to help people change their health habits through cognitive-behavioral techniques (such as self-monitoring, stimulus control, and self-reinforcement) and prevent relapse.

4. Although not everyone engages in unhealthy behavior, all of us experience **stress.** Early accounts of stress focused on physiological reactions: the **fight-or-flight response,** in which an organism is aroused to either attack a threatening invader or to flee; and the **general adaptation syndrome,** which describes three phases of mobilizing and responding to stress. The latter account holds that prolonged or repeated exposure to stress will cause wear and tear on the system. But neither hypothesis takes psychological factors into account. Today there is increasing recognition that our responses to stress vary, depending on the person

and the stressful event. Thus the psychological view defines *stress* as that which an individual appraises as harmful, threatening, or challenging.

5. A number of studies in the field of psychoneuroimmunology suggest that the experience of stress can affect our **immunocompetence,** the measure of how well the immune system protects our bodies from illness. Lowered immunity has been found in people experiencing a wide range of stressful conditions, from unhappy marriages to daily hassles.

6. Some researchers seeking to find the link between stress and illness have focused on *major life events,* such as the death of a spouse, divorce, or retirement. Other researchers have tried to identify the types of events that lead to stress and illness. There is some evidence that the cumulative effects of chronic stress, or even daily hassles, takes a toll on health. Research also shows that uncontrollable situations are usually more stressful than controllable ones. Studies of elderly residents of nursing homes have found that giving the residents more control over their lives increases well-being and may even increase longevity. But however one conceptualizes stress in life, it is important to remember that most people do *not* become ill after experiencing stress.

7. Still other researchers have investigated the reasons why some individuals are more vulnerable to stress and illness than others. This research focuses on personality traits. Studies have shown that the hostile component of Type A personality increases the risk of coronary heart disease. Pessimism (a tendency to see problems as global and insoluble, and to blame oneself) may also increase our propensity for illness in times of stress. In general, optimists have been found to have better health over their lifetime, and to recovery more quickly from illness, than do pessimists. But taking this finding too literally can lead to unrealistic, maladaptive optimism and also to "blaming the victim."

8. The relationship between stress and illness is complex. One must take into account the possibilities of a direct connection (perhaps through the immune system), preexisting vulnerabilities (especially personality traits), changes in health behavior under stress, an increased tendency to seek medical care ("illness behavior"), and interactions among two or more of these variables.

9. The process of **coping** with stress, managing the external and internal demands that are appraised as taxing, takes two forms: *problem-solving efforts,* geared to direct and constructive action; and *emotion-focused efforts,* putting the emphasis on regulating the emotional consequences of a stressful event. Within these two categories are many distinct coping strategies. Eight common ones are confrontative coping (meeting a challenge head-on), seeking social support, planful problem solving, self-control, distancing oneself from the event and its consequences, positive reappraisal, accepting responsibility, and escape or avoidance. Vigilant strategies seem to be more successful than avoidant ones, and venting emotions appears to promote health more than keeping them bottled up.

10. How we manage stress depends a great deal on our *social support* system, the people around us who let us know they love and care for us. Having social ties makes us more able to cope with stress and its effects, although the number of ties seems to be less important than the closeness of those ties. Social support takes three general forms: tangible assistance, information, and emotional support.

11. Techniques in stress management are directed at those who suffer from, or are at risk for, stress-related illnesses and disorders. Programs in stress management may include cognitive-behavioral techniques, **biofeedback** (the process of monitoring bodily functions and learning to control them), relaxation techniques, and aerobic exercise.

SUGGESTED READINGS

Frank, A. W. (1991). *At the will of the body: Reflections on illness.* Boston: Houghton Mifflin. This personal account from a patient who suffered a heart attack and cancer is an enlightening tale of the many repercussions of serious illness. The author conveys his anger at the medical field for not acknowledging the human aspect of the disease process. He suggests that doctors need to place greater emphasis on empathizing with their patients' distress.

Friedman, H. S. (1991). *The self-healing personality.* New York: Henry Holt. This provocative book examines the link between health and personality with its review of recent scholarly research. The author discusses findings that have implications for what people should do to maintain their health.

Taylor, S. E. (1989). *Positive illusions.* New York: Basic Books. In this book, Taylor presents research illustrating that illusions may be important in maintaining physical and mental health. This view is intriguing because it runs counter to the popular belief that distorted perceptions of reality are a sign of mental illness. Taylor shows that in many situations, such distortions are adaptive and necessary.

PSYCHOLOGICAL DISORDERS

A twenty-four-old man, armed with a .44-caliber revolver, cruises a New York City neighborhood late at night, looking for "pretty girls" to shoot. When he is finally captured by police after a year-long search, he has killed six people and wounded seven others. He says that "demons" drove him to commit these crimes.

A middle-aged businessman, fed up with his stressful job, his hour-long commute, and the demands of his suburban life-style, packs a small bag and flees to the mountains, where he settles in an abandoned cabin, determined to live in isolation.

A young woman who showed great academic promise in high school begins to have difficulty with her studies in college. She believes that she is constantly behind in her work and will not be able to catch up, no matter how hard she tries. She feels lonely and becomes increasingly depressed and withdrawn.

A widely acclaimed young pianist, winner of many awards, begins to suffer inexplicable attacks of "nerves" whenever he has to play before an audience. This anxiety becomes increasingly intense and develops into waves of panic. Eventually the very thought of performing in public becomes so terrifying that the pianist's career is jeopardized.

How many of these people have a psychological disorder? Do all of them need psychiatric help? How would trained professionals diagnose their conditions? And what kinds of therapy might they recommend? These are the questions we will be addressing in this chapter and the next, which deal with psychological disorders and their treatments. We begin this chapter by exploring how psychologists define psychological disorders. We then examine some major perspectives on the causes of disorders and investigate how disorders are currently classified. Finally, we describe the symptoms of some major psychological disorders, as well as the insights about them that current theories and research provide.

DEFINING PSYCHOLOGICAL DISORDERS

Psychologists and psychiatrists define psychological disorders by evaluating behavior according to certain criteria. One criterion is violation of widely accepted

Part of the definition of psychological disorders is the extent to which a person deviates from generally accepted social expectations. But that alone is not enough for a diagnosis. Does this woman need psychiatric treatment or a place to live? Or both?

social expectations. A woman who walks around her neighborhood wearing a heavy coat in summer and screaming insults at strangers would, by this measure, be considered disordered. She is violating social expectations regarding dress and polite behavior. Her actions are also statistically rare, another criterion for defining a disorder.

But deviation from statistical norms and violation of social expectations are not always enough to identify a psychological disorder. One reason is that what is statistically rare and socially unexpected can vary so much with time and place. For instance, worshiping ancestral ghosts is uncommon in American culture and violates our expectations, so in our society it would be considered symptomatic of a disorder. In other societies, however, ancestor worship is widespread, and the person who practices it in no way seems odd. Should a psychological disorder depend so much on where a person lives? Many psychologists feel that, to some extent, it should not.

Nor should a definition of a psychological disorder fail to take into account that some unusual behaviors have very positive outcomes. What about the divorced father of thirty years ago who wanted custody of his young children? At the time, his behavior was both statistically rare and opposed to social expectations, but few people then or now would consider him disordered. The same could be said about people throughout history who have pursued unconventional but worthwhile goals. Much of society's vitality comes from those who venture beyond the norms, striking out in new directions. To label all such actions disorders would be to discourage many valuable innovations. Labeling all such actions disorders would also force us to say that people are disordered when they defy social norms because of moral convictions. Consider citizens of Nazi Germany who actively resisted their government's efforts to exterminate Jews. Although they were few in number and violated social expectations, they were certainly not people whom we would call disordered.

A way around these problems is to add to our definition of a psychological disorder some widely accepted standards of what is psychologically "unhealthy." These would include persistent emotional pain and suffering, behaving in a way that is disturbing to others, failing to perform ordinary day-to-day activities, and being irrational or excessively lacking in self-control. Our earlier example of the man who heard voices urging him to kill fits several of these standards. His thoughts and actions were irrational, lacked any semblance of self-restraint, and were highly disturbing to everyone but himself. Similarly, the young pianist who was so terrified that he could no longer perform in public was causing himself enormous emotional pain and distress, and was unable to carry out his normal activities. Thus, according to prevailing standards of mental health, both these people are, for different reasons, considered to have psychological disorders.

Of course, any standard of mental health we use has limitations by itself. Emotional pain and suffering, for example, by itself is insufficient to indicate a psychological disorder. The person who goes through life with little anxiety and upset is not necessarily well adjusted. There are times when great emotional distress is the expected reaction, as when a parent experiences the death of a child. The person who remains indifferent in such a situation can hardly be considered normal. In fact, lack of emotional responsiveness and concern for other people is a symptom of some serious psychological disorders. And even milder lack of distress is not *necessarily* healthy. Some psychologists believe that we cannot grow and reach our full potentials without sometimes taking steps that will be upsetting to us. From this perspective, painful choices are an essential part of achieving self-fulfillment. Other prevailing standards of mental health face similar limitations when used alone.

Thus, no single way of defining a psychological disorder is adequate by itself. We need to apply several yardsticks before labeling a behavior as disordered. The more of these criteria apply to a given way of thinking and acting, the more certain we can be that the label "disorder" is justified. Statistical rarity, violation of social norms, and meeting prevailing standards of what constitutes poor mental health can all help us to distinguish psychologically normal from psychologically disordered behavior. But even so, there is not always universal agreement as to where this line should be drawn. Mental health is best viewed as a continuum. At the extreme ends of that continuum, normality and abnormality are easy to distinguish. In the middle range, however, one condition shades gradually into the other, making it harder to differentiate between the two.

PERSPECTIVES ON PSYCHOLOGICAL DISORDERS

Over the years, many theories have been proposed to explain psychological disorders. The idea that madness results from possession by devils dates back to ancient times. Archeologists have found skulls of Stone Age people with surgical holes chipped in

Until well into the seventeenth century, ignorance and superstition about the causes of abnormal behavior gave rise to a variety of bizarre and sometimes cruel treatments. The contraptions shown in this 1596 German engraving are being used by quacks to drain harmful thoughts from one patient's abdomen and to distill them from another patient's brain.

them—apparently to let out the evil spirits. Exorcism of demons by prayers, potions, and often physical torture was fairly common during the Middle Ages. Such practices demonstrate that people's views about the causes of abnormal behavior often determine how the mentally disturbed are treated.

In the following sections we will review some current perspectives on the causes of psychological disorders. We will see how theories about causes help suggest treatments. Of course, prevailing theories about causes and widely used treatments need not always be related. Today, for instance, biological factors (such as biochemical imbalances) are considered major causes of schizophrenia, but drugs that affect biochemistry are not the only treatment for this disorder. Schizophrenia is also treated with therapies that focus on such things as improving communications in the family. This is true even though faulty family communications is not the major reason that schizophrenia arises in the first place. With this in mind, let us turn to the various perspectives on psychological disorders.

According to learning theorists, cooperative and antisocial behaviors are learned in the same ways. Thus, children may learn that cooperating with another child is as effective as assaultive behavior in getting attention from adults—or they may learn the reverse.

THE BIOLOGICAL PERSPECTIVE

Physicians in ancient Greece were among the first to identify a set of strange symptoms that occurred mainly in women. The patient would suffer headaches and dizzy spells, accompanied by inexplicable aches and pains. Suddenly, part of the body might become paralyzed, or just as suddenly the patient might go blind or lose her voice. The Greeks named this condition "hysteria" because they believed it was caused by the effects of a wandering uterus (the Greek word for uterus is *hystera*). To the Greeks, the uterus was a separate living organism that could roam about the body, wreaking havoc wherever it went. Although this theory of a wandering uterus seems silly to us today, it shows that for thousands of years people have wondered if abnormal behavior might be caused by some biological dysfunction.

The **biological perspective** gained strength in the late nineteenth century, when researchers discovered that some baffling mental disorders could be traced to specific diseases of the brain. The most dramatic of these discoveries was the finding that **general paresis**—an irreversible deterioration of all mental and physical processes—is in fact the final stage of the venereal disease called syphilis (the stage at which the syphilitic microorganisms deeply penetrate the brain and other body organs). Following this discovery, optimism ran high that medical science would someday conquer all mental and emotional disorders.

Today biological researchers are using modern technology to explore the brains of mentally disturbed people. They believe that abnormalities in the workings of chemicals in the brain called neurotransmitters may contribute to many psychological disorders. For example, overactivity of the neurotransmitter dopamine, perhaps caused by an overabundance of certain dopamine receptors in the brain, has been linked to the bizarre symptoms of schizophrenia (Wong et al., 1986). As yet, however, biological researchers have not found organic causes for most mental disorders. This is not to say that such causes do not exist. With further advances in technology, scientists may find more biological factors underlying abnormal behavior.

PSYCHOLOGICAL PERSPECTIVES

Despite the fact that the biological perspective has been very influential, few people believe that most mental and emotional disorders are strictly biological in origin. A large number of mental health professionals place great emphasis on psychological factors, such as emotional conflict, inappropriate learning, and self-defeating ways of thinking. In this chapter we will examine three psychological perspectives: the psychoanalytic, the learning, and the cognitive behavioral perspectives. Because these overlap with theories of personality discussed in Chapter 13, we will only summarize them briefly here.

As we learned in Chapter 13, Sigmund Freud, the founder of the **psychoanalytic approach,** believed that the human psyche consists of three interacting forces: the *id* (a pool of biological urges), the *ego* (which mediates between the id and reality), and the *superego* (which represents society's moral standards). Abnormal behavior, in Freud's view, is caused by the ego's inability to manage the conflict between the opposing demands of the id and the superego. Especially important is failure to manage the conflict between the id's sexual impulses during childhood and society's sexual morality. Although later psychoanalytic thinkers have tended to place less emphasis on the id's sexual urges, they too believe that how people resolve emotional conflicts during childhood affects their thoughts and behaviors for the rest of their lives. Through **psychoanalysis**—a deep probing of people's current thoughts and feelings for clues to their unconscious conflicts—it is hoped that patients will gain critical insights into the roots of their problems, insights that might ultimately make them psychologically healthier.

In sharp contrast to psychoanalytic thinkers, proponents of the **learning perspective** argue that most mental and emotional disorders arise not from unresolved psychic conflicts, but rather from inadequate or inappropriate learning. Learning theorists believe that people acquire abnormal behaviors through the various kinds of learning we discussed in Chapter 6. Therapies based on this perspective are designed to undo past lessons that have instilled inappropriate behaviors and to provide new lessons that will foster more desirable responses.

The earliest therapies based on learning theories were not concerned particularly about what a person *thought*, as long as that person's undesirable responses were reduced. But today, many psychologists recognize the importance of thoughts, or cognitions, in shaping behavior. Those who take a **cognitive perspective** on abnormality say that the quality of our internal dialogue—whether we accept or berate ourselves, build ourselves up or tear ourselves down—has a profound effect on our mental health. Consider a student who fails a difficult exam, decides that he does not have the brains for college, becomes depressed, and gives up trying. To stop his self-defeating actions, he must first stop attributing his failure to lack of ability. Cognitive therapies focus specifically on changing such negative cognitions to help people break free of maladaptive behaviors.

OTHER PERSPECTIVES

Two other perspectives on psychological disorders consider the social world in which a disturbed person lives. These are the interpersonal or family-systems perspective and the sociocultural perspective.

The **interpersonal** or **family-systems perspective** sees psychological disorders as arising partly from a person's network of social relationships. One of the most crucial of these networks is the family, especially to a young child. In fact, this perspective

According to the sociocultural approach to psychology, the high incidence of serious mental disorders among members of the lowest socioeconomic groups is primarily caused by the stresses in their environments.

developed from the experiences of psychotherapists who treated children. They found that they often had to extend their search for causes, as well as their efforts at treatment, to a young client's parents and siblings. Today this perspective includes a variety of ideas about how the family can disrupt normal development.

The **sociocultural perspective** argues that the roots of mental disturbance often lie in such social ills as poverty, poor nutrition, inadequate housing, crime, and discrimination. The primary evidence in support of this view is the generally higher rate of serious mental disorders (such as schizophrenia and alcoholism) among the lowest socioeconomic classes. This pattern may be due to higher levels of stress among the poor, less effective strategies for coping with stress, and greater reluctance to seek treatment for psychological problems.

COMBINING PERSPECTIVES

The different perspectives on psychological disorders are not mutually exclusive. Often we get our richest insights into the causes of a disorder by combining several viewpoints. Many clinicians today are trying to develop integrated models of abnormal behavior—models that incorporate elements from numerous theoretical approaches (Liem, 1980).

One such model, very popular in recent years, is the **diathesis–stress model.** This approach maintains that for various reasons, a given individual may have a predisposition or diathesis to develop a certain mental disorder. Whether or not this disorder actually develops then depends on the environmental stresses the person experiences. This model suggests that preventive treatment can be targeted to people who, as a result of their genetic makeup or other factors, are at risk for developing a given disorder.

CLASSIFYING PSYCHOLOGICAL DISORDERS

Classifying psychological disorders involves identifying sets of symptoms that tend to occur together. Each set of symptoms forms a *syndrome.* Thus, when we talk about schizophrenia, mania, or depression, we are talking about syndromes that clinicians have classified on the basis of their observations.

Why bother classifying psychological disorders? What purposes does it serve? First, a classification system gives mental health professionals a shorthand way of communicating among themselves. When a diagnosis of bipolar disorder is made, for instance, this single term provides a summary of the patient's major symptoms. Second, a classification system helps to suggest effective treatments. By grouping together people with the same symptoms, clinicians can analyze the kinds of treatments that work best for that particular group. This knowledge can then be applied to other cases of the same disorder. Third, a classification system enables the pooling of research data on abnormal behaviors. Without one, researchers would have no way of knowing when they were studying the same or different disorders. Finally, a classification system aids in making predictions. It can provide information about the likelihood of a given disorder, about which people are most susceptible to it, and about how the condition is likely to progress.

The classification system on which virtually all mental health care professionals rely is the *Diagnostic and Statistical Manual of Mental Disorders,* third edition, revised (*DSM-III-R*), published by the American Psychiatric Association in 1987. It contains a detailed list of the major mental disorders and their symptoms. Because such classification systems are based on professionals' current judgments, they tend to change over time. For example, in the first two editions of *DSM,* homosexuality was considered a disorder, but in 1973 the American Psychiatric Association voted to strike it from the manual. *DSM-III* (published in 1980) included only a category called ''ego-dystonic homosexuality,'' which applied exclusively to homosexuals who are disturbed by their sexual orientation. Finally, in *DSM-III-R,* all mention of homosexuality as a diagnostic category was removed.

DSM-III-R recommends a very thorough approach to the evaluation of psychiatric patients. It calls for assessment in terms of five dimensions, or ''axes.'' Axis I lists the clinical syndromes, that is, the problems that lead people to seek psychotherapy. Most serious disorders, such as major depression and schizophrenia, are on Axis I. Axis II refers to ''background'' problems that may contribute to the person's psychopathology. Such problems are typically long-standing and include maladaptive personality traits (for example, compulsiveness and overdependency) as well as developmental problems (language difficulties, for instance). On Axis III the client is evaluated for physical illnesses or conditions that may be related to the psychological symptoms. Axis IV specifies the level of stress in the person's current life, for stress is often linked directly to psychological problems. Finally, Axis V assesses the highest level of functioning the client has shown in the last year—at work, at home, with friends, and in leisure activities. This highest level of functioning is often a good indication of the person's chances for recovery.

Although the American Psychiatric Association has worked hard to produce the most useful diagnostic manual it can, there are still those who criticize classification systems. These critics say that diagnostic labels obscure individual differences in people. One schizophrenic is not identical to every other schizophrenic, they argue, just as one person with severe depression is not exactly like all others. When we try to fit every psychiatric patient into a category, we may inadvertently lose valuable information about each person (Mirowsky and Ross, 1989). And, say critics, giving patients diagnoses can affect not only their self-perceptions but also how others perceive them

(Rosenhan, 1973). When people are labeled schizophrenic, for instance, others expect odd behavior from them and so may interpret *any* unusual action as a sign of mental illness. Given such problems, some critics have even suggested that we would be better off eliminating psychiatric categories altogether.

Most psychologists do not agree with this position. They believe that some diagnosis of mental disorders is essential if our knowledge is to expand (Swartz et al., 1989; Tweed and George, 1989). How, they ask, are we to investigate the effectiveness of treatments for schizophrenia, depression, alcoholism, and so forth without diagnostic labels? Without these labels we would be hard-pressed even to identify a sample population to study. Supporters of psychiatric classification also point out that the *DSM-III-R* system has reasonably good reliability. This means that there is substantial agreement among clinicians as to what is and is not an instance of a particular disorder. There is greater reliability in the diagnosis of some disorders, such as mental disorders and substance use disorders, than of others, such as personality disorders. Whether the *DSM-III-R* system is also valid— that is, whether it accurately classifies what it intends to classify—is more of an open issue. But even if some problems of validity exist in the current system, most psychologists do not want to discard it entirely. Most feel that the benefits of classification far outweigh the drawbacks.

The rest of this chapter explores some of the major disorders listed in *DSM-III-R*. As you read about these disorders, you may be tempted to conclude that some of them apply to people you know, perhaps even to yourself. Be cautious in making such amateur diagnoses, however. It is often quite common for normal people to suffer mild, temporary versions of syndromes we describe. In such cases, professional help is not usually needed. It is only when symptoms become severe and persistent, when they interfere with ordinary life and cause distress in people, that professional help is considered essential.

ANXIETY DISORDERS

Anxiety disorders, as the name suggests, are characterized by anxiety—emotional distress caused by feelings of vulnerability, apprehension, or fear. Some people try to cope with these feelings through ritualized behaviors that may reduce the anxiety somewhat, though never completely. Others try to avoid

The *DSM III-R* classification system helps mental health care professionals distinguish between people who are responding—perhaps ineffectively—to everyday stress and those who are suffering from a major psychological disorder.

situations that trigger the anxiety, but this can interfere greatly with normal life. Here we examine five anxiety disorders, beginning with panic disorder.

PANIC DISORDER

Mr. Wright, a man of 35, was referred to hospital because of a "dizzy turn" which he had experienced during his work as a laborer. He had had similar attacks in the past but, with each one, the associated feelings of panic became more acute. . . .

[Later] he began to complain of pressure in the front of his head and uncontrollable trembling and palpitations. He became more and more dependent on his wife and would go nowhere without her . . . .This meant of course that he had to give up work. (McCulloch and Prins, 1975, p. 54)

Panic disorder is often accompanied by agoraphobia (Greek for "fear of the marketplace"). Victims are so terrified of experiencing a panic attack in public that they become virtual prisoners in their own homes. They may be unable to go outside for months or even years at a time.

People who suffer **panic disorder** experience sudden, inexplicable attacks of intense fear which last for a number of minutes or sometimes even hours. The victims may have difficulty breathing; feel very nauseated, numb, or dizzy; sweat, tremble, or choke for no reason; have chest pains, heart palpitations, hot or cold flashes, and an overwhelming terror of dying or going crazy. Such panic attacks occur in roughly 1 percent of both men and women (Meyers et al., 1984). (Actually, many more people suffer from panic attacks, but they seek emergency coronary care rather than psychiatric treatment.) Often, panic disorder is accompanied by **agoraphobia,** an intense fear of being in places that are hard to escape from quickly or without embarrassment, or where help would not be available if a panic attack occurred (such as outside the home alone or in a bus, train, or car). It is also

common for panic disorder to be accompanied by depression (Breier et al., 1986). Since panic disorder tends to run in families and is more commonly shared by identical twins (who have the same genetic make-up) than by nonidentical twins or other siblings, researchers suspect that it may have a biological cause (Crowe et al., 1987).

PHOBIC DISORDERS

When irrational fear is focused on some specific object or situation (other than the fear of having a panic attack), it is called a **phobia.** (The term comes from the Greek word for "fear.") Sometimes people fear doing something in public that will humiliate them. For instance, there are people who are terrified that they will lose their voice when speaking in front of others. Such groundless fears in social situations are called *social phobias.* Phobias can involve nonsocial fears as well. These are called *simple phobias.* For example, some phobics are terrified of enclosed places (claustrophobia), others of heights (acrophobia), other of particular kinds of animals (dogs, insects, snakes, mice). Table 16.1 lists some additional phobias that clinicians have encountered. About 6 percent of the population suffer from phobias, with women having a substantially higher rate (8%) than men (3.4%) (Meyers et al., 1984). Ironically, these people know that their fear is unreasonable and excessive yet they are still unable to stop it. They try as best they can to avoid the feared stimulus, but this is sometimes difficult. The following case of a simple phobia is fairly typical.

> The client was a 30-year-old male who reported intense fear of crossing bridges and of heights. The fear had begun 3 years earlier when he was driving over a large suspension bridge while feeling anxious due to marital and career conflicts. Looking over the side he had experienced intense waves of fear. From that time onward his fear of bridges had become progressively more severe. At first, only bridges similar to the original were involved, but slowly the fear generalized to all bridges. Concurrently, he developed a fear of heights. Just before he came for treatment, he had been forced to dine with his employer in a restaurant atop a 52-story building. He had developed nausea and diarrhea and had been unable to eat. [Subsequently, he] decided to seek treatment. (Hurley, 1976, p. 295)

Several explanations of phobias have been proposed. Freudians have argued that a phobia develops as a defense mechanism against some unacceptable id impulse the ego is trying to control. The ego displaces anxiety over the impulse onto some symbolically related object or event. Thus, a man with a bridge phobia may be defending against a suicidal urge to jump off high places. In contrast, learning theorists believe that many phobias result from a combination of classical and operant conditioning. A boy bitten by a dog may thereafter fear dogs because he associates them with the fear-arousing stimulus of a painful bite. This is an instance of classical conditioning. The boy may then learn to reduce his fear by avoiding dogs as much as possible. This is an operantly conditioned response maintained by its reinforcing consequences (the reduction of anxiety). But what about phobias that arise in the absence of any incident that threatens real harm? Most people with a snake phobia, for instance, have never been bitten by a snake. Some psychologists believe that the human brain may be *prepared* to learn a fear of certain stimuli, such as dogs or snakes, probably because these animals resemble ancient predators. Significantly, it is much easier to establish conditioned arousal to the sight of snakes previously paired with electric shock than it is to establish conditioned arousal to the sight of, say, human faces (Ohman et al., 1975). So perhaps a propensity to certain types of phobias is partly innate. At the same time, observational learning may play a role in acquiring phobias (Bandura, 1986). A girl who repeatedly hears her mother express a fear of heights may imitate that response and express the same fear.

GENERALIZED ANXIETY DISORDER

Far less common than phobias is **generalized anxiety,** a state of persistent apprehension without good cause. People who have this disorder worry constantly for no apparent reason. They may worry that something terrible is going to happen to their children, even though the children are not in any danger. They may worry that they will be unable to pay their monthly bills, even though they have sufficient money in the bank. When asked why they have these worries, they are unable to give rational answers. The worries are simply there, plaguing them all the time.

Symptoms of tension often occur with generalized anxiety disorder. The victims may be so preoccupied with their worries that they cannot concentrate on anything else, becoming forgetful and

TABLE 16.1 Common Phobias

Phobia	Feared Object or Situation
Acrophobia	High places
Claustrophobia	Enclosed places
Ergasiophobia	Work
Gamophobia	Marriage
Haphephobia	Being touched
Hematophobia	Blood
Monophobia	Being alone
Ocholophobia	Crowds
Xenophobia	Strangers

disorganized (Barlow et al., 1986). They may also be irritable and tired, with sore, aching muscles, especially of the shoulders and neck. And yet they often have trouble sleeping at night. Dizziness, nausea, excessive sweating, shortness of breath, heart palpitations, a dry mouth, and difficulty swallowing are other common complaints. All are signs of a body under prolonged stress.

According to the psychoanalytic perspective, generalized anxiety disorder arises from an unconscious conflict between sexual or aggressive id impulses and the ego's fear that these impulses will be punished. This unconscious conflict leads to chronic worry and tension without knowing why, a condition that Freud called "free-floating anxiety." A very different explanation comes from the cognitive perspective. It focuses on the inability to control negative life events. Research shows that when people feel powerless to eliminate a painful stimulus, they tend to become very upset and give up trying to cope. In time they may develop a chronic feeling of helplessness accompanied by persistent anxiety and tension. Later in this chapter you will see how these same feelings may contribute not only to generalized anxiety but also to major depression.

OBSESSIVE-COMPULSIVE DISORDER

An **obsession** is an unwanted thought or image that keeps intruding into consciousness, one that the person often realizes is senseless but still cannot dismiss. The most common obsessions are recurring thoughts of violence (such as imagining killing a loved one), contamination (dwelling on getting infected with germs), and doubt (wondering whether you have done something you should have done, such as turning off the stove before leaving for vacation).

For some students, carefully lining up pens may be a form of procrastination—putting off studying just one more minute. For other people, however, the need for such orderliness is a compulsion so strong that it interferes with normal functioning.

A **compulsion** is a repetitive behavior that people feel compelled to do even though they realize it is senseless or being performed excessively. Obsessions and compulsions are often closely related, because obsessive thinking can lead to compulsive behavior. Examples are the person who is obsessed with the thought of germs and so cleans everything repeatedly, and the person who is plagued by doubts of having locked the doors and so checks them over and over, dozens of times a day. An obsession, of course, need not always be the cause of a compulsion. Sometimes compulsive people are simply following rigid rules of their own making. Here is an extreme case:

> Mr. B was unmarried, aged 45, and had a 30-year history of obsessive-compulsive problems. . . . [His] basic problem was a compulsion to be slow, meticulous, and

ritualistic, especially when dressing, washing, shaving, cleaning his teeth and combing his hair. . . . For instance, cleaning his teeth involved 192 slow meticulous brush strokes for each application of toothpaste and for each rinse. . . . Bathing would take him up to three hours with half an hour spent in rinsing the bath before filling it and half an hour rinsing the bath afterwards. Every action was performed in a slow meticulous manner reminiscent of the care taken by a bomb disposal expert. (Hodgson and Rachman, 1976, p. 29)

Obsessions can occur without compulsions. For instance, a young man may find that each time he is attracted to a woman, he becomes obsessed with the question of whether to call her for a date. If he calls and is rejected, he will feel devastated; if he does not call, he has no chance at all. He sees one side of the issue and then the other, never able to come to a decision. Over and over he ruminates on the pros and cons in an exhausting pattern of perpetual uncertainty.

Psychologists have offered several theories to account for obsessions and compulsions, which in mild forms are fairly common. In the psychoanalytic view, both are seen as symptoms of underlying psychological conflicts. For instance, compulsive hand washing would be interpreted as a combination of fixation and reaction formation, where the ego is defending itself against the anal desire to be messy and destructive. The learning view, in contrast, focuses on how compulsions can provide negative reinforcement by reducing anxiety. When anxious people discover that some behavior, such as washing their hands, leads to a reduction of anxiety, this response is strengthened. The relief, of course, is only temporary, so the behavior must be repeated over and over. Reduction of anxiety cannot account for obsessions, however, for obsessive thinking typically *raises* anxiety. Some learning theorists argue that obsessions arise when people experience a disturbing thought, the kind of thought that all of us have occasionally (Rachman and Hodgson, 1980). While a normal person would probably dismiss such a thought, an obsessive might become extremely concerned and make an active effort to inhibit such thoughts in the future. In fact, their efforts to inhibit them may simply cause the thoughts to intrude into consciousness even more (Wegner et al., 1987). This raises their anxiety, and a vicious cycle sets in. Finally, the biological

The full extent of post-traumatic stress disorder among combat soldiers in Operation Desert Storm will not be known for a long time. Many victims do not seek professional help for years, and some never do.

perspective looks to abnormalities in the brain that may contribute to obsessions and compulsions. Significantly, identical twins are more likely to *both* show **obsessive-compulsive disorders** than nonidentical twins are. What the identical twins may have inherited is a tendency toward emotional overarousal, with an anxiety disorder then being triggered by unusual life stress (Turner et al., 1985). Alternatively, obsessive-compulsives may suffer from overactivity in certain parts of the brain involved in filtering out irrelevant stimuli and persisting at tasks (Baxter et al., 1987).

POST-TRAUMATIC STRESS DISORDER

One [Vietnam] veteran had warned his close friend, the squad medic, not to go near a crying baby lying in a village road until they had checked the area. In his haste to help the child, the medic raced forward and "was blown to bits" along with the child, who had been booby-trapped. The veteran came into treatment three years later . . . because he was made fearful and anxious by his eight-month-old daughter's crying. He had been unable to pick her up or hold her since her birth despite his conscious wish to "be a good father." (Haley, 1978, p. 263)

This man was diagnosed as having **post-traumatic stress disorder (PTSD),** a state of anxiety, depression, and psychological "numbing" that follows exposure to a severe trauma, such as war, rape, the violent death of a loved one, or a catastrophic natural disaster. Post-traumatic stress disorder may be immediate or delayed, as in the case of this Vietnam veteran. Victims complain of tension, insomnia, and trouble concentrating, plus a feeling that they are remote from others and that life has lost its meaning. Involuntary mental "flashbacks" are also typical, often accompanied by recurrent nightmares in which the trauma is relived. A situation that triggers recollection of the trauma—such as the Vietnam veteran hearing his daughter cry—can intensify the symptoms. Post-traumatic stress disorder can be extremely long-lasting. In studies of survivors of Nazi concentration camps and soldiers returning from war, large percentages still have symptoms twenty, thirty, even forty years later (Krystal, 1968; Kluznik et al., 1986). Unfortunately, many people exposed to events that can cause this disorder never seek professional help (Lehman et al., 1987).

One group of people who have experienced unusual trauma are women who have been raped. Soon after the attack they often display many of the symptoms of post-traumatic stress. They are highly anxious, often reporting stomach pains, headaches,

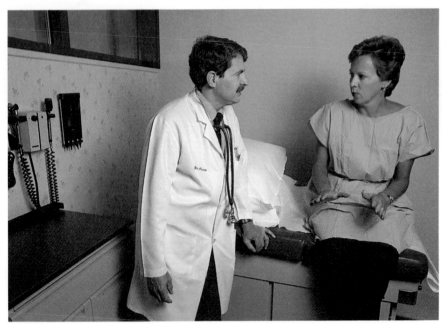

It is normal to be concerned about one's health, but people suffering from hypochondriasis are irrationally convinced that they have a serious illness, in spite of doctors' reassurances that they are perfectly healthy.

jumpiness, insomnia, and other signs of tension. Many relive the rape over and over, in their waking hours and in their dreams. Women who were awakened by their rapist often keep waking up at that same hour every night, bathed in sweat and screaming from a terrifying rape nightmare. Some develop phobias related to the trauma. A woman raped in a parking garage, for instance, may feel intense fear just from standing at the entrance to such a building. These symptoms can endure for a very long time. In one study, 25 percent of rape victims still had not recovered even four to six years after the trauma (Meyer and Taylor, 1986).

Of course, not everyone who experiences a trauma responds with the symptoms of post-traumatic stress. The most important factor differentiating those who do from those who do not is the severity of the trauma involved (Foy et al., 1987, in press). Apparently, some events are *so* traumatic they seem able to trigger symptoms of PTSD in virtually anyone. If so, should we consider the symptoms of post-traumatic stress "abnormal" behavior? Psychologists are still debating this question. Whatever their answer, inclusion of the disorder in *DSM-III-R* has helped enable treatment for thousands of people.

SOMATOFORM DISORDERS

The distinguishing characteristic of a **somatoform disorder** is the presence of one or more symptoms of what seems like a physical dysfunction, but for which there is no identifiable organic cause. Patients may complain of stomach pains, for example, but doctors find nothing to explain this problem. There is, however, a strong indication that the symptoms are related to psychological conflicts. (Note that somatoform disorders are not the same as psychosomatic illnesses. The latter are real physical problems that have a psychological component, such as ulcers caused by stress.) This does not mean that the person with a somatoform disorder is just pretending to be ill. These people have no sense whatsoever that their minds could be creating the symptoms. To them, the symptoms are absolutely real. Of the several types of somatoform disorders, we will discuss two: hypochondriasis and conversion disorder.

HYPOCHONDRIASIS

People who suffer from **hypochondriasis** are persistently fearful that they have contracted some terrible, often fatal disease. The hypochondriac spends much of life scrutinizing bodily functions for signs of serious illness. The minor aches, pains, bumps, and bruises that are impossible to avoid are immediately taken as signs of some dreaded malady in its early stages. Thus, simple headaches are interpreted as symptoms of a brain tumor, an occasional cough as a sign of lung cancer. You might think that when medical tests reveal the hypochondriac's fears to be groundless, the person's anxiety would end. But it does not. The typical hypochondriac refuses to believe a doctor's reassurance; he or she is certain that the feared illness is lurking, and that the doctor has simply failed to recognize it. Many hypochondriacs go from doctor to doctor with the same minor ailments, always receiving the same reassurances yet never finding any relief from their irrational fears.

Little is known about the causes of hypochondriasis. One hypothesis is that, for some hypochondriacs, reports of physical symptoms may be substitutes for expressing emotional pain. An aching shoulder, for example, may be easier to talk about than the pain of a son's failure to telephone home. Alternatively, the attention a hypochondriac gets from doctors, and perhaps from family and friends, may function to reinforce the chronic fears the person expresses.

CONVERSION DISORDER

People suffering a **conversion disorder** manifest what appears to be a genuine physical dysfunction. They suddenly become blind, deaf, paralyzed, or lose sensation in a part of the body, usually in a stressful situation. Yet there is no organic basis for the condition. It is purely psychological in origin—what the ancient Greeks called "hysteria." Conversion disorder was fairly common at the turn of the century, but today it is much rarer. One exception is a relatively high incidence of it among combat soldiers during wartime. Interestingly, conversion symptoms often disappear as suddenly as they appeared. Many "miracle" cures in which the paralyzed suddenly leave their wheelchairs or the deaf suddenly hear may involve conversion disorders.

Conversion disorders reduce anxiety in the people who suffer them. Typically, they make it impossible for the person to engage in some activity that

formerly caused distress. The student who fears she will fail a crucial exam becomes blind and can no longer study. The soldier who has had a brush with death develops a paralyzed arm and can no longer fire a rifle. The anxiety-reducing role of these ailments is suggested by the calm manner in which many people with conversion disorders accept their disabilities.

Several theories have been offered to explain conversion symptoms. Freud argued that they are defenses against forbidden urges. For instance, guilt over an urge to strike one's parents might result in paralysis of the arm. Learning theorists stress the rewards of conversion symptoms: they enable people to reduce anxiety and escape onerous duties, while at the same time gaining sympathy from others. Family-system theorists broaden the search for causes by trying to discover whether a conversion disorder is serving some useful role within the family. Consider a woman who developed conversion blindness when her husband retired (Haley, 1973). Her condition helped him cope with the difficult transition from his demanding job to a less active role at home. Caring for her and running the household made him feel useful. When she began to recover, he became depressed, and he felt better only after she suffered a relapse. According to the interpersonal or family-systems perspective, then, a conversion disorder may be a way of helping other family members to function. The victim, however, may pay a high price for giving this assistance.

DISSOCIATIVE DISORDERS

The **dissociative disorders** affect psychological rather than physical functioning. A part of the self is split off, or dissociated, so that personal memory or identity is disturbed. Dissociative disorders include psychogenic amnesia, psychogenic fugue, and multiple personality.

PSYCHOGENIC AMNESIA

Psychogenic amnesia is the partial or total forgetting of past experiences after some stressful event. Unlike amnesia that has an organic basis, psychogenic amnesia is caused strictly by a psychological trauma. For instance, a man who saw his child killed by a hit-and-run driver may be unable to remember anything from the time of the accident until several days later. Less commonly, the man may remember bits and pieces of the blacked-out period. He might recall, for example, sitting in the hospital waiting room and the fact that one of the doctors had a thick black moustache. Least common of all is psychogenic amnesia in which a person's whole life is blacked out following a trauma. But interestingly, even when this extensive memory loss occurs, the person always remember *some*thing from the past. A woman may not recognize her family, for instance, but she may remember how to knit. Because psychogenic amnesia is related to severe trauma, it is usually quite rare, except in wartime and during natural disasters.

PSYCHOGENIC FUGUE

Psychogenic fugue (from the Latin word for "flight") is another relatively rare dissociative disorder. Victims of it walk away from their homes and their identities for a period of time. That period may be hours, days, months, or even years. In some cases, the person takes up an entirely new life. The recovered fugue victim usually recalls nothing of what happened during the fugue state. The following case is fairly typical.

> A young married woman, chronically unhappy and in conflict over her marriage, occasionally wandered from her home in the daytime and got lost, much as unhappy little children do. She would suddenly "come to" far from home, and with no memory of having left it. (Cameron, 1963, p. 339)

MULTIPLE-PERSONALITY DISORDER

A more extreme form of dissociation, called **multiple-personality disorder,** has been widely publicized in the films *Sybil* and *The Three Faces of Eve.* The person (more often a female) evolves two or more separate personalities, each well defined. Often the personalities contrast sharply. Eve, for example, expressed both the "good girl" personality of Eve White and the naughty, uninhibited personality of Eve Black. The transition from one personality to another is usually rapid, often in a matter of seconds. Sudden-

ly the person's voice and facial expressions change as the next personality emerges. It is common for someone with this disorder to harbor as many as ten distinctive personalities.

The personalities tend to form three clusters: demure, shy, withdrawn (called the "core" personality, since this is the personality most people recognize); aggressive, violent, promiscuous; and level-headed, rational. Some psychologists note the eerie similarity between these three clusters and Freud's concepts of superego, id, and ego, respectively.

Typically, the personality that approaches a therapist for treatment has little or no knowledge that the other personalities exist. Instead, the person is troubled by gaps in time about which he or she has no recollection. Friends may report that the person sometimes acts oddly (a normally demure woman may be seen swearing at a cab driver or drinking heavily in a bar). Yet the person cannot recall doing these out-of-character things. Signs of the personality switch may be noticed, however. A nonsmoker, for example, may discover cigarette butts in a living room ashtray that were not there the night before. Interestingly, the other personalities may know of one another to varying degrees. Sometimes they think of each other as friends and sometimes as adversaries.

The start of multiple-personality disorder is almost always during childhood, typically in response to severe abuse, often sexual. Most cases, however, do not come to a therapist's attention until adulthood. Traditionally, multiple-personality disorder has been considered very rare, but recent reports suggest it is more common than was formerly thought. It should not be mistaken for schizophrenia, which we will discuss later in the chapter.

MOOD DISORDERS

Most of the time, the moods we feel are related to what is happening in our lives. We become elated if we win a lottery and dejected if we fail an exam. At other times, however, we feel marvelous or miserable for no apparent reason. People with **mood disorders** experience much the same thing, but their moods are more intense and they tend to last for longer periods. As a result, their emotions come to distort their entire outlook and to interfere greatly with their normal lives. Mental health professionals identify two major types of mood disorders: **depressive disorders,** in which a sad, discouraged mood is the major symptom; and **bipolar disorders,** in which there are both periods of depression and periods of excessive elation, called mania.

DEPRESSIVE DISORDERS

MAJOR DEPRESSION

One type of depressive disorder is **major depression,** a condition characterized by one or more *episodes of deep sadness and despair,* each of which persists virtually all day long for a period of at least two weeks. People with major depression describe themselves as down, discouraged, and hopeless. They lose interest in formerly pleasurable activities; many say they just do not care about anything anymore.

People with major depression also display a number of other symptoms, several of which must be present before this diagnosis is given. One of these is a significant *loss of energy.* Many people with major depression feel perpetually tired; even the slightest exertion exhausts them. In keeping with this chronic fatigue, depressed people frequently show a *slowing down of behavior.* Posture may become stooped, movements labored, and speech filled with pauses. The opposite may also occur, however. Some depressed people act *agitated;* they pace, wring their hands, and rub their clothing. Depressives also tend to have *difficulties thinking.* They cannot concentrate or remember well; they have great trouble making decisions. Frequently there is an *eating disturbance* too (loss of appetite or marked overeating), as well as *problems in sleeping* (insomnia or a tendency to sleep for hours on end). Many depressives suffer an *exaggerated sense of worthlessness.* They see no virtues in themselves; they greatly magnify their failures; they are convinced that they are utterly hopeless cases. Such feelings can easily lead to a final symptom of depression: *recurring thoughts of death and suicide.*

Some of these symptoms, of course, are ones that many people experience when they are "low" or "blue." But for someone with major depression the symptoms are far more intense (Eastwood et al., 1985). People with major depression may also fail to "bounce back" quickly. The disorder lasts an average of three to six months, depending on its severity. Relapses are also common, occurring in about 50 percent of patients within two years after recovery

Major depression is a specific mood disorder with many criteria for exact diagnosis. Its symptoms go far beyond the state most of us are in when we say we're "depressed."

from a major depressive episode. Those who have already had several such episodes, who are currently under unusual stress, and who lack emotional support from their families are especially prone to relapse (Belsher and Costello, 1988). Here is how one woman described what it is like to spiral downward into a major depression:

> I began not to be able to manage as far as doing the kinds of things that I really had always been able to do easily, such as cook, wash, take care of the children, play games, that kind of thing. . . . I think one of the most frightening aspects at the beginning was that time went so slowly. It would seem sometimes that at least an hour had gone by and I would look at my watch and it would only have been three minutes. And I began not to be able to

concentrate. . . . I couldn't even read any more. And if awakened early . . . I sometimes would lie in bed two hours trying to make myself get up because I just couldn't put my feet on the floor. Then when I did, I just felt that I couldn't get dressed. And then, whatever the next step was, I felt I couldn't do that. (From "Depression: The Shadowed Valley," from the series *The Thin Edge,* © 1975 by the Educational Broadcasting Corporation.)

DYSTHYMIA

Major depression is characterized by acute episodes of sadness that last for several months and then go away, sometimes reoccuring and sometimes not. In contrast, there is also a chronic form of depression, one that endures for years at a time. This condition is called **dysthymia.** The diagnosis of dysthymia is given if depression persists for at least two years without any periods of remission that last for over two months. The most common form of dysthymia involves early onset of the disorder. The person suffers life-long negative moods either persistently or with periods of normal mood lasting a few days or weeks at a time. Dysthymia is a particularly severe form of depressive disorder (Klein et al., 1988). It sometimes occurs among people who also experience periodic episodes of major depression. The prognosis for people with major depression and dysthymia has been found to be especially poor (Keller et al., 1982).

DEPRESSION AND SUICIDE

Given the despair of depression and its often long duration, it is not surprising that some depressed people eventually attempt suicide. In one study of depressed patients studied for a year, 10 percent made at least one suicide attempt (Shapiro and Keller, 1981). There are nearly 30,000 officially recorded suicides a year in America, and the actual number is probably closer to 100,000. For those Americans aged fifteen to twenty-four, suicide is now the second most common cause of death, surpassed only by accidents (Harvard Medical School, 1986; National Center for Health Statistics, 1988). Although three times more men kill themselves than women, three times more women than men *attempt* suicide. Apparently, men typically choose more lethal methods, such as shooting or hanging themselves, whereas women usually use less effective methods, such as sleeping pills (Holden, 1986).

Many common beliefs about suicide are nothing more than myths. For example, there is little truth to the widespread notion that people who attempt suicide and fail are not "serious" about wanting to die. Approximately 2 percent of those who make nonfatal suicide attempts will make a second, completed attempt within a year. Another 10 to 40 percent will go on to a second failed attempt, and some of them, ultimately, to a completed one (Hirsch et al., 1982). There is also little truth to the common assumption that those who talk about committing suicide seldom go ahead and do it. About 70 percent of people who commit or attempt suicide tell others their intentions beforehand (Mishara, 1982; Stengel, 1964). Nor is it true that depressed people whose symptoms begin to improve run a lesser risk of suicide. Ironically, it is when depression begins to lift that people may find the energy and resolve to carry out a suicidal wish (Shneidman, 1973). The widespread belief that one should steer depressed people *away* from talk of suicide, for fear that it will only strengthen their desire, is incorrect as well. Letting despondent people talk about their suicidal wishes may actually help them to overcome these thoughts (Harvard Medical School, 1986). At the very least, such discussions can enable concerned others to estimate just how close to suicide a depressed person is. Getting professional help can be critical to saving the person's life (Beck et al., 1979; Fawcett, n.d.).

What are the signs to look for to help prevent a suicide? The clearest signs are statements that communicate the person's intentions, either directly or indirectly. If someone you know who is under stress ever mentions suicide to you, talks about not being able to "take things" any longer, or discusses actions that imply suicide is being considered (saving up sleeping pills, for instance), do not assume that these are just rash statements. Seek qualified help even if you have to break a confidence. Also be on the lookout for changes in behavior that may signal a suicide decision. If a depressed person suddenly starts to put affairs in order, gives away prized possessions, or has a lift in spirits for no apparent reason, the person may well have decided that suicide is the "answer."

EXPLAINING DEPRESSION

Because so many people suffer from it, depression has been called the common cold of mental illness. In total, an estimated 70 percent of women and over 40 percent of men will experience some form of depres-

The recent alarming increase in suicide among adolescents means that friends and relatives must be more alert to the signs that a depressed person is considering suicide, and must be prepared to seek a qualified mental health care professional's help in preventing the person from going through with it.

sion before age sixty-five (McGuffin and Katz, 1989). The rate of depression has also been rising during this century, and the disorder has been appearing at an increasingly early age (Klerman et al., 1985). Since depression is such a widespread problem, we will devote more space to its causes than we will to the causes of other disorders.

THE PSYCHOANALYTIC PERSPECTIVE

Psychoanalytic thinkers have offered several explanations for depression. One was first proposed by Karl Abraham (1911, 1916), a student of Freud's, and later elaborated by Freud himself (1917). It holds that depression arises from feelings of anger toward a parent or other attachment figure who has died or otherwise abandoned the person. This anger produces guilt, so the person turns it inward, experiencing it as self-loathing, which then brings about depression.

Has research supported this psychoanalytic theory of depression? Although a link between depression and unexpressed anger often does exist, there is little evidence that this anger arose in the way that Freud contended. Many contemporary researchers therefore believe that a second line of psychoanalytic thinking is more promising (Stricker, 1983). This view holds that depression is a reaction to the loss of something deeply valued by a person whose need to be taken care of as an infant was not adequately met (through neglect or the death of a parent, for instance). Such people become fixated on the issue of

dependency and the need for love. So later in life, when something valued is taken from them, they feel unbearably vulnerable and are plunged into depression. In keeping with this theory, depressed people are more likely than others to have experienced the death of a parent during childhood (Barnes and Prosen, 1985). Moreover, depressive episodes are often triggered by critical losses in a person's life— divorce, the death of a loved one, being fired from a job, and so forth (Paykel, 1979). There is also evidence that people who are very dependent on others are particularly prone to feeling depressed over losses in their interpersonal relationships (Hammen et al., 1985). It is as if they are especially sensitive to rejection or abandonment by others and so readily become depressed when these type of events occur.

THE LEARNING PERSPECTIVE

Learning theorists have also offered several theories of depression. Peter Lewinsohn (1974) has argued that depression can arise when a person's behavior no longer elicits the rewards it once did. This loss of rewards is often related to some change in the person's social environment—perhaps the death of a loved one, perhaps loss of or retirement from a job. Suddenly the person is placed in a new situation where he or she no longer receives love and approval from others. Without these rewards, the person gives up trying and becomes depressed and withdrawn. This only worsens the problem, however, for withdrawing from others virtually guarantees that few pleasures will be experienced, and so the depression deepens. If forced into social situations (made to go to a party, for instance), depressed people usually lack the motivation and skills to interact and enjoy themselves. In Lewinsohn's view, they must be *helped* to become involved in rewarding social activities. In this way, the negative cycle maintaining their depression can be broken.

THE COGNITIVE PERSPECTIVE

Lewinsohn focuses on the depressed person's behavior and how it fails to achieve necessary rewards. Cognitive theorists, in contrast, focus on the negative ways that depressed people think about themselves and their lives. Two psychologists who take a cognitive perspective are Aaron Beck and Martin Seligman.

Beck's Cognitive View   Beck (1974, 1985) argues that depressed people have negative schemas about themselves, the world, and the future ("I'm unlikeable; nothing ever goes right; tomorrow will be just as bad as today"). They also commit errors in logic when they interpret *why* things happen. They tend to confirm their negative schemas by using irrelevant information, taking small details out of context, overgeneralizing from single incidents, or minimizing the importance of positive events. Consider one depressed patient's assessment of her therapist's behavior. If the therapist arrived late, she heaped the blame onto herself ("He doesn't want to see me; I'm too hopeless"). Yet if the therapist was early, she also blamed her own shortcomings ("I'm so sick he has to rush to the office"). Beck believes that such distorted thinking is a major factor causing and maintaining depression. To lift depression, he argues, we must help people break free of these negative outlooks and ways of reasoning.

IN DEPTH

Seligman's Theory of "Learned Helplessness"

Martin Seligman and his colleagues have gathered further evidence that negative interpretations of events may indeed be linked to depression. Because Seligman's work provides such a good example of how theories of depression evolve, we will explore his research in depth.

THE INITIAL STUDIES

Seligman's research began with some unusual experiments on dogs (Seligman et al., 1968). He exposed one group of dogs to a long series of electric shocks from which they could not escape. Later, when these same dogs were placed in another situation where they *could* escape shocks by jumping to one side, they tended not to do so. Instead, most lay down motionless, passively enduring as many shocks as the experimenter chose to give. This was not true of a second group of dogs that had *not* received the earlier shocks. Animals in this second group invariably managed to jump and escape the pain. Moreover, the two groups of dogs differed markedly in their postexperimental behavior. Those in the first group seemed to display symptoms of depression—lethargy, inactivity, loss of appetite— while those in the second group did not.

Seligman concluded that the differences between the groups stemmed from what they had learned. Animals in the first group had initially learned that they were helpless to control the shocks, and so continued to act helplessly in the second stage of the experiment, when the shocks *were* controllable. Such "learned helplessness," Seligman speculated, may be an important cause of depression in humans. When people are unable to influence a situation that is important to them, they may not only give up trying to change that situation, they may also become depressed and show little initiative in new situations where success might be possible.

CRITICISMS, ALTERNATIVES, AND FURTHER RESEARCH

Seligman's original theory and research generated much controversy. Critics charged that learned helplessness alone cannot explain the many variations in depression. Why do some depressed people constantly blame themselves while others do so much less often? Why are some depressive episodes so severe and prolonged while others are much shorter and milder?

As a result of these and other criticisms, Seligman and his colleagues modified their original theory (Abramson et al., 1978). They argued that uncontrollable outcomes alone do not determine the nature and magnitude of human depression. The way a person *explains* these outcomes also plays a crucial part. Consider three types of people. The first type attributes undesirable outcomes to temporary external causes. Such people may feel dejected for a time, but they will not reproach themselves. Their chances for bouncing back are good. The second type of person attributes undesirable outcomes to personal inadequacies. Such people will probably experience depression accompanied by guilt and self-blame. The third type of person not only attributes negative outcomes to personal shortcomings but also sees those shortcomings as *enduring* traits. Such people will probably experience the severest depression because they see themselves as persistently inadequate, inevitably prone to failure and rejection.

To gather support for this revised theory, Seligman and his colleagues developed a questionnaire that assesses how people explain negative life events. Using this questionnaire, they have found that many depressed people *do* attribute negative events to stable traits in themselves, while nondepressed people generally do not. Moreover, this style of explanation often *precedes* depression; it is not always the result of an emotionally dejected state. In one study, for instance, people's tendency to attribute negative events to their own stable traits could be used to predict subsequent bouts of depression even though some of these people were not yet depressed when their explanatory style was assessed (Zullow and Seligman, 1985).

Seligman's theory is similar to Beck's in that both suggest that negatively distorted ways of thinking can cause depression. Not all psychologists agree with this perspective, however. Some point to findings which suggest that depressed people's thinking may not be as distorted as Seligman and Beck believe (Coyne and Gotlib, 1983). For instance, compared with other people, those who are depressed are indeed more apt to feel they cannot control negative outcomes, just as Seligman contends. But Seligman may be wrong in assuming that this is because they *imagine* less control than they actually have. Research shows that the depressed are sometimes more realistic in estimating their degree of control over outcomes than nondepressed people are (Alloy and Abramson, 1979). Similarly, depressed people rate themselves as having poorer social skills than other people do; they seem to have the negative self-schemas that Beck says they do. But are these schemas distortions of reality, as Beck suggests? Perhaps not, for unbiased observers agree with the low social-skill ratings that depressed people give themselves (Lewinsohn et al., 1980). Thus, it may simply be that when de-

People with a negatively distorted way of thinking may attribute a bad event, such as a failing grade on an exam, to enduring character flaws.

pressed people view themselves and events negatively, they are making fairly accurate assessments based on the information they have. The lives of depressed people *are* going badly, and their own actions and lack of effort are often involved in the bad experiences they have (Coyne and Gotlib, 1983). If this is so, is it right to say that a distorted view of the world is causing their depression?

But Seligman responds that it may not matter how realistic or unrealistic the views of depressed people are. If, for whatever reason, people think that their own enduring faults cause negative events, this style of thinking is apt to bring on intense and long-lasting dejection. Is Seligman right in making this assumption? The evidence is mixed. In one study, several hundred college students taking an introductory psychology course were assessed for their style of explaining negative events (Metalsky et al., 1987). Shortly thereafter they received their grades on the midterm exam. Most of those who did poorly on the exam became depressed, regardless of how they explained the low score. A negative way of thinking, it seemed, was *not* the major cause of their depression. But the students who *stayed* depressed for longer than just a few days were those who were prone to blame their own enduring faults for the bad things that happened to them. Apparently, when people with this negative outlook experience upsetting events, they often respond with a more intense and prolonged dejection than other people do.

Critics of the learned helplessness view are not satisfied, however. Some ask if a tendency to blame oneself for negative outcomes typically *precedes* depression, as Seligman suggests. Although some studies have supported this contention, other studies have not. In one, for example, patients were assessed at two different times: first while in the midst of a major depression, and later when ready to be discharged from the hospital (Hamilton and Abramson, 1983). During the first assessment, many showed the typical depressive style of attributing causes (placing blame for negative outcomes on persistent shortcomings in themselves); but in the second assessment this tendency had largely disappeared. These findings call into question Seligman's idea that a negative attributional style promotes depression, rather than the other way around. It seems more accurate to say that attributional style interacts with a person's mood, each being capable of influencing the other. If this is so, attributional style is a *contributor* to depression, but not its major cause.

Such findings have encouraged another revision of the learned helplessness theory (Abramson et al., 1989). In this version, a depressive style of attributing causes is just one of several cognitive tendencies that make a person vulnerable to depression. Another is the tendency to cast oneself in a negative light—that is, to form the negative self-schemas that Aaron Beck talks about. A third is the tendency to assume that negative events will have *severe* consequences, that they are capable of virtually crippling a person's life. Such outlooks make it likely that when some stress occurs a person will see things as hopeless, give up trying to change them, and lapse into depression.

PATTERNS AND CONCLUSIONS

Cognitive factors cannot be ignored if we are to fully understand the causes of depression. Today

researchers are examining many different styles of thinking to discover which are related to severe downturns in mood. For instance, when women experience sadness, they often ruminate about it more than men do, which may only serve to intensify and prolong the problem. Men, in contrast, are more inclined to shake off negative feelings by getting involved in some physical activity, such as playing sports or building something. This positive response could help explain why only half as many men as women suffer depression (Nolen-Hoeksema, 1987). Of course, such theories have not yet been proven. Studies are needed, especially longitudinal ones, to help pinpoint the various cognitive factors involved in depression (Downey et al., 1991). At the same time, we must try to determine how these various cognitive factors interact with one another and with other significant forces to bring on serious depression.

THE BIOLOGICAL PERSPECTIVE

Some of these other forces are undoubtedly biological ones. We know this partly from studies of how depression runs in families. For instance, depressed adults who were adopted as infants are more likely to come from biological families with a high incidence of depression than nondepressed adoptees are (Wender et al., 1986). How many times more likely often depends on the severity of the depression involved, with the more severe cases appearing to have a stronger genetic component. It is as if severely depressed adoptees have inherited certain biological traits that make them more susceptible to depression. Similarly, identical twins are significantly more likely to *both* suffer major depression than are fraternal twins (who have on average only half their genes in common) (Allen, 1976; McGuffin and Katz, 1989). Although part of the reason for this pattern could be that parents treat identical twins more similarly than fraternal twins, this is probably not the whole explanation. Inherited biological traits are also implicated.

Researchers wonder what these inherited traits might be. Clues have led to a focus on brain chemicals. For instance, in the 1950s, doctors treating people for tuberculosis tried a drug called iproniazid. It did not cure the disease, but it did brighten the mood of tuberculosis patients, who are often depressed. This discovery helped researchers develop a number of new antidepressant drugs. At about the same time, doctors discovered that a drug called reserpine, used to reduce hypertension (high blood pressure), could also be used to calm highly agitated behavior in seriously disturbed mental patients. Unfortunately, about 15 percent of the time, it had an unwanted side effect: it caused serious depression, sometimes to the point of suicide (Lemieux et al., 1965).

What effects could these various drugs be having on the brain? Researchers found that the new antidepressant drugs (called tricyclics and MAO inhibitors) increased the levels of two neurotransmitters: norepinephrine, which is intimately involved in arousal; and serotonin, which plays a role in emotion and motivation. Interestingly, reserpine was found to have the opposite effect on these two neurotransmitters: it *reduced* the levels of both. So perhaps, researchers reasoned, depression arises when the amounts of norepinephrine and serotonin in the brain drop below some critical levels.

But further research showed that the answer was not this simple. Although depressed patients did seem to have low levels of serotonin, many did not appear to have chronically low levels of norepinephrine (McNeal and Cimbolic, 1986; Muscettola et al., 1984). Does this mean that serotonin depletion alone is the major cause of depression? No. Once again, the answer is not this easy. If depletion of serotonin is the cause of most depressions, then antidepressant drugs, which raise serotonin levels quickly, would show their therapeutic effects right away. But they do not. Instead, it takes between ten and fourteen days for antidepressants to work. What's more, antidepressants stop boosting neurotransmitter levels after they have been taken for a few days. At this point, the amounts of epinephrine and serotonin in the brain fall back to their previous levels. Nevertheless, a week or so later, mood begins to lift. Clearly, something more than just an increase in neurotransmitter levels must be causing this antidepressant effect (Heninger et al., 1983).

Researchers are not yet sure what that something more is. Currently, they are investigating whether antidepressant drugs might gradually cause changes in synapses within the brain that could account for the elevation in mood they produce (Lloyd, 1989). The results of this research may reveal more about the biological factors involved in depression.

THE INTERPERSONAL OR FAMILY-SYSTEMS PERSPECTIVE

Though biological factors seem to play a role in producing and maintaining the symptoms of depression, how others respond to a depressed person may also be significant. According to this perspective, depression is not just something that arises *within* a person; it has important origins in interpersonal relationships too. When someone begins to have depressive symptoms (sadness, tiredness, apathy, and so on), others may react negatively (Coyne, 1976a, 1976b). Although they may try to reassure the person and offer some support, their concern is not always genuine. Frequently, their true feelings show in rejection and avoidance. The depressed person, of course, perceives these negative feelings and responds with greater depression. This only heightens the reaction of others, and they withdraw all the more. Soon a vicious cycle sets in.

In an interesting experiment designed to test the theory that others are often hostile and rejecting toward depressed people, forty-five normal subjects spoke by telephone to either a depressed or a nondepressed person. Those who spoke to a depressed person reported feeling more depressed themselves after the conversation, and they also reported increased hostility. What's more, they expressed much less willingness than the other subjects did to talk with the same person again (Coyne, 1976b). These findings contrast sharply with the view of many cognitive theorists that the depressed person's negative perceptions are largely distortions of reality. Apparently, depressed people often do live in a world where others respond to them negatively. This could easily be a factor contributing to their disturbance, perhaps perpetuating a depression that originally arose for other reasons.

But what exactly does a depressed person do that elicits negative reactions? In a study similar to the one just described, researchers watched while female college students talked to either a depressed or a nondepressed classmate (Gotlib and Robinson, 1982). Compared with the nondepressed classmates, those who were depressed were more negative in their conversational styles. They made more negative remarks and showed less concern and sympathy for their partners. They also smiled less, talked more monotonously, and were generally less animated and pleasant. Not surprisingly, the young women who had to interact with these depressed students quickly responded in kind. Within the first three minutes of the conversation, they too were smiling less and making more negative comments than were those talking to nondepressed classmates.

But such laboratory studies have been criticized for focusing on how strangers react to depressed

This painting, *Misery,* by the Spanish artist Monturiol Nonell (1876–1911), eloquently portrays the sadness and despair of major depression.

people, rather than observing the reactions of family members and friends (Doerfler and Chaplin, 1985). Wouldn't those who are emotionally close to a depressed person be more sympathetic? Family-system theorists argue that though this may be true, there is probably a limit to the patience that even close relatives and friends have for depression. As time goes on and the depression continues, people who were at first concerned and sympathetic may gradually become annoyed. Perhaps they grow tired of offering support and getting none in return (Ziomek and Coyne, 1983). In any case, their negative reaction may serve to deepen the depression.

COMBINING PERSPECTIVES

In summary, there are probably many causes of depression, any number of which can work together to produce depressive symptoms (Akiskal, 1979; Akiskal and McKinney, 1973, 1975). One case might be triggered by biological changes and then made worse by negative thinking and other people's negative reactions. Another case might begin with some distressing life event, which in turn sets in motion both a negative outlook and a physiological reaction that intensifies the problem. Because the roots of

depression are many and complex, a combination of different perspectives helps us to understand it.

BIPOLAR DISORDERS

MANIC-DEPRESSION

In 5 to 10 percent of cases, depressive symptoms are only half the problem. Some depressed people also suffer from **mania,** which is characterized by one or more *periods of exaggerated elation.* The syndrome of depression combined with mania is known as **bipolar disorder.** It affects about 1 percent of the population. Some individuals experience mania without depression, but this appears to be quite rare.

A manic episode has other symptoms besides exaggerated elation. The emotional high is sometimes mixed with intense *irritability,* especially when others try to restrain the manic person. Another common symptom is *hyperactivity.* The manic may plunge headlong into a string of ambitious projects—composing music, writing film scripts, designing a new missile to be sold to the Pentagon—even though the person has never before shown any talent in these areas. This hyperactive behavior is related to a *decreased need for sleep.* Many manics carry on their feverish activities with only a few hours' rest each night. Typically, too, the manic displays *constant talkativeness*. Manics tend to talk rapidly, loudly, and endlessly. Often they are impossible to interrupt. This abnormality in speech may partly reflect the fact that many manics experience the sensation of "racing" thoughts, a sensation clinically referred to as *flight of ideas*. Another common manic symptom is great *distractibility*. In conversation the typical manic leaps from topic to topic. Many manics also show enormously *inflated self-esteem*. They are convinced that they are brilliant, irresistibly attractive, and superior to everyone they meet. This greatly distorted self-image is undoubtedly related to a final manic symptom: *reckless behavior*. Many manics go on extravagant buying sprees, invest the family savings in foolhardy business ventures, or commit sexual indiscretions, all without the slightest awareness that these behaviors could have disastrous results.

You might think that from the victim's viewpoint, mania is an exhilarating experience—a feeling of being invincible, all-powerful, and all-wise. In milder forms of the disorder, this is precisely how the person *does* feel. The problem is that mania often escalates to such feverish heights that the person is totally and frighteningly out of control. Here is how one woman described the terrible transition from relatively mild mania (called hypomania) to much more severe symptoms:

> [*Hypomania*] At first when I'm high it's tremendous . . . ideas are fast . . . like shooting stars you follow 'til brighter ones appear . . . all shyness disappears, the right words and gestures are suddenly all there . . . uninteresting people, things become intensely interesting. Sensuality is pervasive, the desire to seduce and be seduced is irresistible. Your marrow is infused with unbelievable feelings of ease, power, well-being, omnipotence, euphoria . . . you can do anything. . . . But somewhere this changes. . . .
> [*Mania*] The fast ideas become too fast and there are far too many . . . overwhelming confusion replaces clarity . . . you stop keeping up with it—memory goes. Infectious humor ceases to amuse—your friends become frightened . . . everything is now against the grain . . . you are irritable, angry, frightened,

uncontrollable and trapped in the blackest caves of the mind—caves you never knew were there. It will never end. (Goldstein et al., 1980)

Not surprisingly, when a full manic episode occurs, the person is severely impaired on the job and in social relationships. Sometimes hospitalization is needed to prevent harm to oneself or others.

Bipolar disorder takes several forms. In some cases either mania or depression predominates. The person suffers many episodes of depression interspersed with a few of mania, or the pattern is reversed. In rarer instances, mania and depression always alternate. Cases have even been observed in which the moods switch regularly on a twenty-four- or forty-eight-hour cycle, suggesting that in these cases the disorder may be linked to the person's physiological rhythms (Bunney et al., 1972; Jenner et al., 1967; Mendels, 1970). Another pattern, also rare, is a simultaneous mixing of manic and depressive symptoms. The person may weep uncontrollably and threaten suicide, yet at the same time display frantic hyperactivity. Often with bipolar disorder the periods of mood disturbance are relatively short and separated by intervals of normal functioning.

Clinicians have found that depression in people with bipolar disorder differs from that of people who suffer major depression alone, with no manic episodes (called **unipolar depression**). For instance, bipolar depression usually starts earlier in life than unipolar depression, and it also is more likely to run in families. In addition, a drug called lithium carbonate is more effective for bipolars who are currently depressed than it is for people suffering an episode of unipolar depression. This suggests that the two forms of depression may have different causes.

CYCLOTHYMIA

Just as there is a chronic but milder form of unipolar depression (dysthymia), so there is also a chronic but milder form of bipolar disorder called **cyclothymia.** In cyclothymia, a person has, over at least a two-year period, numerous episodes of hypomania and numerous episodes of depression (not severe enough to be labeled major depressions, but disturbing nonetheless). There may be some periods of normal mood occurring in between, but these never last more than two months. Overall, the person seems on an endless treadmill of mood upswings and downturns.

EXPLAINING BIPOLAR DISORDERS

We do not yet have all the pieces to the puzzle of bipolar disorders, but biological factors are strongly implicated. Blood relatives of bipolars are much more likely to also have this condition than other people are (McGuffin and Katz, 1989). Studies of one set of relatives with a very high incidence of bipolar depression showed that most of those who suffered it had two defective genes on chromosome eleven (Egeland et al., 1987). So perhaps an inherited biochemical defect is involved in manic-depression. The brain of a manic-depressive may "overcorrect" for emotional highs and lows by producing too much of the chemicals that normally neutralize mood extremes (Wehr et al., 1987). Biochemical studies of the processes whereby mania switches to depression and depression to mania may shed more light on the causes of this disorder.

SEASONAL AFFECTIVE DISORDER

Another type of mood disturbances are those related to changes in the seasons, called **seasonal affective disorder.** These can vary from mild to extreme depending on the person. In one survey of over 400 people living in Maryland, 92 percent reported seasonal changes in mood and behavior, and 27 percent said that these changes created at least some problems for them. For somewhere between 4 and 10 percent of the sample, the problems were severe enough to cause significant impairment in the person's daily life (Kasper et al., 1989).

There are two types of seasonal affective disorders (Wehr and Rosenthal, 1989). In one, the more common, depression occurs in the winter. In the other, less common, there is summertime depression. Interestingly, the symptoms accompanying sadness and dejection tend to differ for winter and summertime depressives. Those who suffer depression in the summer typically have trouble sleeping, lose their appetites, and lose weight. Winter depressives, in contrast, usually do the opposite: they oversleep, overeat, have cravings for carbohydrate-rich foods, and typically gain weight (Wurtman and Wurtman, 1989). What happens to these people when spring or autumn roles around and their depressive symptoms lift? Often, their moods turn buoyant, sometimes developing into mania.

These seasonal moods must somehow be governed by changes in the natural environment. For wintertime depression, a triggering factor appears to be deficiency of sunlight as the days grow shorter. Significantly, this condition is more frequent, longer lasting, and more severe the higher the latitude at which people live (the higher the latitude, the fewer hours of sunlight a day during the winter months). Also, when people who suffer winter depression travel south in winter (where days are longer), their depressive symptoms improve; and when they travel north in winter (where days are shorter), their depressive symptoms worsen (Rosenthal et al., 1986). These findings have led to the use of artificial sunlight as a form of treatment for wintertime depression (Hellekson et al., 1986; Lewy et al., 1987). People who suffer from it extend the length of their days by exposure to bright "grow" lights, typically during the predawn or evening hours. The cause of summertime depression is more in doubt, but heat may be a precipitating factor. This condition is more frequent, longer lasting, and more severe at lower latitudes, where temperatures are hotter. Significantly, exposure to cold can help to lift the symptoms of summertime depression (Wehr et al., 1987, 1989).

Why would our moods be responsive to such factors as temperature and light? Some psychologists think these reactions are similar to the adaptations than many other animal species make as the seasons change (Wehr and Rosenthal, 1989). For instance, at different times of the year various animal species become more or less active (some even hibernate), eat a great deal or reduce their diets, gain weight or lose weight, and so forth. Perhaps humans respond to the changing seasons in a parallel way, some more so than others. Those who are affected to a major degree and become clinically depressed or manic may simply represent extreme cases of this common response (Kasper et al., 1989).

SCHIZOPHRENIA

Schizophrenia affects about 1 percent of the general population, but it accounts for half of all those committed to mental hospitals (Taube and Rednick, 1973; von Korff et al., 1985). **Schizophrenia** is a severe disorder with bizarre symptoms. In the acute phase of this disease, its victims are unable to function normally, either at work or in their social lives. The condition is also very resistant to treatment. Even with modern drug therapy, little more than a third of all schizophrenics manage to recover (Stephens,

Many people who are affected by the winter type of seasonal mood disorder get relief from their depressive symptoms by sitting in front of a light, which mimics sunlight, for several hours each day.

1978). The following case illustrates what an active phase of schizophrenia is like:

> Six months before his admission Arnold began to scream while at work with no apparent provocation, turned off all the machinery, and continually interfered with the work of others. When his supervisor reprimanded him, Arnold told him to go to hell, and was fired. He claimed that he could see his mother's body floating in the air. . . . Four months before his admission he broke in the door of his home with an ax and threatened the members of his family. He was arrested for this, but released soon thereafter. On the day before his admission he threatened to burn the house, and then broke into his father's room and said, "You have got to kill me or I will kill you. Tonight the time is up." Faced with this choice his father had Arnold arrested again. The next morning Arnold told the police, "I see a whole bunch of dead people sitting here now. They run about my cell at night like crazy men, pulling me around. I hear them whispering to me." He was then committed to the local state hospital.
>
> On admission he was quiet and indifferent to his commitment. His conversation and behavior were childish and marked by foolish and inappropriate laughter. At first he thought it was "awful to be among so many crazy people" but shortly thereafter he realized that it was quite a joke, and laughed heartily about his fate. He felt that the attendants were going to kill him, but laughed foolishly while telling of his fears. . . . He experienced a series of vivid hallucinations, including feeling a man's claws on this throat, although he did not see or hear the man, feeling electricity jar him, seeing ghosts haunting him, seeing blue shadows going around and red shadows going up and down through the air, and seeing wingless female spirits flying through the air. (Zax and Stricker, 1963, pp. 101–102)

We say that Arnold was in an active phase of schizophrenia because his disordered thoughts and bizarre behaviors were so acute. Such an active phase is typically preceded by a period during which behavior progressively deteriorates, becoming more and more peculiar. Following an active episode, a schizophrenic usually enters a residual phase, when symptoms lessen but are still present. Generally, each residual phase is followed by another active episode, and so schizophrenia continues, often throughout the person's life. Arnold's case is fairly typical in that his first schizophrenic symptoms appeared in early adulthood. Although the disorder may also begin in middle or later life, it is more likely to start during or soon after adolescence.

SYMPTOMS OF SCHIZOPHRENIA

The name "schizophrenia" was coined by the Swiss psychiatrist Eugen Bleuler (1911) and comes from the Greek words *schizein,* meaning "split," and *phren,* meaning "mind." Bleuler referred not to a splitting of personality into several parts, as occurs in multiple-personality disorder, but to a breaking of connections among various psychological functions. Emotions, for example, may be split from perception and thus be totally inappropriate to the situation. *DSM-III-R* lists a number of disturbances in thought, emotion, perception, and behavior, most of which must be present for at least six months for the diagnosis of schizophrenia to be given.

Prominent among these are *disturbances in the content of thought,* especially the experience of **delusions**—irrational beliefs held despite overwhelming evidence that these beliefs are wrong. Schizophrenic delusions take several forms. People suffering delusions of grandeur believe that they are some famous person, such as Napoleon or Jesus Christ. Delusions of persecution involve the belief that others, often extraterrestrial beings or secret agents, are plotting against you or controlling your thoughts and actions. Schizophrenics often contend that their thoughts are being stolen or broadcast aloud, or that "foreign" thoughts are being inserted into their heads.

Schizophrenics also suffer *disturbances in the form of thought.* For instance, their thoughts tend to be very loosely related. They leap from one idea to another even though the two ideas are only vaguely connected. As a result, their speech is very disjointed. Here is one example:

> I have just looked up "simplicity" and the dictionary says "sim—one, plicare—to fold, one fold." I told Dr. H. that I dreamed he returned to me the story I sent him which he had folded six times when I had folded it once making it double. Jesus said that the sheep he called would make one fold. I thought at the time that the Latin for six is sex, and that the number of the Beast is 666. Is sex then beastly? I think I will leave you to puzzle out the difference between 6 and 666 and 6 fold in substitution of one fold; for the number of the Beast is a mystery. (Mayer-Gross et al., 1969, p. 267)

Here the speaker moves from a fold in a piece of paper to a sheepfold, from the number 6 to the Latin word for six (*sex*), and from there to the nature of sexual intercourse. Such rambling associations are not characteristic of normal speech.

Schizophrenic speech is abnormal, too, in its poverty of content. A schizophrenic can talk for a very long time and yet say almost nothing. The person speaks in vague abstractions or dwells on tiny details which require many words but convey little information. Schizophrenic speech may also contain many stereotyped phrases, monotonous repetitions, made-up words, and words thrown in just because they rhyme with something else.

In addition to their thought disorders, schizophrenics have *disturbances of perception.* They report auditory, visual, olfactory, and sometimes tactile hallucinations. Arnold's visions of ghosts and spirits and his feelings of being choked and jolted by electricity are quite characteristic. Very often, too, schizophrenics hear voices commenting on their actions, repeating their thoughts aloud, or telling them what to do.

Disturbances of emotion are also typical of schizophrenics. Their emotional responses are either inappropriate or peculiarly blunted. A schizophrenic may laugh when told of a favorite relative's death, get angry when given a present, or show no emotion at all on either occasion. At the same time, schizophrenics have difficulty reading the emotions of others (Feinberg et al., 1986). Even when someone is obviously sad, annoyed, surprised, or frightened, a schizophrenic may hardly notice.

Another schizophrenic symptom is *disturbance in the sense of self.* Schizophrenics are often deeply perplexed about who they are and the meaning of their existence. If they think that other people's thoughts are being inserted into their heads, they may become confused over the boundaries between the self and others.

At the same time, schizophrenics usually suffer *disturbances in volition*—that is, in the ability to initiate plans and carry out goal-directed activities. They appear to lack interest and motivation. Often they seem unable to follow a course of action to its logical conclusion.

TABLE 16.2   Symptoms of Four Subtypes of Schizophrenia

Subtype	Symptoms
Disorganized (hebephrenic) schizophrenia	Most severe disintegration of personality. Most common symptoms are frequent or constant incoherent speech and odd affect, such as laughing or crying at inappropriate times. Disorganized hallucinations and delusions are present.
Catatonic schizophrenia	Characterized either by excessive, sometimes violent, motor activity or by a mute, unmoving, stuporous state. Some catatonic schizophrenics alternate between these two extremes, but often one or the other behavior pattern predominates.
Paranoid schizophrenia	Characterized by delusions of persecution, grandeur, or both. Paranoid schizophrenics trust no one and are constantly watchful, convinced that others are plotting against them. They may seek to retaliate against supposed tormentors.
Undifferentiated schizophrenia	Characterized by hallucinations, delusions, and incoherence without meeting the criteria for the other types or showing symptoms characteristic of more than one type.

Not surprisingly, schizophrenics have *disturbances in interpersonal relationships.* They tend to become preoccupied with their own inner worlds and to avoid involvement with others. Some even act as if other people do not exist at all. There are also schizophrenics who show the opposite tendency. They press themselves on others, intrude upon strangers, and seem oblivious to the fact that excessive closeness makes normal people uncomfortable.

Finally, schizophrenics have *disturbances in motor behavior.* Some act very bizarrely, such as banging their heads against a wall. More often, they simply behave in ways that are inappropriate to the situation or extremely repetitive. One patient may spend hours rubbing his forehead or slapping his leg; another may sit all day on a couch tracing the pattern of the fabric with her finger. In some cases there is no physical movement. The patient remains in one position for hours at a time, responding neither to people nor to things. This condition is called a **catatonic stupor.**

SUBTYPES OF SCHIZOPHRENIA

We have talked so far as if most schizophrenics are very much alike, but this is not the case. There are several subtypes of this disorder, each with a different set of symptoms. Table 16.2 describes four of the subtypes listed in *DSM-III-R.* The first three were proposed many years ago by the German psychiatrist Emil Kraepelin. The difference between catatonic

schizophrenia and the others is great, both behaviorally and in terms of treatment.

A newer classification system divides schizophrenics into three categories: those with *positive or active symptoms* (behavioral excesses such as hallucinations, delusions, and bizarre actions like headbanging), those with *negative or passive symptoms* (behavioral deficits such as social withdrawal, lack of interest in pleasurable activities, lack of emotional responses, and lack of movement), and those with *mixed symptoms* (some negative, some positive) (Andreasen and Losen, 1982). Researchers suspect that each of these three subtypes may have different biological causes, as we will discuss shortly.

EXPLAINING SCHIZOPHRENIA

Schizophrenia remains one of the most puzzling of all the mental disorders. Insights into its causes have come very slowly. Here we examine the most prominent perspectives on the disorder.

THE BIOLOGICAL PERSPECTIVE

Studies of schizophrenics have consistently shown that this disorder runs in families—that is, blood relatives of schizophrenics are more likely to develop the condition than people from families free of schizophrenia (Gottesman et al., 1987). Does this mean that schizophrenia is caused in part by an

an area intimately involved in attention and emotion, it is possible that overactivity of these neurons could produce schizophrenic symptoms. But exactly what is entailed in this overactivity is not yet known. One theory is that schizophrenics have an excess amount of dopamine; another is that their dopamine receptors are unusually sensitive; and a third is that they have an abnormally large number of such receptors (Lee and Seeman, 1977; Meltzer and Stahl, 1976; Wong et al., 1986). The problem with all of these theories is that the data supporting them have not always been consistent. Researchers have not yet found a single abnormal trait related to dopamine activity that *all* schizophrenics share (*Schizophrenia Bulletin*, 1982).

This fact has led some investigators to suspect that what we label a single disorder—schizophrenia—may in fact be several disorders, each with its own causes. Schizophrenia with "positive" or "active" symptoms (such as hallucinations and delusions) may be linked to dopamine overactivity, for it responds quite well to phenothiazines (Haracz, 1982). In contrast, schizophrenia with "negative" or "passive" symptoms (such as blunted emotions and social withdrawal) usually does not respond to phenothiazines, and so it is probably *un*related to dopamine. This second type of schizophrenia, however, may be tied to structural damage in the brain. For instance, many schizophrenics who do not improve with drug therapy have enlarged cerebral ventricles (fluid-filled brain regions), which suggests that their brain tissue has atrophied (Brown et al., 1986). The more enlarged the cerebral ventricles are, the more social isolation and other passive symptoms the patients tend to show (Andreasen et al., 1982). At the same time, schizophrenics with passive symptoms often have smaller frontal lobes than normal people do, as well as signs of degenerated neurons, especially in the cerebral cortex (Andreasen et al., 1986; Benes, 1986). All this implies that they suffer a different disorder (or set of disorders) than schizophrenics with active symptoms do.

Much more research needs to be done before we can draw any firm conclusions about the biological causes of schizophrenia. Today investigation proceeds along several fronts. In addition to studying dopamine activity, scientists are also exploring the possible involvement of other neurotransmitters, including serotonin, norepinephrine, and some of the neuropeptides. Some researchers continue to explore structural defects in the brains of schizophrenics,

Some schizophrenic people exhibit catatonia, a state in which they remain in the same position for hours and do not respond to any external stimuli.

inherited genetic defect? To find out, some researchers have conducted studies that compare the incidence of schizophrenia in identical and fraternal twins. The results of one such study are shown in Figure 16.1. When one identical twin develops schizophrenia, the other is five times more likely than a fraternal twin to develop the disorder too (Ban, 1973). Other studies of twins have likewise suggested that genes play a role in schizophrenia (Gottesman and Shields, 1972; Gottesman et al., 1982).

In searching for the biological factors that schizophrenics inherit, researchers have again looked to neurotransmitters (Valenstein, 1978). Drugs called phenothiazines, which are highly effective in reducing certain symptoms of schizophrenia, block the uptake of the neurotransmitter dopamine at its receptor sites in the brain (Creese et al., 1975). Since many dopamine neurons branch into the limbic forebrain,

FIGURE 16.1   Schizophrenia in biological relatives. A concordance rate of 100 percent would mean that if one member of the biologically related pair is schizophrenic, the other person will be, too. Note that if an identical twin is schizophrenic, the concordance rate is far higher than it is among fraternal twins. (*After Gottesman, 1978./© 1978. Used by permission of John Wiley & Sons, Inc.*)

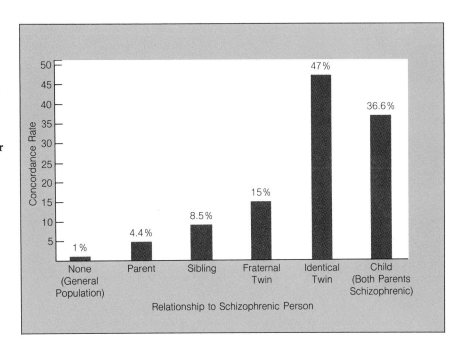

THE INTERPERSONAL OR FAMILY-SYSTEMS PERSPECTIVE

But though biological factors seem to be a major cause of schizophrenia, environmental factors must contribute too. If schizophrenia were entirely a matter of biological inheritance, the second in a pair of identical twins would *always* develop the disorder if the first twin did. This, however, is not what happens. Instead, the second twin succumbs only 40 to 50 percent of the time, suggesting important environmental influences that the two twins do not always share.

Some psychologists think that maladaptive patterns of family interaction are among the environmental factors helping to trigger schizophrenic breakdowns. Studies show that the highest relapse rates, with the most severe recurring symptoms, are often found among discharged schizophrenics who re-

while others are looking into the possibility that a virus infection, a toxin, or a deficiency in the person's immune system might be involved (Mednick et al., 1988; Schmeck, 1986). When the mystery of schizophrenia is finally solved, it will probably be found that many biochemical and structural factors contribute to this disorder's varied and severe symptoms.

turned to the care of their families rather than living alone. It seems as if the family might be aggravating the disorder. But what aspects of family life are involved?

One factor seems to be high **expressed emotion** —that is, an emotionally charged atmosphere in the home, especially characterized by an overbearing involvement with the patient, coupled with much hostility and criticism (Hooley, 1985). (See Table 16.3 for a comparison of statements made by family members judged high or low in expressed emotion.) One study found that 55 percent of schizophrenics who returned to a home high in expressed emotion suffered a relapse within nine months. In contrast, only 16 percent of those who returned to a home low in expressed emotion suffered a relapse in the same time period (Brown et al., 1972). Fortunately, relatives of schizophrenics can often be taught to lower their levels of expressed emotion (Falloon, 1988). When this is done, relapse rates are substantially reduced (Leff et al., 1982). Relapse rates can also be reduced by instructing patients to spend less time with family members who are high in expressed emotion.

Other family traits that may contribute to schizophrenia have to do with the relationship between the parents. After studying the families of schizophrenics

TABLE 16.3   Statements by Relatives of Schizophrenics Showing High and Low Expressed Emotion

High expressed emotion. Note the intrusiveness and negative tone of the feelings they express toward the patient:	"I always say, 'why don't you pick up a book, do a crossword or something like that to keep your mind off it.' *That's* even too much trouble."
	"I've tried to jolly him out of it and pestered him into doing things."
	"He went round the garden 90 times, in the door, back out the door. I said 'Have a chair, sit out in the sun.' Well, he nearly bit my head off."
Low expressed emotion. Note their low-key acceptance of the patient's behavior:	"I know it's better for her to be on her own, to get away from me and try to do things on her own."
	"Whatever she does suits me."
	"I just tend to let it go because I know that when she wants to speak she will speak."

Source: Hooley, 1985.

for several years, one group of researchers concluded that they tend to fall into one of two types: the "schismatic family," which is split by intense parental conflict, and the "skewed family," in which one parent totally submits to the domineering, often disturbed behavior of the other (Lidz, 1973; Lidz et al., 1957). In either family the children tend to grow up confused and uncertain, feelings that might contribute to a schizophrenic breakdown.

Abnormal communications within the family may be involved in schizophrenia too. When members of a schizophrenic's family speak to one another, their exchanges are often vague, muddled, and fragmented, and they tend to have trouble maintaining a shared focus of attention (Lewis et al., 1981; Rodnick et al., 1984; Wynne et al., 1975). We do not yet know if these abnormal communications are a cause or an effect of schizophrenia. It could be that just by virtue of living with a disturbed person, family communications become disturbed (Liem, 1974). More research is needed before this issue of cause and effect can be resolved. At the same time, we need to determine if these abnormal patterns of communication are unique to the families of schizophrenics or if they occur in the families of people with other mental disorders as well.

THE SOCIOCULTURAL PERSPECTIVE

Researchers have wondered if the stress of poverty could also contribute to schizophrenia (Kohn, 1973). After all, given enough stress, virtually anyone may start to show disorders of thought, perception, and emotion. The chronic hardship of being poor might therefore take a serious toll on people's mental health. In addition, living in poverty can lead to a fatalistic attitude that makes effective coping with stress all the harder (Kohn, 1973). These factors could help explain the higher incidence of schizophrenia in lower social classes.

But though this reasoning is plausible, we again have a problem untangling cause and effect. Wouldn't people who are schizophrenic and unable to hold down a good job naturally drift downward on the socioeconomic ladder? If so, many schizophrenics would end up in the ranks of the poor, and poverty would be a *result* of the disorder, not a cause of it. Research suggests that both lines of influence are probably at work here (Turner and Wagonfeld, 1967). While poverty can be the result of schizophrenia, the stress of poverty can also cause symptoms of schizophrenia to emerge.

COMBINING PERSPECTIVES: THE DIATHESIS–STRESS MODEL

Many factors, both biological and environmental, can apparently increase a person's risk of developing schizophrenia. The interaction of these factors has been described in the diathesis–stress model. Here a person is said to have a certain degree of biological predisposition toward schizophrenia, most

TABLE 16.4   Symptoms of Personality Disorders

Disorder	Symptoms
Paranoid personality disorder	Pervasive and long-standing suspiciousness and mistrust of people; hypersensitivity and difficulty in getting along with others
Schizotypal personality disorder	Eccentricities of thinking, perception, communication, and behavior, not severe enough to be schizophrenic
Schizoid personality disorder	Social withdrawal and lack of normal emotional relationships with others
Avoidant personality disorder	Hypersensitivity to rejection and unwillingness to enter into relationships; social withdrawal despite a desire for interaction, and low self-esteem
Dependent personality disorder	Failure to assume responsibility for major areas of one's life; reliance on others to make important decisions; lack of self-esteem
Borderline personality disorder	Instability in behavior, mood, and self-image
Histrionic personality disorder	Overly reactive behavior; exaggerated expressions of emotion seemingly "performed" for an audience
Narcissistic personality disorder	Grandiose sense of self-importance; preoccupation with fantasies of unlimited success; exhibitionistic need for constant admiration
Obsessive-compulsive personality disorder	Preoccupation with rules, order, organization, efficiency, and detail; rigidity and inability to express warm emotions or take pleasure in normally pleasurable activities
Passive-aggressive personality disorder	Indirectly expressed resistance to demands for adequate activity or performance in personal relations and on the job
Antisocial personality disorder	Chronic and continuous behavior that violates the rights of others; inability to form attachments or (often) to succeed in an occupation. Onset before age fifteen

Source: Bootzin and Acocella, 1988, pp. 259–266.

likely genetically inherited. This is the diathesis side of the model. The other side is the role played by life stresses, such as a troubled family environment, or the hardships of poverty. A person with a strong biological predisposition toward schizophrenia would need very few life stresses to trigger the disorder. In contrast, a person with a weak biological predisposition would need many external pressures to develop schizophrenic symptoms; and a person with *no* biological predisposition would probably never suffer the disorder at all (Gottesman and Shields, 1982).

A study of adopted children supports the diathesis–stress model (Tienari et al., 1987). Youngsters born to schizophrenic mothers (and so apt to have a schizophrenic predisposition) had more signs of mental illness if they lived in a troubled adoptive family. In contrast, among children born to *non*schizophrenic mothers, a maladjusted adoptive family was *un*related to poor mental health. Often, then, both a genetic predisposition (a diathesis) *and* a stressful environment are needed for schizophrenic symptoms to surface (Gottesman and Bertelsen, 1989). Since stress

is what ultimately pushes many genetically vulnerable people over the edge, improving the ability to cope with stress may be one of the best defenses against schizophrenic breakdowns (Zubin and Spring, 1977).

PERSONALITY DISORDERS

Personality disorders are deep-seated maladaptive patterns of relating to others. Often the disturbed person does not even recognize there is a problem. The maladaptive behaviors are so deeply ingrained that they are accepted as familiar traits. This acceptance is frequently accompanied by a lack of desire to change, for personality disorders typically cause more distress to others than they do to the people who have them. Table 16.4 lists eleven personality disorders and their primary symptoms. Space allows us to look in more detail at only three of these: antisocial personality disorder (the most serious and extensively studied), narcissistic personality disorder, and borderline personality disorder.

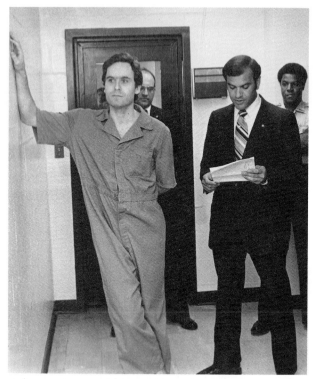

Besides leading stunted, troubled lives themselves, sociopaths like serial murderer Ted Bundy disrupt or destroy the lives of others.

ANTISOCIAL PERSONALITY DISORDER

The **antisocial personality,** or **sociopath,** has a history of antisocial acts, beginning in childhood or adolescence and continuing into adulthood. These people follow their impulses without consideration for others and without experiencing guilt or remorse. They seem to have no conscience and to lack many normal emotions. About 4 percent of American males and 1 percent of American females have this disorder (Robins et al., 1984).

Signs of an antisocial personality become apparent before the age of fifteen. The condition is not diagnosed as an antisocial disorder until age eighteen; it is referred to as conduct disorder in individuals younger than eighteen. The youngster has serious conduct problems, such as truancy, running away from home, fighting, cruelty, destruction of property, stealing, and habitual lying. Similar problems contin-

ue in adulthood, revealing themselves in a number of the following ways: impulsiveness, recklessness, blatant disregard for the truth, excessive irritability and aggression, repeated violations of the law, irresponsible parenting, inability to hold a steady job, failure to honor financial obligations, and incapacity for normal friendship or love.

Psychologists have debated the causes of antisocial personality disorder. Psychoanalytic thinkers believe that sociopaths are products of rejecting parents. If there is no love between parent and child, the child is unlikely to adopt the parents' moral values and so develop a conscience. Studies provide some support for this explanation. Lack of parental affection is a recurring theme in the histories of people with antisocial personality disorder (McCord and McCord, 1964). So are lack of parental supervision and discipline, conflict between the parents, and a father who is antisocial too (McCord, 1979; Robbins, 1966). This last factor—an antisocial father—suggests that antisocial tendencies may be both learned and inherited (Cloninger and Gottesman, 1987). Children could learn antisocial behavior by observing a father's irresponsible actions. The youngsters' misconduct could then be reinforced because it gains them attention they cannot get in other ways. Biological theorists add to this equation the idea that sociopaths may be born with certain physiological traits that make them prone to develop antisocial behavior patterns. Among these is a chronic underarousal of the autonomic nervous system, which is greatly involved in emotional responses (Hare, 1970). This could explain why the sociopath needs to gratify impulses, behave recklessly, and commit crimes for thrills—presumably to boost arousal to a more optimal level. At the same time, chronic underarousal could explain why sociopaths are unresponsive to certain kinds of punishments (electric shock, for example) that make normal people very upset (Kykken, 1957; Schachter and Latané, 1964). Sociopaths seek to *compensate* for underarousal, so they may actually view emotionally arousing punishments positively.

NARCISSISTIC PERSONALITY DISORDER

People with **narcissistic personality disorder** have an overblown sense of their own importance and describe themselves in grandiose terms. Yet underneath their self-aggrandizement, narcissists have very fragile self-esteem. They greatly fear failure and are highly sensitive to criticism. They crave the attention and admiration of others and are constantly trying to impress. They cannot empathize with others' feelings and tend to exploit friendships for their own ends. They are always envying those who seem smarter, more handsome, or more successful than themselves. Some psychologists believe that this disorder develops when parents fail to give children the love, respect, and empathy they need. Personal shortcomings therefore make the children feel vulnerable and they seek unending approval from others (Benjamin, 1987; Kohut, 1978). This theory, however, has not been confirmed. Although narcissism seems to be increasing in our society, we are not yet sure what factors predispose a person to it.

BORDERLINE PERSONALITY DISORDER

The principal feature of **borderline personality disorder** is instability in self-image, interpersonal relations, and mood. These people are highly uncertain about who they are, what their values and goals are, and who their friends ought to be. When they do form relationships, they are usually intense and stormy, characterized by great highs and lows. One day the friend or lover will be idealized and pursued, the next day scorned and rejected. And yet if someone threatens to abandon a person with borderline personality disorder, that person will make frantic efforts to keep the relationship intact. The moods of a person with this disorder are also erratic. They change rapidly from normal to very depressed, irritable, or anxious, and then back again. Often the person complains of chronic feelings of emptiness and boredom, which may help explain why he or she often follows self-damaging impulses, such as spending sprees, sexual indiscretions, or binges of drug abuse. As with narcissism, we do not yet know what causes a borderline personality to develop. The condition, however, tends to run in families, and is more prevalent among women than among men (Baron et al. 1985; McGlashan, 1983).

PSYCHOACTIVE SUBSTANCE USE DISORDERS

A psychoactive substance is any chemical that can alter a person's thoughts, moods, perceptions, and

Alcohol abuse is believed to be involved in half of all traffic accidents in the United States.

behaviors. This includes a wide variety of recreational drugs, including alcohol, marijuana, LSD, cocaine, and amphetamines. Of these, alcohol is by far the most widely used in our society. That is why we have chosen to focus on it here.

ALCOHOL DEPENDENCE AND ABUSE

The social use of alcohol to modify mood and behavior is widely considered appropriate and normal in our society. A great many people have a few drinks when at a party or when relaxing with friends and family after a busy day. But for millions of Americans alcohol consumption has expanded far beyond this moderate recreational use. These people suffer from alcohol dependence and abuse, the most widespread **psychoactive substance use disorders** in America.

Alcohol dependence involves an inability to limit drinking, even if there is a desire to do so. Alcohol-dependent people are often aware that drinking is causing them serious problems in their social and occupational lives, and yet they are powerless to change their drinking habits. Frequently, they are intoxicated or "hung over" when expected to fulfill some major obligation, such as going to work, showing up for an exam, or taking care of their children. They also tend to develop tolerance for the drug, meaning that they need more and more of it to achieve the same high. Refraining from alcohol may cause withdrawal symptoms (trembling, sweating, anxiety, and in severe cases hallucinations). Alcohol-dependent people are commonly called alcoholics. **Alcohol abusers,** in contrast, are people who are not alcoholics, but who still have a drinking problem. For instance, the college student who binges on alcohol every few weekends, to the point of missing classes the following Monday mornings, but who has no other troubles related to the drug, would be diagnosed an alcohol abuser.

About 13 percent of Americans will at some point in their lives have a problem with drinking (Robins et al., 1984). Currently, between 10 and 15 million people in this country meet the definition of alcohol-dependent. Perhaps as many as 35 million others experience negative effects as a result of these problem drinkers. One Gallup poll indicated that fully a third of all American families have experienced difficulties related to alcohol use (Saxe et al., 1983). Although alcohol dependence is more common among adult males, it is on the rise among women as well as teenagers (Becker and Kronus, 1977).

Alcoholism takes a staggering toll economically, medically, and socially (Saxe et al., 1983). Our nation loses as much as $120 billion annually as a result of alcohol dependence, a large proportion of which comes from the sharp decline in the alcoholic's productivity on the job. In addition, an estimated 15 percent of all the dollars Americans spend on health care are used to treat medical problems related to alcohol dependence. Prolonged alcoholism can cause irreparable liver damage, brain dysfunction, and cardiovascular disease. Not surprisingly, the life expectancy of an alcoholic is ten to twelve years shorter than that of the average person. Alcoholism is also frequently implicated in a long list of legal and social

problems. It is estimated that half of all traffic accidents, two-fifths of all family court cases, a third of all suicides, and sizable proportions of assaults, rapes, and murders involve the use of alcohol (Eckardt et al., 1981; NIAAA, 1983). Yet the vast majority of problem drinkers—an estimated 85 percent—receive no treatment.

EXPLAINING ALCOHOLISM

What are the causes of alcoholism? Some psychoanalysts have argued that it may arise in people who as babies develop a conflict over the need for oral gratification. These infants may be uncertain whether food will be given or withheld, and so come to feel abnormally dependent as well as highly anxious. As adults, they may reveal this fixation in such "oral behaviors" as drinking. Interestingly, alcoholics also tend to be heavier smokers than nonalcoholics, smoking presumably being another way to gratify oral needs (Maletzky and Klotter, 1974). Psychoanalytic thinkers have also suggested that heavy alcohol use may be a way of combating low self-esteem and acquiring an illusion of mastery and power. The aggressiveness of some intoxicated alcoholics is said to be an expression of this quest for self-importance and control. But the psychoanalytic prediction that alcoholics will have similar personalities *before* the onset of the disorder has not always been supported (Saxe et al., 1983). Many kinds of people fall prey to alcoholism, suggesting causes other than personality traits.

Learning theorists argue that these causes lie in the rewards of drinking, especially a reduction in tension that alcohol consumption can bring. According to this view, many people start to drink to alleviate stress. At first their cares and worries *do* lessen, so drinking is reinforced. But the more people drink, the greater is the likelihood that their problems will only increase. This is partly because excessive drinking creates additional troubles at home and on the job. It is also because excessive drinking is often done alone, when people have no companions to distract them from worries and cares. As a result, they may dwell on their problems even more than usual and the problems seem worse (Steele and Josephs, 1988; Steele et al., 1986). The additional stress created leads to even heavier drinking and a vicious cycle soon sets in.

Several lines of evidence seem to support this tension-reduction theory. For example, the more stresses there are in a given community (high crime rate, high divorce rate, low income, poor housing, and so forth), the more widespread alcoholism is (Linsky et al., 1985). Similarly, when people who have recovered from alcoholism have a relapse, it is often when very stressful events occur in their lives (Marlatt and Gordon, 1980). This suggests that a need for tension reduction may encourage drinking.

But experiments testing the tension-reduction theory have not always been favorable to it. While subjects under stress do sometimes drink more than nonstressed subjects do, at other times they drink the same amount or even significantly less (Higgins and Marlatt, 1973, 1975; Holroyd, 1978; Marlatt et al., 1975). In one study, for instance, students were led to believe they had done well or poorly on a difficult test, and then were given a chance to drink (Volpicelli et al., 1982). Those who thought they had done well (the low-stress subjects) actually drank *more* than those who thought they had done poorly (the high-stress subjects). It was as if *relief from* tension, not tension itself, fostered drinking in this instance. Such findings have led to the theory that a desire to drink may be related to a drop in the activities of the brain's endorphins, neurotransmitters that serve to reduce pain and elevate mood (Volpicelli, 1987). During stress, the body responds by boosting endorphin levels; after stress, endorphin levels drop. Drinking at this point may be a way of compensating for endorphin reduction, for alcohol seems to stimulate endorphin receptors.

Psychologists have proposed other biological theories of why people drink to excess. One is that some people inherit a neurological defect that alcohol partly corrects (Tarter et al., 1985). This idea is supported by the finding that alcohol consumption reverses certain abnormal neurological symptoms in men at high risk for becoming alcoholics (Hegedus et al., 1984; Schuckit, 1987). People at high risk for alcoholism may also have inherited a tolerance for the drug: they may be able to drink more than other people without experiencing ill effects (Schuckit and Gold, 1988). This would allow them to consume the amounts of alcohol needed to become alcoholics.

Although all these biological theories are still speculative, we have reason to believe that *something* biological may be encouraging alcoholism, especially in males born to parents with a history of continual drinking and antisocial behavior. These boys run a much higher than normal risk of becoming alcoholics too, even when they are adopted into families where alcohol is *not* abused. Those who do become alcoholics seem to have developed a form of the disorder with a very strong genetic component. In addition, there is probably another form of alcoholism that is more heavily influenced by environmental factors (Cloninger et al., 1985). Because of this diversity of causes, clinicians today use many approaches in treating alcoholism. We will say more about these approaches in the next chapter.

SUMMARY

1. Various criteria can be used to assess the abnormality of any behavior. Among them are deviation from statistical norms, conformity to social values, and comparison with some absolute standard of mental health.
2. The **biological perspective** sees abnormal behavior as caused by physical dysfunctions in the body, while the various psychological perspectives see it as caused by factors that arise from a person's experiences. These experiences include emotional conflicts (prominent in the **psychoanalytic approach**), inappropriate learning (central to the **learning perspective**), and maladaptive thinking (the focus of the **cognitive perspective**). In addition, there are perspectives on abnormality that look beyond the individual for causes. These are the **interpersonal** or **family-systems perspective,** which sees abnormal behavior as involving the important relationships in a person's life; and the **sociocultural perspective,** which sees the roots of mental disturbance in social ills such as poverty.
3. A widely used system for classifying mental disorders is contained in the *Diagnostic and Statistical Manual of*

Mental Disorders, third edition, revised (*DSM-III-R*), published by the American Psychiatric Association. Although such classification systems have their critics, it is hard to imagine treatment of the mentally disturbed without them.

4. **Anxiety disorders** are characterized by emotional distress due to feelings of vulnerability, apprehension, or fear. In **panic disorder** a person suffers sudden, inexplicable attacks of intense fear, which are truly terrifying. In **phobic disorders** there is one particular stimulus, such as dogs or high places, that is fear-arousing. In **generalized anxiety disorder,** a person is constantly in a state of apprehension over groundless worries. In **obsessive-compulsive disorder,** anxiety arises over senseless, unwanted thoughts that keep intruding into consciousness (**obsessions**). The person may feel compelled to perform some behavior over and over (a **compulsion**) in an effort to temporarily reduce anxiety. Finally, **post-traumatic stress disorder** is a state of anxiety, depression, and psychological numbing that follows exposure to a severe trauma, such as warfare, rape, or a catastrophic natural disaster.

5. A **somatoform disorder** is characterized by some physical ailment with no organic cause. In **hypochondriasis,** the person is persistently fearful of having some terrible disease, despite doctors' assurances that no physical illness exists. In **conversion disorder,** psychological distress produces what appears to be a genuine physical dysfunction (paralysis or blindness, for instance) even though there is no organic cause.

6. **Dissociative disorders** involve a splitting off (dissociation) of a part of one's personality, so that memory or identity is disturbed. Victims of **psychogenic amnesia** forget all or part of their personal past, while victims of **psychogenic fugue** flee their current identity for a time. Victims of **multiple-personality disorder** develop two or more distinct personalities, which may contrast sharply.

7. There are two classes of **mood disorders: depressive disorders** (in which a sad, discouraged mood is the major symptom) and **bipolar disorders** (in which there are both periods of depression and periods of excessive elation, called **mania**). One type of depressive disorder, called **major depression,** is characterized by acute episodes of deep despondency and despair. Another type is a milder, more chronic form of depression, called **dysthymia.** Finally, there is **seasonal affective disorder,** in which mood disturbances are related to changes in the seasons.

8. **Schizophrenia** is characterized by severe disorders of thought (such as **delusions** and disjointed trains of thinking), of perception (especially hallucinations), and of emotion (inappropriate or blunted feelings). There are also severe disturbances in the sense of self, in volition (difficulty initiating and carrying out plans), in interpersonal relationships (avoidance of others of overintrusiveness), and in motor behavior (extremely repetitive actions or no movement at all). Schizophrenics are unable to cope with most of life's ordinary demands.

9. **Personality disorders** are deeply ingrained maladaptive patterns of behavior that are often more distressing to others than they are to the people who have them. The most serious is **antisocial personality disorder,** characterized by a history of impulsive, irresponsible behavior and total disregard for others. People with **narcissistic personality disorder** have an overblown sense of their own importance and are constantly trying to gain others' attention and admiration. People with **borderline personality disorder** are highly unstable in their self-images, interpersonal relations, and moods.

10. People have a **psychoactive substance use disorder** when they have trouble refraining from the use of a psychoactive drug, even though that drug is causing them serious social, occupational, or medical problems. The most widespread psychoactive substance use disorders in America are **alcohol dependence** and **alcohol abuse.**

SUGGESTED READINGS

Bootzin, R. R., and Acocella, J. R. (1988). *Abnormal psychology* (5th ed.). New York: Random House. A comprehensive textbook that describes the principal psychological disorders and the major perspectives on them.

Bradfield, S. (1990). *The history of luminous motion.* New York: Vintage. This novel examines the life of a precocious and possibly psychotic eight-year-old boy who is being raised by a manic-depressive mother. The book provides a penetrating look at the problems faced by children with mentally disturbed parents.

Gottesman, I. I. (1990). *Schizophrenia genesis: The origins of madness.* New York: W. H. Freeman. The author reviews current research on schizophrenia, with a focus on the genetic and environmental factors implicated in its onset and course. He discusses the issues and controversies associated with diagnosis of the disorder as well as ethical issues pertaining to genetic counseling and national policies.

Porter, R. (1990). *A social history of madness.* New York: Dutton-Obelisk. In this collection of case studies, the history of the insane asylum is told from the point of view of the inmates.

Prochaska, J. O. (1984). *Systems of psychotherapy: A transtheoretical analysis* (2nd ed.). Homewood, IL: Dorsey Press. This book describes one case (an obsessive-compulsive woman) through twelve different theoretical approaches. It is very interesting, vivid, and engaging.

Seligman, M. E. P. (1991). *Learned optimism.* New York: Knopf. This lively and engaging book blends science with practical advice on how people can modify pessimistic ways of thinking that can hold them back and detract from their quality of life.

Spitzer, R. L., Skodol, A. E., Gibbon, M., and Williams, J. B. W. (1986). *A psychiatrist's casebook.* New York: Warner Books. This collection of case studies gives examples of most major psychological disorders. The discussion of each case includes diagnostic criteria and recommended forms of therapy.

Styron, W. (1990). *Darkness visible: A great writer's battle with depression.* New York: Random House. In this book, the author provides a moving account of the agonies he experienced in his struggle to overcome depression.

CHAPTER 17

APPROACHES TO TREATMENT

Anyone who has ever tried to calm a distraught person or bolster a friend who is feeling depressed has used techniques akin to those of psychotherapy. But the professional therapist comes armed with tactics that the average person lacks. For the professional, intuitions about what might help to ease psychological disturbance are supplemented by methods that have often been put to systematic tests. **Psychotherapy,** then, is a series of interactions between one person professionally trained in alleviating psychological problems and another who is suffering from them. It aims to change undesirable ways of thinking, feeling, and acting, and to improve the troubled person's ability to handle stress. If you seek psychotherapy, you will find that it is offered by a variety of mental health professionals with different training (see Table 17.1).

In recent years psychotherapy has rapidly expanded and diversified. Freudian psychoanalysis, which once dominated the field, now coexists with newer therapeutic approaches—especially behavior and cognitive-behavior therapies, humanistic therapies, and family therapies. Each of these general approaches, in turn, has spawned a host of specific treatments, so that today more than a hundred different psychotherapies exist. And as it expanded, psychotherapy has gained increased acceptance, to the point that most of the stigma once attached to it has disappeared.

In this chapter we will explore some of the many available treatments for psychological disorders, including psychoanalytic therapies, humanistic therapies, behavior and cognitive-behavior therapies, family-systems therapies, and other group approaches to treatment. We will also examine various biological treatments, all of which attempt to alter the physiological workings of the brain. These include psychosurgery, electroconvulsive shock therapy, and the use of psychoactive drugs.

It is very valuable to know the difference between the various forms of treatment available for psychological disorders. Some treatments are more effective than others for particular kinds of problems. For instance, to cure a bed-wetting problem in a school-age child, certain types of behavior therapy work very well and very quickly. Unfortunately, most people who seek help for psychological disorders do not even know that different approaches to treatment exist. Knowing about these different approaches can save a person time and effort, as well as the disappointment of trying a therapy that turns out not to be right for that particular person's needs.

TABLE 17.1   Mental Health Professionals

Clinical psychologists: Doctorates in psychology who have been trained in psychological treatments and interventions.

Psychiatrists: Physicians (M.D.'s) who have been clinically trained in diagnosing and treating mental illness.

Psychoanalysts: Professionals (usually psychiatrists) with advanced training in psychoanalysis, which includes being psychoanalyzed oneself.

Counseling psychologists: Those with a Ph.D. in counseling psychology. These therapists are trained to treat relatively mild problems of social and emotional adjustment.

Psychiatric social workers: Those with a master's degree in social work who handle cases involving people with psychiatric disorders.

Of course, most contemporary therapists do not adhere rigidly to only one form of treatment. Most are to some extent eclectic: They use a variety of approaches and techniques depending on the particular problems and needs of the client. Thus, some behavioral psychologists are integrating elements of psychoanalytic theory into their treatments. Similarly, some family therapists are using behavioral strategies. We will return to eclecticism in the treatment of psychological disorder a little later in this chapter.

PSYCHOTHERAPIES

PSYCHOANALYTIC THERAPIES

The oldest form of psychotherapy practiced today is Freudian **psychoanalysis.** For a variety of reasons, few contemporary therapists still follow Freud's doctrines faithfully. For one thing, traditional psychoanalysis is a very long and expensive process, one that most people cannot afford. Consequently, many psychoanalytically oriented therapists, while still striving for insights into unconscious conflicts and motives, have substantially shortened the total time a person spends in psychotherapy. Freud's influence on the treatment of disorders has been enormous, however. So we will examine Freudian psychoanalysis in some

detail before describing the more modern approaches that have developed from it.

FREUDIAN PSYCHOANALYSIS

According to Freud, the major purpose of psychoanalysis is to make people aware of unconscious motives and conflicts that influence their behavior. Freud's experiences with his patients led him to conclude that the source of most disorders is the anxiety felt when unconscious and unacceptable id impulses threaten to break into conscious awareness. To deal with this threat, the person resorts to defense mechanisms, especially to *repression*—a pushing back of shameful thoughts and desires into the unconscious. (See Chapter 13 for a discussion of Freudian defense mechanisms.) But while id impulses can be temporarily hidden, they cannot be banished entirely. As a result, the ego constantly has to work to keep these impulses from surfacing. Freud believed that the best treatment is to bring the forbidden thoughts and desires into consciousness so that the patient can finally confront them. The thoughts and desires can then be "worked through," or explored rationally to facilitate understanding and change. According to Freud, this process should gradually reduce anxiety and free psychic energy for more constructive purposes.

Freud and his followers developed several techniques to draw troublesome urges and feelings out of the unconscious and into consciousness. One is **free association.** The patient lies on a couch, which helps to loosen conscious restraints, and says whatever comes to mind. No thought is to be willfully censored; no logical structure is imposed on the flow of ideas. The therapist listens, rarely interrupting. In time, clues to unconscious thoughts will begin to surface.

Freud's second source of clues to the contents of the unconscious was **dream analysis.** He believed that during sleep restraints are again loosened. But even in sleep, according to Freud, the unconscious is censored, with forbidden thoughts appearing only in symbolic form. Thus, every dream has its **manifest content** (its plot or story line) and its **latent content** (its symbolic meanings), which exposes unconscious conflicts. Recall from Chapter 5 the dream of one woman who had just had a baby. She dreamed that she had given birth to two boys and that one had died (the manifest content). The symbolic meaning (latent content) might be that this new mother felt ambivalent toward her real child, whom she both wanted and didn't want. During psychoanalysis, free association is sometimes used to help a person gain insight into the hidden meaning of a dream. Here is one example of how this process works:

"Well," she said, "this is what I dreamed. . . . I was in what appeared to be a ballroom or a dance hall, but I knew it was really a hospital. A man came up to me and told me to undress, take all my clothes off. He was going to give me a gynecological examination. I did as I was told but I was very frightened. While I was undressing, I noticed that he was doing something to a woman at the other end of the room. She was sitting or lying in a funny kind of contraption with all kinds of levers and gears and pulleys attached to it. I knew that I was supposed to be next, that I would have to sit in that thing while he examined me. Suddenly he called my name and I found myself running to him. The chair or table—whatever it was—was now empty, and he told me to get on it. I refused and began to cry. It started to rain—great big drops of rain. He pushed me to the floor and spread my legs for the examination. I turned over on my stomach and began to scream. I woke myself up screaming."

Following the recital Laura lay quietly on the couch, her eyes closed, her arms crossed over her bosom.

"Well," she said after a brief, expectant silence, "what does it mean?"

"Laura," I admonished, "you know better than that. Associate, and we'll find out."

"The first thing I think of is Ben," she began. "He's an intern at University, you know. I guess that's the doctor in the dream—or maybe it was you. Anyhow, whoever it was, I wouldn't let them examine me."

"Why not?"

"I've always been afraid of doctors . . . afraid they might hurt me."

"How will they hurt you?"

"I don't know. By jabbing me with a needle, I guess. . . ."

"What about gynecological examinations?"

"I've never had one. I can't even bear to think of someone poking around inside me." Again silence; then, "Oh," she said, "I see it now. It's sex I'm afraid of. The doctor in the dream *is* Ben. He wants me to have intercourse, but it scares me and I turn away from him. That's true. . . ."

"But why, Laura?"

"I don't know," she cried, "I don't know. Tell me."

"I think the dream tells you," I said.

"The dream I just told you?"

"Yes. . . . There's a part of it you haven't considered. What comes to your mind when you think of the other woman in the dream, the woman the doctor was examining before you?"

"The contraption she was sitting in," Laura exclaimed. "It was like a —wheel chair—my mother's wheel chair! Is that right?"

"Very likely," I said.

"But why would he be examining her? What would that mean?"

"Well, think of what that examination signified for you."

"Sex," she said. "Intercourse—that's what it means. So that's what it is—that's what it means! Intercourse put my mother in the wheel chair. It paralyzed her. And I'm afraid that's what it will do to me. So I avoid it—because I'm scared it will do the same thing to me. . . ." (Lindner, 1954, pp. 93–95)

In fact, the mother's paralysis was totally unrelated to sex. But Laura had unconsciously connected her mother's condition with the muffled cries and moans that, as a child, she had heard through the walls during her parents' lovemaking.

Naturally, the conscious confrontation of thoughts such as these is not pleasant. As patients near exposure of particularly painful thoughts and feelings, they may show signs of **resistance,** or attempts to block treatment. They may avoid talking about certain topics, pause frequently, or report that their minds are blank. They may even launch into lengthly monologues about irrelevant subjects, such as world politics. The therapist's interpretation of resistance is an important part of treatment, for it helps the patient to see unconscious motives at work.

As psychoanalysis progresses, patients may transfer to the therapist the emotions they felt toward people who were important in their childhood, par-

"IT'S A VERY STRONG CASE OF TRANSFERENCE. I'VE PICKED UP ALL YOUR NEUROSES."

gains in self-knowledge and emotional awareness among individuals who have been through psychoanalysis. There is some consensus that the treatment is most appropriate for clients with anxiety disorders; those with severe psychopathology, such as schizophrenia, tend to do less well. In addition, since psychoanalysis is based on talk and insight, it tends to work best for those who are articulate and well educated (Luborsky and Spence, 1978).

Critics have maintained that traditional psychoanalysis is geared toward "YAVIS" clients—those who are *y*oung, *a*ttractive, *v*erbal, *i*ntelligent, and *s*uccessful, and who are often less in need of help than less advantaged people. Pointing to the duration of this treatment and the expense of going through analysis, critics question the value of psychoanalysis as a general treatment. Critics also point to the absence of carefully controlled, scientific studies demonstrating the effectiveness of long-term, intensive psychoanalytic treatment (Bower, 1991). Of course, systematic research on classical psychoanalysis is extremely difficult to conduct, given the practical obstacles involved in launching a controlled study that would span several years (Garfield and Bergin, 1986).

ticularly their parents. Thus, the therapist may become the target of dependency, hostility, or whatever other feelings lie at the core of the person's problem. Throughout this process of **transference,** the therapist tries to remain a "blank screen" onto which the patient can project childhood conflicts. With the therapist's help, the patient can then begin to acknowledge his or her distorted perceptions, putting things ultimately into a more mature perspective. Such analysis of transference, in fact, is considered the key to successful psychoanalysis. Only in this way can the patient's unconscious conflicts be fully understood and resolved.

Evaluating Long-Term Psychoanalytic Treatment

Among psychotherapists today, there are few issues as controversial as whether classical psychoanalytic psychotherapy is effective. Psychoanalysis has many proponents, among them many "graduates" of analysis who strongly believe that their lives have been fundamentally altered by the process. There is a wealth of clinical case study data reporting enormous

OTHER PSYCHOANALYTIC TREATMENTS

Some of Freud's earliest associates, such as Carl Jung and Alfred Adler, began to modify psychoanalytic theory even as Freud was formulating it. As a result of their disagreements with Freud, these former disciples developed variations on Freud's therapeutic techniques. Later psychoanalytic thinkers carried these innovations still further. Unlike Freud, who maintained that all psychic energy originates in the id, many of the post-Freudian psychoanalytic theorists have argued that the ego possesses substantial energy of its own. As therapists, they have therefore tried to help clients strengthen the ego and develop a firm, well-integrated, autonomous self-identity. Two ego psychologists, whose ideas we discussed in Chapter 13, are Erik Erikson and Heinz Hartmann. Other post-Freudians have stressed the importance of a person's style of relating to others. In this view, faulty relationships with others not only contribute to psychological problems but are the key defining features of all psychological disturbance. This theme can be seen in the writings of Karen Horney, discussed in Chapter 13.

An important merging of this focus on the ego with an emphasis on social relationships is represented by object relations theory (Klein, 1967; Kohut, 1971). This approach stresses the importance of a child's early attachments to the development of the child's sense of self and to subsequent interpersonal relationships.

Because few clients can afford long-term, intensive psychoanalytic psychotherapy, most psychoanalytically oriented therapists do not practice standard psychoanalysis exclusively. Particularly among followers of "neo-Freudians" such as Karen Horney, ego psychologists such as Erik Erikson and Heinz Hartman, and objects relations theorists such as Kohut and Klein, there has been a major effort to develop time-limited, briefer forms of psychoanalytic therapy that may last no more than thirty to fifty sessions. The general psychoanalytic framework still remains, with the therapist uncovering unconscious motives, breaking down defenses, and dealing with the client's resistance. But some of the classic Freudian procedures are missing. The couch is usually dispensed with; most clients now sit up and talk with the therapist face to face. The therapist also takes a more active role, advising, interpreting, and directing. Moreover, a modern psychoanalytic therapist tends to place more emphasis on present problems and relationships than did the classic Freudians.

In recent years, there has been considerable research on the efficacy of brief psychoanalytic therapy, usually called "psychodynamic" or "dynamic" psychotherapy (Koss et al., 1986). Brief dynamic therapy has been shown to be effective for a wide variety of specific problems, including posttraumatic stress disorder, grief, and personality disorders (Goldfried et al., 1990).

HUMANISTIC THERAPIES

Like psychoanalytic therapies, **humanistic therapies** are based on the belief that psychological problems can be treated by giving people insight into needs and motives they may not be aware of. But humanistic therapists flatly reject the determinism implicit in psychoanalysis. Freud viewed troubled people as victims of childhood conflicts over which they could exert very little control. A major tenet of humanism, in contrast, is freedom of choice. Humanistic therapists maintain that a person is ultimately free to make the choices that affect who he or she becomes. Their goal is to liberate the client's innate tendencies toward self-actualization and growth. Although there are many different kinds of humanistic treatments, we will discuss just two: the client-centered therapy of Carl Rogers and gestalt therapy.

ROGERS' CLIENT-CENTERED THERAPY

The best known of the humanistic treatments is Carl Rogers's **client-centered therapy,** in which the therapist helps clients to clarify their true feelings and to come to value who they really are. A central assumption of client-centered therapy is that people have problems in living because others impose on them unreasonable **conditions of worth.** That is to say, parents, peers, and spouses withhold respect and affection until a person acts in ways that conform to *their* expectations of what is appropriate and good, even though that style of behavior may be out of keeping with the person's true self. Thus, a sensitive teenager may have to deny his sensitivity and behave in artificially aggressive ways in order to gain approval from his peers. The result is profound unhappiness and a stifling of self-actualization.

To free the person from unreasonable conditions of worth, the client-centered therapist establishes a warm and accepting environment. He or she never disapproves of what the client does or thinks. In fact, the therapist repeatedly supports the client, offering what Rogers calls **unconditional positive regard** (a liking for the client that is not conditional upon the client acting in a certain way). The therapist also shows *accurate empathy* for the client's feelings and tries to "mirror" them. *Mirroring* does not mean just parroting what the client says. It means restating the client's feelings, genuinely trying to adopt the client's perspective, in order to show that the therapist understands and accepts the client's point of view. As a result, the client feels able to express emotions more freely.

The following excerpt from a therapy session illustrates this technique. The client here is a college student plagued by feelings of inferiority:

Client: Well, it happened again yesterday. I got back that exam in American Lit.
Therapist: I see.
Client: Just like before. I got an A all right—me and eight others. But on the third question the instructor wrote a comment that I could have

"THIS IS THERAPY, MR. DOANE. ONE CAN'T PLEAD THE FIFTH."

been a little clearer or else could have given more detail. The same old crap. I got an A all right, but it's pretty damn clear that I'm like a machine that can generate correct answers without ever understanding. That's it. I memorize, but there's no spark, no creativity. Boy! . . .

Therapist: Even though you got an A you are not satisfied.
Client: That's right. Never satisfied. I could get 42 A-pluses and never feel good. I hate myself . . .

(Phares, 1979)

Here the therapist's mirroring of the young man's dissatisfaction with his performance conveys understanding of the client's feelings and encourages him to elaborate on them. Notice especially how the therapist accepts the client's unhappiness despite his A grade. He doesn't try to dissuade the client from this viewpoint, and he doesn't express disapproval. This nonjudgmental attitude is considered vital if the client is ever to break free of unreasonable conditions of worth.

But mirroring a client's feelings, called **primary empathy,** is only a first step in Rogers's client-centered therapy. The ultimate goal is to bring the client to a new, more productive view of the self. To do this, the therapist gradually begins to suggest what might be causing the client's problems, while still showing an understanding of the client's point of view. This is called **advanced empathy.** For the

young man with feelings of inferiority, advanced empathy would involve helping him to see how others have imposed on him unreasonable conditions of worth, which in turn have made him feel inadequate. The therapist begins to do this right after the young man states that he hates himself for his lack of potential.

Therapist: Yeah. I guess you really felt people put you down because of this lack of potential?
Client: Boy, did they! Especially my folks. They never really said so, but I could tell from the way they acted. . . .
Therapist: And this made you feel sort of worthless? . . .
Client: That's right.

(Phares, 1979)

It is hoped that when these new insights are fully established, the client can shed his need to become the "perfect son" to please his parents. Instead, he can develop pride in the many things he has already accomplished and acquire a sense that he is indeed a capable person. Client-centered therapy holds that advanced empathy is of central importance, for without a new perspective on their lives, troubled people can never overcome their negative feelings.

GESTALT THERAPY

Frederick (Fritz) Perls, who developed **gestalt therapy,** was originally trained as a psychoanalyst. From his Freudian roots, Perls derived the belief that psychological problems arise from repressed and unresolved conflicts—conflicts that must be uncovered and somehow worked through. But Perls saw past conflicts as important only as they bear on a person's present. Like other humanistic therapists, Perls also believed that people must take responsibility for their own feelings and actions. Perls saw all people as ultimately free to decide for themselves whether past conflicts will be allowed to hamper current interpersonal relationships.

Perls adopted the German term *Gestalt,* which means "whole," because his therapy aims at making a person more integrated or psychologically whole. To this end, Perls tried to help his clients shed their old defenses, release their pent-up feelings, increase their self-awareness, and open their blocked potential for growth. He emphasized being in touch with one's immediate feelings, expressing them honestly as they are felt, and accepting responsibility for them. Perls and other gestalt therapists have used a variety of tactics to accomplish these goals. For one thing, the client is encouraged to use the first person singular (I, me, mine) and the active voice (I am, I do, I feel) to show that he or she takes responsibility for feelings and actions. The client says, for example, "I am angry" rather than "Don't you think I have a right to be annoyed?" (Levitsky and Perls, 1970). Sometimes, too, clients are asked to assume responsibility in no uncertain terms. After expressing some truth about themselves, they are to add the emphatic statement "and I take responsibility for that."

Other gestalt exercises are designed to heighten awareness of important psychological conflicts. The client may be asked to voice a conversation between opposing parts of the self. The ambitious, competitive side of the self, for example, may talk with the side that lacks confidence. Each side is to express itself forcefully, as if arguing with the other. Out of such role-playing dialogues an integration of opposing forces may emerge, one that is psychologically healthier than either of the initial forces. The client may also be asked to engage in a dialogue with some emotionally significant person who is not actually present. The aim here is to take care of "unfinished business," to bring unresolved issues with that person to some kind of closure. The following excerpt from a gestalt therapy session illustrates several of these strategies:

Therapist: Tom, what are you experiencing now?
Patient: Anger.
Therapist: Where do you feel this anger?
Patient: [indicating chest] Here, and [indicating hands] here.
Therapist: Just stay with the feeling, and let it increase. And you may get more in touch with it if you breathe deeply, in your abdomen, and let a sound come out when you exhale. . . .
Patient: [breathing abdominally] Ooooh! ooooh! ooooh!
Therapist: What is that experience?
Patient: Anger, resentment.
Therapist: Will you address that resentment to somebody?
Patient: Mother, I resent you . . . everything about you.
Therapist: Specify your resentment.
Patient: I . . . I resent you for making me dependent on you.
Therapist: Tom, how is your voice?
Patient: It's . . . it's a whine.
Therapist: Will you own your voice? Take responsibility?
Patient: I . . . I'm whining. . . . I'm whining.
Therapist: Do that. Whine to your mother, and experience

yourself doing that.
Patient: [whining voice; reaching out with hands] Mother . . . Please . . . please let me go . . . please turn me loose.

(Phares, 1979, p. 374)

This approach, with its emphasis on the expression of pent-up feelings, has had considerable influence on other therapies, particularly group therapies. The gestalt approach has also attracted many adherents, possibly because modern society discourages the expression of intense feelings in most contexts. Research in support of gestalt therapy is now beginning to appear (Johnson and Greenberg, 1985).

BEHAVIOR AND COGNITIVE-BEHAVIOR THERAPIES

Behavior therapies involve applying experimentally derived principles of learning to change maladaptive thoughts, feelings, and behaviors. At first, this primarily meant applying the principles of classical and operant conditioning. But in recent years this group of therapies has diversified to include approaches based on principles of observational learning, social learning, and cognitive learning. One of the most important developments in behavior therapy was the integration of the cognitive point of view. Generally, practitioners of cognitive-behavior therapy try to change their clients' thinking processes in order to change their feelings and their behavior. The cognitive point of view has gained widespread attention in behavior therapy (Dryden and Golden, 1986).

Despite their diversity, however, behavior and cognitive-behavior therapies share a number of features. For one thing, they are all based on the assumption that the same learning principles that govern other behavior, such as modeling and conditioning, are also responsible for abnormal behavior. No deep probing of unconscious conflicts is thought to be needed. Instead, the therapist focuses on the problems that the client reports and on how new learning can be used to alleviate these problems. For the cognitive-behavior therapist, changing maladaptive thoughts and feelings is central to effective treatment. But both behavior and cognitive-behavior therapists take a client's cognitions at face value rather than as defenses against unconscious urges. They also participate very actively in the therapeutic process. Rather than listening to clients recall their childhood experiences, describe their dreams, and

In systematic desensitization, the client is trained in techniques for remaining relaxed while being exposed to increasingly frightening aspects of the anxiety-provoking situation. Eventually, an acrophobic person, say, is able to overcome his or her fear of high places.

free-associate, they ask direct questions and give explicit advice and instructions (Sloane et al., 1975). They also focus more on the current factors maintaining the client's problem, and less on the past factors that may originally have encouraged it.

Many behavior and cognitive-behavior therapies are believed to be effective largely because their step-by-step approach enables clients to gain a sense of self-efficacy, a feeling of mastery over the situation (Bandura, 1977a). With each step in the treatment, the person learns "I can do that" and thus acquires the confidence needed to try the next, more advanced step. These repeated successes, in turn, are not only intrinsically rewarding, they also reinforce expectations of future success, thereby encouraging perseverance.

In the following sections we will explore a number of behavior and cognitive-behavior therapies. First we will cover some treatments based on classical and operant conditioning. Then we will examine some approaches based on modeling and cognitive learning principles.

THERAPIES BASED ON CLASSICAL AND OPERANT CONDITIONING

Exposure-Based Treatments As you learned in Chapter 6, classical conditioning involves the repeat-ed pairing of a neutral stimulus with another stimulus that evokes some involuntary response. Gradually, the formerly neutral stimulus by itself comes to elicit that same response. In John B. Watson's experiment with little Albert, for instance, a frightening noise was repeatedly paired with the presentation of a laboratory rat until eventually the rat alone came to elicit fear. In most cases a classically conditioned response will extinguish if the conditioned stimulus and the unconditioned stimulus are not paired at least occasionally. But in classically conditioned fears like little Albert's, the conditioned stimulus (in Albert's case, the rat) may be so terrifying that it is hard for the person to "unlearn" the deeply ingrained association. This is why behavior therapist Joseph Wolpe (1958, 1973, 1976) developed the technique for treating phobias called systematic desensitization.

Systematic desensitization is a type of exposure to a feared stimulus. It is based on the principle that anxiety and relaxation are incompatible, so people can be taught to be less anxious about something by learning to relax when confronting it. Exposure-based procedures are effective treatments for anxiety disorders such as agoraphobia, obsessive compulsive disorder, and simple phobias (Barlow, 1988; Barlow and Cerny, 1988). Exposure involves having the individual confront his or her feared stimulus in a structured manner. For example, agoraphobics may be treated by exposing them to real-life crowds and public places. The exposure can be sudden or more drawn out, very intense or less intense, prolonged or brief. The evidence suggests that exposure is more effective if it is intense and prolonged, because this enables the client to experience the arousal and then habituate to it (Barlow and Waddell, 1985). Therapists can assist in this process by accompanying their clients during exposure. Because exposure can be extremely unpleasant until habituation is reached, the rapport with the therapist can be important in encouraging the client to stay in treatment. Suppose a client is anxious about flying in airplanes. The therapist begins by asking the person to describe what part of the experience of flying is most frightening, what part is slightly less frightening, what part only moderately frightening, and so on. The therapist then arranges these situations in a hierarchy from most to least fear arousing. Here is a hypothetical example:

1. Experiencing midair turbulence
2. Taking off
3. Taxiing down the runway
4. Boarding the plane
5. Waiting to get on the plane
6. Riding to the airport in a car
7. Buying an airline ticket

The client is next taught a technique of deep muscle relaxation. When this is mastered, the therapist asks the person to imagine the least frightening scene in the hierarchy while staying relaxed. When the client can do so, the procedure is repeated with the next highest item on the list. Eventually, the client is able to imagine the most frightening scene without becoming afraid. This procedure also makes the client less anxious when encountering the feared situation in real life. Often, however, the best results are obtained when real-life desensitization is added. The person with a fear of flying, for instance, after successfully imagining midair turbulence while staying relaxed, would take a real flight on a plane, possibly accompanied by the therapist. The therapist would help the client stay relaxed during all the various stages of the flight. In this way, the phobic person confronts the feared situation firsthand, and in doing so learns, it is hoped, that the fear was groundless. Systematic desensitization has been extensively tried and evaluated. It has been found to be effective for phobias (Kazdin and Wilson, 1978; Rimm and Masters, 1979).

One of the best-known examples of an exposure treatment is Barlow's treatment program for women with agoraphobia (a fear of crowds, public places, and open spaces). The treatment involves group meetings with agoraphobics and their spouses. At these meetings, individuals are encouraged to make gradual forays away from home. Spouses are taught to provide support for these exposures, and client's experiences are discussed at weekly group meetings. Sixty to seventy percent of agoraphobics show marked improvement following this treatment (Barlow & Waddell, 1985).

One of the most important new trends in the development of treatment for anxiety disorders is the combination of exposure and relaxation training with training in cognitive restructuring. Some investigators maintain that cognitive distortions play an important role in perpetuating anxiety disorders. Initial signs of anxiety may be misinterpreted by the client —for example, in a panic attack, clients who are unable to get their breath may become extremely frightened and think they are dying. This misinterpretation of the initial anxiety reaction can result in a further increase in anxiety and panic. Recent research suggests that treatments that combine exposure with relaxation, breathing retraining, cognitive restructuring, and simulation of the sensations of panic attacks within the session for practice in coping can virtually eliminate panic attacks (Barlow, 1988; Beck, 1988). If these initial results are replicated, we will have witnessed a major breakthrough in the treatment of anxiety disorders (Goldfried et al., 1990).

Finally, supplementing exposure with medication can be highly effective in helping people who suffer from avoidance and panic disorders (Telch, Agras, Bar, Taylor, Roth, & Gallen, 1985). Recent evidence also suggests that exposure, when followed by a drug called chlomapramine, may greatly reduce the obsessional thoughts and ritualistic behaviors of people with obsessive-compulsive disorder (Goldfried et al., 1990).

Aversion Conditioning Another therapeutic technique derived from conditioning principles is **aversion conditioning.** In this approach, the problem behavior, or cues related to it, is repeatedly paired with an aversive stimulus (electric shock, for instance, or a drug that induces vomiting). This aversive stimulus serves as a punishment which suppresses the unwanted behavior. At the same time, the person acquires a negative emotional or physiological reaction (fear, nausea) just by being in the presence of cues associated with the problem behavior. This involuntary negative reaction, which is classically conditioned, further deters the person from performing the undesired behavior.

To understand aversion conditioning more fully, consider how it has been tried in the treatment of alcoholism (Nathan, 1976). The look, taste, and smell of alcohol are repeatedly paired with a drug that causes vomiting and so evokes intense feelings of nausea and revulsion. Usually the drug is given immediately before a drink, or is mixed with it, so that the two stimuli occur close together. After a sufficient number of pairings, the person responds to alcohol alone as he or she does to the drug—with strong feelings of nausea at the very sight or smell of it. Other problem behaviors for which aversion therapy has been tried include smoking, overeating, self-mutilation in autistic children, and various sexual deviances, such as exhibitionism.

Aversion conditioning is seldom used alone. For one thing, there is debate over how long the learned avoidance response lasts. After therapy, the new response may quickly extinguish and old behaviors may reemerge (Wilson, 1987). In addition, aversion conditioning, by itself, does not tell people what to do *instead of* the old, unwanted behaviors. For these reasons, it is almost always used with other, more positive forms of treatment (Mahoney and Arnkoff, 1978). A person undergoing aversion conditioning for alcoholism, for example, would also be given instructions on appropriate drinking behavior, explicit guidelines on how to refuse a drink, and so forth. But even when used with other procedures, controversy surrounds the ethics of aversion conditioning. Should therapists inflict pain and discomfort on people, even with their consent? This ethical issue has generally made aversion conditioning a last-resort treatment.

Time Out   A less controversial way of suppressing an unwanted behavior is to withdraw rewards whenever that behavior occurs. This is the basic procedure involved in the form of contingency management known as **time out.** Time out is often used with children who persist in doing something that is dangerous to themselves or to others, or that for some other reason is intolerable. It involves following the undesirable behavior with a period of time away from positive reinforcement. Gradually, the unwanted response should then extinguish, making it easier to use positive reinforcement to encourage desirable behavior.

Time out is clearly related to the old-fashioned remedy of sending misbehaving children to their rooms. However, several procedures that govern time out make it more effective than the typical parent-imposed exile. First, the therapist sets clear rules as to when time out will be administered (when the child throws a tantrum, for instance, or bites another person). The child is carefully informed of these rules, and they are always strictly enforced. Second, the place to which the child is sent for a time-out session, while never intrinsically frightening, contains *no* rewards. There are no toys or books or tapes there, none of the pleasant distractions usually found in a child's own room. Third, the amount of time a child spends in time out is carefully regulated. A timer is usually set, and when the buzzer sounds, time out is over as long as the child has cooperated with the procedure. Generally, a time-out session is quite brief. A minute for every year of age is a common rule of thumb. Finally, the adult who imposes time out does so dispassionately, not with annoyance. This is because some children find *any* attention—even anger—a form of reinforcement.

This last requirement is one of the things that makes it hard for many parents to use time out effectively. When a child who is placed in time out begins to scream loudly, or perhaps starts to kick or throw things, the parents may lose their patience and speak harshly to the child. The child is then gratified by having successfully manipulated the parents and so is apt to continue resisting. Experts usually recommend that resistance on the part of the child should be calmly met with extra minutes in time out or, if that doesn't work, with the addition of a back-up consequence, such as removal of a favorite toy or privilege for a day. But in all cases the consequences should be imposed *calmly*, and the child should know the rules beforehand. Many parents also have trouble being consistent in using time out, because often the problem behavior occurs at "inconvenient" times. For instance, the child who kicks his brother when the siblings are late for school may be let off "just this once" so as not to miss the school bus. In this situation, the child is learning to time his misbehavior to avoid negative consequences. Some parents also abandon time out prematurely because it seems that their child's misbehavior is actually getting worse. This perception is often correct. An operant response that has previously been rewarded in some way typically intensifies when rewards are suddenly withdrawn. In this case, the parents must stay with the time-out procedure until the unwanted behavior finally extinguishes.

Token Economies   Other therapies based on contingency management involve systematically rewarding desirable behavior. One example is the **token economy,** developed more than twenty years ago (Ayllon and Azrin, 1968). In this procedure, specific behaviors immediately earn a person "tokens" (poker chips, slips of paper, or whatever) that can be exchanged for rewards (candy, magazines, television privileges, and so forth). Token economies have been used successfully in many settings: classrooms, residential programs for juvenile offenders, institutions for the mentally retarded, hospitals wards for schizophrenics, to name just a few (Fixsen et al., 1976; Kazdin, 1977). One major study found that a token economy in combination with individual behavior therapy resulted in greater improvement in a group of chronic schizophrenics than did either of two alternative treatment programs (Paul and Lentz, 1977). The schizophrenic patients who experienced the token economy made significant gains in self-care, table manners, housekeeping efforts, social interaction, and vocational skills. Many were able to leave the hospital for community placements, such as group homes and halfway houses, and some were even able to live largely on their own. All this wasn't due just to the token economy. The individual behavior therapy played an important part as well. The token economy, however, according to the researchers, was instrumental in getting the attention of these severely disturbed patients, especially at the start of the program.

But what happens when people leave the setting where a token economy was used? Don't they just gradually revert back to their old, undesirable behaviors? Not necessarily, if the contingency management program has been carefully planned. First, therapists can select target behaviors (those to be rewarded with tokens) that either are reinforcing in their own right (such as interaction with others) or will naturally be reinforced by social approval (such as improved personal hygiene). Second, as the patients acquire the desired behaviors, the therapists can increasingly use social approval rather than tokens to reward them. This strategy brings the reward structure closer to that found in the "outside" world. Third, arrangements can often be made to continue systematic reinforce-

ment outside an institution (for instance, by training family members to reward target behaviors). And fourth, people can be taught to provide their own reinforcement (such as treating themselves to a movie as a reward for looking for a job). These tactics seem to be effective. Compared with traditional hospital care, institutional programs that systematically reward positive behaviors not only increase patients' likelihood of being discharged, they also decrease their chances of being admitted again (Kazdin and Wilson, 1978).

Of course, no one says that a token economy is a cure for schizophrenia or other severe psychological disorders. Chronic schizophrenics who participate in a token economy are usually still abnormal in many ways. But they tend to function more effectively than severely disturbed people without this form of treatment. It is therefore surprising that relatively few mental hospitals use the token economy in their therapeutic programs (Boudewyns et al., 1986).

THERAPIES BASED ON MODELING

Although therapies based on contingency management are widely used today, it is important to remember that rewards and punishments are not always needed for learning to occur. Often we learn simply through *observation*, with no overt rewards or punishments being meted out. When we come to shape our own behavior on the basis of what others do, we are said to be acquiring new behaviors through **modeling.** Of course, we are far more likely to imitate behavior that we see rewarded than behavior that we see punished.

Deliberate modeling has been successfully put to therapeutic uses. It has proved particularly effective in treating phobias. Sometimes the client merely watches another person (either live or on film) interacting with the feared object. For instance, Albert Bandura and his coworkers have had much success eliminating dog phobias in children by having the phobic youngsters observe a fearful child who first approaches a dog, then pets it, and finally plays with it (Bandura et al., 1967). In a variation of this technique, called **participant modeling,** the therapist first models the feared activity for the client and then guides the client through a series of gradual steps culminating in the modeled behavior. In one study, for example, Bandura and others led people with snake phobias from first thinking about snakes, to

Desensitization techniques can help a phobic person conquer an intense fear of snakes.

looking at a snake in a cage, to approaching the snake, to touching it through the wires of its cage, and finally to holding it (Bandura et al., 1969). The researchers found that participant modeling was more effective in ridding people of this fear than either symbolic modeling (watching a model on film) or systematic desensitization. Other research has yielded similar results (Rimm and Mahoney, 1969; Thase and Moss, 1976).

Of course, phobias are not the only disorders for which therapies based on modeling are used. Even disorders as severe as schizophrenia have been helped by such treatments. In one study, researchers asked chronic schizophrenics to pretend that they were in various social situations and to act as people in that situation should (Bellack et al., 1976). At first the schizophrenics performed very poorly. They did not seem to know what feelings or behaviors were appropriate to the situations they were acting out. Then they were given training which included modeling of the appropriate responses by a therapist. When given these models to imitate, and when encouraged

with praise for successes, all of the patients did much better. Apparently, even people with severe psychological disorders can improve their social skills partly through modeling (Wallace and Liberman, 1985).

THERAPIES BASED ON COGNITIVE RESTRUCTURING

In therapies based on classical and operant conditioning, and even in some of those based on modeling, the main emphasis has traditionally been on changing people's overt behavior. In fact, in the days when behavior therapy began, practitioners virtually ignored people's thoughts and feelings, assuming that they should not be the main focus of treatment. In recent years all this has changed, however. It is now widely recognized that how people interpret events around them, perceive themselves, and judge their own abilities is central to their mental health. If people are having problems in living, proponents of this view hold, it is because they are caught in an insidious web of negative, self-defeating thoughts. Such maladaptive thoughts are learned, just like maladaptive behaviors, and so can be changed through appropriate relearning. Therapies with a stress on teaching new, healthier ways of thinking—that is, on restructuring a person's negative cognitions—are called **cognitive-behavior therapies.**

Perhaps the oldest cognitive-behavior treatment is **rational-emotive therapy (RET),** developed by Albert Ellis (1962). Ellis argues that thousands of people lead unhappy lives because of irrational beliefs that color their interpretations of events. Thus, it is not failure itself that is psychologically damaging, but failure screened through the irrational belief that one must excel at everything. Similarly, it is not rejection by itself that causes depression, but rejection filtered through the irrational belief that one must be loved by everyone. Ellis's strategy is to make people aware of the irrationality of many of their views and to replace these old problem-causing outlooks with more realistic ones. In particular, he focuses on changing the maladaptive statements that people say to themselves ("I can't do anything right!" said to oneself when something small goes wrong; "Everyone must think I'm boring!" said to oneself when a new acquaintance turns away and talks to someone else at a party). Rational-emotive therapy has proved to be effective in reducing anxiety in stressful situations, and it may also be useful in treating excessive anger as well as depression (Haaga and Davison, 1989).

Somewhat similar in approach is Donald Meichenbaum's **self-instructional training** (Meichenbaum, 1977). Meichenbaum thoroughly instructs his clients on how to think rational and positive thoughts in stressful situations instead of plunging into the old, self-defeating internal monologues. For instance, a student who always becomes very nervous when taking exams is apt to think like this:

> I'm so nervous, I'm afraid I'll forget the most important material. The teacher will read this test and think I'm an idiot. If I get a D on this test, I'll have to get a B on the final just to get a C for the course. I *know* everybody here studied more than I did, which will shoot the curve way up. If I don't get an A in this course, I may as well forget about graduate school. . . .

Of course, this pattern of thought makes the student even more nervous and so even less likely to do well on the exam. Meichenbaum's remedy is to teach the client new, more positive internal monologues to replace the negative ones. For the anxious student, a new monologue might be:

> I'm going to take slow, deep breaths and keep myself calm. All I have to do is be calm and take my time. . . . Just consider the questions one by one. I spent a fair amount of time studying for this test and I'm going to take each question in turn and be calm while I'm thinking about the answer. I'm an intelligent, competent person, and that fact is not altered by whatever grade I get on this test.

This approach has been particularly useful in helping people to control their anger. Figure 17.1 gives some internal monologues that people have used.

The concept of self-instructional training, or training in problem-solving skills, has been gaining in popularity since it was originally introduced (D'Zurillo, 1986). Such training focuses on teaching general coping skills that can be applied to a variety of problem situations (e.g., giving a speech or meeting new people) and to situations that require increased self-control (eliminating excessive smoking, drinking, or eating, for example). Over the past decade, research has accumulated which demonstrates the effectiveness of this treatment in dealing with a wide variety of stressful situations and difficult life circumstances (Goldfried et al., 1990).

Another treatment that focuses on restructuring a person's negative ways of thinking is Aaron Beck's **cognitive therapy.** Like Ellis, Beck holds that emotional problems are caused primarily by irrational thoughts, or schemas. In analyzing the roots of depression, for instance, Beck argues that this disorder arises from three types of negative thoughts: (1) persistent self-devaluation, (2) negative interpretations of events, and (3) a pessimistic outlook on the future (Beck et al., 1979). In Beck's view, when people interpret trivial setbacks as substantial, read disparagement into innocuous comments made by others, and criticize themselves harshly for things they cannot possibly control, they are more vulnerable to depression.

To change such cognitions, Beck questions clients in such a way that they themselves discover the irrationality of their thinking. This makes the therapist and client partners in the effort to uncover the maladaptive nature of the patient's thoughts. Beck also encourages unconvinced clients to try doing things that will test the validity of their negative assumptions and in doing so prove them wrong. Here is one example of how Beck leads a woman to begin seeing both the senselessness of her belief that she needs her husband in order to be happy and the fact that she has nothing to lose by trying divorce:

Therapist: Why do you want to end your life?

Patient: Without Raymond, I'm nothing. . . . I can't be happy without Raymond. . . . But I can't save our marriage.

Therapist: What has your marriage been like?

Patient: It's been miserable from the very beginning. . . . Raymond has always been unfaithful. . . . I have hardly seen him in the past five years.

Therapist: You say that you can't be happy without Raymond. . . . Have you found yourself happy when you are with Raymond?

Patient: No, we fight all the time and I feel worse.

Therapist: You say you are nothing without Raymond. Before you met Raymond, did you feel you were nothing?

Patient: No, I felt I was somebody.

Therapist: If you were somebody before you knew Raymond, why do you need him to be somebody now?

Patient: [Puzzled] Hmmm. . . .

Therapist: If you were free of the marriage, do you think that men might be interested in you—knowing that you were available?

Preparing for a Provocation

This could be a rough situation, but I know how to deal with it.
I can work out a plan to handle this. Easy does it.
Remember, stick to the issues and don't take it personally.
There won't be any need for an argument. I know what to do.

Impact and Confrontation

As long as I keep my cool, *I'm* in control of the situation.
You don't need to prove yourself. Don't make more out of this than you have to.
There is no point in getting mad. Think of what you have to do.
Look for the positives and don't jump to conclusions.

Coping with Arousal

Muscles are getting tight. Relax and slow things down.
Time to take a deep breath. Let's take the issue point by point.
My anger is a signal of what I need to do. Time for problem-solving.
He probably wants me to get angry, but I'm going to deal with it constructively.

Subsequent Reflection

a. Conflict unresolved

Forget about the aggravation. Thinking about it only makes you upset.
Try to shake it off. Don't let it interfere with your job.
Remember relaxation. It's a lot better than anger.
Don't take it personally. It's probably not so serious.

b. Conflict resolved

I handled that one pretty well. That's doing a good job!
I could have gotten more upset than it was worth.
My pride can get me into trouble, but I'm doing better at this all the time.
I actually got through that without getting angry.

FIGURE 17.1   Examples of statements that individuals rehearsed to manage the anger they anticipated before, during, and after a confrontation. *(Reprinted by permission of Dr. Ray Novaco, University of California, Irvine.)*

Patient: I guess that maybe they would be.

Therapist: Is it possible that you might find a man who would be more constant than Raymond?

Patient: I don't know. . . . I guess it's possible. . . .

Therapist: Then what have you actually lost if you break up the marriage?

Patient: I don't know.

Therapist: Is it possible that you'll get along better if you end the marriage?

Patient: There is no guarantee of that.

Therapist: Do you have a *real marriage*?

Patient: I guess not.

Therapist: If you don't have a real marriage, what do you actually lose if you decide to end the marriage?

Patient: [Long pause] Nothing, I guess.

(Beck, 1976, pp. 289–291)

Research has shown that Beck is correct about the negative schemas of depressed people. The depressed do typically devalue themselves, and the more self-inadequacies that they see, the more persistent their depression tends to be (Dent and Teasdale, 1988). The depressed also interpret events more negatively than other people do, just as Beck contends. In one study, depressed college students were more apt than nondepressed ones to inflate the importance of a test they were told they had done poorly on (Wenzlaff and Grozier, 1988). They seemed inclined to see things as worse than they really were.

Is Beck's method of treating these negative schemas effective? Research suggests that it is. For instance, one recent meta-analysis found that Beck's cognitive-behavior therapy resulted in a greater degree of positive change in depressed patients than did drug treatments, behavioral approaches, or other forms of psychotherapy (Dobson, 1989). Not all researchers agree with this conclusion, however, especially with the idea that Beck's approach is superior to drug treatments for relatively severe depression (Elkin et al., 1989). We need more evidence to resolve the issue. Nevertheless, Beck's cognitive therapy has an excellent record of success.

But how exactly does cognitive therapy help to lift depression? Do new, more rational ways of thinking bring about improvements in mood? Or does an elevated mood make a person think more positively? No one is sure. Interestingly, although people who undergo cognitive therapy end up thinking more positively than before, so do people who undergo drug treatment for depression (Hollon and Beck, 1986; Rush et al., 1982). So perhaps cognitive change is a mediator of *all* therapeutic improvement in depression, by whatever means. Future research may some day give us answers.

One of the most important new trends in the development of treatment for anxiety disorders is the combination of exposure and relaxation training with training in cognitive restructuring. Some investigators maintain that cognitive distortions play an important role in perpetuating anxiety disorders. Initial signs of anxiety may be misinterpreted by the client —for example, in a panic attack, clients who are unable to get their breath may become extremely frightened and think they are dying. This misinterpretation of the initial anxiety reaction can result in a further increase in anxiety and panic. Recent research suggests that treatments that combine exposure with relaxation, breathing retraining, cognitive restructuring, and simulation of the sensations of panic attacks within the session for practice in coping can virtually eliminate panic attacks (Barlow, 1988; Beck, 1988). If these initial results are replicated, we will have witnessed a major breakthrough in the treatment of anxiety disorders (Goldfried et al., 1990).

OPTIMISM PESSIMISM REALITY

FAMILY-SYSTEMS THERAPIES

Family-systems therapies grew out of the recognition that people have psychological problems not in isolation, but rather within a social context. One of the most important social contexts in most people's lives is the family. Interpersonal relations within the family may not only contribute to the onset of a psychological problem, they may also help maintain that problem once it has developed. Changing maladaptive patterns of interaction within families has therefore become an important area of treatment. In doing so, therapists view the family not simply as a collection of people, but rather as an organized system, with each person playing specific roles in relation to the others. From this perspective, it makes sense to treat the family as a unit. Sometimes that unit consists of a married (or cohabiting) couple. Other times the unit is broadened to include the couple's children, or maybe even other relatives, such as the couple's parents. Whoever seems to be involved in the maladaptive patterns of behavior is included in a family-systems approach to treatment.

Treating an entire family to alleviate psychological problems has been used for a variety of disorders, including childhood conduct disorders, anorexia, schizophrenia, depression, alcoholism, and agoraphobia (Falloon et al., 1982, 1985; Haley, 1980; Jacobson et al., 1989). Overall, this approach seems to be quite effective when compared with both individual forms of treatment and with no-treatment controls (Hazelrigg et al., 1987).

Family therapy involves examining the roles played by the various family members and altering the negative and inappropriate behavior that often accompanies these roles. This group is using a technique called "sculpture therapy." Family members assume the position that expresses their role and feelings within the family.

There are no set procedures involved in family-systems treatments; different family-systems therapists take different approaches. One approach is strategic, in that it focuses on getting family members to perform various therapeutic tasks. Usually, these tasks revolve around improving faulty communications within the family. Unfortunately, simply explaining to family members that they are not communicating well is often not enough. Patterns of family interaction are deeply entrenched and very resistant to change. In fact, direct attempts to change an unwanted behavior may only trigger resistance and intensify the problem. How, then, can a family therapist intervene successfully?

A frequently used strategy is called **paradoxical intention.** In one form of it, the therapist requests that a person with negative symptoms go right on displaying those symptoms, perhaps even more forcefully than before. This paradoxical request is often presented to the family as a necessary first step in gaining control over the problem ("If you can learn to turn the symptoms on, you can learn to turn them off"), or the symptoms may be "reframed" in positive terms ("Your angry outbursts show that you are really in touch with your feelings and able to express yourself freely; go ahead and give vent to your anger some more"). But the real reason for this paradoxical tactic is to place the person with the symptoms in a bind (Stanton, 1981). Imagine a family that comes for treatment because of a teenage daughter's delinquent behavior (Haley, 1980). In the therapy session the daughter becomes so disruptive that no interaction is possible. The family therapist unexpectedly *praises* her for expressing her feelings so openly and freely and instructs her to do so again, as loudly as she can. Suddenly the girl is placed in a position where her uncooperative behavior no longer has its desired effect. If she is disruptive, she is following the therapist's directives and presumably acting in a beneficial way. If she quiets down and behaves normally, she is showing unwanted improvement and allowing the session to proceed. The confusion that results from this psychological dilemma can promote important insights into family relationships and lead to new, more positive means of communication among the family members.

How effective are approaches based on paradoxical intent as a form of therapy? In one meta-analysis, they were found to be as effective as many other therapeutic procedures immediately after treatment, and even *more* effective than the others a month later. Apparently, paradoxical interventions have good long-term results (Shoham-Salomon and Rosenthal, 1987). The results are especially good when a paradoxical intervention reframes the client's negative behaviors in a positive way (such as telling the disruptive teenager that her outbursts are in fact good). Changing the meaning of negative behaviors in this manner seems to erode some of their foundations.

Another approach to family-systems therapy is a behavioral one, in which the stress is on teaching family members to reinforce and encourage positive interactions. Consider behavioral therapy for a troubled marriage. The therapist assumes that the higher the rate of positive interactions the partners experience, the more satisfaction they will feel about their relationship (Wood and Jacobson, 1985). One way to increase positive interactions is to institute "caring days" (Stuart, 1976). The husband agrees to do nice things for the wife on one day, with no demands of anything immediately in return, and the wife agrees to do nice things for the husband on another day, again with no expectations of immediate "payback." If the positive feelings created by these reciprocal caring behaviors are reinforcing, then, in time, the couple can begin to exchange caring behaviors in a more natural, give-and-take way. Of course, behavioral principles of learning can also be applied to other family problems. For instance, a family therapist with a behavioral orientation often teaches parents how to change unwanted behaviors in their children through programs of reinforcement (Patterson, 1974).

The behavioral approach to family therapy has a reasonably good record of success. When used for marital therapy, for instance, about half the couples who complete treatment improve their relationship enough so as to no longer be considered distressed (Baucom and Epstein, 1990). But the average couple treated with behavior therapy alone comes to feel that their marriage is just satisfactory, not exceptionally good (O'Leary and Smith, 1991). This is one reason why, in recent years, behavioral family therapy has expanded to include cognitive restructuring as well. Research suggests that this cognitive component can often significantly enhance the effectiveness of a behavioral approach to family treatment (Baucom, 1985; Baucom and Lester, 1986). For some family therapists today, cognitive restructuring has become the primary focus.

This cognitive restructuring involves teaching family members how to change negative ways of thinking that are giving rise to problems. For instance, a wife who assumes that "men are only interested in sex" may judge many of her husband's motives unfairly and cause conflict in their marriage. Similarly, a husband who believes it is strictly a woman's job to care for home and family will probably cause marital stress if his wife also works outside the home. Helping these people adopt more realistic assumptions and standards is one way to reduce family tension and strife (Jordan and McCormick, 1987). Another way is to help family members correctly attribute causes to one another's behavior. Members of troubled families very often assume that each other's negative actions are the result of undesirable personality traits rather than caused simply by situational pressures (Fincham et al., 1987; Fincham and Bradbury, 1988). For instance, the parents of a three-year-old who frequently has tantrums might conclude that he is by nature high-strung and temperamental, instead of looking for inadvertent rewards that are reinforcing his negative behavior. Helping these parents to attribute causes properly is a first step toward solving their problem.

Family therapists with a psychoanalytic orientation take a different tactic. They try to uncover unconscious wishes, fears, and conflicts stemming from a person's early relationships, especially with parents. These early relationships may be negatively affecting current family relations. For instance, a man whose need for maternal love was not fully met as a child may seek excessive mothering from his wife, whom he unconsciously identifies with his mother. Psychoanalytically oriented family treatment involves searching for such hidden motives so that they can be rationally analyzed and begin to lose their power of control (Wachtel and Wachtel, 1986). Usually family members are seen together, so the therapist can observe their patterns of interaction and obtain clues about their unconscious feelings and desires.

One recent study found psychoanalytically oriented family therapy to be more effective than behavior therapy in reducing marital conflict over the long run (Snyder et al., 199?). Of twenty-six couples who completed behavior therapy, ten divorced in the first four years following treatment, compared with only one out of twenty-nine couples who completed psychoanalytic therapy. Moreover, the psychoanalytically treated couples who remained married reported less conflict than did the behaviorally treated couples who remained married. Since these results show up only after a posttreatment period of several years, you can see the importance of conducting long-term

Group therapy brings together people with a common problem, such as obesity, so that they can offer one another advice, understanding, and encouragement.

studies to evaluate psychotherapies. Of course, it remains to be seen if these interesting results can be replicated by other researchers. Perhaps if the behavioral treatments assessed in future studies include specific training in communication skills, as well as cognitive restructuring, improvements would be maintained over a longer period of time.

OTHER GROUP THERAPIES

Family therapy is only one kind of group approach to treatment. When therapy is applied not just to an individual but to an interacting collection of people, it is called **group therapy.** Therapeutic groups often consist of people who initially are strangers to each other. So why are they treated together? One reason is that people with similar problems often benefit from one another as well as from a therapist. From one another they learn that their problems are not unique, that there are others who understand and can provide emotional support. They can also learn how to handle their problems by listening to the advice directed toward other group members. Group therapy is particularly useful in treating interpersonal problems, for it offers opportunities for people to interact and work toward building more effective relationships. Group therapy is economical as well. Since the therapist's time is devoted to several clients

at once, more people can be treated at a lower fee per person.

There are many kinds of group therapy, far more than we can cover here. Each of the individual therapies we have discussed has produced one or more forms of group therapy. Thus, there are psychoanalytic therapy groups, behavior and cognitive-behavior therapy groups, and humanistic (especially gestalt) therapy groups. Other kinds of group therapy draw their approaches from several theoretical schools of thought. In the following sections we will focus on two kinds of popular treatment groups: behavior and cognitive-behavior therapy groups, and self-help groups.

BEHAVIOR AND COGNITIVE-BEHAVIOR THERAPY GROUPS

In behavior and cognitive-behavior therapy groups, experimentally derived principles of learning are applied to maladaptive thoughts, feelings, or behaviors that members of the groups all share. For instance, people with a certain kind of phobia (such as a dog phobia or a fear of flying), who suffer the same social anxiety (speaking in public, for example), who want to gain more self-control over a behavior such as eating or smoking, or who feel they need training in particular social skills might choose a therapy group which has a behavioral orientation.

Consider behaviorally oriented groups for social-skills training. Many people feel deficient in certain social abilities, such as interviewing for a job or making conversation with people they don't know well. In a behavior therapy group they can practice these skills with others who also feel that they lack in them. Although a therapist helps to model appropriate behavior, points out mistakes, and gives constructive advice as well as praise for successes, the members of the group also perform these roles for one another—ideally, in a way that is emotionally understanding and supportive. For example, in a group to train people in the social skill of self-assertion, the therapist would present group members with hypothetical situations in which a person has to make a point in a persuasive way. The group members are to act out these hypothetical dramas in ways that are appropriately self-assertive without generating anxiety or fear of offending others. In the process they comment on each other's performance and make constructive suggestions. Group members also discuss their efforts to be assertive in real-life situations, often role-playing to help learn how they might have performed better. Studies suggest that this form of treatment can be quite successful for certain kinds of problems (Rose, 1986).

SELF-HELP GROUPS

A fast-growing phenomenon in recent years has been the **self-help group**—a group of people who share a particular problem and meet to discuss it among themselves, without the active involvement of a professional therapist (Lieberman and Borman, 1979). The most familiar, and to some extent the inspiration for all such groups, is Alcoholics Anonymous (AA), established by two recovering alcoholics in 1935. AA members freely admit to and discuss their problem drinking, offering one another encouragement and advice regarding how to refrain from alcohol use and avoid an alcoholic relapse. Mutual understanding and support is the hallmark of the organization. Members can call on one another for assistance at any hour of the day or night. Many problems lend themselves to a similar kind of treatment. Self-help groups have been formed by widows, single parents, cancer patients, overeaters, smokers, drug addicts, child-abusing parents, and former mental patients, to name just a few.

Hoping to enhance the confidence and self-esteem of troubled teenagers by roughing it in the outdoors, this social rehabilitation group is preparing for a cross-country trip in covered wagons.

There is evidence that self-help groups can be very effective (e.g., Emerick, 1987; Spiegel et al., 1981). This effectiveness is probably due to a number of factors (Dunkel-Schetter and Wortman, 1987). One is the shared experiences and feelings among members of the group. Because members of self-help groups have all been through the same things, they can understand each other's problems and can reach out in ways that outsiders may find difficult. In addition, communication with others in the same situation provides other benefits. Members of self-help groups can model their behavior after those who are coping effectively. They can also exchange practical information; for example, former alcoholics can discuss how to cope with social pressure to drink, and cancer patients can discuss what they should tell their children or coworkers about their illness. Members of self-help groups can learn as well that what they feel is normal in their situation. Widows, for instance, can learn from one another that it is normal to feel angry at their spouse for "abandoning" them. Finally, there is the sense of companionship and belonging that self-help groups bring. Members no longer feel alone in coping with their troubles. They have something to counteract the sense of isolation that problems in living often bring.

Of course, not all problems are alleviated by self-help groups. In one study of parents who had experienced the sudden loss of a child, participation in both a self-help group and professional psychotherapy still did not result in improvement in either mental health or social functioning after a full year (Videka-Sherman and Lieberman, 1985). Apparently, some situations are so difficult to handle that even the support of sympathetic others is not enough to ease the pain.

COMBINING PSYCHOTHERAPIES: ECLECTIC APPROACHES

Combining different types of psychotherapy to improve the effectiveness of treatment is becoming increasingly common among mental health professionals. In the mid-1980s some 30 to 40 percent of clinicians reported that they took an eclectic approach to treatment (Norcross, 1986). Today that percentage is probably even higher. Eclectic therapists believe that openness to different approaches allows them to tailor a treatment program to the many different needs of each patient.

Even approaches that seem very different in their underlying assumptions about psychological disorders can be successfully combined in an eclectic form of treatment. Consider the combination of behavior therapies and psychoanalytic ones. Behavior therapies focus on overt behavior and current thoughts and feelings, whereas psychoanalytic therapies look for deeper, unconscious conflicts rooted in childhood experiences. Yet these two approaches to treatment are no longer considered mutually exclusive. A number of prominent psychotherapists have explored the ways psychoanalytic and behavior therapies can be integrated to enrich the overall treatment provided (Messer and Arkowitz, 1984; Wachtel, 1977, 1982).

Take the case of Joe M., who comes to a psycholanalyst because he has problems dealing with women (Davison and Neale, 1990). He thinks women take advantage of him because they see him as weak and unassertive. He is even suspicious of friendly overtures from women, whom he considers condescending and manipulative. Analysis reveals a deeply repressed anger toward his mother, who mistreated his father when Joe was a child. Joe's meek and deferential behavior toward women developed as a

defense against this anger. But meekness encourages women to take advantage of him, thereby confirming his belief that women are generally domineering and hurtful.

After psychoanalytic therapy has helped Joe gain insight into the causes of his problem with women, behavioral techniques can help him to alter his *current* maladaptive thoughts and behaviors, replacing them with psychologically healthier ones. For example, the therapist might use assertiveness training to help Joe interact more confidently with women. Once he begins to see that every encounter with a woman need not leave him feeling "pushed around," his negative expectations about women will start to diminish.

Still other approaches to treatment could further assist Joe in resolving his problem with women. For instance, gestalt techniques could help him to express his pent-up anger toward his mother, rather than letting it continue to affect his life. Similarly, if Joe is having marital troubles because of his feelings about women, he and his wife could be treated together, as a family therapist would do. The point is that no approach to treatment should be disregarded if it seems likely to alleviate a problem. This means that in some cases psychotherapies should be combined with biological treatments as well.

BIOLOGICAL TREATMENTS

Some psychological disorders are associated with changes in the delicate chemical balance of the brain. Some neurotransmitters may be in short supply, while others may be too abundant. Some receptors may be underactive, while others are overactive. Some psychologists believe that the best way to treat psychological disorders is by influencing these various changes in the brain. One treatment that attempts to do this is light therapy for seasonal affective disorder, discussed in Chapter 16. Three others are psychosurgery, electroconvulsive shock therapy, and therapies using psychoactive drugs. All attempt to affect the brain's intricate neural systems.

PSYCHOSURGERY

Psychosurgery is the most extreme of the biological treatments. It is a high-risk surgical procedure with irreversible effects. In 1935 Egas Moniz and Almeida Lima developed a procedure known as prefrontal

The novel and film *One Flew over the Cuckoo's Nest* depicted the abuse of psychosurgery as a punishment for unruly patients. While such surgical techniques were overused in the past, they are applied today under strict guidelines and only as a last resort.

lobotomy, in which a surgical instrument was inserted between the brain's frontal lobes and the thalamus, and the instrument was then rotated to destroy tissue. Moniz and Lima expected the interruption in communication between these two areas of the brain to reduce the impact of disturbing stimuli on patients who were chronically agitated or violent. Over the next twenty years other methods of psychosurgery evolved, and thousands of operations may have been performed. Some severely disturbed patients were helped by these procedures, but many were left in lethargic states, others became childlike in their behavior, and still others died on the operating table.

The psychosurgical techniques of the 1940s and 1950s have been abandoned in favor of operations that destroy very small amounts of brain tissue in precise locations (Valenstein, 1973, 1980). Fewer than a hundred such operations are performed each year in the United States, and these are done only after all other treatment options have been exhausted (Donnelly, 1985). In cases of severe depression or intractable obsessive-compulsive disorder, psychosurgery is sometimes effective as a treatment of last resort (Bridges and Bartlett, 1977; Tippin and Henn, 1982). It may also help in reducing manic episodes in people with severe and chronic manic-depression (Lovett and Shaw, 1987; Poynton et al., 1988; Sachdev et al., 1990). But it is now used only under the most stringent safeguards to protect the rights and the welfare of the patient.

ELECTROCONVULSIVE THERAPY

Shock treatment, as **electroconvulsive therapy (ECT)** is commonly called, has proven extremely effective in the treatment of severe depression that fails to respond to antidepressant drugs. It is particularly useful for depression that is triggered by some physiological change, not by a negative event in the afflicted person's life (National Institute of Mental Health, 1985; Scovern and Kilmann, 1980). It is also most effective when the depression has persisted for less than two years—that is, when the problem is not exceptionally long-term and chronic (Black et al., 1989). Although we do not know exactly how, ECT appears to cause a net increase in the brain's level of norepinephrine (Lerer et al., 1986).

Each year an estimated 30,000 to 50,000 Americans receive ECT (Beck and Cowley, 1990). The procedure they undergo is quite simple. Over a period of several weeks, the patient receives a series of brief electric shocks of approximately 70 to 130 volts in intensity. This is enough to induce convulsions similar to epileptic seizures. It is the convulsion, not the electrical current, that produces the therapeutic effect. Although it sounds painful, ECT as it is now administered entails very little discomfort. The patient is first given a sedative and is then injected with a muscle relaxant to prevent involuntary movements that could cause physical injury. Shortly after the shock is given, the patient awakens with no memory of the treatment. Some patients experience more extensive memory loss as a result of ECT, but usually this negative side effect is only temporary. In some cases, however, memory impairment can last for years, which is a major reason why doctors are so cautious about using shock treatment. The method is sometimes used to treat suicidal people, because it works more quickly than most antidepressant drugs. One alternative to ECT is antidepressant drugs used in combination with another drug called lithium (Barry, 1989). This combined drug treatment can sometimes lift depression more quickly than ECT can.

DRUG THERAPIES

Psychoactive drugs, most of which have been introduced in the past few decades, are now the most common form of biological treatment. The drugs developed to treat anxiety, schizophrenia, depression, mania, and other psychological disorders have many benefits. For one thing, **drug therapy** is available to all patients, not just to those who have the time and money for extended psychotherapy. Drugs have also proven useful in some cases where no other therapies have worked. For instance, before the introduction of antipsychotic drugs, some schizophrenic patients spent virtually their whole lives confined to mental hospitals. Today, with drugs to help control their symptoms, many schizophrenics are able to live successfully in the care of their families, or even on their own. In the following sections we will take a look at some of the drugs that have influenced this revolution in treatment, beginning with those used to alleviate anxiety.

ANTIANXIETY DRUGS

Commonly known as minor tranquilizers, **antianxiety drugs** sedate—that is, they have a general calming effect; some can also cause drowsiness. Since many people experience anxiety, tension, and difficulty sleeping at one time or another, these drugs are widely used. Family doctors often prescribe them for

people who, though not undergoing psychological treatment, are having trouble coping during difficult periods in their lives.

There are three kinds of antianxiety drugs: barbiturates, propanediols, and benzodiazepines. The barbiturates have long been used as sleeping medications, and years ago, before alternatives were developed, they were also used to ease stress and tension. But a barbiturate overdose can be deadly, particularly if mixed with alcohol, which is why so many doctors started prescribing the propanediols when they were introduced in the 1950s. The propanediols, such as Miltown and Equanil, soothe anxiety by reducing muscle tension. Even more recent antianxiety drugs are the benzodiazepines, such as Valium, Librium, Xanax, and Klonopin. For many people, they reduce anxiety without seriously impairing alertness and concentration. The benzodiazepines work by enhancing activity of the neurotransmitter GABA, which in turn inhibits certain neurons and dampens excitement of the central nervous system (Bender, 1990). Because benzodiazepines bind to specific receptors in the brain, there must be a naturally occurring neurotransmitter, similar in chemical structure, that has essentially the same anxiety-reducing effects.

In the mid-1970s, the benzodiazepine Valium was the most widely prescribed drug of any kind in the United States. Sales of it have dropped since then, but it is still used every day by millions of Americans. Critics charge that many people abuse Valium by taking it to avoid dealing with the stresses in their lives. There are also questions about Valium's long-term effectiveness. Nevertheless, Valium remains the most widely prescribed tranquilizing drug in this country.

Today two high-potency benzodiazepines, Xanax and Klonopin, are widely used to treat panic disorder, characterized by sudden, inexplicable attacks of intense fear. Klonopin has some advantages over Xanax in that its effects are longer lasting (so fewer doses can be taken in a day), and it is an easier drug to withdraw from when treatment is discontinued. Both, however, tend to produce very positive results in many of those who suffer from panic disorder (Tesar, 1990). Of course, Xanax and Klonopin, like all drugs, have potential negative side effects, so their continued use must be monitored closely. They also can be dangerous when combined with other depressant drugs, such as alcohol.

Another anxiety disorder, obsessive-compulsive disorder, is currently being treated not with antianxiety drugs, but rather with one of two antidepressant medications, Anafranil and Prozac. For up to two-thirds of those with obsessions and compulsions who take Anafranil, the recurring negative thoughts they cannot get out of their minds are significantly reduced and the accompanying anxiety lessens. When used in combination with behavior therapy, compulsive-ritualistic behaviors can also be alleviated (Rasmussen and Eisen, 1989). Anafranil mainly enhances the actions of the neurotransmitter serotonin, suggesting that a serotonin dysfunction may be involved in many cases of obsessive-compulsive disorder (Bender, 1990). Prozac also works primarily by boosting serotonin activity, which is why it too was tried as a treatment for obsessive-compulsive disorder (Levine et al., 1989). Anafranil and Prozac were originally developed as treatments for depression. It is to this therapeutic use that we now turn.

MOOD-REGULATING DRUGS

Antidepressant drugs were discovered by accident in 1952. Irving Selikof and his colleagues were treating tuberculosis patients with a drug called Iproniazid when they noticed that it produced an elevation in mood. Further research led to the discovery that Iproniazid is an *MAO inhibitor,* a drug that stops the action of an enzyme (monoamine oxidase) that normally breaks down the neurotransmitters norepinephrine and serotonin, and so halts their actions. Thus, an MAO inhibitor has the effect of enhancing the activity of norepinephrine and serotonin. Pharmaceutical companies have developed a number of MAO inhibitors (Marplan, Nardil, Parnate) that are effective in reducing depression. They have also developed a class of antidepressants called *tricyclics* because of their three-ringed molecular structure. Examples are Elavil and Tofranil. Tricyclics work by blocking the reuptake of norepinephrine and serotonin by the neurons that normally store them, thus increasing the action of these chemicals at their receptor cites in the brain. Unfortunately, MAO inhibitors and tricyclics can cause negative side effects, some of which are quite serious. These include dry mouth, dizziness, blurred vision, unwanted weight gain, and, for MAO inhibitors, a dangerous rise in blood pressure when dietary restrictions are not followed.

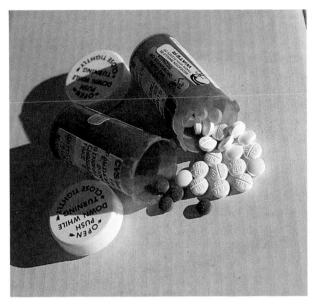

Antianxiety drugs, when prescribed judiciously and taken under careful supervision, are very helpful in relieving symptoms of distress while allowing the patient to continue normal activities.

A second generation of antidepressant drugs, with a variety of chemical structures, has recently been introduced, including Asendin, Dysyrel, and Prozac, among others. Most of these have the advantage of reducing the negative side effects that the tricyclics and MAO inhibitors can cause. Prozac has been so effective in this regard that it is now the nation's most prescribed antidepressant (Mandos et al., 1990). It works by blocking reuptake of serotonin, while having little effect on norepinephrine. Because it is less toxic in overdose than the older antidepressants, doctors can prescribe it without constantly monitoring the patient's blood to see if the dosage is right. However, Prozac may have side effects of its own, including headaches, nausea, insomnia, nervousness, and weight loss. But many patients feel these are easier to endure than their former depression. The long-term effects of Prozac still need to be determined.

Scientists have also discovered a drug that can be used to treat bipolar mood disorders (alternating episodes of mania and depression). This is **lithium,** a metallic substance found in tiny amounts in water throughout the world. A lithium maintenance program can substantially reduce the frequency and severity of abnormal mood swings without diminishing a person's capacity for normal emotional responses (Prien et al., 1984). Apparently, lithium somehow allows the body to reassert its own normal regulation of emotional ups and downs (Shou, 1988; Siever and Davis, 1985). Like other psychiatric drugs, however, lithium can have negative side effects, including upset stomach, hand tremors, and increased urination. If its level in the blood becomes too high, it can also adversely affect the thyroid gland and kidneys, and even cause death (Lydiard and Gelenberg, 1982). For this reason, patients who take the drug must have their dosage carefully monitored. Lithium can also be toxic to an unborn fetus, especially during the first three months of fetal development (Cohen et al., 1988). Consequently, doctors do not prescribe it to pregnant women unless an untreated bipolar disorder would put the woman and her baby at even greater risk.

ANTIPSYCHOTIC DRUGS

The most popular **antipsychotic drugs** are the phenothiazines, including Thorazine and Stelazine, which are widely used in the treatment of schizophrenia. Antipsychotic drugs help alleviate *active* psychotic symptoms, such as extreme agitation, bizarre behaviors, hallucinations, and delusions. They are not effective in treating *passive* symptoms, including social withdrawal, emotional unresponsiveness, and lack of interest in pleasurable activities. In fact, drug treatments may even exacerbate passive psychotic symptoms, because some of the negative side effects of antipsychotic drugs (sluggishness, lethargy) are similar to these symptoms (Diamond, 1985). Partly as a result of this problem, antipsychotic drugs are generally used together with psychotherapies aimed at improving both the patient's social interactions and aspects of his or her family environment that may encourage relapse.

To reduce the risk of relapse, antipsychotic drugs must be taken even during the residual phase of schizophrenia, when psychotic symptoms lessen. The drugs' negative side effects, therefore, are extremely important, for an antipsychotic drug maintenance program can continue for years. The side effect of chronic apathy and lack of interest in life can become psychologically numbing. As one patient described it:

> On Thorazine everything's a bore. Not a bore, exactly. Boredom implies impatience. You can read comic books and *Reader's Digest* forever. You can tolerate talking to jerks forever. Babble, babble, babble. The weather is dull, the flowers are dull, nothing's very impressive. Musak, Bach, Beatles, Lolly and the Yum-Yums, Rolling Stones. It doesn't make any difference. . . . What the drug is supposed to do is keep away hallucinations. What I think it does is just fog up your mind so badly you don't notice the hallucinations or much else. (Vonnegut, 1975, pp. 196–197)

Antipsychotic drugs can also have negative physical side effects. Often they produce what is known as pseudoparkinsonism, or a cluster of symptoms similar to those of Parkinson's disease. These symptoms, which include uncontrollable hand tremors, stiffened muscles, a shuffling gait, and drooling, may continue for up to a year after drug therapy is stopped. Some patients also experience dizziness, fainting, nausea, diarrhea, blurred vision, heightened sensitivity to sunlight, and other physical ailments. More serious still is an often irreversible condition called **tardive dyskinesia,** which develops in some patients who take the drugs for prolonged periods or in high doses. Symptoms include grotesque movements of the face—grimaces, lip smacking, cheek puffing, and protrusions of the tongue. Some victims, acutely embarrassed by these uncontrollable behaviors, avoid all contact with other people, becoming social isolates (Widroe and Heisler, 1976). Tardive dyskinesia occurs in at least 10 to 20 percent of patients taking antipsychotic drugs and at least 40 percent of elderly patients who have taken these drugs for years (Task force on tardive dyskinesia, 1980).

Not surprisingly, when schizophrenics leave a hospital setting, they often stop taking a prescribed antipsychotic to avoid the negative side effects. But unfortunately, they still need the drug to help prevent a relapse. This makes it especially important to find ways of reducing the unwanted side effects that antipsychotic drugs can have. Doctors try to do so by using the lowest possible dose for controlling the psychotic symptoms. They also carefully monitor the patient's reactions to the medication and may try different antipsychotic drugs to find one that is less aversive to the particular person.

A relatively new antipsychotic drug, called Clozaril, is unusual in that it does not cause the involuntary movements that other antipsychotics can cause. It has also been very effective in treating cases of schizophrenia that were previously resistant to drug treatments (Bablenis et al., 1989). It can, however, be highly toxic in overdose, so its use is restricted (Benecke et al., 1988). Clozaril probably has fewer side effects than other antipsychotic drugs because it works more selectively in the brain. (Remember from Chapter 16 that schizophrenia seems to be caused partly by overactivity of the neurotransmitter dopamine.) Whereas other antipsychotics block dopamine receptors in *several* parts of the brain (in the limbic system where it blocks bizarre thoughts and emotions and in the basal ganglia of the forebrain where it interferes with normal body movements), Clozaril works more specifically on the limbic system alone (Baldessarini, 1985; Weintraub and Evans, 1989). Scientists are hopeful that other, less toxic antipsychotics with this same selectivity will soon be developed.

EVALUATING THE EFFECTIVENESS OF TREATMENTS

Throughout this chapter we have mentioned studies suggesting that various forms of treatment are effective. But are some treatments more helpful than others for certain kinds of psychological disorders? Do some produce faster or more long-lasting results? And what about the *overall* effectiveness of available treatments? Can more improvement be expected from undergoing psychotherapy or taking a psychoactive drug than would occur with just the passage of time?

These are more difficult questions to answer than you might think. Many different studies have been conducted to evaluate the effectiveness of treatments for psychological disorders, and often these studies have had conflicting results. To summarize the results of a large number of studies and draw an overall conclusion, researchers often turn to meta-analyses, which was discussed in Chapter 2. Using meta-analysis, one group of researchers found that the average person who undergoes psychotherapy is better off than a full 80 percent of those who remain untreated (Smith and Glass, 1977; Smith et al., 1981). Many other meta-analyses have likewise shown that treatment for a psychological disorder brings about significantly more improvement than just letting "time" do the healing.

In recent years researchers have broadened their efforts to evaluate the effectiveness of treatments for

Antipsychotic drugs, because they are so powerful, must be monitored especially carefully through blood tests and other techniques for confirming that the dosage is appropriate.

psychological disorders. They want to know not just whether treatment is better than no treatment at all, but also which particular treatments are best for which disorders (Goldfried et al., 1990). This they do mainly by conducting studies in which clients with a certain disorder are randomly assigned to different forms of treatment or to a no-treatment control group. One such study, conducted by the National Institute of Mental Health (NIMH), investigated the effectiveness of three different types of treatment for depression: Beck's cognitive therapy, a contemporary psychodynamic treatment focusing on current problems and interpersonal relationships, and treatment with a tricyclic antidepressant drug (imipramine)

(Elkin et al., 1989; Imber et al., 1990). It found that, after sixteen weeks, there were no significant differences in effectiveness among the three forms of treatment. There was some evidence that the interpersonal therapy and the drug therapy were more effective than a control condition in which clients were treated with a placebo drug. This was not the case, however, when the researchers evaluated the relative effectiveness of the three treatments for people whose depression was relatively severe. In the case of moderately severe depression, the drug treatment seemed to work faster and was more effective than either of the two psychotherapies.

This is not to say that psychotherapy should be abandoned for moderately severe cases of depression in favor of an antidepressant drug. For one thing, more information is needed on the long-term effectiveness of drug treatments for depression—whether they protect against further episodes of depression as well as psychotherapies do. Since drugs do not teach people how to cope with stress, it makes sense that depressed patients treated only with drugs might be more vulnerable to future depression (Kupfer and Frank, 1987; Simons et al., 1986). In addition, the drug treatment group in the NIMH study was not completely without psychological intervention. The doctors who administered the antidepressant had a warm, sympathetic relationship with the patients. They gave them attention, encouragement, and emotional support, which could well have played some role in relieving their depressive symptoms. For these reasons, few clinicians advocate using antidepressant drugs alone (Bender, 1990). Most feel that drug treatment *combined* with psychotherapy is the most promising approach for both relieving current depression and preventing depressive relapses (Kupfer et al., 1989).

The final verdict on the relative effectiveness of drug treatments and psychotherapies is by no means in. More research needs to be done before we have all the answers, not only regarding depression, but regarding other disorders as well. Many such studies are now underway or in the planning stages (Sargent, 1990). Moreover, once we know which treatment or combination of treatments is most effective for which disorders, we still need to learn *how* therapeutic change occurs. This knowledge can help clinicians make their approaches to treatment even more effective than they are now (Bender, 1990).

IN DEPTH

Treating Suicidal People

Dear Jim:

I've just emptied 40 capsules and put the powder in a glass of water. I'm about to take it. I'm scared and I want to talk to someone but I just don't have anybody to talk to. I feel like I'm completely alone and nobody cares. I know our breakup was my fault, but it hurts so bad. Nothing I do seems to turn out right, but nothing. My whole life has fallen apart.

I've thought about all of the trite phrases about how it will get brighter tomorrow and how suicide is copping out and really isn't a solution, and maybe it isn't, but I hurt so bad. I just want it to stop. I feel like my back is up against the wall and there is no other way out.

Dear Daddy:

Please don't grieve for me or feel that you did something wrong, you didn't. I'll leave this life loving you and remembering the world's greatest father.

I'm sorry to cause you more heartache, but the reason I can't live anymore is because I'm afraid. Afraid of facing my life alone without love. No one ever knew how alone I am. No one ever stood by me when I needed help. No one brushed away the tears. I cried for "help" and no one heard.

These suicide notes left by college students tell of the deep despair and anguish that can prompt people to take their own lives. You have probably read that suicide is on the rise among young people. Among Americans ages 15 to 19 its incidence has increased three- to fourfold (several thousand Americans in this age group kill themselves every year) (Himmelhoch, 1987). On American college campuses yearly over 10,000 students attempt suicide, and many of them succeed (National Center for Health Statistics, 1988). What's more, official statistics on suicide probably greatly underestimate it, for many people officially killed by "accidents" are in fact suicide victims. In one study, nearly a third of over 900 college students surveyed said they had at least thought about committing suicide (Westefeld and Furr, 1987).

Why do people sometimes conclude that death is preferable to life? And how can we help such people get through this crisis without acting on their suicidal thoughts? Answers to these questions are so important that we will explore them in depth.

THE INITIAL STUDIES

The earliest studies into the causes of suicide searched for social-psychological factors that correlate with it. In the late nineteenth century the French sociologist Émile Durkheim conducted extensive research of this type (Durkheim, 1897). He found, among other things, that Protestants committed suicide three times more often than Catholics and Catholics more often than Jews. Single people killed themselves more often than married people, who in turn had a higher suicide rate than married people with children. Durkheim wondered what could cause these patterns. He hypothesized that suicide is encouraged when a person has few social ties, or only very weak ones. Jews, Durkheim reasoned, are a more closely knit religious group than Catholics, and Catholics a more closely knit group than Protestants. Similarly, married people, especially those with children, have more social ties than those who are single. In short, the more socially isolated a person is, the greater that person's vulnerability to suicide. Modern research lends support to this view. Being single, widowed, divorced, or separated, living alone, and lacking other people for emotional support all place a person at a higher than average risk of suicide (Hawton, 1987). A sense of social isolation is clearly expressed in both the suicide notes presented at the beginning of this "In Depth."

Durkheim's research also revealed that the suicide rate increases during times of rapid economic change. He hypothesized that sudden, dramatic disruptions in people's lives are very disorienting and can make vulnerable people more prone to suicide. Contemporary research also supports this aspect of Durkheim's theory. People who suffer sudden reversals in health or economic status have a higher than average incidence of suicide (Brown and Sheran, 1972; Whitlock, 1986; Hawton, 1987).

Another factor that increases a person's risk of suicide is an interpersonal loss of some kind, such as the death of a loved one or the breakup of a marriage (Bunch, 1972). Breaking up with a girlfriend or boyfriend is a common precipitating factor among high school and college students (Westefeld and Furr, 1989). Sigmund Freud proposed a theory of suicide that involves interpersonal losses. He argued that when people lose a person whom they both love and hate, and some of whose traits they have unconsciously incorporated into themselves, they may direct repressed hostility toward that person inward, sometimes to the point of self-destruction. It is hard to prove or disprove this view of suicide. One pioneering analysis of suicide notes revealed that people who kill themselves don't usually express outright hostility either toward a loved one or toward themselves (Tuckman et al., 1959). This fact alone does not discredit Freud's theory, however, for if anger and hostility are repressed they are not apt to be stated directly in a consciously written note. They might, however, be indirectly stated. For example, the suicide letter to "Daddy" at the start of this section implies a deep and poignant disappointment in the father, who apparently, like others, was not there when his daughter needed him. This deep disappointment is ambivalently mixed with expressions of love.

In more modern times E. Schneidman (1969) has proposed that people who kill themselves see it as a release from psychological anguish they can no longer endure. (The suicide letter to "Jim" expresses such anguish well.) Consistent with this view, researchers have found that the anguish of depression is one of the most important factors increasing a person's risk of suicide. About half of all those who kill themselves suffer depression. Especially important is the sense of hopelessness that is often part of depression. There is a stronger correlation between suicidal wishes and measures of hopelessness than between suicidal wishes and measures of any other symptom of depression (Beck, 1967). Hopelessness is also a better predictor of who will ultimately commit suicide than are either overall level of depression or the degree to which a person thinks about suicide (Beck et al., 1985). Interestingly, a longitudinal study of people with severe depression or bipolar disorder suggests that anxiety-related symptoms, such as excessive worrying, severe insomnia, and lack of concentration, may be even more predictive of suicide than hopelessness and suicidal wishes (Fawcett et al., 1990).

Finally, in Shneidman's view, people who kill themselves are often those who have so narrowed

In the novel and movie *Ordinary People,* a teenager becomes suicidal after a boating accident in which his brother died. During psychotherapy, he gradually acknowledges and overcomes the intense guilt he felt at having survived.

their perceived range of solutions to problems that they see "no other way out." (The writer of the "Dear Jim" letter is again a good example.) In support of this view, other researchers have found that many suicide victims do indeed have impaired problem-solving abilities. Often they show inflexibility and "tunnel vision" in coping with challenges and dilemmas (Linehan et al., 1987; Patsiokas et al., 1979; Schotte and Clum, 1987).

Table 17.2 summarizes the social-psychological risk factors for suicide that we have been discussing, and also includes some others (such as having communicated a suicidal wish, having made a previous suicide attempt, or having a psychiatric condition other than depression). These factors are additive: the more of them a person has, the greater the chances that he or she will commit suicide.

These social-psychological risk factors for suicide readily suggest a form of treatment: reducing or eliminating those factors that are capable of being changed. For instance, a therapist might reduce impaired problem-solving ability in a suicidal patient by helping that person overcome "tunnel vision" and imagine solutions other than dying. Shneidman has relied heavily on this tactic in his own clinical practice. He reports that even though suicidal patients may not immediately accept an alternative solution, just making a list of potential ones can open their minds to the possibility of

other options, and so weaken their suicidal leanings (Shneidman, 1987). Aaron Beck has used a similar tactic in his approach to suicide prevention, but takes it one step further. Not only does he get suicidal patients to consider other solutions to their problems, he also encourages them to cognitively rehearse how those other solutions might be carried out (Beck et al., 1979; Rush and Beck, 1978). This helps them to gain confidence that alternative solutions are in fact possible.

Beck also deliberately tries to reduce a suicidal person's sense of hopelessness (expressed in such statements as "Nothing ever goes right for me," "I can't possibly achieve what I want," and "My problems are unsolvable"). This he does by pointing to evidence that contradicts hopelessness—occasions when things *have* gone right, goals *have* been reached, and problems *have* been solved. By helping people see that a totally hopeless view is irrational, death becomes a less desirable option. Deep despair and hopelessness are also frequently treated with antidepressant drugs. If these are ineffective, deeply depressed people who are dangerously suicidal are often given shock treatments (electroconvulsive therapy). The rapid treatment of anxiety symptoms, through the use of antianxiety drugs, may substantially reduce suicide rates among individuals with severe depression or bipolar disorder (Fawcett et al., 1990).

**TABLE 17.2   Risk Factors Associated
with Suicide**

- Social isolation (living alone; single, widowed, divorced; weak ties to relatives and friends)
- Recent interpersonal loss (death of loved one; end of an important relationship)
- Sudden economic downturn (unemployment; bankruptcy)
- Ill health (especially a chronic illness)
- Psychiatric condition (depression; schizophrenia; personality disorder; alcoholism or other drug abuse)
- Sense of hopelessness
- Anxiety-related symptoms (excessive worrying, severe insomnia, panic attacks, lack of concentration)
- Impaired problem solving (tunnel vision; inflexible thinking)
- Previous suicide attempt
- Communication to others of a wish to die
- Family history of suicide or attempted suicide
- Gender (males 3:1)

Finally, having people stay involved with a suicidal patient is another aspect of contemporary treatment, aimed at overcoming the social isolation that can raise the risk of suicide (Himmelhoch, 1987). Clinicians usually schedule frequent therapy sessions, remain accessible to the patient by phone, and may also hospitalize the person so that he or she does not remain alone. If the patient is not hospitalized, it is also common to enlist the help of relatives or friends to monitor the person's psychological state and to "be there" when needed. In this way, the therapist helps to strengthen the patient's social network. There is also evidence that continued contact with a therapist after the crisis is over can help reduce the recurrence of suicidal episodes (Allebock and Allgulander, 1990).

CRITICISMS, ALTERNATIVES, AND FURTHER RESEARCH

Despite the success of these treatments with specific individuals, they do not seem to be reducing the overall suicide rate. In fact, the *overall* rate of suicide has remained much the same for the last forty years. It is still about 12 in every 100,000 despite all our modern treatment efforts. What is wrong then? Why aren't they more effective?

One answer is that many of those who need help most (those who are strongly suicidal and have formulated a lethal plan) are not getting it (Diekstra, 1989). Once a person has decided that suicide is the "only answer," thinking is usually too impaired for him or her to seek treatment. Relatives and friends, moreover, often misread the signs of impending suicide. They do not encourage or insist on treatment until it is too late. When you add to this the fact that in modern society some of the factors that encourage suicide may be increasing (social isolation, disruptive life changes), it does not seem so surprising that the suicide rate stays constant despite effective treatments.

But some psychologists contend that there are other explanations for the stable suicide rate. They say that our current treatments focus mainly on reducing the social-psychological factors that have long been known to be related to suicide. But, these psychologists argue, social-psychological factors alone cannot identify those who will actually commit suicide. Those at high risk according to these criteria do not always kill themselves, and some of those who do kill themselves seemed at relatively low risk. What we need, these critics say, is a better marker of who is truly suicidal.

That marker may turn out to be a biochemical one. Recent research has found that people who die of suicide have significantly reduced levels of the neurotransmitter serotonin in certain parts of their brains compared with people of similar age and background who have died of other causes (Stanley and Stanley, 1990). Moreover, these reduced levels of serotonin are found in suicide victims regardless of whatever other psychiatric diagnosis they might have (depression, schizophrenia, personality disorder, alcoholism, drug abuse). Interestingly, too, serotonin levels fluctuate during the year and are at their lowest during the spring. This is also the time of year when the suicide rate is highest (Brewerton, 1989).

These findings have important implications for treatment (Stanley and Stanley, 1989). They suggest that we should not treat suicidal tendencies as just a symptom of some other disorder (primarily depression). Instead, it may be more accurate to treat it as a separate disorder with a strong biological component, one that can occur simultaneously with a number of other psychiatric conditions. This is not to say we should ignore the social-psychological factors involved in suicide, nor should we deemphasize treating the other disorders that often accompany it. It is simply to say that in thinking of suicide as a separate and distinct problem, we can better develop treatments to prevent it. The psychotherapy part of this treatment can probably remain much as it is, but drug treatment should probably focus on rectifying serotonin depletions specifically (rather than serotonin *and* norepinephrine, as most current antidepressant drugs do).

PATTERNS AND CONCLUSIONS

Therapists are often successful in preventing suicide, and future approaches to treatment may prove even more effective (Lieberman and Eckman, 1981; Patsiokas and Clum, 1985). Suicidal people *can* be helped to see other ways of dealing with their problems. Does this mean we should insist that they receive professional help? Surprisingly, not all clinicians think so, at least not in every case. Thomas Szasz is one who believes that no one should be forced to accept treatment that he or she does not want, even someone who is suicidal. According to Szasz, people have a right to end their own lives if

that is what they truly wish to do (Szasz, 1986).

But most other clinicians disagree strongly with Szasz's position. They argue that suicidal people do not have a right to inflict a lifetime of sorrow on loved ones left behind (Holmes, 1987). They also point out that the suicidal person's ability to think rationally is greatly reduced (Clum, 1987). How can we fail to intervene when thinking is so impaired? Significantly, many formerly suicidal people who have been forced into treatment later say they are glad that others stepped in during the crisis (Mather, 1987). Suicide victims, in other words, are often ambivalent about dying and long for someone to help them (both the letters at the start of this "In Depth" expressed this common view). From this perspective, it is imperative that we know how to identify suicidal people and that we assist them in getting professional help. With over a half million attempted suicides yearly in the United States, you stand a good chance of someday knowing (even being close to) a suicidal person yourself.

SUMMARY

1. **Psychotherapy** is a systematic series of interactions between a person who is trained in alleviating psychological problems and another who is suffering from them. These interactions are structured by both theories and scientific findings as to why such disturbances occur.

2. In Freudian **psychoanalysis,** the goal is to bring unconscious conflicts into consciousness, where they can be worked through and resolved. Various techniques are used to accomplish this aim, among them **free association** and **dream analysis.** Newer psychoanalytic treatments differ from Freudian psychoanalysis in several ways. For instance, the newer approaches are briefer, with the therapist taking a more active role in advising and directing the client.

3. **Humanistic therapies** are a diverse group of treatments that aim at liberating a person's innate tendencies toward self-actualization and growth. Carl Rogers's **client-centered therapy** tries to free people from the unreasonable **conditions of worth** imposed by others. The therapist creates a warm and empathic environment in which the client can come to understand and to value the true self. **Gestalt therapy,**

another humanistic treatment, emphasizes the need to release pent-up emotions and to take responsibility for one's actions.

4. **Behavior** and **cognitive-behavior therapies** involve applying experimentally derived principles of learning to change maladaptive thoughts, feelings, and behaviors. Some of the techniques used (including **systematic desensitization, aversion conditioning, time out,** and **token economies)** are based on principles of classical and operant conditioning. Others (such as **participant modeling** to treat phobias) are based on principles of modeling and observational learning. Still others [including **rational-emotive therapy (RET), self-instructional training,** and Beck's **cognitive therapy]** are based on cognitive learning principles.

5. **Family-systems therapies** treat psychological problems by trying to change maladaptive patterns of interaction within a person's family. Family-systems therapies often involve all the members of a family, not just those who are displaying the unwanted symptoms. Different family therapists take different approaches, including a strategic approach (which fo-

cuses heavily on changing faulty family communications), a behavioral approach, a cognitive restructuring approach, and a psychoanalytic orientation.

6. Family therapy is just one form of treatment in which more than one client may be involved. In recent decades other **group therapies** have become widely used. Among those currently most popular are behavior and cognitive-behavior therapy groups and **self-help groups.**

7. Many contemporary psychotherapists use more than one approach to treating psychological disorders. These therapists are to some extent eclectic, combining different kinds of approaches and methods depending on the particular problems and needs of the client.

8. Biological treatments attempt to alleviate psychological disorders by altering the delicate balance of the brain's neural systems. One contemporary biological treatment is **psychosurgery,** a treatment of last resort. It involves destroying small amounts of brain tissue in very precise locations in order to relieve chronic and severe symptoms. Another biological treatment, **electroconvulsive therapy (ECT),** uses electric shock to induce a brief convulsion similar to an epileptic seizure. For reasons still unknown, this brief convulsion can relieve severe depression.

9. A third category of biological treatment is **drug therapy. Antianxiety drugs** are widely used by people who are having trouble coping with situational stress.

Antidepressant drugs, especially in combination with psychotherapy, are quite effective in combating depression. **Lithium** works well in controlling abnormal mood swings, from mania to depression, without diminishing a person's capacity for normal emotional responses. Finally, **antipsychotic drugs** are widely used in the treatment of schizophrenia.

10. Numerous studies have shown that treatment for a psychological disorder brings about significantly more improvement than just letting "time" do the healing. In recent years researchers have broadened their efforts to evaluate the effectiveness of treatments for psychological disorders by exploring which particular treatments are best for which disorders.

11. Ideas about the causes of a psychological problem can suggest forms of treatment for it. For instance, identification of social-psychological factors that increase the risk of suicide (such as social isolation, impaired problem-solving ability, and a sense of hopelessness) have given rise to therapies that try to reduce these factors. Examples are strengthening a person's social network to overcome social isolation, pointing out alternative solutions to improve problem solving, and demonstrating the irrationality of negative thinking to combat hopelessness. These approaches to treatment may be made even more effective if they are combined with drugs that counteract the reduced levels of serotonin that suicide victims have been found to have.

SUGGESTED READINGS

Beck, A. T., and Emery, G. (1985). *Anxiety disorders and phobias: A cognitive perspective.* New York: Basic Books. The authors discuss how the principles of cognitive therapy may be successfully applied to anxiety disorders such as panic disorder, agoraphobia, social anxiety, and phobias. They also present a broad overview of the components of cognitive therapy.

Bender, K. J. (1990). *Psychiatric medications.* Newbury Park, CA: Sage. This book provides information on the use of medication for psychological problems. It describes when medications are indicated, the mechanisms of drug actions, side effects, dosage levels, and generic and brand names.

Hyman, J. W. (1990). *The light book: How natural and artificial light affect our health, mood and behavior.* New York: Tarcher/St. Martin's. The author discusses the effects of light on emotions and behavior. Those suffering from seasonal affective disorder will find suggestions for easing its impact.

Sacks, O. (1987). *Awakenings.* New York: HarperCollins. Dr. Oliver Sacks describes his work with patients suffering from a severe neurological disorder. With the use of the drug L-Dopa, these patients, previously considered hopeless cases, experienced radical, although temporary, changes.

Steketee, G., and White, K. (1990). Oakland, CA: New Harbinger Publications, *When once is not enough.* People who have obsessive compulsive disorder or just an interest in the topic will find this detailed description of current treatment both informative and useful. It can be used as a self-help guide or in conjunction with therapy.

Yalom, I. D. (1989). *Love's executioner, and other tales of psychotherapy.* New York: Basic Books. Includes ten fascinating vignettes, each focusing on therapy with a different client. Readers will discover what therapy is like and how it affects the therapist as well as the client.

CHAPTER 18

ATTITUDES AND SOCIAL PERCEPTION

A riot has broken out in a maximum-security prison. Inmates have gained control of one of the cell blocks and have gone on a rampage of destruction to protest overcrowded conditions. How will the authorities react? Will they quell the rebellion brutally—without concern for how many inmates are injured? Or will they take a more restrained approach? To answer these questions, you might want to know more about the personalities of the prison guards and the warden. Are they harsh and callous, punitive and quick to anger, or are they more humane, even tempered, and rational? As logical as it seems to seek this information before predicting how the incident will end, social psychological research has taught us that such differences may not matter at all. Indeed, in some situations a person's dispositions and behaviors are quite unrelated (Ross and Nisbett, 1991). What can matter far more than our personal qualities are the social circumstances in which we may find ourselves.

This central tenet of social psychology was dramatically illustrated in a classic study of the effects of prison life on people's behavior. Philip Zimbardo and his colleagues created a mock prison in the basement of a university building during summer session (1972, 1973). Student volunteers were given extensive personality tests, and only those judged to be mature and emotionally stable were invited to participate. Half were randomly assigned the role of prisoner, and half the role of guard. Then the study began. Only six days later, however, Zimbardo was forced to call off the study because the students' behavior had become too frighteningly real. Those acting as guards were using their power harshly and arbitrarily. Those acting as prisoners had either been reduced to servile robots or had developed symptoms of severe anxiety. Apparently, these perfectly normal college students, assigned to their roles by the flip of a coin, had become the people their social circumstances told them they ought to be.

This is the fascinating insight of social psychology. How people think, feel, and act is not simply the result of their personalities and predispositions. Their behavior is also shaped to a very large degree by the social situations in which they find themselves. What others around us are doing, thinking, and feeling, and how they structure the environment, all have a marked impact on our thoughts, emotions, and behaviors. Social psychologists investigate these powerful situational forces. They seek to understand how we all are influenced by the presence and actions of others, either actual, imagined, or implied (Allport, 1985).

Many sexually active teenagers don't use condoms, even though they are aware that they are risking unwanted pregnancies and sexually transmitted diseases. One reason for this seemingly reckless behavior is that emotional factors—such as embarrassment and shyness—can overwhelm the cognitive components of their attitude toward condoms.

The subject of social psychology is so broad that we will devote two chapters to it. This chapter explores how people and the social environments they create often shape our innermost thoughts and feelings. We discuss social influences on our attitudes, the impressions we form of others, our ideas about why others act in the ways they do, and how we come to love or hate other people. Then, in Chapter 19, we examine how social forces influence behavior. Here we look at pressures to conform to group norms, to obey those in authority, to adhere to social roles, and to follow the lead of others in a variety of circumstances. As you will see repeatedly in both these chapters, human thoughts, feelings, and actions do not originate solely from within. They are also products of the social situations in which we find ourselves.

ATTITUDES

People have attitudes toward just about everyone and everything, from Madonna to Queen Elizabeth, from chocolate ice cream to nuclear reactors. An **attitude** is a disposition to respond favorably or unfavorably toward some person, thing, event, place, idea, or situation (often called an **attitude object**) (Chaiken and Stangor, 1987; Zanna and Rempel, 1988). Attitudes, in other words, are the thoughts and feelings that encourage us to act as if we like or dislike something. Sometimes people dismiss attitudes as unimportant by saying: "That's just your opinion." But attitudes can be a matter of life or death (Flora et al., 1989). Your attitudes toward diet and exercise, drinking and smoking, using seatbelts, and having safe sex affect how long and how well you are apt to live.

COGNITIONS, FEELINGS, AND BEHAVIORS

Psychologists think of attitudes as having three components: what you think or believe about something (the cognitive component), how you feel about it (the emotional component), and how you act toward it (the behavioral component). Sometimes these three components are consistent with each other. For instance, if people think that the death penalty serves as a deterrent to murder (the cognitive component), and they get angry when they hear that a murderer has been granted parole (the emotional component), they are likely to vote for a political candidate who supports capital punishment (the behavioral component).

The three components of an attitude are not *always* consistent, however (Breckler, 1983, 1984). For example, although more than 90 percent of Americans know that smoking causes lung cancer and heart disease (the cognitive component), about 30 percent of Americans still smoke (the behavioral component) (Shopland and Brown, 1987). Some of them even smoke despite negative feelings toward cigarette use (the emotional component). Similarly, although most teenagers believe that contraceptives can guard against unwanted pregnancy, roughly a third of American teenagers who are sexually active do not use contraceptives (Flora et al., 1989). And these are not isolated examples. The correlation between the cognitive and emotional components of an attitude and a person's behavior is surprisingly weak. Knowing what someone thinks and feels about an issue does not enable one to predict very accurately how that person will act (Wicker, 1969). An important question is why this happens: Why are people's thoughts and feelings sometimes at odds with their behaviors? Why, if you *know* something is dangerous, do you sometimes do it anyway? Why do you sometimes even do things that you *dislike* doing?

One reason is that although attitudes can exert a strong influence on behavior, so can many other powerful forces (Cooper and Croyle, 1984; Fishbein and Ajzen, 1975). These forces include social norms and values as well as specific circumstances that pressure people to act in particular ways. Consider the pressures encouraging teenagers *not* to use contraceptives. Acquiring contraceptives can be embarrassing for an adolescent, and there is always the fear that parents will find out. Teenage girls also worry that having contraceptives may make them seem promiscuous to boys. Boys, for their part, are often concerned that, in fumbling for a condom, they will show their sexual inexperience. In addition, both sexes may be too embarrassed to discuss contraception with each other. The result of these converging pressures is a good deal of unprotected sex and unwanted pregnancies.

Notice how, in the case of using contraceptives, different sets of beliefs and feelings are related to a single behavior. A girl may have positive feelings about avoiding pregnancy but negative ones about looking promiscuous. A boy may be fearful of fathering a child but may very much want to look sexually experienced. Thus, behavior that *seems* inconsistent with a person's beliefs and feelings may actually be more consistent than it appears at first glance, once you know the full range of a person's opinions. To increase the accuracy with which behavior can be predicted from a person's opinions, it is best to solicit beliefs and feelings that are as *specifically* relevant as

possible to the behavior of interest (Ajzen and Fishbein, 1980). For instance, to predict contraceptive use among teenagers, you should not ask "Do you favor contraception?" (too general), but rather, "Do you favor using contraceptives despite the inconvenience and embarrassment it may cause you and despite the potential effects on how other people view you?"

To further increase the accuracy with which beliefs and feelings can predict behavior, it is best to consider opinions that are clearly and strongly held. Weak and vague opinions are seldom very good predictors of how you will decide to act in a given situation. In contrast, when you know exactly how you think and feel about something, and when those thoughts and feelings are very prominent in your mind, you are very apt to act in ways consistent with your views (Fazio, 1990).

This was suggested in a study in which students at the University of Minnesota were questioned about their beliefs and feelings toward affirmative-action employment policies (Snyder and Swann, 1976). Two weeks later the students were invited to serve as jurors on a sex-discrimination case. Only those who were first asked to take a few minutes to think about their views on affirmative action delivered verdicts that were consistent with the opinions they had expressed before. Apparently, the reminder made those opinions more prominent and so encouraged verdicts that aligned with them.

Social psychologists have tried to identify real-life factors that help to make beliefs and feelings clearer and stronger, and so more apt to influence behavior. One of these factors is the personal relevance of the issue (Sivacek and Crano, 1982). Consider a study in which college students read a statement that advocated a new policy at their campus (either a parking fee or a mandatory senior exam) (Leippe and Elkin, 1987). Some were told that the policy might be enacted the following year (high personal relevance), while others were told that any decision would not be implemented for another six years (low personal relevance). The students were then asked to express their thoughts and feelings about the policy, after which they were given time to think it over more fully. Those for whom the policy had personal relevance thought more about the issue than the other students did, which probably helped to make their opinions clearer, stronger, and more salient. Later they were over three times more likely to *act* on those opinions by writing to the school administration and voicing their views.

Tobacco companies are experts at persuasion, but as information about the dangers of smoking accumulates, counterpersuasion —both formal and informal—has become more prevalent.

Knowledge about an issue is another factor that seems to help promote behaviors consistent with beliefs and feelings. In one study, for example, college students who were the most knowledgeable about conservation were also the most likely to act on their stated feelings toward it when given the chance to sign a pro-conservation petition and to participate in a recycling project (Kallgren and Wood, 1986). Knowledgeability probably has its effects partly by enhancing the clarity and strength of beliefs and feelings, just as personal relevance does. The more knowledgeable you are about a topic, the clearer your opinions tend to be, and also the stronger your feelings pro or con. This makes you all the more likely to act in ways that match your views. Being informed about an issue is even more apt to influence behavior when knowledge is gained from firsthand experience (Fazio and Zanna, 1981). For instance, beliefs and feelings about smoking are better predictors of whether or not a certain teenager will start to smoke if that teenager has had a great deal of firsthand experience with smokers (Sherman et al., 1982).

EXPLAINING ATTITUDE CHANGE

Never a day goes by that someone doesn't try to persuade you of something. Every year American advertisers spend more than $50 billion to change consumers' attitudes. Political candidates spend another half a billion dollars yearly to convince us to vote for them (McGuire, 1985). In addition, there are countless public interest efforts at persuasion. The Surgeon General warns us that smoking is hazardous to our health; environmental groups exhort us to recycle cans and bottles; the National Safety Council urges us to buckle up our seatbelts. Even everyday conversations with people we encounter are filled with attempts to change attitudes. All together, the average adult is exposed to as many as 1,500 persuasive messages a day (Schultz, 1982). No wonder social psychologists have devoted so much time to studying this topic.

Psychologists are interested in both the conditions under which people are persuaded to change their attitudes and the conditions under which they resist attitude change. Two perspectives have shed light on these important issues: the persuasive communications approach and the cognitive consistency view.

PERSUASIVE COMMUNICATIONS AND ATTITUDE CHANGE

The **persuasive communications** approach to attitude change began during World War II, when the War Department asked psychologist Carl Hovland

During the 1988 presidential campaign, Republican candidate George Bush repeatedly accused his Democratic opponent, Michael Dukakis, of being unpatriotic and "soft" on national security because he proposed cuts in defense spending. Dukakis's aides arranged for him to be photographed in an Army tank in order to demonstrate his "toughness." Dukakis would have been better advised to counter Bush's attack directly rather than symbolically.

and his colleagues to help design persuasive messages to be used in the training and morale boosting of troops. After the war, Hovland continued his work at Yale University (Hovland et al., 1949, 1957). He and his colleagues tried to identify the characteristics of a persuasive message—one that will get people to attend to, comprehend, be swayed by, remember, and act on the basis of the message.

The Source of the Message Some of these characteristics have to do with the source of the message. For instance, a message is often more persuasive when it comes from an expert source—that is, from someone who knows a lot about the topic (Hass, 1981; Kelman and Hovland, 1953). This is especially true when the listener is not very involved in the issue, and so may be willing to accept the expert's opinion without giving it much thought (Chaiken, 1980).

A message is also more persuasive when it comes from someone who seems honest and sincere (McGuire, 1985). Such trustworthiness is partly inspired by the absence of ulterior motives (McGinnies and Ward, 1980). This is why TV commercials sometimes use the "hidden camera" technique. If a shopper who is unaware that she is being filmed praises a detergent's cleaning power, viewers are more likely to believe what she says.

Body language also plays a part in making words seem honest and persuasive. When someone looks you right in the eye, you are more likely to believe that the person has nothing to hide. This is why many politicians prefer to use a teleprompter mounted right on the camera: it allows them to avoid averting their eyes in order to read the speech. Averting the eyes is one body cue that can suggest deception. Another is constantly smiling and nodding the head, or making unnecessary mouth movements, such as nervously biting the lips (Feldman et al., 1978; Kraut, 1978). Hand gestures can suggest deception too. People who frequently finger their hair or touch their faces when trying to persuade are often suspected of being dishonest (Knapp et al., 1974; McClintock and Hunt, 1975).

The Content of the Message It is not only who talks and how they talk that can make a message persuasive, but also what is conveyed. For instance, do you think it is a good idea to ignore an opponent's arguments when trying to present your own view, as if to say that the opponent's charges are not worth your time and attention? Michael Dukakis tried to do this in the 1988 presidential campaign. He ignored George Bush's TV ads implying that he was soft on crime, weak on environmental issues, and less patriotic than Bush. Dukakis should have taken a lesson from social psychologists. Failure to respond to Bush's charges was perceived as weakness, even by those who considered the charges false. It is usually wiser to acknowledge and counter an opponent's claims directly. This is especially true if the opponent's views are well known or controversial (Hass and Linder, 1972). It is even more important to answer the opposition when listeners are well educated and knowledgeable about the topic and when they are initially against your position (Hovland et al., 1949). Advertisers are increasingly recognizing this fact. Whereas twenty years ago they carefully avoided mentioning competing products, today many of them address the competition head-on (McGuire, 1985).

What about fear appeals that try to change our beliefs and behaviors, the kinds of appeals often used to convince us not to do dangerous or unhealthy things (such as failing to use seatbelts, having unsafe sex, smoking, drinking and driving, or abusing drugs). Do you think that fear appeals would be persuasive? Many people do, which is why the results of a classic experiment are surprising. In this study, researchers showed people one of three presentations on oral hygiene. The low-fear appeal simply stated that failure to brush can lead to tooth decay and gum disease; the mild-fear appeal illustrated these conditions with pictures of mild infection and decay; and the high-fear appeal showed hideous color slides of rotting teeth and diseased gums, which, the message warned, could ultimately lead to kidney damage, paralysis, and blindness. Contrary to what the researchers expected, the appeal that aroused the *most* fear was the *least* effective in changing behavior.

Why wasn't the high-fear appeal more effective? One reason is that fear promotes attitude change, but only up to a point. After that point, fear interferes with attention and learning. In one study, for instance, people who were highly anxious about getting cancer were much poorer at attending to an article that explained how regular check-ups can help detect cancer in its early, often curable stages (Jepson and Chaiken, 1986). Overall, they were also less persuaded by the article's message. Apparently, when people are very frightened about a subject, they either "turn off" to messages about it in order to reduce the threat, or they become so nervous when confronted with the message that they cannot pay attention very well.

Another reason why fear appeals can sometimes be ineffective is that fear alone may not be enough to change behavior. People need concrete, personalized information about what the risks are. The more personal the appeal, the more likely people are to be persuaded (Weinstein, 1989). Thus, a description of one man's struggle with lung cancer will probably be more persuasive about the dangers of smoking than will gory full-color pictures of diseased lungs, or statistics about the large number of deaths from lung cancer each year. In addition, people need to know specific steps that can be taken to avoid the feared outcome, and they must believe that they are capable of taking those steps themselves (Leventhal and Nerenz, 1983; Rogers and Mewborn, 1976). This point was illustrated by a study of efforts to get eighth graders to stop smoking (Evans, 1980). Messages about the dangers of smoking were seldom enough to change behavior. The teenagers also needed specific information on how to resist peer pressure to smoke, because peer pressure plays a critical role in maintaining the behavior.

New Directions in Persuasive Communications Research Over decades, researchers collected a great quantity of information about the characteristics of persuasive appeals that tend to promote attitude change. But the problem was that none of these characteristics was influential all of the time. Sometimes a certain trait, such as an expert source, could prompt people to change their opinions, but other times it had very little effect, or no effect at all. There were also times when persuasive appeals seemed to foster an enduring attitude change, and other times when the attitude change was short-lived and superficial. What was needed was an overall theory explaining why such differences occurred.

Richard Petty and John Cacioppo (1986) have been leaders in this effort. They argue that there are two routes through which persuasive communications can affect attitude change. One is the *route of systematic analysis*. It involves attending to central aspects of the message (such as the accuracy of the information and the logic of the arguments), thinking about them carefully, weighing their merits, and so forth, in order to come to a sound conclusion. Persuasion that occurs through systematic analysis tends to be very strong and enduring.

But people do not always analyze carefully when assessing persuasive appeals. Sometimes they just don't care about the issue enough to waste much time and effort on it. Other times, they aren't knowledgeable enough about the subject to evaluate the mes-

Through his optimistic, sincere manner and his reliance on slogans and anecdotes, President Ronald Reagan indirectly encouraged Americans to rely on the heuristic route to forming opinions about his administration's policies.

sage's content well. Still other times, there is so much information to consider that it seems overwhelming. In such cases people tend to use the *heuristic route* to persuasion. Heuristics, as you know from Chapter 8, are short-cut, rule-of-thumb strategies for processing information. Just as we have heuristics for making other kinds of judgments, we have them for judging the worth of persuasive appeals. When you say to yourself, "That person's an expert, so he's apt to be right" or "Everyone else here agrees with that viewpoint (listen to the applause), so it's probably valid," you are using heuristics to come to a conclusion about an attempt at persuasion. Such heuristics focus on peripheral cues in the message, cues that can be assimilated very easily and quickly. Not surprisingly, when persuasion occurs through the heuristic route, it is often rather weak and changeable.

This two-route theory of persuasion helps to explain some interesting findings. For example, when people are not motivated to analyze a message systematically, even a poorly argued appeal can often persuade them, as long as there are peripheral cues that encourage attitude change (Zimbardo and Leippe, 1991). This is why campaign strategists spend so much time working on the peripheral cues that surround their candidates' messages. They are hop-

ing that the audience will use the heuristic route and be influenced by peripheral factors such as physical attractiveness or an upbeat tone. And often, this is exactly what does happen. For instance, in the ten presidential elections from 1948 to 1984, the candidate with the most optimistic tone won in all but one of the races (Zullow et al., 1988). Perhaps we live in an era when the complexity of issues makes systematic analysis of them too overwhelming for many voters. Or perhaps modern campaign strategists give us little more than peripheral cues to consider. In any case, persuasion through the heuristic route is widespread in our society. This is not to say that heuristics cannot be valuable rule-of-thumb tools. But too much reliance on them can sometimes lead to flawed judgments.

COGNITIVE CONSISTENCY AND ATTITUDE CHANGE

Another major approach to attitude change involves the concept of **cognitive consistency**—the tendency of people to keep their various cognitions in relative agreement with one another. Several cognitive consistency theories of attitude change have been proposed, each with distinctive features. All, however, are based on the belief that perceived *in*consistency among our cognitions makes us feel uncomfortable and motivates us to reduce this state of tension.

The Theory of Cognitive Dissonance   One of the most influential cognitive consistency perspectives is cognitive dissonance theory, proposed more than thirty years ago by Leon Festinger (1957). **Cognitive dissonance** is the unpleasant state of tension that develops when people are aware of holding two inconsistent thoughts simultaneously. Cognitive dissonance might arise if you tell yourself you want to save money, but then go out and spend $50 on compact disks; if you claim to be concerned about the environment but don't make any efforts to recycle anything; or if you say you are in love but often think of other people when you are with the person you claim to love. Cognitive dissonance most often occurs when the cognitive component of an attitude clashes with behavior. According to Festinger, this produces a state of extreme discomfort. You can reduce the dissonance and relieve the tension in one of two main ways: either change your behavior, or change your beliefs.

Take the case of a man who is president of a company that manufactures cigarettes. He will probably experience dissonance if he believes himself to be a moral person and also believes that smoking causes heart disease and cancer. His two inconsistent cognitions are: "I am a kind, well-intentioned person, yet by manufacturing cigarettes I am contributing to the premature deaths of thousands of people." To reduce this dissonance, the man is not likely to convince himself that he is uncaring and ruthless, nor is he likely to give up his job. Instead, he will probably modify his cognitions concerning the dangers of cigarettes or the effects of his producing them. He could minimize the link between smoking and fatal illness ("Most of those studies were done when cigarettes had more tar and nicotine than they do now"). Or he could add positive cognitions to counterbalance his negative ones ("Cigarettes may create health problems, but they also reduce stress and makes life more enjoyable"). Or he could downplay the importance of the dissonance-arousing behavior ("If smokers didn't buy my cigarettes, they'd just buy someone else's").

Researchers have created cognitive dissonance in the laboratory by getting people to act in ways that are inconsistent with one of their opinions. Suppose one person is paid a great deal of money to say something he or she does not believe, while another person is paid very little to do so. Which one would you expect to experience cognitive dissonance, and what would be the result? See if your answers agree with the findings in the following classic experiment (Festinger and Carlsmith, 1959).

Subjects were asked to perform an exceedingly boring task: either turning the pegs in a pegboard a quarter turn each and then repeating the procedure many times, or lining up spools in a tray, dumping them out, and lining them up again and again. When each subject finally finished, the experimenter confided that he was actually investigating the effects of preconceptions on performance. Would the subject help out by telling the next subject that the study had been fun and exciting? The researcher offered some of the subjects $1 and others $20 to tell this lie. (A third group, the control group, merely did the task and were not asked to do any lying.) All of the experimental subjects complied with the researcher's request. Then each subject was asked to evaluate the experimental task. Those who had been paid $20 for telling the lie (and those who had not had to lie at all) rated the job as boring—which by objective standards it certainly was. But those who had been paid only $1 to tell the same lie disagreed. They said that the experimental task had in fact been fairly enjoyable!

Why did the $1 subjects rate an intrinsically boring task quite favorably? According to dissonance theory, saying something you do not believe causes psychological discomfort *unless* you have an adequate justification, such as a large fee—and $20 was a substantial sum in 1959. Thus, unlike the subjects offered $20, those offered only $1 had insufficient means to justify the lie to themselves. As a result, they experienced dissonance and responded by convincing themselves that the task had not been so boring after all.

These results have practical implications. They suggest that the *greater* the reward for engaging in a disliked behavior, the *less* the likelihood that attitudes will change to justify that behavior. For instance, when a girl who hates schoolwork is offered $10 for a good report card, she may decide that she is working for the money and continue to dislike studying. If she is offered only $1, however, she may experience cognitive dissonance and resolve it by convincing herself that studying isn't really so bad. The same logic can be applied to the use of punishment. If you

Workers in a factory that discharges its waste into a nearby river may experience cognitive dissonance: they are opposed to water pollution, yet they work for a company that causes it. Some may find the conflict unbearable and quit their jobs, while others may resolve it by assigning the blame to the company's management.

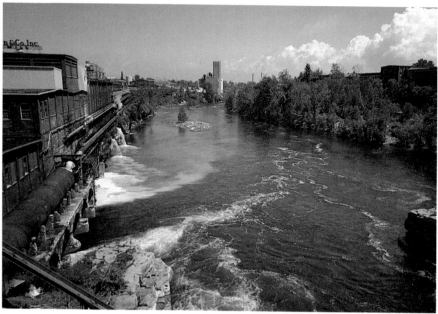

want to convince a preschooler not to play with the stereo set, threatening severe punishment is probably the wrong approach. It may temporarily reduce the unwanted behavior out of fear of the consequences, but it probably will not produce lasting attitude change. A better tactic is to use only a mild threat. Then the child will have less external justification for avoiding the stereo and so be more apt to decide that playing with it is not that much fun after all. The validity of this approach has been demonstrated in several experiments (Carlsmith, 1963; Freedman, 1965). For instance, preschoolers who are told that they will be severely punished for playing with a very attractive toy are more likely to play with that toy when left alone with it later than are children who are threatened with only mild punishment for defiance.

But despite evidence supporting the theory of cognitive dissonance, it has been criticized (Chapanis and Chapanis, 1964; Rosenberg, 1965). Some have argued that the findings can be explained in other ways. One alternative explanation is *impression-man-agement theory* (Baumeister, 1982). It holds that people in cognitive dissonance studies change their attitudes or behavior not because inconsistency makes them feel uncomfortable, but simply because they want to *appear* consistent so as to make a good impression on the experimenter. For example, sub-jects in the boring-task experiment might have said the task was interesting because they didn't want the experimenter to think they would lie for only a dollar. Another alternative explanation is *self-affirmation the-ory* (Steele, 1988). It holds that those who convinced themselves the boring task was really fun were trying to avoid the damaged self-image that would result from knowing they had deliberately lied to another person.

These criticisms of and alternatives to traditional cognitive dissonance theory have inspired researchers to conduct better, more sophisticated studies on the topic. Many of these studies have continued to sup-port the cognitive dissonance concept, but they have shown that cognitive dissonance occurs in more restricted circumstances than originally believed. For instance, we now know that cognitive dissonance arises only when behavior is voluntary and when the person feels responsible for it (Collins and Hoyt, 1972). It also requires negative consequences of some kind, either for oneself or for others. In short, cogni-tive inconsistency, by itself, is not enough to foster dissonance (Scher and Cooper, 1989). A number of factors must work together in order for dissonance to occur. Some researchers have even questioned whether cognitive inconsistency is a necessary ingre-dient in a dissonance-arousing situation (Cooper and

Fazio, 1989). They suggest that it is the guilt or remorse people feel when they are responsible for some negative outcome that often fosters attitude change (Scher and Cooper, 1989). Future researchers may help us to better understand exactly what psychological processes are involved in cognitive dissonance studies.

Bem's Self-Perception Theory Another problem with dissonance theory has been the difficulty of measuring the state of psychological tension that dissonance presumably creates. How do we know, some psychologists have asked, that such a state of tension necessarily arises? Couldn't attitude change be produced in cognitive dissonance experiments without such inner conflict? Daryl Bem (1967) is one researcher who thinks that it could be and often is.

Bem's **self-perception theory** begins by asking how we come to know the attitudes of other people. The answer is often through inference. For instance, if we observe shoppers in a supermarket buying a certain brand of coffee and we see that the brand is not on sale, we are likely to conclude that these people must like the way this coffee tastes. If, however, we observe shoppers in a television commercial eagerly buying the same product, we are not likely to make the same inference about their attitudes. These paid actors have an ulterior motive that ordinary shoppers do not. Both behavior and the situation must therefore be considered when the opinions of others are assessed.

Bem goes on to argue that we often use this same strategy to assess our own attitudes. At times, he says, we are not very sure of our own opinions. As a result, we must look to our behavior and the circumstances surrounding it to "know" what it is we feel. Suppose that someone asks you if you like lamb stew, a question to which most people don't have a ready answer because they don't eat lamb stew very often. You might think to yourself: "I ate a large serving of lamb stew a few weeks ago even though I wasn't very hungry. I guess I must like lamb stew quite a bit." Bem argues that the $1 subjects in the boring-task experiment may also have been unsure of their opinions because of the conditions the experimenters had created. If so, they would probably have asked themselves this: "What must my attitude toward this task be if, for only a dollar, I was willing to tell another person it was fun? I guess my feelings must be *somewhat* positive." Notice how, in this case, there is

no feeling of psychological discomfort fostering attitude change, as cognitive dissonance theory proposes. Instead, people faced with an ambiguous situation simply infer their own attitudes by examining their behavior and the surrounding circumstances. They do this in exactly the same dispassionate way as when they infer the feelings of others.

How valid is Bem's reinterpretation of cognitive dissonance studies? Research suggests that it may not always be accurate. When attitudes and behavior are inconsistent, people *do* often experience an uncomfortable state of arousal, as dissonance theory predicts (Croyle and Cooper, 1983). In such situations, the theory of cognitive dissonance is probably a better explanation than Bem's.

But Bem's self-perception theory nicely explains other attitude changes that cognitive dissonance theory cannot. For instance, when people are rewarded for doing something they already like to do (that is, for doing something *consistent* with their feelings), their interest in the activity may actually decline (Deci and Ryan, 1980; Ross and Fletcher, 1985). Consider one experiment in which nursery school children who enjoyed drawing with felt-tip pens were told that they would be given a special prize for using these pens to draw a picture. The children complied, but a week later their interest in felt-tip pens had decreased markedly. This drop in interest did not occur among children who had been asked to draw a picture for *no* external reward (Lepper et al. 1973). Why lose interest in something that gives you pleasure just because you are rewarded for it? Bem would argue that people reason: "If I'm being rewarded for doing X, maybe I'm only doing it for the reward. Maybe I don't really like X that much after all."

This intriguing application of self-perception theory has stimulated research into ways to maximize people's intrinsic motivation (Lepper and Greene, 1978). Apparently, the effect of rewards depends on the meaning we attach to them (Ross and Fletcher, 1985). If rewards are given as an acknowledgment of competence, they can actually *increase* intrinsic motivation by making us feel good about our abilities (Deci and Ryan, 1980).This is probably why praise, a verbal acknowledgment of good work, often leads to enhanced interest (Johnson et al., 1978). In contrast, when we view a reward as the primary reason for doing something, our intrinsic motivation is apt to suffer (Deci and Ryan, 1985). In this case we are convincing ourselves that we do not really like something as much as we thought, because the situation in which we acted suggests another explanation (we were *paid* to do it).

By the same token, we can convince ourselves to adopt a new opinion just by observing ourselves act in ways consistent with that view (as long as we do not have any obvious external pressures to do so.) In one study, for instance, people read a description of a man and then described him to another person (Higgins and Rholes, 1978). When told that the other person liked the man they were about to describe, they painted a favorable portrait of him; and when told that the other person *dis*liked the man, they described him negatively. It seems that most of us are audience pleasers: we automatically (even unconsciously) slant what we say to be in line with what others *want* to hear. Now, how do you think the subjects in this study rated the man they had described when later asked their *own* opinions of him? Because they lacked a good reason for the slant of their earlier description, they convinced themselves that what they said must have been what they *really* felt. Those who had spoken favorably about the man said that they did indeed like him, while those who had spoken *un*favorably said that they *dis*liked him. Apparently, in some situations, "saying is believing."

This finding has important implications. It seems that just by getting people to act in a certain way (without too much external pressure), they may go on to convince themselves that they feel positively about what they are doing. Suppose you want to convince school-age children to have positive attitudes toward members of other races. Should you lecture them on the "Golden Rule" and the value of brotherly love? You could, but it may be more effective to get them to *act* in helpful, cooperative ways in interracial groups. Since we tend to like those we are nice to, not just the other way around, such interracial cooperation should help to foster positive feelings among the races. (Cook, 1985).

SOCIAL COGNITION

When Sherlock Holmes first met Dr. Watson, he knew in an instant that Watson had just come from Afghanistan, even though Watson had not mentioned this fact. Watson was astonished. How could Holmes, a stranger, know this about him? To Holmes the answer

was simple. He knew Watson was a doctor, and his military bearing made him clearly an army physician. A tanned and haggard face suggested recent hardship in a hot, sunny climate, and an injured left arm (Watson held the arm stiffly) implied a battle wound of some kind. Since the British at the time were fighting in Afghanistan, Watson most likely had just returned from there.

Few of us are as clever as Sherlock Holmes at deducing information about a person from a few simple clues. But all of us engage in a good deal of detective work in our efforts to try to understand what people are like. This process involves **social cognition,** which has been defined as how people make sense of other people and themselves (Fiske and Taylor, 1991). In the following sections we will take a look at two aspects of it. The first is how we form impressions of other people. The second is how we attribute causes to people's behavior.

FORMING IMPRESSIONS

A new tenant moves into the apartment next door to yours. He is about twenty, probably a student, and so big and brawny that he looks like a bull in human clothing. His hair is cut short in a military style. His nose is large, his forehead narrow, his eyes close-set. As you watch him carrying a set of barbells up the front steps, you decide that he is definitely an unintelligent "jock." And so you ignore him, except for a curt "Hi" when you meet by chance in the hall. Six months later you are astounded to learn that your neighbor, a philosophy major, has been elected to Phi Beta Kappa.

Does it surprise you that people form opinions of others on the basis of so little evidence? Probably not. We all constantly size up strangers on the basis of scanty information. What may surprise you, however, are some of the factors that influence these impressions. For instance, traits that we perceive first often count the most, which is called the **primacy effect.** In one classic study, people were presented with the two paragraphs shown in Figure 18.1, which describe a young man named Jim (Luchins, 1957). Those who read only paragraph A saw Jim as extroverted and friendly. Those who read only paragraph B saw him as introverted and shy. How do you think people viewed Jim when they were asked to read *both* paragraphs? Usually, the order of presentation governed their impressions. Most of those who read the

A Jim left the house to get some stationery. He walked out into the sun-filled street with two of his friends, basking in the sun as he walked. Jim entered the stationery store, which was full of people. Jim talked with an acquaintance while he waited for the clerk to catch his eye. On his way out, he stopped to chat with a school friend who was just coming into the store. Leaving the store, he walked toward school. On his way out he met the girl to whom he had been introduced the night before. They talked for a short while, and then Jim left for school.	**B** After school Jim left the classroom alone. Leaving the school, he started on his long walk home. The street was brilliantly filled with sunshine. Jim walked down the street on the shady side. Coming down the street toward him, he saw the pretty girl whom he had met on the previous evening. Jim crossed the street and entered a candy store. The store was crowded with students, and he noticed a few familiar faces. Jim waited quietly until the counterman caught his eye and then gave his order. Taking his drink, he sat down at a side table. When he had finished his drink he went home.

FIGURE 18.1 How do first impressions strike us? Quite powerfully, suggests the Luchins experiment. How do you picture Jim after reading paragraph A, then paragraph B? Do you see him differently after reading the paragraphs in reverse order? *(From Luchins, 1957.)*

"extroverted" paragraph first perceived Jim as basically outgoing, while most of those who read the "introverted" paragraph first saw Jim as essentially a loner.

Why does initial information often dominate our impressions? One reason is a simple shift in attention (Belmore, 1987; Zanna and Hamilton, 1977). When you first meet someone, your interest is piqued to find out what that person is like. Then later, once you feel you have gotten some answers, your attention to the person may flag and you stop acquiring new information. This "turning off" to new information is especially likely when you do not have the time or motivation to probe beneath the surface (Kruglanski and Freund, 1983). Another reason for the primacy effect is the fact that initial information can influence how you interpret additional information that comes to light (Higgins and Bargh, 1987). Bits of data that do not fit your first impression may simply be discounted as atypical. For instance, if you have decided that Jim is basically friendly, you may assume that he just has a problem on his mind if you later see him avoiding other people.

THE INFLUENCE OF SCHEMAS

This last explanation of the primacy effect suggests the importance of schemas, which we have talked about at many points in this book. A *schema* is an integrated set of cognitions about objects, people, or events, which we use to help interpret new information. There are several different kinds of schemas related to people. A **person schema** is a set of logically integrated ideas about what a particular person is like, which we use to help us interpret the meaning of that person's behavior. For instance, if you think that a particular person is a liar, an opportunist, and a cheat, you would probably decide he is stealing something if you saw him looking through your tape collection. A **self-schema,** in contrast, is an integrated set of cognitions about what you yourself are like (Markus, 1977). Your self-schema may be similar or dissimilar to how other people view you. A **social stereotype** is another kind of schema, one about a *group* of people. It is a set of beliefs about how members of that group think and act, beliefs that are often widely shared, but not substantiated.

Why do we develop schemas about people? Part of the reason probably has to do with our limited information-processing capabilities. Because of these limitations, we must find ways to simplify screening the many pieces of information we receive about any given topic. As a result, we fall back on schemas, focusing on some facts and largely ignoring others. This strategy allows us to avoid becoming so overwhelmed by information that no decision, solution, or judgment is possible. Not surprisingly, schemas are often used the most when we have the least amount of time in which to assess something thoroughly (Gibbons and Kassin, 1987).

But though schemas save us cognitive effort, they also pose some risks. For one thing, when the information we gather about someone is sketchy, we tend to fill in missing details based on our schemas, even though these schemas may not be accurate (Bower et al., 1979; Cantor and Mischel, 1977). This is precisely what happened in our earlier example of the muscular new neighbor who was assumed to be unintelligent on the basis of his looks. A schema was used to fill in details that turned out to be wrong.

Just as a schema can affect the details we attribute to a person, it can also affect what we remember about him or her (Markus and Zajonc, 1985). In one study, for instance, people saw a film of a woman and her husband having dinner (Cohen, 1981). Those who were told that the woman was a waitress tended to remember that she drank beer and owned a TV set (traits consistent with a waitress schema), whereas those who were told that the woman was a librarian tended to remember that she wore glasses and listened to classical music (traits consistent with a librarian schema).

But just because you come across an example that does not match one of your schemas (such as a librarian who attends rock concerts), this does not mean that you are apt to change your schema to suit the new information. Schemas are often very resistant to change, particularly those we have held a long while (Fiske and Neuberg, 1990; Higgins and Bargh, 1987). This was shown in a study in which people who had firmly-held schemas regarding the value of capital punishment were asked to evaluate two studies on the subject, one that supported their view, and another that opposed it (Lord et al., 1979). You might think that opposing evidence would weaken an existing schema, but this is not what happened. Existing schemas tended to become even more firmly en-

trenched, despite the fact that one of the studies presented disconfirming data. Apparently, people managed to find flaws in the study that opposed their schema, while accepting at face value the study that supported their view. As a result, they felt they had an even stronger reason for thinking that their original schema was right. This study clearly shows the power of schemas. By filtering information through a schema and casting it in that schema's light, we can make ourselves see even contradictory data as supportive of our views.

The tendency of people to seek out information that confirms their existing schemas has been called **confirmatory hypothesis testing** (Higgins and Bargh, 1987). A schema is essentially a hypothesis about what something is like, and people test that hypothesis by comparing it with real-life observations. The problem is that people "stack the deck" in favor of confirming their schemas by selectively attending to supporting information while ignoring contradictory data (or skewing it to make it seem less problematic). The result is reinforcement of the existing schema, making it even more resistant to change.

But though schemas tend to resist change, they are not immutable. We do sometimes revise our schemas, especially when exposed to much contradictory evidence spread out over a number of occasions (Weber and Crocker, 1983). Consider again our earlier example of forming a snap impression of your new neighbor as a "dumb jock." If you heard classical music coming from his apartment one night, you might dismiss this crack in your schema. ("Maybe someone else is staying there.") But if you heard classical music almost every night, often saw him in the library, noticed that he subscribed to intellectual publications, and several times ran into him at a foreign film, you would begin to reconsider your schema. And so it is with schemas about categories of people, such as racial stereotypes. We tend to dismiss one person who does not fit the stereotype as "the exception that proves the rule." But meeting a number of people who do not conform to our expectations has more of an impact.

THE EFFECTS OF PRIMING

You are home alone, watching a murder mystery on TV. You hear a stair creak, a window rattle. When the dog barks, you jump up and run to the front door to make sure it is locked. The stair has always creaked,

How would your first impression of these two women be affected if you had been "primed" with a description of them as roommates? Sisters? Lovers?

the window has always rattled, and your dog is a notorious loudmouth. But the movie has "primed" you to pay attention to these noises and reinterpret them as signs of an intruder. Such **priming** involves the unconscious activation of a schema, which then encourages ideas associated with that schema to come readily to mind (Fiske and Taylor, 1991). In this case, the movie activated your "murder mystery" schema, which includes the concepts of strange noises and dogs barking warnings in the night.

We can also be primed to perceive a new acquaintance in a certain way if a particular schema has been activated before we meet the person (Higgins and Bargh, 1987; Wyer and Srull, 1986). In one study, for instance, people were shown a list of positive traits (such as "brave" and "persistent"), and others a list of negative traits (such as "foolish" and "stubborn") (Higgins et al., 1977). Then, in a supposedly unrelated test of reading comprehension, they learned about Donald, a man who enjoyed shooting rapids, who drove in a demolition derby, and who was planning to learn to sky dive. Those who had been primed with positive traits generally saw Donald as adventurous and liked him; those who had been primed with negative traits generally saw him as reckless, a person to avoid. Apparently, people can be primed to have favorable or unfavorable impressions of others, even though they are not aware that

priming has occurred. Priming words can even be presented so briefly that people say they cannot read them, but unconsciously the priming process still takes place (Erdley and D'Agostino, 1988). Interestingly, priming can affect a person's judgments and actions up to a week after the prime is encountered (Sinclair et al., 1987). With so much time in which a prime can exert its influence, it has ample opportunity to color social perceptions.

Moods and emotions can also prime our reactions to other people. For instance, if you are elated about having finished your last exam of the semester (and you think you did well), you will be primed to have a good time at a party you go to and to like virtually everyone you meet there. If, on the other hand, you go to the party angry because of a fight with your girlfriend or boyfriend (whom you suspect of seeing someone else), you are primed to see others in a hostile light.

Priming is a "behind-the-schemes" form of influence (Bargh, 1989). Usually, we are completely unaware that a previously activated schema is affecting what we think and do (Chaiken et al., 1989; Gilbert, 1989). Suddenly we simply make an association, and because that association comes to mind so readily, it may foster false confidence that our thinking must be right.

This is not to say that we cannot resist the effects

of priming. With deliberate effort we can reject automatic acceptance of a prime-activated schema and examine hard evidence instead (Bargh, 1989). This is more likely under certain conditions, however. For example, if you are highly motivated to be accurate in your judgment about a person (if a great deal is at stake), you will probably look beyond a prime-activated schema. The same is true when you know you will be held accountable for the judgment you make (Fiske and Taylor, 1991).

SELF-FULFILLING PROPHECIES

You have seen that in forming impressions of people we sometimes make incorrect assumptions based on the schemas we hold. Then we often cling to those incorrect assumptions, despite contradictory information. This in itself is unfortunate. But consider the further effects of incorrect impressions. If you mistakenly perceive someone to be aloof, for example, you are likely to be standoffish in response. This behavior, in turn, may cause the person to behave coolly, thus "confirming" your evaluation. Through your own behavior, in other words, you may encourage the very aloofness that you expected. Your once erroneous belief has become a reality, a **self-fulfilling prophecy.**

Self-fulfilling prophecies have been demonstrated in a number of provocative experiments (e.g., Miller and Turnbull, 1986; Rosenthal, 1966). In one of them, college men and women were asked to "get to know one another" through a ten-minute phone conversation (Snyder et al., 1977). The men were given a profile of their future "phonemate," including a photograph. Some of the photographs showed a woman who was extremely attractive; others, an unattractive woman. In fact, the photographs were not of the future phonemates at all, but had simply been randomly assigned to the women. The men did not know this, however, and they responded as expected. Those who thought they were talking to an attractive woman were friendlier, funnier, and sexier than those who thought they were talking to an unattractive woman. And, most important, the women responded in kind. Those who had been cast as attractive were judged by unbiased listeners to be poised and outgoing, while those who had been cast as homely were judged to be awkward and withdrawn. Apparently, each woman took her cue from her partner's behavior: she became the person he

expected her to be. A substantial amount of research on self-fulfilling prophecies suggests that such effects are common (Fiske & Taylor, 1991).

ATTRIBUTING CAUSES TO BEHAVIOR

Evaluating other people certainly does not end with the formation of first impressions. Even when we know another person quite well, we often want to find out why that person is acting in a certain way. If we can attribute an action to some enduring cause (a stable personality trait, for instance), we add some predictability to our social world. We gain confidence that under similar conditions, this particular person will act much the same way again. Fritz Heider (1944, 1958), the first psychologist to study **causal attribution**—how people attribute causes to behavior—believed that all of us are constantly searching for relatively stable factors underlying other people's actions. Our ability to find such factors makes our social environment seem less random and chaotic.

But the problem is that attributing causes to behavior is not always easy. Often we must decide among several very plausible explanations. When a student tells a professor how much he likes her organic chemistry course, does he really mean what he is saying, or is he trying to wheedle a favorable recommendation for medical school? Such ambiguity may even arise when we are assessing our own motives, as we saw earlier with regard to Daryl Bem's views. It was Bem's work, in fact, that helped focus social psychologists' attention on the general process of making causal inferences.

In studying how people attribute causes to behavior, researchers have raised two main questions: First, what information do we look to in drawing causal inferences? And second, what kinds of errors do we typically make as we go about this process? In the following sections we will explore some answers to both of these intriguing questions.

APPROACHES TO DRAWING
CAUSAL INFERENCES

There have been two influential theories about how people infer the cause of others' behavior. One, proposed by Jones and Davis (1965), focuses on the kinds of behaviors to which people attend when they make causal attributions. Not all behaviors are equally informative, Jones and Davis argue. Some are so common, so socially expected, that they reveal very little about a person. If, for example, a political candidate smiles broadly while shaking hundreds of hands, do you immediately assume that he is a genuinely warm and friendly person? Probably not, because these behaviors are widely expected of people who are seeking public office. It is behavior that is in some way *unexpected* that provides the greatest insight into a person's nature.

Another influential theory of how people make causal attributions was suggested by Harold Kelley (1967, 1971). Kelley's theory is not incompatible with Jones and Davis's; it simply focuses on different aspects of the attribution process. Kelley argues that when we infer the cause of behavior, we tend to compare people's present actions with their past ones, as well as with how others act in similar circumstances.

To explain Kelley's theory more fully, suppose a friend drags you to her dorm party. Soon after you arrive, a classmate named Harry walks over to you and starts "coming on." Why is he behaving this way? Is it something about Harry? (Maybe he's perpetually "on the make.") Something about you? ("Am I especially attractive tonight?") Or something about the situation? ("Maybe Harry's had too much to drink.") To find out, Kelley says, you'd first consider the factor of *consistency*. Has Harry behaved this way in other settings? If so, you have some evidence that Harry is the kind of guy who is always coming on to women. To help confirm this theory, you might next consider the factor of *consensus* by comparing Harry's behavior to that of other men. Do most other men behave toward women the way Harry does? If so, you may conclude that Harry is just being one of the pack. If not, you have added reason to believe that a special personality trait prompts Harry to act as he does. Finally, you may consider the issue of *distinctiveness*. Is Harry's attention directed exclusively toward you? What if several friends all tell you that Harry has used the same line on them ("I've been wanting to meet you since the first time I saw you")? In this case, you are very apt to decide that Harry is perpetually "on the make" and therefore a man whom women should avoid.

Like Jones and Davis's view of how people attribute causes to behavior, Kelley's view has also been confirmed through research (Hazelwood and Olson, 1986; Hewstone and Jaspers, 1987; McArthur, 1972). Notice how both these theories have a similar notion about how people approach the problem of causal attribution. Both assume that we infer the causes of behavior in highly logical ways. We screen available evidence, eliminate that which is questionable, and conduct further tests to prove or disprove hypotheses. In these respects we behave much like amateur scientists.

ATTRIBUTION BIASES

As amateurs, however, we have our limitations. Despite our frequent successes at attributing causes to behavior, we also make attribution errors. And the errors we make are seldom haphazard. We are prone to very systematic attribution biases (Nisbett and Ross, 1980; Ross and Nisbett, 1991).

The Fundamental Attribution Error   Probably the most common attribution error is the tendency to see others' behavior as caused by their personalities rather than by external forces. If you see a woman acting rudely, you are much more inclined to infer that she is rude by nature than that her actions arise from unusual circumstances. This tendency is so powerful that it can cause you to overlook even quite strong situational pressures. For example, even when people know that an essay writer has been assigned to take a certain point of view, they assume that the essay reflects the writer's true opinions (Gilbert and Jones, 1986). This tendency to attribute others' behavior to their inner dispositions is so pervasive that it has been called the **fundamental attribution error** (Ross, 1977).

Why do we make this mistake so often? One reason may be that our attention is usually drawn to whatever is most salient—that is, to whatever is most distinctive in relation to its surroundings, and therefore tends to stand out (Bargh, 1984; Fiske and Taylor, 1991). We can see a person performing a behavior, but many situational factors are invisible. So when we are wondering about the causes of a behavior, we tend to focus on the person doing the acting, or more specifically on that person's nature. This is a quick, automatic kind of attribution. It occurs without giving the matter much thought.

Of course, we are also sometimes capable of looking deeper for causes. Some psychologists have argued that causal attribution can be a two-step process (Gilbert, 1989). First, we almost always make a quick attribution that assigns the cause to the

The fundamental attribution error—that another person's behavior is caused by personality factors rather than by the external circumstances—is especially common in dating situations. The man may think the woman is not interested in him, whereas she is actually just preoccupied with a personal problem.

person. For instance, an instructor who notices a student yawning will probably assume at first glance that the student is bored and poorly motivated. But then she may adjust her initial judgment in light of what she knows about the situation. ("He told me he's working evenings; his paper is due today; maybe he was up all night.") The second step requires a higher order of reasoning and deliberate, conscious effort, so it is not always taken. This is particularly true when we are busy or distracted, as we are in many social situations (Gilbert et al., 1988). The instructor who noticed the student yawning was also proceeding with her lecture, registering a raised hand in the back of the room, keeping an eye on the clock, reaching for the chalk, and wondering if her husband will remember to pick up dessert for the dinner party they are giving that night. Such cognitive "busyness" may help encourage the fundamental attribution error. In contrast, when we have time to assess surrounding circumstances more fully, we are less likely to make this mistake. The fundamental attribution error is also less likely when we know we are going to be held accountable for our judgments and decisions, and when something we want or need depends on the person whose behavior we are seeking to explain (Neuberg, 1989; Tetlock, 1989). In these cases, responsibility and self-interest prod us into taking the second cognitive step.

The Actor-Observer Bias One odd thing about the fundamental attribution error is that we tend to avoid it when thinking about our *own* behavior; then we look to situational causes, *not* to personality factors (Jones and Nisbett, 1971). Thus, there can be a marked difference in how actors and observers explain the same behavior. To the observer a behavior seems to arise from the actor's disposition, whereas to the actor the same behavior may appear to be caused by the surrounding circumstances. This common difference in attributions is called the **actor-observer bias.** Sometimes it can cause interpersonal conflict (Kelley, 1979). For example, parents may attribute a son's poor grades to his laziness (a personality factor), while the son may feel that the real blame lies in a heavy course load (a situational cause). Awareness of the actor-observer bias could help both parties be more sensitive to the other's point of view.

If you think you are immune to the actor-observer bias, take the test in Figure 18.2. You will probably feel that your friend's behavior is more stable than your own, as reflected in the higher score you give your friend. This is because you attribute your friend's behavior largely to a stable disposition, while you see your own behavior as depending more on the situation. One possible reason has to do with differences in knowledge. An actor has extensive knowledge of his or her own behavior and how it has

First, rate a friend of yours on the following characteristics using the scale that follows. Then go back and do the same for yourself.

	Friend	Self
Aggressive	_____	_____
Introverted	_____	_____
Thoughtful	_____	_____
Warm	_____	_____
Outgoing	_____	_____
Hard driving	_____	_____
Ambitious	_____	_____
Friendly	_____	_____
Total	_____	Total _____

Rating Scale

−2	Definitely does not describe
−1	Usually does not describe
0	Sometimes describes, sometimes not
+1	Usually describes
+2	Definitely describes

Now, go back, ignore the pluses and minuses, and total up the two columns.

FIGURE 18.2 Who has the more stable personality—you or a friend? First, rate a friend of yours on the following characteristics using the accompanying scale. Then go back and do the same for yourself. Now, go back, ignore the pluses and minuses, and total up the two columns. *(From Fiske and Taylor, 1984.)*

varied in different situations. An observer, in contrast, has seen the actor in far fewer circumstances and so is apt to think that current behavior is highly typical.

The Self-Serving Bias Does the actor-observer bias always occur? No, not always. Sometimes actors are strongly motivated to attribute causes to themselves. When the outcome of a behavior is favorable, people are usually quick to claim personal responsibility. It is when an outcome is *unfavorable* that people are more apt to pin the blame on circumstances. For instance, when students do well on an exam, they usually credit themselves ("I always knew I was intelligent"); but when they do poorly, they usually fault someone or something else ("The instructor doesn't like me"; "The questions were full of tricks") (Whitley and Frieze, 1985). Similarly, in competitive games, winners usually attribute the results to skill, while losers usually attribute them to luck (Stephan et al., 1979). People also tend to overestimate their own contribution when a joint effort succeeds. For example, each co-author of a successful publication usually thinks that he or she put in the most work (Ross and

Sicoly, 1979). This tendency to take credit for successes and find situational excuses for failure has been aptly called the **self-serving bias.**

One way to make the self-serving bias especially convincing is to publicly announce before you attempt an activity how handicapped you are by negative circumstances. You won't play well in the tennis match because your knee is injured. You're bound to do poorly on your final exam because you didn't have much time to study. Stephan Berglas and Edward Jones (1978) have called this *self-handicapping*. In order to protect your self-esteem, you claim to be starting out at a disadvantage. The self-handicap provides an alibi for poor performance, and makes good performance seem all the more likely to be due to extraordinary personal ability.

In some cases people may actively sabotage their own performance—by not preparing as much as they could, not trying as hard as they might, or starting slowly so as not to create great expectations (Baumgardner and Brownlee, 1987). Consider an experiment at Duke University (Berglas and Jones, 1978). Students were asked to participate in a study on

Those who fish for sport are notorious for their self-serving bias, boasting of their skill when they land a big one, but blaming "the one that got away" on the weather, the time of day, the water temperature, or any number of other external conditions.

"drugs and intelligence." After a first round of exceedingly difficult questions, the students were told they had done extremely well. For the next round they were offered a choice of two drugs: "Actavil," which was said to boost intellectual performance, and "Pandocrin," which was said to lower it. Which did the students choose? Most picked the drug that lowered performance, because it gave them an excuse if they didn't perform as well as they had before. Even tennis champion Martina Navratilova has admitted to such self-handicapping. After losing to some young players, she confessed that she was afraid to play her best for fear that if she lost again she would have to attribute the cause to herself. "I was scared to find out if they could beat me when I'm playing my best," she said, "because if they can, then I am finished" (Frankel and Snyder, 1987).

Psychologists are divided on the question of whether these strategies are adaptive or maladaptive. On the one hand are those who say that self-serving attributions and self-handicapping protect our self-esteem. They insulate us from anxiety in competitive situations and help us avoid depression when our performance is not good (Snyder and Higgins, 1988; Taylor and Brown, 1988). On the other hand are those who argue that these strategies backfire in the long run (Nisbett and Ross, 1980). Self-handicapping may protect us from losing face, but it can also "protect"

us from doing our best. If we don't really try hard, if we create obstacles that can serve as excuses, we will never know how well we might have done. In addition, when we attribute *all* successes to ourselves, we may find it impossible to live up to our overblown self-image. Blaming all our failures on circumstances can have equally negative effects. It can blind us to important shortcomings in ourselves and make it hard for us to learn from our mistakes. As a result, we may be destined to keep repeating the same failures.

ATTRACTION, FRIENDSHIP, AND LOVE

Forming impressions and attributing causes to behavior are processes that apply to everyone we meet. Liking and loving, in contrast, are selective. Few people become our close friends, and fewer still spark that special, intense feeling we call romantic love. Forming friendships and falling in love are among life's most enriching experiences. What light can psychologists shed on friendship and love?

WHAT PROMOTES ATTRACTION?

You have accepted a job in a city halfway across the country. You are excited about the new career opportunity, but a little worried about your social life. How

Many college activities promote attraction between people. Rehearsing for a play, for instance, brings the student actors into frequent, close contact, and they are likely to have a great deal in common. Both these factors—proximity and similarity—are crucial ingredients of friendship and love.

will you make friends? Will you meet "Mr. or Ms. Right"? Social psychology cannot tell you whether you will find the love of your life in Cleveland, but it can tell you what factors will tend to attract you to other people.

PHYSICAL ATTRACTIVENESS

Although most people end up with romantic partners who are roughly equal in attractiveness to themselves, physical beauty is still a social magnet that draws us to other people and encourages us to like them. This was demonstrated in a classic experiment (Walster et al., 1966). Over 700 college freshman attended a computer-dating dance that promised to match dates on the basis of shared interests. Each person was assessed for physical attractiveness, intelligence, and personality traits, but the dates were then assigned completely at random. After the dance the researchers asked participants to rate their computer date. They found that the only factor that consistently influenced a date's rating was that person's physical attractiveness. Intelligence and personality hardly mattered at all. If you are thinking that looks may count a lot at first, but that other factors become important later, you are being too idealistic. In another study, students were paired at random for

a series of five dates, and the importance of physical attractiveness to them actually increased over time (Mathes, 1975).

What is it about beautiful people that so attracts us to them? One is our tendency to associate beauty with a host of positive traits (sensitivity, kindness, intelligence, being interesting to talk to, strength, poise, sociability, good health, sexual responsiveness) and only a relatively few negative characteristics (vanity and conceit, for example) (Cunningham, 1986; Dion et al., 1972; Hatfield and Sprecker, 1986). Moreover, not only do we attribute many desirable traits to beautiful people, we also think positively about those who *associate* with the beautiful (Sigall and Landy, 1973). If a man is going with a very beautiful woman, we assume that he must be special; after all, she could have any man she wants. One reason for our pursuit of beautiful people, then, may be that associating with them enhances our own social status.

If our pursuit of beauty was solely an effort to enhance our social status, however, physical attractiveness would be as important to us in the choice of a same-sex friend as it is in the choice of a mate. But it isn't (Feingold, 1988). Undoubtedly, we gravitate to beautiful potential mates also because we find them sexually arousing. Interestingly, men are more attracted to beautiful mates than women are. For women, the economic status of a man they are romantically involved with is equally, if not more, important (Buss, 1988).

PROXIMITY AND EXPOSURE

Another important ingredient in interpersonal attraction is proximity, or nearness. People are most apt to like, and even to marry, someone who lives near them, sits near them in class, or works near them at the office. In a classic study of this effect, researchers surveyed married couples in a student housing complex (Festinger et al., 1950). The closer to each other that people lived, the more likely they were to become friends. Moreover, couples assigned apartments near busy areas (by the mailboxes, for example) tended to be more popular than those assigned to more secluded places.

These results were undoubtedly related to the frequency with which the people involved saw one another. Apparently, just repeated exposure to another person can create positive feelings. Consider an experiment in which students were told they were participating in a study on taste (Saegert et al., 1973). They were shuttled in and out of small cubicles, where they tasted and rated different liquids, and in the process encountered a number of other people, although they were not permitted to talk to them. Later, the subjects tended to express the greatest liking for those people they had encountered the most often.

Why do people tend to like those they see repeatedly? One possible explanation is that as we become more familiar with a person, that person grows more predictable and less potentially threatening. Though we may never come to love another person solely through repeated exposure, we may at least feel comfortable in that person's presence. This feeling of comfortable familiarity is a basis on which we can begin to build a friendship.

SIMILARITY

Folk wisdom holds that "birds of a feather flock together" but also that "opposites attract." Which is right? More often the first, research shows. We tend to like people who are similar to us—in age, ethnic background, level of education, socioeconomic status, values and attitudes, personality traits, even in habits

such as cigarette smoking and physical characteristics such as height and weight (Buss, 1985).

It is not exactly clear why like attracts like. One possibility is that similar people enjoy each other's company because they confirm each other's values and opinions (Arrowood and Short, 1973; Sanders, 1982). It is not much fun being with someone who constantly criticizes our taste, disagrees with our ideas, and challenges our beliefs. Similarity also paves the way for shared activities (whether discussing Plato or going bowling), and shared activities are another foundation on which to build friendship.

PERCEPTIONS OF MUTUAL LIKING

Finally, we are also attracted to people who seem to like us in return, who appear to reciprocate our feelings. This sets the stage for positive interactions that can help a friendship form. In one study, for instance, college students who were led to believe that another person liked them disclosed more about themselves to that person, spoke to him or her in a more pleasant way, and disagreed with the person less often (Curtis and Miller, 1986). These behaviors, in turn, encouraged similar responses from the other person, and led that person to actually develop a liking for the first.

Conversely, when we think another person does *not* like us, we are not likely to pursue a friendship. This is unfortunate when the other person is not really unfriendly, just shy. For many shy people, expectations that social interactions will be unpleasant are confirmed because of their own shy behavior (Jones and Carpenter, 1986; Leary, 1983). They feel awkward and inhibited in social situations and so tend to be passive and unresponsive. Other people may interpret these behaviors as rejection, and so reciprocate with aloofness or avoidance. In this way a self-fulfilling prophecy develops. The prophecy *can* be broken, however. One group of researchers found that shy people can gain increased social confidence and skill by following a simple social script: "Find out as much as you can about another person" (Leary et al., 1988).

LOVE

Love is an intense positive feeling toward another person, the strongest positive feeling we can experience (Liebowitz, 1983). Although being in love sometimes puts us on an emotional roller coaster, most people would not trade the experience of love for anything. Soon we will take a look at why people fall in love, and what makes love last. But first let us examine several kinds of love relationships.

TYPES OF LOVE

Just as there are differences in all kinds of human relationships, there are differences in love relationships. Psychologist Robert Sternberg (1986) has identified three components of loving: *intimacy* (the feeling of closeness and connectedness that allows two people to confide in one another); *passion* (the drive to be physically united); and *commitment* (the decision to be and stay together). According to Sternberg, best friends have a relationship based on intimacy and commitment, but no passion—what Sternberg calls "companionate love." Passion without intimacy or commitment produces "infatuated love," a torrid but shallow and short-lived affair. Commitment without passion or intimacy is "empty love," as in a marriage where the partners have grown distant from each other but still stay together. "Consummate love," which combines intimacy, passion, and commitment, is in Sternberg's view the most difficult to achieve and maintain.

People often wonder if romantic love passes through stages, much as people pass through stages of life. According to this view, a romantic love based on strong physical attraction often develops first. This **passionate love** is characterized by emotional highs and lows. The lovers vacillate between feelings of tenderness and desire, joy and despair, anxiety and relief, trust and jealousy. They feel that they cannot live without each other. If passionate love is initially lacking intimacy and commitment, it is the infatuated love in Sternberg's model. But then, if intimacy and commitment develop, the relationship becomes consummate love. Passion is hard to sustain indefinitely, however. Gradually, as the love relationship ages, passion often fades and leaves the couple with the intimacy and commitment of **companionate love.** Companionate love is the warm, affectionate bond between two people who are deeply committed to each other. The lovers feel at home with one another. They are partners who share their thoughts, their feelings, and their lives (Hatfield, 1988). An alternative view is that passionate love and companionate love usually have different origins, with most couples experiencing only one kind of love or the other.

IN DEPTH

What Helps Love Last?

The power of a glance has been so much abused in love stories that it has come to be disbelieved in. Few people dare now to say that two beings have fallen in love because they looked at each other. Yet it is in this way that love begins, and in this way only. The rest is only the rest, and comes afterwards. Nothing is more real than those great shocks which two souls give each other in exchanging this spark. (Victor Hugo, *Les Miserables*)

Though Hugo's romantic thunderbolt sounds appealing, for many men and women, falling in love takes a slower course. In one survey of more than 200 engaged college students, only 8 percent of the men and 5 percent of the women reported feeling strong physical attraction for their partner within the first day or two after they met—a far cry from widespread love at first sight. For most of these couples, mutual love developed slowly over several months (Rubin, 1973).

But regardless of whether love grows from one passionate glance or takes its time, what helps it last? We know from previous chapters that maintaining close, satisfying relationships can influence not only our happiness but our mental and physical health. Therefore, we will pursue this question in depth.

THE INITIAL STUDIES

When two people begin dating, friends pull out their crystal ball, declaring: "They're perfect for each other!" or "It will *never* last." Social psychologists also try to predict whether love will last, but their predictions are based on research. Typically, couples are interviewed and tested when they start dating, then are recontacted later. Couples who have stayed together are compared to those who have broken up. In this way, psychologists have identified a number of factors that improve the chances that a love relationship will last.

The more alike two romantic partners are, the more apt they are to stay together. Relationships in which the partners are well matched for age, intelligence, educational plans, physical attractiveness, and so forth have a better than average chance of surviving (Hill et al., 1976). Closeness is also important: couples who stay together tend to spend a lot of time together, to engage in many shared

Romeo and Juliet are Western literature's best-known example of passionate love, or love at first sight. Shown here is the balcony scene from Franco Zeffirelli's film version of Shakespeare's play.

activities, and to consider each other when making everyday plans and decisions (Berg and McQuinn, 1986; Berscheid et al., 1989). For such couples, the enjoyment of being together tends to increase with time.

Personality factors seem to matter too. Certain traits can affect how people behave toward a romantic partner, how they perceive themselves and are perceived by that person, and their partner's satisfaction with the relationship. Among the traits most important to maintaining a relationship is empathy (a feeling of compassion and sympathy for the other person). Women, even more than men, want a partner who is a good listener and able to talk about his feelings (Davis and Oathout, 1987).

CRITICISMS, ALTERNATIVES, AND FURTHER RESEARCH

The initial studies on what makes love endure focused exclusively on what the partners are like—their interests, similarities, etc., at present. In contrast, Phillip Shaver and Cindy Hazan believed that the personal qualities most important to fostering a lasting love relationship have to do with a person's attachment style, which is formed during infancy. According to these investigators, people who experienced loving and dependable relationships during their infancy and childhood tend to have schemas about love and commitment that serve as solid foundations for building stable new ties. Shaver and Hazan strongly believe that the style of attachment which a person develops in infancy often affects that person's love relationships throughout life.

Shaver and Hazan gathered evidence for this view by asking adults to fill out a questionnaire about themselves, their love lives, and their childhoods (Shaver and Hazan, 1985, 1987; Shaver et al., 1988). (A sample question is shown in Figure 18.3). The researchers found that adults' styles of romantic love closely paralleled the three attachment patterns seen in human infants. The patterns of infancy are *secure attachment* (characterized by trust in the parent's availability), *anxious-avoidant attachment* (characterized by avoidance of the parent when the child is upset and associated with a parent who is hostile or indifferent), and *anxious-ambivalent attachment* (characterized by ambivalence toward the parent in stressful situations and associated with a parent whose caregiving is inconsistent).

In what ways did the love lives of Shaver and Hazan's adults mirror these early attachment patterns? *Secure* adults, like secure infants, generally trusted the people they loved, and they viewed themselves as worthy of being loved. They found it

Question: Which of the following best describes your feelings?

A.   I find it relatively easy to get close to others and am comfortable depending on them and having them depend on me. I don't often worry about being abandoned or about someone getting too close to me.

B.   I am somewhat uncomfortable being close to others; I find it difficult to trust them completely, difficult to allow myself to depend on them. I am nervous when anyone gets too close, and often, love partners want me to be more intimate than I feel comfortable being.

C.   I find that others are reluctant to get as close as I would like. I often worry that my partner doesn't really love me or won't want to stay with me. I want to merge completely with another person, and this desire sometimes scares people away.

The first type of attachment style is described "secure," the second as "avoidant," and the third as "anxious/ambivalent."

FIGURE 18.3   Attachment styles: the romantic style we have as adults is strongly influenced by the kind of attachment styles we had as infants. The following items are taken from a questionnaire administered to adults. *(From Shaver et al., 1988, reprinted by permission of Yale University Press.)*

relatively easy to get close to someone else, and rarely worried about being abandoned. Most described their parents as caring and responsive. *Avoidant* adults, in contrast, feared closeness and were very distrustful of others. Many claimed not to believe in romantic love or the need for it, as if they were trying to compensate for deep insecurities. Often they reported that their parents were cold and rejecting. Finally, *ambivalent* adults were preoccupied with finding "real" love, but painfully unable to do so. They were constantly falling in and out of love, and their love lives were characterized by emotional extremes and self-doubts. Often they described their parents in both positive and negative terms, suggesting inconsistent parenting. Interestingly, research evidence suggests that once a person develops a certain style of attachment to others, that style tends to endure.

But how could attachment patterns of infancy affect our love relationships as adults? John Bowlby (1969, 1973, 1980) suggests that babies develop an "inner working model" or schema of what the self and others are like. This model is not fixed for life, of course, but it *can* become a self-fulfilling prophecy. A person who expects rejection, for instance, may behave so defensively—being jealous and distrustful at every step—that rejection becomes more likely.

Another factor affecting the longevity of a relationship that has generated a great deal of recent interest is the way in which the partners attribute causes to each other's behavior (Bradbury and Fincham, 1990). Happy couples tend to attribute each other's positive actions to enduring dispositions, while excusing negative actions as due to extenuating circumstances. Unhappy couples, in contrast, tend to attribute negative actions to enduring dispositions and positive ones to temporary situations (Holtzworth-Munroe and Jacobson, 1985). Thus, if a wife spends too much money on a new outfit, her husband will tend to attribute it to irresponsibility, not the situational demands of an important job interview. And if the husband offers to take his wife out to dinner, the wife may conclude that he feels guilty about something, not that he is being thoughtful. It is easy to see how this pattern of attribution can ruin a relationship. No matter how hard one person tries to please the other, the other person usually fails to see the effort as an act of love.

What about disagreements and arguments between couples? Can't they ruin a relationship too? Surprisingly, no, as long as the partners do not become stubborn or defensive. In fact, open expression of feelings during conflict between lovers or spouses may even be good for the relationship (Gottman and Krokoff, 1989). For instance, a wife's satisfaction with her marriage tends to increase when she expresses anger during arguments with her husband. It is when the wife becomes sad or fearful and the husband whiney or withdrawn that marital satisfaction tends to drop. Apparently, keeping the peace by remaining silent takes a greater toll on a relationship than letting emotions out. When negative feelings are harbored, they tend to fester and grow.

Persistent racial prejudice gives rise to senseless acts like the murder of Yusuf Hawkins, who was killed just for being a young black man visiting a white neighborhood.

CONCLUSIONS

At present, most of the research on love relationships focuses on how peoples' expectations and assumptions about their partner's behavior will influence the course of the relationship. Unlike the earlier studies on similarity and attraction, the more recent research has important implications for how relationships can be improved. As we saw in Chapter 17, forms of marital therapy that attempt to change partners' underlying assumptions and expectations are especially promising. Of course, styles of attachment that were formed at a very early age may be very difficult to change. But people can be helped in romantic relationships by discovering how their behavior toward a lover may be shaped by the treatment they received from parents or other adult authority figures many years ago.

THE PSYCHOLOGY OF PREJUDICE

In the summer of 1989, four black teenagers answered an ad for a used car, price: $500. The owner lived in Bensonhurst, a mostly white, mostly Italian, working-class section of Brooklyn, New York. On the same night, a young white woman in Bensonhurst was celebrating her eighteenth birthday. She had told a former boyfriend that she had invited many of her black and Hispanic friends, and he had better look out. Soon after they exited the subway, the four black teenagers, looking only for a car, were confronted by a mob of some forty white youths, wielding baseball bats and a gun, and shouting "They're here. They're here. Blacks are here." Moments later one of the black teenagers—sixteen-year-old Yusuf Hawkins—lay dead in the street, shot twice through the chest. Later, when black leaders organized protest marches through the community, they were met by residents holding up watermelons and shouting racial slurs. Hardly anyone in Bensonhurst would talk to police who were investigating the murder. "Yusuf Hawkins died of racism in the first degree," declared New York's Mayor David Dinkins. "That's a crime far more common than most of us have been willing to admit" (*The New York Times*, May 18, 1990, p. B3).

Racism is just one form of social **prejudice,** an inflexible negative attitude toward members of a minority group, based on erroneous or incomplete information. This definition of prejudice stresses three things. First, prejudice involves hostile and negative feelings, usually toward an entire group of people. Second, these feelings are unwarranted; they are based on faulty or partial information. And third, prejudice is peculiarly resistant to change, even in the face of strong contradictory evidence. Because social prejudices are so widespread and can cause so much harm to their targets, psychologists believe it is critically important to study and understand them.

The cognitive component of social prejudices is social **stereotypes**—that is, preconceived ideas about what members of a particular group are like. Social stereotypes are essentially group schemas, as we mentioned before. To some extent such stereotyping is an inevitable part of trying to understand and simplify our complex social world. But stereotypes, unfortunately, can become so ingrained that we accept them without question. Thus, we may assume that anyone who has a certain trait (femaleness, for example) *necessarily* has a whole range of other traits (docility, emotionalism, lack of managerial skills) stereotypically associated with the first. As a result, stereotypes blind us to individual differences. Even favorable stereotypes are unjust, because they ignore each person's uniqueness. Of course, the stereotypes involved in social prejudices are by definition *unfavorable*, which is why they support and help maintain a dislike of the target group. Negative stereotypes can easily become abusive when they are used to justify **discrimination,** the behavioral expression of prejudice. For instance, the stereotype of blacks as less intelligent than whites has been used to justify denying blacks equal opportunities for education and employment.

But how can stereotypes be maintained in the face of so much evidence that they are overgeneralizations? The answer lies partly in the way human memory works. Remember from our earlier discussion of schemas that people filter new information through existing knowledge and beliefs. We often reinterpret or ignore anything that does not meet our expectations. And anything that *does* confirm our expectations usually makes a strong impression on us. As a result, we tend to think our stereotypes are far more valid than they actually are. There is no truth, for instance, in the common assumption that women are unreliable employees because they inevitably leave to marry or have children. Yet many people are convinced that this misconception is correct, partly because they selectively remember behavior that conforms to it (Fiske and Taylor, 1991).

Of course, some pieces of contradictory information are too obvious to ignore (the woman who stays with a company for many years and rises to a position of status and power, the black man who eventually

becomes a Supreme Court justice). How does the prejudiced person explain these things? One way is to create subcategories within a stereotype. For example, a person who believes that all athletes are "dumb jocks" might have a subcategory for tennis players, who seem more intelligent than the "typical" athlete. Similarly, a person whose stereotype of blacks centers around muggers might have a subcategory for middle-class blacks who are more law-abiding. When these people meet someone who does not match their general stereotype, they assign them to the subcategory.

At first glance, subcategorizing may seem to be a "breakthrough" in stereotyped thinking: the person does not think that *all* blacks, *all* Asians, *all* athletes, or *all* gays are alike. But in practice, subcategorizing helps prejudiced people continue to see the world in prejudiced ways. Subcategories allow them to accommodate contradictory information without changing their basic, negative schema of the minority group. People who do not match the stereotype are dismissed as "the exception that proves the rule." This way of thinking has been found to be quite common (Deaux, 1976; Fiske and Taylor, 1991).

Two of the most widespread prejudices throughout the world are **racism** (prejudice directed toward members of certain racial groups) and **sexism** (prejudice directed toward one sex, almost always women). Although racism and sexism have many things in common, they are distinctive enough to consider separately.

RACISM

The murder in Bensonhurst described at the beginning of this section was part of a rising wave of racial hate crimes that took the United States by surprise in the late 1980s. Relatively rare in the 1970s and early 1980s, racially motivated attacks have become more and more common. Racial and ethnic violence also flared in the Soviet Union and Eastern Europe, where riots between Azerbaijanis and Armenians, Czechs and Slovaks, Romanians and Hungarians killed scores in 1989–1990, and anti-Semitic attacks were on the rise.

Particularly disturbing is the increase in racial incidents on college campuses. At the University of Massachusetts in Amherst, ten students were injured in a black–white brawl following a World Series game. Students at the University of Wisconsin held a mock slave auction. A black cadet at a military academy in South Carolina withdrew after white students dressed in Ku Klux Klan garb broke into his room and burned a paper cross. Racial or ethnic incidents were reported on 115 American campuses in 1989 alone. When *The New York Times* asked students at twenty schools about major problems on their campus, racism headed the list (October 8, 1989). The National Study of Black College Students found that 80 percent of black undergraduates experienced some form of discrimination during their college years (*The Wall Street Journal,* April 3, 1987). And racism need not be blatant to cause people distress. As a student at MIT explained, ''It's like you are the last person picked as a lab partner, or someone will lean over you and ask the person sitting next to you what the professor said—like you wouldn't have understood it'' (*The Wall Street Journal,* April 3, 1987).

THE DYNAMICS OF CONTEMPORARY RACISM

Polls consistently show that the majority of white Americans support racial equality—up to a point (National Research Council, 1989). For example, nearly all whites believe that blacks (and other racial and ethnic minorities) should have equal opportunity in education, employment, and housing. But far fewer support programs designed to promote racial equality (such as affirmative action, school busing, and open-housing laws). Similarly, the majority of whites endorse racial integration, but when certain boundaries are crossed—when racial contact is too frequent or too close or when too many blacks are involved—they back off. For example, although most white Americans wouldn't think twice about sitting next to a black person on a bus, they might feel uncomfortable dancing with a black person, or going to a restaurant in which nearly all the patrons are black. There is also a significant minority of whites who still hold extremely negative stereotypes about members of other races and who seek to maintain strict social distance from them. Thus, half of whites disapprove of interracial marriage, a third do not want blacks in their neighborhoods, and 20 percent would not send their children to an integrated school (Dovidio and Gaertner, 1986).

Many psychologists believe that the overt racism of the past has been replaced by a new form of *disguised racism* (Katz and Hass, 1988; Kinder and

Racist incidents are on the rise on U.S. college campuses, but as awareness of the problem spreads, efforts to address the issue are also increasing.

Sears, 1981). According to this view, many white Americans are ambivalent about blacks. They believe in racial equality and feel sympathetic toward blacks because of their past and present hardships. But at the same time, they feel that blacks violate such traditional American values as self-reliance, discipline, and hard work. They believe that blacks are largely responsible for their own problems, because they lack ambition, fail to take advantage of opportunities, engage in criminal behavior, abuse drugs and alcohol, have children outside marriage, and so forth. Of course, the majority of whites today are not willing to admit to these views. In fact, many bend over backwards to appear nonracist. But their prejudices are revealed in subtle ways.

In one study, for instance, white students saw lists of positive and negative adjectives, such as clean and ambitious versus stupid and lazy (Dovidio et al.,

1986). Each adjective was paired with either the word *whites* or the word *blacks.* The students' task was to press a button if they thought the words went together. Although the students did not express racial stereotypes in their overt responses, the results were subtly suggestive of them. The students were *quicker* to press the button when saying that a positive trait fit whites than when saying that a positive trait fit blacks. These different reaction times can be explained if deep inside these students harbored schemas of blacks that were less favorable than their schemas of whites.

How do whites handle conflict between egalitarian values and negative feelings toward blacks? How do they resolve the cognitive dissonance? One way is to maintain social distance (Dovidio and Gaertner, 1986). By avoiding blacks they can avoid confronting their racial prejudices. Another way is to express their prejudices only when doing so can be justified in nonracial terms. This second tactic was demonstrated in a study in which white college students were asked to give electric shocks to another student as part of what was described as a biofeedback study (Rogers and Prentice-Dunn, 1981). (Actually, the recipients of the shocks were accomplices in the experiment, and the electrical current was never really turned on.) Significantly, when a black accomplice was insulting to the person delivering the shocks, that person usually delivered more intense shocks than when a white accomplice was similarly rude. It was as if in this situation, where hostility was justified, these white students took the chance to express their racial animosities.

EXPLAINING RACISM

Psychologists have offered many theories to explain why racism develops. Some have argued that certain personality traits may incline people toward racial bigotry. Research into this topic began at the University of California's Berkeley campus (Adorno et al., 1950). Investigators there identified an **authoritarian personality,** characterized by rigid adherence to conventional values, a preference for strong, antidemocratic leaders, and fear and hatred of almost anyone who is different from oneself. They found that many people with this personality type had experienced harsh discipline as children and had parents who frequently withdrew their love and made them feel insecure. The children were consequently very

dependent on their parents, but also very angry toward them. Afraid to express these feelings, they presumably became angry, fearful adults who displaced their repressed hostilities toward their parents onto a much "safer" target: members of minority groups, who were too powerless to retaliate.

But as interesting as this psychoanalytic theory of racial prejudice is, social psychologists do not believe it can fully explain racism. Racial bigotry and hatred are far too widespread to be caused by aberrant personality development alone. For instance, although South Africans who most strongly support apartheid often have authoritarian traits, there are also many other advocates of this policy who are *not* authoritarian (van Staden, 1987). Clearly, there must be social situational factors that foster racial prejudice as well. Social psychologists have devoted a great deal of effort to identifying what these factors are.

One social psychological theory holds that prejudice results when people are in strong competition with each other. A classic study conducted some forty years ago gathered evidence in support of this view (Sherif and Sherif, 1953). Twelve-year-old boys attending summer camp were assigned to one of two groups, the Red Devils or the Bulldogs. After a period of friendly cooperation between the groups, the researchers began to pit them against each other in a series of intensely competitive games. The result was a great deal of intergroup hostility. Apparently, fierce competition can indeed promote prejudice.

Frustration over losing something valued (such as a desirable prize or the self-esteem of winning) can help explain this link between competition and prejudice. When people are frustrated by adverse conditions they cannot change, they often vent their anger and aggression on the most readily available scapegoat. This tendency has been demonstrated experimentally (Miller and Bugelski, 1948). Researchers measured subjects' attitudes toward various minority groups and then placed them in a frustrating situation: they denied them the chance to see an interesting movie, requiring instead that they complete a long series of difficult tests. When asked again to express their attitudes toward the same minorities, most subjects showed significant increases in prejudice. No such increases were found among control subjects, who had not experienced frustration.

But competition and frustration over losing something valued cannot be the only situational factors promoting racial prejudices. Members of the *same* racial group also compete, and sometimes cause each other frustration, and yet their hatreds tend to be directed outward toward other races. What prompts this tendency to vent hostilities on "outsiders"? One answer lies in the way we perceive **in-groups** (those groups with which we identify) and **out-groups** (those groups to which we don't belong). We tend to see our in-groups as collections of varied individuals, partly because we have had so much experience with many different members of these groups. As a result, when one member of the same group angers another, the first tends to differentiate, not generalize. ("That guy's just a bad apple.") In contrast, we tend to see an out-group as an undifferentiated mass, partly because we have had so little experience with its members. Consequently, when we encounter out-group members we don't like, we tend to generalize to *all* members of those groups and form group stereotypes.

This tendency to see "them" as all alike and "us" as differentiated is revealed in many ways. For example, white Americans speak of "black leaders," whom they presume speak for *all* black Americans. When these black leaders disagree on an issue, whites consider it news: the "black community" is divided. But they would never think of referring to President Bush as a "white leader," as if he spoke for all white Americans. Nor are whites surprised when "white leaders" in Congress disagree among themselves. They think of whites as individuals, not a racial category. Indeed, "they"—members of a racial out-group—even look alike to us (Quattrone, 1986). Whites find it easier to identify white faces they have seen before in a group photo. Likewise, blacks find it easier to identify black faces. To a large degree it is also true that "all Chinese look alike" to a Caucasian. But so do all Caucasians look alike to an Asian. Such stereotyped, categorical thinking tends to dehumanize members of racial out-groups and make them ready targets of prejudice.

But what does it do for us to disparage an out-group? What do we gain from this kind of thinking? An interesting answer is provided by **social identity theory** (Tajfel, 1982). It holds that each of us has an individual identity, based on our personal attributes and achievements. But each of us also has a social identity, based on membership in social groups. To a large extent our self-esteem derives from how we evaluate our in-groups in relation to our out-groups. Thus, we tend to see members of our

One of history's most appalling instances of scapegoating occurred in the 1930s and 1940s, when Adolf Hitler's propaganda apparatus succeeded in persuading many European gentiles that Jews were to blame for all the economic, political, and social problems of the time. This pre–World War II poster in Vienna depicts a stereotyped image of a sinister-looking, money-hungry Jew.

in-groups as more attractive, likeable, and successful, and to favor members of our in-groups at the expense of out-group members, because this boosts our self-esteem. When our self-esteem is low, we may "take it out" on out-groups. In one study, for instance, some students were made to feel very embarrassed by contriving to have them knock over a large, neatly ordered stack of computer cards, said to be part of an important project (Meindl and Lerner, 1985). These same students later expressed harsher feelings toward members of an ethnic out-group than did control subjects who had not experienced a blow to their self-esteem.

Finally, people may simply learn racial prejudice as a cultural norm, passed on from generation to generation. As such, racism is taught to children by their elders, in the same way any other widely shared attitude is. In keeping with this view, children's racial attitudes *do* tend to match those of their parents (Ashmore and DelBoca, 1976). Children, for their part, may internalize prevailing racial biases because in doing so they are rewarded with the approval of others, or with self-approval for thinking as they believe a person "ought" to think. There is also a natural tendency to avoid those we are taught to dislike, which creates social distance that further fosters racial fears and suspicions.

COMBATTING RACISM

How can racial prejudice be reduced? Somehow people must look beyond their racial stereotypes and stop seeing in people of other races only what they *expect* to see. Somehow they must assimilate new information that disconfirms their stereotypes, so that eventually they will discard those stereotypes in favor of more positive schemas (Devine, 1989). Simply increasing contact among the races may not be enough to accomplish this goal (Fiske and Neuberg, 1990). Because stereotypes are so resistant to change, only interracial contact under certain conditions will help reduce prejudice (Stuart, 1979).

One of these conditions is equal status. If whites encounter blacks only in low-status roles such as porter, janitor, and domestic servant, traditional stereotypes will probably persist. It is when members of different races find themselves *similar* in status, background, and values that traditional stereotypes are most likely to break down. It also helps if interracial contact enables people to get to know one another well. For instance, simply living next door to a minority family may not reduce prejudice unless the two families become involved with one another. This can sometimes be encouraged by the existence of norms that prescribe friendliness and courtesy. If the belief that neighbors should act "neighborly" overrides all others, prejudice may decline.

Situations that encourage cooperation and interdependence (rather than competition) have been shown to be highly effective in decreasing prejudice. This was shown in a study of children in newly integrated fifth- and sixth-grade classrooms (Aronson and Osherow, 1980). Psychologists set up special interracial study groups in which each child contributed part of the lesson. All the children consequently

had to cooperate with each other in order to pass their exams. The results were dramatic. Within about a week, most of the children had abandoned the old racial put-downs in favor of much more positive interactions. Equally good results occurred in a more recent study in which highly prejudiced white women were paid to work with a black confederate on an "important project" (Cook, 1985). The cooperative interactions continued two hours a day for three weeks. At the end of the study, the women were much less prejudiced than they had been, and this drop in prejudice endured even months later. In contrast, a control group of women who were equally high in prejudice to start with showed no such decline in their negative attitudes toward blacks. Apparently, then, the right circumstances can help people to overcome racial prejudice.

Some new research by Fletcher Blanchard (1991) suggests that people who are antiracist and are willing to speak up about their convictions can help establish the sort of climate that will discourage acts of racism. In 1989 at Smith College, anonymous notes containing statements of racial hatred were sent to four black students. Several months later, this ugly incident was the focus of Blanchard's study. A young woman who said she was conducting an opinion poll for her psychology class approached 144 Smith College students, individually, as they were walking across campus. Each time, a second student, who was actually a confederate of the researcher, was stopped and asked to participate. Both students were asked how they felt the college should respond to the notes, and the confederate always answered first. If she condemned racism with an answer like "Whoever wrote those notes should be expelled," the student reacted similarly. But if she condoned racism—for example, by suggesting that the students must have done something to deserve the notes—students were less likely to condemn the acts and sometimes even expressed approval of the notes. The study emphasizes the importance of an aggressive policy against racist acts.

SEXISM

Throughout recorded history women have been viewed as weak and inferior to men. Both the Bible and the Koran (the sacred book of the Muslim religion) are filled with references to man's moral and intellectual preeminence. When God banished Adam

The male view of women as intellectually inferior was so widely held that even after the hard-fought Nineteenth Amendment gave women the right to vote in 1920, many men found the idea hilarious.

and Eve from the Garden of Eden, he did so for Eve's supposed moral weakness and disobedience. Even men of the eighteenth-century Enlightenment, who advocated sweeping social reforms, were unwilling to view women as equals. Females "must be trained to . . . master their own caprices," wrote the French philosopher Rousseau, "and to submit themselves to the will of others." This strong prejudice against women continued for generations.

Even today in the United States, a nation that we consider progressive, it is women who continue to carry out such tasks as shopping, cooking, and housekeeping, despite the fact that most also hold down full-time jobs outside the home (Rochschild, 1989). Even in families where the husband and wife are both professionals, the wife assumes more responsibility for household tasks and does the lion's share of child rearing (Biernat and Wortman, 1991). In the paid-job market, men continue to hold most of the high-status, high-paying jobs. For instance, while some 15 percent of male workers work in managerial positions, only 7 percent of female workers do (Bureau of the Census, 1982). This is true despite the lack of any concrete evidence that women are less capable leaders than men (Spence et al., 1985). Many employers simply refuse to consider women for higher-status positions that are traditionally filled by men. In one study, for

instance, researchers sent fictional résumés to real employers (Glick et al., 1988). The applicant, a recent college graduate, was named either Kate or Ken Norris. Some résumés described Kate or Ken's previous experience as working in a sporting goods store and on a grounds-maintenance crew, and serving as captain of a basketball team. The employers were asked, among other things, if they would consider the applicant for the position of sales manager at a machinery company (a traditionally "male" job). Most said they would interview Ken but not Kate, even though the two had identical backgrounds.

In other parts of the world, moreover, the economic position of women is far worse than in the United States. Although women constitute one-half of the world's population, they contribute two-thirds of the total working hours, earn one-tenth of all the income, and own only one-hundredth of all the property. What could possibly justify such unequal treatment of women?

SEX STEREOTYPES

The answer lies in widespread stereotypes. Even though the behavioral differences between the sexes are very small, most people believe they are substan-

On TV as in real life, gender stereotypes are slow to change. Fictional newswoman Murphy Brown (portrayed by Candice Bergen) and her guest star, real-life news anchorwoman Connie Chung, are evidence that it has become more acceptable for female characters to be over forty and to pursue careers—but they still have to be beautiful.

tial. For instance, when asked to describe the personality of the "average" man, people tend to view him as active, aggressive, independent, dominant, competitive, ambitious, and a good decision maker, all the traits we associate with competency (Romer and Cherry, 1980). Men "take charge" and "get things done"; they are considered "natural" leaders. The "average" woman, in contrast, is seen as much the opposite. She is believed to be passive, unaggressive, uncompetitive, dependent, submissive, low in ambition, and a generally poor decision maker—in short, a "natural" subordinate. Despite changes in men's and women's roles in recent decades, these sex stereotypes survive (Martin, 1987).

Not only do they survive, they begin to influence parents and children right from birth. The parents of

newborn girls describe their babies as smaller, softer, weaker, more delicate, and more fine-featured than do the parents of newborn boys (Rubin et al., 1974; Spence et al., 1985). In fact, those differences are more perceived than real. Nevertheless, most parents soon begin to act on these stereotypes, as we saw in Chapter 10. Although sometimes unaware of what they are doing, they teach their children a host of traditional assumptions about what boys and girls are like.

Gender differentiation occurs at every stage of development and in virtually every setting and activity. Consider the example of computers. Computer literacy will be essential for tomorrow's workers, yet the majority of computer and video games are designed with boys in mind. In school, computer programming is usually treated as a branch of math, which parents and teachers alike tend to see as a male preserve (Chipman et al., 1985). When forty-three educators were asked to design a computer program to teach grammar to seventh graders, they used questions and examples that appeal to boys (even though thirty-four of the educators were themselves female) (Huff and Cooper, 1987).

In addition to learning gender stereotypes from the adults they interact with, children learn them from the mass media as well. On prime-time TV, there are distinct differences in the way men and women are portrayed (Signorielli, 1989). Female characters are nearly always young and attractive. Until recently, women were rarely shown working outside the home; if they did work, they were usually single or divorced. In the last few years, some shows —"Cosby," "thirtysomething," and "LA Law," for example—have portrayed women's attempts to combine work and family responsibilities. But for the most part, women are shown as struggling to cope with the simultaneous demands of their careers and family life. In contrast, men on prime-time shows tend to be older, wealthier, and more powerful. They appear to meet the demands of work and family with relatively little effort. Many commercials also continue to portray traditional sex roles. Nine times out of ten, the narrator of an ad—the voice of authority—is a man (Bretl and Cantor, 1988). Does viewing these sex stereotypes really have an impact on how children think? Very likely it does. For instance, several studies have found that the more TV young adolescent girls watch, the more stereotyped their conceptions of the two sexes, and the lower their self-confidence (Geis et al., 1984; Morgan, 1982). Of course, it could be that girls with very stereotyped views of men and women are drawn to entertainment that confirms those stereotypes. But at the very least, exposure to sex stereotypes on television is probably helping to reinforce traditional gender-role schemas.

WHY DO SEX STEREOTYPES ENDURE?

Why do sex stereotypes endure in a society that claims to adhere to egalitarian values and has even passed laws against sex discrimination? Earlier in the chapter we noted that even when evidence contradicts stereotypes, people will still use the evidence to confirm the stereotypes. Take the case of a woman who rises to a position of influence in a firm. Because others at her level are primarily men, her "femaleness" is very salient. When other people want to explain the woman's behavior, this salient feature is often the first thing they think of. Thus, if the woman is perceptive enough to forsee some critical problem, her male colleagues may attribute her insight to "woman's intuition." Or if the woman delays in making a decision for valid reasons, the men may nonetheless interpret her behavior as feminine indecisiveness. In these ways, the men confirm their stereotyped views, and so the stereotypes endure despite the woman's capabilities in a high-level job.

Sex stereotypes also endure because social situations often encourage people to act in ways consistent with those stereotypes. For example, women have been found to eat less when they are with a man, apparently because eating a lot is considered unfeminine, and women think that men like "femininity" (Gilbert et al., 1981; Mori et al., 1987). Significantly,

the more attractive the man she is with, the less a woman will eat!

This finding suggests that people shape the gender roles they play to suit their social situations. A woman who is submissive and coy on a date is perfectly capable of adopting a "take-charge" approach when organizing a group of children for an outing. Similarly, a man who acts "macho" with his football buddies can be "sweet" and gentle when he visits his elderly grandmother. It all depends on the situation. But the problem is that because of the way men's and women's work has traditionally been divided, the two sexes typically find themselves in roles that call for gender-stereotyped behaviors (Eagly, 1987). In our society, for instance, the construction and finance industries are dominated by men, while women are more apt to provide services (nurse, teacher, waitress, mother, homemaker). Thus, men are often called upon to wield physical or economic power, while women are expected to show patience and concern for others. Over time we come to believe that the actors are truly "living" their parts, that men are dominant and women caring "by nature."

This cycle, of course, is self-perpetuating. We place people in certain roles, they act accordingly, and then we use those actions as evidence that people's roles are "right" for them. As a result, we steer future generations into the same roles, and the pattern repeats itself. The perpetuation of sexism, then, is a complex process. A full explanation of it must include all the social psychological processes we have described here.

SUMMARY

1. Social psychologists believe that the presence and behavior of other people strongly influence how we think and act. One area they investigate is **attitudes** —dispositions to respond favorably or unfavorably toward some person, thing, event, place, idea, or situation. How attitudes can be changed is a topic that has generated much research. One approach has been to study **persuasive communications,** messages deliberately intended to change attitudes. Some messages are more persuasive than others because of differences in such things as their content and source. Sometimes people carefully analyze central aspects of a message before deciding to accept or reject it. Other

times they take a short-cut (heuristic) route to persuasion, and focus on peripheral factors such as how much applause the speaker is getting. Persuasion through the heuristic route is more likely when people lack the time, knowledge, or motivation to consider an issue closely.

2. Another approach to studying attitude change involves the concept of **cognitive consistency,** the tendency to seek compatibility among our various thoughts and behaviors. When such compatibility is lacking, people can experience psychological discomfort, or **cognitive dissonance,** which they then try to reduce, either by changing attitudes or behavior. One

alternative to cognitive dissonance theory is **self-perception theory.** It holds that in situations of potential cognitive inconsistency, we are often unsure what our true attitudes are. In such cases we simply infer non-dissonance-arousing attitudes by interpreting our own behavior in light of the circumstances that surround it.

3. The process of trying to make sense of other people is called **social cognition.** One aspect of social cognition is forming impressions of others. Often we do this on the basis of very little information. Traits that we perceive first often count the most, called the **primacy effect.** One explanation of the primacy effect is that initial information is used to form a schema of what someone is like. This schema is then used to screen additional information, and so new information tends to be skewed to match the original view. Sometimes we are so sure that the schemas we have formed of people are right, we act toward them in ways that make them *confirm* those schemas, thus creating **self-fulfilling prophecies.**

4. **Priming** occurs when someone encounters stimuli that activate a certain schema, and the schema is then used to interpret (sometimes unfairly) new, unrelated information. For instance, a woman who has just seen a movie about rape, and so is primed with a rape schema, is apt to look suspiciously at all the men she sees when walking alone at night. Priming is a behind-the-scenes form of influence. Usually, we are completely unaware that a previously activated schema is affecting what we think and do.

5. People often try to figure out the causes of others' behavior, a process called forming **causal attribution.** Jones and Davis argue that behavior that is in some way unexpected provides the greatest insight into a person's nature. Kelley believes that we can sometimes attribute the cause even of ambiguous behavior if we have time to analyze the nature of the behavior carefully. (Is it consistent? Shared by others? Confined only to certain situations?)

6. Frequently we make errors in causal attributions. The **fundamental attribution error** refers to the tendency when interpreting others' behavior to give too much weight to personality factors and not enough to situational ones. We do not usually do this when assessing our own behavior, however. When we are the actor (as opposed to the observer), we are much more likely to consider the situation when making causal inferences. This is called the **actor-observer bias.**

One exception is the inclination to take personal credit for things that go well, called the **self-serving bias.**

7. Social psychologists have also studied interpersonal attraction, friendship, and love. They have found that people are drawn to each other for a variety of reasons, including physical attractiveness, proximity and repeated exposure, perceptions of mutual liking, and similarities in attitudes, habits, and backgrounds. Similarity between two people can also help to make a love relationship last. So can certain personality traits, such as empathy for others, a "forgiving" way of attributing causes to a loved one's behavior (seeing extenuating circumstances for undesirable actions), and a generally secure, trusting style of relating to other people. This last factor may be heavily influenced by experiences in infancy.

8. People are also capable of forming social **prejudices,** inflexible, negative attitudes toward members of a minority group based on erroneous or incomplete information. The cognitive component of social prejudices are social **stereotypes,** preconceived ideas about what members of minority groups are like. Stereotypes are often used to justify **discrimination,** the behavioral expression of prejudice.

9. **Racism** is prejudice toward members of racial groups other than one's own. Often the overt racism of the past is being replaced by a new form of *disguised racism.* People bend over backwards to appear non-racist, but their prejudices are revealed in subtle ways. Causes of lingering racism may include **authoritarian personality** traits, strong intergroup competition (which may also involve frustration), perceptions of **in-groups** and **out-groups,** the self-esteem derived from devaluating out-groups, and the tendency of racial prejudice to be learned as a cultural norm. Psychologists have found that one of the best ways to combat racism is to encourage participation in cooperative activities with someone of another race.

10. **Sexism,** or prejudice toward one sex (almost always women), has existed throughout recorded history. Even today in democratic nations, people hold negative stereotypes about women. Children learn these stereotypes from their parents and other adults, from their peers, and from the mass media. The stereotypes endure partly because those who hold them tend to focus on confirming information and ignore contradictory evidence (or discount it as exceptions). Gender stereotypes also survive because social tradi-

tions often place men and women in roles where sex-typed behaviors are called for. Observers then make the fundamental attribution error: they assume that the behaviors they see are caused by the "inner natures" of the two sexes, rather than by situational forces.

SUGGESTED READINGS

Aronson, E. (1984). *The social animal* (4th ed.). New York: Freeman. This book, which won an American Psychological Association National Media award, is an engaging, easy-to-read introduction to social psychology.

Fiske, S., and Taylor, S. (1991). *Social cognition.* New York: McGraw-Hill. A scholarly yet readable discussion of major topics in the field of social cognition, including attribution, schemas, and social inferences.

Hatfield, E., and Specher, S. (1986). *Mirror, mirror . . . The importance of looks in everyday life.* New York: SUNY Press. In this excellent, popular book, social psychologists describe and analyze the importance attributed to physical attractiveness.

Ross, L., and Nisbett, R. E. (1991). *The person and the situation.* New York: McGraw-Hill. An excellent, brief introduction to the field of social psychology. Citing many examples acress cultures and history, the authors explain how powerful social forces interact with our personal psyches to shape our beliefs, our behavior, and our lives.

Zimbardo, P., and Leippe, R. (1991). *Attitudes and attitude change.* This book combines a discussion of classic research with contemporary findings to provide an engaging overview of the field of attitude change.

CHAPTER 19

SOCIAL INFLUENCE AND HUMAN BEHAVIOR

On March 16, 1968, three platoons of American soldiers, known collectively as Charlie Company, swept into the South Vietnamese village of My Lai and killed several hundred unarmed civilians—women, children, and old men. Although the civilians offered no resistance, the Americans set fire to huts, drove the fleeing villagers into open areas, and began to shoot everyone. Some of the men reported that they followed the orders of their leader, Lieutenant William Calley. Others said they simply followed the example of others. Most of the soldiers joined in the shooting; of those who did not fire, not one attempted to stop the slaughter. They stood by as bodies piled up in ditches and the village burned to the ground.

When reports of the massacre reached the United States, most Americans were outraged. How could these soldiers—normal, decent, "all-American boys" —have committed such an atrocity? The investigation that followed revealed that the soldiers of Charlie Company had sustained heavy casualties since arriving in Vietnam only a month earlier. Frightened by the dangers of entering My Lai, which was thought to be an enemy stronghold, upset by the loss of their comrades, and eager for revenge, the soldiers apparently shot without thinking.

The My Lai massacre was one of America's darkest moments in the long and controversial Vietnam war. It is a disturbing illustration of the social psychological perspective we introduced in Chapter 18. How people think and act is not just a product of their inner dispositions. The men of Charlie Company were probably not cruel and without conscience, as many people thought (recall the fundamental attribution error we discussed in Chapter 18). It is more accurate to say that these were basically ordinary people responding to very extraordinary circumstances. In fact, there is a good chance that you would have responded in much the same way. This chapter examines some of the powerful social forces that psychological research shows can sometimes make people behave in ways they would never expect.

Whereas Chapter 18 focused primarily on how social circumstances shape people's attitudes, perceptions, and feelings, this chapter focuses mainly on how social situations influence the way people *act*. We begin with two behavioral patterns of major concern to social psychologists: conformity and obedience. Provocative findings in both these areas explain much about the events at My Lai. We then turn to the topic of human groups and their influence. If you have ever wondered how prisoners of war can be brainwashed, some of your questions will be answered here. Final-

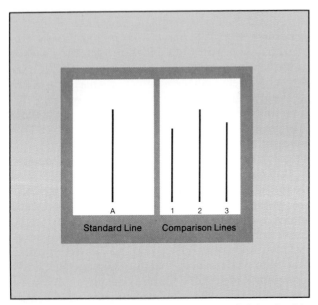

FIGURE 19.1 The stimuli in a single trial in Asch's experiment. The subject must state which of the comparison lines he or she judges to be the same length as the standard. The discrimination is easy to make: control subjects (those who made the judgments without any group pressure) chose line 2 as correct more than 99 percent of the time. (*After Asch, 1951.*)

ly, we examine the causes of both aggression and altruism. You will find that many social forces that influence people can be harnessed for good or ill.

GOING ALONG WITH OTHERS

Most Americans insist that if they had lived in Germany during World War II, they would never have gone along with Adolf Hitler's policy of exterminating the Jews. Could the Germans who not only accepted this policy but actively helped to carry it out all have been mentally deranged and sadistic, as our attributional biases lead us to suspect? As in the case of the My Lai massacre, the answer is "no." Some social forces are powerful enough to make average people publicly support a view they may not really believe in or commit an act that in other circumstances they would consider morally indefensible. To understand what these powerful social forces are, we will investigate three behaviors: conformity, obedience, and compliance.

CONFORMING TO PREVAILING NORMS

Conformity is the tendency to shift one's opinions or actions to correspond with those of other people because of implicit or explicit social pressure (Kiesler and Kiesler, 1969). The extreme example of conformity at My Lai occurred under the fear, stress, and confusion of battle. As one soldier put it, "I looked around and saw everyone shooting. I didn't know what to do, so I started shooting" (*Time*, December 5, 1969). Although the consequences of conformity are seldom this devastating, essentially the same psychological process underlies many of the choices we make every day. Have you ever found yourself ridiculing an acquaintance because others whom you admire were making fun of that person? Note that when you conform, you are not necessarily convinced that what you are saying or doing is right. You may even feel that your actions are wrong. But you feel more strongly that others expect or demand that you do it, or say it, their way.

While we can all find instances of conformity in our lives, just how powerful or extensive is the behavior? One social psychologist, Solomon Asch, decided to find out in a classic series of experiments (1951). If you had been a subject in one of Asch's studies, this is what would have happened: You and seven other students report to a classroom for an experiment on visual judgment. The experimenter displays two large white cards like the ones shown in Figure 19.1. On one card is a single vertical line, which is to serve as a standard. On the other card are three vertical lines of different lengths. You are simply to determine which of the three lines is the same length as the standard line.

The experiment opens uneventfully. The subjects give their answers in the order in which they are seated, you being next to last. On the first trial, everyone chooses the correct line. The second set of cards is shown, and once again the choice is unanimous. The judgments are easy, and you settle in for what you expect will be a rather boring experiment. On the third trial, however, something strange happens. The first person says that line 1 matches the standard, even though it is obvious to you that line 2 is the correct choice. The second person unhesitatingly agrees that line 1 is the right answer, and so do the third, fourth, fifth, and sixth subjects. Now it is your turn, and you are faced with a dilemma. Your own eyes unmistakenly tell you that line 2 is the correct response, but six other people have unanimously and

These photographs were taken during Asch's experiment on conformity. Number 6 is the only real subject; the others are confederates of the experimenter (seen at the right in the upper-left photograph). The subject listens to the others express identical judgments that differ from his own. He shows uneasiness at his dilemma: should he express the judgment he knows to be correct and risk being different from the group, or should he conform to the group's judgment?

confidently selected line 1. What should you do? Stand alone as a minority of one, or go along with the unanimous majority?

A surprising number of Asch's subjects went along with the majority's choice of an incorrect answer. The other participants in the studies were, of course, confederates of the experimenter, and the experiment consisted of twelve "critical" trials, in which the unanimous majority agreed on an obviously wrong answer, interspersed with many trials in which the other participants chose the correct line. Out of all the answers to critical trials given by a total of fifty subjects, about a third were conforming responses and two-thirds were independent. Roughly *70 percent* of the subjects conformed at least once. Twenty-five percent of the subjects were always independent, while only 5 percent were always conforming. Thus, independence prevailed overall, but the amount of yielding was significant, especially when one considers how easy the task was. A comparison group, which gave its answers in writing in private, made very few errors in judging the lines.

FACTORS INFLUENCING CONFORMITY

Several factors have been found to influence how conforming a subject is in an experiment. One factor is the extent of agreement among the participants. Asch found that when just one confederate out of six gave the correct answer, the proportion of conforming responses on the part of subjects dropped dramatically to only 5 percent (Asch, 1956). Another factor influencing conformity is previous exposure to dissenters. In one experiment, subjects had a chance to observe a lone dissenter in a study of color discrimination. In a subsequent experiment, these same subjects exhibited their own independence by deviating from a unanimous incorrect choice 76 percent of the time. Those subjects in this experiment who had *not* witnessed the dissenter conformed 70 percent of the time (Nemeth and Chiles, 1988). Anonymity also appears to reduce conformity. When people are allowed to sit in a private compartment and indicate their answer by pressing a button, they conform much less frequently (Deutsch and Gerard, 1955).

But it is not just the situation that leads to conformity. Personal traits, too, make us more or less likely to conform. Those who are high in self-doubt conform significantly more than those who are self-confident (Campbell et al., 1986). Being lower in status than other group members, or having generally low self-esteem, or knowing that you will have to interact with group members in the future can all make a person more likely to conform (Aronson and

Osherow, 1980; Dittes and Kelley, 1956; Raven and French, 1958).

The conformity of subjects in Asch's experiment can be described as an outward yielding to the group consensus, while inwardly retaining one's own opinions (Kelman, 1958, 1961). The major motivation for this yielding is fear of negative consequences—in this case, appearing foolish by deviating from the majority view. From comments made by Asch's subjects in postexperiment interviews, it is clear that many realized their conforming answers had been wrong, but they did not want to appear as "misfits" or stick out like a "sore thumb." One subject reported: "If I'd been first I probably would have responded differently" (Asch, 1956, p. 31). This was his way of saying that he knew perfectly well what the correct answers were, but he was still unable to contradict the group. Such findings have relevance to the My Lai incident. The soldiers of Charlie Company knew that their actions violated guidelines they had learned during their training. But this knowledge did not prevent them from killing the villagers. Even when conformity leads to extremely negative consequences, the tendency to conform remains strong.

How powerful are the negative consequences of not going along? In Hitler's Germany, it was commonly understood that those who opposed, resisted, or interfered with Hitler's policy of persecuting the Jews could lose their lives. But we do not live in Nazi Germany. Were Asch's nonconforming subjects really made to feel so psychologically uncomfortable? What actually happens to people who do not go along with the group? Research shows that the negative outcomes are often greater than many people think. The nonconformist is usually ostracized in subtle and not-so-subtle ways. For instance, when conventionally and unconventionally dressed college students asked shoppers in a supermarket to change a dime for two nickels, the unconventional-looking students were much more likely to be refused (Raymond and Unger, 1972). The desire to stay in the good graces of a crowd may explain the behavior of referees during professional basketball games. During one recent season, referees called fewer fouls on the star players of the Los Angeles Lakers when they were playing at home (2.4 fouls per game) than when they were playing away (3.1 fouls per game). Nonstar players were called for the same number of fouls at home and away (Lehman and Reifman, 1987).

Other types of conformity make this subject even more complex (Kelman, 1958, 1961). In addition to an outward yielding to avoid negative consequences, there is conformity through **identification,** the tendency to go along with others because we admire and wish to be like them. A young German soldier who treats Jewish prisoners cruelly because he wants to be similar to officers he respects is conforming through identification. Conformity can also involve **internalization,** or coming to accept others' views and actions as appropriate and right. If the young German soldier not only mimics his superiors' actions but actually believes that their cruelty toward Jews is justified, his conformity is partly a matter of internalized prejudices. These different types of conformity help us to predict how enduring a person's behavior is likely to be. For instance, the person who is merely complying will probably stop if the threat of negative consequences is lifted. In contrast, the person who is conforming because of internalization is much more likely to continue the behavior in question, even when he or she is alone or when there is no external pressure to do so.

Some people with a strong need for self-expression will take the opportunity *not* to conform in social influence situations. This expression of individuality is most likely to occur when it is possible for one to come up with a new solution and not simply agree or disagree with a majority's findings (Santee and Maslach, 1982). In that case the dissent can take some creative forms. A profile of those who were found to be "creative dissenters" in a conformity study showed certain common characteristics: high self-esteem, low anxiety in social situations, and willingness to stand out in a crowd (Maslach et al., 1985). On average, men are more likely than women to express dissent, perhaps because they tend to equate competence with "standing out." Women, on the other hand, tend to associate cooperation and agreement with competence. For them, a conforming response may be a more positive way of expressing themselves than dissent (Santee and Jackson, 1982).

Although the consequences of conformity can be brutal, as at My Lai and in Nazi Germany, more recent political events have shown the positive side of conformity (Zimbardo and Leippe, 1991). As more and more people in Eastern European countries took to the streets to protest repressive Communist regimes, the pressure to join in won over many fence straddlers until a "critical mass" was reached that was able to topple the rulers. Conformity, then, can encourage people to perform socially valued acts. It can also fulfill such important personal needs as the need to be liked and accepted. As one social psychologist has commented, "The person who refused to accept anyone's word of advice on any topic whatsoever would probably make just as big a botch of life . . . as the person who always conformed" (Collins, 1970, p. 21).

OBEYING ORDERS: DOING THE UNTHINKABLE

Obedience, following the specific commands of a person in authority, differs from conformity in that it is a response to *explicit* instructions, not just to implicit social pressures. Sometimes obedience serves constructive purposes. Society could not function if most people disobeyed the laws requiring them to pay their taxes or to stop at traffic lights. But at other times obedience demands that people do things they feel are wrong. Such destructive obedience was the focus of investigations by social psychologist Stanley Milgram (1963, 1965b). Milgram's research has shown that many "average" people—people who think they would never participate in brutality—might nevertheless inflict severe pain on their fellow humans if an authority figure told them to do so.

THE MILGRAM STUDIES

Milgram's subjects were men of different ages and occupations, but all had one thing in common: they had answered a request for people to participate in a study on learning at Yale University (Milgram, 1963). Upon arriving at the laboratory, each man was introduced to his supposed cosubject, a mild-mannered, likable man of about fifty, who was actually a confederate in the experiment. The two were asked to draw lots to determine who would be the "teacher" and who would be the "learner." The drawing was rigged so that the real subject always became the teacher.

The experimenter, a stern man in a gray laboratory coat, then explained the purpose and procedure of the study. The experiment, he said, was designed to investigate the effects of punishment on learning. The teacher was to read a list of word pairs to the learner,

who was supposed to memorize them. Then the teacher was to test the learner. Since the teacher and the learner would be in adjoining rooms, the learner was to indicate his choice of the correct word by pressing a button on a panel before him. This would activate a corresponding light on the teacher's control panel.

Every time the learner made a mistake, the teacher was to punish him by administering electric shock from an authentic-looking shock generator. The generator had thirty clearly marked voltage switches, ranging from 15 to 450 volts. Labels under the switches indicated the intensity of the shock, beginning with slight shock and progressing through moderate, strong, very strong, intense, extremely intense, and severe (also marked "Danger"), and ending with the most severe of all, ominously labeled "XXX." With each additional mistake the learner made, the teacher was to increase the shock by one level, or 15 volts.

Everyone then proceeded to the room where the learner would sit. The teacher watched as the learner was strapped into a chair and an electrode (presumably connected to the shock generator) was attached to his wrist. The teacher and the experimenter then went to the generator room, where the teacher was given a "sample shock" of 45 volts from a concealed battery. The generator itself was a phony, incapable of producing anything except buzzing and clicking sounds. For the teacher, however, the sample shock "proved" the authenticity of the machine. The learning trials were now ready to begin.

The experimental plan called for the learner to make many mistakes, requiring the teacher to administer increasingly severe shocks. If the teacher proceeded up to 300 volts (the highest level in the "intense shock" range), the learner would pound on the wall in protest. At 315 volts ("extremely intense shock") the learner would pound loudly again and then fall silent. After this, no more lights would flash on the teacher's panel in answer to his word-pair questions. If the teacher asked how to proceed in this situation, the experimenter would instruct him to treat the absence of a response as a wrong response and continue raising the voltage. If at any point the teacher asked to stop the procedure, the experimenter would tell him to continue, with a number of standardized commands ranging from a stern "Please go on" to an emphatic "You have no choice, you *must* go

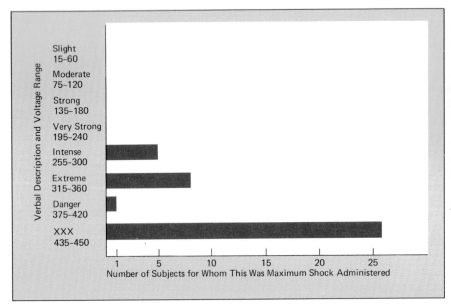

FIGURE 19.2   Results of Stanley Milgram's classic experiment on obedience. Subjects were told to administer increasing amounts of shock to a "learner" on the pretext that scientists were studying the effects of punishment on learning. Of forty experimental subjects, all administered shocks scaled "intense" or higher, and only fourteen refused to go all the way to the most severe, "XXX" shock level. (*After Milgram, 1963.*)

on." If the teacher still refused to obey, the experiment would immediately end.

How long do you think most subjects continued to deliver what they believed to be painful and increasingly dangerous electric shocks to a defenseless victim? When Milgram posed this question to a group of psychology majors, they confidently predicted that few, if any, subjects would go beyond the "very strong shock" level; that is, they would never get to the point where the learner had to pound on the wall for release. A group of psychiatrists offered similar opinions. They felt that only 4 percent of the subjects would continue to shock the learner when he failed to respond (at 315 volts), and that less than 1 percent would administer the highest possible shock. Most people agree with these predictions, which is why the true results are so disturbing. Out of a total of forty subjects, twenty-six, or 65 percent, obeyed the experimenter all the way to the very highest voltage level (see Figure 19.2).

These men were not sadists. In fact, most showed signs of severe emotional strain and psychological conflict during the experiment. They trembled, stuttered, groaned, perspired heavily, bit their lips, laughed nervously, and dug their fingernails into their palms. They frequently asked if they might please stop. But when the experimenter asked them to continue, they obeyed him. As one observer who watched the proceedings through a one-way mirror related:

> I observed a mature and initially poised businessman enter the laboratory smiling and confident. Within 20 minutes he was reduced to a twitching, stuttering wreck, who was rapidly approaching a point of nervous collapse. He constantly pulled on his earlobe and twisted his hands. At one point he pushed his fist into his forehead and muttered: "Oh God, let's stop it." And yet he continued to respond to every word of the experimenter and obeyed to the end. (quoted in Milgram, 1963, p. 377)

Milgram's sample was not at all unrepresentative. His ad did not, just by chance, attract an unusual number of men who were unable to defy authority. Milgram's results have been replicated many times in about half a dozen different countries, with women as subjects as well as men. Very reliably, roughly two-thirds obey the experimenter to the end (Manell, 1971; Milgram, 1974).

Milgram (1965b, 1974) designed a series of follow-up experiments in an effort to find out what factors might lessen such an extraordinary degree of obedience. He discovered that as auditory, visual, and physical contact with the victim increased, the maxi-

FIGURE 19.3 This graph of the results of some of Milgram's studies on obedience shows that the closer the subject was to the victim, the less the amount of shock he was willing to administer, despite the experimenter's demands that he continue. As proximity increased, compliance decreased. (*After Milgram, 1974.*)

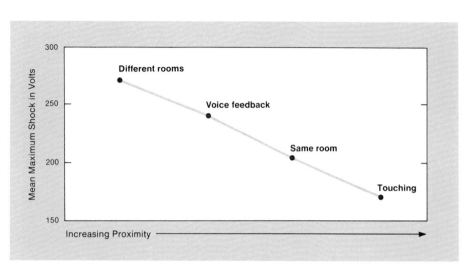

mum shock that the subjects delivered decreased (see Figure 19.3). Obedience also dropped sharply when the experimenter left the room and gave his orders by telephone. Only 22 percent obeyed to the end when the experimenter was not present. It is also easier to disobey an authority when others provide models of defiance. Only 10 percent obeyed to the end after the subjects observed two coteachers refuse to proceed. When the illusion of unanimity is broken, people tend to stop going along with a response that is clearly wrong. This stresses the importance of speaking out when we observe some injustice. Not only may we help the victim in such cases, we may also prompt others to follow our lead (Hollander, 1975).

THE ETHICS OF MILGRAM'S STUDIES

Milgram's experiment raised an explosive controversy over the ethics of his procedures. Critics charged that, without forewarning and prior permission, Milgram knowingly exposed people to enormous stress and may have caused them long-term psychological harm (Baumrind, 1964). Subjects who followed the experimenter's commands to the very end learned a disturbing fact about themselves: they were willing to obey an authority figure even if it meant performing a callous and inhumane act. Might not some subjects find this revelation difficult to live with? At the very least, might it not injure their self-concepts? According to Bem's self-perception theory, discussed in Chapter 18, people who observe themselves acting cruelly in the absence of sufficient external pressures may conclude that they must be less sensitive than they formerly thought. In addition, might not participation in Milgram's experiments reduce a person's trust of legitimate authorities encountered in the future? After all, a Yale psychologist had duped them into acting immorally.

Milgram, however, flatly denied that his procedures caused any lasting harm (Milgram, 1964, 1968, 1974). He pointed out that all his sessions ended with a thorough debriefing, in which the experimenter explained that shocks had never really been given and took care to reassure obedient subjects that their behavior had been entirely normal. As a result of these measures, Milgram argued, no subject left the laboratory in a continuing state of anxiety. Moreover, follow-up questionnaires indicated that most of the subjects (84 percent) were glad to have participated in Milgram's research because they learned something important about human behavior. And as for damaging subjects' ability to trust legitimate authorities in the future, Milgram argued that skepticism toward authorities who require us to act cruelly is a very valuable thing.

What the Asch and Milgram Studies Mean Both the Asch and the Milgram studies yielded important information about human behavior. It appears that our inner moral sense is vulnerable to external pressure and that, in fact, the influence of others can override our convictions. The cruelty exhibited by the subjects of the Milgram experiment was the result of

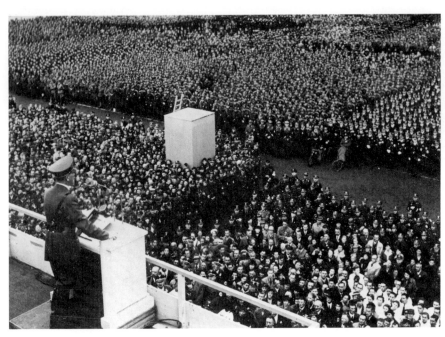

The atrocities committed by ordinary Germans during Adolf Hitler's Third Reich prompted social psychologists to intensify their research into obedience and conformity.

greater social pressure than was exerted on the subjects in Asch's conformity studies. Milgram's subjects did not set out to be cruel, but they did respond to the power of the experimenter's commands, which were apparently more influential than the pleas of the victims for release. Obedience took precedence over the desire to avoid doing harm.

A more recent experiment shows that obedience is still a very relevant social phenomenon. Two Dutch psychologists devised an experiment that called for subjects to disrupt an employment test being taken by an applicant for a job, ultimately causing the applicant to fail the test (Meeus and Raaijmakers, 1986, 1987). The subjects were told that the experiment was to test the effects of stress on the applicants, but in fact the experimenters were interested in how far the subjects would follow orders. The subjects were asked to send fifteen derogatory computer messages that made the applicant progressively more tense, irritable, and despairing. Despite finding their task very disagreeable, 90 percent of the subjects complied to the end. These subjects justified their actions by transferring responsibility for them to the experimenters. The lessons of the Milgram studies and subsequent experiments on obedience should teach us to be wary of authority figures (including political leaders) and alert us to the potential for destructiveness that lies within ourselves. Milgram explained the fundamental lesson of his study: "Ordinary people,

simply doing their jobs, and without any particular hostility on their part, can become agents in a terrible destructive process" (Milgram, 1974, p. 6).

Common Compliance Techniques   Have you ever said "yes" to a sales pitch when you did not really want the product? Have you agreed to join a committee and then a moment later been annoyed with yourself for saying "yes"? If so, you have experienced **compliance**—the act of going along with an *explicit request* from someone who does not hold any particular authority over you. Why do people comply, sometimes against their own better judgment? Psychologists have found that the answer lies largely in how they are approached. Certain techniques can even sway someone who "knows better." Social psychologists have studied these techniques by observing those who make their living getting others to comply with their requests or plans, including fundraisers, car salespersons, and con artists of various kinds. One psychologist even took an automobile sales training course to get a firsthand look at the techniques used (Cialdini, 1988).

One compliance technique uses what is called the **foot-in-the-door phenomenon.** It involves first making a very small request that someone is almost sure to comply with (the foot in the door, so to speak), and then requesting something much more demanding. People who go along with the first request tend to comply with the second one too. In one study of this technique, a researcher telephoned housewives, ostensibly as part of a consumer survey (Freedman and Fraser, 1966). If a woman agreed to talk with the researcher, she was asked eight simple questions about the soaps she used. Then, three days later, the researcher called the same women and asked if a team of half a dozen men could come to their homes to count and classify all the household products. The same intrusive request was made of another group of women who had not complied with the earlier, much smaller survey. The women who had first agreed to the small request were two times more likely than the other women to agree to the larger request. Other researchers have conducted studies that confirm these findings, even among young children (Dillard et al., 1984; Eisenberg et al., 1987).

Why should this be? Perhaps, once people agree to one request, their attitudes toward agreeing change and they come to perceive themselves as individuals who cooperate with others or are committed to what they have begun (Dejong and Musilli, 1982; Freedman and Fraser, 1966). Companies seek to induce such an attitude change in people through the ads they send to potential customers. By making small requests, such as asking potential buyers to scratch a card to see if they have won a prize or to place a token on an order blank, they hope ultimately to commit the consumer to buying the product.

Robert Cialdini and his colleagues (1975) tried reversing the foot-in-the-door technique by first making an impossibly large request and then following up with a much more realistic one. In one study, for instance, some subjects were asked to escort disadvantaged children on a two-hour trip to the zoo. Only 32 percent agreed. Other subjects were first asked to make a two-*year* commitment as a volunteer counselor for delinquent youth. All of them refused. But when later asked if they could at least serve as an escort on a two-hour trip to the zoo, nearly 56 percent agreed. This approach has been called the **door-in-the-face technique,** because the person asked to do the favor seems at first to be slamming the door in the face of the requester. The technique apparently works because most people feel obligated to make mutual concessions: if the requester accepts the first rejection without argument, the person being asked feels obligated to agree to the smaller request.

A third compliance technique is based on the **low-ball phenomenon,** reportedly used by new-car salespeople. A salesperson who uses this technique talks a customer into buying a car at a very good price. Once the customer is ready to sign the sales contract, the salesperson eliminates the price advantage, typically by saying that "the boss" has disallowed the deal because "we'd be losing money." Those in the automobile sales business say that more customers will stand by their decision to buy the car—even though it is now more costly—than would have bought it if the actual price had been divulged at the beginning. Cialdini and his colleagues (1978) demonstrated the low-ball phenomenon in a series of experiments. In one study, college students were invited to participate in an experiment on thinking processes. Of those who were first told that the experiment was to be held at an inconveniently early hour (7 A.M.), only 24 percent agreed to participate and showed up for the appointment. But more than twice that number (53 percent) showed up if they had agreed to participate first and *then* were told the time of the appointment. Apparently, once people have made a commitment, they often feel compelled to go through with it even when key conditions change.

Another technique is one we are all familiar with—the **that's-not-all technique.** How often have you been offered something for sale, and before you had a chance to reply "yes" or "no," the seller "sweetens" the deal by reducing the price or giving two for the price of one? The apparent concession is one the seller had intended to make all along, but the buyer is not supposed to know that. The idea behind this technique is that one concession deserves another (and who can resist a "bargain"?). In a study of the technique, Jerry Burger (1986) set up a booth at a fair where he sold cupcakes. The first customers were told that the cupcakes cost 75 cents; later customers were given a price of $1, but before they could reply, the seller "reduced" the price to 75 cents. Sales increased from 44 to 73 percent as a result of this technique.

Techniques of compliance are not always as harmless as these examples suggest. The same idea of escalating commitment was used to devastating effect in Milgram's experiments on obedience. It is unlikely that many subjects would have administered the most severe shock on the first learning trial, but by starting with mild shocks and gradually strengthening the commitment, the experimenter brought about complete obedience. Torturers have been trained with the same step-by-step approach—first assigned to guard prisoners, then to make arrests, then told to hit the prisoner occasionally, with the last steps being observation and then torture (Haritos-Fatouros, 1988).

THE SOCIAL SIGNIFICANCE OF GROUPS

What constitutes a group? Do passengers on a bus make a group? How about two people who regularly play tennis together? In social psychological terms, the first example would not qualify as a group, but the second would. To be a **group,** a collection of two or more people must meet three criteria (McGrath, 1984; Shaw, 1976). First, members must interact regularly in fairly structured and predictable ways. Second, they must share one or more specific goals, aimed at satisfying certain mutual needs. And finally, members must identify themselves as part of a whole, sharing to some extent a common fate.

Groups can influence human behavior in countless ways. In this chapter we will focus on just a few. First, we will look at how the roles people play in groups can lead them to think and act in ways they might never imagine themselves capable of. Second, we will examine how merely being in a group or in the presence of a group can affect the quality of people's performances and decisions. Finally, we will take a look at the conditions that permit minorities within a group to have a powerful influence over the majority members.

HOW GROUP ROLES SHAPE THOUGHT AND BEHAVIOR

Psychologists have noticed that people often seem to "fit" the roles they play within a group. The clergyman, for instance, is often paternal; the drill sergeant, demanding; the bureaucrat, inflexible; the college professor, intellectual. Although you may think that people fall into roles that suit their inner natures, this is not always the case. Often, it is the role that shapes the person, not the other way around. There is no better illustration of this fundamental fact than a study conducted by psychologist Philip Zimbardo and his colleagues (Zimbardo et al., 1972, 1973).

Zimbardo set out to examine how the prison roles of inmate and guard affect how people in these roles behave. As we briefly mentioned in Chapter 18, he set up his own "mock" prison in the basement of a Stanford University building during summer session. More than seventy-five young men, mostly college students on vacation, volunteered to participate in the paid, two-week simulation of prison life. Of these, Zimbardo selected twenty-one for their emotional stability and maturity. He randomly assigned ten to the role of prisoner and eleven to the role of guard. The guards were given no instructions other than the general need to maintain "law and order."

To make the simulation as authentic as possible, prisoners were "arrested" at their homes and "booked" at the Palo Alto police station by actual police officers. They were then taken to the so-called Stanford County Prison. There they were issued uniforms and ushered into sparsely furnished cells. The first day passed without incident, but on the second day the prisoners staged a surprise revolt. This episode marked a critical turning point in the participants' behavior. After quelling the rebellion by threatening the prisoners with billy clubs and spraying them with fire extinguishers, the guards began to use their power harshly and arbitrarily. They created petty rules and demanded that the prisoners follow them to the letter. They made the inmates perform meaningless, exhausting, degrading chores, and repeatedly ridiculed and demeaned them. The reaction of the prisoners was equally disturbing. Five of them developed such severe anxiety symptoms that they had to be released from the study. The other five were reduced to servile robots. After only six days, Zimbardo was forced to abandon the research; it had become too real.

How can we explain such alarming behavior? The participants had been screened for emotional stability, so we can be reasonably sure they were not psychologically disturbed before the study began. And each person was randomly assigned to his role, so there were no consistent personality differences between the two groups at the start. Zimbardo concluded that the outcome must have been caused by the power of prison roles. The demands of being an inmate or a guard became so dominant that the subjects' personalities temporarily changed. As one ex-prisoner told an interviewer: "I began to feel that I was losing my identity. The person I call [subject's real name] . . . was distant from me, was remote, until finally I wasn't that. I was 416—I was really my number." If a normal, well-adjusted young man can be this transformed by the part he is playing in a psychological study, it is likely that many roles in real life can also exert an enormous influence on us.

Zimbardo admits that his study created an ethical dilemma similar to the one raised by Milgram's obedience research: does the study justify the poten-

 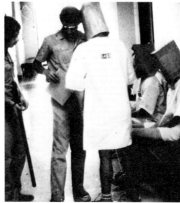 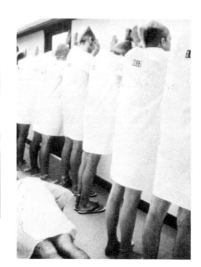

Life inside "Stanford County Prison" during Zimbardo's study of the effect of inmate and guard roles on student volunteers' behavior.

tially harmful effects on the participants? In an effort to avoid any long-term harm to his subjects, Zimbardo "debriefed" them extensively at the end of the project, encouraging them to vent their feelings. Subsequent questionnaires, interviews, and group reunions suggest that the subjects recovered reasonably well from the experience. Zimbardo argues that although the emotional price paid for this research was indeed high, the information gained was very important (Zimbardo et al., 1972). For one thing, it provided dramatic evidence that a prison environment can be socially destructive, regardless of the prior personalities of people who find themselves there. Zimbardo has made a great effort to communicate his findings to a wide audience, including prison administrators and inmates, legislators, other government officials, and the public in general. In this way he hopes to make the high price paid for his data socially worthwhile (Zimbardo, 1975).

GROUP EFFECTS ON PROBLEM SOLVING AND PERFORMANCE

Clearly, group roles shape our actions. What effects, if any, do groups have on our performance and problem-solving abilities? Does working within a group or in the presence of others help us to produce a better product? Or do people usually do their best when working alone?

SOCIAL FACILITATION

One of the earliest experiments in social psychology showed that people perform simple motor tasks faster when they compete with one another than when they merely race the clock (Triplett, 1898). Several decades later, psychologist Floyd Allport arrived at similar findings concerning simple cognitive tasks. People solving multiplication problems or generating word associations performed better in the presence of four or five others, even though each worked independently (Allport, 1920, 1924). Allport called the tendency for the presence of others to improve people's performance **social facilitation.** Even lower animals show this effect at times. For instance, in one experiment, individual ants worked harder at digging tunnels (they moved more dirt) when they worked in groups of two or three than when they worked alone (Chen, 1937).

But the findings on social facilitation were not in complete agreement. People trying to learn complex mazes usually did better when alone. And in experiments with birds, performance on certain tasks seemed to be inhibited by the presence of other birds. Somehow these contradictory findings needed to be reconciled. But how?

Psychologist Robert Zajonc (1965, 1966) proposed one way. He argued that many of the contradictions could be eliminated if we assume that the presence of others increases a person's motivation or

The presence of an audience can enhance a good pool player's performance, but onlookers can make an unskilled player perform as though he or she had never held a cue before.

drive. Studies had already demonstrated that when drive increases, subjects tend to perform the most well-learned, "automatic" responses they know— their so-called dominant responses. To this Zajonc added the observation that dominant responses sometimes facilitate, but at other times hinder the performance of a task. More specifically, when a person is confronted with very familiar tasks (such as simple arithmetic) to which the solutions are well known, increased drive should improve performance because the dominant responses are correct. In contrast, when people are faced with difficult tasks they have not yet mastered (such as solving a complex maze), increased drive should hinder performance because the dominant responses are usually inappropriate. Subsequent research has tended to support Zajonc's model of social facilitation (Guerin, 1986; Schmitt et al., 1986).

Zajonc's model has many practical applications. People who are very familiar with and skillful at the tasks they are performing—professional athletes, musicians, or actors, for example—are likely to do better in front of an audience than when they are alone. Beginning pianists and actors, however, are in a different situation. They are likely to become rattled by the presence of others, fall back on their still underdeveloped "instincts," and so perform more poorly than they would alone. In one study support-

ing this idea, the experimenters had four confederates closely observe college students who were playing pool. The results bore out Zajonc's theory: When the good players were shooting before the audience of four, their accuracy increased from 71 to 80 percent. Conversely, the accuracy of the poor players being watched fell from 36 to 25 percent (Michaels et al., 1982).

Psychologists are still trying to determine just what it is about the presence of others that causes an increase in drive. One idea is that we simply become more alert and aroused when other people are around, especially if they are strangers (Guerin, 1986). Another possibility is that the presence of others arouses evaluation apprehension, which heightens our drive. Male joggers have been found to increase their speed when encountering a woman seated in the grass facing them; their performance was unaffected if the woman's back was turned (Worringham and Messick, 1983). The self-consciousness associated with evaluation apprehension may, however, interfere with behaviors that are best performed without thinking, such as throwing free throws in a basketball game (Mullen and Baumeister, 1987). Finally, increased drive may result from a desire to overcome the distractions that the presence of others creates (Baron, 1986). On easy tasks, we may compensate for the distractions by trying harder and possibly improving our performance. On hard tasks, in contrast, distractions may make the tasks even harder to perform. Which explanation seems most likely? That depends on the situation, and there may be situations in which all three explanations have some validity.

SOCIAL LOAFING

Do you think you would perform better as an anonymous part of a group than as an individual? After all, you would have the benefit of a team effort and the comfort of not being scrutinized individually. In fact, however, these factors often have the opposite effect: most people tend to slack off when part of a group, a behavior known as **social loafing.** If you think back to group projects that you have been part of, you no doubt can point to some team members who contributed very little or less than they were capable of (you might even point to yourself). Social loafing is in many ways the mirror image of social facilitation: social facilitation improves our performance because it spotlights individual effort, whereas in situations of social loafing, our performance is pooled with that of others and is not individually identifiable.

Social loafing was discovered in experiments conducted in the 1880s by the French agricultural engineer Max Ringelmann. He found that in simple tasks calling for a collective effort, such as pulling a rope or pushing a cart, individual output declined from what people could do on their own (Ringelmann, 1913). The term *social loafing* was coined nearly one hundred years later by Bibb Latané and his colleagues, who conducted an experiment with similar results (Latané et al., 1979). They blindfolded college students and equipped them with earphones that gave off a staticlike noise. The students were then asked to yell as loudly as they could. Some students were asked to do this on their own; others were told to perform the task as part of a group; and still others *thought* they were in a group but were in fact alone. The subjects who were alone yelled louder than those in either of the other two experimental conditions, showing evidence of social loafing in group situations.

More than four dozen studies have replicated these results and show that loafing increases as the size of the group increases (Jackson and Williams, 1988). The evaluation apprehension that increases

drive in individual efforts does not seem to work in group efforts; when individuals can get lost in the crowd, they do not feel accountable for their contributions and so are not concerned about being evaluated. One way to control social loafing, then, is to get people to be more aware of their performance, perhaps by comparing it to some standard, such as a norm or how others in the group are doing (Harkins and Szymanski, 1987, 1988, 1989). Another way is to have others evaluate the individual efforts within a group; coaches do this by going over videotapes of games and pinpointing individual performances. Other conditions that can minimize social loafing include being engaged in tasks that are challenging or involving (Brickner et al., 1986), believing that one's teammates are working hard as well (Zaccaro, 1984), feeling committed to the group, and being rewarded for group success (Hackman, 1986).

DECISION MAKING IN GROUPS

Pressures to conform are especially powerful in small, close-knit groups (Blake and Mouton, 1979). When a small, cohesive group becomes so concerned with maintaining unanimity that its members can no longer appraise alternatives realistically, it has fallen victim to a phenomenon that social psychologist Irving Janis (1982, 1985) calls **groupthink.**

A classic case of groupthink occurred during John F. Kennedy's presidency, preceding what has come to be known as the Bay of Pigs fiasco. In the early part of 1961, President Kennedy and his inner circle of foreign policy advisers decided unanimously to use Cuban exiles trained by the Central Intelligence Agency to invade Fidel Castro's Cuba. Foreseeing an easy victory, the group failed to appreciate many obvious and vital factors, such as the size, strength, and loyalty of Castro's troops and the morale of the invaders. Within three days of the landing at the Bay of Pigs, 1,200 of the exile-soldiers had been captured and some 200 killed. "How," President Kennedy asked after the fiasco was over, "could we have been so stupid?"

Another disastrous group performance was the decision-making process that sent the space shuttle *Challenger* on its fatal journey in January 1986 (Magnuson, 1986). Engineers at the companies that manufactured the rocket's boosters and the orbiter warned their company managers and NASA officials of the danger of launching in subzero temperature. But

President John F. Kennedy and his advisers worked together closely—perhaps too closely. Their group solidarity, lack of dissent, and feelings of invincibility gave rise to the "groupthink" that resulted in the Bay of Pigs fiasco in 1961.

NASA pressed the managers to authorize the already much-delayed launch of *Challenger*. Overruling the engineers, the managers agreed to go ahead. In fact, the NASA executive who made the final decision to launch was never even told of the engineers' objections.

Janis maintains that, in each of these situations, poor decision making occurred because of several powerful conditions within the groups. For one thing, the groups were generally highly cohesive. In such groups, Janis argues, members often feel a strong compulsion to avoid disrupting group unity and the positive feelings it creates. As a result, they tend to convince themselves that all the group's decisions are sound, a major symptom of groupthink. Such self-imposed censorship fosters what Janis calls an *illusion of unanimity*. Members of the team assume that anyone who remains silent during policy talks must be in complete accord. This, of course, may not be the case. But once an illusion of unanimity is established, it helps convince the members that their plan must be right.

Strong cohesiveness can impair group decisions in yet another way. The close camaraderie that often arises within such groups can create feelings of euphoria and an *illusion of invulnerability*. By this, Janis means that close-knit groups sometimes come to believe that they will always be successful, no matter what the odds. As one member of Kennedy's

inner circle recalled: "It seemed that, with John Kennedy leading us and with all the talent he had assembled, nothing could stop us" (quoted in Janis, 1982, p. 35).

Janis does not argue that these negative tendencies occur in *all* close-knit groups. Only those that meet other conditions as well are likely to fall prey. According to Janis, a highly cohesive group that is insulated from other decision-making bodies, that lacks established procedures for searching out and appraising various options, and that is headed by a strong-minded, respected leader is the one most susceptible to groupthink. Another condition that may help lead to groupthink is stress generated by how difficult the decision is or by time pressure (Callaway et al., 1985), as in the case of the *Challenger* launch. At least one researcher, however, finds structural conditions (as in the nature of the group) far more predictive of groupthink than situational conditions, such as time pressure (McCauley, 1989).

How can close-knit groups avoid succumbing to groupthink? Janis has offered several suggestions (Janis, 1982a; Janis and Mann, 1977). These prescriptions go beyond just avoiding the conditions conducive to groupthink; they actually establish the norm for a no-holds-barred, critical debate (McCauley, 1989). First, the group leader should instruct the group about the consequences of groupthink and encourage members to express any doubts without fear of disapproval. The leader should maintain an impartial stance while others are airing their views. The members need to be encouraged to consider all alternatives and to evaluate them critically. Dividing the members into separate units, each of which considers the issues independently, can increase the range of options generated by the group as a whole. At least one member at every group meeting should adopt the role of "devil's advocate," challenging majority preferences. Outside experts with differing views should be invited to address the group, and the members should be encouraged to discuss the deliberations with colleagues whose opinions they value.

Listing all the advantages and disadvantages of each alternative can also provide a helpful perspective (Janis, 1972). The effect of overconfidence was significantly decreased in a study in which subjects were asked to list the reasons why they might be wrong about their decisions and then given a chance to make corrections (Koriat et al., 1980). Once a decision has been reached, a "second chance" meeting should be held where any lingering doubts can be aired. A tactic called *anticipated regret* (Janis and Mann, 1977) asks the group members to imagine how the decision might be viewed from some future vantage point: will they be likely to regret their decision?

Minority Influence The story of groups is not just about how groups influence the individual. Many crucial points in history have turned on how one person or a minority of persons influenced the larger group. Think of what Galileo or Martin Luther or Martin Luther King, Jr. were able to accomplish, despite being members of a distinct minority to begin with. Ralph Waldo Emerson attributed great power to minorities: "If the single man plant himself indomitably on his instincts, and there abide, the huge world will come round to him."

The secret of minority influence is expressed in Emerson's sentiment: the minority view must be indomitable and abiding. One study found that a minority that consistently identifies blue slides as green will sometimes win over members of the majority, but if the minority occasionally wavers and calls one-third of the blue slides blue, virtually no member of the majority will agree with the wrong judgments (Moscovici, 1985; Moscovici et al., 1969). A minority that is highly visible and is able to create conflict in the group also tends to be influential, because these qualities focus attention on the minori-ty position (Moscovici and Mugny, 1983). Once majority members start to consider other positions, the norm of conformity has been broken and it is easier to get people to shift their views.

Majorities and minorities influence people in different ways (Moscovici and Personnaz, 1980). People tend to simply conform to a majority view, out of intimidation or fear of rejection. But a minority view piques their interest; they are not concerned about rejection, which allows them to think more deeply about the issue of disagreement and attempt to discover *why* the minority holds a contrary opinion. This can result in a real attitude change on the part of the majority member, and not just an outward compliance.

Charlan Nemeth (1979) holds that the differences in how majorities and minorities influence us extend to the way we process information. The intimidating majority view leads to superficial processing —focusing on the majority position without considering other aspects of the issue. Minorities, on the other hand, stimulate the kind of deep thinking that comes up with creative decisions and novel solutions. Studies of group problem solving show that, while majorities elicit greater compliance, minorities do induce people to devise original and accurate solutions to problems (Nemeth and Kwan, 1986; Nemeth and Wachtler, 1983). A study on jury deliberation also showed that minorities stimulate decisions of high quality (Cowan et al., 1984). Nemeth's intriguing ideas are the subject of increasing research attention (Chaiken and Stangor, 1987).

The force of a minority conviction can have a stunning impact on a group—whether it is a jury or an entire society—but there is often a price to be paid for such courage. Nemeth (1979) found that out when she planted a minority of two on a simulated jury: the two were invariably disliked, even though they often got the majority to rethink their positions. Other experiments have also shown that going against the majority can be a painful experience (Levine, 1989).

AGGRESSION

Each year more than 6 million Americans are the victims of violent crime, which includes murder, rape, robbery, and aggravated assault (Langan and Innes, 1985). From 1977 to 1986, the number of violent crimes increased by some 50 percent *(The*

As public displays of aggression and rates of violent crime increase in our society, psychologists are urgently studying the various possible causes, biological and social.

World Almanac, 1988). Of these crimes, the greatest number occur in families through child abuse or neglect, spouse abuse, and other forms of domestic violence (Straus et al., 1980; Widom, 1989). Violent crimes are easy to identify as acts of aggression. But would a person with the AIDS virus who deliberately does not practice safe sex be considered aggressive? Would incessantly nagging and criticizing a spouse or child be counted as an act of aggression? Throwing a tennis racket? Giving a boxing opponent a black eye? Executing a prisoner? Killing an animal? Committing suicide? Only the first two of these situations fit our definition of **aggression:** behavior that is directed toward intentionally injuring another person who does not wish to be hurt (Baron, 1977; Krebs and Miller, 1985). Keep in mind that the injury can be psychological as well as physical.

Not all acts of aggression are contemptible. Sometimes we must be aggressive in standing up for what we think is right or in protecting ourselves or others. In wartime, aggression gets rewarded with medals of honor. The kind of aggression we are concerned with here is excessive and unprovoked hostile behavior. What factors make so many people overly aggressive? In the sections that follow, we will see that biological dispositions, social learning, and emotional states, especially frustration, all help account for the disturbingly high level of aggression in our society today.

FACTORS AFFECTING AGGRESSION

BIOLOGICAL INFLUENCES

Freud thought that aggression is part of our nature—"an innate, independent, instinctual disposition in man" (1930, p. 102). Aggressive energy, he argued, builds up within people and demands some form of release, often called a **catharsis.** This release can be direct, as when we shout in anger or hit someone. It can also be vicarious, as when we cheer contestants in a boxing match. In either case, however, Freud believed that such cathartic behaviors reduce aggressive drive.

Building on Freud's idea that aggression is innate, researchers in the field of **sociobiology** seek to discover the biological factors that underlie social behavior in all animal species, including human beings (Wilson, 1975, 1978). Sociobiologists believe that some of our behavioral inclinations—such as the tendency to respond aggressively when we are threatened—may be a direct outgrowth of the way the human brain and nervous system are structured. As such, these inclinations are part of our genetic inheritance, retained by natural selection because they helped our ancestors survive.

The Nobel-prize-winning ethologist Konrad Lorenz has described this evolutionary process in some detail. Lorenz argues that all animals have a "fighting instinct" directed toward members of their own species (Lorenz, 1974). This instinct, he maintains, has great survival value. For example, aggressive contests over mates ensure that the strongest males will father the most offspring, thus improving the species as a whole. But Lorenz believes that violence has become a problem for humans partly because, unlike many animal species, our ancestors never evolved the innate inhibition against *killing* members of their own species. They developed artificial means of aggression (spears, guns, bombs, etc.) faster than they could develop natural inhibitions of aggression against their own kind. In effect, cultural evolution has outpaced biological evolution. But at the same time, modern civilization demands that humans suppress their aggressive urges. Lorenz believes that if expression of the fighting instinct is repeatedly prohibited in any animal, aggressive impulses build up and may eventually be discharged in particularly vicious ways. This, Lorenz proposes, helps explain our periodic outbreaks of extreme violence.

Aggression, then, appears to be a universal biological trait. But if so, how can we explain the great differences among people in their display of aggressiveness? At the same time, those individuals who do behave aggressively are fairly consistent in their behavior, even if it may be expressed in different ways at different ages: a child who repeatedly bites other children at age five may hit at age ten and use a weapon at age twenty. The differences *among* individuals and the consistency *within* individuals suggest to some observers that aggressiveness is a genetic, inheritable trait. Studies of aggressiveness in twins turned up a correlation of .40 for identical twins (who share the same genetic makeup) and a correlation of only .04 for fraternal twins (who share only about 50% of their genes) (Rushton et al., 1986). While such evidence leads some social scientists to conclude there is a major genetic component to aggression (Tellegen et al., 1988; Wilson and Herrnstein, 1985), others require more data to be convinced (Kamin, 1986).

Are sex differences in aggression attributable to biological effects? Many studies have confirmed that while men and women differ little in verbal aggression, males are distinctly more *physically* aggressive than females (Deluty, 1985; Eagly and Steffen, 1986.) The vast majority of violent crimes are committed by men (Federal Bureau of Investigation, 1987). It is possible that the higher level of male sex hormones in men is linked to physical aggression or that the male physique, with its greater bulk and muscle, allows men to be more aggressive. Another possibility, however, is that greater aggressiveness is associated with the higher social status that men in most cultures enjoy (White, 1983). Thus men grow up learning that it is acceptable and safe to display their aggressiveness, while women, feeling less power in their position, are socialized to restrain their aggressive tendencies (Perry et al., 1986).

SOCIAL LEARNING INFLUENCES

Most social scientists agree that aggressive behavior can be *learned*. Research has shown that even in lower animals many responses once considered purely "instinctive" are actually learned responses. For instance, young cats do not hunt rats solely through instinct. They learn this behavior by watching older cats (Kuo, 1930). In humans, the influence of learning is even more extensive. This is why social learning theories of aggression have generated so much interest. These theories by no means invalidate the inborn component of aggression; they merely add to our knowledge of the expression of aggressive behavior.

According to social learning theories, people learn how to injure others through exposure to violent models and by having aggression positively reinforced (Bandura, 1977c). The power of models to elicit aggressive behavior was demonstrated in a classic experiment (Bandura et al., 1961). Nursery school students observed one of two adults: one adult ignored a 5-foot inflated "Bobo" doll while playing quietly with a Tinkertoy set; the other adult abused the doll. The violent model's attack was unlike anything that normal preschoolers do spontaneously. The model punched the doll in the face, beat it over the head with a mallet, tossed it angrily in the air, and kicked it about the room, punctuating these assaults with cries of "Sock him in the nose!" . . . "Kick him!" . . . "Pow!" When the children were later given access to a Bobo doll under mildly frustrating conditions, those exposed to the violent model behaved much more aggressively than those exposed to the subdued model. Furthermore, the children who had witnessed the violent model tended to imitate that person's behavior. They punched, hammered, tossed, and yelled right down to the final kick and last emphatic "Pow!"

Are these boys exhibiting a biological predisposition toward aggression, or have they learned aggressive behavior from social experiences?

Exposure to aggressive models, then, appears both to reduce inhibitions against aggression and to suggest specific aggressive acts. Indeed, Bandura suggests that one way models may instigate aggression is to indicate, implicitly or explicitly, that such behavior is an appropriate, desirable, or permissible response (Bandura, 1977c). But we should not underestimate the influence of the *non*aggressive model. Observing such a model provides another option for action and may serve to strengthen a person's resistance to aggression. An angry person who observes someone acting calmly and reasonably is likely to cool off rather than strike out (Baron, 1983a).

What factors affect the degree to which a person is likely to imitate aggression? One important influence is the presence of rewards or punishments. In a follow-up study, Bandura (1965) found that children are much less likely to imitate a model who is punished for aggression. The inhibiting effect of punishment, however, is complex. Generally, several conditions have to be met for fear of punishment to work: there must be alternative ways to obtain what the aggressive individual wants; the punishment must be perceived as quick and certain; the individual must not be extremely angry and must believe that the punisher has the right to deliver punishment (Baron, 1983a). Moreover, as soon as the threat of punishment is removed, a person may reenact observed aggression, especially if the potential rewards for doing so are great. And research shows that most

aggression is extremely rewarding. In one study nearly 80 percent of children's physical and verbal assaults produced highly positive results for the aggressor (Patterson et al., 1967). Sometimes these rewards were tangible (such as obtaining a desirable toy), other times they were social (winning the admiration of peers), still other times they were internal (boosting the child's sense of power), and at times all three types of rewards were received.

One of the most controversial issues surrounding the social learning of aggression is the effect of widespread violence seen on television, a topic we explored in depth in Chapter 2. Children watch an average of thirty hours of television each week (Tangeney and Feshbach, 1988), and eight out of every ten TV programs contain violence (Gerbner et al, 1986). That constitutes a rather heavy dose of violent modeling. Defenders of television programming argue that, for the most part, exposure to TV violence has a positive effect. They say it offers viewers a catharsis, a release of pent-up hostility. But others argue that TV violence has a far more negative influence. They believe that popular programs provide people with models of destructive behavior. Young children, these critics charge, are especially vulnerable. They are likely to imitate the violent behavior of their TV heroes, whose aggressive acts are usually rewarded.

Although findings regarding the impact of TV violence have not always been in agreement, most studies to date support television's critics. It is clear that people who witness aggressive acts on television sometimes imitate them shortly thereafter (Baron, 1977; Liebert et al., 1973; Parke et al., 1977). Some correlational studies indicate that the TV violence does not necessarily trigger direct imitation but just generally raises the level of aggressive behavior. For instance, heavily publicized prizefights tend to be followed by significantly higher levels of homicide in the general population (Phillips, 1983, 1986).

What is perhaps most disturbing is that TV violence has a desensitizing effect: the more we see of it, the more we become inured to it. The result is that people are more accepting of actual aggressive behavior and less likely to be upset by it (Cline et al., 1973; Thomas, 1982). We will see the consequences of that desensitization later in the "In Depth" discussion of violence against women.

THE INFLUENCE OF FRUSTRATION

Social learning theories provide great insight into how people acquire a repertoire of aggressive behaviors and how their performance of these behaviors is shaped by rewards and punishments. But social learning theories say nothing about the relationship between a person's emotional state and the amount of aggression that he or she shows. For instance, many highly aggressive acts seem to occur because of intense or prolonged frustration. Can we make any generalizations about the link between frustration and aggression?

Many years ago, psychologist John Dollard and his colleagues took the extreme position that "aggression is *always* a consequence of frustration" and that "frustration *always* leads to some form of aggression" (Dollard et al., 1939, p. 1). By **frustration** they meant unanticipated interference with any goal-directed behavior. Thus, when people are thwarted in their attempts to obtain food or shelter, sex or sleep, love or recognition, they become aggressive. This is not to say that they immediately lash out at the cause of their frustration. An aggressive response, Dollard argued, can be delayed, disguised, transferred to other people and objects (displaced), or otherwise deflected from its immediate and logical goal. Nevertheless, frustration in Dollard's view always leads to some kind of behavior aimed at releasing aggressive urges.

Critics were quick to question Dollard's **frustration–aggression hypothesis.** Aggression, they said, is only one of many possible reactions to frustration. For example, some people withdraw when their ef-

forts are thwarted, and others simply work harder to achieve their goal. Other critics have found that, contrary to what Dollard suggested, frustration is not the only cause of anger and aggression. In interviews about their real-life experiences of anger, people report becoming angry for a variety of reasons, including injury to their pride or self-esteem and violation by others of accepted social norms (Averill, 1982, 1983). Finally, some critics maintain that frustration produces aggression only when the goal appears to have been interfered with unjustifiably or when the frustrated person feels personally affronted (Averill, 1982; Dodge, 1986; Weiner, 1985).

In reviewing the studies on frustration and aggression, Leonard Berkowitz (1989) finds the core proposition of the Dollard analysis valid but would modify it to state that frustrations generate aggression only to the extent that they are *felt as unpleasant.* Frustrations are aversive events, and the more negative feelings they produce, the more likely they are to instigate aggression. Berkowitz expands on this idea by proposing that any kind of negative feelings—sadness and depression as well as hostility and irritability—will produce anger and aggressive behavior (Finman and Berkowitz, 1989).

IN DEPTH

Pornography: What Is Its Relationship to Rape?

The statistics are startling:

Three out of four women will be the target of at least one violent crime in their lifetimes (*Newsweek,* July 23, 1990, p. 50).

A reported rape is committed every six minutes (FBI Uniform Crime Reports, 1971–1988). Yet only 5 percent of all rapes are reported to the police; 42 percent are never revealed to anyone (Koss et al., 1987).

Rape has increased four times as fast as the overall crime rate in the last ten years (*Newsweek,* July 23, 1990, p. 46, citing a report of the Senate Judiciary Committee hearings on violent crime).

A random survey of female residents of Charleston County, South Carolina, found that close to 15 percent had experienced one or more attempted or completed sexual assaults; 5 percent had been raped (Kilpatrick et al., 1985).

College students are a high risk group for rape since they fit in the age range for the bulk of rape victims and offenders. One study of the college population

Exposure to violent pornography tends to increase men's aggressive sexual behavior and attitudes toward women. Should films like these be banned?

revealed that 15 percent of the women had been raped and 12 percent were victims of an attempted rape. Nearly 54 percent of the women experienced some form of sexual victimization, ranging from unwanted fondling to rape (Koss et al., 1987).

And their attackers are not likely to be lurking strangers. Sexual violence is so pervasive it must take place within the everyday interaction of "normal" men and women (Johnson, 1980). In fact, the most likely scenario for a rape is within a close relationship, which may help explain why so many rapes go unreported. Many social scientists are convinced that rape is actually "rooted in the dominant norms of our culture" (Miller and Moran, 1989). It is the dark side of a socialization process that cultivates a dominant and aggressive male sexuality and a submissive, passive female sexuality.

Various studies have shown the extent to which normal males are willing to engage in sexual coercion. Twelve percent of male college students in one survey acknowledged that they used strong physical force or violence to try to engage in a sex act against their partner's will (Sigelman et al., 1984). In another survey 15 percent of college men reported having forced intercourse at least once; personality and attitude tests revealed that this group had particularly negative feelings toward women (Rapaport and Burkhart, 1984). Other sur-

veys have found that 35 percent of the college male respondents admitted that they might rape a woman if they were absolutely sure of not being caught (Malamuth, 1981; Stille et al., 1987). Typically those men are aggressive toward women in both the laboratory and on dates. And they are particularly likely to do so if they frequently watch pornography (Malamuth, 1984, 1989). Does this mean that pornography causes rape? To illuminate this issue we will take an in-depth look at research on the effects of pornography.

THE INITIAL STUDIES

Pornography is material designed to sexually arouse its viewers or readers. The sexual revolution of the last decade has led to changes in what is portrayed in pornographic magazines and films. Since "ordinary" sex is no longer considered to be a taboo subject, pornographers have gone to new lengths to titillate their readers and viewers. The recent trend in pornography involves the depiction of violence against women as an integral part of sex—including rape, torture, beating, and bondage. In response to these trends, feminists have raised questions about the impact of viewing such material (Lerman, 1978–1979).

Since most pornography is directed toward heterosexual males, it is particularly important to learn how such material affects their attitudes toward women. Certain links are clear. Any type of arousal increases the likelihood of angry aggression (Zillman, 1983), and for heterosexual males, sexual arousal automatically puts the focus on women. Many studies have shown that men aroused by pornographic material tend to be aggressive toward women. Edward Donnerstein and a colleague (Donnerstein and Barrett, 1978) designed an experiment in which male subjects were first angered by either a male or female confederate of the experimenter and were subsequently shown a nonviolent pornographic film. After seeing the film, the subjects took part in a "learning" experiment in which they had an opportunity to deliver shocks to the confederate who had angered them. The men were more aggressive toward the confederate than control subjects who saw a neutral film, and they were equally aggressive toward the male and female confederates. But what if social restraints on male aggression against females were loosened by repeated opportunities to retaliate against someone who angered them? Would the male subjects then be more aggressive toward the female confederate? Donnerstein and John Hallam (1979) constructed another experiment giving the subjects two chances to show their aggression after seeing pornographic films. As expected, the subjects were more aggressive toward the female confederate than the male confederate on the second opportunity to retaliate.

What we learn from these experiments is that pornographic material does arouse aggression in males and that this aggression is *gender-specific*— that is, directed against women—when social restraints on male-to-female aggression are reduced.

What effect does long-term exposure to pornographic material have on arousal and aggression? Does it loosen restraints against violence toward women? In one experiment Dolf Zillmann and Jennings Bryant (1984) showed thirty-six X-rated films to one group of male and female college students, eighteen of the films to another group, and no film or neutral films to a control group over a course of six weeks. The results were somewhat surprising. The more pornographic films the students saw, the *less* aroused they were by them and the *less* aggressively they behaved. In fact, those students who had seen thirty-six X-rated films were less aggressive in response to provocation than were the control-group students. Becoming habituated to pornography apparently decreases its power to arouse, which may cut back on aggression. Does this mean that we should inoculate males against aggression toward women by showing *more* rather than less pornography?

An additional result of the experiment would argue that we should not. Three weeks after seeing the last film the *attitudes* of the students were examined. When asked their opinion about a rape trial, both the male and female students who had seen the pornographic films recommended lighter sentences for the rapist than did control subjects, and they expressed less support for the women's liberation movement. The male subjects had more callous attitudes toward women than the control males. Thus, while actual aggressive behavior may have decreased as a consequence of the repeated exposure to pornography, the attitudes that might restrain aggression were diminished. Becoming desensitized to the consequences of aggression opens the door to later acts of aggression (Thomas, 1982).

The results of research on **violent pornography,** material that combines sexual explicitness with violence, are even more disturbing. Typically, films combining sex and violence show a woman being attacked by a rapist, fighting him off at first, but then getting aroused and begging for more. Not only do such films generate high arousal, they also elicit aggressive thoughts that are specifically directed toward women. In several studies, men who watched violent pornography increased their aggression toward women, while their aggression toward men was about the same as after watching nonviolent pornography (Donnerstein et al., 1987; Linz et al., 1987).

Researchers are specifically interested in knowing whether such movies perpetuate men's belief in the **rape myth**—the idea that women mean "yes" when they say "no" and in fact ask for and secretly wish for rape. Men who subscribe to the rape myth are likely to see nothing wrong with inappropriate sexual behavior, beginning with forcing a kiss on a woman (Margolin, Miller, and Moran, 1989).

Can violent pornography reinforce the rape myth? Two investigators studied the effect of such films on male attitudes (Malamuth and Check, 1981). They arranged for some college students to see two commercial films (*Swept Away* and *The Getaway*) that showed women sexually aroused by an assailant; a control group of students watched two

The rape myth has been the subject of popular movies, as well as pornographic ones. In *The Accused*, a group of men claim that a woman's seductive behavior was reason enough to rape her.

movies without sexual content. Several days later all the students filled out a questionnaire in class that measured their attitudes about violence toward women and beliefs about rape. Those male students who had seen the sexually violent films were more tolerant of rape and more likely to agree that women enjoyed rape than were the students who saw the other films.

A similar study (Malamuth and Check, 1985) revealed that false beliefs about rape were likely to be increased as a result of watching movies with sexually violent content, especially among men who had already expressed aggressive attitudes toward women. Former Surgeon General C. Everett Koop put the matter this way in commenting on his report on pornography and public health (Mulvey and Haugaard, 1986):

> Impressionable men—many of them still in adolescence—see this material and get the impression that women like to be hurt, to be humiliated, to be forced to do things they do not want to do, or to appear to be forced to do things they really do want to do. It is a false and vicious stereotype that leads to much pain and even death for victimized women. (Koop, 1987, p. 945)

Concluding that many forms of pornography produce antisocial effects expressed in increased violence against women, the Attorney General's Commission on Pornography (1986) recommended legal action: stricter enforcement of existing obscenity laws and consideration of additional legal measures. But some social scientists challenge both these conclusions and recommendations, as we will now see.

CRITICISMS, ALTERNATIVES, AND FURTHER RESEARCH

Daniel Linz and his colleagues argue that getting rid of pornography will not solve the problem of violence against women (Linz et al., 1987). They contend that the message of violence against women gets across loud and clear in material that is not sexually explicit or "pornographic" according to the obscenity laws. Consider, for example, the Malumud and Check experiment in which the males who were aggressive toward women had watched commercially successful R-rated films with nonexplicit depictions of sexual violence. Another researcher who has analyzed the content of videos found more examples of forced sex or overt aggression in *non*pornographic videos than in the X-rated ones (Palys, 1986). And an analysis of detective magazines found that the covers of 76 percent of them showed domination of women; 38 percent depicted women in bondage (Dietz et al., 1986).

Among the many stories of brutality or indifference to the suffering of others, occasionally an episode of unselfish heroism emerges to remind us that altruism remains an enduring human trait. The efforts of hundreds of volunteers to rescue Jessica McClure, a nineteen-month-old girl who fell into a narrow well in 1987, made headlines around the world.

The pervasiveness of the message of violence against women in the culture led Linz and his colleagues (1987) to question the appropriateness of singling out sexually explicit pornographic material for legal action.

PATTERNS AND CONCLUSIONS

The point that Linz and colleagues make, then, is that the perpetuation of the rape myth and of sexual violence is not the exclusive domain of legally obscene materials. The mass media is saturated with ideas of violence against women, and to legislate against them would be impractical as well as potentially harmful to the rights of free expression.

Their recommendation is to *educate* the public to combat the negative images of women and to allow people to make wiser choices and be more critical consumers of the mass media. Thus, those who write and produce TV shows, screenplays, books, magazine articles, and so on should recognize the dangers of conveying messages of sexual violence, and the public should be aware that the rape myth is itself a myth that grossly distorts women's reactions to rape. More and more researchers are concluding that it is negative attitudes toward women, more than any brief arousal from pornographic material, that motivate sexual aggres-

sion against women (Demaré et al., 1988; Malamuth and Briere, 1986). The danger of violent pornography is in its power to perpetuate those negative attitudes. Ultimately, the public needs to be disabused of the rape myth and convinced that sexually violent images demean not only those who are portrayed but also those who watch them (Donnerstein et al., 1987).

ALTRUISM

One year after a band of teenage boys brutally beat and raped a jogger in New York's Central Park, several young men made the headlines for a very different reason: they had risked their lives to rescue five young children who were locked in a burning car. None of the youths knew the children, but they responded unhesitatingly to their distress, despite warnings from bystanders that the car might blow up at any moment. Some people make their living by helping others—firefighters and emergency medical workers, for example—and they do not demand high salaries for doing good. Many people help others for no money at all: they tutor schoolchildren, assist in hospitals, visit AIDS patients, bring meals to the elderly, donate blood. Just as psychologists have tried to understand the causes of aggression, so have they also investigated the causes of **altruism,** unselfish concern for others.

FACTORS AFFECTING ALTRUISM

The idea that human beings are genetically programmed to help one another—that we have altruistic instincts—has received much attention (Dawkins, 1975; Wilson, 1975). Rushton's twin studies have found genetic correlations of altruism as well as of aggressiveness (Rushton et al., 1986). However, most social scientists reject the notion that altruism is strongly influenced by heredity. Such an explanation seems insufficient to explain the great variations in altruistic tendencies that we repeatedly observe. It seems clear that both learning and situational pressures must also play a part. Social psychologists seek to discover the conditions in people's lives that encourage or inhibit the helping response.

INFLUENCES ON BYSTANDER INTERVENTION IN EMERGENCIES

In the summer of 1990, a six-year-old Italian girl became a symbol of shame for her nation. Vanessa Moretti and her father were on their way to the beach when her father suffered a fatal heart attack while driving in a tunnel. Before dying, he managed to pull the car over. Vanessa got out of the car to seek help but was repeatedly knocked down by gusts from the speeding cars. For the next half hour, bleeding and in tears, she stumbled along more than a mile of open highway. Hundreds of cars passed by before a motorist pulled over. It was the start of summer holidays, and as one Italian paper noted, "along the happy road of vacation there were no scheduled stops for attending to the pain of others" (C. Haberman, *The New York Times,* July 19, 1990, p. 1).

Many years earlier another highly publicized case of bystander apathy became the catalyst for research into how to account for why people do or do not help others. At about 3 A.M. in a middle-class area of Queens, a borough of New York City, a young woman named Kitty Genovese was savagely attacked outside her apartment building when she arrived home from work. As the victim screamed for help, at least thirty-eight neighbors looked out their windows, but not one came to her aid. The attack continued for more than thirty minutes before Kitty Genovese died of multiple stab wounds.

The Genovese murder caused a sensation in the press. How could people be so apathetic, so indiffer-

ent to another's pain? Many saw it as a classic illustration of urban callousness, of city dwellers' reluctance to "get involved." Yet investigation revealed that the witnesses to Kitty Genovese's murder had been far from indifferent. Her neighbors did not just close their blinds and go back to bed. They stood and watched transfixed, "unable to act but unwilling to turn away" (Latané and Darley, 1976, pp. 309–310). What prevented them from acting? Research on bystander intervention indicates that a number of powerful social forces operate in any emergency situation, and some of these strongly inhibit helping.

John Darley and Bibb Latané, who have studied bystander intervention extensively, argue that the act of aiding the victim in an emergency is the result of many events and choices, all of which are *less* likely to occur in the presence of others (Darley and Latané, 1968). First, the bystander must notice that something unusual is occurring: the event must intrude on his or her private thoughts. But the problem here is that most people consider it bad manners to watch the actions of others closely, especially those of strangers. So people in a crowd tend to tune out sights and sounds and stare straight ahead. This decreases the likelihood that an individual immersed in a group will even notice the signs of a possible emergency.

Noticing signs is not enough. A bystander must also determine whether this particular event is serious enough to warrant intervention. This decision is often far from easy, for most of the signs that suggest an emergency are ambiguous. Cries for help from the next apartment might be genuine, or they might be coming from a TV set. When others are present, most of us think twice before rushing to the rescue, because we are concerned about appearing foolish if no emergency exists. So we adopt an air of calm indifference while looking around to see how others are reacting. Since everyone else may be trying to appear indifferent as well, each bystander may be taken in by the others' nonchalance and led—or misled—to define the situation as a nonemergency (Latané et al., 1981).

But even if a bystander notices an event and labels it an emergency, the presence of others may *still* decrease that person's chances of intervening. Being in a group tends to dilute our sense of personal responsibility. We conclude that others have as much obligation to respond as we do. As a result, everyone hesitates, wondering who should step forward, until it is too late to do anything. This diffusion of responsibility may have occurred among witnesses to the Kitty

Genovese murder. Onlookers may have reasoned that someone else had undoubtedly already summoned help.

To test whether diffusion of responsibility does indeed occur during emergencies, Darley and Latané (1968) staged an incident. College students who had volunteered for an experiment were ushered into private rooms containing earphones and a microphone. The study was said to involve a group discussion about personal problems caused by life in a high-pressure urban environment. Subjects learned that the talk would take place over an intercom system, to preserve anonymity, and that the experimenter would not be listening in. Each subject was led to believe that one, two, or five other people were participating in the discussion, but in fact all voices except the true subject's were prerecorded.

The first speaker, in the course of talking of the pressures of living in New York City, acknowledged that he suffered nervous seizures under severe stress. When it was his turn to speak again, he began to stutter and fumble for words, simulating the onset of a seizure. Within a few minutes he was choking and pleading for help. How do you think the subjects who overheard this performance reacted? As predicted by Darley and Latané, the larger the perceived group, and therefore the greater the potential diffusion of responsibility, the less likely a subject was to summon help. Of those who thought they were alone, 85 percent reported his plight, whereas only 62 percent of those who thought there was one other bystander did so, and only 31 percent of those who thought there were four other bystanders. Thus, the tendency for feelings of personal responsibility to decline as groups grow larger seemed to be quite strong.

What people call bystander apathy may not be apathy at all. In the experiment just described, those who failed to report the seizure were anything but indifferent. Many showed signs of extreme anxiety as they considered what to do. Their failure to intervene seemed not so much a decision against responding as a state of *in*decision. The typical bystander in an emergency, Darley and Latané argue, is "an anguished individual in genuine doubt, concerned to do the right thing but compelled to make complex decisions under pressure of stress and fear. His reactions are shaped by the actions of others—and all too frequently by their inaction" (Darley and Latané, 1968, p. 300.)

These findings are pessimistic about the prospects of receiving help when many bystanders are present. But do the social forces they describe *always* operate in groups that witness an emergency? Fortunately, the answer seems to be "no." When the signs of an emergency are unambiguous and observers can see whether or not help has been sent for, a victim may be more likely to receive aid in the presence of a sizable group than when few bystanders are watching (Solomon et al., 1978). This was demonstrated in an emergency staged on a subway train in New York City (Piliavin et al., 1969). In 70 percent of the trials, bystanders immediately came to the aid of a young man who suddenly collapsed onto the floor. And the helping response was quicker when seven or more people were present than when only one, two, or three people were in the car. Why this should be so is not clear. Perhaps once it is obvious that helping is the "right" reaction, a larger group increases the pressure to conform to this ethical norm.

OTHER INFLUENCES ON HELPING BEHAVIOR

Besides studying the factors affecting bystander intervention in emergencies, social psychologists have also studied the influences on other forms of helping, such as giving to charities or doing favors for people. Their research has shown that many factors can boost or inhibit helping responses. We will explore just a few.

Mood and Level of Stress   When we feel good, we are very likely to do good. Charity drives at Christmas seem to be based on the principle that people are more generous when they are in a holiday mood. Social psychologists have confirmed this tendency in experimental situations. For example, Alice Isen and Paula Levin (1972) induced positive moods in subjects by leaving change in the coin return of a public telephone. They then watched to see whether those who found the money would help a confederate who dropped a pile of papers outside the phone booth. Those who had been made happy by finding the money were more likely to offer assistance than were control subjects who found no money. Even a mood raiser as simple as sunny skies and pleasant weather can increase a person's tendency to help others (Cunningham, 1979). There are two possible explanations for this "good mood" effect: (1) people want to continue in a good frame of mind, which is supported by positive behavior; and (2) the good mood evokes positive thoughts which lead to good deeds (Carlson et al., 1988).

Psychologists have confirmed the truth of the saying "Christmas is a time for giving." The holiday atmosphere tends to make people feel good, and being happy encourages generosity.

Does this mean that being in a *bad* mood inhibits helping? To the contrary, it appears that we are increasingly likely to help others, under certain circumstances, when we are feeling unhappy (Carlson and Miller, 1987). The **negative state relief model** holds that we seek relief from negative moods by doing something positive, something that will lift our own spirits (Cialdini et al., 1973). This model suggests that the motivation for helping is primarily self-serving (Cialdini et al., 1987).

The Empathy–Altruism Hypothesis So far it seems as if helping is a matter of egotism: we help others because it makes us feel good. Aren't we ever motivated by genuine *unselfish* concern for others, regardless of our own level of personal distress? Psychologist C. Daniel Batson says "yes" (Batson, 1987). He bases his theory on the existence of empathy, experiencing another's emotional condition as if it is one's own. According to Batson, to the extent that we feel empathy with another we will engage in altruistic helping.

Batson devised a number of experiments that set up empathic concern in subjects and then sorted out their motives for helping: were they interested primarily in reducing their own distress or in reducing another's distress? The key factor in these experiments was the difficulty of escaping from a helping situation. Batson theorized that people high in empathic concern would help others even when it was easy to escape from the situation—in other words, when a means of relieving one's own distress was available. If you were to participate in one of these experiments, this is how it would work: You show up at a laboratory to take part in an investigation of task performance under unpleasant conditions. You are introduced to a fellow subject (actually a confederate of the experimenter), and you draw lots to see which of you will do a task while receiving random shocks and which will observe. The drawing is rigged so that you will be the observer. While observing the confederate on closed circuit TV, you see her become increasingly uncomfortable with the shocks and hear her describe to the experimenter a traumatic experience with an electric fence that she had as a child. She is ready to go on, but the experimenter hesitates and asks if you would be willing to trade places.

How you react at this point depends on how Batson has varied the conditions of the experiment. You were told at the outset either that the woman receiving shocks had personal values and interests close to your own or that they were quite different from yours. This established your level of empathic concern: if you think the confederate is like yourself, you would feel more empathy for her. Batson also varied the conditions by which you could escape. You might have been told that you could leave after only two trials of shocks (easy-escape condition), or that you had to stay for all ten trials and either volunteer to take some shocks yourself or continue to watch the subject suffer (difficult-escape condition). The experimenter asks you if you will trade places after two trials. How do you think you would react under these conditions?

The results of Batson's experiment (Batson et al., 1981) closely matched his predictions. An overwhelming percentage of subjects high in empathy acted to help the confederate in both the easy- and difficult-escape conditions. Even a majority of those low in empathy offered to trade places when escape was difficult. Only those who measured low in empathy *and* who were offered an easy escape were not likely to trade places when they could escape. Those with little empathetic concern chose to do so, while those with high empathetic concern were willing to help. Batson concluded from these findings that true altruistic behavior, as measured by empathy, does exist.

Critics of Batson's hypothesis offer other reasons why people might help in these situations. They might be motivated by a desire to avoid social disapproval for not helping (Archer, 1984), or they might want to lift their own mood (consistent with the negative relief model) (Schaller and Cialdini, 1988). Even Batson considered whether the empathic individuals were perhaps tending to their own internal needs, such as feeding pride or avoiding shame or guilt. But Batson tested these possibilities in another series of experiments and rejected them in favor of his empathy–altruism hypothesis (Batson et al., 1988). He also tested the possibility of negative relief and found that wanting (Batson et al., 1989). Batson's conclusions and the increasing acceptance of them among social psychologists are important: they give hope for society, for it seems we are not inevitably selfish individuals.

Belief in a Just World   Another factor affecting altruism is belief in a just world—the conviction that, in the long run, wrongdoing will be punished and good deeds will be rewarded (see Figure 19.4). Research suggests that this belief is very common among both children and adults (Lerner et al., 1976). Psychologist Melvin Lerner has argued that people with a strong belief in a just world may be motivated to try to restore justice when innocent people suffer.

1. Movies in which good triumphs over evil are unrealistic.
2. Students almost always deserve the grades they receive in school.
3. Although evil men may hold political power for a while, in the general course of history good wins out.

FIGURE 19.4   Items from the Just-World Scale. The scale is composed of two types of statements: those like item 1, with which people who believe in a just world tend to disagree; and statements like items 2 and 3, with which those holding just-world convictions would probably agree. (*From Rubin and Peplau, 1973, p. 79.*)

They may also perform altruistic acts in anticipation of receiving some reward in return for their kindness. In one series of experiments, Zuckerman (1975) found that when students were asked two days before a final exam to help a person with research or to serve as a reader for the blind, the strong believers in a just world were more likely than others to comply with the request. According to Zuckerman, these students reasoned that if they did something kind for another person, they would be repaid with success on their exam. Significantly, these strong believers were no more likely than others to perform a favor when final exams were five months away.

Belief in a just world, however, is a two-edged sword (Lerner, 1974). Sometimes this conviction prompts people to derogate the victims of misfortune. To understand why, suppose you saw people suffering through no fault of their own. Suppose further that there was nothing that could be done to right this injustice. If you strongly believed that life was fair, such misfortune would be highly upsetting to your view of the nature of things. In order to deal with this challenge to your belief in a just world, you might come to view the victims in a negative light, enabling you to conclude that they *deserve* their suffering.

Studies provide evidence that people do reason this way. Subjects in experiments will derogate the personal qualities of a fellow subject who is assigned to receive painful electric shocks, even if it is clear that the assignment occurred by chance (Lerner, 1970; Lerner and Matthews, 1967; Lerner and Simmons, 1966). Outside the laboratory, people have been

es than of inner dispositions. Very few personality traits have been found to be consistently related to altruistic behaviors. In one study that compared people who had intervened to stop a crime with people who had not, the researchers could not distinguish the helpers from the nonhelpers on tests measuring "humanitarianism" and "social responsibility" (Huston et al., 1981). What mattered was whether the person felt competent to handle such a situation. Thus, the demands of a particular incident can overpower the tendency to act on one's "nature."

A similar study used seminary students as subjects, just the type we could expect to act as "good Samaritans" (Darley and Batson, 1973). The students were asked to participate in an experiment in another building. Half the students were told that they were late and everyone was waiting for them to start the experiment; the other half were told that they were early so they could take their time proceeding to the other building. En route, each student encountered a man slumped in a doorway. Did both late-comers and early birds stop to help the man? Sixty-three percent of the early students did, but only 10 percent of the late students stopped. We can assume that the inner dispositions of the two types of subjects did not differ significantly, but the situational factors did. It seems that being in a hurry can prevent us from following natural inclinations to help another. This is the central message of social psychology: how we act is shaped to a large extent by the social situations in which we find ourselves.

THE CONSEQUENCES OF HELPING

WHY HELPING FAILS

People offer help with the expectation that it will do some good, but surprisingly often it backfires. Social psychologists wonder what it is about helping efforts that can sometimes cause more harm than good. Philip Brickman and his colleagues (1982) have proposed several answers. One is that help givers often assume that the recipients of their aid are far less competent than they really are. As a result, they may deny the recipients the opportunity to master useful skills. B. F. Skinner offers this example: "We watch a child tying a shoelace and grow jittery, and to escape from our jitteriness we 'help' the child tie the lace. In doing so we destroy one chance to learn to tie

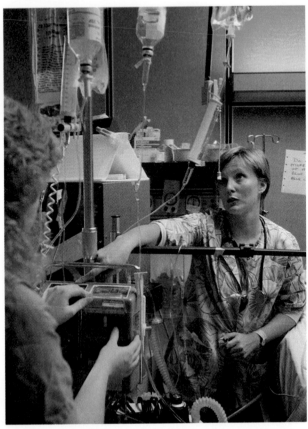

People in the helping professions are subject to extremely high levels of stress. They often literally hold the lives of others in their hands. This life-or-death responsibility makes them especially susceptible to burnout.

found to blame, derogate, and shun victims of violent crime or those who suffer psychological disorders (Farina et al., 1971; Symonds, 1975). For example, a person who has been raped or mugged may receive censure from friends ("You should have known better than to walk in that neighborhood alone") instead of sympathy.

How Important Are Inner Dispositions? You may have wondered why no mention has been made of inner dispositions in this discussion of altruism. Surely a primary reason for either altruistic or selfish acts must be a person's underlying character traits. Yet research shows that this common-sense judgment is much less true than people think. The "good Samaritan" is often more the product of circumstanc-

shoes" (Skinner, 1978). The same thing may happen when a well-meaning person leaps to assist someone physically disabled every time he or she seems to be having trouble. Although the help is well-intentioned, the disabled person has no chance to learn how to handle everyday problems alone.

A related difficulty is that when the help giver does too much for the recipient, the recipient may come to assume that all the gains he or she makes are due to the help giver's efforts. This attribution can be very self-defeating. Studies show that people are much more likely to continue working to overcome a problem when they believe that whatever gains they make are attributable to *themselves* (Brickman et al., 1982; Chambliss and Murray, 1979; Liberman, 1978). This is because attributing gains to the self tends to build confidence that one can cope with a problem effectively (Coates et al., 1983). Subsequently, the person is much more apt to take the initiative, persevere, and overcome obstacles.

THE HELPING ROLE: BURNOUT

People who make helping their profession—doctors, clinical psychologists, nurses, social workers—sometimes reach the point of burnout. **Burnout** is a debilitating psychological state in which the help giver emotionally withdraws from the job of helping. As motivation drops, the person becomes apathetic and may suffer a decline in self-esteem. Decreased concern for clients is another symptom of burnout, as help givers lose their idealism and become pessimistic. Often they detach themselves from their clients as people, seeing them instead as "cases" to be treated in dehumanizing ways. Increased irritability and anger often accompany these changed outlooks. Burnout victims may rationalize their failures by attributing them to the people they are supposedly trying to help. Like the stereotype of the hardened bureaucrat, they also tend to become mechanical and very resistant to innovation (Edelwich and Brodsky, 1980; Maslach, 1976).

What causes burnout? Consistent with the social psychological perspective, burnout has less to do with personality factors than with situational ones. One obvious situational pressure is overwork. Help givers with heavy caseloads and limited community resources may try to avoid feeling guilty and frustrated by distancing themselves from clients (Chenriss et al.,

1976). Another contributing factor may be the unrealistic expectations with which many helping professionals begin their careers. The hard reality they discover once they are on the job can lead to early disillusionment (Cherniss et al., in press). Finally, there are the emotional demands of being in a helping profession. For example, clients give therapists much more negative than positive feedback (Rodin, 1985). One solution to the suffering that comes with empathizing with clients is to become emotionally detached, providing services in an uninvolved manner (Edelwich and Brodsky, 1980). However, Kevin Corcoran (1989) finds that it is not empathy *per se* that is associated with burnout, but empathy in which there is a total loss of emotional separation from the person needing help—that is, the helpers feel the needy person's emotions as their own and not *as if* they were their own.

What can be done to alleviate burnout? Helping professionals should try to develop realistic outlooks on their jobs: working conditions will probably never be perfect, many clients will make progress only in very small steps, and some will never make any progress at all (Edelwich and Brodsky, 1980). Then helping professionals can begin to set priorities for putting their limited resources to use. By giving more responsibility for improvements to their clients, they can often reduce their own workloads and emotional burdens. At the same time, the clients will be more apt to acquire a sense of confidence that they can control their own destinies and help solve their own problems. This can greatly increase a helping professional's success rate and so make his or her work more satisfying (Edelwich and Brodsky, 1980). Sometimes simple changes in work requirements can also boost job satisfaction. In one study, for instance, the outlooks of child-care workers improved significantly just by assigning each person a small number of children to look after rather than having the entire staff share responsibility for *all* the youngsters (Pines and Maslach, 1978). Finally, research shows that burnout is less likely among professionals who can discuss their problems candidly with one another and who can reduce interactions with clients when stress becomes too great (Baslach, 1976; Wortman and Dunkel-Schetter, 1979). Thus, maintaining a proper balance between concern for clients and personal needs seems to be an important factor in avoiding burnout.

SUMMARY

1. Social pressure often induces **conformity,** a shifting of our opinions or actions to correspond with those of other people. In some cases of conformity we may outwardly yield to a group consensus while inwardly retaining our own opinions. In other situations, the conformity is more extreme: we actually embrace new values through **identification** or **internalization.**

2. Research on **obedience**—following the explicit instructions of a person in authority—has shown that many of us are willing to obey orders even when our actions might harm other people. Although this research remains controversial, Milgram's basic finding that people are susceptible to destructive obedience has not been refuted.

3. Another form of going along with others is **compliance**—the act of acceding to an explicit request from someone who does not hold any particular authority. Common techniques used to obtain compliance include the **foot-in-the-door phenomenon,** the **door-in-the-face technique,** the **low-ball phenomenon,** and the **that's-not-all technique.**

4. A **group** is a collection of two or more people who interact regularly, share specific goals, and identify themselves as part of a whole. The role we play within a group can be very powerful in changing our behavior, as Zimbardo's mock prison study showed.

5. Being among others may enhance our ability to perform some tasks, an effect known as **social facilitation.** But if our effort in a group is anonymous and we rely too much on the contribution of others, we may tend to slack off, a behavior known as **social loafing.** Pressures to conform are particularly powerful in small, close-knit groups, where we may fall victim to **groupthink,** a mode of decision making characterized by suppression of alternative views and distorted appraisals of reality. Occasionally, a minority can change the views of a majority in a group, but only when the minority view is unwavering and highly visible.

6. Excessive interpersonal **aggression** is a fundamental problem among human beings. Freud and Lorenz have argued that our aggressive drives are innate. Freud believed that aggressive drives demand some form of release, or **catharsis;** Lorenz maintains that the "fighting instinct" has survival value. **Sociobiology** suggests that biological factors such as the structure of the human brain and nervous system may be partly responsible for aggression.

7. Social learning theorists have shown that aggression can be learned from violent models and positive reinforcement of aggressive behavior. **Frustration,** or unanticipated interference with goal-directed behavior, can also play a role in promoting aggression. According to Dollard's **frustration–aggression hypothesis,** aggression in some form is always a consequence of frustration. Critics, however, maintain that aggression is only one of many possible reactions to frustration and that sources other than frustration can cause anger and aggression. Berkowitz modifies Dollard's hypothesis to state that frustrations generate aggression only to the extent they are felt as unpleasant.

8. **Violent pornography,** material that combines sexual explicitness with violence, is highly arousing and elicits negative emotions and aggressive thoughts directed specifically toward women. Because sexually violent material is increasingly common in movies, books, and magazines that are not considered pornographic under the obscenity laws, relying on legal action may not solve the problem of violence against women. For that reason some psychologists think the only solution is to educate the public to become more critical consumers of the mass media.

9. Whether we display **altruism,** unselfish concern for others, depends on many factors, including the nature of the event demanding our response, the number of other people present, our emotional state at the time, the amount of stress present, the degree to which the situation seems just or unjust, and our beliefs. Acts of altruism and helping behavior seem to depend more on external circumstances than on inner dispositions.

10. Many helping efforts are unsuccessful. Those receiving help may come to depend too much on the help givers or become resentful of the help, and help givers may reach a point of **burnout**—emotional withdrawal from the job of helping. Overwork, unrealistic expectations, and the emotional demands of the helping profession may all contribute to burnout.

SUGGESTED READINGS

Aronson, E. (1988). *The social animal* (5th ed.). New York: Freeman. This book, which won an American Psychological Association National Media Award, is an engaging, easy-to-read introduction to the topics central to social psychology.

Baron, R. (1977). *Human aggression.* New York: Plenum. This very readable introduction to research on aggression discusses social, environmental, and individual determinants of aggression and techniques for controlling or preventing aggression.

Hunt, M. (1990). *The compassionate beast: What science is discovering about the humane side of mankind.* New York: Morrow. Hunt, a science writer, draws from new research in social psychology to clarify such mysteries as why Kitty Genovese was murdered, and why people risked their lives during World War II by hiding Jews from the Nazis.

Kelman, H. C., and Hamilton, V. L. (1989). *Crimes and obedience: Toward a social psychology of authority and responsibility.* New Haven, CT: Yale University Press. A social psychologist and a sociologist analyze the My Lai massacre, Watergate, and the Iran–Contra affair, presenting a major analysis of the rationale behind illegal acts ordered by authority.

Milgram, S. (1974). *Obedience to authority.* New York: Harper & Row. The reader is invited to observe as Milgram works methodically and creatively through his series of eighteen obedience experiments, searching for an explanation of destructive obedience.

Rushton, J., and Sorrentino, R. (Eds.) (1981). *Altruism and helping behavior.* Hillsdale, NJ: Lawrence Erlbaum. This collection of essays by researchers in the field of prosocial behavior discusses the ways in which such behavior develops, the effects of various circumstances surrounding the helping incident, and the relationship of individual characteristics to helping behavior.

GLOSSARY

The boldface number after each entry refers to the chapter in which the term is discussed.

accommodation In Piaget's theory, the modification of old ways of thinking to incorporate new knowledge and information. **9**

acetylcholine (Ach) A neurotransmitter found in various parts of the peripheral nervous system, in the spinal cord, and in specific regions of the brain. **3**

action potential An abrupt change in a cell's polarity which temporarily makes the cell's interior positive and the cell's exterior negative. This change travels the length of a neuronal axon. **3**

action tendencies How we are likely to act. **11**

active memory Another name for short-term memory. **7**

actor-observer bias The tendency to attribute one's own behavior to environmental causes, rather than some enduring personality trait. **18**

adrenalin See **epinephrine. 3**

adrenals A pair of endocrine glands located above the kidneys that affect the body's reaction to stress as well as produce sex hormones and numerous other hormonelike chemicals. **3**

advanced empathy A later stage in client-centered therapy in which the therapist gradually begins to suggest what might be causing the client's problems, while still showing a deep understanding of the client's point of view. **17**

afferent pathways Nerve pathways leading toward the central nervous system. **3**

afterimage A visual impression that lasts after removal of the stimulus that caused it. **4**

aggression Behavior that is directed toward intentionally injuring another person. **19**

agnosia The inability to recognize some properties or class of objects. **4**

agoraphobia An intense fear of being in places that are hard to escape from quickly or without embarrassment, or where help would not be readily available. **16**

alcohol abuser A person who is not an alcoholic (alcohol-dependent), but who does have a drinking problem. **16**

alcohol dependence Any problem involvement with alcohol; psychological and physical addiction to alcohol. **16**

alcoholic blackout Fragmentary or even total loss of memory for events that occur while drinking. **5**

algorithm A precisely stated set of rules or procedures for solving problems of a particular kind. **8**

all-or-none response The firing of an axon once the stimulus threshold is reached, regardless of the amount of stimulation. **3**

alpha waves Moderately slow brain waves that occur when a person relaxes with eyes closed. **5**

altruism Unselfish concern for others. **19**

amnesia, psychogenic A dissociative disorder involving the partial or total forgetting of past experiences after some stressful event. **16**

amplitude The intensity of a sound wave, or amount of pressure it exerts, as measured by the distance of the wave's peaks and valleys from a baseline of zero. Amplitude determines loudness. **4**

amygdala One of the three interrelated structures of the limbic system; the others are the hippocampus and septal area. **3**

anal stage According to Freud, the second psychosexual stage (occurring during the second year of life) during which bowel control is accomplished and pleasure focused on the function of elimination. **13**

androgens Sex hormones secreted by the adrenal glands that are involved in the development of male sex characteristics. **3**

anorexia nervosa A condition affecting mainly teenage women characterized by an obsession with the subject of obesity and weight control. **12**

anterograde amnesia A form of amnesia that affects memory only for new events and information, *not* for things stored in the past. **7**

antianxiety drug Commonly known as a minor tranquilizer, this type of drug reduces excitability and causes drowsiness. **17**

antidepressant drug Any mood-regulating drug effective in treating certain types of depression; known as the tricyclics because of their three-ringed molecular structure. **17**

antipsychotic drug Any major tranquilizer used to alleviate extreme agitation and hyperactivity in psychotic patients. **17**

antisocial personality (sociopath) A person who follows his or her impulses without consideration for the rights or feelings of others, and with no guilt or remorse. **16**

anvil One of a set of three tiny, interconnected bones in the middle ear that transmit sound from the eardrum to the cochlea. **4**

anxiety A state of psychic distress which, according to Freud, occurs when the ego loses its struggle to reconcile the divergent demands of the id, the superego, and reality. **13**

anxiety disorders The group of mental disorders (panic attacks, phobias, obsessions, and compulsions) characterized by emotional distress caused by feelings of vulnerability, apprehension, or fear. **16**

anxious attachment The type of bond between infant and care giver characterized by the expectation that the care giver will be inaccessible at times and somewhat unresponsive and ineffective. **10**

applied science The deliberate use of research findings to solve some practical problem or to improve the quality of human life. **1**

artificial intelligence (AI) An expanding subfield of cognitive psychology, with links to biology, computer science, mathematics, and linguistics, that explores complex models of human mental processes. **1, 8**

assimilation   In Piaget's theory, the incorporation of new information into old ways of thinking or behaving. **9**

associative learning   Learning that certain events are connected with one another. **6**

attachment   The special bond between an infant and his or her primary care giver. **10**

attitude   An association between some person, thing, event, idea, or situation and an evaluation of it. **18**

attitude object   The target of an attitude; that person, thing, event, idea or situation that we have a disposition to evaluate in a particular way. **18**

auditory canal   The passageway that extends from the opening of the outer ear to the eardrum. **4**

auditory nerve   Neural impulses, triggered by movement of hair cells, travel via this nerve to the brainstem, ascend through the thalamus to the auditory cortex where the perception of sound and its patterns begins. **4**

authoritarian   A parenting style, characterized by harsh controlling behavior, lack of responsiveness to a child's wishes, and inflexible thinking. **10**

authoritarian personality   An individual who shows rigid adherence to conventional values about authority and morality, as well as a preference for strong, antidemocratic leaders. **18**

authoritative   A parenting style, identified by D. Baumrind, characterized by responsiveness, coupled with firmness in setting limits, and flexibility in thinking. **10**

automatic encoding   Memory encoding that seems to happen with no deliberate effort. **7**

autonomic nervous system   The division of the peripheral nervous system that controls the internal muscles (blood vessels, heart, intestines) and the glands. **3**

availability heuristic   An approach people use to judge odds involving the assessment of the probability of an uncertain event to occur according to the ease with which past examples come to mind. **8**

aversion conditioning   A therapeutic technique which attempts to reduce the frequency of deviant behavior by pairing an aversive stimulus, such as a loud noise, with the cues related to the deviant behavior, thereby making the cues themselves become aversive. **17**

avoidance learning   A cause and effect relationship whereby learning takes place through avoiding the stimulus. It can be established through negative reinforcement. **6**

axon   The long extension of a neuron that usually transmits impulses away from the cell body. **3**

backward conditioning   Presenting the unconditioned stimulus before the conditioned stimulus, thereby reversing the usual order. **6**

backward search   A heuristic in which a person begins at the end (or resolution) of a problem and then works backward in order to discover the steps involved. **8**

basic anxiety   According to Horney, the helplessness and insecurity a child feels when parents' behavior is indifferent, disparaging, and erratic. **13**

basic hostility   According to Horney, a child's feeling of deep resentment toward parents who arouse the child's basic anxiety. **13**

basic science   The study of a subject or discipline without regard to whether that study will have immediate practical effects. **1**

basilar membrane   An elastic membrane in the inner ear which helps transmit sound waves to the auditory nerve. **4**

behavior modification   The conscious use of operant conditioning principles to change human behavior. **6**

behavior therapy   The application of learning theory and other experimentally derived psychological principles to the task of changing problem behavior. **17**

behavioral assessment   A type of personality assessment that seeks to measure objectively both environmental contingencies and people's responses to them. **14**

behavioral genetics   The study of the relative contributions of environmental and heredity factors to differences in human thought and behavior. **9**

behavioral measures   Objective, quantifiable measures of a subject's behavior. **2**

behaviorist   A psychologist who stresses the study of observable behavior and accounts for such behavior in terms of an association that the organism has learned in the past. **1**

behaviorist approaches   The methods of understanding personality that view the development and functioning of the personality as a set of learned responses, not as something that results from unconscious conflicts and urges. **1, 13**

beta waves   Rapid or high-frequency brain waves common when a person is fully awake and alert. **5**

bi-directional influence   The mutual affects of parent and child on each other, as each responds to the other. **10**

binocular disparity   The difference between the retinal images of the two eyes. **4**

binocular neurons   Neurons in the brain's visual regions that receive input from both eyes. **4**

biofeedback   The use of monitoring instruments to give a person a continuous flow of information about his or her own physiological responses in order to control them. **15**

biological approach   A perspective on personality that focuses on behavior patterns that may be a result of adaptive pressures that existed in our evolutionary past, which holds that personality traits might be to some degree genetically determined, and that some personality traits might be due to differences in physiological functioning. **13**

biological perspective   An approach which views psychological disorders as arising from physical disfunctions in the body, and therefore as forms of illness. **16**

biomedical model   The traditional view of illness as a purely biological malfunction, which can be explained and treated without reference to the victim's psychological state or social situation. **15**

biopsychosocial model   A multi-approach view of illness which suggests that treatment requires consideration of the biological, psychological, and social causes. The basis for the field of health psychology. **15**

bipolar cells   Cells in the eye that are stimulated by rods or cones and in turn stimulate ganglion cells. **4**

bipolar (manic-depressive) disorder   A psychological disorder characterized by the episodic nature of extremes of mood. **16**

blocking   Occurs when prior conditioning to one stimulus prevents conditioning to another. **6**

borderline personality disorder   A personality disorder characterized by instability in self-image, interpersonal relations, and mood. **16**

bottom-up processing   See **data-driven processing. 4**

bulimia   An eating disorder which involves periodic gorging alternating with purging to avoid gaining weight. **12**

burnout   A syndrome among some service professionals characterized by apathy and a decline in self-esteem, loss of concern for clients, rationalizing failure by attributing it to clients, irritability and anger, and resistance to change. **19**

Cannon-Bard theory   The view, developed by W. B. Cannon and his associate L. L. Bard, that the basis of emotion lies in the central nervous system, specifically in the thalamus. **11**

case study   Intensive investigation and in-depth analysis of a single individual. **2**

castration anxiety   According to Freud, the fear a young boy experiences that his father will punish him for his Oedipal longings by cutting off his penis. **13**

CAT scan   Computerized transaxial tomography, a rapidly rotating X-ray beam that takes pictures of the brain from hundreds of different positions. **3**

catatonic stupor   Remaining in one position for hours, responding neither to people nor to things; a condition schizophrenics sometimes display. **16**

catharsis   Release of built-up aggressive drive or energy. **15, 19**

causal attribution   How people attribute causes to behavior. **18**

cell body   Region of the neuron which contains the cell nucleus and all other life-sustaining systems of the cell. **3**

central core   A major brain area involved in the control of functions basic to survival. **3**

central fissure   The separation between the frontal lobe and the parietal lobe of the brain's cortex. **3**

central nervous system (CNS)   The ultimate control center of all human behavior, consisting of the brain and the spinal cord. **3**

central tendency   A middle value (such as a mean, median, or mode) of a set of scores. **2**

cerebellum   Located to the rear of the pons, it coordinates voluntary movement of the skeletal muscles and regulates physical balance. **3**

cerebral cortex.   See **cortex. 3**

cerebral hemispheres   Also the forebrain. The two large structures lying above the brain's central core that are involved in learning, speech, reasoning, and memory. **3**

chaining   Learning a sequence of operant behaviors which eventually ends in a primary reward. **6**

chromosome   Thread-shaped structures within the cell nucleus that carry the organism's genes. **9**

chunking   Perceiving related items as a larger unit or cluster; used to increase the capacity of normal short-term memory. **7**

ciliary muscles   Muscles in the eye that change the shape of the lens for focus. **4**

circadian rhythm   Naturally occurring daily cycle of the body. **5**

circle of emotions   A model which holds that emotions vary along two primary dimensions: pleasant-to-unpleasant and high-to-low activation. **11**

classical (or Pavlovian) conditioning   A process of learning discovered by Ivan Pavlov in which a conditioned stimulus (CS) repeatedly presented with an unconditioned stimulus (UCS) that normally evokes an involuntary response, develops into a learned or conditioned response even in the absence of the CS. **6**

classically conditioned response   Behavior that results when a neural stimulus is repeatedly paired with another stimulus that evokes an involuntary response, such as emotions or physical reflexes. **6**

client-centered therapy   Carl Rogers' system of psychotherapy, based on the belief that the client is responsible for his or her own potential and self-actualization, and in which the therapist creates an atmosphere of acceptance and helps clients to clarify their true feelings. **17**

clinical psychologist   Doctorates in psychology who have been trained in psychological treatments and interventions. Those with a Ph.D., instead of a Psy.D., also have training in doing research. **17**

clinical psychology   The diagnosis and treatment of behavioral disorders. **1**

cochlea   The spiral-shaped part of the inner ear containing the receptors for hearing. **4**

cochlear implant   A surgical procedure in which microelectrodes are surgically positioned at various points along the cochlea. This procedure is designed to help people with neural deafness. **4**

cognition   The process of organizing information in our minds to help accomplish some desired end. **1**

cognitive appraisal theory   A theory which holds that emotions arise from how we appraise events in our environment in relation to our short- and long-term goals and our abilities and resources for coping. **11**

cognitive arousal theory   A theory developed by Stanley Schacter and Jerome Singer, which holds that we interpret physiological arousal by reading cues in our environment. **11**

cognitive behavior therapy   Therapy that attempts to change clients negative thought patterns. **17**

cognitive consistency   The tendency of people to keep their various cognitions in relative agreement with one another. **18**

cognitive dissonance   The theory advanced by Leon Festinger that people are motivated by the need to achieve consistency between their attitudes and their behavior. **18**

cognitive learning   Learning that involves forming expectations and mental schemas of objects and events. **6**

cognitive perspective   An approach to understanding abnormality through consideration of the role of patterns of thought in manifestations of abnormality. **1, 16**

cognitive psychologist   A professional who studies the mental processes, or cognitions, in order to understand human behavior. **1**

cognitive therapy   A variation of cognitive restructuring therapy developed by Beck in which patients are questioned in such a way that they themselves discover the irrationality of their thoughts. **17**

companionate love   The warm, affectionate bond between two people who are deeply committed to each other. **18**

compliance   Outwardly seeming to yield to pressure while actually maintaining one's own opinions. **19**

compulsion   An act of irrational behavior that the person seems unable to control. **16**

computer-assisted instruction   See **programmed instruction. 6**

concept   A mental construct that enables a person to classify objects by the characteristics they share with other objects. **8**

concepts of conservation   The recognition that certain features of things (such as quantity) remain the same despite changes in other features (such as external appearance). **9**

conceptually driven processing   Knowledge stored in the brain that influences what we hear, see, and feel. **4**

concrete-operational period   The third stage of Piaget's theory of intellectual growth (which usually comprises the elementary-school years), during which a child begins to think logically—but only in regard to concrete objects. **9**

concrete operations   Logical operations that involve reversible transformations of concrete objects and events. **9**

concurrent validity   The type of validity a test has if results can be correlated with another criterion that is immediately available. **14**

conditional positive regard   According to Rogers, the withholding of love and praise from a child unless he or she conforms to parental and social standards. **13**

conditioned operant response   Results from a learned association between a particular action and a desirable consequence. **6**

conditioned response (CR)   A response to a previously neutral stimulus learned through association in the process of conditioning. **1**

conditioned stimulus (CS)   The stimulus which elicits a new response as a result of the conditioning process. **6**

conditions of worth   Rogers' term for the strong ideas children hold about which thoughts and behaviors will bring positive regard and so are desirable and "good." **13, 17**

conduction deafness   Malfunctions of the outer or middle ear that impair the ear's ability to mechanically amplify sound waves, e.g., wax buildup in the ear canal. **4**

cones   Receptor cells in the retina that are sensitive to color and that are used primarily for daytime or high-light-intensity vision. **4**

confabulation   The manufacture of an item in memory to replace one that a person is unable to retrieve. **7**

confirmatory hypothesis testing   The tendency of people to seek out information that confirms their existing schemas. **18**

conformity   The tendency to shift one's opinions or actions to correspond with those of other people because of implicit or explicit social pressure. **19**

connectionist framework   A view of cognitive processes that emphasizes the connections between stimuli and responses, between the cognitive system's inputs and outputs. **7**

consciousness   An active awareness of the many thoughts, images, perceptions, and emotions that occupy one's mind at any given time. **5**

consolidation   The process of a series of solidifying events occurring when a memory is acquired enabling it to become fixed in long-term memory. **7**

constituent   A group of words that make sense together. **8**

constructivist view   See **indirect perspective. 4**

contingency contracting   A behavioral technique in which a person makes a contract with another individual detailing the rewards or punishments contingent on succeeding or failing to make a behavior change. **15**

contingency management   An operant-conditioning therapy that seeks to increase desirable behaviors by reinforcement and to decrease undesirable ones by punishment or withdrawal of rewards. **6**

continuity   A gestalt principle of organization proposing that items will be perceived as belonging together if they appear to form a single, continuous grouping. **4**

continuous reinforcement schedule   The providing of reinforcement each time the subject exhibits the desired behavior. **6**

contralateral control   A basic principle of brain organization where the motor cortex of the right hemisphere controls movement on the left side of the body and the left hemisphere controls right-side movement. **3**

control group   In an experiment, subjects who experience all the same conditions as experimental subjects *except* the key factor that is being evaluated. **2**

conventional level   According to Kohlberg, the stage in moral development during which a child adheres to rules to win the approval of others, and is inclined to follow the dictates of established authority. **10**

conversion disorder   The loss of a sensory or motor function without organic impairment, usually following some traumatic event. **16**

coping   The process of managing the internal and external demands that one appraises as taxing or overwhelming. **15**

cornea   The tough, transparent, curved outer covering of the front of the eyeball which admits light into the interior of the eye. **4**

corpus callosum   The large cable of nerve cells connecting the two cerebral hemispheres of the brain. **3**

correlation coefficient   A numerical value that indicates the strength and direction of the relationship between two variables. **2**

correlation research   A research design used to find out the extent to which two variables are related when a true experiment is not feasible. **2**

cortex   The covering of gray matter of the cerebral hemisphere. Much of the "higher-order" processing occurs here, relating to learning, speech, reasoning, and memory. **3**

counseling psychologist   A professional trained to help individuals deal with mild problems of social and emotional adjustment. **1, 17**

counterconditioning   Reduction or elimination of a classically conditioned response. See also **systematic desensitization. 6**

criterion validity   The type of validity a test has if a person's score on it can be correlated with some other yardstick of what is being measured. **14**

cross-sectional study   A study in which the population is divided into subgroups on the basis of certain criteria, the subgroups are randomly sampled, and the members of each sample are then surveyed, tested, or observed. **2**

cyclothymia   A chronic form of bipolar disorder (manic-depression). **16**

data-driven processing   Information flowing from our sense organs to the brain. **4**

daydream   A train of thought that departs from a person's immediate situation and whatever tasks are at hand. **5**

decay theory   The view that memories simply fade away with the passage of time if they are not renewed through periodic use. **7**

deep processing   Mental activity, also called elaborative rehearsal, which facilitates the transfer of information from short-term to long-term memory storage by emphasizing the meaning of a stimulus. **7**

defense mechanism   According to Freudian theory, a mental strategy that the ego uses to block harmful behavior and thus reduce anxiety. **13**

delta sleep   The deepest stage of sleep when delta waves occupy more than 50 percent of a sleeper's EEG. **15**

delta waves   Very slow brain waves that predominate during deep sleep. **5**

delusion   An irrational belief held despite overwhelming evidence to the contrary. **16**

demand characteristic   In an experiment, any clue felt by the subjects about the response they think the researcher wants them to make. **2**

dendrites   The short, branched extensions of a neuron that usually carry neural impulses toward the cell body. **3**

denial   According to psychoanalytic theory, a defense mechanism which involves a refusal to acknowledge some threat. **13**

dependent variable   A factor that is expected to change when the independent variable is manipulated. **2**

depolarization   A decrease in the electrical imbalance associated with the resting state. **3**

depressant   A chemical that suppresses nerve impulses, such as alcohol. **5**

depression, major   A depressive disorder characterized by one or more episodes of deep sadness and despair, each of which persists virtually all day long for a period of at least two weeks. **16**

depressive disorders   Mood disorders in which a sad, discouraged mood is the major symptom. **16**

depth perception   The ability to see the world in three dimensions and tell how far away an object is. **4**

descriptive statistics Statistical methods used to summarize a vast amount of data in forms that are brief and easy to understand. **2**

developmental psychology The branch of psychology that describes and explains the patterns of growth and systematic changes that occur in human beings throughout the life cycle, from conception to death. **1, 9**

diathesis-stress model A theory that the interaction of factors such as biological predisposition combined with life stress may cause schizophrenia. **16**

dichotic listening A technique, developed by E. C. Cherry, involving the simultaneous input of different information into each ear. **7**

dichromat A person who is partially color blind because of the lack or loss of one of the three forms of iodopsin normally found in the cones. **4**

direct perspective A theory of perception that sensory data presented to the eyes is passed to the brain which automatically structures the data into a meaningful whole. **4**

discrimination The behavioral expression of prejudice. **18**

discrimination training A procedure used to teach an animal to respond only to a specific stimulus by presenting similar stimuli which will not elicit a reward. **6**

discriminative stimulus The stimulus which elicits the reward in discrimination training. **6**

dispersion The degree of scatter among the individual numbers of a set of numbers. **2**

displacement According to psychoanalytic theory, a defense mechanism that involves the transfer of unacceptable feelings from their appropriate target to a "safer" object. **13**

dissociation A split in consciousness whereby certain thoughts, feelings, and behaviors operate independently from others; one theory of what happens in hypnosis. **5**

dissociative disorder A psychological disorder that involves the splitting off of a part of the personality so that personal memory or identity is disturbed. **16**

divergent thinking The ability to generate many different answers to a question. **8**

DNA (deoxyribonucleic acid) A long, spiral-shaped complex molecule composed of subunits of chemical structures, the sequence of which determines the genetic information carried by the chromosome. **9**

door-in-the-face technique A compliance strategy in which a smaller counter request is made in response to a refusal of a larger request. **19**

double-blind technique A procedure in which neither the experimenter nor the subjects know who has been assigned to the experimental group or who is acting as a control. **2**

dream analysis A technique used in psychoanalytically oriented therapy in which the hidden meaning of a dream can be brought to light, and unconscious wishes, fantasies, and conflicts can be explored. **17**

drive State of biological need that motivates an animal to act to reduce tension. **12**

drive-reduction theory A theory of motivation developed by behaviorist Clark Hull and others which states that biological needs are the basic motivators of action. **12**

drug Any substance that can alter the functioning of a biological system. **5**

drug therapy The treatment of psychological disorders through the administration of drugs. **17**

dysthymia A chronic form of depression, one that endures for years at a time. **16**

eardrum A thin membrane between the outer and inner ear that responds to changes in air pressure by vibrating, thus amplifying sound. **4**

ecological validity The issue concerning research methods suggesting that conditions in a laboratory experiment may not always mirror those in real-life settings. **2**

educational psychologist A researcher who specializes in analyzing and improving formal education and other aspects of the learning process. **1**

effector cells Cells specialized for contracting muscles and for stimulating glandular secretions. **3**

efferent pathways Nerve pathways leading away from the central nervous system. **3**

effortful encoding A deliberate attempt to put something into memory. **7**

ego According to Freud, the part of the psyche that mediates transactions between the external environment and the demands of the id and the superego; the ego operates on the reality principle. **13**

egocentric Among young children, the belief that everyone views the world from the same perspective as the child does. **9**

ego psychologist A psychoanalytic investigator who considers herself or himself a Freudian but who elaborates on Freud's theory, emphasizing ego functions. **13**

eidetic images Visual images that persist with incredible clarity and detail for a minute or two before they fade. **7**

elaborative rehearsal See **deep processing**. **7**

electroconvulsive therapy (ECT) A form of biological therapy used to treat depression in which an electric current is passed through the brain, causing a convulsion which is therapeutic. **17**

electroencephalogram (EEG)   Tracings of brain-wave patterns made by an electroencephalograph. **5**

emotion   A reaction pattern that includes physiological changes, expressive behaviors, and states of feeling, arising involuntarily in response to a challenging situation. **11**

empathy   The experiencing of another's emotional condition as if it is one's own. **19**

empiricist view   A theory of perceptual development, linked to the indirect or constructivist perspective, which holds that perceptual processes are learned from sensory experience. **4**

encoding   The act of converting sensory stimuli into a form that can be placed in memory, often using old information to analyze or to manipulate the data. **7**

encoding strategy   Any tactic such as verbally naming or labeling objects and mentally picturing words used to take information into short-term memory. **7**

endocrine glands   Those glands that produce hormones and secrete them into the bloodstream. **3**

endogenous opioids   Chemicals that occur naturally within the central nervous system and that have molecular structures which are very similar to those of morphine and other opium-based narcotics **3**

environment   In psychology, the external surroundings in which a person lives and the internal makeup of a person's body. **9**

environmental psychology   The field of study which focuses on the interrelationships between people and their physical and social surroundings. **1**

epinephrine   Also adrenalin. This hormone prepares the body to deal with stress by producing various physiological changes. **3**

episodic memories   Recollections of events an individual has personally experienced. **7**

equilibration   In Piaget's theory, the process by which development is achieved by attempting to reach a balance between assimilation and accommodation. **9**

erectile failure   A sexual dysfunction that occurs in men characterized by the inability to achieve or maintain an erection. **12**

escape learning   A cause and effect relationship whereby learning is achieved through escaping the stimulus. It can be established through negative reinforcement. **6**

evolutionary psychology   A field of psychology that focuses on the genetic bases of animal and human social behaviors. **12**

excitement phase   The first stage of the sexual response cycle, characterized by increased breathing, heart rate, and muscular tension in both women and men. **12**

executive control structures   Case's term for the child's current ways of representing the world coupled with the child's current strategies for dealing with specific kinds of problems. **9**

expectancy-value model   The explanation of motivation that takes into account both the expectancy of achieving a particular goal and the value placed upon it. **12**

experiment   A research method designed to answer questions about causes. **2**

experimental group   Those subjects experiencing the experimental condition. **2**

experimental psychologist   A psychologist who studies one of several "basic" processes, such as sensation, perception, or learning, shared by a variety of animal species. **1**

experimental psychology   The approach to psychology in which psychologists use experimentation to gather data on the basic processes shared by many animal species. **1**

expressed emotion   The amount of criticism and hostility directed toward schizophrenics by other people, especially from within families. **16**

extinction   The slow weakening and eventual disappearance of a conditioned response. **6**

facial feedback   The hypothesis that facial expressions play a key role in initiating or at least modulating the experience of emotion. **11**

factor   A basic ability. **14**

factor analysis   A statistical technique used by researchers to determine which groups of scores on mental tests tend to cluster together. They then explain each cluster by assuming some basic ability, or underlying factor. **13, 14**

family/systems perspective   A method of understanding psychological problems through study of the network of human relationships important in a person's life. **16**

family-systems therapy   Psychotherapy which stresses the importance of altering family roles and patterns of communication that maintain maladaptive behavior. **17**

feature-based model   The model of concept formation which holds that one tests hypotheses regarding which features of a stimulus define it as a member of a category. **8**

field experiment   An experiment which has been designed and conducted in a natural setting. **2**

figure   Section of the perceptual field which represents objects. **4**

figure and ground   See **figure**; **ground. 4**

fight-or-flight response   A physiological reaction to stress in which an organism is aroused either to attack a threatening invader or to flee. **15**

fixation   In psychoanalysis, a state of arrested development where an individual remains "locked" in a particular psychological battle and expresses this conflict symbolically. **13**

fixed-interval schedule A partial reinforcement schedule in which a reward is given for the first correct response after a certain time interval. **6**

fixed-ratio schedule A partial reinforcement schedule in which a reward is given after a specified number of responses. **6**

foot-in-the-door phenomenon A tendency to comply with a larger request if a person has previously agreed to a smaller one. **19**

forced observation The tendency of people to perceive the world according to their unique vocabulary and the structural rules of their language. **8**

forebrain See **cerebral hemispheres. 3**

form perception The ability to detect unified patterns in a mass of sensory data. **4**

formal-operational period The last stage of Piaget's theory of intellectual growth (from adolescence through adulthood), during which a person learns to think simultaneously about many systems of operations and to think hypothetically. **9**

formal operations Piaget's term for the cognitive changes in adolescence marking the onset of adult-like thinking, characterized by the ability to think hypothetically and in abstract terms. **9**

forward conditioning Presenting the conditioned stimulus slightly before the unconditioned stimulus in order to create the perception of a contingency. **6**

fovea A pit-like depression near the center of the retina, densely packed with cones but no rods, that provides a person's sharpest, most detailed vision. **4**

free association A psychoanalytic technique for exploring the unconscious through a patient's unrestrained expression of thoughts that occur spontaneously. **1, 17**

frequency The number of compression-rarefaction cycles that occur per second. The frequency of a sound wave corresponds to the pitch one hears. **4**

frequency theory The theory of pitch that argues that the basilar membrane vibrates in exactly the same frequency pattern as the original sound wave, thus pitch is determined by the frequency per second of neural impulses sent to the brain. **4**

frontal lobe The portion of each cerebral hemisphere that is concerned with the regulation of voluntary movements. (See **motor cortex.**) **3**

frustration Interference with any goal-directed behavior. **19**

frustration-aggression hypothesis Dollard's theory that aggression is always a consequence of frustration, and frustration always leads to some form of aggression. **19**

fugue, psychogenic A dissociative disorder; a total abdication of one's home and identity. People suffering from this disorder may be absent from their home for hours or years, and recall nothing of what happened in the fugue state. **16**

fully functioning Rogers' term for people who, because they have learned conditions of worth that are few and reasonable, are open to a wide range of feelings and behaviors. **13**

functional fixedness The tendency to overlook novel uses for things. **8**

functionalism The view, influenced by Darwin's theories and expounded chiefly by William James, that psychological processes have adaptive functions that allow the human species to survive and that these processes are more important to investigate than the mind's structure. **1**

fundamental attribution error The tendency to overestimate the role of dispositional rather than situational factors in judging the behavior of others. **18**

fundamental needs In Maslow's hierarchy, those needs associated with physical requirements, such as satisfying thirst and hunger, and those related to obtaining a safe environment. **13**

g factor Spearman's term for general intellectual ability. **14**

ganglia Bundles of neurons that process information. **3**

ganglion cells Nerve tissue cells of the eye that form the fibers of the optic nerve. **4**

gate-control theory The theory asserting that the sensation of pain depends on the balance of activity between large- and small-diameter (A and C) nerve fibers within the spinal cord. **4**

gender role The pattern of behavior generally associated with masculinity or femininity. **10**

general adaption syndrome As outlined by Hans Selye, the set of physiological responses that is evoked by all unusually demanding stresses, pleasurable as well as painful, on the body. **15**

general paresis The final stage of syphilis characterized by irreversible deterioration of all mental and physical processes. **16**

generalization gradient The decreasing tendency to display a conditioned response as the resemblance between a new stimulus and a conditioned one becomes weaker. **6**

generalized anxiety Diffuse and persistent fears that are impossible to manage through avoidance. **16**

genes The inherited set of developmental instructions within the cell nucleus that are the basic units for the transmission of hereditary characteristics. **9**

genital stage According to Freud, the fifth psychosexual stage (occurring from puberty on), during which the sexual focus shifts from autoeroticism to sexual intercourse. **13**

gestalt A meaningful pattern that the brain constructs from sensory information; also meaning "whole," as in psychotherapy that aims at making a person psychologically "whole" or integrated. **4**

gestalt psychology The approach to psychology maintaining that what emerges from perception of individual pieces of information is a whole that is greater than the sum of its parts. **4**

gestalt therapy Psychotherapy that emphasizes the present and attempts to make a client **whole** by ridding him or her of defenses, increasing awareness, and releasing pent up feelings. **17**

glia Also neuroglia. Cells that hold neurons in place, carry nutrients to them, repair and protect them, and aid in the propagation of impulses. **3**

gonads Glands that secrete sex hormones. The female gonads are the ovaries, which secrete estrogen and progesterone. The male gonads are the testes, which secrete testosterone. **3**

graded potentials Changes in electrical potential of dendrites in proportion to the amount of stimulation being received. **3**

grasping reflex The infant's tendency to cling tightly to any small object placed in one of his or her hands. **9**

ground The part of the perceptual field that represents space between objects. **4**

group A collection of people who regularly interact with one another in a structured way, are oriented toward specific goals, and who have a feeling of group identity and solidarity. **19**

group therapy The type of treatment in which therapists work with an interacting collection of people rather than with individuals. **17**

groupthink A term coined by Janis describing the mode of decision making whereby a small, cohesive group becomes so concerned with maintaining unanimity that it can no longer appraise alternatives realistically. **19**

growth cone A club-like extension at the growing tip of an axon or dendrite in an immature neuron, from which many hair-like filaments extend. **3**

growth hormone The hormone produced by the pituitary gland which plays a key role in physical development. **3**

habituation A simple form of learning in which the response to a given stimulus grows weaker and weaker the more that stimulus is presented. **9**

hair cells Cells containing hair-like projections that are receptors for hearing in the inner ear. **4**

hallucinogen A drug that produces hallucinations and impaired thinking. **5**

hammer One of a set of three tiny, interconnected bones in the middle ear that transmit sound from the eardrum to the cochlea. **4**

happiness An enduring, positive emotional state that includes quiet contentment with one's life as well as active pleasures and achievements. **11**

Hawthorne effect The phenomenon in which subjects behave in unusual ways simply because they are part of a scientific study. **2**

health psychology A subfield that identifies and treats the psychological factors related to mental and physical health. **1, 15**

heredity In psychology, the characteristics transmitted by the genes a person was born with. **9**

heritability factor An estimate of genetic contributions to the individual differences in people who belong to the same population. **14**

heuristic A technique for discovering information; a so-called rule-of-thumb strategy in problem solving. **8**

hidden observer A phenomenon that occurs under hypnosis in which two parts of consciousness seem to split so that one part is unaware of the feelings or actions of the other. **5**

hierarchy of needs Maslow's concept that all humans face a series of needs in life, and that needs at more basic levels must be met before the person can go on to fulfill higher-level needs. **13**

hindbrain An area in the brain's central core consisting of the medulla, the pons, the reticular formation, and the cerebellum. **3**

hippocampus One of three interrelated structures of the limbic system; the others are the septal area and the amygdala. **3**

hormones Chemical substances produced by the endocrine system that circulate through the bloodstream and regulate physiological activities. **3**

humanistic approach A method of understanding personality that emphasizes the human potential for growth, creativity, and spontaneity, and that stresses the importance of an individual's subjective experience of the world. **1, 13**

humanistic therapy Treatment aimed at liberating the client's innate tendencies toward self-actualization and growth. **17**

hyperpolarization An increase in the electrical imbalance associated with the resting state. **3**

hypnotic susceptibility A measurable trait used to classify how easily a person can be hypnotized. **5**

hypochondriasis Psychological disorder characterized by persistent and irrational fear of having a disease despite reassurance from doctors that no physical illness exists. **16**

hypothalamus A structure located below the thalamus which regulates the body's internal environment and acts to maintain balance within the body. **3**

hypothesis A proposition or idea that one sets out to test. **2**

id According to Freud, the impulsive and unconscious part of the psyche which operates via the pleasure principle toward the gratification of instinctual drives. **13**

identification According to Freud, a method of reducing the anxiety produced by the Oedipus conflict by categorizing oneself as psychologically similar to the parent of one's own sex, and therefore adopting the parent's gender role as one's own. In social psychology, the tendency to go along with others because we admire and wish to be like them. **10, 19**

identity An individual's sense of personal uniqueness and continuity. **10**

identity crisis A concept, introduced by Erikson, that describes the chaos that results, often in adolescence, from not having a clear sense of self regarding goals, interests, place in the family, role in society, etc. **10**

immune system The body's "surveillance system," which guards the body against foreign invaders (called antigens). **15**

immunocompetence The measure of how well the immune system protects the body from illness. **15**

incentive The expectation of receiving a reward or punishment that stimulates or maintains goal-directed behavior. **12**

independent variable A factor that an experimenter deliberately manipulates. **2**

indirect perspective A theory of perception that all we process directly are sensory cues that additional information stored in memory enables us to make sense of the cues. **4**

industrial and organizational psychologist A psychologist who studies all aspects of the relationship between people and their workplace. **1**

infantile amnesia The failure of people to retain episodic memories from infancy. **9**

inferential statistics Statistical methods used to conclude whether the data tend to support a researcher's original hypothesis, or whether the results could have occurred by chance alone. **2**

inferiority complex Adler's theory that all children are born with a deep sense of inferiority because of their small size, physical weakness, and lack of knowledge and power in the adult world. **13**

information-processing system In psychology, an analogy borrowed from computer science, that suggests the mind takes in information, processes it, and produces outputs in the form of ideas, words, and behaviors. **1**

information-processing view of intelligence An approach to studying intelligence which looks closely at *how* people think and reason intelligently. **14**

in-groups Those groups with which one identifies. **18**

inhibited ejaculation A sexual dysfunction characterized by the man's inability to ejaculate during sex with a partner. **12**

insomnia Difficulty falling asleep or staying asleep all night. **5**

instinctive drift A reversion to a genetically based behavior that competes with a learned behavior. **6**

instincts Innate, internal forces, characteristic of a species, which propel individuals to behave in broadly predictable ways. **12**

intelligence The capacities to acquire and retain knowledge and to understand concepts and relationships. **14**

intelligence quotient (IQ) A measure of an individual's mental development obtained by dividing a person's mental age (the average age of children who obtain a particular score on an intelligence test) by a person's chronological age and multiplying by 100. **14**

intensity In light, how densely photons in a light wave are packed. In sound, the amount of pressure a sound wave exerts. **4**

interactionist view A theory of perceptual development which holds that both the interaction of inherited biological factors *and* experience are necessary for the perceptual processes to unfold. **4**

interference The fading of memory due to the inevitable confusion encountering subsequent similar experiences. **7**

internal consistency The characteristic of a test that yields the same responses from people to items that measure the same thing; see **split halves**. **14**

internalization Incorporation of society's values into the self or personality to such an extent that violation of these standards produces a sense of guilt. **10, 19**

interneurons The neurons that connect neurons to each other and integrate the activities of the sensory and motor neurons. **3**

interpersonal perspective See **family/systems persective**. **16**

intrinsic motivation The internal satisfaction of acting competently that explains behavior. **12**

intrinsic reinforcement and punishment Those self-reactions such as self-esteem and self-reproach that affect a person's learning and behavior. **6**

invertebrates Animals without backbones. **3**

iodopsin A light-sensitive chemical pigment found in the retina's cone cells. **4**

ions Electrically charges particles. **3**

iris A ring of pigmented tissue that gives the eye its color, which expands and contracts the pupil to control the amount of light that enters the eye. **4**

James-Lange theory The view of William James and Carl Lange that the perception of stimuli in the environment triggers bodily changes that produce the actual experience of emotion. **11**

just noticeable difference From Weber's law, formulated by Gustav Fechner, the minimum difference between two stimuli that can be accurately perceived. **4**

Kaufman Assessment Battery for Children (K-ABC) An intelligence test that minimizes cultural bias by lessening the impact of language ability on scores and by separating problem-solving ability from acquired knowledge. **14**

Korsakoff's syndrome An acute condition of the memory caused by excess alcohol whereby the person can remember almost nothing about events that occurred since the disorder set in. **5**

Krause bulbs Receptors believed to be responsible for the sensation of cold. **4**

latency stage According to Freud, the fourth stage of psychosexual development (occurring from age five or six until the start of puberty), during which sexual impulses are repressed while the child learns social and cognitive skills. **13**

latent content In psychoanalysis, the symbolic meanings of dreams that expose unconscious wishes. **5, 17**

latent learning Learning in which knowledge of a new behavior is not demonstrated until an incentive to do so arises. **6**

lateral fissure The top boundary of each temporal lobe of the brain's cortex. **3**

lateralized brain structures Structures that appear on one side of the brain but not the other. **3**

lateralized functions A term used to describe the human brain, in which different sides control different behavioral functions. **3**

law of effect Thorndike's theory that responses that lead to satisfying consequences will be strengthened and are likely to be repeated, whereas responses that lead to unsatisfying consequences will be weakened and are unlikely to occur again. **6**

learned motive See **secondary drive. 12**

learning A relatively permanent change in performance potential that arises from experience. **6**

learning perspective An approach to understanding abnormal behavior which notes that we learn abnormal behaviors much as we learn normal ones—through modeling, classical conditioning, operant conditioning, and so on. **16**

lens In vision, a transparent, elastic structure that allows the eye to adjust its focus in accordance with an object's distance. **4**

light and shadow Depth cues processed by the way our brain organizes and gives meaning to sensory information. When the bottom of something is in shadow, you see it as projecting forward; and when, conversely, the top is in shadow, you see it as recessed. **4**

limbic system The innermost borders of the cerebral hemispheres which are involved in emotion, motivation, and sexual and feeding behavior. **3**

linear perspective The impression of depth created by the convergence of parallel lines as they recede into the distance; a monocular depth cue. **4**

linguistic relativity hypothesis Whorf's notion that language heavily influences thought. **8**

linguistic universals Features found in all languages as a result of shared human characteristics of thought. **8**

lithium A drug used to treat both manic and bipolar affective disorders. **17**

localization of function The principle that different parts of the brain are involved in different behaviors. **3**

longitudinal study A study in which the same group of people is examined over a number of years. **2**

long-term memory The storage of information for an indefinite period of time to be used over and over again. **7**

low-ball phenomenon A compliance strategy based on the idea that a person's decision to perform a certain act often holds even if that action becomes more costly. **19**

lucid dream Nighttime fantasy in which the dreamer clearly perceives that he or she is only dreaming, yet the dream continues. **5**

maintenance rehearsal See **shallow processing. 7**

major depression See **depression, major. 16.**

mania A prolonged state of elation and feverish activity often mixed with intense irritability. **16**

manic-depressive disorder See **bipolar disorder. 16**

manifest content In psychoanalysis, dream material recalled and reported by the dreamer; the plot or story line of the dream. **5, 17**

mean The arithmetic average of a set of numbers. **2**

means–end analysis A heuristic by which means are sought that will move the problem solver closer to the goal. **8**

measures of variability Statistical techniques for expressing the spread of numbers in a frequency distribution. **2**

median The number that falls in the exact middle of a distribution of numbers arranged from highest to lowest. **2**

mediation A focusing of attention on a single stimulus, thus restricting sensory input and producing an altered state of consciousness. **5**

medulla The part of the hindbrain that controls autonomic activities, such as circulation and breathing, and is also involved in chewing, salivation, and facial movements. **3**

meiosis The process of sperm and egg cell division during which chromosome pairs are split, rearranged, and distributed to two daughter cells. **9**

menarche The start of the menstrual cycle. **10**

mental set   The inclination to repeat a solution that has worked in the past. See also **set**. **8**

mental strategies   Testing techniques used to identify the defining features of unfamiliar concepts, according to Bruner. **1**

mentally retarded   The term applied to a person whose general intelligence has from childhood been significantly below average and who has trouble functioning in normal everyday settings. **14**

meta-analysis   A sophisticated statistical method by which the results of many studies are combined to give the average value (as a single score) of a therapy's success. **2, 16**

metacognition   The ability to monitor one's own thoughts. **9**

method of loci   A mnemonic device involving the association of items to be remembered with a series of places, or loci, that are already firmly fixed in memory. **7**

midbrain   A small area in the brain's central core above the hindbrain containing centers for visual and auditory reflexes. **3**

Minnesota Multiphasic Personality Inventory (MMPI)   An objective personality test, designed to provide a detailed list of a subject's personality traits based on his or her answers to a series of over 550 statements. **14**

misinformation acceptance   The adoption into one's memory of later-learned, incorrect information. **7**

mnemonic devices   Memory aids that improve recall ability, including method of loci, key word system, and eidetic imagery. **7**

mode   The number or score that is most frequently obtained in a distribution. **2**

modeling   The process by which someone learns a new behavior by observing other people perform that behavior. **17**

monochromat   A person whose cones contain only one form of iodopsin and who thus sees shades of gray. **4**

mood disorders   People with mood disorders can feel intensely marvelous or miserable for long periods of time and for no apparent reason. As a result, their emotions come to distort their entire outlook and interfere greatly with their normal lives. **16**

mood-congruent recall   A bias in retrieving memories where a positive mood may act to screen out negative thoughts and situations, and vice versa. **7**

mood-dependent memory   Memory that is easier to retrieve when the person is in the psychological state in which the information was originally stored. **7**

morphemes   The smallest combinations of speech sounds that have meaning in a given language. **8**

motion parallax   The differences in the relative movement of retinal images that occur when we change position. **4**

motivated forgetting   The forgetting of information because we want to, either consciously or unconsciously. **7**

motivation   Those factors that arouse, sustain, and direct behavior toward attainment of some goal. **12**

motor cortex   The area of the brain's frontal lobe next to the central fissure, concerned primarily with the regulation of voluntary movements. **3**

motor neurons   The neurons that carry signals from the central nervous system to the muscles and glands. **3**

MRI   Magnetic resonance imaging, a diagnostic technique that uses magnetic fields to provide data about the chemical contents and environments of cells. **3**

multiple personality disorder   An extreme form of dissociation in which a person's personality structure divides into two or more complete identities, each well defined and distinct from the others. **16**

myelin sheath   The fatty, whitish substance around an axon. **3**

narcissistic personality disorder   A personality disorder characterized by an overblown sense of one's own importance. **16**

narcolepsy   A condition in which a wide-awake person loses muscle control and lapses into sleep. **5**

nativist theories   The view of Noam Chomsky and others which holds that language acquisition is controlled by the genetically programmed development of certain neural circuits in the brain. **9**

nativist view   The view of perceptual development, linked to the direct perspective, which holds that perceptual processes are accounted for partly by learning and partly by the ways in which sensory systems work. **4**

natural concepts   Categories used in daily thought to classify objects. They are thought to be encoded through prototypes, not a list of defining features. **8**

naturalistic observation   The study of subjects in a natural setting without interference or distraction from the investigator. **2**

need for achievement   The motivation to achieve; those high in this need persist longer and do better on difficult tasks and are apt to set realistic and challenging goals. **12**

negative correlation   The relationship between two variables in which a high incidence of one is accompanied by a low incidence of the other. **2**

negative reinforcement   Reinforcement that strengthens a response because the response removes some painful or unpleasant stimulus or enables the individual to avoid it. **6**

negative state relief model   A model of behavior which holds that we seek relief from negative moods by doing something positive, something that will lift our own spirits. **19**

nerve cord   A tubular bundle of nerve cells that runs the length of the body, one on each side. **3**

nerves   Bundles of neurons that transmit messages by electrochemical impulses from one part of the body to another. **3**

network models of memory   Theories that the ideas and concepts stored in memory are linked by means of their relationship. The idea that memory can be dependent on mood or emotion is one such model. **7**

neural deafness   A hearing disorder resulting from damage to the basilar membrane and hair cells. **4**

neurobiological perspective   One of the five perspectives to dominate psychology in the twentieth century explains thoughts, feelings, and behaviors in terms of the workings of the brain and nervous system. **1**

neurons or nerve cells   Cells specialized for conducting signals from one part of the body to another; they connect receptor cells to effector cells and integrate their activities. **3**

neuropeptides   A class of brain chemicals first identified as hormones and now considered neurotransmitters. **3**

neuropsychologists   A psychologist who studies how basic processes are controlled by the nervous system, of which the brain is the central part. **1**

neurotransmitter   A chemical substance which diffuses across synapses and activates receptor sites on adjacent cells. **3**

node of Ranvier   A gap in the myelin sheath of an axon that helps speed the action potential impulses. **3**

noise   Irrelevant competing stimuli that limit the sensory capacities.

non-REM sleep   All the stages of sleep, collectively, when rapid eye movement (REM) is absent. **5**

nonverbal communication   Facial expressions, body movements, and pitch and tone of voice, both inherited and learned, that express emotion; sometimes called body language. **11**

noradrenalin   See **norepinephrine. 3**

norepinephrine   Also called noradrenalin. A hormone that plays a role in adapting the body to stress. **3**

norm(s)   An unstated expectation or explicit standard for behavior that members of a group share. In testing, the descriptive statistics such as the range of scores on a test and percentage of test takers who earned scores at various levels. **14**

normal curve   A line graph of a distribution having a bell-shaped curve. **2**

normal distribution   A statistical distribution showing a normal curve. **2**

obedience   Following the explicit commands of a person in authority. **19**

object relations theory   An approach to the ego that emphasizes the importance of early attachments to the development of the child's ego, the child's feelings about the self, and later interpersonal relationships. **13**

observational learning   The process of learning how to act by watching the behavior of others. **6, 13**

obsession   A recurring irrational thought, one that the person recognizes as senseless and tries to suppress but cannot. **16**

occipital lobes   A rear portion of each cerebral hemisphere, concerned with the reception and analysis of visual information. **3**

Oedipus conflict   According to Freud, the tendency of children to see themselves as rivals of the same-sex parent for the affection of the parent of the opposite sex. When resolved, the conflict leads to adoption of the values of the same-sex parent. **10**

olfaction   The sense of smell. **4**

olfactory bulbs   The part of the brain at the forward base of the cerebral hemispheres that receives nerve impulses concerning smell from the nose and relays them to other parts of the brain. **4**

olfactory membranes   Membranes that line the roof of the nasal passages and contain many receptor cells. **4**

operant behaviors   Actions that an organism emits spontaneously, of its own accord. **6**

operant conditioning   Learning to either make or withhold a particular response because of its consequences. **6**

opponent-process model   The model of emotional response which holds that a negative emotion triggers a positive emotion, and vice versa. If the original emotion is removed, the opposite emotion will temporarily overwhelm the organism. **12**

opponent-process theory   The theory of color vision proposed by Hering that states that there are four primary colors which, when linked in complementary pairs in the brain, form ''opponent'' systems. One opponent system contains cells that are stimulated by red and inhibited by green and others that are stimulated by green and inhibited by red. In a second opponent system, yellow and blue similarly act in opposition to each other. A third opponent system is achromatic and enables the perception of brightness. **4**

optic nerve   The nerve which carries visual information from the eye to the brain. **4**

optimum level of arousal   The level of cortical stimulation at which an organism's goal-directed behaviors are most effective. **12**

oral stage   According to Freud, the first psychosexual stage (occurring during the first year of life) in which sexual pleasure is focused on the month's activities. **13**

orgasmic phase   The third stage of the sexual response cycle characterized by strong muscle contractions, rise in blood pressure and heartbeat, and extremely heightened arousal accompanied by feelings of intense pleasure as muscle tension is released. **12**

out-groups   Those groups to which one does not belong. **18**

oval window   A membrane between the middle ear and the inner ear that transmits sound to the cochlea. **4**

overregularization   The tendency of preschoolers to overextend a grammatical rule to instances where it does not apply. **9**

Pacinian corpuscles   Receptors deep under the skin surface sensitive to pressure within muscles and internal organs. **4**

panic disorder   An anxiety disorder in which the sufferer experiences sudden, inexplicable attacks of intense fear which last for minutes or even hours. **16**

papillae   The bumpy, hill-like projections on the top surface of the tongue that contain the taste buds. **4**

paradoxical intervention   A technique used in family therapy in which the therapist demands that a person with negative symptoms continues to display or even intensify those symptoms, as a first step in gaining control over the problem. **17**

parasympathetic nervous system   The division of the autonomic nervous system that dominates under conditions of relaxation and tends to conserve the body's energy. **3**

parietal lobes   A portion of the cerebral hemisphere, behind the frontal lobes on the opposite side of the cortex's central fissure, concerned with skin senses and the sense of body position. **3**

partial overlap   The illusion, created when one object partially covers another, that the covered object is farther away. **4**

partial reinforcement schedule   Reinforcing a desired behavior only part of the time. **6**

participant modeling   A therapeutic technique in which the therapist serves as a model by performing activities feared by a patient and then guiding the client through a series of steps culminating in the same activity. **17**

participant observation   A form of naturalistic observation in which an investigator joins an existing group in order to record thoughts and feelings accessible to only group members. **2**

passionate love   Romantic love, based on strong physical attraction and characterized by emotional highs and lows. **18**

peace psychology   The study of how war, especially nuclear war, can be avoided. **1**

peg word system   A mnemonic device that involves associating items to be learned with appropriate key words that are easily visualized. **7**

perception   The process whereby the brain gives order and meaning to the sensations it receives. **4**

perceptual constancy   The tendency of the brain to perceive objects with stable properties even though the visual images received are constantly changing. **4**

perceptual grouping   The concept by which gestalt psychologists explain relationships among sensory stimuli. The chief principles of grouping are proximity, continuity, and similarity, which may all be integrated by another principle—simplicity. **4**

perceptual illusion   A perception not in accord with the true characteristics of an object. **4**

perceptual set   A frame of mind that "sets" or readies a person to perceive stimuli in a certain way. **4**

peripheral nervous system   The branch of the nervous system that conveys signals from the body's sensory receptors to the central nervous system and transmits messages back to the muscles and glands. **3**

permissive   A parenting style characterized by responsiveness, coupled, however, with a failure to set firm limits or to require age-appropriateness behavior. **10**

person schema   A set of logically integrated ideas about what a particular person is like, which we use to help us interpret the meaning of that person's behavior. **18**

personality   The set of relatively stable and distinctive styles of thought, behavior, and emotional response that characterize a person's adaptations to surrounding circumstances. **13**

personality development   The emergence of distinctive styles of thought, feeling, and behavior which makes each human being a distinct individual. **10**

personality disorders   Deep-seated maladaptive patterns of relating to others that cause distress either to the victim, those around the victim, or both. **16**

personality psychologist   A psychologist who describes and explains individual differences in behavior. **1**

personnel psychology   A subfield of industrial and organizational psychology that is concerned with screening, hiring, assigning, and promoting employees. **1**

persuasive communication   A message consciously intended to persuade or to promote attitude change. **18**

PET scan   Positron emission tomography, a technique that allows researchers to trace the path of a radioactive substance through the brain from outside the skull. **3**

phallic stage   According to Freud, the third psychosexual stage (occurring to the third to fifth or sixth year of life), during which a child struggles with identification with the same-sex parent. **13**

phobia   An excessive and irrational fear of particular objects or situations. **16**

phoneme   Category or class of slightly varying sounds that speakers of a language perceive as linguistically similar. **8**

photon   A subatomic particle of light radiation. **4**

physiological assessment   Measures that provide objective, quantitative data on phenomena associated with particular psychological states, such as sleep, that are difficult to assess in other ways. **2**

pinna   The projection of skin-covered cartilage visible on the outside of the head, through which sound enters the outer ear. **4**

pituitary   A small endocrine gland at the base of the brain which controls a wide range of bodily functions, and which has been called the "master gland." **3**

placebo   A substance that has no physiological effect. **2**

placebo drinking   A technique for controlling alcohol consumption in which a person drinks only nonalcoholic beverages that look like alcoholic drinks, or alternates between alcoholic and nonalcoholic beverages. **15**

plateau stage   The second stage of the sexual response cycle, characterized by heightened arousal. **12**

pleasure principle   According to psychoanalytic theory, the principle of mental functioning of the id whereby physical tensions are reduced by gratification of instinctual drives without regard to logic, reality, or morality. **13**

polarized   Describing cells that are negatively charged inside and positively charged outside. **3**

polygraph   Often called a lie detector, this instrument monitors the physiological changes (blood pressure, heart rate, and the like) that accompany emotion. **11**

pons   The structure of the brain which transmits information about body movement from the higher brain centers and spinal cord to the cerebellum, and is vital in integrating movements between the right and left sides of the body. **3**

positive correlation   The relationship between two variables in which a high incidence of one is accompanied by a high incidence of rank on the other. **2**

positive reinforcement   The strengthening of a conditioned response because the response is followed by a positive or pleasant stimulus. **6**

postconventional level   According to Kohlberg, the final stage in moral development, during which a person recognizes that universal ethical principles can transcend specific societal laws. Failure to adhere to these principles brings self-condemnation. **10**

posttraumatic stress disorder (PTSD)   A state of anxiety, depression, and psychological "numbing" following exposure to a severe trauma. **15, 16**

pragmatics   The field that studies the implicit understandings people have about how language should be used in different social contexts. **8, 9**

preconventional level   According to Kohlberg, the early stage in moral development during which a child adheres to the rules of society because he or she fears the consequences of breaking them. **10**

predictive validity   The type of validity a test has if results can be correlated with people's future performance. **14**

prejudice   A negative and inflexible attitude toward members of a minority group based on erroneous or incomplete information. **18**

premature ejaculation   A common sexual complaint characterized by ejaculation before both partners are mutually satisfied. **12**

preoperational period   The second stage of Piaget's theory of intellectual growth (from age two through six) during which a child understands complex events but cannot use mental operations or coordinate thoughts into logical systems. **9**

prepared learning   Learning for which an organism is biologically predisposed. **6**

primacy effect   The principle that information perceived first tends to outweigh later information; this explains the strength of first impression. **18**

primary drive   A state of physiological tension that arises from needs built into the body's system. **12**

primary empathy   The first step in client-centered therapy during which the therapist mirrors a client's feelings. **17**

primary erectile failure   A sexual dysfunction in which the man has never been able to have an erection. **12**

primary orgasmic dysfunction   A sexual dysfunction in which the woman has never experienced an orgasm. **12**

primary reinforcer   A reinforcer that satisfies some basic biological need and can thus be used to establish and maintain a conditioned response. **6**

primary sexual characteristics   The physical features of gender identity involved in reproduction, such as the sex organs. **10**

priming   The unconscious activation of a schema, which then encourages ideas associated with that schema to come readily to mind. **18**

proactive interference   The fading of memory or confusion that occurs when material learned earlier interferes with recall of material learned later. **7**

probability   The likelihood of a particular event or response occurring. **2, 8**

procedural memories   Learned associations between stimuli and responses that allow a person to easily perform motor skills. **7**

programmed instruction   Instruction which emphasizes reinforcement by providing the student with immediate feedback for every response. Information is presented sequentially in small segments, and the learner does not proceed to a new unit until the learning of the present one is demonstrated. **6**

projection   According to psychoanalytic theory, a defense mechanism that involves the unknown attribution of one's own objectionable impulses to other people. **13**

projective tests   Tests in which personality characteristics are revealed by the way a subject responds to and interprets ambiguous material, such as an inkblot or ambiguous scene in a picture. **14**

propositions   Unitary ideas that combine to yield the meaning of a sentence. **8**

prototype   An example that best illustrates a concept; the means by which natural concepts are thought to be encoded in memory. **8**

proximity   The principle of gestalt psychology that stimuli close together tend to be seen as a group. **4**

psychiatric nurse   A registered nurse who has specialized in psychiatric care as part of the nursing degree. **17**

psychiatric social worker   A person who has a master's degree in social work and who specializes in psychiatric social work. **17**

psychiatrist   A medical doctor who specializes in the diagnosis and treatment of mental disorders. **1, 17**

psychoactive drug   A drug that interacts with the central nervous system to alter a person's mood, perception, mode of thinking, and behavior. **5**

psychoanalysis   Freudian psychotherapy which employs techniques such as an analysis of dreams and free association to unlock the thoughts and feelings of the unconscious and break their power to control behavior. **1, 13, 16, 17**

psychoanalyst   Usually a psychiatrist (although sometimes a lay person or psychologist) who has had advanced training in psychoanalysis and who has been psychoanalyzed as part of that training. **1, 17**

psychoanalytic approach   Method of understanding personalitiy initiated by Freud that emphasizes childhood experiences as critically important in shaping adult personality. **1, 13, 16**

psychogenic amnesia   See **amnesia, psychogenic. 16**

psychogenic fugue   See **fugue, psychogenic. 16**

psychoimmunology   A subfield of psychology that examines how psychological factors alter the immune system and ultimately increase the risk of immune system-related diseases such as AIDS, cancer, arthritis, infections, and allergies. **15**

psychological needs   In Maslow's hierarchy, all higher-level needs, including the needs to belong, to be loved, to achieve competence and recognition, and to attain self-actualization. **13**

psychology   The science that studies behavior and mental processes. **1**

psychopharmacology   The study of the link between drugs and behavior. **1**

psychosurgery   The removal or destruction of parts of the brain for the purpose of altering behavior. **17**

psychotherapy   A series of systematic verbal and emotional interactions, involving primarily talk, between a person who is trained to aid in alleviating psychological problems and someone who is suffering from them. **17**

puberty   The period marking the start of adolescence during which a person's reproductive organs become capable of functioning and secondary sex characteristics develop. **10**

punishment   A consequence that produces suppression or decrease in frequency of the behavior that caused it. **6**

pupil   The opening in the center of the eye through which light enters and travels to the retina. **4**

quasi-experiment   A research design that approximates, but does not meet, the requirements of a true experiment because the investigator has far less control over variables or cannot randomly assign subjects to conditions. **2**

racism   Prejudice directed toward members of certain racial groups. **18**

random sample   A sample in which every member of the population has an equal chance of being included. **2**

range   The difference between the highest and lowest scores of a set of scores. **2**

rational-emotive therapy (RET)   Albert Ellis's method of therapy, which seeks to replace irrational, problem-provoking outlooks with more realistic ones. **17**

reaction formation   According to psychoanalytic theory, a defense mechanism that involves the replacement of an anxiety-producing impulse or feeling with its direct opposite. **13**

reaction range   The range of social and developmental possibilities that depend on the person's experiences. **10**

reality principle   The operating principle of the ego based on the need for gratification of instinctual drives to be curbed by the realistic demands of the environment; gratification is thereby modified or delayed to insure the safety of the individual. **13**

recall   The retrieval of specific pieces of information from long-term memory, usually guided by retrieval cues. **7**

receptor cells   Cells embedded in the sense organs that are sensitive to various types of stimulation from the environment. **3**

recognition   Consideration of a particular stimulus and decision about whether it matches something stored in long-term memory. **7**

reflex arc   The simplest type of circuit between neurons, linking a sensory input to a motor response. **3**

regression   According to psychoanalytic theory, a defense mechanism whereby a person made anxious by threatening thoughts and feelings behaves in ways characteristic of an earlier period of life. **13**

rehearsal   The conscious repetition of information in an effort to retain it in short-term memory, usually involving speech. **7**

reinforcement (reward)   A consequence that produces repetition or increase in frequency of the behavior that caused it. **6**

relative closeness to the horizon   Objects that are closer to the horizon are generally seen as more distant; a monocular depth clue. **4**

relative size   Of two objects thought to be the same size, the one that casts the smaller retinal image is perceived to be farther away; a monocular depth cue. **4**

reliability   An essential criterion in determining the value of a test. A test is reliable if it yields, upon repetition, similar results for different parts of the test, for scoring by different judges, and for the same test administered to the same person at two different times. **2, 14**

REM rebound   Compensation for lost REM sleep on one night by more REM sleep the next night. **5**

REM sleep   A stage of sleep when a person experiences rapid eye movement. Vivid dreaming appears to take place primarily during episodes of REM sleep. **5**

replication   Reconstruction of the basic features of a study to see if the results are similar. **2**

representational thought   The ability to recognize things mentally when they are not physically present. **9**

representative sample   A sample in which important subgroups are represented according to their incidence in the population as a whole. **2**

representativeness heuristic   A heuristic by which given information is matched with a stereotype. **8**

repression   The psychological defense mechanism, first described by Freud, by which people push unacceptable, anxiety-provoking thoughts and impulses into their unconscious to avoid confronting them directly. **7, 12, 13**

resistance   Attempts by a client in therapy to block treatment. **17**

resolution stage   The final stage of the sexual response cycle characterized by the gradual reduction of heart rate, blood pressure, and muscle tension as the body returns to normal. **12**

resting potential   The electrical imbalance that occurs across the cell membrane when a cell is polarized; in this state, the nerve cell membrane is negatively charged inside and positively charged outside. **3**

restrained eaters   People who may be "starving" themselves from their bodies' point of view in order to achieve thinness, and who would gain a great deal of weight if they "let themselves go" regarding eating. **12**

reticular formation   Clusters of neurons and nerve fibers that extend from the spinal cord to the thalamus, acting as a sentry system to arouse the forebrain and also affecting the sleep-waking cycle. **3**

retina   The light-sensitive inner surface of the eyeball. The retina is a predominantly neural structure consisting of several layers, including a layer of rods and cones. **4**

retroactive interference   The fading of memory or confusion that occurs when information learned later interferes with information learned earlier. **7**

retrograde amnesia   A form of amnesia which involves a memory loss for only a segment of the past, not for the recollection of new events. **7**

rhodopsin   The deep red pigment in the rods of the eye. **4**

rods   Long, thin receptor cells in the periphery of the retina that are sensitive to light of low intensity and that function in dim light and nighttime vision. **4**

rooting reflex   The infant's tendency to turn the head toward any object that gently touches a cheek. This response helps the child locate a nipple for feeding. **9**

Rorschach Inkblot Test   During this test, developed in 1921 by Hermann Rorschach, a subject's responses to ambiguous inkblots are studied for their emotional expression, their focus, and their recurring patterns. **14**

sample   A selected segment of the available data that is representative of the whole. **2**

scanning hypothesis   The theory, proposed by William Dement, that rapid eye movements accompanying dreams may be due to the dreamer "watching" the activity in the dream. **5**

schedule of reinforcement   The way in which rewards are given for appropriate behavior. **6**

schema   A key set of cognitions, or mental representation, of objects and events against which incoming data is compared and interpreted. **1, 13**

schizophrenia   Any of a group of psychoses characterized by disorders of attention or perception, profound disturbances in thinking, inappropriate emotional reactions, disturbed motor behavior, and social withdrawal. **16**

school psychology   An applied field of psychology which is concerned with problem behavior and learning difficulties among elementary and secondary students. **1**

Scholastic Aptitude Test (SAT)   A verbal and mathematical test developed by the College Entrance Examination Board and designed to measure "aptitude for college studies." **14**

script   The schema of routine events that can be expected in a particular situation. **8**

seasonal mood disorders   Mood disturbances related to changes in the seasons. **16**

secondary drive   Also termed learned motive; a state of physiological tension learned through association with primary drives and their reduction. **12**

secondary erectile failure   A condition in which the man has problems maintaining an erection in some situations. **12**

secondary orgasmic dysfunction   A condition in which the woman may sometimes experience orgasm, but not with her primary sexual partner or during intercourse. **12**

secondary (or conditioned) reinforcer   A stimulus which signals that a primary reinforcer is on the way. **6**

secondary sexual characteristics   The physical features of gender identity not directly involved with reproduction, such as the development of pubic hair, changes in voice, etc. **10**

secure attachment   The type of bond between infant and care giver characterized by the expectation that the care giver will be available and responsive. **10**

selective attention   The brain's ability to screen out some information entering a particular sensory channel and focus primarily on only one aspect of information entering the same channel. **7**

self-actualization   According to Rogers, the striving for the fulfillment of one's own capabilities and potential. **1, 13**

self-efficacy   The feeling people have of being able to deal effectively with a situation. **13**

self-fulfilling prophecy   The phenomenon whereby investigators' expectations influence their findings. **2, 18**

self-help group   A group of people who share a particular problem and meet to discuss it among themselves, without the active involvement of professional therapists. **17**

self-instructional training   Donald Meichenbaum's version of cognitive therapy in which clients make a conscious effort to think rational and positive thoughts in stressful situations. **17**

self-perception theory   Bem's theory that people infer their attitudes by observing their own behavior and the circumstances surrounding it, much as they infer the attitudes of others. **18**

self-report tests, or self-reports   A method of measuring variables by recording and tallying the responses of subjects to questions about how they thought, felt, or were inclined to act in a given situation; also, written records by clients of their problem behaviors and situations. **2, 14**

self-schema   An integrated set of cognitions about what you yourself are like. In social cognitive theory, an organized set of knowledge about the self that guides perception and interpretation of information in social situations. **13, 18**

self-serving bias   The tendency of an individual to take credit for successes and to find situational excuses for failures. **18**

semantic approach   The theory that listeners form hypotheses about the meaning of sentences by hearing key content words in a given context. **8**

semantic memories   Mental representations of objects, states, and qualities in a person's world. **7**

senile plaques   Insoluble clumps in the brain, consisting of a certain protein surrounded by degenerating axon terminals and glial cells. Senile plaques are a characteristic of Alzheimer's disease. **3**

sensation   The process whereby stimulation of receptor cells in various parts of the body sends nerve impulses to the brain. **4**

sensorimotor period   The first stage of Piaget's theory intellectual growth (from birth to about two years), during which an infant learns through perceiving sensations and physical actions. **9**

sensory adaptation   Reduced ability of a sensory system to provide information after prolonged, constant stimulation. **4**

sensory deprivation   Drastic reduction of exposure to stimuli for a prolonged period. **12**

sensory memory   The momentary lingering of sensory information one experiences after a stimulus has been removed. **7**

sensory neurons   The neurons that carry information from the sense organs to the central nervous system. **3**

sensory overload   Intense bombardment of the senses with numerous stimuli. **12**

sensory threshold   Minimum stimulus needed to produce a detectable sensation. **4**

septal area   One of three interrelated structures of the limbic system; the others are the hippocampus and amygdala. **3**

set   A fixed pattern of thought, behavior, or response; a predictable sequence of motor-neuron activity; also a predictable response pattern to a specific event. See also **mental set. 15**

setpoint   The level of fat that the brain considers normal. When body fat goes significantly above setpoint, loss of appetite sets in; when body fat falls significantly below it, hunger takes over. **12**

sexism   Prejudice directed toward one sex, almost always toward women. **18**

sexual dysfunction   Any persistent or recurring problem that prevents a person from engaging in sexual relations or from reaching orgasm during sex. **12**

sexual response cycle   The sequence of four physiological stages of human sexual response identified by Masters and Johnson. **12**

shallow processing   Mental activity, also known as maintenance rehearsal, that is inattentive, shallow, and concerned only with superficial features of a stimulus without consideration of the *meaning* of the stimulus; this information can only be maintained in short-term memory. **7**

shaping   A method developed by B. F. Skinner in which an animal is systematically reinforced for displaying closer and closer approximations of the desired response. **6**

short-term memory   The conscious retention of recently encountered things or of information retrieved from long-term storage for very short periods. **7**

short-term storage space   Case's term for the memory capacity available to think actively about problems and work out solutions. **9**

signal detection theory Theory summarizing the factors that influence the ability to detect sensory stimuli. **4**

similarity A gestalt principle of organization proposing that objects will be perceived as groups if they are similar in shape, color, texture, etc. **4**

single-blind technique A procedure in which the experimenter knows who is in the experimental group and who is in the control group but the subjects do not. **2**

Skinner box A small compartment that provides a controlled setting in which an animal may be trained to perform a specific behavior for a reward; sometimes called an operant chamber. **6**

sleep apnea A biological factor in insomnia; when muscles of the throat relax and shut off air passages, repeated shortages of oxygen cause the sleeper to awake and gasp for air. **5**

social cognition The process of organizing information about other people in our minds, so that we may understand them. **18**

social cognitive approach A perspective on personality that is based on the principles of learning and information processing and that focuses on the different ways in which individuals interpret events, and how these interpretations shape their styles of coping with the problems of everyday life. **13**

social development How a person's interactions and relationships with others change as that person grows older. **10**

social facilitation The phenomenon that occurs when a person's performance improves because of the presence of others. **19**

social identity theory A theory which holds that each of us has an individual identity, based on our personal attributes and achievements, but each of us also has a social identity, based on membership in social groups. **18**

social learning theory The belief of cognitive psychologists that a great deal of learning is accomplished by observation of other people's behavior, often in the absence of reinforcement. **6**

social loafing The tendency of many people to slack off when they are part of a group. **19**

social psychologist A psychologist who studies how environmental factors, especially the presence of others, influences individual perception, belief, motivation, and behavior. **1**

Social Readjustment Rating Scale (SRRS) A table developed by Holes and Rahe of 43 common life events, ranking their stress value (in numerical life-change units) according to the degree of adjustment required. **15**

social smile One aspect of infant behavior, triggered by the sight of the human face, by which the infant enhances its prospects for survival by attracting the attention of the care giver. **10**

social stereotype A set of beliefs about how members of a group think and act, beliefs that are widely shared but not substantiated. **18**

socialization The process of learning the values and expectations of one's society. **10**

sociobiology The systematic study of the biological basis of all social behavior. **19**

sociocultural perspective An approach to understanding mental disturbance through a study of the social context in which that person lives, considering such social factors as poverty and discrimination. **16**

sociopath See **antisocial personality. 16**

somatic nervous system The division of the peripheral nervous system that controls the skeletal muscles. **3**

somatoform disorder A physical ailment, or fear of such ailment, that has no organic cause. **16**

somatosensory cortex The forward part of the parietal lobes that function as the primary receiving area for the skin senses and for the sense of body position. **3**

split halves A procedure for randomly dividing a test into two halves, and comparing subjects and scores on both halves to measure a test's reliability. **14**

spontaneous recovery The temporary reappearance of an extinguished response when an organism is returned to the original learning situation. **6**

standard deviation A measure of variability showing average extent to which all the numbers in a particular set vary from the mean. **2**

standardization The administering of a test to a group which is considered representative of those for whom the test is designed, to determine the normative distribution of the test. **14**

Stanford-Binet test The Stanford University revision of Binet's test; currently employed, usually with children, to judge intelligence by verbal and performance tests grouped according to the subjects' age levels. **14**

statistical significance The level of probability that the results of an experiment occurred solely by chance; a convention for deciding when to reject chance as the explanation of results. **2**

statistics Mathematical methods for assessing and presenting data in summary form. **2**

stereotype A cluster of preconceived beliefs and expectations about the way members of a group think and act. **18**

stimulant A drug that produces physiological and mental arousal by stimulating the central nervous system. **5**

stimulus Any form of energy to which an organism is capable of responding. **4**

stimulus control The stimulus prevailing at the time of reinforcement which will come to control the organism's response. **6**

stimulus discrimination   The expression of a learned response only to a particular stimulus. **6**

stimulus generalization   The performance of a learned response in the presence of similar stimuli. **6**

stirrup   One of a set of three tiny, interconnected bones in the middle ear that transmit sound from the eardrum to the cochlea. **4**

strategies   In social cognitive theory, the specific techniques or procedures people use to work on their life tasks. **13**

stress   In psychology, anything that a person appraises as harmful, threatening, or challenging. **15**

Strong-Campbell Interest Inventory (SCII)   A test designed to measure a subject's pattern of interests in order to aid in occupational choices. **14**

structuralism or structural psychology   Developed by Wilhelm Wundt, the study of how the basic units of human consciousness form the organization, or structure, of the mind. **1**

subgoal analysis   A heuristic by which a problem is analyzed into a set of manageable smaller problems called subgoals. **8**

subjective contours   Lines or shapes that appear to be present but are not physically there. **4**

sublimation   According to psychoanalytic theory, a defense mechanism that involves the redirecting of forbidden impulses toward more socially acceptable goals. **12, 13**

subliminal perception   The brain's ability to register a stimulus presented so briefly or weakly that it cannot be consciously perceived. **4**

superego   According to Freud, the partially unconscious part of the psyche that incorporates parental and social standards of morality and that acts to prohibit thoughts and actions that express instinctual drives. **10, 13**

superstitious behavior   Behavior that is strengthened or weakened because by chance it happens to precede reinforcement or punishment. **6**

survey   An attempt to estimate the opinions, characteristics, or behaviors of a particular population by investigation of a representative sample. **2**

sympathetic nervous system   The division of the autonomic nervous system that mobilizes the body's resources in an emergency or stress situation. **3**

synapse   The area surrounding a synaptic cleft, including the tip of the axon on one side and the receiving cell's membrane on the other. **3**

synaptic clefts   The tiny gaps that separate neuronal axons from adjacent cells. **3**

syntactic approach   The theory that listeners derive from syntactic clues when they analyze and interpret sentences. **8**

syntax   The rules of a language which determine how words are combined into grammatical phrases and sentences. **8**

System of Multicultural Pluralistic Assessment (SOMPA)   A ''culture-free'' intelligence test developed by Jane Mercer for minority-group children. It consists of a standard IQ test, a one-hour interview with a child's parents, and a complete medical examination for the test taker. **14**

systematic desensitization   A technique in behavioral therapy for reducing anxiety or removing phobias by pairing muscle relaxation with the presentation of potentially threatening objects or situations in hierarchical order, from least to most feared. **6, 17**

tardive dyskinesia   Uncontrollable physical behaviors, including grotesque facial movements, that are an apparently irreversible side effect of prolonged use of antipsychotic drugs; sometimes associated with brain damage. **17**

target organs   Specific organs affected by hormones circulating in the bloodstream. **3**

tasks   In social cognitive theory, the goals we set for ourselves, the ideals for which we strive. **13**

taste buds   Tiny organs located in the surface layer of the tongue that are the receptors for taste. **4**

tectorial membrane   A relatively rigid membrane in the inner ear which helps transmit sound waves to the auditory nerve. **4**

telegraphic speech   The tendency of very young children to construct short sentences made up entirely of nouns and action verbs, without articles, conjunctions, or modifiers, for example, ''car go.'' **9**

temperament   A relatively stable behavioral disposition that can be seen in an individual's behavior. **10**

temporal lobes   The area of each cerebral hemisphere, concerned with hearing and visual processing. **3**

teratogens   Substances that raise the risk of developmental abnormalities. **9**

test-retest   A procedure for administering a test to the same people on more than one occasion to measure its reliability. **14**

texture gradient   An influence on depth perception in which highly textured near objects appear coarser, and more distant ones appear finer. **4**

thalamus   A structure above the midbrain that relays information from the sensory organs to the cerebral cortex. **3**

that's-not-all technique   A compliance strategy in which a small, usually preplanned, concession is made to ''sweeten'' a deal. **19**

Thematic Apperception Test (TAT)   A projective psychological test in which a subject's responses to a series of cards with ambiguous scenes are analyzed on an individual basis. **14**

theory An attempt to fit all the known, relevant facts into a logical explanation. 1

theta waves Slow brain waves that occur at the beginning of sleep. 5

thyroid gland Located in the neck, this endocrine gland secretes hormones that help regulate the body's metabolism. 3

thyroxin A hormone secreted by the thyroid gland which plays an important role in regulating the body's metabolism. 3

time out An operant-conditioning therapy technique that involves following undesirable behavior with a period of time away from positive reinforcement. 17

time-series A design in which the researcher repeatedly observes or measures the dependent variable both before and after the independent variable changes. 2

tip-of-the-tongue phenomenon The experience of feeling as though something is stored somewhere in one's memory but cannot be located quickly. 7

token economy A structured environment in which objects such as poker chips are used as rewards that may be exchanged by patients for desired activities or objects; a technique used in operant-conditioning therapies. 6, 17

top-down processing See **conceptually driven processing.** 4

trait According to Guilford, any relatively enduring way in which one individual differs from another. 13

trait theory Method of understanding personality that organizes human behavior according to characteristics, or traits, that distinguish a person and can be objectively measured. 13

transference The transfer to the analyst of feelings of love and hostility that were originally directed toward a client's parents or other authority figures; a basic feature of psychoanalysis. 17

trichromat A person whose cones contain three distinct forms of iodopsin and thus has normal color vision. 4

trichromatic theory The theory of color vision that only three different types of color receptors in the eye (blue, green, and red) are necessary for detecting every color on the visible spectrum. 4

Type A personality A label for people who display an excessive competitive drive, aggressiveness, hostility, and impatience, and are prone to heart disease. 13

Type B personality A label for people who are calmer and more relaxed than Type A personalities and also less susceptible to heart disease. 13

unconditional positive regard Acceptance and support that a therapist following Carl Rogers' approach would give to a client regardless of what he or she said or did. 17

unconditioned response (UCR) A response elicited by an unconditioned stimulus without any form of learning. 6

unconditioned stimulus (UCS) A stimulus that elicits an unconditioned response without any form of learning. 6

unconscious A term used by Freud for the region of the mind not directly accessible to normal awareness. 1

unipolar depression Major depression without manic episodes. 16

utility The value one places on potential outcomes in a decision-making situation. 8

vaginismus A sexual dysfunction of women characterized by involuntary muscle spasms that cause the vagina to shut tightly so that penetration by a penis is extremely painful or impossible. 12

validity An essential criterion in determining the value of a test. A test is valid if it measures what it is supposed to measure. 2, 14

variable-interval schedule An unpredictable and irregular partial reinforcement schedule in which there is no perceived relationship between the time elapsed and the frequency of rewards. 6

variable-ratio schedule An unpredictable and irregular partial reinforcement schedule in which there is no perceived relationship between the number of responses and the number of rewards. 6

variables Factors capable of change. 2

vertebrae Bony segments that form a spinal column and protect the cells of the nervous system. 3

vertebrates Animals with backbones. 3

vicarious reinforcement and punishment Environmental consequences following the behavior of others that affects how an observer will behave. 6

volley principle The theory that explains why people can hear high-frequency sound by assuming that the frequency of neural firing that the brain detects is determined not by the rate of firing of single neurons but rather by groups of neurons. 4

wavelength The distance between the crest of one light wave and the crest of the next; the determinant of color. 4

Weber's law Formulated by Gustav Fechner, this law states that the amount by which a stimulus must be increased to produce a "just noticeable difference" in sensation is always a constant proportion of the initial stimulus intensity. 4

Wechsler scales The Wechsler Adult Intelligence Scale (WAIS), the Wechsler Intelligence Scale for Children (WISC), and the Wechsler Preschool and Primary Scale of Intelligence (WPPSI). Along with the Stanford-Binet, these are the most frequently used individual intelligence tests; they differ from the Stanford-Binet in several ways, primarily in yielding not a single IQ score but separate scores for each subtest. 14

white matter The myelinated axons of the nervous system. 3

working memory Another name for short-term memory. 7

REFERENCES

The number in brackets at the end of each entry refers to the chapter of the text in which that work is cited.

Aber, J. L., and **Allen, J. P.** (1987). Effects of maltreatment on young children's socioemotional development: An attachment theory perspective. *Developmental Psychology, 23*(3), 406–414. [10]

Abraham, K. (1911). Notes on psychoanalytic investigation and treatment of manic-depressive insanity and allied conditions. In D. Bryan and A. Strachey (Trans.), *Selected Papers of Karl Abraham, M.D.* London: Hogarth Press, 1948. [16]

Abraham, K. (1916). The first pregenital stage of the libido. In D. Bryan and A. Strachey (Trans.), *Selected Papers of Karl Abraham, M.D.* London: Hogarth Press, 1948. [16]

Abramson, L. Y., Metalsky, G. I., and **Alloy, L. B.** (1989). The hopelessness theory of depression: A metatheoretical analysis with implications for psychopathology research. *Psychological Review.* [16]

Abramson, L. Y., Seligman, M. E. P., and **Teasdale, J. D.** (1978). Learned helplessness in humans: Critique and reformulation. *Journal of Abnormal Psychology, 87,* 49–74. [16]

Ackroyd, P. (1984). *T. S. Eliot: A Life.* New York: Simon and Schuster. [11]

Acredolo, L. P., and **Hake, J. L.** (1982). Infant perception. In B. B. Wolman (Ed.), *Handbook of Developmental Psychology.* Englewood Cliffs, NJ: Lawrence Erlbaum. [4]

Adair, J. G. (1984). The Hawthorne effect: A reconsideration of the methodological artifact. *Journal of Applied Psychology, 69,* 334–345. [2]

Adams, D. B., Gold, A. R., and **Burt, A. D.** (1978). Rise in female-initiated sexual activity at ovulation and its suppression by oral contraceptives. *New England Journal of Medicine, 299,* 1145–1150. [12]

Adams, J. A. (1980). *Learning and Memory: An Introduction* (rev. ed.). Homewood, IL, Dorsey Press. [7]

Adams, J. D. (1978). Improving stress management: An action-research based OD intervention. In W. W. Burke (Ed.), *The Cutting Edge.* La Jolla, CA: University Associates. [15]

Adelmann, P. K., and **Zajonc, R. B.** (1989). *Annual Review of Psychology, 40,* 249–280. [11]

Adler, A. (1930). Individual psychology. In C. A. Murchison (Ed.), *Psychologies of 1930* (pp. 395–405). Worcester, MA: Clark University Press. [13]

Adler, A. (1936). On the interpretation of dreams. *International Journal of Individual Psychology, 1,* 3–16. [5]

Adler, J., and **Gosnell, M.** (1982, December 13). What it means to be fat. *Newsweek,* pp. 84–90. [12]

Adler, N. E. (1991). Unpublished Arrowhead talk. [15]

Adler, N. E. (in press). Abortion as a model of crisis and loss: An examination of empirical evidence. In W. H. Filipp, L. Montada, and M. Lerner (Eds.), *Life Crises and Experiences of Loss in Adulthood.* Morristown, NJ: Lawrence Erlbaum. [15]

Adler, N. E., David, H. E., Major, B. N., Roth, S. H., Russo, N. F., and **Wyatt, G. E.** (1990, April 6). Psychological responses after abortion. *Science, 248,* 41–44. [15]

Adorno, T. W., Frenkel-Brunswick, E., Levinson, D. J., and **Sanford, R. N.** (1950). *The Authoritarian Personality.* New York: Harper & Row. [18]

AERA, APA, NCME. (1985). *Standards for Educational and Psychological Testing.* Washington, DC: American Psychological Association. [14]

Ainsworth, M. D. S. (1989, April). Attachments beyond infancy. *American Psychologist, 44*(4), 709–716. [10]

Ainsworth, M., Bleher, M., Waters, E., and **Wall, S.** (1978). *Patterns of Attachment.* Hillsdale, NJ: Lawrence Erlbaum. [10]

Ajzen, I., and **Fishbein, M.** (1980). *Understanding Attitudes and Predicting Social Behavior.* Englewood Cliffs, NJ: Prentice-Hall. [18]

Akabas, M. H., Dodd, J., and **Al-Awqati, Q.** (1988). A bitter substance induces a rise in intercellular calcium in a subpopulation of rat taste cells. *Science, 242,* 1047–1050. [4]

Akiskal, H. S. (1979). A biobehavioral approach to depression. In R. A. Depue (Ed.), *The Psychobiology of the Depressive Disorders.* New York: Academic Press. [16]

Akiskal, H. S., and **McKinney, W. T., Jr.** (1973). Depressive disorders: Toward a unified hypothesis. *Science, 182,* 20–29. [16]

Akiskal, H. S., and **McKinney, W. T., Jr.** (1975). Overview of recent research in depression. *Archives of General Psychiatry, 32,* 285–305. [16]

Alba, J. W., and **Hasher, L.** (1983). Is memory schematic? *Psychological Bulletin, 93*(2), 203–231. [7]

Albert, R. S. (1980). Family positions and the attainment of eminence. *Gifted Child Quarterly, 24,* 87–95. [14]

Alkon, D. L. (1984). Calcium mediated reduction of ionic currents: A biophysical memory trace. *Science, 226,* 1037–1045. [7]

Allen, M. G. (1976). Twin studies of affective illness. *Archives of General Psychiatry, 33,* 1476–1478. [16]

Alloy, L. B., and **Abramson, L. Y.** (1979). Judgment of contingency in depressed and nondepressed: Sadder but wiser? *Journal of Experimental Psychology: General, 108,* 441–485. [16]

Allport, F. H. (1920). The influence of the group upon association and thought. *Journal of Experimental Psychology, 3,* 159–182. [19]

Allport, F. H. (1924). *Social Psychology.* Boston: Houghton Mifflin. [19]

Allport, G. W. (1937). *Personality: A Psychological Interpretation.* New York: Holt, Rinehart and Winston. [13]

Allport, G. W. (1961). *Pattern and Growth in Personality.* New York: Holt, Rinehart and Winston. [13]

Allport, G. W. (1966). Traits revisited. *American Psychologist, 21,* 1–10. [13]

Allport, G. W., and **Odbert, H. S.** (1936). Trait-names: A psycho-texical study. *Psy-*

chological Monographs, 47 (Whole No. 211). [13]

Allport, G. W., and **Postman, L. J.** (1947). *The Psychology of Rumor.* New York: Holt. [7]

Alper, T. G. (1974). Achievement motivation in college women: A now-you-see-it-now-you-don't phenomenon. *American Psychologist, 29,* 194–203. [12]

American Cancer Society. (1989). *Cancer facts and figures—1989.* Atlanta: Author. [15]

American Psychiatric Association (1980). *Diagnostic and Statistical Manual of Mental Disorders* (3rd ed.). [DSM-III]. Washington, DC: Author. [16]

American Psychological Association (1968). By-laws of the American Psychological Association. *1968 Directory.* Washington, DC: Author. [1]

American Psychological· Association. (1990). Ethical principles of psychologists. *American Psychologist, 45,* 390–395. [2]

American Psychological Association, Ethics Committee. (1988). Trends in ethics cases, common pitfalls, and published resources. *American Psychologist, 43,* 564–572. [2]

Amoore, J. E., Johnston, J. W., Jr., and **Rubin, M.** (1964). The stereochemical theory of odor. *Scientific American, 210,* 42–49. [4]

Anand, B. K., and **Brobeck, J. R.** (1951). Localization of a "feeding center" in the hypothalamus of the rat. *Proceedings of the Society for Experimental Biological Medicine, 77,* 323–324. [12]

Anand, B. K., Chhina, G. S., and **Singh, B.** (1961). Some aspects of electroencephalographic studies in yogis. *Electroencephalography and Clinical Neurophysiology, 13,* 452–456. [5]

Anastasi, A. (1976). *Psychological Testing.* (4th ed.). New York: Macmillan. [14]

Anderson, K. J. (1990). Arousal and the inverted-U hypothesis: A critique of Neiss's "Reconceptualizing arousal." *Psychological Bulletin, 107,* 96–100. [12]

Anderson, R. C., and **Prichert, J. W.** (1978). Recall of previously unrecallable

information following a shift in perspective. *Journal of Verbal Learning and Verbal Behavior, 17,* 1–12. [7]

Andison, F. S. (1977). TV violence and viewer aggression: A cumulation of study results 1956–1976. *Public Opinion Quarterly, 41,* 314–331. [2]

Andreasen, N. C. (1988, March 18). Brain imaging: Applications in psychiatry. *Science, 239,* 1381–1388. [3]

Andreasen, N. C., Nasrallah, H. A., Dunn, V., Olson, S. C., Grove, W. M., Ehrhardt, J. C., Coffman, J. A., and **Crossett, J. H.** (1986). Structural abnormalities in the frontal system in schizophrenia: A magnetic resonance imaging study. *Archives of General Psychiatry, 43*(2), 136–144. [16]

Andreasen, N. C., and **Olsen, S.** (1982). Negative versus positive schizophrenia: Definition and validation. *Archives of General Psychiatry, 39,* 789–794. [16]

Andreasen, N. C., Smith, M. R., Jacoby, C. G., Dennert, J. W., and **Olsen, S. A.** (1982). Ventricular enlargement in schizophrenia: Definition and prevalence. *American Journal of Psychiatry, 139*(3), 292–302. [16]

Andrews, E. A., and **Braveman, N. S.** (1975). The combined effects of dosage level and interstimulus interval on the formation of one-trial poison-based aversions in rats. *Animal Learning and Behavior, 3,* 287–289. [6]

Andrews, F. M., and **Withey, S. B.** (1976). *Social Indicators of Well-Being: Americans' Perceptions of Life Quality.* New York: Plenum Press. [11]

Angier, N. (1991, May 29). Study says anger troubles women denied abortions. *The New York Times,* p. C10. [15]

Angier, R. P. (1927). The conflict theory of emotion. *American Journal of Psychology, 39,* 390–401. [11]

Archer, R. L. (1984). The farmer and the cowman should be friends: An attempt at reconciliation. *Psychological Journal of Personality and Social Psychology, 46,* 709–711. [19]

Armstrong, R. H. (1965, March). *Gastric Secretion During Sleep and Dreaming.* Paper

presented at the annual meeting of the Association for the Psychophysiological Study of Sleep, Washington, DC. [5]

Aronfreed, J. (1969). The concept of internalization. In D. A. Goslin (Ed.), *Handbook of Socialization Theory and Research.* Chicago: Rand McNally. [10]

Aronson, E. (1976). *The Social Animal* (2nd ed.). San Francisco: W. H. Freeman. [14]

Aronson, E., and **Osherow, N.** (1980). Cooperation, prosocial behavior, and academic performance: Experiments in the desegregated classroom. In L. Bickman (Ed.), *Applied Social Psychology Annual* (Vol. 1). Beverly Hills, CA: Sage Publications. [18, 19]

Arrowood, J., and **Short, J. A.** (1973). Agreement, attraction, and self-esteem. *Canadian Journal of Behavioral Science, 5,* 242–252. [18]

Asch, S. E. (1951). Effects of group pressure upon the modification and distortion of judgments. In H. S. Guetzkow (Ed.), *Groups, Leadership, and Man: Research in Human Relations.* Pittsburgh: Carnegie Press. [19]

Asch, S. E. (1956). Studies of independence and conformity: A minority of one against a unanimous majority. *Psychological Monographs, 70* (9, Whole No. 416). [19]

Ashmore, R. D., and **Del Boca, F. K.** (1976). Psychological approaches to understanding intergroup conflicts. In P. A. Katz (Ed.), *Towards the Elimination of Racism.* Elmsford, NY: Pergamon Press. [18]

Aslin, R. N., Pisoni, D. B., and **Jusczyk, P. W.** (1983). Auditory development and speech perception in infancy. In P. Mussen (Ed.), *Handbook of Child Psychology* (Vol. 2). New York: Wiley. [9]

Athanasiou, R., Oppel, W., Michelson, L., Unger, Y., and **Yager, M.** (1973). Psychiatric sequelae to term birth and induced early and late abortion: A longitudinal study. *Family Planning Perspectives, 5,* 227–231. [15]

Atkinson, J. W. (Ed.). (1958). *Motives in Fantasy, Action, and Society.* Princeton, NJ: Van Nostrand Reinhold. [12]

Atkinson, J. W. (1964). *An Introduction*

to Motivation. Princeton, NJ: Van Nostrand Reinhold. [12]

Atkinson, J. W., and Litwin, G. H. (1960). Achievement motive and test anxiety conceived as motive to approach success and motive to avoid failure. *Journal of Abnormal and Social Psychology, 60,* 52–63. [12]

Atkinson, J. W., and Raynor, J. O. (Eds.). (1974). *Motivation and Achievement.* Washington, DC: Winston. [12]

Attorney General's Commission on Pornography (1986). *Final Report of the Attorney General's Commission on Pornography* (Report No. 027–000–01259–1). Washington, DC: U.S. Government Printing Office. [19]

Ault, R. L. (1983). *Children's Cognitive Development* (2nd ed.). Oxford: Oxford University Press. [9]

Averill, J. R. (1982). *Anger and Aggression: An Essay on Emotion.* New York: Springer-Verlag. [19]

Averill, J. R. (1983, November). Studies on anger and aggression: Implications for theories of emotion. *American Psychologist,* pp. 1145–1160. [19]

Axelrod, S., and Apsche, J. (Eds.). (1983). *The Effects of Punishment on Human Behavior.* New York: Academic Press. [6]

Ayllon, T., and Azrin, N. H. (1968). *The Token Economy: A Motivational System for Therapy and Rehabilitation.* New York: Appleton-Century-Crofts. [17]

Ayres, C. E. (1921). Instinct and capacity: I. The instinct of belief in instincts. *Journal of Philosophy, 18,* 561–566. [12]

Bablenis, E., Weber, S. S., and Wagner, R. L. (1989). Clozapine: A novel antipsychotic agent. *DICP The Annals of Pharmacotherapy, 23,* 109–115. [17]

Baddeley, A. (1982). *Your Memory: A User's Guide.* New York: Macmillan. [7]

Baer, J. D., Kivlahan, D. R., Fromme, K., and Marlatt, G. A. (1989). Secondary prevention of alcohol abuse with college student populations: A skills-training approach. In G. Howard (Ed.), *Issues in Alcohol Use and Misuse by Young Adults.* Notre Dame, IN: Notre Dame University. [15]

Bahrick, H. P. (1984). Semantic memory content in permastore: Fifty years of memory for Spanish learned in school. *Journal of Experimental Psychology: General, 113*(1), 1–37. [7]

Baillargeon, R. (1987). Object permanence in 3½- and 4½-month-old infants. *Developmental Psychology, 23*(5), 655–664. [9]

Baillargeon, R., Spelke, E., and Wasserman, S. (1985). Object permanence in five-month-old infants. *Cognition, 20,* 191–208. [9]

Baldessarini, R. J. (1977). *Chemotherapy in Psychiatry.* Cambridge, MA: Harvard University Press. [17]

Baldessarini, R. J. (1985). Drugs and the treatment of psychiatric disorders. In A. G. Gilman, L. S. Goodman, T. W. Rall, and F. Murad (Eds.), *The Pharmacological Basis of Therapeutics* (7th ed., pp. 387–445). New York: Macmillan. [17]

Baltes, P. B., Reese, H. W., and Nesselroade, J. R. (1977). *Life-Span Developmental Psychology: Introduction to Research Methods.* Monterey, CA: Brooks/Cole. [2]

Baltes, P. B., and Schaie, K. W. (1974). Aging and IQ: The myth of the twilight years. *Psychology Today, 7,* 35–40. [9]

Ban, T. (1973). *Recent Advances in the Biology of Schizophrenia.* Springfield, IL: Charles C. Thomas. [16]

Bandura, A. (1965). Influence of models' reinforcement contingencies on the acquisition of imitative responses. *Journal of Personality and Social Psychology, 1,* 589–595. [19]

Bandura, A. (1977a). Self-efficacy: Toward a unifying theory of behavioral change. *Psychological Review, 84,* 191–215. [6, 13, 17]

Bandura, A. (1977b). *Social Learning Theory.* Englewood Cliffs, NJ: Prentice-Hall. [6, 13]

Bandura, A. (1977c). Psychological mechanism of aggression. *Conference on Human Ecology: Claims and Limits of a New Discipline.* Bad Homburg, West Germany. [19]

Bandura, A. (1982). Self-efficacy mechanism in human agency. *American Psychologist, 37,* 122–147. [13]

Bandura, A. (1986). *Social Foundations of Thought and Action: A Social Cognitive Theory.* Englewood Cliffs, NJ: Prentice-Hall. [6, 13, 15, 16]

Bandura, A., Blanchard, E. B., and Ritter, B. (1969). Relative efficacy of desensitization and modeling approaches for inducing behavioral, affective, and attitudinal changes. *Journal of Personality and Social Psychology, 13,* 173–199. [17]

Bandura, A., Grusec, J. E., and Menlove, F. L. (1967). Vicarious extinction of avoidance behavior. *Journal of Personality and Social Psychology, 5,* 16–23. [17]

Bandura, A., Ross, D., and Ross, S. (1961). Transmission of aggression through imitation of aggressive models. *Journal of Abnormal and Social Psychology, 63,* 575–582. [2, 10, 19]

Banks, M. S., and Salapatek, P. (1983). Infant visual perception. In P. Mussen (Ed.), *Handbook of Child Psychology* (4th ed., Vol. 2). M. M. Haith and J. Campos (Eds.), *Infancy and Developmental Psychology* (pp. 435–571). New York: Wiley. [9]

Bargh, J. A. (1989). Conditional automaticity: Varieties of automatic influence in social perception and cognition. In J. S. Uleman and J. A. Bargh (Eds.), *Unintended Thought.* New York: Guilford (pp. 3–51). [18]

Barlow, D. H. (1986). Causes of sexual dysfunction: The role of anxiety and cognitive interference. *Journal of Counseling and Clinical Psychology, 54,* 140–148. [12]

Barlow, D. H. (1988). *Anxiety and Its Disorders.* New York: Guilford. [17]

Barlow, D. H., Blanchard, E. B., Vermilyea, J. A., Vermilyea, B. B., and DiNardo, P. A. (1986). Generalized anxiety and generalized anxiety disorder: Description and reconceptualization. *American Journal of Psychiatry, 143,* 40–44. [16]

Barlow, D. H., and Cerny, J. A. (1988). *Psychological Treatment of Panic.* New York: Guilford. [17]

Barlow, D. H., and **Waddell, M. T.** (1985). Agoraphobia. In D. H. Barlow (Ed.), *Clinical Handbook of Psychological Disorders.* New York: Guilford. [17]

Barlow, H. B., and **Mollon, J. D.** (Eds.). (1982). *The Senses.* Cambridge: Cambridge University Press. [4]

Barnes, G. E., and **Prosen, H.** (1985). Parental death and depression. *Journal of Abnormal Psychology, 94,* 64–69. [16]

Baron, J., (1985). *Rationality and Intelligence.* Cambridge, England: Cambridge University Press. [14]

Baron, R. A. (1977). *Human Aggression.* New York: Plenum. [19]

Baron, R. A. (1983). The control of human aggression: An optimistic perspective. *Journal of Social and Clinical Psychology, 1,* 97–119. [19]

Baron, R. S. (1986). Distraction-conflict theory: Progress and problems. In L. Berkowitz (Ed.), *Advances in Experimental Social Psychology.* Orlando, FL: Academic Press. [19]

Bartlett, F. C. (1932). *Remembering: A Study in Experimental and Social Psychology.* London: Cambridge University Press. [1, 7]

Bartoshuk, L. M. (1974). Taste illusions: Some demonstrations. *Annals of the New York Academy of Sciences, 237,* 279–285. [4]

Bartoshuk, L. M. (1988). Taste. In R. C. Atkinson, R. J. Hernstein, L. Gardner, and R. D. Luce (Eds.), *Stevens' Handbook of Experimental Psychology* (2nd ed., Vol. 1, pp. 461–502). New York: Wiley. [4]

Bates, J. E. (1987). Temperament in infancy. In J. D. Osofsky (Ed.), *Handbook of Infant Development* (2nd ed., pp. 1101–1149). New York: Wiley. [10]

Batson, C. D. (1987). Prosocial motivation: Is it ever truly altruistic? In L. Berkowitz (Ed.), *Advances in Experimental Personality* (Vol. 20). San Diego: Academic Press. [19]

Batson, C. D., Batson, J. G., Griffitt, C. A., Barrientos, S., Brandt, J. R., Sprengelmeyer, P., and **Bayly, M. J.** (1989). Negative-state relief and the empathy-altruism hypothesis. *Journal of Personality and Social Psychology, 56,* 922–933. [19]

Batson, C. D., Duncan, B. D., Ackerman, P., Buckley, T., and **Birch, K.** (1981). Is empathic emotion a source of altruistic motivation? *Journal of Personality and Social Psychology, 40,* 290–302. [19]

Batson, C. D., Dyck, J. L., Brandt, J. R., Batson, J. G., Powell, A. L., McMaster, M. R., and **Griffitt, C.** (1988). Five studies testing two new egoistic alternatives to the empathy-altruism hypothesis. *Journal of Personality and Social Psychology, 55,* 52–57. [19]

Baucom, D. H., and **Lester, G. W.** (1986). The usefulness of cognitive restructuring as an adjunct to behavioral marital therapy. *Behavior Therapy, 17,* 385–403. [17]

Baum, A., and **Valins, S.** (1977). *Architecture and Social Behavior: Psychological Studies of Social Density.* Hillsdale, NJ: Lawrence Erlbaum. [15]

Baumeister, A. A. (1987, August). Mental retardation: Some conceptions and dilemmas. *American Psychologist, 42(8),* 796–800. [14]

Baumeister, R. F. (1982). A self-presentational view of social phenomena. *Psychological Bulletin, 91,* 3–26. [18]

Baumeister, R. F., and **Scher, S. J.** (1988). Self-defeating behavior patterns among normal individuals: Review and analysis of common self-destructive tendencies. *Psychological Bulletin, 104,* 3–22. [15]

Baumgardner, A. H., and **Brownlee, E. A.** (1987). Strategic failure in social interaction: Evidence for expectancy disconfirmation process. *Journal of Personality and Social Psychology, 52,* 525–535. [18]

Baumrind, D. (1964). Some thoughts on the ethics of research: After reading Milgram's "Behavioral study of obedience." *American Psychologist, 19,* 421–423. [19]

Baumrind, D. (1967). Child care practices anteceding three patterns of preschool behavior. *Genetic Psychology Monographs, 75,* 43–88. [10, 13]

Baumrind, D. (1977, March 17). *Socialization Determinants of Personal Agency.* Paper presented at the biennial meetings of the Society for Research in Child Development, New Orleans. [13]

Baumrind, D. (1984, March). *Family Socialization and Development Competence Project (FSP).* Paper presented to the Program in Social Ecology, University of California, Irvine. [10]

Baxter, L. R., Phelps, M. E., Mazziotta, J. C., Guze, B. H., Schwartz, J. M., and **Selin, C. E.** (1987). Local cerebral glucose metabolic rates in obsessive-compulsive disorder: A comparison with rates in unipolar depression and normal controls. *Archives of General Psychiatry, 44,* 211–218. [16]

Beach, F., and **Merari, A.** (1970). Coital behavior in dogs: V. Effects of estrogen and progesterone on mating and other forms of social behavior in the bitch. *Journal of Comparative and Physiological Psychology Monograph, 70(1) Pt. 2,* 1–22. [12]

Beach, L. R., Campbell, F. L., and **Townes, B. D.** (1979). Subjective utility and the prediction of birth-planning decisions. *Organizational Behavior and Human Performance, 24,* 18–28. [8]

Beaumont, J. G., Young, A. W., and **McManus, I. C.** (1984). Hemisphericity: A critical review. *Cognitive Neuropsychology, 1(2),* 191–212. [3]

Beck, A. T. (1967). *Depression: Clinical, Experimental and Theoretical Aspects.* New York: Hoeber. [17]

Beck, A. T. (1974). The development of depression: A cognitive model. In R. J. Friedman and M. M. Katz (Eds.), *The Psychology of Depression: Contemporary Theory and Research.* Washington, DC: Winston-Wiley. [16]

Beck, A. T. (1976). *Cognitive Therapy and the Emotional Disorders.* New York: International Universities Press. [17]

Beck, A. T. (1988). Cognitive approaches to panic disorder: Theory and therapy. In S. Rachman and J. D. Masur (Eds.), *Panic: Psychological Perspectives.* Hillsdale, NJ: Lawrence Erlbaum. [17]

Beck, A. T., Kovacs, M., and **Weissman, A.** (1979). Assessment of suicidal intention: The scale for suicide ideation. *Journal of Clinical and Consultant Psychology, 47,* 243–252. [16]

Beck, A. T., Rush, A. J., Shaw, B. F., and

Emery, G. (1979). *Cognitive Therapy of Depression.* New York: Guilford. [17]

Beck, A. T., Steer, R. A., Kovacs, M., and Garrison, B. (1985). Hopelessness and eventual suicide: A 10 year prospective study of patients hospitalized with suicidal indeation. *American Journal of Psychiatry, 145,* 559–563. [17]

Beck, A. T. et al. (1985). Treatment of depression with cognitive therapy and amitriptyline. *Archives of General Psychiatry, 42*(2), 142–148. [16]

Beck, M., and Cowley, G. (1990, March 26). Beyond lobotomies. *Newsweek,* p. 44. [17]

Becker, C., and Kronus, S. (1977). Sex and drinking patterns: An old relationship revisited in a new way. *Social Problems, 24,* 482–497. [16]

Beckham, E. E., and Leber, W. R. (1985). *Handbook of Depression.* Homewood, IL: Dorsey Press. [11]

Bedford, V. H. (1989). Ambivalence in adult sibling relationships. *Journal of Family Issues, 10,* 211–224. [14]

Beebe, B., Alson, D., Jaffe, J., Feldstein, S., and Crown, C. (1988). Vocal congruence in mother-infant play. *Journal of Psycholinguistic Research, 17*(3), 245–259. [9]

Beecher, H. K. (1959). *Measurement of Subjective Responses.* New York: Oxford University Press. [4]

Begley, S. (1989, August 14). The stuff that dreams are made of. *Newsweek,* pp. 41–44. [5]

Bekesy, G. von. (1959). Synchronism of neural discharges and their demultiplication in pitch perception on the skin and in learning. *Journal of the Acoustical Society of America, 31,* 338–349. [4]

Bellack, A. S., Hersen, M., and Turner, S. M. (1976). Generalization effects of social skills training in chronic schizophrenics: An experimental analysis. *Behaviour Research and Therapy, 14,* 391–398. [17]

Belli, R. F. (1989). Influences of misleading postevent information: Misinformation interference and acceptance. *Journal of Experimental Psychology: General, 118*(1), 72–85. [7]

Bellugi, U. (1964, November). *The Emergence of Inflections and Negative Systems in the Speech of Two Children.* Paper presented at the meeting of the New England Psychological Association. [9]

Bellugi, U. (1970). Learning the language. *Psychology Today, 4,* 32–35ff. [9]

Belsher, G., and Costello, C. G. (1988). Relapse after recovery from unipolar depression: A critical review. *Psychological Bulletin, 104*(1), 84–96. [16]

Belsky, J. (1988). The effects of infant day care reconsidered. *Early Childhood Quarterly, 3,* 235–272. [10]

Belsky, J., Fish, M., and Isabella, R. (1991). Continuity and discontinuity in infant negative and positive emotionality: Family antecedents and attachment consequences. *Developmental Psychology, 27,* 421–431. [10]

Belsky, J., and Isabella, R. (1988). Maternal, infant, and social-contextual determinants of attachment security. In J. Belsky and T. Nezworski (Eds.), *Clinical Implications of Attachment* (pp. 41–94). Hillsdale, NJ: Lawrence Erlbaum. [10]

Bemis, K. M. (1978). Current approaches to the etiology and treatment of anorexia nervosa. *Psychological Bulletin, 85,* 593–617. [12]

Bender, K. J. (1990). *Psychiatric Medications: A Guide for Mental Health Professionals.* Newbury Park, CA: Sage Publications. [17]

Benecke, R., Conrad, B., and Klingelhofer, J. (1988). Successful treatment of tardive and spontaneous dyskinesia with corticosteroids. *European Neurology, 28,* 146–149. [17]

Benjamin, L. S. (1987). The use of the SASB dimensional model to develop treatment plans for personality disorders. I: Narcissism. *Journal of Personality Disorders, 1*(1), 43–70. [17]

Bennett, W., and Gurin, J. (1982). *The Dieter's Dilemma.* New York: Basic Books. [12]

Benson, K., and Feinberg, I. (1977). The beneficial effects of sleep in an extended Jenkins and Dallenbach paradigm. *Psychophysiology, 14,* 375–383. [7]

Berg, J. H., and McQuinn, R. D. (1986). Attraction and exchange in continuing and noncontinuing relationships. *Journal of Personality and Social Psychology, 50*(5), 942–952. [18]

Berglas, S., and Jones, E. E. (1978). Drug choice as a self-handicapping strategy in response to noncontingent success. *Journal of Personality and Social Psychology, 36,* 405–417. [18]

Berkman, L. F., and Syme, S. L. (1979). Social networks, host resistance, and mortality: A nine-year followup study of Alameda County residents. *American Journal of Epidemiology, 109,* 186–204. [15]

Berkowitz, L. (1989). Frustration-aggression hypothesis: Examination and reformulation. *Psychological Bulletin, 106,* 59–73. [19]

Berkowitz, L., and Geen, R. G. (1966). Film violence and cue properties of available targets. *Journal of Personality and Social Psychology, 3,* 525–530. [18]

Berkowitz, L., and Lepage, A. (1976). Weapons as aggression-eliciting stimuli. *Journal of Personality and Social Psychology, 7,* 202–207. [18]

Berkowitz, R., Eberlein-Vries, R., Kuipers, L., and Leff, J. (1984). Educating relatives about schizophrenia. *Schizophrenia Bulletin, 10,* 418–429. [16]

Berlin, B., and Kay, P. (1969). *Basic Color Terms: Their Universality and Evolution.* Berkeley: University of California Press. [8]

Berlyne, D. E. (1950). Novelty and curiosity as determinants of exploratory behaviour. *British Journal of Psychology, 41,* 68–80. [12]

Berlyne, D. E. (1960). *Conflict, Arousal, and Curiosity.* New York: McGraw-Hill. [12]

Bernard, L. L. (1924). *Instinct.* New York: Holt. [12]

Bernstein, I. L. (1978). Learned taste aversions in children receiving chemotherapy. *Science, 200,* 1302–1303. [6]

Bernstein, I. L. (1985). Learned food aversions in the progression of cancer and its treatment. *Annals of the New York Academy of Sciences, 443,* 365–380. [6]

Bernstein, I. L. (1986). Food aversion learning: A role in cancer anorexia. *Nutrition and Behavior, 3,* 117–127. [6]

Bernstein, I. L., Webster, M. M., and Bernstein, I. D. (1982). Food aversions in children receiving chemotherapy for cancer. *Cancer, 50,* 2961–2963. [6]

Berscheid, E., Snyder, M., and Omoto, A. M. (1989). The Relationship Closeness Inventory: Assessing the closeness of interpersonal relationships. *Journal of Personality and Social Psychology, 57*(5), 792–807. [18]

Bertenthal, B. I., and Fischer, K. W. (1978). The development of self-recognition in the infant. *Developmental Psychology, 14,* 44–50. [10]

Bevan, W. (1964). Subliminal stimulation: A pervasive problem for psychology. *Psychological Bulletin, 61,* 89–99. [4]

Bexton, W. H. (1953). *Some Effects of Perceptual Isolation in Human Beings.* Unpublished doctoral dissertation. McGill University, Montreal. [12]

Bexton, W. H., Heron, W., and Scott, T. H. (1954). Effects of decreased variation in the sensory environment. *Canadian Journal of Psychology, 8,* 70–76. [12]

Biederman, I., Glass, A. L., and Stacy, E. W., Jr. (1973). Searching for objects in real-world scenes. *Journal of Experimental Psychology, 97,* 22–27. [4]

Biederman, I., Mezzanotte, R. J., and Rabinowitz, J. C. (1982). Scene perception: Detecting and judging objects undergoing relational violations. *Cognitive Psychology, 14,* 143–177. [4]

Biederman, I., Mezzanotte, R. J., Rabinowitz, J. C., Francolini, C. M., and Plude, D. (1981). Detecting the unexpected in photointerpretation. *Human Factors, 23,* 153–164. [4]

Biederman, I., Rabinowitz, J. C., Glass, A. L., and Stacy, E. W., Jr. (1974). On the information extracted from a glance at a scene. *Journal of Experimental Psychology, 103,* 597–600. [4]

Biernat, M., and Wortman, C. B. (in press). The sharing of home responsibilities between professionally-employed women and their husbands. [1]

Black, D. W., Winokur, G., and Nasarallah, A. (1989). Illness duration and acute response in major depression. *Counseling Therapy, 5,* 338–343. [17]

Blake, R., and Hirsch, H. V. B. (1975). Deficits in binocular depth perception in cats after alternating monocular deprivation. *Science, 190,* 1114–1116. [4]

Blake, R. R., and Mouton, J. (1979). Intergroup problem solving in organizations: From theory to practice. In W. Austin and S. Worchel (Eds.), *The Social Psychology of Intergroup Relations.* Monterey, CA.: Brooks/Cole. [19]

Blanchard, M., and Main, M. (1979). Avoidance of the attachment figure and social-emotional adjustment in day-care infants. *Developmental Psychology, 15,* 445–446. [10]

Blaney, P. H. (1986). Affect and memory: A review. *Psychological Bulletin, 99*(2), 229–246. [7]

Blascovich, J. (1990). Individual differences in physiological arousal and perception of arousal: Missing links in Jamesian notions of arousal-based behavior. *Personality and Social Psychology Bulletin, 16*(4), 665–675. [11]

Blehar, M. C. (1974). Anxious attachment and defensive reactions associated with day care. *Child Development, 45,* 683–692. [10]

Bleuler, E. (1950). *Dementia Praecox or the Group of Schizophrenias* (1911). J. Sinkin (Trans.). New York: International Universities Press. [16]

Block, J. (1971). *Lives Through Time.* Berkeley, CA: Bancroft Books. [13]

Block, J., and Block, J. (1980). The role of ego-control and ego resiliency in the organization of behavior. In W. A. Collins (Ed.), *The Minnesota Symposium on Child Psychology* (Vol. 13). Hillsdale, NJ: Lawrence Erlbaum. [13]

Bloom, B. (1985). *Developing Talent in Young People.* New York: Ballantine. [9]

Bloom, K. (1988). Quality of adult vocalizations affects the quality of infant vocalizations. *Journal of Child Language, 15,* 469–480. [9]

Bloom, K., Russell, A., and Wassenberg, K. (1987). Turn taking affects the quality of infant vocalizations. *Journal of Child Language, 14,* 211–227. [9]

Bloom, L. M. (1970). *Language Development: Form and Function in Emerging Grammars.* Cambridge, MA: MIT Press. [9]

Bloomfield, H. H., and Kory, R. B. (1976). *Happiness: The TM Program, Psychiatry and Enlightenment.* New York: Dawn Press/Simon and Schuster. [5]

Blumberg, B. D., Golbus, M. S., and Hanson, K. H. (1975). The psychological sequelae of abortion performed for a genetic indication. *American Journal of Obstetrics and Gynecology, 122,* 799–808. [15]

Blumenthal, A. L. (1985). Wilhelm Wundt: Psychology as the propaedeutic science. In C. E. Buxton (Ed.), *Points of View in the Modern History of Psychology.* New York: Academic Press. [1]

Boden, M. (1981). *Artificial Intelligence and Natural Man.* New York: Basic Books. [1]

Bolles, R. C. (1975). *Theory of Motivation* (2nd ed.). New York: Harper & Row. [12]

Bolles, R. C., and Fanselow, M. S. (1982). Endorphins and behavior. *Annual Review of Psychology, 33,* 87–101. [3]

Booth-Kewley, S., and Friedman, H. S. (1987). Psychological predictors of heart disease: A quantitative review. *Psychological Bulletin, 101,* 343–362. [13]

Bootzin, R. R., and Acocella, J. R. (1988). *Abnormal Psychology: Current Perspectives* (5th ed.). New York: Random House. [16]

Bothwell, R. K. (1989, August). *Hypnosis and Episodic Recall.* Paper presented at annual meeting of the American Psychological Association, New Orleans. [5]

Bouchard, C., Tremblay, A., Despres, J.-P., Nadeau, A., Lupien, P. J., Theriault, G., Dussault, J., Moorjani, S., Pinault, S., and Fournier, G. (1990, May 24). The response to long-term overfeeding in identical twins. *The New England Journal of Medicine, 322,* 1477–1482. [12]

Bouchard, T. J., Jr., Lykken, D. T., McGue, M., Segal, N. L., and Tellegen, A. (1990,

October 12). Sources of human psychological differences: The Minnesota study of twins reared apart. *Science, 250,* 223–228. [9]

Bouchard, T. J., and McGue, M. (1990, March). Genetic and rearing environmental influences on adult personality: An analysis of adolescent twins reared apart. *Journal of Personality, 58,* 263–292. [10]

Boudewyns, P. A., Fry, T. J., and Nightingale, E. J. (1986). Token economy programs in VA medical centers: Where are they today? *The Behavior Therapist, 9,* 126–127. [17]

Bower, B. (1991). Science and clinical tradition clash amid new insights into depression. *Science News, 139,* 56–57. [17]

Bower, G. H. (1972). A selective review of organizational factors in memory. In E. Tulving and W. Donaldson (Eds.), *Organization of Memory.* New York: Academic Press. [7]

Bower, G. H. (1981). Mood and memory. *American Psychologist, 36,* 129–148. [7]

Bower, G. H., Black, J., and Turner, T. (1979). Scripts in text comprehension and memory. *Cognitive Psychology, 11,* 177–220. [18]

Bower, G. H., and Mayer, J. D. (1985). Failure to replicate mood-dependent retrieval. *Bulletin of the Psychonomic Society, 23,* 39–42. [7]

Bower, G. H., Monteiro, K. P., and Gilligan, S. G. (1978). Emotional mood as a context of learning and recall. *Journal of Verbal Learning and Verbal Behavior, 17,* 573–585. [7]

Bower, G. H., and Morrow, D. G. (1990). Mental models in narrative comprehension. *Science, 247,* 44–48. [8]

Bowers, K. S. (1983). *Hypnosis for the Seriously Curious.* New York: Norton. [5]

Bowlby, J. (1969). *Attachment and Loss* (Vol. 1). New York: Basic Books. [10, 18]

Bowlby, J. (1973). Separation, anxiety, and anger. *Attachment and Loss* (Vol. 2). New York: Basic Books. [18]

Bowlby, J. (1980). Loss, sadness, and depression. *Attachment and Loss* (Vol. 3). New York: Basic Books. [18]

Bowlby, J. (1982). *Attachment and Loss* (2nd ed.). New York: Basic Books. [12]

Boynton, R. M. (1988). Color vision. *Annual Review of Psychology, 39,* 69–100. [4]

Bradbard, M. R., Martin, C. L., Endsley, R. C., and Halverson, C. F. (1986). Influence of sex stereotypes on children's exploration and memory: A competence versus performance distinction. *Developmental Psychology, 22*(4), 481–486. [10]

Bradbury, T. N., and Fincham, F. D. (1990). Attributions in marriage: Review and critique. *Psychological Bulletin, 107,* 3–33. [18]

Bradshaw, J. C., and Nettleton, N. C. (1974). Articulatory interference and the mown-down heterophone effect. *Journal of Experimental Psychology, 102,* 88–94. [8]

Brainerd, C. J. (1978). The stage question in cognitive-developmental theory. *The Behavioral and Brain Sciences, 1,* 173–213. [9]

Bransford, J. D., and Johnson, M. K. (1973). In W. G. Chase (Ed.), *Visual Information Processing.* New York: Academic Press. [7]

Bransford, J. D., and Stein, B. S. (1984). *The Ideal Problem Solver: A Guide for Improving Thinking, Learning, and Creativity.* New York: W. H. Freeman. [8]

Brazelton, T. B., and Cramer, B. G. (1990). *The Earliest Relationship.* New York: Addison-Wesley. [10]

Breckler, S. J. (1983). *Validation of Affect, Behavior and Cognition Distinct Components of Attitudes.* Unpublished dissertation, Ohio State University, Columbus. [18]

Breckler, S. J. (1984). Empirical validation of affect, behavior, and cognition as distinct components of attitudes. *Journal of Personality and Social Psychology, 47,* 1191–1205. [18]

Breier, A., Charney, D. S., and Heninger, G. R. (1986). Agoraphobia with panic attacks. *Archives of General Psychiatry, 43,* 1029–1036. [16]

Breland, K., and Breland, M. (1961). The misbehavior of organisms. *American Psychologist, 61,* 681–684. [6]

Bremer, J. (1959). *Asexualisation: A Fol-low-Up Study of 244 Cases.* New York: Macmillan. [12]

Bretl, D. J., and Cantor, J. (1988). The portrayal of men and women in U.S. television commercials: A recent content analysis and trends over 15 years. *Sex Roles, 18,* 595–609. [18]

Brewer, W. F., and Nakamura, G. V. (1984). The nature and functions of schemas. In R. S. Wyer and T. K. Srull (Eds.), *Handbook of Social Cognition* (Vol. 1, pp. 119–160). [7]

Brewerton, T. D. (1989). Seasonal variation of serotonin function in humans: Research and clinical implications. *Annals of Clinical Psychiatry, 1* 153–164. [17]

Brickman, P. (1978). *Happiness: Can We Make It Last?* Unpublished paper, Northwestern University. [11]

Brickman, P., and Campbell, D. T. (1971). Hedonic relativism and planning the good society. In M. H. Appley (Ed.), *Adaptation Level Theory.* New York: Academic Press. [11]

Brickman, P., Coates, D., and Janoff-Bulman, R. (1978). Lottery winners and accident victims: Is happiness relative? *Journal of Personality and Social Psychology, 36,* 917–927. [11]

Brickman, P., Rabinowitz, V. C., Karuza, J., Coates, D., Cohn, E., and Kidder, L. (1982). Models of helping and coping. *American Psychologist, 37,* 368–384. [19]

Brickner, M. A., Harkins, S. G., and Ostrom, T. M. (1986). Effect of personal involvement: Thought-provoking implications for social loafing. *Journal of Personality and Social Psychology, 51,* 763–769. [19]

Bridges, P. K., and Bartlett, J. R. (1977). Psychosurgery: Yesterday and today. *British Journal of Psychiatry, 131,* 249–260. [17]

Brigham, C. C. (1923). *A Study of American Intelligence.* Princeton: Princeton University Press. [14]

Broadbent, D. E. (1958). *Perception and Communication.* London: Pergamon Press. [7]

Brody, L. R., Zelazo, P. R., and Chaika, H. (1984). Habituation–dishabituation to speech in the neonate. *Developmental Psychology, 20,* 114–119. [9]

Brooks-Gunn, J., and **Furstenberg, F. F.** (1989). Adolescent sexual behavior. *American Psychologist, 44*(2), 249–257. [10]

Brown, A. L., and **Kane, M. J.** (1988). Preschool children can learn to transfer: Learning to learn and learning from example. *Cognitive Psychology,* 493–523. [9]

Brown, G. W., Birley, J. L. T., and **Wing, J. K.** (1972). Influence of family on the course of schizophrenic disorders: A replication. *British Journal of Psychiatry, 121,* 241–258. [16]

Brown, G. W., and **Harris, T.** (1978). *Social Origins of Depression: A Study of Psychiatric Disorders in Women.* New York: Free Press. [15]

Brown, J. (Ed.). (1976). *Recall and Recognition.* London: Wiley Interscience. [7]

Brown, J. A. (1958). Some tests of the decay theory of immediate memory. *Quarterly Journal of Experimental Psychology, 10,* 12–21. [7]

Brown, J. D., and **Seigel, J. M.** (1988). Exercise as a buffer of life stress: A prospective study of adolescent health. *Health Psychology, 57,* 1103–1110. [15]

Brown, L. T. (1984). Misconceptions about psychology aren't always what they seem. *Teaching of Psychology, 11,* 75–78. [1]

Brown, R. (1973). *A First Language: The Early Stages.* Cambridge, MA: Harvard University Press. [9]

Brown, R., and **Bellugi, U.** (1964). Three processes in the child's acquisition of syntax. *Harvard Educational Review, 34,* 133–151. [9]

Brown, R., Cazden, C., and **Bellugi-Klima, U.** (1968). The child's grammar from I to III. In J. P. Hill (Ed.), *Minnesota Symposium on Child Development* (Vol. 2, pp. 28–73). Minneapolis: University of Minnesota Press. [9]

Brown, R., Colter, N., Corsellis, J. A., Crow, T. J., Frith, C. D., Jagoe, R., Johnstone, E. C., and **Marsh, L.** (1986). Postmortem evidence of structural brain changes in schizophrenia. Differences in brain weight, temporal horn area, and parahippocampal gyrus compared with af-

fective disorder. *Archives of General Psychiatry, 43*(1), 36–42. [16]

Brown, R., and **McNeill, D.** (1966). The "tip of the tongue" phenomenon. *Journal of Verbal Learning and Verbal Behavior, 5,* 325–337. [7]

Brown, T. R., and **Sheran, T. J.** (1972). Suicide prediction: A review. *Life-Threatening Behavior, 2,* 67–98. [17]

Brownell, K. D., Marlatt, G. A., Lichtenstein, E., and **Wilson, G. T.** (1986). Understanding and preventing relapse. *American Psychologist, 41,* 765–782. [15]

Bruch, H. (1980). *The Golden Cage: The Enigma of Anorexia Nervosa.* New York: Random House. [12]

Bruner, J. S., Goodnow, J. J., and **Austin, G. A.** (1956). *A Study of Thinking.* New York: Wiley. [7]

Brunnquell, D., Crichton, L., and **Egeland, B.** (1981). Maternal personality and attitude in disturbances of child rearing. *American Journal of Orthopsychiatry, 51,* 680–691. [10]

Bryan, J. H. (1975). Children's cooperation and helping behaviors. In E. M. Hetherington (Ed.), *Review of Child Development Research* (Vol. 5). Chicago: University of Chicago Press. [10]

Buck, R. (1976). A test of nonverbal receiving ability: Preliminary studies. *Human Communication Research, 2,* 162–171. [11]

Buck, R. (1985). Prime theory: An integrated view of motivation and emotion. *Psychological Review, 92,* 389–413. [11]

Buck, R. (1990). William James, the nature of knowledge, and current issues in emotion, cognition, and communication. *Personality and Social Psychology Bulletin, 16*(4), 612–625. [11]

Buckhout, R., Eugenio, P., Licitra, T., Oliver, L., and **Kramer, T. H.** (1982, August). Hypnosis and Eyewitness Memory: The Effects of Unintentional Bias. Paper presented at the annual meeting of the American Psychological Association, Washington, DC. [5]

Bunch, J. (1972). Recent bereavement in relation to suicide. *Journal of Psychosomatic Research, 16,* 361–366. [17]

Bunney, W. E., Jr., Murphy, D. L., Goodwin, F. K., and **Borge, G. F.** (1972, September). The "switch process" in manic-depressive illness: A systematic study of sequential behavior changes. *Archives of General Psychiatry, 27,* 295–302. [16]

Burger, J. M. (1986). Increasing compliance by improving the deal: The that's-not-all technique. *Journal of Personality and Social Psychology, 51,* 277–283. [19]

Burgess, A. W., and **Holmstrom, L. L.** (1974). Rape trauma syndrome. *American Journal of Psychiatry, 131,* 981–986. [11]

Burgess, A. W., and **Holmstrom, L. L.** (1978). Recovery from rape and prior life stress. *Research in Nursing and Health, 1,* 165–174. [11]

Buss, D. M. (1985). Human mate selection. *American Scientist, 73,* 47–51. [18]

Buss, D. M. (1988). Love acts: The evolutionary biology of love. In R. J. Sternberg and M. L. Barnes (Eds.), *The Psychology of Love* (pp. 100–118). New Haven: Yale University Press. [18]

Buss, D. M. (1990). Toward a biologically informed psychology of personality. *Journal of Personality, 58*(1), 1–16. [13]

Buss, D. M. (in press). Evolutionary personality psychology. *Annual Review of Psychology.* [12]

Butcher, J. N., Dahlstrom, W. G., Graham, J. R., Tellegen, A., and **Kaemmer, B.** (1989). *Manual for Restandardized Minnesota Multiphasic Personality Inventory; MMPI-2.* Minneapolis: University of Minnesota Press. [14]

Bylinsky, G. (1986, January 20). Medicine's next marvel: The memory pill. *Fortune,* pp. 68–71. [3]

Byrne, D., and **Kelley, K.** (1984). Introduction: Pornography and sex research. In N. M. Malamuth and E. Donnerstien (Eds.), *Pornography and Sexual Aggression.* Orlando, FL: Academic Press. [19]

Cabanac, M. (1971). The physiological role of pleasure. *Science, 173,* 1103–1107. [12]

Cacioppo, J. T., Petty, R. E., Losch, M. E., and **Kim, H. S.** (1986). Electromyographic activity over facial muscle regions can differentiate the valence and intensity of affective reactions. *Journal of Personality and Social Psychology, 50,* 260–268. [11]

Cacioppo, J. T., and **Tassinary, L.** (1990). *Principles of Psychophysiology: Physical, Social, and Inferential Elements.* Cambridge: Cambridge University Press. [11]

Cain, W. S. (1988). Olfaction. In R. C. Atkinson, R. J. Hernstein, L. Gardner, and **R. D. Luce (Eds.),** *Stevens' Handbook of Experimental Psychology* (2nd ed., Vol. 1, pp. 409–460). New York: Wiley. [4]

Calhoun, L. G., Kahn, A., Selby, J. W., and **Magee, D. L.** (1985). Victim emotional response: Effect on social reaction to victims of rape. *British Journal of Social and Clinical Psychology.* [11]

Callaway, M. R., Marriott, R. G., and **Esser, J. K.** (1985). Effects of dominance on group decision making: Toward a stress-reduction explanation of groupthink. *Journal of Personality and Social Psychology, 49,* 949–952. [19]

Camara, K. A., and **Resnick, G.** (1988). Interparental conflict and cooperation: Factors moderating children's post-divorce adjustment. In E. M. Hetherington and J. D. Arasteh (Eds.), *Impact of Divorce, Single Parenting, and Stepparenting on Children* (pp. 169–195). Hillsdale, NJ: Lawrence Erlbaum. [10]

Cameron, N. (1963). *Personality Development and Psychopathology.* Boston: Houghton Mifflin. [16]

Campbell, A., Converse, P. E., and **Rogers, W. L.** (1976). *The Quality of American Life: Perceptions, Evaluations and Satisfactions.* New York: Russell Sage Foundation. [11]

Campbell, A. M. G., Evans, M., Thomson, J. L., and **Williams, M. J.** (1971). Cerebral atrophy in young cannabis smokers. *Lancet, 2,* 1219–1224. [1]

Campbell, D. T. (1978). Measuring the effects of social innovations by means of time series. In J. M. Tanur et al. (Eds.), *Statistics: A Guide to the Unknown* (pp. 159–169). San Francisco, CA: Holden-Day. [2]

Campbell, D. T., and **Stanley, J. C.** (1966). Experimental and quasi-experimental designs for research on teaching. In *Experimental and Quasi-Experimental Designs for Research.* Chicago: Rand McNally. (Reprinted from N. L. Gage [Ed.], *Handbook of Research on Teaching,* 1963, pp. 171–246). [2]

Campbell, J. B., and **Hawley, C. W.** (1982). Study habits and Eysenck's theory of extroversion-introversion. *Journal of Research in Personality, 16,* 139–146. [13]

Campbell, J. D., Tesser, A., and **Fairey, P. J.** (1986). Conformity and attention to the stimulus: Some temporal and contextual dynamics. *Journal of Personality and Social Psychology, 51,* 315–324. [19]

Campos, J. J., Barrett, K., Lamb, M., Goldsmith, H., and **Stenberg, C.** (1983). Socioemotional development. In P. Mussen (Ed.), *Handbook of Child Psychology* (4th ed., Vol. 2): M. M. Haith and J. Campos (Eds.), *Infancy and Developmental Psychology* (pp. 783–915). New York: Wiley. [10]

Canestrari, R. E., Jr. (1963). Paced and self-paced learning in young and elderly adults. *Journal of Gerontology, 18,* 165–168. [9]

Cannell, C. G., and **Kahn, R. L.** (1968). Interviewing. In G. Lindzey and E. Aronson (Eds.), *Handbook of Social Psychology: Research Methods* (Vol. 2). Reading, MA: Addison-Wesley. [2, 7]

Cannon, W. B. (1927). The James-Lange theory of emotions: A critical examination as an alternative theory. *American Journal of Psychology, 39,* 106–124. [11]

Cannon, W. B. (1929). *Bodily Changes in Pain, Hunger, Fear, and Rage* (2nd ed.). New York: Appleton-Century. [11]

Cannon, W. B. (1932). *The Wisdom of the Body.* New York: Norton. [15]

Cannon, W. B., and **Washburn, A. L.** (1912). An explanation of hunger. *American Journal of Physiology, 29,* 441–454. [12]

Cantor, N. (1990, June). From thought to behavior: "Having" and "doing" in the study of personality and cognition. *American Psychologist, 45*(6), 735–750. [13]

Cantor, N. (in press). Social psychology and social biology: What can we leave to evolution? *Motivation and Emotion.* [12]

Cantor, N., and **Mischel, W.** (1977). Traits as prototypes: Effects on recognition memory. *Journal of Personality and Social Psychology, 35,* 38–48. [18]

Caplan, P. J., MacPherson, G. M., and **Tobin, P.** (1985). Do sex-related differences in spatial abilities exist? A multilevel critique with new data. *American Psychologist, 40,* 786–799. [9]

Carlson, M., Charlin, V., and **Miller, N.** (1988). Positive mood and helping behavior: A test of six hypotheses. *Journal of Personality and Social Psychology, 55,* 211–229. [19]

Carlson, M., and **Miller, N.** (1987). Explanation of the relation between negative mood and helping. *Psychological Bulletin, 102,* 91–108. [19]

Carmichael, L., Hogan, H. P., and **Walter, A. A.** (1932). An experimental study of the effect of language on the reproduction of visually perceived form. *Journal of Experimental Psychology, 15,* 73–86. [7]

Carr, D., Bullen, B., Krinar, G., Arnold, M., Rosenblatt, M., Beitins, I. Z., Martin, J. B., and **McArthur, J. W.** (1981). Physical conditioning facilitates the exercise-induced secretion of beta-endorphin and beta-lipotropin in women. *New England Journal of Medicine, 305,* 560–563. [3]

Carr, W. J., and **Caul, W. F.** (1962). The effect of castration in rats upon the dissemination of sex odors. *Animal Behavior, 10,* 20–27. [11]

Carrol, E. N., Zuckerman, M., and **Vogel, W. H.** (1982). A test of the optimal level of arousal theory of sensation seeking. *Journal of Personality and Social Psychology, 42,* 572–575. [11]

Cartwright, R. D. (1979). The nature and function of repetitive dreams: A survey of speculation. *Psychiatry, 42,* 131–137. [5]

Case, R. (1985). *Intellectual Development: Birth to Adulthood.* New York: Academic Press. [9]

Cattell, R. B. (1959). Anxiety, extroversion, and other second order personality factors in children. *Journal of Personality, 27,* 464–476. [13]

Cattell, R. B. (1971). *Abilities: Their*

Structure, Growth, and Action. Boston: Houghton Mifflin. [14]

Ceci, S. J., and **Liker, J. K.** (1986). A day at the races: A study of IQ, expertise, and cognitive complexity. *Journal of Experimental Psychology, 115*(3), 255–266. [14]

Ceniti, J., and **Malamuth, N. M.** (1984). Effects of repeated exposure to sexually violent or non-violent stimuli on sexual arousal to rape and nonrape depictions. *Behavioral Research Therapy, 22,* 535–548. [12]

Centers for Disease Control (1989). Surgeon General's report on smoking: Reducing health consequences of smoking: 25 years of progress, 1964–1989. Washington, DC: Central Office for Health Promotion and Education on Smoking and Health, U.S. Government Printing Office. [15]

Chaiken, S. (1980). Heuristic versus systematic information processing and the use of source versus message cues in persuasion. *Journal of Personality and Social Psychology, 39,* 752–766. [18]

Chaiken, S., Liberman, A., and **Eagly, A. H.** (1989). Heuristic and systematic information processing within and beyond the persuasion context. In J. S. Uleman and J. A. Bargh (Eds.), *Unintended Thought* (pp. 212–251). New York: Guilford. [18]

Chaiken, S., and **Stangor, C.** (1987). Attitudes and attitude change. *Annual Review of Psychology, 38,* 575–630. [18, 19]

Chambliss, C. A., and **Murray, E. J.** (1979). Efficacy attribution, locus of control, and weight loss. *Cognitive Therapy and Research, 3,* 349–353. [19]

Chang, T. M. (1986). Semantic memory: Facts and models. *Psychological Bulletin, 99*(2), 199–220. [7]

Chan-Palay, V., and **Palay, S. L.** (Eds.). (1984). *Coexistence of Neuroactive Substances in Neurons.* New York: Wiley. [3]

Chapanis, N. P., and **Chapanis, A. C.** (1964). Cognitive dissonance: Five years later. *Psychological Bulletin, 61,* 1–22. [18]

Charlesworth, W. R., and **Dzur, C.** (1987). Gender comparisons of preschoolers' behavior and resource utilization in group problem-solving. *Child Development, 58,* 191–200. [10]

Chase, M. H., and **Morales, F. R.** (1983). Subthreshold excitatory activity and motoneuron discharge during REM periods of active sleep. *Science, 221,* 1195–1198. [5]

Chassin, L., and **Sherman, S.** (1985). Adolescents' Changing Relationships with Parents and Peers: A Cohort Sequential Study. Paper presented at the biennial meeting of the Society for Research in Child Development, Toronto. [10]

Chen, S. C. (1937). Social modification of the activity of ants in nest-building. *Physiological Zoology, 10,* 420–436. [19]

Cherniss, C., Egnatios, E. S., and **Wacker, S.** (1976). Job stress and career development in new public professionals. *Professional Psychology, 7,* 428–436. [19]

Cherniss, C., Egnatios, E. S., Wacker, S., and **O'Dowd, B.** (in press). The professional mystique and burnout in public sector professionals. *Social Policy.* [19]

Cherry, E. C. (1953). Some experiments on the recognition of speech with one and two ears. *Journal of the Acoustical Society of America, 25,* 975–979. [7]

Cherry, F., and **Deaux, K.** (1975, May). *Fear of Success vs. Fear of Gender-Inconsistent Behavior: A Sex Similarity.* Paper presented at the meeting of the Midwestern Psychological Association, Chicago. [12]

Cheseman, J., and **Merikle, P. M.** (1985). Word recognition and consciousness. In D. Besner, T. G. Waller, and G. E. MacKinnon (Eds.), *Reading Research: Advances in Theory and Practice* (Vol. 5). New York: Academic Press. [4]

Chi, M. T. H. (1978). Knowledge structures and memory development. In R. S. Siegler (Ed.), *Children's Thinking: What Develops?* Hillsdale, NJ: Lawrence Erlbaum. [8]

Chi, M. T. H., and **Ceci, S. J.** (1986). The restructuring of knowledge in memory development. In H. W. Reese and L. P. Lipsitt (Eds.), *Advances in Child Development and Behavior* (Vol. 22, pp. 1–42). [9]

Chi, M. T. H., Glaser, R., and **Reese, E.** (1982). Expertise in problem solving. In R. J. Sternberg (Ed.), *Advances in the Psychology of Human Intelligence* (Vol. 1, pp. 7–76). Hillside, NJ: Lawrence Erlbaum. [8]

Children's Defense Fund. (1987). *A Children's Defense Budget, FY 1988: An Analysis of Our Nation's Investment in Children.* Washington, DC: Author. [10]

Chomsky, N. (1972). *Language and Mind.* New York: Harcourt Brace Jovanovich. [7, 9]

Chomsky, N. (1979). *Language and Responsibility.* New York: Pantheon. [9]

Churchland, P. S., and **Sejnowski, T. J.** (1988, November 4). Perspectives on cognitive neuroscience. *Science, 242,* 741–745. [3]

Chwalisz, K., Diener, E., and **Gallagher, D.** (1988). Autonomic arousal feedback and emotional experience: Evidence from the spinal cord injured. *Journal of Personality and Social Psychology, 54*(5), 820–828. [11]

Cialdini, R. B., Cacioppo, J. T., Bassett, R., and **Miller, J. A.** (1978). Low-ball procedure for producing compliance: Commitment then cost. *Journal of Personality and Social Psychology, 36,* 463–476. [19]

Cialdini, R. B., Darby, B. L., and **Vincent, J. E.** (1973). Transgressional altruism: A case for hedonism. *Journal of Personality and Social Psychology, 9,* 502–516. [19]

Cialdini, R. B., Schaller, M., Houlihan, D., Arps, K., Fultz, J., and **Beaman, A. L.** (1987). Empathy-based helping: Is it selflessly or selfishly motivated? *Journal of Personality and Social Psychology, 52,* 749–758. [19]

Cialdini, R. B., Vincent, J. E., Lewis, S. K., Catalan, J., Wheeler, D., and **Darby, L.** (1975). Reciprocal concessions procedure for inducing compliance: The door-in-the-face technique. *Journal of Personality and Social Psychology, 31,* 206–215. [19]

Cicchetti, D., and **Beeghly, M.** (in press). Down syndrome: A developmental perspective. Cambridge: Cambridge University Press. [9]

Cicchetti, D., and **Sroufe, L.** (1978). An organizational view of affect: Illustration from the study of Down's syndrome infants. In M. Lewis and L. Rosenblum (Eds.), *The Development of Affect.* New York: Plenum. [9]

Clark, E. (1983). Meanings and concepts. In P. Mussen (Ed.), *Handbook of*

Child Psychology (4th ed., Vol. 3): J. H. Flavell and E. Markman (Eds.), *Cognitive Development*. New York: Wiley. [9]

Clarke-Stewart, A. (1982). *Day Care.* Cambridge, MA: Harvard University Press. [10]

Clarke-Stewart, A. (1989). Infant day care: Maligned or malignant? *American Psychologist, 44*(2), 266–273. [10]

Clarke-Stewart, A., and Fein, G. (1983). Early childhood programs. In P. Mussen (Ed.), *Handbook of Child Psychology* (4th ed., Vol. 2): M. M. Haith and J. Campos (Eds.), *Infancy and Developmental Psychobiology* (pp. 917–1000). New York: Wiley. [10]

Clarke-Stewart, A., Thompson, W., and Lepore, S. (1989, April). *Manipulating Children's Interpretations through Interrogation.* Paper presented at the meeting of the Society for Research in Child Development, Kansas City, MO. [2]

Cline, V. B., Croft, R. G., and Courrier, S. (1973). Desensitization of children to television violence. *Journal of Personality and Social Psychology, 27*, 360–365. [19]

Cloninger, C. R., and Gottesman, I. I. (1987). Genetic and environmental factors in antisocial behavior disorders. In S. Mednick, T. Moffitt, and S. Strack (Eds.), *The Causes of Crime: New Biological Approaches.* Cambridge: Cambridge University Press.

Clum, G. A. (1987, September). Abandon the suicidal?: A reply to Szasz. *American Psychologist, 42*, 883–885. [17]

Coates, D., Renzaglia, G. J., and Embree, M. C. (1983). When helping backfires: Help and helplessness. In J.•D. Fisher, A. Nadler, and B. DePaulo (Eds.), *New Directions in Helping* (Vol. 1). New York: Academic Press. [19]

Coates, D., Wortman, C. B., and Abbey, A. (1979). Reactions to victims. In I. H. Frieze, D. Bar-Tal, and J. S. Carroll (Eds.), *New Approaches to Social Problems.* San Francisco: Jossey-Bass. [11]

Cobb, S. (1976). Social support as a moderator of life stress. *Psychosomatic Medicine, 38*, 300–314. [15]

Cochran, S. D., and Mays, V. M. (in press). AIDS-related sexual behavior and

disclosure: Is it safe if you ask? *New England Journal of Medicine.* [15]

Cohen, F., Kearney, K. A., Zegans, L. S., Kemeny, M. E., Neuhaus, J. M., and Stites, D. P. (1989). *Acute Stressors, Chronic Stressors, and Immunity and the Role of Optimism as a Moderator.* Manuscript submitted for publication. [15]

Cohen, L., Rosenbaum, J. F., and Heller, V. (1988). Prescribing lithium for pregnant women. *American Journal of Psychiatry, 145*, 772–773. [17]

Cohen, L., and Roth, S. (1984). Coping with abortion. *Journal of Human Stress, 10*(3), 140–145. [15]

Cohen, L. J. (1981). Can human irrationality be experimentally demonstrated? *Behavior and Brain Science, 4*, 317–331. [18]

Cohen, N. J., and Corkin, S. (1981). The amnesic patient H. M.: Learning and retention of a cognitive skill. *Neuroscience Abstracts, 7*, 235. [7]

Cohen, S., and Lichtenstein, E. (1989). Partner behaviors that support quitting smoking. *Journal of Consulting and Clinical Psychology.* [15]

Cohen, S., and Wills, T. A. (1985). Stress, social support, and the buffering hypothesis. *Psychological Bulletin, 98*, 310–357. [15]

Cohn, T. E., and Lasley, D. J. (1986). Visual sensitivity. *Annual Review of Psychology, 37*, 495–521. [4]

Cole, R. A., and Jakimic, J. (1980). A model of speech perception. In R. A. Cole (Ed.), *Perception and Production of Fluent Speech.* Hillsdale, NJ: Lawrence Erlbaum. [8]

Collias, N. E. (1956). The analysis of socialization in sheep and goats. *Ecology, 37*, 228–239. [2]

Collins, B. E. (1970). *Social Psychology.* Reading, MA: Addison-Wesley. [19]

Collins, B. E., and Aspinwall, L. G. (1989, May). *Impression Management in Negotiations for Safer Sex.* Paper presented to the Second Iowa Conference on Personal Relationships, Iowa City, IA. [15]

Collins, B. E., and Hoyt, M. F. (1972). Personal responsibility-for-consequences: An integration and extension of the forced

compliance literature. *Journal of Experimental Social Psychology, 8*, 558–593. [18]

Collins, R. L., and Marlatt, G. A. (1981). Social modeling as a determinant of drinking behavior: Implications for prevention and treatment. *Addictive Behaviors, 6*, 233–239. [2]

Collins, R. L., Taylor, S. E., and Skokan, L. A. (1990). A better world or a shattered vision? Changes in perspectives following victimization. *Social Cognition.* [15]

Colt, W. D., Wardlaw, S., and Frantz, A. (1981). The effect of running on plasma beta-endorphin. *Life Science, 28*, 1637–1640. [3]

Coltheart, M. (1989, November 10). Cognition and its disorders. *Science, 246*, 827–828. [3]

Combs, B. J., Hales, D. R., and Williams, B. K. (1980). *An Invitation to Health.* Menlo Park, CA: Benjamin/Cummings. [5]

Comfort, A. (1971). Likelihood of human pheromones. *Nature, 230*, 432–433. [12]

Committee on Government Operations, House of Representatives. (1989, December 11). *The Federal Role of Determining the Medical and Psychological Impact of Abortion on Women,* 101st Congress, 2nd session. House Report 101–392. [15]

Condry, J., and Condry, S. (1976). Sex differences: A study of the eye of the beholder. *Child Development, 47*, 812–819. [10]

Condry, J., and Dyer, S. (1976). Fear of success: Attribution of cause to the victim. *Journal of Social Issues, 32*, 63–83. [12]

Conger, J. (1977). *Adolescence and Youth: Psychological Development in a Changing World.* New York: Harper & Row. [10, 13]

Conley, J. J. (1985). Longitudinal stability of personality traits: A multitrait-multimethod-multioccasion analysis. *Journal of Personality and Social Psychology, 49*, 1266–1282. [13]

Cook, M. L., and Peterson, C. (1986). Depressive irrationality. *Cognitive Therapy and Research, 10*, 293–298. [15]

Cook, N. M. (1989). The applicability of verbal mnemonics for different populations: A review. *Applied Psychology, 3*, 3–22. [7]

Cook, S. W. (1985). Experimenting on social issues: The case of school desegregation. *American Psychologist, 40,* 452–460. [18]

Cooper, H. (1986). In R. Feldman (Ed.), *Social Psychology Applied to Education.* Cambridge, England: Cambridge University Press. [2]

Cooper, J., and **Croyle, T.** (1984). Attitudes and attitude change. *Annual Review of Psychology, 35,* 395–426. [18]

Cooper, J., and **Fazio, R. H.** (1989). Research traditions, analysis, and synthesis: Building a faulty case around misinterpreted theory. *Personality and Social Psychology Bulletin, 15*(4), 519–529. [18]

Coopersmith, S. (1967). *The Antecedents of Self-Esteem.* New York: W. H. Freeman. [13]

Corcoran, K. J. (1989). Interpersonal stress and burnout: Unraveling the role of empathy. *Journal of Social Behavior and Personality, 4,* 141–144. [19]

Coren, S., Porac, C., and **Ward, L. M.** (1979). *Sensation and Perception.* New York: Academic Press. [4]

Costa, P. T., Jr., and **McCrae, R. R.** (1980a). Still stable after all these years: Personality as a key to some issues in adulthood and old age. In P. B. Baltes and O. G. Brim, Jr. (Eds.), *Life-Span Development and Behavior,* New York: Academic Press. [10]

Costa, P. T., and **McCrae, R. R.** (1980b). Influence of extraversion and neuroticism on subjective well-being: Happy and unhappy people. *Journal of Personality and Social Psychology, 38,* 668–678. [11]

Costa, P. T., and **McCrae, R. R.** (1986). Personality stability and its implications for clinical psychology. *Clinical Psychology, 6*(5), 407–423. [11]

Cowan, W. M., Fawcett, J. W., Dennis, D. M., and **Stanfield, B. B.** (1984). Regressive events in neurogenesis. *Science, 225,* 1258–1265. [3, 19]

Coyne, J. (1976a). Toward an interactional description of depression. *Psychiatry, 39,* 14–27. [16]

Coyne, J. (1976b). Depression and the response of others. *Journal of Abnormal Psychology, 85,* 186–193. [16]

Coyne, J. C., and **Gotlib, I. H.** (1983). The role of cognition in depression: A critical appraisal. *Psychological Bulletin, 94*(3), 472–505. [16]

Craig, R. L., and **Siegel, P. S.** (1979). Does negative affect beget positive affect? A test of the opponent-process theory. *Bulletin of the Psychonomic Society, 14,* 404–406. [12]

Craik, F. I. M., and **Byrd, M.** (1982). Aging and cognitive deficits: The role of attentional resources. In F. I. M. Craik and S. E. Trehub (Eds.), *Advances in the Study of Communication and Affect: Aging and Cognitive Processes* (Vol. 8, pp. 191–211). New York: Plenum. [9]

Craik, F. I. M., and **Lockhart, R. S.** (1972). Levels of processing: A framework for memory research. *Journal of Verbal Learning and Verbal Behavior, 11,* 671–684. [7]

Craik, F. I. M., and **Simon, E.** (1980). Age differences in memory: The roles of attention and depth of processing. In L. W. Poon et al. (Eds.), *New Directions in Memory and Aging.* Hillsdale, NJ: Lawrence Erlbaum. [9]

Crapo, L. (1985). *Hormones: The Messengers of Life.* New York: W. H. Freeman. [3]

Crawford, H. J. (1985, August). *Cognitive Flexibility, Dissociation, and Hypnosis.* Presidential address presented to the meeting of the Hypnosis Division of the APA, Los Angeles, CA. [5]

Creese, I., Burt, D. R., and **Snyder, S. H.** (1975). Brain's dopamine receptor—labeling with [dopamine-H_3] and [H_{21} operidol-H_3]. *Psychopharmacology Communications, 1,* 663–673. [16]

Crépault, C., Abraham, G., Porto, R., and **Couture, M.** (1977). Erotic imagery in women. In R. Gemme and C. C. Wheeler (Eds.), *Progress in Sexology* (pp. 267–283). New York: Plenum. [12]

Crépault, C., and **Couture, M.** (1980). Men's erotic fantasies. *Archives of Sexual Behavior, 9,* 565–582. [12]

Critchlow, B. (1986). The powers of John Barleycorn: Beliefs about the effects of alcohol on social behavior. *American Psychologist, 41,* 751–764. [5]

Crockenberg, S. (1986, April). *Maternal Anger and the Behavior of Two-Year-Old Children.* Paper presented at the International Conference on Infant Studies, Beverly Hills, CA. [10]

Cronbach, L. J. (1975). Five decades of public controversy over mental testing. *American Psychologist, 30,* 1–14. [14]

Crouse, J., and **Trusheim, D.** (1988). *The Case Against the SAT.* Chicago: University of Chicago Press. [14]

Croyle, R. T., and **Cooper, J.** (1983). Dissonance arousal: Physiological evidence. *Journal of Personality and Social Psychology, 45,* 782–791. [18]

Cummings, E. M. (1980). Caregiver stability and day care. *Developmental Psychology, 16,* 31–37. [10]

Cunningham, M. R. (1979). Weather, mood, and helping behavior: Quasi-experiments with the Sunshine Samaritan. *Journal of Personality and Social Psychology, 37,* 1947–1956. [19]

Cunningham, M. R. (1986). Measuring the physical in physical attractiveness: Quasi-experiments on the sociobiology of female facial beauty. *Journal of Personality and Social Psychology, 50,* 925–935. [18]

Curtis, R. C., and **Miller, K.** (1986). Believing another likes or dislikes you: Behaviors making the beliefs come true. *Journal of Personality and Social Psychology, 51,* 284–290. [18]

Curtiss, S. (1977). *Genie: A Psycholinguistic Study of a Modern-Day "Wild Child."* New York: Academic Press. [2, 9]

Czeisler, C. A., Moore-Ede, M. C., and **Coleman, R. M.** (1982, July 30). Rotating shift work schedules that disrupt sleep are improved by applying circadian principles. *Science, 217,* 460–463. [12]

Dagg, P. K. B. (1991). The psychological sequelae of therapeutic abortion—denied and completed. *American Journal of Psychiatry, 148*(5), 578–585. [15]

Dakof, G. A., and **Taylor, S. E.** (1990). Victims' perceptions of social support:

What is helpful from whom? *Journal of Personality and Social Psychology, 58,* 80–89. [15]

Damasio, A. R., Damasio, H., and van Hoesen, G. W. (1982). Prosopagnosia: Anatomic basis and behavioral mechanisms. *Neurology, 32,* 331–341. [4]

Damon, W. (1977). *The Social World of the Child.* San Francisco: Jossey-Bass. [10]

Damon, W. (1983). *Social and Personality Development,* New York: Norton. [10]

Daniels, D., Dunn, J., Furstenberg, F., and Plomin, R. (1985). Environmental differences within the family and adjustment differences within pairs of adolescent siblings. *Child Development, 56,* 764–774. [10]

Darley, C. F., Tinklenberg, J. R., Roth, W. T., Hollister, L. E., and Atkinson, R. C. (1973). Influence of marihuana on storage and retrieval processes in memory. *Memory and Cognition, 1,* 196–200. [5]

Darley, J. M., and Batson, C. D. (1973). From Jerusalem to Jericho: A study of situational and dispositional variables in helping behavior. *Journal of Personality and Social Psychology, 27,* 100–119. [19]

Darley, J. M., and Latané, B. (1968). Bystander intervention in emergencies: Diffusion of responsibility. *Journal of Personality and Social Psychology, 8,* 377–383. [1, 19]

Daro, D. (1988). *Confronting Child Abuse: Research for Effective Program Design.* New York: Free Press. [10]

Darwin, C. (1896). *The Expression of the Emotions in Man and Animals.* London: Murray. [11]

Datan, N., Rodeheaver, D., and Hughes, F. (1987). Adult development and aging. *Annual Review of Psychology, 38,* 153–180. [9]

David, H., Dytrych, Z., Matejeck, Z., and Schüller, V. (1988). *Born Unwanted: Developmental Effects of Denied Abortion.* New York: Springer. [15]

David, H., Rasmussen, N., and Holst, E. (1981). Postpartum and postabortion psychotic reactions. *Family Planning Perspectives, 13*(2), 88–93. [15]

Davidson, R. (1984). *Emotion, Cognition, and Behavior.* New York: Cambridge University Press. [11]

Davidson, R. J., Ekman, P., Saron, C. D., Senulis, J., and Friesen, W. (1990). Approach/withdrawal and cerebral asymmetry: Emotional expression and brain physiology I. *Journal of Personality and Social Psychology, 58,* 330–341. [11]

Davidson, R. J., and Fox, N. A. (1989). Frontal brain asymmetry predicts infants' response to maternal separation. *Journal of Abnormal Psychology, 98,* 127–131. [11]

Davis, J. D., Gallagher, R. J., Ladove, R. F., and Turansky, A. J. (1969). Inhibition of food intake by a humoral factor. *Journal of Comparative and Physiological Psychology, 67,* 407–414. [12]

Davis, M. H., and Oathout, H. A. (1987). *Journal of Personality and Social Psychology, 53*(2), 397–410. [18]

Davis, P. J. (1987). Repression and the inaccessibility of affective memories. *Journal of Personality and Social Psychology, 53,* 585–593. [13]

Davis, P. J., and Schwartz, G. E. (1987). Repression and the inaccessibility of affective memories. *Journal of Personality and Social Psychology, 52,* 155–162. [13]

Davis, R. C., Carafolo, L., and Kveim, K. (1959). Conditions associated with gastrointestinal activity. *Journal of Comparative and Physiological Psychology, 52,* 466–475. [12]

Davison, G. C., and Neale, J. M. (1990). *Abnormal Psychology* (5th ed.). New York: Wiley. [17]

Daw, N. W. (1968). Colour-coded ganglion cells in the goldfish retina: Extension of their receptive fields by means of new stimuli. *Journal of Physiology* (London), *197,* 567–592. [4]

Dawes, R. M. (1988). *Rational Choice in an Uncertain World.* San Diego: Harcourt, Brace, Jovanovich. [8]

Dawkins, E. (1975). *The Selfish Gene.* New York: Oxford University Press. [19]

Deaux, K. (1976). Sex: A perspective on the attribution process. In J. H. Harvey, W. J. Ickes, and R. F. Kidd (Eds.), *New Direc-*

tions in Attribution Research (Vol. 1). Hillsdale, NJ: Lawrence Erlbaum. [18]

Deaux, K. (1985). Sex and gender. *Annual Review of Psychology, 36,* 49–81. [12]

De Casper, A., and Fifer, W. (1980). Of human bonding: Newborns prefer their mothers' voices. *Science, 208,* 1174–1176. [9]

De Casper, A., and Spence, M. J. (1986). Prenatal maternal speech influences newborns' perception of speech sounds. *Infant Behavior and Development, 9,* 133–150. [9]

Deci, E. L., and Ryan, R. M. (1980). The empirical exploration of intrinsic motivational processes. In L. Berkowitz (Ed.), *Advances in Experimental Social Psychology* (Vol. 13). New York: Academic Press. [12, 18]

De Groot, A. D. (1965). *Thought and Choice in Chess.* The Hague: Mouron. [7]

Deguchi, H., Fujita, T., and Sato, M. (1988). Reinforcement control of observational learning in young children: A behavioral analysis of modeling. *Journal of Experimental Child Psychology, 46,* 362–371. [6]

Deitz, P. E., Harry, B., and Hazelwood, R. R. (1986). Detective magazines: Pornography for the sexual sadist? *Journal of Forensic Sciences, 31*(1), 197–211. [19]

DeJong, W., and Musilli, L. (1982). External pressure to comply: Handicapped versus nonhandicapped requesters and the foot-in-the-door phenomenon. *Personality and Social Psychology Bulletin, 8,* 522–527. [19]

Dekker, J., and Everaerd, W. (1989). Psychological determinants of sexual arousal: A review. *Behavioral Research Therapy, 27,* 353–364. [12]

DeLoache, J. S., and Todd, C. M. (1988). Young children's use of spatial categorization as a mnemonic strategy. *Journal of Experimental Child Psychology, 46,* 1–20. [9]

DeLongis, A., Coyne, J. C., Dakof, G., Folkman, S., and Lazarus, R. S. (1982). Relationship of daily hassles, uplifts, and major life events to health status. *Health Psychology, 1,* 119–136. [15]

Deluty, R. H. (1985). Consistency of assertive, aggressive, and submissive behavior for children. *Journal of Personality and Social Psychology, 49,* 1054–1065. [19]

Demare, D., Briere, J., and **Lips, H. M.** (1988). Violent pornography and self-reported likelihood of sexual aggression. *Journal of Research in Personality, 22,* 140–153. [19]

Dembroski, T. M., and **Costa, P. T., Jr.** (1987). Coronary prone behavior: Components of the Type A pattern and hostility. *Journal of Personality, 55*(2), 211–235. [13]

Dembroski, T. M., and **MacDougall, J. M.** (1985). Beyond global Type A: Relationships of paralinguistic attributes, hostility, and anger-in to coronary heart disease. In T. Field, P. McAbe, and N. Schneiderman (Eds.), *Stress and Coping* (pp. 223–242). Hillsdale, NJ: Lawrence Erlbaum. [13]

Dembroski, T. M., and **Williams, R. B.** (1989). Definition and assessment of coronary-prone behavior. In N. Schneiderman, P. Kaufman, and S. M. Weiss (Eds.), *Handbook of Research Methods in Cardiovascular Behavioral Medicine.* New York: Plenum. [13]

Dement, W. C. (1960). Dream deprivation. *Science, 132,* 1420–1422. [5]

Dement, W. C. (1969). The biological role of REM sleep. In A. Kales (Ed.), *Sleep Physiology and Pathology.* Philadelphia: Lippincott. [5]

Dement, W. C. (1976). *Some Must Watch While Some Must Sleep: Exploring the World of Sleep.* New York: Norton. [5]

Dent, J., and **Teasdale, J. D.** (1988). Negative cognition and the persistence of depression. *Journal of Abnormal Psychology, 97,* 29–34. [17]

Denton, G. G. (1971). *The Influence of Visual Pattern on Perceived Speed.* Crowthorne, England: Road Research Library. [4]

Dermer, M., Cohen, S. J., and **Anderson, E. A.** (1978). *Evaluative Aspects of Life as a Function of Vicarious Exposure to Hedonic Extremes.* Unpublished paper, University of Wisconsin, Milwaukee. [11]

Der Simonian, R., and **Laird, N. M.** (1983). Evaluating the effect of coaching on SAT scores: A metanalysis. *Harvard Educational Review, 53,* 1–15. [14]

Deutsch, H. (1945). *The Psychology of Women: A Psychoanalytic Interpretation.* New York: Grune & Stratton. [15]

Deutsch, M., and **Gerard, H. B.** (1955). A study of normative and informational influences on social judgment. *Journal of Abnormal and Social Psychology, 51,* 629–636. [19]

DeValois, R. L., and **DeValois, K.** (1975). Neural coding of color. In E. C. Carterette and M. P. Friedman (Eds.), *Handbook of Perception* (Vol. 5, pp. 117–166). New York: Academic Press. [4]

Devine, P. G. (1989). Stereotypes and prejudice: Their automatic and controlled components. *Journal of Personality and Social Psychology, 56,* 5–18. [18]

Dhanens, T. P., and **Lundy, R. M.** (1975). Hypnotic and waking suggestions and recall. *International Journal of Clinical and Experimental Hypnosis, 23,* 68–79. [5]

Diamond, B. (1969, September). Interview regarding Sirhan Sirhan. *Psychology Today,* pp. 48–55. [7]

Diamond, M. (1984, November). A love affair with the brain. *Psychology Today,* pp. 62–73. [3]

Diamond, R. (1985). Drugs and quality of life: The patient's point of view. *Journal of Clinical Psychiatry, 46,* 29–35. [17]

Dickinson, A. Expectancy theory in animal conditioning. In S. B. Klein and R. R. Mowrer (Eds.), *Contemporary Learning Theory: Pavlovian Conditioning and the State of Traditional Learning Theory.* Hillsdale, NJ: Lawrence Erlbaum. [6]

DiClemente, R. J., Zorn, J., and **Temoshok, L.** (1986). Adolescents and AIDS: A survey of knowledge, attitudes and beliefs about AIDS in San Francisco. *American Journal of Public Health, 87,* 1443–1445. [15]

Diekstra, R. F. W. (1989). Suicidal behavior in adolescents and young adults: The international picture. *Crisis, 10,* 16–35. [17]

Diener, E. (1984). Subjective well-being. *Psychological Bulletin, 95,* 542–575. [11]

Diener, E., Horowitz, J., and **Emmons, R. A.** (1985). Happiness of the very wealthy. *Social Indicators Research, 16,* 263–274. [11]

Diener, E., Sandvik, E., and **Pavot, W.** (1989). Happiness is the frequency, not intensity, of positive versus negative affect. In F. Strack, M. Argyle, and N. Schwarz (Eds.), *The Social Psychology of Subjective Well-Being.* [11]

Dienstbier, R. A. (1978). Emotion-attribution theory: Establishing roots and exploring future perspectives. In S. Murray and R. Levine (Eds.), *Nebraska Symposium on Motivation* (pp. 237–306). Lincoln: University of Nebraska Press. [11]

Digman, J. M. (1990). Personality structure: Emergence of the five-factor model. *Annual Review of Psychology, 41,* 417–440. [13]

Dillard, J. P., Hunter, J. E., and **Burgoon, M.** (1984). Sequential-request persuasive statements: Meta-analysis of foot-in-the-door and door-in-the-face. *Human Communication Research, 10,* 461–488. [19]

Dimberg, U. (1990). Facial electromyography and emotional reactions. (For Distinguished Early Career Contribution to Psychophysiology: Award Address, 1988.) *Psychophysiology, 27*(5), 481–494. [11]

Dimberg, U., and **Ohman, A.** (1983). The effect of directional facial cues on electrodermal conditioning to facial stimuli. *Psychophysiology, 20,* 160–167. [11]

Dinan, T. G., and **Barry, S.** (1989). A comparison of electroconvulsive therapy with a combined lithium and tricyclic combination among depressed tricyclic nonresponders. *Acta. Psychiatr. Scand., 80,* 97–100. [17]

Dion, K., Berscheid, E., and **Walster, E.** (1972). What is beautiful is good. *Journal of Personality and Social Psychology, 24,* 285–290. [18]

Dishman, R. K. (1982). Compliance/adherence in health related exercise. *Health Psychology, 1,* 237–267. [15]

Dittes, J., and **Kelley, II.** (1956). Effects of different conditions of acceptance upon conformity to group norms. *Journal of Abnormal and Social Psychology, 53,* 100–107. [19]

Dixon, N. F. (1971). *Subliminal Perception: The Nature of a Controversy.* London: McGraw-Hill. [4]

Dobson, K. S. (1989). A meta-analysis of the efficacy of cognitive therapy for depression. *Journal of Counseling and Clinical Psychology, 57,* 414–419. [17]

Dodd, J., and **Jessell, T. M.** (1988, November 4). Axon guidance and the patterning of neuronal projections in vertebrates. *Science, 242,* 692–699. [3]

Dodge, K. A. (1986). Social information-processing variables in the development of aggression and altruism in children. In C. Zahn-Waxler, E. M. Cummings, and R. Iannoti (Eds.), *Altruism and Aggression: Biological and Social Origins.* Cambridge, England: Cambridge University Press. [19]

Doerfler, L. A., and **Chaplin, W. F.** (1985). Type III error in research on interpersonal models of depression. *Journal of Abnormal Psychology, 94,* 227–230. [16]

Dohrenwend, B. S., Dohrenwend, B. P., Dodson, M., and **Shrout, P. E.** (1984). Symptoms, hassles, social supports, and life events: Problem of confounded measures. *Journal of Abnormal Psychology, 93,* 222–230. [15]

Dollard, J., Doob, L. W., Miller, N. E., Mowrer, O. H., and **Sears, R. R.** (1939). *Frustration and Aggression.* New Haven: Yale University Press. [19]

Donnelly, J. (1985). Psychosurgery. In H. I. Kaplan and B. J. Sadock (Eds.), *Comprehensive Textbook of Psychiatry* (4th ed., p. 1563). Baltimore: Williams and Williams. [17]

Donnerstein, E., and **Barrett, G.** (1978). The effects of erotic stimuli on male aggression towards females. *Journal of Personality and Social Psychology, 36,* 180–188. [19]

Donnerstein, E., and **Hallam, J.** (1978). Facilitating effects of erotica on aggression against women. *Journal of Personality and Social Psychology, 36,* 1270–1277. [19]

Donnerstein, E., Linz, D., and **Penrod, S.** (1987). *The Question of Pornography.* New York: Free Press. [19]

Dormen, L., and **Edidin, P.** (1989, August). Original spin. *Psychology Today,* pp. 47–52. [8]

Dornbusch, S. M. (1974). To try or not to try. *Stanford Magazine, 2,* 51–54. [12]

Dovidio, J. F., Evans, N., and **Tyler, R. B.** (1986). Racial stereotypes: The contents of their cognitive representations. *Journal of Experimental Social Psychology, 22,* 22–37. [18]

Dovidio, J. F., and **Gaertner, S. L.** (Eds.) (1986). *Prejudice, Discrimination, and Racism.* New York: Academic Press. [18]

Downey, G., Silver, R., and **Wortman, C. B.** (1991). Reconsidering the attribution-adjustment relation: Coping with the loss of an infant from SIDS. *Journal of Personality and Social Psychology.* [16]

Drewnowski, A., Hopkins, S. A., and **Kessler, R. C.** (1988). The prevalence of bulimia nervosa in the U.S. college student population. *American Journal of Public Health, 78,* 1322–1325. [12]

Dryden, W., and **Golden, W. L.** (Eds.). (1986). *Cognitive Behavioral Approaches to Psychotherapy.* London: Harper & Row. [17]

Duffy, E. (1957). The psychological significance of the concept of "arousal" or "activation." *Psychological Review, 64,* 265–275. [12]

Duncan, C. P. (1949). The retroactive effect of electroshock on learning. *Journal of Comparative and Physiological Psychology, 42,* 32–44. [7]

Duncker, K. (1945). On problem-solving. (L. S. Lees, Trans.). *Psychological Monographs, 58*(270). (Original work published 1935.) [8]

Dunkel-Schetter, C., and **Wortman, C. B.** (1982). The interpersonal dynamics of cancer: Problems in social relationships and their impact on the patient. In H. Freedman (Ed.), *Interpersonal Issues in Health Care* (pp. 69–100). New York: Academic Press. [11, 17]

Dunn, J. (1988). Mothers and siblings: Connections between three family relationships. In R. Hinde and J. Stevenson-Hinde (Eds.), *Towards understanding families.* Cambridge, England: Cambridge University Press. [9]

Dunn, J., and **Plomin, R.** (1990). *Separate Lives: Why Siblings Are So Different,* New York: Basic Books. [10, 14]

Dunn, J., and **Stocker, C.** (1989). *Stability and Change in Sibling Relationships between Early and Middle Childhood.* Manuscript. [10]

Dupont, R. L. (1988). The counselor's dilemma: Treating chemical dependence at college. In T. M. Rivinus (Ed.), *Alcoholism/Chemical Dependency and the College Student* (pp. 41–61). New York: Haworth Press. [15]

Durkheim, E. (1897/1951). *Suicide: A Study of Sociology* (J. A. Spaulding and G. Simpson, Trans.). New York: Free Press. [17]

Dusek, D., and **Girdano, D. A.** (1987). *Drugs: A Factual Account.* New York: Random House. [5]

Dutta, R., Schulenberg, E., and **Lair, T. J.** (1986, April). *The Effect of Job Characteristics on Cognitive Abilities and Intellectual Flexibility.* Paper presented at the annual meeting of the Eastern Psychological Association, New York. [9]

Dweck, C. S. (1975). The role of expectations and attributions in the alleviation of learned helplessness. *Journal of Personality and Social Psychology, 31,* 674–685. [1, 12]

Dweck, C. S., Davidson, W., Nelson, S., and **Enna, B.** (1978). Sex differences in learned helplessness: II. The contingencies of evaluative feedback in the classroom; and III. An experimental analysis. *Developmental Psychology, 14,* 268–276. [12, 15]

Dweck, C. S., and **Goetz, M.** (1978). Attributions and learned helplessness. In J. Harvey, W. Ickes, and R. F. Kidd (Eds.), *New Directions in Attribution Research* (Vol. 2). Hillsdale, NJ: Lawrence Erlbaum. [12]

Dweck, C. S., Goetz, T. E., and **Strauss, N.** (1980). Sex differences in learned helplessness: IV. An experimental and naturalistic study of failure generalization and its mediators. *Journal of Personality and Social Psychology, 38,* 441–452. [12]

Dweck, C. S., and **Leggett, E. L.** (1988). A social-cognitive approach to motivation and personality. *Psychological Review, 95,* 256–273. [12]

Dweck, C. S., and **Reppucci, N. D.** (1973). Learned helplessness and reinforcement responsibility in children. *Journal of Personality and Social Psychology, 25,* 109–116. [1]

D'Zurilla, T. J. (1986). *Problem Solving Therapy.* New York: Springer. [17]

Eagly, A. H. (1987). *Sex Differences in Social Behavior: A Social Role Interpretation.* Hillsdale, NJ: Lawrence Erlbaum. [18]

Eagly, A. H., and **Steffen, V. J.** (1986). Gender and aggressive behavior: A meta-analytic review of the social psychology literature. *Psychological Bulletin, 100,* 309–330. [19]

Eastwood, M. R., Whitton, J. L., Kramer, P. M., and **Peter, A. M.** (1985). Infradian rhythms: A comparison of affective disorders and normal persons. *Archives of General Psychiatry, 42,* 297–299. [16]

Ebbinghaus, H. (1913). *Memory: A Contribution to Experimental Psychology* (H. A. Roger and C. E. Bussenius, Trans.). New York: Teachers College. (Original work published 1885.) [7]

Eccles, J. E. (1983). *Sex Differences in Achievement Patterns.* Presented at the Nebraska Symposium on Motivation, Lincoln, NE. [12]

Eccles, J. E., Adler, T., and **Meece, J. L.** (1984). Sex differences in achievement: A test of alternative theories. *Journal of Personality and Social Psychology, 46,* 26–43. [12]

Eccles (Parsons), J., Adler, T. F., Futterman, R., Goff, S. B., Kaczala, C. M., Meece, J. L., and **Midgley, C.** (1983). Expectations, values, and academic behaviors. In J. T. Spence (Ed.), *Achievement and Achievement Motivation* (pp. 75–146). San Francisco: W. H. Freeman. [9]

Eccles, J. S. (1985). Why doesn't Jane run? Sex differences in educational and occupational patterns. In F. D. Horowitz and M. O'Brien (Eds.), *The Gifted and Talented: Developmental Perspectives* (pp. 251–295). Washington, DC: American Psychological Association. [14]

Eccles, J. S. (1987). Gender roles and women's achievement-related decisions. *Psychology of Women Quarterly, 11*(2), 135–171. [12]

Eckardt, M. J., Hartford, T. C., Kaelber, C. T. et al. (1981). Health hazards associated with alcohol consumption. *JAMA, 246,* 648–666. [16]

Eckenrode, J. (1984). Impact of chronic and acute stressors on daily reports of mood. *Journal of Personality and Social Psychology, 46,* 907–918. [15]

Edelman, G. M. (1987). *Neural Darwinism: The Theory of Neuronal Group Selection.* New York: Basic Books. [3]

Edelson, E. (1983, July–August). Scanning the body magnetic. *Science, 83,* pp. 60–65. [3]

Edelwich, J., and **Brodsky, A.** (1980). *Burnout: Stages of Disillusionment in the Helping Professions.* New York: Human Sciences Press. [19]

Educational Testing Service. (1980). *Test Scores and Family Income.* Princeton, NJ: Author. [14]

Edwards, B. (1979). *Drawing on the Right Side of the Brain.* Los Angeles, CA: J. P. Tarcher. [3]

Egeland, B. (1991, February). Paper presented at the annual meeting of the American Association for the Advancement of Science, Washington, DC. [10]

Egeland, J. A., Gerhard, D. S., Pauls, D. L., Sussex, J. N., Kidd, K. K., Allen, C. R., Hostetter, A. M., and **Housman, D. E.** (1987). Bipolar affective disorders linked to DNA markers on chromosome 11. *Nature, 325,* 783–787. [16]

Eibl-Eibesfeldt, I. (1970). *Ethology: The Biology of Behavior.* (E. Klinghammer, Trans.). New York: Holt, Rinehart and Winston. [11]

Eibl-Eibesfeldt, I. (1975). *Ethology: The Biology of Behavior.* New York: Holt, Rinehart and Winston. [12]

Eichorn, D., Hunt, J., and **Honzik, M. P.** (1981). Experience, personality, and IQ: Adolescence to middle age. In D. Eichorn, J. Clausen, N. Haan, M. Honzik, and P. Mussen (Eds.), *Present and Past in Middle Life.* New York: Academic Press. [9]

Eimas, P. D., Siqueland, E. R., Jusczyk, P. and **Vigorito, J.** (1971). Speech perception in infants. *Science, 171,* 303–306. [9]

Eisdorfer, C., Axelrod, S., and **Wilkie, F.** (1963). Stimulus exposure time as a factor in serial learning in an aged sample. *Journal of Abnormal and Social Psychology, 67,* 594–600. [9]

Eisenberger, R., Cotterell, N., and **Marvel, J.** (1987). Reciprocation ideology. *Journal of Personality and Social Psychology, 53,* 743–750. [19]

Ekman, P. (1982). *Emotion in the Human Face* (2nd ed.). New York: Cambridge University Press. [11]

Ekman, P. (1985). *Telling Lies: Clues to Deceit in the Marketplace, Marriage, and Politics.* New York: Norton. [11]

Ekman, P., and **Friesen, W. V.** (1969). The repertoire of nonverbal behavior categories, origins, usage, and coding. *Semiotica, 1,* 49–98. [11]

Ekman, P., and **Friesen, W. V.** (1974). Detecting deception from body or face. *Journal of Personality and Social Psychology, 29,* 288. [11]

Ekman, P., and **Friesen, W. V.** (1986). A new pan-cultural facial expression of emotion. *Motivation and Emotion, 10,* 159–169. [11]

Elias, J. Z. (1989). The changing American scene in the use of projective techniques: An overview. *British Journal of Projective Psychology, 34*(2), 31–39. [14]

Eliot, R. S., and **Buell, J. C.** (1983). The role of the central nervous system in sudden cardiac death. In T. M. Dembroski, T. Schmidt, and G. Blunchen (Eds.), *Behavioral Bases of Coronary-Prone Behavior.* New York: Krager. [13]

Elkin, I., Shea, M. T., Watkins, J. T., Imber, S. D., Sotsky, S. M., Collins, J. F., Glass, D. R., Pilkonis, P. A., Leber, W. R., Docherty, J. P., Fiester, S. J., and **Parloff, M. B.** (1989). National institute of mental health treatment of depression collaborative research program. *Archives of General Psychiatry, 46,* 971–982. [17]

Elkind, D. (1961). Children's discovery of the conservation of mass, weight, and volume: Piaget replications studies II. *Journal of Genetic Psychology, 98,* 37–46. [9]

Elkind, D. (1981). *Children and Adolescents: Interpretive Essays on Jean Piaget.* New York: Oxford University Press. [15]

Ellis, A. (1962). *Reason and Emotion in Psychotherapy.* Secaucus, NJ: Lyle Stuart. [17]

Ellis, H. C., and **Hunt, R. R.** (1989).

Fundamentals of Human Memory and Cognition (4th ed.). Dubuque: Brown. [7]

Emerick, C. D. (1987). Alcoholics anonymous: Affiliation processes and effectiveness as treatment. *Alcoholism: Clinical and Experimental Research, 11,* 416–423. [17]

Emmons, R. A., and Diener, E. (1985). Factors predicting satisfaction judgments: A comparative examination. *Social Indicators Research, 16,* 157–167. [11]

Empson, J., and **Clarke, P.** (1970). Rapid eye movements and remembering. *Nature, 227,* 287–288. [5]

Engen, T., Lipsitt, L. P., and **Kaye, H.** (1963). Olfactory responses and adaptation in the human neonate. *Journal of Comparative and Physiological Psychology, 56,* 73–77. [9]

Epstein, A. N., and **Teitelbaum, P.** (1962). Regulation of food intake in the absence of taste, smell and other oropharyngeal sensations. *Journal of Comparative and Physiological Psychology, 55,* 753–759. [12]

Epstein, S. (1979). The ecological study of emotions in humans. In K. Blankstein (Ed.), *Advances in the Study of Communication and Affect.* New York: Plenum. [13]

Epstein, S. (1983). Aggregation and beyond: Some basic issues on the prediction of behavior. *Journal of Personality, 51,* 360–392. [13]

Erber, J. T., Herman, J., and **Botwinick, J.** (1980). The effects of encoding instructions on recall and recognition memory. *Experimental Aging Research, 6,* 341–348. [9]

Erdelyi, M. H. (1985). *Psychoanalysis: Freud's Cognitive Psychology.* New York: W. H. Freeman. [5]

Erdelyi, M. H., and **Kleinbard, J.** (1978). Has Ebbinghaus decayed with time? The growth of recall (hyperamnesia) over days. *Journal of Experimental Psychology: Human Learning and Memory, 4,* 275–289. [5]

Erdley, C. A., and **D'Agostino, P. R.** (1988). Cognitive and affective components of automatic priming effects. *Journal of Personality and Social Psychology, 54,* 741–747. [18]

Erickson, R. P. (1984). On the neural bases of behavior. *American Scientist, 72,* 233–241. [4]

Ericsson, K. A., Chase, W. G., and **Faloon, S.** (1980). Acquisition of a memory skill. *Science, 208,* 1181–1182. [7]

Erikson, E. H. (1950). *Childhood and Society.* New York: Norton. [10]

Eron, L. D. (1982). Parent-child interaction, television, violence, and aggression of children. *American Psychologist, 37*(2), 197–211. [2]

Ervin, S. (1964). Imitation and structural change in children's language. In E. H. Lenneberg (Ed.), *New Directions in the Study of Language.* Cambridge, MA: MIT Press. [9]

Evans, J. St. B. T. (1982). On statistical intuitions and inferential rules: A discussion of Kahneman and Tversky. *Cognition, 12,* 319–323. [8]

Evans, R. (1980). Behavioral medicine: A new applied challenge to social psychologists. In L. Bickman (Ed.). *Applied Social Psychology Annual* (Vol. 1). Beverly Hills, CA: Sage Publications. [18]

Everly, G. S., Jr. *A Clinical Guide to the Treatment of the Human Stress Response.* New York: Plenum. [15]

Eysenck, H. J. (1967). *The Biological Basis of Personality.* Springfield, IL: Charles C. Thomas. [12]

Eysenck, H. J. (1970). *The Structure of Human Personality.* London: Methuen. [13]

Fabricius, W. V., and **Wellman, H.** (1983). Children's understanding of retrieval cue utilization. *Developmental Psychology, 19,* 14–21. [9]

Falloon, I. R. (1988). Behavioral family management in coping with functional psychosis: Principles, practice, and recent developments. *International Journal of Mental Health, 17*(1), 35–47. [16]

Falloon, I. R. H., Boyd, J. L., McGill, C. W., Razani, J., Moss, H. B., and **Gilderman, A. N.** (1982). Family management in the prevention of exacerbation of schizophrenia: A controlled study. *New England Journal of Medicine, 306,* 1437–1440. [17]

Falloon, I. R. H., Boyd, J. L., McGill, C. W., Williamson, M., Razani, J., Moss, H. B., Gilderman, A. N., and **Simpson, G. M.** (1985). Family management in the prevention of morbidity of schizophrenia. *Archives of General Psychiatry, 42,* 887–896. [17]

Fancier, R. E. (1985). *The Intelligence Men: Makers of the IQ Controversy.* New York: Norton. [14]

Farina, A., Gliha, D., Boudreau, L. A., Allen, J. G., and **Sherman, M.** (1971). Mental illness and the impact of believing others know about it. *Journal of Abnormal Psychology, 77,* 1–5. [19]

Fawcett, J. (undated). *Before It's Too Late: What to Do When Someone You Know Attempts Suicide.* American Association of Suicidology, prepared in cooperation with Merck, Sharp and Dohme Health Information Services, West Point, PA. [15]

Fazio, R. H. (1990). Multiple processes by which attitudes guide behavior: The MODE model as an integrative framework. In M. P. Zanna (Ed.), *Advances in Experimental Social Psychology* (Vol. 23, pp. 75–109). New York: Academic Press. [18]

Fazio, R. H., and **Zanna, M. P.** (1981). Direct experience and attitude-behavior consistency. In L. Berkowitz (Ed.), *Advances in Experimental Social Psychology, 14,* 161–202. New York: Academic Press. [18]

Fechner, G. T. (1860). *Elemente der Psychophysik.* Leipzig: Breitkopf und Härtel. [4]

Federal Bureau of Investigation. (1987). Uniform crime reports: Arrests, by sex. In *The World Almanac and Book of Facts* (p. 820). New York: World Almanac. [19]

Feinberg, I., and **Fein, G.** (1982, February 26). Computer-detected patterns of electroencephalographic delta activity during and after extended sleep. *Science, 215,* 1131–1133. [5]

Feinberg, T. E., Rifkin, A., Schaffer, C., and **Walker, E.** (1986). Facial discrimination and emotional recognition in schizophrenia and affective disorders. *Archives of General Psychiatry, 43,* 276–279. [16]

Feingold, A. (1988, February). Cognitive gender differences are disappearing. *American Psychologist, 43*(2), 95–103. [9]

Feldman, R. S., Devin-Sheehan, L., and Allen, V. L. (1978). Nonverbal clues as indicators of verbal dissembling. *American Educational Research Journal, 15,* 217–231. [18]

Felton, B. J., Revenson, T. A., and Hinrichsen, G. A. (1984). Stress and coping in the explanation of psychological adjustment among chronically ill adults. *Social Science and Medicine, 18,* 889–898. [15]

Fennema, E., and Sherman, J. (1977). Sex-related differences in mathematics achievement, spatial visualization and affective factors. *American Educational Research Journal, 14,* 51–71. [12]

Fennema, E., and Sherman, J. (1978). Sex-related differences in mathematics achievement and related factors: A further study. *Journal for Research in Mathematics Education, 9,* 189–203. [12]

Festinger, L. (1957). *A Theory of Cognitive Dissonance.* Stanford, CA: Stanford University Press. [18]

Festinger, L., and Carlsmith, J. M. (1959). Cognitive consequences of forced compliance. *Journal of Abnormal and Social Psychology, 58,* 203–210. [18]

Festinger, L., Riecken, II. W., and Schachter, S. (1956). *When Prophecy Fails.* Minneapolis: University of Minnesota. [2]

Festinger, L., Schachter, S., and Back, K. (1950). *Social Pressures in Informal Groups: A Study of Human Factors in Housing.* New York: Harper & Row. [18]

Field, T. M., Woodson, R., Greenberg, R., and Cohen, D. (1982). Discrimination and imitation of facial expressions by neonates. *Science, 218,* 179–181. [9]

Figley, C. R. (1989). *Helping Traumatized Families.* San Francisco: Jossey-Bass. [10]

Fillion, T. J., and Blass, E. M. (1986, February 14). Infantile experience with suckling odors determines adult sexual behavior in male rats. *Science, 231,* 729–731. [12]

Fincham, F. D., Beach, S., and Nelson, G. (1987). Attribution processes in distressed and nondistressed couples: 3. Causal and responsibility attributions for spouse and behavior. *Cognitive Therapy and Research, 11,* 71–86. [17]

Fincham, F. D., and Bradbury, T. (1988). The impact of attributions in marriage: Empirical and conceptual foundations. *British Journal of Clinical Psychology, 27,* 77–90. [17]

Fine, A. (1986, August). Transplantation in the central nervous system. *Scientific American,* pp. 52–58B. [3]

Fingerer, M. (1973). Psychological sequelae of abortion: Anxiety and depression. *Journal of Community Psychology, 1,* 221–225. [15]

Finman, R., and Berkowitz, L. (1989). Some factors influencing the effect of depressed mood on anger and overt hostility toward another. *Journal of Research in Personality, 23,* 70–84. [19]

Fischer, C. L., Daniels, J. C., Levin, S. L., Kimzey, S. L., Cobb, E. K., and Ritzman, W. E. (1972). Effects of the spaceflight environment on man's immune system: II. Lymphocyte counts and reactivity. *Aerospace Medicine, 43,* 1122–1125. [15]

Fishbein, M., and Ajzen, I. (1975). *Belief, Attitude, Intention, and Behavior: An Introduction to Theory and Research.* Reading, MA: Addison-Wesley. [17]

Fisher, A. E. (1956). Maternal and sexual behavior induced by intracranial chemical stimulation. *Science, 124,* 228–229. [12]

Fisher, A. E. (1967). Chemical stimulation of the brain. In *Psychobiology: The Biological Bases of Behavior.* San Francisco: W. H. Freeman. [12]

Fisher, S., and Greenburg, R. P. (1977). *The Scientific Credibility of Freud's Theories and Therapy.* New York: Basic Books. [13]

Fiske, S. T., and Taylor, S. E. (1984). *Social Cognition.* New York: Random House. [18]

Fixsen, D. L., Phillips, E. A., and Wolf, M. M. (1976). The teaching-family model of group home treatment. In W. E. Craighead, A. E. Kazdin, and M. J. Mahoney (Eds.), *Behavior Modification: Principles, Issues, and Applications.* Boston: Houghton Mifflin. [17]

Flaherty, C. F. (1985). *Animal Learning and Cognition.* New York: Knopf. [6]

Flavell, J. H. (1986). Development of children's knowledge about the appearance–reality distinction. Distinguished Scientific Contributions Award Address. *American Psychologist, 41,* 418–425. [1]

Flavell, J. H., Shipstead, S. G., and Croft, K. (1978). Young children's knowledge about visual perception: Hiding objects from others. *Child Development, 49,* 1208–1211. [9]

Flavell, J. H., and Wellman, H. M. (1977). Meta-memory. In R. V. Kail, Jr., and J. W. Hagen (Eds.), *Perspectives on the Development of Memory and Cognition* (pp. 3–33). Hillsdale, NJ: Lawrence Erlbaum. [9]

Fleming, I., Baum, A., Davidson, L. M., Rectanus, E., and McArdle, S. (1987). Chronic stress as a factor in physiologic reactivity to challenge. *Health Psychology, 6,* 221–237. [15]

Flora, J. A., Maibach, E. W., and Maccoby, N. (1989). The role of the media across four levels of health promotion intervention. *Annual Review of Public Health, 10,* 181–201. [18]

Flynn, J. P., Vanegas, H., Foote, W., and Edwards, S. (1970). Neural mechanisms involved in a cat's attack on a rat. In R. E. Whalen (Ed.), *Neural Control of Behavior* (pp. 135–173). New York: Academic Press. [11]

Folkman, S., Lazarus, R. S., Dunkel-Schetter, C., DeLongis, A., and Gruen, R. J. (1986). Dynamics of a stressful encounter: Cognitive appraisal, coping, and encounter outcomes. *Journal of Personality and Social Psychology, 50,* 992–1003. [15]

Fordyce, M. W. (1988). A review of results on the happiness measures: A 60-second index of happiness and mental health, *Social Indicators Research, 20,* 355–381. [11]

Fordyce, W. E. (1988, April). Pain and suffering: A reappraisal. *American Psychologist, 43*(4), 276–283. [4]

Forehand, R., Long, N., and Brody, G. (1988). Divorce and marital conflict: Relationship to adolescent competence and adjustment in early adolescence. In E. M. Hetherington and J. D. Arasteh (Eds.), *Impact of Divorce, Single Parenting, and Stepparenting on Children* (pp. 155–167). Hillsdale, NJ: Lawrence Erlbaum. [10]

Foulkes, D. (1964). Theories of dream formation and recent studies of sleep consciousness. *Psychological Bulletin, 62,* 236–247. [5]

Fowles, D. C., Christie, M. J., Edelberg, R., Grings, W. W., Lykken, D. T., and **Venables, P. H.** (1981). Public recommendations for electrodermal measurements. Committee Report. *Psychophysiology,* pp. 232–239. [11]

Fox, L. H., and **Washington, J.** (1985). Programs for the gifted and talented: Past, present, and future. In F. D. Horowitz and M. O'Brien (Eds.), *The Gifted and Talented: Developmental Perspectives* (pp. 197–221). Washington, DC: American Psychological Association. [14]

Foy, D. W., Carroll, E. M., and **Donahoe, C. P.** (in press). Etiological factors in the development of PTSD in clinical samples of combat veterans. *Journal of Consulting and Clinical Psychology.* [16]

Foy, D. W., Resnick, H. S., Sipprelle, R. C., and **Carroll, E. M.** (1987). Premilitary, military, and postmilitary factors in the development of combat-related posttraumatic stress disorder. *Behavior Therapist, 10,* 3–9. [16]

Frankel, M. T. (1988). Sex differences. In D. F. Bjorklund (Ed.), *Children's Thinking: Developmental Functions and Individual Differences* (pp. 285–299). Pacific Grove, CA: Brooks/Cole. [9]

Frankenburg, W. K. (1978). Denver Developmental Screening Test. Denver: University of Colorado Medical Center.

Frederiksen, N., (1986). Toward a broader conception of human intelligence. *American Psychologist, 41*(4), 445–452. [14]

Freedman, J. L. (1965). Long-term behavioral effects of cognitive dissonance. *Journal of Experimental Social Psychology, 1,* 145–155. [18]

Freedman, J. L. (1984). Effect of television violence on aggressiveness. *Psychological Bulletin, 96,* 227–246. [2]

Freedman, J. L., and **Fraser, S. C.** (1966). Compliance without pressure: The foot-in-the-door technique. *Journal of Personality and Social Psychology, 4,* 195–202. [19]

Freud, S. (1900). *The Interpretation of Dreams* (J. Strachey, Ed. and Trans.). New York: Avon, 1980. [5, 13]

Freud, S. (1917). Mourning and melancholia. In E. Jones, M.D. (Ed.), *Collected Papers* (Vol. 4, pp. 152–170). London: Hogarth Press/Institute of Psycho-Analysis, 1950. [16]

Freud, S. (1920). *Beyond the Pleasure Principle* (J. Strachey, Ed. and Trans.). New York: Norton, 1975. [13]

Freud, S. (1923). *The Ego and the Id.* London: Hogarth Press, 1947. [13]

Freud, S. (1925). Some physical consequences of the anatomical distinction between the sexes. In J. Strachey (Ed. and Trans.). *The Complete Psychological Works: Standard Edition* (Vol. 19, pp. 258, 327). New York: Norton, 1976. [13]

Freud, S. (1930). *Civilization and Its Discontents* (J. Strachey, Ed. and Trans.). New York: Norton, 1963. [13, 19]

Freud, S. (1935). *A General Introduction to Psychoanalysis.* New York: Washington Square Press. [13]

Friedman, M., and **Rosenman, R. H.** (1974). *Type A Behavior and Your Heart.* New York: Knopf. [13]

Friedman, M., Thoresen, C. E., Gill, J. J., Ulmer, D., Thompson, L., Powell, L., Price, A., Elek, S. R., Rabin, D. D., Breall, W. S., Piaget, G., Dixon, T., Bourg, E., Levy, R., and **Tasto, D. I.** (1984). Feasibility of altering Type A behavior pattern after myocardial infarction. *Circulation, 66,* 83–92. [13]

Fries, J. F., and **Crapo, L. M.** (1981). *Vitality and Aging: Implications of the Rectangular Curve.* San Francisco: W. H. Freeman. [9]

Frieze, I. H., Parsons, J. E., Johnson, R. B., Ruble, D. N., and **Zellman, G. L.** (1979). *Women and Sex Roles: A Social Psychological Perspective.* New York: Norton. [12]

Frijda, N. H. (1986). *The Emotions.* New York: Cambridge University Press. [11]

Frijda, N. H. (1988). The laws of emotion. *American Psychologist, 43*(5), 349–358. [11]

Frijda, N. H., Kuipers, P., and **ter Schure, E.** (1989). Relations among emotion, appraisal, and emotion action tendencies. *Journal of Personality and Social Psychology, 57*(2), 212–228. [11]

Frye, J. S., and **Stockton, R. A.** (1982). Discriminant analysis of posttraumatic stress disorder among a group of Viet Nam veterans. *American Journal of Psychiatry, 139,* 52–56. [15]

Furstenberg, F. F. (1988). Child care after divorce and remarriage. In E. M. Hetherington and J. D. Arasteh (Eds.), *Impact of Divorce, Single Parenting, and Stepparenting on Children* (pp. 245–261). Hillsdale, NJ: Lawrence Erlbaum. [10]

Gackenbach, J., and **Bosveld, J.** (1989, October). Take control of your dreams. *Psychology Today,* pp. 27–32. [5]

Gale, A. (1969). "Stimulus hunger": Individual differences in operant strategy in a button-pressing task. *Behaviour Research and Therapy, 7,* 263–274. [13]

Galin, D., and **Ornstein, R. E.** (1975). Hemispheric specialization and the duality of consciousness. In H. J. Widroe (Ed.), *Human Behavior and Brain Function,* Springfield, IL: C. C. Thomas. [3]

Gallup Organization, Inc. (1979). *Women's Attitudes Regarding Breast Cancer.* Survey conducted for the American Cancer Society. [15]

Gangestad, S. W., and **Simpson, J. A.** (1990, March). Toward an evolutionary history of female sociosexual variation. *Journal of Personality, 58*(1), 69–96. [13]

Garbarino, J., and **Garbarino, A.** (1986). *Emotional Maltreatment of Children.* Chicago: National Commission for Prevention of Child Abuse. [10]

Garbarino, J., Guttman, E., and **Seeley, J. W.** (1986). *The Psychologically Battered Child,* San Francisco: Jossey-Bass. [10]

Garcia, J., Hankins, W. G., and **Rusiniak, K. W.** (1974). Behavioral regulation of the milieu interne in man and rat. *Science, 185,* 824–831. [6]

Garcia, J., Kimeldorf, D. J., and **Hunt, E. L.** (1961). The use of ionizing radiation as a motivating stimulus. *Psychological Review, 68,* 383. [6]

Garcia, J., Kimeldorf, D. J., Hunt, E. L., and **Davies, B. P.** (1956). Food and water consumption of rats during exposure to gamma radiation. *Radiation Research, 4,* 33–41. [6]

Garcia, J., and **Koelling, R. A.** (1966). Relation of cue to consequence in avoidance learning. *Psychonometric Science, 4,* 123–124. [6]

Gardner, B. T., and **Gardner, R. A.** (1972). Two-way communication with an infant chimpanzee. In A. M. Schrier and F. Stollnitz (Eds.), *Behavior of Nonhuman Primates* (Vol. 4). New York: Academic Press. [8]

Gardner, E. (1975). *Fundamentals of Neurology.* Philadelphia: W. B. Saunders. [3]

Gardner, H. (1982). *Developmental Psychology* (2nd ed.). Boston: Little, Brown, 1982. [8]

Gardner, H. (1983). *Frames of Mind: The Theory of Multiple Intelligences.* New York: Basic Books. [14]

Gardner, H. (1985). *The Mind's New Science.* New York: Cambridge University Press. [9]

Gardner, L. I. (1972). Deprivation dwarfism. *Scientific American, 227,* 76–82. [9]

Garfield, S. L., and **Bergin, A. E.** (Eds.). (1986). *Handbook of Psychotherapy and Behavior Change* (3rd ed.). New York: Wiley. [17]

Gazzaniga, M. S. (1989, September 1). Organization of the human brain. *Science, 245,* 947–952. [3]

Geer, J. H., and **Head, S.** (1990). The sexual response system. In J. T. Cacioppo and L. G. Tassinary (Eds.), *Principles of Psychophysiology: Physical, Social, and Inferential Elements.* Cambridge: Cambridge University Press. [12]

Geisler, C. (1986). Repression: A psychoanalytic perspective revisited. *Psychoanalysis and Contemporary Thought, 8*(2), 253–298. [13]

Geldard, F. A. (1972). *The Human Senses* (2nd ed.). New York: Wiley. [4]

Gelman, D. (1989, August 14). Dreams on the couch. *Newsweek,* pp. 45–47. [5]

Gelman, R. (1972). Logical capacity of very young children: Number invariance rules. *Child Development, 43,* 75–90. [9]

Gerbner, G., and **Gross, L.** (1976, Spring). Living with television: The violence profile. *Journal of Communications, 26,* 172–199. [6]

Gerbner, G., Gross, L., Morgan, M., and **Signorielli, N.** (1986). Living with television: The dynamics of the cultivation process. In J. Bryant and D. Zillman (Eds.), *Perspectives on Media Effects.* Hillsdale, NJ: Lawrence Erlbaum. [19]

Geschwind, N. (1979). Specialization of the human brain. *Scientific American, 241,* 180–199. [3]

Gevarter, W. B. (1985). *Intelligent Machines: An Introductory Perspective on Artificial Intelligence and Robotics.* Englewood Cliffs, NJ: Prentice-Hall. [4]

Ghiselin, B. (Ed.). (1952). *The Creative Process.* Berkeley: University of California Press. [8]

Giantonio, G. W., Lund, N. L., and **Gerall, A. A.** (1970). Effects of diencephalic and rhinencephalic lesions on the male rat's sexual behaviour. *Journal of Comparative Physiological Psychology, 73,* 38–46. [12]

Gibbons, F. X., and **Kassin, S. M.** (1987). Information consistency and perceptual set: Overcoming the mental retardation "schema." *Journal of Applied Social Psychology, 17,* 810–827. [18]

Gibbs, J., and **Schnell, S.** (1986, April). *Moral Development Versus Socialization: A Critique of the Controversy.* Paper presented at the biennial meeting of the Society for Research in Child Development, Toronto. [10]

Gibson, J. J. (1950). *The Perception of the Visual World.* Boston: Houghton Mifflin. [4]

Gibson, J. J. (1966). *The Senses Considered as Perceptual Systems.* Boston: Houghton Mifflin. [4]

Gibson, J. J. (1979). *The Ecological Approach to Visual Perception.* Boston: Houghton Mifflin. [4]

Gigerenzer, G., Hell, W., and **Blank, H.** (1988). Presentation and content: The use of base rates as a continuous variable. *Journal of Experimental Psychology: Human Perception and Performance, 14,* 513–525. [8]

Gilbert, D. T. (1989). Thinking lightly about others: Automatic components of the social inference process. In J. S. Uleman and J. A. Bargh (Eds.), *Unintended Thought* (pp. 189–211). New York: Guilford. [18]

Gilbert, D. T., and **Jones, E. E.** (1986). Perceiver-induced constraint: Interpretations of self-generated reality. *Journal of Personality and Social Psychology, 50,* 269–280. [18]

Gilbert, D. T., Pelham, B., and **Krull, D.** (1988). *Journal of Personality and Social Psychology, 54*(5), 733–740. [18]

Gilbert, L. A., Waldroop, J. A., and **Deutsch, C. J.** (1981). Masculine and feminine stereotypes and adjustment: A reanalysis. *Psychology of Women Quarterly, 5,* 790–794. [18]

Gilligan, C. (1977). In a different voice: Women's conceptions of self and of morality. *Harvard Educational Review, 47,* 481–517. [10]

Gilligan, C. (1982). *In a Different Voice: Psychological Theory and Women's Development.* Cambridge, MA: Harvard University Press. [10]

Gilligan, C. (1989). *Mapping the Moral Domain.* Cambridge, MA: Harvard University Press. [10]

Gilligan, S. G., and **Bower, G. H.** (1984). Cognitive consequences of emotional arousal. In C. Izard, J. Kagan, and R. Zajonc (Eds.), *Emotions, Cognitions, and Behavior.* New York: Cambridge University Press. [7]

Glantz, M. D. (Ed.). (1984). *Correlates and Consequences of Marijuana Use.* Washington, DC: Department of Health and Human Services. [5]

Glaser, R., Kiecolt-Glaser, J. K., Stout, J. C., Tarr, K. L., Speicher, C. E., and **Holliday, J. E.** (1985). Stress-related impairments in cellular immunity. *Psychiatry Research, 16,* 233–239. [15]

Glaser, R., Rice, J., Speicher, C. E., Stout, J. C., and **Kiecolt-Glaser, J. K.** (1986). Stress depresses interferon production by leukocytes concomitant with a decrease in natural killer cell activity. *Behavioral Neuroscience, 100,* 675–678. [15]

Glasgow, R. E., and **Lichtenstein, E.** (1987). Long-term Effects of behavioral smoking cessation interventions. *Behavior Therapy, 18,* 297–324. [15]

Glenberg, A., Smith, S. M., and Green, C. (1977). Type I rehearsal: Maintenance and more. *Journal of Verbal Learning and Verbal Behavior, 11,* 403–416. [7]

Glenn, N. D., and Weaver, C. N. (1981). The contribution of marital happiness to global happiness. *Journal of Marriage and the Family, 43,* 161–168. [11]

Glick, I. O., Weiss, R. S., and Parkes, C. M. (1974). *The First Year of Bereavement.* New York: Wiley. [11]

Glisky, E. L., Schacter, D. L., and Tulving, E. (1986). Computer learning by memory-impaired patients: Acquisition and retention of complex knowledge, *Neuropsychologia, 24,* 313–328. [3]

Goddard, G. V. (1964). Functions of the amygdala. *Psychological Bulletin, 62,* 89–109. [3]

Goddard, G. V. (1980). Component properties of the memory machine: Hebb revisited. In P. W. Jusczyk and R. M. Klein (Eds.), *The Nature of Thought: Essays in Honour of D. O. Hebb* (pp. 231–247). Hillsdale, NJ: Lawrence Erlbaum. [7]

Gold, R. G., and Gold, S. R. (1982). Sex differences in actual daydream content. *Journal of Mental Imagery, 6,* 109–112. [5]

Goldberger, L. (1982). Sensory deprivation and overload. In L. Goldberger and S. Breznitz (Eds.), *Handbook of Stress: Theoretical and Clinical Aspects.* New York: Free Press. [12]

Goldfried, M. R., Greenberg, L. S., and Marmar, C. (1990). Individual psychotherapy: Process and outcome. *Annual Review of Psychology, 41,* 659–688. [17]

Goldsmith and Campos. (1991). *Child Development,* 1944–1964. [10]

Goldstein, E. B. (1984). *Sensation and Perception* (2nd ed.). Belmont, CA: Wadsworth. [5]

Goldstein, M. J., Baker, B. L., and Jamison, K. R. (1980). *Abnormal Psychology: Experiences, Origins and Interventions.* Boston: Little, Brown. [16]

Goleman, D. (1977). *The Varieties of the Meditative Experience.* New York: Dutton. [5]

Goleman, D. Studies on development of empathy challenge some old assumptions. *The New York Times.* [2]

Goodenough, F. L. (1932). Expression of the emotions in a blind-deaf child. *Journal of Abnormal and Social Psychology, 27,* 328–333. [11]

Goodman, C. S., and Bastiani, M. J. (1984). How embryonic nerve cells recognize one another. *Scientific American, 251,* 58–66. [3]

Gordon, M. (1991). *Good Boys and Dead Girls.* New York: Viking. [15]

Gordon, W. C. (1989). *Learning and Memory.* Pacific Grove, CA: Brooks/Cole. [6]

Gortmaker, S. L., Eckenrode, J., and Gore, S. (1982). Stress and the utilization of health services: A time series and cross-sectional analysis. *Journal of Health and Social Behavior, 23,* 25–38. [15]

Gotlib, I. H., and Robinson, L. A. (1982). Responses to depressed individuals: Discrepancies between self-reports and observer-rated behavior. *Journal of Abnormal Psychology.* [16]

Gottesman, I. (1978). Schizophrenia and genetics: Where are we? Are you sure? In L. C. Wynne, R. L. Cromwell, and S. Matthysse (Eds.), *The Nature of Schizophrenia: New Approaches to Research and Treatment.* New York: Wiley. [16]

Gottesman, I. I., and Bertelsen, A. (1989, October). *Confirming Unexpressed Genotypes for Schizophrenia, Archives of General Psychiatry, 46,* 867–872. [16]

Gottesman, I. I., McGuffin, P., and Farmer, A. E. (1987). Clinical genetics as clues to the "real" genetics of schizophrenia. *Schizophrenia Bulletin, 13,* 23–47. [16]

Gottesman, I., and Shields, J. (1976). A critical review of recent adoption, twin and family studies of schizophrenia: Behavioral genetics perspectives. *Schizophrenia Bulletin, 2*(3), 360–398. [16]

Gottesman, I., and Shields, J. (1982). *Schizophrenia and Genetics: A Twin Study Vantage Point.* New York: Academic Press. [16]

Gottesman, I. I., Shields, J., and Hanson, D. R. (1982). *Schizophrenia: The Epigenetic Puzzle.* New York: Cambridge University Press. [16]

Gould, J. L. (1986). The biology of learning. *Annual Review of Psychology, 37,* 163–192. [6]

Gould, R. L. (1972). The phases of adult life: A study in developmental psychology. *American Journal of Psychiatry, 129,* 521–531. [10]

Gould, R. L. (1978). *Transformations.* New York: Simon and Schuster. [10]

Gould, S. J. (1985, June). The median isn't the message. *Discover,* pp. 40–42. [2]

Graf, P., and Schacter, D. L. (1985). Implicit and explicit memory for new associations in normal and amnesic subjects. *Journal of Experimental Psychology: Learning, Memory, and Cognition, 11,* 501–518. [7]

Graham, K. R. (1986). Explaining "virtuoso" hypnotic performance. *Behavioral and Brain Sciences, 9*(3), 473–474. [5]

Gray, S. H. (1982). Exposure to pornography and aggression toward women: The case of the angry male. *Social Problems, 29,* 387–398. [12]

Greco, C., Rovee-Collier, C., Hayne, H., Griesler, P., and Earley, L. (1986). Ontogeny of early event memory: I Forgetting and retrieval by 2- and 3-month olds. *Infant Behavior and Development, 9,* 441–460. [9]

Green, D. M., and Swets, J. A. (1966). *Signal Detection Theory and Psychophysics.* New York: Wiley. [4]

Greenberg, M. A., and Stone, A. A. (1990). Writing about disclosed versus undisclosed traumas: Health and mood effects. *Health Psychology, 9,* 114–115. [15]

Greenberg, P. F. (1977). The thrillseekers. *Human Behavior, 6,* 17–21. [12]

Greenough, W. T. (1986). What's special about development? Thoughts on the bases of experience-sensitive synaptic plasticity. In W. T. Greenough and J. M. Juraska (Eds.), *Developmental Neuropsychology* (pp. 387–408). New York: Academic Press. [3]

Greenwald, A. G., Spangenberg, E. R., Pratkanis, A. R., and Eskenazi, J. (1991). Double-blind tests of subliminal self-help audiotapes. *Psychological Science, 2,* 119–122. [4]

Gregory, R. L. (1970). *The Intelligent Eye.* New York: McGraw-Hill. [4]

Gregory, R. L. (1973). *Eye and Brain: The Physiology of Seeing.* New York: McGraw-Hill. [4]

Gribbin, K., Schaie, K. W., and **Parham, I. A.** (1980). Complexity of life style and maintenance of intellectual abilities. *Journal of Social Issues, 36,* 47–61. [9]

Grisham, J. C. (1987, June). "Hypnotically Refreshed" Testimony. *APA Monitor,* p. 41. [5]

Grossman, H. J. (1983). *Classification in Mental Retardation.* Washington, DC: American Association of Mental Deficiency. [14]

Grossman, S. P. (1975). Role of the hypothalamus in the regulation of food and water intake. *Psychological Review, 82,* 200–224. [12]

Gruber, H. (1981). *Darwin on Man* (2nd ed.). Chicago: University of Chicago Press. [8]

Guerin, B. (1986). Mere presence effects on humans: A review. *Journal of Personality and Social Psychology, 22,* 38–77. [19]

Guilford, J. P. (1959). *Personality.* New York: McGraw-Hill. [13]

Guilford, J. P. (1967). *The Nature of Human Intelligence.* New York: McGraw-Hill. [8]

Guilford, J. P. (1982). Cognitive psychology's ambiguity: Some suggested remedies. *Psychological Review, 89,* 48. [14]

Gur, R. C., and **Reivich, M.** (1980). Cognitive task-effects on hemispheric blood flow in humans: Evidence for individual differences in hemispheric activation. *Brain and Language, 9,* 78–92. [3]

Gurin, G., Veroff, J., and **Feld, S.** (1960). *Americans View Their Mental Health: A Nationwide Interview Survey.* New York: Basic Books. [11, 16]

Haaga, D. A., and **Davisson, G. C.** (1989). Outcome studies of rational-emotive therapy. In M. E. Bernard and R. DiGiuseppe (Eds.), *Inside Rational-Emotive Therapy.* New York: Academic Press. [17]

Haber, R. N. (1969). Eidetic images. *Scientific American, 220,* 36–44. [6]

Haber, R. N. (1979). Twenty years of haunting eidetic imagery: Where's the ghost? *The Behavioral and Brain Sciences, 2,* 583–629. [6]

Hackman, J. R. (1986). The design of work teams. In J. Lorsch (Ed.), *Handbook of Organizational Behavior.* Englewood Cliffs, NJ: Prentice-Hall. [19]

Haley, J. (1973). *Uncommon Therapy.* New York: Norton. [16]

Haley, J. (1980). *Leaving Home: The Therapy of Disturbed Young People.* New York: McGraw-Hill. [17]

Haley, S. A. (1978). Treatment implications of post-combat stress response syndromes for mental health professionals. In C. R. Figley (Ed.), *Stress Disorders Among Vietnam Veterans.* New York: Brunner/Mazel. [16]

Hall, C. S., and **Van de Castle, R. L.** (1966). *The Content Analysis of Dreams.* New York: Appleton-Century-Crofts. [5]

Hall, J. A., Rosenthal, R., Archer, D., Di Matteo, M. R., and **Rogers, P. L.** (1978, May). Decoding wordless messages. *Human Nature,* pp. 68–75. [11]

Hamburg, D. A., and **Adams, J. E.** (1967). A perspective on coping behavior: Seeking and utilizing information in major transitions. *Archives of General Psychiatry, 17,* 277–284. [13]

Hamburg, D. A., and **Takanishi, R.** (1989, May). Preparing for life: The critical transition to adolescence. *American Psychologist, 44,* 825–827. [10]

Hamilton, E. W., and **Abramson, L. Y.** (1983). Cognitive patterns and major depressive disorder: A longitudinal study in a hospital setting. *Journal of Abnormal Psychology, 92,* 173–184. [16]

Hammen, C., Marks, T., Mayol, A., and **de Mayo, R.** (1985). Depressive self-schemas, life stress, and vulnerability to depression. *Journal of Abnormal Psychology, 94*(3), 308–319. [16]

Hansen, R. D., and **Hansen, C. H.** (1988). Repression of emotionally tagged memories: The architecture of less complex emotions. *Journal of Personality and Social Psychology, 55*(5), 811–818. [13]

Haracz, J. H. (1982). The dopamine hypothesis: An overview of studies with schizophrenic patients. *Schizophrenia Bulletin, 8,* 438–469. [16]

Hardaway, R. A. (1990). Subliminally activated symbiotic fantasies: Facts and artifacts. *Psychological Bulletin, 107,* 177–195. [5]

Harding, H. C. (1967). Hypnosis in the treatment of migraine. In J. Lassner (Ed.), *Hypnosis and Psychosomatic Medicine.* New York: Springer-Verlag. [12]

Hare, R. D. (1970). *Psychopathy: Theory and Research.* New York: Wiley. [16]

Hargadon, F. (1981). Tests and college admissions. *American Psychologist, 36,* 1112–1119. [14]

Hariton, E. B., and **Singer, J. L.** (1974). Women's fantasies during sexual intercourse: Normative and theoretical implications. *Journal of Consulting and Clinical Psychology, 42,* 313–322. [12]

Haritos-Fatouros, M. (1988). The official torturer: A learning model for obedience to the authority of violence. *Journal of Applied Social Psychology, 18,* 1107–1120. [19]

Harkins, S. G., and **Szymanski, K.** (1987). Social loafing and social facilitation: New wine in old bottles. In C. Hendrick (Ed.), *Group Processes and Intergroup Relations: Review of Personality and Social Psychology* (Vol 9). Newbury Park, CA: Sage Publications. [19]

Harkins, S. G., and **Szymanski, K.** (1988). Social loafing and self-evaluation with an objective standard. *Journal of Experimental Social Psychology, 24,* 354–365. [19]

Harkins, S. G., and **Szymanski, K.** (1989). Social loafing and group evaluation. *Journal of Personality and Social Psychology, 56,* 934–941. [19]

Harkness, S. (1980). The cultural context of child development. In C. M. Super and S. Harkness (Eds.), *New Directions for Child Development.* No. 8. *Anthropological Perspectives on Child Development* (pp. 7–13). San Francisco: Jossey-Bass. [10]

Harlow, H. F. (1953). Mice, monkeys, men, and motives. *Psychological Review, 60*, 23–32. [12]

Harlow, H. F. (1958). The nature of love. *American Psychologist, 13*, 673–685. [10]

Harlow, H. F., and **Harlow, M. K.** (1966). Learning to love. *American Scientist, 54*, 244–272. [10, 11]

Harlow, H. F., and **Harlow, M. K.** (1969). Effects of various mother–infant relationships on rhesus monkey behaviors. In B. M. Foss (Ed.), *Determinants of Infant Behavior* (Vol. 4, pp. 15–36). London: Methuen. [10]

Harlow, H. F., Harlow, M. K., and **Meyer, D. R.** (1950). Learning motivated by a manipulation drive. *Journal of Experimental Psychology, 40*, 228–234. [12]

Harris, L., and Associates (1986). *American Teens Speak: Sex, Myths, TV, and Birth Control. The Planned Parenthood Poll.* New York: Planned Parenthood Federation of America. [10]

Harris, R. J. (1977). Comprehension of pragmatic implications in advertising. *Journal of Applied Psychology, 62*, 603–608. [8, 9]

Hartmann, E., Backeland, F., and **Zwilling, G.** (1975). Psychological differences between long and short sleepers. *Archives of General Psychiatry, 32*, 765–777. [5]

Hartshorne, H., and **May, M. A.** (1928). *Studies in the Nature of Character,* (Vol. 1): *Studies in Deceit.* New York: Macmillan. [13]

Harvard Medical School. (1986). Suicide—Part II. *Mental Health Letter, 2*(8), 1–4. [16]

Hasher, L., and **Zacks, R. T.** (1984, December). Automatic processing of fundamental information: The case of frequency occurrence. *American Psychologist, 39*, 1372–1388. [7]

Hass, R. G. (1981). Effects of source characteristics on cognitive responses in persuasion. In R. E. Petty, T. M. Ostrom, and T. C. Brock (Eds.), *Cognitive Responses in Persuasion.* Hillsdale, NJ: Lawrence Erlbaum. [18]

Hass, R. G., and **Linder, D. E.** (1972). Counterargument availability and the effects of message structure on persuasion. *Journal of Personality and Social Psychology, 23*, 219–233. [18]

Hatch, T. C., and **Gardner, H.** (1986). From testing intelligence to assessing competencies: A pluralistic view of intellect. *Roeper Review, 8*(3), 147–150. [14]

Hatfield, E., and **Sprecher, S.** (1968). *Mirror, Mirror . . . The Importance of Looks in Everyday Life.* New York: SUNY Press. [18]

Hatton, G. I. (1985). Reversible synapse formation and modulation of cellular relationships in the adult hypothalamus under physiological conditions. In C. W. Cotman (Ed.), *Synaptic Plasticity* (pp. 373–404). London: Guilford Press. [3]

Hauri, P. (1982). *The Sleep Disorders* (2nd ed., pp. 1–20, 21–27, 36–37, 52–56). Kalamazoo, MI: Upjohn Corp. [5]

Hawton, K. (1987). Assessment of suicide risk. *British Journal of Psychiatry, 150*, 145–153. [17]

Hayes, K. J., and **Hayes, C.** (1951). The intellectual development of a home-raised chimpanzee. *Proceedings of the American Philosophical Society, 95*, 105–109. [8, 9]

Hazan, C., and **Shaver, P.** (1987). Romantic love conceptualized as an attachment process. *Journal of Personality and Social Psychology, 57*, 731–739. [18]

Hazelrigg, M. D., Cooper, H. M., and **Borduin, C. M.** (1987). Evaluating the effectiveness of family therapies: An integrative review and analysis. *Psychological Bulletin, 101*, 428–442. [17]

Hazelwood, J. D., and **Olson, J. M.** (1986). Covariation information, causal questioning, and interpersonal behavior. *Journal of Experimental Social Psychology, 22*, 276–291. [18]

Hebb, D. (1955). Drives and the CNS. *Psychological Review, 62*, 243–253. [12]

Hebb, D. O. (1949). *Organization of Behavior.* New York: Wiley. [7]

Hebb, D. O. (1972). *Textbook of Psychology.* Toronto: Saunders. [7]

Heckhausen, H. (1977). Achievement motivation and its constructs: A cognitive model. *Motivation and Emotion, 1*, 283–329. [12]

Hedge, A., Erikson, W., and **Rubin, G.** (1990, November). *Work and Well-Being: An Agenda for the 90s.* Paper presented at an APA conference, Washington, DC. [1]

Hedges, L., and **Olkin, I.** (1985). *Statistical Methods for Meta-Analysis,* New York: Academic Press. [2]

Hefner, R. S., and **Hefner, H. E.** (1983). Hearing in large and small dogs: Absolute thresholds and size of the tympanic membrane. *Behavioral Neuroscience, 97*, 310–318. [4]

Heider, F. (1944). Social perception and phenomenal causality. *Psychological Review, 51*, 358–374. [18]

Heider, F. (1958). *The Psychology of Interpersonal Relations.* New York: Wiley. [18]

Hellekson, C. J., Kline, J. A., and **Rosenthal, N. E.** (1986). Phototherapy for seasonal affective disorder in Alaska. *American Journal of Psychiatry, 143*, 1035–1037. [16]

Heller, W. (1990). The neuropsychology of emotion: Developmental patterns and implications for psychopathology. In N. L. Stein, B. Leventhal, and T. Trabasso (Eds.), *Psychological and Biological Approaches to Emotion* (pp. 167–211). Hillsdale, NJ: Lawrence Erlbaum. [11]

Hellige, J. B., Bloch, M. I., and **Taylor, A. K.** (1988). Multitask investigation of individual differences in hemispheric asymmetry. *Journal of Experimental Psychology: Human Perception and Performance, 14*(2), 176–187. [3]

Helmrath, T. A., and **Steinitz, E. M.** (1978). Death of an infant: Parental grieving and the failure of social support. *Journal of Family Practice, 6*, 785–790. [11]

Helson, H. (1964). *Adaptation-level theory.* New York: Harper & Row. [11]

Heninger, G. R., Charney, D. S., and **Menkes, D. B.** (1983). Receptor sensitivity and the mechanisms of action of antidepressant treatment. In P. J. Clayton and J. E. Barrett (Eds.), *Treatment of Depression:*

Old Controversies and New Approaches. New York: Raven Press. [16]

Herman, C. P., and **Mack, D.** (1975). Restrained and unrestrained eating. *Journal of Personality, 43,* 647–660. [12]

Herman, C. P., and **Polivy, J.** (1975). Anxiety, restraint, and eating behavior. *Journal of Abnormal Psychology, 84,* 666–672. [12]

Herman, C. P., and **Polivy, J.** (1980). Restrained eating. In A. J. Stunkard (Ed.), *Obesity.* Philadelphia: W. B. Saunders. [12]

Hetherington, A. W., and **Ranson, S. W.** (1940). Hypothalamic lesions and adiposity in the rat. *The Anatomical Record, 78,* 149–172. [12]

Hetherington, E. M. (1988). Parents, children, and siblings six years after divorce. In R. Hinde and J. Stevenson Hinde (Eds.), *Relations between Relationships within Families.* Oxford: Oxford University Press. [10]

Hetherington, E. M. (1989). Coping with family transitions: Winners, losers, and survivors. *Child Development, 60,* 1–14. [10]

Hetherington, E. M., Stanley-Hagan, M., and **Anderson, E. R.** (1989, February). Marital transitions: A child's perspective. *American Psychologist, 44*(2), 303–312. [10]

Hewstone, M., and **Jaspers, J.** (1987). Covariation and causal attribution: A logical model of the intuitive analysis of variance. *Journal of Personality and Social Psychology, 53,* 663–672. [18]

Hibscher, J. A., and **Herman, C. P.** (1977). Obesity, dieting, and the expression of "obese" characteristics. *Journal of Comparative and Physiological Psychology, 91,* 374–380. [12]

Higbee, K. L. (1988). Practical aspects of mnemonics. In M. M. Gruenberg, P. E. Morris, and R. N. Sykes (Eds.), *Practical Aspects of Memory: Current Research and Issues* (Vol. 2, pp. 409–414). New York: Wiley. [7]

Higgins, E. T., and **Bargh, J. A.** (1987). Social cognition and social perception. *Annual Review of Psychology, 38,* 369–425. [18]

Higgins, E. T., Rohles, W. S., and **Jones, C. R.** (1977). Category accessibility and impression formation. *Journal of Experimental Social Psychology, 13,* 141–154. [18]

Higgins, R. L., and **Marlatt, G. A.** (1973). Effects of anxiety arousal on the consumption of alcohol by alcoholics and social drinkers. *Journal of Consulting and Clinical Psychology, 41,* 426–433. [16]

Higgins, R. L., and **Marlatt, G. A.** (1975). Fear of interpersonal evaluation as a determinant of alcohol consumption in male social drinkers. *Journal of Abnormal Psychology, 84,* 644–651. [16]

Higgins, S. T. (1989, August). *Intranasal Cocaine: Effects on Learning and Performance in Humans.* Paper presented at the annual meeting of the American Psychological Association, New Orleans. [5]

Hilgard, E. R. (1965). *Hypnotic Susceptibility.* New York: Harcourt Brace Jovanovich. [5]

Hilgard, E. R. (1973). A neodissociation interpretation of pain reduction in hypnosis. *Psychological Review, 80,* 396–411. [5]

Hilgard, E. R. (1975). Hypnosis. *Annual Review of Psychology, 26,* 19–44. [5]

Hilgard, E. R., Morgan, A. H., and **Macdonald, H.** (1975). Pain and dissociation in the cold pressor test: A study of hypnotic analgesia with "hidden reports" through automatic key-pressing and automatic talking. *Journal of Abnormal Psychology, 84,* 280–289. [5]

Hilgard, J. R. (1970). *Personality and Hypnosis: A Study of Imaginative Involvement.* Chicago: University of Chicago Press. [5]

Hilgard, J. R. (1974). Imaginative involvement: Some characteristics of the highly hypnotizable and the nonhypnotizable. *International Journal of Clinical and Experimental Hypnosis, 22,* 128–156. [5]

Hill, C. T., Rubin, Z., and **Peplau, L. A.** (1976). Breakups before marriage: The end of 103 affairs. *Journal of Social Issues, 32,* 147–168. [18]

Hill, W. F. (1985). *Learning: A Survey of Psychological Interpretations* (4th ed.). New York: Harper & Row. [6]

Hillenberg, J. G., and **DiLorenzo, T. M.** (1987). Stress management training in health psychology practice: Critical clinical issues. *Professional Psychology: Research and Practice, 18*(4), 402–404. [15]

Himmelhoch, J. M. (1987). Lest treatment abet suicide. *Journal of Clinical Psychiatry, 48,* 44–54. [17]

Hirsch, S. R., Walsh, C., and **Draper, R.** (1982). Parasuicide: A review of treatment intervention. *Journal of Affective Disorders, 4,* 299–311. [16]

Hite, S. (1987). *Women and Love: A Cultural Revolution.* New York: Knopf. [2]

Hobson, J. A. (1988). *The Dreaming Brain.* New York: Basic Books. [5]

Hobson, J. A., and **McCarley, R. W.** (1977). The brain as a dream state generator: An activation-synthesis hypothesis of the dream process. *American Journal of Psychiatry, 134,* 1335–1348. [5]

Hodgson, R., and **Rachman, S.** (1976). The modification of compulsive behavior. In H. J. Eysenck (Ed.), *Case Studies in Behaviour Therapy.* Boston: Routledge and Kegan Paul. [16]

Hoebel, B. G., and **Teitelbaum, P.** (1962). Hypothalamic control of feeding and self-stimulation. *Science, 135,* 375–377. [12]

Hoffman, M. L. (1970). Conscience, personality, and socialization techniques. *Human Development, 13,* 90–126. [13]

Hoffman, M. L. (1976). Empathy, role-taking, guilt, and development of altruistic motives. In T. Lickona (Ed.), *Moral Development and Behavior: Theory, Research and Social Issues.* New York: Holt, Rinehart and Winston. [10]

Hoffman, M. L., and **Saltzstein, H. D.** (1967). Parent discipline and the child's moral development. *Journal of Personality and Social Psychology, 5,* 45–57. [10]

Hogan, R. (1975). Theoretical egocentrism and the problem of compliance. *American Psychologist, 30,* 533–540. [10]

Hogarth, R. (1981). Beyond discrete biases: Functional and dysfunctional aspects of judgmental heuristics. *Psychology Bulletin, 90,* 197. [8]

Hohmann, G. W. (1966). Some effects of spinal cord lesions on experienced emotional feelings. *Psychophysiology, 3,* 143–156. [11]

Hokfelt, T., Johansson, O., and Goldstein, M. (1984). Chemical anatomy of the brain. *Science, 225,* 1326–1334. [3]

Holahan, C. J., and Moos, R. H. (1987). Personal and contextual determinants of coping strategies. *Journal of Personality and Social Psychology, 52,* 946–955. [15]

Holahan, C. K., Holahan, C. J., and Belk, S. S. (1984). Adjustment in aging: The roles of life stress, hassles, and self-efficacy. *Health Psychology, 3,* 315–328. [15]

Holbrook, J. M. (1983). CNS stimulants. In G. Bennett, et al. (Eds.), *Substance Abuse: Pharmacological, Developmental, and Clinical Perspectives.* New York: Wiley. [5]

Holden, C. (1987, May 8). Female math anxiety on the wane. *Science, 236,* 660–661. [9]

Holden, C. (1989, January 6). Universities fight animal activists. *Science, 243,* 17–19. [2]

Hollander, E. P. (1975). Independence, conformity, and civil liberties: Some implications from social psychological research. *Journal of Social Issues, 31,* 55–67. [19]

Hollon, S. D., and Beck, A. T. (1986). Cognitive and cognitive–behavioral therapies. In S. L. Garfield and A. E. Bergin (Eds.), *Handbook of Psychotherapy and Behavior Change* (3rd ed.). New York: Wiley. [17]

Holmes, C. B. (1987, September). Comment on Szasz's view of suicide prevention. *American Psychologist, 42,* 881–882. [17]

Holmes, D. S. (1984). Meditation and somatic arousal reduction: A review of the experimental evidence. *American Psychologist, 39,* 1–10. [5]

Holmes, J., and Gregersen, M. I. (1974). Life change and illness susceptibility. In B. S. Dohrenwend and B. P. Dohrenwend (Eds.), *Stressful Life Events: Their Nature and Effects.* New York: Wiley. [15]

Holmes, T. H., and Rahe, R. H. (1967). The social readjustment rating scale. *Journal of Psychosomatic Research, 11,* 213–218. [15]

Holroyd, K. A. (1978). Effects of social anxiety and social evaluation on beer consumption and social interaction. *Journal of Studies on Alcohol, 39,* 737–744. [16]

Holstein, C. B. (1976). Irreversible, stepwise sequence in the development of moral judgment: A longitudinal study of males and females. *Child Development, 47,* 31–61. [10]

Holtzworth-Munroe, A., and Jacobson, N. S. (1985). Causal attribution of married couples: When do they search for causes? What do they conclude when they do? *Journal of Personality and Social Psychology, 48,* 1398–1412. [18]

Hooley, J. M. (1985). Expressed emotion: A review of the critical literature. *Annual Review of Psychology, 5,* 119–139. [16]

Hoon, P. W., Bruce, K., and Kinchloe, B. (1982). Does the menstrual cycle play a role in sexual arousal? *Psychophysiology, 19,* 21–26. [12]

Hopson, J. L. (1988, July/August). A pleasurable chemistry. *Psychology Today,* pp. 28–33. [3]

Horn, J. L. (1982). The aging of human abilities. In B. B. Wolman (Ed.), *Handbook of Developmental Psychology,* Englewood Cliffs, NJ: Prentice-Hall. [14]

Horner, M. S. (1970). Femininity and successful achievement: A basic inconsistency. In J. M. Bardwicks, E. Douvan, M. Horner, and D. Gutmann (Eds.), *Feminine Personality and Conflict.* Monterey, CA: Brooks/Cole. [12]

Horney, K. (1945). *Our Inner Conflicts.* New York: Norton. [13]

Horney, K. (1967). *Feminine Psychology.* New York: Norton. [13]

Horowitz, F. D., and O'Brien, M. (1986). Gifted and talented children: State of knowledge and directions for research. *American Psychologist, 41*(10), 1147–1152. [14]

Hothersall, D. (1984). *History of Psychology.* New York: Random House. [1]

House, J. S. (1981). *Work Stress and Social Support.* Reading, MA: Addison-Wesley. [15]

House, J. S. (1987). Chronic stress and chronic disease in life and work: Conceptual and methodological issues. *Work and Stress, 1,* 129–140. [15]

House, J. S., Umberson, D., and Landis, K. R. (1988). Structures and processes of social support. *American Review of Sociology, 14,* 293–318. [15]

Hovland, C. I., Janis, I. J., and Kelley, H. H. (1953). *Communication and Persuasion.* New Haven: Yale University Press. [18]

Hovland, C. I., Lumsdaine, A. A., and Sheffield, F. D. (1949). *Studies in Social Psychology in World War II, Vol. 3: Experiments in Mass Communication.* Princeton: Princeton University Press. [18]

Howard, D. (1983). *Cognitive Psychology: Memory, Language and Thought.* New York: Macmillan. [8, 9]

Howes, C. (1990). Can the age of entry into child care and the quality of child care predict adjustment in kindergarten? *Developmental Psychology, 26,* 292–303. [10]

Howes, C., and Eldredge, R. (1985). Responses of abused, neglected, and nonmaltreated children to the behaviors of their peers. *Journal of Applied Developmental Psychology, 6,* 261–270. [10]

Howes, C., and Rubenstein, J. L. (1981). *Determinants of Toddler Experience in Day Care: Social-Affective Style of Age of Entry and Quality of Setting.* Unpublished manuscript, University of California at Los Angeles. [10]

Hrudova, L. et al. (1987). Forward and backward conditioning of vasomotor reactions: A comparison. *Activitas Nervosa Superior, 29,* 153–158. [6]

Hubel, D. H., and Wiesel, T. N. (1959). Receptive fields of single neurons in the cat's striate cortex. *Journal of Physiology, 148,* 574–591. [4]

Hubel, D. H., and Wiesel, T. N. (1979). Brain mechanisms of vision. *Scientific American, 241,* 150–162. [4]

Hudspeth, A. J. (1985, November 15). The cellular basis of hearing: The biophysics of hair cells. *Science, 230,* 745–752. [4]

Huesman, L. R., and **Eron, L. D.** (1983). Factors influencing the effect of television violence on children. In M. J. A. Howe (Ed.), *Learning from Television: Psychological and Educational Research* (pp. 153–177). London: Academic Press. [2]

Huff, C., and **Cooper, J.** (1987). Sex bias in educational software: The effects of designers' stereotypes on the software they design. *Journal of Applied Social Psychology, 17,* 519–532. [18]

Hughes, J. R. (1984). Psychological effects of habitual aerobic exercise: A critical review. *Preventive Medicine, 13,* 66–78. [15]

Hughes, J. R., Casal, D. C., and **Leon, A. S.** (1986). Psychological effects of exercise: A randomized cross-over trial. *Journal of Psychosomatic Research, 30,* 355–360. [15]

Hull, C. L. (1943). *Principles of Behavior.* New York: Appleton. [11]

Hull, J. G., and **Bond, C. F., Jr.** (1986). Social and behavioral consequences of alcohol consumption and expectancy: A meta analysis. *Psychological Bulletin, 99,* 347–360. [5]

Hultsch, D. F., Hertzog, C., and **Dixon, R. A.** (1987). Age differences in metamemory: Resolving the inconsistencies. *Canadian Journal of Psychology, 41*(2), 193–208. [9]

Hunt, M. (1982). *The Universe Within.* New York: Simon and Schuster. [8, 9]

Hurley, A. D. (1976). Unsystematic desensitization using pleasurable images to inhibit anxiety. *Journal of Behavior Therapy and Experimental Psychiatry, 7,* 295. [16]

Hurvich, L. M., and **Jameson, D.** (1957). An opponent-process theory of color vision. *Psychological Review, 64,* 384–404. [4]

Huston, T. L., Ruggiero, M., Conner, R., and **Geis, G.** (1981). Bystander intervention into crime: A study based on naturally occurring episodes. *Social Psychology Quarterly, 44,* 14–23. [19]

Huttenlocher, J., and **Presson, C. C.** (1979). The coding and transformation of spatial information. *Cognitive Psychology, 11,* 375–394. [9]

Hyde, J. S. (1981). How large are cognitive gender differences? A meta-analysis using w^2 and d. *American Psychologist, 36,* 892–901. [9]

Hyde, J. S., and **Linn, M. C.** (Eds.). (1986). *The Psychology of Gender: Advances Through Meta-Analysis.* Baltimore: Johns Hopkins University Press. [9]

Imber, S., Pilkonis, P., Sotsky, S., Elkin, I. et al. (1990, June). Mode-specific effects among three treatments for depression. *Journal of Consulting and Clinical Psychology, 58*(3), 352–359. [17]

Imperato-McGinley, J., Peterson, R. E., Gautier, T., and **Sturla, E.** (1979). Androgens and the evolution of male gender identity among male pseudo-hermaphrodites with 5-reductase deficiency. *New England Journal of Medicine, 300,* 1233–1270. [10]

Ingvar, D. H. (1985). "Memory of the future": An essay on the temporal organization of conscious awareness. *Human Neurobiology, 4,* 127–136. [3]

Irwin, M., Daniels, M., Smith, T. L., Bloom, E., and **Weiner, H.** (1987). Impaired natural killer cell activity during bereavement. *Brain, Behavior, and Immunity, 1,* 98–104. [3]

Isaacson, R. L. (1964). Relation between achievement, test anxiety, and curricular choices. *Journal of Abnormal and Social Psychology, 68,* 447–452. [12]

Isen, A. M., and **Levin, P. F.** (1972). Effect of feeling good on helping: Cookies and kindness. *Journal of Personality and Social Psychology, 21,* 384–388. [11, 19]

Isen, A. M., Shalker, T. E., Clark, M., and **Karp, L.** (1978). Affect, accessibility of material in memory, and behavior: A cognitive loop? *Journal of Personality and Social Psychology, 36,* 1–12. [11]

Iversen, L. L. (1979). The chemistry of the brain. *Scientific American, 241,* 134–149. [3, 5]

Izard, C. E. (1971). *The Face of Emotion.* New York: Appleton-Century-Crofts. [11]

Izard, C. E. (1984). Emotion-cognition relationships and other human develop-ment. In C. E. Izard, J. Kagan, and R. B. Zajonc (Eds.), *Emotion, Cognitions and Behavior.* New York: Cambridge University Press. [11]

Izard, C. E. (1990a). The substrates and functions of emotion feelings: William James and current emotion theory. *Personality and Social Psychology Bulletin, 16*(4), 626–635. [11]

Izard, C. E. (1990b). Facial expressions and the regulation of emotions. *Journal of Personality and Social Psychology, 58*(3), 487–498. [11]

Izard, C. E., Hembree, E. A., Dougherty, L. M., and **Spizzari, C. C.** (1983). Changes in facial expressions of 2- to 19-month-old infants following acute pain. *Developmental Psychology, 19,* 418–426. [11]

Jackson, J. M., and **Williams, K. D.** (1988). *Social Loafing: A Review and Theoretical Analysis.* Unpublished manuscript, Fordham University. [19]

Jakobson, R. (1982). Einstein and the science of language. In G. Holton (Ed.), *Albert Einstein—Historical and Cultural Perspectives.* Princeton: Princeton University Press. [6]

James, W. (1890). *The Principles of Psychology* (Vol. 2). New York: Holt. [1, 4, 11]

Jameson, D., and **Hurvich, L.** (1989). Essay concerning color constancy. *Annual Review of Psychology, 40,* 1–22. [4]

Janis, I. L. (1972). *Victims of groupthink: A psychological study of foreign policy decisions and fiascoes.* Boston: Houghton Mifflin. [1, 19]

Janis, I. L. (1982). Counteracting the adverse effects of concurrence-seeking in policy-planning groups: Theory and research perspectives. In H. Brandstatter and J. Davis (Eds.), *Group Decision Making* (European Monographs in Social Psychology, No. 25). [19]

Janis, I. L. (1985). Sources of error in strategic decision making. In J. M. Pennings (Ed.), *Organizational Strategy and Change.* San Francisco: Jossey-Bass. [19]

Janis, I. L., and **Mann, L.** (1977). *Decision making: A Psychological Analysis of Conflict,*

Choice, and Commitment. New York: Free Press. [19]

Janowitz, H. D. (1967). Role of gastrointestinal tract in the regulation of food intake. In C. F. Code (Ed.), *Handbook of Physiology: Alimentary Canal* (Vol. 1, pp. 219–224). Washington, DC: American Physiological Society. [12]

Janowitz, H. D., and **Grossman, M. I.** (1949). Some factors affecting the food intake of normal dogs and dogs with esophagostomy and gastric fistula. *American Journal of Physiology, 159,* 143–148. [12]

Janowitz, H. D., and **Grossman, M. I.** (1951). Effect of prefeeding, alcohol and bitters on food intake of dogs. *American Journal of Physiology, 164,* 182–186. [12]

Janz, N. K., and **Becker, M. H.** (1984). The health belief model: A decade later. *Health Education Quarterly, 11,* 1–47. [15]

Jarvik, L. F. (1975). Thoughts on the psychobiology of aging. *American Psychologist,* 576–583. [9]

Jenkins, J. G., and **Dallenbach, K. M.** (1924). Oblivescence during sleep and waking. *American Journal of Psychology, 35,* 605–612. [7]

Jenner, F. A., Gjessing, L. R., Cox, J. R., Davies-Jones, A., and **Hullin, R. P.** (1967). A manic-depressive psychotic with a 48-hour cycle. *British Journal of Psychiatry, 113,* 859–910. [16]

Jensen, A. R. (1969). How much can we boost I.Q. and scholastic achievement? *Harvard Educational Review, 39,* 1–123. [14]

Jepson, C., and **Chaiken, S.** (1986). *The Effect of Anxiety on the Systematic Processing of Persuasive Communications.* Paper presented at the annual meeting of the American Psychological Association, Washington, DC. [18]

Johansson, G., and **Vallbo, A. B.** (1983). Tactile sensory coding in the glabrous skin of the human hand. *Trends in Neuroscience, 6,* 27–32. [4]

John, E. R., Prichep, L. S., Fridman, J., and **Easton, P.** (1988, January 8). Neurometrics: Computer-assisted differential diag-

nosis of brain dysfunctions. *Science, 239,* 162–169. [2, 3]

Johnson, A. G. (1980). On the prevalence of rape in the United States. *Signs: Journal of Women in Culture and Society, 6,* 136–146. [19]

Johnson, C. M., Bradley-Johnson, S., McCarthy, R., and **Jamie, M.** (1984). Token reinforcement during WISC-R administration. *Applied Research on Mental Retardation, 5,* 43–52.

Johnson, G. (1987, August). Memory: Learning how it works. *The New York Times Magazine.* [7]

Johnson, S. M., and **Greenberg, L. S.** (1985). Differential effects of experiential and problem-solving interventions in resolving mental conflict. *Journal of Consulting and Clinical Psychology, 53,* 175–184. [17]

Johnston, E., and **Donoghue, J. R.** (1971). Hypnosis and smoking: A review of the literature. *American Journal of Clinical Hypnosis, 13,* 265–272. [5]

Johnston, L., O'Malley, P., and **Bachman, J.** (1986). *Drug use among American high school students, college students, and other young adults: National trends through 1985.* Washington, DC: National Institute on Drug Abuse. [15]

Jones, E. E., and **Davis, K. E.** (1965). From acts to dispositions: The attribution process in person perception. In L. Berkowitz (Ed.), *Advances in Experimental Social Psychology* (Vol. 2, pp. 219–266). New York: Academic Press. [18]

Jones, E. E., and **Nisbett, R. E.** (1971). *The Actor and Observer: Perceptions of the Causes of Behavior.* New York: General Learning Press. [18]

Jones, G. V. (1988). Analyzing memory blocks. In M. M. Gruenberg, P. E. Morris, and R. N. Sykes (Eds.), *Practical Aspects of Memory: Current Research and Issues* (Vol. 1, pp. 215–220). New York: Wiley. [7]

Jones, L. V., and **Appelbaum, M. I.** (1989). Psychometric methods. *Annual Review of Psychology, 40,* 23–43.

Jones, M. C. (1924). The elimination of children's fears. *Journal of Experimental Psychology, 7,* 382–390. [6]

Jones, M. C. (1974). Albert, Peter and John B. Watson. *American Psychologist, 29,* 581–583. [6]

Jones, R. A. (1985). *Research Methods in the Social and Behavioral Sciences.* Sunderland, MA: Sinauer Assoc. [2]

Jones, W. H., and **Carpenter, B. N.** (1986). Shyness, social behavior, and relationships. In W. H. Jones, J. M. Cheek, and S. R. Briggs (Eds.), *Shyness: Perspectives on Research and Treatment* (pp. 227–238). New York: Plenum. [18]

Jones-Witters, P., and **Witters, W.** (1983). *Drugs and Society: A Biological Perspective.* Monterey, CA: Wadsworth. [5]

Jonides, J., Kahn, R., and **Rozin, P.** (1975). Imagery instructions improve memory in blind subjects. *Bulletin of the Psychonomic Society, 5,* 424–426. [7]

Jordan, H. A. (1969). Voluntary intragastric feeding: Oral and gastric contributions to food intake and hunger in man. *Journal of Comparative and Physiological Psychology, 68,* 498–506. [12]

Jordan, T. J., and **McCormick, N. B.** (1987, April). *The Role of Sex Beliefs in Intimate Relationships.* Paper presented at the annual meeting of the American Association of Sex Educators, Counselors, and Therapists, New York. [17]

Josephson, W. L. (1987). Television violence and children's aggression: Testing the priming social script and disinhibition predictions. *Journal of Personality and Social Psychology, 53*(5), 882–890. [2]

Jouvet, M. (1967). The stages of sleep. *Scientific American, 216,* 62–72. [5]

Julesz, B. (1984). A brief outline of the textron theory of human vision. *Trends in Neuroscience, 7,* 41–45. [4]

Jung, C. G. (1953). *Collected Works.* H. Read, M. Fordham, and G. Adler (Eds.). (R. F. C. Hull, Trans.). Princeton, NJ: Princeton University Press. [13]

Kagan, J. (1984). *The Nature of the Child.* New York: Basic Books. [10]

Kagan, J., Kearsley, R. B., and **Zelazo, P. R.** (1978). *Infancy: Its Place in Human*

Development. Cambridge, MA: Harvard University Press. [9, 10]

Kail, R. (1990). *The Development of Memory in Children.* New York: W. H. Freeman. [9]

Kail, R., and **Pellegrino, J. W.** (1985). *Human Intelligence: Perspectives and Prospects.* New York: W. H. Freeman. [14]

Kaiser, R. B. (1970). *R. F. K. Must Die: A History of the Robert Kennedy Assassination and Its Aftermath.* New York: Dutton. [7]

Kalat, J. W., and **Rozin, P.** (1971). Role of interference in taste-aversion learning. *Journal of Comparative and Physiological Psychology, 77,* 53–58. [6]

Kales, A., Hoedemaker, F., Jacobson, A., and **Lichtenstein, E.** (1964). Dream deprivation: An experimental reappraisal. *Nature, 204,* 1337–1338. [5]

Kaltreider, N. B., Goldsmith, S., and **Margolis, A.** (1979). *American Journal of Obstetrics and Gynecology, 135,* 235. [15]

Kaltreider, N. B., Wallace, A., and **Horowitz, M. J.** (1979). A field study of the stress response syndrome: Young women after hysterectomy. *Journal of the American Medical Association, 242,* 1499–1503. [11]

Kamin, L. J. (1974). The science and politics of I.Q. *Social Research, 41*(3), 387–425. [14]

Kamin, L. J. (1986). Is there crime in the genes? The answer may depend on who chooses what evidence. *Scientific American, 254*(2), 22–27. [19]

Kaminoff, R. D., and **Proshansky, H. M.** (1982). Stress as a consequence of the urban physical environment. In L. Goldberger and S. Breznitz (Eds.), *Handbook of Stress: Theoretical and Clinical Aspects.* New York: Free Press. [12]

Kandel, E. R. (1979). Small systems of neurons. *Scientific American, 241,* 67–76. [7]

Kandel, E. R. (1984). Steps toward a molecular grammar for learning: Explorations into the nature of memory. In K. J. Isselbacher (Ed.), *Medicine, Science & Society Symposia Celebrating the Harvard Medical School Bicentennial.* New York: Wiley. [7]

Kangas, J., and **Bradway, K.** (1974). Intelligence at middle age: A thirty-eight-year follow-up. *Developmental Psychology, 5,* 333–337. [9]

Kanizsa, G. (1976). Subjective contours. *Scientific American, 234,* 48–52. [4]

Kaplan, J. (1988, November 11). The use of animals in research. *Science, 243,* 839–940. [2]

Kaplan, R. M. (1982). Nader's raid on the testing industry: Is it in the best interest of the consumer? *American Psychologist, 37,* 15–23. [14]

Kasamatsu, A., and **Hirai, T.** (1966). An electroencephalographic study on the Zen meditation (Zayen). *Folia Psychiatrica et Neurologica Japonica, 20,* 315–366. [5]

Kasper, S., Wehr, T. A., Bartko, J. J., Gaist, P. A., and **Rosenthal, N. E.** (1989, September). Epidemiological findings of seasonal changes in mood and behavior. *Archives of General Psychiatry, 46,* 823–833. [16]

Katz, H., and **Beilin, H.** (1976). A test of Bryant's claims concerning the young child's understanding of quantitative invariance. *Child Development, 47,* 877–880. [9]

Katz, I., and **Hass, R. G.** (1988). Racial ambivalence and American value conflict: Correlational and priming studies of dual cognitive structures. *Journal of Personality and Social Psychology, 55,* 893–905. [18]

Katz, M. L. (1973). *Female Motive to Avoid Success: A Psychological Barrier or a Response to Deviancy?* Princeton, NJ: Educational Testing Service. [12]

Kaye, K., and **Marcus, J.** (1978). Imitation over a series of trials without feedback: Age six months. *Infant Behavior and Development, 1,* 141–155. [9]

Kazdin, A. E. (1977). *The Token Economy: A Review and Evaluation.* New York: Plenum. [17]

Kazdin, A. E., and **Wilson, G. T.** (1978). *Evaluation of Behavior Therapy: Issues, Evidence, and Research Strategies.* Cambridge, MA: Ballenger. [17]

Keating, D. P. (1980). Thinking processes in adolescence. In J. Adelson (Ed.), *Handbook of Adolescent Psychology.* New York: Wiley. [9]

Keating, D. P. (1988). Byrnes' reformulation of Piaget's formal operations. *Developmental Review, 8,* 376–384. [9]

Keesey, R. E., and **Powley, T. L.** (1986). The regulation of body weight. *American Review of Psychology, 37,* 109–133. [12]

Kelley, H. H. (1967). Attribution theory in social psychology. In D. Levine (Ed.), *Nebraska Symposium of Motivation* (Vol. 15, pp. 192–238). Lincoln: University of Nebraska Press. [18]

Kelley, H. H. (1971). *Attribution in Social Interaction.* Morristown, NJ: General Learning Press. [18]

Kelley, H. H. (1979). *Personal Relationships.* Hillsdale, NJ: Lawrence Erlbaum. [18]

Kelling, S. T., and **Halpern, B. P.** (1983). Taste flashes: Reaction times, intensity, and quality. *Science, 219,* 412–414. [4]

Kelly, D. D. (1981). Somatic sensory system. 4. Central representations of pain and analgesia. In E. R. Kandel and J. H. Schwartz (Eds.), *Principles of Neural Science* (2nd ed.). New York: Elsevier. [4, 5]

Kelly, G. (1955). *The Psychology of Personal Constructs.* New York: Norton. [13]

Kelman, H. C. (1958). Compliance, identification, and internalization: Three processes of attitude change. *Journal of Conflict Resolution, 2,* 51–60. [19]

Kelman, H. C. (1961). Processes of opinion change. *Public Opinion Quarterly, 25,* 57–78. [19]

Kelman, H. C., and **Hovland, C. I.** (1953). "Reinstatement" of the communicator in delayed measurement of opinion change. *Journal of Abnormal and Social Psychology, 48,* 327–335. [18]

Kemeny, M. E., Cohen, R., Zegans, L. S., and **Conant, M. A.** (1989). Psychological and immunological predictors of genital herpes recurrence. *Psychosomatic Medicine, 51,* 195–208. [15]

Kemper, T. D. (1978). *A Social Interaction Theory of Emotions.* New York: Wiley. [11]

Kendzierski, D. (1990). Exercise self-schemata: Cognitive and behavioral correlates. *Health Psychology, 9,* 69–82. [15]

Kennell, J. H., Jerauld, R., Wolfe, H., Chesler, D., Kreger, N. C., McAlpine, W., Steffa, M., and Klaus, M. H. (1974). Maternal behavior one year after early and extended post-partum contact. *Developmental Medicine and Child Neurology, 16,* 172–179. [2]

Kety, S. S. (1979). Disorders of the human brain. *Scientific American, 241,* 202–214. [3]

Kiecolt-Glaser, J. K., Garner, W., Speicher, C., Penn, G. M., Holliday, J., and Glaser, R. (1984). Psychosocial modifiers of immunocompetence in medical students. *Psychosomatic Medicine, 46,* 7–14. [15]

Kiecolt-Glaser, J. K., Glaser, R., Shuttleworth, E., Dyer, C. S., Ogrocki, P., and Speicher, C. E. (1987). Chronic stress and immunity in family caregivers of Alzheimer's disease victims. *Psychosomatic Medicine, 49,* 523–535. [15]

Kiecolt-Glaser, J. K., Glaser, R., Williger, D., Stout, J., Messick, G., Sheppard, S., Ricker, D., Romisher, S. C., Briner, W., Bonnell, G., and Donnerberg, R. (1985). Psychosocial enhancement of immunocompetence in a geriatric population. *Health Psychology, 4,* 25–41. [15]

Kiecolt-Glaser, J. K., Kennedy, S., Malkoff, S., Fisher, L., Speicher, C. E., and Glaser, R. (1988). Marital discord and immunity in males. *Psychosomatic Medicine, 50,* 213–229. [15]

Kiesler, C. A., and Kiesler, S. B. (1969). *Conformity.* Reading, MA: Addison-Wesley. [19]

Kihlstrom, J. F. (1984). Conscious, subconscious, unconscious: A cognitive perspective. In K. S. Bowers and D. Meichenbaum (Eds.), *The Unconscious Reconsidered* (pp. 149–211). New York: Wiley. [5]

Kihlstrom, J. F. (1985). Hypnosis. *Annual Review of Psychology, 36,* 385–418. [5]

Kihlstrom, J. F. (1986). Strong inferences about hypnosis. *The Behavioral and Brain Sciences, 9*(3), 474–475. [5]

Kihlstrom, J. F. (1987, September 18). The cognitive unconscious. *Science, 237,* 1445–1452. [4]

Kilpatrick, D. G., Best, C. L., Veronen, L. J., Amick, A. E., Villeponteaux, L. A., and Ruff, G. A. (1985). Mental health correlates of criminal victimization: A random community survey. *Journal of Consulting and Clinical Psychology, 53,* 866–873. [19]

Kimble, G. A. (1989, March). *American Psychologist, 44*(3), 491–499. [2]

Kinder, D. R., and Sears, D. O. (1981). Prejudice and politics: Symbolic racism versus racial threats to the good life. *Journal of Personality and Social Psychology, 40,* 414–431. [18]

Kinsbourne, M. (1982). Hemispheric specialization and the growth of human understanding. *American Psychologist, 37,* 411–420. [3]

Kinsey, A. C., Pomeroy, W. B., and Martin, C. E. (1948). *Sexual Behavior in the Human Male.* Philadelphia: W. B. Saunders. [2]

Kinsey, A. C., Pomeroy, W. B., Martin, C. E., and Gebhard, P. H. (1953). *Sexual Behavior in the Human Female.* Philadelphia: W. B. Saunders. [2]

Kintsch, W., and Kennan, J. (1974). The psychological reality of text bases. In W. Kintsch (Ed.), *The Representation of Meaning in Memory.* Hillsdale, NJ: Lawrence Erlbaum. [8, 9]

Kivilan, D. R., Coppel, D. B., Fromme, K., Williams, E., and Marlatt, G. A. (1989). Secondary prevention of alcohol-related problems in young adults at risk. In K. D. Craig and S. M. Weiss (Eds.), *Prevention and Early Intervention: Biobehavioral Perspectives.* New York: Springer. [15]

Klanderman, J., Devine, J., and Mollner, C. (1985). The K-ABC: A construct validity study with WISC-R and Stanford-Binet. *Journal of Clinical Psychology, 41,* 273–281. [14]

Klaus, M. H., Jerauld, R., Kreger, N. C., McAlpine, W., Steffa, M., and Kennell, J. H. (1972). Maternal attachment: Importance of the first post-partum days. *New England Journal of Medicine, 286,* 460–463. [2]

Klaus, M. H., and Kennell, J. H. (1976). *Maternal–Infant Bonding.* St. Louis: C. V. Mosby. [2]

Klein, D. N., Clark, D. C., Dansky, L., and Margolis, E. T. (1988). Dysthymia in the offspring of parents with primary unipolar affective disorder. *Journal of Abnormal Psychology, 97,* 265–274. [16]

Klein, G. S. (1967). Peremptory ideation: Structure and force in motivated ideas. In R. Jessor and S. Feshback (Eds.), *Cognition, Personality, and Clinical Psychology.* San Francisco: Jossey-Bass. [13, 17]

Klein, S. B. (1991). *Learning Principles and Applications* (2nd Ed.). New York: McGraw-Hill. [6]

Kleinginna, P. R., Jr., and Kleinginna, A. M. (1981). A categorized list of emotion definitions, with suggestions for a consensual definition. *Motivation and Emotion, 5,* 355. [11]

Kleitman, N. (1969). Basic rest-activity cycle in relation to sleep and wakefulness. In A. Kales (Ed.), *Sleep: Physiology and Pathology.* Philadelphia: Lippincott. [5]

Klerman, G. L., Lavori, P. W., Rice, J., Reich, T., Endicott, J., Andreason, N. C., Keller, M. B., and Hirshfield, R. M. A. (1985, July). Birth cohort trends in rates of major depressive disorder among relatives of patients with affective disorder. *Archives of General Psychiatry, 42,* 689–693. [16]

Kliegl, R., Smith, J., and Baltes, P. B. (1989). Testing-the-limits and the study of adult age differences in cognitive plasticity of a mnemonic skill. *Developmental Psychology, 25*(2), 247–256. [9]

Klineberg, O. (1938). Emotional expression in Chinese literature. *Journal of Abnormal and Social Psychology, 33,* 517–520. [11]

Klinger, E. (1987, October). The power of daydreams. *Psychology Today,* pp. 37–44. [5]

Kluckhohn, C., and Murray, H. A. (1953). Personality formation: The determinants. In C. Kluckhohn, H. A. Murray, and D. M. Schneider (Eds.), *Personality in Nature, Society, and Culture* (pp. 53–67). New York: Knopf. [13]

Klüver, H., and Bucy, P. C. (1939). Preliminary analysis of function of the temporal lobes in monkeys. *Archives of Neurology and Psychiatry, 42*, 979–1000. [3]

Kluznik, J. C., Speed, N., Van Valkenburg, C., and Magraw, R. (1986). Forty-year follow-up of United States prisoners of war. *American Journal of Psychiatry, 143*(11), 1443–1446. [16]

Knapp, M. L., Hart, R. P., and Dennis, H. S. (1974). An exploration of deception as a communication construct. *Human Communication Research, 1*, 15–29. [18]

Knittle, J. L., and Hirsch, J. (1968). Effect of early nutrition on the development of rat epididymal fat pads: Cellularity and metabolism. *Journal of Clinical Investigation, 47*, 2091. [12]

Kobasigawa, A. (1974). Utilization of retrieval cues by children in recall. *Child Development, 45*, 127–134. [9]

Kohlberg, L. (1963). The development of children's orientation toward a moral order: 1. Sequence in the development of moral thought. *Vita Humana, 6*, 11–33. [10]

Kohlberg, L. (1969). Stage and sequence: The cognitive-developmental approach to socialization. In D. A. Goslin (Ed.), *Handbook of Socialization and Research* (pp. 347–480). Chicago: Rand McNally. [10]

Kohn, M. L. (1973). Social class and schizophrenia: A critical review and a reformulation. *Schizophrenia Bulletin, 7*, 60–79. [16]

Kohn, P. M. and Coulas, J. T. (1985). Sensation-seeking, augmenting-reducing, and the perceived and preferred effects of drugs. *Journal of Personality and Social Psychology, 48*, 99–106. [12]

Kohut, H. (1971). *The Analysis of the Self.* New York: International Universities Press. [13, 17]

Kohut, H. (1978). *The Search for Self.* New York: International Universities Press. [16]

Kohut, H., and Wolfe, E. S. (1978). The disorders of self and their treatment: An outline. *International Journal of Psychoanalysis, 59*, 413–425. [13]

Kolata, G. (1984). Studying in the womb. *Science, 225*, 302–303. [9]

Kolb, B. (1989, September). Brain development, plasticity, and behavior. *American Psychologist, 44*(9), 1203–1212. [3]

Kolb, B., and Whishaw, I. Q. (1990). *Fundamentals of human neuropsychology* (3rd ed.). New York: W. H. Freeman. [3]

Koop, C. E. (1987). Report of the Surgeon General's Workshop on Pornography and Public Health. *American Psychologist, 42*, 944–945. [19]

Korchin, S. J., and Schuldberg, D. (1981). The future of clinical assessment. *American Psychologist, 36*, 1147–1158. [14]

Koriat, A., Lichtenstein, S., and Fischoff, B. (1980). Reasons for confidence. *Journal of Experimental Psychology: Human Learning and Memory, 6*, 107–118. [19]

Korn, J. H., and Bram, D. R. (1988, December). What is missing in the method section of *APA Journal* articles? *American Psychologist*, pp. 191–192. [2]

Koshland, D. E. (1989, March 10). Animal rights and animal wrongs. *Science, 243*, 1253. [2]

Koss, M. P., and Butcher, J. N. (1986). Research on brief psychotherapy. In S. L. Garfield and A. E. Bergin (Eds.), *Handbook of Psychotherapy and Behavior Change* (3rd ed.). New York: Wiley. [17]

Koss, M. P., Gidycz, C. A., and Wisniewski, N. (1987). The scope of rape: Incidence and prevalence of sexual aggression and victimization in a national sample of higher education students. *Journal of Consulting and Clinical Psychology, 55*, 162–170. [19]

Krasner, L. (1978). The future and the past in the behaviorism–humanism dialogue. *American Psychologist, 33*, 799–804. [13]

Kraut, R. E. (1978). Verbal and nonverbal cues in the perception of lying. *Journal of Personality and Social Psychology, 36*, 380–391. [18]

Krebs, D. L., and Miller, D. T. (1985). Altruism and aggression. In G. Lindsey and E. Aronson (Eds.), *Handbook of Social Psychology* (3rd ed.). Reading, MA: Addison-Wesley. [19]

Kroger, W. S., and Douce, R. G. (1979). Hypnosis in criminal investigation. *International Journal of Clinical and Experimental Hypnosis, 27*, 358–374. [5]

Kroll, N. E. A., Schepeler, E. M., and Angin, K. T. (1986). Bizarre imagery: The misremembered mnemonic. *Journal of Experimental Psychology: Learning, Memory, and Cognition, 12*(1), 42–53. [7]

Kromer, L. F., Bjorklund, A., and Stenevi, U. (1981a). Innervation of embryonic hippocampal implants by regenerating axons of cholinergic septal neurons in the adult rat. *Brain Research, 210*, 153–171. [3]

Kromer, L. F., Bjorklund, A., and Stenevi, U. (1981b). Regeneration of the septo-hippocampal pathways in adult rats is promoted by utilizing embryonic hippocampal implants as bridges. *Brain Research, 210*, 173–200. [3]

Kruglanski, A. W., and Freund, T. (1983). The freezing and unfreezing of lay inferences: Effects on impressional primacy, ethnic stereotyping, and numerical anchoring. *Journal of Experimental and Social Psychology, 19*, 448–468. [18]

Krystal, H. (1968). *Massive Psychic Trauma.* New York: International University Press. [16]

Kübler-Ross, E. (1969). *On Death and Dying.* New York: Macmillan. [11]

Kuczaj, S. (1982). *Language Development: Syntax and Semantics* (Vol. 1). Hillsdale, NJ: Lawrence Erlbaum. [9]

Kuhn, D., Langer, J., Kohlberg, L., and Haan, N. S. (1977). The development of formal operations in logical and moral judgment. *Genetic Psychology Monographs, 95L*, 97–188. [10]

Kulik, J. A., Bangert-Drowns, R. L., and Kulik, C. C. (1984). The effectiveness of coaching for aptitude tests. *Psychological Bulletin, 95*, 179–188. [14]

Kulik, J. A., and Mahler, H. I. M. (1989). Social support and recovery from surgery. *Health Psychology, 8*, 221–238. [15]

Kunst-Wilson, W., and Zajonc, R. (1980). Affective discrimination of stimuli that cannot be recognized. *Science, 207*, 557–558. [4]

Kuo, Z. Y. (1930). The genesis of the cat's

responses to the rat. *Journal of Comparative Psychology, 11,* 1–35. [19]

Kupfer, D. J., and **Frank, E.** (1987). Relapse in recurrent unipolar depression. *American Journal of Psychiatry, 144,* 86–88. [17]

Kupfer, D. J., Frank, E., and **Perel, J. M.** (1989). The advantage of early treatment intervention in recurrent depression. *Archives of General Psychiatry, 46,* 771–775. [17]

Kurtines, W., and **Grief, E. B.** (1974). The development of moral thought: Review and evaluation of Kohlberg's approach. *Psychological Bulletin, 81,* 453–470. [10]

Kuwada, J. Y. (1986). Cell recognition by neuronal growth cones in a simple vertebrate embryo. *Science, 233,* 740–746. [3]

La Berge, S. P. (1981, January). Lucid dreaming: Directing the action as it happens. *Psychology Today,* pp. 48–57. [5]

Labov, W., and **Fanshel, D.** (1977). *Therapeutic Discourse: Psychotherapy as Conversation.* New York: Academic Press. [8]

Laird, J. D. (1974). Self-attribution of emotion: The effects of expressive behavior on the quality of emotional experience. *Journal of Personality and Social Psychology, 29,* 475–486. [11]

Laird, J. D. (1984). The real role of facial response in the experience of emotion: A reply to Tourangeau and Ellsworth, and others. *Journal of Personality and Social Psychology, 47,* 909–917. [11]

Lamb, M. E. (1981). The development of father–infant relations. In M. E. Lamb (Ed.), *The Father's Role in Child Development* (rev. ed.). New York: Wiley. [10]

Lamb, M. E. (1986). The father's role in a changing world. In M. Lamb (Ed.), *The Father's Role: Applied Perspectives.* New York: Wiley. [10]

Lamb, M. E., and **Campos, J.** (1982). *Development in Infancy.* New York: Random House. [11]

Lamb, M. E., and **Hwang, C. P.** (1982). Maternal attachment and mother–neonate

bonding: A critical review. In M. E. Lamb and A. L. Brown (Eds.), *Advances in Developmental Psychology* (Vol. 2, pp. 1–39). Hillsdale, NJ: Lawrence Erlbaum. [2]

Lancet, D. (1984). Molecular view of olfactory reception. *Trends in NeuroSciences, 7,* 35–36. [4]

Landon, P. B., and **Suedfeld, P.** (1972). Complex cognitive performance and sensory deprivation: Completing the U-curve. *Perceptual and Motor Skills, 34,* 601–602. [12]

Landsman, T. (1974). The humanizer. *American Journal of Orthopsychiatry, 44,* 345–352. [13]

Lang, P. J., Rice, D. G., and **Sternbach, R. A.** (1972). The psychophysiology of emotion. In N. S. Greenfield and R. A. Sternbach (Eds.), *Handbook of Psychophysiology.* New York: Holt, Rinehart and Winston. [11]

Langan, P. A., and **Innes, C. A.** (1985). *The Risk of Violent Crime.* Bureau of Justice Statistics Special Report, NCJ-97119. Washington, DC: U.S. Government Printing Office. [19]

Lange, C. G., and **James, W.** (1922). *The Emotions* (I. A. Haupt, Trans.). Baltimore: Williams and Wilkins. [11]

Langer, E. J. (1989). *Mindfulness.* Reading, MA: Addison-Wesley. [8]

Langer, E. J., and **Rodin, J.** (1976). The effects of choice and enhanced personal responsibility for the aged: A field experiment in an institutional setting. *Journal of Personality and Social Psychology, 34,* 191–198. [15]

Langer, E. J., Rodin, J., Beck, P., Weinman, C., and **Spitzer, L.** (1979). Environmental determinants of memory improvement in late adulthood. *Journal of Personality and Social Psychology, 37,* 2003–2013. [10]

Langley, P., Simon, H. A., Bradshaw, G. L., and **Sytkow, J. M.** (1987). *Scientific Discovery.* Cambridge: MIT Press. [8]

Langston, C. A., and **Cantor, N.** (1989). Social anxiety and social constraint: When making friends is hard. *Journal of Personality and Social Psychology, 56*(4), 649–661. [13]

Lanyon, R. I., and **Lanyon, B.** (1978). *Behavior Therapy: A Clinical Introduction.* Reading, MA: Addison-Wesley. [6, 16]

LaPiere, R. T. (1934). Attitudes vs. actions. *Social Forces, 13,* 230–237. [4, 17]

Larsen, R. J. (1987). The stability of mood variability: A spectral analytic approach to daily mood assessments. *Journal of Personality and Social Psychology, 52*(6), 1195–1204. [11]

Larsen, R. J., and **Diener, E.** (1985). An evaluation of subjective well-being measures. *Social Ind., 17*(1), 1–17. [11]

Larsen, R. J., and **Diener, E.** (1987). Affect intensity as an individual difference characteristic: A review. *Journal of Research in Personality, 21,* 1–39. [11]

Larsen, R. J., and **Diener, E.** (in press). Promises and problems with the circumplex model of emotion. *Review of Personality and Social Psychology, 13.* [11]

Larsen, R. J., and **Ketelaar, T.** (1989). Extraversion, neuroticism and susceptibility to positive and negative mood induction procedures. *Journal of Personality and Individual Differences, 10*(12), 1221–1228. [11]

Larsen, R. J., and **Ketelaar, T.** (in press). Personality and susceptibility to positive and negative emotional states. *Journal of Personality and Social Psychology.* [11]

Larsen, R. J., and **Sinnet, L. M.** (in press). Meta-analysis of experimental manipulations: Some factors affecting the Velten Mood Induction Procedure. *Personality and Social Psychology Bulletin.* [11]

Lashley, K. S. (1929). *Brain Mechanisms and Intelligence.* Chicago: University of Chicago Press. [3]

Lassen, N. A., Ingvar, D. H., and **Skinhoj, E.** (1978). Brain function and blood flow. *Scientific American, 239,* 62–71. [3]

Latané, B., and **Darley, J. M.** (1968). Group inhibition of bystander intervention in emergencies. *Journal of Personality and Social Psychology, 10,* 215–221. [1]

Latané, B., and **Darley, J. M.** (1976). *Help in a Crisis: Bystander Response to an Emergency.* Morristown, NJ: General Learning Press. [19]

Latané, B., Nida, S. A., and Wilson, D. W. (1981). The effects of group size on helping behavior. In J. P. Rushton and R. M. Sorrentino (Eds.), *Altruism and Helping Behavior: Social, Personality, and Developmental Perspectives.* Hillsdale, NJ: Lawrence Erlbaum. [19]

Latané, B., Williams, K., and Harkins, S. (1979). Many hands make light the work: The causes and consequences of social loafing. *Journal of Personality and Social Psychology, 37,* 822–832. [19]

Lau, R. R., Kane, R., Berry, S., Ware, J., and Roy, D. (1980). Channeling health: A review of televised health campaigns. *Health Education Quarterly, 7,* 56–89. [15]

Laurence, J. R., and Perry, C. (1983). "Hidden Observer" phenomenon in hypnosis: An experimental creation? *Journal of Personality and Social Psychology, 44,* 163–169. [5]

Lavie, P., and Kripke, D. F. (1981). Ultradian circa 1 1/2 hour rhythms: A multioscillatory system. *Life Sciences, 29,* 2445–2450. [5]

Lawson, N. C. (1976). *Depression After Spinal Cord Injury: A Multimeasure Longitudinal Study.* Unpublished doctoral dissertation, University of Houston. [11]

Lazarus, A. (1985). Psychiatric sequelae of legalized first trimester abortion. *Journal of Psychosomatic Obstetrics and Gynecology, 4,* 144–150. [15]

Lazarus, R. (1966). *Psychological Stress and the Coping Process.* New York: McGraw-Hill. [15]

Lazarus, R. S. (1990). Constructs of the mind in adaptation. In N. L. Stein, B. Leventhal, and T. Trabasso (Eds.), *Psychological and Biological Approaches to Emotion* (pp. 3–20). Hillsdale, NJ: Lawrence Erlbaum. [11, 15]

Lazarus, R. S., Cohen, J. B., Folkman, S., Kanner, A., and Schaefer, C. (1980). Psychological stress and adaptation: Some unresolved issues. In H. Selve (Ed.), *Guide to Stress Research.* New York: Van Nostrand Reinhold. [13]

Lazarus, R. S., and Folkman, S. (1984). *Stress, Appraisal, and Coping.* New York: Springer.

Lazarus, R. S., and Folkman, S. (in press). Coping and adaptation. In W. D. Gentry (Ed.), *The Handbook of Behavioral Medicine.* New York: Guilford Press. [15]

Lazarus, R. S., and Launier, R. (1978). Stress-related transactions between person and environment. In L. A. Pervin and M. Lewis (Eds.), *Internal and External Determinants of Behavior.* New York: Plenum. [15]

Leary, M. R. (1983). *Understanding Social Anxiety: Social, Personality, and Clinical Perspectives.* Beverly Hills, CA: Sage Publications. [18]

Leary, M. R., Kowalski, R. M., and Bergen, D. J. (1988). Interpersonal information acquisition and confidence in first encounters. *Personality and Social Psychology Bulletin, 14,* 68–77. [18]

Leavitt, F. (1974). *Drugs and Behavior.* Philadelphia: W. B. Saunders. [5]

Lee, T., and Seeman, P. (1977). Dopamine receptors in normal and schizophrenic human brains. *Society for Neuroscience Abstracts* (Vol. 3, p. 443). Bethesda, MD: Society for Neuroscience. [16]

Leff, J., Kuipers, L., Berkowitz, R., Eberlein-Vries, R., and Sturgeon, D. (1982). A controlled trial of social intervention in the families of schizophrenic patients. *British Journal of Psychiatry, 141,* 121–134. [16]

Lefrançois, G. R. (1982). *Psychological Theories and Human Learning* (2nd ed.). Monterey, CA: Brooks/Cole. [6]

Lehman, A. K., and Rodin, J. (1989). Styles of self-nurturance and disordered eating. *Journal of Consulting and Clinical Psychology, 57,* 117–122. [12]

Lehman, D. R., and Reifman, A. (1987). Spectator influence on basketball officiating. *Journal of Social Psychology, 127,* 673–675. [19]

Lehman, D. R., Wortman, C. B., and Williams, A. F. (1987). Long-term effects of losing a spouse or child in a motor vehicle crash. *Journal of Personality and Social Psychology, 52,* 218–231. [11, 16]

Lehmann, E., Beeler, G. W., and Fender, D. H. (1967). EEG responses during the observation of stabilized and normal ret-inal images. *Electroencephalograph and Clinical Neurophysiology, 22,* 136–142. [5]

Leibowitz, M. R. (1983). *The Chemistry of Love.* Boston: Little, Brown. [18]

Leippe, M. R., and Elkin, R. A. (1987). When motives clash: Issue involvement and response involvement as determinants of persuasion. *Journal of Personality and Social Psychology, 52,* 269–278. [18]

Lemieux, G., Davignon, A., and Genest, J. (1965). Depressive states during Rauwolfia therapy for arterial hypertension. *Canadian Medical Association Journal, 74,* 522–526. [16]

Lenard, H. G., and Schulte, F. L. (1972). Polygraphsleep study in cranioagus twins. (Where is the sleep transmitter?) *Journal of Neurology, Neurosurgery, and Psychiatry, 35,* 756–762. [15]

Lepper, M. R., and Greene, D. (Eds.). (1978). *The Hidden Cost of Reward.* Hillsdale, NJ: Lawrence Erlbaum. [18]

Lepper, M. R., Greene, D., and Nisbett, R. E. (1973). Undermining children's intrinsic interest with extrinsic reward: A test of the "overjustification" hypothesis. *Journal of Personality and Social Psychology, 28,* 129–137. [18]

Lerer, B., Weiner, R. D., and Belmaker, R. H. (1986). *ECT: Basic Mechanisms.* Washington, DC: American Psychiatric Press. [17]

Lerman, L. (1978–1979). Preface to violent pornography: Degradation of women versus right of free speech. *New York University Review of Law and Social Change, VIII*(2), 181–189. [19]

Lerner, M. J. (1970). The desire for justice and reaction to victims. In J. R. Macaulay and L. Berkowitz (Eds.), *Altruism and Helping Behavior.* New York: Academic Press. [19]

Lerner, M. J. (1974). Social psychology of justice and interpersonal attraction. In T. Huston (Ed.), *Foundations of Interpersonal Attraction.* New York: Academic Press. [19]

Lerner, M. J., and Matthews, G. (1967). Reactions to suffering of others under conditions of indirect responsibility. *Journal of*

Personality and Social Psychology, 5, 319–325. [19]

Lerner, M. J., Miller, D. T., and **Holmes, J.** (1976). Deserving and the emergence of forms of justice. In L. Berkowitz and E. Walster (Eds.), *Advances in Experimental Social Psychology.* New York: Academic Press. [19]

Lerner, M. J., and **Simmons, C. H.** (1966). Observer's reaction to the "innocent victim": Compassion or rejection? *Journal of Personality and Social Psychology, 4,* 203–210. [19]

Levenson, R. W., Ekman, P., and **Friesen, W. V.** (1990). Voluntary facial action generates emotion-specific autonomous nervous system activity. *Psychophysiology, 27*(4), 363–382. [11]

Leventhal, H., and **Nerenz, D. R.** (1983). A model for stress research with some implications for the control of stress disorders. In D. Meichenbaum and M. E. Jaremko (Eds.), *Stress Reduction and Prevention.* New York: Plenum. [18]

Levine, J. M. (1989). Reaction to opinion deviance in small groups. In P. Paulus (Ed.), *Psychology of Group Influence: New Perspectives.* Hillsdale, NJ: Lawrence Erlbaum. [19]

Levine, R., Hoffman, J. S., Knepple, E. D., and **Kenin, M.** (1989). Long-term fluoxitine treatment of a large number of obsessive compulsive patients. *Journal of Clinical Psychopharmacology, 9,* 281–283. [17]

Levinson, D. J., with **Darrow, C. N., Klein, E. B., Levinson, M. H.,** and **McKee, B.** (1978). *The Seasons of a Man's Life.* New York: Knopf. [10]

Levinson, S. C. (1983). *Pragmatics.* New York: Cambridge University Press. [8, 9]

Levitsky, A., and **Perls, F. S.** (1970). The rules and games of gestalt therapy. In J. Fagan and I. L. Sheperd (Eds.), *Gestalt Therapy Now.* Palo Alto, CA: Science and Behavior Books. [17]

Levy, J. (1985, May). Right brain, left brain: Fact and fiction. *Psychology Today,* pp. 38–44. [3]

Levy, S. M., Herberman, R. B., Lee, J. K., Lippman, M. E., and **d'Angelo, T.** (1989). Breast conservation versus mastectomy: Distress sequelae as a function of choice. *Journal of Clinical Oncology, 7,* 367–375. [15]

Lewin, K. (1951). *Field Theory in the Social Sciences.* New York: Harper. [12]

Lewinsohn, P. H. (1974). A behavioral approach to depression. In R. J. Friedman and M. M. Katz (Eds.), *The Psychology of Depression: Contemporary Theory and Research.* Washington, DC: Winston-Wiley. [16]

Lewinsohn, P. M., Mischel, W., Chaplin, W., and **Barton, R.** (1980). Social competence and depression: The role of illusionary self-perceptions. *Journal of Abnormal Psychology, 89,* 203–212. [16]

Lewis, J. M., Rodnick, E. H., and **Goldstein, M. J.** (1981). Intrafamilial interactive behavior, parental communication deviance, and risk for schizophrenia. *Journal of Abnormal Psychology, 90,* 448–457. [16]

Lewy, A. J., Sack, R. I., Miller, L. S. et al. (1987). Antidepressant and circadian phase-shifting effects of light. *Science, 235,* 352–354. [16]

Liberman, A. M., and **Mattingly, I. G.** (1989, January 27). A specialization for speech perception. *Science, 243,* 489–494. [8]

Liberman, B. L. (1978). The role of mastery in psychotherapy: Maintenance of improvement and prescriptive change. In J. D. Frank, R. Hoehn-Saric, D. D. Imber, B. L. Liberman, and A. R. Stone (Eds.), *The Effective Ingredients of Successful Psychotherapy.* New York: Brunner-Mazel. [19]

Liberman, R. P., and **Eckman, T.** (1981). Behavior therapy vs. insight-oriented therapy for repeated suicide attempters. *Archives of General Psychiatry, 38,* 1126–1130. [17]

Lieberman, M. A., and **Borman, L.** (1979). *Self-help Groups for Coping With Crisis.* San Francisco: Jossey-Bass. [17]

Liebert, R. M., and **Baron, R. A.** (1972). Some immediate effects of televised violence on children's behavior. *Developmental Psychology, 6,* 469–475. [2]

Liebert, R. M., Neale, J. M., and **Davidson, E. S.** (1973). *The Early Window: Effects of Television on Children and Youth.* Elmsford, NY: Pergamon Press. [19]

Liebowitz, H. W., and **Owens, D. A.** (1986, January). We drive by night. *Psychology Today,* pp. 55–58. [4]

Liem, J. H. (1974). Effects of verbal communications of parents and children: A comparison of normal and schizophrenic families. *Journal of Consulting and Clinical Psychology, 42,* 438–450. [16]

Liem, J. H. (1980). Family studies schizophrenia: An update and commentary. In S. J. Keith and L. R. Mosher (Eds.), *Special Report: Schizophrenia, 1980* (pp. 82–108). Washington, DC: U.S. Government Printing Office. [16]

Lindner, R. (1954). *The Fifty-Minute Hour.* New York: Holt, Rinehart and Winston. [17]

Lindsay, P. H., and **Norman, D. A.** (1977). *Human Information Processing: An Introduction to Psychology* (2nd ed.). New York: Academic Press. [7]

Lindsley, D. B. (1951). Emotion. In S. S. Stevens (Ed.), *Handbook of Experimental Psychology.* New York: Wiley. [12]

Linehan, M. M., Camper, P., Chiles, J. A., Strosahal, K., and **Shearin, E. S.** (1987). Interpersonal problem solving and parasuicide. *Cognitive Therapy and Research, 11,* 1–12. [17]

Linn, R. L. (1982). Admissions testing on trial. *American Psychologist, 37,* 279–291. [14]

Linn, R. L. (1986). Educational testing and assessment: Research needs and policy issues. *American Psychologist, 41*(10), 1153–1160. [14]

Linton, M. (1978, July). I remember it well. *Psychology Today,* pp. 81–86. [7]

Linton, M. (1982). Transformations of memory in everyday life. In Ulric Neisser (Ed.), *Memory Observed* (pp. 77–91). New York: W. H. Freeman. [7]

Linz, D., Donnerstein, E., and **Adams, S. M.** (1989, Summer). Physiological desensitization and judgments about female victims of violence. *Human Communications Research, 15*(4), 509–522. [2]

Linz, D., Donnerstein, E., and Penrod, S. (1987). The findings and recommendations of the Attorney General's Commission on Pornography: Do the psychological "facts" fit the political fury? *American Psychologist, 42,* 946–953. [19]

Livingston, M. S. (1988). Art, illusion, and the visual system. *Scientific American, 258,* 78–85. [4]

Livingston, M. S., and Hubel, D. H. (1987). Psychophysical evidence for separate channels for the perception of form, color, movement, and depth. *Journal of Neuroscience, 7,* 3416–3468. [4]

Lloyd, K. G. et al. (1989). The GABAergic hypothesis of depression. *Progress in Neuro-Psychopharmacology and Biological Psychiatry, 13*(3–4), 341–351. [16]

Locke, A. (1980). *The Guided Reinvention of Language.* London: Academic Press. [8]

Loeb, G. E. (1985, February). The functional replacement of the ear. *Scientific American,* pp. 104–111. [4]

Loehlin, J. C., Horn, J. M., and Willerman, L. (1981). Personality resemblance in adoptive families. *Behavior Genetics, 11,* 309–330. [10]

Loftus, E. F. (1975). Leading questions and the eyewitness report. *Cognitive Psychology, 7,* 560–572. [2]

Loftus, E. F. (1979). *Eyewitness Testimony.* Cambridge, MA: Harvard University Press. [7]

Loftus, E. F., and Greene, E. (1980). Warning: Even memory for faces may be contagious. *Law and Human Behavior, 4,* 323–334. [7]

Loftus, E. F., and Hoffman, H. G. (1989). Misinformation and memory: The creation of new memories. *Journal of Experimental Psychology: General, 118*(1), 100–104. [7]

Loftus, E. F., Levidow, B., and Duensing, S. (1991). Who remembers best?: Individual differences in memory for events that occurred in a science museum. *Applied Cognitive Psychology, 5.* [9]

Loftus, E. F., Miller, D. G., and Burns, H. J. (1978). Semantic integration of verbal information into a visual memory. *Journal of Experimental Psychology, 4,* 19–31. [2, 7]

Loftus, G. R., and Loftus, E. F. (1983). *Mind at Play: The Psychology of Video Games.* New York: Basic Books. [6]

Logue, A. W. (1986). *The Psychology of Eating and Drinking.* New York: W. H. Freeman. [12]

Logue, A. W. (1991). *The Psychology of Eating and Drinking: An Introduction* (2nd ed.). New York: W. H. Freeman. [12]

Loomis, J. M., and Lederman, S. J. (1986). Tactile perception. In R. B. Kenneth, L. Kaufman, and J. P. Thomas (Eds.), *Handbook of Perception and Human Performance* (Vol. 2, pp. 1–4). New York: Wiley. [4]

Lopes, L. L. (1989, January 15). *The Rhetoric of Irrationality.* Paper presented at AAAS meeting, San Francisco. [8]

LoPiccolo, J., and Stock, W. E. (1986). Treatment of sexual dysfunction. *Journal of Consulting Psychology, 54,* 158–167. [12]

Lorenz, K. (1974). *The Eight Deadly Sins of Civilized Man* (Marjorie Kerr-Wilson, Trans.). New York: Harcourt Brace Jovanovich. [19]

Lovett, L. M., and Shaw, D. M. (1987). Outcome in bipolar affective disorder after stereotactic tractotomy. *British Journal of Psychiatry, 151,* 113–116. [17]

Luborsky, L., and Spence, D. P. (1978). Quantitative research on psychoanalytic therapy. In S. L. Garfield and A. E. Bergin (Eds.), *Handbook of Psychotherapy and Behavior Change: An Empirical Analysis* (2nd ed.). New York: Wiley. [17]

Luce, G. G. (1971). *Body Time.* New York: Random House. [5]

Luce, R. D., and Krumhansl, C. L. (1988). Measurement, scaling, and psychophysics. In R. C. Atkinson, R. J. Hernstein, L. Gardner, and R. D. Luce, (Eds.), *Stevens' Handbook of Experimental Psychology* (2nd ed., Vol. 1, pp. 3–74). New York: Wiley. [4]

Luchins, A. S. (1946). Classroom experiments on mental set. *American Journal of Psychology, 59,* 295–298. [8]

Luchins, A. S. (1957). Primacy-recency in impression formation. In C. I. Hovland (Ed.), *The Order of Presentation in Persuasion* (pp. 33–61). New Haven: Yale University Press. [18]

Luria, A. R. (1968). *The Mind of a Mnemonist* (Lynn Solotaroff, Trans.). New York: Basic Books. [7]

Luria, A. R. (1973). *The Working Brain* (Basil Haigh, Trans.). London: Penguin Books. [4]

Luria, Z., and Herzog, E. (1985, April). *Gender Segregation Across and Within Settings.* Paper presented at the biennial meeting of the Society for Research in Child Development, Toronto. [10]

Lydiard, R. B., and Gelenberg, A. J. (1982). Hazards and adverse effects of lithium. *Annual Review of Medicine, 33,* 327–344. [17]

Lykken, D. T. (1957). A study of anxiety in the sociopathic personality. *Journal of Abnormal and Social Psychology, 55,* 6–10. [16]

Lynch, G. (1984, April). A magical memory tour. *Psychology Today,* pp. 28–39. [7]

Lynch, G., and Baudry, M. (1984). The biochemistry of memory: A new and specific hypothesis. *Science, 224,* 1063. [7]

Lynn, S. J., and Rhue, J. W. (1988, January). Fantasy proneness: Hypnosis, developmental antecedents, and psychopathology. *American Psychologist, 43*(1), 35–44. [5]

Maccoby, E. E. (1988). Gender as a social category. *Developmental Psychology, 24,* 755–765. [10]

Maccoby, E. E., and Jacklin, C. N. (1974). *The Psychology of Sex Differences.* Stanford, CA: Stanford University Press. [9, 10]

Maccoby, E. E., and Jacklin, C. N. (1987). Gender segregation in childhood. In H. Reese (Ed.), *Advances in Child Behavior and Development* (Vol. 20). [10]

Maccoby, E. E., and Martin, J. (1983). Socialization in the context of the family. In P. Mussen (Ed.), *Handbook of Child Psychology* (4th ed., Vol. 4), E. M. Hetherington (Ed.), *Socialization, Personality, and Social Development.* New York: Wiley. [10]

Macfarlane, A. (1977). *The Psychology of Childbirth*. Cambridge, MA: Harvard University Press. [9]

MacKinnon, D. W. (1962). The nature and nurture of creative talent. *American Psychologist, 17*, 484–495. [13]

MacKinnon, D. W. (1965). Personality and the realization of creative potential. *American Psychologist, 20*, 273–281. [13]

Mackintosh, N. J. (1983). *Conditioning and Associative Learning: Oxford Psychology Series, No. 3*. Oxford, England: Claredon Press. [6]

MacNichol, E. F., Jr. (1964). Three-pigment color vision. *Scientific American, 211*, 48–56. [4]

Maddi, S. (1976). *Personality Theories: A Comparative Analysis* (3rd ed.). Homewood, IL: Dorsey Press. [13]

Maddison, D., and **Walker, W. L.** (1967). Factors affecting the outcome of conjugal bereavement. *British Journal of Psychiatry, 113*, 1057–1067. [11]

Madsen, K. B. (1959). *Theories of Motivation: A Comparative Study of Modern Theories of Motivation*. Copenhagen: Munksgaard. [12]

Magnuson, E. (1986, March 10). "A serious deficiency": The Rogers Commission faults NASA's "flawed" decision-making process. *Time* (international ed.), pp. 40–42. [19]

Mahler, M. S. (1968). *On Human Symbiosis and the Vicissitudes of Individuation: Infantile Psychosis*. New York: International Universities Press. [13]

Mahler, M. S., Pine, F., and **Bergman, A.** (1975). *The Psychological Birth of the Human Infant*. New York: Basic Books. [10, 13]

Mahoney, M. J., and **Arnkoff, D.** (1978). Cognitive and self-control therapies. In S. L. Garfield and A. E. Bergin (Eds.), *Handbook of Psychotherapy and Behavior Change: An Empirical Analysis* (2nd ed.). New York: Wiley. [17]

Maier, N. R. F. (1931). Reasoning in humans. *Journal of Comparative Psychology, 12*, 181–194. [8]

Main, M., and **George, C.** (1985). Responses of abused and disadvantaged toddlers to distress in age-mates: A study in the day-care setting. *Developmental Psychology, 21*, 407–412. [10]

Mair, R. G., Gesteland, R. C., and **Blank, D. L.** (1982). Changes in morphology and physiology of olfactory receptor cilia during development. *NeuroScience, 7*, 3091–3103. [4]

Major, B., Mueller, P., and **Hildebrandt, K.** (1985). Attributions, expectations and coping with abortion. *Journal of Personality and Social Psychology, 48*(3), 585–599. [15]

Malamuth, N. M. (1981). Rape fantasies as a function of exposure to violent sexual stimuli. *Archives of Sexual Behavior, 10*, 33–47. [19]

Malamuth, N. M. (1984). Aggression against women: Cultural and individual causes. In N. M. Malamuth and E. Donnerstein (Eds.), *Pornography and Sexual Aggression*. Orlando, FL: Academic Press. [19]

Malamuth, N. M. (1989). The attraction to sexual aggression scale: Part one. *Journal of Sex Research, 25*. [19]

Malamuth, N. M., and **Check, J. V. P.** (1981). The effects of mass media exposure on acceptance of violence against women: A field experiment. *Journal of Research in Personality, 15*, 436–446. [19]

Malamuth, N. M., and **Check, J. V. P.** (1985). The effects of aggressive pornography on beliefs in rape myths: Individual differences. *Journal of Research in Personality, 19*, 299–320. [19]

Malamuth, N. M., Check, J. V. P., and **Brier, J.** (1986). Sexual arousal in response to aggression: Ideological, aggressive, and sexual correlates. *Journal of Personality and Social Psychology, 50*, 330–350. [19].

Maletzky, B. M., and **Klotter, J.** (1974). Smoking and alcoholism. *American Journal of Psychiatry, 131*(4), 445–447. [16]

Malpass, R. S., and **Devine, P. G.** (1981). Guided memory in eyewitness identification research. *Journal of Applied Psychology, 66*, 343–350. [5]

Malsbury, C. W. (1974). Facilitation of male rat copulatory behaviour by electrical stimulation of the medial preptic area. *Physiology and Behavior, 7*, 797–805. [12]

Maltz, D. N., and **Borker, R. A.** (1983). A cultural approach to male-female miscommunication. In J. A. Gumperz (Ed.), *Language and Social Identity* (pp. 195–216). New York: Cambridge University Press. [10]

Mandler, G. (1984). *Mind and Body*. New York: Norton. [5]

Mandos, L., Clary, C., and **Schweizer, E.** (1990, February). Prescribing practices for fluoxetine: A brief survey. *Journal of Clinical Psychopharmacology, 10*, 74–75. [17]

Marañon, G. (1924). Contribution à l'etude de l'action emotive de l'adrenaline. *Revue Francaise d'Endocrinologie, 2*, 301–325. [11]

Maratsos, M. (1983). Some current issues in the study of the acquisition of grammar. In P. Mussen (Ed.), *Handbook of Child Psychology* (4th ed., Vol. 3), J. H. Flavell and E. Markman (Eds.), *Cognitive Development* (pp. 707–786). New York: Wiley. [9]

Marcel, A. (1983). Conscious and unconscious perception: An approach to the relation between phenomenal experience and perceptual process. *Cognitive Psychology, 15*, 238–300. [4]

Margolin, L., Miller, M., and **Moran, P.** (1989). When a kiss is not just a kiss: Relating violations of consent in kissing to rape myth acceptance. *Sex Roles, 20*, 231–243. [19]

Mark, V. H., and **Ervin, F. R.** (1970). *Violence and the Brain*. New York: Harper & Row. [11]

Markman, E. (1977). Realizing that you don't understand: A preliminary investigation. *Child Development, 48*, 986–992. [9]

Markus, H. (1977). Self-schemata and processing information about the self. *Journal of Personality and Social Psychology, 35*(2), 63–78. [13]

Markus, H., and **Nurius, P.** (1987). Possible selves. *American Psychologist, 41*(9), 954–969.

Markus, H., and **Zajonc, R. B.** (1985). The cognitive perspective in social psychology. In G. Lindsey and E. Aronson

(Eds.), *Handbook of Social Psychology* (3rd ed.). Reading, MA: Addison-Wesley. [18]

Marlatt, G. A., and **George, W. H.** (1988). Relapse prevention and the maintenance of optimal health. In S. Shumaker, E. Schron, and J. K. Ockene (Eds.), *The Adoption and Maintenance of Behaviors for Optimal Health.* New York: Springer. [16]

Marlatt, G. A., Kosturn, C. F., and **Lang, A. R.** (1975). Provocation to anger and opportunity for retaliation as determinants of alcohol consumption in social drinkers. *Journal of Abnormal Psychology, 84,* 652–659. [16]

Marlatt, G. A., and **Nathan, P. E.** (Eds.). (1978). *Behavioral Approaches to Alcoholism.* New Brunswick, NJ: Rutgers Center for Alcohol Studies. [2]

Marlatt, G. A., and **Rohsenow, D. J.** (1981, December). The think-drink effect. *Psychology Today,* pp. 60–70. [5]

Martin, C. L., and **Halverson, C. F., Jr.** (1981). A schematic processing model of sex typing and stereotyping in children. *Child Development, 52,* 1119–1134. [10]

Martin, G., and **Pear, J.** (1983). *Behavior Modification: What It Is and How It Works* (2nd ed.). Englewood Cliffs, NJ: Prentice-Hall. [6]

Martindale, C. (1981). *Cognition and Consciousness.* Homewood, IL: Dorsey Press. [12]

Marx, J. L. (1988, August 19). Sexual responses are—almost—all in the brain. *Science, 241,* 903–904. [3]

Marx, J. L. (1989, March 31). Brain protein yields clues to Alzheimer's disease. *Science, 243,* 1664–1666. [3]

Maslach, C. (1976). Burned-out. *Human Behavior, 5,* 16–22. [19]

Maslach, C., Stapp, J., and **Santee, R. T.** (1985). Individuation: Conceptual analysis and assessment. *Journal of Personality and Social Psychology, 49,* 729–738. [19]

Maslow, A. H. (1954). *Motivation and Personality.* New York: Harper & Row. [13]

Maslow, A. H. (1966). *The Psychology of Science: A Reconnaissance.* New York: Harper & Row. [13]

Maslow, A. H. (1968). *Toward a Psychology of Being* (2nd ed.). New York: Van Nostrand Reinhold. [13]

Maslow, A. H. (1971a). *The Farther Reaches of the Human Mind.* New York: Viking. [13]

Maslow, A. H. (1971b). Some basic propositions of a growth and self-actualization psychology. In S. Maddi (Ed.), *Perspectives on Personality.* Boston: Little, Brown. [13]

Masten, A. S. (1986, August). *The Patterns of Adaptation to Stress in Middle Childhood.* Paper presented at the meeting of the American Psychological Association, Washington, DC. [10]

Masters, J. C., Burish, T. G., Hollon, S. D., and **Rimin, D. C.** (1987). *Behavior Therapy: Techniques and Empirical Findings.* San Diego: Harcourt, Brace, Jovanovich. [6]

Masters, W. H., and **Johnson, V. E.** (1966). *Human Sexual Response.* Boston: Little, Brown. [12]

Masters, W. H., and **Johnson, V. E.** (1970). *Human Sexual Inadequacy.* Boston: Little, Brown. [12]

Mather, D. B. (1987, September). The case against preventing suicide prevention: Comments on Szasz. *American Psychologist, 42,* 882–883. [17]

Mathes, E. W. (1975, November). The effects of physical attractiveness and anxiety on heterosexual attraction over a series of five encounters. *Journal of Marriage and Family,* pp. 769–773. [18]

Matlin, M. (1983). *Cognition.* New York: Holt, Rinehart and Winston. [8]

Matlin, M. (1989). *Cognition* (2nd ed.). New York: Holt, Rinehart and Winston. [8]

Matthews, K., and **Haynes, S. G.** (1986). Type A behavior pattern and coronary risk: Update and critical evaluation. *American Journal of Epidemiology, 123,* 923–960. [13]

Matthies, H. (1989). Neurobiological aspects of learning and memory. *Annual Review of Psychology, 40,* 381–404. [7]

Maugh, T. H., II. (1982). Marijuana "justifies serious concern." *Science, 215,* 1488–1490. [5]

May, R. (1982). The problem of evil: An open letter to Carl Rogers. *Journal of Humanistic Psychology, 22,* 10–21. [13]

Mayer, J. (1952). The glucostatic theory of regulation of food intake and the problem of obesity. *Bulletin of the New England Medical Center, 14,* 43–49. [12]

Mayer, J. D., and **Bremer, D.** (1985). Assessing mood with affect-sensitive tasks. *Journal of Personality Assessment, 49*(1), 95–99. [11]

Mayer, R. E. (1983). *Thinking, Problem Solving, Cognition.* New York: W. H. Freeman. [8]

Mayer-Gross, W., Slater, E., and **Roth, M.** (1969). *Clinical Psychiatry.* Baltimore: Williams & Wilkins. [16]

McAdams, D. P. (1988a). Biography, narrative, and lives: An introduction. *Journal of Personality, 56*(1), 1–18. [13]

McAdams, D. P. (1988b). *Power, Intimacy, and the Life Story: Personological Inquiries into Identity.* New York: Guilford. [13]

McAdams, D. P. (1990). *The Person: An Introduction to Personality Psychology.* San Diego: Harcourt Brace Jovanovich.

McArthur, L. A. (1972). The how and what of why: Some determinants and consequences of causal attribution. *Journal of Personality and Social Psychology, 22,* 171–193. [18]

McBurney, D. H., and **Collings, V. B.** (1984). *Introduction to Sensation/Perception* (2nd ed.). Englewood Cliffs, NJ: Prentice-Hall. [4]

McCartney, K., Scarr, S., Phillips, D., Grajek, S., and **Schwarz, J. C.** (1982). Environmental differences among day care centers and their effect on children's development. In E. F. Zigler and E. W. Gordon (Eds.), *Day Care: Scientific and Social Policy Issues.* Boston: Auburn House. [10]

McCauley, C. (1989). The nature of social influence in groupthink: Compliance and internalization. *Journal of Personality and Social Psychology, 57,* 250–260. [19]

McClelland, D. C. (1955). Some social consequences of achievement motivation. In M. R. Jones (Ed.), *Nebraska Symposium on Motivation 1955.* Lincoln: University of Nebraska Press. [12]

McClelland, D. C. (1973). Testing for competence rather than for "intelligence." *American Psychologist*, 1–14. [14]

McClelland, D. C. (1978). Managing motivation to expand human freedom. *American Psychologist*, 201–210. [12]

McClelland, D. C. (1985). *Human Motivation*. Glenview, IL: Scott, Foresman. [12]

McClelland, D. C., Atkinson, J. W., Clark, R. W., and **Lowell, E. L.** (1953). *The Achievement Motive*. New York: Appleton-Century-Crofts. [12]

McClelland, D. C., Atkinson, J. W., Clark, R. W., and **Lowell, E. L.** (1976). *The Achievement Motive* (2nd ed.). New York: Irvington. [12]

McClelland, D. C., and **Winter, D. G.** (1969). *Motivating Economic Achievement*. New York: Free Press. [12]

McClelland, J. L. (1988). Connectionist models and psychological evidence. *Journal of Memory and Language, 27*, 107–123. [7]

McClintock, C. C., and **Hunt, R. G.** (1975). Nonverbal indicators of affect and deception in an interview setting. *Journal of Applied Psychology, 5*, 54–67. [18]

McCloskey, M., and **Zaragoza, M.** (1985). Misleading postevent information and memory for events: Arguments and evidence against memory impairment hypothesis. *Journal of Experimental Psychology: General, 114*(1), 1–16. [7]

McCord, W., and **McCord, J.** (1964). *The Psychopath: An Essay on the Criminal Mind.* New York: Van Nostrand-Reinhold. [16].

McCrae, R. R. (1989). Why I advocate the five factor model: Joint factor analyses of the NEO-PI with other instruments. In D. M. Buss and N. Cantor (Eds.), *Personality Psychology: Recent Trends and Emerging Directions* (pp. 237–245). New York: Springer-Verlag. [13]

McCrae, R. R., and **Costa, P. T., Jr.** (1984). *Emerging Lives, Enduring Dispositions: Personality in Adulthood.* Boston: Little, Brown. [10]

McCrae, R. R., and **Costa, P. T., Jr.** (1988, June). Recalled parent-child relations and adult personality. *Journal of Personality, 56*(2), 417–434. [10]

McCulloch, J. W., and **Prins, H. A.** (1975). *Signs of Stress.* London: Collins. [16]

McDonald, K. (1985, June 5). Changes in facial expression can alter a person's moods. *Chronicle of Higher Education.* p. 15. [11]

McDonald, K. (1988, July/August). Mending the brain. *Psychology Today*, pp. 44–49. [3]

McDougall, W. (1908). *Social Psychology.* New York: Putnam's. [12]

McEwan, N. H., and **Yuille, J. C.** (1982, June). *The effect of hypnosis as an interview technique on eyewitness memory.* Paper presented at the annual meeting of the Canadian Psychological Association, Montreal. [5]

McGinnies, E., and **Ward, C. D.** (1980). Better liked than right: Trustworthiness and expertise as factors in credibility. *Personality and Social Psychology Bulletin, 6*, 467–472. [18]

McGrath, J. E. (1984). *Groups: Interaction and Performance.* Englewood Cliffs, NJ: Prentice-Hall. [19]

McGuffin, P., Bebbington, P., and **Katz, R.** (1989). The Camberwell Collaborative Depression Study: III. Depression and adversity in the relatives of depressed controls: Reply. *British Journal of Psychiatry, 154*, 565. [16]

McGuire, W. J. (1985). Attitudes and attitude change. In G. Lindsey and E. Aronson (Eds.), *Handbook of Social Psychology* (3rd ed., pp. 233–346). Reading, MA: Addison-Wesley. [18]

McKean, K. (1985, April). Of two minds: Selling the right brain. *Discover*, pp. 34–40. [3]

McKinnon, W., Weisse, C. S., Reynolds, C. P., Bowles, C. A., and **Baum, A.** (1989). Chronic stress, leukocyte subpopulations, and humoral response to latent viruses. *Health Psychology, 8*, 389–402. [15]

McKoon, G., Ratcliff, R., and **Dell, G. S.** (1986). A critical evaluation of the semantic–episodic distinction. *Journal of Experimental Psychology: Learning, Memory, and Cognition, 12*(2), 295–306. [7]

McNeal, E. T., and **Cimbolic, P.** (1986). Antidepressants and biochemical theories of depression. *Psychological Bulletin, 99*, 361–374. [16]

McNeill, D. (1966). Developmental psycholinguistics. In F. L. Smith and G. A. Miller (Eds.), *The Genesis of Language: A Psycholinguistic Approach.* Cambridge, MA: MIT Press. [9]

Mead, M. (1935). *Sex and Temperament in Three Primitive Societies.* New York: Morrow. [10]

Meaney, M. J., Aitken, D. H., van Berkel, C., Bhatnagar, S., and **Sapolsky, R. M.** (1988, 12 February). Effects of neonatal handling on age-related impairments. *Science, 239*, 766–768. [9]

Medin, D. L., and **Smith, E. E.** (1984). Concepts and concept formation. *Annual Review of Psychology, 35*, 113–138. [8]

Mednick, S. A., Machon, R., Huttunen, M. O., and **Bonett, D.** (1988). Fetal viral infection and adult schizophrenia. *Archives of General Psychiatry, 45*, 189–192. [16]

Meeus, W. H. J., and **Raaijmakers, Q. A. W.** (1986). Administrative obedience: Carrying out orders to use psychological-administrative violence. *European Journal of Social Psychology, 16*, 311–324. [19]

Meeus, W. H. J., and **Raaijmakers, Q. A. W.** (1987). Administrative obedience as a social phenomenon. In W. Doise and S. Moscovici (Eds.), *Current Issues in European Social Psychology* (Vol. 2, pp. 183–230). Cambridge, England: Cambridge University Press. [19]

Mehrabian, A. (1972). *Nonverbal Communication.* Hawthorne, NY: Aldine-Atherton. [11]

Meichenbaum, D. H. (Ed.). (1977). *Cognitive Behavior Modification: An Integrative Approach.* New York: Plenum. [15, 17]

Meichenbaum, D. H., and **Deffenbacher, J. L.** (1988). Stress inoculation training. *Counseling Psychologist, 16*(1), 69–90. [15]

Meichenbaum, D. H., and **Turk, D.** (1982). Stress, coping, and disease: A cognitive-behavioral perspective. In R. W. J. Neufield (Ed.), *Psychological Stress and Psychopathology.* New York: McGraw-Hill. [15]

Meindl, J. R. and **Lerner, M. J.** (1985). Exacerbation of extreme responses to an out-group. *Journal of Personality and Social Psychology, 47,* 71–84. [18]

Meisami, E. (1978). Influence of early anosmia on the developing olfactory bulb. *Progress in Brain Research, 48,* 211–230. [3]

Melges, F. T., Tinklenberg, J. R., Hollister, L. E., and **Gillespie, H. K.** (1970). Marihuana and temporal disintegration. *Science, 168,* 1118–1120. [5]

Melges, F. T., Tinklenberg, J. R., Hollister, L. E., and **Gillespie, H. K.** (1971). Marihuana and the temporal span of awareness. *Archives of General Psychiatry, 24,* 564–567. [5]

Melton, G., and **Gray, J.** (1988). Ethical dilemmas in AIDS research: Individual privacy and public health. *American Psychologist, 43,* 60–64. [2]

Meltzer, H. Y., and **Stahl, S. M.** (1976). Dopamine hypothesis of schizophrenia— Review. *Schizophrenia Bulletin, 2,* 19–76. [16]

Meltzoff, A. N., and **Moore, M. K.** (1977). Imitation of facial and manual gestures by human neonates. *Science, 198,* 75–78. [9]

Meltzoff, A. N., and **Moore, M. K.** (1983). Newborn infants imitate adult facial gestures. *Child Development, 54,* 702–709. [9]

Melzack, R., and **Woll, P. D.** (1965). Pain mechanisms: A new theory. *Science, 150,* 971–979. [4]

Mendels, J. (1970). *Concepts of Depression.* New York: Wiley. [16]

Mercer, J. (1979). *Technical Manual: SOMPA (System of Multicultural Pluralistic Assessment).* New York: Psychological Association. [14]

Merikle, P. M. (1988, winter). Subliminal auditory messages: An evaluation. *Psychology and Marketing, 5*(4), 355–372. [4]

Merton, R. K., and **Kitt, A. S.** (1950). Contributions to the theory of reference group behavior. In R. K. Merton and P. F. Lazarsfeld (Eds.), *Continuities in Social Research: Studies in the Scope and Method of "The American Soldier."* New York: Free Press. [11]

Mervis, C. B., Catlin, J., and **Rosch, E.** (1976). Relationships among goodness-of-example, category norms, and word frequency. *Bulletin of the Psychonomic Society, 7,* 283–284. [8]

Messick, S. (1980). Test validity and the ethics of assessment. *American Psychologist, 35,* 1012–1027. [14]

Messick, S., and **Jungeblut, A.** (1981). Time and method in coaching for the SAT. *Psychological Bulletin, 89,* 191–216. [14]

Metalsky, G. I., Haberstadt, L. J., and **Abramson, L. Y.** (1987). Vulnerability and invulnerability to depressive mood reactions: Toward a more powerful test of the diathesis-stress and causal mediation components of the reformulated theory of depression. *Journal of Personality and Social Psychology, 52,* 386–393. [16]

Meyer, C. B., and **Taylor, S. E.** (1986). Adjustment to rape. *Journal of Personality and Social Psychology, 50,* 1226–1234. [16]

Michael, R. P., and **Keverne, E. B.** (1968). Pheromones in the communication of sexual status in primates. *Nature, 218,* 746–749. [12]

Michael, R. P., Keverne, E. B., and **Bonsall, R. W.** (1971). Pheromones: Isolation of male sex attractants from a female primate. *Science, 172,* 964–966. [12]

Michaels, J. W., Blommel, J. M., Brocata, R. M., Linkous, R. A., and **Rowe, J. S.** (1982). Social facilitation and inhibition in a natural setting. *Replications in Social Psychology, 2,* 21–24. [19]

Midgley, C., Feldlaufer, H., and **Eccles, J. S.** (1989). Student/teacher relations and attitudes toward mathematics before and after the transition to junior high school. *Child Development, 60* (4), 981–992. [12]

Miers, M. L. (1985). Current NIH perspectives on misconduct in science. *American Psychologist, 40,* 831–835. [2]

Milgram, S. (1963). Behavioral study of obedience. *Journal of Abnormal and Social Psychology, 67,* 371–378. [1, 2, 19]

Milgram, S. (1964). Issues in the study of obedience: A reply to Baumrind. *American Psychologist, 19,* 848–852. [19]

Milgram, S. (1965a). Liberating effects of group pressure. *Journal of Personality and Social Psychology, 1,* 127–134. [19]

Milgram, S. (1965b). Some conditions of obedience and disobedience to authority. In I. D. Steiner and M. Fishbein (Eds.). *Current Studies in Social Psychology* (pp. 243–262). New York: Holt, Rinehart and Winston. [19]

Milgram, S. (1968). Some conditions of obedience and disobedience to authority. *Human Relations, 18,* 56–76. [19]

Milgram, S. (1974). *Obedience to Authority.* New York: Harper & Row. [19]

Miller, D. J. (1978). Effects of noise on people. In E. C. Carterette and M. P. Friedman (Eds.), *Handbook of Perception* (Vol. 4). New York: Academic Press. [4]

Miller, D. T., and **Turnbull, W.** (1986). Expectancies and interpersonal processes. In M. R. Rosenzweig and L. W. Porter (Eds.), *Annual Review of Psychology* (Vol. 37, pp. 233–256). Palo Alto, CA: Annual Review. [18]

Miller, G. A. (1956). The magical number seven, plus or minus two: Some limits on our capacity for processing information. *Psychological Review, 63,* 81–97. [6]

Miller, G. A. (1962). *Psychology.* New York: Harper & Row. [14]

Miller, G. A. (1981). *Language and Speech.* New York: W. H. Freeman. [8, 9]

Miller, G. A., Galanter, E., and **Pribram, K. H.** (1960). *Plans and the Structure of Behavior.* New York: Holt, Rinehart and Winston. [1]

Miller, G. A., and **Glucksberg, S.** (1988). Psycholinguistic aspects of pragmatics and semantics. In R. C. Atkinson and R. J. Hernstein, in G. Lindzey and R. D. Luce (Eds.), *Stevens Handbook of Experimental Psychology* (2nd ed., Vol. 2, pp. 417–472). New York: Wiley. [8]

Miller, G. R., and **Burgoon, J. K.** (1982). Factors affecting assessments of witness credibility. In N. L. Kerr and R. M. Bray (Eds.). *The Psychology of the Courtroom.* New York: Academic Press. [11]

Miller, L. L., and **Branconnier, R. J.** (1983). Cannabis: Effects on memory and the cholinergic limbic system. *Psychological Bulletin, 93,* 441–456. [5]

Miller, L. L., Cornett, T. L., Brightwell, D. R., McFarland, D. J., Drew, W. G., and Winkler, A. (1977). Marijuana: Effects on storage and retrieval of prose material. *Psychopharmacology, 51,* 311–316. [5]

Miller, L. L., Cornett, T. L., and McFarland, D. J. (1978). Marijuana: An analysis of storage and retrieval deficits in memory with the technique of restricted reminding. *Pharmacology Biochemistry and Behavior, 8,* 327–332. [5]

Miller, N. E. (1985). The value of behavioral research on animals. *American Psychologist, 40,* 423–440. [2]

Miller, N. E., and Bugelski, R. (1948). Minor studies of aggression: II. The influence of frustrations imposed by the in-group on attitudes expressed toward outgroups. *Journal of Psychology, 25,* 437–452. [18]

Miller, S. A. (1976). Nonverbal assessment of conservation of number. *Child Development, 47,* 722–728. [9]

Miller, W. (1975). Psychological deficit in depression. *Psychological Bulletin, 82,* 238–260. [9]

Milner, B. (1976). CNS maturation and language acquisition. In H. Whitaker and H. A. Whitaker (Eds.), *Studies of Neurolinguistics* (Vol. 1). New York: Academic Press. [9]

Mineka, S., Suomi, S. J., and DeLizio, R. (1981). Multiple separations in adolescent monkeys: An opponent-process interpretation. *Journal of Experimental Psychology, 110,* 56–85. [12]

Mirowsky, J., and Ross, C. E. (1989, March). Psychiatric diagnosis as reified measurement. *Journal of Health and Social Behavior, 30,* 11–25. [16]

Mischel, W. (1968). *Personality and Assessment.* New York: Wiley. [13]

Mischel, W. (1976). *Introduction to Personality* (2nd ed.). New York: Holt, Rinehart and Winston. [13]

Mischel, W. (1981). *Introduction to Personality* (3rd ed.). New York: Holt, Rinehart and Winston. [13]

Mishara, B. L. (1982). College students' experiences with suicide and reactions to suicidal verbalizations: A model for prevention. *Journal of Community Psychology, 10,* 142–150. [16]

Mishkin, M., and Appenzeller, T. (1987). The anatomy of memory. *Scientific American, 256,* 80–89. [3]

Moldofsky, H., and Scarisbrick, P. (1976, January/February). Induction of neurasthenic musculoskeletal pain syndrome by selective sleep stage deprivation. *Psychosomatic Medicine, 38*(1), 35–44. [5]

Mollon, J. D. (1982). Color vision. *Annual Review of Psychology, 33,* 41–85. [4]

Monahan, L., Kuhn, D., and Shaver, P. (1974). Intrapsychic versus cultural explanations of the "fear of success" motive. *Journal of Personality and Social Psychology, 29,* 60–64. [12]

Money, J., and Ehrhardt, A. A. (1972). *Man and Woman, Boy and Girl.* Baltimore: Johns Hopkins University Press. [12]

Monge, R., and Hultsch, D. (1971). Paired associate learning as a function of adult age and the length of anticipation and inspection intervals. *Journal of Gerontology, 26,* 157–162. [9]

Monnier, M., Boehmer, A., and Scholer, A. (1976). Early habituation, dishabituation, and generalization induced in visual center by color stimuli. *Vision Research, 16,* 1497–1504. [9, 12]

Monroe, S. M. (1983). Major and minor life events as predictors of psychological distress: Further issues and findings. *Journal of Behavioral Medicine, 6,* 189–205. [15]

Montgomery, G. (1989, March). The mind in motion. *Discover, 10,* 58–68. [3]

Moore, D. S. (1979). *Statistics: Concepts and Controversies.* New York: W. H. Freeman. [2]

Moore, T. E. (1982). Subliminal advertising: What you see is what you get. *Journal of Marketing, 46,* 38–47. [4]

Moore, T. E. (1988, winter). The case against subliminal manipulation. *Psychology and Marketing, 5*(4), 297–316. [4]

Mori, D., Chaiken, S., and Pliner, P. (1987). "Eating lightly" and the self-presentation of femininity. *Journal of Personality and Social Psychology, 53,* 693–702. [18]

Morris, N. M., and Udry, J. R. (1978). Pheromonal influences on human sexual behavior: An experimental search. *Journal of Biosocial Science, 10,* 147–157. [12]

Morrison, F. J., Giordani, B., and Nagy, J. (1977). Reading disability: An information processing analysis. *Science, 199,* 77–79. [7]

Morse, R. C., and Stoller, D. (1982, September). The hidden message that breaks habits. *Science Digest,* p. 28. [4]

Moscovici, S. (1985). Social influence and conformity. In G. Lindsey and E. Aronson (Eds.), *Handbook of Social Psychology* (3rd ed.). Reading, MA: Addison-Wesley. [9, 19]

Moscovici, S., Lage, S., and Naffrechoux, M. (1969). Influence of a consistent minority on the responses of a majority in a color perception task. *Sociometry, 32,* 365–380. [19]

Moscovici, S., and Mugny, G. (1983). Minority influence. In P. Paulus (Ed.), *Basic Group Process.* New York: Springer-Verlag. [19]

Moscovici, S., and Personnaz, B. (1980). Studies in social influence vs. minority influence and conversion behavior in a perceptual look. *Journal of Experimental Social Psychology, 16,* 270–283. [19]

Moses, S. (1991, January). Major revision of SAT goes into effect in 1994. *APA Monitor,* p. 35. [14]

Moskowitz, D. S., Schwarz, J. C., and Corsini, D. A. (1977). Initiating day care at three years of age: Effects on attachment. *Child Development, 48,* 1271–1276. [10]

Moss, H. A. (1967). Sex, age, and state as determinants of mother–infant interaction. *Merrill-Palmer Quarterly of Behavior and Development, 13,* 19–36. [10]

Moss, R. B., Moss, H. B., and Peterson, R. (1989). Microstress, mood, and natural killer-cell activity. *Psychosomatics, 30,* 279–283.

Mowbray, C. T. (1988). Post-traumatic therapy for children who are victims of violence. In F. M. Ochberg (Ed.), *Post-Traumatic Therapy and Victims of Violence* (pp. 196–212). New York: Brunner/Mazel.

Mowrer, O., and **Mowrer, W.** (1930). Enuresis: A method for its study and treatment. *American Journal of Orthopsychiatry, 8,* 436–459. [6]

Muir, D., and **Field, J.** (1979). Newborn infants orient to sound. *Child Development, 50,* 431–436. [8]

Mullen, B., and **Baumeister, R. F.** (1987). Group effects on self-attention and performance: Social loafing, social facilitation, and social impairment. In C. Hendrick (Ed.), *Group Processes and Intergroup Relations: Review of Personality and Social Psychology* (Vol. 9). Newbury Park, CA: Sage Publications. [19]

Mulvey, E. P., and **Haugaard, J. L.** (1986, August 4). *Report of the Surgeon General's Workshop on Pornography and Public Health.* Washington, DC: U.S. Department of Health and Human Services, Office of the Surgeon General. [19]

Murray, H. A. (1959). Vicissitudes of creativity. In H. H. Anderson (Ed.), *Creativity and Its Cultivation.* New York: Harper & Row. [8]

Muscettola, G., Potter, W. Z., Pickar, D., and **Goodwin, F. K.** (1984). Urinary 3-methoxy-4-hydroxyphenylglycol and major affective disorders. *Archives of General Psychiatry, 41,* 337–342. [16]

Mussen, P., Honzik, M., and **Eichorn, D.** (1982). Early adult antecedents of life satisfaction at age 70. *Journal of Gerontology, 37,* 315–322. [10]

Mussen, P. H., and **Eisenberg-Berg, N.** (1977). *The Roots of Caring, Sharing, and Helping: The Development of Prosocial Behavior in Children.* San Francisco, CA: W. H. Freeman. [13]

Muter, P. (1980). Very rapid forgetting. *Memory and Cognition, 8,* 174–179. [7]

Myers, D. G., and **Ridl, J.** (1979, August). Can we all be better than average? *Psychology Today,* pp. 89–98. [2, 7]

Myers, J. K., Weissman, M. M., Tischler, G. L., Holzer, C. E., Leaf, P. J., Orvaschel, H. A., Anthony, J. C., Boyd, J. H., Burke, J. E., Kramer, M., and **Stoltzman, R.** (1984). Six-month prevalence of psychiatric disorders in three communities: 1980–1982. *Archives of General Psychiatry, 41,* 959–967. [16]

Nairn, A., and Associates. (1980). *The Reign of ETS: The Corporation That Makes Up Minds.* Washington, DC: Nader. [14]

Nathan, P. E. (1976). Alcoholism. In H. Leitenberg (Ed.), *Handbook of Behavior Modification and Behavior Therapy.* Englewood Cliffs, NJ: Prentice-Hall. [17]

Nathans, J. (1989, February). The genes for color vision. *Scientific American, 260,* 42–49. [4]

National Academy of Sciences. (1982a). *Ability Testing: Uses, Consequences, and Controversies.* A. K. Wigdor and W. R. Gardner (Eds.). Washington, DC: National Academy Press. [14]

National Academy of Sciences. (1982b). *Marijuana and Health.* Washington, DC: National Academy Press. [5]

National Center for Health Statistics (1988). Advance report of final mortality statistics, 1986. *NCHS Monthly Vital Statistics Report, 37* (Suppl. 6). [16, 17]

National Institute of Alcohol Abuse and Alcoholism (NIAAA). (1982). *Alcohol and Health Monograph Nos. 1, 2, 3, 4.* Washington, DC: Department of Health and Human Services. [5]

National Institute of Mental Health (NIMH). (1985). *Mental Health, United States.* Washington, DC: U.S. Government Printing Office. [17]

Natsoulas, T. (1983). Concepts of consciousness. *The Journal of Mind and Behavior, 4,* 13–59. [5]

Navarro, M. (1991, March 4). Life salvaged, now savored: Living longer with AIDS. *The New York Times,* pp. A1, B6. [15]

Needleman, H. L., Schell, M. A., Bellinger, D., Leviton, A. and **Allred, E. N.** (1990, January 11). The long-term effects of exposure to low doses of lead in children: An 11 year follow-up report. *The New England Journal of Medicine, 322*(2), 85–88.

Neiss, R. (1988). Reconceptualizing arousal: Psychobiological states in motor performance. *Psychological Bulletin, 103,* 345–366. [12]

Neiss, R. (1990). Ending arousal's reign of error: A reply to Anderson. *Psychological Bulletin, 107,* 101–105. [12]

Nelson, K. (1973). Structure and strategy in learning to talk. *Monographs of the Society for Research in Child Development, 38*(1–2). [9]

Nelson, K. (1977). Facilitating children's syntax acquistion. *Developmental Psychology, 13,* 101–107. [9]

Nelson, K. (1981). Individual differences in language development: Implications for development and language. *Developmental Psychology, 17*(2), 170–187. [9]

Nemeth, C. (1979). The role of an active minority in intergroup relations. In W. G. Austin and S. Worchel (Eds.), *The Social Psychology of Intergroup Relations.* Monterey, CA: Brooks/Cole. [19]

Neuberg, S. L. (1989). The goal of forming accurate impressions during social interactions: Attenuating the impact of negative expectancies. *Journal of Personality and Social Psychology, 56,* 374–386. [18]

Neugarten, B. L. (1976). Adaptation and the life cycle. *The Counseling Psychologist, 6,* 16–20. [9]

Newberger, C., Melnicoe, L., and **Newberger, E.** (1986). The American family in crisis: Implications for children. *Current Problems in Pediatrics, 16,* 674–721. [10]

Newell, A., and **Simon, H. A.** (1972). *Human Problem Solving.* Englewood Cliffs, NJ: Prentice-Hall. [1, 8]

Nichols, J. G. (1975). Causal attributions and other achievement-related cognitions: Effects of task outcomes, attainment value and sex. *Journal of Personality and Social Psychology, 31,* 379–389. [12]

Nisbett, R. E. (1972). Hunger, obesity, and the ventromedial hypothalamus. *Psychological Review, 79,* 433–453. [12]

Nisbett, R. E., Fong, G. T., Lehman, D. R., and **Cheng, P. W.** (1987). Teaching reasoning. *Science, 238,* 625–631. [8]

Nisbett, R. E., and **Ross, L.** (1980). *Human Inference: Strategies and Shortcomings of Social Judgment.* Englewood Cliffs, NJ: Prentice-Hall. [18]

Nisbett, R. E., and **Wilson, T.** (1977). Telling more than we know. *Psychological Review, 84,* 231–259. [8, 12]

Nolen-Hoeksema, S. (1987). Sex differences in unipolar depression: Evidence and theory. *Psychological Bulletin, 101,* 259–282. [16]

Nolen-Hoeksema, S., Girgus, J. S., and Seligman, M. E. P. (1989, August). *Predictors of the Onset and Course of Depression in Children.* Paper presented at the annual convention of the American Psychological Association, New Orleans, LA. [10]

Norcross, J. C. (1986). *Handbook of Eclectic Psychotherapy.* New York: Brunner/Mazel. [17]

Notarius, C. I., Wemple, C., Ingraham, L. J., Burns, T. J., and **Kollar, E.** (1982). Multichannel responses to an interpersonal stressor: Interrelationships among facial display, heart rate, self-report of emotion, and threat display. *Journal of Personality and Social Psychology, 43,* 400–408. [11]

O'Brien, D. F. (1982). The chemistry of vision. *Science, 218,* 916–966. [4]

Oden, M. H. (1968). The fulfillment of promise: Forty-year follow-up of Terman gifted group. *Genetic Psychology Monographs, 7,* 3–93. [14]

Öhman, A., Erixon, G., and **Löfberg, I.** (1975). Phobias and preparedness: Phobic versus neutral pictures as conditional stimuli for human autonomic responses. *Journal of Abnormal Psychology, 84,* 41–45. [16]

Olds, J., and **Milner, P.** (1954). Positive reinforcement produced by electrical stimulation of septal area and other regions of the rat brain. *Journal of Comparative and Physiological Psychology, 47,* 419–427. [3]

O'Leary, K. D., and **Smith, D. A.** (1991). Marital interactions. *Annual Review of Psychology, 42,* 191–212. [17]

Orne, M. T. (1962). On the social psychology of the psychological experiment: With particular reference to demand characteristics and their implications. *American Psychologist, 17,* 776–783. [2]

Orne, M. T., Soskis, D. A., Dinges, D. F., and **Orne, E. C.** (1984). Hypnotically induced testimony. In G. L. Wells and E. F. Loftus (Eds.), *Eyewitness Testimony: Psychological Perspective* (pp. 171–213). Cambridge University Press. [5]

Ornstein, R. (1977). *The Psychology of Consciousness* (2nd ed.). New York: Harcourt Brace Jovanovich. [3, 5]

O'Rourke, K. (1986). *Medical Ethics Common Ground for Understanding.* St. Louis, MO: Catholic Health Association of the U. S. [13]

Oscar-Berman, M., and **Ellis, R. J.** (1987). Cognitive deficits related to memory impairments in alcoholism. *Recent Development in Alcoholism, 5,* 59–80. [5]

Osofsky, J., and **Osofsky, H.** (1972). The psychological reaction of patients to legalized abortion. *American Journal of Orthopsychiatry, 42,* 48–59. [15]

Paivio, A. (1971). *Imagery and Verbal Process.* New York: Holt, Rinehart and Winston. [7]

Palmore, E., and **Kivett, V.** (1977). Change in life satisfaction: A longitudinal study of persons aged 46–70. *Journal of Gerontology, 32,* 311–316. [11]

Palys, T. S. (1986). Testing the common wisdom: The social content of video pornography. *Canadian Psychology, 27,* 22–35. [19]

Panksepp, J. (1982). Toward a general psychobiological theory of emotions. *The Behavioral and Brain Sciences, 5,* 407–467. [11]

Panksepp, J. (1986). The neurochemistry of behavior. *Annual Review of Psychology, 37,* 77–107. [3, 5]

Papez, J. W. (1937). A proposed mechanism of emotion. *Archives of Neurology and Psychiatry, 38,* 725–743. [11]

Papoušek, H. (1969). Individual variability in learned responses in human infants. In R. J. Robinson (Ed.), *Brain and Early Behavior: Development in the Fetus and Infant.* (pp. 251–266). London: Academic Press. [9]

Parke, R. D., Berkowitz, L., Leyens, J. P., West, S. G., and **Sebastian, R. J.** (1977). Some effects of violent and nonviolent movies on the behavior of juvenile delinquents. In L. Berkowitz (Ed.), *Advances in Experimental Social Psychology* (Vol. 10, pp. 135–172). New York: Academic Press. [2, 19]

Parker, E. S., Birnbaum, I. M., and **Noble, E. P.** (1976). Alcohol and memory: Storage and state dependency. *Journal of Verbal Learning Behavior, 15,* 691–702. [5]

Parker, E. S., and **Noble, E. P.** (1977). Alcohol consumption and cognitive functioning in social drinkers. *Journal of Studies on Alcohol, 36,* 1224–1232. [5]

Parker, K. C. H., Hanson, R. K., and **Hunsley, J.** (1988). MMPI, Rorschach, and WAIS: A meta-analytic comparison of reliability, stability, and validity. *Psychological Bulletin, 103*(3), 367–373. [14]

Parkes, C. M. (1972). Components of the reaction to loss of a limb, spouse, or home. *Journal of Psychosomatic Research, 16,* 343–349. [11]

Parkes, C. M. (1975). Unexpected and untimely bereavement: A statistical study of young Boston widows and widowers. In B. B. Schoenberg, I. Gerber, A. Wiener, A. H. Kutscher, D. Peretz, and A. C. Carr (Eds.), *Bereavement: Its Psychosocial Aspects.* New York: Columbia University Press. [11]

Parkes, C. M., and **Weiss, R. S.** (1983). *Recovery From Bereavement.* New York: Basic Books. [11]

Parkin, A. J. (1984). Levels of processing, context, and facilitation of pronunciation. *Acta Psychologia, 55,* 19–29. [7]

Patsiokas, A., and **Clum, G. A.** (1985). Effects of psychotherapeutic strategies in the treatment of suicide attempters. *Psychotherapy: Theory, Research, and Practice, 22,* 281–290. [17]

Patsiokas, A., Clum, G., and **Luscomb, R.** (1979). Cognitive characteristics of suicide attempters. *Journal of Consulting and Clinical Psychology, 47,* 478–484. [17]

Patterson, G. R. (1974). Interventions for boys with conduct problems: Multiple settings, treatments, and criteria. *Journal of Consulting and Clinical Psychology, 42,* 471–481. [17]

Patterson, G. R., Littman, R. A., and **Bricker, W.** (1967). Assertive behavior in children: A step toward a theory of aggression. *Monographs of the Society for Research in Child Development, 32* (Serial No. 113). [19]

Pattison, E. M. (1977). *The Experience of Dying.* Englewood Cliffs, NJ: Prentice-Hall. [11]

Paul, G. L., and **Lentz, R. J.** (1977). *Psychosocial Treatment of Chronic Mental Patients: Milieu Versus Social-Learning Programs.* Cambridge, MA: Harvard University Press. [17]

Pavlov, I. P. (1927). *Conditioned Reflexes* (G. V. Anrep, Trans.). London: Oxford University Press. [6]

Pavot, W., Diener, E., and **Fujita, F.** (1990). Extroversion and happiness. *Journal of Personality and Individual Differences, 11*(12), 1299–1306. [11]

Paykel, E. S. (1979). Recent life events in the development of depressive disorders. In R. A. Depue (Ed.), *The Psychology of the Depressive Disorders: Implications for the Effects of Stress.* New York: Academic Press. [16]

Pearlin, L. I., and **Schooler, C.** (1978). The structure of coping. *Journal of Health and Social Behavior, 19*, 2–21. [15]

Pearlman, C. A. (1982). Sleep structure variation and performance. In W. B. Webb (Ed.), *Biological Rhythms, Sleep and Performance* (pp. 143–173). New York: Wiley. [12]

Penfield, W. (1969). Consciousness, memory, and man's conditioned reflexes. In K. H. Pribram (Ed.), *On the Biology of Learning* (pp. 127–168). New York: Harcourt Brace Jovanovich. [7, 12]

Penick, S., Smith, G., Wienske, K., and **Hinkle, L.** (1963). An experimental evaluation of the relationship between hunger and gastric motility. *American Journal of Physiology, 205*, 421–426. [12]

Pennebaker, J. W., Colder, M., and **Sharp, L. K.** (1990). Accelerating the coping process. *Journal of Personality and Social Psychology, 58*(3), 528–537. [11]

Pennebaker, J. W., Hughes, C. F., and **O'Heeron, R. C.** (1987). The psychophysiology of confession: Linking inhibitory and psychosomatic processes. *Journal of Personality and Social Psychology, 52*(4), 781–793. [11]

Peplau, L. A. (1976). Impact of fear of success and sex-role attitudes on women's competitive achievement. *Journal of Personality and Social Psychology, 34*, 561–568. [12]

Peplau, L. A., and **Gordon, S. L.** (1985). Women and men in love: Gender differences in close heterosexual relationships. In R. K. Unger and B. S. Wallston (Eds.), *Women, Gender, and Social Psychology* (pp. 357–391). Hillsdale, NJ: Lawrence Erlbaum. [2]

Perlmutter, M. (1983). Learning and memory through adulthood. In M. W. Riley, B. B. Hess, and K. Bond (Eds.), *Aging in Society: Selected Reviews of Research.* Hillsdale, NJ: Lawrence Erlbaum. [9]

Perlmutter, M., and **Mitchell, D. B.** (1982). The appearance and disappearance of age differences in adult memory. In F. Craik and S. Trehub (Eds.), *Aging and Cognitive Processes.* New York: Plenum. [9]

Perloff, L. S. (1987). Social comparison and illusions of invulnerability. In C. R. Snyder and C. R. Ford (Eds.), *Coping with Negative Life Events: Clinical and Social Psychological Perspectives.* New York: Plenum. [15]

Perrett, D. I., Mistlin, A. J., and **Chitty, A. J.** (1987). Visual neurones responsive to faces. *Trends in Neuroscience, 10*(9), 358–364. [3]

Perri, M. G., McAllister, D. A., Gange, J. J., Jordan, R. C., Mcadoo, W. G., and **Nezu, A. M.** (1988). Effects of four maintenance programs on the long-term management of obesity. *Journal of Consulting and Clinical Psychology, 56*, 529–534. [12]

Perry, D. G., Perry, L. C., and **Rasmussen, P.** (1986). Cognitive social learning mediators of aggression. *Child Development, 57*, 700–711. [19]

Pervin, L. A. (1984). *Personality: Theory, Assessment, and Research.* (4th ed.). New York: Wiley. [13]

Pervin, L. A. (1989). *Personality: Theory and Research* (5th ed.). New York: Wiley. [14]

Petersen, A. C. (1989). *Developmental Transitions and Adolescent Mental Health.* Paper presented at the annual meeting of the American Psychological Association, New Orleans, LA. [10]

Peterson, C., Seligman, M. E. P., and **Vaillant, G. E.** (1988). Pessimistic explanatory style is a risk factor for physical illness: A thirty-five-year longitudinal study. *Journal of Personality and Social Psychology, 55*, 23–27. [15]

Peterson, L. R., and **Peterson, M.** (1959). Short-term retention of individual verbal items. *Journal of Experimental Psychology, 58*, 193–198. [7]

Petty, R. E., and **Cacioppo, J. T.** (1981). *Attitudes and Persuasion: Classic and Contemporary Approaches.* Dubuque, IA: William C. Brown. [18]

Phares, E. J. (1979). *Clinical Psychology: Concepts, Methods, and Profession.* Homewood, IL: Dorsey Press. [17]

Phelps, C. H. et al. (in press). *Neurobiology of Aging.* [3]

Phillips, D. P. (1983). The impact of mass media violence on U.S. homicides. *American Sociological Review, 48*, 560–568. [19]

Phillips, D. P. (1986). Natural experiments on the effects of mass media violence on fatal aggression: Strength and weaknesses of a new approach. In L. Berkowitz (Ed.), *Advances in Experimental Social Psychology* (Vol. 19, pp. 207–250). New York: Academic Press. [19]

Phillips, S., with **King, S.,** and **Du Bois, L.** (1978). Spontaneous activities of female versus male newborns. *Child Development, 49*, 590–597. [10]

Piaget, J. (1952). *The Origins of Intelligence in Children* (M. Cook, Trans.). New York: International Universities Press. [1]

Piaget, J. (1954). *The Construction of Reality in the Child* (M. Cook, Trans.). New York: Basic Books. [1]

Piaget, J. (1969). *The Child's Conception of Physical Causality.* Totowa, NJ: Littlefield, Adams. (Original work published 1930). [9]

Piaget, J., and **Inhelder, B.** (1956). *The Child's Conception of Space.* London: Routledge & Kegan Paul. [9]

Piaget, J., and **Inhelder, B.** (1969). *The Psychology of the Child.* New York: Basic Books. [9]

Piliavin, I. M., Rodin, J., and Piliavin, J. A. (1969). Good Samaritanism: An underground phenomenon? *Journal of Personality and Social Psychology, 13*, 289–299. [19]

Piliavin, J. A., and Piliavin, I. M. (1972). Effect of blood on reactions to a victim. *Journal of Personal and Social Psychology, 23*, 353–361. [2]

Pinel, J. P. J. (1990). *Biopsychology.* Boston: Allyn and Bacon. [3]

Pines, A., and Maslach, C. (1978). Characteristics of staff burnout in mental health settings. *Hospital and Community Psychiatry, 29*, 233–237. [19]

Pines, M. (1981, September). The civilizing of Genie. *Psychology Today,* pp. 28–34. [2]

Pines, M. (1982, February). Baby, you're incredible. *Psychology Today,* pp. 48–53. [9]

Piotrowski, C., and Keller, J. W. (1989). Use of assessment in mental health clinics and services. *Psychological Reports, 64*, 1298. [14]

Piotrowski, C., and Keller, J. W. (in press). Psychological testing in outpatient mental health facilities: A national study. *Professional Psychology: Research and Practice.* [14]

Plomin, R. (1987, March 27). Nature, Nurture and Human Development. Presented as a Science and Public Policy Seminar sponsored by the Federation of Behavioral, Psychological and Cognitive Sciences. [9]

Plomin, R. (1989, February). Environment and genes: Determinants of behavior. *American Psychologist, 44*(2), 105–111. [9]

Plunkett, J. W., Klein, T., and Meisels, S. J. (1988). The relationship of preterm infant-mother attachment to stranger sociability at three years. *Infant Behavior and Development, 11*, 83–96. [10]

Plutchik, R., and Ax, A. F. (1967). A critique of "determinants of emotional state" by Schachter and Singer (1962). *Psychophysiology, 4*, 79–82. [11]

Polivy, J., and Herman, C. P. (1985). Dieting and binging: A causal analysis. *American Psychologist, 40*, 193–201. [12]

Polivy, J., Herman, C. P., Hackett, R., and Kuleshnyk, I. (1986). The effects of self-attention and public attention on eating in restrained and unrestrained subjects. *Journal of Personality and Social Psychology, 50*, 1253–1260. [12]

Pollack, I., and Pickett, J. M. (1964). Intelligibility of excerpts from fluent speech: Auditory vs. structural context. *Journal of Verbal Learning and Verbal Behavior, 3*, 79–84. [8]

Portnoy, F., and Simmons, C. (1978). Day care and attachment. *Child Development, 49*, 239–242. [10]

Posner, M. I. (1973). *Cognition: An Introduction.* Glenview, IL: Scott, Foresman. [8]

Posner, M. I., Petersen, S. E., Fox, P. T., and Raichle, M. E. (1988, June 17). Localization of cognitive operations in the human brain. 240, 1627–1631. [3]

Poynton, A., Bridges, P. K., and Bartlett, J. R. (1988). Resistant bipolar affective disorder treated by stereotactic subcaudate tractotomy. *British Journal of Psychiatry, 152*, 354–358. [17]

Prechtl, R. R. (1982). Regressions and transformations during neurological development. In T. G. Bever (Ed.), *Regression in Mental Development: Basic Phenomena and Theories* (pp. 103–116). Hillsdale, NJ: Lawrence Erlbaum. [9]

Premack, D. (1971a). Language in the chimpanzee? *Science, 172*, 808–822. [8]

Premack, D. (1971b). On the assessment of language competence in the chimpanzee. In A. M. Schrier and F. Stollnitz (Eds.). *Behavior of Nonhuman Primates* (pp. 185–228). New York: Academic Press. [8]

Premack, D. (1976). Language and intelligence in ape and man. *American Scientist, 64*, 674–683. [8]

Premack, D. (1983). Animal cognition. *Annual Review of Psychology, 34*, 351–362. [8]

Pribram, K. H. (1981). Emotions. In S. B. Filskov and T. J. Boll (Eds.), *Handbook of Clinical Neuropsychology.* New York: Wiley. [11]

Prien, R. F., Kupfer, D. J., Mansky, P. A., Small, J. G., Tuason, V. B., Voss, C. B., and Johnson, W. E. (1984). Drug therapy in the prevention of recurrences in unipolar and bipolar affective disorders. *Archives of General Psychiatry, 41*, 1096–1104. [17]

Privette, G., and Landsman, T. (1983). Factor analysis of peak performance: The full use of potential. *Journal of Personality and Social Psychology, 44*, 195–200. [11]

Putnam, W. H. (1979). Hypnosis and distortions in eyewitness memory. *International Journal of Clinical and Experimental Hypnosis, 27*, 437–448. [5]

Quattrone, G. A. (1986). On the perception of a group's variability. In S. Worchel and W. G. Austin (Eds.), *Psychology of Intergroup Relations* (2nd ed.). Chicago: Nelson Hall. [18]

Quinn, M. E., Fontana, A. F., and Reznikoff, M. (1987). Psychological distress in reaction to lung cancer as a function of spousal support and coping strategy. *Journal of Psychosocial Oncology, 4*, 79–90. [15]

Rachlin, H. (1985). Pain and behavior. *The Behavioral and Brain Sciences, 8*, 43–83. [4]

Rachman, S. J., and Hodgson, R. J. (1980). *Obsessions and Compulsions.* Englewood Cliffs, NJ: Prentice-Hall. [16]

Radke-Yarrow, M., and Zahn-Waxler, C. (1984). Roots, motives, and patterns in children's prosocial behavior. In E. Staub, D. Bar-Tal, J. Karylowski, and J. Reykowski (Eds.), *Development and Maintenance of Prosocial Behavior.* New York: Plenum. [10]

Ramachandran, V. S. (1988, August). Perceiving shape from shading. *Scientific American, 259*, 76–83. [4]

Rapaport, K., and Burkhart, B. R. (1984). Personality and attitudinal characteristics of sexually coercive college males. *Journal of Abnormal Psychology, 93*, 216–221. [19]

Rassmussen, S. A., and Eisen, J. L. (1989). Clinical features and phenomenology of obsessive compulsive disorder. *Psychiatric, 19*, 67–73. [17]

Ratcliff, R., and McKoon, G. (1978). Priming in item recognition: Evidence for the propositional structure of sentences. *Journal of Verbal Learning and Verbal Behavior, 17,* 403–417. [8]

Raven, B. H., and **French, J.** (1958). Legitimate power, coercive power, and observability in social influence. *Sociometry, 21,* 83–97. [19]

Ray, C. C. (1991, May 7). Eliminating alcohol. *The New York Times,* p. C8. [15]

Raymond, B. J., and **Unger, R. K.** (1972). "The apparel oft proclaims the man": Cooperation with deviant and conventional youths. *Journal of Social Psychology, 87,* 75–82. [19]

Reason, J., and **Lucas, D.** (1984). Using cognitive diaries to investigate naturally occurring memory blocks. In J. E. Harris and P. E. Morris (Eds.), *Everyday Memory, Actions and Absent-Mindedness* (pp. 53–70). London: Academic Press. [7]

Reason, J., and **Mycielska, K.** (1982). *Absent Minded? The Psychology of Mental Lapses and Everyday Errors.* Englewood Cliffs, NJ: Prentice-Hall. [7]

Reed, G. M. (1989). *Stress, Coping, and Psychological Adaptation in a Sample of Gay and Bisexual Men with AIDS.* Unpublished doctoral dissertation, University of California, Los Angeles. [15]

Reedy, M. N., Birren, J. E., and **Schaie, K. W.** (1981). Age and sex differences in satisfying love relationships. *Human Development, 24,* 52–66. [10]

Reeke, G. N., Jr., and **Edelman, G. M.** (1988). Real brains and artificial intelligence. *Daedalus, 117,* 143–173. [3]

Reese, W. H., and **Rodeheaver, D.** (1985). Problem-solving and complex decision-making. In J. E. Birren and K. W. Schaie (Eds.), *Handbook of the Psychology of Aging* (2nd ed.). New York: Van Nostrand Reinhold. [9]

Reeves, R. (1983, December). George Gallup's nation of numbers. *Esquire,* pp. 91–96. [2]

Reinisch, J., and **Beasley, R.** (1980). *The Kinsey Institute New Report on Sex.* New York: St. Martin's Press. [2]

Renault, B., Ragot, R., LeSevere, N., and **Remond, A.** (1982). Onset and offset of brain events as indices of mental chronometry. *Science, 215,* 1413–1415. [3]

Renken, B., Egeland, B., Marvinney, D., Mangelsdorf, S., and **Sroufe, L. A.** (1989). Early antecedents of aggression and passive-withdrawal in elementary school. *Journal of Personality, 57,* 257–282. [10]

Rensberger, B. (1985, May 30). Feigned emotion often becomes real. *Washington Post,* p. A7. [11]

Reschly, D. J. (1981). Evaluation of the effects of SOMPA measures on classification of students as mildly mentally retarded. *American Journal of Mental Development. 86*(1), 16–20. [14]

Rescorla, R. A. (1968). Probability of shock in the presence and absence of CS in fear conditioning. *Journal of Comparative and Physiological Psychology, 66,* 1–5. [6]

Rescorla, R. A. (1988, March). Pavlovian conditioning: It's not what you think it is. *American Psychologist, 43,* 151–160. [6]

Revusky, S. H., and **Bedarf, E. W.** (1967). Association of illness with prior ingestion of novel foods. *Science, 155,* 219–220. [6]

Rice, M. L. (1989, February). Children's language acquisition. *American Psychologist, 44*(2), 149–156. [9]

Rimm, D. C., and **Mahoney, M. J.** (1969). The application of reinforcement and participant modeling procedures in the treatment of snake-phobic behavior. *Behavior Research and Therapy, 7,* 369–376. [17]

Rimm, D. C., and **Masters, J. C.** (1979). *Behavior Therapy: Techniques and Empirical Findings.* New York: Academic Press. [17]

Ringelmann, M. (1913). Research on animate sources of power: The world of man. *Annales de l'Institute National Agronomique,* 2e serie—tome XII, 1–40. [19]

Risberg, J., Halsey, J. H., Wills, E. L., and **Wilson, E. M.** (1975). Hemispheric specialization in normal man studied by bilateral measurements of the regional cerebral blood flows: A study with the 133 Xe inhalation technique. *Brain, 98,* 511–524. [3]

Riskind, J. H. (1984). They stoop to conquer: Guiding and self-regulatory functions of physical posture after success and failure. *Journal of Personality and Social Psychology, 47,* 479–493. [11]

Ritter, W., Simson, R., Vaughan, H. G., Jr., and **Macht, M.** (1982). Manipulation of event-related potential manifestations of information processing stages. *Science, 218,* 909–910. [3]

Robins, L. N., Helzer, J. E., Weissman, M. M., Orvaschel, H., Gruenberg, E., Burke, J. D., and **Reiger, D. A.** (1984). Lifetime prevalence of specific psychiatric disorders in three sites. *Archives of General Psychiatry, 41,* 942–949. [16]

Rock, I. (1984). *The Logic of Perception.* Cambridge, MA: MIT Press. [4]

Rodgers, J. (1984). Targets in the brain. *Mosaic* (National Science Foundation Publication No. 5, Vol. 15). Washington, DC: US Government Printing Office. [3]

Rodgers, J. E. (1982). The malleable memory of eyewitnesses. *Science Digest, 3,* 32–35. [7]

Rodin, J. (1979). Obesity: Why the losing battle? *JSAS: Catalog of Selected Documents in Psychology, 9,* 17. [12]

Rodin, J. (1981). Current status of the internal-external hypothesis of obesity. *American Psychologist, 36,* 361–372. [12]

Rodin, J., and **Langer, E. J.** (1977). Long-term effects of a control-relevant intervention with the institutionalized aged. *Journal of Personality and Social Psychology, 35,* 897–902. [15]

Rodin, J., and **Plante, T.** (1989). The psychological effects of exercise. In R. S. Williams and A. Wallece (Eds.), *Biological effects of physical activity* (pp. 127–137). Champaign, IL: Human Kinetics. [15]

Rodnick, E. H., Goldstein, M. J., Lewis, J. M., and **Doane, J. A.** (1984). Parental communication style, affect, and role as precursors of offspring schizophrenia-spectrum disorders. In N. F. Watt, E. J. Anthony, L. C. Wynne, and J. E. Rolf (Eds.), *Children at Risk for Schizophrenia: A Longitudinal Perspective* (pp. 81–92). Cambridge: Cambridge University Press. [16]

Roe, A. (1946). The personality of artists. *Educational Psychology Measurement, 6,* 401–408. [8]

Roe, A. (1953). *The Making of a Scientist.* New York: Dodd, Mead. [8]

Roediger, H. L., and Payne, D. G. (1982). Hypermnesia: The role of repeated testing. *Journal of Experimental Psychology: Learning, Memory, and Cognition, 8,* 66–72. [5]

Rogers, C. R. (1951). *Client-Centered Therapy: Its Current Practice, Implications, and Theory.* Boston: Houghton Mifflin. [13]

Rogers, C. R. (1961). *On Becoming a Person: A Therapist's View of Psychotherapy.* Boston: Houghton Mifflin. [13]

Rogers, C. R. (1963). The actualizing tendency in relation to "motives" and to consciousness. In M. R. Jones (Ed.), *Nebraska Symposium on Motivation* (pp. 1–24). Lincoln: University of Nebraska Press. [13]

Rogers, C. R. (1970). *On Becoming a Person: A Therapist's View of Psychotherapy* (2nd ed.). Boston: Houghton Mifflin. [13]

Rogers, C. R. (1971). A theory of personality. In S. Maddi (Ed.), *Perspectives on Personality.* Boston: Little, Brown. [13]

Rogers, C. R. (1981). Rollo May: Man and philosopher. *Perspectives, 2*(1). [13]

Rogers, C. R. (1985). Toward a more human science of the person. *Journal of Humanistic Psychology, 25,* 7–24. [13]

Rogers, C. R., and Dymond, R. F. (Eds.). (1954). *Psychotherapy and Personality Change.* Chicago: University of Chicago Press. [13]

Rogers, R. W., and Mewborn, C. R. (1976). Fear appeals and attitude change: Effects of a threat's noxiousness, probability of occurrence, and the efficacy of coping responses. *Journal of Personality and Social Psychology, 34,* 54–61. [18]

Rogers, W. (1984). Changing health-related attitudes and behavior: The role of preventive health psychology. In J. H. Harvey, E. Maddux, R. P. McGlynn, and C. D. Sloltenberg (Eds.), *Social Perception in Clinical and Counseling Psychology* (Vol. 2, pp. 91–112). Lubbock, TX: Texas Technical University Press. [15]

Rollin, E. B. (1985). The moral status of research animals in psychology. *American Psychologist, 40,* 920–926. [2]

Romer, N., and Cherry, D. (1980). Ethnic and social class differences in children's sex-role concepts. *Sex Roles, 6,* 246–263. [18]

Rosch, E. (1978). Principles of categorization. In E. Rosch and B. B. Lloyd (Eds.), *Cognition and Categorization.* New York: Wiley. [8]

Rose, S., Gottfried, A., and Bridger, W. (1981a). Cross-modal transfer and information processing by the sense of touch in infancy. *Developmental Psychology, 17,* 90–98. [9]

Rose, S., Gottfried, A., and Bridger, W. (1981b). Cross-modal transfer in 6-month-old infants. *Developmental Psychology, 17,* 661–669. [9]

Rose, S. D. (1986). Group methods. In F. H. Kanfer and A. P. Goldstein (Eds.), *Helping People Change: A Textbook of Methods.* Elmsford, NY: Pergamon. [17]

Rosen, B. C., and D'Andrade, R. (1959). The psychological origins of achievement motivations. *Sociometry, 22,* 185–218. [12]

Rosenberg, M. J. (1965). When dissonance fails: On eliminating evaluation apprehension from attitude measurement. *Journal of Personality and Social Psychology, 1,* 28–42. [18]

Rosenfield, P., Lambert, N. M., and Black, A. (1985). Desk arrangement effects on pupil classroom behavior. *Journal of Educational Psychology, 77,* 101–108. [1]

Rosenhan, D. L. (1973). On being sane in insane places. *Science, 179,* 250–258. [16]

Rosenman, R. H. (1978). The interview method of assessment of the coronary-prone behavior pattern. In T. M. Dembroski, S. M. Weiss, J. L. Shields, S. G. Haynes, and M. Feinleib (Eds.), *Coronary-Prone Behavior* (pp. 55–70). New York: Springer-Verlag. [13]

Rosenman, R. H., Brand, R. J., Jenkins, C. D., Friedman, M., Straus, R., and Wurm, M. (1975). Coronary heart disease in the Western Collaborative Group Study: Final follow-up experience of 8½ years. *Journal*

of the *American Medical Association, 233,* 872–877. [13]

Rosenthal, N. E., Carpenter, C. J., James, S. P., Parry, B. L., Rogers, S. L. B., and Wehr, T. A. (1986). Seasonal affective disorder in children and adolescents. *American Journal of Psychiatry, 143,* 356–358. [16]

Rosenthal, R. (1966). *Experimenter Effects in Behavioral Research.* New York: Appleton-Century-Crofts. [2, 18]

Rosenthal, R. (1984). *Meta-Analysis Procedures for Social Research.* Beverly Hills, CA: Sage Publications. [2]

Rosenthal, R., Archer, D., Di Matteo, M. R., Koivumaki, J. H., and Rogers, P. L. (1974, September). Body talk and tone of voice: The language without words. *Psychology Today,* pp. 64–68. [11]

Rosenzweig, M. R., Bennett, E. L., and Diamond, M. C. (1972). Brain changes in response to experience. *Scientific American, 226,* 22–29. [3]

Rosenzweig, M. R., and Leiman, A. L. (1989). *Physiological Psychology* (2nd ed.). New York: McGraw-Hill. [3, 5]

Rosnow, R. L., and Rosenthal, R. (1989, October). Statistical procedures and the justification of knowledge in psychological science. *American Psychologist, 44*(10), 1276–1284. [2]

Ross, A. (1981). *Child Behavior Therapy.* New York: Wiley. [6]

Ross, L. (1977). The intuitive psychologist and his shortcomings: Distortions in the attribution process. In L. Berkowitz (Ed.). *Advances in Experimental Social Psychology.* New York: Academic Press. [18]

Ross, L., and Nisbett, R. E. (1991). *The Person and the Situation: Perspectives of Social Psychology,* New York: McGraw-Hill. [18]

Ross, M., and Fletcher, G. J. O. (1985). Attribution and social perception. In G. Lindsey and E. Aronson (Eds.), *Handbook of Social Psychology* (3rd ed., pp. 73–122). Reading, MA: Addison-Wesley. [18]

Ross, M., and Sicoly, F. (1979). Egocentric biases in availability and attribution. *Journal of Personality and Social Psychology, 37,* 322–336. [18]

Rothbart, M. K. (1986). Longitudinal observation of infant temperament. *Developmental Psychology, 22*(3), 356–365. [10]

Rotter, J. (1954). *Social Learning and Clinical Psychology.* Englewood Cliffs, NJ: Prentice-Hall. [13]

Rovee-Collier, C. (1990). *Infant Memory.* Paper presented at the annual meeting of the American Psychological Association, Boston. [9]

Rubin, D. C. (1985, September). The subtle deceiver: Recalling our past. *Psychology Today,* pp. 38–46. [7]

Rubin, J. L., Provenzano, F. J., and **Luria, Z.** (1974). The eye of the beholder: Parents on sex of newborns. *American Journal of Orthopsychiatry, 44,* 512–519. [18]

Rubin, Z. (1973). Liking and loving: Patterns of attraction in dating relationships. In T. L. Huston (Ed.), *Foundations of Interpersonal Attraction.* New York: Academic Press. [18]

Ruderman, A. J., and **Grace, P. S.** (1988). *Addictive Behavior, 13,* 359–368. [12]

Ruggiero, L., Williamson, D., Davis, C. J., Schlundt, D. G., and **Carey, M. P.** (1988). Forbidden food survey: Measure of bulimics's anticipated emotional reactions to specific foods. *Addictive Behaviors, 13,* 267–274. [12]

Rumbaugh, D. M., Gill, T. V., and **von Glaserfeld, E. C.** (1963). Reading and sentence completion by a chimpanzee. *Science, 182,* 731–733. [8]

Rush, A. J., and **Beck, A. T.** (1978). Cognitive therapy of depression and suicide. *American Journal of psychotherapy, 32,* 201–219. [17]

Rush, A. J., Beck, A. T., Kovacs, M., Weisenberger, J., and **Hollon, S. D.** (1982). Comparison of the effects of cognitive therapy on hopelessness and self-concept. *American Journal of Psychiatry, 139,* 862–866. [17]

Rushton, J. P., Rulker, D. W., Neale, M. C., Nias, D. K. B., and **Eysenck, H. J.** (1986). Altruism and aggression: The heritability of individual differences. *Journal of Personality and Social Psychology, 50,* 1192–1198. [19]

Russell, J. A. (1980). A circumplex model of affect. *Journal of Personality and Social Psychology, 39*(6), 1161–1178. [11]

Russell, J. A., Lewicks, M., and **Niit, T.** (1980). A cross-cultural study of a circumplex model of affect. *Journal of Personality and Social Psychology, 57*(5), 848–856. [11]

Russo, J. E., Krieser, G., and **Miyashita, S.** (1975). An effective display of unit price information. *Journal of Marketing, 39,* 11–19. [8]

Rutter, M. (1987). Psychosocial resilience and protective mechanisms. *American Journal of Orthopsychiatry, 57*(3), 316–331. [10]

Rychlak, J. F. (1986). The logic of consciousness. *British Journal of Psychology, 77,* 257–267. [5]

Sachdev, P., Smith, J. S., and **Matheson, J.** (1990). Is pschosurgery antimanic? *Biological Psychiatry, 27,* 363–371. [17]

Sacks, O. (1987). *The Man Who Mistook His Wife for a Hat.* New York: Harper and Row. [3]

Saegert, S., Swap, W. C., and **Zajonc, R. B.** (1973). Exposure, context, and interpersonal attraction. *Journal of Personality and Social Psychology, 25,* 234–242. [18]

Sampson, E. E. (1978). Scientific paradigms and social values: Wanted—a scientific revolution. *Journal of Personality and Social Psychology, 36,* 1332–1343. [10]

Sampson, H. (1965). Deprivation of dreaming sleep by two methods. *Archives of General Psychiatry, 13,* 79–86. [5]

Sanders, G. S. (1982). Social comparison as a basis for evaluating others. *Journal of Research in Personality, 16,* 21–31. [18]

Sandvik, E., Diener, E., and **Larsen, R. J.** (1985). The opponent process theory and affective reactions. *Motivation and Emotion, 9,* 407–418. [12]

Santee, R. T., and **Jackson, S. E.** (1982). Sex differences in the evaluative implications of conformity and dissent. *Social Psychology Quarterly, 45,* 121–125. [19]

Santee, R. T., and **Maslach, C.** (1982). To agree or not to agree: Personal dissent amid social pressure to conform. *Journal of Personality and Social Psychology, 42,* 690–700. [19]

Santrock, J., and **Bartlett, J.** (1986). *Developmental Psychology: A Life-Cycle Perspective.* Dubuque, IA: W. C. Brown. [10]

Sarbin, T. R., and **Coe, W. C.** (1972). *Hypnosis: A Social Psychological Analysis of Influence Communication.* New York: Holt, Rinehart and Winston. [5]

Sargent, M. (1990, June). Panic disorder. *Hospital and Community Psychiatry, 41,* 621–623. [17]

Savage-Rumbaugh, E. S., Pate, J. L., Lawson, J., Smith, S. T., and **Rosenbaum, S.** (1983a). Can a chimpanzee make a statement? *Journal of Experimental Psychology: General, 112,* 457–492. [8]

Savage-Rumbaugh, E. S., Romski, M. A., Sevcik, R., and **Pate, J. L.** (1983b). Assessing symbol usage versus symbol competency. *Journal of Experimental Psychology: General, 112,* 508–512. [8]

Saxe, L., Dougherty, D., Esty, K., and **Fine, M.** (1983). *Health Technology Case Study 22: The Effectiveness and Costs of Alcoholism Treatment.* Washington, DC: Office of Technology Assessment. [16]

Scarr, S. (1984a). *Mother Care/Other Care.* New York: Basic Books. [10]

Scarr, S. (1984b, May). (Interviewed by E. Hall). What's a parent to do? *Psychology Today.* pp. 58–63. [10]

Scarr, S., Phillips, D., and **McCartney, K.** (1989, November). Working mothers and their families. *American Psychologist, 44*(11), 1402–1409. [10]

Scarr, S., Weber, P. L., Weinberg, R. A., and **Wittig, M. A.** (1981). Personality resemblance among adolescents and their parents in biologically-related and adoptive families. *Journal of Personality and Social Psychology, 40,* 885–898. [10]

Scarr, S., and **Weinberg, R. A.** (1976). IQ test performance of black children adopted by white families. *American Psychologist, 3,* 726–739. [14]

Scarr-Salapatek, S. (1971). Unknowns in the IQ equation. *Science, 174,* 1223–1228. [14]

Schachter, S. (1959). *The Psychology of Affiliation.* Stanford, CA: Stanford University Press. [2]

Schachter, S. (1964). The interaction of cognitive and physiological determinants of emotional state. In L. Berkowitz (Ed.). *Advances in Experimental Social Psychology* (pp. 48–81). New York: Academic Press. [11]

Schachter, S. (1971a). *Emotion, Obesity, and Crime.* New York: Academic Press. [11]

Schachter, S. (1971b). Some extraordinary facts about obese humans and rats. *American Psychologist, 26,* 129–144. [11]

Schachter, S., Goldman, R., and **Gordon, A.** (1968). The effects of fear, food deprivation, and obesity on eating. *Journal of Personality and Social Psychology, 10,* 91–97. [12]

Schachter, S., and **Singer, J. E.** (1962). Cognitive, social and physiological determinants of emotional state. *Psychological Review, 69,* 379–399. [11]

Schaefer, C., Coyne, J. C., and **Lazarus, R. S.** (1981). The health-related functions of social support. *Journal of Behavioral Medicine, 4,* 381–406. [15]

Schaie, K. W. (1984). The Seattle longitudinal: A 21 year exploration in the development of psychometric intelligence. In K. W. Schaie (Ed.), *Longitudinal Studies of Adult Psychological Development.* New York: Guilford Press. [9]

Schaie, K. W. (1989). The hazards of cognitive aging. *Gerontologist, 29*(4), 484–493. [9]

Schaie, K. W. (1990). The optimization of cognitive functioning in old age: Predictions based on cohort-sequential and longitudinal data. In P. B. Baltes and M. M. Baltes (Eds.), *Longitudinal Research and the Study of Successful (Optimal) Aging.* Cambridge: Cambridge University Press. [9]

Schaie, K. W., and **Willis, S.** (1986). Can decline in intellectual functioning be reversed? *Developmental Psychology, 22,* 223–232. [9]

Schaller, M., and **Cialdini, R. B.** (1988). The economics of empathic helping: Support for a mood management motive. *Journal of Experimental Social Psychology, 24,* 163–181. [19]

Schank, R., and **Abelson, R.** (1977). *Scripts, Plans, Goals, and Understanding.* Hillsdale, NJ: Lawrence Erlbaum. [8]

Scheier, M. F., and **Carver, C. S.** (1985). Optimism, coping, and health: Assessment and implications of generalized outcome expectancies. *Health Psychology, 4,* 219–247. [15]

Scheier, M. F., Weintraub, J. K., and **Carver, C. S.** (1986). Coping with stress: Divergent strategies of optimists and pessimists. *Journal of Personality and Social Psychology, 51,* 1257–1264. [15]

Scheir, M. F., Matthews, K. A., Owens, J., Magovern, G. J., Sr., Lefbvre, R. C., Abbott, R. A., and **Carver, C. S.** (1989). Dispositional optimism and recovery from coronary artery bypass surgery: The beneficial effects on physical and psychological well-being. *Journal of Personality and Social Psychology, 57,* 1024–1040. [15]

Scher, S. J., and **Cooper, J.** (1989). Motivational basis of dissonance: The singular role of behavior consequences. *Journal of Personality and Social Psychology, 56,* 899–906. [18]

Schmeck, H. M., Jr. (1984, March 27). Implant brings sound to deaf and spurs debate over its use. *New York Times,* pp. C1+. [4]

Schmeck, H. M., Jr. (1986, March 18). Schizophrenia focus shifts to dramatic changes in brain. *New York Times,* pp. C1, C3. [16]

Schmitt, B. H., Gilovich, T., Goore, N., and **Joseph, L.** (1986). Mere exposure and social facilitation: One more time. *Journal of Experimental Social Psychology, 22,* 242–248. [19]

Schneider, A. M., and **Tarshis, B.** (1986). *An Introduction to Physiological Psychology* (3rd ed.). New York: Random House. [5]

Schneider, S. (1988). Attitudes toward death in adolescent offspring of Holocaust survivors: A comparison of Israeli and American adolescents. *Adolescence, 23,* 703–710. [14]

Schneider-Helmert, D. (1985). Clinical evaluation of SDIP. In A. Wauguier, J. M. Monti, and M. Radulovacki (Eds.), *Sleep, Neurotransmitters, and Neuromodulators* (pp. 279–291). New York: Raven. [5]

Schneider-Rosen, K., and **Cicchetti, D.** (1984). The relationship between affect and cognition in maltreated infants: Quality of attachment and the development of visual self-recognition. *Child Development, 55,* 648–658. [10]

Schoen, L. S., and **Badia, P.** (1984). Facilitated recall following REM and NREM naps. *Psychophysiology, 21,* 299–306. [7]

Schotte, D., and **Clum, G. A.** (1987). Problem-solving skills in suicidal psychiatric patients. *Journal of Consulting and Clinical Psychology, 55,* 49–54. [17]

Schulz, R. (1976). Effects of control and predictability on the physical well-being of the institutionalized aged. *Journal of Personality and Social Psychology, 33,* 563–573. [15]

Schwartz, J. L. (1987). *Review and Evaluation of Smoking Cessation Methods: The United States and Canada* (NIH Publication #87–2940). Washington, DC: U.S. Department of Health and Human Services. [15]

Schwartz, R. (1984). Body weight regulation. *University of Washington Medicine, 10,* 16–20. [12]

Schwartz, R. G., and **Leonard, L. B.** (1984). Words, objects, and actions in early lexical acquisition. *Journal of Speech and Hearing Research, 27,* 119–127. [9]

Schwarz, N., and **Strack, F.** (1990). Evaluating one's life: A judgmental model of subjective well-being. In F. Strack, M. Argyle, and N. Schwarz (Eds.), *The Social Psychology of Well-Being.* Oxford: Pergamon. [11]

Scovern, A. W., and **Kilmann, P. R.** (1980). Status of electroconvulsive therapy: Review of the outcome literature. *Psychological Bulletin, 87,* 260–303. [17]

Sears, D. O. (1986). College sophomores in the laboratory: Influences of a narrow data base on psychology's view of human nature. *Journal of Personality and Social Psychology, 51*, 515–530. [2]

Sears, R. R. (1977). Sources of life satisfaction of the Terman gifted men. *American Psychologist, 32*, 119–128. [10]

Sedlack, A. (1989, April). *National Incidence of Child Abuse and Neglect.* Paper presented at the biennial meeting of the Society for Research in Child Development, Kansas City. [10]

Sejnowski, T. J., Koch, C., and **Churchland, P. S.** (1988, September 9). Computational neuroscience. *Science, 241*, 1299–1306. [3]

Sekular, R., and **Blake, R.** (1990). *Perception* (2nd ed.). New York: McGraw-Hill. [4]

Seligman, M. E. P., Maier, S. F., and **Geer, J.** (1968). The alleviation of learned helplessness in the dog. *Journal of Abnormal Psychology, 78*, 256–262. [16]

Selman, R. L. (1976). Toward a structural analysis of developing interpersonal relations concepts. In A. Pick (Ed.), *Minnesota Symposia on Child Psychology* (Vol. 10). Minneapolis: University of Minnesota. [10]

Selman, R. L. (1980). *The Growth of Interpersonal Understanding.* New York: Academic Press. [10]

Selman, R. L., and **Byrne, D.** (1974). A structural-developmental analysis of levels of role-taking in middle childhood. *Child Development, 45*, 803–806. [10]

Selye, H. (1956). *The Stress of Life.* New York: McGraw-Hill. [15]

Senden, M. von (1960). *Space and Sight: The Perception of Space and Shape in the Congenitally Blind Before and After Operation* (P. Heath, Trans.). New York: Free Press. [4]

Shallice, T. (1988). *From Neuropsychology to Mental Structure.* New York: Cambridge University Press. [3]

Shapiro, C. M., Bortz, R., Mitchell, D., Bartel, P., and **Jooste, P.** (1981). Slow-wave sleep: A recovery period after exercise. *Science, 214*, 1253–1354. [5]

Shapiro, R. W., and **Keller, M. B.** (1981). Initial six-month follow-up of patients with major depressive disorder: A prelimi-

nary report from the NIMII Collaborative Study of the Psychobiology of Depression. *Journal of Affective Disorders, 3*, 205–220. [16]

Shatz, M., and **Gelman, R.** (1973). The development of communication skills: Modifications in the speech of young children as a function of listener. *Monographs of the Society for Research in Child Development, 38*, 1–37. [9]

Shaver, J. P., and **Strong, W.** (1976). *Facing Value Decisions: Rationale-Building for Teachers.* Belmont, CA: Wadsworth. [10]

Shaver, P., and **Hazan, C.** (1985). Incompatibility loneliness, and "limerence." In W. Ickes (Ed.), *Compatibility and Incompatibility in Relationships* (pp. 163–184). New York: Springer-Verlag. [18]

Shaver, P., Hazan, C., and **Bradshaw, D.** (1988). Love as attachment: The integration of three behavioral systems. In R. J. Sternberg and M. L. Barnes (Eds.), *The Psychology of Love.* New Haven: Yale University Press. [18]

Shaw, M. E. (1976). *Group Dynamics: The Psychology of Small Group Behavior* (2nd ed.). New York: McGraw-Hill. [19]

Sheehan, P. W., and **Tilden, J.** (1984). Real and simulated occurrences of memory distortion in hypnosis. *Journal of Abnormal Psychology, 93*(1), 47–57. [5]

Sherif, M., and **Sherif, C. W.** (1953). *Groups in Harmony and Tension.* New York: Harper & Row. [18]

Sherman, S. J., and **Corty, E.** (1984). Cognitive heuristics. In R. S. Wyer and T. K. Srull (Eds.), *Handbook of Social Cognition* (Vol. 1, pp. 189–286). Hillsdale, NJ: Lawrence Erlbaum. [8]

Sherman, S. J., Presson, C. C., Chassin, L., Bensenberg, M., Corty, E., and **Olshavsky, R. W.** (1982). Smoking intentions in adolescents. *Personality and Social Psychology Bulletin, 8*, 376–383. [18]

Shevrin, H. (1988). Unconscious conflict: A convergent psychodynamic and electrophysiological approach. In M. Horowitz, (Ed.), *Psychodynamics and Cognition* (pp. 117–167). Chicago: University of Chicago Press. [13]

Shevrin, H. (1990). Subliminal perception and repression. From J. L. Singer (Ed.), *Repression and Dissociation: Implications for Personality Theory, Psychopathology, and Health* (pp. 103–119). Chicago: University of Chicago Press. [13]

Shields, J. (1976). Heredity and environment. In H. J. Eysenck and G. D. Wilson (Eds.), *A Textbook of Human Psychology.* Baltimore: University Park Press. [13]

Shneidman, E. S. (1973). *Deaths of Man.* New York: Quadrangle. [16]

Shneidman, E. S. (1976). A psychological theory of suicide. *Psychiatric Annals, 6*, 51–66. [17]

Shneidman, E. S. (1987). A psychological approach to suicide. In G. R. VandenBos and B. K. Bryant (Eds.), *Cataclysms, Crises, and Catastrophes: Psychology in Action.* Washington, DC: American Psychological Association. [17]

Shoham-Salomon, V., and **Rosenthal, R.** (1987). Paradoxical interventions: A meta-analysis. *Journal of Consulting and Clinical Psychology, 55*, 22–28. [17]

Shopland, D. R., and **Brown, C.** (1987). Toward the 1990 objectives for smoking: Measuring the progress with 1985 NHIS data. *Public Health Reports, 102*, 68–73. [18]

Shou, M. (1988). Lithium treatment of manic depressive illness. *Journal of the American Medical Association, 259*, 1834–1836. [17]

Shreve, A. (1982, November 21). Careers and the lure of motherhood. *New York Times Magazine*, pp. 38–42. [10]

Shucard, D. W., Cummins, K. R., and **McGee, M. G.** (1984). Event-related potentials differentiate normal and disabled readers. *Brain and Language, 21*, 318–334. [3]

Shusterman, L. R. (1979). Predicting the psychological consequences of abortion. *Social Science and Medicine, 13A*, 683–689. [15]

Sieber, J. E., and **Stanley, B.** (1988, January). Ethical and professional dimensions of socially Sensitive Research. *American Psychologist, 43*(1), 49–55. [2]

Siegal, M. (1987). Are sons and daughters treated more differently by fathers than by mothers? *Developmental Review, 7,* 183–209. [10]

Siegel, L. S. (1988). Agatha Christie's learning disability. *Canadian Psychology, 29*(2), 213–216. [6]

Siegel, R. K. (1977). Hallucinations. *Scientific American, 237,* 132–140. [5]

Siegler, R. S. (1986). *Children's Thinking* (2nd ed.). Englewood Cliffs, N.J.: Prentice-Hall. [9]

Siever, L. J., and **Davis, K. L.** (1985). Overview: Toward dysregulation hypothesis of depression. *American Journal of Psychiatry, 142,* 1017. [17]

Sigall, H., and **Landy, D.** (1973). Radiating beauty: The effects of having a physically attractive partner on person perception. *Journal of Personality and Social Psychology, 28,* 218–224. [18]

Signorielli, N. (1989). Television and conceptions about sex roles: Maintaining conventionality and the status quo. *Sex Roles, 21,* 341–360. [18]

Silveira, J. (1971). Incubation: The effect of interruption timing and length on problem solution and quality of problem processing. Unpublished doctoral dissertation, University of Oregon. [8]

Silver, J., and **Rutishauser, U.** (1984). Guidance of optic axons *in vivo* by a preformed adhesive pathway or neuroepithelial effect. *Developmental Biology, 106,* 485. [3]

Silver, R. L., Boon, C., and **Stones, M. H.** (1983). Searching for meaning in misfortune: Making sense of incest. *Journal of Social Issues, 39*(2), 81–102. [10]

Silver, R. L., and **Wortman, C. B.** (1980). Coping with undesirable life events. In J. Garber and M. E. P. Seligman (Eds.), *Human Helplessness: Theory and Applications* (pp. 279–375). New York: Academic Press. [11, 15]

Silverman, L. H. (1976). The further use of the subliminal psychodynamic activation method for the experimental study of the clinical theory of psychoanalysis: On the specificity of the relationship between symptoms and unconscious conflicts. *Psy-chotherapy: Theory, Research, and Practice, 13*(1), 2–16. [13]

Silverman, L. H. (1982). A comment on two subliminal psychodynamic activation studies. *Journal of Abnormal Psychology, 91*(2), 126–130. [13]

Simmons, F. B., Epley, J. M., Lummis, R. C., Guttman, N., Frishkopf, L. S., Harmon, L. D., and **Zwicker, E.** (1965). Auditory nerve: Electrical stimulation in man. *Science, 148,* 104–106. [4]

Simon, H., and **Gilmartin, K.** (1973). A simulation of memory for chess positions. *Cognitive Psychology, 5,* 29–46. [7]

Simon, N., and **Senturia, A.** (1966). Psychiatric sequelae of abortion. *Archives of General Psychiatry, 15,* 378–389. [15]

Simons, A. D., Murphy, G. E., Levine, J. L., and **Wetzel, R. D.** (1986). Cognitive therapy and pharmacotherapy for depression. Sustained improvement over one year. *Archives of General Psychiatry, 43,* 43–48. [17]

Simonton, D. K. (1988). *Scientific Genius: A Psychology of Science.* Cambridge University Press. [8]

Simonton, D. K. (1989, February 6). The surprising nature of scientific genius. *The Scientist.* [8]

Simpson, E. L. (1974). Moral development research: A case study of scientific cultural bias. *Human Development, 17,* 81–106. [10]

Sinclair, R. C., Mark, M. M., and **Shotland, R. L.** (1987). Construct accessibility and generalizability across response categories. *Personality and Social Psychology Bulletin, 13,* 239–252. [18]

Singer, D. G., and **Benton, W.** (1989, October). Caution: Television may be hazardous to a child's mental health. *Developmental and Behavioral Pediatrics, 10*(5), 259–261. [2]

Singer, W. (1986). Neuronal activity as a shaping factor in postnatal development of visual cortex. In W. T. Greenough and J. M. Jurasko (Eds.), *Developmental Neuropsychobiology* (pp. 271–293). New York: Academic Press. [4]

Singular, S. (1982, October). A memory for all seasonings. *Psychology Today,* pp. 54–63. [7]

Sivacek, J., and **Crano, W. D.** (1982). Vested interest as a moderator of attitude-behavior consistency. *Journal of Personality and Social Psychology, 43,* 210–221. [18]

Skinner, B. F. (1938). *The Behavior of Organisms: An Experimental Analysis.* New York: Appleton-Century-Crofts. [1, 6]

Skinner, B. F. (1948). *Walden Two.* New York: Macmillan. [1]

Skinner, B. F. (1953). *Science and Human Behavior.* New York: Macmillan. [6]

Skinner, B. F. (1978). The ethics of helping people. In L. Wispe (Ed.), *Sympathy, Altruism, and Helping Behavior.* New York: Academic Press. [19]

Skinner, B. F. (1983, January). Utopia or disaster. (Interview conducted by L. Rosenthal.) *Science Digest,* pp. 14–15, 103–104. [6]

Skinner, B. F. (1985). Cognitive science and behaviourism. *British Journal of Psychology, 76,* 291–301. [6]

Sloane, R. B., Staples, F. R., Cristal, A. H., Yorkston, W. J., and **Whipple, K.** (1975). *Psychotherapy vs. Behavior Therapy.* Cambridge, MA: Harvard University Press. [17]

Slobin, D. I. (1972, July). Children and language: They learn the same way all around the world. *Psychology Today,* pp. 71–74ff. [9]

Slobin, D. I. (1973). Cognitive prerequisites for the development of grammar. In C. A. Ferguson and D. I. Slobin (Eds.), *Studies of Child Language Development.* New York: Holt, Rinehart and Winston. [9]

Slobin, D. I. (1982). Universal and particular in the acquisition of language. In L. Gleitman and E. Wanner (Eds.), *Language Acquisition: The State of the Art.* New York: Cambridge University Press. [9]

Slovic, P., Fischhoff, B., and **Lichtenstein, S.** (1976). Cognitive processes and societal risk taking. *Oregon Research Institute Monograph, 15.* [8]

Slovic, P., Fischhoff, B., and **Lichtenstein, S.** (1977). Behavioral decision theory. *Annual Review of Psychology, 28,* 1–39. [8]

Slovic, P., Fischhoff, B., and Lichtenstein, S. (1980, June). Risky assumptions. *Psychology Today*, pp. 44–48. [8]

Smead, V. S. (1988). Trying too hard: A correlate of eating related difficulties. *Addictive Behaviors, 13*, 307–310. [12]

Smith, C. A. (1989). Dimensions of appraisal and physiological response in emotion. *Journal of Personality and Social Psychology, 56*, 339–353. [11]

Smith, C. A., and Ellsworth, P. C. (1985). Patterns of cognitive appraisal in emotion. *Journal of Personality and Social Psychology, 48*, 813–838. [11]

Smith, E. E., and Medin, D. L. (1981). *Categories and Concepts.* Cambridge, MA: Harvard University Press. [8]

Smith, M. C. (1983). Hypnotic memory enhancement of witnesses: Does it work? *Psychological Bulletin, 94*, 387–407. [5]

Smith, M. L., and Glass, G. V. (1977). Meta-analysis of psychotherapy outcome studies. *American Psychologist, 32*, 752–760. [17]

Smith, M. L., Glass, G. V., and Miller, R. L. (1981). *The Benefits of Psychotherapy.* Baltimore, MD: Johns Hopkins University Press. [17]

Smith, P. K., and Daglish, L. (1977). Sex differences in parent and infant behavior in the home. *Child Development, 48*, 1250–1254. [10]

Smith, R. H., Diener, E., and Wedell, D. H. (1989). *Journal of Personality and Social Psychology, 56*(3), 317–325. [11]

Smith et al. (1991). *Journal of Behavioral Medicine* (article on negative health effects of hostility). [1]

Smolak, L. (1986). *Infancy.* Englewood Cliffs, NJ: Prentice Hall. [9, 10]

Smothers, R. (1991, February 26). Waiting enters a new phase at the home of the 101st Airborne. *The New York Times*, p. A17. [15]

Snyder, C. R., and Higgins, R. L. (1988). Excuses: Their effective role in the negotiation of reality. *Psychological Bulletin, 104*, 23–35. [18]

Snyder, D. K. et al. (1991, February).
Journal of Consulting and Clinical Psychology. [17]

Snyder, F. (1970). The phenomenology of dreaming. In L. Madow and L. H. Snow (Eds.). *The Psychodynamic Implications of the Physiological Studies on Dreams.* Springfield, IL: Charles C. Thomas. [5]

Snyder, M., Berscheid, E., and Glick, P. (1985). Focusing on the exterior and the interior: Two investigations of the initiation of personal relationships. *Journal of Personality and Social Psychology, 48*, 1427–1439. [1]

Snyder, M., Tanke, E. D., and Berscheid, E. (1977). Social perception and interpersonal behavior: On the self-fulfilling nature of social stereotypes. *Journal of Personality and Social Psychology, 35*, 656–666. [18]

Snyder, S. H. (1980). *Biological Aspects of Mental Disorder.* New York: Oxford University Press. [3]

Snyder, S. H. (1984). Drug and neurotransmitter receptors in the brain. *Science, 224*, 22–31. [3]

Snyderman, M., and Rothman, S. (1987). Survey of expert opinion on intelligence and aptitude testing. *American Psychologist, 42*, 137–144. [14]

Solomon, L. Z., Solomon, H., and Stone, R. (1978). Helping as a function of number of bystanders and ambiguity of emergency. *Personality and Social Psychology Bulletin, 4*, 318–321. [19]

Solomon, R. L. (1980). The opponent-process theory of acquired motivation: The costs of pleasure and the benefits of pain. *American Psychologist, 35*, 691–712. [12]

Solomon, R. L., and Corbit, J. D. (1974). An opponent-process theory of motivation. *Psychological Review, 81*, 119–145. [12]

Spanos, N. P. (1986). Hypnotic behavior: A social-psychological interpretation of amnesia, analgesia, and "trance logic." *Behavioral and Brain Sciences, 9*(3), 449–467. [5]

Spanos, N. P., Gwynn, M. I., Comer, S. L., Baltruweit, W. J., and de Groh, M. (1989). Are hypnotically induced pseudo-memories resistant to cross-examination?
Law and Human Behavior, 13(3) 271–289. [5]

Spanos, N. P., and Hewitt, E. C. (1980). The hidden observer in hypnotic analgesia: Discovery or experimental creation? *Journal of Personality and Social Psychology, 39*, 1201–1214. [5]

Spearman, C. (1927). *The Abilities of Man.* New York: Macmillan. [14]

Speisman, J., Lazarus, R. S., Mordkoff, A., and Davidson, L. (1964). Experimental reduction of stress based on ego defense theory. *Journal of Abnormal and Social Psychology, 68*, 367–380. [15]

Spence, J. T., Deaux, K., and Helmreich, R. L. (1985). Sex roles in contemporary American society. In G. Lindsey and E. Aronson (Eds.), *Handbook of Social Psychology* (3rd ed.). Reading, MA: Addison-Wesley. [18]

Spencer, Jr., D. G., Yaden, S., and Lal, H. (1988). Behavioral and physiological detection of classically-conditioned blood pressure reduction. *Psychopharmacology*, 25–28. [6]

Spenner, K., and Featherman, D. L. (1978). Achievement ambitions. *Annual Review of Sociology, 4*, 373–420. [12]

Sperling, G. (1960). The information available in brief visual presentation. *Psychological Monographs, 74* (Whole No. 498). [7]

Sperry, R. W. (1976). Changing concepts of consciousness and free will. *Perspective in Biology and Medicine, 20*, 9–19. [5]

Sperry, R. W. (1982). Some effects of disconnecting the cerebral hemispheres. *Science, 217*, 1223–1226. [3]

Spiegel, D., Bloom, J. R., Kraemer, H. C., and Gottheil, E. (1989, October 14). Effect of psychosocial treatment on survival of patients with metastatic breast cancer. *The Lancet*, 888–891. [2]

Spiegel, D., Bloom, J., and Yalom, I. (1981). Group support for patients with metastatic cancer. *Archives of General Psychiatry, 38*, 527–533. [17]

Spiegel, H. (1970). A single-treatment method to stop smoking using ancillary self-hypnosis. *International Journal of Clinical Hypnosis, 18*, 235–250. [5]

Springer, S., and **Deutsch, G.** (1985). *Left Brain, Right Brain* (rev. ed.). New York: W. H. Freeman.

Springer, S. P., and **Deutsch, G.** (1989). *Left Brain, Right Brain* (3rd ed.). San Francisco, CA: W. H. Freeman. [3]

Sprinthall, N., and **Collins, W. A.** (1984). *Adolescent Psychology.* New York: Addison-Wesley.

Squire, L. R. (1986). Mechanisms of memory. *Science, 232,* 1612–1619. [3, 7]

Squire, L. R. (1987). *Memory and Brain,* New York: Oxford University Press. [7]

Sroufe, L. A. (1988). The role of infant–caregiver attachment in development. In J. Belsky and T. Nezworski (Eds.), *Clinical Implications of Attachment* (pp. 18–40). Hillsdale, NJ: Lawrence Erlbaum. [10]

Sroufe, L. A., and **Cooper, R. G.** (1988). *Child Development: Its Nature and Course.* New York: Knopf. [10]

Sroufe, L. A., Fox, N., and **Pancake, V.** (1983). Attachment and dependency in developmental perspective. *Child Development, 54,* 1615–1627. [10]

Staddon, J. E. R., and **Ettinger, R. H.** (1989). *Learning: An introduction to the Principles of Adaptive Behavior.* San Diego: Harcourt Brace Jovanovich. [6]

Stanley, J. C. (1983, February). Education in the fast lane: Methodological problems of evaluating its effects. *Evaluation News,* pp. 28–46. [14]

Stanley, M., and **Stanley, B.** (1989, Spring). Biochemical studies in suicide victims: Current findings and future implications. *Suicide and Life-Threatening Behavior, 19,* 30–42. [17]

Stanley, M., and **Stanley, B.** (1990, April). Postmortem evidence for serotonin's role in suicide. *Journal of Clinical Psychiatry, 51,* 22–28. [17]

Stanton, M. D. (1981). Strategic approaches to family therapy. In A. Gurman and D. P. Kniskern (Eds.). *Handbook of Family Therapy* (p. 361). New York: Brunner/Mazel. [17]

Steele, C. M., Southwick, L., and **Pagano, R.** (1986). Drinking your troubles away: The role of activity in mediating alcohol's reduction of psychological stress. *Journal of Abnormal Psychology, 95,* 173–180. [16]

Stein, M. I. (1956). A transactional approach to creativity. In C. W. Taylor (Ed.), *The 1955 University of Utah Research Conference on the Identification of Creative Scientific Talent.* Salt Lake City: University of Utah Press. [8]

Steinberg, L. (1986). Latchkey children and susceptibility to peer pressure: An ecological analysis. *Developmental Psychology, 22,* 433–439. [10]

Steinberg, L., and **Belsky, J.** (1990). *Infancy, Childhood, and Adolescence: Development in Context.* New York: McGraw-Hill. [9]

Stelmack, R. M. (1990, March). Biological bases of extroversion: Psychophysiological evidence. *Journal of Personality, 58*(1), 293–311. [13]

Stenberg, C. R., and **Campos, J. J.** (1990). The development of anger expressions in infancy. In N. L. Stein, B. Levanthal, and T. Trabasso (Eds.), *Psychological and Biological Approaches to Emotion* (pp. 247–282). Hillsdale, NJ: Lawrence Erlbaum. [11]

Stengel, E. (1964). *Suicide and Attempted Suicide.* Baltimore, MD: Penguin. [16]

Stephens, J. H. (1978). Long-term prognosis and followup in schizophrenia. *Schizophrenia Bulletin, 4,* 25–46. [16]

Stern, M. J., Pascale, L., and **McLoone, J. B.** (1976). Psychosocial adaptation following an acute myocardial infarction. *Journal of Chronic Diseases, 29,* 513–526. [13]

Stern, W. (1910). Abstracts of lectures on the psychology of testimony and on the study of individuality. *American Journal of Psychology, 21,* 270–282. [14]

Sternberg, R. J. (1984). *Beyond IQ: A Triarchic Theory of Human Intelligence.* New York: Cambridge University Press. [14]

Sternberg, R.J. (1985). Human intelligence: The model is the message. *Science, 230,* 1111–1118. [14]

Sternberg, R. J. (1986). A triangular theory of love. *Psychological Review, 93,* 119–135. [18]

Sternberg, R. J. (1988). Mental self-government: A theory of intellectual styles and their development. *Human Development, 31,* 197–224. [14]

Sternberg, R. J., Conway, B. E., Ketron, J. L., and **Berstein, M.** (1981). Peoples's conceptions of intelligence. *Journal of Personality and Social Psychology, 41,* 37–55. [14]

Sternberg, R. J., and **Davidson, J. E.** (1982, June). The mind of the puzzler. *Psychology Today,* pp. 37–44. [8]

Sternberg, R. J., and **Gastel, J.** (1989). Coping with novelty in human intelligence: An empirical investigation. *Intelligence, 13,* 187–197. [14]

Stevens, C. F. (1979). The neuron. *Scientific American, 241,* 55–65. [3]

Stocker, C., Dunn, J., and **Plomin, R.** (1989). Sibling relationships: Links with child temperament, maternal behavior, and family structure. *Child Development, 60,* 715–727. [10]

Stolz, W. (1967). A study of the ability to decode grammatically novel sentences. *Journal of Verbal Learning and Verbal Behavior, 6,* 867–873. [8]

Stone (1987). Event content in a daily survey is differentially associated with concurrent mood. *Journal of Personality and Social Psychology, 52*(1), 56–58. [11]

Strack, F., Martin, L. L., and **Stepper, S.** (1988). *Journal of Personality and Social Psychology, 54*(5), 768–777. [11]

Straus, M. A., Gelles, R. J., and **Steinmetz, S. K.** (1980). *Behind closed doors: Violence in the American family.* Garden City, NY: Anchor Books. [19]

Streissguth, A. P., Barr, H. M., Sampson, P. D., Darby, B. L. et al. (1989). IQ at age four in relation to maternal alcohol use and smoking during pregnancy. *Developmental Psychology, 25*(1), 3–11. [14]

Streissguth, A. P., Martin, D. C., Barr, H. M., Sandman, B. M., Kirchner, G. L., and **Darby, B. L.** (1984). Intrauterine alcohol and nicotine exposure: Attention and reaction time in 4-year-old children. *Developmental Psychology, 20,* 533–541. [9]

Stricker, G. (1983). Some issues in psychodynamic treatment of the depressed patient. *Professional Psychology: Research and Practice, 14*, 209–217. [15]

Strickland, B. R. (1987, December). On the threshold of the second century of psychology. *American Psychologist, 42*(12), 1055–1056. [1]

Stroop, J. R. (1935). Studies of interference in serial verbal reactions. *Journal of Experimental Psychology, 18*, 643–662. [7]

Stuart, R. B. (1976). An operant interpersonal program for couples. In D. H. L. Olson (Ed.), *Treating Relationships*. Lake Mills, Iowa: Graphic Publishing Company. [17]

Stunkard, A. J., Harris, J. R., Pedersen, N. L., and McClearn, G. E. (1990). The body-mass index of twins who have been reared apart. *The New England Journal of Medicine, 322*, 1483–1487. [12]

Stuss, D. T., and Benson, D. F. (1984). Neuropsychological studies of the frontal lobes. *Psychological Bulletin, 95*, 3–28. [3]

Suedfeld, P. (1975). The benefits of boredom: Sensory deprivation reconsidered. *American Scientist, 63*, 60–69. [12]

Sugarman, S. (1983). Why talk? Comment on Savage-Rumbaugh et al. *Journal of Experimental Psychology: General, 112*(4). 493–497. [8]

Suls, J., and Mullen, B. (1981). Life events, perceived control and illness: The role of uncertainty. *Journal of Human Stress, 7*(2), 30–34. [15]

Swanbrow, D. (1989, August). The paradox of happiness. *Psychology Today*, pp. 37–39. [11]

Swartz, M., Carroll, B., and Blazer, D. (1989, March). In response to "Psychiatric Diagnosis as Reified Measurement. *30*, 33–34. [16]

Sweet, W. H., Ervin, F., and Mark, V. H. (1969). The relationship of violent behavior to focal cerebral disease. In S. Garattini and E. Sigg (Eds.), *Aggressive Behavior*. New York: Wiley. [11]

Swets, J. A. (1961). Is there a sensory threshold? *Science, 134*, 168–177. [4]

Symonds, M. (1975). Victims of violence: Psychological effects and aftereffects. *American Journal of Psychoanalysis, 35*, 19–26. [19]

Szasz, T. S. (1961). *The Myth of Mental Illness: Foundations of a Theory of Personal Conduct*. New York: Harper & Row. [15]

Szasz, T. (1986, July). The case against suicide prevention. *American Psychologist, 41*, 806–812. [17]

Tajfel, H. (1982). Social Identity and Intergroup Relations. Cambridge, England: Cambridge University Press. [18]

Tangney, J. P., and Feshbach, S. (1988). Children's television viewing frequency: Individual differences and demographic correlates. *Personality and Social Psychology Bulletin, 14*, 145–148. [19]

Tanner, J. M. (1982). *Growth at Adolescence* (2nd ed.). Oxford: Scientific Publications. [10]

Tart, C. T. (1970). Marijuana intoxication: Common experiences. *Nature, 226*, 701–704. [5]

Task Force on Tardive Dyskinesia. (1980). *American Psychiatric Association Task Force Report* (No. 18, p. 44). Washington, DC: American Psychiatric Association Press. [17]

Taube, C. A., and Rednick, R. (1973). *Utilization of Mental Health Resources by Persons Diagnosed with Schizophrenia*. (DHEW Publication No. [HSM] 72–9110). Rockville, MD: National Institute of Mental Health. [16]

Tavris, C. (1982). *Anger: The Misunderstood Emotion*. New York: Simon and Schuster. [6, 11]

Tavris, C. (1987, September 27). Old age is not what it used to be. *New York Times Magazine, Part 2 (Good Health)*, pp. 24–25, 91–92. [9]

Taylor, S., and Thompson, S. (1981). *Stalking the Elusive "Vividness" Effect*. Unpublished manuscript, University of California at Los Angeles. [8]

Taylor, S. E. (1991). *Health Psychology* (2nd ed.). New York: McGraw-Hill. [15]

Taylor, S. E., and Brown, J. D. (1988). Illusion and well-being: A social psycho-

logical perspective on mental health. *Psychological Bulletin, 103*, 193–210. [18]

Taylor, S. E., Wood, J. V., and Lichtman, R. R. (1983). It could be worse: Selective evaluation as a response to victimization. *Journal of Social Issues, 39*, 19–40. [11]

Teasdale, J. D., and Fogarty, F. J. (1979). Differential effects of induced mood on retrieval of pleasant and unpleasant events from episodic memory. *Journal of Abnormal Psychology, 88*, 248–257. [7]

Teghtsoonian, R. (1971). On the exponents in Stevens' law and the constant in Ekman's law. *Psychological Review, 78*, 71–80. [4]

Telch, M. J., Agras, W. S., Barr Taylor, C., Roth, W. T., and Gallen, C. C. (1985). Combined pharmacological and behavioral treatment for agoraphobia. *Behavioral Research Therapy, 23*, 325–335. [17]

Tellegen, A., Lykken, D. T., Bouchard, T. J., Wilcox, K. J., Segal, N. L., and Rich, S. (1988). Personality similarity in twins reared apart and together. *Journal of Personality and Social Psychology.*

Tenopyr, M. L. (1981). The realities of employment testing. *American Psychology, 36*(51), 1120–1127. [14]

Terman, L. M. (1916). *The Measurement of Intelligence*. Boston: Houghton Mifflin. [14]

Terrace, H. S. (1979, November). How Nim Chimpsky changed my mind. *Psychology Today*, pp. 65–76. [8]

Tesar, G. E. (1990, May). High-potency benzodiazepines for short-term management of panic disorder: The U. S. experience. *Journal of Clinical Psychiatry* (Suppl.), *51*, 4–10. [17]

Tesser, A. (1985). Some effects of self-evaluation maintenance cognition and action. In R. M. Sorrentino and E. T. Higgins (Eds.)., *The Handbook of Motivation and Cognition: Foundations of Social Behavior*. New York: Guilford. [12]

Tetlock, P. E. and Boerrger, R. (1989). Accountability: A social magnifier of the dihition effect. *Journal of Personality and Social Psychology, 57*, 388–398. [18]

Thase, M. E., and Moss, M. K. (1976).

The relative efficacy of covet modeling procedures and guided participant modeling on the reduction of avoidance behavior. *Journal of Behavior Therapy and Experimental Psychiatry, 7*, 7–12. [17]

Thomas, A., Chess, S., and **Birch, H.** (1970). The origin of personality. *Scientific American, 223*, 102–109. [13]

Thomas, M. H. (1982). Physiological arousal, exposure to a relatively lengthy aggressive film, and aggressive behavior. *Journal of Research in Personality, 16*, 72–81. [19]

Thompson, J. K., Jarvie, G. J., Lahey, B. B., and **Cureton, K. J.** (1982). Exercise and obesity: Etiology, physiology, and intervention. *Psychological Bulletin, 91*, 55–79. [13]

Thompson, L. J. (1971). Language disabilities in men of eminence. *Journal of Learning Disabilities, 4*, 39–50. [6]

Thompson, R. F. (1985). *The Brain: An Introduction to Neuroscience.* New York: W. H. Freeman. [3, 5]

Thompson, R. F. (1986). The neurobiology of learning and memory. *Science, 233*, 941–947. [3, 7]

Thompson, R. F. (1988). Brain substrates of learning and memory. In T. Boll and B. K. Bryant (Eds.), *Clinical Neuropsychology and Brain Function: Research, Measurement and Practice,* (pp. 61–83). Washington, DC: American Psychological Association. [2, 7]

Thompson, R. F., with **McCormick, D. A., Lavoid, D. G., Clark, G. A., Kettner, R. E.,** and **Mauk, M. D.** (1983). The engram found? Initial localization of the memory trace for a basic form of associative learning. In J. M. Sprague and A. N. Epstein (Eds.), *Progress in Psychobiology and Physiological Psychology.* (Vol. 10, pp. 167–196). New York: Academic Press. [7]

Thoresen, C. E., and **Mahoney, M. J.** (1974). *Behavioral Self-Control.* New York: Holt. [15]

Thorndike, E. L. (1898). *Animal intelligence. Psychological Review Monograph, 2.* [6]

Thorndike, E. L. (1932). *The Fundamentals of Learning.* New York: Teachers College. [6]

Thorndike, R. L., Hagen, E. P., and **Sattler, J. M.** (1986). *Stanford-Binet Intelligence Scale* (4th ed.). Chicago: Riverside. [14]

Thorne, B. (1986). Boys and girls together, but mostly apart: Gender arrangements in elementary schools. In W. W. Hartup and Z. Rubin (Eds.), *Relationships and Development.* Hillsdale, NJ: Lawrence Erlbaum. [10]

Thurstone, L. L. (1938). *Primary Mental Abilities.* Chicago: University of Chicago Press. [14]

Tienari, P., Sorri, A., Lahti, I., Naarala, M. N., Wahlberg, E., Moring, J., Pohjola, J., and **Wynne, L. C.** (1987). Genetic and psychosocial factors in schizophrenia: The Finnish adoptive family study. *Schizophrenia Bulletin, 13*, 477–484. [16]

Timberlake, W., and **Lucas, G. A.** (1984). Behavior systems and learning: From misbehavior to general principles. In S. B. Klein and R. R. Mowrer (Eds.), *Contemporary Learning Theories: The Impact of Biological Constraints on Learning.* Hillsdale, NJ: Lawrence Erlbaum. [6]

Tinklenberg, J. R. (1971). A clinical view of the amphetamines. *American Family Physician, 4*, 82–86. [5]

Tippin, J., and **Henn, F. A.** (1982). Modified leucotomy in the treatment of intractable obsessive neurosis. *American Journal of Psychiatry, 139*, 1601–1603. [17]

Tolman, E. C. (1959). Principles of purposive behavior. In S. Koch (Ed.), *Psychology: A Study of Science* (Vol. 2). New York: McGraw-Hill. [12]

Tolman, E. C., and **Honzik, C. H.** (1930). *Introduction and Removal of Reward and Maze Performance in Rats.* University of California Publications in Psychology, 4, 257–275. [6]

Tomarken, A. J., Davidson, R. J., and **Henriques, J. B.** (1990). Resting and frontal brain asymmetry predicts affective responses to films. *Journal of Personality and Social Psychology, 59*(4), 791–801. [11]

Tomkins, S. S. (1962). *Affect, Imagery, Consciousness: Vol. 2. The Negative Affects.* New York: Springer. [11]

Tomkins, S. S. (1980). Affect as amplification: Some modifications in theory. In R. Plutchik and H. Kellerman (Eds.), *Emotion: Theory, Research, and Experience: Vol. 1. Theories of Emotion* (pp. 141–164). New York: Academic Press. [11]

Tonkova-Yampol'skaya, R. V. (1973). Development of speech intonation in infants during the first two years of life. In C. A. Ferguson and D. I. Slobin (Eds.), *Studies of Child Language Development* (pp. 128–138). New York: Holt, Rinehart and Winston. [9]

Tracy, K. (1984). Staying on topic: An explication of conversational relevance. *Discourse Processes, 7*, 337–464. [8]

Trask, C. H., and **Cree, E. M.** (1962). Oximeter studies on patients with chronic obstructive emphysema, awake and during sleep. *New England Journal of Medicine, 266*, 639–642. [5]

Treadway, M., and **McCloskey, M.** (1989). Effects of racial stereotypes on eyewitness performance: Implications of the real and rumoured Allport and Postman studies. *Applied Cognitive Psychology, 3*, 53–63. [7]

Treisman, A. M. (1960). Contextual cues in selective listening. *Quarterly Journal of Experimental Psychology, 12*, 242–248. [7]

Treisman, A. M. (1964). Verbal cues, language and meaning in selective attention. *American Journal of Psychology, 77*, 206–219. [7]

Treisman, A. M. (1986). Features and objects in visual processing. *Scientific American, 255*(5), 114B–125. [4]

Tresemer, D. W. (1974, March). Fear of success: Popular, but unproven. *Psychology Today*, pp. 82–85. [12]

Tresemer, D. W. (1977). *Fear of Success.* New York: Plenum. [12]

Triplett, N. (1898). The dynamogenic factors in pacemaking and competition. *American Journal of Psychology, 9*, 507–533. [19]

Truax, C. B., Wargo, D. G., Frank, J. D., Imber, S. D., Battle, C. C., Hoehn-Saric, R., Nash, E. H., and **Stone, A. R.** (1966). Therapist empathy, genuineness, and warmth and patient therapeutic outcome.

Journal of Consulting Psychology, 30, 395–401. [13]

Tuckman, J., Kleiner, R. J., and Lavell, M. (1959). Emotional content of suicide notes. *American Journal of Psychiatry, 116,* 59–63. [17]

Tulving, E. (1985). How many memory systems are there? *American Psychologist, 40*(4), 385–398. [7]

Tulving, E., and Pearlstone, Z. (1966). Availability versus accessibility of information in memory for words. *Journal of Verbal Learning and Verbal Behavior, 5,* 381–391. [7]

Tunstall, O., Gudjonsson, G., Eysenck, H., and Haward, L. (1982). Professional issues arising from psychological evidence presented in court. *Bulletin of the British Psychological Society, 35,* 329–331. [14]

Turk, D. C., Meichenbaum, D. H., and Berman, W. H. (1979). Application of biofeedback for the regulation of pain: A critical review. *Psychological Bulletin, 86,* 1322–1338. [15]

Turner, R. J., and Wagonfeld, M. O. (1987). Occupational mobility and schizophrenia. *American Sociological Review, 32,* 104–113. [16]

Turner, S. M., Beidel, D. C., and Nathan, R. S. (1985). Biological factors in obsessive-compulsive disorders. *Psychological Bulletin, 97,* 430–450. [16]

Tversky, A., and Kahneman, D. (1971). Belief in the law of small numbers. *Psychological Bulletin, 76,* 105–110. [8]

Tversky, A., and Kahneman, D. (1973). Availability: A heuristic for judging frequency and probability. *Cognitive Psychology, 5,* 207–232. [8]

Tversky, A., and Kahneman, D. (1981). The framing of decisions and the psychology of choice. *Science, 211,* 453–458. [8]

Tversky, A., and Kahneman, D. (1983). Extensional versus intuitive reasoning: The conjunction fallacy in probability judgment. *Psychological Review, 90,* 293–315. [7]

Tversky, B., and Tuchin, M. (1989). A reconciliation of the evidence on eyewitness testimony: Comments on McCloskey and Zaragoza. *Journal of Experimental Psychology: General, 118*(1), 85–90. [7]

Tweed, D. L., and George, L. K. (1989, March). A more balanced perspective on "Psychiatric Diagnosis as Reified Measurement." *30,* 35–37. [16]

Tyhurst, J. S. (1951). Individual reactions to community disaster. *American Journal of Psychiatry, 10,* 746–769. [12]

Ullman, M. (1962). Dreaming, life-style, and physiology: A comment on Adler's view of the dream. *Journal of Individual Psychology, 18,* 18–25. [5]

Umberson, D. (1987). Family status and health behaviors: Social control as a dimension of social integration. *Journal of Health and Social Behavior, 28,* 306–319. [15]

U.S. Bureau of the Census. (1982). Statistical Abstract of the United States: 1982–1983 (103rd ed.). Washington, DC: U.S. Government Printing Office. [18]

Vaillant, G. (1977) *Adaption to Life.* Boston: Little, Brown. [10]

Valenstein, E. S. (1973). *Brain Control: A Critical Examination of Brain Stimulation and Psychosurgery.* New York: Wiley. [17]

Valenstein, E. S. (1978, July). Science-fiction fantasy and the brain. *Psychology Today,* pp. 28–39. [16]

Valenstein, E. S. (1980). *The Psychosurgery Debate.* San Francisco: W. H. Freeman. [17]

Valois, P., Desharnais, R., and Godin, C. (1988). A comparison of the Fishbein and Ajzen and the Triandis attitudinal models for the prediction of exercise intention and behavior. *Journal of Behavioral Medicine, 11,* 459–472. [15]

Vandell, D. L., and Corasaniti, M. A. (1990, Fall). Child care and the family: Complex contributors to child development. *New Directions for Child Development, 49,* 23–37. [10]

Van Dyke, C., and Byck, R. (1982). Cocaine. *Scientific American, 44,* 132–141. [5]

Van Orden, G. C., Johnston, J. C., and Hale, B. L. (1989). Word identification in reading proceeds from spelling to sound to meaning. *Journal of Experimental Psychology: Learning, Memory, and Cognition, 14*(3), 371–386. [8]

Van Osdol, W. R., and Shane, D. G. (1977). *An Introduction to Exceptional Children.* Dubuque, IA: William C. Brown. [14]

Vaughan, E. (1977). Misconceptions about psychology among introductory psychology students. *Teaching of Psychology, 4,* 138–141. [1]

Vaughn, B. E., Gove, F. L., and Egeland, B. (1980). The relationship between out-of-home care and the quality of infant mother attachment in an economically disadvantaged population. *Child Development, 51,* 1203–1214. [10]

Velten, E. (1968). A laboratory task for induction of mood states. *Behavior Research and Therapy, 6,* 473–483. [11]

Videka-Sherman, L., and Lieberman, M. (1985). The effects of self-help and psychotherapy intervention on child loss: The limits of recovery. *American Journal of Othropsychiatry, 55,* 70–82. [17]

Vogel, G. (1975). A review of REM deprivation. *Archives of General Psychiatry, 32,* 749–761. [5]

Vogel, G., Thurmond, A., Gibbons, D., Sloan, K., Boyd, M., and Walker, M. (1975). Sleep reduction effects on depressive syndromes. *Archives of General Psychiatry, 32,* 765–777. [5]

Von Korff, M., Nestadt, G., Romanoski, A., Anthony, J., Eaton, W., Merchant, A., Chahal, R., Kramer, M., Folstein, M., and Gruenberg, E. (1985). Prevalence of treated and untreated DSM-III schizophrenia: Results of a two-stage community survey. *Journal of Nervous and Mental Disease, 173,* 577–581. [16]

Vonnegut, M. (1975). *The Eden Express.* New York: Praeger. [17]

Wachtel, E. F., and Wachtel, P. L. (1986). *Family Dynamics in Individual Psychotherapy: A Guide to Clinical Strategies.* New York: Guilford. [17]

Wachtel, P. (1977). *Psychoanalysis and Behavior Therapy.* New York: Basic Books. [17]

Wachtel, P. L. (1982). Vicious circles: The self and the rhetoric of emerging and unfolding. *Contemporary Psychoanalysis, 18,* 259–273. [17]

Wachter, K. W. (1988). Disturbed by meta-analysis? *Science, 241,* 1407–1408. [2]

Wadden, T. A., Stunkard, A. J., and **Liebschutz, J.** (1988). *Journal of Consulting and Clinical Psychology, 56,* 925–928. [12]

Wagenaar, W. (1986). My memory: A study of autobiographical memory over six years. *Cognitive Psychology, 18,* 225–252. [7]

Wagenaar, W. A. (1988). People and places in my memory: A study on cue specificity and retrieval from autobiographical memory. In M. M. Gruenberg, P. E. Morris, and R. N. Sykes (Eds.), *Practical Aspects of Memory: Current Research and Issues* (Vol. 1, pp. 228–233). New York: Wiley. [7]

Wald, G. (1968). Molecular basis of visual excitation. *Science, 162,* 230–239. [4]

Waldrop, M. M. (1984). Artificial intelligence in parallel. *Science, 225,* 608–610. [1]

Waldrop, M. M. (1985). Machinations of thought. *Science 85, 6,* 38–45. [7]

Waldrop, M. M. (1987). The workings of working memory. *Science, 237,* 1564–1567. [7]

Waldrop, M. M. (1988a). Toward a unified theory of cognition. *Science, 241,* 27–29. [8]

Waldrop, M. M. (1988b). Soar: A unified theory of cognition? *Science, 241,* 296–298. [8]

Walker-Andrews, A. S., and **Gibson, E. J.** (1987). What develops in bimodal perception? In L. P. Lipsitt and C. K. Rovee-Collier (Eds.), *Advances in Infancy Research* (Vol. 4). Norwood, NJ: Ablex. [9]

Wall, J. T. (1988). Variable organization in cortical maps of the skin as an indication of the lifelong capacities of circuits in the mammalian brain. *Trends in Neuroscience, 12,* 549–557. [4]

Wall, P. D., and **Sweet, W. H.** (1967). Temporary abolition of pain in man. *Science, 155,* 108–109. [4]

Wallace, B., and **Fisher, L. E.** (1987). *Consciousness and Behavior* (2nd ed.). Boston: Allyn and Bacon. [5]

Wallace, C. J., and **Liberman, R. P.** (1985). Social skills training for patients with schizophrenia: A controlled clinical trial. *Psychiatry Research, 15,* 239–247. [17]

Wallace, R. K., and **Benson, H.** (1972). The physiology of meditation. *Scientific American, 226,* 84–90. [12]

Wallach, H., and **Slaughter, V.** (1988). The role of memory in perceiving subjective contours. *Perception and Psychophysics, 43,* 101–106. [4]

Wallerstein, J. S. (1988). *Second Chances: Men, Women and Children a Decade after Divorce.* Ticknor and Fields: New York. [10]

Wallerstein, J. S., and **Blakeslee, S.** (1989). *Second Chances: Men, Women, and Children a Decade after Divorce.* New York: Ticknor & Fields. [15]

Wallston, B. S., Alagna, S. W., DeVellis, B. McE., and **DeVellis, R. F.** (1983). Social support and physical health. *Health Psychology, 2,* 367–391. [15]

Walster, E., Aronson, V., Abrahams, D., and **Rottman, L.** (1966). Importance of physical attractiveness in dating behavior. *Journal of Personality and Social Psychology, 4,* 508–516. [18]

Wardle, J., and **Beales, S.** (1988). Control and loss of control over eating: An experimental investigation. *Journal of Abnormal Psychology, 97,* 35–40. [12]

Warr, P. (1978, February). Study of psychological well-being. *British Journal of Psychology, 69,* 111–121. [11]

Warren, R. M. (1970). Perceptual restoration of missing speech sounds. *Science, 167,* 392–393. [8]

Wason, P., and **Johnson-Laird, P. N.** (1972). *Psychology of Reasoning: Structure and Content.* Cambridge, MA: Harvard University Press. [9]

Waters, E., Wippman, J., and **Sroufe, L. A.** (1979). Attachment, positive affect, and competence in the peer group: Two studies in construct validation. *Child Development, 50,* 821–829. [10]

Watkins, L. R., and **Mayer, D. J.** (1982). Organization of endogenous opiate and nonopiate pain control systems. *Science, 216,* 1185–1192. [3]

Watson, D., Clark, L. A., and **Tellegren, A.** (1988). Development and validation of brief measures of positive and negative affect: The PANAS Scales. *Journal of Personality and Social Psychology, 54(6),* 1063–1070. [11]

Watson, D., and **Tellegren, A.** (1985). *Psychological Bulletin, 98(2),* 219–235. [11]

Watson, J. B. (1924). *Behaviorism.* New York: People's Institute. [1]

Watson, J. B., and **Rayner, R.** (1920). Conditioned emotional reactions. *Journal of Experimental Psychology, 3,* 1–14. [6]

Watson, J. S. (1972). Smiling, cooing, and "the game." *Merrill-Palmer Quarterly of Behavior and Development, 18,* 323–339. [9]

Webb, E. J., Campbell, D. T., Schwartz, R. D., and **Sechrest, L.** (1966). *Unobtrusive Measures: Nonreactive Research in the Social Sciences.* Chicago: Rand McNally. [2]

Webb, W. B. (1975). *Sleep: The Gentle Tyrant.* Englewood Cliffs, NJ: Prentice-Hall. [5]

Webb, W. B., and **Agnew, H.** (1970). Sleep characteristics of long and short sleepers. *Science, 168,* 146–147. [5]

Weber, R., and **Crocker, J.** (1983). Cognitive processes in the revision of stereotypic beliefs. *Journal of Personality and Social Psychology, 45,* 961–977. [18]

Wechsler, D. (1949). *Wechsler Intelligence Scale for Children.* New York: Psychological Corporation. [14]

Wechsler, D. (1955). *Wechsler Adult Intelligence Scale Manual.* New York: Psychological Corporation. [14]

Wechsler, D. (1967). *Wechsler Preschool and Primary Scale of Intelligence.* New York: Psychological Corporation. [14]

Wegman, M. E. (1986). Annual summary

of vital statistics—1985. *Pediatrics, 79*(6), 817–827. [10]

Wegner, D. M. et al. (1987). Paradoxical effects of thought suppression. *Journal of Personality and Social Psychology, 53*(1), 5–13. [16]

Wehr, T. A., Giesen, H. A., Schulz, P. M. et al. (1989). Summer depression: Description of the syndrome and comparison with winter depression. In N. E. Rosenthal and M. Blehar (Eds.), *Seasonal Affective Disorder and Phototherapy*. New York: Guilford. [16]

Wehr, T. A., and Rosenthal, N. E. (1989, July). Seasonality and affective illness. *American Journal of Psychiatry, 146*(7), 829–839. [16]

Wehr, T. A., Sack, D. A., and Rosenthal, N. E. (1987). Seasonal affective disorder with summer depression and winter hypomania. *American Journal of Psychiatry, 144*, 1602–1603. [16]

Weil, A. T., and Zinberg, N. E. (1969). Acute effects of marijuana on speech. *Nature, 222*, 434–437. [5]

Weiner, B. (1972). *Theories of Motivation: From Mechanism to Cognition*. Chicago: Markham. [12]

Weiner, B. (Ed.).(1974). *Achievement Motivation and Attribution Theory*. Morristown, NJ: General Learning Press. [12]

Weiner, B. (1980). *Human Motivation*. New York: Holt, Rinehart and Winston. [12]

Weiner, B. (1985). An attributional theory of achievement motivation and emotion. *Psychological Review, 92*, 548–573. [19]

Weiner, B., Heckhausen, H., Meyer, W. U., and Cook, R. C. (1972). Causal ascriptions of achievement behavior: A conceptual analysis of effort. *Journal of Personality and Social Psychology, 21*, 239–248. [12]

Weinstein, N. D. (1980). Unrealistic optimism about future life events. *Journal of Personality and Social Psychology, 39*, 806–820. [15]

Weinstein, N. D. (1982). Unrealistic optimism about susceptibility to health prob-

lems. *Journal of Behavioral Medicine, 5*, 441–460. [15]

Weinstein, N. D. (1989). Effects of personal experience on self-protective behavior. *Psychological Bulletin, 105*(1), 31–50. [18]

Weintraub, M., and Evans, P. (1989). Clozapine: A neuroleptic agent for selected schizophrenics and patients with tardive dyskinesia. *Hospital Formulary, 24*, 16–27. [17]

Weisberg, R. W. (1986). *Creativity: Genius and Other Myths*. New York: W. H. Freeman. [8]

Weisenberg, M. (1977). Pain and pain control. *Psychological Bulletin, 84*, 1008–1044. [15]

Weisenberg, T., and McBride, K. E. (1935). *Aphasia: A Clinical and Psychological Study*. New York: Commonwealth Fund. [3]

Wellman, H., Collins, J., and Glieberman, J. (1981). Understanding the combination of memory variables: Developing conceptions of memory limitations. *Child Development, 52*, 1313–1317. [9]

Wellman, H. M. (1987). The early development of memory strategies. In F. Weinert and M. Perlmutter (Eds.), *Memory Development: Universal Changes and Individual Differences*. Hillsdale, NJ: Lawrence Erlbaum. [9]

Wender, P. H., Kety, S. S., Rosenthal, D., Schulsinger, F., Ortman, J., and Lunde, I. (1986). Psychiatric disorders in the biological and adaptive families of adaptive individuals with affective disorders. *Archives of General Psychiatry, 43*, 923–929. [16]

Wender, P. H., Rosenthal, R., Kety, S., Schulsinger, S., and Welner, J. (1974). Cross fostering: A research strategy for clarifying the role of genetic and experimental factors in the etiology of schizophrenia. *Archives of General Psychology, 30*, 121–128. [15]

Wenzlaff, R. M., and Grozier, S. A. (1988). Depression and the magnification of failure. *Journal of Abnormal Psychology, 97*, 90–93. [17]

Werner, E. E. (1987). Vulnerability and

resiliency in childhood at risk for delinquency: A longitudinal study from birth to young adulthood. In J. D. Burchard and S. M. Burchard (Eds.), *Prevention of Delinquent Behavior* (pp. 68–84) Beverly Hills, CA: Sage Publications. [10]

Werner, H., and Siqueland, E. R. (1978). Visual recognition memory in the preterm infant. *Infant Behavior and Development, 1*, 79–94. [9]

Wessels, N. K. (1988). *Biology*. New York: Random House. [3]

Westefeld, J. S., and Furr, S. R. (1987). Suicide and depression among college students. *Professional Psychology: Research and Practice, 18*, 119–123. [17]

Westen, D., Ludolph, P., Lerner, H., Ruffins, S. et al. (1990). Object relations in borderline adolescents. *Journal of the American Academy of Child and Adolescent Psychiatry, 29*, 338–348. [14]

Wetzel, C. D., Janowsky, D. S., and Clopton, P. L. (1982). Remote memory during marijuana intoxication. *Psychopharmacology, 76*, 278–281. [5]

Wetzler, S. (1985). Mood state-dependent retrieval: A failure to replicate. *Psychological Reports, 65*, 759–765. [7]

Wever, E. G., and Bray, C. W. (1937). The perception of low tones and the resonance-volley theory. *Journal of Psychology, 3*, 101–114. [4]

Whalen, R. E., and Simon, N. G. (1984). Biological motivation. *Annual Review of Psychology, 35*, 257–276. [12]

White, F. J., and Appel, J. B. (1982). Lysergic acid diethylamide (LSD) and lisuride: Differentiation of their neuropharmacological actions. *Science, 216*, 535–537. [5]

White, H. R. (1988). Longitudinal patterns of cocaine use among adolescents. *American Journal of Drug Alcohol Abuse, 14*(1), 1–15. [5]

White, R. W. (1959). Motivation reconsidered: The concept of competence. *Psychological Review, 66*, 297–333. [12]

Whitehorn, D., and Burgess, P. R. (1973). Changes in polarization of central branches of myelinated mechanoreceptor and nociceptor fibers during noxious and innocuous stimulation of the skin. *Journal of Neurophysiology, 36,* 226–237. [4]

Whitehouse, P. J., Price, D. L., Struble, R. G., Clark, A. W., Coyle, J. T., and DeLong, M. R. (1982). Alzheimer's disease and senile dementia: Loss of neurons in the basal forebrain. *Science, 215,* 1237–1239. [3]

Whitley, B. E., Jr., and Frieze, I. H. (1985). Children's causal attributions for success or failure in achievement settings. A meta-analysis. *Journal of Education Psychology, 77,* 608–616. [18]

Whitlock, F. A. (1986). Suicide and physical illness. In A. Roy (Ed.), *Suicide.* Baltimore: Williams and Wilkins. [17]

Whorf, B. L. (1956). Science and linguistics. In J. B. Carroll (Ed.), *Language, Thought, and Reality: Selected Writings of Benjamin Lee Whorf* (pp. 207–219). Cambridge, MA: MIT Press. [8]

Wicker, A. W. (1969). Attitudes versus action: The relationship of verbal and overt behavioral responses to attitude objects. *Journal of Social Issues, 25,* 41–43. [18]

Widom, C. S. (1989). Does violence beget violence? A critical examination of the literature. *Psychological Bulletin, 106,* 3–28. [19]

Widom, C. S. (1991, February). Paper presented at the annual meeting of the American Association for the Advancement of Science, Washington, DC. [10]

Widroe, H. J., and Heisler, S. (1976). Treatment of tardive dyskinesia. *Diseases of the Nervous System, 37,* 162–164. [17]

Wiener, H. (1966). External chemical messengers, 1: Emission and reception in man. *New York State Journal of Medicine, 66,* 3153–3170. [12]

Williams, M. D. (1976). *Retrieval From Very Long-Term Memory.* Unpublished doctoral dissertation. University of California at San Diego. [7]

Williamson, D. A., Davis, C. J., Goreczny, A. J., and Blouin, D. C. (1988). Body-image disturbances in bulimia nervosa: Influences of actual body size. *Journal of Abnormal Psychology, 98,* 87–99. [12]

Wills, T. A. (1981). Downward comparison principles in social psychology. *Psychological Bulletin, 90,* 245–271. [11, 13]

Wilson, E. O. (1975). *Sociobiology: The New Synthesis.* Cambridge, MA: Harvard University Press. [19]

Wilson, E. O. (1978). *On Human Nature.* Cambridge, MA: Harvard University Press. [19]

Wilson, G. (1978). Introversion/extroersion. In H. London and J. E. Exner (Eds.), *Dimensions of Personality* (pp. 217–261). New York: Wiley. [13]

Wilson, G. T. (1982). From experimental research to clinical practice: Behavior therapy as a case study. In R. M. Adams, N. J. Smelser, and D. J. Treiman (Eds.), *Behavioral and Social Science Research: A National Resource* (Part II). Washington, DC: National Academy Press. [6]

Wilson, G. T. (1987). Chemical aversion conditioning as a treatment for alcoholism: A re-analysis. *Behaviour Research and Therapy, 25,* 503–516. [17]

Wilson, J. R., and Plomin, R. (1986). Individual differences in sensitivity and tolerance to alcohol. *Social Biology, 32,* 162–168. [5]

Winocur, G. (1984). Memory localization in the brain. In L. R. Squire and N. Butters (Eds.), *Neuropsychology of Memory* (pp. 122–133). New York: Guilford. [7]

Winograd, E., and Soloway, R. (1986). On forgetting the location of things stored in special places. *Journal of Experimental Psychology: General, 115,* 366–372. [1]

Winston, P. H., and Prendergast, C. A. (Eds.). (1984). *The A1 Business: Commercial Uses of Artificial Intelligence.* Cambridge, MA: MIT Press. [1]

Winterbottom, M. R. (1958). The relation of need for achievement to learning experiences in independence and mastery. In J. W. Atkinson (Ed.), *Motives in Fantasy, Action and Society.* New York: Van Nostrand. [12]

Winters, K. C., Newmark, C. S., Lumry, A. E., Leach, K., and Weintraub, S. (1984). MMPI code types characteristic of DSM-III schizophrenics, depressives, and bipolars. *Journal of Clinical Psychology, 4,* 382–386. [14]

Winters, K. C., Newmark, C. S., Lumry, A. E., Leach, K., and Weintraub, S. (1985). MMPI codetypes characteristic of DSM-III schizophrenics, depressives, and bipolars. *Journal of Clinical Psychology, 41,* 382–386. [14]

Wise, L., Steel, L., and MacDonald, C. (1979). *Origins and Career Consequences of Sex Differences in High School Mathematics Achievement.* Prepared for the National Institute of Education, Washington, DC. [12]

Wise, R. A., and Rompre, P-P. (1989). Brain dopamine and reward. *Annual Review of Psychology, 40,* 191–225. [3]

Wittgenstein, L. (1963). *Tractatus Logico-Philosphicus* (2nd ed.). New York: Humanities Press. (Original work published 1922). [8]

Wolf, F. M. (1986). *Meta-Analysis: Quantitative Methods for Research Synthesis,* Beverly Hills, CA: Sage Publications. [2]

Wolff, P. H. (1969). The natural history of crying and other vocalizations in early infancy. In B. M. Foss (Ed.), *Determinants of Infant Behavior* (Vol. 4). London: Methuen. [9]

Wolpe, J. (1958). *Psychotherapy by Reciprocal Inhibition.* Stanford, CA: Stanford University Press. [17]

Wolpe, J. (1973). *The Practice of Behavior Therapy* (2nd ed.). Elmsford, NY: Pergamon Press. [17]

Wolpe, J. (1976). *Theme and Variations: A Behavior Therapy Casebook.* Elmsford, NY: Pergamon Press. [17]

Wong, D. F., Wagner, H. N., Jr., Tune, L. E., Dannals, R. F., Pearlson, G. D., Links, J. M., Tamminga, C. A., Broussolle, E. P., Ravert, H. A., Wilson, A. A., Toung, J. K. T., Malat, J., Williams, J. A., O'Tuama, L. A., Snyder, S. H., Kuhar, M. J., and Gjedde, A. (1986). Positron emission tomography reveals elevated D^2 dopamine receptors in drug-naive schizophrenics. *Science, 234,* 1558–1563. [16]

Wong, E., and Weisstein, N. (1982). A new perceptual context-superiority effect: Line segments are more visible against a figure than against a ground. *Science, 218,* 587–589. [4]

Wood, G. (1983). *Cognitive Psychology: A*

Skills Approach. Monterey, CA: Brooks/Cole. [8]

Wood, L. F., and **Jacobson, N. S.** (1985). Marital distress. In D. H. Barlow (Ed.), *Clinical Handbook of Psychological Disorders.* New York: Guilford. [17]

Woody, C. D. (1986). Understanding the cellular basis of memory. *Annual Review of Psychology, 37,* 433–493. [7]

Woody, E. Z., Costanza, P. R., Liefer, H., and **Conger, J.** (1981). The effects of taste and caloric perceptions on the eating behavior of restrained and unrestrained subjects. *Cognitive Therapy and Research, 5*(4), 381–390. [12]

Woolsey, C. N. (1961). Organization of the cortical auditory system. In W. A. Rosenblith (Ed.), *Sensory Communication.* New York: Wiley. [3]

The World Almanac. (1988). New York: Pharos Books. [19]

Worringham, D. J., and **Messick, D. M.** (1983). Social facilitation of running: An unobtrusive study. *Journal of Social Psychology, 121,* 23–29. [19]

Wortman, C. B., and **Dunkel-Schetter, C.** (1979). Interpersonal relationships and cancer: A theoretical analysis. *Journal of Social Issues, 35,* 120–154. [19]

Wortman, C. B., and **Lehman, D. R.** (1985). Reactions to victims of life crises: Support attempts that fail. In I. G. Sarason and B. R. Sarason (Eds.), *Social Support: Theory, Research, and Applications.* Dordrecht, Netherlands: Martinus Nijhoff. [15]

Wortman, C. B., and **Silver, R. C.** (1989). The myths of coping with loss. *Journal of Consulting and Clinical Psychology, 57,* 349–357. [11]

Wortman, C. B., and **Silver, R. C.** (in press). Effective mastery of bereavement and widowhood: Longitudinal research. In P. B. Baltes and M. M. Baltes (Eds.), *Successful Aging: Research and Theory.* London: Cambridge University Press. [11]

Wortman, C. B., Silver, R. C., and **Kessler, R. C.** (in press). The meaning of loss and adjustment to bereavement. In M. S. Stroebe, W. Stroebe, and R. O. Hansson (Eds.), *Bereavement: A Sourcebook of Research and Intervention.* London: Cambridge University Press. [15]

Wright, L. (1988). The Type A behavior pattern and coronary heart disease. *American Psychologist, 43*(1), pp. 2–14. [13]

Wundt, W. (1904). *Principles of Physiological Psychology* (5th ed.). New York: Macmillan. (Original work published 1874). [1]

Wurtman, R. J. and **Wurtman, J. J.** (1989, January). Carbohydrates and depression. *Scientific American,* pp. 68–75. [16]

Wyer, R. S., Jr., and **Srull, T. K.** (1986). Human cognition in its social context. *Psychological Review, 93,* 322–359. [18]

Wynne, L. C., Singer, M. T., Bartko, J. J., and **Toohey, M. L.** (1975). Schizophrenics and their families: Recent research on parental communication. In J. M. Tanner (Ed.), *Psychiatric Research: The Widening Perspective.* New York: International Universities Press. [16]

Yarrow, M. R., Scott, P., and **Waxler, C. Z.** (1973). Learning concern for others. *Developmental Psychology, 8,* 240–260. [13]

Yee, D. K., and **Eccles, J. S.** (1988). Parent perceptions and attributions for children's math achievement. *Sex Roles, 19*(5–6), 317–333. [12]

Youngblade, L. M., and **Belsky, J.** (1989). Child maltreatment, infant-parent attachment, security, and dysfunctional peer relationships in toddlerhood. *TECSE, 9,* 1–15. [10]

Yussan, S. R., and **Berman, L.** (1981). Memory predictions for recall and recognition in first, third, and fifth grade children. *Developmental Psychology, 17,* 224–229. [9]

Zabin, L. S., Hirsch, M. B., and **Emerson, M. R.** (1989). *Family Planning Perspectives, 12,* 248. [15]

Zaccaro, S. J. (1984). Social loafing: The role of task attractiveness. *Personality and Social Psychology Bulletin, 10,* 99–106. [19]

Zajonc, R. B. (1965). Social facilitation. *Science, 149,* 269–274. [19]

Zajonc, R. B. (1966). *Social Psychology: An Experimental Approach.* Belmont, CA: Wadsworth. [19]

Zajonc, R. B. (1980). Feeling and think-ing: Preferences need no inferences. *American Psychologist, 35,* 151–175. [11]

Zajonc, R. B. (1984). On the privacy of affect. *American Psychologist, 39*(2), 117–123. [11]

Zajonc, R. B. (1986). The decline and rise of scholastic aptitude scores: A prediction derived from the confluence model. *American Psychologist, 41*(8), 862–867. [14]

Zajonc, R. B., Murphy, S. T., and **Inglehart, M.** (1989). Feeling and facial efference: Implications of the vascular theory of emotion. *Psychological Review, 99*(3), 395–416. [11]

Zanna, M. P., and **Hamilton, D. L.** (1977). Further evidence for meaning change in impression formation. *Journal of Experimental Social Psychology, 13,* 224–238. [18]

Zanna, M. P., and **Rempel, J. K.** (1988). Attitudes: A new look at an old concept. In D. Bar-Tal and A. Kruglanski (Eds.), *The Social Psychology of Knowledge.* New York: Cambridge University Press. [18]

Zaragoza, M. S., and **Koshmider, J. W.** (1989). Misled subjects may know more than their performance implies. *Journal of Experimental Psychology: Learning, Memory, and Cognition, 15*(2), 246–255. [7]

Zax, M., and **Stricker, G.** (1963). *Patterns of Psychopathology.* New York: Macmillan. [16]

Zeki, S. (1980, April 3). Representation of colours in the cerebral cortex. *Nature, 284,* 412–418. [4]

Zelig, M., and **Beidleman, W. B.** (1981). The investigative use of hypnosis: A word of caution. *International Journal of Clinical and Experimental Hypnosis, 29*(4), 401–412. [5]

Zigler, E., and **Seitz, V.** (1982). Social policy and intelligence. In R. J. Sternberg (Ed.), *Handbook of Human Intelligence.* Cambridge: Cambridge University Press.

Zillman, D. (1983). Arousal and aggression. In R. G. Geen and E. Donnerstein (Eds.), *Aggression: Theoretical and Empirical Review,* New York: Academic Press. [19]

Zillman, D., and **Bryant, J.** (1984). Effects of massive exposure to pornography. In N. M. Malamuth and E. I. Donnerstein (Eds.), *Pornography and Social Aggression.*

(115–138). New York: Academic Press. [19]

Zimbardo, P. G. (1975). Transforming experimental research into advocacy for social change. In M. Deutsch and H. Hornstein (Eds.), *Applying Social Psychology: Implications for Research, Practice, and Training.* Hillsdale, NJ: Lawrence Erlbaum. [19]

Zimbardo, P. G., Andersen, S. M., and Kabat, L. G. (1981). Paranoia and deafness: An experimental investigation. *Science, 212,* 1529–1531. [2]

Zimbardo, P. G., Haney, C., and Banks, W. C. (1973, April 8). A Pirandellian prison. *New York Times Magazine,* pp. 38–60. [18,19]

Zimbardo, P. G., Haney, C., Banks, W. C., and Jaffe, D. (1972). *The Psychology of Imprisonment: Privation, Power, and Pathology.* Unpublished paper, Stanford University. [18, 19]

Zimbardo, P. G., and Leippe, M. R. (1991). *The psychology of attitude change and social influence.* New York: McGraw-Hill. [18, 19]

Ziomek, M., and Coyne, J. C. (1983). *Depression and Supportive Behavior.* Unpublished manuscript, University of California at Berkeley. [16]

Zola-Morgan, S., Squire, L., and Mishkin, M. (1982). The neuroanatomy of amnesia: Amygdala-hippocampus versus temporal stem. *Science, 218,* 1337–1339. [3]

Zubin, J., and Spring, B. (1977). Vulnerability—a new view of schizophrenia. *Journal of Abnormal Psychology, 86,* 103–126. [16]

Zuckerman, M. (1960). The effects of subliminal and supraliminal suggestions on verbal productivity. *Journal of Abnormal and Social Psychology, 60,* 404–411. [4]

Zuckerman, M. (1975). Belief in a just world and altruistic behavior. *Journal of Personality and Social Psychology, 31,* 972–976. [19]

Zuckerman, M. (1978, February). The search for high sensation. *Psychology Today,* pp. 30–46, 96, 99. [12]

Zuckerman, M. (1979). *Sensation Seeking: Beyond the Optimal Level of Arousal.* Hillsdale, NJ: Lawrence Erlbaum. [12]

Zuckerman, M., and Lubin, B. (1985). *Manual for Multiple Affect Adjective Check List—Revised.* San Diego, CA: Educational and Industrial Testing Service. [11]

Zukin, S. R., and Zukin, R. S. (1979). Specific phencyclidine-3 binding in rat central nervous system. *Proceedings of the National Academy of Sciences, 10,* 5372–5376. [5]

Zullow, H. M., Oettingen, G., Peterson, C., and Seligman, M. E. P. (1988). Pessimistic explanatory style in the historical record. *American Psychologist, 43,* 673–682. [18]

CREDITS

Photographs

Photo Works. **497:** Georges Merillon/Gamma Liaison. **498:** Will & Deni McIntyre/Photo Researchers. **501:** D. & I. MacDonald/The Picture Cube. **503:** Will & Deni McIntyre/Photo Researchers. **505:** Bernice Jones. **508:** Scala/Art Resource. **511:** Arlene Collins/Monkmeyer Press. **514:** Grunnitus/Monkmeyer Press. **518:** UPI/Bettmann Newsphotos. **519:** Carol Lee/The Picture Cube. **528:** Sidney Harris. **530:** Harley Schwadron. **532:** Jacques M. Chenet/Woodfin Camp. **536:** Innervisions. **539:** Sidney Harris. **540:** Leif Skoogfors/Woodfin Camp. **542:** Michael Abramson/Woodfin Camp. **543:** E. Williamson/The Picture Cube. **545:** The Museum of Modern Art Film Stills Archive. **547:** Stan Aggie/Picture Group. **549:** Custom Medical Stock Photo. **552:** Everett Collection. **558:** Barbara Burnes/Photo Researchers. **560:** Elyse Rieder/The Photo Works. **561:** AP/Wide World Photos. **563:** UPI/Bettmann Newsphotos. **565:** Dan Budnik/Woodfin Camp. **570:** Deborah Davis/PhotoEdit. **573:** Greg Gawlowski/Photo 20–20. **575:** Farrell Grehan/Photo Researchers. **576:** Sepp Seitz/Woodfin Camp. **579:** Movie Still Archives. **581:** AP/Wide World Photos. **583:** Peter Yates/Picture Group. **585:** The Bettmann Archive. **587:** Historical Picture Service. **588:** CBS, 1990. **595:** William Vandivert. **600:** The Bettmann Archive. **603:** courtesy Professor Philip G. Zimbardo. **604:** R. Rowan/Photo Researchers. **606:** UPI/Bettmann Newsphotos. **608:** Anthony Johnson/The Picture Cube. **610:** Barbara Laing/Picture Group. **612:** Gerald Fritz/The Stock Solution. **614:** Everett Collection. **615:** Larry Kolvoord/Black Star. **618:** Tim Eagan/Woodfin Camp. **620:** Terry Wild Studio.

Figures and Tables

Pages 74 and **75:** Figures 3.8 and 3.9, from *Biology* by Wessels. Random House, Copyright (c) 1988. Used by permission of McGraw-Hill, Inc. **85:** Figure 3.13, reprinted with permission of Macmillan Publishing Company from *The Cerebral Cortex of Man* by Wilder Penfield and Theodore Rasmussen. Copyright (c) 1950 Macmillan Publishing Company; copyright renewed (c) 1978 Theodore Rasmussen. **90:** Table 3.1, summarized from *Fundamentals of Human Neuropsychology*, 3rd ed., by Bryan Kolb and Ian Q. Wishaw. Copyright (c) 1990 by W. H. Freeman and Company. Used by permission. **111:** Figure 4.8, from *Perception*, 2nd ed., by Sekuler and Blake. McGraw-Hill, Copyright (c) 1990. Used by permission of McGraw-Hill, Inc. **117:** Figure 4.10, from I. Darian-Smith, A. Goodwin, M. Sugitani, and J. Heywood, "The Tangible Features of Textured Surfaces: Their Representation in the Monkey's Somatosensory Cortex," in G. Edelman, W. E. Gall, and M. W. Cowan, eds., *Dynamic Aspects of Neocortical Functions*, Wiley, 1984. Used by permission of The Neurosciences Research Foundation, Inc., and Ian Darian-Smith. **120:** Figure 4.11, from *Journal of Psychology*, vol. 39 (1955), pp. 157–160. Reprinted with permission of the Helen Dwight Reid Educational Foundation. Published by Heldref Publications, 4000 Albemarle St., N.W., Washington, D.C. 20016. Copyright (c) 1955. **122:** Figure 4.13, from "Subjective Contours" by Gaetano Kanizsa. Copyright (c) 1976 by Scientific American, Inc. All rights reserved. **125:** Figure 4.17, adapted from *Perception*, 2nd ed., by Sekuler and Blake. McGraw-Hill, Copyright (c) 1990. Used by permission of McGraw-Hill, Inc. **142:** Figure 5.3, adapted from *Physiological Psy-*

chology, 2nd ed, by Rosenzweig and Leiman. McGraw-Hill, Copyright (c) 1990. Used by permission of McGraw-Hill, Inc. **149:** Figure 5.4, Copyright (c) April 4, 1983, U.S. News & World Report. **154:** Figure 5.5, *Triangle*, Sandoz Journal of Medical Science, vol. 2, 3, 1955, Copyright (c) 1955 Sandoz Ltd Basle, Switzerland. **160:** Figure 6.3, adapted from *Learning and Memory*, by W. C. Gordon. Copyright (c) 1983 by Wadsworth, Inc. Used with the permission of Brooks/Cole Publishing Company, Pacific Grove, CA 93950. **205:** Figure 7.7, from *The Psychology of Rumor* by Gordon W. Allport and Leo Postman, copyright (c) 1947 and renewed 1975 by Holt, Rinehart and Winston, Inc., reprinted by permission of the publisher. **228:** Figure 8.8, adapted from "Classroom Experiments on Mental Sets," by A. S. Luchins, in *American Journal of Psychology*, vol. 59 (1946). Copyright (c) 1946, 1974 by the Board of Trustees of the University of Illinois. Used by permission of the University of Illinois Press. **230:** Figure 8.9, from J. L. Adams, *Conceptual Blockbusting*, Copyright (c) 1990 by James L. Adams. Used by permission of Addison-Wesley Publishing Co., Inc. Reading, MA. **260:** Table 9.1 from "The Denver Developmental Screening Test" by W. K. Frankenburg and J. B. Dodds, *Journal of Pediatrics*, vol. 71, no. 2 (1967), pp. 181–191, as adapted in *A Child's World*, 5th ed., by D. E. Papalia and S. W. Olds, McGraw-Hill, Copyright (c) 1990. Used by permission of William K. Frankenburg, M.D., and McGraw-Hill, Inc. **264:** Figure 9.2, illustration from *The Essential Piaget* edited by Howard E. Gruber and J. Jacques Voneche. Copyright (c) 1978 by Basic Books, Inc. Reprinted by permission of Basic Books, Inc., a division of HarperCollins Publishers. **269:** Table 9.2, from *Infancy, Childhood and Adolescence* by L. Steinberg and J. Belsky. McGraw-Hill, Copyright (c) 1990. Used by permission of McGraw-Hill, Inc. **278:** Figure 9.7, from "Sex Differences" by M. T. Frankel, in *Children's Thinking: Developmental Functions and Individual Differences*, ed. by D. F. Bjorklund. Copyright (c) 1988. Used by permission of Brooks/Cole Publishing Co. **286:** Table 10.1, adapted from *Child Development* by L. A. Sroufe and R. G. Cooper, Knopf, Copyright (c) 1988. Used by permission of McGraw-Hill, Inc. **301:** Table 10.2, adapted from *Separate Lives: Why Siblings Are So Different* by Judy Dunn and Robert Plomin. Copyright (c) 1991 by Basic Books, Inc. Reprinted by permission of Basic Books, Inc., a division of HarperCollins Publishers. **322:** Figure 11.1. Used by permission of Randy J. Larsen, Ph.D. **330:** and **333:** Figures 11.3 and 11.5, from "Promises and Problems with the Circumplex Model of Emotion," by Larsen and Diener, in *Review of Personality and Social Psychology*, 13. Copyright (c) 1992 by Sage Publications, Inc. **331:** Figure 11.4, reprinted with permission from *Behavior Research and Therapy*, vol. 6, "A Laboratory Task for Induction of Mood States" by E. Velten. Copyright (c) 1968, Pergamon Press. **358** Figure 12.1, from "The Physiological Role of Pleasure" by M. Cabanac, in *Science*, vol 173. Copyright (c) 1971 by the AAAS. Used by permission of the AAAS and Prof. M. Cabanac. **364:** Table 12.1, from "Anxiety, Restraint, and Eating Behavior," by Peter Herman and Janet Polivy, in *Journal of Abnormal Psychology*, vol. 84. Copyright (c) 1975 by the American Psychological Association. Reprinted by permission. **376:** Table 12.2, from "The Search for High Sensation," by M. Zuckerman, in *Psychology Today*, February 1978. **399:** Table 13.1, from L. A. Pervin, *Personality: Theory, Assessment, and*

NAME INDEX

SUBJECT INDEX

unconditional, 529–530
Positive reinforcement, 172
Positron emission tomography (PET) scan, 80
Possible selves, 408
Postconventional level, 307–308
Posttraumatic stress disorder (PTSD), 473, 497–498
Practice, stress management and, 481
Pragmatics, 243–244, 272
Preconventional level, 306–307
Prediction as goal of psychology, 16–17
Predictive validity, 423
Prefrontal areas, 85
Prefrontal lobotomy, 544–545
Prejudice, 581–589
Premature ejaculation, 369
Preoperational period, 261
Preoptic region, sexual responsiveness and, 367
Prepared learning, 180
Prespeech communication, 269–270
Pressure sense, 116–117
Primacy effect, 567–568
Primary appraisal, 345
Primary drives, 356
Primary empathy, 530
Primary erectile failure, 369
Primary orgasmic dysfunction, 369
Primary reinforcer, 176
Primary sexual characteristics, 309
Priming, impression formation and, 569–571
Proactive interference, 213
Probability, 50
  decision making and, 233
  judging, 235–238
Problem-directed coping, 476
Problem solving, 222–232
  by computer, 229–231
  creative, 231–232
  deciding solutions are satisfactory and, 229
  devising solution strategies and, 224–229
  group effects on shaping of, 603–607
  planful, coping with stress and, 477
  presentation of problem and, 223–224
Problem-solving abilities, intelligence and, 424
Procedural memories, 197–198
Profile of Nonverbal Sensitivity (PONS), 328
Programmed instruction, 177–178
Progressive relaxation, stress management and, 481
Project Head Start, IQ and, 441

Projection, 390
Projective tests, 444–446
Propanediols, 546
Propositions, 241–242
Prototype, 221–222
Proximity:
  attraction and, 577
  love and, 578–579
  perceptual grouping and, 122–123
Prozac, 547
Pseudoparkinsonism, 548
Psyche, structure of, 388–389
Psychiatrists, 22–23
Psychoactive drugs, 148–155, 546–549
  neurotransmitters and, 69
Psychoactive substance abuse, 519–521
  (See also Alcoholism)
Psychoanalysis, 11, 23, 526–529
  Freudian, 526–528
  long-term, evaluating, 528
  memory and, 215
  other, 528–529
Psychoanalytic perspective, 9, 11–12
  on alcoholism, 520
  on depression, 503
  on family therapy, 541–542
  on forgetting, 214
  on gender role development, 303–304
  on moral development, 306
  of motivation, 355–356
  on personality, 386–396
  on psychological disorders, 490–491
  on social and personality development, 285, 287
Psychoanalytic theories:
  evaluating, 395–396
  Freudian, 387–392
  other, 392–395
Psychobiography, theory of, 412–413
Psychodynamic psychotherapy, 529
Psychogenic amnesia, 499–500
Psychogenic fugue, 500
Psychological benefits, of meditation, 156–157
Psychological disorders, 486–522
  anxiety, 493–498
  biological perspective on, 490
  classifying, 492–493
  combining perspectives on, 492
  definition of, 487–489
  dissociative, 499–500
  interpersonal perspective on, 491
  of mood, 500–510
  of personality, 517–519
  psychoactive substance abuse and, 519–521
  psychological perspectives on, 490–491

sociocultural perspective on, 491–492
  somatoform, 498–499
  treatment of (see Biological treatments; Psychotherapy)
  (See also Schizophrenia)
Psychological factors, pain and, 117
Psychological needs, 411–412
Psychology:
  careers in, 17–25
  definition of, 3
  eclectic approach to, 14–16
  emergence of, 8–9
  fields of specialization in, 17–24
  goals of, 16–17
  as means of promoting human welfare, 6–7
  reasons to study, 24–25
  as science, 3–6
  in twentieth century, 9–14
Psychoneuroimmunology, 324–325, 465
Psychopharmacology, 18
  (See also Drug therapy)
Psychophysiological approach:
  evaluating, 416–417
  to personality, 416
Psychosexual development, stages of, 391–392
Psychosurgery, 544–545
Psychotherapy, 525–544
  behavior and cognitive-behavior therapies, 178–179, 531–539
  eclectic approaches to, 544
  family-systems, 539–542
  group, 542–544
  humanistic, 529–531
  psychoanalytic, 526–529
  psychodynamic, 11, 23, 215, 529
PTSD (posttraumatic stress disorder), 473, 497–498
Puberty, 309–310
Punishments, 172
  as incentives, 357–358
  intrinsic, 185
  in observational learning, 185
  using to change behavior, 179
  vicarious, 185
Pupil (of eye), 103

Quasi-experimental designs, 36–37

Race, IQ differences and, 438–443
Racism, 581–586
  combatting, 586
  disguised, 583–584
  dynamics of, 583–584
  theoretical explanations of, 584–586